GARDENS
OF ENGLAND & WALES

1993

**A GUIDE TO OVER 3,000 GARDENS
THE MAJORITY OF WHICH ARE NOT NORMALLY
OPEN TO THE PUBLIC**

THE NATIONAL GARDENS SCHEME CHARITABLE TRUST
HATCHLANDS PARK, EAST CLANDON, GUILDFORD, SURREY GU4 7RT
TEL 0483 211535   FAX 0483 211537

Contents

©The National Gardens Scheme 1993

All rights reserved. No part of this publication may be reproduced or transmitted in any form by any means electronic or mechanical including photocopying, recording or any other information storage and retrieval system without prior written permission from the publisher.

Published by the National Gardens Scheme, Hatchlands Park, East Clandon, Guildford, Surrey GU4 7RT

Editor: Lt Col D G Carpenter (Retd.)

Designed by Jonathan Newdick.

Cover illustration of Dallam Tower, Cumbria by Val Biro

A catalogue record for this book is available from the British Library.

Typeset in Linotron Bell Centennial by Land & Unwin (Data Sciences) Limited, Bugbrooke.

Text printed and bound by Benham & Company, Colchester.

Cover and colour section printed by George Over Limited, Rugby.

ISBN 0-900558-25-3 ISSN 0141-2361

GARDEN LOVERS' HOLIDAYS

WHERE
DORSET · DEVON
MEETS

Philip and Ian, our award-wining chefs, prepare superb meals each day with a tempting choice of dishes. Twice weekly we dine by candlelight with our resident pianist softly playing in the background.

Fairwater Head – a welcoming country house, w twenty luxury *en suite* bedrooms, comfortable lounges, award-winning gardens, and magnificei views across the Axe Valley. Guests return year after year to enjoy the peace and tranquillity an caring family hospitality.

In springtime and in autumn we visit famous homes and gardens by luxury coach, with talks

Guests at Clapton Court

experts, and plants to take hom You can also plan your own programme by reading our new brochure, which gives a guide tc nearby gardens, National Trust properties, and the Lyme Regis coast.

This year we plan to visit 'Rosemoor', the new R.H.S. gard with breaks of particular interes in bridge, history, wine-tasting antiques, craft, and classical mu

FAIRWATER HEAD COUNTRY HOUSE HOTEL
Hawkchurch, Near Axminster, Devon, EX13 5TX
Telephone: (0297) 678349   AA★★★RAC

The National Gardens Scheme Charitable Trust

'The Gardens Scheme' was started at the suggestion of Miss Elsie Wagg, a member of the council of the Queen's Nursing Institute, as part of a national memorial to Queen Alexandra whose deep and sympathetic interest in district nursing was well known.

Although this country was renowned for its gardens, few people had the opportunity to see them, so that when 600 were opened in 1927 the response was such that the experiment became an English institution. The Scheme, now called the **National Gardens Scheme Charitable Trust**, has continued and expanded ever since, in 1992 raising more than £1.200,000 from over 2,900 gardens.

The National Gardens Scheme helps many deserving causes, the first call on its funds being in support of its original beneficiary, the **Queen's Nursing Institute** for the relief of district and other nurses in need – be this caused by old age, difficulties through illness or the stress and pressure of their work.

Since 1949 a contribution has been made to the **Gardens Fund of The National Trust** to help maintain gardens of special historic or horticultural interest. In 1984 the increasing popularity of the Scheme made it possible to extend further its charitable work by assisting the **Cancer Relief Macmillan Fund** with funds for training **Macmillan Nurses** in the continuing care of the terminally ill. In 1986 the Scheme took on the charitable work previously organised by Gardeners' Sunday in aid of the **Gardeners' Royal Benevolent Society** and the **Royal Gardeners' Orphan Fund**.

Many other national and local charities also benefit from the Scheme, since garden owners may, if they so wish, allocate an agreed proportion of the proceeds of an opening for the National Gardens Scheme to another charity. The names of these additional charities are published in the descriptive entries for the gardens.

We wish to emphasise that the majority of the gardens listed are privately owned and are only opened on the dates shown in the text through the generosity of the owners wishing to support this charity. These gardens are **NOT OPEN** to the public on other dates except by prior agreement.

The Chairman and Council wish to express their deep gratitude to all those whose generous support of the National Gardens Scheme makes it possible to help these most worth-while charities. Please help us to help others by visiting as many gardens as you can.

Thank you for your support.

Garden Statuary
& Architectural Items

at Sotheby's Country House Saleroom in Sussex

25TH & 26TH MAY 1993
28TH SEPTEMBER 1993

If you wish to enter items in these sales or would like a free valuation, please send a photograph with details. We can also advise on the removal and transport of heavy or awkward items from your property.

After the Antique: A white marble figure of the Apollo Belvedere, 55ins high. Sold in September 1992 for £3,850.

For further information or catalogue enquiries, please contact James Rylands, Sotheby's, Summers Place, Billingshurst, West Sussex RH14 9AD. *Tel:* (0403) 783933 or Jennifer Cox, Sotheby's, 34 - 35 New Bond Street, London W1A 2AA. *Tel:* (071) 408 5217.

THE WORLD'S LEADING FINE ART AUCTION HOUSE

SOTHEBY'S
FOUNDED 1744

Patron, President and Council of The National Gardens Scheme Charitable Trust

Relevant organisations and publications

Historic Houses Castles and Gardens in Great Britain and Ireland, 1993 edition
Published by Professional Publications, Reed Information Services Limited, Windsor Court, East Grinstead House, East Grinstead, West Sussex. Price £7.45 at W.H. Smith, National Trust Shops and all leading booksellers in Great Britain and Ireland. Published annually in January in full colour throughout, it gives details of over 1,300 houses, castles and gardens open to the public.

The National Trust
Certain gardens opened by The National Trust are opened in aid of the National Gardens Scheme on the dates shown in this book. Information about the regular opening of these gardens is given in the 1993 *Handbook for Members and Visitors* (issued free to members), published by The National Trust (£3.95 plus 70p for postage; subject to alteration) and obtainable from 36 Queen Anne's Gate, London SW1H 9AS or from any National Trust Property. The National Trust Gardens Handbook (£3.95) provides more detailed information on the Trust's gardens, sold in bookshops & National Trust shops.

Scotland's Gardens Scheme
Raises funds through the opening of gardens for the Queen's Nursing Institute (Scotland), the Gardens Fund of The National Trust for Scotland and over 150 other charities nominated by the garden owners. Handbook with all details of openings published mid-February. Tours: two six-day coach tours. Free brochure available. Handbook (£2.50 inc. p & p) from Scotland's Gardens Scheme, 31 Castle Terrace, Edinburgh EH1 2EL Telephone 031-229 1870.

The National Trust for Scotland
Established in 1931. In its care are over 100 properties. As well as castles, cottages, mountains, islands and historic sites, the Trust has in its care 24 major Scottish gardens. The National Trust for Scotland, 5 Charlotte Square, Edinburgh EH2 4DU Telephone 031-226 5922

The Ulster Gardens Scheme
A list of the private gardens open to the public under the Ulster Gardens Scheme can be obtained from: The Public Affairs Manager, The National Trust, Rowallane, Saintfield, Co. Down, BT24 7LH. Telephone Saintfield (0238) 510721

The Automobile Association Guide to Britain
2000 Days out in Britain gives details of more than 2,000 places of interest in England, Wales, Scotland, Channel Islands and Northern Ireland. Available from AA bookshops and all good booksellers. Price £3.99.

The Historic Houses Association
Represents over 1,300 private owners of historic houses and outstanding gardens. The HHA is particularly concerned with the problem of funding gardens. It runs the Christie's/HHA Garden of the Year Award; helps administer a scheme for training gardeners and organises periodic seminars. A quarterly magazine is available to members and friends of the Historic Houses Association and on subscription. HHA, 2 Chester Street, London SW1X 7BB. Telephone 071-259 5688.

Irish Heritage Properties (HITHA)
Publishes annually an illustrated booklet with information on over 50 properties. Available from Irish Heritage Properties, 3a Castle Street, Dalkey, Co. Dublin. Telephone Dublin 2859633.

The Automobile Association
The AA has kindly arranged for information on gardens open for the Scheme to be available from their local offices.

The Royal Automobile Club
The RAC has kindly arranged that their RAC Touring Information Department (081-686 0088) can provide details of locations of gardens open for the Scheme.

INSPIRATION FOR GARDENERS

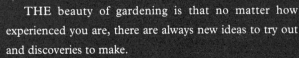

A special invitation to join The Royal Horticultural Society

THE beauty of gardening is that no matter how experienced you are, there are always new ideas to try out and discoveries to make.

For thousands of gardeners, membership of the RHS is the best possible source of inspiration.

Join us and you can enjoy unlimited free admission to the Society's gardens at Wisley, Rosemoor and, new for 1993, Hyde Hall in Essex – as well as seven other famous gardens up and down the country.

There is also privileged admission to flower shows – such as the Chelsea Flower Show, the brand new International Spring Gardening Fair at Wembley, the Malvern Spring Gardening Show and the Harrogate Spring and Autumn Flower Shows – as well as over 250 lectures and demonstrations around the country.

Best of all, every month you receive your own copy of the Society's famous journal, *The Garden* - required reading for serious gardeners all over the world.

Help secure the future of Britain's great gardening heritage

The many benefits of membership are only half the story. As a Member, you can help the Society's work as well.

In our gardens we care for definitive collections of flowers, fruit and vegetables, and conduct a busy programme of trials and research. Education is important too: our efforts range from training young horticulturists to offering advice to tens of thousands of gardeners every year.

As a registered charity, the RHS relies entirely on the money we can raise ourselves to continue these initiatives; and your subscription is a vital contribution.

Please help us by joining the Society or enrolling a friend as a Member today.

Join today, or introduce a friend – and save £3

Normally the first year of RHS membership costs £27 (£22 plus a £5 enrolment fee). But, as a special introduction to the Society for readers of the National Garden Scheme's *Gardens of England and Wales*, you can join or, if your are already a Member, enrol a friend, for just £24.

All you have to do is complete and return the form below. If you are enrolling a friend, please complete the form with your own name and address and enclose a separate sheet with the new Member's details.

Application for RHS membership

TO: The Royal Horticultural Society, Membership Department, PO Box 313, Vincent Square, London SW1P 2PE. Tel: 071-834 4333

If you would prefer not to cut this coupon, please write to us with your details, being sure to mention that you are a *Gardens of England and Wales* reader.

☐   I would like to join the Society at the special introductory rate of £24 for the year.

☐   I would like to enrol a friend as a Member. I enclose their name and address on a separate sheet.

Name . . . .

Address . . . .

. . . . *Postcode* . . . .

Please make your cheque payable to The Royal Horticultural Society. If you have enrolled a friend, the new Member's pack and card will be sent to you to pass on.   Code 107

Royal Gardens

SANDRINGHAM HOUSE AND GROUNDS Norfolk
By gracious permission of Her Majesty The Queen, the House and grounds at Sandringham will be open (except when Her Majesty The Queen or any members of the Royal Family are in residence) on the following days:
From 11th April to 3rd October inclusive daily.
Please note that the **house only** will be **closed** to the public from 19 July to 7th August inclusive and that the house and grounds will be closed from 23rd July to 4th August inclusive. Coach drivers and visitors are advised to confirm these closing and opening dates nearer the time.
Hours
Sandringham House: 11 (12 noon on Sundays) to 4.45; Sandringham grounds: 10.30 (11.30 on Sundays) to 5.
Admission Charges
House and grounds: adults £3, OAPs £2.00, children £1.50. Grounds only: adults £2, OAPs £1.50; children £1.00. It is not possible to purchase a ticket to visit the house only. Admission to the museum is free. Advance party bookings will be accepted. There are no reductions in admission fees for parties. Picnicking is not permitted inside the grounds. Dogs are not permitted inside the grounds. Free car and coach parking.
Sandringham Church
This will be open as follows, subject to weddings, funerals and special services: when the grounds are open as stated above, hours 11-5 April to September, 1-5 during October. At other times of the year the church is open by appointment only.
Enquiries
The Public Enterprises Manager, Estate office, Sandringham or by telephone 9-1, 2-4.30 Monday to Friday inclusive on King's Lynn 772675.
Sandringham Flower Show
This will be held on Wednesday 28th July.

FROGMORE GARDENS Berkshire
By gracious permission of Her Majesty The Queen, the Frogmore Gardens, Windsor Castle, will be open from 10.30-7 on the following days:
Wednesday May 5 and Thursday May 6.
Coaches by appointment only: apply to the National Gardens Scheme, Hatchlands Park, East Clandon, Guildford, Surrey, GU4 7RT (Telephone 0483 211535) stating whether May 5 or 6, and whether morning or afternoon. Admission £1.50 accompanied children free. Dogs not allowed. Royal mausoleum also open, free of charge, both days. Entrance to gardens and mausoleum through Long Walk gate. Visitors are requested kindly to refrain from entering the grounds of the Home Park. Light refreshments will be available at the free car park (near the outer gate to the gardens).

FROGMORE HOUSE Berkshire
Also open but not for NGS. Entrance only from Frogmore Gardens. Admission Adults £2.50, over 60's £2, under 17 £1.50, children under age of 8 not admitted.

BARNWELL MANOR Northamptonshire
By kind permission of Their Royal Highnesses Princess Alice Duchess of Gloucester and the Duke and Duchess of Gloucester, the gardens at Barnwell Manor will be open from 2.30-6 on:
Sundays 9th and 23rd May. Admission £1, children free.

 # The National Trust

ONCE AGAIN, money raised by the National Gardens Scheme has helped the National Trust to preserve some of this country's finest gardens and to train the gardeners of the future. In 1993 you can see the National Gardens Scheme's money at work:

- Glendurgan in Cornwall, where the famous maze is being replanted
- Calke Abbey in Derbyshire where a vinery is being put back into the old physic garden
- Uppark in West Sussex, where the garden, devastated during the fire and subsequent rebuilding works, is being replanned
- Cliveden in the Thames Valley, where the 'secret' rose garden created for Lord Astor by Sir Geoffrey Jellicoe is being given new life.

In 1993 two gardeners, placed at Coleton Fishacre in Devon and Trengwainton, Cornwall, complete a training and work experience programme thanks to finance from the National Gardens Scheme.

Thank you for your continuing support

General Information

‡ following a garden name in the Dates of Opening list indicates that those gardens sharing the same symbol are nearby and open on the same day. ‡‡ indicates a second series of nearby gardens open on the same day.

¶   Opening for the first time.

❀   Plants/produce for sale if available.

&   Gardens with at least the main features accessible by wheelchair.

✗   No dogs except guide dogs but otherwise dogs are usually admitted, provided they are kept on a lead. Dogs are not admitted to houses.

●   Gardens marked thus, which open throughout the season, give a guaranteed contribution from their takings to the National Gardens Scheme.

▲   Where this sign appears alongside dates in the *descriptive* entry for a garden it denotes that this garden will be open in aid of the National Gardens Scheme on the dates shown, but that this garden is *also open* regularly to the public on *other days*. Details of National Trust gardens can also be found in the *National Trust Gardens Handbook;* see page 9.

Children All children must be accompanied by an adult.

Additional charities nominated by owner Where the owners of 'private' gardens (not normally open to the public) have nominated some other charity to receive an agreed share from an opening for the National Gardens Scheme, the name of the other charity is included in the descriptive entry as (Share to ....).

Distances and sizes In all cases these are approximate.

Open by appointment Please do not be put off by this notation. The owner may consider his garden too small to accommodate the numbers associated with a normal opening or, more often, there may be a lack of car parking space. It is often more rewarding than a normal opening as the owner will usually give a guided tour of the garden. Any size of party is normally welcome from 2 upwards.

Coach parties Please, by appointment only unless stated otherwise.

Houses Not open unless this is specifically stated; where the house or part-house is shown an additional charge is usually made.

Tea When this is available at a garden the information is given in capitals, e.g. TEAS (usually with home-made cakes) or TEA (usually with biscuits). There is, of course, an extra charge for any refreshments available at a garden. Any other information given about tea is a guide only to assist visitors in finding somewhere in the area for tea.

Buses Continuance of many bus services is a matter of considerable uncertainty, especially on Sundays. It is strongly recommended that any details given in this guide be checked in advance.

National Trust Members are requested to note that where a National Trust property has allocated an opening day to the National Gardens Scheme which is one of its normal opening days, members can still gain entry on production of their National Trust membership card (although donations to the Scheme will be welcome). Where, however, the day allocated is one on which the property would *not* normally be open, then the payment of the National Gardens Scheme admission fee will be required.

Professional photographers Photographs taken in a garden may not be used for sale or reproduction without the prior permission of the garden owner.

Lavatories Private gardens do not normally have outside lavatories. Regretably, for security reasons, owners have been advised not to admit visitors into their houses to use inside toilets.

ENGLAND

Avon

Hon County Organiser:	Mrs J A Heaford, Bellevue, Publow, nr Pensford, Bristol, BS18 4HP Tel 0761 490271
Assistant Hon County Organisers:	Mrs Audrey Holliman, 252 Down Road, Portishead, Bristol BS20 8HY Tel 0275 843568
	Mrs Sally Sparks, Pine Leigh, Church Road, Leigh Woods, Bristol BS8 3PG Tel 0272 730066
Avon Leaflet:	Mrs Jean Damey, 2 Hawburn Close, Bristol BS4 2PB Tel 0272 775587
Hon County Treasurer:	J A Heaford, Esq.

DATES OF OPENING

By appointment
For telephone numbers and other details see garden descriptions

Algars Manor, Iron Acton
Alwih Cottage, Alverston
Brewery House, Southstoke
Church Farm, Lower Failand
Jasmine Cottage, Clevedon
23 Kelston Road, Bath
The Manor House,
    Walton-in-Gordano
Madron, Bathford
Orchard House, Claverton
Sherborne Garden, Litton
Springfield Barn, Upton Cheyney
Stanton Prior Gardens, nr Bath
University of Bristol Botanic Gardens
Urn Cottage, Charfield
Vine House, Henbury

Regular openings
For details see garden descriptions

Jasmine Cottage, Clevedon. Every
    Thurs April 15 to Aug 26
The Manor House,
    Walton-in-Gordano. Every Weds
    and Thurs April 14 to Sept 16 &
    Oct 20 to Nov 4
Sherborne Garden, Litton. Suns,
    Mons June 14 to Sept 6
Stanton Prior Gardens, nr Bath.
    Thurs April 8 to Sept 30

---

13 March Saturday
    Langford Court, Langford
14 March Sunday
    Langford Court, Langford

21 March Sunday
    Tockington Gardens
28 March Sunday
    Jasmine Cottage, Clevedon
4 April Sunday
    Brook Cottage, Upper Langford
    23 Kelston Road, Bath
11 April Sunday
    Algars Manor & Algars Mill, Iron
      Acton
    Bedford House, Clevedon
    Coley Court, Coley, East
      Harptree ‡
    Sherborne Garden, Litton ‡
12 April Monday
    Algars Manor & Algars Mill, Iron
      Acton
    Bedford House, Clevedon
    The Manor House,
      Walton-in-Gordano
17 April Saturday
    Vine House, Henbury
18 April Sunday
    Bourne House, Burrington
    Crowe Hall, Widcombe
    Vine House, Henbury
24 April Saturday
    Brackenwood Garden Centre,
      Portishead
25 April Sunday
    Brackenwood Garden Centre,
      Portishead
    Jasmine Cottage, Clevedon
26 April Monday
    Brackenwood Garden Centre,
      Portishead
27 April Tuesday
    Brackenwood Garden Centre,
      Portishead
28 April Wednesday
    Brackenwood Garden Centre,
      Portishead
    Portland Lodge, Almondsbury

2 May Sunday
    Coombe Dingle Gardens, Bristol
    Goldney Hall, Bristol
    The Manor House,
      Walton-in-Gordano
3 May Monday
    Coombe Dingle Gardens,
      Bristol
    The Manor House,
      Walton-in-Gordano
5 May Wednesday
    Orchard House, Claverton
16 May Sunday
    Algars Manor & Algars Mill, Iron
      Acton ‡
    Severn View, Grovesend,
      Thornbury ‡
    West Tyning, Beach
17 May Monday
    Algars Manor & Algars Mill, Iron
      Acton
19 May Wednesday
    Orchard House, Claverton
    Windmill Cottage, Backwell
22 May Saturday
    Lower Failand Gardens, Bristol
23 May Sunday
    Barrow Court, Barrow Gurney
    Lower Failand Gardens, Bristol
    Severn View, Grovesend,
      Thornbury
30 May Sunday
    Bedford House, Clevedon ‡
    Jasmine Cottage, Clevedon ‡
    Severn View, Grovesend,
      Thornbury
    The Urn Cottage, Charfield
    Vine House, Henbury
31 May Monday
    Bedford House, Clevedon
    Vine House, Henbury
2 June Wednesday
    Orchard House, Claverton

6 June Sunday
Churchill Court, Churchill
Clifton Gardens, Bristol
Crowe Hall, Widcombe
Hazel Cottage, Lower Hazel
The Manor House,
    Walton-in-Gordano
Severn View, Grovesend,
    Thornbury
13 June Sunday
Harptree Court, East Harptree
Severn View, Grovesend,
    Thornbury
Sherborne Garden, Litton
16 June Wednesday
Orchard House, Claverton
Windmill Cottage, Backwell
19 June Saturday
Brewery House, Southstoke
20 June Sunday
Badminton House, Badminton
Bedford House, Clevedon
Doynton House, Doynton ‡
Gardener's Cottage, Upton
    Cheyney ‡
Highfield House, Chew Magna
23 June Wednesday
Tockington Gardens

24 June Thursday
Windmill Cottage, Backwell
27 June Sunday
Brooklands, Burnett
Church Farm, Lower Failand
Jasmine Cottage, Clevedon
30 June Wednesday
Brooklands, Burnett
1 July Thursday
Windmill Cottage, Backwell
10 July Saturday
Brewery House, Southstoke
11 July Sunday
23 Kelston Road, Bath
Stanton Drew Gardens, nr
    Bristol
University of Bristol Botanic
    Garden
16 July Friday
Windmill Cottage, Backwell
17 July Saturday
Publow Gardens, Publow
18 July Sunday
Publow Gardens, Publow
25 July Sunday
Jasmine Cottage, Clevedon ‡
The Manor House,
    Walton-in-Gordano ‡

29 July Thursday
Windmill Cottage, Backwell
1 August Sunday
Stanton Prior Gardens, nr Bath
Tranby House, Whitchurch, Bristol
8 August Sunday
Dyrham Park, Chippenham
20 August Friday
Windmill Cottage, Backwell
29 August Sunday
Jasmine Cottage, Clevedon ‡
The Manor House,
    Walton-in-Gordano ‡
30 August Monday
The Manor House,
    Walton-in-Gordano
12 September Sunday
Jasmine Cottage, Clevedon
University of Bristol Botanic
    Garden
15 September Wednesday
Tockington Gardens
19 September Sunday
Tockington Gardens
29 September Wednesday
Windmill Cottage, Backwell
10 October Sunday
Sherborne Garden, Litton

DESCRIPTIONS OF GARDENS

Algars Manor & Algars Mill ❀ Iron Acton 9m N of Bristol. 3m W of Yate Sodbury. Turn S off Iron Acton bypass B4059, past village green, 200yds, then over level Xing (Station Rd). TEAS **Algars Manor**. *Combined adm £1.50 Chd 20p. Easter Sun, Mon April 11, 12; Sun, Mon May 16, 17 (2-6)*
Algars Manor ❀ (Dr & Mrs J M Naish) 3-acre woodland garden beside R Frome; mill-stream; native plants mixed with azaleas, rhododendrons, camellias, magnolias, eucalyptus. Picnic areas. Early Jacobean house (not open) and old barn. *Also by appt* **Tel 0454 228372**
Algars Mill (Mr & Mrs J Wright) entrance via Algars Manor. 2-acre woodland garden beside R. Frome; spring bulbs, shrubs; early spring feature of wild Newent daffodils. 300-400 yr old mill house (not open) through which mill-race still runs

¶**Alwih Cottage** &❀ (Y E Buckoke) Shellards Lane Alveston. 3m SE of Thornbury, 10m N of Bristol. Take 'The Street leading to Shellards Lane' off the A38 immediately opp The Alveston House Hotel. Signposted Itchington. 1.7m down the lane. ⅓-acre landscaped garden with interesting trees, shrubs, herbaceous borders and a gravel garden planted with herbs. TEAS by arrangement. *Adm £1 OAP's 50p Chd free. By appt only Feb to end Oct. Parties welcome, maximum 4 cars.* **Tel 0454 412124**

Badminton &❀ (The Duke & Duchess of Beaufort) 5m E of Chipping Sodbury. Large garden designed four years ago. Still in the process of being created. Mixed and herbaceous borders; many old-fashioned and climbing roses;

conservatories and orangery; walled kitchen garden recreated in Victorian style ¼m from house with a new glass house. TEAS. *Adm £1.50 OAPs/Chd £1 under 10 free. Sun June 20 (2-6)*

Barrow Court ❀ Barrow Gurney 5m SW Bristol. From Bristol take A370 and turn E onto B3130 towards Barrow Gurney; immediate right, Barrow Court Lane, then ½m, turn R through Lodge archway. 2 acres of formal gardens, designed by Inigo Thomas in 1890. Architectural garden, with sculpture and pavilions; arboretum; on going renovations to paths; stonework, replanted yew hedging and parterres. C17 E-shaped house (not open). Parking limited. TEAS. *Adm £1 Chd 50p. Sun May 23 (2-6)*

Bedford House ✗❀ (Mrs M D Laverack) 16 Wellington Terrace, Clevedon. 12m W of Bristol (Junction 20 off M5). Follow signs to seafront and Pier. From Pier, turn N up Marine Parade into Wellington Terrace (B3124). No 16 is on L (sea) side. A terraced cliff garden overlooking the Bristol Channel, designed to suit steep contours and its setting in a splendid seascape; also illustrates gardening in sea winds. Steep steps down to each terrace, also enjoyable from above. Featured on HTV. TEAS. *Adm £1 Chd free. Easter Sun, Mon, April 11, 12 Sun, Bank Hol Mon, May 30, 31, Sun June 20 (2-6)*

Bourne House &✗❀ (Mr & Mrs Christopher Thomas) 12m S Bristol. N of Burrington. Turning off A38 signposted Blagdon-Burrington; 2nd turning L. 4 acres, and 2 paddocks. Stream with waterfalls & lily pond; mature trees, and shrubs. Herbaceous border, roses; bulbs. Teas at Burrington Combe Cafe (1m). *Adm £1 Chd free. Sun April 18 (2-6)*

Brackenwood Garden Centre Woodland Garden ⚅❀ (Mr & Mrs John Maycock) 131 Nore Rd, Portishead. From Bristol A369 (10m). M5 Junc 19. Walk lies behind Brackenwood Garden Centre open daily 9-5. **Tel 0275 843484**, 1m from Portishead on coast rd to Clevedon. Woodland garden covering 6 acres and rising steeply through heavy woodland with superb views over the Bristol Channel to Wales and The Severn Bridge. Rhododendrons and Camellias provide a foil to Japanese Maples, rare trees and shrubs, woodland pools, black swans, bluebells and primroses add to the unspoilt beauty of the woodland. TEAS. *Adm £1 Chd 50p. Sat, Sun, Mon, Tues, Wed April 24, 25, 26, 27, 28 (9-5) (Sun 10-5)*

Brewery House ⚅❀ (John and Ursula Brooke) 2½m S of Bath off A367, L onto B3110, take 2nd R to Southstoke or bus to Cross Keys. House is ¼m down Southstoke Lane. Please park where signed and walk down. ⅔-acre garden on 2 levels. Fine views; top garden walled. Many unusual plants, species and other clematis. Vegetable garden with raised beds. Water garden. All organic. Partly suitable for wheelchairs. TEAS in aid of Southstoke Village Hall. *Adm 80p Chd free. Sats June 19 July 10 (2-6). Also open by appt May & Sept* **Tel 0225 833153**

Brook Cottage ᬗ⚅❀ (Mr & Mrs J S Ledbury) Upper Langford. 13m S Bristol on A368 NW of Burrington Combe, adjacent to the Blagdon Water Garden Centre. Mature garden of 2½ acres with stream. Interesting collection of trees, shrubs and spring bulbs. Walled garden with good selection of fruit trees. TEAS in aid of St John's Church. *Adm £1 Chd free. Sun April 4 (2-6)*

Brooklands ⚅❀ (Mr & Mrs Patrick Stevens) Burnett. 2m S Keynsham on B3116. Turn R into Burnett Village. 1½-acre garden; mature trees and variety of ornamental shrubs; rose garden; herbaceous border; recent planting of shrub roses; fine views of distant Mendip Hills. TEAS in aid of St Michaels Church, Burnett. *Adm £1 Chd free. Sun June 27 (10-6) Wed June 30 (2-7)*

¶**Churchill Court** ᬗ⚅❀ (Mr & Mrs J Murray) Church Lane, Churchill. 15m SW of Bristol on A38. Churchill Court lies between the comprehensive school and St John's Church in Church Lane. 1m from Churchill traffic lights. 2 acres of garden around an historically interesting house set against a backdrop of a Norman Church. Herbaceous borders, rock garden, rose garden, hardy fuchsia garden, range of unusual trees and shrubs, interesting mature specimen trees, organic kitchen garden feature in this beautiful setting. TEAS in aid of St John's Church Kneeler Project. *Adm £1.50 Chd free. Sun June 6 (2-6)*

Clifton Gardens Bristol. Close to Clifton Suspension Bridge. *Combined adm £1.50 Chd 25p. Sun June 6 (2-6)*
  9 Sion Hill ⚅❀ (Mr & Mrs R C Begg) Entrance from Sion Lane. Small walled town garden, densely planted; climbing & herbaceous plants; herb garden; old roses

Regular Openers. Too many days to include in diary. Usually there is a wide range of plants giving year-round interest. See head of county section for the name and garden description for times etc.

¶**16 Sion Hill** ᬗ⚅ (Drs Cameron and Ros Kennedy) Entrance via green door in Sion Lane, at side of No 16. Small pretty town garden with pond, several interesting shrubs and trees
17 Sion Hill ᬗ⚅❀ (Mr & Mrs P Gray) Entrance from Sion Lane. Town garden with trees and shrubs. TEAS in aid of Clifton and Hotwells Improvement Society (Lookout Scheme)

Coley Court ⚅❀ (Mrs M J Hill) Coley, East Harptree, 8m N of Wells. Take B3114 through East Harptree, turn L, signed Coley and Hinton Blewitt. From A39 at Chewton Mendip take B3114, 2m, sign on right, Coley, Hinton Blewitt, follow lane 400yds to white house on left before bridge. 1-acre; open lawn, stone walls, spring bulbs; 1-acre old Somerset orchard. Early Jacobean house (not open). TEA. *Adm 70p Chd 30p. Sun April 11 (2-6)*

Coombe Dingle Gardens ᬗ 4m NW of Bristol centre. From Portway down Sylvan Way, turn left into the Dingle and Grove Rd. From Westbury-on-Trym, Canford Lane sharp right at beginning of Westbury Lane. From Bristol over Downs, Parrys Lane, Coombe Lane; turn left and sharp right into the Dingle and Grove Rd. TEAS **Hillside**. *Combined adm £1 Chd free (Share to Friends of Blaise). Sun, Mon May 2, 3 (2-6)*
  Hillside ᬗ (Mrs C M Luke) 42 Grove Rd. 2 acres late Georgian lay-out. Victorian rose garden; fine trees, shrubs. Walled kitchen garden
  Pennywell ❀ (Mr & Mrs D H Baker) Grove Rd. 2 acres; varied collection trees and shrubs inc 50ft span flowering cherry; rockery, organic kitchen garden. Views over adjoining Blaise Castle Estate, Kingsweston Down and the Trym Valley. Exhibition of sculpture by Mary Donington. Plant stall (in aid of Friends of Blaise)

Crowe Hall (John Barratt Esq) Widcombe. 1m SE of Bath. Left up Widcombe Hill, off A36, leaving White Hart on right. Large varied garden; fine trees, lawns, spring bulbs, series of enclosed gardens cascading down steep hillside. Italienate terracing and Gothick Victorian grotto contrast with park-like upper garden. Dramatic setting, with spectacular views of Bath. DOGS welcome. TEAS. *Adm £1 Chd 30p. Suns May 9, 23 Aug 15, for NGS Suns April 18, June 6 (2-6)*

Doynton House ᬗ❀ (Mrs C E Pitman) Doynton. 8m E of Bristol, ¾m NE of A420 at E end of Wick. Mature, old-fashioned 2-acre garden with herbaceous borders, shrubs and lawns. TEAS. *Adm £1 Chd 20p. Sun June 20 (2-6)*

Dyrham Park ⚅❀ (The National Trust) 8m N of Bath. 12m E of Bristol. Approached from Bath-Stroud Road (A46), 2m S of Tormarton interchange with M4, exit 18. Situated on W side of late C17 house. Herbaceous borders, yews clipped as buttresses, ponds and cascade, parish church set on terrace. Niches and carved urns. Long lawn to old west entrance Deer Park. TEAS. *Adm incl house £4.70 Chd £2.30. Sun Aug 8 (12-5)*

¶**Gardener's Cottage** ⚅❀ (Mr & Mrs M J Chillcott) Wick Lane, Upton Cheyney. 6m NW of Bath; 8m SE of Bristol off A431, turn L near Bitton signposted Upton Cheyney; ¾m up Brewery Hill, first turning L after Upton

Inn, parking at Upton Inn. 1-acre part walled garden, formerly kitchen garden of early C18 manor house, redesigned by present owners within the last 6 yrs with shrubs, herbaceous borders, pergolas, clematis and roses. Also large pond and rock garden, bog area and other water features. TEAS. *Adm £1 Chd free. Sun June 20 (2-6)*

Goldney Hall ❦ (University of Bristol) Lower Clifton Hill, Bristol. At top of Constitution Hill, Clifton. 9-acre Grade II Outstanding Garden, developed 1731–68 by Thomas Goldney, Bristol merchant; fine period grotto; terrace, bastion, tower, orangery and parterre; old-world garden with many species of the period. Cream TEAS in orangery. *Adm £1.50 OAPs/Chd 75p (Share to Goldney Restoration Fund). Sun May 2 (2-6)*

Harptree Court &❦ (Mr & Mrs Richard Hill) East Harptree, 8m N of Wells via A39 Bristol Rd to Chewton Mendip; then B3114 to East Harptree, gates on left. From Bath via A368 Weston-super-Mare Rd to West Harptree. Large garden; fine old trees in lovely setting; woodland walks; handsome stone bridge; subterranean passage, Doric temple, lily pond and paved garden. TEAS. *Adm £1 Chd free. Sun June 13 (2-6)*

Hazel Cottage ❦ (Dr & Mrs Brandon Lush) Lower Hazel 700 yds W of Rudgeway from A38; 10m N of Bristol. ½-acre cottage garden in rural setting with wide variety of plants and shrubs including alpines and some unusual varieties. TEAS. *Adm £1 Chd free (Share to Bristol Research into Alzheimer's and Care of the Elderly). Sun June 6 (2-6)*

¶**Highfield House** &❦ (Mr & Mrs R A Webb) Chew Magna. 7m S Bristol. A37 Bristol-Wells Rd; at top of Pensford Hill take B3130 to Chew Magna and proceed to top of High Street. Large C19 garden extensively replanted during the last 4 yrs by the present owners. Mixed shrub and herbaceous borders; open lawns containing some unusual specimens. Fine stone-walled vegetable and flower garden; other interest-small flock of pedigree Hampshire Downs. TEAS. *Adm £1 Chd free. Sun June 20 (2-6)*

Iford Manor see Wiltshire

Jasmine Cottage ❦❦ (Mr & Mrs Michael Redgrave) 26 Channel Rd, Clevedon. 12m W of Bristol (junction 20 off M5). Follow signs to seafront and Pier, continue N on B3124, past Walton Park Hotel, turn R at St Mary's Church. Garden ⅓-acre created for interest in all seasons by owners from a wooded shelter belt. Old-fashioned roses; pergola; mixed shrub borders; island beds; pond and potager. Development continues with new plantings of unusual herbaceous, tender perennials and climbers. Featured in HTV News and BBC Points West. TEAS. *Adm £1 Chd free. Suns March 28, April 25, May 30, June 27, July 25, Aug 29, Sept 12 (2-6) Every Thurs April 15 to Aug 26 (2-5.30). Open by appt* Tel Clevedon (0275) 871850

23 Kelston Road ❦❦ (Basil Williams) 3m NW of Bath on A431 to Bitton. ⅓-acre terraced plantsman's garden on 4 levels; replanted since 1982; bulbs, rockery, herbaceous, old-fashioned roses, vegetables; acid beds; greenhouse; conservatory; good views. Featured on Channel 4 TV Oct 91. TEAS. Please observe parking advice. *Adm £1 Chd 60p (Share to All Saints Church, Weston). Suns, April 4, July 11 (2-6). Also by appt* Tel 0225 423904

Langford Court &❦❦ (Sir John & Lady Wills) Langford. 11m S of Bristol on A38, drive gates off Langford Lane, signed Burrington. To the N of the A38. Large garden in lovely setting; fine old trees; topiary; orangery; shrubs; daffodils and crocuses. TEAS in aid of St Peter's Hospice Bristol. *Adm £1 Chd free. Sat, Sun March 13, 14 (2-5)*

Lower Failand Gardens &❦ Lower Failand, 6m SW of Bristol. Take B3128 out of Bristol to Clevedon Rd. Via Clerk-Combe Hill, turn right down Oxhouse Lane opp garage; or turn off M5 Junc 19 towards Bristol. 1st R through Portbury, turn left into Failand Lane.

Church Farm (Mr & Mrs N Slade) L past Church then R into private rd. House is 1st R. Parking adj to Church. 3-acre small holding garden started in 1974; run on organic principles; large collection clematis, unusual plants and trees. TEAS May 22, 23 only. *Adm £1 Chd 25p (Share to Intermediate Technology). Sat, Sun May 22, 23; Sun June 27 (2-5.30). Also open by appt* Tel 0275 373033

Failand Court (Mr & Mrs B Nathan) 1m along Oxhouse Lane. Park in Oxhouse Lane and at church. 1¼-acre mature garden originally landscaped by Sir Edward Fry. Further developed by Miss Agnes Fry. Interesting trees, shrubs and vegetable garden. TEAS. *Adm £1 Chd 25p. Sat Sun May 22, 23 (2-5.30)*

¶**Madron** ❦❦ (Mr & Mrs Martin Carr) Ostlings Lane, Bathford. Approx 3½m, E of Bath close to A4. At Batheaston roundabout take A363 Bradford-upon-Avon Rd; then 1st turning L, Ostlings Lane is immediately on R alongside Crown Inn. At top of short rise 100yds stone pillars on L are entrance to Madron-second house on L along drive. Park in village. 1¼-acre garden created over 9 yrs from a derelict hillside overlooking the Avon valley and surrounding hills. Borders and banks with shrubs, hardy and tender perennials, with particlar emphasis on plant and colour associatons; newly created water garden, all set amidst fine lawns with conifer and deciduous trees. Featured in Practical Gardening, April 1992. TEAS by arrangement. *Adm £1 Chd free. Thurs, June, July, Aug by prior appt only (2.30-5.30)* Tel 0225 859792

The Manor House &❦❦ (Mr & Mrs Simon Wills) Walton-in-Gordano, 2m NE of Clevedon. Entrance on N side of B3124, Clevedon to Portishead Rd, just by houses on roadside nearest Clevedon. Clevedon-Portishead buses stop in Village. 4-acres; plantsman's garden, featured in 'Country Life' 1989, trees, shrubs, herbaceous, bulbs and alpines, mostly labelled. Coaches by appt only. TEAS (Suns, Mons only) (in aid of St Peters Hospice Bristol). *Adm £1, Acc. chd under 14 free (Share to St Peter's Hospice, Bristol). April 14 to Sept 16 and Oct 20 to Nov 4 every Wed & Thurs (10-4); Mon April 12; Sun, Mon May 2, 3, Suns June 6, July 25, Aug 29, Mon Aug 30 (2-6). Open by appt all year.* Tel 0275 872067

By Appointment Gardens. See head of county section

Orchard House ✿✿ (Rear-Adm & Mrs Hugh Tracy) Claverton, 3½m from Bath on A36; follow signpost to Claverton Village. Or ½m down hill from American Museum. Bus stop Claverton. 2½-acre plantsman's garden; botanical interest combined with attractive and informal layout; collections of alpines, ground-cover, silver plants; rock gardens, herbaceous borders, lawns, shrubs, views. Small Nursery. *Adm £1 Chd free. Weds May 5, 19, June 2, 16, (2-6). Groups welcome by appt May to Sept* Tel 0225 465650

Portland Lodge ✿✿ (Mr & Mrs F S Jennett) 8 Knole Close. About 1m from Almondsbury interchange. Turn off A38 to Lower Almondsbury on Over Lane, right at War Memorial, left into Pound Lane and left again into Knole Close. Small, windswept hillside garden with panoramic views over R. Severn. Designed by owner since 1979 to create a sheltered haven. Garden has 3 levels; circular lawns and densely planted mixed borders of small trees, shrubs and perennials. Gravel used to improve drainage on heavy clay soil. *Adm £1 Chd free (Share to Meal-A-Day Fund). Wed April 28*

¶Publow Gardens ੬✿✿ 7m S of Bristol. A37 Bristol-Wells to Pensford Bridge. Turn L off A37 and L again into Publow Lane and ½m to Publow Church. TEAS at The Old Vicarage in aid of All Saints, Publow. *Combined adm £1.50 Chd free. Sat, Sun July 17, 18 (2-5)*
  ¶Bellevue (Mr & Mrs J A Heaford) opp The Old Vicarage. Mature 1¼-acre garden with brook below steep bank; wide variety of plants; trees, shrubs and vegetables, extensively replanted by present owners since 1980. Some streamside and bank planting with moisture loving and drought tolerant plants
  ¶The Old Vicarage ✿✿ (Mr & Mrs D Woodford) 2-acre mature garden in lovely setting adjacent to C14 church. Open lawns, mixed borders, pretty walled garden and large orchard. Many stone features

Severn View ✿✿ (Mr & Mrs Eric Hilton) Grovesend, 1½m E of Thornbury. On A38 on Bristol side of Wye Vale Nurseries. (Grovesend is postal address, but ignore signpost to it) 1-acre; notable for large rock garden with wide range of alpine plants, many rare, grown in screes, raised beds, troughs, rock walls, peat beds etc. Also shrubs, herbaceous borders; 3 alpine houses and many frames. Fine views of Severn Valley. *Adm 80p Acc chd free (Share to Thornbury Hospital). Suns May 16, 23, 30, June 6, 13 (2-6)*

Sherborne Garden (Pear Tree House) ੬✿ (Mr & Mrs John Southwell) Litton. 15m S of Bristol, 7m N of Wells. On B3114 Litton to Harptree, 7m past Ye Olde Kings Arms. 3½ acres landscaped into several gardens of distinctive character; cottage garden; rock garden; large ponds with moisture gardens; pinetum; mixed wood. Collection of hollies (190 varieties); acers, birches; species roses. Featured on TV 'Gardeners World'. Picnic area. TEA. *Adm £1.50 Chd free. Suns, Mons June 14 to Sept 6. For NGS Sun, April 11, Homemade TEAS on Sun June 13, Oct 10 (11-6.30). By appt; parties by arrangement* Tel 0761 241220

Regular Openers. See head of county section.

Springfield Barn ✿✿ (Mr & Mrs H Joseph Woods) Upton Cheyney, Bitton, 5m NW of Bath; 8m SE of Bristol. A431 Bath-Bristol turn off for Upton Cheyney. 500yds approx on R beyond row of cottages. 1¼-acre garden, started 1960, designed and planted with up to six hundred species, many from own propagation, by present owners. Many unusual plants. Seen in Bristol Evening Post and featured on HTV. TEAS by arrangement. *Adm £1 Chd 25p. By appt May to Sept. Parties, horticultural societies, school parties particularly welcome.* Tel 0272 322129

¶Stanton Drew Gardens ੬✿ 7m S Bristol A37 Bristol-Wells; at top of Pensford Hill take B3130 to Chew Magna. After 1m turn towards Stanton Drew at thatched round house. Cautiously negotiate humpbacked bridge and the gardens are just after the bridge. Parking is supervised. TEAS in aid of Village Funds. *Combined adm £1.50 Chd free. Sun July 11 (12-6)*
  ¶Rectory Farm House (Dr & Mrs J P Telling) ½-acre garden surrounding C15 Church House later used as a farmhouse. Garden completely redesigned and replanted over the past 18 mths. Trees, shrubs, mixed borders, pond and new rock garden
  Stanton Court (Dr R J Price & Partners) A new garden established from 1986 to complement the recreational needs of a Nursing Home. Ideal for disabled visitors. Access for elderly persons a priority. Our aim is minimal maintenance with maximum variety. The wide range of plants have been largely donated by the locality. Pond; terrace garden; patio; large sweeping borders; cut flower beds and fruits in season. Mature copper beech and cedars

Stanton Prior Gardens ੬✿✿ 6m from Bath on A39 Wells Rd; at Marksbury turn L to Stanton Prior; gardens either side of Church. Ploughmans lunch & cream TEAS. *Combined adm £1.50 Chd free. Every Thurs April 8 to Sept 30 (12-5) for NGS Sun Aug 1 (11-5); and by appt all year* Tel 0761 470384
  Church Farm (Mr & Mrs L Hardwick) Herbaceous borders, open lawn, rock garden, wild area with ¼-acre pond; ducks and geese
  The Old Rectory (Lt Col & Mrs Patrick Mesquita) 1-acre garden incl mediaeval pond. Landscaped and replanted since 1983, with unusual shrubs and plants, apple and pear arches and pergola with white roses and clematis
  9 Stanton Prior ✿ (Mrs J Groom) Small cottage garden created in 1987. Rockeries, mixed borders, pond

Tockington Gardens ੬ 10m N of Bristol. From A38, turn L signposted Tockington/Olveston after bridging M4. R at Triangle in Tockington and L 50yds on — Old Down Hill. L at top of hill then immediate R. Alternatively follow brown signs to Oldown. TEAS available at Kitchen Garden. *Combined adm £1.50 OAP 70p Chd free (Share to ERIC and Bristol Age Care Concern). Combined open days Sun March 21, Sept 19, Weds June 23, Sept 15 (2-6)*
  Old Down House (Mr & Mrs Robert Bernays) 5-acres divided into small formal and informal gardens by hedges and walls; topiary, shrubs; azaleas, rhododendrons, camellias; extensive lawns; rock garden; fine trees (weeping beeches etc); herbaceous borders, semi-wild areas, fine views to Severn and Welsh Hills

The Brake ❀ (Mr & Mrs M Romain) Vicarage Lane. 1½-acres with fine views of Severn Estuary; various organic methods used; long mixed borders with emphasis on plants that thrive on dry, exposed hillside; woodland garden with interesting ground cover, bulbs, cyclamen

¶**Tranby House** ✿❀ (Paul & Jan Barkworth) Norton Lane, Whitchurch. ½m S of Whitchurch Village. Leave Bristol on A37 Wells Rd, through Whitchurch Village 1st turning on R, signposted Norton Malreward. Parking in field at junction of A37 and Norton Lane. Garden is 200yds along Norton Lane. 1¼-acre informal garden, designed and planted to encourage wildlife. Includes trees, shrubs, flower borders, ponds and meadow area; flowers from the garden are pressed and used to create pressed flower pictures. Partly suitable for wheelchairs. TEA. *Adm £1 Chd free (Share to Avon Wildlife Trust). Sun Aug 1 (2-6)*

University of Bristol Botanic Garden ♿✿❀ Bracken Hill, North Rd, Leigh Woods, 2m W of Bristol. From Bristol via Clifton cross suspension bridge North Rd is 1st right. 5-acre garden with about 4,000 species illustrating diversity of the plant kingdom; special collections of hebe, cistus, ferns, sempervivum, many British plants; 5,000sq ft of glass; large rock garden. TEAS. *Adm £1 Chd 50p (Share to Friends of Bristol University Botanic Garden). ▲Suns July 11, Sept 12 (2-5) also by appt all year* **Tel 0272 733682**

The Urn Cottage ✿❀ (Mr A C & Dr L A Rosser) 19 Station Road, Charfield. 3m W of Wotton-under-edge and 3m E of M5 exit 14. In Charfield turn off main road at the The Railway Tavern, then 400 yds on L: short walk from car park. ¾-acre cottage gdn made from scratch by owners since 1982 and still developing. Natural materials used throughout to compliment stone built cottage and country setting. Wide variety of plants, mixed borders with colour groupings, herbaceous border, herb bed, small streamside gardens, vegetables. TEAS. *Adm £1 Chd 10p. Sun May 30 (12-6) Parties by appt all year* **Tel 0453 843156**

Vine House ♿❀ (Prof & Mrs T F Hewer) Henbury, 4m N of Bristol. Bus stop: Salutation Inn, Henbury, 50yds. 2-acres; trees, shrubs, water garden, bulbs, naturalised garden landscaped and planted by present owners since 1946. *Adm £1 OAPs/Chd 50p (Share to Friends of Blaise). Sat, Sun, April 17, 18; Sun, Mon, May 30, 31 (2-6); also by appt all year* **Tel Bristol 0272 503573**

West Tyning ♿❀ (Mr & Mrs G S Alexander) Beach. From Bath (6m) or Bristol (7m) on A43l. From Bitton village turn N up Golden Valley, signposted Beach. Continue up lane for 2m to Wick–Upton Cheyney Crossroads, turn R up Wick Lane for 200 yards. Parking in adjacent field. 1¼-acre garden, much altered through the years since 1986 aiming for a more informal woodsey look, easy plants. New shrubs, trees, roses, geraniums and other ground cover. Rock garden, curved mixed borders, woodland garden with stone paths and circular beds, planting continuing in newly cleared copse. TEAS. *Adm £1 Chd free. Sun May 16 (2-6)*

Windmill Cottage ✿❀ (Alan & Pam Harwood) Hillside Rd, Backwell. 8m SW of Bristol. Take A370 out of Bristol to Backwell, ½m past Xrds/traffic lights, turn L into Hillside Rd. Parking available in Backwell recreation area, on R hand side of main rd (10 min walk). Hillside Rd is single track lane with no parking (unless by prior arrangement or special reasons). Parking also at New Inn. Into a 2-acre plot put a plentiful variety of plants, add to this a pinch of knowledge and a sprinkling of wildflowers, together with a reasonable amount of ground cover; blend in some colour and a generous dash of fragrance. Bind the whole thing together with a large collection of clematis, balanced with a proportion of vegetables. A good supply of enthusiasm to be added at regular intervals, allow to develop over a period of 8 to 10 yrs, adjusting quantities as the ingredients mature and set into a rocky outcrop. TEAS. *Adm £1 Chd 50p. Weds May 19, June 16, Sept 29 (2-5); Thurs June 24, July 1, 29 (6.30-9); Fris July 16, Aug 20 (2-5). Groups welcome by appt* **Tel 0275 463492**

Bedfordshire

Hon County Organiser: Mrs S Whitbread, The Mallowry, Riseley, Bedford MK44 1EF

DATES OF OPENING

By appointment
For telephone numbers and other details see garden descriptions

88 Castlehill Rd, Middle End, Totternhoe

Seal Point, Luton

Regular opening
For details see garden descriptions

Toddington Manor, Toddington

April 4 Sunday
Broadfields, Keysoe Row

April 11 Sunday
King's Arms Path Gardens, Ampthill

April 25 Sunday
Howard's House, Cardington
Woburn Abbey, Woburn

May 16 Sunday
Odell Castle, nr Bedford
May 23 Sunday
Aspley Guise Gardens,
Bletchley
May 30 Sunday
88 Castlehill Rd, Middle End,
Totternhoe
Seal Point, Luton
Woodleys Farm House,
Melchbourne

June 6 Sunday
Southill Park, nr Biggleswade
June 13 Sunday
Toddington Manor, Toddington
Woburn Abbey, Woburn
June 20 Sunday
Grove Lodge, 6 Deepdale, Potton
Odell Castle, nr Bedford
July 4 Sunday
88 Castlehill Rd, Middle End,
Totternhoe

Luton Hoo Gardens, Luton
July 11 Sunday
47 Hexton Rd, Barton-le-Clay
The Rectory, Barton-le-Clay
Wayside Cottage, Barton-le-Clay
July 17 Saturday
Broadfields, Keysoe Row
August 1 Sunday
Toddington Manor, Toddington

DESCRIPTIONS OF GARDENS

Aspley Guise Gardens 2m SW of M1 (Exit 13) towards Woburn Sands. Entrance from Church Rd. *Combined adm £2 Chd ½ price. Sun May 23 (2-6)*
    Aspley House ✕❀ (Mr & Mrs C I Skipper) House on E side of village. 5 acres; shrubs and lawns. William and Mary house (not open). TEA
    The Rookery ✕ (C R Randall Esq) 5 acres; rhododendrons and woodland

Broadfields & (Mr & Mrs Izzard) Keysoe, Row East. Leave Bedford on Kimbolton Rd B660 approx 8½m. Turn R at Keysoe Xrds by White Horse public house ½m on right. 3 acres of herbaceous borders; mature trees; shrubs; vegetable and fruit gardens. TEAS. *Adm £1 Chd 50p. Sun April 4, Sat July 17 (2-6)*

¶88 Castlehill Road ✕❀ (Chris & Carole Jell) Middle End, Totternhoe. 2m W of Dunstable, R turn off B489 Aston-Clinton Rd. Fronting main rd approx ½m through village. Elevated position with fine views across Aylesbury Vale and Chilterns. Adjoining Totternhoe Knolls Nature Reserve. ½-acre, S sloping on limestone and clay, entirely created by owners. Plantsman garden for all seasons; designed as small gardens within a garden since 1986; shrubs; climbers and herbaceous. TEAS. *Adm £1 Chd free. Suns May 30, July 4 (2-6). Also by appt Tel 0525 220780*

¶Grove Lodge & (Peter Wareing & Jean Venning) 6 Deepdale, Potton. 2m E of Sandy on 1042 towards Potton, past RSPB Reserve, downhill to Xrds. L at 'Locomotive' - lane to TV mast; first house on R. 1½-acre sandy hillside garden; conifers; heathers, shrubs, incl rhododendrons, climbing roses, herbaceous border, orchard with wild flowers, rockery banks with pond. TEAS in aid of R.A.T.S. *Adm £1 Chd 50p. Sun June 20 (2-6)*

¶47 Hexton Road &❀ (Mrs S H Horsler) Barton-le-Clay. 6m N of Luton on the B655 Barton-le-Clay to Hitchin Rd (Hitchin 5m). Set in ¼ acre cottage garden with mixed borders. *Adm £1 Chd 50p. Sun July 11 (2-6)*

Howard's House (Humphrey Whitbread Esq) Cardington. 2m SE of Bedford. Walled and flower gardens; flowering cherries and clematis. Tea Bedford. *Adm £1 Chd 50p. Sun April 25 (2-6)*

King's Arms Path Gardens Ampthill Town Council (Mrs N W Hudson) Ampthill. Entrance opp. Market Sq. Ampthill, down Kings Arms Yard. Small woodland garden of about 1½ acres created out of derelict ground by plantsman the late William Nourish. Trees, shrubs, bulbs. Maintained by 'The Friends of the Garden.' TEAS. *Adm 50p Chd 15p. For NGS Sun April 11 (2.30-5)*

Luton Hoo Gardens ✕ (The Wernher Family) Luton; entrance at Park St gates. Bus: Green line 707, 717, 727 London-Luton Garage: London Country 321 Watford-Luton via St Albans to Luton Garage. Landscape garden by Capability Brown. House built by Robert Adam in 1767. Wernher Collection. Restaurant. NO DOGS. TEAS. *Adm gardens only £1.85 OAP £1.60 Chd 60p. For NGS Sun July 4 (2-6)*

Odell Castle (The Rt Hon Lord Luke) NW of Bedford. From A6 turn W through Sharnbrook; from A428, N through Lavendon and Harrold. Station: Bedford 10m. Terrace and lower garden down to R. Ouse. House built 1962 on old site, using original stone. TEAS. *Adm £1 Chd free. Suns May 16, June 20 (2-6)*

The Rectory & (Canon Peter Whittaker) Barton-Le-Clay. Barton-Le-Clay is 6m N of Luton. From A6 turn E on to B655 then to Church Rd. Bus Bedford to Luton. 2 acres with background of Chilterns; moat, rockery, mature trees,lawns; overlooked by C12 church. TEA. *Adm £1 Chd 50p. Sun July 11 (2-6)*

Seal Point (Mrs Danae Johnston) 7 Wendover Way. In NE Luton, turning N off Stockingstone Rd into Felstead Way. ⅔ acre, plantswoman's garden on sloping site designed for privacy plus views, water, trees, shrubs, climbers and herbaceous. 'Gardeners World' '86. 'Practical Gardening' Oct 89. TEAS. *Adm £1 Chd 20p. Sun May 30 (2-6) also open by appointment Tel 0582 26841*

Southill Park &❀ (Mr & Mrs S C Whitbread) 5m SW of Biggleswade. Large garden, rhododendrons, renovated conservatory. *Adm £1 Chd 50p. Sun June 6 (2-6).*

Toddington Manor &❀ (Sir Neville & Lady Bowman-Shaw) 1m NW of Toddington, 1m from M1 (exit 12); 1st right in village (signed Milton Bryan); house ½m on right. Restored by present owners; 2 ponds plus stream running through garden; large woods with 2 lakes; rare breeds centre for cattle (3 breeds), sheep (7 breeds), goats (2 breeds), vintage tractor collection (some working), cricket match on private pitch. TEAS. *Adm £2 Chd £1. Every Bank Hol Mons and 3rd Sat in month May to Sept. For NGS Suns June 13, Aug 1 (12-6)*

¶**Wayside Cottage** & (Mr Denis Hibburd) Barton-le-Clay. On sharp bend halfway round Manor Rd which goes from Bedford Rd to Hexton Rd. Bedford Rd goes E. Hexton Rd goes N. ⅓ acre of undulating gardens with lawns, paving stone features round an old world cottage. Trees and herbaceous border, water garden, summer house and other hidden corners. *Adm £1 Chd 50p. Sun July 11 (2-6)*

Woburn Abbey ⚘ (The Marquess of Tavistock) Woburn. Woburn Abbey is situated 1½m from Woburn Village, which is on the A4012 almost midway from junctions 12 and 13 of the M1 motorway. 22 acres of private garden originally designed by Wyattville, with recent restoration of the The Duchess' rose garden. Unique hornbeam maze with C18 temple by Chambers. TEAS. *Adm £1 Chd free. Suns April 25, June 13 (11-5.30)*

Woodleys Farm House &⚘❀ (Hon Mrs Hugh Lawson Johnston) Melchbourne. Leave A6 10m N of Bedford, or 4m S of Rushden. House reached by lime avenue before reaching village of Melchbourne. Small garden 1½ acres, with roses, lawns, shrubs and herbaceous plants. TEAS. *Adm £1 Chd free. Sun May 30 (2-6)*

By Appointment Gardens. These owners do not have a fixed opening day usually because they do not like crowds or have insufficient parking space. Owner will often give guided tour.

Berkshire

Hon County Organiser:　　　Mrs M A Henderson, Ridings, Kentons Lane, Wargrave, RG10 8PB
Asst Hon County Organisers:　(Central) Mrs J Granville, Holly Copse, Goring Heath, Nr Reading
　　　　　　　　　　　　　　The Hon Mrs C Willoughby, Buckhold Farm, Pangbourne
　　　　　　　　　　　　　　(NW) Mrs G Elmes, Stable Cottage, Donnington Grove, Newbury, RG14 2LA
　　　　　　　　　　　　　　(SW) Mrs P Meigh, Fishponds, West Woodhay, Nr Newbury
Hon County Treasurer:　　　Michael Payne, Scotlands Farm, Cockpole Green, Nr Wargrave, RG10 8QP

DATES OF OPENING

By appointment
For telephone numbers and other details see garden descriptions

Blencathra, Finchampstead
Hurst Lodge, nr Reading
Jasmine House, nr Windsor
Meadow House, nr Newbury
Simms Farm House, Mortimer, nr Reading

Regular openings
For details see garden description
Meadow House, nr Newbury. Every Wed May 12 to Aug 11 except June 23

February 24 Wednesday
　The Old Rectory, Burghfield, nr Reading
March 7 Sunday
　Old Rectory Cottage, nr Pangbourne
March 21 Sunday
　Foxgrove, Enborne, nr Newbury
March 31 Wednesday
　The Old Rectory, Burghfield, nr Reading

April 4 Sunday
　Foxgrove, Enborne, nr Newbury
　Old Rectory Cottage, nr Pangbourne
　Welford Park, nr Newbury
April 11 Sunday
　Kirby House, Inkpen,
　West Woodhay House, Inkpen
April 12 Monday
　Swallowfield Park, nr Reading
April 18 Sunday
　Blencathra, Finchampstead
　Folly Farm, nr Reading
April 25 Sunday
　Odney Club, Cookham
　The Old Rectory, Farnborough, Wantage
April 28 Wednesday
　The Old Rectory, Burghfield, nr Reading
May 2 Sunday
　Oakfield Gardens, nr Mortimer
　The Old Mill, Aldermaston
May 3 Monday
　Foxgrove, Enborne, nr Newbury
May 5 Wednesday
　Frogmore Gardens, Windsor
May 6 Thursday
　Frogmore Gardens, Windsor
May 9 Sunday
　Bussock Wood, nr Newbury
　Jasmine House, nr Windsor

Old Rectory Cottage, nr Pangbourne
　Scotlands, Cockpole Green
　Silwood Park, Ascot
May 16 Sunday
　Alderwood House, Greenham Common
　Finchampstead Gardens
　Hurst Lodge, nr Reading ‡
　The Old Rectory, Farnborough, Wantage
　Reynolds Farm, nr Twyford ‡
　Sunningdale Park, Ascot
May 23 Sunday
　Aldermaston Park, Aldermaston
　Bear Ash, Hare Hatch, nr Wargrave
　Beenham House, Beenham
　Blencathra, Finchampstead ‡
　Fox Steep, Crazies Hill
　Silwood Park, Ascot
　Stone House, Brimpton
　Wasing Place, Aldermaston
　Whiteknights, The Ridges, Finchampstead ‡
May 26 Wednesday
　The Old Rectory, Burghfield, nr Reading
May 30 Sunday
　Little Bowden, Pangbourne
　Simms Farm House, Mortimer, nr Reading

May 31 Monday
Combe Manor, Newbury
Folly Farm, nr Reading
Fox Hill, Inkpen,
June 5 Saturday
Englefield House, Theale
June 6 Sunday
Alderwood House, Greenham
Common
Englefield House, Theale
Mariners, Bradfield
Waltham Place, White Waltham
June 12 Saturday
Eton College, Windsor
June 13 Sunday
Basildon Park, Reading
Chieveley Gardens, nr Newbury
Peasemore Gardens
The Priory, nr Reading
Swallowfield Park, nr Reading
June 20 Sunday
Heads Farm, Chaddleworth
Meadow House, nr Newbury
Old Rectory Cottage, nr
Pangbourne

Summerfield House, Crazies Hill,
nr Wargrave
June 23 Wednesday
Rooksnest, Lambourn
June 27 Sunday
Alderwood House, Greenham
Common
Folly Farm, nr Reading
Hazelby House, nr Newbury
The Old Rectory, Farnborough,
Wantage ‡
Woolley Park, nr Wantage ‡
June 30 Wednesday
The Old Rectory, Burghfield, nr
Reading
July 4 Sunday
Stanford Dingley Village Gardens
July 11 Sunday
Chieveley Manor, nr Newbury
The Harris Garden, Reading
Little Bowden, Pangbourne ‡
Old Rectory Cottage, Pangbourne ‡
Wasing Place, Aldermaston
July 18 Sunday
Ockwells Manor, Maidenhead ‡

Stone House, Brimpton
Waltham Place, White Waltham ‡
July 25 Sunday
Bussock Mayne, nr Newbury
July 28 Wednesday
The Old Rectory, Burghfield, nr
Reading
August 25 Wednesday
The Old Rectory, Burghfield, nr
Reading
September 12 Sunday
Hurst Lodge, nr Reading
September 29 Wednesday
The Old Rectory, Burghfield, nr
Reading
October 3 Sunday
Scotlands, Cockpole Green
October 10 Sunday
Foxgrove, Enborne, nr
Newbury
October 17 Sunday
Silwood Park, Ascot
October 27 Wednesday
The Old Rectory, Burghfield, nr
Reading

DESCRIPTIONS OF GARDENS

Aldermaston Park ⅄❀ (Blue Circle Industries plc) Newbury 10m W; Reading 10m E; Basingstoke 8m S. 137-acres, surrounding Victorian Mansion (1849) with modern offices making interesting contrast of architecture. Fine trees; specimen rhododendrons and shrubs; large lawns; lakeside walk. TEA. *Adm £1 Chd 50p. Sun May 23 (10-4)*

Alderwood House ⅄❀ (Mr & Mrs P B Trier) Greenham Common. S of Newbury take A 339 towards Basingstoke for approx 3m. Turn L towards the Main Gates of RAF Greenham Common. Turn R immediately before gate along gravel path to house. Interesting 2½-acre garden started in 1904. On many levels with a number of rare trees and shrubs. Old roses, herbaceous border, conservatory and fine vegetable garden. TEAS. *Adm £1 Chd 50p. Suns May 16, June 6, 27 (2-6)*

Basildon Park ⅄ (Lord & Lady Iliffe; The National Trust) Lower Basildon, Reading. Between Pangbourne and Streatley, 7m NW of Reading on W of A329. Private garden designed and planted by Lady Iliffe with help of Lanning Roper. Mainly old roses but other interesting plants constantly being added by owner. TEAS in NT house. *Adm 50p.* ▲*For NGS Sun June 13 (2-6)*

Bear Ash ⅄❀ (Lord & Lady Remnant) Hare Hatch, 2m E of Wargrave. ½m N of A4 at Hare Hatch, between Reading and Maidenhead. 2-acres; charming garden overlooking parkland; new lake; silver and gold planting; shrub and specie roses. TEAS. *Adm £1 Chd free. Sun May 23 (2-6)*

Beenham House ⅄❀ (Prof & Mrs Gerald Benney) Beenham. ½-way between Reading and Newbury, 1m N of A4; entrance off Webbs Lane. 21 acres of grounds and garden; old Lebanon cedars, oaks, hornbeams; recent plantings. Good views of park and Kennett Valley. Regency house (not open). Coach parties by appt. TEAS. *Adm £1 Chd free (Share to St Mary's Church, Beenham). Sun May 23 (2-6)*

Blencathra ⅄❀ (Dr & Mrs F W Gifford) Finchampstead. Entrance from private drive at the NW end of Finchampstead Ridges on B3348 between Finchampstead War Memorial and Crowthorne Station. Parking on joint private drive or The Ridges. Disabled passengers may alight near the house. 11-acre garden which present owners started in 1964, is still being developed. Many varied mature trees; lawns; heathers; rhododendrons; azaleas; wide range of conifers; three small lakes and stream; bog areas and spring bulbs. Interesting throughout year. TEA. *Adm £1.50 Chd free. Suns April 18, May 23 (2-6) also open by appt - parties welcome.* **Tel 0734 734563** *see also* **Whiteknights**

¶**Bussock Mayne** ⅄ (Mr & Mrs C Povey) Snelsmore Common. 3m N of Newbury on B4494. A variety of specimen trees, herbaceous beds, shrubs, fine rock and water garden. Use of swimming pool and tennis court. Set in 5 acres. TEAS. *Adm £1 Chd 50p. Sun July 25 (2-6)*

Bussock Wood ❀ (Mr & Mrs W A Palmer) Snelsmore Common. 3m N of Newbury. On B4494 Newbury-Wantage Rd. Bluebells, fine trees and views; sunken garden with lily pond. Early Briton Camp. TEAS. *Adm 50p Chd 20p (Share to Winterbourne Parish Church). Sun May 9 (2-6)*

Chieveley Gardens ᴄ⚥ 5m N Newbury. Take A34 N, pass under M4, then L to Chieveley. Follow rd into High St. Chieveley House on R, Maypole Cottage further on L. *Combined adm £1 Chd free. Sun June 13 (2-6)*

Chieveley House (Lord & Lady Goff) Large walled garden containing substantial trees, yew hedges; herbaceous borders; sunken water garden. Listed house (not open). TEAS

Maypole Cottage (The Misses B & R Hartas Jackson) Attractive small garden, owner maintained with shrubs and plants of botanical interest

Chieveley Manor ᴄ⚥❀ (Mr & Mrs C J Spence) 5m N Newbury. Take A34 N pass under M4, then left to Chieveley. After ½m left up Manor Lane. Large garden with fine view over stud farm. Walled garden containing borders, shrubs and rose garden. Listed House (not open). TEAS. *Adm £1 Chd free (Share to St Mary's Church Chieveley). Sun July 11 (2-6)*

Cobwood House, Newbury see Hampshire

¶**Combe Manor** (Lady Mary Russell) Combe. Approx 10m from Newbury or from Andover. From M4 in Hungerford, turn L after passing under railway bridge; over cattle grid onto Hungerford Common; turn R 400 yds later and follow signs to Inkpen; pass The Swan on L, bear R at junction and then almost immediately L to Combe Gibbet and Combe. The Manor stands ½m from the village beside the church. 2 acres of lawns, borders, roses, shrubs and fruit trees. Walled garden with C17 gazebo. C11 church adjoining will be open. Teas at Fox Hill. *Combined adm with Fox Hill £1.50 Chd free. Mon May 31 (2-6)*

Englefield House ⚥❀ (Mr & Mrs W R Benyon) nr Theale. Entrance on A340. 7-acres of woodland garden with interesting variety of trees; shrubs; stream and water garden; formal terrace with fountain and borders. Commercial garden centre in village. Deer park. Part of garden suitable for wheelchairs. Home made TEAS Long Gallery NGS days only. Open every Mon all year, (10-dusk). *Adm £1.50 Chd free (Share to St Mark's Church).* ▲*For NGS Sat, Sun, June 5, 6 (2-6)*

Eton College Gardens ⚥❀ (Provost & Fellows). Stations: Windsor ¾m Eton ½m. Bus: Green Line 704 & 705 London-Windsor 1m. Luxmoore's Garden is an island garden created by a housemaster about 1880; reached by beautiful new bridge; views of college and river. Provost's and Fellows' Gardens adjoin the ancient buildings on N and E sides. Parking off Slough Rd, signposted. TEAS in aid of Datchet PCC. *Combined adm £1 Chd 20p. Sat June 12 (2-6)*

Finchampstead Gardens are situated near the Finchampstead Ridges which is a National Trust beauty spot on the B3348 between Finchampstead War Memorial and Crowthorne Station. Car parking on The Ridges or National Trust car park (Wellingtonia Ave). *Combined adm £1.50 Chd free. Sun May 16 (2-6)*

Ridgeways ᴄ⚥❀ (Mr & Mrs R R Hart) at The Ridges end of Wellingtonia Avenue on S side. 2½-acres with wide variety trees, rhododendrons, azaleas; ornamental ponds. No dogs. TEAS. *Adm £1 Chd free*

Half Way Tree ᴄ⚥❀ (Mr & Mrs J C Tanner) halfway along Wellingtonia Avenue on N side, near National Trust Car Park. 4-acre garden & woodland; rhododendrons, alpines, bog garden. Greenhouses mainly cacti, succulents. *Adm £1 Chd free*

Folly Farm ᴄ⚥ (The Hon Hugh & Mrs Astor) Sulhamstead, 7m SW of Reading. A4 between Reading/Newbury (2m W of M4 exit 12); take rd marked Sulhamstead at Mulligans Restaurant 1m after Theale roundabout; entrance 1m on right, through BROWN gate marked 'Folly Farm Gardens'. One of the few remaining gardens where the Lutyens architecture remains intact. Garden, laid out by Gertrude Jekyll, has been planted to owners' taste, bearing in mind Jekyll and Lutyens original design. Raised white garden, sunken rose garden; spring bulbs; herbaceous borders; ilex walk; avenues of limes, yew hedges, landscaped lawn areas, formal pools. Some recent simplifications and new planting. House (not open). TEAS. *Adm £1.50 Chd free (Share to West Berkshire Marriage Guidance Trust). Sun April 18, Mon May 31, Sun June 27 (2-6)*

Foxgrove ᴄ⚥❀ (Miss Audrey Vockins) Enborne, 2½m SW of Newbury. From A343 turn right at 'The Gun' 1½m from town centre. Bus: AV 126, 127, 128; alight Villiers Way PO 1m. Small family garden; interesting foliage plants, troughs, spring bulbs, naturalised in orchard; double primroses, snowdrop species and varieties; peat bed; adjoining nursery. Autumn opening for cyclamen, colchicums, nerines. TEAS. *Adm £1 Chd free. Suns March 21, April 4, Oct 10, Mon May 3 (2-6)*

¶**Fox Hill** ᴄ❀ (Mrs Martin McLaren) Inkpen. Between Hungerford and Newbury, turn off A4 at sign saying Kintbury & Inkpen. Drive into Kintbury. Turn L by shop onto Inkpen Rd. After approx 1m, turn R at Xrds. After passing village signpost saying Inkpen, turn 1st L down bridleroad. Garden 2nd on L. Car park in field. 3-acre garden, blossom, bulbs, many interesting shrubs. Newly planted. Small formal garden and duck pond. TEAS. *Combined adm with* **Combe Manor** *£1.50 Chd free. Mon May 31 (2-6)*

Fox Steep ᴄ⚥❀ (Juddmonte Farms) Crazies Hill. Midway between Henley-on-Thames and Wargrave. 2m E of Henley on A423; take turning at top of hill to Cockpole Green. From Knowl Hill on A4 and Wargrave follow Cockpole Green signs. Old well-established 4-acre garden provides pretty setting for Elizabethan timbered house, formerly an Inn; associated with Gertrude Jekyll. TEA. *Adm £1 Chd free. Sun May 23 (2-6)*

Frogmore Gardens ᴄ⚥ (by gracious permission of Her Majesty The Queen) Windsor Castle; entrance via Park St gate into Long Walk (follow AA signs). Visitors are requested kindly to keep on the route to the garden and not stray into the Home Park. Station and bus stop Windsor (20 mins walk from gardens); Green Line bus no 701, from London. Limited parking for cars only (free) Large garden with lake and lovely trees. The Royal Mausoleum, within the grounds, will also be open free of charge. Refreshment tent in car park on Long Walk (from where there is a 5 min walk to the gardens). **Coaches by**

appointment only (apply to NGS, Hatchlands Park, East Clandon, Guildford, Surrey GU4 7RT enc. s.a.e. or **Tel 0483 211535** stating whether May 6 or 7; am or pm). *Adm £1.50 Chd free. Wed May 5, & Thurs May 6 (10.30-7; last adm 6.30)*

The Harris Garden & Experimental Grounds ♿⚘❀ (University of Reading, School of Plant Sciences) Whiteknights, Reading RG6 2AS. Turn R just inside Pepper Lane entrance to University campus. 12-acre research and teaching garden extensively redeveloped since 1989. Rose gardens; shrub rose, herbaceous and annual borders, winter garden, bog garden, herb garden, walled garden etc. Gertrude Jekyll border new in 1993. Extensive glasshouses. Most plants labelled. TEAS. *Adm £1 Chd free. Sun July 11 (2-6)*

Hazelby House ♿⚘ (Mr & Mrs M J Lane Fox) North End, 6m SW of Newbury. Take R turn to Ball Hill off A343 just outside Newbury; approx ¼m beyond Ball Hill on rd to Kintbury. Exceptional 5-acre garden featured in numerous books and articles. TEAS. *Adm £1.50 Chd 75p. Sun June 27 (2-6.30)*

Heads Farm ♿⚘❀ (Mr & Mrs Thomas Egerton) Chaddleworth. Turn off A338 1m N of Great Shefford. Go up hill and take 1st L to Chaddleworth. Heads Farm is ½m on L. 8m from Wantage. Pretty 1½-acre garden with fine downland views. Paeonies; fine yews, beech hedges. Herbaceous borders. Shrub roses and white rose garden. TEAS. *Adm £1 Chd free (Share to St Andrew's Church). Sun June 20 (2-6)*

Highclere Castle, nr Newbury see Hampshire

Hurst Lodge ♿❀ (Mr & Mrs Alan Peck) In Hurst village on A321 Twyford to Wokingham Rd. An old garden 5 acres, spring flowers and bulbs, camellias, magnolias, rhododendrons, hydrangeas. TEAS. *Adm £1 Chd 20p.* Also open **Reynolds Farm** *(May only)* Suns May 16, Sept 12 (2-5.30). By appt **Tel 0734 341088**

Jasmine House ❀ (Mr & Mrs E C B Knight) Hatch Bridge, 2m W of Windsor. On A308 Windsor-Maidenhead opp Windsor Marina; follow signs from new roundabout by Jardinerie Garden Centre. ⅓-acre garden designed for all-year interest with conifers (over 150 different), dwarf rhododendrons, heather beds; hostas; sink gardens; trees notable for decorative bark; ornamental pools; collection of Bonsai. Garden featured in RHS Journal (March 1979); 'The Gardens of Britain' & 'Mon Jardin et Ma Maison' (Feb '82). TEAS Country Gardens Garden Centre (1m). *Adm £1 Chd free. Sun May 9 (2-6)* Also by appt **Tel 0753 841595**

Kirby House ♿❀ (Richard Astor Esq) Turn S off A4 to Kintbury; L at Xrds in Kintbury towards Combe. 2m out of Kintbury. Turn L immediately beyond Crown & Garter. House and garden at bottom of hill. 4 acres in beautiful setting; bulbs and blossom and many mature trees C18 brick house (not open). TEAS at **West Woodhay House**. *Combined adm with* **West Woodhay House** *£2 Chd 25p. Sun April 11 (2-6)*

Little Bowden ♿❀ (Geoffrey Verey Esq) 1½m W of Pangbourne on Pangbourne-Yattendon Rd. Large garden with fine views; woodland walk, azaleas, rhododendrons, bluebells. Heated swimming pool 20p extra. TEAS. *Adm £1 Chd free. Suns May 30, July 11 (2.30-6)*

Mariners ❀ (Mr & Mrs W N Ritchie) 7m W of Reading. From Theale (M4 exit 12 take A340) towards Pangbourne 1st L to Bradfield. Pass through wood and turn L by farm. 1st R after War Memorial into Mariners Lane. 1-acre charming well designed garden, owner maintained; made from heavy clay field, now matured; large variety of plants; herbaceous and shrub border; rose, clematis; silver leaved plants. TEAS & ice cream. *Adm £1 Chd 20p. Sun June 6 (2-6)*

Meadow House ♿⚘❀ (Mr & Mrs G A Jones) Ashford Hill is on the B3051 8m SE of Newbury. Take turning at SW end of village signposted Wolverton Common and Wheathold. Meadow House on R approx 300 yds along lane. Approx 1½-acre plantsman's garden created over the last 8 years. Pond with waterside planting; beds; many unusual plants. TEAS NGS day only. *Adm £1.25 Chd free (Share to Newbury Victim Support). Sun June 20, every Wed May 12 to Aug 11 (excl June 23) see* **Hampshire** *(2-6) and by appt.* **Tel 0734 816005** *(2-6)*

Oakfield Gardens ❀ nr Mortimer 6m SW of Reading. From Reading take smaller roundabout turn R for Grazeley Green, Wokenfield and Mortimer. TEAS provided by Royal British Legion. *Combined adm £1.50 Chd free. Sun May 2 (2-6)*
> **Oakfield** (Sir Michael & Lady Milne-Watson) Lovely spring garden, daffodils, camellias, magnolias, flowering prunus; large lake and woodland walks
> **The Stables** (Mr & Mrs Andrew Milne-Watson) Interesting shrub garden

¶Ockwells Manor ♿❀ (Mr & Mrs B P Stein) Maidenhead. Exit 8/9 off M4. A423M towards Henley. 1st slip rd to L to Cox Green and White Waltham. R at 1st roundabout. L at 2nd roundabout. Follow rd to end and turn R. 3½ acres of formal garden around mediaeval Manor House. Listed grade 1 (not open); walled garden; clipped yews; small maze; lime avenue; swimming pool; peacocks, ornamental ducks and geese; farm animals; woodland walk. TEAS. *Adm £1.50 Chd free. Sun July 18 (2-6)*

Odney Club ♿❀ (John Lewis Partnership) Cookham. Car park in grounds. 120 acres; lawns, garden and meadows on R. Thames; specimen trees. Cream TEAS River Room. *Adm £1.50 Chd free (Share to Sue Ryder Foundation). Sun April 25 (2-6)*

The Old House, Silchester see Hampshire

The Old Mill ♿ (Mrs E M Arlott) Aldermaston. On A4 between Reading and Newbury, take A340 then follow signs. 7 acres; lawns; walks; flower beds; shrubs; R. Kennet flows through with sluices and hatches. Fine Old Mill House (not open). TEAS. *Adm £1 Chd free. Sun May 2 (2-6)*

By Appointment Gardens. See head of county section

Old Rectory Cottage &♠ (Mr & Mrs A W A Baker) Tidmarsh, ½m S of Pangbourne, midway between Pangbourne and Tidmarsh turn E down narrow lane; left at T-junction. Medium-sized garden; wild garden; small lake; unusual plants; spring bulbs; shrubs; lilies; roses; geraniums; sorbus avenue; rose hedge. Arab horses, ornamental ducks, pheasants, white doves. Featured in many Gardening books. *Adm £1 Chd free (Share to BBONT). Suns March 7, April 4, May 9, June 20, July 11 (2-6)*

The Old Rectory, Burghfield &&♠ (Mr & Mrs R R Merton), 5m SW of Reading. Turn S off A4 to Burghfield village; right after Hatch Gate Inn; entrance on R. Medium-sized garden; herbaceous and shrub borders; roses, hellebores, lilies, many rare and unusual plants collected by owners from Japan and China; old-fashioned cottage plants; autumn colour. Georgian house (not open). *Adm 50p Chd 10p (Share to Save the Children & NCCPG Local Group). The last Weds of every month except Nov-Dec & Jan (11-4)*

The Old Rectory, Farnborough &♠ (Mrs Michael Todhunter) 4m SE of Wantage. From B4494 Wantage-Newbury Rd, 4m from Wantage turn E at sign for Farnborough. Outstanding garden with unusual plants: fine view; old-fashioned roses; collection of small flowered clematis; herbaceous borders. Beautiful house (not open) built c.1749. Teas in village. *Adm £1.50 Chd free (Share to All Saints, Farnborough). Suns April 25, May 16, June 27 (2-6)*

Peasemore Gardens 7m N of Newbury on A34 to M4 junction 13. N towards Oxford then L signed Chievely. Through Chievely and onto Peasemore. TEAS. *Combined adm £1 Chd free. Sun June 13 (2-6)*
    The Old Rectory, Peasemore &♠ (Mr & Mrs I D Cameron) Georgian house with fine trees in lovely setting. Shrub roses, peonies, large rose border and herbaceous border
    Paxmere House &♠ (The Hon Mrs John Astor) Opposite The Old Rectory. 2-acre cottage garden. Roses, shrubs, etc
    ¶**Peasemore House** & (Mr & Mrs Richard W Brown) Passed 3 thatched cottages on R entering Peasemore. Garden on R behind flint and brick wall. 2½ acres traditional garden with lovely trees, shrubs and roses with extensive views over arable downland

The Priory &♠ (O W Roskill Esq) Beech Hill, 9m S of Reading. Turn off at Spencers Wood PO Bus: 411, 412 from Reading. C14 Benedictine priory largely rebuilt 1648. Branch of Loddon flows through garden. Probably laid out in C17. Lawns, herbaceous borders, shrubs; kitchen garden. Teas in village in aid of Beech Hill Church. *Adm £1 Chd 20p. Sun June 13 (2-6)*

Reynolds Farm &♠ (Christopher & Dawn Wells) Hurst, 3m S of Twyford. From Hurst Lodge turn L; after ¾m take 1st left; entrance 200 yds on L. Small garden of weekend cottage, designed for minimal maintenance and maximum effect; interesting collection of shrubs and plants. Teas at **Hurst Lodge**. *Adm £1 Chd free. Sun May 16 (2-5.30)*

Rooksnest &♠ (Dr & Mrs M D Sackler) Earls Court Farm, Lambourne Woodlands. Situated approx 3m from the A338 (Wantage) Rd along the B4000. Nearest village, Lambourne. Rooksnest signposted on the B400 in both directions, ie whether approaching from Lambourne or from the A338. Approx 10-acre exceptionally fine traditional English garden. Recently restored with help from Arabella Lennox-Boyd. Includes terraces; rose garden; lilies; herbaceous borders; Victorian herb garden; many specimen trees and fine shrubs. TEA. *Adm £1.50 Chd 25p. Wed June 23 (2-5)*

Scotlands &♠ (Mr Michael & the Hon Mrs Payne) Cockpole Green. Midway between Henley-on-Thames and Wargrave. 2m E of Henley on A423; take turn at top of hill to Cockpole Green. 4 acres; clipped yews; shrub borders; grass paths through trees to woodland and pondgardens with Repton design rustic summer house. Rocks with waterfall. Featured in 'New Englishwoman's Garden' by R. Verey, English Gardens 1988 by Peter Coats. TEAS. *Adm £1.50 Chd free. Suns May 9, Oct 3 (2-5)*

Silwood Park & (Imperial College) Ascot. 1½m E of Ascot in the junction of A329 and the B383. Access from the B383 200 metres N of the Cannon Inn. 240 acres of parklands and natural habitats, surrounding fine C19 house by Waterhouse, architect of the Natural History Museum. Japanese garden under restoration; pinetum; young arboretum specialising in oaks and birches. Two nature walks (1m & 2m) through oak and beech woodland to lake. TEAS in conservatory. *Adm £1 Chd 50p. Suns May 9, 23; Oct 17 (2-6)*

Simms Farm House &&♠ (H H Judge Lea & Mrs Lea) Mortimer, 6m SW of Reading. At T-junction on edge of village, from Grazeley, turn R uphill; L by church into West End Rd; at next Xrd L down Drury Lane; R at T-junction. 1-acre garden with mixed shrub borders, small rockery; Bog garden; formal pond; unusual plants. Lovely view. TEA. *Adm 70p Chd 30p. Sun May 30 (2-6); also by appt* Tel 0734 332360

Stanford Dingley Village Gardens &&♠ Between Reading and Newbury. Pretty village with ancient Church and bridge over River Pang. Parking in field. *Combined adm £1 Chd 50p. Sun July 4 (2-6) including:*
    Bradfield Farm (Mr & Mrs Newton) ½-acre. Wide variety of plants. Further 5-acres mixed broadleaf planting in 1990
    The Manor House ♠ (Mr & Mrs Park) Close to church, 3-acre garden planted informally; water gardens. TEAS

Stone House &♠ (Mr & Mrs Nigel Bingham) Brimpton 6m E of Newbury. Turn S off A4 at junction by Coach & Horses, signed Brimpton and Aldermaston. ½m W of T junction by War Memorial signed Newbury. Medium-sized garden in attractive park; naturalised bulbs; rhododendrons; water garden; extensive collection plants and shrubs; walled kitchen garden; picnic area. TEA. *Adm £1 Chd free (Share to Brimpton Church). Suns May 23, June 18 (2-6)*

Regular Openers. See head of county section.

Summerfield House 🌺 (Mr & Mrs R J S Palmer) Crazies Hill. Midway between Henley-on-Thames and Wargrave. 2m E of Henley on A423, take turn at top of hill signed Cockpole Green, then turn R at Green. Garden opp village hall. 7 acres, herbaceous and shrub borders, many recently planted rare trees, large working greenhouse, 1½-acre lake completed 1989. House (not open) formerly Henley Town Hall, originally constructed in 1760 in centre of Henley and moved at end of C19. *Adm £1 Chd under 12 free. Sun June 20 (2-6)*

Sunningdale Park 🌿🌺 (Civil Service College) Ascot. 1½m E of Ascot off A329 at Cannon Inn or take Broomhall Lane off A30 at Sunningdale. Over 20 acres of beautifully landscaped gardens laid out by Capability Brown. Terrace garden and victorian rockery designed by Pulham incl cave and water features. Lake area with paved walks; extensive lawns with specimen trees and flower beds; impressive massed rhododendrons. Beautiful 1m woodland walk. TEAS. *Adm £1.50 Chd 50p. Sun May 16 (2-5)*

Swallowfield Park 🌿🌿 (Country Houses Association) 5m S between Reading and Wokingham on A33 under M4; 2m then L to Swallowfield. Entrance by Village Hall. Landscaped garden, exceptionally fine trees including cedars; ancient yew tree walk, small lake, massed rhododendrons; distinguished house built 1689 (not open). TEAS. *Adm £1.50 Chd 50p (Share to Country House Association). Mon April 12, Sun June 13 (2-5)*

Waltham Place 🌿🌺 White Waltham. 3½m S of Maidenhead. Exit 8/9 on M4, then A423(M) or M40 exit 4 then A404 to A4 Maidenhead exit and follow signs to White Waltham. 40 acres woodland, lake and gardens with magnificent trees, bluebells, rhododendrons; interesting long borders; walled garden; kitchen garden; glasshouses. Plants well labelled. Organic farm and gardens. TEAS. *Adm £2 Chd 50p (Share to Helen House Hospice). Suns June 6, July 18 (2-7)*

> **By Appointment Gardens.** These owners do not have a fixed opening day usually because they do not like crowds or have insufficient parking space. Owner will often give guided tour.

Wasing Place 🌿🌺 (Sir William Mount) Aldermaston, SE of Newbury. Turn S off A4 at Woolhampton; or 3m E take A340 to Aldermaston. ½m drive. Large garden; unusual shrubs and plants, rhododendrons; azaleas; lawns, walled and kitchen garden; greenhouses, herbaceous borders, magnificent cedars. C12 church. TEAS in aid of St Nicholas Church, Wasing. *Adm £1 Chd free. Suns May 23, July 11 (2-6)*

Welford Park 🌿🌺 (Mrs J L Puxley) 6m NW of Newbury. Entrance on Newbury/Lambourn Rd (fine gates with boot on top). Spacious grounds; spring flowers; walk by R. Lambourn. Queen Anne house (not open). TEA. *Adm £1 Chd free (Share to Welford Church). Sun April 4 (2-5)*

West Silchester Hall, nr Reading see Hampshire

West Woodhay House 🌿🌺 (J R Henderson Esq) 6m SW of Newbury. From Newbury take A343. At foot of hill turn R for East Woodhay and Ball Hill. 3½m turn L for West Woodhay. Go over Xrds in village, next fork R past Church. Gate on L. Parkland; large garden with bulbs, roses, shrubs, lake, woodland garden. Large walled kitchen garden, greenhouses. TEAS. *Combined adm £2 Chd 25p (Share to West Woodhay Church)* with **Kirby House.** *Sun April 11 (2-6)*

Whiteknights 🌿 (Mr & Mrs P Bradly) Finchampstead. Midway along Finchampstead Ridges on B3348 between Finchampstead War Memorial and Crowthorne Station. 2½ acres, lawns, Japanese water garden, dwarf conifers, interesting plantings, small vegetable garden. TEA at **Blencathra**. *Adm 80p Chd free (Share to Guide Dogs for the Blind). Combined adm with* **Blencathra** *£2.20. Sun May 23 (2-6)*

Woolley Park 🌿🌺 (Mr & Mrs Philip Wroughton) 5m S of Wantage on A338 turn L at sign to Woolley. Large park, fine trees and views. Two linked walled gardens beautifully planted. Teas close to Old Rectory, Farnborough. *Adm £1. Sun June 27 (2-6)*

Buckinghamshire

Hon County Organiser:	Mrs Peter Toynbee, The Old Vicarage, Brill, Aylesbury HP18 9RP Tel 0844 237 064
Assistant Hon County Organisers:	Mrs D W Fraser, The Old Butcher's Arms, Dark Lane, Oving, Aylesbury HP22 4HP Tel 0296 641026 Mrs C S Sanderson, Wellfield House, Cuddington, Aylesbury HP18 0BB Tel 0844 291626
Hon County Treasurer:	Peter Toynbee Esq.

DATES OF OPENING

By appointment

For telephone numbers and other details see garden descriptions

Blossoms, nr Great Missenden
Brill Gardens, nr Thame
Charlton, Dorney Reach, nr
  Maidenhead
Dorneywood Garden, Burnham
  (By written appt only)
Garden Cottage, Farnham Royal
Great Barfield, High Wycombe
Hall Barn, Beaconsfield
Harewood, Chalfont St Giles
The Manor Farm, Little Horwood, nr
  Winslow
The Manor House, Bedlow, nr
  Aylesbury
The Manor House, Princes
  Risborough
Pasture Farm, Longwick, nr Princes
  Risborough
Springlea, Seymour, Marlow
Walmerdene, Buckingham
The Wheatsheaf Inn, Weedon

February 21 Sunday
Great Barfield, High Wycombe
March 7 Sunday
Campden Cottage, Chesham Bois
March 28 Sunday
Greenlands, nr Henley on Thames
April 4 Sunday
Ascott, nr Leighton Buzzard
April 9 Friday (Good Friday)
Turn End, Haddenham
April 11 Sunday (Easter Sunday)
Chetwode Manor, Buckingham
Overstroud Cottage, Gt
  Missenden ‡
Peppers, Gt Missenden ‡
Quoitings, Marlow
April 17 Saturday
Kincora, Beaconsfield
April 18 Sunday
Campden Cottage, Chesham
  Bois ‡
Kincora, Beaconsfield ‡
The Old Vicarage, Padbury
Oving Gardens, nr Aylesbury
Spindrift, Jordans, Beaconsfield ‡
April 25 Sunday
Long Crendon Gardens, nr
  Thame ‡
Nether Winchendon House, nr
  Aylesbury ‡
May 2 Sunday
Garden Cottage, Farnham
  Royal ‡
Harewood, Chalfont St Giles ‡

The Manor House, Bledlow, nr
  Aylesbury ‡‡
Overstroud Cottage, Gt Missenden
Pasture Farm, Longwick, nr
  Princes Risborough ‡‡
May 3 Monday (Bank Hol)
Garden Cottage, Farnham Royal
Great Barfield, High Wycombe
The Manor Farm, Little Horwood,
  nr Winslow
May 9 Sunday
Campden Cottage, Chesham
  Bois ‡
Cliveden, Taplow
The Manor House, Princes
  Risborough
Overstroud Cottage, Gt
  Missenden ‡
Quainton Gardens, Nr
  Aylesbury ‡‡
Winslow Hall, Winslow ‡‡
May 16 Sunday
Chicheley Hall, Newport
  Pagnell
Chalfont St Giles Gardens
Springlea, Seymour, Marlow
Turn End, Haddenham
May 18 Tuesday
Stowe Landscape Gardens,
  Buckingham
May 23 Sunday
The Edge, Chalfont St Giles ‡
Favershams Meadow, Gerrards
  Cross ‡
Oving Gardens, nr Aylesbury
May 30 Sunday
Garden Cottage, Farnham Royal
May 31 Monday
Garden Cottage, Farnham Royal
Gracefield, Lacey Green
June 6 Sunday
The Old Rectory, Cublington
Overstroud Cottage, Gt
  Missenden ‡
Springlea, Seymour, Marlow
Weir Lodge, Chesham ‡
June 9 Wednesday
Spindrift, Jordans, Beaconsfield
June 13 Sunday
Ascott, nr Leighton Buzzard
Campden Cottage, Chesham
  Bois ‡
Cuddington Gardens, nr Thame ‡‡
Favershams Meadows, Gerrards
  Cross ‡
The Manor House, Princes
  Risborough ‡‡
Tythrop Park, nr Thame ‡‡
Whitchurch Gardens, Nr Aylesbury
June 16 Wednesday
Cuddington Gardens, nr Thame
June 19 Saturday
The Old Vicarage, Padbury ‡
Walmerdene, Buckingham ‡

June 20 Sunday
Chalfont St Giles Gardens ‡
Claydon House, Middle
  Claydon ‡‡
Gipsy House, Gt Missenden ‡
Hillesden House, nr
  Buckingham ‡‡‡
Little Linford Gardens, nr
  Newport Pagnell ‡‡‡‡
Long Crendon Gardens, nr Thame
Loughton Village Gardens, Milton
  Keynes ‡‡‡‡
The Manor House, Bledlow, nr
  Aylesbury
The Old Vicarage, Padbury ‡‡‡
Overstroud Cottage, Gt
  Missenden ‡
Quainton Gardens, Nr
  Aylesbury ‡‡
Walmerdene, Buckingham ‡‡‡
June 23 Wednesday
Quainton Gardens, Nr Aylesbury
June 27 Sunday
Cheddington Gardens, Leighton
  Buzzard
The Edge, Chalfont St Giles
The Manor House, Hambleden
Pasture Farm, Longwick, nr
  Princes Risborough ‡
River Cottage, Radclive, nr
  Buckingham ‡‡
Turn End, Haddenham ‡
Westcott House, Gawcott, nr
  Buckingham ‡‡
June 28 Monday
River Cottage, Radclive, nr
  Buckingham ‡
Westcott House, Gawcott, nr
  Buckingham ‡
July 4 Sunday
Great Barfield, High Wycombe
Watercroft, Penn
July 10 Sunday
Bucksbridge House, Wendover
Kincora, Beaconsfield
July 11 Sunday
Bucksbridge House, Wendover
Campden Cottage, Chesham Bois ‡
Flint House, Penn Street,
  Amersham ‡
Kincora, Beaconsfield ‡‡
Newton Longville Gardens,
  Milton Keynes
Watercroft, Penn ‡‡
July 18 Sunday
Hughenden Manor, High
  Wycombe ‡
Prestwood Gardens, nr Gt
  Missenden ‡
Ravenstone House, nr Olney
Springlea, Seymour, Marlow
July 25 Sunday
The Manor Farm, Little Horwood,
  nr Winslow

The Manor House, Princes Risborough ‡
Nether Winchendon House, nr Aylesbury ‡

July 28 Wednesday
Spindrift, Jordans, Beaconsfield

August 8 Sunday
Campden Cottage, Chesham Bois

August 15 Sunday
Pollards, Whiteleaf, nr Princes Risborough

August 22 Sunday
Peppers, Gt Missenden

August 29 Sunday
Heron Path House, Wendover

August 30 Monday
Heron Path House, Wendover
Spindrift, Jordans, Beaconfield

September 5 Sunday
Cliveden, Taplow
Overstroud Cottage, Gt Missenden
Quoitings, Marlow
West Wycombe Park, West Wycombe

September 12 Sunday
Pasture Farm, Longwick, nr Princes Risborough ‡
Springlea, Seymour, Marlow
Turn End, Haddenham ‡

September 19 Sunday
Campden Cottage, Chesham Bois

September 26 Sunday
Great Barfield, High Wycombe

DESCRIPTIONS OF GARDENS

Ascott ♿✻❀ (Sir Evelyn and Lady de Rothschild; The National Trust) Wing, 2m SW of Leighton Buzzard, 8m NE of Aylesbury via A418. Bus: United Counties 141 Aylesbury-Leighton Buzzard. Beautiful surroundings and layout. Garden part formal, part natural; many specimen trees, shrubs, naturalised bulbs, sunken garden; lily pond. Tea Mentmore Village. *Adm £3 Chd £1.50 Under 5 free. Suns April 4, June 13 (2-6). Last adm 5pm*

Blossoms ♿✻❀ (Dr & Mrs Frank Hytten) Cobblers Hill, 2½m NW of Great Missenden by Rignall Road (signed to Butlers Cross) to King's Lane (1½m) then to top of Cobblers Hill, R at yellow stone marker and in 50yds R at stone marked Blossoms. Map ref SP874034. 4-acre garden begun as hill-top fields in 1923, plus 1-acre beechwood. Lawns, trees, old apple orchard, small lake, water gardens, woodland, troughs, scree garden and several patios. Large areas of bluebells, wild daffodils, fritillaria and other spring bulbs. Flowering cherries and many interesting trees including small collections of acer, eucalyptus and salix; foliage effects throughout the year. TEAS. *Adm £1.50. Open by appt only* **Tel 02406 3140**

Brill Gardens ✻ 7m N of Thame. Turn off B4011, Thame-Bicester; or turn off A41 at Kingswood; both marked to Brill. TEA. *Collecting Box. By appt this year only, daily April to end Sept. Ring any no below*

Commoners ✻ (Mr & Mrs R Wickenden) Tram Hill. Under ¼-acre; low walled old cottage garden; alpines, shrubs, herbaceous, many plants from seed and cutting. Views in all directions. **Tel 0844 237418**

Old Farm (Dr & Mrs Raymond Brown) The Common. ½-acre established garden around 3 terraces of old shrub roses; secluded position with high open views over Otmoor; kitchen garden; soft fruit; mature and younger trees; interesting shrubs; small pond; conservatory added to C17 stone and brick cottage (not open) **Tel 0844 238 232**

14 The Square ✻ (Mrs Audrey Dyer) Tiny paved garden with hand made pots. Culinary and fragrant herbs and plants to attract wildlife

56 Windmill Street ❀ (Mr & Mrs C D Elliott) Pocket handkerchief walled clay garden featuring imaginative use of space; mixed borders in raised beds include interesting foliage, uncommon plants. Pergola, patio, many containers. **Tel 0844 237407**

Bucksbridge House ♿✻❀ (Mr & Mrs J Nicholson) Heron Path, Wendover. ½m S of Wendover. Chapel Lane is 2nd turn on L off A413 towards Amersham. House is on L at bottom of lane. Georgian house with established 2-acre garden; large herbaceous border, unusual shrubs, roses, laburnum arches, an ornamental vegetable garden and 2 well stocked greenhouses. Also available pots, bird baths and sculptures by Frances Levy. TEAS. *Adm £1 Chd 30p. Sat, Sun July 10, 11 (2-6)*

Campden Cottage ✻❀ (Mrs P Liechti) 51 Clifton Rd, Chesham Bois, N of Amersham. From Amersham-on-the-Hill take A416; after 1m turn R (E) at Catholic Church. From Chesham take A416; and first turning L after beech woods. ½-acre derelict garden, restored by owner since 1971; plantsman's garden of year-round interest; fine collection of unusual and rare plants. Hellebores in March. Featured on TV 'Gardeners' World' and in 'The New Englishwoman's Garden' 1987 and the 'Good Gardens Guide 1993'. Please use car park signed on main road. Teas Old Amersham. No push chairs. *Adm £1 Chd free. Suns March 7, April 18, May 9, June 13, July 11, Aug 8, Sept 19, (2-6). Also by appt for parties with TEAS. No coaches.* **Tel 0494 726818**

Chalfont St Giles Gardens Off A413. Teas at Gardens Ass Club House School Lane. *Combined adm £1.50 or £1 per garden. Suns May 16, June 20 (2-6)*

Concordia ✻❀ (Mr & Mrs D E Cobb) 76 Deanway, Chalfont St Giles. Limited parking in Deanway. From car park in Chalfont St Giles follow signs. A small challenging garden on a difficult sloping site. Herbaceous and shrub borders; rock garden; fruit trees; collection of unusual orchids

Halfpenny Furze ♿✻❀ (Mr & Mrs R Sadler) Mill Lane, Chalfont St Giles. From London take A413 signed Amersham. Mill Lane is ½m past mini roundabouts at Chalfont St Giles. Limited parking in Mill Lane, 1-acre plantsman's garden on clay: part woodland (rhododendrons, azaleas, acers, magnolias, cercis, cercidiphyllum) part formal (catalpa, cornus, clerodendrum unusual shrubs, roses and mixed borders)

Regular Openers. Too many days to include in diary. Usually there is a wide range of plants giving year-round interest. See head of county section for the name and garden description for times etc.

Charlton ❀ (Mrs L Rutterford) 5 Harcourt Rd, Dorney Reach, nr Maidenhead. Turn S off A4 approx 3m E of Maidenhead into Marsh Lane (signposted Dorney Reach) continue 1m; Harcourt Road is 2nd on R over motorway bridge. Approx ¾-acre garden on light free draining soil organically cultivated and designed to provide interest throughout the year. Mixed borders with variety of shrubs, hardy perennials, climbers and annuals; small pond, vegetables, fruit and greenhouse. (Suitable for wheelchairs if dry). TEA. *Adm £1. By appt only all year.* **Tel 0628 24325**

Cheddington Gardens 11m E of Aylesbury; turn off B489 at Pitstone. 7m S of Leighton Buzzard; turn off B488 at Cheddington Station. Teas on the green. *Combined adm £2 Chd free (Share to Methodist Chapel and St Giles Church. Cheddington). Sun June 27 (2-6)*

   Chasea (Mr & Mrs A G Seabrook) Small garden on clay; assorted tubs and baskets round pool on patio; shrubs and conifers
   Cheddington Manor ⚘ (Mr & Mrs H Hart) 3½-acres; small lake and moat in informal setting, roses, herbaceous border, and interesting mature trees
   1 The Green (Mr R Aslett) Very small cottage garden 50′ × 20′; climbers, window boxes, pool and collection of fuchsias
   The Old Reading Room &❀ (Mr & Mrs W P Connolley) ⅓-acre cottage garden; shrubs, perennials, bedding and small fern collection; trees incl ginkgo biloba
   Rose Cottage &⚘❀ (Mr & Mrs D G Jones) ¼-acre cottage garden planted for all year interest with accent on colour; old roses; small scree area with unusual plants and conservatory
   21 Station Road & (Mr & Mrs P Jay) ½-acre informal garden with wildflower conservation area; herbaceous and shrub borders; herbs and kitchen garden
   ¶Woodstock Cottage ⚘ (Mr & Mrs D Bradford) 42 High Street. Delightful cottage garden with rear courtyard and patio

Chetwode Manor &⚘ (Mrs J E H Collins) 5m SW of Buckingham via A421. Turn E by Newton Purcell railway bridge; after 1½ m turn L at T junction; turn R in 100yds; garden 200yds on R. Medium-sized garden, large mixed borders, shrubs & ground cover plants; old roses, fine osmarea hedge; spring bulbs, C17 Manor House (not open). TEA. *Adm £1 Chd free. Sun Apr 11 (2-6)*

Chicheley Hall &⚘ (The Trustees of the Hon Nicholas Beatty & Mrs John Nutting) Chicheley, on A422 between Bedford and Newport Pagnell; E of Newport Pagnell and 3m from junc 14 of M1. Georgian House (open) set in spacious lawns, herbaceous borders, roses on mellowed brick walls; woodland planted with bulbs; formal lake attributed to London & Wise 1709 after Hampton Court. TEAS. *Adm £1.50 Chd 50p.* ▲*Sun May 16 (2.30-5)*

Claydon House &❀ (Sir Ralph & Lady Verney; National Trust) Middle Claydon. 8m S of Buckingham. From Aylesbury take A413 N to Winslow, then follow signs to middle Claydon and NT sign Claydon House. From Buckingham take A413 S and turn R at Padbury. Claydon House was given to the National Trust by Sir Ralph and Lady Verney in 1957. The garden, a mass of bulbs in spring, consists of shrub beds and an old walled garden devoted to old-fashioned roses and sun loving plants; through its circular moon door can be seen a wild flower meadow whose colours change through the season, and which contains rare annuals and perennials. Beyond is a 2-acre walled kitchen garden run as a commercial organic nursery being restored to its Victorian glory. Pot plants on sale. Organic shop open. Cream TEAS. *Adm £1.* ▲*Sun June 20 (1-5)*

Cliveden &⚘❀ (The National Trust) 2m N of Taplow. A number of separate gardens within extensive grounds, first laid out in the C18 incl water garden, rose garden; herbaceous borders; woodland walks and views of the Thames. Suitable for wheelchairs only in part. TEAS. *Adm grounds only £3.50 Chd £1.75. Suns May 9; Sept 5 (11-6)*

Cuddington Gardens 3½m NE Thame or 5m SW of Aylesbury off A418. Best kept village winners 1992. Gardens signed in village. TEAS on Sun June 13 at various venues in aid of Darby & Joan & Village Hall Restoration Fund. TEA on Wed June 16. Parking at **The Old Rectory** on Aylesbury side of village). *Combined adm £2 Chd free. Sun, Wed June 13, 16 (2-6)*

   Church Cottage & (Mr & Mrs Alan Grey) Colourful village garden with trees; shrubs and annuals. Mixed border. Small water garden
   ¶1 Great Stone Cottages (Mr & Mrs P Wenham) Entry to the garden is from the drive in Holly Tree Lane. Long, narrow cottage garden divided into several sections, each with its own character. They contain ponds and fountains with patio, shrub, alpine, herb, heather and vegetable areas
   The Old Post & (Mr & Mrs R Fleming) ½-acre family garden planted for year round interet. new rose and wisteria colonnade, Wychert wall, shrub, herbaceous and mixed borders; shady beds and vegetables
   The Old Rectory ⚘ (Mr & Mrs R J Frost) Former Victorian rectory with stunning views over Winchendon valley. 2-acre garden bounded by mature trees, laid out with beds of mixed shrubs; rockery; herbaceous island bed; paved rose garden with fish pond; pavilion. Variety of planted containers including mangers around courtyard
   The Platt & (The Misses Corby) Mixed herbaceous and annual border; roses; soft fruits and vegetables. Paved area with varieties of thyme
   Tibby's Cottage & (Mrs Rosalind Squire) Cottage garden surrounding 400-yr-old picturesque thatched cottage. Natural stream running through to pool and bog garden. Lovely view to Nether Winchendon
   Tyringham Hall & (Mr & Mrs Ray Scott) Water and bog garden, patios and lawns surround mediaeval house. Dell with well and waterfall between Tyringham Hall and **Tibby's Cottage**

By Appointment Gardens. These owners do not have a fixed opening day usually because they do not like crowds or have insufficient parking space. Owner will often give guided tour.

Dorneywood Garden ᴅ⚘❀ (The National Trust) Dorneywood Rd, Burnham. From Burnham village take Dropmore Rd, and at end of 30mph limit take R fork into Dorneywood Rd. Dorneywood is 1m on R. From M40 junction 2, take A355 to Slough then 1st R to Burnham, 2m then 2nd L after Jolly Woodman signed Dorneywood Rd. Dorneywood is about 1m on L. 6-acre country garden with shrubs, rose garden, mixed borders and dell. TEAS. *Adm £2 Chd free. Garden open by written appt only on Weds July 7, 14, Sats Aug 7, 21 (2-6). Apply to the Secretary, Dorneywood Trust, Dorneywood, Burnham, Bucks SL1 8PY*

The Edge ⚘❀ (Mr & Mrs D Glen) London Rd, Chalfont St Giles. Garden is ¼m towards Chalfont St Peter from The Pheasant Xrds on A413 nr Kings Rd. Georgian cottage with landscaped garden of ¾ acre, created by owners. Partially enclosed with walls and yew hedges, interesting shrubs incl magnolias, white judas tree, wisterias, climbing and shrub roses. TEAS. *Adm £1 Chd free. Suns May 23, June 27 (2-6)*

¶Favershams Meadow ᴅ⚘ (Mr & Mrs H W Try) 1½m W of Gerrards Cross on A40. Turn N into Mumfords Lane opp lay-by with BT box. Garden ¼m on R. 1½ acre garden started in 1989. Mixed herbaceous, knot, parterre and rose gardens; blue and white borders around gazebo; brick paved vegetable garden; views to Bulstrode Park. TEAS in aid of the Red Cross and The Wexham Gastrointestinal Trust. *Adm £1.50 Chd free. Suns May 23, June 13 (2-6)*

Flint House ᴅ⚘ (Mr & Mrs David White) Penn Street Village, 2m SW of Amersham. Turn S off A 404 into village opp church. Parking in church car park. 1½-acre garden surrounding C19 flint vicarage; herbaceous borders, shrubs and climbing roses, raised alpine bed, newly planted herb garden; urns and rose 'hoops' beside tennis court. TEA. *Adm £1 Chd 20p. Sun July 11 (2-6)*

Garden Cottage ᴅ❀ (Mrs Pauline Sheppey) Farnham Royal. 3m NW of Slough; on A355 turn W at Farnham Royal along Farnham Lane towards Burnham; then 2nd R and 1st L into East Burnham Lane. Informal 1-acre country garden. Wide range of plants particularly herbaceous. Year-round colour, form and foliage. Yew hedges, mixed borders, raised beds, heather garden. Nursery adjoining. Cream TEAS by Thames Valley Hospice. Plants and local produce for sale. *Adm £1 Chd free. Suns, Mons May 2, 3, 30, 31 (10-6) by appt all year Tel 0753 642243*

Gipsy House ⚘ (Mrs F Dahl) Gt Missenden. A413 to Gt Missenden. From High St turn into Whitefield Lane, continue under railway bridge. Large Georgian house on R with family additions. York stone terrace, pleached lime walk to writing hut; shrubs, roses, herbs, small walled vegetable garden, orchard and gipsy caravan for children. Limited access for wheelchairs. Teas locally. *Adm £1.20 Chd 30p (Share to Roald Dahl Foundation). Sun June 20 (2-5.30)*

Regular Openers. See head of county section.

Gracefield ᴅ❀ (Mr & Mrs B Wicks) Lacey Green. Take A4010 High Wycombe to Aylesbury Rd. Turn R by Red Lion at Bradenham, up hill to Walters Ash; L at T-junc for Lacey Green. Brick and flint house on main rd beyond church facing Kiln Lane. 1½-acre mature garden; many unusual plants, trees, mostly labelled; orchard, soft fruit, shrub borders, rockery; plants for shade, sink gardens. Two ponds. Plants for sale if available. TEAS. *Adm £1.20 Chd free. Bank Hol Mon May 31 (2-6). Parties by written appt May to Sept*

Great Barfield ᴅ⚘❀ (Richard Nutt Esq) Bradenham, A4010 4m NW of High Wycombe 4m S of Princes Risborough. At Red Lion turn into village and turn R. Park on green. Walk down No Through Road. 1½-acre garden, designed for views, lay out, contrast and colour, as background for unusual plants. Michael Gibson in 'The Rose Gardens of England' says that it is a plantsman's garden in the best possible sense of the term and not to be missed to see how all plants should be grown to the best advantage. Feb now not only famous for snowdrops and hellebores but willows and a variety of bulbs; drifts of crocus; May unique collections of Pulmonarias and Bergenias; also red Trilliums now naturalised. July old-fashioned and climbing roses, Lilies including naturalised. L. martagon. Sept considerable collection of colchicum, autumn colour and Sorbus berries. NCCPG national collection of leucojum (spring & early May); celandine (early May); iris unguicularis. Sales of unusual plants. TEAS. *Adm £1 Chd under 16 free (Share to Friends of St Botolphs Church). Sun Feb 21 (2-5), Mon May 3 (2-6), Sun July 4 (2-6) Sun Sept 26 (2-5). Also by appt Tel 0494 563741*

Greenlands ᴅ⚘❀ (Henley The Management College) 2m E of Henley-on-Thames on A4155 Marlow Rd. Easy access from M4 & M40 via A404 turning off onto A4155 for Marlow. Garden of 30 acres, mainly lawn sweeping down to R. Thames. Very fine mature cedars, oaks and other species, spring bulbs. Recently restored sunken garden and fountain. TEAS. *Adm £1.50 Chd free. Sun March 28 (2-6)*

Hall Barn (Lt. Col. The Lord & Lady Burnham) Lodge gate 300 yds S of Beaconsfield Church in town centre. One of the original gardens opening in 1927 under the National Gardens Scheme, still owned by the Burnham family. A unique landscaped garden of great historical interest, laid out in the 1680's. Vast 300-yr-old curving yew hedge. Extensive replanting in progress after severe gale damage. Formal lake. Long avenues through the Grove, each terminating in a temple, classical ornament or statue. Obelisk with fine carvings in memory of Edmund Waller's grandson who completed the garden about 1730. *Garden open by written appointment only. Applications to Lady Burnham, Hall Barn, Beaconsfield, Buckinghamshire HP9 2SG*

Harewood ᴅ⚘❀ (Mr & Mrs John Heywood) Harewood Rd, Chalfont St Giles. Chalfont and Latimer Met Line tube station ¾m. From A404 Amersham-Rickmansworth Rd, at mini roundabout in Little Chalfont village turn S down Cokes Lane. Harewood Rd is 200yds on L. 1-acre; fine yew and box hedges; established conifers; wide variety unusual shrubs and hardy plants; old roses; many climbers incl roses, clematis, wisterias; pool, sink gardens; planted for year-round interest. Emphasis on foliage and colour contrast. Cream TEAS. *Adm £1.50 Chd free (Share to Arthritis & Rheumatism Council). Sun May 2 (2-5). Also by appt* Tel 0494 763553

Heron Path House &⚭❀ (Mr & Mrs Bryan C Smith) Chapel Lane. ½m S of Wendover off A413. Chapel Lane 2nd turn on L; house at bottom. 2½-acre garden featuring immaculate lawns, brilliant bedding displays and hanging baskets of fuchsias, geraniums etc; shrub borders, rockery, pond and greenhouse. TEAS. *Adm £1.50 Chd 50p (Share to The Wendover Society and RUKBA). Sun, Mon Aug 29, 30 (2-6)*

Hillesden House &⚭❀ (Mr & Mrs R M Faccenda) Hillesden, 3m S of Buckingham via Gawcott. Follow Hillesden signs after Gawcott on Calvert Rd. 6 acres developed since 1978 from virgin land on site of C16 Manor House by superb Perpendicular Church 'Cathedral in the Fields'; large lawns, shrubberies; rose, alpine and foliage gardens; interesting clipped hedges; conservatory; large lakes and deer park; commanding views over countryside. TEAS. *Adm £1.30 Chd under 12 free (Share to Hillesden Church). Sun June 20 (2-6)*

Hughenden Manor &⚭❀ (The National Trust) 1½m N of High Wycombe on W side of Great Missenden Rd A4128; (Grid ref: SU866955 on OS sheet 165). 5 acres with lawns, terraced garden, herbaceous border, formal annual bedding, orchard and woodland walks. The Trust has undertaken restoration work in accordance with photographs taken at the time of Disraeli's death. Teas available from Hughenden Church House. *Adm House & Garden £3.30 Chd £1.65. Sun July 18 (12-6)*

Kincora &⚭❀ (Mr & Mrs J A K Leslie) 54 Ledborough Lane. Take M40 or A40 to Beaconsfield, then Amersham Rd (A355) 1m, turn L at sign for New Town and Model Village. Parking next turning L after 14th lamppost. 2-acre garden; borders, mixed bedding, wild area and containers surrounding swimming pool. TEAS. *Adm £1 Chd free (Share to Ioian Rennie Hospice). Sats, Suns April 17, 18, July 10, 11 (2-6)*

Little Linford Gardens &⚭❀ 2m N of Newport Pagnell between Gayhurst & Haversham overlooking Great Ouse valley. Flower display in beautiful C13/14 village church. TEAS in aid of Little Linford Church. *Combined adm £1.20 Chd free (Share to Little Linford Church). Sun June 20 (2-6)*

    Elmwood House (Mr & Mrs Peter Tinworth) 1¾-acre country garden, sloping site on 3 levels. Collection of old roses; mature trees; shrubs; flower borders; orchard and vegetable garden; conservatory and small pond

    Hall Farm (Hon Richard & Mrs Godber) 3-acre hilltop farmhouse garden created over last 14 yrs. Mixed borders; trees and shrubs. Special planting for exposed area. Walled garden with converted barn and conservatory; secluded swimming pool with sun loving plants. Also kitchen garden, herbs; orchard and new water garden

Long Crendon Gardens 2m N of Thame B4011 to Bicester. TEAS. *Combined adm £2 Chd free (Share to Long Crendon Day Centre)*
Sun April 25 (2-6)
    Manor House & (Sir William & Lady Shelton) turn R by church; house through wrought iron gates. 6-acres; lawns sweep down to 2 ornamental lakes; each with small island, willow walk along lower lake with over 20 varieties of willow; fine views towards Chilterns. House (not open) 1675. TEAS
    The Old Crown ⚭ (Mr & Mrs R H Bradbury) 100yds past Chandos Inn. 1 acre on steep SW slope. Old-fashioned and other roses and climbers. Flowering shrubs, herbaceous plants. Spring bulbs, assorted colourful containers in summer; small vegetable patch
    Old Post House (Mr & Mrs Nigel Viney) In the picturesque High St at corner of Burts Lane. Attractive cottage garden. Interesting shrubs, and planting. Small produce stall
    Springfield Cottage &❀ (Mrs Elizabeth Dorling) 6 Burts Lane. ⅓-acre secluded garden planted for all-year-round foliage and easy maintenance
Sun June 20 (2-6)
    Baker's Close ⚭ (Mr & Mrs P Vaines) 2-acre garden on SW slope. Partly walled it incl courtyard, terraced lawns, rockery with pond, roses, shrubs, herbaceous plantings and wild area
    48 High Street &❀ (Mr & Mrs John Allerton) ¼-acre village garden; colourful herbaceous borders, shrubs, old-fashioned roses; vegetables. TEAS
    8 Ketchmere Close &⚭❀ (Mr & Mrs A Heley) 1991 and 1992 award winner incl Booker Garden Centre Competition for the best kept garden under 100ft in Buckinghamshire. Colourful split level garden with extensive views. Wide range of shrubs, conifers, rockery and water feature
    Manor House & (Sir William & Lady Shelton) Description with April opening
    The Old Crown ⚭ (Mr & Mrs R H Bradbury) Description with April opening
    Windacre &❀ (Mr & Mrs K Urch) 62 Chilton Rd. 1-acre; roses, shrubs, orchard, main features sunken lawns and trees. TEAS

¶**Loughton Village Gardens** 1m W of Milton Keynes City Centre. 3m S of Stony Stratford and 3m N of Bletchley off Watling Street; or Junction 14 M1 or A5 to Portway roundabout on H5 Portway and follow signs. TEAS and plant sales in aid of Parish Church and the Apert's Syndrome Support Group. *Combined adm £1.50 Acc chd free. Sun June 20 (1.30-6)*
    ¶**Cell Farm Cottage** &⚭❀ (Mr & Mrs D J Oakley) 1 The Green. C16 cottage, ¼-acre garden. Project started in 1990; site shared with livery stables; shrubs, perennials, climbing roses, containers. Garden dominated by 40′ chestnut tree
    ¶**Fullers Barn** &⚭❀ (Mr & Mrs John Walker) The Green. ⅓ acre bordered on one side by stream, and surrounded by parkland. Planted 4 yrs ago on a clay farm yard now a family garden. Borders, pond, shrubs, raised beds and vegetables, fruit trees and greenhouse
    ¶**2 The Green** ⚭ (Mr & Mrs A Cirigliano) 150′ x 20′ colourful village garden. Pool, borders, containers and productive vegetable garden; limited space fully used

¶The Old School ⚘ (Mr & Mrs George Button) School Lane. 3½-acre garden developed over 10 yrs. Ornamental pond, orchard, wild area, shrubs interestingly planted, herbaceous border

¶5 School Lane ⚲⚘ (Miss Hanna Bird) Small cottage garden in rural setting by the church

The Manor Farm ⚲⚘⚘ (Mr & Mrs Peter Thorogood) Little Horwood sign-posted 2m NE Winslow off A413. 5m E Buckingham and 5m W Bletchely turning S off A421. Hilltop farmhouse garden on acid clay, laid out and replanted 1986. Wide range of alpines and plantsman's plants for year round interest in colour, form and foliage; good roses, 100' hosta border, herbaceous, wild flower meadow, damp garden, lovely views. Cream TEAS and stalls. *Adm £1.50 Chd free (Share to Royal Agricultural Benevolent Institute for disabled and displaced farmers and farm managers). Bank Hol Mon May 3, Sun July 25 (2-6). By appt April to Sept* **Tel 029671 4758**

The Manor House, Bledlow ⚲⚘⚘ (The Lord & Lady Carrington) ½m off B4009 in middle of Bledlow village. Station: Princes Risborough, 2½m. Paved garden, parterres, shrub borders, old roses and walled kitchen garden. House (not open) C17 & C18. Water and species garden with paths, bridges and walkways, fed by 14 chalk springs. Also a new 2-acre garden with sculptures and landscaped planting. Partly suitable wheelchairs. TEA May, TEAS June only. *Adm £2 Chd free. Suns May 2, June 20 (2-6); also by appt May to Sept (2-4.30)*

The Manor House, Hambleden ⚘ (Maria Carmela, Viscountess Hambleden) Hambleden. NE of Henley-on-Thames, 1m N of A4155. Conservatory; shrubs and old-fashioned rose garden. Teas at Hambleden Church *Adm £1 Chd 10p. Sun June 27 (2-6)*

The Manor House, Princes Risborough ⚲⚘ (Mr & Mrs R Goode) From High Wycombe take A4010 to Princes Risborough. Turn L down High St. L at Market Square and bear R. The Manor House is R of church; public car park beyond. From Aylesbury-Thame follow signs to town centre and turn R at Market Square. 2 acres surrounding C17 house (not open); large walled garden designed by NT in 1972 with pond, box balls and mixed borders; orchard, with blue and white borders leading to gazebo; small formal walled rose garden and woodland area with wildlife pond. TEAS July only. *Adm £1 Chd 20p (Share to the National Asthma Campaign). Suns May 9, June 13, July 25 (2-6). Also by appt at weekends only April to Sept* **Tel 08444 3168**

Nether Winchendon House ⚲⚘ (Mr & Mrs R Spencer Bernard) Nether Winchendon, 5m SW of Aylesbury; 7m from Thame. Picturesque village, beautiful church. 5 acres; fine trees, variety of hedges; naturalised spring bulbs; shrubs; herbaceous borders. Tudor manor house (not open) home of Sir Francis Bernard, last British Governor of Massachusetts. TEA weather permitting. *Adm £1.30 Chd under 15 free.* ▲*Suns April 25, July 25 (2-5.30)*

┌─────────────────────────────────────┐
│ **By Appointment Gardens.** See head of │
│ county section │
└─────────────────────────────────────┘

¶Newton Longville Gardens ⚲⚘ 1½m SW Bletchley off A421 Buckingham-Bletchley (Milton Keynes). Flower and country craft festival in St Faith's Church. Craft stalls in village hall. TEAS. *Combined adm £2 Chd free (Share to St Faith's Church). Sun July 11 (2-6)*

¶Church End ⚲ (Mr & Mrs M Rutherford) Secluded garden approx ½ acre, shrubs, herbaceous, large lily pond with fish. Prize winning fruit and vegetable area

¶11a Drayton Road ⚲ (Mr & Mrs A Lay) ½-acre long narrow rear garden. Interesting lay-out. Herbaceous and shrub borders open into fruit and vegetable areas.

¶69 Drayton Road (Mr & Mrs O Schneidau) Beautifully landscaped cottage garden with many interesting features. A large pond, shrubs, annuals and herbaceous perennials

¶The Old Rectory ⚲ (Mr & Mrs J Clarke) Garden of approx ½ acre created over last 11 yrs surrounding C18 house. Mature Tulip tree supporting kiftsgate rose thought to be planted to commemorate the Battle of Waterloo. Shrub and herbaceous borders, series of small ponds leading to larger lily pond

¶3 School Drive ⚲ (Mr & Mrs Hand) Patio with water feature and steps leading to small garden and attractively shaped lawn with surrounding borders. Pergola with climbers; plants in containers. Winner of Best Kept part of Garden competition 1992 (Village competition)

¶64 Westbrook End (Mr & Mrs J Blackhall) 2-acre terraced garden. Three ponds and woodland area. ⅓ acre organic fruit and vegetables. Apiary may be viewed at own risk on application to owner

The Old Rectory, Cublington ⚲⚘⚘ (Mr & Mrs J Naylor) 7m SW of Leighton Buzzard. From Aylesbury via A418 towards Leighton Buzzard; after 4½m turn L (W) at Xrds. Follow signs to Aston Abbots, then Cublington. 2-acre country garden with herbaceous border, rosebeds, shrubs and mature trees; vegetables; ponds, climbing plants. TEAS. *Adm £1 Chd free. Sun June 6 (2-5)*

The Old Vicarage, Padbury ⚲⚘⚘ (Mr & Mrs H Morley-Fletcher) Padbury 2m S of Buckingham on A413 follow signs in village. 2½ acres on 3 levels; flowering shrubs and trees; rose garden, new parterre. Display collection of hebes; pond and sunken garden. Fine views. Teas in church behind house (June only). *Adm £1 Chd free (Share to League of Friends of Buckingham Hospital). Sun April 18 (2-5), Sat, Sun June 19, 20 (2-6). Also open in June only* **Walmerdene**, *Buckingham 2m*

Overstroud Cottage ⚲⚘ (Mr & Mrs J Brooke) The Dell, Frith Hill. Amersham 6m Aylesbury 10m. Turn E off A413 at Gt Missenden onto B485 Frith Hill to Chesham. White Gothic cottage set back in layby 100yds up hill on L. Parking on R at Parish Church. Cottage originally C16 hospital for Missenden Abbey. 1-acre garden on two levels carved from chalk quarry. Winter/spring garden with hellebores, bulbs and winter flowering shrubs; borders of different colour schemes; collection of old-fashioned herb and species roses and traditional cottage plants; herb and sink gardens. Not suitable for children or push chairs. Teas at Parish Church. *Adm £1 Chd 50p (Share to Parish Church Fabric Fund and Save the Children Fund). Suns April 11, May 2, 9, June 6, 20, Sept 5 (2-6)*

Oving Gardens 5m NW of Aylesbury sign-posted off A 413 at Whitchurch. Also sign-posted 1m E of Waddesdon off A41. Garden pots and bird baths by Frances Levy. TEAS. Disabled parking in centre of village. *Combined adm £2 Chd free. Suns April 18, May 23 (2-6)*

Manor Close ዿ❀ (Mr & Mrs R J Hawkins) Manor Road. Mature, established garden of 1½-acres herbaceous borders; brick pathways; many spring bulbs; spectacular views over countryside. *New books stall in May*

Milton Cottage ❀ (Mr & Mrs G Harrington) The Green. Garden on two levels with step feature; small pond; arches, planted for colour and foliage effect. House is copy of Milton's Cottage at Chalfont St Giles. *(Not open April 18)*

The Old Butchers Arms ዿ❀❀ (Mr & Mrs Denys Fraser) Dark Lane. ¼-acre sloping chalk garden. Featuring unusual plants mostly labelled. Arches, paving, small scree garden. Many clematis and roses. Garden featured in BBC's Gardener's World magazine. TEAS

The Old School House ዿ (Mr & Mrs M Ryan) Playground now a walled garden. Small courtyard with rockery; orchard with daffodils and lovely views

Wall Cottage ❀ (Mr & Mrs L Libson) Manor Road. A small, mature and secluded dry walled cottage garden on two levels, mixed borders

Pasture Farm ዿ❀❀ (Mr & Mrs R Belgrove) Thame Rd. Longwick, nr Aylesbury. 1 m W of Longwick on the Thame Rd. A4129. 4m E of Thame. Farm entrance 50yds from layby. Garden at top of farm track. ½-acre labelled plantswoman's garden. Herbaceous border, rockery. White garden with shrubs, perennials, bulbs and annuals. Many plants for sale incl unusual white varieties. TEAS. *Adm £1 Chd free. Suns May 2, June 27, Sept 12 (2-6). Also by appt* Tel 08444 3651

¶Peppers ዿ❀❀ (Mr & Mrs J Ledger) 4 Sylvia Close, Gt Missenden. A413 Amersham to Aylesbury Rd. At Great Missenden by-pass turn at sign Great & Little Kingshill (Chiltern Hospital). After 400yds turn L, Nags Head Lane. After 300yds turn R under railway bridge. Sylvia Close 50yds on R. Approx 1 acre. Wide variety of plants, shrubs, trees, inc uncommon conifers, collection of acers, unusual containers, spring and autumn colour. TEA. *Adm £1 Chd free. Easter Sun April 11, Sun Aug 22 (10-5)*

¶Pollards ዿ (Mr & Mrs George Baker) Upper Icknield Way. ¾m NE of Princes Risborough via A4010; turn up Peters Lane at Monks Risborough. 1½-acre garden on chalk; formal and informal beds; orchard, vegetables and herbs; good views. TEAS. *Adm £1 Chd free. Sun Aug 15 (2-6)*

¶Prestwood Gardens ❀ From Amersham or Aylesbury turn off A413 at Gt Missenden. Take A4128 to High Wycombe through Prestwood. At end of High St as rd bears L go straight on. Anchor Cottage is adjoining Pinecroft on R hand side in Honor End Lane. Parking in public car park in High St, 300yds. Teas at Hughenden Church House. Combined *Adm £1 Chd free (Share to Save the Children Fund). Sun July 18 (2-6)*

¶Anchor Cottage (Group Captain & Mrs D L Edwards) ¼-acre garden with colour for all seasons. Pergola, pond, roses, shrubs and shade loving plants

¶Pinecroft (Mrs B Checkley & Mrs Smith) An enthusiast's very small and wide garden. Good use made of difficult shaped area with features

Quainton Gardens 7m NW of Aylesbury. Nr Waddesdon turn N off A41. *Combined adm £2 Chd free*

Sun May 9 (2-6)

Cross Farmhouse ዿ❀ (Mr & Mrs E Viney) 1 acre of undulating terrain formed 12 yrs ago from a farmyard and farmer's vegetable patch. Now a mature garden with landscaped pond and bank, old fruit trees, shrubs and bulbs for a long season of interest

¶Doddershall Park ዿ❀ (Mr & Mrs Christopher Prideaux) Medium-sized romantic garden, mixed borders, trees and shrubs. 2 large stretches of water part of old moat surrounding C16/17 Manor house. TEAS

Hatherways ዿ❀ (Mr & Mrs D Moreton) A cottage garden which has gradually emerged from a near wilderness. Bog garden, some interesting shrubs, herbaceous plants and bulbs. Plant stall in aid of the NSPCC

Sun June 20, Wed June 23 (2-6)

Brudenell House ዿ❀ (Dr & Mrs H B Wright) Church St (opp. Church). 2-acre garden surrounding old rectory. Interesting mature trees, large herbaceous/shrub borders; rose garden, fruit and vegetables. TEAS Sun June 20, TEA Wed June 23

Capricorner ዿ❀ (Mr & Mrs A Davis) Small garden created in former stable yard since 1986, planted for year round interest with many scented plants; wild garden evolving; views

Thorngumbald ዿ❀ (Mr & Mrs J Lydall) Cottage garden heavily planted wioth wide selection of old-fashioned plants, organicallyl grown; small pond, conservatory; attempts to encourage wild life

Quoitings ዿ❀❀ (Kenneth Balfour Esq) Oxford Rd, Marlow, 7m E of Henley, 3m S of High Wycombe; at Quoiting Sq, in Marlow turn N out of West St (A4155); garden 350yds up Oxford Rd on L. 2½-acres secluded garden with wide range of conifers and magnificent trees incl tulip, lime and pomegranate. Grand display of self propagated tulips and polyanthus followed by colourful mixed flower and dahlia beds; lawns; ha-ha; vistas. C17/18 house (not open) formerly home of Historiographer Royal to William IV and Queen Victoria. Brass Band. TEAS. *Adm £1.50 Chd free. Sun April 11 (1-5). Sun Sept 5 (1-6)*

Ravenstone House ዿ❀ (Mr & Mrs R Jackson) Ravenstone, nr Olney. 4m N of Newport Pagnall. Take B526, turn R in Gayhurst, then L past gravel pit. 3rd house on R in village. Approx 3 acres of mixed borders and shrubs. Rock garden, 2 ponds. Sun loving plants round swimming pool, colourful containers. Small kitchen garden. *Adm £1 Chd free. Sun July 18 (2-5)*

River Cottage ❀❀ (Mrs P Hancock) Radclive. 1½m W of Buckingham, lies down narrow lane between A422 Buckingham-Brackley Rd. A421 Buckingham-Oxford Rd nr Buckingham Garden Centre. ¼-acre cottage garden developed since 1987. Many unusual plants; shrubs and climbers. Further ¼-acre wild garden to river being developed. (Plants proceeds to BNO Group Hardy Plant Society). *Adm £1 Chd free. Sun, Mon June 27, 28 (2-5).* **Westcott House, Gawcott** *also open 1m away*

Spindrift &&& (Mr & Mrs Eric Desmond) Jordans, 3m NE of Beaconsfield. From A40, midway between Gerrards Cross and Beaconsfield turn N into Potkiln Lane; after 1m turn L into Jordans village; at far side of green turn R. Garden for all seasons; acid loving shrubs; herbaceous borders, hosta and hardy geranium collection; vines, pools, solar greenhouse, terraced vegetables and fruit garden on hill. Dell, specimen trees. Clematis, unusual shrubs and hardy plants. Partly suitable for wheelchairs. Member of Wellesborne Vegetable Research Assoc. TEAS. *Adm £1 Chd under 12 25p. Suns April 18, Weds June 9, July 28, Mon Aug 30 (2-5); also by appt for parties* Tel 02407 3172

Springlea &&& (Mr & Mrs M Dean) Seymour Plain. 1m from Marlow, 2½m from Lane End off B482. From Lane End pass Booker airfield on L then in 1m pass Seymour Court, L at pillar-box on grass triangle. ⅓-acre secluded garden backed by beechwoods; all year interest, featuring 60′ herbaceous border against high brick wall, pond, rockery, bog garden, rhododendrons, clematis, arch walkway, unusual plants and shrubs. Racing pigeon loft. 1991 and 1992, award winner incl Booker Garden Centre competition for most unusual best kept garden over 100′ in Buckinghamshire. *Adm £1 Chd free. Suns May 16, June 6, July 18, Sept 12 (2-6). Also by appt March to October* Tel 0628 473366

¶**Stowe Landscape Gardens** (The National Trust) 3m NW of Buckingham via Stowe Ave. Follow brown NT signs. One of the supreme creations of the Georgian era; the first, formal layout was adorned with many buildings by Vanbrugh, Kent and Gibbs; in the 1730s Kent designed the Elysian Fields in a more naturalistic style, one of the earliest examples of the reaction against formality leading to the evolution of the landscape garden; miraculously, this beautiful garden survives; its sheer scale must make it Britain's largest work of art. TEAS. *Adm £3.50 Chd £1.75. Tues May 18 (10-5)*

Turn End &&& (Mr & Mrs Peter Aldington) Townside, Haddenham. From A418 turn to Haddenham between Thame (3m) and Aylesbury (6m). Turn at Rising Sun into Townside. BR Hadd and Tham Parkway. This acre seems much more. Through archways and round corners are several secret gardens. A sweeping lawn bounded by herbaceous beds and a wooded glade with snowdrops, narcissi and bluebells. Old roses, iris and climbers abound. A sunny gravel garden has raised beds, alpine troughs and sempervivum pans. The house designed and built by the owners encloses a courtyard and fish pool. Featured in 'Country Life', 'The Garden', 'Practical Gardening'. Homemade TEAS. *Adm £1.20 Chd 40p (Share to HDA Haddenham Helpline & Aylesbury Advocates). Fri April 9, Suns May 16 (House open) June 27, Sept 12 (2-6) Groups by appt at other times.* Tel 0844 291383

Tythrop Park &&& (Mr & Mrs Jeremy Cotton) Kingsey 2m E of Thame, via A4129; lodge gates just before Kingsey. 4 acres. Replanting of wilderness. Walled kitchen garden, fully productive. Muscat and black (Muscat) d'Hamburg vine propagated from vine at Hampton Court 150yrs ago in vine house. Courtyard now planted as grey garden. Newly planted parterre to South of Carolean house (not open); stable block recently restored. TEA. *Adm £1.50 Chd free. Sun June 13 (2-6)*

Walmerdene && (Mr & Mrs M T Hall) 20 London Rd Buckingham. From Town Centre take A413 (London Rd). At top of hill turn R. Park in Brookfield Lane. Cream House on corner. Small town garden, unusual plants mostly labelled; bulbs; herbaceous; euphorbias; climbing and shrub roses; clematis; sink garden; small pond; white and yellow border; small conservatory and grapehouse. TEAS. *Adm £1 Chd free Sat, Sun June 19, 20 (2-6) also by appt* Tel 0280 817466. *Also open* **Old Vicarage, Padbury** *2m*

Watercroft and Watercroft Cottage && (Mr & Mrs P Hunnings) Penn 3m N of Beaconsfield on B474, 600yds past Penn Church. Medium-sized garden on clay; white flowers, new herb garden, rose walk, weeping ash; kitchen garden; wild flower meadow. New planting and pond, plants and Honey for sale. C18 house, C19 brewhouse (not open). TEAS in aid of Penn Church Heating Fund. *Adm £1 Chd 30p. Suns July 4, 11 (2-6)*

Weir Lodge && (Mr & Mrs Mungo Aldridge) Latimer Rd Chesham. Approx 1m SE of Chesham. Turn L from A416 along Waterside at junction of Red Lion St and Amersham Rd. From A404 Rickmansworth Amersham Rd turn R at signpost for Chenies and Latimer and go for 4m. Parking at Weir House Mill (McMinns) dangerous turning. ¾-acre garden on bank of R. Chess. Recovered from dereliction in 1983 by owners. Stream and ponds with planted banks. Gravelled terrace with sun loving plants. Assorted containers; shrub and mixed beds; wild flowers. Mature trees incl fine beeches in adjoining paddock. TEAS in aid of Chesham Society. *Adm £1 Chd free. Sun June 6 (2-6)*

Westcott House && (Mr & Mrs H S Hodding) Gawcott. 2m S of Buckingham off A421 Buckingham to Oxford Rd. House on corner of Radclive Rd. ½-acre cottage garden; shrubs, herbaceous plants, alpines; small collection of bonsais; two peat beds. *Adm £1 Chd free (Share to Holy Trinity Church, Gawcott Restoration Fund). Sun, Mon June 27, 28 (2-5).* **River Cottage, Radclive** *with plant stall also open 1m away*

West Wycombe Park && (Sir Francis Dashwood; The National Trust). West Wycombe. 3m W of High Wycombe on A40. Bus: from High Wycombe and Victoria. Landscape garden; numerous C18 temples and follies incl Temple of the Winds, Temple of Venus, Temple of Music. Swan-shaped lake, with flint bridges and cascade. *Adm (grounds only) £2.50 Chd £1.25 Sun Sept 5 (2-5)*

The Wheatsheaf Inn &&& (Mrs W Witzmann) Weedon. 2m N of Aylesbury off A413 Buckingham-Aylesbury rd. Black and White thatched Tudor Inn opp 15′ brick wall of 'Lilies'. Parking in courtyard and village. Since 1985 3 acres of field turned into a formal, flower and wild garden; with pond, roses, shrubs, perennials, spring bulbs, heather, conifers. Badminton and croquet lawn. Year round interest and fine views. Front has a preservation 400-yr-old walnut probably planted when the Old Wheatsheaf Coaching Inn was built. Many other old trees incl. hazel Grove for thatching. *Adm £1 Chd free. By appt only.* Tel 0296 641 581

¶**Whitchurch Gardens** 4m N of Aylesbury on A413 TEAS at Priory Court. Combined *Adm £1.50 Chd free. Sun June 13 (2-6)*

¶**Bay Cottage** ✲ (Mr & Mrs D Sharpe) Very small walled garden with patio built by owner with clever use of stonework. Colourful containers

¶**Church View Barn** ✲ (Mr & Mrs J Manson) Converted barn with partly walled garden designed by owners in 1992. Many climbers, roses, rockery and herbaceous border. Good views

¶**Fielding House** ♿ (Mr & Mrs W Hartman) ¼-acre partly walled cottage garden. Good views towards Waddesdon. Crafts for sale

¶**29 High Street** ❀ (Mrs S R Ward) Small sloping village garden. Variety of plants chosen mainly for their resistance to exposed site. Good views

¶**Mullions** ✲ (Dr & Mrs L I Holmes-Smith) ⅓ acre picturesque cottage garden behind C17 cottage. 2 ponds and garden on 3 terraces

¶**The Old Cottage** ♿✲ (Mr & Mrs R Gwynne-Jones) ¾-acre cottage garden. herbaceous border, herbs, good views. Path to Whittle Hole Spring.

¶**Priory Court** ♿❀ (Mr & Mrs H Bloomer) ⅔-acre partly walled former C17 rectory garden. Herbaceous and mixed borders, roses and herbs. Wild shady areas, vegetables and fruit. TEAS

Winslow Hall ♿✲ (Sir Edward & Lady Tomkins) On A413 10m N of Aylesbury, 6m S of Buckingham. Free public car park. Large garden with interesting shrubs and trees. *Adm £1.50 Chd free. Sun May 9 (2-5)*

Cambridgeshire

Hon County Organisers:
South: Lady Nourse, North End House, Grantchester CB3 9NQ
North: Mrs M Thompson, Stibbington House, Wansford, Peterborough PE8 6JS Tel 0780 782043

Assistant Hon County Organisers:
South: John Drake Esq., Hardwicke House, Highditch Road, Fen Ditton Tel 022 052 246
Timothy Clark Esq, Nether Hall Manor, Soham, Ely CB7 5AB Tel 0353 720269

Hon County Treasurer (North Cambridgeshire): Michael Thompson Esq.

DATES OF OPENING

By appointment
For telephone numbers and other details see garden descriptions

Chippenham Park, nr Newmarket
Docwra's Manor, Shepreth
Hardwicke House, Fen Ditton
83 High Street, Harlton
Lane End, Orton Longueville
Nuns Manor, Frog End, Shepreth
Padlock Croft, West Wratting
Scarlett's Farm, West Wratting
19 Swaynes Lane, Comberton
Tetworth Hall, nr Sandy
Weaver's Cottage, Streetly End, West Wickham

Regular opening
For details see garden descriptions

The Crossing House, Shepreth
Docwra's Manor, Shepreth. Every Mon, Wed, Fri and selected Suns

April 4 Sunday
Chippenham Park, nr Newmarket
King's College Fellows' Garden, Cambridge
Trinity College Fellows' Garden, Cambridge

April 16 Friday
Wimpole Hall, Royston

April 18 Sunday
Bartlow Park, Linton
Barton Gardens, Cambridge

May 3 Monday
Waterbeach Gardens, nr Waterbeach

May 16 Sunday
Docwra's Manor, Shepreth

May 22 Saturday
Padlock Croft, West Wratting
Scarlett's Farm, West Wratting
Weaver's Cottage, Streetly End, West Wickham

May 23 Sunday
Tetworth Hall, nr Sandy

May 29 Saturday
Island Hall, Godmanchester

May 30 Sunday
Hardwicke House, Fen Ditton
Tetworth Hall, nr Sandy

June 6 Sunday
Ely Gardens
Leckhampton, Cambridge
Nuns Manor, Frog End, Shepreth
Thorpe Hall, Peterborough

June 13 Sunday
The Bell School of Languages, nr Cambridge

June 17 Thursday
Bainton House, nr Stamford

June 19 Saturday
Burghley House, Stamford

June 20 Sunday
Burghley House, Stamford
Chippenham Park, nr Newmarket
Elm House, Elm, nr Wisbech
Fen Ditton Gardens, Fen Ditton
Grantchester Gardens, Grantchester
Hardwicke House, Fen Ditton
Madingley Hall, Cambridge
19 Swaynes Lane, Comberton

June 23 Wednesday
Milton, Peterborough

June 26 Saturday
Padlock Croft, West Wratting
Peckover House, Wisbech
Scarlett's Farm, West Wratting

Weaver's Cottage, Streetly End,
West Wickham
June 27 Sunday
Inglethorpe Manor, nr Wisbech
Upton Gardens, nr Peterborough
West Wratting Park, West Wratting
July 4 Sunday
Clare College, Fellows' Garden,
Cambridge
July 10 Saturday
Christ's College, Cambridge
Emmanuel College Gardens &
Fellows' Garden, Cambridge
July 11 Sunday
Anglesey Abbey, Cambridge
83 High Street, Harlton

Melbourn Bury, Royston
Melbourn Lodge, Royston
Nuns Manor, Frog End, Shepreth
July 17 Saturday
Padlock Croft, West Wratting
Scarlett's Farm, West Wratting
Weaver's Cottage, Streetly End,
West Wickham
July 18 Sunday
Pampisford Gardens, nr
Cambridge
Stibbington Gardens, nr
Peterborough
July 25 Sunday
King's College Fellows' Garden,
Cambridge

August 1 Sunday
Wytchwood, Great Stukeley
August 8 Sunday
Abbots Ripton Hall, Huntingdon
August 14 Saturday
Peckover House, Wisbech
August 15 Sunday
Anglesey Abbey, Cambridge
Robinson College, Grange Road,
Cambridge
September 5 Sunday
18 Cattels Lane, Waterbeach
Docwra's Manor, Shepreth
October 13 Wednesday
Milton, Peterborough

DESCRIPTIONS OF GARDENS

Abbots Ripton Hall ✻ (Lord De Ramsey) Abbots Ripton. Past Huntingdon on A1 signposted Abbots Ripton. In village turn L on B1090, 500 yards turn L into Hall Lane. 7½-acre garden containing many fine old trees; shrubs rose circle and grey border designed by Humphry Waterfield. Oldest rose in garden is called rosa shailers white; osmarea burkwoodii hedge; arboretum with very rare trees planted by Humphrey Waterfield; large rosa chinensis mutabilis. Although most of the plants in the garden are named, the Head Gardener is available to answer your questions. TEAS in aid of local charities. *Adm £2 Chd £1. Sun Aug 8 (2-6)*

Anglesey Abbey ৬✻❀ (The National Trust) 6m NE of Cambridge. From A45 turn N on to B1102 through Stow-cum-Quy. 100 acres surrounding an Elizabethan manor created from the remains of an abbey founded in reign of Henry I. Garden created during last 50 years; avenues of beautiful trees; groups of statuary; hedges enclosing small intimate gardens; daffodils and 4,400 white and blue hyacinths (April); magnificent herbaceous borders (June). Lunches & TEAS. *Adm garden only £3 Chd £1.50. Suns July 11, Aug 15 (11-5.30)*

¶**Bainton House** ৬✻ (Major W & Hon Mrs Birkbeck) Stamford. 4m E of Stamford on B1443 in Bainton Village. Turn N at Bainton Church. Entrance 400yds on the L. Approx 3 acres mature garden, shrubs, mixed borders, wild flowers and woodland. TEAS. *Adm £1 Chd free. Thurs June 17 (2-5.30)*

Bartlow Park ৬❀ (Brig & Mrs Alan Breitmeyer) 1½m SE of Linton. 6m NE of Saffron Walden; 12m SE of Cambridge; from A604 at Linton turn SE for Bartlow. Bus: Cambridge-Haverhill; alight Bartlow Xrds, 300yds. Medium-sized garden around house built 1964 in fine natural landscape of mature trees; spring bulbs, flowering shrubs and recently planted ornamental trees, with emphasis upon best contrasting foliage effects, set around lawns and formal rose beds. TEAS. *Adm £1.70 Chd free (Share to Bartlow Church Restoration Fund). Sun April 18 (2-6)*

Barton Gardens 3½m SW of Cambridge. Take A603, in village turn right for Comberton Rd. TEA. *Combined adm £1 Chd 25p (Share to GRBS). Sun April 18 (2-5)*
  The Gables ❀ (P L Harris Esq) 11 Comberton Rd. 2-acre old garden, mature trees, ha-ha, spring flowers
  Garden House ৬❀ (John Wheeldon Esq) Comberton Rd. Mixed domestic. *(Share to Cancer Research Campaign)*
  14 Haslingfield Road ৬ (J M Nairn Esq) Orchard, lawns, mixed domestic
  31 New Road (Dr D Macdonald) Cottage garden
  Orchard Cottage, 22 Haslingfield Road ৬❀ (Mr & Mrs W R Spencer) Interesting mixed domestic. ½-acre garden with alpine greenhouse and raised vegetable beds
  The Seven Houses ৬❀❀ (GRBS) Small bungalow estate on left of Comberton Rd. 1½-acre spring garden; bulbs naturalised in orchard. Gift stall
  Townsend (B R Overton Esq) 15a Comberton Rd. 1-acre; lawns, trees, pond; extensive views

The Bell School of Languages ❀❀ Red Cross Lane, Hills Rd, Cambridge. In SE Cambridge close to new Addenbrooke's Hospital on A604. Car park. Bus: Eastern Counties 185, 186, 193 to Hospital island; 113 passes gates (Haverhill bus). Large garden; herbaceous borders; summer bedding plants; fine trees and view. TEAS. *Adm £1 Chd free. Sun June 13 (2-5.30)*

Burghley House ৬❀ (Lady Victoria Leatham) Stamford Lincs. 1½m SW of Stamford signposted. Large 'Capability Brown' Parkland Garden; lake; small areas of formal planting House also open. TEAS. *Adm £1 Chd 50p (5 to 14). Sat, Sun June 19, 20 (11-4)*

Chippenham Park ৬ (Mr & Mrs Eustace Crawley) Chippenham. 5m NE of Newmarket 1m off A11. Walled parkland with mature and newly planted rare trees, large lake with 3 islands. 7 acres of gardens and woods containing roses, mixed borders of some rare shrubs and perennials and unusual trees. The spring gardens around the lake are dramatically beautiful and becoming more so after extensive replantings. The summer gardens too have been greatly extended and replanted in recent years. TEAS. *Adm £1.50 Chd free (Share to St Margaret's Church, Chippenham). Suns April 4, June 20 (2-6). Also by appt 0638 720221*

| Regular Openers. See head of county section. |

Christ's College &⚘ (Fellows) Cambridge. Large college garden near city centre; some form of garden since C16; present design from mid C19; 'Milton's Mulberry Tree'; large herbaceous borders and mature trees. *Adm £2 Chd 50p. Sat July 10 (2-6)*

Clare College, Fellows' Garden &⚘ (Master & Fellows) Cambridge. The Master and Fellows are owners of the Fellows' Garden which is open; the Master's garden (nearby) is not open to the public. Approach from Queen's Rd or from city centre via Senate House Passage, Old Court and Clare Bridge. 2 acres; one of the most famous gardens on the Cambridge Backs. TEAS. *Adm £1 Chd under 13 free. Sun July 4 (2-6)*

The Crossing House & (Mr & Mrs Douglas Fuller and Mr John Marlar) Meldreth Rd, Shepreth, 8m SW of Cambridge. ½m W of A10. King's Cross-Cambridge railway runs alongside garden. Small cottage garden with many old-fashioned plants grown in mixed beds in company with modern varieties; shrubs, bulbs, etc, many alpines in rock beds and alpine house. *Collecting box. Visitors welcome any day of the year* Tel Royston 261071

Docwra's Manor &⚘❀ (Mrs John Raven) Shepreth, 8m SW of Cambridge. ½m W of A10. Cambridge-Royston bus stops at gate opposite the War Memorial in Shepreth. 2-acres of choice plants in series of enclosed gardens. Small nursery for hardy plants. TEA May 16, Sept 5 only. In aid of Shepreth Church Funds. *Adm £1.50 Chd free. All year Mon, Wed, Fri (10-4), Suns April 4, May 2, June 6, July 4, Aug 1, Oct 3 (2-5), also Bank Hol Mons (10-4). Proceeds for garden upkeep. Also by appt.* Tel 0763 261473, 261557, 260235. *For NGS Suns May 16, Sept 5 (2-6)*

Elm House &⚘❀ (Mr & Mrs D G Bullard) 2m S of Wisbech. Turn off A1101 onto B1101 to Elm Village. House on left, 200 yds before the Church. Georgian fronted C17 House (not open); lawns with trees; old-fashioned walled garden; mixed borders - perennials and shrubs, young arboretum. Free car park in field. TEAS in aid of All Saints Church, Elm. *Adm £1 Chd free. Sun June 20 (2-5.30)*

Ely Gardens &⚘ 14 miles N of Cambridge on A10. *Combined adm £2 Chd 50p. Single garden £1 (Share to Old Palace Sue Ryder Home). Sun June 6 (2.30-5.30)*
    58 Barton Road (Ms R Sadler) A small garden specialising in wildlife conservation
    The Bishops House To right of main Cathedral entrance. Walled garden, former cloisters of monastery. Mixed herbaceous, box hedge, rose garden, kitchen garden
    31 Egremont St (Mr & Mrs J Friend-Smith) A10 Lyn Road out of Ely. 2nd left. Approx 1-acre. Lovely views of cathedral, mixed borders, cottage garden. Ginkgo tree, tulip tree and many other fine trees
    Old Bishops Palace 1½ acres with small lake, iris walk and herbaceous border wonderfully restored by two expert volunteers to its original C17. Famous for its Plane tree – oldest and largest in country. TEAS. *(Share to Old Palace Sue Ryder Home)*
    The Old Guildhall, 48 St Mary's St (Mr & Mrs J Hardiment) Interesting walled garden with unusual plants

¶43 Prickwillow Road (Mr & Mrs P J Stanning) Designed ½-acre garden with many interesting and unusual plants

Emmanuel College Garden & Fellows' Garden &⚘ in centre of Cambridge. Car parks at Parker's Piece and Lion Yard, within 5 mins walk. One of the most beautiful gardens in Cambridge; buildings of C17 to C20 surrounding 3 large gardens with pools; also herb garden; herbaceous borders, fine trees inc Metasequoia glyptostroboides. On this date access allowed to Fellows' Garden with magnificent Oriental plane and more herbaceous borders. Teashops in Cambridge. *Adm £1 Chd free. Sat July 10 (2.30-5.30)*

Fen Ditton Gardens ⚘❀ 3½m NE of Cambridge. From A45 Cambridge-Newmarket rd turn N by Borough Cemetary into Ditton Lane; or follow Airport sign from bypass. *Combined adm £1.50 Chd 50p (Share to Sue Ryder Foundation). Suns June 20 (2-5.30)*
    Hardwicke House ⚘❀ (Mr L & Mr J Drake) 2 acres designed to provide shelter for plants on exposed site; divided by variety of hedges; species roses; rare herbaceous plants; home of national collection of aquilegias, collection of plants grown in this country prior to 1650. Please park in road opposite. *Also by appt* Tel 022 052 246
    The Old Stables (Mr & Mrs Zavros) Large informal garden; old trees, shrubs and roses; many interesting plants, herbs and shrubs have been introduced. House (not open) converted by owners in 1973 from C17 stables
    The Rectory (Revd & Mrs L Marsh) New garden being laid out around new rectory. Visitors invited to inspect progress over next few years as owners wish to continue their support for the NGS.

Grantchester Gardens. ❀ 2m SW of Cambridge. A10 from S, left at Trumpington (Junction 11, M11). M11 from N, left at Junc 12. Palestrina Singers will be performing at the Old Vicarage. Craft Fair at Manor Farm, quality handmade goods; wooden toys; pottery, stained glass; glass blowing demonstration; honey and demonstrations of beekeeping. Plant stall by Cambridge City Council (John Hobson) and Art exhibition at North End House. TEAS. *(Share to Grantchester Church). Sun June 20 (2-6)*
    Balls Grove ⚘ (Mr & Mrs R H Barnes) An organic conservation garden consisting of a vegetable garden, lawns with perennial beds and shrubs; 2 ponds; small copse with some interesting, mature trees
    43 Broadway &⚘ (Mr & Mrs R Hill) 2 separate footpaths from Broadway. 1-acre lawns and formal garden with trees and alpine sink gardens; rest paddock backing onto farm meadows
    Home Grove & (Dr & Mrs C B Goodhart) 1-acre mature, orchard-type garden with shrub roses. Specimen trees and lawns and carefully planned kitchen garden
    North End House &⚘ (Sir Martin & Lady Nourse) 1 acre, newly laid out; shrub and herbaceous borders; old-fashioned roses; water garden and rockery. Small conservatory. Art exhibition
    The Old Mill (Jeremy Pemberton Esq) ½-acre on both sides of Mill Race in attractive rural setting. The Old Mill, mentioned in Rupert Brooke's poem 'Grantchester', was burnt down in 1928

The Old Vicarage ⅋✗❀ (Lord & Dr Archer) 2½ acres; house dating from C17; informal garden laid out in mid C19 with C20 conservatory; lawn with fountain; ancient mulberry tree; many other interesting trees incl cut-leaf beech; beyond garden is wilderness leading to river bank bordered by large old chestnut trees immortalised by Rupert Brooke, who lodged in the house 1910–1912

Hardwicke House ✗❀ (Mr L & Mr J Drake) 2 acres designed to provide shelter for plants on exposed site; divided by variety of hedges; species roses; turkish and rare herbaceous plants; home of national collection of aquilegias, collection of plants grown in this country prior to 1650. Please park in road opposite. *Adm £1.50 Chd 50p (Share to Sue Ryder Foundation). Suns May 30, June 20 (2- 5.30). Also by appt* Tel **022 052 246**

83 High Street, Harlton ⅋✗❀ (Dr Ruth Chippindale) 7m SW of Cambridge. A603 (toward Sandy); after 6m turn left (S) for Harlton. ⅓-acre interesting design which includes many different features, colours and a wide diversity of plants. TEAS. *Adm 70p Chd 30p (Share to Harlton Church Restoration Fund). Sun July 11 (2-6); also by appointment* Tel **0223 262170**

¶**Inglethorpe Manor** ✗❀ (Mr & Mrs Roger Hartley) Emneth, near Wisbech. 2m S of Wisbech on A1101. 200yds on L beyond 40mph derestriction sign. Entrance opp Ken Rowe's Garage. Large garden with interesting mature trees incl giant wellingtonia, lawns, mixed and herbaceous borders, shrub roses, rose walk and lakeside walk. Victorian house (not open). Plants for sale and TEAS in aid of NSPCC. *Adm £1. Sun June 27 (2-6)*

Island Hall ⅋✗❀ (Mr Christopher & The Hon Mrs Vane Percy) Godmanchester. In centre of Godmanchester next to car park, 1m S of Huntingdon (A1) 15m NW of Cambridge (A604). Station: Huntingdon (1m). An important mid-C18 mansion of great charm owned and being restored by an award winning Interior Designer. Tranquil riverside setting with ornamental island forming part of the grounds. The 1-acre garden has been reclaimed from neglect and from the Nissen huts put there when the house was requisitioned in World War II. Formal shaped borders planted with different box are either side of the gravel terrace. The gaps have been filled with pyramids of fastigiate yew. New shrubberies have been planted with a walk through to white and blue borders, with urns, hedges and good vistas. The Island is being cleared and wild flowers encouraged. An exact replica of the original Chinese bridge over the millstream was completed in 1988. TEAS in aid of Godmanchester Church Organ Restoration Fund. *Adm £1.50. Sat May 29 (2-5)*

King's College Fellows' Garden ⅋✗❀ Cambridge. Fine example of a Victorian garden with rare specimen trees. Colour booklet available £1.50, free leaflet describing numbered trees. TEAS. *Adm £1 Chd free. Suns April 4, July 25 (2-6)*

By Appointment Gardens. Avoid the crowds. Good chance of a tour by owner. See garden description for telephone number.

Lane End ✗❀ (Mr & Mrs R M Bulkeley) 9 St Botolph Lane Orton Longueville. 2m W of Peterborough, just off A1139 (was A605) 2½m E of intersection with A1. Approaching from W take second R after junction with Nene Parkway, just before Texaco garage (hidden entrance, narrow private road). Lane End is last house on L. Designer's small garden of ⅙-acre containing unusual plants in a variety of habitats; small trees; shrub roses; herbaceous and mixed borders, pond, scree bed. Emphasis on organic gardening and encouraging wildlife. *Adm £1 Chd free. By appt only* Tel **0733 231177**

Leckhampton ⅋✗ (Corpus Christi College) 37 Grange Rd, Cambridge. Grange Rd is on W side of Cambridge and runs N to S between Madingley Rd (A1303) and A603; drive entrance opp Selwyn College. 10 acres; originally laid out by William Robinson as garden of Leckhampton House (built 1880); George Thomson building added 1964 (Civic Trust Award); formal lawns, rose garden, small herbaceous beds; extensive wild garden with bulbs, cowslips, prunus and fine specimen trees. TEAS. *Adm £1 Chd free. Sun June 6 (2-6)*

Madingley Hall Cambridge ✗ (University of Cambridge) 4m W, 1m from M11 Exit 13. C16 Hall set in 7½ acres of attractive grounds. Features include landscaped walled garden with hazel walk, borders in individual colours and rose pergola. Meadow, topiary and mature trees. TEAS. *Adm £1 Chd free. (Share to Madingley Church Restoration Fund) Sun June 20 (2.30-5.30)*

Melbourn Bury ⅋✗❀ (Mr & Mrs Anthony Hopkinson) 2¼m N of Royston; 8m S of Cambridge; off the A10 on edge of village, Royston side. 5 acres; small ornamental lake and river with wildfowl; large herbaceous border; fine mature trees with wide lawns and rose garden. TEAS in aid of WI. *Combined adm with* **Melbourn Lodge** *£1 Chd free. Sun July 11 (2-6)*

Melbourn Lodge ⅋✗❀ (J R M Keatley Esq) Melbourn 3m N of Royston, 8m S of Cambridge. House in middle of Melbourn village. 2-acre garden maintained on 9 hrs work in season. C19 grade II listed house (not open). TEAS at Melbourne Bury. *Combined adm with* **Melbourn Bury** *£1 Chd free. Sun July 11 (2-6)*

Milton ⅋✗ (Countess Fitzwilliam) nr Peterborough. Entrance to park 1½m W of Peterborough city centre; off Bretton Way which leads from Thomas Cook roundabout on A47. Approx 8 acres of pleasure grounds designed by Humphrey Repton in 1791, with orangery by John Carr of York; walled garden with herbaceous borders and shrubs designed by Percy Caine in the 1950's. TEA. *Adm £2 Chd free. Weds June 23, (2-6) Oct 13 (2-5)*

Nuns Manor ⅋✗❀ (Mr & Mrs J R L Brashaw) Shepreth nr Royston Herts. 8m SW of Cambridge 200 yds from A10 Melbourn-Shepreth Xrds. C16 farmhouse surrounded by 2-acre garden (extended 1987); interesting plants, large pond, woodland walk, kitchen garden. Mixed and herbaceous borders. *Adm £1 Chd free. Suns June 6, July 11 (2-6); also by appt May to Aug* Tel **0763 260313**

Padlock Croft ♿✿❀ (Mr & Mrs P E Lewis) West Wratting. From dual carriageway on A604 between Linton and Horseheath take turning N (Balsham W Wratting); Padlock Road is at entry to village. Plantsman's organic garden of ⅔-acre, home of the National Campanula Collection; mixed borders, troughs, alpine house etc. inc rare plants; rock and scree gardens; newly formed potager with raised beds. TEA. *Combined Adm £1.50 Chd 50p with* **Scarletts Farm** *and* **Weavers Cottage.** *Sats May 22, June 26, July 17 (2-7); also by appt* **Tel 0223 290383**

Pampisford Gardens ♿✿❀ 8m S of Cambridge on A505. TEAS at the Old Vicarage (in aid of RDA). *Combined adm £1.50 Chd free. Sun July 18 (2-5.30)*
  The Dower House (Dr & Mrs O M Edwards) 7 High Street. Medieval house surrounded by well designed and interesting garden
  Glebe Crescent A group of pensioners houses with very colourful small gardens. No 5 won the 1st prize for best kept small garden in S Cambs
  The Old Vicarage (Mr & Mrs Nixon) Next to Church in village. 2½-acres; mature trees; shrub and herbaceous borders with good ground cover plants; small Victorian style conservatory planted with rare species

Peckover House ✿ (The National Trust) Wisbech. In centre of Wisbech town, on N bank of R Nene (B1441). Garden only open. 2-acre Victorian garden; rare trees, inc maidenhair (Ginkgo), tulip trees etc. Many old-fashioned roses and colourful borders. Orange trees growing in well-stocked greenhouse. TEAS. *Adm £1 Chd 50p.* ▲*Sats June 26, Aug 14 (2-5.30)*

Robinson College ♿✿❀ (Warden & Fellows) Cambridge. Gardens surround the College and are enclosed by Grange Rd, Adams Rd, Sylvester Rd and Herschel Rd, ½m W of the centre of Cambridge. Access is by Porters' Lodge on Grange Rd and Thorney Creek Gate Herschel Rd, (off Grange Rd). Ample parking in surrounding roads. From M11 turn E at junction 12 (A 603) and then turn L into Grange Rd after ½m. 8-acre garden created 1979 by landscaping several Edwardian gardens. The site is bisected by the Bin Brook, with a pool at its centre. Since 1982 there has been a programme of planting. Gardens contain a wide range of trees, notably snake bark maples (acer spp), parrotia persica, sequoiadendron giganteum pendulum and celtis australis. Also numerous shrubs; cistus sp., ceanothus impressus, southmead and blue mound, as well as other plants from the Mediterranean and New Zealand. The constraints on the site make it necessary to exploit a wide range of shade-tolerant species. Tea. *Adm £1 Chd free. Sun Aug 15 (2-6)*

Scarlett's Farm ♿✿❀ (Mr & Mrs M Hicks) Padlock Rd, West Wratting. From dual carriageway on A604 between Linton and Horseheath taking turning N (W Wratting 3½); Padlock Road is at entry to village. Scarlett's Farm at end of Padlock Road. ⅓-acre mixed garden brought back from state of neglect since 1984. Shrubs, herbaceous, roses, annuals, small deep bed vegetable area. TEAS. *Combined adm £1.50 Chd 50p with* **Padlock Croft** *and* **Weavers Cottage.** *Sats May 22, June 26, July 17 (2-6); also by appt* **Tel 0223 290812**

Stibbington Gardens ✿ 8m W of Peterborough off the A1. Stibbington House & 107 Elton Rd are W of A1 on B671 Elton Rd S of Wansford Old Castle Farmhouse is in Stibbington Village E of A1. Signed Stibbington from A1. TEAS at Stibbington House. *Combined adm £1.50 Chd free. Sun July 18 (2-6)*
  107 Elton Road (Mr & Mrs J Ferris) 1 acre, comprising lawns with many roses; mainly annuals and dahlias; enclosed with mature trees
  ¶**Old Castle Farmhouse** ♿ (Mr & Mrs J M Peake) Cul-de-sac S of church. Mainly lawn and shrubs with pond, garden borders a small backwater of R Nene and covers approx 2 acres
  Stibbington House (Mr & Mrs Michael Thompson) Wansford. Approx 3 acres of trees, shrubs, mixed borders, lawns running down to mill stream (River Nene), site of old paper mill. Longhorn cattle in field

¶**19 Swaynes Lane** ♿✿❀ (Dr & Mrs Lyndon Davies) Comberton. 5m W of Cambridge. From M11 take exit 12 and turn away from Cambridge on A603. Take first R B1046 through Barton to Comberton; follow signs from Xrds. Garden of approx ½ acre attractively planted with wide range of flowering plants framed by foliage and shrubs. Gravel bed and troughs give contrast; vegetable garden. TEAS. *Adm £1 Chd 50p (Share to Herbal Research). Sun June 20 (2-5.30); also by appt* **Tel 0223 264159 and 262686**

Tetworth Hall ❀ (Lady Crossman) 4m NE of Sandy; 6m SE of St Neots off Everton-Waresley Rd. Large woodland and bog garden; rhododendrons; azaleas, unusual shrubs and plants; fine trees. Queen Anne house (not open). TEA in aid of Waresley Church. *Adm £1 Chd free. Suns May 23, 30 (2-6.30), also by appt April 15 to June 15* **Tel 0767 50212**

Thorpe Hall ♿✿❀ (Sue Ryder Foundation) Longthorpe Rd, Longthorpe, Peterborough. 1m W of Peterborough city centre. Thorpe Hall 1665 Grade I house in Grade II listed garden with original walls; gate piers; urns and niches. Unique garden in course of replanting. Victorian stone parterre; iris collection; rose garden and 1850 herbaceous borders. TEAS. *Adm Garden only £1 Chd 50p (Share to Sue Ryder Foundation). Sun June 6 (2-5.30)*

Trinity College, Fellows' Garden ♿✿ Queen's Road, Cambridge. Garden of 8-acres, originally laid out in the 1870s by W.B. Thomas; lawns with mixed borders, shrubs, specimen trees. Drifts of spring bulbs. *Adm £1 Chd free. Sun April 4 (2-6)*

¶**Upton Gardens** ✿❀ 5m W of Peterborough. Turn off A47 between Castor and Wansford at roundabout signed Upton. TEAS. *Combined adm £1 Chd free. Sun June 27 (2-5)*
  ¶**Model Farm** (Mr & Mrs M F Longfoot) Farmhouse garden with walled kitchen garden. Many shrubs and perennials giving colour and interest. TEAS
  Rose Cottage (Mr & Mrs K W Goodacre) Small cottage garden; pond; herbs; octagonal greenhouse; many varieties of plants and shrubs giving colour

---

Regular Openers. See head of county section.

Waterbeach Gardens ✂ Cambridge 7m N of Cambridge on E of A10, well signed. Flower Festival, crafts, toilets and Teas at St Johns Chruch in aid of Church funds. *Combined adm £1 Chd free. Mon May 3 (2-6)*

45 Bannold Road ♿ (Mr & Mrs K Knight) Rockery, raised bed of ericaceous plants and shrubs, small vegetable area, rose beds

90 Bannold Rd ❀ (Mr & Mrs R L Guy) Feature front garden of coloured barks (rubus bifloris) etc. Small garden to rear

18 Cattels Lane ♿❀ (Mr & Mrs Vincent) Model vegetable garden with fruit trees, small pond and rockery, greenhouse, shrubs. *Also open Sun Sept 5 (2-6) Adm 50p Chd free*

Weaver's Cottage ♿✂ (Miss Sylvia Norton) Streetly End, West Wickham. From dual carriageway on A604 between Linton and Horseheath take turning N (W Wratting 3½m then 1st turning R (Streetly End 1¼m). Keep L at triangle. Weaver's Cottage is 5th on the R. ½-acre garden planted for fragrance with bulbs; shrubs; herbs; perennials; honeysuckle; old shrub and climbing roses. National Lathyrus Collection. TEA. *Combined adm £1.50 Chd 50p with* **Padlock Croft** *and* **Scarletts Farm**. *Sats May 22, June 26, July 17 (2-6). Visitors welcome any time by appt* **Tel 0223 892399**

West Wratting Park ♿✂❀ (Mr & Mrs Henry d'Abo) 8m S of Newmarket. From A11, between Worsted Lodge and Six Mile Bottom, turn E to Balsham; then N along B1052 to West Wratting; Park is at E end of village. Georgian house (orangery shown), beautifully situated in rolling country, with fine trees; rose and herbaceous gardens; walled kitchen garden. TEAS. *Adm £1 Chd free. Sun June 27 (2-7)*

Wimpole Hall ♿✂ (National Trust) Arrington. 5m N of Royston signed off A603 to Sandy 7m from Cambridge or off A1198. Part of 350-acre park. Vivid show of many varieties of daffodils is main attraction in April; fine trees and marked walks in park. Pre-booked guided tours only available 11.00, 15.00 hrs given by Head Gardener. TEA. *Adm £1.50 Chd free. ▲Fri April 16 (10.30-5)*

¶Wytchwood ✂❀ (Mr & Mrs David Cox) Gt Stukeley. 2m N of Huntingdon. Turn off B1043 into Owl End by Great Stukeley village hall. Parking at village hall and in Owl End. 1 acre year round interest. Lawns, shrubs, perennial plants, trees, pond, roses, area of wild plants and grasses. Vegetables and rare poultry. Last year (1992) this garden finished in the top ten of Gardener Of The Year competition. Sponsored by Garden News and Thompson and Morgan Seeds. TEA. *Adm £1 Chd 50p. Sun Aug 1 (2-5.30)*

Cheshire & Wirral

Hon County Organiser: Nicholas Payne Esq, The Mount, Whirley, Macclesfield, Cheshire, SK11 9PB
Assistant Hon County Organisers: Mrs T R Hill, Salterswell House, Tarporley, Cheshire CW6 OED
Mrs N Whitbread, Lower Huxley Hall, Hargrave, Chester, CH3 7RJ

DATES OF OPENING

By appointment
For telephone numbers and other details see garden descriptions

Cherry Hill, Malpas
The Old Hall, Willaston
Orchard Villa, Alsager
5 Pine Hey, Neston
85 Warmingham Road, Coppenhall
Wood End Cottage, Whitegate
Woodsetton, Alsager

Regular openings
For details see garden descriptions

Arley Hall, Northwich. Every Tues to Sun & Bank Hols April to Oct
Capesthorne, Macclesfield. April to Sept incl; various times see text
Cholmondeley Castle Gardens, Malpas. Suns and Bank Hols April 4 to Oct 17
Dunge Farm Gardens, Kettleshulme. Daily May to Sept
Lyme Park, Disley, Stockport. Open daily
Norton Priory, Runcorn. All year for various days see text
Peover Hall, Knutsford. Mons & Thurs May to Oct excluding Bank Hols
The Quinta, Swettenham. Daily April to Oct

April 4 Sunday
The Well House, Tilston

April 11 Sunday
The Old Hall, Willaston
Penn, Alderley Edge
Poulton Hall, Bebington

April 12 Monday
Penn, Alderley Edge

April 18 Sunday
Woodsetton, Alsager

April 25 Sunday
Penn, Alderley Edge

May 2 Sunday
Tushingham Hall, Whitchurch

May 3 Monday
Orchard Villa, Alsager

May 9 Sunday
5 Pine Hey, Neston
The Quinta, Swettenham
The Well House, Tilston

May 16 Sunday
Dorfold Hall, Nantwich
Rode Hall, Scholar Green
Willaston Grange, S Wirral

May 19 Wednesday
Cherry Hill, Malpas

The Quinta, Swettenham

May 23 Sunday
Hare Hill Gardens, Over
Alderley ‡
Manley Knoll, Manley
Penn, Alderley Edge ‡

May 24 Monday
Penn, Alderley Edge

May 26 Wednesday
Dunge Farm Gardens,
Kettleshulme
Reaseheath, nr Nantwich

May 29 Saturday
Peover Hall, Knutsford

May 30 Sunday
Bolesworth Castle, Tattenhall
Peover Hall, Knutsford

May 31 Monday
Ashton Hayes, Chester
Penn, Alderley Edge

June 2 Wednesday
Reaseheath, nr Nantwich

June 5 Saturday
The Old Parsonage, Arley Green

June 6 Sunday
Henbury Hall, Nr Macclesfield
35 Heyes Lane. Timperley
Little Moreton Hall, Congleton
The Old Hall, Willaston
The Old Parsonage, Arley Green
Orchard Villa, Alsager

June 9 Wednesday
Reaseheath, nr Nantwich

June 12 Saturday
Arley Hall & Gardens,
Northwich

June 13 Sunday
Norton Priory, Runcorn
Poulton Hall, Bebington
85 Warmingham Road,
Coppenhall

June 16 Wednesday
Reaseheath, nr Nantwich

June 19 Saturday
Lyme Park, Disley, Stockport

June 20 Sunday
Lyme Park, Disley, Stockport
5 Pine Hey, Neston
Rosewood, Puddington
Woodsetton, Alsager

June 23 Wednesday
Cherry Hill, Malpas
Reaseheath, nr Nantwich

June 26 Saturday
Ness Gardens, Ness

June 27 Sunday
Burton Village Gardens,
Burton

June 28 Monday
Tatton Park, Knutsford

June 30 Wednesday
Reaseheath, nr Nantwich

July 7 Wednesday
Reaseheath, nr Nantwich

July 9 Friday
Dunham Massey, Altrincham

July 11 Sunday
35 Heyes Lane. Timperley
Newbold, Bruera, nr Saighton
Wood End Cottage,
Whitegate

July 14 Wednesday
Reaseheath, nr Nantwich

July 18 Sunday
The Mount, Whirley ‡
5 Pine Hey, Neston
Whirley Hall, Macclesfield ‡

July 21 Wednesday
Reaseheath, nr Nantwich

July 28 Wednesday
Reaseheath, nr Nantwich

August 4 Wednesday
Capesthorne, Macclesfield
Ness Gardens, Ness

August 8 Sunday
Dunge Farm Gardens,
Kettleshulme

August 14 Saturday
Cholmondeley Castle Gardens,
Malpas

August 30 Monday
Thornton Manor, Wirral

DESCRIPTIONS OF GARDENS

Arley Hall & Gardens &❀ (Hon M L W Flower), 6m W of Knutsford. 5m from M6 junc 19 & 20 & M56 junc 9 & 10. 12 acres; gardens have belonged to 1 family over 500 yrs; great variety of style and design; outstanding twin herbaceous borders (one of earliest in England); unusual avenue of clipped Ilex trees, walled gardens; yew hedges; shrub roses; azaleas, rhododendrons; herb garden; scented garden; woodland garden and walk. Arley Hall and Private Chapel also open. Lunches and light refreshments (in C16 converted barn adjacent to earlier 'Cruck' barn). Gift shop. *Adm Gardens & Chapel only £2.60, Chd under 17 £1.30. Hall £1.60 extra; Chd 80p under 5 free (Share to Cheshire Red Cross Society). April to Oct every Tues to Sun inc & Bank Hols (12-5) last adm to gardens 4.30. For NGS Sat June 12 (12-5). Special rates and catering arrangements for pre-booked parties.* **Tel 0565 777353**

Ashton Hayes (Michael Grime Esq) Chester. Midway between Tarvin and Kelsall on A54 Chester-Sandiway rd; take B5393 N to Ashton and Mouldsworth. Approach to Ashton Hayes can be seen halfway between Ashton and Mouldsworth. The ¾m drive is beside former lodge. About 12 acres, including arboretum and ponds. Predominantly a valley garden of mature trees and flowering shrubs. Great variety of azaleas and rhododendrons; notable embothrium. TEAS. *Adm £1.50 OAPs £1 Chd 50p (Share to Church of St John the Evangelist, Ashton Hayes). Mon May 31 (2-6)*

Bolesworth Castle &❀❀ (Mr & Mrs A G Barbour) Tattenhall. Enter by lodge on A41 1m N of Broxton roundabout. Landscape with rhododendrons, trees, shrubs and borders. TEAS. *Adm £1.75 Chd 75p (Share to Harthill & Burwardsley Churches). Sun May 30 (2-5.30)*

Burton Village Gardens ❀❀ 9m NW of Chester. Turn off A540 at Willaston-Burton Xrds (traffic lights) and follow rd for 1m to Burton. *Combined adm £1.50 Chd free (Share to St Johns Hospice). Sun June 27 (2-6)*
    Bank Cottage (Mr & Mrs J R Beecroft) Small, very colourful, mixed cottage garden with old roses backing on to village cricket ground
    Briarfield (Mr & Mrs P Carter) About an acre of rare trees and shrubs in woodland setting close to **Rake House**
    Rake House (Mr & Mrs R I Cowan) TEAS only in enclosed sandstone courtyard, with pond, relaid with original cobbles and York stone, opp the College. Short woodland trail to and from **Lynwood**
    Lynwood ❀ (Mr & Mrs P M Wright) On the fringe of the village on the Neston Road. ⅓-acre garden with shrub borders; rockery, pond with waterfall, pergola, arbour with climbers, heathers and alpines

---

By Appointment Gardens. These owners do not have a fixed opening day usually because they do not like crowds or have insufficient parking space. Owner will often give guided tour.

Capesthorne & (Mr & Mrs W A Bromley-Davenport) 5m W of Macclesfield. 7m S of Wilmslow on A34. Bus stop: Capesthorne (Congleton to Manchester route). Medium-sized garden; daffodil lawn; azaleas, rhododendrons; flowering shrubs; herbaceous border; lake and pool. Georgian chapel built 1722 on view. Hall open for viewing from 2pm until 4pm (extra charge). Illustrated book on garden/woodland walks available at £1. Historic parks and gardens. TEAS and LUNCHES. Free car park. *Adm garden £2 OAPs £1.75 Chd 50p; Hall extra £2 OAPs £1.75 Chd 50p. Combined tickets £3.50, £3, £1. Suns April to Sept inc; Wed May to Sept inc Tues & Thurs June to July; also Good Fri & Bank hols. For NGS Wed Aug 4 (12-6)*

Cherry Hill &❀ (Mr & Mrs Miles Clarke) 2m W of Malpas signed from B5069 to Chorlton. Massed bulbs in spring; walks through pine woods and rhododendrons to trout lake; walled garden, herbaceous borders, shrub roses. Ornamental vegetable garden. TEAS in attractive house overlooking Welsh mountains. Cricket ground. *Adm £2 Chd 50p (Share to Hospice of the Good Shepherd). Weds May 19, June 23 (2-6.30). Parties by appt March to July* Tel 0948 860355

Cholmondeley Castle Gardens &❀ (The Marchioness of Cholmondeley) Malpas. Situated off A41 Chester-Whitchurch Rd and A49 Whitchurch-Tarporley Rd. Romantically landscaped gardens full of variety. Azaleas, rhododendrons, flowering shrubs, rare trees, herbaceous borders and water garden. Lakeside picnic area, gift shop, rare breeds of farm animals. Ancient Private Chapel in the Park. Tearoom offering light lunches etc. *Adm gardens only £2.50 OAPs £1.50 Chd 75p. Open Suns and Bank Hols only April 4 to Oct 17 (12-5.30). Weekday visits accepted by prior arrangement. Reduced rate for coach parties. For NGS Sat Aug 14 (12-5.30)* Tel 0829 720383 *or* 720203

Dorfold Hall ❀❀ (Mr & Mrs Richard Roundell) 1m W of Nantwich on A534; between Nantwich and Acton. 18-acre garden with formal approach; lawns and recently planted woodland and water gardens. TEAS in aid of Acton Parish Church. *Adm £1.50 Chd 75p. Sun May 16 (2-5.30)*

¶Dunge Farm Gardens ❀❀ (Mr & Mrs David Ketley) Kettleshulme. Take B5470 rd from Macclesfield. Kettleshulme is 6m from Macclesfield. Turn R in village signed Goyt Valley and in ½m at Xrds, turn R down lane to Dunge Farm. Surrounded by romantic hills and set in 5½ acres, at 1000ft, this is the highest garden in Cheshire; mature trees, woodland, stream with waterfall, bog gardens, herbaceous borders, species rhododendrons, magnolias, acers and mechonopsis. Yr-round interest, an oasis in the Pennine foothills. TEAS. *Adm £2 Chd 50p. Open daily May 1 to Sept 30 (10.30-4.30) Wed May 26, (10.30-4.30). For NGS Sun Aug 8 (10.30-4.30)*

Dunham Massey &❀❀ (The National Trust) Altrincham. 3m SW of Altrincham off A56. Well signed. Garden over 20 acres, on ancient site with moat lake, mount and orangery. Mature trees and fine lawns with extensive range of shrubs and herbaceous perennials suited to acid sand, many planted at waterside. Set in 350 acres of deer park. TEAS. *Adm £2 Chd £1 (car entry £2). ▲For NGS Fri July 9 (12-5)*

Hare Hill Gardens &❀ (The National Trust) Over Alderley. Between Alderley Edge and Prestbury, turn off N at B5087 at Greyhound Rd (118:SJ85765). Bus: Cheshire E17 Macclesfield–Wilmslow (passing BR Wilmslow and Prestbury) to within ¾m. Stations: Alderley Edge 2½m, Prestbury 2½m. Attractive spring garden featuring a fine display of rhododendrons and azaleas. A good collection of hollies and other specimen trees and shrubs. The 10-acre garden includes a walled garden which hosts many wall shrubs including clematis and vines. The borders are planted with agapanthus (African lily) and geraniums. *Adm £2 Chd £1. ▲For NGS Sun May 23 (10-5.30)*

Henbury Hall &❀ (Mr & Mrs Sebastian de Ferranti) nr Macclesfield. 2m W of Macclesfield on A537 rd. Turn down School Lane, Henbury at Blacksmiths Arms: East Lodge on R. Large garden with lake, beautifully landscaped and full of variety. Azaleas, rhododendrons, flowering shrubs, rare trees, herbaceous borders. *Adm £2 Chd 50p. Sun June 6 (2.30-6)*

¶35 Heyes Lane (Mr & Mrs David Eastwood) Timperley. Heyes Lane is a turning off Park Road (B5165) 1m from the junction with the A56 Altrincham-Manchester Rd 1½m N of Altrincham. Or from A560 turn W in Timperley Village for ¼m. Newsagents shop on corner. A small suburban garden 30' × 90' on sandy soil maintained by a keen plantswoman member of the Organic Movement (HDRA). An all-year-round garden; trees; small pond; greenhouses; fruit and vegetables with a good collection of interesting and unusual plants. *Adm £1 Chd free. Suns June 6, July 11 (2-6)*

Little Moreton Hall &❀❀ (The National Trust) Congleton. On A34, 4m S of Congleton. 1½-acre garden surrounded by a moat and bordered by yew hedges, next to finest example of timber-framed architecture in England. Herb and historic vegetable garden, orchard and borders. Knot garden based on design in 'The English Gardener' published by Leonard Meager in 1670, though probably Elizabethan in origin. Adm includes entry to the Hall with optional free guided tours. Wheelchairs and electric mobility vehicle available. Disabled toilet. Picnic lawns. Shop and restaurant serving coffee, lunches and afternoon teas. TEAS. *Adm £3.50 Chd 1.75. ▲For NGS Sun June 6 (12-5)*

¶Lyme Park (Stockport Metropolitan Borough Council - The National Trust) Disley. 6m SE of Stockport just W of Disley on A6 rd. 17-acre garden retaining many original features from Tudor and Jacobean times; high Victorian style bedding; a Dutch garden; a Gertrude Jekyll style herbaceous border; an Edwardian rose garden and many other features. Also rare trees, a wild flower area and lake. Guided tours June 19, 20, at 2pm, 3pm, 4pm. Donations to NGS. *Adm £3.20 per car, pedestrians free. Open all year except Dec 25, 26. (11-5) summer; (11-4) winter. Sat, Sun June 19, 20 (11-5)*

Manley Knoll & (Mrs D G Fildes) Manley, NE of Chester. Nr Mouldsworth. B5393. Quarry garden; azaleas and rhododendrons. TEAS. *Adm £1 Chd 25p. Sun May 23 (2-6.30)*

The Mount &⋇ (Mr & Mrs Nicholas Payne) Whirley. The Mount is situated about 2m due W of Macclesfield along A537 rd. Opp Blacksmiths Arms at Henbury, go up Pepper St, turn L into Church Lane which becomes Anderton Lane in 100yds. The Mount is about 200yds up Anderton Lane on L. Adequate parking. The garden is approx 1½ acres and is of architectural character with hedges, terraces and walls. About ¼-acre of rhododendrons, azaleas, roses, herbaceous and some bedding plants; and also interesting trees including eucryphia nymansensis, fern leaved beech and sciadopitys. The garden is very much compartmentalized with lawns; shrubberies; herbaceous border; swimming pool and short vista of Irish Yews. TEAS. *Adm £1.50 Chd 50p. Sun July 18 (2.30-6)*

Ness Gardens &⋇❀ (University of Liverpool) Neston. Between Neston and Burton, 10m NW of Chester; 4m from end of M56; signed A540 and A550. 45 acres of landscaped gardens. Notable collection of rhododendrons, azaleas, camellias, magnolias, cherries, rowans, birches, conifers, roses, primulas, lilies, etc. Large rock and alpine garden; terrace gardens; herbaceous borders; plants for autumn and winter colour; conservatory and greenhouses; woodland and water gardens; laburnum arch. Tree and nature trails; Chinese plants collected by George Forrest. Children's play and picnic area (no ball games). Parts of the gardens suitable for wheelchairs. Free parking for over 1000 cars. Licensed refreshment rooms, gift shop. TEAS. *Adm £3 Chd (10-18)/OAP £2, Family £7. For NGS Sat June 26, Wed Aug 4 (9.30-5)*

Newbold &⋇❀ (Mrs J N Davies-Colley) Bruera nr Saighton. 5m SE of Chester. From A41 Chester-Whitchurch. Turn W at Hatton Heath towards Bruera, entrance on L approx 1m. Old garden; rare trees. clipped yews; vistas. TEAS. *Adm £1.50 Chd 50p (Share to Bruera Church). Sun July 11 (2-6)*

Norton Priory &❀ (Norton Priory Museum Trust Ltd) Tudor Road, Manor Park, Runcorn. Runcorn New Town 1m, Warrington 5m. From M56 Junc 11 turn for Warrington and follow signs. From Warrington take A56 for Runcorn and follow signs. 16 acres well established woodland gardens; Georgian summerhouses; rock garden and stream glade; 3-acre walled garden of similar date (1760s) recently restored. Georgian and modern garden designs; fruit training; rosewalk; colour borders; herb garden, cottage garden and exhibition. Priory remains of museum also open. *Adm All-in-ticket £2.40 Concessions £1.20. Daily April to October (12-5) weekends and bank hols (12-6) Nov to March (12-4) (Walled garden closed Nov-Feb). For NGS Sun June 13 (12-6)*

The Old Hall &⋇❀ (Dr & Mrs M W W Wood) Hadlow Rd, Willaston S Wirral, 8m NW of Chester on village green. ¾-acre; mixed border; interesting plants; daffodils; winter flowering shrubs and colour. C17 house. TEAS, June 6 only. *Adm £1.50 Chd 50p (Share to Muscular Dystrophy Group). Easter Suns April 11, June 6 (2-6); also by appt Tel 051 327 4779*

The Old Parsonage &❀ (The Hon Michael & Mrs Flower) Arley Green; 5m NNE of Northwich and 3m Great Budworth; 6m W Knutsford; 5m from M6 juncs 19, 20 and M56 juncs 9, 10. Follow signposts to Arley Hall and Gardens and at central crossroad follow notices to The Old Parsonage. The Old Parsonage lies across park at Arley Green, a cluster of old buildings in a very attractive rural setting beside a lake. 2-acre garden has old established yew hedges sheltering herbaceous and mixed borders, shrub roses and climbers, a newly planted woodland garden and pond, with some unusual young trees and foliage shrubs. Waterplants, rhododendrons, azaleas, meconopsis. Plant stall. *Adm £1.50 Chd 75p. (Share to Red Cross). Visitors will be admitted to Arley Hall Gardens (teas, plants, shop available) at concessionary rate (£1.50 Chd under 17 75p) on production of their Old Parsonage ticket. Sat, Sun June 5, 6 (2-6)*

Orchard Villa ⋇❀ (Mr & Mrs J Trinder) 72 Audley Rd, Alsager. At traffic lights in Alsager town centre turn S towards Audley, house is 300 yds on R beyond level crossing. Long and narrow, this ⅓-acre has been designed to grow a wide range of herbaceous plants, iris and alpines in features such as scree, peat, raised, light and shade beds. TEAS. *Adm £1 Chd Free. Bank Hol Mon May 3, Sun June 6 (1.30-5); also by appt May to Aug Tel 0270 874833*

Penn &⋇❀ (R W Baldwin Esq) Macclesfield Rd, Alderley Edge. ¾m E of Alderley Edge village, on B5087, Alderley Edge-Macclesfield rd. Turn left into Woodbrook Rd for car parking. 2½ acres; April entries especially for magnolias, camellias, earlier rhododendrons incl. blue and yellow. May entries for azaleas and rest of rhododendrons (up to 500 species and hybrids) and perhaps meconopsis. Partly suitable for wheelchairs. TEA. *Adm £1.50 OAPs £1 Chd 50p. Suns April 11, 25, May 23; Mons April 12, May 24, 31 (2-5.30)*

Peover Hall &⋇❀ (Randle Brooks Esq) Over Peover. 3m S of Knutsford on A50, Lodge gates by Whipping Stocks Inn. 15-acres. 5 walled gardens: lily pond, rose, herb, white and pink gardens; C18 landscaped park, moat, C19 dell, rhododendron walks, large walled kitchen garden, Church walk, purple border, blue and white border, pleached lime avenues, fine topiary work. Dogs in park only. TEAS. *Adm £1.50 Chd 50p. Mons & Thurs (2-5) May to Oct. NOT Bank Hols. Other days by appt for parties. For NGS Sat, Sun May 29, 30 (2-6)*

5 Pine Hey &⋇❀ (Mr & Mrs S J Clayton) Neston. A540 Chester to Hoylake Road. Turn off at the Shrewsbury Arms (Roast Inn) traffic lights towards Neston. Turn R at T-junction drive through Neston past cross on the left, then fork L at the Methodist Church/Brewer Arms continue along Leighton Rd, past the old Windmill and Earl Drive on the L. Pine Hey is the next on L. The garden covers approx. ¾ acre and is laid out informally with different areas, inluding a copse, new water garden, stream and lawns each with its own character. The main objective is to make it an all-year garden, and there is an element of surprise when first entering. TEAS (in aid of RNLI Neston and Parkgate Branch). *Adm £1.50 Chd free (Share to Walton Pain Relief Foundation and Wirral Methodist Housing Assoc.). Sun May 9, June 20, July 18 (2-5); also by appt May 9 to July 18 Tel 051 336 3006*

Poulton Hall &⋪ (The Lancelyn Green Family) Poulton Lancelyn, 2m from Bebington. From M53, exit 4 towards Bebington; at traffic lights (½m) right along Poulton Rd; house 1m on right. 2½ acres; lawns, ha-ha, wild flower meadow, shrubbery, walled gardens. TEAS. *Adm £1.50 Chd 20p. Suns April 11, June 13 (2-6)*

The Quinta &⋪ (Sir Bernard & Lady Lovell) Swettenham. Turn E off A535 at Twemlow (Yellow Broom Cafe) and follow signs to Swettenham. 10-acre garden with extensive collection of trees and shrubs leading to woodland walks overlooking the Dane Valley and to the thirty-nine step descent to Swettenham brook. TEA Suns & Bank Hols only. *Adm £2 Acc Chd free. Open daily April 1 to Oct 31 (2-6). For NGS Sun May 9, Wed May 19 (2-6)*

Reaseheath ⋪⊛ (Reaseheath College) nr Nantwich. 1½m N of Nantwich on the A51. The Gardens, covering 12 acres, are based on a Victorian Garden surrounding Reaseheath Hall and contain many mature trees of horticultural interest. The gardens are used as a teaching resource. There are specialised features of particular interest including, glasshouses; model fruit garden; rose garden; woodland garden; lakeside bog garden and extensive shrub borders, lawns and sports facilities. TEA. *Collecting Boxes. Weds May 26, June 2, 9, 16, 23, 30, July 7, 14, 21, 28 (2-4)*

Rode Hall ⊛ (Sir Richard & Lady Baker Wilbraham) Scholar Green National Grid reference SJ8157 5m SW of Congleton between A34 and A50. Terrace and rose garden with view over Humphrey Repton's landscape is a feature of Rode gardens, as is the Victorian wild flower garden with a grotto and the walk to the lake past the old Stew pond. Other attractions include a restored ice house and working walled kitchen garden. TEAS. *Adm £1.50 Chd 50p (House extra £2) (Share to All Saints Church, Odd Rode and St Mary's Church Astbury). Sun May 16 (2-5.30)*

Rosewood ⋪⊛ (Mr & Mrs A Dodd) Tranmore Farm, Puddington. Grid Ref: SJ 37SW-327 735 7.5m N of Chester, Ness Gardens 2m. Puddington is located 1½m from A540 NW of Two Mills junction with A550. Look out for car parking signs on entering village. Converted farm building in rural hamlet with 1 acre of new trees; shrubs; lake and mixed herbaceous started from rough field and farmyard. Work commenced on small area in 1982 with further cultivation of the whole area since then. The garden demonstrates various ages of development. TEAS. *Adm £1.50 Chd free. Sun June 20 (2-6)*

Tatton Park &⋪⊛ (Cheshire County Council: The National Trust) Knutsford. Well signposted on M56 junction 7 and from M6 junction 19. 2½m N of Knutsford. Gardens contain many unusual features and rare species of plants, shrubs and trees. Considered to be the very finest and most important of all gardens within The National Trust they rank among England's 'Top Ten'. Features include orangery by Wyatt, fernery by Paxton, Japanese, Italian and rose gardens. Greek monument and African hut. Hybrid azaleas and rhododendrons, swamp cypresses, tree ferns, tall redwoods, bamboos and pines. An exotic garden offering a new and delightful surprise round every corner, a palimpsest of 200 years develop-

ment by the Egerton family. The Tatton Garden Society part of the garden will also be open. TEAS. *Adm £2.50 Group £1.80 Chd £1.70 Group £1.30.* ▲*For NGS Mon June 28 (10.30-5)*

Thornton Manor ⊛ (The Viscount Leverhulme) Thornton Hough, Wirral. From Chester A540 to Fiveway Garage; turn right on to B5136 to Thornton Hough village. From Birkenhead B5151 then on to B5136. From M53, exit 4 to Heswall; turn left after 1m. Bus: Woodside-Parkgate; alight Thornton Hough village. Large garden of all year round interest. TEAS. Free car park. *Adm £1.50 OAPs/Chd 50p. Bank Hol Mon Aug 30 (2-7)*

Tushingham Hall (Mr & Mrs P Moore Dutton) 3m N of Whitchurch. Signed off A41 Chester-Whitchurch Rd; Medium-sized garden in beautiful surroundings; bluebell wood alongside pool; ancient oak, girth 26ft. TEA. *Adm £1.50 Chd 30p. (Share to St Chad's Church, Tushingham). Sun May 2 (2-6.30)*

¶85 Warmingham Road ⋪⊛ (Mr & Mrs A Mann) Coppenhall. Approx 3m N of Crewe town centre towards Warmingham Village. Close by White Lion Inn, Coppenhall. ⅓-acre plantsman's garden, with shrubs, perennial borders, raised beds, troughs, rock garden, peat garden, pond and greenhouse with cacti and succulents. Speciality alpines. TEA. *Adm £1 Chd free. Sun June 13 (12-5). By appt May to Sept* Tel 0270 582030

The Well House ⋪⊛ (Mrs S H French-Greenslade) Tilston, nr Malpas. 12m S of Chester, follow signs to Tilston from A41 S of Broxton roundabout, taking Malpas Rd through Tilston. House and antique shop on dangerous bend. Parking if possible in a field or on roadside. Approx ¾-acre small cottage garden, divided by a natural stream. Land over the stream, only acquired autumn 1990, is reached by a bridge; all plantings still very young. Attractive summerhouse, tiny pond and pumped waterfall. Winding paths through variety of small areas; herbs; shrubs and secret garden. At its best when the many bulbs are out in the spring. TEAS. *Adm £1.50 Chd 25p. Suns April 4, May 9 (2-6)*

¶Whirley Hall &⋪ (Sir William & Lady Mather) Macclesfield. O.S. sheet 118 map ref 875746. The Hall is N of Knutsford Rd (A537) to Macclesfield going E, take the 2nd turning L after Monks Heath traffic lights up Whirley Lane. The Hall is 1m on L. Going W out of Macclesfield, 70 yds after Broken Cross fork R along Birtes Rd, the Hall is 1¼m on R. 1½ acres of lawns, shrubs, borders, flagged terraces and kitchen garden. *Adm £1.50 Chd 50p. Sun July 18 (2.30-6)*

Willaston Grange & (Sir Derek and Lady Bibby) Willaston. A540 Chester to West Kirby until opposite the new Elf Garage. Proceed down B5151 Hadlow Road, towards Willaston. Borders, rock garden, vegetable garden, orchard, about 3 acres. Special feature-woodland walk. TEAS. *Adm £1.50 OAPs £1 Chd free. Sun May 16 (2-6)*

By Appointment Gardens. Avoid the crowds. Good chance of a tour by owner. See garden description for telephone number.

Wood End Cottage ✿✿ (Mr & Mrs M R Everett) Grange Lane, Whitegate. Turn S off A556 (Northwich/Chester) to Whitegate village, opp school follow Grange Lane for 300 yds. ½-acre sloping to a natural stream; developed as a plantsman's garden. Mature trees; herbaceous; clematis; raised beds. TEAS. Plant stall. *Adm £1.50 Chd 50p (Share to British Epilepsy Assoc). Sun July 11 (2-6); also by appt in May, June, July* **Tel 0606 888236**

Woodsetton ✿✿ (Mr & Mrs Eric Barber) Alsager. At town centre follow B5078, take third turning L into Pikemere Road and then second turning on R. Approx 1-acre, interesting plants; trees; shrubs; rhododendrons; large natural wildlife pool, scree and alpines. TEAS. *Adm £1 Chd free (Share to St. Lukes Hospice 'Grosvenor House', Winsford, Cheshire). Suns April 18, June 20 (2-6) also by appt May, June, July* **Tel 0270 877623**

Clwyd

See separate Welsh section beginning on page 274

Cornwall

Hon County Organiser:	G J Holborow Esq, Ladock House, Ladock, Truro, Cornwall Tel 0726 882274
Assistant Hon County Organisers:	Mrs W Eliot (Publicity) Tregye Cottage, Carnon Down, Truro TR3 6JH Tel 0872 864739
	Mrs D Morison (W Cornwall) Boskenna, St Martin, Manaccon, Helston Tel 0326 231 210
	Mrs Richard Jerram (N Cornwall) Trehane, Trevanson, Wadebridge Tel 0208 812523
Cornwall Leaflet	Tony Shaw Esq, Rope House, Cliff Street, Mevagissey, nr St Austell, Cornwall PL26 6QL Tel 0726 842819
Hon County Treasurer:	Mrs Cynthia Bassett, 5 Athelstan Park, Bodmin, PL31 1DS Tel 0208 73247

DATES OF OPENING

By appointment
For telephone numbers and other details see garden descriptions

Chyverton, Zelah
The Hollies, Grampound, nr Truro
Trelean, St Martin-in-Meneage
Trevegean, Heamoor
Woodland Garden, Garras

Regular openings
For details see garden descriptions

Carwinion, Mawnan Smith. Daily April to Oct
Headland, Polruan-by-Fowey. Every Thurs June to Sept

Ken Caro, Bicton, nr Liskeard. Every Sun, Mon, Tues, Wed April 11 to June 30, Weds only July & Aug
Penjerrick Garden, Budock nr Falmouth. Every Weds & Suns March 1 to Sept 30
Trebah, Mawnan Smith. Daily throughout the year
Tregrehan, Par. Mid March to end June, and Sept, Weds to Suns
Trewithen, nr Truro. Mon to Sat March 1 to Sept 30
Woodland Garden, Garras. Sats April 10 to Oct 30

April 4 Sunday
Penjerrick Garden, Budock nr Falmouth
Tremeer Gardens, St Tudy

April 10 Saturday
Bosloe, Mawnan Smith
April 11 Sunday (Easter Sunday)
Porthpean House, St Austell
Trelissick, Feock
April 18 Sunday
Oak Tree House, Perran-ar-Worthal
Penwarne nr Falmouth
April 25 Sunday
Polgwynne, Feock
St Michael's Mount, Marazion
May 2 Sunday
Estray Parc, Penjerrick
May 9 Sunday
Boconnoc, Nr Lostwithiel
Cotehele House, St Dominick
Pinetum, Harewood
Tregrehan, Par

May 16 Sunday
Bosvigo House, Truro
Helland Bridge Pottery, nr Bodmin
Loveny, St Neot
The Old Mill Herbary, Helland
Bridge
Pinetum, Harewood
May 19 Wednesday
Peterdale, Millbrook
May 20 Thursday
Headland, Polruan
May 23 Sunday
Carclew Gardens,
Perran-ar-Worthal
Lanhydrock, Bodmin
May 27 Thursday
Headland, Polruan
May 30 Sunday
Lamorran House, St Mawes
June 6 Sunday
Northwood Farm, St Neot

The Old Barn, St Neot
June 13 Sunday
Creed House, Creed, Grampound
Higher Truscott, nr Launceston
The Hollies, Grampound, nr Truro
Trerice, nr Newquay
Trevegean, Heamoor
June 17 Thursday
Ince Castle Gardens, Saltash
June 20 Sunday
Mary Newman's Cottage,
Saltash
The Old Vicarage, Marazion,
Penzance
Tregilliowe Farm, Penzance
June 23 Wednesday
The Old Vicarage, Marazion,
Penzance
June 26 Saturday
Berriow Bridge and Middlewood
Gardens, nr Launceston

June 27 Sunday
Berriow Bridge and Middlewood
Gardens, nr Launceston
Roseland House, Chacewater
July 2 Friday
Prideaux Place, Padstow
July 9 Friday
Prideaux Place, Padstow
July 11 Sunday
Peterdale, Millbrook
Roseland House, Chacewater
July 18 Sunday
Pine Lodge Gardens, Cuddra, St
Austell
Tregilliowe Farm, Penzance
August 8 Sunday
Pinetum, Harewood
September 26 Sunday
Trebartha, nr Launceston
October 24 Sunday
Trelean, St Martin-in-Meneage

DESCRIPTIONS OF GARDENS

¶**Berriow Bridge & Middlewood Gardens** ⚘✿ Hillbrooke. OS map ref: SX 273752 Situated where B3254 crosses R Lynher between Launceston & Liskeard. Park at Berriow Bridge where tickets & map available. In a lovely valley below Bodmin Moor, several gardens show a variety of landscape styles from small cottages with secret & surprising gardens, roses, unusual plants, streams & natural stone, to a larger riverside garden with sculptures and woodland walk. (Featured on TV). TEAS in aid of North Hill Village Hall. *Combined adm £2 Chd free. Sat, Sun June 26, 27 (2-6)*

Boconnoc ✿✿ (Mr & Mrs J D G Fortescue) 2m S of A390. On main rd between middle Taphouse and Downend garage, follow signs. Privately owned gardens covering some 20 acres, surrounded by parkland and woods. Magnificent old trees, flowering shrubs and views. TEAS. *Adm £1.50 Chd Free (Share to Boconnoc Church Window Fund). Sun May 9 (2-6)*

Bosloe ✿ (The National Trust) Mawnan Smith, 5m S of Falmouth. In Mawnan Smith, take Helford Rd and turn off for Durgan. Medium-sized garden; fine view of R Helford. *Adm £1 Chd free. Sat April 10 (2-5)*

Bosvigo House ✿⚘✿ (Mr & Mrs M Perry) Bosvigo Lane. ¾m from Truro centre take Redruth Rd at Highertown, turn R before Shell garage down Dobbs Lane. After 400yds entrance to house is on L, after nasty L-hand bend. 3-acre garden still being developed surrounding Georgian house (not open) and Victorian conservatory. Series of enclosed and walled gardens with mainly herbaceous plants for colour and foliage effect. Woodland walk. Many rare and unusual plants. Partly suitable for wheelchairs. TEAS, served in servants' hall on charity Suns only. *Adm £1.50 Chd 50p. For NGS Sun May 16 (2-5)*

Carclew Gardens ✿⚘✿ (Mrs Chope) Perran-ar-Worthal, nr Truro. From A39 turn E at Perran-ar-Worthal. Bus: alight Perran-ar-Worthal 1m. Large garden, rhododendron species; terraces; ornamental water. TEAS. *Adm £1.50 Chd 50p (Share to Barristers Benevolent Fund). Sun May 23 (2-5.30)*

Carwinion (Mr H A E Rogers) Mawnan Smith via Carwinion Rd. An unmanicured or permissive valley garden of some 10 acres with many camellias, rhododendrons and azaleas flowering in the spring. Apart from an abundance of wild flowers, grasses, ferns etc, the garden holds the premier collection of temperate bamboos in the UK. TEAS. *Adm £1 Chd 50p. Open daily April to Oct (2-5.30)*

Chyverton (Mr & Mrs N T Holman) Zelah, N of Truro. Entrance ¾m SW of Zelah on A30. Georgian landscaped garden with lake and bridge (1770); large shrub garden of great beauty; outstanding collection magnolias acers, camellias, rhododendrons, primulas, rare and exotic trees and shrubs. Visitors personally conducted by owners. *Adm £2.50 (£2 for parties over 20 persons) Chd & Students £1. By appt only weekdays March to June* **Tel 0872 540324**

Cotehele House ✿⚘✿ (The National Trust) 2m E of St Dominick, 4m from Gunnislake (turn at St Ann's Chapel); 8m SW of Tavistock; 14m from Plymouth via Tamar Bridge. Terrace garden falling to sheltered valley with ponds, stream and unusual shrubs. Fine medieval house (one of the least altered in the country); armour, tapestries, furniture. Lunches and TEAS. *Adm house, garden & mill £5 Chd £2.50; garden, grounds & mill £2.50 Chd £1.50 Sun May 9 (11-5.30)*

> **By Appointment Gardens.** These owners do not have a fixed opening day usually because they do not like crowds or have insufficient parking space. Owner will often give guided tour.

¶**Creed House** ⚘✿❀ (Mr & Mrs W R Croggon) Creed. From the centre of Grampound on A390 (halfway between Truro & St Austell). Take rd signposted to Creed. After 1m turn L opposite Creed Church and the garden is on L. Parking in lane. 5-acre landscaped Georgian Rectory garden. Tree collection; rhododendrons; sunken alpine and formal walled herbaceous gardens. Trickle stream to ponds and bog. Natural woodland walk. Restoration began 1974 – continues & incl recent planting. TEAS. *Adm £1.50 Chd free. Sun June 13 (2-5.30)*

¶**Estray Parc** ✿ (Mr & Mrs J M Williams) Penjerrick. Leave Penjerrick main entrance on R follow the rd towards Mawnan Smith until entrance to The Home Hotel on L. Directly opp turn R and follow the signs. In 1983 most of this 3-acre garden was a bramble thistle infested field. A considerable variety of plants have been introduced and continuous grass cutting has produced passable sloping lawns interspersed by a large collection of trees and shrubs. *Adm £1 OAPs/Chd 50p Sun May 2 (2-6)*

Headland ✿ (Jean & John Hill) Battery Lane, Polruan. On E of Fowey estuary; leave car in public park; walk down St Saviour's Hill, turn left at Coast Guard office. 1¼-acre cliff garden with sea on 3 sides; mainly plants which withstand salty gales but incl sub-tropical. Spectacular views of Coast; cove for swimming. Cream TEAS. *Adm £1 Chd 50p. Open every Thurs June, July, Aug, Sept. For NGS Thurs May 20, 27 (2-8)*

¶**Helland Bridge Pottery** ⚘✿ (Paul & Rone Jackson) Helland Bridge, Bodmin. 2m N of Bodmin off A30. Follow signs to Helland, next to R Camel. 1½ acre garden 2 ¼-acre meadow. Family garden comprising bog garden, ponds, river frontage; borders, orchard and vegetable garden. Pottery open. *Combined adm with **The Old Mill Herbary** £2 Chd 50p Sun May 16 (2-5)*

¶**Higher Truscott** ✿❀ (Mr & Mrs J C Mann) St Stephens. 3m NW of Launceston between St Stephens & Egloskerry. Signposted. All the year round elevated garden of 1 acre in a natural setting. Trees, shrubs, climbers; herbaceous plants & alpines, (many unusual). Splendid views. Ornamental vegetable garden. TEAS. *Adm £1 Chd free. Sun June13 (2-6)*

The Hollies ⚘✿❀ (Mr J & Mrs N B Croggon) Grampound, nr Truro. In centre of village on Truro-St Austell rd. 2-acre garden of unusual design; unusual mixed planting of trees, shrubs and alpines. TEAS. *Adm £1 Chd 50p. Sun June 13 (2-5.30); also by appt April-Sept* **Tel 0726 882474**

Ince Castle Gardens & Grounds ❀ (Patricia, Viscountess Boyd of Merton) 5m SW of Saltash. From A38, at Stoketon Cross take turn signed Trematon, Elmgate. 5-acres with lawns and ornamental woods; shell house and dovecote. TEA. *Adm £1.50 Chd free. Thurs 17 June (2-6)*

● **Ken Caro** ✿❀ (Mr & Mrs K R Willcock) Bicton, Pensilva, 5m NE of Liskeard. From A390 to Callington turn off N at Butchers Arms, St Ive; take Pensilva Rd; at next Xrds take rd signed Bicton. 2 acres mostly planted in 1970; well-designed and labelled plantsman's garden; rhododendrons, flowering shrubs, conifers and other trees; herbaceous borders. Panoramic views. Collection of waterfowl and aviary birds. *Adm £1.50 Chd 50p. April 11 to June 30 every Sun, Mon, Tues, Wed; Weds only July, Aug (2-6). Groups by appt* **Tel 0579 62446**

Lamorran House ✿ (Mr & Mrs Dudley-Cooke) Upper Castle Rd, St Mawes. First turning R after garage; signposted to St. Mawes Castle. House ½m on L. Parking in rd. 4-acre sub-tropical hillside garden with beautiful views to St Anthonys Head. Extensive water gardens in Mediterranean and Japanese settings. Large collection of rhododendrons, azaleas, palm trees, cycads, agaves and many S hemisphere plants and trees. TEAS. *Adm £2 Chd Free. Sun May 30 (10.30-5)*

Lanhydrock ⚘✿❀ (The National Trust) Bodmin, 2½m on B3268. Station: Bodmin Parkway 1¾m. Large-sized garden; formal garden laid out 1857; shrub garden with good specimens of rhododendrons and magnolias and fine views. Lunches and TEAS. Closed Mondays. *Adm house & garden £5 Chd £2.50; garden only £2.60 Chd £1.30. Sun May 23 (11-5.30; last adm to house 5)*

Loveny, St Neot (Mr & Mrs J G Thompson) Take rd L of the London Inn. Up steep hill. L past school. Follow NGS posters. Park in lane. Riverside gdn with mature trees and shrubs; interesting waterside plants. TEAS. *Adm £1 Chd free. Sun May 16 (2-6)*

Mary Newman's Cottage ✿❀ (Tamar Protection Society) Culver Rd, ¼m from Saltash town centre; park on waterfront. Cottage garden with herbaceous, annuals and herbs. Overlooks R Tamar and Bridges. Recently restored C15 cottage, former home of Sir Francis Drake's first wife. TEAS. *Adm £1 Chd free (Share to Tamar Protection Society). Sun June 20 (2-6)*

Northwood Farm, St Neot ✿ (Mr & Mrs P K Cooper) take rd out of village to Wenmouth Cross. L and first R. Follow very narrow rd and NGS posters to Farm on R. House & garden on site of a China Clay Dri used 150 yrs ago. House rebuilt from barn and garden from old sunken pits still being developed. Discovery of several natural springs led to creation of ponds now with collection of water birds. TEA. *Combined adm with **The Old Barn** £1.50, Chd free. Sun June 6 (2-5.30)*

Oak Tree House ❀ (Mr & Mrs R H C Robins) Perran-ar-Worthal, nr Truro. Turn R off A39 Truro-Falmouth rd after Norway Inn; signed Perranwell. House on R corner. A medium sized, sheltered and mature garden several levels planted with camellias, rhododendrons and other spring flowers. TEAS. *Adm £1 Chd 50p. Sun April 18 (2-6)*

The Old Barn, St Neot ⚘❀ (Mr & Mrs H S Lloyd) nr Liskeard. Turn R by garage, down lane to Holy Well. Cross field. 1st on L. Park in field. Riverside garden, mature trees, shrubs; mixed perennials, roses, clematis, pelargoniums, lawns, pond with water lilies. TEAS. *Combined adm with **Northwood Farm** £1.50 Chd free. Sun June 6 (2-5.30)*

The Old Mill Herbary ♿❀ (Mr & Mrs R D Whurr) Helland Bridge, Bodmin. OS Map Ref SX065717. Approx 4 acres semi-wild garden; natural woodland walks, alongside R Camel. Many wild flowers; adjacent Camel trail. Extensive planted display of culinary, medicinal and aromatic herbs; shrubs; climbing and herbaceous plants. Active mill leat, water garden, raised patio pond with aquatics, Koi and other fish. Statuary, small raised alpine gardens. Treneague camomile lawn. A specialist's garden of historical and botanical interest. TEAS. *Combined adm with Helland Bridge Pottery* £2 Chd 50p. ▲*For NGS Sun May 16 (2-5)*

¶**The Old Vicarage** ♿❀ (Dr & Mrs Senior) Marazion. 3½m E of Penzance on hillside W end of Marazion. Marazion to Penzance coast rd - end of town bear R edge of marsh. Keep R up hillside, garden 800yds on R; limited parking in narrow lane. Large car parks W Marazion. ½-acre garden started 1964, overplanted by optimistic owners fantasizing Mediterranean climate. A plantsman's garden. TEAS in aid of Cancer Relief. *Adm* £2 *Chd free. Sun, Wed June 20, 23 (2-6)*

Penjerrick Garden ❀ (Rachel Morin) Budock. 3m SW of Falmouth between Budock and Mawnan Smith. Entrance at junction of lanes opp. Penmorvah Manor Hotel. Parking on verge along drive. Room to park one coach at gate. 15-acre garden of historical and botanical interest. Home of Barclayi and Penjerrick rhododendron hybrids. The upper garden with lovely view to the sea, contains many rhododendrons, camellias, magnolias, azaleas, bamboos, tree ferns and magnificent trees. The lower luxuriant valley garden features ponds in a wild woodland setting. *Adm* £1 *Chd 50p (Share to Cornwall Garden Trust)*. ▲*For NGS Sun April 4 (11-5). Guided tours* Tel 0326 250074 *Jane Bird*

Penwarné ♿⚥ (Mr & Mrs H Beister) 3¼m SW of Falmouth. 1½m N of Mawnan. Garden with many varieties of flowering shrubs, rhododendrons, magnolias, New Zealand shrubs, formal and informal garden; walled garden. Ornamental ducks. *Adm* £1 *Chd 50p. Sun April 18 (2-5)*

Peterdale ⚥❀ (Mrs Ann Mountfield) Millbrook. Via Torpoint Ferry travelling W A374 to Antony; 1st L at main junction signed Millbrook, along new rd to Southdown. 1st L at new roundabout, straight ahead up St Johns Rd. Peterdale last bungalow on L. Small garden started 1980 from field; designed and created by owner on different levels; interesting collection of shrubs, trees, herbaceous plants combined with several mini lawns. TEAS. *Adm* £1.50 *Chd free Wed May 19 Sun July 11 (10-4)*

Pine Lodge Gardens ♿⚥❀ (Mr & Mrs R H J Clemo) Cuddra. On A390 E of St Austell between Holmbush and Tregrehan. Follow signs. 6 acres garden set in 16 acres natural woodland. Wide range well-labelled rare plants, shrubs in herbaceous borders using original designs and colour combinations. Rhododenderons, camellias, specimen trees. Many interesting features, incl bog garden, fish pond. TEAS. *Adm* £2 *Chd free. Sun July 18 (1-5)*

Regular Openers. See head of county section.

¶**Pinetum** ♿⚥❀ (Mr & Mrs G R Craw) Harewood. 6m SW of Tavistock. From A390 Tavistock-Callington Rd proceed towards Calstock. After 1m follow sign to Harewood Parish Church. At church continue straight on. 3rd house on R. Parking in lane (with care). 2 acres with unusual and specimen pine trees, unusual shrubs, conifers; camellias, rhododendrons and herbaceous borders. TEAS. *Adm* £1 *Chd free. Suns May 9, 16, Aug 8 (2-6)*

Polgwynne ♿⚥❀ (Mr & Mrs P Davey) Feock. 5m S of Truro via A39 (Truro-Falmouth rd) and then B3289 to 1st Xrds: straight on ½m short of Feock village. 3½-acre garden and grounds. Fruit and vegetable garden, woodlands extending to shore of Carrick Roads; magnificent Ginkgo Biloba (female, 12′ girth) probably the largest female ginkgo in Britain; other beautiful trees; many rare and unusual shrubs. Lovely setting and view of Carrick Roads. TEAS. *Adm* £1.50 *Chd free. Sun April 25 (2-5.30)*

Porthpean House ♿❀ (Christopher Petherick Esq) 2m SE of St Austell. Take turning off A390 signed Porthpean, left after Mount Edgcumbe Hospice down Porthpean Beach Rd, large white house at very bottom of hill. 3-acre garden adjoining seashore, panoramic views, planted 1950s; varied and outstanding collection of camellias, rhododendrons and azaleas; special feature a hillside covered with primroses and daffodils. TEAS. *Adm* £1.50 *Chd free.* ▲*For NGS Sun April 11 (2-5)* Tel 0726 72888

¶**Prideaux Place** ♿ (Mr & Mrs Prideaux-Brune) Padstow. On the edge of Padstow follow brown signs for Prideaux Place, from ring rd (A389). Surrounding Elizabethan house the present main grounds were laid out in the early C18 by Edmund Prideaux. Ancient deer park with stunning views over Camel estuary; victorian woodland walks currently under restoration. Newly restored sunken formal garden. A garden of vistas. Cream TEAS. *Adm* £1.50 *Chd free. Fris July 2, 9 (1.30-5)*

Roseland House ❀ (Mr & Mrs Pridham) Chacewater, nr Truro. Situated in Chacewater 4m W of Truro, at Truro end of main st. Parking in village car park (100 yds) or surrounding roads. 1-acre garden, with a large range of plants, some unusual, many scented, most plants in the garden propagated for sale. Garden is divided into several different areas, with pond, old orchard and Victorian conservatory (open). TEAS. *Adm* £1.50 *Chd free. Suns June 27, July 11 (2-5)* Tel 0872 560451

St Michael's Mount ⚥❀ (The Rt Hon Lord St Levan; The National Trust) Marazion. ½m from shore at Marazion by Causeway; otherwise by ferry. Flowering shrubs; rock plants; castle walls; fine sea views. TEAS. *Adm Castle & gardens* £3, *Chd* £1.50 *(under 16)*. ▲*Sun April 25 (10.30-4.45)*

● **Trebah** ❀ (Trebah Garden Trust) 1m SW of Mawnan Smith and 500 yards W. of Glendurgan, 4m SW of Falmouth. Excellent parking (free) and access for coaches. 25-acre S. facing breathtaking ravine garden, planted in 1850's by Charles Fox. The extensive collection of rare and mature trees and shrubs incl glades of huge tree ferns over 100 years old and sub-tropical exotics. Hydrangea collection covers 2½ acres. Water garden with waterfalls and rock pool stocked with mature Koi Carp. A magical garden of unique beauty for the plantsman, the artist and the family. Play area and trail for children. Use of private beach. Tea/Coffee and light refreshments. *Adm £2.50 Chd and disabled £1. Open every day throughout year (10.30-5 last admission). For special arrangements* **Tel 0326 250448)**

Trebartha (The Latham Family) North Hill, SW of Launceston. Nr junction of B3254 & B3257. Wooded area with lake surrounded by walks of flowering shrubs; woodland trail through fine woods with cascades and waterfalls; American glade with fine trees. TEAS. *Adm £1.50 Chd 50p (Share to North Hill Parish Church Roof Fund). Sun Sept 26 (2-6)*

¶**Tregilliowe Farm** ୧୫ (Mr & Mrs J Richards) Penzance-Hayle A30 Rd from Penzance turn R at Crowlas Xrds. After approx 1m turn sharp L on to St Erth Rd. 2nd farm lane on R. 2-acre garden still developing. Herbaceous beds with wide range of perennials and grasses. Raised Mediterranean bed. Further areas being developed. TEAS June in aid of Cancer Relief Macmillan Fund. July in aid of St Julias Hospice. *Adm £1 Chd free. Suns June 20, July 18 (2-6)*

Tregrehan ୧୫ (Mr T Hudson) Tregrehan. Entrance on A390 opp Britannia Inn 1m W of St Blazey. Access for cars and coaches. Garden largely created since early C19. Woodland of 20 acres containing fine trees, award winning camellias raised by late owner and many interesting plants from warm temperate climes. Show greenhouses a feature containing softer species. TEA. *Adm £2 Chd 75p. Mid March to end June, and Sept Weds to Suns.* ▲*For NGS Sun May 9 (10.30- 5)*

Trelean ❀ (Sqn-Ldr G T & Mrs Witherwick) St Martin-in-Meneage. 8m E of Helston. From Helston take St Keverne rd B3293; after 4m turn L for Mawgan then follow signs. Medium-sized valley garden of 3 acres. Contained within 20 acres of natural woodland. A ¼m Helford riverside walk with a freshwater, fern-clad stream discharging onto beach. A plantsman's domain, purpose planted for autumn colour, yet of all seasons interest. Autumn colour film show. TEAS. *Adm £1.25 Chd Free. Sun Oct 24 (12-5). Also by appt (owner conducted tour)* **Tel 0326 231255** *(evenings)*

Trelissick ୧୫❀ (The National Trust; R Spencer Copeland Esq) Feock, 4m S of Truro, nr King Harry Ferry. On B3289. Large garden; superb view over Falmouth harbour. Georgian house (not open). Through courtesy of Mr Copeland NGS visitors offered access to private terrace 50p. TEAS. *Adm £3 Chd £1.50* ▲ *For NGS Sun April 11 (1-5.30)*

Tremeer Gardens St Tudy, 8m N of Bodmin; W of B3266, all roads signed. 7-acre garden famous for camellias and rhododendrons with water; many rare shrubs. *Adm £1 Chd 50p. Sun April 4 (2-6)*

Trerice ୧୫❀ (The National Trust) Newlyn East 3m SE of Newquay. From Newquay via A392 and A3058; turn right at Kestle Mill (NT signposts). Small manor house, rebuilt in 1571, containing fine plaster ceilings and fireplaces; oak and walnut furniture and tapestries. Lunches & TEAS. *Adm house & garden £3.60 Chd £1.80.* ▲*Sun June 13 (11-5.30)*

Trevegean ୫❀(Mr & Mrs E C Cousins) 9 Manor Way. Take Penzance by-pass; take first L off roundabout towards Treneere and Heamoor. Sharp R turn for Manor way. ⅓-acre divided into series of enclosed areas; planting some formal, informal, herb garden, shrubs and perennials; connected by brick and slab paths some edged with box. TEAS. *Adm £1 Chd free (Share to St Julias Hospice Hayle). By appt only April 1 to July 31. For NGS Sun June 13 (2-5)* **Tel 0736 67407**

● **Trewithen** ୧୫ (A M J Galsworthy Esq) Truro. ½m E Probus. Entrance on A390 Truro-St Austell Rd. Signposted. Large car park. Internationally renowned garden of 30 acres laid out by Maj G Johnson between 1912 & 1960 with much of original seed and plant material collected by Ward and Forrest. Original C18 walled garden famed for towering magnolias and rhododendrons; wide range of own hybrids. Flatish ground amidst original woodland park. TEAS *Adm £2 Chd £1. Mon to Sat March 1 to Sept 30 (10-4.30) Special arrangements for coaches Mrs Norman* **Tel 0726 882763**

●**Woodland Garden** ୫❀ (Mr & Mrs N Froggatt) Or Helston/St Keverne Rd B3293, turn R ¼m past Garras village at Woodland Garden sign. Entrance on R after ½m. Informal 2½-acre garden in wooded valley, planted in the last 14 years with camellias, rhododendrons, magnolias, trees and shrubs, primulas and many unusual plants. Planting and development continue. Lovely spring succession of wild daffodils, primroses and then blue bells. Small pond and stream. ¼-mile walk to 9 acres or Goonhilly Downs, an impressive area of heathers (especially the Erica Vagans, best July-Sept). Dogs only allowed on Downs. *Adm £1 Chd free. Sats April 10 to Oct 30 (2-5). Also by appt.* **Enquiries Tel 032622-295**

Cumbria

Hon County Organiser: (South) Mrs R E Tongue, Paddock Barn, Winster, Windermere LA23 3NW
Assistant Hon County Organiser: (North) Mrs Julian Fraser, Ormside Hall, Ormside, Appleby CA16 6EJ

DATES OF OPENING

by appointment
For telephone numbers and other details see garden descriptions

The Beeches, Houghton, nr Carlisle
Rydal Mount, Eskdale Green, nr Gosforth

Regular openings
For details see garden descriptions

Brockhole, Windermere. Daily 1 April to 3 Nov
Holehird, Windermere. Daily
Holker Hall & Gardens, Cark-in-Cartmel. Suns to Fris April 1 to Oct 31
Hutton-in-the-Forest, Penrith. Daily except Sats
Levens Hall, Kendal. Daily except Fris and Sats April 1 to Sept 30
Lingholm, Portiscale. Daily April 1 to October 31
Muncaster Castle, Ravenglass. Daily

April 18 Sunday
Corrie, Watermillock, Penrith
April 26 Monday
Levens Hall, Kendal
May 2 Sunday
Dallam Tower, Milnthorpe
The Nook, Helton
Rydal Mount, Eskdale Green, nr Gosforth
May 5 Wednesday
Lingholm, Portiscale
Rydal Mount, Eskdale Green, nr Gosforth
May 8 Saturday
Acorn Bank, Temple Sowerby, nr Penrith
May 9 Sunday
Stagshaw, Ambleside
May 13 Thursday
Muncaster Castle, Ravenglass
May 15 Saturday
Nunwick Hall, Great Salkeld, nr Penrith
May 16 Sunday
Browfoot, Skelwith Bridge, Ambleside ‡
Castletown House
Copt Howe, Chapel Stile ‡
Fell Yeat, Kirkby Lonsdale ‡‡
Halecat, Witherslack ‡‡
Hutton-in-the-Forest, Penrith
Lindeth Fell Country House, Bowness
Nunwick Hall, Great Salkeld, nr Penrith
May 22 Saturday
Curlew Crag, Crosthwaite
May 23 Sunday
Brockhole, Windermere ‡‡
Copt Howe, Chapel Stile ‡
Curlew Crag, Crosthwaite ‡‡
Fellside, Millbeck
High Beckside Farm, Cartmel
St Anne's, Great Langdale ‡
May 29 Saturday
Holehird, Windermere
May 30 Sunday
Matson Ground, Bowness-on-Windermere
June 6 Sunday
Hazelmount
Stagshaw, Ambleside ‡
Station House, Lamplugh, nr Workington
Yews, Bowness-on-Windermere ‡
June 12 Saturday
Rannerdale Cottage
June 13 Sunday
Palace How, Loweswater ‡
Rannerdale Cottage ‡
June 20 Sunday
Dallam Tower, Milnthorpe
Fell Yeat, Kirkby Lonsdale
Hutton-in-the-Forest, Penrith
June 23 Wednesday
Scarthwaite, Grange-in-Borrowdale
June 26 Saturday
Acorn Bank, Temple Sowerby, nr Penrith
June 27 Sunday
Askam Hall, Penrith
High Cleabarrow, Windermere
Scarthwaite, Grange-in-Borrowdale
July 3 Saturday
Sizergh Castle, nr Kendal
July 4 Sunday
Whitbysteads, Askham
July 18 Sunday
Dallam Tower, Milnthorpe ‡
Halecat, Witherslack ‡
Holehird, Windermere
July 31 Saturday
Acorn Bank, Temple Sowerby, nr Penrith
August 4 Wednesday
Lingholm, Portiscale
August 25 Wednesday
Rydal Mount, Eskdale Green, nr Gosforth
September 5 Sunday
Brockhole, Windermere ‡
Matson Ground, Bowness-on-Windermere ‡
September 27 Monday
Levens Hall, Kendal

DESCRIPTIONS OF GARDENS

Acorn Bank ♿✲❀ (The National Trust), Temple Sowerby. 6m E of Penrith on A66; ½m N of Temple Sowerby. Bus: Penrith-Appleby or Carlisle-Darlington; alight Culgaith Rd end. Medium-sized walled garden; fine herb garden; orchard and mixed borders; wild garden with woodland/riverside walk. Dogs on leads only woodland walk. *Adm £1.50 Chd 80p. April 1 to Oct 31 daily (10-5). For NGS Suns May 9, June 27, Aug 1 (10-5)*

Askham Hall ✲❀ (The Earl & Countess of Lonsdale) 5m S of Penrith. Turn off A6 for Lowther and Askham. Askham Hall is a pele tower, incorporating C14, C16 and early C18 elements in courtyard plan. Formal outlines of garden with terraces of herbaceous borders and original topiary, probably from late C17. Shrub roses and recently created herb garden. Kitchen garden. TEA. *Adm £1 Chd free (Share to Askham & Lowther Churches). Sun June 27 (2-5.30)*

Regular Openers. See head of county section.

The Beeches ⚭❀ (Mr & Mrs J B McKay Black) 42 The Green, Houghton. 2m NE of Carlisle. Leave M6 at junction 44. Take B6264 (Brampton & Carlisle Airport). After 1m turn R over M6 into village. Parking in lay-by on R at end of village green. The Beeches is 10 yards further. Plantsman's garden approx ¾-acre. Herbaceous, mixed borders, raised beds of alpines, peat garden, troughs and pool. Many dwarf bulbs in Spring. Alpine house and frame. Good collections of hostas and dwarf rhododendrons. *Adm £1 Chd free. By appointment only* Tel 0228 22670

¶**Brockhole** ⅄ (Lake District National Park) Windermere. 2m NW of Windermere on A591 between Windermere and Ambleside. 10 acres formal gardens, designed by Thomas Mawson. Acid soils and mild aspect, many unusual or slightly tender plants, shrub roses, herbaceous borders, scented garden. 20 acres informal grounds, wide variety of trees and shrubs. Picnic area, adventure playground, boat trips on Lake Windermere. Garden walks. Plant sales NGS days only. TEAS. *Adm Free (Pay & display car parking charges only). Suns May 23, Sept 5 (10-5)*

Browfoot ⅄❀ (Mr Trevor Woodburn) Skelwith Bridge 2½m SW of Ambleside on A593. Turn down lane at Skelwith Bridge. Woodland garden developed by owner; rhododendrons; azaleas; species trees and natural rock garden. Approx 2 acres. Parking & TEAS provided by and in aid of the Community Centre. *Adm £1 Chd 40p. Sun May 16 (12.30-5.30)*

Castletown House ⅄❀ (Mr & Mrs Mounsey-Heysham) Rockcliffe. 5m NW of Carlisle. ¾m from Rockcliffe. The garden is situated above the River Eden, with outstanding rhododendrons and azaleas. A formal garden with shrubs, many bulbs and primulas. There is also a working walled garden. TEAS. *Adm £1 Chd 50p. Sun May 16 (2-5)*

Copt Howe ❀ (Professor R N Haszeldine) Chapel Stile. Great Langdale ¼m W of Chapel Stile on B5343 from Ambleside. Parking at adjacent Harry Place Farm, short walk up drive. Buses from Ambleside. 2-acre plantsman's garden reaching maturity, with new areas under development. Extensive collections of acers (especially Japanese), camellias, azaleas, rhododendrons, rare shrubs and trees, perennials; herbaceous and bulbous species; alpines and trough gardens; dwarf and large conifers; Japanese and Himalayan plants. Magnificent views. TEAS. *Adm £1.50 Chd free (Share to Langdales Society May 16, Friends of the Lake District May 24). Suns May 16, 24 (10-5.30)*

¶**Corrie** ⅄❀ (Mrs Derek Pattinson) Watermillock. From Penrith and M6 Junction 40 take A66 towards Keswick (W ½m). Turn L at roundabout for Ullswater A592. At head of lake turn R, 2m passing Brackenrigg Hotel. Bottom of hill on L opp telephone box. From Patterdale pass Leeming House Hotel and continue approx 1m passing 2 white houses on L of roadside. Garden on R on next corner. A 5-acre garden constructed 5 years ago with daffodils and shrubs. Magnificent views of Ullswater. TEAS. *Adm £1 Chd 50p. Sun April 18 (2-5)*

Curlew Crag ❀ (Mrs K M Lawson) Crosthwaite, Kendal. Kendal 5m, Windermere 5m, Levens Bridge 8m. Just off A5074 follow signs from Crosthwaite P.O. Medium-sized garden. Year-round interest, especially early spring for naturalized bulbs, May to June for rhododendrons, camellias, azaleas and June to July for 'old' shrub roses. A knot-garden, woodland and lovely views. TEA. *Adm £1 Chd 50p (Share to Crosthwaite Recreation Ground). Sat, Sun, May 22, 23 (2-5.30)*

Dallam Tower ⅄❀ (Brigadier & Mrs C E Tryon-Wilson) Milnthorpe, 7m S of Kendal. 7m N of Carnforth, nr junction of A6 and B5282. Station: Arnside, 4m; Lancaster, 15m. Bus: Ribble 553, 554 Milnthorpe-Lancaster via Arnside, alight at Lodge Gates. Medium-sized garden; natural rock garden, waterfalls, fine display of rambler and polyanthus roses; wood walks, lawns, shrubs. *Adm 80p Chd free. Suns May 2, June 20, July 18 (2-5)*

Fell Yeat ⅄❀❀ (Mr & Mrs O S Benson) Casterton, nr Kirkby Lonsdale. Approx 1m E of Casterton Village on the rd to Bull Pot. Leave A65 at Devils Bridge, follow A683 for a mile, take the R fork to High Casterton at the golf course, straight across at two sets of Xrds, the house is immediately on the L about ¼m from no through rd sign. 1-acre informal country garden with mixed borders, herbaceous, old roses, small fernery, herb garden and small pond. Extensive views of the Lune Valley from a still developing garden. TEAS (in aid of NCCPG). *Adm £1 Chd free. Suns May 16, June 20 (2-5.30)*

Fellside ❀ (Mr & Mrs C D Collins) Millbeck, 2m N of Keswick. Turn off A591 Keswick-Bassenthwaite rd opp sign to Millbeck (2m from Keswick); at T-junc in Millbeck village turn right; garden 300yds on left. 1-acre, informal, shrub garden; 300 varieties of rhododendrons, camellias, azaleas, on steep terraced site. Pretty glen with beck; magnificent views of Derwent Water and Bassenthwaite. Tea John Gregg, The Cottage, Millbeck or The Old Mill (Nat Trust) Mirehouse. *Adm 60p Chd 30p. Sun May 23 (2-5.30)*

Halecat ⅄❀ (Mrs Michael Stanley) Witherslack, 10m SW of Kendal. From A590 turn into Witherslack at start of dual Carriageway (signposted Witherslack); left in township and left again, signpost 'Cartmel Fell'; lodge gates on left (map ref. 434834). Medium-sized garden; mixed shrub and herbaceous borders, terrace, sunken garden; gazebo; daffodils and cherries in Spring, over 70 different varieties of hydrangea; beautiful view over Kent estuary to Arnside. Nursery garden attached. TEA. *Adm 60p Chd free (Share to Leukaemia Campaign). Suns May 16, July 18 (2-5)*

Hazelmount ⅄❀❀ (Mrs J Barratt) Thwaites, Millom, 2m from Broughton-in-Furness off A595 up hill after crossing Duddon River Bridge. 5-acre woodland garden, small lake with stream; spring display of species rhododendrons, azaleas and flowering shrubs. Mature trees and exceptional views of Duddon Estuary and sea. TEAS. *Adm £1 Chd free (Share to NSPCC). Sun June 6 (2-5.30)*

┌─────────────────────────────────────┐
By Appointment Gardens. See head of county section
└─────────────────────────────────────┘

¶**High Beckside Farm** ⚹ (Mr & Mrs P J McCabe) Cartmel. 1¾m N of Cartmel. Take the Haverthwaite Rd, from the PO in the village. A newly created conservation area, a wild garden with ponds, waterfalls, waterfowl; flowering bushes and a number of rare trees. An arboretum in the very early stages of formation. 11 acres of wild flowers on a hillside with fine views. A small house garden. Approx ¼m from house to conservation area. Stout shoes. TEA. *Adm £1 Chd 25p. Sun May 23 (12-5)*

High Cleabarrow ঌ⚹❀ (Mr & Mrs R T Brown) 3m SE of Windermere off B5284 Crook to Kendal Rd (nr Windermere Golf Course). 1½-acre newly designed and planted garden comprising wide variety of herbaceous, old-fashioned roses, shrubs, unusual plants on different levels; woodland area. TEAS. *Adm £1 Chd 50p. Sun June 27 (1.30-5.30)*

Holehird (Lakeland Horticultural Society) ⚹ Patterdale Road, Windermere. ½m N of Windermere town on A591. Turn R onto A592 to Patterdale. Garden signposted on R ¾m on A592. Car park along private drive. The garden of nearly 5 acres is set on a hillside with some of the best views in Lakeland, with a great diversity of plants that grow well in this area, incl alpine and heather beds and a collection of rhododendrons and azaleas. The walled garden is mostly herbaceous. National collections of astilbes, polystichum, ferns and hydrangeas. Partially suitable wheelchairs. Garden always open. *Entrance by donation £1 Chd free. Warden available throughout summer (11-5). Coach parties by appointment, guides available Tel 05394 46008. For NGS Sat May 29, Sun July 18 (10-5)*

Holker Hall & Gardens ঌ⚹❀ (Lord & Lady Cavendish) Cark-in-Cartmel. 4m W of Grange-over-Sands. 12m W of M6 (junction 36). 24 acres of magnificent formal and woodland gardens associated with Joseph Paxton & Mawson. Rare trees, shrubs, exotic flowering trees, magnolias and rose garden. Water features incl superb limestone cascade. New elliptical formal garden and rhododendron and azalea arboretum. Winners of Christies - H.H.A. Garden of the Year Award (1991). C19 Wing of Holker Hall, Motor Museum, Patchwork & Quilting Display, Kitchen Exhibition, Adventure Playground, Deer Park, Shop & Cafeteria. *Garden tours Mons 11.30am & 2.30pm. Discounted Adm & catering to groups 20+ by prior arrangement. The Garden Festival June 6. Adm prices not available at time of going to press. Sun to Fris April 1 to Oct 31 (10.30-6 last entry 4.30).*

Hutton-in-the-Forest (Lord Inglewood) 5m NW of Penrith. 3m from exit 41 of M6. Magnificent grounds with C18 walled flower garden, terraces and lake. C19 Low garden, specimen trees and topiary; woodland walk and dovecote. Mediaeval House with C17, C18 and C19 additions. TEAS. *Adm £1.50 grounds, £3 house & grounds chd free grounds £1 house & grounds. Grounds open daily all year except Sats (11-5) House and tea room open Thurs, Fris, Suns (1-4) from Easter to Oct 3 and all Bank Hol Mons. For NGS Suns May 16, June 20 (11-5)*

Levens Hall ঌ⚹❀ (C H Bagot Esq) 5m S of Kendal on Milnthorpe Rd (A6); Exit 36 from M6. 10 acres inc famous topiary garden and 1st ha-ha laid out by M Beaumont in 1694; magnificent beech circle; formal bedding; herbaceous borders. Elizabethan mansion, added to C13

pele tower, contains superb panelling, plasterwork and furniture. Steam collection illustrating history of steam 1830-1920. Only gardens suitable for wheelchairs. *Adm House & Garden £3.80 OAPs £3.30 Chd £2.20. Garden only £2.50 OAPs £2.30 Chd £1.50. Reduction for groups. April 1 to Sept 30. House and garden, gift shop, tearoom. children's play area, picnic area. Sun, Mon, Tues, Wed, Thurs house (11-4.30), grounds (10-5), steam collection (2-5). Closed Fri & Sat. For NGS Mons April 26, Sept 27 (10.30-5)*

Lindeth Fell Country House Hotel ঌ (Air Commodore & Mrs P A Kennedy) 1m S of Bowness on A5074. 6-acres of lawns and landscaped grounds on the hills above Lake Windermere, probably designed by one of the Mawson school around 1907; majestic conifers and specimen trees best in spring and early summer with a colourful display of rhododendrons, azaleas and Japanese maples; grounds offer splendid views to Coniston mountains; rose garden and herbaceous border newly developed. TEAS in hotel. *Adm £1 Chd free. Sun May 16 (2-5)*

Lingholm ঌ⚹❀ (The Viscount Rochdale) Keswick. On W shore of Derwentwater; Portinscale 1m; Keswick 3m. Turn off A66 at Portinscale; drive entrance 1m on left. Ferry: Keswick to Nicol End, 10 mins walk. Bus: Keswick to Portinscale, 1m; 'Mountain Goat' minibus service from town centre passes drive end. Formal and woodland gardens; garden walk 1m; rhododendrons, azaleas, etc. Spring daffodils, autumn colour. Plant centre. Free car park. TEAS. *Adm £2.50 (incl leaflet) Chd free. April 1 to Oct 31 daily. For NGS Weds May 5, Aug 4 (10-5)*

¶**Matson Ground** ঌ⚹❀ (Matson Ground Settlement) Windermere. From Kendal turn R off B5284 signposted Heathwaite, 100 yds after Windermere Golf Club entrance. Lane joins another in ¼m. Continue straight on. Garden is on L after ¼m. From Bowness turn L onto B5284 from A5074. After ¾m turn L at Xrds follow sign to Heathwaite. Garden on L ¾m along lane. A watercourse flows through the ornamental garden ending at a large pond in the wild garden of meadow grassland with spring bulbs and later wild flowers. Azaleas and rhododendrons, large mixed shrub/herbaceous borders and some very imaginative topiary work. Landscape designer John Brookes has been behind much of the recent changes in the garden. There is also a ½-acre walled kitchen garden being run on organic methods with greenhouses and a dovecote. Adjacent to the ornamental garden is a 2-acre amenity woodland. TEAS. *Adm £1 Chd 50p. Suns May 30, Sept 5 (10-5)*

Muncaster Castle ঌ❀ (Mrs P R Gordon-Duff-Pennington) 1m E of Ravenglass, 17m SW of Whitehaven on A595. 77 acres; famous large collection of species rhododendrons, azaleas and camellias, some unique in UK; arboretum; historic and scenic site at foot of Eskdale. Owl centre. Giftshop. Also extensive garden centre. Coach parties and schools by appt. Special arrangements for disabled at front gate. CAFE. *Castle, Garden and Owl Centre Adm £4.50 Chd £2.50 Family (2+2) £12; Garden and Owl Centre Adm £2.90 Chd £1.60 Family (2+2) £8; Parties £3.50 Chd £1.95 Gardens and Owl Centre open all year. Castle open daily from Mar 28 to Oct 31 except Mons (also open all Bank Hol Mons). Castle (1-4) garden and Owl Centre (11-5). For NGS Thurs May 13 (11-5)*

The Nook ৬❀ (Mr & Mrs P Freedman) Helton. Penrith N 5m. From B5320, take signs to Askham-Haweswater. Turn R into Helton. ½-acre terraced rock garden, beds and tubs, alpines, ornamental pool, goldfish, bog plants, fruit and herb garden; magnificent views over River Lowther and parkland. Homemade jam and chutney for sale. TEAS. *Adm £1 Chd free. Sun May 2 (11-4)*

Nunwick Hall ⚘❀ (Mr & Mrs C M & Mr O H Thompson) On outskirts of Great Salkeld, 5½m NE of Penrith. Parkland and walks to the River Eden. 7 acres of garden, with terrace, a parterre, lawns with rose garden, borders and large Victorian rockery. The original walled garden has flowers, fruit, vegetables and an orchard. Picnics in park. TEAS. *Adm £1.60 Chd under 12 free (Share to St Cuthbert's Church, Great Salkeld). Sat, Sun May 15, 16 (2-5)*

Palace How ৬⚘❀ (Mr & Mrs A & K Johnson) Brackenwaite, Loweswater, 6m SE of Cockermouth on B5292 and B5289 or from Keswick 10m over Whinlatter Pass, through Lorton village, follow signs for Loweswater. 1-acre 9yr-old well established garden in damp hollow surrounded by mountains. Many unusual trees and shrubs especially rhododendrons and acers. Pond with varied bog plants; iris; candelabra primulas and Himalayan poppies. Roses and alpines. TEA. *Adm £1.20 Chd free (Share to Allerdale Disability Association). Sun June 13 (10-4)*

Rannerdale Cottage ৬❀ (The McElney Family) Buttermere. 8m S of Cockermouth, 10m W of Keswick. ½-acre cottage garden with beck and woodland walk overlooking Crummock Water, splendid mountain views. Herbaceous, shrubs, roses, perennial geraniums, tree peonies, pond with fish. TEAS. *Adm £1 Chd free. Sat, Sun June 12, 13 (11-5)*

Rydal Mount ❀ (Don & Toni Richards) Eskdale Green. Turn off A595 where signed 6m to Eskdale Green Village. Turn sharp R opp Woodall Stores. 2nd house on R. 1½-acre garden on natural rock facing SW. Primarily heathers and tree heaths with a selection of shrubs; small trees including eucalyptus and American blueberries; water garden. TEAS. *Adm 50p Chd 30p (Share to West Cumbria Hospice at Home). Sun May 2; Weds May 5, Aug 25 (2-5) Also by appt* **Tel 09467 23267**

St Anne's ❀ (Mr & Mrs R D Furness) Great Langdale. 5m from Ambleside on B5343. Follow signs for Langdale/Old Dungeon Ghyll. At Skelwith Bridge take R hand fork and at Elterwater take R hand. Through Chapel Stile, ¾m on L hand side travelling W. 3-acre partial woodland with established variety of conifers and trees, azaleas and rhododendrons. Natural rock faces with alpines, streams and rocky paths. Magnificent views Langdales. Partially suitable for wheelchairs. *Adm £1 Chd free. Sun May 23 (12-5)*

Scarthwaite ⚘ (Mr & Mrs E C Hicks) Grange-in- Borrowdale. From Keswick take B5289 to Grange; cross bridge, house ¼m on L. Ferns, cottage garden plants and many others closely packed into ⅓ acre. *Adm 80p Accompanied chd free. Wed June 23, Sun June 27 (2-5)*

Sizergh Castle ⚘❀ (The National Trust) nr Kendal. Close to and W of the main A6 trunk road, 3m S of Kendal. An approach road leaves A6 close to and S of A6/A591 interchange. ⅔-acre Limestone Rock Garden is the largest owned by the National Trust; it has a large collection of Japanese maples, dwarf conifers, hardy ferns, primulas, gentians and many other perennials and bulbs; water garden with bog and aquatic plants; on walls around main lawn are shrubs and climbers, many half-hardy; rose garden contains specimen roses along with shrubs, climbers, ground cover and lilies; also wild flower banks, herbaceous border, crab apple orchard with spring bulbs and 'Dutch' garden. *Castle & gdn adm £3.30 Chd £1.70; gdn adm £1.70 Chd 90p. For NGS Sat July 3 (12.30-5.30)*

Stagshaw ❀ (The National Trust) ½m S of Ambleside. Turn E off A 591, Ambleside to Windermere rd. Bus 555 Kendal-Keswick alight Waterhead. Woodland gdn incl fine collection of rhododendrons and azaleas. Ericaceous trees & shrubs incl magnolias, camellias, embothriums & a newly planted heather garden. Views over Windermere. *Adm £1 Chd 50p. For NGS Suns May 9, June 6 (10-5.30)*

Station House ৬❀ (Mr & Mrs G Simons) Wright Green. Lamplugh approx 6m from Workington, Whitehaven and Cockermouth signposted off A5086 Lilyhall-Workington from Cockermouth-Egremont Rd ½m under disused railway line from Workington-Whitehaven A595 at Leyland roundabout take rd signposted Branthwaite-Loweswater. 2-acre garden created over site of disused railway line and station. Features shrubs and trees; vegetable and fruit garden. TEAS. *Adm 50p Chd 25p. Sun June 6 (10.30-4.30)*

Whitbysteads ⚘❀ (The Hon Mrs Anthony Lowther) Askham nr Penrith 8m from Penrith. Turn R at Eamont Bridge off the A6. Turn L at Y fork after Railway Bridge signed Askham. Through village, turn R at Queen's Head. 1-acre garden on several levels surrounding farmhouse on edge of fells, featuring wide variety shrub roses, unusual herbaceous plants and geraniums. Pergola; fountain. Magnificent views over Eden Valley. TEA. *Adm £1 Chd free (Share to St Michael & All Angels Church, Lowther). Sun July 4 (2-5)*

Yews ⚘❀ (Sir Oliver & Lady Scott) Windermere. Bus: Ulverston-Bowness, alight Middle Entrance Drive, 50 yds. Medium-sized formal Edwardian garden; fine trees, ha-ha, herbaceous borders. TEAS. *Adm £1 Chd free (Share to Marie Curie Cancer Care). Sun June 6 (2-5.30)*

❀

Derbyshire

Hon County Organiser:	Mr & Mrs R Brown, 210 Nottingham Rd, Woodlinkin, Langley Mill, Nottingham NG16 4HG Tel 0773 714903
Hon County Treasurer:	Mrs G Nutland, 29 Kimberley Rd, Nuthall, Nottingham

DATES OF OPENING

By appointment
For telephone numbers and other details see garden descriptions

Bath House Farm, Ashover
Cherry Tree Cottage, Hilton
Dam Farm House, Ednaston
Darley House, nr Matlock
Gamesley Fold Cottage, Glossop
The Limes, Apperknowle
23 Mill Lane, Codnor
Oaks Lane Farm, Brockhurst
57 Portland Close, Mickleover
Thatched Farm, Radbourne
Valezina Hillside, Heage

Regular openings
For details see garden descriptions

Lea Gardens. Daily March 20 to July 31
Renishaw Hall, nr Sheffield. Suns &
    Thurs May 2 to July 29

April 12 Monday
Renishaw Hall, nr Sheffield
April 18 Sunday
Meynell Langley, Kirk Langley ‡
57 Portland Close, Mickleover
Radburne Hall, nr Derby ‡
Shottle Hall Guest House, Belper
April 25 Sunday
Dam Farm House, Ednaston
Fir Croft, Calver, nr Bakewell
May 9 Sunday
Cherry Tree Cottage, Hilton
Gamesley Fold Cottage, Glossop
The Limes, Apperknowle
Yeldersley Hall, Ashbourne
May 16 Sunday
Broomfield College, Morley

Dam Farm House, Ednaston
Fir Croft, Calver, nr Bakewell
The Limes, Apperknowle
210 Nottingham Road, Woodlinkin
May 23 Sunday
Cherry Tree Cottage, Hilton
Dove Cottage, Clifton
The Limes, Apperknowle
May 27 Thursday
Kedleston Hall, Derby
May 30 Sunday
Bath House Farm, Ashover
Dam Farm House, Ednaston
Fir Croft, Calver, nr Bakewell
The Limes, Apperknowle
57 Portland Close, Mickleover
Thatched Farm, Radbourne
June 5 Saturday
The Old Post Office, Risley
June 6 Sunday
Bramley Hall Cottage, Apperknowle
Gamesley Fold Cottage, Glossop
Hope Gardens
The Old Slaughterhouse, Shipley Gate
Prospect House, Swanwick
Quarndon Hall, Derbyshire
June 13 Sunday
Birchwood Farm, Coxbench
Dam Farm House, Ednaston
The Poplars, Derby
Thatched Farm, Radbourne
June 17 Thursday
The Poplars, Derby
June 20 Sunday
Bramley Hall Cottage, Apperknowle
Cherry Tree Cottage, Hilton
Dove Cottage, Clifton
Fir Croft, Calver, nr Bakewell
The Poplars, Derby

June 26 Saturday
Mount Cottage, Ticknall
June 27 Sunday
Dam Farm House, Ednaston
Mount Cottage, Ticknall
210 Nottingham Road, Woodlinkin ‡
Prospect House, Swanwick ‡
Tudor House Farm, Kirk Langley
July 4 Sunday
Locko Park, Spondon
23 Mill Lane, Codnor
Oaks Lane Farm, Brockhurst
The Old Slaughterhouse, Shipley Gate
Thatched Farm, Radbourne
July 8 Thursday
Oaks Lane Farm, Brockhurst
July 10 Saturday
Tissington Hall, nr Ashbourne
July 11 Sunday
Lea Hurst, nr Matlock
The Limes, Apperknowle
July 18 Sunday
Bath House Farm, Ashover
Hardwick Hall
159 Longfield Lane, Ilkeston
July 25 Sunday
Dove Cottage, Clifton
The Limes, Apperknowle
23 Mill Lane, Codnor
July 28 Wednesday
Calke Abbey, Ticknall
August 1 Sunday
Davlyn, 31 The Crescent, Breaston
August 15 Sunday
Bramley Hall Cottage, Apperknowle
Dove Cottage, Clifton
August 30 Monday
Tissington Hall, nr Ashbourne

DESCRIPTIONS OF GARDENS

Bath House Farm ♿♣❀ (Mr & Mrs Hetherington) Ashover. 4½m N of Matlock on A632 Chesterfield Rd. Take lst R after leaving village of Kelstedge and next R at T-junction. Overlooking Ashover and with extensive views this recently landscaped garden has a wide variety of heathers and mixed borders and a large water feature with waterfall, pond and stream surrounded by well chosen plants and rare shrubs and trees. Home-baked TEAS. *Adm £1 Chd free (Share to West Derby Federal Self Help Group mentally ill). Suns May 30, July 18 (11.30-4). Also by appt June to Aug Tel 0246 590562*

¶**Birchwood Farm** ❀♣ (Mr & Mrs S Crooks) Coxbench. 5m N Derby, from A38 take B6179 by Little Chef, through Little Eaton, till 1st Xrds, turn L then R over the railway crossing and take the rd to Holbrook, drive 100yds on L. Car parking in field at top of drive. ⅓-acre garden enclosed within old brick and stone walls. This garden is for plant enthusiasts, the wide range of herbaceous plants include hardy geraniums, hostas, penstemons, silver plants, campanulas, delphiniums, English roses. The garden is surrounded by woods and includes a pond. TEA. *Adm £1 Acc chd free. Sun June 13 (2-5.30)*

Bramley Hall Cottage ❀ (Mr & Mrs G G Nicholson) Chapel Lane, Apperknowle. 5m N of Chesterfield, from Unstone turn E for 1m to Apperknowle. 1¼ acres, informal plantsman's garden with beautiful view. Wide range of unusual shrubs many with golden or variegated foliage, hostas, lewisias and over 50 clematis. Herbaceous and heather beds, ground cover, secret garden, English rose bed. Long hydrangea walk and stream garden, hardy fuchsias (40 varieties - Aug opening) TEAS. *Adm £1 Chd free. Suns June 6, 20, Aug 15 (2-5)*

Broomfield College ♿✿❀ Morley on A608, 4m N of Derby and 6m S of Heanor. Landscaped garden of 10 ha; shrubs, trees, rose collection, herbaceous borders; glasshouses; display fruit and vegetable gardens. TEAS. *Adm £1 Chd 20p. Sun May 16 (12-4.30)*

Calke Abbey ♿✿ (The National Trust) Ticknall. 9m S of Derby on A514 between Swadlincote and Melbourne. Extensive walled gardens constructed in 1773. Divided into flower garden, kitchen garden and physic garden. Restoration commenced in 1987. Surrounding the walled garden the pleasure ground has been re-fenced and replanting is underway. Ruined orangery is subject to recent fundraising appeal. TEAS. *Adm £2 Chd £1. Wed July 28 (11-5)*

Cherry Tree Cottage ✿❀ (Mr & Mrs R Hamblin) Hilton. 7m W of Derby, turn off the A516 opp The Old Talbot Inn in village centre. Parking - small public car park in Main St. Additional parking Hilton Village Hall, Eggington Road. A plant lover's C18 cottage garden, about ⅓-acre with herbaceous borders; large herb garden; small pool and scree garden. Many unusual and interesting plants; collections of snowdrops, specie aquilegias, old dianthus and hellebores. Featured in Small Gardens summer 1990, 'Gardeners World' April 1991 and Good Garden Guide. *Adm 60p Chd free (Share to The Sue Ryder Home Staunton Harold). Suns May 9, 23 June 20 (2-5) also by appt April, May, June and July weekdays only* **Tel 0283 733778**

Dam Farm House ♿✿❀ (Mrs J M Player) Yeldersley Lane, Ednaston, 5m SE of Ashbourne on A52, opp Ednaston Village turn, gate on right 500 yds. 2-acre garden beautifully situated contains mixed borders, scree. Unusual plants have been collected many are propagated for sale. TEAS (some Suns). *Adm £1 Chd 25p (Share to Leukemia Research, Red Cross). Suns April 25, May 16, 30, June 13, 27 (1.30-4.30). Visitors and groups are welcome by appt* **Tel 0335 60291**

Darley House ♿✿❀ (Mr & Mrs G H Briscoe) Darley Dale, 2m N of Matlock. On A6 to Bakewell. 1½ acres; originally set out by Sir Joseph Paxton in 1845; being restored by present owners; many rare plants, trees; balustrade and steps separating upper and lower garden, a replica of Haddon Hall. As featured on BBC 'Gardeners World'. Picture Gallery. Plants and extensive range of seeds available. TEA. *Adm £1 Chd free. Open by appt April 24 to Sept 26* **Tel 0629 733341**

Davlyn 31 The Crescent ❀ (Dave & Lynda Melbourne) Breaston. Directly on A6005 between Long Eaton and Draycott. 2m from M1 exit no 25. ⅓-acre cottage garden. Winner of 1990 Erewash Gardens competition. A surprise round every corner of this delightful garden with herbaceous borders; hosta beds; pergolas; arbours; two ponds; bog garden; Japanese garden surrounded by red trellis containing bridge and Buddha; vegetable plot; 3 greenhouses, window boxes, hanging baskets; stone trough. The garden is an extension of their home. TEA. *Adm £1 Chd free. Sun Aug 1 (10-5)*

Dove Cottage ✿❀ (Mr & Mrs S G Liverman) Clifton. 1½m SW of Ashbourne. ¾-acre garden by R. Dove extensively replanted and developed since 1979. Emphasis on establishing collections of hardy plants and shrubs incl alchemillas, alliums, berberis, geraniums, euphorbias, hostas, lilies, variegated and silver foliage plants inc astrantias. Interesting gooseberry cordon hedges est over 25 yrs. Featured in Living Magazine 1991. TEA. *Adm £1 Chd free (Share to British Heart Foundation). Suns May 23, June 20, July 25, Aug 15 (1.30-5)*

Fir Croft ✿❀ (Dr & Mrs S B Furness) Froggatt Rd, Calver, Via Sheffield. 4m N of Bakewell; between Q8 filling station and junction of B6001 with B6054. Plantsman's garden; rockeries; water garden and nursery; extensive collection (over 2000 varieties) of alpines, conifers. New tufa and scree beds. *Collection box. Nursery opens every Sat, Sun, Mon (1-6) March to Dec. Adjacent garden for NGS Suns April 25, May 16, 30, June 20 (2-6)*

¶**Gamesley Fold Cottage** ✿❀ (Mr & Mrs G Carr) Glossop. Off Glossop-Marple Rd nr Charlesworth, turn down the lane directly opp St Margaret's School, Gamesley. White cottage at the bottom. Old-fashioned cottage garden down a country lane with lovely views of surrounding countryside. A spring garden planted with herbaceous borders, wild flowers and herbs in profusion to attract butterflies and wildlife. Plants and seeds for sale. TEA. *Adm £1 Chd free. Suns May 9, June 6 (1-4). Visitors & groups welcome by appt April, May, June* **Tel 04578 67856**

Hardwick Hall ♿✿❀ (The National Trust) Doe Lea, 8m SE of Chesterfield. S of A617. Grass walks between yew and hornbeam hedges; cedar trees; herb garden; herbaceous borders. Finest example of Elizabethan house in the country; very fine collection of Elizabethan needlework, tapestry. Restaurant in Old Kitchens. TEAS on days the Hall is open. *Adm garden only £2 Chd £1. Sun July 18 (12-5.30)*

¶**Hope Gardens** ✿❀ Hope Village is on A625 about 15m W of Sheffield. Maps will be available showing the location of gardens in the village. A group of small gardens of differing types. Many have interesting plants and all have good views. Tickets and maps will be available either from the village hall or from individual gardens. Teas available in the village. *Combined adm £2 Chd 50p (Share to St Peter's Church, Hope). Sun June 6 (2-6)*

Regular Openers. Too many days to include in diary. Usually there is a wide range of plants giving year-round interest. See head of county section for the name and garden description for times etc.

Kedleston Hall &✿ (The National Trust) 3m NW of Derby. Signposted from junction of A38/A52. 12-acre garden. A broad open lawn, bounded by a ha-ha, marks the C18 informal garden. A formal layout to the W was introduced early this century when the summerhouse and orangery, both designed by George Richardson late C18, were moved to their present position. The gardens are seen at their best during May and June when the azaleas and rhododendrons are one mass of colour. The Long Walk, a woodland walk of some 3m, is bright with spring flowers. TEA. *Adm £1.50 Chd 75p. Thurs May 27 (11-5)*

● **Lea Gardens** &✿ (Mr & Mrs Tye) Lea, 5m SE of Matlock off A6. A rare collection of rhododendrons, azaleas, kalmias, alpines and conifers in a delightful woodland setting. Light lunches, TEAS, home-baking. Coaches by appt. *Adm £2 Chd 50p daily. Daily March 20 to July 31 (10-7)*

¶**Lea Hurst (Residential Home)** ✿✿ (Royal Surgical Aid Society) Holloway. 6m SE of Matlock off A6, nr Yew Tree Inn, Holloway. Former home (not open) of Florence Nightingale. 5-acre garden consisting of rose beds, herbaceous borders, new shrubbery incl varieties, ornamental pond, all set in beautiful countryside. TEAS. *Adm £1 Chd free (Share to RSAS). Sun July 11 (2-5)*

The Limes &✿ (Mr & Mrs W Belton) Crow Lane, Apperknowle, 6m N of Chesterfield; from A6l at Unstone turn E for 1m to Apperknowle; 1st house past Unstone Grange. Bus: Chesterfield or Sheffield to Apperknowle. 2½ acres with herbaceous borders, lily ponds, roses and flowering shrubs, scree beds & rockeries; hundreds of naturalised daffodils and formal bedding with massed bedding of pansies in the spring, geraniums and bedding plants in summer. Putting green and large natural pond with ducks and geese. Nature trail over 5 acres. Home-made TEAS. *Adm £1 Chd 25p. Suns May 9, 16, 23, 30; July 11, 25 (2-6). Coach and private parties on other days, evening visits welcome by appt* **Tel 0246 412338**

Locko Park ✿ (Capt P J B Drury-Lowe) Spondon, 6m NE of Derby. From A52 Borrowash bypass, 2m N via B6001, turn to Spondon. Large garden; pleasure gardens; rose gardens. House by Smith of Warwick with Victorian additions. Chapel, Charles II, with original ceiling. TEAS. *Adm 60p Chd 30p. Sun July 4 (2-6)*

159 Longfield Lane &✿✿ (David & Diane Bennett) Ilkeston (Stanton side) off Quarry Hill, opp Hallam Fields Junior School. A large, informal over-flowing garden that works for its owners with fruit, vegetables, shrubs, flowers, two small fish ponds and a conservatory. A strong emphasis on texture, colour and lots of unexpected corners. Home-made TEAS. *Adm £1 Chd free. Sun July 18 (2-6)*

Meynell Langley &✿ (Godfrey Meynell Esq) Between Mackworth and Kirk Langley on A52 Derby-Ashbourne rd. Turn in at green iron gate by grey stone lodge on N side of road. Trees, lawns, daffodils, lake, views. TEAS in Regency country house. *Adm £1.50 Chd 50p (Share to Church Urban Fund). Sun April 18 (2-6)*

¶**23 Mill Lane** &✿ (Mrs S Jackson) Codnor. 12m NW of Nottingham. A610 Ripley 10m N of Derby, A38 Ripley. 2 car parks nearby. Lawns, herbaceous borders, small pond, waterfall; fruit trees; clematis. 2nd prize Amber Valley 'Best Kept Garden' competition 1992. TEA. *Adm £1 Chd free. Suns July 4, 25 (11-6) Also by appt June to Sept* **Tel 0773 745707**

Mount Cottage ✿✿ (Mr & Mrs J T Oliver) 52 Main Street, Ticknall, 9m S Derby, adjacent entrance Calke Abbey NT and Wheel Public House. Medium-sized cottage garden, herbaceous borders, shrubs, lawns, small pool area, numerous roses, surrounding C18 cottage. TEAS. *Adm 50p Chd 25p. Sat, Sun June 26, 27 (11-5)*

210 Nottingham Rd (Mr & Mrs R Brown) Woodlinkin. 12m NW of Nottingham, nr Codnor; A610. ½-acre; collections of old, modern shrub and climbing roses; geraniums; hellebores; shrubs; small trees. TEA. *Adm £1 Chd free. Suns May 16, June 27 (2-5)*

Oaks Lane Farm ✿✿ (Mr & Mrs J R Hunter) Brockhurst, Ashover nr Chesterfield. At Kelstedge 4m from Matlock on A632 Chesterfield Rd, just above Kelstedge Inn, turn L up narrow rd, then turn R ½m, garden is 150yds on R. Partly suitable for wheelchairs. ¾-acre informal plantsman's garden in beautiful situation with herbaceous borders, natural streams and pond. Many varieties of hostas, euphorbia and old-fashioned roses. TEA. *Adm £1 Chd free. Sun, Thurs July 4, 8 (11-5). Also by appt* **Tel 0246 590324**

¶**The Old Post Office** ✿ (Mr & Mrs R N Wilson) Risley. Halfway between Derby and Nottingham on B5010. 1m from M1 junction 25, walk down lane marked 'Public Footpath'. ¾-acre garden in conservation area, adjacent to C16 church, interesting variety of trees, shrubs and perennials; mature cactus and succulent collection; pond, brook. Cream Teas in aid of Treetops Hospice at Village Hall nearby. *Adm 75p Chd free. Sat June 5 (2-6)*

The Old Slaughterhouse ✿✿ (Robert & Joyce Peck) Shipley Gate. 1m S of Eastwood, take Church St from Sun Inn traffic lights, and over A610, L to narrow rd to Shipley Boat Inn; parking near Shipley Lock (Erewash Canal) and Inn. ¾-acre long, narrow garden, restored from overgrown ash tip since 1984; 200-yrs-old stone aqueduct over river; over 400 trees planted; hard and soft surfaces; division into 'rooms'; wide variety of planting; hidden pond; pleasant extra walks in Erewash Valley (canal and river sides). TEAS. *Adm £1 Chd free (Share to Heanor Hospital League of Friends June 6, Erewash Canal Assoc July 4). Suns June 6, July 4 (2-6)*

¶**The Poplars** &✿✿ (The Clemson Family) Derby. Off A6 N of Derby. (200yds S of The Broadway Inn and opp N end of Belper Rd.) ½m N of cathedral. ¼-acre garden; design dates from 1882; many original features. Variety of herbaceous plants, shrubs, herbs, fruit. *Adm £1 Chd free. Suns June 13, 20, Thurs June 17 (2-6)*

By Appointment Gardens. Avoid the crowds. Good chance of a tour by owner. See garden description for telephone number.

57 Portland Close ✗❀ (Mr & Mrs A L Ritchie) Mickleover. Approx 3m W of Derby, turn R off B5020 Cavendish Way then 2nd L into Portland Close. Small plantsman's garden, wide variety of unusual bulbs, alpines and herbaceous plants. Special interest in sink gardens, hostas, named varieties of primulas (single and double); auriculas (show, border, alpine and doubles), violas and cyclamen. Featured in 'Good Garden Guide'. *Adm 50p Chd free. Sun April 18, May 30 (2-5.30); also by appt* **Tel 0332 515450**

Prospect House ꝭ✗❀ (Mr & Mrs J W Bowyer) 18 Pentrich Rd, Swanwick; turn at traffic lights A61 to B6016 Pentrich. Park main rd. ¾-acre; conifers, shrubs, herbaceous plants, cordyline palms, carpet bedding with sedums, sempervivums, echeverias; collection cacti; succulents, shrub and leaf begonia, abutilons various; rock plants; geraniums; pelargoniums, hostas. Greenhouses; kitchen garden. TEA. *Adm 50p Chd 10p. Suns June 6, 27 (1-6)*

Quarndon Hall ꝭ✗❀ (N A Bird) Quarndon. Off A6 between Duffield and Allestree; car parking at Joiners Arms. 3-acre old established garden in process of replanting; emphasis on unusual shrubs, trees and rhododendrons. Further 3 acres being laid out including rockeries, waterfalls, Italian and secret gardens. TEA. *Adm £1.50 Chd free (Share to Quarndon Parish Church). Sun June 6 (1-6)*

Radburne Hall ꝭ✗ (Maj & Mrs J W Chandos-Pole) Kirk Langley, 5m W of Derby. W of A52 Derby-Ashbourne Rd; off Radburne Lane. Large landscape garden; large display of daffodils; shrubs; formal rose terraces; fine trees and view. Hall (not open) is 7-bay Palladian mansion built c1734 by Smith of Warwick. Ice-house in garden. *Adm £1 Chd 50p. Sun April 18 (2.30-6)*

Renishaw Hall ꝭ❀ (Sir Reresby & Lady Sitwell) Renishaw. Renishaw Hall is situated equidistant 6m from both Sheffield and Old Chesterfield on A616 2m from its junction with M1 at exit 30. Italian style garden with terraces, old ponds, yew hedges and pyramids laid out by Sir George Sitwell C1900. Interesting collection of herbaceous plants and shrubs; nature trail. Shop provides wine, souvenirs, antiques. TEAS. *Adm £2 OAPs £1 Chd 50p. Mon April 12, Thurs May 6, 13, 20, 27, June 3, 10, 17, 24, July 1, 8, 15, 22, 29, Suns May 2, 9, 16, 23, 30, June 6, 13, 20, 27, July 4, 11, 18, 25 (2-5)*

Regular Openers. See head of county section.

Shottle Hall Farm Guest House ꝭ❀ (Mr & Mrs P Matthews) Belper. Off B5023 Duffield to Wirksworth Rd. 200yds N of Xrds (Railway Inn) with A517 Ashbourne to Belper Rd. 2½ acres natural garden featuring shrubs; roses; bedding plants; bulbs; small herbaceous border and lawns. Cream TEAS. *Adm £1 Chd under 12 free. Sun April 18 (2-5)*

Thatched Farm ꝭ✗❀ (Mr & Mrs R A Pegram) Radbourne. Exit A52 Derby-Ashbourne Road. 2m N of Derby Ring Road. 2-acre plantsman's garden in parkland setting. Alpines, bulbs, trees, shrubs, perennials and roses including rowans, willows and primulas; half hardy perennials; conservatory fully planted. C17 House. TEAS. *Adm £1 Chd free. Sun May 30 (Share to Relate), Sun June 13 (Share to Gloucestershire Old Spots Pigs), Sun July 4 (Share to St Andrews Church) (2-6). Also by appt* **Tel 0332 824507**

Tissington Hall ꝭ✗ (Sir Richard FitzHerbert, Bt) N of Ashbourne. E of A515. Large garden; roses, herbaceous borders. Tea available in village. *Adm £1 Chd free. Sat July 10, Mon Aug 30 (2-5)*

Tudor House Farm ✗❀ (Mr & Mrs G Spencer) Kirk Langley. 4½m N of Derby on A52 Ashbourne Rd. Take turning opp Meynell Arms Hotel, garden 400yds on R. ¼-acre garden on two levels. Mixed beds of shrubs and perennials; small fish and lily pond; heathers and alpine troughs. TEAS. *Adm 75p Chd free. Sun June 27 (2-5)*

¶**Valezina Hillside** ✗❀ (Mr & Mrs P Bowler) Heage. Between Ripley and Belper, further details on arranging appt. A butterfly/wildlife garden of ½ acre adjacent to open countryside. In parts steeply sloping, can be slippery. Mini-habitats incl a buddleia wilderness and wildlife pond. A hillside meadow and woodland garden are overlooked by a cottage garden rich in butterfly nectar plants. Essentially kept wild (but controlled) in order to maintain a permanent breeding habitat for over 20 species of butterfly who have been encouraged to stay since 1985. Totally informal with a profusion of wild flowers. TEAS. *Adm £1 Chd free. By appt only May to Sept. Butterflies most numerous in July and Aug* **Tel 0773 853099**

Yeldersley Hall ꝭ✗ (Mr & Mrs Rex Sevier) 2m SE of Ashbourne on A52. 4 acres of pleasure grounds in the course of restoration, retaining original Victorian layout. Many rarities, rhododendrons, azaleas, bulbs and interesting herbaceous borders; much recent replanting under direction of Brian Davis. TEAS. *Adm £1 Chd free. Sun May 9 (2-6)*

❀

Devon

Ion County Organiser: Mervyn T Feesey Esq., Woodside, Higher Raleigh Rd, Barnstaple

DATES OF OPENING

By appointment
For telephone numbers and other details see garden descriptions

Addisford Cottage, nr Dolton
Andrew's Corner, nr Okehampton
Avenue Cottage, Ashprington
11 Beaumont Road, Plymouth. June only
Bickham Barton, Roborough. To end of June
Blackpool House, Stoke Fleming
Bramble Cottage, West Hill
Bundels, Sidbury
Burrow Farm Garden, Dalwood
Castle Tor, Torquay
Cleave House, Okehampton
Court Hall, North Molton
The Croft, Yarnscombe
Croftdene, Ham Dalwood
Crosspark, Northlew
The Downes, Monkleigh
1 Feebers Cottage, Westwood
Fernwood, Ottery St Mary
Fore Stoke Farm, Holne, nr Ashburton
Garden House, Torquay
The Glebe House, Whitestone
Gratton's Field Cottage, Northlew
Higher Spriddlestone, Brixton
Holywell, Bratton Fleming
Kingswear, Ridley Hill Gardens
Little Upcott Gardens, Marsh Green
The Lodge, Mannamead, Plymouth
Lower Coombe Royal, Kingsbridge
The Moorings, nr Lyme Regis
16 Moorland View, Derriford, Plymouth
Mulberry House, Barbican Terrace, Barnstaple
The Old Mill, Blakewell
The Old Rectory, Clayhidon
The Old Rectory, Woodleigh
The Orchard, Kenn
Orchard Cottage, Exmouth
38 Phillipps Avenue, Exmouth
The Pines, Salcombe
Quakers, Membury
51 Salters Road, nr Exeter
Setts, Bovey Tracey
Shallowford Lodge, Great Torrington
Silver Copse, nr Marsh Green
Sowton Mill, Dunsford
41 Springfield Close, Plymstock
Stanewood, nr Tiverton

Topsham Gardens, 20 Monmouth Avenue
Vicar's Mead, East Budleigh
Warren Cottage, nr Ermington
Weetwood, nr Honiton
Westpark, Yealmpton
Withleigh Farm, nr Tiverton

Regular openings
For details see garden descriptions

Alleron, Loddiswell, nr Kingsbridge. March to Oct
Avenue Cottage, Ashprington. Tues to Sat March 31 to Sept 30
Bicton College of Agriculture. Open Mon to Fri all year
Burrow Farm Garden, Dalwood. Daily April 1 to Sept 30
Clovelly Court, Clovelly. Every Thurs April 29 to Sept 23
Crosspark, Northlew. Fris, Suns, Easter & May Bank Hols March 26 to Aug 15
Docton Mill & Gardens, nr Hatland. Daily March to Sept
The Downes, Monkleigh. Daily Fri April 9 to Sun June 13
Fernwood, Ottery St Mary. Daily April 9 to End of May
The Garden House, Yelverton. Daily March 1 to Oct 31
Gidleigh Park, Chagford. Daily all year Mon to Fri except Bank Hols
Hill House, nr Ashburton. Open all year
Little Upcott Gardens, Marsh Green. Mons May, June, July & Aug
Marwood Hill, nr Barnstaple. Daily except Christmas Day
Plant World, nr Newton Abbot. Open daily
Rosemoor Garden, Great Torrington. Open daily all year
Wylmington Hayes, nr Honiton. Easter Weekend & Every Sun & Bank Hol Mons until the end of Aug

February 7 Sunday
Hill House, nr Ashburton
March 21 Sunday
Bickham House, Kenn, nr Exeter
Westpark, Yealmpton
March 24 Wednesday
Bickham House, Kenn, nr Exeter

Westpark, Yealmpton
March 28 Sunday
Bickham Barton, Roborough
Glebe Cottage, nr Warkleigh
April 4 Sunday
Bickham Barton, Roborough
Higher Knowle, Lustleigh
Holywell, Bratton Fleming
Kingswear, Ridley Hill Gardens
Mothecombe House, Holbeton
38 Phillipps Avenue, Exmouth
April 9 Friday
Gratton's Field Cottage, Northlew
The Pines, Salcombe
Wylmington Hayes, nr Honiton
April 10 Saturday
The Pines, Salcombe
Wylmington Hayes, nr Honiton
April 11 Sunday
Bickham Barton, Roborough
Bundels, Sidbury
Gratton's Field Cottage, Northlew
Higher Knowle, Lustleigh
Holywell, Bratton Fleming
The Moorings, nr Lyme Regis
Penrose, Crediton
38 Phillipps Avenue, Exmouth
The Pines, Salcombe
Silver Copse, nr Marsh Green
Vicar's Mead, East Budleigh
Wylmington Hayes, nr Honiton
April 12 Monday
Bickham Barton, Roborough
1 Feebers Cottage, Westwood
Higher Knowle, Lustleigh
The Moorings, nr Lyme Regis
The Pines, Salcombe
Silver Copse, nr Marsh Green
Wylmington Hayes, nr Honiton
April 14 Wednesday
Bundels, Sidbury
Holywell, Bratton Fleming
April 15 Thursday
Bundels, Sidbury
Whitmore, nr Chittlehamholt
April 18 Sunday
Bickham Barton, Roborough
Bickham House, Kenn, nr Exeter
Higher Knowle, Lustleigh
Holywell, Bratton Fleming
Kingswear, Ridley Hill Gardens
Meadowcroft, Plympton
April 21 Wednesday
Bickham House, Kenn, nr Exeter
April 25 Sunday
Andrew's Corner, nr Okehampton
Bickham Barton, Roborough
Chevithorne Barton, nr Tiverton

Coleton Fishacre, Kingswear
Hartland Abbey, nr Bideford
Higher Knowle, Lustleigh
Holywell, Bratton Fleming
Killerton Garden, Broadclyst
16 Moorland View, Derriford,
Plymouth
38 Phillipps Avenue, Exmouth
Valley House, nr Axminster

April 28 Wednesday
Bicton College of Agriculture

April 29 Thursday
1, Feebers Cottage, Westwood
Greenway Gardens, Churston
Ferrers

May 1 Saturday
Mothecombe House, Holbeton
The Old Glebe, Eggesford

May 2 Sunday
Bickham Barton, Roborough
Bramble Cottage, West Hill
Hamblyn's Coombe, Dittisham
Higher Knowle, Lustleigh
Holywell, Bratton Fleming
Kings Gatchell, Higher Metcombe
The Lodge, Mannamead, Plymouth
Meadowcroft, Plympton
The Moorings, nr Lyme Regis
Mothecombe House, Holbeton
The Old Glebe, Eggesford
Topsham Gardens, nr Exeter
Valley House, nr Axminster
Vicar's Mead, East Budleigh

May 3 Monday
Bickham Barton, Roborough
Bramble Cottage, West Hill
Hamblyn's Coombe, Dittisham
Higher Knowle, Lustleigh
Kings Gatchell, Higher Metcombe
The Moorings, nr Lyme Regis
The Old Glebe, Eggesford
Topsham Gardens, nr Exeter

May 5 Wednesday
Holywell, Bratton Fleming

May 6 Thursday
Greenway Gardens, Churston
Ferrers

May 8 Saturday
Dartington Hall Gardens, nr
Totnes
Garden House, Torquay

May 9 Sunday
Andrew's Corner, nr Okehampton
Bickham Barton, Roborough
Castle Drogo, Exeter
Dartington Hall Gardens, nr
Totnes
Garden House, Torquay
Higher Knowle, Lustleigh
Holywell, Bratton Fleming
Knightshayes Gardens, nr Tiverton
The Orchard, Kenn
Penrose, Crediton
38 Phillipps Avenue, Exmouth

Woodside, Barnstaple

May 12 Wednesday
Meadowcroft, Plympton

May 15 Saturday
Garden House, Torquay
Pleasant View Nursery, nr
Newton Abbot
The Quoin, Bigbury

May 16 Sunday
Arlington Court, nr Barnstaple
Bickham House, Kenn, nr Exeter
Bickham Barton, Roborough
The Cider House, Yelverton
Cleave House, Okehampton
Delamore, Cornwood
Fast Rabbit Farm, Ash Cross
1, Feebers Cottage, Westwood
Garden House, Torquay
Glebe Cottage, nr Warkleigh
The Glebe House, Whitestone
Higher Knowle, Lustleigh
Higher Warcombe, nr Kingsbridge
Holywell, Bratton Fleming
Jenarl, Stoke Fleming
Little Southey, nr Culmstock
Pleasant View Nursery, nr
Newton Abbot
Saltram House, nr Plympton
Sampford Peverell Gardens:
Challis & Millstream Cottage

May 19 Wednesday
Bickham House, Kenn, nr Exeter
Bicton College of Agriculture

May 22 Saturday
Ottery St Mary Gardens
The Quoin, Bigbury
Scypen, Ringmore
Setts, Bovey Tracey
Withleigh Farm, nr Tiverton
Wolford Lodge, nr Honiton

May 23 Sunday
Addisford Cottage, nr Dolton
Andrew's Corner, nr Okehampton
Bickham Barton, Roborough
Bundels, Sidbury
Castle Drogo, Exeter
Chivithorne Barton, nr Tiverton
Coleton Fishacre, Kingswear
Delamore, Cornwood
The Glebe House, Whitestone
Higher Knowle, Lustleigh
Holywell, Bratton Fleming
Kerscott House, nr Swimbridge
The Lodge, Mannamead,
Plymouth
Mardon, Moretonhampstead
Meadowcroft, Plympton
The Orchard, Kenn
Ottery St Mary Gardens
38 Phillipps Avenue, Exmouth
The Rectory, Aveton Gifford, nr
Kingsbridge
Sampford Peverell Gardens:
Challis & Millstream Cottage

Setts, Bovey Tracey
Starveacre, Dalwood, nr
Axminster
Withleigh Farm, nr Tiverton

May 26 Wednesday
Bundels, Sidbury

May 27 Thursday
Bundels, Sidbury

May 28 Friday
The Pines, Salcombe

May 29 Saturday
Little Upcott, Marsh Green
The Pines, Salcombe

May 30 Sunday
Addisford Cottage, nr Dolton
Bickham Barton, Roborough
Bramble Cottage, West Hill
Croftdene, Ham, Dalwood
Glebe Cottage, nr Warkleigh
The Glebe House, Whitestone
Gorwell House, nr Barnstaple
Higher Knowle, Lustleigh
Holywell, Bratton Fleming
Kings Gatchell, Higher Metcombe
Lee Ford, Budleigh Salterton
Little Upcott, Marsh Green
Mardon, Moretonhampstead
Meadow Court, Slapton
The Moorings, nr Lyme Regis
The Old Parsonage, Warkleigh
The Pines, Salcombe
Robin Hill, Exeter
Silver Copse, nr Marsh Green
Starveacre, Dalwood, nr
Axminster
Twitchen Mill, nr South Molton
Vicar's Mead, East Budleigh

May 31 Monday
Addisford Cottage, nr Dolton
Bickham Barton, Roborough
Bramble Cottage, West Hill
The Croft, Yarnscombe
Higher Knowle, Lustleigh
Kings Gatchell, Higher Metcombe
The Moorings, nr Lyme Regis
The Pines, Salcombe
Silver Copse, nr Marsh Green

June 2 Wednesday
Higher Lukesland, nr Ivybridge

June 5 Saturday
Farrants, Kilmington
Pleasant View Nursery, nr
Newton Abbot

June 6 Sunday
Andrew's Corner, nr Okehampton
Bickham Barton, Roborough
The Bungalow, North Tawton
The Cider House, Yelverton
Farrants, Kilmington
1, Feebers Cottage, Westwood
Glebe Cottage, nr Warkleigh
The Glebe House, Whitestone
Gratton's Field Cottage, Northlew
Higher Warcombe, nr Kingsbridge

Jenarl, Stoke Fleming
Little Webbery, Alverdiscott
Mardon, Moretonhampstead
Meadow Court, Slapton
The Old Mill, Blakewell nr
  Barnstable
The Old Vicarage, Shute
Overbecks, Salcombe
Pleasant View Nursery, nr
  Newton Abbot

June 9 Wednesday
Addisford Cottage, nr Dolton
Bicton College of Agriculture
Bramble Cottage, West Hill
The Old Vicarage, Shute
Scypen, Ringmore

June 12 Saturday
Bovey Tracey Gardens
Bramble Cottage, West Hill
Farrants, Kilmington

June 13 Sunday
Addisford Cottage, nr Dolton
Bovey Tracey Gardens
Bramble Cottage, West Hill
Cleave House, Okehampton
The Croft, Yarnscombe
Farrants, Kilmington
Fast Rabbit Farm, Ash Cross
Fore Stoke Farm, Holne
The Glebe House, Whitestone
Mothecombe House, Holbeton
The Old Vicarage, Shute
38 Phillipps Avenue, Exmouth
Riversbridge, nr Dartmouth
Sowton Mill, Dunsford
Topsham Gardens, 20,
  Monmouth Ave

June 16 Wednesday
Cleave House, Okehampton
The Old Vicarage, Shute

June 19 Saturday
Bundels, Sidbury
Little Upcott, Marsh Green

June 20 Sunday
Addisford Cottage, nr Dolton
Andrew's Corner, nr
  Okehampton
Bickham Barton, Roborough
Bickham House, Kenn, nr Exeter
Bundels, Sidbury
The Glebe House, Whitestone
Gratton's Field Cottage, Northlew
Little Upcott Gardens, Marsh
  Green
The Rectory, Aveton Gifford
Riversbridge, nr Dartmouth
Saltram House, nr Plympton
Vicar's Mead, East Budleigh
Warren Cottage, nr Ermington
Woodside, Barnstaple

June 23 Wednesday
Bickham House, Kenn, nr Exeter
Bundels, Sidbury
Warren Cottage, nr Ermington

June 24 Thursday
Bundels, Sidbury

June 26 Saturday
Barton House, Nymet Rowland

June 27 Sunday
Addisford Cottage, nr Dolton
Barton House, Nymet Rowland
Court Hall, North Molton
The Croft, Yarnscombe
1, Feebers Cottage, Westwood
Fore Stoke Farm, Holne
Glebe Cottage, nr Warkleigh
The Glebe House, Whitestone
Gorwell House, nr Barnstaple
Heddon Hall, Parracombe
Holywell, Bratton Fleming
Kerscott House, nr Swimbridge
Mulberry House, Barnstaple
The Old Parsonage, Warkleigh
Overbecks, Salcombe
38 Phillipps Avenue, Exmouth
41 Springfield Close, Plymstock
Twitchen Mill, nr South Molton
Vicar's Mead, East Budleigh

June 28 Monday
Barton House, Nymet Rowland

July 1 Thursday
Whitmore, nr Chittlehamholt

July 4 Sunday
The Bungalow, North Tawton
Croftdene, Ham Dalwood
The Glebe House, Whitestone
Knightshayes Gardens, nr Tiverton
Mulberry House, Barnstaple
Sowton Mill, nr Dunsford
Vicar's Mead, East Budleigh

July 10 Saturday
Pleasant View Nursery, nr
  Newton Abbot
Silver Copse, nr Marsh Green

July 11 Sunday
Addisford Cottage, nr Dolton
Arlington Court, nr Barnstaple
The Croft, Yarnscombe
The Glebe House, Whitestone
Heddon Hall, Parracombe
Killerton Garden, Broadclyst
Pleasant View, nr Newton Abbot
Robin Hill, Exeter
Sampford Peverell Gardens
Silver Copse, nr Marsh Green

July 14 Wednesday
Addisford Cottage, nr Dolton
Bicton College of Agriculture
The Garden House, Yelverton
Knightshayes Gardens, nr Tiverton

July 17 Saturday
Little Upcott, Marsh Green

July 18 Sunday
Addisford Cottage, nr Dolton
Andrew's Corner, nr Okehampton
Bickham House, Kenn, nr Exeter
1, Feebers Cottage, Westwood
Hill House, nr Ashburton

Little Upcott, Marsh Green
Portington, nr Lamerton
Sampford Peverell Gardens
Woodside, Barnstaple

July 21 Wednesday
Bickham House, Kenn, nr Exeter

July 24 Saturday
Garden House, Torquay

July 25 Sunday
Addisford Cottage, nr Dolton
The Croft, Yarnscombe
Garden House, Torquay
Glebe Cottage, nr Warkleigh
Gorwell House, nr Barnstaple
Hill House, nr Ashburton
Portington, nr Lamerton

July 26 Monday
Fardel Manor, nr Ivybridge

July 31 Saturday
Topsham Gardens: Clyst Cottage

August 1 Sunday
Glebe Cottage, nr Warkleigh
Hill House, nr Ashburton
Kerscott House, nr Swimbridge
41 Springfield Close, Plymstock
Topsham Gardens: Clyst Cottage

August 7 Saturday
Pleasant View, nr Newton Abbot

August 8 Sunday
The Croft, Yarnscombe
Gratton's Field Cottage, Northlew
Hill House, nr Ashburton
The Lodge, Mannamead,
  Plymouth
Pleasant View, nr Newton Abbot

August 11 Wednesday
The Garden House, Yelverton

August 15 Sunday
Bickham House, Kenn, nr Exeter
Glebe Cottage, nr Warkleigh
Gratton's Field Cottage, Northlew
Hill House, nr Ashburton
Penrose, Crediton

August 18 Wednesday
Bickham House, Kenn, nr Exeter
Bicton College of Argiculture

August 22 Sunday
The Old Mill, Blakewell, nr
  Barnstaple

August 28 Saturday
Barton House, Nymet Rowland

August 29 Sunday
Barton House, Nymet Rowland
Glebe Cottage, nr Warkleigh

August 30 Monday
Barton House, Nymet Rowland
The Croft, Yarnscombe
Silver Copse, nr Marsh Green

September 4 Saturday
Pleasant View, nr Newton Abbot

September 5 Sunday
1, Feebers Cottage, Westwood
Gorwell House, nr Barnstaple
Kerscott House, nr Swimbridge

Pleasant View, nr Newton Abbot
September 8 Wednesday
Bicton College of Agriculture
September 19 Sunday
Bickham House, Kenn, nr Exeter
Glebe Cottage, nr Warkleigh
The Old Parsonage, Warkleigh

September 22 Wednesday
Bickham House, Kenn, nr Exeter
September 26 Sunday
1, Feebers Cottage, Westwood
Glebe Cottage, nr Warkleigh
October 10 Sunday
1, Feebers Cottage, Westwood

October 17 Sunday
Starveacre, Dalwood, nr
Axminster
November 7 Sunday
The Moorings, nr Lyme Regis

DESCRIPTIONS OF GARDENS

Addisford Cottage *⊁❀* (Mr & Mrs R J Taylor) West Lane, Dolton. ½m W of Dolton. From village centre past Royal Oak for ½m to bottom of valley, gate on R across ford. Typical Devon thatched cottage with 1-acre garden in wooded valley. Stream, pond, ornamental waterfowl. Wide selection of hardy plants. Limited parking at cottage. TEAS. *Adm £1 Chd free. Suns, Mon May 23, 30, 31, Wed June 9, July 14, Suns June 13, 20, 27, July 11, 18, 25 (11-5). Also by appt* **Tel 08054 365**

¶Alleron ⅄❀ (Mr & Mrs Jeremy Davies) Loddiswell. Turn off Loddiswell-S Brent rd, just N of Lodd Village. Follow signed lane, across T-junction and take L fork down bumpy private drive. Drive slowly, large car park at rear. 3-acre informal garden in lovely wooded valley, streams, lakes, bog plants, spring bulbs, autumn colours, old roses and some herbaceous. Walk around lovely wood, beautiful in bluebell season. Unique circular walled garden, thatched topping to walls, possibly dating early C19, origin unknown. Picnic area, ample car parking. Stone Butter house with own spring water. Cream TEAS. *Adm £1 OAP 75p Chd 50p (Share to NGS). Open daily March to Oct incl (11 - dusk). Parties by arrangement*

Andrew's Corner ⅄⊁❀ (H J & Mr & Mrs R J Hill) Belstone, 3m E of Okehampton signed to Belstone. Parking restricted but may be left on nearby common. Plantsmans garden 1,000ft up on Dartmoor, overlooking Taw Valley; wide range unusual trees, shrubs, herbaceous plants for year round effect inc alpines, rhododendrons, bulbs, dwarf conifers; well labelled. TEAS. *Adm 60p Chd 30p. Suns April 25; May 9, 23; June 6, 20; July 18; (2.30-6); also by appt* **Tel 0837 840332**

Arlington Court ⅄⊁ (The National Trust) Shirwell, nr Barnstaple. 7m NE of Barnstaple on A39. Rolling parkland and woods with lake. Rhododendrons and azaleas; fine specimen trees; small terraced Victorian garden with herbaceous borders and conservatory. Regency house containing fascinating collections of objet d'art. Carriage collection in the stables. Restaurant. *Adm garden only £2.40 Chd £1.20. Suns May 16, July 11 (11-5.30)*

Avenue Cottage ⅄ (Mr R J Pitts & Mr R C H Soans) Ashprington. A381 from Totnes to Kingsbridge. 3m SE Totnes from centre of village past church for 300yds, drive on R. 11-acres of garden with woodland walks and ponds. Part of C18 landscape garden undergoing recreation by designers/plantsmen, garden guide available. *Adm £1 Chd 25p. Collecting box. Tues to Sat March 31 to Sept 30 (11-5). Other times by appt* **Tel 0803 732769.** *No coaches*

Barton House *⊁❀* (Mr and Mrs A T Littlewood) Nyme Rowland. 9m NW of Crediton. Follow signs to Nyme Rowland from A377 at Lapford or B3220 at Aller Bridge Garden opposite C15 church. 1-acre garden designed an maintained by owners. Beautiful views to Dartmoor. Ind vidual areas developed with varied character. Herbs pond; herbaceous; yew garden; ferns, grotto, roses an fountain pool. TEAS. *Adm £1 Chd 50p (Share to St Ba tholomew's Church, Nymet Rowland). Sats, Suns, Mor June 26, 27, 28, Aug 28, 29, 30 (2-6)*

41 Beaumont Road *⊁* (Mr & Mrs A J Parsons) St Judes Plymouth. ½m from city centre, 100yds from Beaumor Park; take Ebrington St exit from Charles X roundabout i city centre. Parking in nearby side rds. Matchbox sizec walled town garden; intensive tub-culture of uncommo shrubs, small trees, climbers; compact and colourful wit roses; pieris, camellias and clematis. Prize winning ga den shown on TSW & Gardener's World. TEA. *Adm 75 Chd 20p. By appt only June* **Tel 0752 668640**

Bickham Barton *⊁❀* (Helen Lady Roborough Roborough, 8m N of Plymouth. Take Maristow turn o Roborough Down, ½-way between Plymouth and Tavis tock, then follow poster directions. Bus stop: Maristow sign on Roborough Down; posters at Maristow turnin 1m from house. Shrub garden; camellias; rhododendrons azaleas; cherries; bulbs; trees. Lovely views. *Adm £ Every Sun March 28 to June 6, Sun June 20; Mons Apr 12, May 3, 31 (2-5.30); also by appt until end of June* **Te Yelverton 852478**

¶Bickham House *⊁❀* (Mr & Mrs John Tremlett) Kenr 6m W of Exeter 1m off A38. Plymouth-Torquay rd leav dual carriage-way at Kennford Services, follow signs t Kenn. 1st R in village, follow lane for ¾m to end of no through rd. Ample parking. No shade for dogs. 5-acr garden in peaceful wooded valley. Lawns, mature tree and shrubs; naturalised bulbs, mixed borders. Conserva tory, small parterre, pond garden; 1-acre walled kitche garden; lake. Cream TEAS. *Adm £1 Chd 50p. Suns Marc 21, April 18, May 16, June 20, July 18, Aug 15, Sept 19 Weds March 24, April 21, May 19, June 23, July 21, Au 18, Sept 22 (2-6)*

Bicton College of Agriculture ⅄⊁❀ (Devon Count Council) Entrance to the College is by Sidmouth Lodge half-way between Budleigh Salterton and Newton Popple ford on A376. Proceed up famous monkey puzzle avenu with fine views of the parkland and trees. From the top c the drive follow signs to garden car park. The gardens ar linked to the old Georgian mansion and extend via the ar boretum to the old walled garden and glasshouses, bein the centre of the Horticultural Dept. Rich variety of plant in beds and borders, laid out for teaching and effect; including NCCPG national collections of agapanthus & pittosporum; arboretum extends for ½m with various trees and shrubs inc magnolia, camellia and flowering cherries. Parking in gardens car park, short walk to gardens. Entrance tickets obtainable at Plant Centre. Garden and arboretum guides available. *Adm £1.50 Chd free. Weds April 28, May 19, June 9, July 14, Aug 18, Sept 8 (11-4.30). Gardens also open Mon to Fri throughout year (11-4.30)*

Blackpool House ✗ (Lady A Newman) Stoke Fleming, 4½m SW of Dartmouth. Opp car park at Blackpool Sands. Shrub garden, on steep hillside, containing many rare, mature and tender shrubs. Beautiful sea views. Tea Blackpool Sands take-away on sands. *Adm £1 Chd free. By appt only, spring & summer* Tel Stoke Fleming 770261

Bovey Tracey Gardens Gateway to Dartmoor. A382 midway Newton Abbot to Moretonhampstead. Teas locally. *Combined adm £1.50 Chd 25p. Sat, Sun June 12, 13 (2-6)*
¶26 **Beckett Road** (Mrs D C Starling) off Coombe Close nr Church. Very small garden with interesting plants
Bibbery ✿ (Misses E & A Hebditch) Higher Bibbery. B3344 to Chudleigh Knighton. Cul-de-sac behind Coombe Cross Hotel. Plantspersons small garden, sheltered corners harbouring interesting shrubs and tender plants. *Also by appt* Tel 0626 833344
Church View ✿ (Mr & Mrs R Humphreys) East Street. B3344 opp St Peter & St Paul's Church. Small garden, but many unusual plants, incl secluded vegetable area. Disabled parking
¶**Fig Tree Cottage** (Kenneth & Marjorie Snook) East Street. Small unpretentious cottage garden reflecting owners interest in plants. Large free car park Mary St 200 yds
Sunnyside (Mr & Mrs Green) Hind Street. Near town centre off A382. Opp Baptist church. Well established enclosed garden; trees and shrubs; herbaceous and colourful conservatory; productive vegetable area. Parking nearby

Bramble Cottage ✗✿ (Captain & Mrs Brian Norton) Lower Broad Oak Rd, West Hill, Ottery St Mary. From A3052 Exeter-Sidmouth rd turn N at Halfway Inn on B3180 for 2m, then right at Tipton Cross, then left fork and continue down hill to turn left at bottom into Lower Broad Oak Rd to second house on right. ¾-acre semi-woodland garden, plus ½-acre woodland, ponds and bog area; interesting shrubs; troughs; primulas a special feature in late spring. Adjoining Kings Gatchell. *Adm 75p Chd 15p. Suns, Mons May 2, 3; 30, 31; Wed June 9, Sat, Sun June 12, 13 (11-5); also by appt May to June* Tel 0404 814642

Bundels ✿ (Mr & Mrs A Softly) Ridgway, Sidbury. From Sidmouth B3175 turn left at free Car Park in Sidbury. From Honiton A375, turn right. Garden 100yds up Ridgway on left. 1½-acre organic garden inc small wood and pond set round C16 thatched cottage (not open); over 100 varieties of old-fashioned and other shrub roses. Typical cottage garden with accent on preservation of wild life. GRBS Gift stall. Teas in village. *Adm 50p Chd 10p. Suns April 11, May 23, June 20; Weds April 14, May 26, June 23; Thurs April 15, May 27, June 24, Sat June 19 (2-6). Also by appt May to July* Tel Sidbury 312

The Bungalow ✗✿ (Dr & Mrs M C Corfield) 9 Bouchers Hill, North Tawton. 6m NE of Okehampton A3072 3m W of Bow. Past clock tower, North Street (between bank & cafe). ¼m up hill sharp L for 100yds. 1-acre garden. Views over Dartmoor, wide variety of shrubs and perennials. Collections of hardy geraniums, ornamental grasses and ground cover plants incl small hebes and potentillas. Pond and bog garden. Colour scheme beds. Some interesting climbers and wall shrubs 100' herbaceous border featured on TSW. TEAS. *Adm £1 Chd 50p. Suns June 6, July 4 (2-6)*

Burrow Farm Garden ✗✿ (Mr & Mrs John Benger) Dalwood, 4m W of Axminster. A35 Axminster-Honiton Rd; 3½m from Axminster turn N near Shute Garage on to Stockland Rd; ½m on right. Secluded 5-acre garden with magnificent views has been planned for foliage effect and includes woodland garden in a dell with rhododendrons, azaleas etc; large bog garden; pergola walk with rose-herbaceous borders. Nursery adjoining. Cream TEAS (Suns, Weds & Bank Hols). *Adm £1.50 Chd 50p. April 1 to Sept 30 daily (2-7). Also mornings by appt* Tel 0404 831285

Castle Drogo ✗✗✿ (The National Trust) Drewsteignton. W of Exeter, S of A30. Medium-sized garden with formal beds and herbaceous borders; shrubs, woodland walk overlooking Fingle Gorge. Wheelchair available. Plant centre. Restaurant. TEAS. *Adm gardens only £2 Chd £1.* ▲*For NGS Suns May 9, 23 (10.30-5.30)*

Castle Tor ✗ (Leonard Stocks) Wellswood, Torquay. From Higher Lincombe Rd turn E into Oxlea Rd. 200yds on right, entrance identified by eagles on gate pillars. Spectacular scenic listed garden superbly designed and laid out under the influence of Lutyens in the mid-30s. Stepped terraces, orangery, paved work and ornamental water. *Adm £1 Chd 25p. By appt only* Tel 0803 214858

¶**Chevithorne Barton** ✗ (Michael Heathcote Amory Esq) Chevithorne. 3m NE of Tiverton. A terraced walled garden and further informal planting in woodland of trees and shrubs incl a National Oak Collection. In spring the garden features magnolias, rhododendrons and azaleas. *Adm £1 Chd 25p (Share to CPRE). Suns April 25, May 23 (2-6)*

The Cider House ✗✿ (Mr & Mrs M J Stone) Buckland Abbey, Yelverton. From A386 Plymouth-Tavistock, 100yds S of Yelverton roundabout follow NT signs to Buckland Abbey. At Xrds before Abbey entrance turn N signed Buckland Monachorum. Drive 200yds on L, or short walk for visitors to Abbey. Peaceful and secluded garden with restrained planting complementing mediaeval house, part of a Cistercian monastery. Terrace borders and herbs, former Abbey walled kitchen garden with fruit, vegetables and flowers. Unspoilt aspect over wooded valley surrounded by NT land. Cream TEAS. *Adm £1 Chd 50p. Suns May 16, June 6 (2-6)*

Cleave House ✿& (Ann & Roger Bowden) Sticklepath, 3½m E of Okehampton on old A30 towards Exeter. Cleave House on left in village, on main road just past small right turn for Skaigh. ½-acre garden with mixed planting for all season interest. National Collection of hostas with 300 varieties, 100 of these are for sale. *Adm 50p. Suns May 16, June 13; Wed June 16 (10.30-5.30). Also by appt April to Oct* Tel 083784 0481

Clovelly Court &✿ (The Hon Mrs Rous) Clovelly. 11m W of Bideford. A39 Bideford to Bude turn at Clovelly Cross Filling Station, 1m lodge gates and drive straight ahead; also 'Long Walk' pedestrian entrance 200yds from top of village (back rd) at large green gate shared with entrance to coastal footpath. 25 acres parkland with beautiful open views through woodlands towards sea. 1-acre walled garden with borders, fruit and vegetables. 500yds walk from village (through green gate) along path lined with ancient trees and rhododendrons. Medieval Manor adjacent C14 Church nr coastline. Free parking in drive. Directions at Garden entrance, blue doors in Church Path. *Adm £1 Chd 20p (Share to NSPCC; Braunton Cheshire Home). April 29 to Sept 23 every Thurs (2-5); coach parties by appt*

Coleton Fishacre ✿ (The National Trust) 2m NE of Kingswear. 20-acre garden planted and developed according to personal taste of the D'Oyly Carte family during 1926-1947 and unaltered by subsequent owners, now under restoration; wide range of tender and uncommon trees and shrubs in spectacular coastal setting. *Adm £2.60 Chd £1.30. Suns April 25, May 23 (10.30-5.30)*

¶**Court Hall** ✿& (Mr & Mrs C Worthington) North Molton. 2½m N from A361 Barnstaple-Tiverton rd. In N Molton drive up the hill into the square with church on your L take the only drive beside the old school buildings and Court Hall is just round the bend. A very small south facing walled garden; large conservatory; rose, clematis, honeysuckle arbours surround a swimming pool garden with tender plants, rock wall and table. *Adm £1 Chd 20p. Sun June 27 (2-6). Also by appt June 1 to July 10* Tel 059 84 224

The Croft &✿& (Mr & Mrs Jewell) Yarnscombe. From A377, 5m S of Barnstaple turning W opposite Chapelton Railway Stn. for 3m. Drive on L at village sign. From B3232 ¼m N of Huntshaw TV mast Xrds, turn E for 2m. 1-acre garden on edge of village with unspoilt distant views to West. Alpine area and wide selection of unusual plants and shrubs. Island beds, much herbaceous material, ponds and bog area. Cream TEAS Bank hols only or by prior arrangement for parties. *Adm £1 Chd free (Share to St. Andrews Church). Mon May 31, Suns June 13, 27; July 11, 25, Aug 8; Mon Aug 30; (2-6). Also by appt* Tel 0769 60535

Croftdene ✿& (Joy and Phil Knox) Ham Dalwood. Between Axminster and Honiton. From A35 3½m W of Axminster turn N nr Shute Garage signed Dalwood and Stockland. Keep L up Stockland Hill until just past television mast. Turn R signed Ham. 1½m to Ham Cross. Park by telephone box. From A30 5m E of Honiton turn R signed Axminster and Stockland 3m to televsion mast turn L to Ham. 1½-acre garden in the making since 1988

with further 1-acre of natural woodland. Wide range of shrubs; herbaceous; ericaceous; alpines; woodland and water plants. Island beds; rock garden; peat beds; stream-side and pond. Featured on TV 'Gardens For All 1991' TEAS at **Burrow Farm**. *Adm 60p Chd 20p. Suns May 30, July 4 (2-6). Also by appt* Tel 040 483 271

Crosspark &✿& (Mrs G West) Northlew. From Okehampton follow A30 for 1m turn R to Holsworthy drive for 6m past Avia Garage turn R signposted Northlew, over bridge, turn L to Kimber, we are 3m along this rd on L, or 2½m from Highampton on the Northlew Rd. 1-acre plantswoman's garden by colour theme; herbaceous borders; ponds, incl wildlife pond; bog garden; rockery heathers and conifers. Wide range of plants. Featured on BBC Gardeners World and ITV. Large variety of unusual plants for sale. TEA. *Adm 75p Chd 20p. Fris, Suns Easter & May Bank Hol Mons. March 26 to Aug 15 (2-6). Also by appt all year, coaches welcome*

Dartington Hall Gardens &✿& (Dartington Hall Trust) Approx 1½m NW of Totnes. From Totnes take A384, turn R at Dartington Parish Church. 28-acre garden surrounds C14 Hall and Tiltyard. Plant sales shop and nursery. *Adm (donation) £2.00 recommended. Sat, Sun May 8, 9 (dawn to dusk)*

Delamore & (Mrs F A V Parker) Cornwood, Ivybridge. A38; leave at turning for Lee Mill and Cornwood 6m E of Plymouth. 4-acre garden with flowering shrubs, lawns and mature trees. Swimming pool available. TEAS. *Adm £1 Chd 50p. Suns May 16, 23 (2-6)*

Docton Mill and Garden ✿& (Mr & Mrs N S Pugh) Spekes Valley nr. Hartland. Off A39: From N Devon via Clovelly Cross & Hartland to Stoke, or from N Cornwall via Kilkhampton to the West Country Inn. On either route turn L and follow Elmscott signs towards Lymebridge in Spekes Valley for 3½m. A garden for all seasons (depicted on BBC TV in Spring, Summer and Autumn) with working water mill dated 1249, situated in one of Devon's outstanding beauty spots where garden blends with natural landscape. Nearly 8 acres of sheltered wooded valley 1500yds from Spekes Mill Mouth coastal waterfalls and beach. Mill pond, leats, trout stream crossed by footbridges and smaller streams. Cultivated areas including bog garden, rockery, outcrops, woodland, and orchard. Displays in their seasons of narcissi, primulas, shrub roses, specimen trees, shrubs and herbaceous plants beside a profusion of wild primroses, bluebells, foxgloves and ferns. Lunch, tea at Hartland Quay. *Adm £1.50 Chd under 16 free. Daily March to Sept (10-5). Parties by prior arrangement* Tel 0237 441 369

The Downes ✿& (Mr & Mrs R C Stanley-Baker) 4½m S of Bideford; 3m NW of Torrington. On A386 to Bideford turn left (W) up drive, ¼m beyond layby. 15 acres with landscaped lawns; fine views overlooking fields and woodlands in Torridge Valley; many unusual trees and shrubs; small arboretum; woodland walks. TEA Sats, Suns only. *Adm £1 Chd 20p. Daily April 9 to June 13 (all day); also by appt June to Sept* Tel Torrington 22244

Regular Openers. See head of county section.

Fardel Manor ઠ৯ (Dr A G Stevens) 1¼m NW of Ivybridge; 2m SE of Cornwood; 200yds S of railway bridge. 5-acre, all organic garden, maintained with conservation and wildlife in mind. Partly reticulated. 2½ acres developed over past 10 years with stream, pond and lake. Also, small courts and walled gardens around C14 Manor, with orangery, herbaceous borders and Italian garden. TEAS. *Adm £1 Chd 50p (Share to Frame). Mon July 26 (11-4.30)*

Farrants ઠ৯ (Mr & Mrs M Richards) Kilmington. 2m W of Axminster. A35, turn S at Kilmington Cross into Whitford Rd; garden about ¼m on left. 1-acre garden with stream planted since 1963; mostly shrubs and ground cover for colour contrast around C16 cottage. *Adm 80p Chd free. Sats, Suns June 5, 6, 12, 13 (2.30-6)* **Tel 0297 32396**

¶Fast Rabbit Farm ৯ (Mr & Mrs Mort) Ash Cross. 1½m from Dartmouth off the Dartmouth-Totnes rd pass park and ride. Turn L at Rose Cottage. Opp direction, from Totnes or Kingsbridge, pass Woodland Park on R, drive past Norton Park on L turn R at Rose Cottage. Newly created garden in sheltered valley with natural stream. Several ponds and lake; partially wooded; rockery; extensively planted; extends 8 acres with new woodland planting and walks being created through woodland at head of valley. Car park. Some level walks. 'Invalids' please phone prior to visit. TEA. *Adm £1 Chd 50p. Suns May 16, June 13 (2-6)*. **Tel 080 421 437**

1 Feebers Cottage ઠ৯ (Mr & Mrs M J Squires) Westwood. 2m NE of Broadclyst from B3181 (formerly A38) Exeter-Taunton, at Dog Village (Broadclyst) bear E to Whimple, after 1½m fork left for Westwood. ⅔-acre cottage garden on level site with wide variety of trees, shrubs, rock-plants, alpines, old-fashioned roses, small pond with water plants. Nursery. Cream TEAS July 18 only, tea and biscuits on other days. *Adm £1 Chd free. Mon, Thurs April 12, 29; Suns May 16; June 6, 27; July 18; Sept 5, 26; Oct 10 (2-6). Also by appt* **Tel Whimple 822118**

Fernwood ৯ (Mr & Mrs H Hollinrake) Toadpit Lane, 1½m W of Ottery St Mary; ¼m down Toadpit Lane (off B3174). 2-acre woodland garden; wide selection of flowering shrubs, conifers and bulbs; species and hybrid rhododendrons and azaleas special feature in spring. *Adm £1 Acc chd free. Open every day from April 9 to end of May all day or by appt* **Tel Ottery St Mary 812820**

Fore Stoke Farm ৯ (Mrs Anne Belam) Holne, nr Ashburton. A small ½-acre garden full of interesting plants; incl roses, clematis, herbaceous, hardy geraniums, campanulas, grasses and many more. All well labelled. 2 ponds. At 900 ft plants must be hardy. Rabbits and ponies to look at. TEA. *Sun June 13* special sale of homegrown plants. Cream TEAS. *Sun June 27. Adm £1 Chd free. (2.30-5.30). Also by appt* **Tel 036 43 394**

Garden House ৯ (Mr & Mrs W Rawson) Lower Warberry Road, Torquay. From harbour, Babbacombe Road, 7th turning left. Garden ½m on L at widening of rd, opp 'Sorento'. 1-acre S sloping with sea view from upper level of garden. Terraced with water garden, featuring lily pond, fountain, waterwheel. Parking on roadway. TEAS. *Adm £1 Chd 50p. Sats, Suns May 8, 9, 15, 16; July 24, 25 (2-6). Also by appt* **Tel 0803 292563**

The Garden House ৯ (The Fortescue Garden Trust) Buckland Monachorum, Yelverton. W of A386, 10m N of Plymouth. 8-acre garden of interest throughout year; inc 2-acre walled garden, one of finest in the country; fine collections of herbaceous and woody plants. Coaches and parties by appt only. TEAS. *Adm £2.50 Chd 50p (Share to NGS). March 1 to Oct 31 daily. For NGS Weds July 14, Aug 11 (10.30-5)*

Gidleigh Park (Paul & Kay Henderson) From Chagford R into Mill St. 150yds, fork R, to bottom of hill then follow sign for 1¾m. 700ft up on edge of Dartmoor, within the National Park, in beautiful surroundings. Tumbling streams with boulders and natural granite outcrops; terrace and parterre with herb garden; extensive natural water garden; woodland walks underplanted with rhododendrons and azaleas; massed bulbs in spring. Park in hotel car park, not in drive. Lunches and cream TEAS £3.50-£8.50. *Adm 50p Chd 25p. Open Mon to Fri except bank hols all year round, tours and parties by prior appt* **Tel Chagford 432367**

Glebe Cottage ৯ (Mrs C Klein) Warkleigh. 5m from South Molton on B3227 to Umberleigh. L at Homedown Xrds towards Chittlehamholt, straight on at next Xrds, 200yds on L, parking at bottom of track. 1-acre cottage garden, S sloping, terraced wide collection of interesting plants in different situations; stumpery with ferns to hot dry garden with mediterranean subjects; bog garden, old roses many primulas and geraniums. Cottage garden favourites alongside rare plants. Wide variety of unusual plants available from adjoining nursery. *Adm £1 Chd free. Suns March 28; May 16, 30; June 6, 27, July 25; Aug 1, 15, 29; Sept 19, 26 (2-5)* **Tel 0769 540 554**

The Glebe House ৯ (Mr & Mrs John West) Whitestone. 4m W of Exeter, adjoining Whitestone Church. (Narrow lanes, unsuitable for coaches). 2½-acre garden. Spring interest, extensive lawns, daffodils and trees (esp. acers, birches and eucalyptus), large heather garden. Summer interest, over 300 varieties of rose (esp. species old-fashioned, modern, shrub and climbing), clematis, honeysuckles. Outstanding views S from Exe estuary to Dartmoor. Former Rectory, part C14 with Georgian frontage (not open). C14 Tithe Barn (Ancient monument). Interesting C13/14 Church adjoins. Parking in lanes around Church. *Adm £1 Chd free (Share to Whitestone Church). Suns May 16, 23, 30; June 6, 13, 20, 27; July 4, 11 (2-5). Also by appt* **Tel 0392 81200**

Gorwell House ઠ৯ (Dr J A Marston) 1m E of Barnstaple centre, on Bratton Fleming rd, drive entrance between two lodges on left. 4 acres of trees and shrubs, walled garden; mostly created since 1982; small temple; summer house with views across estuary to Lundy and Hartland Point. TEAS. *Adm £1 Chd free (Share to Barnstaple Parish Church Organ Appeal). Suns May 30; June 27; July 25; Sept 5 (2-6)*

Gratton's Field Cottage ✿❀ (Mrs C F Luxton) Northlew. 8m W of Okehampton. Northlew Square towards Highampton. ½m from village on L. Small cottage garden; spring bulbs; shrubs; fuchsias; fish pond. Recent additional tree and shrub planting. TEA. *Adm 50p. Easter Fri, Sun April 9, 11, Suns June 6, 20, Aug 8, 15 (11-5). By appt* **Tel 0409 221361**

Greenway Gardens ❀ (Mr & Mrs A A Hicks) Churston Ferrers, 4m W of Brixham. From B3203, Paignton-Brixham, take rd to Galmpton, thence towards Greenway Ferry. Partly suitable for wheelchairs 30 acres; old-established garden with mature trees; shrubs; rhododendrons, magnolias and camellias. Recent plantings; commercial shrub nursery. Woodland walks by R. Dart. Limited parking. TEA and biscuits. *Adm £1 Chd 50p. Thurs April 29, May 6 (2-6)* **Tel 0803 842382**

¶**Hamblyn's Coombe** (Capt R S McCrum Ret'd) Dittisham. From B3207 to Dittisham, turn sharp R at Red Lion Inn, along The Level. After public car park on L fork R up steep private rd. Field car park signposted at top. 10 min very pretty walk to garden. 7 acres sloping steeply to R Dart, with dramatic view across river to Greenway House. Extensive recent planting of trees and shrubs; wild meadows and mature broad leaf woods. Woodland walks, stream and ponds and long river foreshore at bottom of garden. Sculpture by Bridget McCrum around garden. Ideal for children and dogs. TEA. *Adm £1 Chd free. Sun, Mon May 2, 3 (2-6)*

Hartland Abbey (Sir Hugh Stucley & the Hon Lady Stucley) Hartland. Turn off A39 W of Clovelly Cross. Follow signs to Hartland through town on rd to Stoke and Quay. Abbey 1m from town on right. 2 woodland shrubberies with camellias, rhododendrons etc; ½m walk to walled gardens; ¾m woodland walk to sea. No picnics please. TEAS. *Adm £1 Chd 50p (Share to St Nectan's Church, Hartland). Sun April 25 (2-5.30)*

¶**Heddon Hall** (Mr & Mrs W H Keatley) Parracombe. 10m NE of Barnstaple off A39. 400 yds N up hill from village centre. Entrance to drive on R. Ample parking 200 yds. Garden of former rectory on edge of Exmoor under restoration extending to 3 acres. Walled garden with formal layout and herbaceous beds; sheltered flower garden; semi shaded S sloping shrubbery with paths leading down to natural stream and water garden. *Adm £1 Chd 50p Suns June 27, July 11 (2-6)*

Higher Knowle (Mr & Mrs D R A Quicke) Lustleigh, 3m NW of Bovey Tracey A382 towards Moretonhampstead; in 2½m L at Kelly Cross for Lustleigh; in ¼m L/R at Brookfield along Knowle Rd; in ½m steep drive on left. 3-acre steep woodland garden; rhododendrons, camellias, magnolias on a carpet of primroses, bluebells; water gardens and good Dartmoor views. Teas in village. *Adm £2 Chd free. Suns April 4, 11, 18, 25; May 2, 9, 16, 23, 30; Mons April 12, May 3, 31 (2-6)*

> **By Appointment Gardens.** These owners do not have a fixed opening day usually because they do not like crowds or have insufficient parking space. Owner will often give guided tour.

Higher Lukesland ♿✿❀ (J Howell) Harford, 1½m N of Ivybridge. Follow sign by London Hotel, in Ivybridge, to Harford, across new rd and railway for 1½m. White entrance gate on right just beyond high stone wall. Parking in field opp gates. Small secluded semi-wild garden in rural setting, on level ground around bungalow; cottage planting at front, wide range unusual foliage shrubs at rear specially grown for floral decoration, some chosen for royal weddings etc. TEA. *Adm 50p Chd 25p (Share to Barnardos). Wed June 2 (2-6)*

Higher Spriddlestone ♿ (Mr & Mrs David Willis) Brixton, nr Plymouth. A379 5m E from Plymouth, S at Martin's Garden Centre sign, ¾m to top of hill, R opp Spriddlestone sign, entrance 50yds on L. 1½-acre developing garden in rural setting. Level area around house, with borders, informal wildlife and kitchen gardens and ponds. Teas at Martin's Garden Centre. *Adm £1 Chd free. By appt only* **Tel 0752 401184**

¶**Higher Warcombe** ✿ (Mr & Mrs A Treverton) Nr Kingsbridge. 2m N of Kingsbridge on the B3194 between Sorley Green Cross and Stumpy Post Cross. Take 1st turning L signposted Warcombe, house and garden approx ½m down lane. 1-acre garden on SW facing slope started in 1982 incl lawns, trees, rhododendrons, shrubs and herbaceous. Two steep banks planted for ground cover are a special feature and there is a pretty courtyard with container planting and a small walled garden. TEAS. *Adm £1 Chd 50p. Suns May 16, June 6 (2-5.30)*

Hill House Nursery & Gardens ♿❀ (Mr & Mrs R Hubbard) Landscove. Between Dartington & Ashburton signed A38 or A384 Buckfastleigh-Totnes. Old Vicarage beside church both designed by John Loughborough Pearson, architect of Truro Cathedral. The 3 acre garden was the subject of 'An Englishman's Garden' by Edward Hyams, a previous owner. Also featured in 'English Vicarages and Their Gardens' and several times on TV. Said by many well known horticulturists to be one of the finest collections of plants anywhere. TEAS. *Adm £1 Chd 25p. Suns Feb 7 (11-4) July 18, 25, Aug 1, 8, 15 (2-5)*

Holywell ✿❀ (Mr & Mrs R Steele) Bratton Fleming. 7m NE of Barnstaple. Turn W beside White Hart Inn (opp White Hart Garage) signed Village Hall. At 300yds fork L for Rye Park. Entrance drive ¼m at sharp L. Parking at house. Garden on edge of Exmoor in woodland setting of mature trees, in all about 25 acres. Stream, ponds and borders. Woodland walk to Lower River meadow and old Lynton Railway Track. Many unusual plants for sale. TEAS. *Adm 50p Chd 25p. Suns April 4, 11, 18, 25; May 2, 9, 16, 23, 30; June 27. Weds April 14; May 5 (2-5). Also by appt* **Tel 0598 710213**

Jenarl ✿ (Robert Eales Esq) Shady Lane, Stoke Fleming. 3m W of Dartmouth A379. From village centre (towards Blackpool sands), 100yds, L into Shady Lane Garden ½m. Parking. 1½-acre sub tropical coastal garden, informal collection of unusual shrubs, bamboos, palms, and water garden. *Adm £1.25 Chd 50p. Suns May 16, June 6 (2-5.30)*

Kerscott House &❀ (Mrs Jessica Duncan) Swimbridge. Barnstaple-South Molton (former A361) 1m E of Swimbridge, R at top of hill, immediate fork L, 100yds on L, 1st gate past house. Developing 6-acre garden surrounding C16 farmhouse in peaceful rural setting. Ornamental trees, wide selection of shrubs, herbaceous and tender perennials, pond and bog garden. Cream TEAS May and June only. *Adm 75p Chd free. Suns May 23, June 27, Aug 1, Sept 5 (2-6)*

Killerton Garden &❀❀ (The National Trust) 8m N of Exeter. Via B3181 Cullompton Rd (formerly A38), fork left in 7m on B3185. Garden 1m follow NT signs. 15-acres of spectacular hillside gardens with naturalised bulbs sweeping down to large open lawns. Delightful walks through fine collection of rare trees and shrubs; herbaceous borders. Wheelchair and 'golf' buggy with driver available. Restaurant. *Adm gardens only £2.80 Chd £1.40.* ▲*For NGS Suns April 25, July 11 (10.30-5.30)*

Kings Gatchell &❀❀ (Mr & Mrs K Adlam) Higher Metcombe. From Exeter, A30 to Airport, pass straight on through Aylesbeare over Tipton Cross, through beech copse (don't bear R), down hill, house on L. Neighbouring Bramble Cottage, West Hill. ⅔-acre wide variety many unusual plants, strong in daphnes, alpines, hebes, ferns (NCCPG collection), smaller rhododendrons, ilex. Greenhouses. *Adm 75p Chd free. Suns, Mons May 2, 3, 30, 31 (11-5)*

¶**Kingswear-Ridley Hill Gardens** ❀ From Torquay and Paignton A379 S towards Brixham, at Hillhead B3205 follow signs to Lower Ferry. At Kingswear one-way circuit up hill to Y fork, L into Higher Contour Rd. ½m keep to R at fork down Ridley Hill. After 100yds turn L into drive. Parking at Mulberry House 100yds on L. From Dartmouth cross river on Lower Ferry. 30yds hard R up Church Hill, 200 yds at 1st junction L into Ridley Hill. A close-knit group of medium-sized terraced gardens in spectacular setting overlooking the Estuary of the R Dart, dating from 2nd half of the C19. Wide range of shrubs, herbaceous perennials and bulbs. Mount Ridley garden features a gauge '0' live steam model railway. TEAS. *Combined adm £2.50 Chd 25p (Share to Army Benevolent Fund). Suns April 4, 18 (2-6)*
  ¶**The Chart House** (Mrs D Curry)
  ¶**The Coach House** (Mrs B Stannard)
  ¶**Mount Ridley** (Mr & Mrs Farmer)
  ¶**Mulberry House** ❀ (Major & Mrs Molloy) *Also open by appt* Tel 0803 752 301
  ¶**Ridley Gate** (Mrs C Byass)

Knightshayes Gardens &❀❀ (The National Trust) 2m N of Tiverton. Via A396 Tiverton-Bampton; turn E in Bolham, signed Knightshayes Court; entrance ½m on left. Large 'Garden in the Wood', 50 acres of landscaped gardens with pleasant walks and views over the Exe valley. Choice collections of unusual plants, inc acers, birches, rhododendrons, azaleas, camellias, magnolias, roses, spring bulbs, alpines and herbaceous borders; formal gardens; Wheelchair available. Restaurant. *Adm garden only £2.80 Chd £1.40.* ▲*Suns May 9, July 4 (10.30-5.30)*

Lee Ford &❀ (Mr & Mrs N Lindsay-Fynn) Budleigh Salterton. Bus:DG, frequent service between Exmouth railway station (3½m) and Budleigh Salterton, alight Lansdowne corner. 40 acres parkland, formal and woodland gardens with extensive display of spring bulbs, camellias, rhododendrons, azaleas and magnolias. Adam pavilion. Picnic area. Car park free. Home made cream TEAS (3-5.30) and charity stalls. *Adm £1.20 OAPs £1 Chd 60p Special rate for groups 20 or more £1 (Share to other charities). Sun May 30 (1.30-5.30); also by prior appt for parties only* Tel 0395 445894

Little Southey &❀❀ (Mr & Mrs S J Rowe) Northcott, Nr Culmstock. Uffculme to Culmstock rd, through Craddock then turn R at 6'6 restriction sign, Little Southey ½m on L. Culmstock to Uffculme turn L at restriction sign to Blackborough, right at Xrds to Northcott. House on R. Young garden surrounding C17 farmhouse. Wide variety of plants grown for round the year interest. Limited parking if wet. Plant sale partly in aid of NCCPG. TEAS. *Adm 75p Chd free. Sun May 16 (2-6)*

Little Upcott Gardens &❀❀ (Mr & Mrs M Jones) Marsh Green signposted off A30 Exeter to Honiton rd 4m E of M5 junction 29. Also signposted off B3180 and then from village. Informal 2-acre garden with many features of visual interest on different levels, featured on TV in 1992. Sensitive combination of plant styles and colour and unusual varieties of conifers, shrubs, perennials and alpine, some of which are available for sale. The original cottage garden is also open and there is a newly landscaped water feature with ornamental ducks. Plenty of seats available and assistance given to disabled incl partially sighted, by prior arrangement. Parties welcomed with cream teas, available by appt. TEAS. *Adm £1 Chd 50p (Share to Cats Protection League, Ottery Branch) Sats, Suns May 29, 30, June 19, 20, July 17, 18. Every Mon May, June, July, Aug (1.30-5.30). Also by appt* Tel 04048 22797

¶**Little Webbery** &❀ (Mr & Mrs J A Yewdall) Webbery Cross, Alverdiscott. Approx 2½m E of Bideford. Accessible either from Bideford (E The Water) along the Alverdiscott Rd or from the Barnstaple to Torrington Rd B3232 taking the rd to Bideford at Alverdiscott and passing through Stoney Cross. Parking adjacent Xrds. Approx 3-acre garden with two large borders near the house with lawns running down a valley, a pond, mature trees on either side and fields below which are separated by a Ha Ha. It has a walled garden to one side with box hedging, which is partly used for fruit, vegetables, and incl a greenhouse; lawns; rose trellises; shrubs and climbing plants. There is a tennis court below and a lake beyond. TEA. *Adm £1 Chd 50p. Sun June 6 (2-6)*

The Lodge &❀ (Mr & Mrs M H Tregaskis) Hartley Ave, Mannamead, Plymouth. 1½m from City Centre via Mutley Plain. Turn right at Henders Corner into Eggbuckland Rd, 3rd right at Tel kiosk to end of cul de sac. ½-acre S sloping aspect with variety of unusual shrubs, conifers, camellias and ground cover plants. Former L.A. Nursery with range of lean-to glasshouses for fruit and tender subjects. Featured on TV 'Gardens For All'. TEA. *Adm £1 Chd 20p (Share to St. Luke's Hospice). Suns May 2, 23, Aug 8 (2-6). Also by appt* Tel Plymouth 220849

Regular Openers. See head of county section.

Lower Coombe Royal ⚘❀ (Mr & Mrs H Sharp) Kingsbridge. ½m N of Kingsbridge on Loddiswell rd. Sign at gate. Historic woodland garden with rhododendrons, camellias, azaleas, magnolias and rare trees; terraces with tender and unusual shrubs; lawns, herbaceous borders; eucalypts. (Commercial shrub nursery open daily.) *Adm 50p Chd 25p. By appt only* Tel **Kingsbridge 853717**

Mardon ⚘ (His Honour & Mrs A C Goodall) ½m from Moretonhampstead, from the Xrds in Moretonhampstead take the Chagford rd A382, then R at once (not sharp R to Church), down hill, over a stream, enter by cattle grid on R before hill. 2-acres with lawns and terrace, rhododendrons; trout pond and streams; fine view of Moretonhampstead church. Teas in Moretonhampstead. *Adm £1 Chd free. Suns May 23, 30; June 6 (2-5.30)*

Marwood Hill ♿❀ (Dr J A Smart) Marwood, 4m N of Barnstaple signed from A361 Barnstaple-Braunton rd. In Marwood village, opp church. 20-acre garden with 3 small lakes. Extensive collection of camellias under glass and in open; daffodils, rhododendrons, rare flowering shrubs, rock and alpine scree; waterside planting; bog garden; many clematis; Australian native plants. National collection astilbe, iris, ensata, tulbaghia. Plants for sale between 11-1 and 2-5. Teas in Church Room (Suns & Bank Hols or by prior arrangement for parties). *Adm £2 OAP £1.50 Acc chd under 12 free. Daily except Christmas Day (dawn-dusk)*

¶**Meadow Court** ♿ (Ken & Heather Davey) Slapton. Entering the village of Slapton from the A379 at the Memorial on the beach. Take 2nd R and 1st L to house and garden in middle of village. Large free parking area. A young level garden of 1 acre created in the last 12 yrs and maintained by the owner. Large pond with waterfall; Gunnera and marginals, water hens nest here. Large lawned area with trees and shrubs; heathers and shrub roses. TEAS. *Adm £1 Chd 25p. Suns May 30, June 6 (2-6)*

Meadowcroft ♿❀ (Mrs G Thompson) 1 Downfield Way, Plympton. From Plymouth left at St Mary's Church roundabout, along Glen Rd, 3rd right into Downfield Drive; garden on right. From A38, Plympton turn-off L at 1st roundabout, R at 2nd down Hillcrest Drive and Glen Rd, L at bottom of hill. Opp Dillons into Downfield Drive. Medium size; stream; rhododendrons, azaleas, trees, flowering shrub borders. TEA. *Adm 60p Chd free. Suns April 18, May 2, 23 Weds May 12 (2-5.30)*

The Moorings ❀ (Mr & Mrs A Marriage) Rocombe, Uplyme, 2m NW of Lyme Regis. A3070 out of Lyme Regis, turn right 150yds beyond The Black Dog; over Xrds, fork right into Springhead Rd; top gate to garden 500yds on left. From Axminster A35; in 2m, 200yds beyond Hunters Lodge (Shell garage on Xrds), fork right twice then straight on 1m, top gate to garden on right. 3-acre peaceful woodland garden, developed since 1965, on hillside with terraced paths, overlooking unspoilt countryside. Fine trees inc many species eucalyptus, unusual pines, nothofagus; flowering shrubs inc some rare; daffodils and other spring flowers, ground cover, many ferns, autumn colour. *Adm 75p Chd free. Suns, Mons April 11, 12; May 2, 3, 30, 31; Sun Nov 7 (11-5). Also by appt* Tel **0297 443295**

16 Moorland View ⚘❀ (Mr & Mrs G E J Wilton) Derriford, Plymouth. From Plymouth or A38 take A386 Tavistock Rd. After Derriford roundabout 1st L into Powisland Drive, 1st R into Roborough Ave, then L at bottom. Garden is approx 4m from Plymouth City centre. Small town garden with variety of plants. A typical lady's garden. TEA. *Adm 50p. Sun April 25 (2-5). Also by appt* Tel **0752 708800**

Mothecombe House ⚘❀ (Mr & Mrs A Mildmay-White) Holbeton, SE of Plymouth 4m. From A379, between Yealmpton and Modbury, turn S for Holbeton. Queen Anne house (not open). Walled gardens, herbaceous borders. Orchard with spring bulbs; camellia walk and flowering shrubs. Newly planted bog garden; streams and pond; bluebell woods leading to private beach. Walk through picturesque thatched cottages to the Old School Teahouse and along the coastal footpath to the stunning Erme Estuary. TEAS. *Adm garden £1.50 Chd free (Share to Holbeton Church). Suns, Sats, April 4 (2-5) May 1, 2; June 13 (2-6)*

Mulberry House ♿ (Dr & Mrs David Boyd) Barbican Terrace, Barnstaple. From the new rd (A361) follow signs to the Barbican Industrial Estate. This takes you L past a corner shop with Benson & Hedges sign down Summerland St. At the end fork R into Barbican Terrace, Mulberry House 2nd entrance on L. Parking at Trinity Churchyard which is also accessible from the south end. 1-acre varied planting; foliage, especially gold and variegated; climbers and shade plants. TEA. *Adm 50p Chd 25p (Share to Trinity Church). Suns June 27, July 4 (2-6). Also by appt* Tel **0271 45387**

The Old Glebe ♿⚘❀ (Mr & Mrs Nigel Wright) Eggesford, 4m SW of Chulmleigh. Turn S off A377 at Eggesford Station (½-way between Exeter & Barnstaple), cross railway and River Taw, drive straight uphill (signed Brushford) for ¾m; turn right into bridle path. 5-acre garden of former Georgian rectory with mature trees and several lawns, courtyard, walled herbaceous borders and a bog garden; emphasis on species and hybrid rhododendrons and azaleas 500 varieties. TEAS. *Adm £1 Chd 20p (Share to The Abbeyfield Chulmleigh). Sat, Sun, Mon May 1, 2, 3 (2-6)*

¶**The Old Mill** ⚘ (Mr & Mrs Shapland) Blakewell Muddiford, nr Barnstaple. ½m N past District hospital off B3230 to Ilfracombe signed Blakewell Fisheries then L again into Fisheries car park. Follow signs to Old Mill along lane to end, parking by Water Wheel on R. 3-acre garden on S facing slope nestles at the rear of a grade 11 listed Mill, surrounded by beautiful countryside views. A variety of conifers, rhododendrons, shrubs, heathers and herbaceous plants; also newly planted lime tree avenue, water gardens and many other interesting features. *Adm 80p Chd free. Suns June 6, Aug 22 (11-5). Also by appt* Tel **0271 75002**

By Appointment Gardens. Avoid the crowds. Good chance of a tour by owner. See garden description for telephone number.

¶**The Old Parsonage** ⚮❀ (Mr & Mrs Alex Hill) Warkleigh. 4m SW South Moulton on B3226 past Clapworthy Mill (Hancocks Cider) R at stone barn signs to Warkleigh. From S through Chittlehamholt then 2nd R at War Memorial. Telephone kiosk marked on OS landranger sheet 180. Young garden of 1 acre around former C16 Parsonage. Herbaceous border at entrance; enclosed terraced garden behind house with wide range of plants and raised beds. Steep slope planted with trees and shrubs for autumn colour. Cream TEAS. *Adm £1 Chd 50p (Share to NCCPG). Suns May 30, June 27, Sept 19 (2-6)*

The Old Rectory, Clayhidon ⚮❀ (Mr & Mrs K J Wakeling) 4m from Wellington via South St or M5 exit 26 for Ford St. House next to Half Moon Inn and Church. 3-acres woodland garden with new plantings amid mature native trees; large numbers of naturalized bulbs mainly daffodils and snowdrops. Walled garden with mixed borders, ponds and rockery. *Adm 60p. Chd 30p. By appt only* Tel 0823 680534

The Old Rectory, Woodleigh ⚭⚮ (Mr & Mrs H E Morton) nr Loddiswell. 3½m N of Kingsbridge E off Kingsbridge- Wrangaton rd at Rake Cross (1m S of Loddiswell). 1½m to Woodleigh. Garden on right in hamlet. C19 Clergymans garden partly enclosed by stone walls; restored and added to by present owners; mature trees with collection of rhododendrons, camellias and magnolias and other shrubs; large numbers of naturalised bulbs especially crocus and daffodils in early March. *Adm 50p Chd 10p. By appt only* Tel Kingsbridge 550 387

The Old Vicarage, Shute ⚮❀ (Mr & Mrs R Ingram) A35 3m W of Axminster, 6m E of Honiton, turn S on B3161 at Shute Garage, sign-posted Shute and Colyton. House on R ⅓m past tall gate pillars at side of rd. Please park in adjacent field. 1-acre garden on sloping site, surrounding stone built house, with lovely open view over Umborne valley to sea. This existing garden is being extended to include adjoining 2-acre field, so there are many features in the making. Terraced rockery, borders, roses old and new, informal shrub plantings. New box parterre. Cream TEAS. *Adm 75p Chd 30p. Suns June 6, 13 (2-5) Weds June 9, 16 (10-5)*

The Orchard ❀ (Mrs Hilda M Montgomery) Kenn. 5m S of Exeter off A38 ¾ acre; mostly trees; variety of conifers, azaleas, camellias, rhododendrons, many shrubs; fishponds and flowerbeds. Masses of spring bulbs. Ample parking nr Church. *Adm £1 OAPs/Chd 50p (Share to Redgate Bird Sanctuary, Exmouth). Suns May 9, 23 (2-5.30); also by appt* Tel Exeter 832530

Orchard Cottage ⚭❀ (Mr & Mrs W K Bradridge) 30, Hulham Rd, Exmouth, From Exeter A376 L into Hulham Road, just before first set of traffic lights. Entrance lane between Nos 26 and 32 Hulham Rd, opp lower end of Phillips Avenue. ¼-acre typical cottage garden. Parking in Hulham Road or Phillips Avenue. *Adm 50p Chd free. By appt only* Tel 0395 278605 *(2.30-5.30)*

¶**Ottery St Mary Gardens** Town maps available at each garden. Suggested car park in Brook St will be signposted. Cream TEAS at Ernespie. *Combined adm £1.50 Chd 50p. Sat, Sun May 22, 23 (2-6)*

¶**Ernespie, Londogs Lane** ⚭ (Dr & Mrs G Ward) Next to Ravenhill, connected by garden gate. South facing hot, dry garden and badger playground, planted for easy care, cutting and continuous colour; rhododendrons, heathers, roses; level terrace. Cream TEAS in aid of Ottery Nursing Care

¶**Little Beaumont, Ridgeway** ⚮ (Mr & Mrs I A Martin) From town centre, pass church on L (Honiton Rd), take 1st R on bend into Ridgeway. Approx 200 yds on R. Partly walled ¼-acre garden with shrubs, trees and herbaceous border

¶**Ravenhill, Londogs Lane** ⚭⚮❀ (Ruth & Guy Charter) Take Sidmouth Rd from town square, 200 yds up Tip Hill turn L up narrow Longdogs Lane, 5th house on R. Medium-sized garden with a wide variety of unusual plants. South aspect, country views; pond; keen NCCPG propagator. Unusual plants for sale

¶**10 Slade Close** ⚮❀ (Betty & Jenny Newell) From town centre take B3174 towards Seaton. Turn R into Slade Rd, then L into Slade Close and R again. Small garden, mixed shrubs, spring flowers, small pond, scree garden

¶**59 Yonder Street** ⚮ (John & Rosemary Maybery) Turn R from Brook St car park. Steps up to garden about 50 yds on R. Tiny town garden in its 3rd yr

Overbecks ⚮ (The National Trust) Sharpitor 1½m SW of Salcombe. From Salcombe or Malborough follow NT signs. 6-acre garden with rare plants and shrubs; spectacular views over Salcombe Estuary. *Adm garden only £2 Chd £1.* ▲*Suns June 6, 27 (10-8 sunset if earlier)*

Penrose ⚮❀ (Mr & Mrs A Jewell) Crediton. A377 main Exeter to Barnstaple road, turn into Park Rd by Hillbrow Residential Home. Garden opp third turning on L. ⅓-acre town garden with small lawns, shrubs and herbaceous borders, pond with waterfall and wishing well, areas for fruit and veg and for growing produce for exhibition. Spring bulbs and summer annuals. TEA. *Adm 50p Chd free. Suns April 11; May 9; Aug 15 (2-5)*

38 Phillipps Avenue ⚭⚮❀ (Mr & Mrs R G Stuckey) Exmouth. From Exeter, turn L into Hulham rd just before 1st set of traffic lights, 1st L into Phillipps Avenue (ample parking). Small, highly specialised alpine and rock garden containing extensive collection of rock plants and miniature shrubs, many rare and unusual; peat bed; scree bed; troughs; New Zealand collection. National NCCPG Helichrysum collection. Small alpine nursery. Teashops Exmouth. *Adm 50p Chd free (Share to NCCPG June 27 only). Suns April 4, 11, 25, May 9, 23; June 13, 27; (2-6). Also by appt* Tel 0395 273636

The Pines (Mr & Mrs R A Bitmead) Main Rd, Salcombe. At junction of Devon and Sandhills rds; lower entrance and parking Sandhills rd. All seasons ¾-acre S facing garden; fine coastal views to Sharpitor Headland and N Sands Valley. Informal garden of surprises; many interesting and unusual shrubs, trees; water gardens; bulbs, camellias, azaleas, heathers. *Adm £1 Chd free. Fris, Sats, Suns, Mons April 9, 10, 11, 12; May 28, 29, 30, 31 (11-5). Also by appt all year* Tel Salcombe 842198

Plant World 🌸 (Ray & Lin Brown) St. Mary Church Rd Newton Abbot. Follow brown signs from A380 Penn Inn Roundabout. Car park on L past Water Gardens. 4-acre Hillside Garden, laid out as a map of the world with native plants. Alpines, especially primulas and gentians, shrubs, herbaceous. Himalayan and Japanese gardens. Comprehensive cottage garden with double primroses, auriculas etc. 3 National Primula Collections. Seen on ITV June 1987. Rare and unusual plants sold in adjacent nursery. Picnic area, viewpoint over Dartmoor and Lyme Bay. Collecting box. *Adm 50p Chd free. Open daily (9-5)* **Tel 0803 872939**

Pleasant View ৬✿🌸 (Mr & Mrs B D Yeo) Two Mile Oak, nr Denbury. 2m from Newton Abbot on A381 to Totnes. R opp 2m Oak Garage signed Denbury. ¾m on L. Large car park. 2-acre plantsman's garden surrounded by open countryside with pleasant views. Wide variety of uncommon shrubs many tender. National Collections of Abelia and Salvia. Plants for sale in adjoining nursery (see advert). *Adm £1 Chd 25p. Sats, Suns May 15, 16, June 5, 6, July 10, 11, Aug 7, 8, Sept 4, 5 (2-6)*

¶**Portington** ✿ (Mr & Mrs A Dingle) Lamerton. From Tavistock B6632 to Launceston. ¼m beyond Blacksmiths Arms, Lamerton, fork L (signed Chipshop). Over Xrds (signed Horsebridge) first L then L again (signed Portington). From Launceston R at Carrs Garage and R again (signed Horsebridge), then as above. Small garden in peaceful rural setting with fine views over surrounding countryside. Mixed planting with shrubs and borders; woodland walk to small lake. TEAS. *Adm £1 Chd 25p. Suns July 18, 25 (2-5.30)*

Quakers ✿🌸 (Mr & Mrs T J Wallace) Membury. 3m NW of Axminster A35 to Honiton, ½m W of Axminster turn N signed Membury. About ½m S of Church, take L turning, past Lee Hill Hotel entrance. Interesting small terraced flower garden around old Quaker Meeting House. Across lane a plantsman's mixed tree and shrub garden leading down to wetland plantings and wooded stream. *Adm £1. Also by appt April to November (11.30-5.30)* **Tel Stockland 312**

¶**The Quoin** ✿🌸 (Bob & Sheila Mousley) Bigbury. A379 Kingsbridge to Plymouth. At Harraton Cross, between Modbury and Aveton Gifford. Take B3392 signposted Burgh Island. In Bigbury turn L, signposted Easton. Pedestrian entrance adjacent to the church of St Lawrence. ⅓-acre developed since 1987 for visual appeal using a wide range of perennials, New Zealanders, grasses etc; pond. TEA. *Adm £1 Chd 50p. Sats May 15, 22 (10-4.30)*

The Rectory ৬ (Mr & Mrs D Lloyd) Aveton Gifford. 4m W of Kingsbridge, A379 on W outskirts of village 200yds beyond Taverners Inn. Entrance to drive opp village sign. 1-acre garden, part woodland with rhododendrons, azaleas and roses. Parking at Village Hall, below house. Disabled ONLY park in driveway. *Adm 50p Chd 25p. Suns May 23, June 20 (2-5.30)*

By Appointment Gardens. See head of county section

Riversbridge (Mr & Mrs Sutton-Scott-Tucker) ½m inland from Blackpool sands and signed from A3122. Small walled gardens adjoining farmyard in lovely unspoilt valley with ponds and stream; herbaceous plants, roses and some unusual shrubs. TEAS. *Adm £1 Chd free. Suns June 13, 20 (2-6)*

Robin Hill ✿ (Dr G Steele-Perkins) Deep Dene Park, Exeter. From Barrack Rd turn W into Wonford Rd; entry to drive on left beyond Orthopaedic Hospital. ½-acre around house on level ground with variety of ornamental trees and shrubs; wall plants, ground cover and small pond. *Adm £1 Chd free. Suns May 30, July 11 (2-6)*

Rosemoor Garden ৬✿🌸 (The Royal Horticultural Society) Great Torrington. 1m SE of Great Torrington on B3220 to Exeter. Original plantsman's garden started in 1959; rhododendrons (species and hybrid), ornamental trees and shrubs; dwarf conifer collection, species and old-fashioned roses; scree and raised beds with alpine plants, arboretum. The Society is expanding the Garden from 8 acres to 40 over the next 15 years. The new Garden already contains 2000 roses in 200 varieties, two large colour theme gardens, herb garden, potager, 200 metres of herbaceous border and a large stream and bog garden. A cottage and a foliage garden open in 1993. The new Visitors Centre contains a restaurant, shop, and plant centre selling interesting and unusual plants. *Adm £2.50 Chd 50p Groups £2 per person. Open daily all year (10-6 April to Sept) collecting box for NGS*

51 Salters Road ✿🌸 (Mrs J Dyke) Exeter. Typical small town garden; specialising in unusual plants inc primulas, auriculas and alpines (owner has for many years been Committee member of Exeter Branch of Alpine Garden Society). *Collecting box for NGS. By personal appt only* **Tel Exeter 76619**

Saltram House ৬✿ (The National Trust) Plympton, 3m E of Plymouth, S of A38, 2m W of Plympton. 8 acres with fine specimen trees; spring garden; rhododendrons and azaleas. C18 orangery and octagonal garden house. George II mansion with magnificent plasterwork and decorations, incl 2 rooms designed by Robert Adam. Wheelchair available. Restaurant. *Adm gardens only £2.20 Chd £1.10.* ▲*For NGS Suns May 16, June 20 (10.30-5.30)*

Sampford Peverell Gardens 6m from Tiverton on A373, 1m from junction 27 on M5. Canal walks. TEAS at Challis. *Combined adm £1.50 Chd 50p (2.30-6.30)*

    Challis 🌸 (Mr & Mrs G Issac) Next to Globe Inn in the centre of the village. A well established garden with trees and shrubs. Large lawned area with flower beds, fish ponds and rockery. Some interesting outbuildings with many hanging baskets in the courtyard. The garden leads directly to the tow path of the Grand Western Canal. TEAS. *Suns May 16, 23, July 11, 18*

    High Cross House ✿🌸 (Mr & Mrs Bowers) Higher Town. Adjacent to Church. ¾-acre garden in sections comprising walled garden, courtyard garden, lawns with beds containing specimen shrubs and herbaceous plants. Large vegetable plot. Garden extends to the canal. *Suns July 11, 18*

Millstream Cottage ✿✾ (Mr Regester & Miss Tully) Higher Town. 1st R after PO (from village centre), cottage at bottom of lane. Young ⅓-acre garden with stream. Raised herb beds, pergola, pond, wild area and vegetable plot. Cordon and fan-trained fruit trees. *Suns May 16, 23, July 11, 18*

Norold ✾ (Mr & Mrs Thorley) Opp Parkway Station Rd. Parking in layby opp. Small Garden with lawns, bedding plants, dahlias, petunias, roses, geraniums, sweet peas, chrysanthemums, antirrhinums, shrubs etc, vegetable area. *Suns July 11, 18*

The Old Rectory ✾ (Janet & Greville Jefcoate) Higher Town. Simple garden around a C16 grade 11 listed Rectory with many different types of roses, herbaceous borders and some shrubs, with lawns, fruit and vegetables, in a beautiful setting in the village centre next to the church. The garden is on two levels, the lower level runs alongside the Grand Western Canal, which is a Country Park. *Suns July 11, 18*

¶**Scypen** ✾ (Mr & Mrs John Bracey) Ringmore. 5m S of Modbury. From A379 Plymouth-Kingsbridge S at Harraton Cross on B3392. R at Pickwick Inn (signed Ringmore). Park in Journey's End car park on L opp church. ½-acre coastal garden still being developed, integrating design, landscaping and mixed planting for year-round effect and to take advantage of lovely views of church, sea and unspoilt Nat. Trust coast and farmland. Salt and wind tolerant plants; silver wedding garden; organic kitchen garden; chamomile and thyme lawns. TEAS. *Adm 50p Chd 25p. Sat May 22, Wed June 9 (2-5)*

Setts (Mrs Jack Cutler) Haytor Rd, Bovey Tracey. 1m W of Bovey Tracy. Take B3344 to Widecombe Rd, after ¼m fork L, garden ¼m on R on Haytor Rd, next door to Edgemoor Hotel. ⅔-acre garden, herbaceous borders, wood containing rhododendrons (species and hybrids), azaleas, camellias, acers etc. *Adm 50p Chd 25p. Sat, Sun May 22, 23 (2-6). Also by appt (Spring, Summer, Autumn)* **Tel 0626 833043**

Shallowford Lodge ✿✾ (Mr & Mrs P J Cull) Great Torrington. ½m E of Torrington on B3227; turn S down Borough rd; left at Junior School; along Caddywell Lane ½m to bottom of hill; (OS map ref 506185). Small woodland garden begun 1970, being extended and planted with rhododendrons, azaleas, magnolias. Some level ground with streams, primulas, wild daffodils and other bulbs; peat garden with collection dwarf rhododendrons. *Adm 50p Chd 25p. By appt only* **Tel 0805 22182**

Silver Copse ✿✾ (Mrs V E Osmond) nr Marsh Green. From Exeter; A30 to Jack-in-the-Green, R to Rockbeare and Marsh Green, L towards Ottery. Garden ¾m on the R. From Sidmouth; A3052 to Half-way Inn. B3180 N for 1½m L at Xrds towards Marsh Green, garden 200yds on L. 3 acres, all seasons garden, wide selection shrubs, rhododendrons, azaleas, ornamental pools and alpines, as shown T.S.W. *Adm 75p Chd free. Suns, Mons April 11, 12; May 30, 31; Sat, Sun July 10, 11, Mon Aug 30 (10-5). Also by appt* **Tel 0404 822438**

Sowton Mill ✿✿✾ (A Cooke and S Newton) nr Dunsford. From Dunsford take B3193 S for ½m. Entrance straight ahead off sharp R bend. From A38 N along Teign Valley for 8m. Sharp R after humpback bridge. 4 acres laid out around former mill, leat and river. Part woodland, ornamental trees and shrubs, mixed borders and scree. Year round interest. TEA. *Adm £1 Chd 50p (Share to Cygnet Training Theatre). Suns June 13, July 4 (2-6). Also by appt* **Tel 0647 52347**

41 Springfield Close ✿✾ (Mr & Mrs Clem Spencer) Plymstock, 4m SE of Plymouth city centre. Leave A379 to Kingsbridge opp Elburton Hotel, follow Springfield Rd across Reservoir Rd, 1st right into Springfield Close. Medium landscaped surburban garden with country atmosphere; wide range of interesting plants, pond, waterfall, doves, exhibition of paintings and woodcraft. TEA. *Adm £1 Chd free. Suns June 27, Aug 1 (11.30-4.30). Also by appt June to Aug* **Tel Plymouth 401052**

Stanewood ✾ (Ian & Joyce Gordon) 2½m from Witheridge on rd to Rose Ash. 2½ acres with shelter belt. April and May polyanthus and rhododendrons in woodland; July, water plants beside stream and lily pond; Sept, hydrangeas. Teas at Southwick Herb Garden nearby. *Adm £1. By appt only* **Tel 0884 860 359**

Starveacre ✿✾ (Mr and Mrs Bruce Archibold) Dalwood. Leave Axminster on A35 travelling W. After 3m (Shute Xrds) turn R at staggered Xrds signposted Dalwood. Follow signs to Dalwood and go through village, over stream, round sharp L bend. Follow road, ignoring left turn, up steep hill and at top turn L. Under pylons and up hill. After crest, take L turn before white 5-bar gate. Starveacre is at end of lane. A plantsmans garden of 5 acres on a hillside facing S and W with superb views. Mixed plantings of rhododendrons, camellias, conifers, acers, magnolias and much more. TEAS. *Adm 80p Chd under 14 free. Suns May 23, 30, Oct 17 (2-5)*

Topsham Gardens 4m from Exeter. Free parking in Holman Way car park. Teas at 20 Monmouth Ave. *Adm 50p each garden Chd free. For shared and other dates see individual gardens*

Clyst Cottage ✿✾ (Alf & Sheila Crouch) Elm Grove Ave. The garden is 250 yds from Holman Way carpark and is reached by turning R out of the car park and crossing the railway via the kissing gate. Elm Grove Ave is opp the end of the lane. This is a ¼-acre carefully landscaped suburban garden which contains many less familiar tender plants & shrubs. *Sun, Mon May 2, 3, Sat, Sun July 31, Aug 1 (2-6)*

¶**4 Grove Hill** ✿✾ (Margaret and Arthur Boyce) Off Elm Grove Rd, opp junction with Station Rd. A small town garden with some rare plants, troughs and screes with alpine plants and unusual bulbs. *Sun Mon May 2, 3 (2-6)*

20 Monmouth Avenue ✿✾ (Anne & Harold Lock) Access to Monmouth Ave by footpath on the L after leaving Holman Way car park. ⅓-acre level garden, wide range of unusual plants and shrubs giving year round effect, mixed curved borders, herbaceous, shrubs and bulbs incl a collection of hardy geraniums and alliums. Some old fashioned roses. Featured on TV 'Gardens For All'. TEAS. *Suns, Mon, May 2, 3, June 13 (2-6). Also by appt* **Tel 0392 873734**

Twitchen Mill &❀ (Mr & Mrs G Haydon) 6m NE of South Molton. A361 S Molton to Taunton, 400yds past caravan site on outskirts of town at top of hill, L signed Twitchen for 5m. Straight on at last fork 200yds before Mill. 1-acre level garden on the foothills of Exmoor, in beautiful wooded valley, bordered with leat and clear water stream. Parking on roadside also in field. TEAS. *Adm £1 Chd free. Suns May 30, June 27 (2-6)*

Valley House ❀❀ (Dr & Mrs M Morgan) Churchill. Axminster to Chard A358 for 1m L after Weycroft Mill, signed Smallridge. 2nd R after Ridgeway Inn to Chardstock and Churchill. 150yds down hill, 1st R into cul-de-sac, house last on L. 1-acre enthusiasts garden on sloping site overlooking open farmland, largely planted since 1980 with ornamental trees, shrubs, bulbs. Includes extensive water garden featuring hostas, astilbes and grasses. Considerate parking in nearby lanes, please. TEAS. *Adm £1 Chd 20p. Suns April 25, May 2 (2-6)*

Vicar's Mead &❀❀ (Mr & Mrs H F J Read) Hayes Lane, East Budleigh, 2m N of Budleigh Salterton. From B3178 (formally A376), Newton Poppleford-Budleigh Salterton, turn off W for East Budleigh; Hayes Lane is opp 'Sir Walter Raleigh'; garden 100yds W of public car park. 3½ acres of informal plantings around a 500yr-old historic former vicarage; wide range of unusual and rare shrubs, trees, bulbs and perennials etc, displayed on a steep terraced escarpment. Hostas and 4 National Collections a feature. Tea in village. *Adm £1 Chd free. Suns April 11, May 2, 30; June 20, 27; July 4 (2-6). Also by appt.* **Tel 03954 42641**

Warren Cottage ❀ (Margaret Jock & Libs Pinsent) Higher Ludbrook, Ermington, Ivybridge. 1¼m E of Ermington on A3121 turn R signed Higher Ludbrook. 1½-acres started from field 1986, with sloping lawn; mixed beds and borders. Small pond with marginals. Some unusual plants. TEAS. *Adm £1 Chd free (Share to Ermington & Ugborough Churches). Sun, Wed June 20, 23 (2-6). Also by appt May to Sept* **Tel Modbury 830698**

Weetwood ❀ (Mr & Mrs J V R Birchall) Offwell, 2m from Honiton. Turn S off A35 (signed Offwell), at E end of Offwell. 1-acre all seasons garden; rhododendrons, azaleas, shrubs, ornamental pools, rock gardens, collection of dwarf conifers. Teashops Honiton. *Adm 50p Chd 10p (Share to The Forces Help Society, Lord Roberts Workshops). By appt only spring, summer & autumn* **Tel 040 483 363**

Westpark &❀❀ (Mr & Mrs D Court) Yealmpton, B3137 E of Plymouth; Xrds centre of village, turn S on Newton Ferrers rd; park end of Torr Lane (Disabled in drive). 1-acre garden in attractive country setting around Victorian house. Mixed plantings of mature trees, shrubs, roses, borders; variety of naturalised spring bulbs. Interesting

late C19 narcissi during April. TEA. *Adm £1 Chd 25p. Sun, Wed, March 21, 24 (2-5.30). Also by appt mid Feb to mid Oct* **Tel 0752 880236**

Whitmore ❀❀ (Mr & Mrs Cyril Morgan) Chittlehamholt. 12m SE Barnstaple, 8m S of S Molton. From the village take rd S past Exeter Inn and High Bullen Hotel; Whitmore is ¼m further on L down long tree-lined drive. 3-acre garden with ponds, stream and herbaceous borders. An interesting collection of trees and shrubs planted mostly for landscape value. Further 3 acres of woodland garden mainly ferns and pleasant sylvan walks. TEAS. *Adm £1 Chd 50p. Thurs April 15, July 1 (2-5)*

Withleigh Farm ❀ (T Matheson) Withleigh village. 3m W of Tiverton on B3137, 10yds W of 'Withleigh' sign, entrance to drive at white gate. Peaceful undisturbed rural setting with valley garden, 12 years in making; stream, pond and waterside plantings; bluebell wood walk under canopy of mature oak and beech; wild flower meadow, primroses and daffodils in spring, wild orchids. TEA. *Adm £1 Chd 25p (Share to Cancer & Arthritis Research). Sat, Sun May 22, 23 (2-5). Also open by appt* **Tel Tiverton 253853**

Wolford Lodge & (The Very Rev. the Dean of Windsor and Mrs Patrick Mitchell) Dunkeswell. Take Honiton to Dunkeswell rd. L at Limer's Cross. Drive ½m on L at white entrance gate and lodge. 4 acres semi-woodland with massed rhododendrons, azaleas and camellias. Distant views to S over unspoilt Devon countryside. Woodland walks. *Adm £1 OAP/Chd 50p. Sat May 22 (2-6)*

Woodside ❀ (Mr & Mrs Mervyn Feesey) Higher Raleigh Rd, Barnstaple. On outskirts of Barnstaple, A39 to Lynton, turn right 300yds above fire station. 2 acres, S sloping; intensively planted; collection of ornamental grasses, bamboos, sedges and other monocots; unusual and rare dwarf shrubs, rock plants and alpines; raised beds, troughs; variegated and peat-loving shrubs, ornamental trees and dwarf conifers, emphasis on foliage; New Zealand collection. *Adm £1 Chd 50p. Suns May 9, June 20, July 18 (2-5.30)*

Wylmington Hayes ❀❀ (Mr and Mrs P Saunders) Wilmington. 5½m N of Honiton on A30. Turn R. Signposted Stockland 3m/Axminster 10m, after 3½m entrance gates on R (before Stockland TV Station). Reclaimed gardens, created in 1911. 83-acres of gardens and woodlands with spectacular hybrid rhododendrons, azaleas, magnolias, camellias, acers. Lakes, ponds, topiary, arboretum, woodland walks with abundant wildlife. Interesting collection of ornamental and domestic waterfowl including black swans. TEAS. *Adm £2.50 Chd £1. Easter Fri, Sat, Sun, Mon April 9, 10, 11, 12; Suns and Bank Hol Mons until end of Aug (2-5). Coaches & parties by appt* **Tel 040 483 751**

Dorset

Hon County Organiser:	Mrs Hugh Lindsay, The Old Rectory, Litton Cheney, Dorchester DT2 9AH Tel (Long Bredy 0308) 482 383
Assistant Hon County Organisers:	Mrs Boileau, Rampisham Manor, Dorchester, DT2 OPT
	Stanley Cherry Esq., Highbury, Woodside Rd, West Moors, Ferndown BH22 0LY Tel Ferndown 874372
	Mrs John Greener, Langebride House, Long Bredy, Dorchester Tel Long Bredy 482 257
	Mrs G D Harthan, Russets, Rectory Lane, Child Okeford, Blandford, DT11 8DT Tel Child Okeford 860703
	Mrs W E Ninniss, 52 Rossmore Road, Parkstone, Poole BH12 3NL
Hon County Treasurer:	Mrs R Patterson, 10 Herringston Road, Dorchester DT1 2BS

DATES OF OPENING

By appointment
For telephone numbers and other details see garden descriptions

Arnmore House, Bournemouth
Bridge House, Portesham
Broadlands, Hazelbury Bryan
Cartref, Stalbridge
Chiffchaffs, Bourton
Corfe Barn, Broadstone
Cox Hill, Marnhull
Domineys Yard, Buckland Newton
Edgeways, Poole
Edmondsham House, Cranborne
Highbury, West Moors
Langebride House, Long Bredy
Little Platt, Plush
Moulin Huet, West Moors
The Old Mill, Spetisbury
The Old Rectory, Fifehead Magdalen
Old Rectory, Seaborough
Orchard House, Portesham
Pumphouse Cottage, Alweston
46 Roslin Road South, Bournemouth
Russets, Child Okeford, nr Blandford
Star Cottage, Wimborne
14 Umbers Hill, Shaftesbury
Welcome Thatch, Witchampton
2 Winters Lane, Portesham
Wincombe Park

Regular openings
For details see garden descriptions

Abbotsbury Gardens, nr Weymouth. March 1 to Oct 31
Broadlands, Hazelbury Bryan. Every Wed June, July & August
Chettle House, nr Blandford. Daily April 9 to Oct 10 except Tues & Sats
Chiffchaffs, Bourton. Open various Suns, Weds and Thurs March 21 to Sept 26
Compton Acres Gardens, Poole. Daily March 1 to end of Oct

Cranborne Manor Gardens, Cranborne. Weds March to Sept incl
Deans Court, Wimborne Minster. Open various Suns, Mons, Thurs, see text
Forde Abbey, nr Chard. Daily
Horn Park, Beaminster. April to Oct Tues, Thurs and 1st and 3rd Suns every month. Also Bank Hol Mons April to Oct 1
Ivy Cottage, Ansty. Every Thurs April to Oct 25
Kingston Maurward Gardens, Dorchester. April to Sept
Langmoore Manor, Charmouth. Suns, Tues, Weds, Thurs & Sats end March to end Oct
Mapperton Gardens, nr Beaminster. Daily March to Oct
Minterne, nr Cerne Abbas. Daily April 1 to Oct 31
The Old Mill, Spetisbury. Every Wed May to Sept
Parnham, Beaminster. Suns, Weds & Bank Hols April 4 to Oct 28
Snape Cottage, Bourton. Every Wed April 7 to Sept 29 (closed Aug)
Stapehill Abbey, Wimborne. Open all year. Closed Mons & Tues
Star Cottage, Wimborne. Sats, Suns & Bank Hols all year
Sticky Wicket, Buckland Newton. Thurs May to Sept

March 14 Sunday
Langebride House, Long Bredy
March 21 Sunday
Frankham Farm, Ryme Intrinseca
Langmoore Manor, Charmouth
March 28 Sunday
Chiffchaffs, Bourton
Langebride House, Long Bredy
April 4 Sunday
Broadlands, Hazelbury Bryan
Frith House, Stalbridge
Harmans Cross Gardens

Stour House, Blandford
April 7 Wednesday
Cranborne Manor Gardens, Cranborne ‡
Edmondsham House, Cranborne ‡
April 9 Friday
Catnap Cottage, Hilton
April 10 Saturday
Ashley Park Farm, Damerham
April 11 Sunday
Aller Green, Ansty ‡
Bexington, Lytchett Matravers
Horn Park, Beaminster
Ivy Cottage, Ansty ‡
The Old Rectory, Litton Cheney
Langebride House, Long Bredy
St Nicholas Close, Wimborne
Snape Cottage, Bourton
Thistledown, Alweston
April 12 Monday
Catnap Cottage, Hilton
Edmondsham House, Cranborne
April 14 Wednesday
Edmondsham House, Cranborne
April 18 Sunday
Boveridge Farm, Cranborne
Cartref, Stalbridge
Domineys Yard, Buckland Newton
Stockford, East Stoke
Thistledown, Alweston
April 21 Wednesday
Edmondsham House, Cranborne
April 25 Sunday
Broadlands, Hazelbury Bryan
Chiffchaffs, Bourton
Corfe Barn, Broadstone
Thistledown, Alweston
April 28 Wednesday
Edmondsham House, Cranborne
May 1 Saturday
Ashley Park Farm, Damerham
May 2 Sunday
Charlton Cottage, Tarrant Rushton
Frankham Farm, Ryme Intrinseca
Mapperton Gardens, nr Beaminster
North Leigh House, nr Wimborne ‡

St Nicholas Close, Wimborne
Snape Cottage, Bourton
Thistledown, Alweston
May 3 Monday
Chiffchaffs, Bourton
Long Ash Cottage, Milton Abbas
Mapperton Gardens, nr
Beaminster
May 9 Sunday
Bexington, Lytchett Matravers
Hilltop Cottage, Woodville
6 Hollands Mead Avenue,
Owermoigne
Kesworth, Wareham
Moulin Huet, West Moors
Stockford, East Stoke
Thistledown, Alweston
May 12 Wednesday
Hilltop Cottage, Woodville
May 13 Thursday
Kingston Maurward Gardens,
Dorchester
May 16 Sunday
Boveridge Farm, Cranborne
Bridge House, Portesham
Broadlands, Hazelbury Bryan
Corfe Barn, Broadstone
2 Curlew Road, Bournemouth
Kesworth, Wareham
Langmoore Manor, Charmouth
Moulin Huet, West Moors
Old Rectory, Seaborough
Smedmore, Kimmeridge
Star Cottage, Wimborne
Thistledown, Alweston
Woodside Lodge, East Lulworth
May 19 Wednesday
Wincombe Park, nr Shaftesbury
May 22 Saturday
Studland Bay House, nr Swanage
May 23 Sunday
Aller Green, Ansty ‡
Cartref, Stalbridge
Eurocentre Language School,
Bournemouth
Highwood Garden, Wareham
Hilton House, Hilton, nr Blandford
Ivy Cottage, Ansty ‡
Moigne Combe, nr Dorchester
Moulin Huet, West Moors
The Old Rectory, Litton Cheney
The Old Rectory, Pulham
52 Rossmore Road, Parkstone
Thistledown, Alweston
May 26 Wednesday
Hilton House, Hilton, nr Blandford
The Old Rectory, Pulham
Studland Bay House, nr Swanage
May 27 Thursday
Melbury House, nr Yeovil
May 29 Saturday
Ashley Park Farm, Damerham
May 30 Sunday
Chiffchaffs, Bourton

Deans Court, Wimborne Minster
Edgeways, Poole
Farriers, Puddletown ‡
Glebe House, East Lulworth
Highwood Garden, Wareham
Horn Park, Beaminster
Moigne Combe, nr Dorchester
Northbrook Farm, Puddletown ‡
46 Roslin Road South,
Bournemouth
Snape Cottage, Bourton
Stockford, East Stoke
Thistledown, Alweston
May 31 Monday
Chiffchaffs, Bourton
Long Ash Cottage, Milton Abbas
46 Roslin Road South,
Bournemouth
June 2 Wednesday
Glebe House, East Lulworth
June 6 Sunday
7 Church Street, Upwey ‡
Conewood, Ferndown
High Hollow, Corfe Mullen
Hilltop Cottage, Woodville
Kingston Lacy, nr Wimborne
Minster
Langebride House, Long Bredy
Langford Farm, Sydling St
Nicholas
Portesham House, Portesham
52 Rossmore Road, Parkstone
Thistledown, Alweston
West Manor, Upwey ‡
Wimborne Minster Model Town &
Gardens
June 9 Wednesday
The Old Rectory, Pulham
The Orchard, Blynfield Gate, nr
Shaftesbury
June 10 Thursday
7 Church Street, Upwey
Melbury House, nr Yeovil
June 12 Saturday
Cranborne Manor Gardens,
Cranborne
Mill Cottage, Burton Bradstock
June 13 Sunday
Bexington, Lytchett Matravers
Boveridge Farm, Cranborne
Charlton Cottage, Tarrant Rushton
Chettle House, nr Blandford
Corfe Barn, Broadstone
Cox Hill, Marnhull
Fernhill Cottage, Witchampton ‡
Fernhill House, Witchampton ‡
Frith House, Stalbridge
High Hollow, Corfe Mullen
Hilton House, Hilton, nr Blandford
The Old Rectory, Fifehead
Magdalen
The Old Rectory, Pulham
Portesham Gardens, Portesham
Snape Cottage, Bourton

Thistledown, Alweston
Welcome Thatch, Witchampton ‡
Weston House, Buckhorn
Weston
Woodside Lodge, East Lulworth
June 16 Wednesday
Cox Hill, Marnhull
Hilton House, Hilton, nr Blandford
The Old Rectory, Pulham
The Orchard, Blynfield Gate
June 17 Thursday
Melbury House, nr Yeovil
Red House Museum and Gardens,
Christchurch
June 19 Saturday
The Manor House, Abbotsbury
Mill Cottage, Burton Bradstock
Three Bays, Beacon Hill
June 20 Sunday
Cox Hill, Marnhull
Fernhill Cottage, Witchampton ‡
Fernhill House, Witchampton ‡
Frankham Farm, Ryme Intrinseca
37 The Glade, Ashley Heath
6 Hollands Mead Avenue,
Owermoigne
The Manor House, Abbotsbury
46 Roslin Road South,
Bournemouth
Star Cottage, Wimborne
Thistledown, Alweston
Three Bays, Beacon Hill
Welcome Thatch, Witchampton ‡
Weston House, Buckhorn Weston
Wimborne Minster Model Town &
Gardens
June 23 Wednesday
The Old Mill, Spetisbury
The Orchard, Blynfield Gate, nr
Shaftesbury
June 24 Thursday
Kingston Maurward Gardens,
Dorchester
June 26 Saturday
Higher Came Farmhouse,
Dorchester
The Manor House, Chaldon
Herring
Rampisham Gardens, Rampisham
June 27 Sunday
Chiffchaffs, Bourton
The Cobbles, Shillingstone
Edgeways, Poole
Farriers, Puddletown
Higher Melcombe, Melcombe
Bingham
Hilton House, Hilton, nr Blandford
Northbrook Farm, Puddletown
The Old Mill, Spetisbury
The Old Parsonage, Kimmeridge
The Old Vicarage, Stinsford
Rampisham Gardens, Rampisham
Snape Cottage, Bourton
Steeple Manor, nr Wareham ‡

June 30 Wednesday
The Old Parsonage, Kimmeridge
The Orchard, Blynfield Gate, nr
  Shaftesbury
July 1 Thursday
Fernhill Cottage, Witchampton
Melbury House, nr Yeovil
July 4 Sunday
7 Church Street, Upwey ‡
The Cobbles, Shillingstone
Corfe Barn, Broadstone
Greenings, Chilfrome
Portland House, Weymouth
West Manor, Upwey ‡
July 7 Wednesday
The Orchard, Blynfield Gate, nr
  Shaftesbury
July 8 Thursday
7 Church Street, Upwey
Fernhill Cottage, Witchampton
Melbury House, nr Yeovil
July 10 Saturday
Domineys Yard, Buckland
  Newton ‡
Sticky Wicket, Buckland Newton ‡
Three Bays, Beacon Hill
July 11 Sunday
Bexington, Lytchett Matravers
Catnap Cottage, Hilton
2 Curlew Road, Bournemouth
Domineys Yard, Buckland
  Newton ‡
37 The Glade, Ashley Heath
6 Hollands Mead Avenue,
  Owermoigne
Oakmead, nr Beaminster
Snape Cottage, Bourton
Sticky Wicket, Buckland Newton ‡
Sturminster Newton Gardens
Three Bays, Beacon Hill
July 14 Wednesday
The Orchard, Blynfield Gate, nr
  Shaftesbury
July 15 Thursday
Fernhill Cottage, Witchampton

2 Winters Lane, Portesham
July 17 Saturday
Three Bays, Beacon Hill
July 18 Sunday
Chettle House, nr Blandford
Edgeways, Poole
Stour House, Blandford
Three Bays, Beacon Hill
July 22 Thursday
Fernhill Cottage, Witchampton
July 25 Sunday
Chiffchaffs, Bourton
37 The Glade, Ashley Heath
7 Highfield Close, Corfe Mullen
Hilltop Cottage, Woodville
Melplash Court, nr Bridport
July 29 Thursday
Fernhill Cottage, Witchampton
August 1 Sunday
7 Church Street, Upwey ‡
Farriers, Puddletown ‡‡
High Hollow, Corfe Mullen ‡
7 Highfield Close, Corfe Mullen ‡
North Leigh House, nr Wimborne
Northbrook Farm, Puddletown ‡
Warmwell House, nr Dorchester
West Manor, Upwey ‡
August 5 Thursday
7 Church Street, Upwey
Fernhill Cottage, Witchampton
August 8 Sunday
Bexington, Lytchett Matravers
Edgeways, Poole
Eurocentre Language School,
  Bournemouth
High Hollow, Corfe Mullen
August 11 Wednesday
Hilltop Cottage, Woodville
August 12 Thursday
Fernhill Cottage, Witchampton
August 15 Sunday
Domineys Yard, Buckland
  Newton ‡
Frith House, Stalbridge
Higher Melcombe, Melcombe

  Bingham
Sticky Wicket, Buckland Newton ‡
Stour House, Blandford
August 19 Thursday
Fernhill Cottage, Witchampton
August 22 Sunday
Hilltop Cottage, Woodville
August 26 Thursday
Fernhill Cottage, Witchampton
August 29 Sunday
Aller Green, Ansty ‡
Chiffchaffs, Bourton
Ivy Cottage, Ansty ‡
Oakmead, nr Beaminster
Rosedene, Bournemouth
August 30 Monday
Chiffchaffs, Bourton
September 5 Sunday
Rosedene, Bournemouth
Wimborne Minster Model Town
  & Gardens
September 12 Sunday
Bexington, Lytchett Matravers
Rosedene, Bournemouth
Thistledown, Alweston
September 19 Sunday
Cartref, Stalbridge
Langmoore Manor, Charmouth
Thistledown, Alweston
September 26 Sunday
Aller Green, Ansty
Chiffchaffs, Bourton
Ivy Cottage, Ansty
Priest's House, Wimborne
October 3 Sunday
Deans Court, Wimborne Minster
October 6 Wednesday
Edmondsham House, Cranborne
October 13 Wednesday
Edmondsham House, Cranborne
October 20 Wednesday
Edmondsham House, Cranborne
Wincombe Park, nr Shaftesbury
October 27 Wednesday
Edmondsham House, Cranborne

DESCRIPTIONS OF GARDENS

● **Abbotsbury Gardens** &.® (Ilchester Estates) 9m NW of Weymouth. 9m SW of Dorchester. From B3157 Weymouth-Bridport, turn off 200yds W of Abbotsbury village, at foot of hill. 20 acres; uniquely mild Mediterranean-type climate, started in 1760 and considerably extended in C19; much replanting during past few years; very fine collection of rhododendrons, camellias, azaleas; wide variety of unusual and tender trees and shrubs. Peacocks. Childrens play area, woodland trail, aviarys and plant centre. TEAS. *Adm £2.90 OAPs £2.30 Chd free, reduced rate in winter. (For party rate* Tel 0305 871387*) March 1 to Oct 31 (10-5); winter (10-3)*

Aller Green ✗ (A J Thomas Esq) Aller Lane, Ansty, 12m N of Dorchester. From Puddletown take A354 to Blandford; After Public House, take 1st left down Long Lane signed Dewlish-Cheselbourne; through Cheselbourne to Ansty then 1st R before Fox Inn down Aller Lane. 1-acre typical Dorset cottage garden; unusual trees, shrubs and perennials in old orchard setting and many perennials grown for Autumn Colour. Garden featured on Channel 4 'Garden Club' 1992. TEAS at Ivy Cottage. *Combined adm with* **Ivy Cottage** *£2 Chd 30p. Suns April 11 (Share to RNLI); May 23 (Share to the Samaritans); Aug 29 (Share to The Dorset Hospice); Sept 26 (Share to the Red Cross) (2-5.30)*

Regular Openers. See head of county section.

Arnmore House ఈ⚘ (Mr & Mrs David Hellewell) 57 Lansdowne Rd, Bournemouth B3064. 1-acre garden combines classical formality with diversity and efficiency; beautiful modern garden, with its Victorian house, created over a period of 25yrs by its owner, well known composer David Hellewell, who has published a booklet describing the garden's evolution; topiary; specimen trees and plants; the garden has been featured in 'Homes & Garden' magazine Nov 1988. *Adm £1 Chd free. By appt* **Tel 0202 551440**

Ashley Park Farm ఈ⚘ (David Dampney Esq). Damerham. Follow yellow signs off B3078, immediately W of village, 5m from Fordingbridge. Newly created gardens of 5 acres with farm and woodland walks. With many interesting trees, an arboretum in the making although now mature enough for visiting, Eucalyptus grove; wild flower meadow. Many exciting plants for south facing walls, borders. TEAS. *Adm £1 Chd free (Share to Damerham Church). For NGS Sats April 10, May 1, 29 (2-5.30). (See also* **Boveridge Farm***)*

Bexington ఈ⚘⚘ (Mr & Mrs Robin Crumpler) Lytchett Matravers. In Lime Kiln Rd, opp old School at west end of village. Colourful garden of ½-acre maintained by owners, with mixed borders of many interesting and unusual plants, heathers and dwarf conifers with shrubs and trees. Planted ditch forms a bog garden of primulas and hostas etc. Part of garden recently reclaimed and planted provides an interesting contrast. TEAS & plant stall for Alzheimer Disease Society & gardening charities. *Adm 70p Chd 20p. Suns April 11, May 9, June 13, July 11, Aug 8, Sept 12 (2-6)*

Boveridge Farm ఈ⚘⚘ (David Dampney Esq) Cranborne. Leave Cranborne on Martin Rd unclass, thence take 2nd right Boveridge Farm. A plantsman's garden of 2 acres on 3 levels, part chalk and part acid; with lawns around old farmhouse, formerly manor house of the Hooper family; in rural surroundings with fine views. Fountain, fern bank and many rare and interesting trees and shrubs. Specimen acer 'Brilliantissimum', prunus 'Shidare Yoshino', prunus 'Pendula Rubra', Paulownia tomentosa. Teas at Ashley Park, Damerham (next village 3m). *Adm £1 Chd free (Share to Cranborne Church). Suns April 18, May 16, June 13 (2-5). (See also* **Ashley Park Farm***)*

Broadlands ఈ⚘⚘ (Mr & Mrs M J Smith) Hazelbury Bryan. 4m S of Sturminster Newton. From A357 Blandford to Sherborne rd, take turning signed Hazelbury Bryan, garden ½m beyond Antelope PH. 2-acre garden in country setting with extensive views, begun in 1975, made and maintained by owners. Island beds; herbaceous borders by colour theme; ornamental woodland underplanted with hellebores, spring bulbs etc; rockery; heathers and conifers; ponds incl one for conservation. Wide range of plants incl magnolias, rhododendrons, hydrangeas and unusual perennials. TEAS every Wed June, July and Aug. *Adm £1.20 Chd with adult free. April 4, 25 (Share to Dorset Trust for Nature Conservation), May 16 (Share to Hazelbury Bryan Village Hall). Open every Wed in June, July and Aug (Share to the NGS) (2-5.30). For NGS Suns April 4, 25, May 16 also by appt* **Tel 0258 817374**

Cartref ⚘⚘ (Nesta Ann Smith) Station Rd, Stalbridge. From A30, S at Henstridge for 1m. Turn L opp Stalbridge PO, House 80 yds on R. Free car park a little further on the R. A plantsman's garden approx ¼-acre, cottage garden plants (old cultivars); raised vegetable beds (organic). Irises, herbs and old roses. TEA. *Adm £1.50 Chd free. Suns April 18, May 23, Sept 19 (10-5) also by appt* **Tel 0963 63705**

Catnap Cottage ఈ⚘⚘ (Mrs M J Phillips) Hilton, Blandford. 1m W from Milton Abbas, 10m SW Blandford. Please park at Hilton church. 2 min walk. Disabled parking at house. 1¼ acres of shady cottage garden, trees, shrubs, perennials and herbs. Planted for all seasons, especially spring. Teas at Milton Abbas. *Adm £1 Chd 50p. Good Friday, Easter Mon April 9, 12 & Sun July 11 (10-5)*

Charlton Cottage ఈ (The Hon Penelope Piercy) Tarrant Rushton. 3m SE of Blandford Forum B3082. Fork L top of hill out of Blandford, R at T-junction, first L to Tarrant Rushton, R in village to last thatched cottage on L of street. Garden on both sides street. Herbaceous borders, shrubs, water garden, views of Tarrant valley. *Adm £1 Chd 25p (Share to Church of England Childrens Society). Suns May 2, June 13 (2-6)*

Chettle House ఈ⚘⚘ (Mr & Mrs Patrick Bourke) Chettle. 6m NE of Blandford Forum on A354 turn L to Chettle, L at tree in village, up hill past church; car park past drive gates. Coach parties. Garden only suitable for wheelchairs. 3 acres with lawns, herbaceous and shrubs. Small vineyard, nursery, art gallery. Queen Anne house open. TEAS usually available. *Adm £1.80 Chd free. April 9 to Oct 10 daily ex Tues and Sats. For NGS Suns June 13, July 18 (11-5)* **Tel 0258 89209**

Chiffchaffs ⚘⚘ (Mr & Mrs K R Potts) Chaffeymoor. Leave A303 (Bourton by pass) at junction signposted Gillingham, Blandford and Bourton at W end of Bourton village. House signposted Chaffeymoor Lane. A garden for all seasons with many interesting plants, bulbs, shrubs, herbaceous border, shrub roses. Attractive walk to woodland garden with far-reaching views across the Blackmore Vale. Shown on TSW 'Gardens for All' October 92, also in Gardeners World magazine Sept 92. Nursery open Tues-Sat and on garden open days. TEAS last Sun and Bank Hol weekends. *Adm £1.50 Chd 50p (Share to St Michael's Church, Penselwood). Open every Sun and Bank Holiday weekend, Weds & Thurs (except for 1st Sunday, Wed & Thurs in each month) from March 21 to Sept 26. For NGS last Sunday and Bank Holiday weekends plus 10% of all receipts (2-5.30). Parties by appt at other times* **Tel 0747 840841**

7 Church Street ఈ⚘⚘ (Ann & Gordon Powell) Upwey, nr Weymouth. ½m from bottom of Ridgeway Hill on A354 Dorchester–Weymouth rd turn R B3159 (Bridport Rd) L turn at bottom of hill. Limited parking for disabled only. 3 acres of mixed planting. Main trees planted 1972 with recent additions of shrubs and perennials. Woodland planted early 50's. Teas at Wishing Well. *Adm Thurs £1 Chd free. Combined adm with* **West Manor** *£2. Suns June 6, July 4, Aug 1, Thurs June 10, July 8, Aug 5 (2-6)*

The Cobbles ✿✸ (Mr & Mrs A P Baker) Shillingstone. 5m NW of Blandford. In middle of village opp Old Ox Inn, Shillingstone. Plantsman's 1½-acre chalk garden round C17 cottage. Borders thickly planted with a mixture of shrubs, herbs, wild flowers, old roses foliage plants & perennials incl many hardy geraniums. Small lake, stream and ditch garden. *Adm £1 Chd free. Suns June 27, July 4 (2.30-5.30)*

● **Compton Acres Gardens** ❀✿✸ Canford Cliffs Road, Poole, Dorset. Signposted from Bournemouth and Poole. Wilts & Dorset Buses 147, 150, 151. Yellow Buses nos 11 & 12 stop at entrance. Reputed to be the finest gardens in Europe incl Japanese, Italian, Rock and Water, Heather Dell Woodland Walk and Sub-Tropical Glen. Magnificent bronze and marble statuary. Large selection of plants and stoneware garden ornaments. Refreshments available. Large free car/coach park. *March 1 to end of Oct daily. 10.30-6.30 last admission 5.45pm.* **Tel 0202 700778**

Conewood ❀✿✸ (Mr & Mrs Alfred Knight) 308 New Rd, Ferndown. 6m N of Bournemouth on A347, between Dormy Hotel and Heddell & Deeks Garage. Colourful and well stocked garden of ⅓ acre with fine selection of plants and shrubs. A special feature is the large pond with Japanese style tea house. Fish may also be viewed from underwater window below the large waterfall. TEA. *Adm 60p Chd 20p. Sun June 6 (10-5)*

Corfe Barn ✿✸ (John & Kathleen McDavid) Corfe Lodge Rd, Broadstone. From main roundabout in Broadstone W along Clarendon Rd, ¾m N into Roman Rd, after 50yds W into Corfe Lodge Rd. ⅔ acre on three levels on site of C19 lavender farm. Informal country garden with much to interest both gardeners and flower arrangers. Parts of the original farm have been incorporated in the design. A particular feature of the garden is the use made of old walls. TEAS. *Adm 50p Chd 25p. Suns April 25, May 16, June 13, July 4 (2-5) also by appt* **Tel 0202 694179**

Cox Hill ❀✿✸ (Capt & Mrs J R Prescott) 3m N of Sturminster Newton, turning L at Walton Elm; 3m E of Stalbridge via Stour River Bridge at Kings Mill. 2 acres with far reaching views over Blackmore Vale. Colour and contrast within secluded areas and lawns, water garden, roses, specimen trees and orchard. TEA. *Adm £1 Chd free (Share to Dorset Red Cross). Suns June 13, 20; Weds June 16 (2-5.30) also by appt May, June & Sept* **Tel 0258 820059**

● **Cranborne Manor Gardens** ❀✿✸ (The Viscount & Viscountess Cranborne) Cranborne. 10m N of Wimborne on B3078. Beautiful and historic gardens laid out in C17 by John Tradescant and enlarged in C20, featuring several gardens surrounded by walls and yew hedges: white garden, herb and mount gardens, water and wild garden. Many interesting plants, with fine trees and avenues. *Adm £2.50 OAPs £2 (Share to NSPCC). Weds March to Sept inc (9-5). For NGS Wed April 7, Sat June 12 (9-5)*

By Appointment Gardens. These owners do not have a fixed opening day usually because they do not like crowds or have insufficient parking space. Owner will often give guided tour.

¶2 Curlew Road ❀✿ (Mr & Mrs Gerald Alford) Strouden Park, Bournemouth. From Castle Lane West turn S into East Way, thence E into Curlew Rd. Small town garden 200' × 30' divided into rooms and linked by arches. Conifers, acers, rhododendrons, clematis; spring and summer bedding; three water features. Winner of Bournemouth in Bloom competition 1991. The owners are seriously disabled and their garden is thus of especial interest to other disabled people. *Adm 50p Chd 20p. Suns May 16, July 11 (2-6)*

Deans Court ❀✿✸ (Sir Michael & Lady Hanham) Wimborne. Just off B3073 in centre of Wimborne. 13 acres; partly wild garden; water, specimen trees, free roaming peacocks, birds. House (open by written appt) originally the Deanery to the Minster. Herb garden with organically grown herb plants for sale. TEAS. *Adm £1.50 Chd 70p. Easter Sun April 11, Suns May 3, Aug 29 (2-6). Easter Mon April 12, Bank Hol Mons May 4, 31, Aug 30 (10-6). Thurs April 1-Sept 30 (2-6). For NGS Suns May 30, Oct 3 (2-6). Groups by arrangement. For other days contact Wimborne TIC* **Tel Wimborne 886116**

Domineys Yard ❀✿ (Mr & Mrs W Gueterbock) Buckland Newton, 11m from Dorchester and Sherborne 2m E of A352 or take B3143 from Sturminster Newton. Take 'no through rd' between church and 'Gaggle of Geese' public house next to phone box. Entrance 200 metres on left. Park in lane. 2½-acre garden on chalk, clay and green sand surrounding C17 thatched cottage with adjacent terraced cottages and gardens, with large kitchen garden and lawn tennis court. Developed over 32 years with unusual plants, shrubs and trees incl camellias, clematis, roses, lilies and other bulbs spring and autumn colour making it a garden for all seasons. July openings only exhibition of flower watercolours by Victoria Fraser and Nicola Leader. Hand turned wooden bowls by Patrick O'Dowd. Ploughman's lunch. TEAS and swimming pool available (11-6). *Adm £1.30 Chd 30p (Share to Leonard Cheshire Foundation Family Support Service). Sat July 10 (11-6), Suns April 18 (2-6), July 11 (11-6), Aug 15 (2-6); also by appt* **Tel 030 05295**

Edgeways ❀✿✸ (Mr & Mrs Gerald Andrew) 4 Greenwood Ave, Poole. From Lilliput Rd nr Compton Acres turn N into Compton Ave, W into Fairway Rd, thence left into Greenwood Ave. Please do not park by roundabout of cul-de-sac. Delightful informal design of ⅓ acre in a mature treed setting, created and maintained by present owners. Emphasis is on plant associations and foliage contrasts forming vistas and year-round living pictures. Bog, water and rock gardens, many choice herbaceous plants. *Adm 80p Chd with adult free. Suns May 30, June 27, July 18, Aug 8 (11.30-5.30), also by appt May to Aug* **Tel 0202 707074**

Edmondsham House ❀✿✸ (Mrs Julia Smith) Edmondsham, nr Cranborne. B3081, turn at Sixpenny Handley Xrds to Ringwood and Cranborne; thereafter follow signs to Edmondsham. Large garden; spring bulbs, trees, shrubs; walled garden with herbaceous border; vegetables and fruit; grass cockpit. Early church nearby. TEAS Easter Mon, TEA Weds. *Adm £1 Chd 50p under 5 free (Share to PRAMA). Mon April 12, Weds April 7, 14, 21, 28; Oct 6, 13, 20, 27 (2-5); also by appt* **Tel 07254 207**

¶**Eurocentre Language School** &✿ (Eurocentres (UK)) 22-28 Dean Park Rd, Bournemouth. Off Wimborne Rd (A347) ¼m N of Richmond Hill roundabout. Series of 4 linked gardens, now being restored to reflect the original surroundings of the late Victorian houses. Mature specimen trees and lawns; rhododendrons, small trees and flowering shrubs; spring and summer bedding, climbers, dahlia borders and small fernery. TEAS. *Adm 60p Chd 30p (Share to Bournemouth General Hospital Scanner Appeal). Suns May 23, Aug 8 (2-6)*

¶**Farriers** &✿ (Mr & Mrs P S Eady) 16 The Moor. On the A354 Puddletown-Blandford Rd opp the rd to Piddlehinton, close to the Blue Vinney Public House, Dorchester 5m. ⅓-acre informal country garden with much to interest gardeners and flower arrangers designed and maintained by owners; shrubs, herbaceous, dahlias, sweet peas, chrysanthemums, vegetable plot, greenhouse with collection of begonias and streptocarpus, pond. *Combined adm with* **Northbrook Farm** *£1 Chd free. Suns May 30, June 27, Aug 1 (2-6)*

Fernhill Cottage ✿✿ (Miss Forwood) Witchampton. 3½m E of Wimborne B3078 L to Witchampton then L up Lower St Blandford Rd, cottage on R 200yds. Small thatched cottage garden, interesting perennials, species and shrub roses. Teas in village. *Adm 50p Chd free (Share to Hahneman & Herbert Hospitals). Suns June 13, 20 and every Thurs July & August (2-5)*

Fernhill House &✿✿ (Mrs Hildyard) Witchampton. 3½m E of Wimborne B3078 L to Witchampton then L up Lower St. Blandford Rd, house on R 200 yds. Herbaceous borders, roses, woodland walk with pond and shrubs. Teas in village. *Adm £1 Chd free (Share to Dorset Respite and Hospice Trust). Suns June 13, 20 (2-5)*

● **Forde Abbey** &✿ (M Roper Esq) 4m SE of Chard. 7m W of Crewkerne; well signed off A30. 30 acres; many fine shrubs and some magnificent specimen trees incl postwar arboretum; herbaceous borders, rock and kitchen gardens; in bog garden one of larger collections Asiatic primulas in SW. Refreshments 11-4.30 during summer. *Adm £3 OAPs £2.60 Chd and wheelchairs free. Open daily all year (10-4.30)*

Frankham Farm &✿ (Mr & Mrs R G Earle) Ryme Intrinseca. A37 Yeovil-Dorchester; 3m S of Yeovil turn E at Xrds with garage; drive ¼m on L. 2 acres started in 1960s; Plantsman's garden with shrubs, trees, spring bulbs, clematis, roses, vegetables & fruit; extensive wall planting. Recently planted unusual hardwoods. TEAS in aid of Ryme Church. *Adm £1 Chd free. Suns March 21, May 2, June 20 (2-5.30)*

Frith House & (Urban Stephenson Esq) Stalbridge. Between Milborne Port & Stalbridge, 1m S of A30. Turn W nr PO in Stalbridge. 4 acres; self-contained hamlet: lawns; 2 small lakes; woodland walks. Terrace in front of Edwardian house, mature cedars; flower borders, excellent kitchen garden. TEAS. *Adm £1 Chd free. Suns April 4, June 13, Aug 15 (2-6)*

37 The Glade ✿ (Mrs Sally Tidd) Ashley Heath. 3m W of Ringwood, leave A31 at roundabout into Woolsbridge Rd; after ¾m left into The Glade. From N may be approached from Ashley Heath PO and Lions Lane. Colourful ⅓-acre garden in a pleasing setting designed, built and maintained by owner. Flower arrangers garden containing a varied collection of foliage plants; climbing plants; shrubs for decorative effect and year round interest; flower borders arranged in colour schemes. *Adm 50p Chd 5p. Suns June 20, July 11, 25 (2-6)*

Glebe House ✿ (Mr & Mrs J G Thompson) East Lulworth. 4m S of Wool 6m W of Wareham. Take Coombe Keynes Rd to East Lulworth. Glebe House just to E of Weld Arms and War Memorial. Shrub garden with lawns; walks and terrace, 2 acres with interesting and varied planting. TEAS. *Adm £1 Chd free (Share to Wool & Bovington Cancer Relief). Sun May 30, Wed June 2 (2-6)*

¶**Greenings** &✿ (Mr & Mrs A D T Philp) 1m NW of Maiden Newton. Chilfrome lies between Maiden Newton and Cattistock. Garden next to church. Park in village. Charming ½-acre garden for plantsman created over the last 4yrs in beautiful setting; herbaceous borders, pond, small rockery. TEAS. *Adm £1 Chd 25p. Sun July 4 (2.30-6)*

Harmans Cross Gardens &✿✿ (Mr & Mrs R F Knight and others). 1½m SE of Corfe Castle village on A351. R at Harmans Cross Village Stores. Car park at Village Hall, Haycrafts Lane. Alternatively by steam train from Swanage. Group of 6 varied gardens with spring bulbs and shrubs and views of Purbeck Hills. TEAS. *Combined adm £1 Chd free (Share to Parkinson's Disease Soc.). Sun April 4 (2-5.30)*

¶**High Hollow** ✿✿ (Paul & Valerie Guppy) 15 Chapel Close, Corfe Mullen. From Wareham Rd W end of village at Naked Cross turn N into Waterloo Rd; after 1m turn E into Chapel Lane, where please park and not in Chapel Close. Beautiful and colourful garden of ¼ acre surrounding bungalow, with many unusual plants and cultivars. Herbaceous border, ferns and roses. The use of water is a special feature. TEAS. *Adm 50p Chd 25p (Share to the Cats Protection League). Suns June 6, 13, Aug 1, 8 (2-5)*

Highbury &✿✿ (Stanley Cherry Esq) West Moors, 8m N of Bournemouth. In Woodside Rd, off B3072 Bournemouth-Verwood rd; last rd at N end of West Moors village. Garden of ½ acre in mature setting surrounding interesting Edwardian house (1909 listed). Many rare and unusual plants and shrubs; herb borders; botanical & horticultural interest for gardeners & plantsmen, with everything labelled. Weather station. Seen on T.V. Featured in detail in Blue Guide Gardens of England. TEAS in orchard when fine. *House and garden, organised parties Adm £1 (incl TEA); Otherwise by appt. Garden only 75p (2-6). April to Sept* **Tel 0202 874372**

Higher Came Farmhouse ✿✿ (Capt & Mrs Randal Macgregor) Dorchester. 2m S of Dorchester. Dorchester By-pass. A354 to Weymouth. 1st turning L (Winterborne Herringston). Give way at Junction; straight on; then follow rd to bottom Came Down Golf Course. House is at end of small farm rd. It will be well signed. Chalk garden planted over the last 7yrs; mixed borders; courtyard. Exuberant planting with emphasis on form, colour and easy maintenance. Mixed borders, clematis, shrub roses, ground cover. TEA. *Adm £1 Chd free (Share to Dorset Respite & Hospice Trust). Sun June 26 (2-6)*

Higher Melcombe ᶳᶳ (Lt Col and Mrs J M Woodhouse) Melcombe Bingham. 11m N of Dorchester. From Puddletown A354 to Blandford. After ½m take turning L (after inn). Follow signs to Cheselbourne then to Melcombe. At Xrds in Melcombe Bingham follow signpost 'Private rd to Higher Melcombe'. 1½-acre garden being redeveloped. Fine views and setting outside Elizabethan house and chapel. New shrubs and bedding plants. Parking adjoining field. TEAS. *Adm £1 Chd free (Share to Joseph Weld Hospice Appeal). TEA Sun June 27, TEAS Sun Aug 15 (2-5.30)*

7 Highfield Close ᶳᶳᶳ (Mr & Mrs Malcolm Bright) Corfe Mullen. From Wareham Rd turn E in Hanham Rd, thence ahead into Highfield Close. Colourful ⅓-acre summer garden designed and made by owners over 15yrs. Bedding plants, fuchsias and pelargoniums interplanted with shrubs; fish pond and ornamental pool. Much to interest gardeners in a small area. TEAS. *Adm 50p Chd 20p. Suns July 25, Aug 1 (2-6)*

Highwood Garden ᶳ (H W Drax Esq) Charborough Park, Wareham, 6m E of Bere Regis. Enter park by any lodge on A31; follow signpost to Estate Office, then Highwood Garden. Large garden with rhododendrons and azaleas in woodland setting. TEAS. *Adm £1 Chd 50p (7-16 yrs) (Share to Red Post Parish). Suns May 23, 30 (2.30-6)*

Hilltop Cottage ᶳᶳ (Mr & Mrs Emerson) approx 5m N Sturminster Newton on B3092 turn R at Stour Provost Xrds, signposted Woodville. After 1¼m a thatched cottage on the R hand side. Parking in lane outside. ¼-acre extremely well stocked informal cottage garden. Includes a small nursery. Enquiries **Tel 074785 512**. TEAS. *Adm 50p Chd free. Suns May 9, June 6, July 25, Aug 22; Weds May 12, Aug 11 (2-6)*

Hilton House ᶳᶳ (Mr & Mrs S Young) 10m SW of Blandford. Take A354 to Winterbourne Whitechurch through Milton Abbas past Milton Abbey, Hilton House is next to the church in Hilton. 3½-acre garden with mature trees and beautiful views. Main planting since 1978. Parking at Hilton House. TEAS Suns only (May 23 in aid of Red Cross, June 13 Multiple Sclerosis, June 27 Joseph Weld Hospice) Tea Weds only. *Adm £1 Chd free. Suns May 23, June 13, 27; Weds May 26, June 16 (2-5.30) Parties by appt* **Tel 0258 880229**

6 Hollands Mead Avenue ᶳᶳ (Mrs J M Baxter) Owermoigne. 6m E of Dorchester on A352, L at sign to Owermoigne village; 2nd L. Delightful ⅕-acre garden made and maintained by owners; planned for year-round colour; good herbaceous perennials, shrubs, collections of heaths, hostas, ferns and alpines. TEAS. *Adm 60p Chd free (Share to West Dorset Hospice). Suns May 9, June 20, July 11 (2-6)*

Horn Park ᶳᶳ (Mr & Mrs John Kirkpatrick) Beaminster. On A3066 1½m N of Beaminster on L before tunnel. Ample parking; toilet; large garden; magnificent views. Listed house built by pupil of Lutyens in 1910 (not open). Wide variety unusual plants & shrubs in terraced, herbaceous, rock, woodland & water gardens; lawns. Woodland walk in spring in bluebell woods; ponds, wild flowers inc orchids. Teas Beaminster & Craft Centre Broadwindsor. *Adm £2. Open every Tues, Thurs & 1st & 3rd Suns every month; also Bank Hol Mons April to Oct 1. For NGS Suns April 11, May 30 (2-6)*

Ivy Cottage ᶳᶳ (Anne & Alan Stevens) Aller Lane, Ansty, 12m N of Dorchester. A354 from Puddletown to Blandford; After pub take 1st L down Long Lane signed Dewlish-Cheselbourne, through Cheselbourne to Ansty then 1st R before Fox Inn, down Aller Lane. 1½-acre excellent plantsman's garden specialising in unusual perennials, moisture-loving plants; specimen trees and shrubs. Featured in the book 'The New Englishwoman's Garden' and in T.S.W. 'Gardens for All' 1988 and TVS 'That's Gardening' 1990. Garden on Channel 4 'Garden Club' 1992. TEAS. *Combined adm with* **Aller Green** *£2 Chd 30p. Sun April 11 (Share to R.N.L.I); Sun May 23 (Share to Samaritans); Sun Aug 29 (Share to The Dorset Hospice); Sun Sept 26 (Share to Red Cross). (2-5.30) Also every Thurs April to Oct 25 (10-5). Parties by appt only* **Tel Milton Abbas 880053**

Kesworth (H J S Clark Esq) 1½m N of Wareham. Turn off A351 almost opp school at Sandford, down Keysworth Drive to level Xing. Grounds incl 600 acre wildlife sanctuary at W end of Poole Harbour suitable for picnics, birdwatching, walks through unspoilt woods and marshes amongst fine wild scenery; herd of Galloway cattle. Elegant and colourful small garden round house. Tea Wareham. *Adm £1 Chd free (Share to Sandford Church). Suns May 9, 16 (12.30-7). Last adm 5.30 pm*

Kingston Lacy ᶳᶳᶳ (The National Trust) 1½m W of Wimborne Minster on the Wimborne-Blandford rd B3082. The setting landscaped in the C18, to W J Bankes's Kingston Lacy House. Magnificent trees planted over 175 years by Royal and famous visitors; avenue of limes and cedars; 9 acres of lawn; Dutch garden; sunken garden laid out to 1906 plans. TEAS and lunches. *Adm House & Garden £5, Gardens £2, Chd half price. For NGS Sun June 6 (11.30-6)*

Kingston Maurward ᶳᶳᶳ A delightful Edwardian garden set in a C18 landscape. E of Dorchester turning off the roundabout at end of Dorchester by-pass A35. Bus alight Stinsford ¼m. Enter grounds through the farm animal park. Kingston Maurward house is a classical Georgian mansion set in gardens laid out in the C18 including a 5-acre lake and overlooks the Dorchester watermeadows. An extensive restoration programme is nearing completion in the Edwardian gardens which are divided by hedges and stone balustrading. Each intimate garden contains a wealth of interesting plants and stone features, including the national collection of salvias and penstemons. In addition an original Elizabethan walled garden is laid out as a demonstration of plants suitable for Dorset. *Adm £2.50 Chd £1.50. Open Easter to end Sept. For NGS Thurs May 13, June 24 (1-5)*

Langebride House ✗ (Maj & Mrs John Greener) Long Bredy. ½-way between Bridport and Dorchester, S off A35, well signed. Substantial old rectory garden with many designs for easier management. 200-yr-old beech trees, bi-colour beech hedge, pleached limes and yew hedges, extensive collections of spring bulbs, bulbarium, herbaceous plants, flowering trees and shrubs. *Adm £1 Chd free (Share to Joseph Weld House). Suns March 14, 28 (2-5), April 11, June 6 (2-6). By appt March to end July* **Tel 0308 482 257**

¶Langford Farm ❀ (Mr & Mrs A J H Du Boulay) Sydling St Nicholas. 6m NW of Dorchester off A37 to Yeovil. Turn R to Sydling St Nicholas after leaving Grimston. 1m and to R. 2½m from Sydling St Nicholas to Dorchester on valley rd. 1m from Frampton over hill and crossing A37. New garden on slope facing SW solid chalk foundation; 2 terraces approx 2 acres including wild water garden; 40 varieties of roses mainly climbing and shrub; pergola and gazebo also pergola round kitchen garden. Garden partly suitable for wheelchairs. TEAS. *Adm £1 Chd free. Sun June 6 (2-5)*

Langmoore Manor ❀ (Mr & Mrs S Connell) Charmouth. A35 W Bridport. Take Lyme Regis exit off the roundabout. 1st house on L. Natural landscape of 18 acres incl woodland, lakes. Colourful kitchen garden; scented courtyard and bog garden and introduction of garden museum. TEAS and light lunches. *Adm £1.80 Chd 50p. Open Suns, Tues, Weds, Thurs and Sats from end March to end Oct (11-5.30). For NGS Suns March 21, May 16, Sept 19 (11-5.30)* **Tel 0297 60229**

Little Platt ♿✗❀ (Sir Robert Williams) Plush, 9m N of Dorchester by B3143 to Piddletrenthide, then 1½m NE by rd signed Plush & Mappowder, 1st house on L entering Plush. 1-acre garden created from a wilderness since 1969; interesting collection of ornamental trees and flowering shrubs, incl several daphnes, spiraeas and viburnums; spring bulbs, hellebores, numerous hardy geraniums and unusual perennials. *Adm £1 Chd free. By appt only March to Aug* **Tel Piddletrenthide 320**

Long Ash Cottage ♿✗❀ (Mr & Mrs A Case) Milton Abbas. 10m From Blandford-Dorchester on A354, 3m from Milbourne St Andrew on Ansty Rd not Milton Abbas Rd. Private ½-acre cottage garden adjoining The Rare Poultry, Pig and Plant Centre, with many unusual and old fashioned flowers. Also exhibition of paintings by botanical artist Susan Goodricke. *Adm 75p Chd 25p. Mons May 3, 31 (2-5.30)*

The Manor House, Abbotsbury ✗ (Mr D Nabarro) Abbotsbury is equidistant (9m) from Dorchester, Weymouth and Bridport. The Manor House is in Church St opp St Nicholas church. Cars can park in the public carpark by the Swan Inn. There is no parking by The Manor House. The gardens extending to 2½ acres were designed in 1988 by Ian Teh. They feature four inter-connecting ponds surrounded by herbaceous borders and a herb garden. The gardens lie below St Catherine's chapel and are in sight of the sea. TEAS. *Adm £1.50 Chd free. Sat, Sun June 19, 20 (2.30-6)*

The Manor House, Chaldon Herring ✗❀ (Dale & Alice Fishburn) 9m E of Dorchester, mid-way between Dorchester-Wareham on A352, turn S at sign to East Chaldon. 2 acres in valley in chalk hills, blends into surroundings; plantsman's garden with many perennials and climbers; small but fine kitchen garden. Home-made TEAS. *Adm £1.50 Chd free (Share to St Nicholas Church, Chaldon Herring). Sat June 26 (4-8)*

Mapperton Gardens ♿✗❀ (Montagu Family) near Beaminster. 6m N of Bridport off A35. 2m SE of Beaminster off B3163. Descending valley gardens beside one of Dorset's finest manor houses (C16-C17) House and garden listed Grade I. Gardens featured in Country Life (Spring 1993) and Discovering Gardens TV series (1990-91). Magnificent walks and views. Fish ponds, orangery, formal Italian-style borders and topiary; specimen trees and shrubs; car park. Upper levels only, suitable for wheelchairs. House open to group tours by appt **Tel 0308 862645**. *Adm garden £2.50 Chd £1.50, under 5 free. March to Oct daily (2-6). For NGS Sun, Mon May 2, 3 (2-6)*

Melbury House ♿✗❀ 6m S of Yeovil. Signed on Dorchester-Yeovil rd. 13m N of Dorchester. Large garden; very fine arboretum; shrubs and lakeside walk; beautiful deer park. Garden only. Last season saw many changes and more are planned for this year. TEAS. *Adm £2 OAPs/Chd £1 (Share to CRMF). Thurs May 27, June 10, 17; July 1, 8 (2-5)*

Melplash Court ♿❀ (Mr & Mrs Timothy Lewis) Melplash. On the A3066 between Beaminster and Bridport, just N of Melplash. Turn W and enter between field gates next to big gates and long avenue of Chestnut trees. Free parking in the field. The gardens were designed by Lady Diana Tiarks and consist of park planting, bog garden, croquet lawn and adjacent borders. Formal kitchen garden and lake, Japanese garden, ponds, stream garden, etc. TEAS in aid of Melplash Church. *Adm £2 Chd free. Sun July 25 (2-6)*

Mill Cottage ♿✗❀ (Mr & Mrs G V G Fowler) Burton Bradstock. From Bridport follow signs S and E B3157 to Burton Bradstock (2½m). Limited parking for elderly and infirm otherwise park in the centre of village and follow signs from Middle St. Young 1-acre garden over-looking watermeadows divided by hedges and walls into series of areas, including flower garden, soft fruit and vegetables all of which are organically grown seen: on TSW 'Gardens for all' Oct 1991. TEAS in aid of National Children's Home. *Adm £1 Chd free. Sats June 12, 19 (2-6)*

● Minterne (The Lord Digby) Minterne Magna. On A352 Dorchester-Sherborne rd. 2m N Cerne Abbas; woodland garden set in a valley landscaped in the C18 with small lakes, cascades and rare trees; many species and hybrid rhododendrons and magnolias tower over streams and water plants. *Adm £2 Accompanied chd and parking free. Open daily April 1 to Oct 31 (10-7)*

By Appointment Gardens. Avoid the crowds. Good chance of a tour by owner. See garden description for telephone number.

Moigne Combe (Maj-Gen H M G Bond) 6m E of Dorchester. 1½m N of Owermoigne turn off A352 Dorchester-Wareham Rd. Medium-sized garden; wild garden and shrubbery; heathers, azaleas, rhododendrons etc; woodland paths and lake walk. Tea Wyevale Garden Centre, Owermoigne. *Adm £1 1st chd 25p thereafter 10p. Suns May 23, 30 (2-5.30)*

Moulin Huet ✗ (Harold Judd Esq) 15 Heatherdown Rd, West Moors. 7m N of Bournemouth. Leave A31 at West Moors Garage into Pinehurst Rd, take 1st R into Uplands Rd, then 3rd L into Heatherdown Rd. thence into cul-de-sac. ⅓-acre garden made by owner from virgin heathland after retirement. Considerable botanical interest; collections of 90 dwarf conifers and bonsai; many rare plants and shrubs; alpines, sink gardens, rockeries, wood sculpture. Featured on TV 'Gardeners World' 1982. Garden News Gardener of the Year Award 1984. *Adm 50p Chd free. Suns May 9, 16, 23 (2-5). Also by appt. Parties welcome* Tel 0202 875760

¶**Northbrook Farm** ᕦ❀ (Shelia & Tim Cox) Take A354 Puddletown to Blandford. After Blue Vinney Public House take 1st L (Long-lane) signed Dewlish-Cheselbourne turn L into farm rd marked Northbrook Farm. ½-acre garden created from a field since 1987, comprising mixed shrub/herbaceous borders in harmonising colours, conifer/heather bed. Unusual plants. *Combined adm with* **Farriers** *£1 Chd free. Suns May 30, June 27, Aug 1 (2-6)*

North Leigh House ❀ (Mr & Mrs Stanley Walker) Colehill, 1m NE of Wimborne. Leave B3073 (formerly A31) nr Sir Winston Churchill public house into North Leigh Lane, thence ¾m. 5 acres of informal parkland with fine trees, small lake, rhododendrons; ornamental shrubs; specimen magnolia grandiflora and Green Brunswick fig; colony of orchis morio and naturalised spring bulbs in lawns; Victorian features include balustraded terrace, fountain pool, walled garden and conservatory, all being restored and maintained by owners. Dogs on leads welcome. Suitable wheelchairs in parts. TEAS. *Adm 75p Chd 25p (Share to Animal Aid, May; Bournemouth & District Animal Ambulance Service Aug). Suns May 2, Aug 1 (2-6)*

Oakmead ᕦ (Mr & Mrs P D Priest) Mosterton. On A3066 Beaminster to Crewkerne in centre of village. Roadside parking. ⅔-acre lawns with well shaped & colourful beds of shrubs, perennials, heathers, roses; unusual plants. *Adm £1 Chd free. Sun July 11, Aug 29 (2-6)*

The Old Mill ᕦ❀ (The Rev & Mrs J Hamilton-Brown) Spetisbury, Spetisbury Village opposite school on A350 3m SE of Blandford. 2 acres mainly water garden by river Stour; small rockery; herbaceous plants. Teas at Marigold Cottage in Spetisbury. *Adm £1 Chd free. Wed June 23, Sun June 27, also every Weds May to Sept (2-5.30) also by appt* Tel 0258 453939

The Old Parsonage ᕦ (Major & Mrs Mansel) Kimmeridge. 7m S of Wareham. Turn W off A351 Wareham-Swanage at sign to Kimmeridge. 1st house on R in Kimmeridge. ½-acre garden newly planted 1989; many unusual perennials and shrubs planned for all year interest; roses; clematis and hydrangeas; pond in lawn; small

vegetable and fruit garden; beautiful sea view; dogs on leads; Teas in village. *Adm 80p Chd 40p. Sun June 27, Wed June 30 (2.15-5.15)*

The Old Rectory, Fifehead Magdalen ᕦ❀ (Mrs Patricia Lidsey) 5m S of Gillingham just S of the A30. Small garden with interesting shrubs and perennials; pond; plant stall. *Adm 80p Chd free. Sun Jun 13 (2-6) also by appt* Tel 0258 820293

The Old Rectory, Litton Cheney ❀ (Mr & Mrs Hugh Lindsay) 1m S of A35, 10m Dorchester. 6m Bridport. Park in centre of village and follow signs. Greatly varied garden with small walled garden recently redesigned; 4 acres beautiful natural woodland on steep slope with streams and ponds, primulas, native plants; wild flower lawn; (stout shoes recommended). TEAS in aid of Dorchester Voluntary Bureau & Red Cross. *Adm £1 Chd 20p. Easter Sun April 11; Sun May 23 (2-5.30)*

The Old Rectory, Pulham ᕦ❀ (Rear Adm Sir John & Lady Garnier) on B3143 turn E at Xrds in Pulham. 13m N of Dorchester. Sherborne and Sturminster Newton both 8m. 3 acres with mature trees and beautiful view; many trees and shrubs, herbaceous borders and shrub roses planted since 1975. Plant stall in aid of Dorset Respite & Hospice Trust. TEAS. *Adm £1.20 Chd free. Suns May 23, June 13; Weds May 26; June 9, 16 (2-7)*

Old Rectory, Seaborough ❀ (Mr & Mrs C W Wright) 3m S of Crewkerne. Take B3165, after derestriction sign 2nd L, ¾m 1st R, then after 2½m second L in village. 2-acre garden constructed since 1967; splendid views; rare trees, conifers, magnolias, flowering shrubs, roses, Himalayan plants, bulbs throughout the year, ferns; over 1000 species and cultivars. TEAS in aid of Church. *Adm £1 Chd 20p. Sun May 16 (2-6); also by appt all year* Tel 0308 68426

¶**The Old Vicarage, Stinsford** ✗❀ (Mr & Mrs Antony Longland) Stinsford. Off roundabout at eastern end of Dorchester by-pass A35. Follow signs for Stinsford Church 400yds. Use church car park. Old Vicarage on L facing church. 1¼ acres restored and replanted since 1986. Herbaceous borders, terrace, lawns, fruit, exuberant pot planting and some unusual plants and shrubs; roses in variety. Thomas Hardy, C Day Lewis and Cecil Hanbury, creator of gardens at La Mortola Italy and Kingston Maurwand, commemorated in church next door. *Adm £1.50 Chd free. Sun June 27 (2-6)*

The Orchard ✗❀ (Mr & Mrs K S Ferguson) Blynfield Gate. 2m W of Shaftesbury on the rd to Stour row. From Shaftesbury take the B3091 to St James's Church then onto the Stour Row Rd. A 3-acre country garden, orchard and meadow on SE slope of Duncliffe Hill. Fine views and plenty of seats. Large variety of plants incl collections of hardy geraniums, campanulas and wild flowers; formal, informal and wild areas to attract butterflies and bees. Small natural pond. Home-made TEAS. *Adm £1.50 to incl descriptive guide and plant information. Chd free (Share to Red Cross). Weds June 9, 16, 23, 30; July 7, 14 (2-6)*

● **Parnham** ⅄ (Mr & Mrs John Makepeace) ½m S of Beaminster on A3066, 5m N of Bridport. 14 acres extensively reconstructed early this century; much variety of form and interest, topiary; terraces; gazebos; spring fed water rills; small lake; fine old trees; grand herbaceous borders featured in Discovering Gardens (1990/91). Old roses in formal front courtyard; riverside walk and woodland; many unusual plants. House (Grade 1 listed, dating from 1540) exhibitions of contemporary craftsmanship, also John Makepeace furniture workshops. Restaurant, coffee, lunches. TEAS. *Adm to whole site £3 Chd 10-15 £1.50 under 10 free. April 4 to Oct 28 every Sun, Wed & Bank Hol incl. Good Friday (10-5). Group visits by appt Tues & Thurs* Tel **0308 862204**

Portesham Gardens 7m W of Weymouth on coast rd, B3157 to Bridport. From Dorchester take A35 W, turn L in Winterborne Abbas and follow signs to Portesham; parking in village. Teas at Millmead Country Hotel. *Combined adm £3. Sun June 13 (2-6)*
   Bridge House Water Garden ✗ (Mr & Mrs G Northcote) Designed and constructed in 1987 in Japanese manner; Publicised in 'Through the Garden Gate' BBC2, 'The Dorset Gardens Guide', and 'Garden Answers!' Principal features: torre-gate stone and ceramic lanterns, 'half-moon' stone and timber bridges, trout stream, borrowed scenery, pine island, waterfall, local stone-walled terraces, over 300 plantings suitable for smaller seaside garden; new rear patio and dry sand/rock garden in low maintenance frontage; garden planning exhibition in studio. *Also open Sun May 16. Adm £1 Chd free. Also by appt April to Sept* Tel **0305 871685**
   Orchard House ⅄✗ (Mr & Mrs F J Mentern) ⅓-acre walled cottage garden; ground cover, herbs; unusual old-fashioned perennials; rockeries and water garden; fruitful veg area, working greenhouses run as a small nursery open daily for charity. *Also by appt* Tel **0305 871611**
   Portesham House ⅄✗ (Mrs G J Romanes) Home of Admiral Sir Thomas Masterman Hardy with 300-yr-old Mulberry tree; over an acre of family garden with excellent modern dry stone walling, old walls and stream. Paeony collection and many unusual trees and shrubs. *Also open Sun June 6 (2-6). Adm £1 Chd free*
   2 Winters Lane ✗ (Mr & Mrs K Draper) Portesham. Winters Lane is signposted in village to Coryates. ¼-acre garden with ponds and water features. Many ideas for smaller gardens such as small herb garden; container garden and dry garden. 30 varieties of clematis and most plants labelled. *Adm 75p Chd free. Sun June 13, Thurs July 15 (2-6), also by appt June and July* Tel **0305 871316**

¶**Portland House** The National Trust (Mr & Mrs A Phillipson) 24 Belle Vue Rd. 1m from Weymouth town centre. Take Portland Rd from town centre; turn L from Rodwell Rd into Bincleaves Rd then into Belle Vue Rd on R. Park in Belle Vue Rd. Over 4 acres of mature trees, lawns, hydrangeas and fuchsias, avenue of palm trees; superb views over Portland harbour (weather permitting) part suitable for wheel chairs. *Adm £1 Chd 50p. Sun July 4 (2-6)*

Priest's House ✗✿ (The Priest's House Museum Trust) 23 High St, Wimborne. Free public car parks nearby. Old 'borough plot' garden of ½ acre, at rear of local museum, in partly C16 town house. Extending to mill stream and containing many unusual plants, trees and exhibits. Tearoom daily. *Adm £1.50 Chd 50p.* ▲*Sun Sept 26 (2-4.30)*

Pumphouse Cottage ✿ (Mr & Mrs R A Pugh) Mundens Lane. Alweston is 3m SE of Sherborne on A3030 to Blandford. Take L turning 50yds after PO marked Mundens Lane. 1st cottage on L. ½-acre cottage garden on several levels with stream, terraces, pergola, large collection of old roses, herbaceous borders, herbs and unusual plants; spring bulbs. *Adm £1 Chd free. By appt Spring and Autumn*

Rampisham Gardens. 9m S of Yeovil take A37 to Dorchester. 7m turn R signed Evershot follow sign-post to Rampisham. 11m NW Dorchester take A37 to Yeovil, 4m turn L A356 signed Crewkerne; at start of wireless masts R to Rampisham. Small unspoilt village deep in rural Dorset with C14 church. Cream TEAS, plant stall and cake stall in aid of Church at **Manor Garden**. *Combined adm £2.50 Chd free. Sat, Sun June 26, 27 (2-6)*
   Broomhill ✗ (Mr & Mrs D Parry) A family garden of 1 acre with unusual trellised entrance leading to mixed borders and island beds with a great variety of plants. The lawns slope down to a large wildlife pond
   Hill View ✗ (Mr & Mrs Childs) Villager's traditional cottage garden, amongst the abundance of vegetables and flowers you will find a bank with fossils and pieces of petrified wood. Plants mainly grown from saved seeds
   The Old Chapel ✗ (Mr & Mrs W Reder) Approx ⅓-acre garden created in 1990 on a bare building site. Based on TV programme 'The Ornamental Kitchen Garden' incl woodland walk with stream and patio gardens
   Rampisham Manor ✗✿ (Mr & Mrs Boileau) Spacious lawns round Manor House, 2½ acres with hedged walks; herbaceous, shrub and formal rose and lavender beds. Ornamental kitchen garden, fine views and full of interest

Red House Museum and Gardens ⅄✗ (The Hampshire Museum Service) Quay Road, Christchurch. Tranquil setting in heart of town's conservation area. Gardens of ½ acre developed from early 1950's to complement Museum; plants of historic interest; herb garden with sunken lawn, south garden with lawns, herbaceous and woodland plants; old rose border. Gardens used as gallery display area for sculpture exhibitions. Admission to Museum and Art Gallery included. *Adm £1 OAP/Chd 60p (under five free) (Share to the Mayor of Christchurch's Appeal of the Year).* ▲*For NGS Thurs June 17 (10-5)*

Rosedene ✗✿ (Mr & Mrs J M Hodges) 98 Hill View Road, Ensbury Park, parallel with and ½m distant from A347 main Wimborne Rd in north Bournemouth. Walled town garden 120ft × 35ft, lined with mature espalier fruit trees, with two greenhouses and 18ft geodesic solar dome together containing seven varieties of grape, fruit being a special interest of the owners. Other houses contain carnations, chrysanthemums and vegetables. Large pool with fish. There is much of interest contained in this small plot. Parts suitable for wheelchairs. *Adm 50p Chd 20p. Suns Aug 29, Sept 5, 12 (2-5)*

46 Roslin Road South &✿❀ (Dr & Mrs Malcolm Slade) Bournemouth. W of N end of Glenferness Ave in Talbot Woods area of Bournemouth. ⅓-acre walled town garden of year round interest. Features include rose pergola, two pools, sunken lawn, with many colourful and mature herbaceous and shrub plantings. Carefully tended fruit and vegetable garden. *Adm 50p Chd 25p. Suns May 30, June 20; Mon May 31 (1.30-5). Also by appt from May to July* Tel 0202 510243

52 Rossmore Road ✿❀ (Mr & Mrs W E Ninniss) Parkstone, Poole. From A348 Poole-Ringwood rd turn SE into Rossmore Rd, thence ¼m. ⅓-acre interesting town garden designed in rooms; containing many rare and unusual plants; small knot garden; scree garden; herb garden. Featured on TVS 'That's Gardening' 1991. TEAS. *Adm 70p Chd 25p. Suns May 23, June 6 (2-6)*

Russets &❀ (Mr & Mrs G D Harthan) Rectory Lane, Child Okeford. 6m NW Blandford via A357 and turn off N at Shillingstone; or from A350 turn W at sign for Child Okeford. Parking space in Rectory Lane (ask nr centre of village). ½-acre plantsman's garden with something of interest at all times. In spring, flowering shrubs and bulbs. In summer shrub roses, perennials and clematis. In autumn clematis, asters and other late flowering perennials. Good autumn colour late Sept and Oct. *Visitors & parties welcome. By appt only April to Oct* Tel Child Okeford 860703

St Nicholas Close &✿ (Mr & Mrs Arthur Thorne) 38 Highland Rd, Colehill, Wimborne. Leave B3073 (formerly A31) at traffic lights turn N into St John's Hill, after small roundabout into Rowlands Hill, after ¼m turn R into Highland Rd and park. The garden is approached on foot, please, by short lane. ⅓-acre created by owners, with specialist collections of unusual species: cultivars of rhododendrons, azaleas, camellias against mature trees, incl eucalyptus. *Adm 50p Chd free. Suns April 11, May 2 (2-6)*

● **Smedmore** &❀ (Dr Philip Mansel) Kimmeridge, 7m S of Wareham. Turn W off A351 (Wareham-Swanage) at sign to Kimmeridge. 2 acres of colourful herbaceous borders; display of hydrangeas; interesting plants and shrubs; walled flower gardens; herb courtyard. *Adm £2 Chd £1. Sun May 16 (2.15-5.15). Enquiries* Tel 0929 480 719

Snape Cottage ✿❀ (Mr & Mrs I S Whinfield) Leave A303 (Bourton By-pass) at junction signposted Gillingham, Blanford and Bourton, Garden at W end of Bourton village lane signed Chaffey moor. Opp Chiffchaffs. ½-acre plantsman's cottage garden with old-fashioned and uncommon plants, most labelled. Beautiful views, wildlife pond. Plants and herbs for sale. Exhibition of handthrown and sculpted pottery on Easter Sun and Mon; also spinning demonstration and working pole-lathe in garden. *Adm £1 Chd free. Suns April 11, May 2, 30; June 13, 27; July 11, also every Weds April 7 to Sept 29 (closed Aug) (2-6). Parties welcome by appt* Tel 0747 840330

Regular Openers. See head of county section.

● **Stapehill Abbey** ✿ Wimborne Rd West, Ferndown. 2½m W of Ferndown on the old A31, towards Wimborne, ½m E of Canford Bottom roundabout. Early C19 Abbey, its gardens and estate restored and renovated to lawns, herbaceous borders; rose and water gardens; victorian cottage garden; lake and orchid house. Mature trees. Busy working Craft Centre; Countryside Museum featuring the National Tractor Collection, all under cover. Refreshments available in former refectory throughout the day. Large free car/coach park. TEAS. *Open daily Easter to Sept (10-5); Oct to Easter (10-4); closed Mons and Tues in winter.* Tel 0202 861686

Star Cottage ✿❀ (Lys de Bray) 8 Roman Way, Cowgrove, Wimborne. Leave B3082 at Hillbutts, 1½m W of Wimborne, thence through Pamphill to Cowgrove. The garden will become another 'living library' of botanical artist and author Lys de Bray FLS, lately of Turnpike Cottage, Wimborne. Visitors will thus have an opportunity of meeting Miss de Bray and of seeing a specialised garden in the making, from the very first stages. The owner is a R.H.S. Gold Medallist whose botanical drawings and paintings are on permanent exhibition in her working studio which is open throughout the year at weekends. *Adm 75p Chd 40p. Garden and Studio open all year. End Oct to end March (2-4). Sats & Suns (2-6). For NGS Suns May 16, June 20 (2-6). Also by appt* Tel 0202 885130

Steeple Manor &✿❀ (Mr Julian & the Hon Mrs Cotterell) Steeple, 5m SW of Wareham in Isle of Purbeck. Take Swanage rd from Wareham, or by-pass, R in Stoborough. Garden designed by Brenda Colvin 1920's round C16/17 Purbeck Stone Manor House (not open); lovely setting in folds of Purbeck hills in small hamlet of Steeple next to ancient church, specially decorated for the occasion. Walls, hedges, enclosed gardens, ponds, stream, bog garden and meadow, collection old roses; many interesting and tender plants and shrubs. Parts garden suitable for wheelchairs. Free parking. Cream TEAS. *Adm £2.50 OAPs £1.25 Chd under 16 free (Share to CRMF). Sun June 27 (2-6)*

Sticky Wicket &✿❀ (Peter & Pam Lewis) Buckland Newton. 11m from Dorchester and Sherborne. 2m E of A352 or take B3143 from Sturminster Newton. T-junction midway Church, School and Gaggle of Geese public house. 1½-acre garden created since 1987, unusual designs, well documented showing wild life interest; fragrant cottage garden planting including many perennials and herbs. Features include the Round Garden, a 'floral tapestry' of gently flowing colours, informal white garden. Featured on TV and in publications including 'English Private Gardens'. TEAS. *Adm £1.25 Chd 50p (Share to Buckland Newton Church). Every Thurs May to Sept incl (10.30-8). Sat, Suns May 30, June 20, Sept 11, 12 (2-6). Parties by app* Tel 03005 476 *For NGS Sat, Sun July 10, 11 (11-6), Sun Aug 15 (2-6)*

Stockford & (Mrs A M Radclyffe) East Stoke, 3½m W of Wareham on A352. Drive marked Stockford almost opp Stokeford Inn. 3 acres of woodland and walled gardens. Very old thatched house. *Adm 50p Chd 25p. Suns April 18, May 9, 30 (2-6)*

Stour House &⚘ (T S B Card Esq) East St, Blandford. On 1-way system, 100yds short of market place. 2½-acre town garden, half on a romantic island in R. Stour reached by a remarkable bridge; bulbs; borders; river views. TEAS. *Adm 60p Chd 20p (Teas and share to Blandford Parish Church, July). Suns April 4, July 18, Aug 15 (2-6)*

¶**Studland Bay House** &⚘ (Mrs Pauline Ferguson) Studland. On B3351 5m E of Corfe Castle. Through village, entrance on R before Studland Bay House. Ample parking (no coaches). From Bournemouth, take Sandbank ferry, 2½m, garden on L after Knoll House Hotel. 6-acre spring garden overlooking Studland Bay. Planted in 1930's on heathland; magnificent rhododendrons, azalea walk, camellias, magnolias, ferns and stream; recent drainage and replanting, garden suitable for wheelchairs. TEAS. *Adm £1.50 Chd free. Sat, Wed May 22, 26 (2-6)*

Sturminster Newton Gardens &⚘ Off A357 between Blandford and Sherborne take turn opp Nat West Bank. Park in car park or behind Stourcastle Lodge. Walk down Penny St for **Ham Gate** and Goughs Close for **Stourcastle Lodge**. TEAS at Ham Gate. *Combined adm £1.50 Chd free. Sun July 11 (2-6)*
   Ham Gate &⚘ (Mr & Mrs H E M Barnes) Informal 2-acre garden with shrubs, trees, lawns running down to R. Stour, pleasant woodland views across water meadows, over the last few years Pam Lewis has helped redesign the garden
   ¶**Stourcastle Lodge** ⚘ (Jill & Ken Hookham-Bassett) A S facing secluded cottage style garden, well stocked with herbaceous plants and shrubs with laid out vegetable garden

¶**Thistledown** ⚘⚘ (Mr & Mrs E G Gillingham) Owlweston 3m SE of Sherborne. From main A3030, turn into Mundens Lane by Oxfords Bakery. Garden 100yds along lane; park in drive, overflow car park opp village hall. 1-acre garden planted for year round interest. Bulbs, conifers, roses, shrubs, trees, herbaceous borders and ponds. *Adm £1 Chd free. Suns April 11, 18, 25, May 2, 9, 16, 23 30, June 6, 13, 20, Sept 12, 19 (2-5.30)*

¶**Three Bays** ⚘⚘ (Mr & Mrs Christopher Garrett) 8, Old Wareham Rd, Beacon Hill, (nr junction with A350) 4m SW of Wimborne. Garden of ½ acre made and maintained by owners. There is a Japanese flavour to the garden, with stone lanterns, dovecot and water features. Fuchsias are a special interest of the owners and there is a covered fuchsia garden. New rose garden for 1993 with 150 plants in 34 varieties. Shrubs and herbaceous borders with much use of sloping site. TEA. *Adm 75p OAPs and Chd 50p (Share to Cancer Research Campaign). Sats, Suns June 19, 20 July 10, 11, 17,18 (10-5). Parties by appt* **Tel 0202 623352**

14 Umbers Hill ⚘⚘ (Mrs K Bellars) Shaftesbury. Take B3091 (Bimport) descend St John's Hill to small Xrds; R into Breach Lane, bear R into Umbers Hill. Small sloping garden with lovely views of Blackmore Vale; large rockery and many stone sinks with variety of rock plants and alpines; over 50 clematis bloom throughout year; hardy ferns; Japanese corner; dwarf conifers and shrubs; small

greenhouse. *Adm 75p Including cup of tea/coffee (Share to Cancer Research Campaign, Shaftesbury Branch). By appt only all year* **Tel Shaftesbury 53312**

Warmwell House &⚘ (Mr & Mrs H J C Ross Skinner) Warmwell. Dorchester rd to Wareham A352 roundabout turn L for Warmwell. Weymouth rd N A353 goes through Warmwell to meet Puddletown-Dorchester rd. Approx 5 acres of garden recently reorganised due to January 1990 storm damage. Much new planting. Old-fashioned Dutch garden. Newly planted maze. TEAS. *Adm £1. Sun Aug 1 (2-5)*

Welcome Thatch ⚘⚘ (Mrs Diana Guy) Witchampton. 3½m E of Wimborne B3078 L to Witchampton. Continue through village past church & shop. Welcome Thatch last but one cottage on R before you reach fields. Varied cottage garden with listed thatched property; small pond, interesting borders. Not suitable for elderly, infirm or young chd. TEA. *Adm 75p Chd free. Suns June 13, 20 (2-6) also by appt* **Tel 0258 840894**

West Manor & (Mr & Mrs R Bollam) Church St, Upwey. ½m from bottom of Ridgeway Hill on A354 Dorchester-Weymouth rd. Turn R on B3159 (Bridport). At bottom of hill turn L, Church St. Limited parking for disabled only. ¾-acre low maintenance garden, worked on organic principles; lawns, borders, shrubs, woodland, small pond and vegetable garden. Teas at Wishing Well. *Combined adm with* **7 Church St** *£2 Chd free. Suns June 6, July 4, Aug 1 (2-6)*

Weston House &⚘⚘ (Mr & Mrs E A W Bullock) Buckhorn Weston. 4m W of Gillingham and 4m SE of Wincanton. From A30 turn N to Kington Magna, continue towards Buckhorn Weston and after railway bridge take L turn towards Wincanton. 2nd on L is Weston House. 1 acre; old roses; herbaceous and shrub beds; lawns; view of Blackmore Vale. TEAS in aid of Buckhorn Weston Parish Church. *Adm £1 Chd free. Suns June 13, 20 (2-6)*

Wimborne Minster Model Town & Gardens &⚘⚘ (The Wimborne Minster Model Town Trust). King St 200 yds W of Minster, opp. public car park. 1½-acre grounds with one-tenth scale models of the town in early fifties, surrounded by landscaped gardens. Herbaceous borders, alpines, herbs, heather and rose gardens, with many rare and unusual plants, with pools and fountain, making a colourful pleasure garden. Many seats and views over Stour valley. Refreshments daily. *Adm £1.75 OAPs £1.50 Chd 75p (5-15) under five free. For NGS Suns June 6, 20, Sept 5 (10-5)*

Wincombe Park ⚘ (The Hon M D Fortescue) 2m from Shaftesbury. Off A350 to Warminster signed to Wincombe and Donhead St Mary. Plantsman's garden surrounding house set in parkland; raised beds, shrubs, perennials; walled kitchen garden; view of valley with lake and woods. Unusual plants for sale. TEAS. *Adm £1.50 Chd free. Weds May 19, Oct 20 (2-5.30), also groups by appt* **Tel 0747 52161**

By Appointment Gardens. See head of county section

Woodside Lodge & (Mr & Mrs K H Lewis) E Lulworth. 5m SW of Wareham just N of B3070 nr village green & telephone box, follow signs. Extends to 1¾ acres graduating from formal to semi wild, with natural pond area; many shrub and tree species with rhododendrons, azaleas, camellias, iris and other herbaceous plants. TEAS in aid of Church. *Adm £1 Chd free (Share to Church Restoration Fund). Suns May 16, June 13 (2-6)*

Co. Durham

Hon County Organiser: Mrs Ian Bonas, Bedburn Hall, Hamsterley, Bishop Auckland DL13 3NN
Tel 0388 88231

DATES OF OPENING

By appointment
For telephone numbers and other details see garden descriptions

St Aidan's College, Durham

Regular openings
For details see garden descriptions

Raby Castle, Staindrop. See text for dates
St Aidan's College, Durham

University of Durham Botanic Garden. Nov 1 to Oct 31

May 30 Sunday
Barningham Park, nr Barnard Castle
Westholme Hall, Winston

June 13 Sunday
Eggleston Hall Gardens, nr Barnard Castle

June 20 Sunday
Low Walworth Hall, Darlington
Westholme Hall, Winston

June 27 Sunday
Brancepeth Gardens, Durham

July 4 Sunday
Merrybent Gardens, nr Darlington

July 11 Sunday
Bedburn Hall, Hamsterley
Westholme Hall, Winston

August 29 Sunday
Westholme Hall, Winston

September 12 Sunday
Westholme Hall, Winston

DESCRIPTIONS OF GARDENS

Barningham Park (Sir Anthony Milbank) 6m S of Barnard Castle. Turn S off A66 at Greta Bridge or A66 Motel via Newsham. Woodland walks, trees and rock garden. House (not open) built 1650. Home-made TEAS. *Adm £1.50 Chd (under 14) 50p. Sun May 30 (1-6)*

Bedburn Hall &❀ (Ian Bonas Esq) Hamsterley, 9m NW of Bishop Auckland. From A68 at Witton-le-Wear, turn off W to Hamsterley; turn N out of Hamsterley-Bedburn and down 1m to valley. From Wolsingham on B6293 turn off SE for 3m. Medium-sized garden; terraced garden on S facing hillside with streams; lake; woodland; lawns; rhododendrons; herbaceous borders; roses. TEAS. *Adm £1 Chd 50p. Sun July 11 (2-6)*

Brancepeth Gardens &❀ 6m SW of Durham on A690 between villages of Brandon and Willington. An attractive sandstone village consisting of a few Georgian and later houses at the gates of the Castle & Church which orginate from late C12. TEAS. *Adm £1.50 Chd 50p. Sun June 27 (2-5.30)*
  Quarry Hill & (Sir Paul Nicholson) Attractive landscaped garden containing many tender and southern hemisphere plantings surrounding Elizabethan house.

Eggleston Hall Gardens &❀❀ (Sir William Gray) Eggleston, NW of Barnard Castle. Route B6278. Large garden with many unusual plants; large lawns, rhododendrons, greenhouses, mixed borders, fine trees, large extension of kitchen garden (all organically grown). Garden centre open. TEAS. *Adm £1.50 Chd 30p. Sun June 13 (2-5.30)*

Low Walworth Hall &❀ (Mr & Mrs Peter Edwards) 3½m W of Darlington, on Staindrop Rd. B6279 (½m drive). Old walled garden; herbaceous borders, shrubs, roses; trout rearing pond. Interesting and varied shrubs and greenhouse plants for sale. Home-made TEAS. *Adm £1.50 Chd 50p (Share to Northumbria Historic Churches). Sun June 20 (2-5.30)*

Merrybent Gardens on A67. 2½m W of Darlington within easy reach of town centre. An opportunity to explore these small varied private gardens close to the R. Tees. TEAS. *Combined adm £1 Chd 50p. Sun July 4 (2-5.30)*
  42 Merrybent (Mr & Mrs D Hunter) A large natural pond with a collection of hostas and ferns
  67 Merrybent (Mr & Mrs C Bennett) An interesting vegetable garden

Regular Openers. See head of county section.

● **Raby Castle** ♿✿ (The Rt Hon The Lord Barnard) Staindrop, NW of Darlington. 1m N of Staindrop on A688 Barnard Castle-Bishop Auckland. Buses: 75, 77 Darlington-Barnard Castle; 8 Bishop Auckland-Barnard Castle; alight Staindrop, North Lodge, ¼m. Large walled garden; informal garden with ericas; old yew hedges; shrub and herbaceous borders; roses. Castle also open, principally C14 with alterations made 1765 and mid-C19; fine pictures and furniture. Collection of horse-drawn carriages and fire engines. Garden only suitable wheelchairs. TEAS at Stables. Special terms for parties on application. *Adm Castle Gardens and carriages £3 OAPs £2.60 Chd £1.30; Gardens & carriages only £1 OAPs/Chd 75p. Sat to Wed April 10 to 14, May 1 to June 30, Weds, Suns only; July 1 to Sept 30 daily (except Sats); also Bank Hol weekends, Sat to Tues (Castle 1-5; garden and park 11-5.30, last adm 4.30); also by appt for parties* Tel Staindrop 60202

St Aidan's College ♿ (By kind permission of the Principal) Durham. 1m from City centre. A1050 N towards Durham City; turn W at South End House, where St Aidan's College signposted. St Aidan's College was designed by Sir Basil Spence and the grounds laid out according to a plan by Prof Brian Hackett about 1966. The maturing garden (3 acres) includes shrub planting, rose beds and raised beds; several specimen trees of interest incl cedrus libani, have been planted. From the garden there are unequalled views of Durham Cathedral, Durham City and Durham University Observatory, designed by Anthony Salvin. In porter's lodge are available, booklets £1 & postcards 20p. *Gardens open all year except Christmas and Easter. Please arrange with Bursar* Tel **091 374 3269** *Donations to NGS*

University of Durham Botanic Garden ♿✿ 1m from centre of Druham. Turn off A167 (old A1) at Cock O'The North roundabout, direction Durham for 1m; turn R into Hollingside Lane (steep narrow angular junction) which is between Grey and Collingwood Colleges; gardens 600yds on R. 18 acres on a beautiful SW facing hillside features 12-yr-old North American Arboretum, woodland and ornamental bog garden, winter heather beds and tropical and desert display glasshouses. The Prince Bishop's garden contains 6 sculptures by Colin Wilbourne. TEAS in Visitor Centre. *Adm £1 Chd 50p. March 1 to Oct 31 (10-5) Nov 1 to Feb 28 every afternoon weather permitting*

Westholme Hall ♿✿ (Capt & Mrs J H McBain) Winston. 11m W of Darlington. From A67 Darlington-Barnard Castle, nr Winston turn N onto B6274. 5 acres of gardens and grounds laid out in 1892 surround the Jacobean house (not open). Rhododendrons, flowering shrubs, mixed borders, old-fashioned rose garden. The croquet lawn leads on to an orchard, stream and woodland. TEAS. *Adm £1 Chd 50p. Suns May 30, June 20, July 11, Aug 29, Sept 12 (2-6)*

Dyfed

See separate Welsh section beginning on page 274

Essex

Hon County Organiser:	Mrs Hugh Johnson, Saling Hall, Great Saling, Braintree CM7 5DT
Assistant Hon County Organiser:	Mrs Rosemary Kenrick, The Bailey House, Saffron Walden CB10 2EA
Hon County Treasurer:	Eric Brown Esq, 19 Chichester Road, Saffron Walden, CB11 3EW

DATES OF OPENING

By appointment
For telephone number and other details see garden descriptions

Beth Chatto Gardens, Elmstead Market
8 Dene Court, Chelmsford
Feeringbury Manor, Feering

The Fens, Langham
Lower Dairy House, Nayland
The Magnolias, Brentwood
Olivers, nr Colchester
Park Farm, Great Waltham
Reed House, Great Chesterford
Saling Hall, Great Saling
Volpaia, Hockley

Regular openings
For details see garden description

Beth Chatto Gardens, Elmstead Market. March 1 to Oct 31, Mons to Sats. Nov 1 to March 1, Mons to Fris. Closed all Bank Hols
Feeringbury Manor, Feering. Weekday mornings May 3 to Aug 27. Closed weekends and Bank Hols

The Fens, Langham. Thurs, Sats,
  March to Aug
Hyde Hall, RHS Garden, Rettendon.
  March 28 to Oct 24 Sats, Suns,
  Weds, Thurs & Bank Hols
Saling Hall, Great Saling. Weds May,
  June & July
Volpaia, Hockley. Thurs, Suns April
  11 to June 27

March 28 Sunday
The Magnolias, Brentwood
April 3 Saturday
Lower Dairy House, Nayland
April 4 Sunday
The Fens, Langham
Lower Dairy House, Nayland
April 10 Saturday
Lower Dairy House, Nayland
April 11 Sunday
Lower Dairy House, Nayland
The Magnolias. Brentwood
Olivers Farm, Toppesfield
Park Farm, Great Waltham
April 12 Monday
Lower Dairy House, Nayland
Park Farm, Great Waltham
April 18 Sunday
Glen Chantry, Wickham Bishops
Saling Hall Lodge, Great Saling
April 24 Saturday
Lower Dairy House, Nayland
April 25 Sunday
The Fens, Langham ‡
Lower Dairy House, Nayland
The Magnolias, Brentwood
Park Farm, Great Waltham
Whalebone House, Langham ‡
April 26 Monday
Park Farm, Great Waltham
May 1 Saturday
Lower Dairy House, Nayland
May 2 Sunday
Glen Chantry, Wickham Bishops
Lower Dairy House, Nayland
The Magnolias, Brentwood
Old Hill House, Aldham
Park Farm, Great Waltham
Warwick House, Great Dunmow
May 3 Monday
Glen Chantry, Wickham Bishops
Lower Dairy House, Nayland
Park Farm, Great Waltham
May 8 Saturday
Lower Dairy House, Nayland
May 9 Sunday
Lower Dairy House, Nayland
Olivers Farm, Toppesfield
May 16 Sunday
6 Fanners Green, Great Waltham ‡

Glen Chantry, Wickham Bishops
The Magnolias, Brentwood
Park Farm, Great Waltham ‡
Saling Hall Lodge, Great Saling
May 17 Monday
6 Fanners Green, Great Waltham
Park Farm, Great Waltham
May 22 Saturday
Lower Dairy House, Nayland
May 23 Sunday
Lower Dairy House, Nayland
May 29 Saturday
Lower Dairy House, Nayland
May 30 Sunday
8 Dene Court, Chelmsford
The Fens, Langham
Folly Faunts House, Goldhanger
Glen Chantry, Wickham Bishops
Lower Dairy House, Nayland
The Magnolias, Brentwood
Park Farm, Great Waltham
Saling Hall Lodge, Great Saling
Warwick House, Great Dunmow
May 31 Monday
Glen Chantry, Wickham Bishops
Lower Dairy House, Nayland
Park Farm, Great Waltham
June 5 Saturday
Lower Dairy House, Nayland
June 6 Sunday
Lower Dairy House, Nayland
Olivers Farm, Toppesfield
Park Farm, Great Waltham
June 7 Monday
Park Farm, Great Waltham
June 12 Saturday
Lower Dairy House, Nayland
Stamps and Crows, Layer Breton
  Heath
Tye Farm, Elmstead Market
June 13 Sunday
8 Dene Court, Chelmsford ‡
Fanners Farm, Great Waltham ‡
6 Fanners Green, Great
  Waltham ‡
Glen Chantry, Wickham Bishops
Lofts Hall, Elmdon, nr Saffron
  Walden
Lower Dairy House, Nayland
The Magnolias, Brentwood
Park Farm, Great Waltham ‡
Stamps and Crows, Layer Breton
  Heath
Warwick House, Great Dunmow
June 14 Monday
Fanners Farm, Great Waltham ‡
6 Fanners Green, Great Waltham ‡
Park Farm, Great Waltham ‡
June 16 Wednesday
Stamps and Crows, Layer Breton
  Heath

June 20 Sunday
Park Farm, Great Waltham
June 21 Monday
Park Farm, Great Waltham
June 26 Saturday
Lower Dairy House, Nayland
June 27 Sunday
Clavering Gardens, nr Saffron
  Walden
8 Dene Court, Chelmsford
Glen Chantry, Wickham Bishops
Lower Dairy House, Nayland
Panfield Hall, nr Braintree
Park Farm, Great Waltham
Saling Hall, Great Saling ‡
Saling Hall Lodge, Great Saling ‡
June 28 Monday
Park Farm, Great Waltham
July 3 Saturday
Lower Dairy House, Nayland
July 4 Sunday
Lower Dairy House, Nayland
July 10 Saturday
Ardleigh Park, Ardleigh
Lower Dairy House, Nayland
July 11 Sunday
Amberden Hall, Widdington
Ardleigh Park, Ardleigh
8 Dene Court, Chelmsford ‡
6 Fanners Green, Great Waltham ‡
The Fens, Langham ‡‡
Glen Chantry, Wickham Bishops
Lower Dairy House, Nayland
Park Farm, Great Waltham ‡
Whalebone House, Langham ‡‡
July 12 Monday
6 Fanners Green, Great Waltham ‡
Park Farm, Great Waltham ‡
July 18 Sunday
The Magnolias, Brentwood
Saling Hall Lodge, Great Saling
July 25 Sunday
8 Dene Court, Chelmsford
Park Farm, Great Waltham
July 26 Monday
Park Farm, Great Waltham
August 1 Sunday
The Magnolias, Brentwood
August 8 Sunday
8 Dene Court, Chelmsford
August 22 Sunday
8 Dene Court, Chelmsford
August 29 Sunday
The Magnolias, Brentwood
September 5 Sunday
Glen Chantry, Wickham Bishops
September 19 Sunday
Glen Chantry, Wickham Bishops
The Magnolias, Brentwood
October 24 Sunday
The Magnolias, Brentwood

DESCRIPTIONS OF GARDENS

Amberden Hall &⚘❀ (Mr & Mrs D Lloyd) Widdington. 6m from Saffron Walden. E off B1383 nr Newport. Follow signs to Mole Hall Wildlife Park. Drive ½m beyond park on R. Medium-sized walled garden with collection of unusual hardy plants, shrubs and ivy allée. Raised vegetable garden. TEAS. *Adm £1.25 Chd free (Share to St Mary's Church, Widdington). Sun July 11 (2-6)*

Ardleigh Park & (Mrs Veronica McKinlay) 3m NE of Colchester, 2m S of Ardleigh, between A137 and B1029. Leave Ardleigh on Station Rd, after 1m turn R into Park Rd. ½m on R. 30 acres of park and garden, with roses, sunken garden, Italian garden with Mediterranean cypresses, and woodland garden. Combined with garden sculpture and art exhibition. TEAS. *Adm £1.50 Chd free. Sat, Sun July 10, 11 (10-6)*

● **Beth Chatto Gardens** &⚘❀ (Mrs Beth Chatto) On A133, ¼m E of Elmstead Market. 5 acres of attractively landscaped garden with many unusual plants, shown in wide range of conditions from hot and dry to water garden. Adjacent nursery open. *Adm £1.50 Chd free. March 1 to Oct 31, every Mon to Sat but closed Bank Hols (9-5); Nov 1 to end of Feb every Mon to Fri but closed Bank Hols (9-4). Parties by appt*

Clavering Gardens &⚘ Clavering. On B1038 7m N of Bishops Stortford. Turn W off B1368 (old A11) at Newport. TEAS in Cricket Pavilion on village green. *Adm £2 Chd free (Share to Clavering Cricket Club Pavilion Appeal). Sun June 27 (2-5.30)*

> **Brooklands** (Mr & Mrs John Noble) Walled garden; herbaceous and shrub borders; rustic rose trellis. 10-year-old arboretum and newly planted orchard. ¾-acre
>
> **Clavering Court** (Mr & Mrs S R Elvidge) Approx 1½ acres fine trees, shrubs and borders. Walled garden, Edwardian greenhouse
>
> **Deers** (Mr & Mrs S Cooke) Shrub and herbaceous borders; ponds; old roses in formal garden; walled vegetable garden; flower meadow; trees. 4 acres. Parking in yard next to house
>
> ¶**24 Pelham Road** ❀ (Mrs J & Mr P Cooper) Modern house with small plant lovers' garden. Herbaceous shrub border, rockeries, bog garden, herbs, annuals, containers, wildlife pond area. Run organically for over 10 yrs
>
> **Piercewebbs** (Mr & Mrs B R William-Powlett) Includes old walled garden, shrubs, lawns, ha ha, yew and stilt hedges, pond and grass tennis court. Extensive views. New trellised rose garden (1992)
>
> **Shovellers** (Miss J & Miss E Ludgate) Stickling Green. 3-acre extended cottage garden, orchard and meadow

¶**8 Dene Court** ⚘❀ (Mrs Sheila Chapman) Chelmsford. W of Chelmsford (Parkway). Take A1060 Roxwell Rd for 1m. Turn R at traffic lights into Chignall Rd, Dene Court 3rd on R. Parking in Chignall Rd. Well maintained and designed compact garden (250 sq yds) circular lawn surrounded by many unusual plants incl wide variety of clematis, roses, salvias, ferns and grasses; ornamental well; three pergolas; rose-covered perimeter wall. *Adm 75p Chd free (Share to Audrey Appleton Trust for the Ter-*

minally Ill). *Suns May 30, June 13, 27, July 11, 25, Aug 8, 22 (2-6). Parties by appt*

Fanners Farm &⚘ (Mr & Mrs P G Lee) 4m N of Chelmsford. In Great Waltham turn into South Street opp Six Bells public house. Garden 1¼m on R. Informal garden of approx 2 acres surrounding C14 house (not open). Conservatory and small collection of vintage cars. TEAS. *Adm 75p Chd free. Sun, Mon June 13, 14 (2-6)*

6 Fanners Green ⚘❀ (Dr & Mrs T M Pickard) 4m N of Chelmsford. In Great Waltham turn into South Street opp Six Bells public house. Garden 1¼m on the R. Small country garden with mixed borders, herb garden and conservatory. *Adm £1 Chd free. Suns, Mons May 16, 17; June 13, 14; July 11, 12 (2-6)*

Feeringbury Manor & (Mr & Mrs G Coode-Adams) Coggeshall Rd, Feering, on rd between Coggeshall and Feering. 7-acre garden bordering R Blackwater. Many unusual plants including wide variety of honeysuckles, clematis, old-fashioned roses; rare bog-loving plants, border ponds and streams; small Victorian water wheel. Contemporary art exhibition in C14 chapel. *Adm £1.50 Chd £1. Weekday mornings May 3 to Aug 27 (8-1) Closed weekends and Bank Hols. Also open by appt* **Tel 0376 561946**

The Fens &⚘❀ (Mrs Ann Lunn) Old Mill Rd, Langham. 5m N of Colchester off A12. Old Mill Rd starts at T-junction with High St and is an extension of Chapel Rd, leading to Boxted-Dedham Rd. Undulating 2-acre cottage garden maintained by owners, with pond; shade and ditch gardens recreated after 1987 storm; primulas and a wide variety of interesting plants; nursery open. TEAS for charity on April 4, May 30 and at **Whalebone House** on April 25, July 11. *Adm £1 Chd 50p. Thurs, Sat March to Aug. Suns April 4, 25, May 30, July 11 (2-5). Also by appt* **Tel 0206 272259**

Folly Faunts House &❀ (Mr & Mrs J C Jenkinson) Goldhanger. Between Maldon and Colchester on B1026; signed ½m from both directions. 5-acre garden and grounds, divided into 5 different types of garden, created from scratch since 1962. During 1989 a further 6 avenues and 12 acres of land have been planted with a wide variety of trees. A large number of unusual and rare trees, shrubs and plants. Large car park. TEAS. *Adm £1.50 Chd 50p. Sun May 30 (2-5)*

Glen Chantry &⚘❀ (Mr & Mrs W G Staines) Wickham Bishops 1½m SE of Witham. Take Maldon Rd from Witham and 1st L to Wickham Bishops: cross narrow bridge over R Blackwater and turn immediately L up track by side of Blue Mills. 3-acre garden with emphasis on mixed borders with unusual perennials, limestone rock gardens with associated water features and heather and conifer beds. Newly planted white garden and foliage beds. Wide range of plants for sale. TEAS in aid of the Malcolm Sargeant Cancer Fund for Children. *Adm £1 Chd 50p. Suns April 18; May 2, 16, 30; June 13, 27; July 11; Sept 5, 19; Mons May 3, 31 (2-5)*

● **Hyde Hall Garden** &⚘❀ (Royal Horticultural Society) Rettendon, 7m SE of Chelmsford; 6m NE of Wickford. Signed from A130/A132. Flowering trees, shrubs, perennials, roses, bulbs, ornamental greenhouses and ponds; all-year-round colour. TEAS. *Adm £2 Chd 6-14 75p. Parties 20+ £1.50. Every Sat, Sun, Wed, Thurs and Bank Hols (11-6) from March 28 to Oct 24*

Lofts Hall &*✿* (Maj & Mrs C R Philipson) Elmdon. 8m E of Royston. 5m W of Saffron Walden off B1039. Large garden, 6 acres; roses; herbaceous and shrub borders; kitchen garden; lake and C16 carp pond. Early C17 dovecote (reputedly 2nd largest in England), stud farm. TEAS. *Adm £1.50 Chd 50p. Sun June 13 (2-6)*

Lower Dairy House &*✿* (Mr & Mrs D J Burnett) 7m N of Colchester off A134. Turn L at bottom of hill before Nayland village into Water Lane, signed to Little Horkesley. Garden ½m on L past farm buildings. Plantsman's garden approx 1½ acres. Natural stream with waterside plantings; rockery and raised beds; lawns; herbaceous borders; roses. Many varieties of shrubs and ground cover plants. Garden made and maintained by owners for year round colour and variety. Good spring bulbs and blossom. Tudor House (not open). TEAS. *Adm £1 Chd 50p. Sats, Suns, Mons April 3, 4, 10, 11, 12, 24, 25; May 1, 2, 3, 8, 9, 22, 23, 29, 30, 31; June 5, 6, 12, 13, 26, 27; July 3, 4, 10, 11 (2-6). Also by appt* Tel **0206 262 220**

The Magnolias *✿* (Mr & Mrs R A Hammond) 18 St John's Ave, Brentwood. From A1023 turn S on A128; after 300 yds R at traffic lights; over railway bridge; St John's Ave 3rd on R. ½-acre well-designed informal garden with particular appeal to plantsmen; good collection spring bulbs; ground-cover; trees and shrubs incl maples, rhododendrons, camellias, magnolias and pieris. Koi ponds and other water interests. TEA. *Adm £1 Chd 50p. Suns March 28; April 11, 25; May 2, 16, 30; June 13; July 18; Aug 1, 29; Sept 19; Oct 24 (10-5). Also by appt for parties March to Oct incl* Tel **0277 220019**

¶**Old Hill House** &*✿* (Mr & Mrs J S d'Angibau) Aldham. On A604, 5m W of Colchester; top of Ford Street Hill. From A12 and A120, turn off at Marks Tey; N past Marks Tey Station, R at Xrds by Aldham Church. 1-acre garden with mixed shrubs and herbaceous borders and formal herb garden, maintained by owners for year round interest. TEAS. *Adm £1 Chd free (Share to NSPCC). Sun May 2 (2-5.30)*

Olivers &*✿* (Mr & Mrs D Edwards) 3m SW of Colchester, between B1022 & B1026 (signposted from both) From Colchester via Maldon Rd, turn L into Gosbecks Rd at Leather Bottle public house; R into Olivers Lane. C18 house (not open) overlooks Roman river valley, surrounded by terrace and yew backed borders; closely planted with wide variety of plants, many unusual and for varying conditions. Lawns; 3 lakes; meadow; woodland with fine trees underplanted with shrubs including rhododendrons and old roses; spring bulbs and bluebells. *Adm £1.50 Chd free. Open all year by appt* Tel **0206 330575**

Olivers Farm &*✿* (Mr & Mrs J G Blackie) Toppesfield. Garden is situated 1½m W of A604 between Great Yeldham and Toppesfield. Last house on L before T-junction, down drive. Nearest town, Halstead 7m. 1½-acre garden

created since 1978. Woodland garden, trees, shrubs, roses and herbaceous. Lime avenue in paddock; C16 farm house (not open). Small vineyard, TEAS. *Adm £1 Chd 50p (Share to Riding for the Disabled). Suns April 11, May 9, June 6 (2-6)*

Panfield Hall &*✿* (Mr & Mrs R Newman) 2m Braintree. Turn N off A120 through Great Saling; R (signed Panfield); 1m on R again; 2m through village, R into Hall Rd. 4-acre garden surrounding house dated 1520 (not open). Monks' stewponds. Shrub borders, herbaceous borders, many old roses. Parterre. Fresh Cream TEAS. *Adm £1 OAP/Chd 50p. Sun June 27 (2-6)*

Park Farm *✿* (Mrs J E M Cowley & Mr D Bracey) Chatham Hall Lane, Great Waltham, 5m N of Chelmsford. From Chelmsford take the B1008 through Broomfield village and carry straight on until you come to Chatham Hall Lane on the L signposted to Howe St. Park Farm is approx ½m on L. 2-acre garden on farmyard site; old-fashioned shrub roses, herbaceous plants, recently planted ponds. TEAS. *Adm 80p Chd 40p. Suns & Mons April 11, 12, 25, 26; May 2, 3, 16, 17, 30, 31; June 6, 7, 13, 14, 20, 21, 27, 28; July 11, 12, 25, 26 (2-6). Groups by arrangement* Tel **0245 360871**

Reed House &*✿* (Mrs W H Mason) Great Chesterford. 4m N of Saffron Walden and 1m S of Stump Cross, M 11. On B184 turn into Great Chesterford High Street. Then L at Crown & Thistle public house into Manor Lane. ¾-acre garden with collection of unusual plants developed in the last 6 years. *Adm £1.50 Chd 50p. Open by appt only* Tel **0799 30312**

Saling Hall &*✿* (Mr & Mrs H Johnson) Great Saling, 6m NW of Braintree. A120; midway between Braintree-Dunmow turn off N at the Saling Oak. 12 acres; walled garden dated 1698; small park with fine trees; extensive new collection of unusual plants with emphasis on trees; water gardens. TEAS Sun only. *Adm £1.50 Chd free (Share to St James's Church, Great Saling). Weds in May, June, July (2-5). Sun June 27 (2-6). Also parties by appt*

Saling Hall Lodge &*✿* (Mr & Mrs K Akers), Great Saling. 6m from Braintree. Turn N off A120 between Braintree and Dunmow at the Saling Oak public house. Drive at end of village on L, please park in village. Well-designed and maintained ½-acre garden with pond, limestone rock garden, small peat garden, tufa bed and sinks. TEA. *Adm 70p Chd free. Suns April 18, May 16, 30, June 27, July 18 (2-5)*

Stamps and Crows &*✿* (Mr & Mrs E G Billington) Layer Breton Heath. 5½m S of Colchester on B1022 take L fork signposted Birch and Layer Breton. Garden on R side of Layer Breton Heath. 2½ acres of moated garden surrounding C15 farmhouse (not open). Herbaceous borders, mixed shrubs, old roses and good ground cover. Recently created formal garden. Fine views towards Layer Marney Tower. TEAS (Sun only). *Adm £1 Chd free (Share to St. Mary's Church, Layer Breton). Sat, Sun, Wed June 12, 13, 16 (2-6)*

Tye Farm ᴋ⚘ (Mr & Mrs C Gooch) On A133 2m from Colchester and ½m before Elmstead Market on the R, (opp end of village to Beth Chatto). About 1 acre incl shrubberies, formal herb garden and large conservatory. *Adm £1.50 Chd 50p. Sat June 12 (2-6)*

● **Volpaia** ⚘ (Mr & Mrs D Fox) 54 Woodlands Rd, Hockley. 2¾m NE of Rayleigh. B1013 Rayleigh-Rochford, turn S from Spa Hotel into Woodlands Rd. On E side of Hockley Woods. 1-acre containing many exotic trees, rhododendrons, camellias besides other shrubs. Carpets of wood anemones and bluebells in spring, underplanting is very diverse esp with woodland, liliaceous plants and ferns. Home of Bullwood Nursery. TEA. *Adm £1 Chd 30p (Share to Essex Group of NCCPG). All Thurs & Suns from April 11 to June 27 (2.30-6). Also by appt* **0702 203761**

> **By Appointment Gardens.** See head of county section

Warwick House ᴋ⚘ (Mr & Mrs B Creasey) Easton Lodge. 1m N of Great Dunmow on B184, take rd to Lt Easton, ½m turn L to Easton Lodge, 1¼m to white gates marked Easton Lodge, through these gardens ½m on right. Originally wing of Easton Lodge, home of Countess of Warwick; old house now demolished and gardens of 1½ acres created since 1972 on much of old house site. Features inc C18 dovecote; conservatory; cobbled, herringbone courtyard with fountain; ponds with koi and water fowl. American Air Force Exhibit. TEA. *Adm £1.50 OAPs £1 Chd 50p (Share to Five Parishes). Suns May 2, 30; June 13 (2-6)*

¶**Whalebone House** ᴋ⚘ (Mr & Mrs W Durlacher) Langham. N on A12 from Colchester, ignore sign to Langham and turn off to Stratford St Mary. 1st L into Dedham Rd, entrance ½m on L at end of thatched pink cottage. 3½-acre garden of well maintained mixed borders with wide variety of shrubs, perennials and trees. TEAS for charity. *Adm £1 Chd 50p. Suns April 25, July 11 (2-6)*

Glamorgan

See separate Welsh section beginning on page 274

Gloucestershire

Hon County Organisers:	Mr & Mrs Witold Wondrausch, The New Inn, Poulton, Cirencester GL7 5JE Tel 0285 850226
Assistant Hon County Organisers:	Guy Acloque Esq, Alderley Grange, Wotton-under-Edge GL12 7QT
	Mrs Barry Dare, Old Mill Dene, Blockley, Moreton-in-Marsh GL56 9HU
	Mrs Clive Davies, Applegarth, Alstone, nr Tewkesbury GL20 8JD
	Mrs Sally Gough, Trevi, Over Old Road, Hartpury GL19 3BJ
	A V Marlow Esq, Greenedge, 32 Dr Browns Road, Minchinhampton GL19 3BT
	Mrs Richard Pile, Ampney Knowle, nr Cirencester GL7 5ED
	Mrs Peregrine Pollen, Norton Hall, Mickleton, nr Chipping Campden GL55 6PU
Hon County Auditor:	H J Shave Esq, ACCA (Bradings) 31 Castle Street, Cirencester GL7 1QD

DATES OF OPENING

By appointment
For telephone numbers and other details see garden descriptions

Ampney Knowle, Barnsley
Beverston Castle, nr Tetbury
Blockley: The Old Bank, Paxton

House, Pear Trees
Bhardonna, nr Newent
Camp Cottage, Highleadon,
The Chipping Croft, Tetbury Gardens
Cirencester Gardens
Cotswold Farm, nr Cirencester
Ewen Manor, nr Cirencester
Gentian Cottage, Stow-on-the-Wold
Grove Cottage, Lower Lydbrook

Hodges Barn, Shipton Moyne
Hunts Court, North Nibley
8 Hyatts Way, Bishops Cleeve
Jasmine House, Bream, nr Lydney
Laurel Cottage, Brockweir Gardens
Lower Meend Gardens: Bank House
The Mill House, Blaisdon
Millend House, nr Coleford
The New Inn, Poulton

The Old Manor, Twyning
Old Mill Dene, Blockley
Orchard Cottage, Gretton
Redwood House, Halmore, Berkeley
The Red House, Staunton
Ryelands House, Taynton
Scrubditch Farm, North Cerney &
  Marsden Manor Gardens, nr
  Cirencester
St Francis, Minchinhampton Gardens
Sunningdale, nr Westbury-on-Severn
153 Thrupp Lane, nr Stroud
Tin Penny Cottage, Whiteway,
  Stroud
Westbury Court Garden
Willow Lodge, Longhope

Regular openings
For details see garden descriptions

Barnsley House, nr Cirencester.
  Mons, Weds, Thurs & Sats
Batsford Park, nr Moreton-in-Marsh.
  Daily March 1 to Oct 31
The Bell House,
  Westbury-on-Severn
Bourton House Garden,
  Bourton-on-the-Hill. Every Thurs &
  Fri May 27 to Sept 30 and June 27
Camp Cottage, Highleadon, nr
  Newent. Every Sun, Tues, Thurs
  April 4 to Sept 30
Cerney House: North Cerney
  Gardens. Every Wed & Sat all
  year
Grove Cottage, Lower Lydbrook,
  Cinderford. Every Sunday March
  7 to Sept 26 except May 9 & 16
Hodges Barn, Shipton Moyne, nr
  Tetbury. Every Mon, Tues & Fri
  April 1 to Aug 1
Lydney Park, Lydney. Every Sun,
  Wed & Bank Hol April 4 to June
  6. Every day May 31 to June 6
Misarden Park, nr Stroud. Every
  Tues, Wed & Thurs April 1 to
  Sept 30
The Old Manor, Twyning. Every Mon
  March 1 to Oct 31
Painswick Rococo Garden,
  Painswick. Every Wed to Sun Feb
  1 to mid-Dec and Bank Hol Mons
Rodmarton Manor, nr Cirencester.
  Sats May 15 to Aug 28
Selsley Herb Farm, nr Stroud.
  April 1 to Sept 30
Sezincote, nr Moreton-in-Marsh.
  Every Thurs, Fri & Bank Hol
  (except Dec)
Stanway House, Winchcombe. Tues
  & Thurs June to Aug
Sudeley Castle, Winchcombe. Daily
  April 1 to Oct 31

Tin Penny Cottage, Whiteway,
  Stroud. For dates see text
Trevi Garden, Hartpury. For dates
  see text

February
Every Wed
  Tin Penny Cottage, Whiteway,
  Stroud
February 4 Thursday
  Home Farm, Huntley, nr Newent
February 18 Thursday
  Home Farm, Huntley, nr Newent
February 21 Sunday
  The Mill House, Blaisdon
March
Every Sun from March 7
  Grove Cottage, Lower Lydbrook,
  Cinderford
Every Mon
  The Old Manor, Twyning
Every Wed
  Tin Penny Cottage, Whiteway,
  Stroud
March 4 Thursday
  Home Farm, Huntley, nr Newent
March 14 Sunday
  Minchinhampton Gardens
  153 Thrupp Lane, nr Stroud
March 18 Thursday
  Home Farm, Huntley, nr Newent
March 25 Thursday
  Trevi Garden, Hartpury
March 28 Sunday
  Brockweir Gardens, nr Chepstow
  Boilingwell, Sudeley Hill, nr
  Winchombe
  Painswick Rococo Garden
April
Every Sun
  Grove Cottage, Lower Lydbrook,
  Cinderford
Every Sun, Tues, Thurs
  Camp Cottage, Highleadon, nr
  Newent
Every Mon
  The Old Manor, Twyning
Every Wed
  Tin Penny Cottage, Whiteway,
  Stroud
Every Thurs
  The Bell House,
  Westbury-on-Severn
  Trevi Garden, Hartpury, nr
  Gloucester
April 1 Thursday
  Home Farm, Huntley, nr Newent
April 4 Sunday
  Ashley Gardens, nr Tetbury
  The Bell House,
  Westbury-on-Severn
  Minchinhampton Gardens
  Misarden Park, nr Stroud

Newark Park, nr
  Wotton-under-Edge
North Rye House, nr
  Moreton-in-Marsh
Ryelands House, Taynton, Newent
Westonbirt Gardens, Tetbury
April 11 Sunday
  The Bell House,
  Westbury-on-Severn
  Bhardonna, nr Newent ‡
  Hodges Barn, nr Tetbury
  Jasmine House, Bream, nr Lydney
  The Old Rectory, Todenham, nr
  Moreton
  Pinbury Park, nr Cirencester
  Redwood House, Halmore,
  Berkeley
  Ryelands House, Taynton,
  Newent ‡
  Willersey House, nr Broadway
  Yew Tree Cottage, Ampney St
  Mary, nr Cirencester
April 12 Monday
  Ashley Manor, Ashley Gardens, nr
  Tetbury
  The Bell House,
  Westbury-on-Severn
  Bhardonna, nr Newent ‡
  Boilingwell, Sudeley Hill, nr
  Winchcombe
  Camp Cottage, Highleadon, nr
  Newent
  Jasmine House, Bream, nr Lydney
  Redwood House, Halmore,
  Berkeley
  Ryelands House, Taynton,
  Newent ‡
  Tin Penny Cottage, Whiteway,
  Stroud
  Willersey House, nr Broadway
April 15 Thursday
  Home Farm, Huntley, nr Newent
April 17 Saturday
  The New Inn, Poulton
  Selsley Herb Farm, nr Stroud
April 18 Sunday
  Beverston Castle, nr Tetbury
  Lydney Park, Lydney
  Malt House Cottage, Icomb, nr
  Stow
  The Mill House, Blaisdon ‡
  Old Mill Dene, Blockley
  Osborne House, Frocester, nr
  Stonehouse
  Ryelands House, Taynton,
  Newent ‡
April 19 Monday
  Beverston Castle, nr Tetbury
April 24 Saturday
  Sudeley Castle, Winchcombe
April 25 Sunday
  Abbotswood, Stow-on-the-Wold
  The Bell House,
  Westbury-on-Severn

Brockweir Gardens, nr
Chepstow
Ryelands House, Taynton, nr
Newent
Stanway House, Winchombe
Tetbury Gardens, The Chipping
Croft
Tin Penny Cottage, Whiteway,
Stroud

April 29 Thursday
Home Farm, Huntley, nr Newent
Jasmine House, Bream, nr Lydney

May
Every Sun, Tues, Thurs
Camp Cottage, Highleadon, nr
Newent ‡
Every Mon
The Old Manor, Twyning
Every Wed
Tin Penny Cottage, Whiteway,
Stroud
Every Thurs
The Bell House,
Westbury-on-Severn
Trevi Garden, Hartpury, nr
Gloucester ‡

May 1 Saturday
Barnsley House, nr
Circencester

May 2 Sunday
Ampney Knowle
The Bell House,
Westbury-on-Severn
Blockley Gardens,
Moreton-in-Marsh
Eastcombe, Bussage and
Brownshill Gardens
Green Cottage, Lydney ‡
Grove Cottage, Lower Lydbrook,
Cinderford
Hodges Barn, nr Tetbury
Jasmine House, Bream, nr
Lydney ‡
Nympsfield Gardens, nr
Nailsworth
Ryelands House, Taynton,
Newent ‡‡
Trevi Garden, Hartpury, nr
Gloucester ‡‡

May 3 Monday
The Bell House,
Westbury-on-Severn ‡
Boilingwell, Sudeley Hill, nr
Winchombe
Camp Cottage, Highleadon, nr
Newent ‡‡
Eastcombe, Bussage and
Brownshill Gardens
Jasmine House, Bream, nr
Lydney ‡
Ryelands House, Taynton,
Newent ‡‡
Tin Penny Cottage, Whiteway,
Stroud

May 5 Wednesday
Lydney Park, Lydney
May 9 Sunday
Abbotswood, Stow-on-the-Wold
Batsford Park, nr
Moreton-in-Marsh
Green Cottage, Lydney
Hidcote Manor Garden, nr
Chipping Campden
The Manor, Boddington
Redwood House, Halmore,
Berkeley
Snowshill Manor, nr Broadway

May 13 Thursday
Home Farm, Huntley, nr Newent
Jasmine House, Bream, nr Lydney

May 15 Saturday
Burnt Norton, nr Chipping
Campden ‡
Hartpury College, nr Gloucester
Kiftsgate Court, nr Chipping
Campden ‡
The New Inn, Poulton

May 16 Sunday
The Bell House,
Westbury-on-Severn ‡
Burnt Norton, nr Chipping
Campden
Chalford Gardens, nr Stroud
Gentian Cottage, Fosse Lane,
Stow
Green Cottage, Lydney ‡
Jasmine House, Bream, nr
Lydney ‡
Lindors Country House, St
Briavels, nr Lydney ‡
Millend House, nr Coleford ‡
Priors Mesne Cottage,
Aylburton ‡
Tin Penny Cottage, Whiteway,
Stroud

May 22 Saturday
Selsley Herb Farm, nr Stroud

May 23 Sunday
The Bell House,
Westbury-on-Severn ‡
Chalford Gardens, nr Stroud ‡‡
Ewen Manor, nr Cirencester
Green Cottage, Lydney ‡
Grove Cottage, Lower Lydbrook,
Cinderford ‡
Lower Meend Gardens ‡
153 Thrupp Lane, nr Stroud ‡‡
Upper Cam Gardens, nr
Dursley
Yew Tree Cottage, Ampney St
Mary, nr Cirencester

May 25 Tuesday
153 Thrupp Lane, nr Stroud

May 27 Thursday
Bourton House,
Bourton-on-the-Hill
Home Farm, Huntley, nr Newent
Jasmine House, Bream, nr Lydney

May 30 Sunday
The Bell House,
Westbury-on-Severn
Bourton House,
Bourton-on-the-Hill ‡
Bourton-on-the-Hill Gardens ‡
Brockweir Gardens, nr
Chepstow ‡‡
Eastington Gardens, nr
Northleach
Gentian Cottage, Fosse Lane,
Stow
Green Cottage, Lydney ‡‡
Grove Cottage, Upper Lydbrook
Cinderford ‡
Hodges Barn, nr Tetbury
Jasmine House, Bream, nr
Lydney ‡‡
Millend House, nr
Coleford ‡‡
Nympsfield Gardens, nr
Nailsworth
The Red House, Staunton, nr
Gloucester
Ryelands House, Taynton,
Newent ‡‡‡
Sunningdale, Grange Court, nr
Westbury ‡‡‡
Willow Lodge, Longhope, nr
Gloucester ‡‡‡

May 31 Monday
The Bell House,
Westbury-on-Severn ‡‡
Brackenbury, Coombe,
Wotton-under-Edge
Camp Cottage, Highleadon, nr
Newent ‡‡
Eastington Gardens, nr
Northleach
Jasmine House, Bream, nr
Lydney ‡
Millend House, nr Coleford ‡
Ryelands House, Taynton, nr
Newent ‡‡
Sunningdale, Grange Court, nr
Westbury ‡‡
Tin Penny Cottage, Whiteway,
Stroud
Willow Lodge, Longhope, nr
Gloucester ‡‡

June
Every Sun
Grove Cottage, Lower Lydbrook,
Cinderford
Every Sun, Tues, Thurs
Camp Cottage, Highleadon, nr
Newent
Every Mon
The Old Manor Twyning
Every Wed
Tin Penny Cottage, Whiteway,
Stroud
Every Thurs
The Bell House,

Westbury-on-Severn
Trevi Garden, Hartpury, nr
Gloucester
June 2 Wednesday
Green Cottage, Lydney
June 3 Thursday
The Old Bank: Blockley Gardens
June 5 Saturday
Barnsley House, nr Circencester
Blundells, Broadwell, nr Stow
Yew Tree House, Twyning,
Tewkesbury
June 6 Sunday
Blundells, Broadwell, nr Stow
Boilingwell, Sudeley Hill, nr
Winchombe
The Chestnuts, nr
Minchinhampton
Cirencester Gardens: Little Tulsa,
38 Cecily Hill
Green Cottage, Lydney
Kemble Gardens, nr Cirencester
North Cerney & Marsden Manor
Gardens
Stanway House, Winchombe
Sunningdale, Grange Court, nr
Westbury
Tetbury Gardens
Yew Tree House, Twyning,
Tewkesbury
June 9 Wednesday
Green Cottage, Lydney
June 10 Thursday
The Old Bank: Blockley Gardens
Jasmine House, Bream, nr Lydney
June 12 Saturday
Rodmarton Manor, nr Cirencester
June 13 Sunday
The Bell House,
Westbury-on-Severn ‡‡‡
Cirencester Gardens: 38 Cecily
Hill
Frampton-on-Severn Gardens
Green Cottage, Lydney ‡
Hunts Court, North Nibley,
Dursley ‡‡
Jasmine House, Bream, nr
Lydney ‡
Malt House Cottage, Icomb
Pitt Court, North Nibley ‡‡
Poulton Gardens, nr Cirencester
The Red House, Staunton, nr
Gloucester
Redwood House, Halmore,
Berkeley
Stancombe Park, Dursley
Sunningdale, Grange Court, nr
Westbury ‡‡‡
Willow Lodge, Longhope, nr
Gloucester ‡‡‡
June 16 Wednesday
Pitt Court, North Nibley
June 17 Thursday
The Old Bank: Blockley Gardens

June 19 Saturday
Kiftsgate Court, nr Chipping
Campden
June 20 Sunday
Adlestrop Gardens, nr Stow ‡‡
Alderley Grange, nr
Wotton-under-Edge ‡
Cirencester Gardens: 38 Cecily
Hill
Cotswold Farm, nr Cirencester
Green Cottage, Lydney ‡‡‡
Hodges Barn, nr Tetbury
Hunts Court, North Nibley ‡
Millend House, nr Coleford ‡‡‡
North Rye House, nr
Moreton-in-Marsh ‡‡
Pitt Court, North Nibley ‡
Rookwoods, Waterlane, nr Bisley
Sunningdale, Grange Court, nr
Westbury ‡‡‡
Tin Penny Cottage, Whiteway,
Stroud
Willow Lodge, Longhope, nr
Gloucester ‡‡‡
Witcombe Gardens, nr Gloucester
June 24 Thursday
The Old Bank: Blockley Gardens
Bourton House, Bourton-on-the-Hill
Jasmine House, Bream, nr Lydney
June 26 Saturday
Selsley Herb Farm, nr Stroud
June 27 Sunday
The Bell House,
Westbury-on-Severn ‡‡‡
Blockley Gardens,
Moreton-in-Marsh
Brackenbury, Coombe,
Wotton-under-Edge ‡
Brockweir Gardens, nr
Chepstow ‡‡
Cirencester Gardens: 38 Cecily
Hill, 20 St Peters Rd
Green Cottage, Lydney ‡‡
Hunts Court, North Nibley ‡
Jasmine House, Bream, nr
Lydney ‡
Stanton Gardens, nr Broadway
Stowell Park, nr Northleach
Sunningdale, Grange Court, nr
Westbury ‡‡‡
Willow Lodge, Longhope, nr
Gloucester
June 30 Wednesday
Daylesford House, nr
Stow-on-the-Wold
July
Every Sun
Grove Cottage, Lower Lydbrook,
Cinderford
Every Sun, Tues, Thurs
Camp Cottage, Highleadon, nr
Newent
Every Mon
The Old Manor, Twyning

Every Wed
Tin Penny Cottage, Whiteway,
Stroud
July 1 Thursday
Trevi Garden, Hartpury, nr
Gloucester
July 4 Sunday
Beverston Castle, nr Tetbury
Boilingwell, Sudeley Hill, nr
Winchombe
Cirencester Gardens: 38 Cecily
Hill
Combend Manor, Elkstone, nr
Cheltenham
Hunts Court, North Nibley
Misarden Park, nr Stroud
Upton Wold, nr Moreton-in-Marsh
Willersey House, nr Broadway
July 5 Monday
Beverston Castle, nr Tetbury
Willersey House, nr Broadway
July 8 Thursday
Jasmine House, Bream, nr Lydney
July 11 Sunday
Broad Campden Gardens, nr
Chipping Campden
Casa Mia, Clifford Manor, nr
Newent
Cirencester Gardens
Hunts Court, North Nibley
Jasmine House, Bream, nr Lydney
Oxwold House, nr Barnsley
Quenington Gardens, nr Fairford
The Red House, Staunton, nr
Gloucester
Redwood House, Halmore, Berkeley
Sezincote, nr Moreton-in-Marsh
Sunningdale, Grange Court, nr
Westbury
Willow Lodge, Longhope, nr
Gloucester
July 15 Thursday
Trevi Garden, Hartpury, nr
Gloucester
July 17 Saturday
The New Inn, Poulton
July 18 Sunday
Campden House, Chipping
Campden
Casa Mia, Clifford Manor, nr
Newent ‡
Cirencester Gardens: 38 Cecily
Hill
The Mill House, Blaisdon ‡
Millend House, nr Coleford
Tin Penny Cottage, Whiteway,
Stroud
Willow Lodge, Longhope, nr
Gloucester ‡
July 22 Thursday
Casa Mia, Clifford Manor, nr
Newent
Jasmine House, Bream, nr
Lydney

July 24 Saturday
Burnt Norton nr Chipping
Campden
Selsley Herb Farm, nr Stroud

July 25 Sunday
Bhardonna, nr Newent ‡
Brackenbury, Coombe,
Wotton-under-Edge
Brockweir Gardens, nr
Chepstow ‡‡
Burnt Norton, nr Chipping
Campden
Casa Mia, Clifford Manor, nr
Newent ‡
Cirencester Gardens: 38 & 40
Cecily Hill
Icomb Place, nr
Stow-on-the-Wold
Jasmine House, Bream, nr
Lydney ‡‡
Sunningdale, Grange Court, nr
Westbury ‡
Willow Lodge, Longhope, nr
Gloucester ‡

July 29 Thursday
Bourton House,
Bourton-on-the-Hill

August
Every Sun
Grove Cottage, Lower Lydbrook,
Cinderford
Every Sun, Tues, Thurs
Camp Cottage, Highleadon, nr
Newent
Every Mon
The Old Manor, Twyning
Every Wed
Tin Penny Cottage, Whiteway,
Stroud

August 1 Sunday
Boilingwell, Sudeley Hill, nr
Winchombe
Cirencester Gardens: 38 Cecily
Hill
Minchinhampton Gardens
Trevi Garden, Hartpury, nr
Gloucester

August 2 Monday
Minchinhampton Gardens

August 5 Thursday
Jasmine House, Bream, nr Lydney
Trevi Garden, Hartpury, nr
Gloucester

August 8 Sunday
Cirencester Gardens: 38 Cecily
Hill
Jasmine House, Bream, nr Lydney
Redwood House, Halmore,
Berkeley

Sunningdale, Grange Court, nr
Westbury ‡
Willow Lodge, Longhope, nr
Gloucester ‡

August 14 Saturday
The New Inn, Poulton

August 15 Sunday
Millend House, nr Coleford
Tin Penny Cottage, Whiteway,
Stroud
Westonbirt Gardens, Tetbury
Willow Lodge, Longhope, nr
Gloucester

August 19 Thursday
Trevi Garden, Hartpury, nr
Gloucester

August 21 Saturday
Kiftsgate Court, nr Chipping
Campden
Selsley Herb Farm, nr Stroud

August 26 Thursday
Bourton House,
Bourton-on-the-Hill
Jasmine House, Bream, nr
Lydney

August 29 Sunday
Brockweir Gardens, nr
Chepstow ‡‡
Bourton House,
Bourton-on-the-Hill ‡
Bourton-on-the-Hill Gardens ‡
Eastington Gardens, nr
Northleach
Jasmine House, Bream, nr
Lydney ‡‡
Sunningdale, Grange Court, nr
Westbury ‡‡

August 30 Monday
Camp Cottage, Highleadon, nr
Newent
Eastington Gardens, nr Northleach
Jasmine House, Bream, nr
Lydney ‡
Sunningdale, Grange Court, nr
Westbury ‡
Tin Penny Cottage, Whiteway,
Stroud

September
Every Sun
Grove Cottage, Lower Lydbrook,
Cinderford
Every Sun, Tues, Thurs
Camp Cottage, Highleadon, nr
Newent
Every Mon
The Old Manor, Twyning
Every Wed
Tin Penny Cottage, Whiteway,
Stroud

September 2 Thursday
Trevi Garden, Hartpury, nr
Gloucester

September 5 Sunday
Boilingwell, Sudeley Hill, nr
Winchcombe
Green Cottage, Lydney ‡
Westbury Court Garden,
Westbury-on-Severn ‡
Westonbirt Gardens, Tetbury

September 9 Thursday
Jasmine House, Bream, nr Lydney

September 11 Saturday
Sudeley Castle, Winchcombe

September 12 Sunday
Green Cottage, Lydney ‡
Jasmine House, Bream, nr
Lydney ‡
Redwood House, Halmore,
Berkeley

September 16 Thursday
Trevi Garden, Hartpury, nr
Gloucester

September 18 Saturday
Selsley Herb Farm, nr Stroud

September 19 Sunday
The Bell House,
Westbury-on-Severn

September 20, 21, 22, 23, 24 & 25
The Bell House,
Westbury-on-Severn

September 26 Sunday
The Bell House,
Westbury-on-Severn
Brockweir Gardens, nr
Chepstow
Tin Penny Cottage, Whiteway,
Stroud

September 30 Thursday
Bourton House,
Bourton-on-the-Hill

October
Every Mon
The Old Manor, Twyning
Every Wed
Tin Penny Cottage, Whiteway,
Stroud

October 3 Sunday
Boilingwell, Sudeley Hill, nr
Winchcombe

October 10 Sunday
Painswick Rococo Garden,
Painswick

November, December 1993 January, February 1994
Every Wed
Tin Penny Cottage, Whiteway,
Stroud

DESCRIPTIONS OF GARDENS

Abbotswood (Dikler Farming Co) 1m W of Stow-on-the-Wold, nr Lower Swell. Beautiful, extensive heather and stream gardens; massed plantings of spring bulbs and flowers; rhododendrons, flowering shrubs, specimen trees; extensive herbaceous borders, roses, formal gardens; fine example of garden landscape. Buses not allowed in grounds. TEAS. Car park free. *Adm £1.50 Chd free. Suns April 25, May 9 (1.30-6)*

Adlestrop Gardens ❀ 3m E of Stow-on-the-Wold, off A436. A delightful small village made famous by Jane Austen and the poet Edward Thomas. A variety of gardens will be on show. Produce and plant stalls in aid of Church Fabric Fund. TEAS partly in aid of village hall. *Adm £1 Chd free. Sun June 20 (2-6)*

Alderley Grange &✿ (Mr Guy & the Hon Mrs Acloque) Alderley, 2m S of Wotton-under-Edge. Turn NW off A46, Bath-Stroud rd, at Dunkirk (2m equidistant Hawkesbury Upton and Wotton-under-Edge). Walled garden with fine trees, roses; herb gardens and aromatic plants. Featured in The Garden, RHS 1991 and TV 'Gardeners World' 1992. *Adm £1.50 Chd free. Sun June 20 (2-6). Parties by appt during June*

Ampney Knowle ❀ (Mr & Mrs Richard Pile) nr Cirencester. 4m NE Cirencester A433/B4425 ¼m S of Barnsley on Ampney Crucis road. Medium-sized garden planted since 1970 with terrace; mixed borders and old shrub roses. Woodland garden with indigenous wild flowers and 40-acre bluebell wood. Picnic site. *Adm £1.50 Chd free. Sun May 2 (12-6). Also by appt* **Tel 0285 740230**

Ashley Gardens 3m NE of Tetbury on A433, turn R through Culkerton to Ashley. *Combined adm £1.50 Chd free (Share to Ashley Church). Sun April 4 (2-6)* **Ashley Manor** *also open April 12 Adm £1.00 Chd free*
    Ashley Grange &✿ (Miss A L Pearson) Old garden of one-time Georgian/Victorian rectory with fine landscape views. Shrubs and herbaceous borders. Sensitively redesigned since 1971 for easier upkeep
    Ashley Manor ✿❀ (Mr & Mrs M J Hoskins) Old garden altered since 1982 with pond garden; mature yew hedges, collection of clematis, climbing and shrub roses, herbaceous border; terrace of herbs; kitchen garden. Typical Cotswold pigeon house and tithe barn. Manor house C15 and early C18 (not open)

Barnsley House &✿❀ (Mrs Rosemary Verey) Barnsley 4m. NE of Cirencester on A433/B4425. Mature garden with interesting collection of shrubs and trees; ground cover; herbaceous borders; pond garden; laburnum walk; knot and herb gardens; formal kitchen garden; C18 summer houses. C17 house (not open). *Adm £2 OAPs £1 Chd free (no charge Dec-Feb). Mons, Weds, Thurs & Sats (10-6). Parties by appt only* **Tel 0285 740281**. *For NGS Sats May 1, June 5 (2-6)*

By Appointment Gardens. These owners do not have a fixed opening day usually because they do not like crowds or have insufficient parking space. Owner will often give guided tour.

Batsford Park ❀ (The Batsford Foundation) 2m NW of Moreton-in-Marsh, A44/A429 intersection. Nearest bus & train Moreton-in-Marsh. Arboretum & wild garden; over 1000 named trees (many rare) and shrubs; magnolias, flowering cherries, bulbs; beautiful views from Cotswold escarpment. House not open. TEAS at Garden Centre open all year round (10-5) Arboretum. *Adm £2 Chd/OAPs and parties £1.50. March 1 to Oct 31 daily (10-5). For NGS Sun May 9 (2-5)*

The Bell House &✿❀ (Mr & Mrs G J Linklater) Westbury-on-Severn. 9m SW of Gloucester close to A48 in village next to Westbury Court Gardens (NT). Painter's garden on dramatic, S-facing, 2 acre site next to unusual church with view to R Severn and Newnham. Fan-shaped garden designed by Jefferies of Cirencester in 1940s with terraces, sweeping lawns and mature trees, many exotic. Long mixed borders, naturalised bulbs, fritillarias, heather and azalea beds. Water gardens with enormous slabs of forest stone. Featured in TV 'Gardeners World' 1991. Permanent exhibition of water colours. Special exhibition of paintings and garden history in Sept. Unusual herbaceous plants incl pentsemons, chimney pots and other artefacts for sale. Morning coffee and TEAS (Suns & Bank Hol Mons only). *Adm £1 Chd 50p (Share to Westbury Church 'Fix the Clock Fund' and Parish Hall Fund). Every Thurs April to June (2-6) Suns April 4, 11, 25, May 2, 16, 23, 30, June 13, 27 (10.30-6) Sept 19 to 26 incl (2-6) Bank Hol Mons April 12, May 3, 31 (10.30-6). Parties by appt* **Tel 0452 760388**

Beverston Castle &✿ (Mrs L Rook) Beverston. 2m W of Tetbury on A4135. Overlooked by romantic C12-15 castle ruin the overflowingly planted paved terrace leads from C17 house across moat to sloping lawn with spring bulbs in abundance and full herbaceous and shrub borders. Large walled kitchen garden and greenhouses. TEA (April 18) TEAS (July 4). Plants for sale July. *Adm £1 Chd 50p (Share to Beverston Church Restoration Fund). Suns, Mons, April 18, 19; July 4, 5 (2-6). Also by written appt all year*

Bhardonna &✿ (Mr & Mrs G W Webb) Ledbury Rd. 1m N of Newent on Ledbury-Dymock road B4215. Landscaped garden of 1½ acres still being developed; shrubs; spring bulbs; borders; fish ponds; collection of horse ploughs. TEA. *Adm 80p Chd free. Sun, Mon April 11, 12, Sun July 25 (2-6). Also by appt May 1 to Sept 30* **Tel 0531 822169**

Blockley Gardens ✿❀ NW of Moreton-in-Marsh. A44 Moreton-Broadway; turning E. TEAS. *Combined Adm £2 or 50p per garden Chd free (Share to Blockley Sports Club Appeal). Suns May 2, June 27 (2-6)*
    Broughton Cottage (Mr & Mrs R A Smeeton) Small garden on steep slope overlooking village
    Elm Barns (Sir Thomas & Lady Skyrme) Shrubs; lawns; pool; beautiful views
    The Garage (Mr & Mrs Stuart-Turner) Unusual garden making the best of a difficult slope; varied plantings
    Grange Cottage (Mrs J Moore) Small garden with unusual plants
    Laggan Cottage (Mr A Corrie) ½-acre sloping garden; mainly shrubs with herbaceous border; fruit trees and lily pond. *Open only May 2*

The Old Bank (Mr & Mrs P de Witt Barton) Small, terraced garden on hillside; courtyard, rock garden, shrubs, roses, clematis and view. Featured in Amateur Gardening May 92. *Also open Thurs June 3, 10, 17, 24 (10-4). Also by appt* Tel **0386 700271**

Old Mill Dene (Mr & Mrs B S Dare) 2½-acre garden with terraced slopes and mill pool, not safe for small children. *Also open Sun April 18 (2-6). Also by appt* Tel **0386 700457**

The Old Mill (Dr J Shackleton Bailey) Garden with millpond, stream, bulbs, flowers and shrubs. *Open only May 2*

The Old Quarry (Mr & Mrs A T Hesmondhalgh) 1-acre landscaped garden in old quarry with grass walks & lovely views

Paxton House (Mr & Mrs Peter Cator) Walled garden on different levels; unusual plants, spring bulbs, shrub roses. *Also by appt* Tel **0386 700213**

Pear Trees (Mrs J Beckwith) Small secluded, walled cottage garden with unusual plants. *Open only June 27. Also open by appt* Tel **0386 700464**

¶**Rodneys** (Mr & Mrs T Q Abell) Newly designed formal walled garden. *May 2 only*

Blundells ⬥❀ (Mr & Mrs Joe Elliott) Broadwell 1m N of Stow-on-the-Wold off A429. Medium-sized garden with large variety of hardy plants and alpines, trees, shrubs, herbaceous borders, roses, lilies, 25 plus old stone sinks and troughs planted with alpines. TEAS. *Adm £1 Chd free (Share to GRBS). Sat, Sun June 5, 6 (2-6)*

Boilingwell ❀ (Canon & Mrs R W Miles) Sudeley 1½m SE of Winchcombe. Take Castle St. out of Winchcombe, or Rushley Lane on Broadway road (signed Guiting Power); ¼m up hill beyond Sudeley Castle North Lodge. 1½-acre garden; a plantsman's paradise richly planted for year round colour and easy maintenance. TEAS. *Adm £1 Chd free (Share to Stanley Pontlarge Church). Suns March 28, June 6, July 4, Aug 1, Sept 5, Oct 3; Bank Hol Mons April 12, May 3 (2-6)*

Bourton House Garden ✄ (Mr & Mrs R Paice) Bourton-on-the-Hill 2m W of Moreton-in-Marsh on A44. When did you last see Graptopetalum paraguayense, Adlumia fungosa and Malus aleta. There is an exciting collection of tender and hardy plants used in a creative and inventive way in colour borders, pots and containers. The evolving 3-acre garden is set round a fine C18 house (not open) and a C16 tithe barn where you can help yourself to tea. *Adm £2 Chd free. Every Thurs & Fri May 27 to Sept 30 & Sun June 27 (12-5). For NGS last Thurs of every month. Also Bank Hol Suns May 30, Aug 29 (1-6) in conjunction with* **Bourton-on-the-Hill Gardens**

Bourton-on-the-Hill Gardens ✄❀ 2m NW Moreton-in-Marsh A44 to Broadway. Wide selection of gardens. Plant stall. TEAS (2-5). *Gardens adm £2.50 (including* **Bourton House** *as above) Chd free (Share to village Old School). Suns May 30, Aug 29 (1-6)*

The Chantry (Mr & Mrs J Coram-James) Large lawns with mixed borders – excellent views

3 Chantry Gardens (Mr & Mrs G Glaser) Small well planned garden with pond

Glebe House (Sir Peter & Lady Herbert) Ex rectory garden. Mixed borders. Views

Hillcrest (Mr & Mrs M Gaden) Small garden, mixed borders

Porch House (Mr & Mrs A Firth) Established terraced garden next to Churchyard

Springwood (Mr & Mrs D Storey) Cottage garden. Mixed borders

Tawnies (Mr & Mrs P Hayes) Raised beds with ericaceous plants. Long lawn

Brackenbury ❀ (Mr & Mrs Peter Heaton) Coombe, 1m NE of Wotton-under-Edge. From Wotton Church ½m on Stroud rd (B4058) turn right (signed Coombe); from Stroud left off B4058, 300yds past Wotton-under-Edge sign; house 300yds on right. ⅔-acre terraced plantsman's and flower arranger's garden; foliage a special feature. Well-maintained mixed borders, cottage garden, pool; 450 different hardy perennials and 130 different shrubs. Fruitcage, vegetables on deep-bed system. Still evolving; National Collection of Erigeron cultivars. Featured in L'Ami des Jardins 1991. Home-made TEAS. *Adm £1 Chd free (Share to Cotswold Care Hospice). Mon May 31, Suns June 27, July 25 (2-6)*

Broad Campden Gardens ⬥✄❀ 5m E of Broadway 1m SE of Chipping Campden. TEAS at Village Hall. *Combined adm £2 or 50p each garden Chd free. Sun July 11 (2-6). Free car park. Coaches by appt only* Tel **0386 840467**

The Angel House (Mr & Mrs Bill Boddington) Garden in old damson and apple orchard, with view of church and C17 and C18 cottages

Briar Hill House (Mr & Mrs Geoffrey Ellerton) Shrubs, roses, heathers and conifers

Cherry Orchard Cottage (Mr & Mrs David Brook) ¾-acre orchard, shrub bank and secret garden

The Farthings (Mr & Mrs John Astbury) Terraced cottage garden

The Malt House (Mr & Mrs Nick Brown) Sheltered garden with small stream, being gradually replanted with shrubs from herbaceous for simplified management

Manor Barn (Mr Michael Miles & Mr Christopher Gurney) 1½-acres. Formal terraces, sweeping cultivated meadow, newly planted woodland and shrubbery, boundary of wandering stream with falls

Norman Chapel (Mr & Mrs Alistair Voaden) 3 acres; trees, shrubs, herbaceous borders, water garden and stream

Old Stones (Mr & Mrs H R Rolfe) A new ¾-acre garden, started 1989. Designed and constructed with the exception of the stone walling by the owners; terraced garden leading down to a stream with lawns, shrubs and roses

Pinders (Mr & Mrs Ian Dunnett) 1-acre garden on several levels, rare shrubs and trees

Sharcomb Furlong (Mr & Mrs Basil Hasberry) ¾-acre; wide range of shrubs, shrub roses and trees

¶**Vine Cottage** (J M Murray) Small cottage garden in idyllic situation. Large selection of roses and herbaceous around a well and lawn

Withy Bank (Mr & Mrs Jim Allen) ½-acre; acers and shrubs

Regular Openers. See head of county section.

¶**Brockweir Gardens** ✗❀ From A466 Chepstow to Monmouth rd, cross R Wye to Brockweir, ¾m uphill take L turning to Coldharbour, L at Xrds. 2m Tintern Abbey. Car park at Laurel Cottage only. TEAS at Laurel Cottage & Fernleigh. *Adm 75p each garden. Suns March 28, April 25, May 30, June 27, July 25, Aug 29, Sept 26 (2-6)*

¶**Fernleigh** (Capt & Mrs J P Gould) Approach on foot from Laurel Cottage. 2½ acres of well established garden situated at an altitude of 500'. Many old trees, camellias and spring bulb collection. A peaceful garden with splendid views across the valley of the R Wye. *Suns March 28, April 25, May 30, Sept 26 only*

Laurel Cottage ৬ (David & Jean Taylor) Informal 1-acre cottage garden with lovely view over Offa's Dyke path. Interesting selection of unusual shrubs and plants. Stone walling, sloping lawn, herbaceous flowers, spring bulbs, small vegetable garden and mini arboretum. *Also by appt* **Tel 0291 689565**

¶**Threeways** (Mr & Mrs Iorwerth Williams) Follow signs from A466 Brockweir Bridge or from B4228 at Hewelsfield Xrds: also on foot from Laurel Cottage. 2-acre garden developed since 1984. Former paddock planted with unusual shrubs and trees. Small woodland area, bog garden and stream. Formal area with water feature and herbaceous borders

Burnt Norton ৬❀ (Earl of Harrowby) 1½m N of Chipping Campden on rd to Mickleton; L into farm lane as rd goes downhill; then through wood for ½m. 16 acres; part formal but mostly wooded garden on Cotswold escarpment. Subject of T.S. Elliot's 'Burnt Norton' quartet. House (not open). TEAS. *Adm £1 Chd free (Share to GRBS, MSS Trust). Sats, Suns May 15, 16; July 24, 25 (2-6)*

Camp Cottage ৬✗❀ (L R Holmes Esq & S O'Neill Esq) Highleadon, nr Newent. 6m NW of Gloucester. From Glos take A40 Ross rd, turn R onto B4215 Newent rd, 2½m along turn R at sign for Upleadon. The cottage is about 100yds up lane on L hand side. A plant lovers C17 cottage garden. ¾-acre approx. Old roses, pergola with arches, climbing plants, many unusual plants including alpines, shrubs, perennials, herbs. Short shrubland walk. Featured on TV 'Gardeners' World' 1990. TEA. *Adm £1 Chd 25p. Suns, Tues & Thurs April 4 to Sept 30. Bank Hol Mons April 12, May 3, 31; Aug 30 (2-6). Also by appt all year* **Tel 0452 790352**

Campden House ৬❀ (Mr & Mrs Philip Smith) Chipping Campden. Drive entrance on Chipping Campden to Weston Subedge rd, about ¼m SW of Campden. 2-acre garden with mixed borders; fine parkland; Manor house with C17 tithe barn in hidden valley. TEAS and plant stall (in aid of the Gloucestershire Macmillan Nurses). *Adm £1 Chd free. Sun July 18 (2-6)*

Casa Mia ৬❀ (Mr & Mrs Bryan Jones) Clifford Manor, Judges Lane. Off B4216 Newent to Huntley rd approx 2½m from Newent turn R signposted May Hill. Garden is on L about ¾m. Enthusiast's 1½-acre garden in lovely setting; mixed herbaceous and shrub borders; mature trees; stream and vegetable garden. TEAS. *Adm 80p Chd free. Suns July 11, 18, 25; Thurs 22 (2-6). Groups by appt July only* **Tel 0452 830404**

¶**Chalford Gardens** ✗ 4m E of Stroud on A419 to Cirencester. Both gardens on Marle Hill high above the Chalford Vale are reached on foot by steep climb from car park on main rd. *Combined adm £1.50 Chd free. Suns May 16, 23 (11-6)*

¶**Brendan House** (Anthony J Ault) Approx 1-acre garden on steep hillside, partly terraced with attractive views to the S and W. Mature trees, ponds

¶**The Old Chapel** (F J & F Owen) Artist's 1-acre Victorian chapel garden on precipitous hillside. A tiered tapestry of herbaceous borders, formal potager, orchard, pond and summer house, old roses. Gothic pergola and rose tunnel, many unusual plants all laid out on terraced S-facing Marle Cliff. Small exhibition of limited edition prints of flowers and gardens in the conservatory

The Chestnuts ✗❀ (Mr & Mrs E H Gwynn) Minchinhampton. From Nailsworth by Avening rd (B4014) L Weighbridge Inn ¼m up hill. From Minchinhampton 1m via New Rd or Well Hill. ⅔-acre walled garden; shrubs; bulbs; roses; clematis; rock garden; pool garden. ⅔-acre arboretum, planted since 1972 with wide variety of unusual trees and shrubs inc many sorbus species and shrub roses. Lovely views of hills, woods and fields. *Adm £1 Chd free (Share to Gloucestershire Wildlife Trust). Sun June 6 (2-6)*

The Chipping Croft – See Tetbury Gardens

Cirencester Gardens. Cecily Hill is on W side of Cirencester near gates into Park and open air swimming pool

Little Tulsa, 38 Cecily Hill ❀ (Fr & Mrs John Beck) Walled garden on two levels packed with 500 different perennials. Featured in many books and on Central TV, Sept 92. Last chance to see this garden before owners move. *Adm 90p Suns June 6, 13, 20, 27; July 4 (2-5). Adm £2 July 11 (2-6). Adm 90p July 18 (2-5.30). Adm £1.20 July 25 (2-5.30). Adm 90p Aug 1, 8 (2-5.30). Chd under 16 free. Also by appt June to mid Aug* **Tel 0285 653778**

40 Cecily Hill. Exhibition of botanical pictures and china by Annette Firth, NDD, SBA. *Suns July 11 (2-6), 25 (2-5.30)*

¶**42 Cecily Hill** (Mr & Mrs Philip Beckerlegge) Medium-sized family garden with good walls. Clematis, roses, herbaceous border; shrubs, rock garden. *Sun July 11 only (2-6)*

Cecily Hill House (Mr & Mrs Rupert de Zoete) Walled town garden with tranquil atmosphere; herbaceous and shrub borders; small ornamental kitchen garden. TEAS by WI. *Sun July 11 only (2-6). Also by appt mid June to July 31* **Tel 0285 653766**

20 St Peter's Road ❀ (Meg and Jeff Blumsom) Off Cricklade St. turn R into Ashcroft Rd then L then R. Small town garden entirely remade without grass; herbaceous, clematis, rockery, pond. Featured in The Gardener, May 91. *Adm 50p Chd free. Suns June 27, July 11 (2-6). Also by appt* **Tel 0285 657696**

By Appointment Gardens. Avoid the crowds. Good chance of a tour by owner. See garden description for telephone number.

Combend Manor ⚭❀ (Mr & Mrs Noel Gibbs) Elkstone. On A417 N of Cirencester turn R signed Elkstone immediately R through pillars 1m on R. 3-acre mature garden in beautiful setting, partly laid out by Gertrude Jekyll; a variety of gardens within the main garden incl arboretum; water garden; old-fashioned roses, heather garden. TEAS. *Adm £1.50 OAP/Chd £1.00 (Share to Elkstone Parish Church). Sun July 4 (2-6)*

Cotswold Farm ⚭ (Major & Mrs P D Birchall) 5m N of Cirencester on A417; signed immediately W of Five Mile House Inn. Cotswold garden in lovely position on different levels with a terrace designed by Norman Jewson in 1938; shrubs, mixed borders, alpine border, spring flowers, shrub roses; walled kitchen garden. *Adm £1.50 Chd free. Sun June 20 (2-6). Also by appt May, June and July* Tel 0285 653856

¶**Daylesford House** ⚭ (Sir Anthony & Lady Bamford) Daylesford. Between Stow-on-the-Wold and Chipping Norton. R turn to village of Daylesford off A436. Through the village to main gate for Daylesford House. Country house walled kitchen garden in the making (since 1990). Orchid house, peach house, working glasshouses. Unusual vegetables, rose terrace, old-fashioned roses, trellis arbours, nuttery, winter garden. Pleasure grounds around Grade I house not open. *Adm £1.50 Chd free (Share to Daylesford Church). Wed June 30 (2-6)*

Eastcombe, Bussage & Brownshill Gardens 3m E Stroud. 2m N of A419 Stroud to Cirencester on turning signposted to Bisley and Eastcombe. Cream TEAS at Eastcombe Village Hall. *Combined adm £2, Chd free (Share to Glos Macmillan Nurses Appeal). Sun, Mon, May 2, 3 (2-6)*
    Eastcombe:
    Ashcroft (Mr & Mrs H T Cornell) Dr Crouch's Rd. Small garden with many bulbs, primulas and year-round colour
    Brewers Cottage ⚭ (Mr & Mrs T G N Carter) Easily managed hillside garden with laburnum covered pergola, shady & sunny borders and a small hidden courtyard. All year colour
    21 Farmcote Close ⚭❀ (Mr & Mrs R Bryant) A housing estate garden, designed with curved beds to soften appearance. Over 300 varieties of interesting perennials, bulbs, shrubs and old roses on various colour themes. Espalier fruit
    Fidges Hill House (Mr & Mrs R Lewis) From building site with knee high weeds to cottage garden in 6 years; secluded and lovely view. No car access, please park in village
    Glenview (Mr & Mrs J Carroll) Dr Crouch's Road. 4-yr-old garden; colour scheme of yellow, blue and white with two exceptions; a 'hot' section is planned
    ¶**Jasmine Cottage** (Mr & Mrs K Hopkins) Colourful cottage garden with view of the beautiful Toadsmoor valley
    Vatch Rise ⚭❀ (Mr & Mrs R G Abbott) Small garden with beautiful view. Extensive and interesting collection of bulbous plants, alpines and unusual perennials

Brownshill:
    Bovey End (Sir Norman & Lady Wakefield) Brownshill. A large, informal garden sloping steeply with beautiful views across the Golden and Toadsmoor Valleys; many trees and shrubs
Bussage:
    ¶**Pine Corner** (Mr & Mrs W Burns-Brown) ¾-acre terraced garden overlooking Toadsmoor Valley. Spring bulbs, shrubs, alpines; kitchen & herb garden
    Redwood ❀ (Mr & Mrs D Collins) Terraced garden with informal lawns and planting; trees; shrubs; bulbs; alpines and vegetable garden with cordon fruit trees
    Spindrift, The Ridge ⚭ (Mr & Mrs B Wilson) Small garden on housing estate devoted largely to plant breeding experiments including a white foxglove mutation

Eastington Gardens 1m SE of Northleach (A40). Charming Cotswold village with lovely views. TEAS at **Middle End**. *Combined adm £1.50 Chd free (Share to Northleach Church). Suns, Mons May 30, 31; Aug 29, 30 (2-6)*
    Bank Cottage (Mr & Mrs E S Holland) Lower End. Colourful cottage garden
    Middle End ❀ (Mr & Mrs Owen Slatter) Medium-sized garden of general interest
    Yew Tree Cottage (M Bottone Esq) Cottage garden with shade-loving plants

Ewen Manor ⚭⚭ (Lady Gibbs) 4m S of Cirencester via A429 3m from Cirencester turn at signpost Ewen 1m. Medium-sized garden; herbaceous border, lily pool, sunken garden, cedar trees, yew hedges, Georgian Cotswold manor (not open). *Adm £1 Chd free. Sun May 23. Also by appt* Tel 0285 770206

Frampton-on-Severn Gardens ⚭ SW of Gloucester nr Stonehouse 2m from M5 junction 13. TEAS in Village Hall in aid of WI. *Adm 60p per garden Chd free (Share to Gloucestershire Wildlife Trust and International League for Protection of Horses and NCCPG, Glos). Sun June 13 (2-6)*
    Buckholt (Brigadier & Mrs C E H Sparrow) 200yds beyond the S end of the village green on the L. Walled garden of about 1-acre, mature trees, shrubs and herbaceous borders, lavender garden with roses
    Frampton Court (Mrs P F S Clifford) L hand side of village green. Fine view of Gothic orangery, 1760, standing at the end of a formal canal with water lilies and mixed shrub border on one side. Mature trees. *Open to groups by appt* Tel 0452 740267
    Frampton Manor (Mr & Mrs Rollo Clifford) R hand side of village green. Fragrant walled garden with yew and lavender hedges. Mixed shrub and herbaceous borders. C15 timbered house, reputed birthplace of 'Fair Rosamund'. *Open to groups by appt*

Gentian Cottage ⚭❀ (Mrs J D Lefeaux) Stow-on-the-Wold. From Bourton on A429 continue N over both sets of traffic lights in Stow - 100yds after second lights turn L into Fosse Lane. Small garden partly replanted during the last few years. Shrubs, bulbs, herbaceous borders — rock plants a speciality, including gentians. *Adm 50p Chd free (Share to Moreton-in-Marsh Hospital League of Friends). Suns May 16, 30 (2-6). Also by appt May to July* Tel 0451 830322

Green Cottage ＆襟 (Mr & Mrs F Baber) At far end of Lydney on A48 Gloucester-Chepstow road turn R up narrow lane immediately after derestriction sign. Garden 50 yds on R. Unsuitable for coaches; will take a minibus. An informal country garden of approx 1 acre with planted stream bank, hostas, iris and cottage garden. Many herbaceous paeonies, incl the National Reference Collection of pre and early post 1900 cultivars (1824-1918). Large wayward specimen of clematis montana 'Rubens' (May). Specie and officinalis paeonies (May). National Collection and other cultivars (June). TEAS Suns only. *Adm £1 Chd 20p. Suns May 2, 9, 16, 23, 30; June 6, 13, 20, 27; Sept 5, 12 (2-6); Weds June 2, 9 (11-5)*

¶**Grove Cottage** 襟襟 (Mr Graham Birkin & Mr Allan Thomas) Forge Hill, Lower Lydbrook. 5m NW of Cinderford. Leave car in public car park, mount facing flight of 104 steps to Forge Hill: garden 2nd L from top step. 2-acre garden on precipitous slope overlooking Wye valley. Many steps and steep paths to negotiate but a garden full of unusual plants and bulbs. Peat beds, pond, bog gardens, raised beds and ¼-acre rockery with many little known alpines. Extensive collection of iris. Not suitable for small children. TEA. *Adm £1 Chd 50p. Every Sun March 7 to Sept 26 (not May 9 and 16) (2-6). Also by appt* Tel 0594 860544

Hartpury College ＆襟襟 Hartpury House, 5m N of Gloucester. Take A4l7 Gloucester-Ledbury; clearly signposted. 14 acres; large lawns; trees, shrubs and terraces; glasshouses; kitchen garden; alpine beds; late Victorian ornamental gardens designed by Thomas Mawrson. TEAS. *Adm £1 Chd free. Sat May 15 (2-5)*

Hidcote Manor Garden ＆襟襟 (The National Trust) 4m NE of Chipping Campden. Series of formal gardens, many enclosed within superb hedges, incl hornbeam on stems. Many rare trees, shrubs, plants. Coffee, lunches and teas. *Adm £4.40 Chd £2.20. Daily except Tues & Fri, April to Oct 31 (11-7); no entry after 6 or an hour before dusk if earlier). For NGS Sun May 9 (11-7); no adm after 6*

Hodges Barn ＆襟 (Mr & Mrs C N Hornby) Shipton Moyne 3m S of Tetbury on Malmesbury side of Shipton Moyne. Very unusual C15 dovecot converted into a family home 55 yrs ago. Cotswold stone walls act as host to climbing and rambling roses, clematis, vines and hydrangeas; and together with yew, rose and tapestry hedges they create the formality of the area around the house; mixed shrub and herbaceous borders, shrub roses and a water garden; woodland garden planted with cherries, magnolias and spring bulbs. Featured in Country Life & House & Garden. Also open; adjoining garden of **Hodges Farmhouse**, by kind permission of Mr & Mrs Clive Lamb. *Combined adm £1.50 Chd free. Mons, Tues & Fris April 1 to Aug 1 (2-5). For NGS Suns Apr 11, May 2, 30 June 20 (2-6). Also by appt: parties welcome, teas by arrangement* Tel 0666 880202

¶**Home Farm** (Mrs T Freeman) Huntley. On the B4216 ½m from the A40 in Huntley travelling towards Newent. The house and gardens are in an elevated position with exceptional views over the Vale of Gloucester and up to the Cotswold escarpment. Over 1m of woodchip paths winding through woods to show carpets of spring flowers. Snowdrops, wood anemones, daffodils, bluebells and orchids. Enclosed garden with heather bed and fern border. One wood recently planted with rhododendrons and azaleas. *Adm £1 Chd free. Thurs Feb 4, 18, March 4, 18, April 1, 15, 29, May 13, 27 (2-dusk)*

Hunts Court ＆襟襟 (Mr & Mrs T K Marshall) North Nibley, Dursley. 2m NW of Wotton-under-Edge. From Wotton B4060 Dursley rd turn R in Nibley at Black Horse; fork L after ¼m. Recently extended 2½-acre garden with unusual shrubs, 400 varieties old roses, herbaceous, and heather beds and lawns set against tree clad hills and Tyndale monument. House (not open) probably birth place of William Tyndale. Picnic area. Home-made TEAS (Suns only) in aid of St Martin's Church. *Adm £1 Chd free. Garden and Nursery open Tues-Sat all year ex Aug; also Bank Hol Mons. For NGS Suns June 13, 20, 27; July 4, 11 (2-6); also by appt* Tel 0453 547440

8 Hyatts Way 襟襟 (Mr & Mrs P M Herbert and Paul Herbert) Bishops Cleeve, 4m N of Cheltenham; take A435 towards Evesham, at roundabout take road to Bishops Cleeve; at Bishops Cleeve turn R past Esso Garage, follow road to school, turn L, then 2nd R. Small plantsman's garden, slightly untidy but featuring over 500 varieties, inc digitalis and salvia species; many other unusual plants and alpines in sinks. *Adm 70p Chd 25p. By appt only April 11 to Aug 8* Tel 0242 673503

Icomb Place 襟 (Mr & Mrs T L F Royle) 4m S of Stow-on-the-Wold; after 2m on A424 Burford rd turn L to Icomb village. 100-year-old sizeable garden extensively restored. Featuring woodland walk through mature & young trees in arboretum; rhododendrons & azaleas; grotto; pools, stream and water garden; parterre; lawned garden with extensive views. C14 manor house (not open). TEAS. *Adm £1.50 Chd 75p (Share to Care Trust). Sun July 25 (2-6)*

Jasmine House ＆襟襟 (V M Bond Esq) Bream. In picturesque Royal Forest of Dean. From Lydney take B4231 Bream rd; in 3 miles turn R to village; immediately after Xrds turn R into concealed lane Blue Rock Crescent opp. school; house 200yds on L. Plantsman's garden of ¾ acre; alpines, fuchsias, bonsai, old-fashioned cottage plants, wild flowers, 2 small ponds, vegetables; many unusual plants. *Adm 75p Chd free. Suns April 11, May 2, 16, 30; June 13, 27; July 11, 25; Aug 8, 29; Sept 12. Bank Hol Mons April 12, May 3, 31; Aug 30, Thurs April 29, May 13, 27, June 10, 24; July 8, 22; Aug 5, 26, Sept 9 (2-6); also by appt all the year. Garden clubs especially welcome* Tel 0594 563688

Kemble Gardens 4m SW of Cirencester on A429 to Malmesbury. TEAS by WI Kemble House. *Combined adm £1.50 Chd free. Sun June 6 (2-6)*

  Kemble House ＆襟 (Mrs Donald Peachey) Large, mature, old-fashioned garden makes a lovely setting for Teas. Garden recovering from neglect following recent ill health

  3 Kemble Park ＆襟 (Mr & Mrs Douglas Milbank) Medium-sized landscaped garden adjacent to converted C18 coachhouse in a charming setting of wood and parkland; lawns; rose beds; herbaceous borders; rockery; shrubs and mature trees

Limes Cottage (Mrs M Brazier) Small walled garden; mixed planting shrubs and herbaceous; shrub roses; troughs; small pond

¶**Old Orchard** (Mr & Mrs J K Johnston) A cottage style garden with herbaceous and shrub areas; roses and clematis; pond and alpines

Kiftsgate Court ✿✿ (Mr & Mrs J G Chambers) 3m NE of Chipping Campden, adjacent to Hidcote Nat Trust Garden. 1m E of A46 and B4081. Magnificent situation and views; many unusual plants and shrubs; tree paeonies, hydrangeas, abutilons, species and old-fashioned roses, inc largest rose in England, R.filipes Kiftsgate. TEAS (May 30 to Aug 31). Buses by appt. *Adm £2.50 Chd £1. Suns, Weds, Thurs & Bank Hols April 1 to Sept 30. Also Sats in June & July (2-6). For NGS (Share to Sue Ryder Home, Leckhampton Court) Sats May 15; June 19, Aug 21 (2-6)*

Lindors Country House ♿✿ (Rosemary Aspinall) St Briavels off B4228 4 miles SW of Coleford & 7 miles W of Lydney. Mature gardens laid out over 100 yrs ago; meandering streams with steps; waterfalls and ponds descend to River Wye; 9-acre tranquil grounds with many non-native trees, shrubs and fine views of Wye Valley. Cream TEAS in marquee. *Adm £1.50 Chd free. Sun May 16 (2-6)*

Lower Meend Gardens ✿✿ 5m NW Lydney nr St Briavels, ½m from St Briavels Castle down B4228 to hairpin bend. Walk of 200 yds from car parking. No coaches. TEA **Brook Cottage** in aid of Cobalt Unit, Cheltenham. *Combined adm £1.50 Chd free. Sun May 23 (11-5)*

Bank House (Mr & Mrs W J Neale) Terraced hillside garden intensively planted with shrubs, herbaceous and alpine plants, troughs. Approx ¼-acre. Rare breed of sheep. Magnificent views of Wye Valley. *By appt June to Sept* Tel 0594 530433

Brook Cottage (Mr & Mrs P Mills) Sloping landscaped gardens with small parterre and other interesting features

¶**The Hampden** (Phillip & Doreen Powell-Tuck) About 1½ acres of wild garden and shrubs, including azaleas and rhododendrons; paddock with ornamental trees

Lydney Park ✿ (Viscount Bledisloe) Lydney. On A48 Gloucester-Chepstow rd between Lydney & Aylburton. Drive is directly off A48. 8 acres of extensive valley garden with many varieties of rhododendron, azaleas and other flowering shrubs; trees and lakes. Garden round house; magnolias and daffodils (April). Roman Temple Site and Museum. Deer park with fine trees. TEAS; also picnic area (in park). *Adm £1.50 Weds £1 (Acc chd & cars free). Easter Sun & Mon; Every Sun, Wed & Bank Hol from Sun April 4 to June 6, but every day Sunday May 31 to June 6 (11-6). For NGS Sun April 18, Wed May 5 (11-6). Also parties by appt* Tel 0594 842844

Malt House Cottage ♿✿ (Mr & Mrs T W Jenkins) Icomb. 3½m S of Stow-on-the-Wold, after 2½m turn L off A424. ½-acre cottage garden in picturesque village. Spring bulbs; shrubs; herbaceous borders; water garden and rockery. TEA. *Adm 80p Chd free. Suns April 18, June 13 (11-6)*

The Manor ♿✿ (Robert Hitchins Ltd) Boddington 3m W of Cheltenham off the A4019 Cheltenham to Tewkesbury rd. After crossing the M5 motorway take first turning L which is signed to Boddington. The Manor is 400 yds on the left along the lane. Old garden altered and restored since 1985 including wild flower woodland walk, mature specimen trees, extensive lawns and lakes with recently planted pineteum and bog garden. Neo-Gothic Manor House (not open). TEAS. *Adm £1 Chd free. Sun May 9 (2-6)*

The Mill House ✿✿ (Mr & Mrs John Chappell) Blaisdon. 10m W of Gloucester, between Huntley on A40 and Westbury-on-Severn on A48. 1-acre garden on gently sloping south-facing site. Special interests include plants associated with the county; large collection of unusual snowdrops and spring flowering plants in old Mill Race. Cottage style herbaceous borders. Featured on TV in 'Gardeners World'. *Adm £1 Chd free (Share to St Michael and All Angels Church, Blaisdon). Suns Feb 21 (12-4) April 18, July 18 (2-6). Also by appt all year, parties welcome* Tel 0452 830522

Millend House ✿✿ (Mr & Mrs J D'A Tremlett) Coleford. 1½m SW out of Coleford on the Newland road, centre of Coleford signposted (Newland 2m). 2-acre hillside garden with picturesque valley views; many varied & interesting herbaceous and shade-loving plants & shrubs. Paths to secluded seating places & through well-maintained wood. Also small vegetable garden & gazebo. TEAS (except on May 30, 31) in aid of Imperial Cancer Research. *Adm £1 Chd free. Suns May 16, 30; Mon May 31; Suns June 20, July 18, Aug 15 (2-6). Groups welcome by appt May 1 to Sept 30*

Minchinhampton Gardens ♿✿✿ Minchinhampton 4m SE Stroud. From Market Sq down High St 100yds; then right at Xrds; 300yds turn left. Free car parking. Over 8 acres of adjacent gardens. Cream TEAS. *Combined adm £1.50 Chd free (Share to Minchinhampton Centre for the Elderly). Suns March 14, April 4, Aug 1, Mon Aug 2 (2-6)*

Derhams House (Mr & Mrs Mark Byng) Garden created since 1957; water garden; shrubs, herbaceous borders; snowdrops and crocus in March

Lammas Park (Mr & Mrs P Grover) Lawns, herbaceous borders, wild garden, restored 'hanging gardens'. Superb views

St Francis (Mr & Mrs Peter Falconer) Garden made in old park round modern Cotswold stone house. Fine beech avenue; terraced garden; trough gardens; bonsai trees; unusual plants; giant snowdrops (spring); C18 ice-house. Picnickers welcome. *Also by appt* Tel 0453 882188

Misarden Park ♿✿✿ (Maj & Mrs M T N H Wills) 7m NE of Stroud. Spring flowers, shrubs, fine topiary (some designed by Edwin Lutyens) and herbaceous borders within a walled garden; roses (recently refurbished); fine specimen trees; C17 manor house (not open) standing high overlooking Golden Valley. Garden featured in 'Country Life' Spring Gardens issue 1992. Garcen Nurseries (under new management). TEAS in aid of Miserden PTA. *Adm £1.50 Chd free. April 1 to Sept 30 every Tues, Wed & Thurs (9.30-4.30). For NGS (Share to St Andrew's Church) Suns April 4, July 4 (2-6)*

The New Inn (Witold & Heather Wondrausch) Poulton. 5m E of Cirencester on A417 opp sign to Quenington (A433). An idiosyncratic collection of plants in ⅔ acre.; spring bulbs, cottagey flowers, climbing plants; wild garden with pond; vegetable patch *Adm £1 Chd free. Sats April 17, May 15, July 17, Aug 14. Also by appt* **Tel 0285 850226**

Newark Park & (Robert Parsons Esq) Ozleworth, 1½m E of Wotton-under-Edge, 1½m S of junc A4135/B4058. Steeply terraced romantic woodland garden in 10 acres around C16 hunting lodge (not open). Spring bulbs and cyclamen on hillside leading down to carp pond and C18 walled garden and summer house. Garden under restoration. Spectacular views. TEAS. *Adm £1 Chd 50p (Share to the Arthritis and Rheumatism Council). Sun April 4 (2-5)*

North Cerney & Marsden Manor Gardens North Cerney, with famous C13 church, 4m N Cirencester on A435 Cheltenham road. **Cerney House** behind church: **Scrubditch Farm** on Woodmancote-Perrots Brook Lane. Woodland walk between the two gardens. **Marsden Manor** on A435 midway between Cirencester and Cheltenham. 1m N of Rendcomb. Entrance just after deer crossing sign. *Combined adm £1.50 Chd £1. Sun June 6 (2-6)*
> **Cerney House** ✗ (Sir Michael & Lady Angus) Large mature garden with trees, shrubs, lawns, old roses, spring bulbs. Herb & rock gardens. Walled garden with herbaceous borders and vegetables. TEAS. *Also open all year every Wed and Sat (2-6)*
> **Scrubditch Farm** &✿ (Mr & Mrs J Herdman) 2-acre informal garden evolved over 30 years from an orchard. Old roses, many interesting trees and shrubs. TEAS. *Also by appt* **Tel 0285 831309**
> ¶**Marsden Manor** ✿ (Mr & Mrs Richard Worsley) A series of characterful gardens and growing areas. Mature herbaceous borders, elevated rose bed; fish pond, large variety of shrubs and trees. Dogs may be walked in scenic woodland grounds along the R. Churn

¶**North Rye House** &✿ (Mr & Mrs Peter Stoddart) Moreton-in-Marsh. On A429 Foss Way halfway between Moreton-in-Marsh and Stow-on-the-Wold. Also signed from Broadwell village. Recently created and still developing 1-acre garden with modern ha-ha designed to blend scenically into its surrounding parkland setting with mature trees. Spring bulbs, mixed borders, shrub roses, alpines and small vegetable garden provide continuous colour and interest. TEAS. *Adm £1 Chd free. Suns April 4, June 20 (2-5)*

Nympsfield Gardens ✗✿ 3m NW of Nailsworth. Signed from B4066 Stroud-Dursley rd. TEAS **Coach House** (May 30). *Combined adm £1.50 Chd free (Share to Nympsfield Village Hall). Suns May 2, 30 (2-6)*
> **Barberi Cottage** ✿ (Mrs F Mack) Small garden with alpines. *May 2, 30*
> **Bath Road Farm** (Mr & Mrs K Wright) Windswept cottage garden under construction; interesting wild plants, pond, vegetables. *May 2, 30*
> **Candle Cottage** (Mr & Mrs A N Pearce) Small landscaped cottage garden. *May 2, 30*
> **The Coach House** (Mr & Mrs R Overton) Small tree-lined garden. Unusual plants all labelled. *May 30 only*

Four Wells (Mr J Price) Small cottage garden. *May 2, 30*
Highlands (Mr & Mrs R Easton) Garden on sloping windswept site. *May 2, 30*
Pen-y-Banc (Mr & Mrs C Ward) adjoining above garden. *May 2, 30*
The Post Office (Mr & Mrs B Westwood) Small garden featuring heathers & violas. *May 2, 30*
White Hart Court (Mr & Mrs M Reynolds) Small formal garden with pool. C 16 Coach House (part open). *May 2, 30*

The Old Manor &✗✿ (Mrs Joan Wilder) Twyning. 3m N of Tewkesbury via A38 to Worcester; follow sign to Twyning; garden opposite T-junction at top end of village. 2 acres, walled garden full of interest. Unusual shrubs, trees, herbaceous, alpines; two areas of developing arboretum; pool; terrace plantings; troughs. Field walks for picnics. Featured in TV 'Gardeners World'. Small nursery, all stock from garden (catalogue 30p and large SAE). TEAS by WI on Bank Hol Mons only. *Adm £1.30 Chd 60p (Share to GRBS & RGOF). Every Mon Mar 1 to Oct 31 (2-5, or dusk if earlier) other days except Suns by appt* **Tel 0684 293516** *evenings*

Old Mill Dene, Blockley ✗✿ (Mr & Mrs B S Dare) School Lane, Blockley. From A44, Bourton-on-the-Hill, take the turn to Blockley. 1m down hill turn left behind 30mph sign, labelled cul de sac. 2½-acre garden with steep lawned terraces facing south and a mill-pool in a frost pocket with stream. Vegetable garden parterre with views over the hills. Dangerous for young children. TEAS. *Adm £1.50 Chd 50p (Share to Gloucestershire Churches Preservation Trust). Sun April 18 (2-6). Also open with* **Blockley Gardens** *Suns May 2, June 27 and by appt* **Tel 0386 700457**

The Old Rectory, Todenham &✿ (Lady Elizabeth Longman) 4m NE of Moreton-in-Marsh. Turn right off A429 at N end of Moreton to Todenham. 1-acre garden replanted and altered since 1980. Shrubs; trees; herbaceous borders; formal kitchen garden; conservatory; pond. TEAS in aid of Todenham Church. *Adm £1 Chd free. Sun April 11 (2-6)*

Orchard Cottage ✗✿ (Rory Stuart Esq) Gretton. 2 miles N of Winchcombe. Up Duglinch Lane beside Bugatti Inn in the middle of Gretton. Approx 400yds up lane turn R after Magnolia Grandiflora and opp black railings. Approx 1½-acres. Romantically overplanted, owner-maintained garden, created largely by the late Mrs Nancy Saunders. Always some interest; many unusual plants. Teas in Winchcombe. *Adm £1. Open all year. By appt only* **Tel 0242 602491**

¶**Osborne House** & (Mr & Mrs G L Atkinson-Willes) Frocester. 2m SW of Stonehouse (or 2m S of M5 junction 13) midway between Eastington and Frocester. 2 acres containing herbaceous and shrub borders, island beds; many spring bulbs; small arboretum planted since 1975 incl collection of birches; climbing plants on house and outbuilding walls. TEAS by WI. *Adm £1 Chd free. Sun April 18 (2-6)*

Oxwold House & (Mr & Mrs James D'Arcy Clark) Barnsley. 4m NE of Cirencester. From A433 Cirencester-Burford rd, on the outskirts of Barnsley, turn L signposted Coln Rogers. 3-acre garden surrounded by parkland with woodland walk; shrubs; trees; herbaceous borders; mature chestnut avenue approach and fine view. TEAS. *Adm £1.50 Chd free. Sun July 11 (2-6)*

Painswick Rococo Garden ✤ (Lord & Lady Dickinson) ½m outside village on B4073. Unique C18 garden restoration from the brief Rococo period combining contemporary buildings, vistas, ponds and winding woodland walks. Coach House restaurant for coffee, lunches, TEAS. 'Present Collection' shop. *Adm £2.40 OAP £2 Chd £1.20. Feb 1 to mid-December. Weds to Sundays and Bank Hol Mons (11-5). Groups by appt* **Tel 0452 813204.** *For NGS Suns March 28, Oct 10 (11-5)*

Pinbury Park & (Mr & Mrs John Mullings) Cirencester 6½m. Signed off Sapperton-Winstone rd between A419 and A417. 5-acres; topiary, yew avenue, lawns, bulbs, impressive view, gazebo. Tudor Manor house (not open) former Royal residence of King Penda. *Adm £1 Chd 50p. Sun April 11 (2-5)*

Pitt Court &✤✤ (Mr & Mrs M W Hall) North Nibley. Turn E off the B4060 at North Nibley past the Black Horse Inn into Barrs Lane. Continue for approx ¾m. A small garden of approx ⅓ acre, interesting use of 'hard' features; paving, dwarf walls, etc. variety of smaller trees, shrubs and herbaceous borders; conifers; lawn and alpine area. Very limited car parking. Teas at **Hunts Court** Suns only open nearby with plenty of parking (½m). *Adm 60p Chd free. Sun June 13, Wed June 16, Sun June 20 (2-6)*

Poulton Gardens &✤ 5m E of Cirencester on A417. Cream TEAS at **Poulton Manor**. *Combined adm £1.50 Chd free. Sun June 13 (2-6)*
   Almas Cottage (Mr & Mrs G Lavin) Tiny garden overflowing with traditional cottage plants
   The New Inn (Mr & Mrs Witold Wondrausch) An idiosyncratic collection of plants in ⅔-acre. *Also open Sats April 17, May 15, July 17, Aug 14. Also by appt* **Tel 0285 850226**
   The Old School (Mr & Mrs Derek Chalk) Small walled garden with interesting shrubs, clematis, roses, herbaceous plants
   Poulton Fields (Lord Wigram) 1m NE of Poulton village. Off Poulton-Bibury rd, between Betty's Grave Xrds and Sunhill Xrds. 2-acre garden within Cotswold walls and beech hedges; herbaceous border; roses and climbers; interesting young trees and shrubs; small vegetable garden. Dogs may be walked in carpark paddock
   Poulton House (Mr & Mrs Tom Boyd) 1½-acre Cotswold garden; herbaceous border, rose border, pond, shrubs, kitchen garden and specimen trees
   Poulton Manor (Mrs Anthony Sanford) 2 acres reconstructed for minimal maintenance; old yew hedges, hornbeam avenue, natural garden, trees, shrubs; walled kitchen garden. Charles II house (not open)
   Sarnia (Mr & Mrs W M Young) ½-acre garden with shrubs and perennials to give colour and interest throughout the year

Priors Mesne Cottage ✤ (Mr & Mrs T F Cox) Aylburton 4m S of Lydney. Take A48 towards Chepstow. In Aylburton take 1st right at The George, Church Rd. 2m up hill to junc, left at sign to Alvington and Woolaston, entrance 1st on right. Woodland walk to remains of romantic 2-acre wild garden with three pools, fine trees, azaleas, bamboos. Subject of book A Gloucestershire Wild Garden 1899 and featured in the film The Assam Garden. *Adm £1 Chd free. Sun May 16 (2-6)*

Quenington Gardens &✤✤ 2m N of Fairford, E of Cirencester. Peaceful riverside village with church renowned for Norman doorways. TEAS in aid of The Home Farm Trust at **The Old Rectory**. *Combined adm £2 Chd free. Sun July 11 (2-6)*
   ¶**Apple Tree Cottage** (Mrs P Butler-Henderson) Interesting small cottage garden protected by its own 'micro-climate' conservatory with unusual plants
   ¶**Court Farm** (Mr & Mrs Frank Gollins) Natural riverside landscape; part of historic grounds of Knights Hospitallers with dovecote, woodland walk and water garden
   ¶**26 The Green** (Miss Sandra Lawrence) Mass of summer flowers on raised bed and patio. Large rockery and pond
   Mallards (Mrs Joyce Roebuck) Summer flowers, large well-stocked fish pond, aquatics and walled vegetable garden
   The Old Rectory (Mr & Mrs David Abel-Smith) Picturesque and varied riverside garden with herbaceous border and wilderness; extensive organic vegetable garden
   Pool Hay (Mr & Mrs A W Morris) Small is beautiful. Picturesque riverside cottage garden
   Quenington House (Mr & Mrs Geoffrey Murray) Walled gardens, pergolas, old shrub roses, wide herbaceous borders. Lots of clematis, salvias and penstemons

The Red House &✤✤ (Mr & Mrs K Turner) Pillows Green, Staunton, 8m NW of Gloucester on A417; from Staunton Xrds ½m off B4208. Split level organic garden and ¾-acre wildlife garden with herbaceous borders; rockery and terrace with containers; also flower meadow C17 House (part open). Garden designed & maintained by owners. All plants for sale grown from garden stock. TEA. *Adm £1 Chd free (Share to Gloucestershire Wildlife Trust). Suns May 30, June 13, July 11 (2-6). Also by appt* **Tel 0452 840505**

¶**Redwood House** &✤✤ (Mr & Mrs Eric Sadler) Halmore. 2½m NE Berkeley and SW Slimbridge. Turn off A38 at The Prince of Wales and follow signs to Halmore. First R out of Halmore into Slimbridge Lane for ½m to garden on L handside of sharp bend. ⅓ acre. 600 different cottage garden perennials and herbs, all labelled; old roses, shrubs and trees planted for scent and wildlife. *Adm 80p Chd free. Sun, Mon, April 11, 12, Suns May 9, June 13, July 11, Aug 8, Sept 12 (2-6) also by appt all year* **Tel 0453 811421**

By Appointment Gardens. Avoid the crowds. Good chance of a tour by owner. See garden description for telephone number.

Rodmarton Manor &⚭✿ (Mr & Mrs Simon Biddulph) Cirencester. Between Cirencester and Tetbury off A433. House designed by Ernest Barnsley. Gardens laid out in the 1920's and made famous by Mary Biddulph during the 1960's-1980's. Eighteen separate areas of distinctive character and incl a wide range of plants, shrubs, topiary, hedging, alpine troughs and the well known herbaceous borders. New planting in progress. TEAS (June 12 only). *Adm £1.50 Chd free. Sats May 15 to Aug 28. Parties by appt only* Tel 0285 841253. *For NGS (Share to Rodmarton PCC) Sat June 12 (2-6)*

Rookwoods (Mr & Mrs R Luard) Waterlane, Oakridge, 5m E of Stroud, 7m W of Cirencester just N of A419. 1¼m SE of Bisley. 3-acre well structured garden with herbaceous borders to colour themes. Pleached Whitebeam around recently designed pool area. Wide variety of old-fashioned and modern climbing and shrub roses (labelled), water gardens and outstanding views. TEAS. *Adm £1 Chd free. Sun June 20 (2-6). Coaches by appt*

Ryelands House ✿ (Capt & Mrs Eldred Wilson) Taynton, 8m W of Gloucester. ½-way between Huntley (A40) and Newent (B4215) on B4216. Fascinating sunken garden, great variety of plants, many rare; trees, shrubs, bulbs, herbaceous borders, species and old roses; waterside plants, pools and herbs. Also unique, very popular woodland and country walk. Outstanding views and abundance of wild flowers; famed for wild daffodils. 2-acre lake in beautiful setting. Good selection plants always for sale. Dogs welcome on walk only. TEAS. *Adm £2 Chd free. Suns April 4, 11, 18, 25, May 2, 30; Mons April 12, May 3, 31 (2-6) also by appt for private parties in April and May* Tel 0452 790251

Selsley Herb Farm &✿ (Peter & Gillian Wimperis) Water Lane. 1½m S of Stroud on B4066 signed to Dursley. Narrow lane just past cattle grid onto Selsley Common. 2½ acres of fragrant garden created from a concrete farmyard and field in 1974 and still being developed; various formal and informal herb gardens, old-fashioned roses, collection of penstemons, bee and butterfly garden mainly planted with collection of buddleia, pond area. Shop and plant sales area. Featured on ITV, BBC TV, National Japanese TV and in many books. Cream TEAS on Sundays and NGS days in garden if sunny or in 400 yr old barn if wet. *Adm £1 Chd, OAP's 50p (Share to All Saints Church, Selsley). April 1 to Sept 30 (10-5 weekdays), (2-5 Suns). For NGS Sats April 17, May 22, June 26, July 24, Aug 21, Sept 18 (10-5)*

Sezincote ✗ (Mr & Mrs David Peake) 1½m SW of Moreton-in-Marsh. Turn W along A44 towards Evesham; after 1½m (just before Bourton-on-the-Hill) take turn left, by stone lodge with white gate. Exotic oriental water garden by Repton and Daniell with lake, pools and meandering stream, banked with massed perennial plants of interest. Large semi-circular orangery, formal Indian garden, fountain, temple and unusual trees of vast size in lawn and wooded park setting. House in Indian manner designed by Samuel Pepys Cockerell was insipiration for Brighton Pavilion. TEAS (July only). *Adm £2.50 Chd £1 under 5 free. Open every Thurs Fri & Bank Hols (except Dec) (2-6). For NGS Sun July 11 (2-6)*

Snowshill Manor ✗ (The National Trust) 3m SW of Broadway. Small terraced garden in which organic and natural methods only are used. Highlights include tranquil ponds, old roses, old-fashioned flowers and herbaceous borders rich in plants of special interest. House contains collections of fine craftmanship incl musical instruments, clocks, toys, bicycles. *Adm house & gdn £4 Chd £2. Family ticket £11. House & garden are open April & Oct Sats, Suns (11-1 & 2-5) Easter Sat to Mon open (11-1 & 2-6); May to end Sept Wed to Sun and Bank Hol Mon (11-1 & 2-6 or sunset if earlier). For NGS Sun May 9 (11-1 & 2-6)*

Stancombe Park &✿ (Mrs B S Barlow) Dursley. ½-way between Dursley and Wotton-under-Edge on B4060. Bus stop: 30yds from gates. 2 gardens; (1) around house. Herbaceous borders. Pleached limewalk. New tree and shrub planting; (2) a short walk along valley descending into the historic Folly Garden. Lake. Temple. Grotto. Tunnels. TEAS. *Adm £2 Chd free (Share to St Cyr Church, Stinchcombe). Sun June 13 (2-6)*

Stanton &✿ Nr Broadway. One of the most picturesque and unspoilt C17 Cotswold villages with many gardens (30 open in 1992) ranging from charming cottage to large formal gardens. Plant stall. Car park £1. TEAS from 3-5.30. *Adm £1.50 Chd free (Share to Stanton Village Church). Sun June 27 (2-6.30)*

Stanway House (Lord Neidpath) 1m E of B4632 Cheltenham-Broadway rd on B4077 Toddington to Stow-on-the-Wold rd. 20 acres of planted landscape in early C18 formal landscape setting. Arboretum, historic pleasure grounds with specimen trees inc pinetum; remains of ornamental canal and cascade; chestnut and oak avenue; folly; daffodils and roses in season. Striking C16 Manor with gatehouse, tithe barn and church. Tea at The Bakehouse, Stanway. *Adm gardens only £1 Chd 50p House and Gardens £2 Chd £1. Also house open Tues & Thurs June to Aug (2-5). For NGS (Share to Wemyss Memorial Hall, Stanway). Suns April 25, June 6 (2-5)*

Stowell Park ✗ (The Lord & Lady Vestey) 2m SW of Northleach. Off Fosseway A429. Large garden, lawned terraces with magnificent views over the Coln Valley. Fine collection of old-fashioned roses and herbaceous plants, with a pleached lime approach to the House. Two large walled gardens contain vegetables, fruit, cut flowers and ranges of greenhouses, also a long rose pergola and wide, plant-filled borders divided into colour sections. House (not open) originally C14 with later additions. TEAS. *Adm £1.50 Chd free (Share to Royal British Legion). Sun June 27 (2-6)*

Sudeley Castle &⚭✿ (Lord and Lady Ashcombe) Winchcombe. The gardens of historic C15 castle, home of Queen Katherine Parr. The Queen's Garden, with double yew hedges, has been replanted with old-fashioned roses, herbs and perennials. Richard III's Banqueting Hall is backdrop for romantic 'ruined' garden while the Tithe Barn displays an impressive collection of species roses. Also formal pools, extensive lawns with fine trees and spring bulbs; magnificent views. 'Sudeley Castle Roses'. Specialist plant centre, with old roses, topiary, herbs and other unusual plants. Restaurant. TEAS. *Garden adm £3.10 Chd £1.40. Open daily April 1 to Oct 31. For NGS Sats April 24, Sept 11 (11-5)*

Sunningdale & ✿✿ (J Mann Taylor Esq) Grange Court. 8m W of Gloucester, 2m NE of Westbury-on-Severn. Turn off A48 at Hunt Hill near Chaxhill. A ¾-acre garden with beds crammed full of choice plants from around the world. Pool and bog garden built into slope and large greenhouse with display beds full of pot plants and climbers. Extensive views across the countryside. The National Collection of Phlomis should be at its best in June. Plant catalogue for sale. Teas in Westbury. *Adm £1 Chd 50p. Sunningdale Season Ticket £2. Sun May 30, Mon 31; Suns June 6, 13, 20, 27, July 11, 25; Aug 8, 29; Mon Aug 30 (2-5). Also open by appointment* Tel 0452 760268

Tetbury Gardens, Tetbury. *Combined adm £1.50 Chd free. Sun June 6 (2-6).* The Chipping Croft. *Adm £1 Sun April 25 (2-6)*

> **The Chipping Croft** ✿ (Dr & Mrs P W Taylor) At bottom of Chipping Hill approached from market place. 2-acre, secluded, walled town garden on three levels, with mature trees, shrubs, herbaceous borders, rose beds and unusual plants; spring blossom and bulbs. A series of formal gardens, incl fruit and vegetables; also a water garden. C17 Cotswold house (not open). TEAS in aid of Action Research for the Crippled Child. *Adm £1 Chd free. Suns April 25, June 6 (2-6). Also by appt* Tel 0666 503178
>
> **The Old Stables** ✗ (Brigadier and Mrs J M Neilson) Enter New Church St B3124 from Long St at Xroads signed to Stroud and Dursley. Turn L at Fire station into Close Gardens. Small walled garden on two levels in old stable yard of a town house. Flowering shrubs; clematis; bonsai; water garden; paved area with alpines in troughs. *Sun June 6 (2-6)*

153 Thrupp Lane ✗✿ (Mr & Mrs D Davies) 1½m E of Stroud. Take A419, Thrupp Lane is on L 1m from Stroud, then ½m along Thrupp Lane. ⅓-acre on sloping site, full of interesting and unusual plants, rockeries, shrubs and ponds - all planted to encourage wild life. Good winter interest. TEAS. *Adm 50p Chd free. Suns March 14 May 23, Tues May 25 (2-6). Also by appt all year* Tel 0453 883580

Tin Penny Cottage ✗✿ (E S Horton) Whiteway, near Miserden, 6m NE Stroud between Birdlip & Stroud on B4070. At Fostons Ash Public House take rd signed Bisley then immediately L to Whiteway ½m; 300yd walk to garden. Enthusiast's medium-sized garden on cold clay. Designed to be visually attractive and grow a wide variety of hardy plants, many rare and unusual, and incl a collection of sempervivum. TEAS in Village Hall Bank Hol Mons and Suns April 25, Aug 15. *Adm £1. Chd free. Weds all year. Bank Hol Mons April 12, May 3, 31, Aug 30. Suns April 25, May 16, June 20, July 18, Aug 15, Sept 26 (2-6) and by appt all year* Tel 0285 821482

Trevi Garden &✿ (Gilbert & Sally Gough) Hartpury 5m NW of Gloucester via A417. In village sharp back right into Over Old Road before War Memorial. 1 acre of gardens within a garden; winding water garden; laburnum/clematis walk, shrubberies, herbaceous borders, collection of hardy geraniums; all year round interest. Garden completely designed and maintained by owners. B & B. TEAS on Suns. *Adm £1 Chd free. Suns May 2; Aug 1 (2-6); also open Thurs March 25; April 1, 8, 15, 22, 29;* May 6, 13, 20, 27; June 3, 10, 17, 24; July 1, 15; Aug 5, 19; Sept 2, 16 (2-6); coaches/groups by appt on other dates Tel 0452 700370

Upper Cam Gardens ✗✿ 1m W of Dursley. Grouped around St George's Church. Upper Cam signposted from B4066. TEAS. *Combined adm £1 Chd free. Sun May 23 (2-6)*

> **Bell Courts** (Mr & Mrs E W V Acton) ¾-acre; shrubs, herbaceous plants and kitchen garden
>
> **Cleveland** (Mr & Mrs R Wilkinson) Small garden on windy site. Shrubs, herbaceous and unusual plants. Vegetable plot
>
> **17 Everlands** (T Edwards) Small new garden, bowl's green; ducks; R Cam flows through the garden
>
> **20a Everlands** (Mr & Mrs A A Pearce) Shrubs, herbaceous plants, rockery, kitchen garden
>
> **Lynwood, 20 Everlands** (Mr & Mrs D G Atkin) ½-acre garden, trees, shrubs, walled vegetable garden. Scree garden with alpines and conifers. Miniature railway for children
>
> **Noggins Hollow** (Mr & Mrs K Hall) Stream-side garden with new herbaceous beds, shrubs & vegetable garden
>
> ¶**16 Springhall** (Old Court) (Mr & Mrs J E Beebee) Mature garden with open aspect. Shrubs, herbaceous and rock plants, pond. Display of complementary stained glass
>
> **The Vicarage** (Rev Chris & Mrs Gill Malkinson) Walled autumn garden recently replanted; trees; shrubs and spring/summer rockery

Upton Wold ✗✿ (Mr & Mrs I R S Bond) 5m W of Moreton-in-Marsh, on A44 1m past A424 junction at Troopers Lodge Garage. Recently created garden architecturally and imaginatively laid out around C17 house with commanding views. Yew hedges; old shrub roses; herbaceous walk; some unusual plants and trees; vegetable garden; pond garden and woodland garden. Cream TEAS. *Adm £1 Chd free (Share to Chipping Norton Theatre Trust). Sun July 4 (10-6)*

Westbury Court Garden & (The National Trust) Westbury-on-Severn 9m SW of Gloucester on A48. Formal Dutch style water garden, earliest remaining in England; canals, summer house, walled garden; over 100 species of plants grown in England before 1700. *Adm £2 Chd £1. April to end Oct. Wed to Sun & Bank Hol Mon (11-6) Closed Good Fri. Other months by appt only. For NGS Sun Sept 5 (11-6)*

Westonbirt Gardens at Westonbirt School & 3m S of Tetbury. A433 Tetbury-Bristol. 22 acres. Formal Victorian Italian garden, terraced pleasure garden, rustic walks, lake recently redredged & stocked with carp. Rare, exotic trees and shrubs. Tea at Hare & Hounds Hotel, Westonbirt ½m, (to book for parties Tel 0666 88233). *Adm £1 Chd 25p. Suns April 4, Aug 15, Sept 5 (2-5.30)*

> **Regular Openers.** Too many days to include in diary. Usually there is a wide range of plants giving year-round interest. See head of county section for the name and garden description for times etc.

Willersey House (Maj-Gen & Mrs David Tabor) 1½m from Broadway on road to Stratford-on-Avon. In Willersey village take first R turn on sharp bend. Entrance 200yds up hill on right. Ornamental ponds; wide variety trees; shrubs, mixed borders surround lovely old Cotswold house. Special features: bulbs April, roses July. TEAS Sun pm only. *Adm £1 Chd 50p. Suns, Mons April 11, 12 (11-6); July 4, 5 (11-7)*

Willow Lodge &✿❀ (Mr & Mrs John H Wood) on A40 between May Hill & Longhope 10m W of Gloucester, 6m E of Ross-on-Wye. 1½-acre plantsman garden with great variety of unusual plants many rare incl shrubs, herbaceous borders, an alpine walk, stream and pool with water features, several greenhouses, vegetable garden; plants labelled, ample parking. Grounds extend to 4 acres with many wild flowers. TEAS. *Adm £1 Chd 20p. Sun & Mon May 30, 31, Suns June 13, 20, 27 July 11, 18, 25, Aug 8, 15 (2-6). Groups welcome. Also by appt* **Tel 0452 831211**

Witcombe Gardens &✿ 4m E of Gloucester on A417 turn R at 12 Bells Inn for Church Cottage and Witcombe Park; ½m on from inn turn L signed **Court Farm House**. TEAS **Witcombe Park**. *Combined adm £1.50 Chd free. Sun June 20 (2-6)*

    Church Cottage &❀ (Sir Christopher & Lady Lawson) Great Witcombe. 2 acres; typical cottage flowers; shrubs; stream and ponds. Soft drinks

Court Farm House &✿❀ (Mr & Mrs Andrew Hope) Little Witcombe. An informal family garden of 1 acre started 10 yrs ago from scratch. Shrubs, roses, herbaceous perennials and self-seeding annuals; wild garden, rock garden, herb garden, scree bed, play area; children welcome

Witcombe Park &✿ (Mrs W W Hicks Beach) Great Witcombe. Medium-sized garden; roses, flowering shrubs and sunken garden set in beautiful Cotswold scenery. (*Share to Gloucestershire Wildlife Trust*)

Yew Tree Cottage ✿❀ (Mrs B Shuker; Kim & Penny Pollit) Ampney St Mary. At E end of Ampney St Peter on A417 from Cirencester fork left at Red Lion, 1st L to Ampney St Mary, then 1st R in village. Medium-sized garden; variety of interesting plants throughout year inc alpines, bulbs, perennials, shrubs, clematis. TEAS (by WI). *Adm £1 Chd free. Suns April 11, May 23 (2-5)*

Yew Tree House &✿❀ (Mr & Mrs J R Bent) Twyning, nr Tewkesbury. Western edge of Twyning village on Brokeridge Common some 500 yds from M50 junction with A38. Approx 2½ acres. Trees, shrubs and water garden. A spring garden with some rare and unusual varieties; collection of new shrub roses. Adjacent to 10-acre naturalised woodland with water features. Free qualified horticultural advice given by Fellow of the Institute of Horticulture. Picnic area. TEAS. *Adm £1 Chd 50p. Sat, Sun June 5, 6 (2-6.30)*

Gwent & Gwynedd

See separate Welsh section beginning on page 274

Hampshire

Hon County Organiser: Mrs T H Faber, The Drove, West Tytherley, Salisbury SP5 1NX

Assistant Hon County Organisers: Mrs G E Coke, Jenkyn Place, Bentley, nr Farnham

Mrs A R Elkington, Little Court, Crawley nr Winchester SO21 2PU

Mrs R J Gould, Ewell House, 44 Belmore Lane, Lymington SO41 9NN

Mrs D Hart Dyke, Hambledon House, Hambledon PO7 4RU

J J Morris Esq, The Ricks, Rotherwick, Nr Basingstoke RG27 9BL

Mrs Miles Rivett-Carnac, Martyr Worthy Manor, nr Winchester SO21 1DY

M H Walford Esq, The White Cottage, Headbourne Worthy, nr Winchester SO23 7LA

Hon County Treasurer: M S Hoole Esq, c/o Lloyds Bank plc, 6 Market Place, Romsey SO51 8YS

DATES OF OPENING

By appointment

For telephone numbers and other details see garden descriptions

Abbey Cottage, Itchen Abbas
Bramdean House, Alresford
Brandy Mount House, Alresford
Broadhatch House, Bentley
Fairfield House, Hambledon
Greatham Mill, Greatham, nr Liss
The Hedges, East Wellow
Hambledon House, Hambledon
Hightown Farm, Ringwood
60, Lealand Road, Drayton
The Little Cottage, Lymington
Little Court, Crawley
Long Thatch, Warnford
The Manor House, Upton Grey
Marycourt, Odiham
Merdon Manor, Hursley
Rotherfield Park, East Tisted
Rowans Wood, Ampfield
Vernon Hill House, Bishop's Waltham
West Silchester Hall
White Windows, Longparish

Regular openings

For details see garden descriptions

Exbury Gardens, nr Southampton. Open daily Feb 27 to Oct 24
Furzey Gardens, Minstead. Daily except Dec 25 & Dec 26
Greatham Mill, Greatham, nr Liss. Suns & Bank Hols, April 11 to end of Sept
Highclere Castle, nr Newbury. Open Weds to Suns July, Aug, Sept. Easter & Bank Hols
Jenkyn Place, Bentley. Thurs to Suns & Bank Hol Mons, April 8 to Sept 12
Little Barn Garden, & Barnhawk Nursery, Woodgreen. April 2 to Oct 24
Lymore Valley Herbs, Milford-on-Sea. Open all year except Dec 25 to March 1
Macpenny Woodland Garden Nurseries, Bransgore. Daily except Dec 25, 26 & Jan 1
Petersfield Physic Garden. Daily except Dec 25 to Sept
Spinners, Boldre. Daily April 20 to Sept, closed Mons & Tues from July 1
Stratfield Saye House, Reading. Open daily (except Fri) May 1 to last Sun in Sept

March 21 Sunday
Bramdean House, Alresford ‡
Brandy Mount House, Alresford ‡
March 27 Saturday
Durmast House, Burley
March 28 Sunday
Broughton Gardens, nr Stockbridge
Eversley Gardens, Eversley
Little Court, Crawley
Mylor Cottage, Droxford
Pennington Chase, Lymington
March 29 Monday
Little Court, Crawley
March 31 Wednesday
Court Lodge, West Meon
April 4 Sunday
Cheriton Cottage, Cheriton, nr Alresford ‡
Court Lodge, West Meon
East Lane, Ovington
Headbourne Worthy Gardens, Winchester
Sowley House, Sowley, Lymington
Tichborne Park, Alresford ‡
Tylney Hall Hotel, Rotherwick
West Tytherley Gardens
April 11 Sunday
Bramdean House, Alresford ‡
Woodcote Manor, Alresford ‡
April 12 Monday
Beechenwood Farm, nr Odiham
Bramdean House, Alresford
April 14 Wednesday
Hall Place, West Meon
Little Court, Crawley
April 18 Sunday
Abbey Cottage, Itchen Abbas
Appleshaw Manor, nr Andover
Ashford Gardens, Steep
Byways, Burley
Crawley Gardens, Crawley ‡
The Old House, Silchester
Paige Cottage, Crawley ‡
Rowans Wood, Ampfield
April 25 Sunday
Belmore Lane Gardens, Lymington
Brandy Mount House, Alresford
60, Lealand Road, Drayton
Rowans Wood, Ampfield
Rumsey Gardens, Clanfield
Vine Cottage, Ewshott
May 2 Sunday
Abbey Cottage, Itchen Abbas ‡
Byways, Burley
Chilland, Martyr Worthy, nr Winchester ‡
The Cottage, Chandlers Ford
The Old House, Silchester
Vernon Hill House, Bishop's Waltham
Vine Cottage, Ewshott

May 3 Monday
Abbey Cottage, Itchen Abbas ‡
Chilland, Martyr Worthy, nr Winchester ‡
The Cottage, Chandlers Ford
Rookley Manor, Upper Somborne
Sadlers Farmhouse, Lymington
Vernon Hill House, Bishop's Waltham
May 5 Wednesday
Exbury Gardens, nr Southampton
The Manor House, Upton Grey
May 9 Sunday
Brandy Mount House, Alresford ‡
Burkham House, nr Alton
Cold Hayes, Steep Marsh
The Dower House, Dogmersfield
Eversley Gardens, Eversley
Tichborne Park, Alresford ‡
May 12 Wednesday
The Manor House, Upton Grey
May 16 Sunday
Ashford Gardens, Steep ‡
Bramdean House, Alresford
Cobwood House, nr Newbury
The Dower House, Dogmersfield
Empshott Grange, nr Selborne
Greatham Mill, Greatham, nr Liss
Hackwood Park (Spring Wood), Basingstoke
Heathlands, 47 Locks Rd, Locks Heath
Lockerley Hall, nr Romsey
North Ecchinswell Farm, nr Newbury
The Old House, Silchester
Petersfield Physic Gardens ‡
Pylewell Park, Lymington
South End House, Lymington
Tylney Hall Hotel, Rotherwick
Vine Cottage, Ewshott
May 19 Wednesday
The Manor House, Upton Grey
May 20 Thursday
The Hedges, East Wellow
May 22 Saturday
3 St Helens Road, Hayling Island
May 23 Sunday
The Cottage, Chandlers Ford
Lithend, Crawley ‡
Fiddlers Cottage, Woodgreen ‡‡
The Hedges, East Wellow
Little Barn Garden, & Barnhawk Nursery, Woodgreen‡‡
Little Court, Crawley‡
Pylewell Park, Lymington‡‡‡
Rowans Wood, Ampfield
Rumsey Gardens, Clanfield
3 St Helens Road, Hayling Island
Walhampton, Lymington ‡‡‡
The Wylds, Liss
May 24 Monday
Lithend, Crawley
Little Court, Crawley

May 26 Wednesday
The Manor House, Upton Grey
May 27 Thursday
The Hedges, East Wellow
May 29 Saturday
Fernlea, Chilworth, Southampton
Lisle Court Cottage, Lymington
Springfield, Hayling Island
May 30 Sunday
Croylands, nr Romsey
Eversley Gardens, Eversley
Hambledon House, Hambledon ‡‡
The Hedges, East Wellow
Lisle Court Cottage, Lymington
Long Thatch, Warnford
Manor Lodge, Crawley
Monxton Gardens, nr Andover
The Old House, Silchester ‡
Pennington Chase, Lymington
Rowans Wood, Ampfield
Springfield, Hayling Island ‡‡‡
Verona Cottage, Hayling
    Island ‡‡‡
West Silchester Hall, nr Reading ‡
White Cottage, Hambledon ‡‡
May 31 Monday
House-in-the-Wood, Beaulieu
Long Thatch, Warnford
Manor Lodge, Crawley
Monxton Gardens, nr Andover
Sadlers Farmhouse, Lymington
June 2 Wednesday
Croylands, nr Romsey
The Manor House, Upton Grey
June 3 Thursday
The Hedges, East Wellow
June 5 Saturday
Durmast House, Burley
June 6 Sunday
Croylands, nr Romsey
The Hedges, East Wellow
Jenkyn Place, Bentley
Robins Return, Hordle, Lymington
June 9 Wednesday
Croylands, nr Romsey
The Manor House, Upton Grey
June 10 Thursday
The Hedges, East Wellow
June 13 Sunday
Cranbury Park, Otterbourne
Croylands, nr Romsey
Droxford Gardens, Droxford
The Hedges, East Wellow
Lithend, Crawley ‡
Little Court, Crawley ‡
Old Timbers, Mill Hill, Alresford
Paige Cottage, Crawley ‡
Pullens, West Worldham, nr Alton
Rosewood Farm, West Tytherley
Roxfords House, Binsted
Vernon Hill House, Bishop's
    Waltham
The Vyne, Sherborne St John
Westbrook House, Holybourne

White Windows, Longparish
June 14 Monday
Lithend Crawley‡
Little Court, Crawley‡
White Windows, Longparish
June 16 Wednesday
Croylands, nr Romsey
The Manor House, Upton Grey
June 20 Sunday
Beechenwood Farm, nr Odiham
Bramdean House, Alresford‡
Bramdean Lodge, Alresford‡
Brandy Mount House, Alresford‡
Broadhatch House, Bentley
Buriton Gardens, Buriton ‡‡‡‡
Byways, Burley
Croylands, nr Romsey
Fairfield House, Hambledon ‡‡‡‡
The Garden House, Lymington ‡‡
Glevins, Lymington‡‡
Hambledon House,
    Hambledon ‡‡‡‡
Hill House, Cheriton, nr
    Alresford‡
Little Barn Garden, & Barnhawk
    Nursery, Woodgreen‡‡‡
Longstock Park Gardens,
    Stockbridge
Merrie Cottage, Woodgreen‡‡‡
The Old Vicarage, Appleshaw
Petersfield Physic Garden ‡‡‡‡
Roxfords House, Binsted
June 21 Monday
Broadhatch House, Bentley
June 23 Wednesday
Croylands, nr Romsey
The Manor House, Upton Grey
June 27 Sunday
Apple Court, nr Lymington
Brocas Farm, Lower Froyle, nr
    Alton
Buriton Gardens, Buriton
Burkham House, nr Alton
Colemore House, nr Alton
Ivalls Farm Cottage, Bentworth
John Hines Studios, Aldershot
60, Lealand Road, Drayton
Marycourt, Odiham‡
Mattingley Gardens, nr Hook
Mottisfont Abbey, nr Romsey
Old Meadows, Silchester
Sadlers Farmhouse, Lymington
Tunworth Old Rectory, nr
    Basingstoke‡
June 30 Wednesday
The Manor House, Upton Grey
July 4 Sunday
Jenkyn Place, Bentley
Marycourt, Odiham
Moundsmere Manor, Preston
    Candover
Somerley, nr Ringwood
Vernons Hill House, Bishop's
    Waltham

July 7 Wednesday
The Manor House, Upton Grey
Marycourt, Odiham
July 10 Saturday
Hinton Ampner, Alresford
July 11 Sunday
Broadhatch House, Bentley
Cold Hayes, Steep Marsh
Hinton Ampner, Alresford
Merdon Manor, Hursley
July 12 Monday
Broadhatch House, Bentley
July 14 Wednesday
The Manor House, Upton Grey
July 17 Saturday
Veronica Cottage, Lymington
July 18 Sunday
Apple Court, nr Lymington
Bramdean House, Alresford ‡
Bramdean Lodge, Alresford ‡
Heathlands, 47 Locks Rd, Locks
    Heath
Veronica Cottage, Lymington
July 21 Wednesday
The Manor House, Upton Grey
July 24 Saturday
12 Rozelle Close, Littleton
July 25 Sunday
Highclere Castle, nr Newbury
John Hines Studios, Aldershot
Lithend, Crawley ‡
Little Court, Crawley ‡
12 Rozelle Close, Littleton
July 28 Wednesday
The Manor House, Upton Grey
August 1 Sunday
Hill House, Old Alresford
Oakley Manor, Church Oakley
August 8 Sunday
Martyr Worthy Gardens, nr
    Winchester
Rumsey Gardens, Clanfield
West Silchester Hall, nr
    Reading
August 15 Sunday
Bramdean House, Alresford ‡
Bramdean Lodge, Alresford ‡
Cheriton Cottage, Cheriton, nr
    Alresford ‡
Highclere Castle, nr Newbury
Little Court, Crawley
August 16 Monday
Little Court, Crawley
August 22 Sunday
Highclere Castle, nr Newbury
August 28 Saturday
Fernlea, Chilworth, Southampton
August 29 Sunday
60, Lealand Road, Drayton
August 30 Monday
John Hines Studios, Aldershot
September 5 Sunday
Highclere Castle, nr Newbury
Wonston Lodge, Wonston

September 12 Sunday
Empshott Grange, nr Selborne
Greatham Mill, Greatham, nr Liss

September 26 Sunday
White Windows,
Longparish

October 24 Sunday
Little Barn Garden, & Barnhawk
Nursery, Woodgreen

DESCRIPTIONS OF GARDENS

Abbey Cottage &⚭❀ (Colonel P J Daniell) Rectory Lane, Itchen Abbas. Turn off B3047 Alresford-Kingsworthy Rd, 1m E of Itchen Abbas. Interesting walled garden and meadow with trees, designed and maintained by owner. *Adm £1 Chd free (Share to Winchester Cathedral). Suns April 18, May 2, Mon May 3 (12-5.30) also by appt* **Tel 0962 779575**

Apple Court & Apple Court Cottage &⚭❀ (Mrs D Grenfell, Mr R Grounds & Mrs M Roberts) Lymington. From the A337 between Lymington and New Milton turn N into Hordle Lane at the Royal Oak at Downton Xrds. Formal 1½-acre garden being created by designer-owners within the walls of former Victorian kitchen garden. Four National Reference Collections incl small leafed hosta. White garden, daylily display borders, collection of ferns and grasses. Small specialist nursery. Adjoining small cottage garden with variegated catalpa. TEAS at Royal Oak, Downton. Cold drinks available. *Adm £1 Chd 25p (Share to All Saints Church, Hordle). Suns June 27, July 18 (2-5.30)*

Appleshaw Manor &⚭ (The Hon Mrs Green) Nr Andover. Take A342 Andover-Marlborough Rd. Turn to Appleshaw 1m W of Weyhill. Fork L at playing field. Entrance on R after ½m next to white Church. 7-acre garden and grounds surrounded by wall. Shrubs, herbaceous, roses, wood garden, arboretum. Notable beech and yew hedges. Spring bulbs. TEA. *Adm £1.50 Chd free (Share to St Peter's Church, Appleshaw). Sun April 18 (2-5)*

Ashford Gardens ⚭ Steep, nr Petersfield. 2m N of Petersfield, off Alresford Rd (no. C18); fork right ½m past Cricketers Inn at Steep. 12 acres set in valley of the Ash under steep wooded hangers of Stoner and Wheatham, described by poet Edward Thomas (who lived for a time at Berryfield before killed in France in 1917). Landscaped pools; waterfalls, beautiful trees; interesting shrubs, banks of azaleas and rhododendrons add colour and variety to this naturally lovely setting. *Combined Adm £1.50 Chd 25p. Suns April 18, May 16 (2-6)*
    Ashford Chace (Ashford Chace Ltd)
    Old Ashford Manor (J Abrahams Esq)

Ashley Park Farm. See Dorset

Beechenwood Farm &⚭❀ (Mr & Mrs M Heber-Percy) Hillside; turn S into King St. from Odiham High St. Turn L after cricket ground for Hillside and follow signs. 2-acre garden; woodland garden with spring bulbs; herb garden; rock garden; orchard and vegetable gardens. WI TEAS. *Adm £1 Chd free. Easter Mon April 12 (2-5); Sun June 20 (2-6)*

Belmore Lane Gardens ⚭❀ Lymington. Go to the Public Car Park behind Waitrose Supermarket. From here exit on foot W entering Belmore Lane. R for No 8, L for 44 & 48. *Combined Adm £1.50 Chd 50p. Sun April 25 (2-5.30)*

Auburn &⚭❀ (Mr & Mrs K R Pooley) 100 yds down the hill on the R immediately S of Ewell House. This ¼-acre garden was, until 1970, part of Ewell House and is now separated by a Sussex brick wall. There are island beds of azaleas, rhododendrons and other shrubs; a pond, terrace, rockeries and a small shrubbery

Ewell House &⚭ (Mr & Mrs R J Gould) 100 yds down on your R. This is a town garden of ⅓ acre and was completely replanned and replanted in 1986. It is acquiring some maturity but considerable new planting is still taking place. There is a variety of shrubs incl camellias and small rhododendrons. Cream TEAS

¶**Rose Cottage** (Capt Carver) A small (60ft × 30ft) walled garden behind the house with access through the integral garage. It contains quite a profusion of trees, shrubs, heathers, climbers and spring bulbs plus a fish pond

Bramdean House ⚭❀ (Mr & Mrs H Wakefield) In Bramdean village on A272. Carpets of spring bulbs. Walled garden with famous herbaceous borders, working kitchen garden, large collection of unusual plants. TEAS. *Adm £ Chd free (Share to Bramdean Parish Church). Mon Apr 12, Suns March 21 April 11, May 16, June 20, July 18 Aug 15, (2-5); also by appt* **Tel 0962 771214**

Bramdean Lodge & (Hon Peter & Mrs Dickinson) Bramdean village nr Alresford, on A272 (car park and TEAS as for Bramdean House). 1¾ acres, walled garden, variety of plants, including more than 80 varieties of clematis. *Adm £1 Chd free. Suns June 20, July 18, Aug 15 (2-5)*

Brandy Mount House &❀ (Mr & Mrs M Baron) Alresford centre, first R in East St before Sun Lane. Please leave cars in Broad St. 1-acre informal plantsman's garden, spring bulbs, hellebores, species geraniums, snowdrop collection, daphne collection, clematis, herbaceous and woodland plants. *Adm £1 Chd free. Suns March 21 April 25, May 9, June 20 (also by appt Saturdays) (2-5)* **Tel 0962 732189**

Broadhatch House &⚭❀ (Bruce & Lizzie Powell) Bentley; 4m NE of Alton; on A31 between Farnham/Alton. Bus AV452; go up School Lane. 3½ acres formal garden, double herbaceous borders; rose gardens, old-fashioned roses; unusual flowering shrubs. Included and illustrated in 'Rose Gardens of England'. *Adm £1.50 Chd free (Share to Basingstoke Wel-Care). Suns June 20, July 11 (2-6) Mons June 21, July 12 (11-6). Also by appt* **Tel 0420 23185**

Brocas Farm &⚭❀ (Mrs A A Robertson) Lower Froyle ½m up road to Lower Froyle from A31 turning just W of Bentley; medium-sized garden with herbaceous; rose and shrub borders; vegetables and arboretum of small trees. TEAS. *Adm £1 Chd 50p (Share to CRMF). Sun June 2 (2-6)*

Broughton Gardens 4m from Stockbridge, 8m from Romsey. From Stockbridge take A30 going W, take L after 1½m and L at T-junction in Broughton. Parking at Broughton House, short walk by Wallop Brook to Grandfathers and Mill House. *Combined adm £2 Chd free. Sun March 28 (2-5.30)*

Broughton House ♿✂❀ (Mrs I Macpherson) Entrance on L off High St beyond church and shop. Medium-sized informal garden with Wallop Brook running through. Peaceful setting with lawns; fine trees; shrub borders; walled garden. TEAS

¶**Grandfathers** ♿ (Col & Mrs T Fitzgibbon) Turn L ½m beyond church into Rookery Lane. Medium-sized garden, mainly trees, shrubs and ground cover plants; spring bulbs

¶**Mill House** ♿✂ (Mr & Mrs E A Waldron) Entrance on same rd, past Rookery Lane. Medium-sized informal garden with riverside walk, spring bulbs, trees and shrubs

Buriton Gardens ❀ 3m S of Petersfield off A3. Beside village pond. TEAS. *Combined Adm £1.50 Chd 25p (Share to St Mary's). Suns June 20, 27 (2-6)*

The Manor House ♿ (C R Wood Esq) One time home of Edward Gibbon, author of 'Decline and Fall of Roman Empire', who describes in his autobiography, the prospect from the garden of the 'long hanging woods which could not have been improved by art or expense'! Walled garden, old-fashioned rose walk; swimming pool. C18 Dovecote

The Old Rectory ♿ (Major & Mrs R A Wilson) Walled garden; old-fashioned roses; herbaceous borders. The house originally Petersfield Manor oldest in the district dating from 1313 (not open)

Whistlers ♿ (Sir William & Lady Vincent) Thatched house 1604; undulating garden with woodland; large pond with island and waterfowl; streams, waterfalls and newly planted water garden; old-fashioned roses, rose pergola and dovecote

Burkham House ♿✂ (Mr & Mrs D Norman) nr Alton. 3m NW of Alton from A339 between Basingstoke and Alton. On Alton side of Herriard, turn off W for Burkham. 10 acres of beautiful mature trees, azaleas, acers, spring flowers, lake, and new arboretum, cottage garden and herbaceous borders. TEAS. *Adm £1 Chd 25p. Suns May 9, June 27 (2.30-5.30)*

Byways ✂❀ (J A F Binny Esq) Castle Hill Lane, Burley, 5m SE of Ringwood. 1m S from centre of Burley on Bransgore Rd. Alpine garden made by the late E.D. Doncaster about 1926; also camellias, magnolias, rhododendrons, roses and other interesting trees and shrubs. Tea Forest Tea House, Burley. *Adm £1 Chd 50p. Suns April 18, May 2, June 20 (2-6)*

Cheriton Cottage ♿✂❀ (Mrs I Garnett-Orme) Cheriton. 3m S of Alresford, B3046 in centre of village. 4-acre garden with chalk stream (R Itchen near source). Trees, shrubs, mixed borders, roses, spring bulbs, lawns. TEAS. *Adm £1 Chd 50p. Suns April 4, Aug 15 (2-5)*

Chilland ♿✂(Mrs L A Impey) Martyr Worthy. Midway between Winchester and Alresford on B3047. Mature garden. Fine situation. Shrub borders designed for foliage colour. Many interesting plants. *Adm £1 Chd free. Sun, Mon May 2, 3 (2-5.30). Also Sun Aug 8 with* **Martyr Worthy Gardens**

Cobwood House ♿✂❀ (Mr & Mrs R F Kershaw) Woolton Hill. Off Newbury-Andover A343. 1st R after Newbury derestriction sign to Ball Hill and East Woodhay. Take next L, after ½m L again, white gate 20yds on L. 2-acre spring garden originally planted by the late Sir Kenneth Swan QC in 1940; rhododendrons, azaleas, camellias, magnolias and other specimen trees and shrubs, vegetable garden. TEAS. *Adm £1 Chd (under 14) free. Sun May 16 (2-5.30)*

Cold Hayes (Mr & Mrs Brian Blacker) Steep Marsh. Turn off A3 (Petersfield bypass) to Steep Marsh. Turn off Petersfield-Alresford Rd 3m from Petersfield. From Steep village observe direction signs. Medium-sized garden; flowering shrubs, trees, beautiful views. TEA. *Adm £1 Chd 25p. Suns May 9, July 11 (2-6)*

Colemore House ♿✂❀ (Mr & Mrs S de Zoete) Colemore. From Alton take A32 S for 4m past Rotherfield Park, turn L ½m on, up small lane marked to Colemore. Garden next door to church. Approx 2-acre garden divided by walls and hedges. Mixed borders, unusual plants; arched apple walk; lawns and mature trees. TEAS. *Adm £1.50 Chd free (Share to Winchester Cathedral Trust). Sun June 27 (2-6)*

The Cottage ♿✂❀ (Mr & Mrs H Sykes) 16 Lakewood Rd, Chandler's Ford. 6m S of Winchester. Leave M3 at junction 12, follow signs to Chandler's Ford. At Hanrahans public house on Winchester Rd, turn W into Merdon Ave, then 3rd rd on L. ¾-acre garden with spring bulbs, camellias, rhododendrons, azaleas, magnolias, conifers, bog garden and ponds. TEAS. *Adm £1 Chd 10p (Share to British Heart Foundation). Suns May 2, 23, Mon May 3 (2-6)*

Court Lodge ✂❀ (Patricia Dale) West Meon. 8m W of Petersfield, S on A32. ¼-acre specialist cottage garden, home of botanical artist Patricia Dale RMS and her husband. Many unusual and old-fashioned plants, grown for professional painting; studio also open with collection of botanical water colour paintings, greeting cards etc. Teas on Sun only, in Church. *Adm 70p Chd 25p. Wed March 31, Sun April 4 (2-6)* **Tel 0730 829473**

Cranbury Park ♿ (Mr & Mrs Chamberlayne-Macdonald) Otterbourne, 5m S of Winchester. 2m N of Eastleigh; main entrance on old A33 between Winchester-Southampton, by bus stop at top of Otterbourne Hill. Entrances also in Hocombe Rd, Chandlers Ford and Poles Lane, Otterbourne. Extensive pleasure grounds laid out in late C18 and early C19; fountains; rose garden; specimen trees; lakeside walk. Family carriages will be on view. TEAS. *Adm £1.50 Chd 50p (Share to St Denys Church, Chilworth). Sun June 13 (2-5)*

Crawley Gardens 5m NW of Winchester, off A272 Winchester-Stockbridge Rd. Gardens signed from centre of village. TEA. *Adm by donations. Sun April 18 (2-5.30)*

The Dower House &✗ (Mr & Mrs R Pearson) 3½ acres. A spring garden mainly lawn. Drifts of bulbs, flowering cherries and shrubs; small courtyard and walled cottage garden

Glebe House & (Lt-Col & Mrs John Andrews) 1½ acres; mainly lawn, bulbs, shrubs and herbaceous borders

Lithend &✗❀ (Mrs F L Gunner) Small cottage garden. *Also open Suns, Mons May 23 (Share to RSPB), 24, June 13, 14, July 25 (2-5.30). Combined adm £1 Chd free with* **Little Court**

Croylands &✗❀ (The Hon Mrs Charles Kitchener) Old Salisbury Lane, Romsey. From Romsey take A3057 Stockbridge Rd, L after 1m at Dukes Head, fork L after bridge, 1m on R. Wheelwright's cottage on Florence Nightingale's Family Estate, surrounded by 2 acres unusual, interesting trees, shrubs and plants. Peony garden. TEAS. *Adm £1 Chd free. Sun May 30, June 6, 13, 20; Weds, June 2, 9, 16, 23 (2-6)*

The Dower House & (Mr & Mrs Michael Hoare) Dogmersfield. Turn N off A287. 6-acre garden including bluebell wood with collection of over 250 varieties of rhododendrons, azaleas, magnolias and other flowering trees and shrubs; fine views. TEAS. *Adm £1.25 Chd free. Suns May 9, 16 (2-6)*

Droxford Gardens 4½m N of Wickham on A32 approx mid-way between Alton-Portsmouth. *Combined adm £2 OAPs £1 Chd 50p 1 garden £1. Sun June 13 (2-6)*

Fir Hill ❀ (Mrs Derek Schreiber) 4½ acres; roses, shrubs, herbaceous and shrub borders. Home-made TEAS. Car park

The Mill House & (Mrs C MacPherson) Garden of 2 acres; shrubs, flower beds, orchard, mill stream, roses, vineyard. Car park

Mylor Cottage &❀ (Dr & Mrs Martin ffrench Constant) ½m S of Droxford on the Swanmore Rd. Car park. Trees, shrubs and herbaceous border. *Also open Sat, Sun March 27, 28 (2-5) see under* **Mylor Cottage**

¶**Durmast House** &✗❀ (Mr & Mrs P E G Daubeney). 1m SE of Burley, nr White Buck Hotel. 4-acre garden designed by Gertrude Jekyll in 1907 in the process of being restored from the original plans. Formal rose garden edged with lavender, 130-yr-old Monterey pine, 100-yr-old cut leaf beech and large choisya. Victorian rockery, lily pond, coach-house, large wisteria and herbaceous border. *Adm £1 Chd 50p (Share to Hampshire Garden Trust and Delhi Women's Assoc Clinic). Sats March 27, June 5 (2.30-5.30)*

East Lane ✗ (Sir Peter & Lady Ramsbotham) Ovington A31 from Winchester towards Alresford. Immediately after roundabout 1m west of Alresford, small sign to Ovington turn sharp L up incline, down small country rd to Ovington. East Lane is the only house on left, 500yds before Bush Inn. 4 acres, spring bulbs, mixed herbaceous and shrubs; woodland; walled rose garden. Terraced water garden. *Adm £1 Chd free. Sun April 4 (2-6)*

Empshott Grange ✗ (Mr & Mrs James Scott) Nr Selborne. 6m SE of Alton. Take B3006 1m out of Selborn turn R towards Empshott Green. Entrance 600yds on Mature family garden on steep wooded hanger wi views to Noar Hill and Hawkley. Walled garden with ori inal greenhouse with vine, fruit, shrubs and trees; 800-y old church adjacent. Teas at Selborne. *Adm £1 Chd fre Suns May 16, Sept 12 (2-5.30)*

Eversley Gardens ❀ On B3016. Signposted from A3 (just west of Blackbush Airport) and from A327 (just be yond cricket ground at Eversley Cross when headed fo Yateley). *Combined adm £1.50 Chd free. Suns March 2 May 9, 30 (2-6)*

Kiln Copse (A Jervis O'Donohoe Trust) 8 acres; da fodil and bluebell wood; foxgloves; good collection rhododendrons; mixed border; roses; natural lak bogside plants, extensive new plantings of shrub rose and perennials

Kiln Copse Cottage Small cottage garden in th grounds of Kiln Copse

Little Coopers (Mr & Mrs J K Oldale) 10-acre garde Drifts of daffodils in March. A woodland walk mea ders through bluebells, rhododendrons, azaleas ar unusual shrubs most of which are labelled. Shaded ▮ mature trees, walk leads to water & bog garden wi ponds and stream, then onto extensive lawn in fro of house surrounded by Mediterranean and rose ga dens. Small Japanese garden by the house. TEAS aid of Arthritis and Rheumatism Research

● **Exbury Gardens** &❀ (Exbury Gardens Trust) Exbur 2½m SE of Beaulieu; 15m SW of Southampton. V B3054 SE of Beaulieu; after 1m turn sharp R for Exbur 200 acres of woodland garden incorporating the Rot schild Collection of azaleas, rhododendrons, magnolia maples and camellias. Luncheons and teas. Plant Cent and Gift Shop. *Spring Season: Feb 27-July 4. Adm m April-early June £3.50 OAPs & groups £3 (OAPs reduce 50p Thurs) Chd 10-16 £2.50. Early/late season prices 5 less. Gardens N of Gilbury Lane Bridge open Summer Ju 5 to Sept 5 Adm adults & parties £1.50 OAPs & Chd 1 16 £1. Autumn Sept 6 to Oct 24. Adm £2 OAPs & grou £1.50. Chd 10-16 £1. Open daily 10-5.30/dusk. For N Wed May 5*

Fairfield House &✗❀ (Mr & Mrs Peter Wake) Hambl don. 10m SW of Petersfield. Hambledon village. Mediur sized garden; large collection of shrub and climbin roses, mixed borders, walled gardens, fine cedar tree TEAS. *Adm £1.50 Chd free. Sun June 20 (2-6). Also op by appt anytime; suitable for groups* Tel 0705 632 431

¶**Fernlea** ✗❀ (Mr & Mrs P G Philip) Chilworth. N Southampton on A27 at junction of M3 and M27, ta A27 towards Romsey. After 1m turn L at Clump Inn. Pr ceed along Manor Rd into Chilworth Drove for about ½ Under restoration from rhododendron ponticum. Habi gardening to encourage native flora and fauna. Bult azaleas, rhododendrons, heathers and mediterrane plants. Specimen trees dating back to mid C19. Set high ground with views to Isle of Wight. Garden merg into woodland. 15 acres in all. Picnics welcome. TE *Adm £1 Chd free. Sats May 29, Aug 28 (10-6).*

Regular Openers. See head of county section.

Fiddlers Cottage ❀ (Group Capt & Mrs Musgrave) Woodgreen. 3m NE of Fordingbridge via A338. Turn E to Woodgreen; bear L in village; R immediately past Horse and Groom, continue for 1¼m; enter through Little Barn Garden; 3 acres of woodland with informal plantings of shrubs; bulbs and ground cover plants; areas of heather mown to replace conventional grass lawns; TEAS. *Adm 60p Chd 25p. Sun May 23 (2-6)*

● **Furzey Gardens** ♿✂❀ (Furzey Gardens Charitable Trust) Minstead, 8m SW of Southampton. 1m S of A31; 2m W of Cadnam and end of M27; 3½m NW of Lyndhurst. 8 acres of informal shrub garden; comprehensive collections of azaleas and heathers; water garden; fernery; summer and winter flowering shrubs. Botanical interest at all seasons. Also open (limited in winter) Will Selwood Gallery and ancient cottage (AD 1560). High-class arts and crafts by 150 local craftsmen. Tea Honey Pot ¼m. *Adm £2.50 OAPs £2 Chd £1.50 March to Oct. £1.50 OAPs £1 Chd 75p winter. Daily except Dec 25 & 26 (10-5; dusk in winter)*

The Garden House ✂ (Mr & Mrs C Kirkman) Lymington. Off Lymington High St opp Woolworths. ¾ acre of walled plantsman's garden with unusual hardy shrubs and perennials, 2 ponds and ornamental kitchen garden. TEAS. *Adm £1 Chd free (Share to Oakhaven Hospice). Sun June 20 (2-6)*

¶**Glevins** ♿✂❀ (Mrs Clarke) Lymington. Situated off Lymington High St. between Lloyds Bank and Nat West Bank. ½-acre small walled garden with wide view of the Solent and Yarmouth I.O.W. Mixed borders, small rockery, conservatory. TEAS. *Adm £1 Chd free. Sun June 20 (2-6)*

Greatham Mill ♿✂❀ (Mrs E N Pumphrey) Greatham, nr Liss. 5m N of Petersfield. From A325, at Greatham turn onto B3006 towards Alton; after 600yds L into 'No Through Rd' lane to garden. Interesting garden with large variety of plants surrounding mill house, with mill stream and nursery garden. *Adm £1 Chd free (Share to Greatham PCC). April 11 to end of Sept every Sun & Bank Hol. For NGS Suns May 16, Sept 12 (2-6). Also by appointment any day* **Tel 0420 538219**

Hackwood Park (The Spring Wood) ✂❀ (The Viscount and Viscountess Camrose) 1m S of Basingstoke. Entrance off Tunworth Rd. Signed from A339 Alton-Basingstoke. 80 acres delightful C17-C18 semi-formal wood with pavilions, walks, glades; magnificent ornamental pools, amphitheatre, interesting trees and bulbs. Home-made TEAS and produce. *Adm £1.50 OAPs 50p (Share to St Leonard's Church, Cliddesden and St Mary's Church, Herriard).* ▲*For NGS Sun May 16 (2-6)*

¶**Hall Place** ♿ (Mr & Mrs Dru Montagu) West Meon. 7m W of Petersfield. From A32 in West Meon, take rd to East Meon, garden on R. Parking in drive. Large collection of rare and unusual daffodils in 8 acres of garden designed by Lanning Roper 30 years ago. Grass walks, spring bulbs, many varieties of trees and shrubs; walled kitchen garden. *Collecting box. Wed April 14 (2-6)*

Hambledon House ✂ (Capt & Mrs David Hart Dyke) Hambledon. 8m SW of Petersfield. In village centre behind George Hotel. Approx 2 acres partly walled garden. Mixed borders; unusual plants. Some borders newly designed and recently planted. TEAS. *Adm £1 Chd 25p. Suns May 30, June 20 (2-6) also by appt* **Tel 0705 632380**

Headbourne Worthy Gardens 2m N Winchester B3420 to Three Maids Hill roundabout, take rd signed The Worthys. Follow 1½m, under railway bridge. *Combined adm £2 Chd free. Sun April 4*

The Manor House ♿✂ (Mr & Mrs P Anker) C17 house, 2 acres spring bulbs and shrubs, recently restored 300-yr-old cob wall. Mature trees and borders

Upper Farm ♿✂ (Mr & Mrs S Browne) Garden comprises 2 parts, an older formal area terraced with mixed borders, and hedged vegetable garden approx 1½ acres. Young woodland garden with wide variety bulbs approx 2½ acres. TEA

Heathlands ♿ (Dr John Burwell) 47 Locks Rd, Locks Heath. Locks Rd runs due S from Park Gate into Locks Heath. No 47 is 1m down on the R hand side (Grid Ref 513 069). 1-acre garden designed & developed by the owner since 1967. An attempt has been made to give year round interest against a background of evergreens & mature trees. Spring bulbs, rhododendrons, paulownias. cyclamen, ferns and some less usual plants. Topiary, small herbaceous border. National Collection of Japanese anemones. TEAS. *Adm £1 Chd free. Suns May 16, July 18 (2-5.30)*

The Hedges ♿✂❀ (Mr & Mrs F J Vinnicombe) E Wellow, 3m from Romsey. At M27 junction 2, take A36 N 2m, turn R into Whinwhistle Rd. Hamdown Cres is 3rd turning on L. ¼ acre densely planted mixture of bulbs; hardy perennials; shrubs and trees including two small ponds. TEA. *Adm 75p Chd free. Thurs May 20, 27 June 3, 10 (11-5); Suns May 23, 30, June 6, 13 (2-5). Also by appt* **Tel 0794 22539**

Highclere Castle ♿✂❀ (The Earl of Carnarvon) Nr Newbury. Entrance on A34 4½m S of Newbury. Spectacular Charles Barry Mansion set in Capability Brown parkland with extensive lawns; specimen trees, orangery; C18 walled garden with yew walks, large areas of herbaceous beds, ornamental trees and shrubs. Gift shop & plant centre, picnic area. TEAS. *Adm £2 (garden only). Open Weds to Suns July, Aug, Sept. Suns & Mons Easter, May & Aug Bank Hols. For NGS Suns July 25, Aug 15, 22, Sept 5 (2-6) last entry 5pm*

Hightown Farm ♿ (Mr & Mrs Oliver Ziegler) Hightown Hill, Ringwood. ½m from Picket Post on A31. From Southampton 1st L after Picket Post, signed Hightown and Crow. Signpost on drive 1st L after 2 cattle grids. From Ringwood turn round and return from Picket Post, then as above. 5 acres of a wide variety of shrubs, border plants and bulbs in season, cyclamen in September. Established and new planting. Picnic area. *Adm £1.50 Chd free. Daily April to Oct incl, noon to 5.30, coaches welcome. By appt only* **Tel 0425 474278**

¶**Hill House, Cheriton** ❀ (Hon Christopher Chetwode) nr Alresford. In centre of Cheriton, turn up Hill Houses Lane. Garden is last house at top. 2½-acre garden and orchard. Wonderful view. 12-yr-old garden on very windy site. TEA. *Adm £1 Chd free. Sun June 20 (2-6)*

Hill House, Old Alresford ❤ (Maj & Mrs W F Richardson) From Alresford 1m along B3046 towards Basingstoke, then R by church. 2 acres of herbaceous border and formal beds set around large lawn; kitchen garden. TEA. *Adm £1 Chd free. Sun Aug 1 (2-6)*

Hinton Ampner ❤❀ (The National Trust) S of Alresford. On Petersfield-Winchester Rd A272. 1m W of Bramdean village. Large garden; formal layout; flowering shrubs and trees; roses. Good views. TEAS. *Adm £2.20 Chd £1.10. Sat, Sun July 10, 11 (1.30-5)*

House-in-the-Wood ❀ (Countess Michalowska) 1½m from Beaulieu; signed from Motor Car Museum, Beaulieu. R turn to Southampton off B3056 Beaulieu-Lyndhurst Rd. 13-acre woodland garden; rhododendrons and azaleas. Coach parties by appt. **Tel Beaulieu 612346.** *Adm £2 Chd 50p. Mon May 31 (2.30-6.30)*

Ivalls Farm Cottage ❀❀ (Major & Mrs Ward) Bentworth. Alton 4½m. Take A339 W from Alton. 4m on turn sharp L to Bentworth. Approx 1 acre, essentially a cottage garden owner maintained. Over 200 roses, small herbaceous borders; pool and wild pond; kitchen garden. TEAS. *Adm £1 Chd free. Sun June 27 (2.30-6.30)*

Jenkyn Place ❤❀❀ (Mrs G E Coke) Bentley. 400yds N of Xrds in Bentley. Heritage sign on A31. Bus: Guildford-Winchester, alight Bentley village, 400yds. Well designed plantsman's garden, many interesting shrubs and perennials, double herbaceous borders. Car park free. Disabled may set down at gates (Coaches only by prior appt). *Adm £2 Chd 75p. Thurs, Fris, Sats, Suns & Bank Hol Mons April 8 to Sept 12 (2-6). For NGS Suns June 6, July 4 plus 5 per cent of other receipts*

John Hines Studios ❀ (Mr John Hine) 2 Hillside Rd, Aldershot. From A31 take 3rd exit off large roundabout on E side of Farnham. Signed Farnborough A325 and Basingstoke A30, at next roundabout take 3rd exit signed Aldershot B3007. After 1m, with railway bridge ahead, rd bends sharply L and becomes Eggars Hill. Hillside Rd is 400yds on L. Garden is 2nd entrance on R. A small newly created courtyard garden (approx 50' x 60') surrounded by a restored C17 barn (open). Garden is planted with a wide range of climbers & herbaceous plants to give maximum colour and interest over a long season. Garden also includes hanging baskets, window boxes, containers and a dovecote. TEAS in traditional English tea room. *Adm £1 Chd 50p. Suns June 27, July 25; Mon Aug 30 (10.30-4.30)*

60 Lealand Road ❤❀❀ (Mr F G Jacob) Drayton. 2m from Cosham E side of Portsmouth. Old A27 (Havant Rd) between Cosham and Bedhampton. Small garden created and designed by owner since 1969. Featured in National Gardening Magazines. A first prize winner in 'The News' Gardening Competitions 1992. Exotic plants (including cacti) with rockery, ponds and dwarf conifers etc. TEA.

Adm 60p Chd 20p. Suns April 25, June 27, Aug 29 (11-5). Also by appt **Tel 0705 370030**

Lisle Court Cottage ❤❀ (The Lady O'Neill of the Maine) Lisle Court Rd, Lymington. From Lymington Pier Station (IOW car ferry) follow rd E for 1m, at small Xrds R; garden within ½m. 2 acres overlooking Solent; borders of hardy and half-hardy shrubs; small woodland garden. *Adm £1 Chd 20p. Sat, Sun May 29, 30 (2-6)*

Lithend ❤❀❀ (Mrs F L Gunner) For direcctions see under Crawley Gardens open April 18. Also open with **Little Court, Crawley** *Combined adm £1 children free. Suns May 23 (Share to RSPB) 24; June 13, 14; July 25 (2-5.30)*

Little Barn Garden & Barnhawk Nursery ❤❀ (Drs R & V A Crawford) Woodgreen. 3m NE of Fordingbridge via A338. Turn E to Woodgreen; bear L in village; R immediately past Horse and Groom, continue for 1¼m; 2½ acres of mature informal garden with all year interest in form, colour and texture; rhododendron; azalea; camellia; magnolia; acer and collector's plants with peat, scree, rock, woodland, bog and water area; Teas nearby. *Garden open to nursery visitors every Fri and Sat (9-5) from April 2 to Oct 24. Adm 60p Chd 25p. For NGS Suns May 23, June 20 and for autumn colour Oct 24 (2-6)*

The Little Cottage (Wing Commander & Mrs Peter Prior) ½m from Lymington on A337 towards Brockenhurst, opp Toll House Inn. ¼ acre being developed into small formal gardens. Five completed - blue and yellow garden connected with laburnum tunnel to a narrow trellised border of blue and white leading to a white courtyard garden with tender white climbers on south facing cottage wall; arches to pink rose garden with lime green foliage and mauve garden with silver foliage. Red garden and apricot and copper garden being developed. *Adm £1. Open by appt May to Sept 30* **Tel Lymington 0590 679395**

Little Court ❤❀❀ (Prof & Mrs A R Elkington) 5m NW of Winchester off A272 in centre of village. A very sheltered 2-acre plantsman's garden on different levels with cob and flint walls. Drifts of naturalised bulbs. Mixed borders with carefully chosen colour themes; formal walled kitchen garden; fine view to the south; bantams and geese. TEA Suns only. *Combined Adm £1 Chd free. Suns, Mons March 28, 29; Wed April 14, Aug 15, 16. With Lithend Suns, Mons May 23 (Share to RSPB), 24, June 13, 14 July 25 (2-5.30). Also by appt* **Tel 0962 776365**

Lockerley Hall ❤ (Mr & Mrs R J Croft) Lockerley. From Romsey take A3057 N, L at Dukes Head A3084 to Dunbridge Station, L to Lockerley and then follow signs to E Tytherley - N from Romsey. Victorian Estate. Extensive grounds under restoration including ornamental orchard kitchen garden, mixed borders, rose garden, water garden, maze, knot garden, parterre, orangery and woodland garden. TEAS. *Adm £1.50 Chd free. Sun May 16 (2-6)*

By Appointment Gardens. These owners do not have a fixed opening day usually because they do not like crowds or have insufficient parking space. Owner will often give guided tour.

Longstock Park Gardens &✿❀ (Leckford Estate Ltd; Part of John Lewis Partnership) 3m N of Stockbridge. From A30 turn N on to A3057; follow signs to Longstock. 7 acres woodland and water garden; extensive collection of aquatic and bog plants. Walk through park from water garden leads to arboretum, herbaceous border. *Adm £1.50 Chd 50p. Sun June 20 (2-5)*

Long Thatch &✿❀ (Mr & Mrs P Short) Warnford. 1m S of West Meon on A32 turn R at George & Falcon, 100 yds turn R at T-junction, continue for ¼m; thatched house on R, parking opp house. 1½-acre garden; many unusual trees; shrubs and herbaceous plants; spring bulbs; collection of hellebores and hostas; bog garden; R Meon flows through garden. *Adm £1 Chd free (Sale of plants to Warnford Church). Sun, Mon May 30, 31 (2-6). Also by appt Societies welcome.* **Tel 0730 829285**

Lymore Valley Herbs &✿❀ (N M Aldridge) Braxton Farm. 3m W of Lymington. From A337 at Everton take turning to Milford-on-Sea, 70 yds on L is Lymore Lane. Turn into Lane and gardens are part of Braxton courtyard down lane on L. Evolving courtyard with raised pool and fountain. New walled garden ¼ acre with Tudor style knot. Herbaceous borders, lawns, spring bulbs, fig and mulberry trees. Rose pillars. Exhibition and sale of local artists work. TEAS. Shop, plants, no dogs in courtyard or walled garden (dog rings & water provided). *Adm 75p Chd free. Open 9-5 all year round except Dec 25 to March 1st*

Macpenny Woodland Garden & Nurseries ❀ (Mr & Mrs T M Lowndes) Burley Road, Bransgore. Midway between Christchurch and Burley. From Christchurch via A35, at Cat and Fiddle turn left; at Xrds by The Crown, Bransgore turn R and on ¼m. From A31 (travelling towards Bournemouth) L at Picket Post, signed Burley; through Burley to Green Triangle then R for Bransgore and on 1m beyond Thorney Hill Xrds. 12 acres; gravel pit converted into woodland garden; many choice, rare plants incl camellias, rhododendrons, azaleas, heathers. Large herbaceous selection. Tea Burley (Forest Tearooms) or Holmsley (Old Station Tea Rooms). *Collecting box. Daily except Dec 25 & 26 and Jan 1. (Mons-Sats 9-5; Suns 2-5)*

The Manor House &❀ (Mr & Mrs J Wallinger) 6m SE of Basingstoke in Upton Grey village on hill immediately above the church. 4-acre garden designed by Gertude Jekyll in 1908: meticulously restored over last 8 yrs to original plans, which will be on display, and with few exceptions plants as she specified: Nuttery, tennis lawn, bowling green, rose garden, formal garden with herbaceous borders and dry stone walling; wild garden with pond. Garden has yet to mature but overall shape and colour are perfectly evident. TEAS. *Adm £1.50 Chd 50p (Share to Hampshire Gardens Trust). Weds May, June & July (2-5); also by appt* **Tel 0256 862827**

Manor Lodge &✿❀ (Mr & Mrs K Wren) Crawley. Signposted from A272 and near the village pond. Walled garden of over 50 roses and mixed plants; converted barn with small garden; large range of shrubs. TEA Sun only. *Adm £1 (Share to WWF). Sun, Mon May 30, 31 (2-5.30)*

Martyr Worthy Gardens Midway between Winchester and Alresford on B3047. Gardens joined by Pilgrims Way through Itchen Valley, approx ½m. TEAS in Village Hall. *Adm £1 per garden Chd free. Sun Aug 8 (2-5.30)*
> **Chilland** & (Mrs L A Impey) Mature garden. Fine situation. Shrub borders designed for foliage colour. Many interesting plants
> **Manor House** &❀ (Cdr & Mrs M J Rivett-Carnac) Large garden, roses, mixed borders, lawns, shrubs & fine trees, next to C12 church

Marycourt &❀ (Mr & Mrs M Conville) Odiham 2m S of Hartley Wintney on A30 or Exit 5 on M3; In Odiham High St. 1-acre garden and paddocks. Old garden roses; shrubs; ramblers dripping from trees. Silver/pink border, long shrubaceous and colourful herbaceous. Dry Stone Wall/alpines thriving. Grade II starred house. *Adm £1 Chd free (Share to Jonathan Conville Memorial Trust). Suns June 27, July 4 (2-6) Wed July 7 (all day) also by appt* **Tel 0256 702100**

Mattingley Gardens &✿ Mattingley. 2½m N of Hook on rd to Reading B3349. Take rd to Mattingley Church. Parking at church. *Combined adm £1 Chd under 12 free. Sun June 27 (2-6)*
> **Mattingley Green Cottage** (Mrs Michael Edwards) Cottage garden maintained by owner, 1½ acres, large herbaceous border. Thatched cottage C14 (not open) overlooking village green and church. TEAS
> **Mattingley Cottage** (Mr & Mrs R Todd) 1-acre informal garden of shrub borders and trees surrounding and disguising tennis court. All planting since 1979. Owner maintained

Meadow House, nr Newbury See Berkshire

Merdon Manor &✿❀ (Mr & Mrs J C Smith) Hursley, SW of Winchester. From A3090 Winchester-Romsey, at Standon turn on to rd to Slackstead; on 2m. Medium-sized garden; fine views; herbaceous border; small formal walled water garden (as seen on TV). TEAS. *Adm £1 Chd 25p. Sun July 11 (2-6); also by appt* **Tel 0962 775215**

Merrie Cottage &✿ (Mr & Mrs C K Thornton) Woodgreen 3m N of Fordingbridge on A338 turn E to Woodgreen. Fork R at PO towards Godshill. Entrance 200 yds on L. Limited parking for disabled or park on common and walk down footpath. 1-acre damp garden on sloping site with interesting varieties. TEAS. *Adm £1 Chd free. Sun June 20 (2-6)*

Monxton Gardens &✿❀ 3m W of Andover, between A303 and A343; in Monxton at Xrds take Abbots Ann Rd. Parking, picnicking, TEAS (if wet in village hall) in aid of Church. *Combined adm £1 Chd 10p. Sun, Mon May 30, 31 (2-5.30)*
> **Field House** (Dr & Mrs Pratt) 2-acre garden made by owners; herbaceous borders, orchard, chalk-pit garden with pond and kitchen garden
> **Hutchens Cottage** (Mr & Mrs R A Crick) ¾-acre cottage garden with old roses, shrubs, mixed thyme and kitchen garden

Mottisfont Abbey Garden &✖❀ (The National Trust) Mottisfont, 4½m NW of Romsey. From A3057 Romsey-Stockbridge turn W at sign to Mottisfont. 4 wheelchairs available at garden. 30 acres; originally a C12 Priory; landscaped grounds with spacious lawns bordering R Test; magnificent trees; remarkable ancient spring pre-dating the Priory; walled garden contains NT's large collection of old-fashioned roses. Tea Mottisfont PO. *Adm £2.50 Chd over 5 £1.25.* ▲*Sun June 27 (12-8.30). Last admission 7.30 pm*

Moundsmere Manor & (Mr & Mrs Andreae) 6m S of Basingstoke on B3046. Drive gates on L just after Preston Candover sign. 20 acres, incl formal rose gardens; herbaceous borders, large greenhouses, unusual trees and shrubs. Coaches by appt. *Adm £1 Chd 50p. Sun July 4 (2-6)*

Mylor Cottage & (Dr & Mrs Martin ffrench Constant) Droxford. ½m S of Droxford on the Swanmore Rd. Car park. Medium sized garden; March: anemone blande, spring bulbs and cherries; June: trees, shrubs and herbaceous border. *Adm £1 Chd free. Sun March 28 (2-5) Sun June 13 open with* **Droxford Gardens** *(2-6)*

¶North Ecchinswell Farm & (Mr & Mrs Robert Henderson) Nr Newbury. Turn S off A339 Newbury-Basingstoke rd. House 1m from turning (sign-posted Ecchinswell and Bishops Green) on L-hand side. Approx 6-acre garden. Shrub borders, woodland garden, small arboretum. *Adm £1 Chd free. Sun May 16 (2.30-5.30)*

Oakley Manor &✖❀ (Mr & Mrs R H Priestley) Oakley. 5m W of Basingstoke. From Basingstoke towards Whitchurch on B3400 turn L at Station Rd ½m W of Newfound and follow signs. Bus no. 55 Basingstoke to Oakley. Large garden, lawn, trees, water garden, borders, rose garden, greenhouses, herb garden, wild conservation area. TEA. Free parking at the Manor. *Adm £1 Chd 50p. Sun Aug 1 (2-5.30)*

The Old House &❀ (Mr & Mrs M Jurgens) Bramley Road, Silchester; entrance next to Silchester (Calleva) Roman Museum. Queen Anne rectory with large garden. Camellias; rhododendrons, azaleas, shrub borders, shrub roses, paddocks, ponds, bluebell woodlands, bog garden. Fine selection of specimen trees and shrubs. Roman town walls and Amphitheatre ¼m; medieval Church. TEAS in aid of church. *Adm £1 Chd 50p (Share to St Mary The Virgin Church, Silchester). Suns April 18, May 2, 16, 30 (2-6)*

¶Old Meadows &✖ (Dr & Mrs J M Fowler) Silchester. Off A340 between Reading and Basingstoke. 1m S of Silchester on rd to Bramley, signposted at Xrds. 5 acres including walled garden with cottage flowers and vegetables. Herbaceous borders, old meadow walk. TEAS. *Adm £1 Chd free (Share to Basingstoke and Alton Cardiac Rehabilitation). Sun June 27 (2-6)*

Old Timbers &✖ (Mr & Mrs J A B Leask) Mill Hill, Alresford, Park in Broad St in town centre; Mill Hill at bottom of Broad St on L. C16 cottage with herbaceous garden. TEAS. *Adm £1 Chd 50p Sun June 13 (2-6)*

The Old Vicarage ✖ (Sir Dermot & Lady De Trafford) Appleshaw. Take A342 Andover to Marlborough Rd, turn to Appleshaw 1m W of Weyhill, fork L at playing field, on L in village by clock. 2-acre walled garden mature trees, bush and rambler roses, shrub borders, shrubs and trees in grass; fruit and herb garden with box hedges. *Adm £1.50 Chd free. Sun June 20 (2-5)*

¶Paige Cottage ❀ (Mr & Mrs T W Parker) Next to Crawley village pond. Signposted from A272. 1 acre of traditional English country garden with large shrub and herbaceous borders and including grass tennis court and walled Italian style swimming pool. Cherry and apple blossom rises above a carpet of many daffodil varieties. These give way to climbing roses. *Adm £1. Suns April 18, June 13 (2-5.30)*

Pennington Chase &✖❀ (Mrs V E Coates) 2m SW Lymington L off A337, at Pennington Cross roundabout. 4 acres, flowering shrubs, azaleas and rhododendrons with some unusual trees in fine state of maturity. TEA. *Adm £1 Chd 50p. Suns March 28, May 30 (2-7)*

Petersfield Physic Garden &✖❀ (Hampshire Gardens Trust) 16 High St, Petersfield. Centre of town. Recreation of C17 garden in ⅔ acre planted in 1989. Features include knot garden; topiary; orchard; shrubs; florist borders and physic beds. *Collecting box. Open daily (not Christmas Day) (9-5). For NGS Suns May 16, June 20 (9-5)*

Pullens &✖❀ (Mr & Mrs R N Baird) W Worldham. From Alton take B3006 SE on the Selborne Rd. After 2½m turn L to W Worldham.By church turn R. Pullen 100yds on R behind wall. Approx 1-acre informal cottage style walled garden to blend with Selborne stone house. Particular emphasis on colour and all year round interest. *Adm £1 Chd free. Sun June 13 (2-6)*

Pylewell Park &❀ (The Lord Teynham) 2½ m E of Lymington beyond IOW car ferry. Large garden of botanical interest; good trees, flowering shrubs, rhododendrons lake, woodland garden. *Adm £1.50 Chd 50p (Share to Wessex Regional Medical Oncology Unit). Suns May 16, 2. (2-6)*

Robins Return &✖❀ (Mr & Mrs J Ingrem) Tiptoe. 2m NE of New Milton. Take B3055, at Xrds by Tiptoe Church Turn into Wootton Rd (signposted to Wootton). Garden 400 yds on L. ⅔-acre garden. Shrubs, roses and herbaceous plants; ornamental pool and rock garden; greenhouses; organic kitchen garden and fruit. Parts of the garden recently redesigned and planted. *Adm £1 Chd over 9 yrs 25p. Sun June 6 (2-5)*

Rookley Manor ❀ (Lord & Lady Inchyra) Upper Som borne. 6m W of Winchester. From A272 Winchester Stockbridge Rd. At Rack and Manger turn L towards Kings Somborne. 2m on R. 2 acres; spring bulbs, flowers and blossom; herbaceous, shrub roses, kitchen garden. TEAS *Adm £1 Chd 20p. Mon May 3 (2-6)*

By Appointment Gardens. See head of county section

¶**Rosewood Farm** ✿ (Mr & Mrs D Bowman) French-moor, West Tytherley. 10m E of Salisbury; 10m NW of Romsey. From A30 4½m W of Stockbridge take turn S signed West Tytherley-Norman Court. Continue through village on rd to West Dean after ½m L signed to French-moor. Attractive 1-acre informal garden with pond, waterfall and unusual plants and shrubs surrounded by lovely views. Adapted from a field 5 yrs ago. TEAS. *Adm £1 Chd 50p. Sun June 13 (2-6)*

Rotherfield Park &❀ (Sir James & Lady Scott) East Tisted, 4m S of Alton on A32. Large garden; walled and rose garden, herbaceous borders; lovely grounds with beautiful trees; pond; greenhouses. Picnickers welcome. TEAS (only when house is open). *Adm House & garden £2.50 Chd free. Garden only £1 Chd free (Share to Rainbow Trust) House and Garden open (2-5) every Bank Hol Sun & Mon from Easter & the first 7 days of June, July, Aug. Garden only Easter to Sept 30 every Thurs, Sun (2-5) (honesty box). Also by appt Tel 042058 204*

Rowans Wood ✿❀ (Mrs D C Rowan) 28 Straight Mile, Ampfield, on A31 (S side); 2m E of Romsey. 2m W of Potters Heron Hotel. Parking on service Rd. 2-acre wood-land garden made and maintained by owners; rhododen-drons, azaleas, camellias, spring bulbs. Foliage and ground cover plants. Over 50 varieties of hosta; fine trees. Considerable new planting as a result of recent hurricane losses. Views. TEAS. *Adm £1 Chd 25p (Share to Winchester & Romsey Branch RSPCA). Suns April 18, 25, May 23, 30 (2-5). Also by appt 0794 513072*

Roxfords House &✿ (Nicolas Wickham Irving Esq) Bin-sted. Next door to Binsted Church, S of Binsted Xrds. Much of the garden has been completely transformed and replanted (with the help of Helen Dorrien Smith) in 1990. Shrubs; trees with charming views down to Sel-borne. TEAS. *Adm £1 Chd free. Suns June 13, 20 (2-5.30)*

¶**12 Rozelle Close** ✿ (Margaret & Tom Hyatt) Littleton. Turn E off A272 Winchester to Stockbridge Rd. Just in-side Winchester 40 mph zone. 1m Hookers Nursery on R. Rozelle Close 150 yds on L just short of Running Horse public house. ⅓-acre spectacular display of herbaceous and 10,000 bedding plants; tubs; troughs; hanging bas-kets; 2 ponds; 3 greenhouses; vegetables. *Donations. Sat, Sun 24, 25 July (9.30-5.30)*

Rumsey Gardens &✿❀ (Mr & Mrs N R Giles) 117 Drift Rd, Clanfield, 6m S of Petersfield. Turn off A3 N of Horn-dean, signed Clanfield. 2 acres; alpine, herbaceous; heather, rhododendrons and wild gardens. Celebrity opening May only. *Adm £1 Chd 50p. Suns April 25, May 23, Aug 8 (11-5)*

¶**Sadlers Farmhouse** &❀ (Nicholas Lock) Lymington. Take A337, S out of Lymington. Turn L at Pennington Cross roundabout. ½m down lane on R. Quantities of rare and half hardy shrubs and trees; herbaceous beds; densely planted in 3 acres. Plantsman's garden created in 1976 by the owner; rhododendrons, camellias, magnolias and acers; spring and summer bulbs. Nursery open. *Adm £1 Chd free. Mons May 3, 31; Sun June 27 (2-6)*

3 St Helens Road &❀ (Mr & Mrs Norman Vaughan) Hayling Island. From Beachlands on seafront, turn R 3rd turning on R into Staunton Avenue, then 1st L. Parking in drive. ⅓-acre ornamental garden with conifers in variety. Interesting trees and shrubs; water garden; old roses. Best Large Garden 1990 and 1992 in 'The News' Best Garden Competition. Featured in 'Amateur Gardening' 1992. TEAS. *Adm by donation. Sat, Sun May 22, 23 (11-6)*

Somerley ✿ (The Earl & Countess of Normanton) 2m N of Ringwood off A338 between Ringwood & Ibsley. Turn to Ellingham Church and follow sign to Somerley House. From bus alight Ellingham Cross, country house garden with herbaceous and rose borders, pergola and herb gar-dens and ornamental kitchen garden and gift shop. Views over R Avon Valley and fine specimen trees in parkland. *Adm £1. Sun July 4 (2-6)*

South End House &✿❀ (Mr & Mrs Peter Watson) Lym-ington. At town centre, turn S opp St Thomas Church 70 yds, or park free behind Waitrose and use walkway. Walled town garden to Queen Anne house. ¼-acre, architecturally designed as philosophers' garden. Pergo-las, trellises and colonnade attractively planted with vines, clematis, wisteria and roses, combine with sculpted awnings to form 'outdoor rooms', enhanced by fountains, music and lights. Wide pavings, easy access, extensive seating. TEAS. *Adm £1 Chd free. Sun, May 16 (2.30-5.30)*

Sowley House &✿❀ (Mr & Mrs O Van Der Vorm) Sow-ley. At Lymington follow signs to I.O.W. ferry. Continue E on this rd past the ferry nearest to the Solent for 3m until Sowley pond on L. Sowley House is opp the pond. Old garden in country setting approx 4-5 acre with lovely far reaching views over the Solent to the I.O.W. Since 1986 the present owners have done a lot of redesigning and replanting. Walled garden, herbaceous and shrub borders, cottage, herb and rock gardens. Orchard, wood-land and bog garden still in the making. Famous for its drifts of daffodils mixed with wild primroses and violets. Stream walk down to the Solent. TEA. *Adm £1.50 Chd free. Sun April 4 (2-5)*

Spinners ✿❀ (Mr & Mrs P G G Chappell) Boldre. Signed off the A337 Brockenhurst Lymington Rd. Garden made by owners. Azaleas, rhododendrons, magnolias, hydran-geas, maples etc interplanted with a wide range of choice herbaceous plants and bulbs. Nursery contains a wide selection of less common and rare hardy plants, trees and shrubs. *Adm £1 Chd under six free. April 20 to Sept 1 daily (10-6) but closed Mons & Tues from July 1. Nursery open all the year and part of garden daily but closed Mons, Tues (exept by appt Tel 0590 673347) July 1 to April 1*

Springfield ✿❀ (Vice-Adm Sir John & Lady Lea) 27 Brights Lane, Hayling Island. From Havant take main rd over Hayling bridge, 3m fork R at roundabout into Manor Rd, Brights Lane ¼m on R. Bus: from Havant, ask for Manor Rd, Hayling Island, alight at Manor Rd PO. ⅓-acre walled cottage garden; mainly mixed borders containing wide variety of labelled plants; vegetables, greenhouses. Partially suited for wheelchairs. *Adm by donation. Sat, Sun May 29, 30 (11-6)*

● **Stratfield Saye House** ఉ (Home of the Dukes of Wellington) Off A33, equidistant between Reading and Basingstoke. House built 1630; presented to the Great Duke in 1817; unique collection of paintings, prints, furniture, china, silver and personal mementoes of the Great Duke. Special Wellington Exhibition; Great Duke's funeral carriage. Wildfowl sanctuary; American, rose and walled gardens and grounds. Refreshments. Also, nearby, Wellington Country Park with woodlands, meadowlands and lake. TEAS. *Adm £4 Chd £2 special rates for 20 or more.* **Tel 0256 882882.** *Open daily (except Fri) 1st May until the last Sun in Sept (11.30-4.30. Last ticket 4)*

Swallowfield Park, nr Reading see Berkshire

Tichborne Park ఉ఻ (Mrs J Loudon) Alresford. 1m S off A31 New Alresford on B 3046. 2m N of the A272 New Cheriton on B 3046. Approx 10-acres. Lake, River Itchen, large lawns, trees, shrubs, daffodils, kitchen gardens, glasshouse. TEAS. *Adm £1 Chd 50p. Suns April 4, May 9 (2-6)*

Tunworth Old Rectory ఉ఻ (The Hon Mrs Julian Berry) 5m SE of Basingstoke. 3m from Basingstoke turn S off A30 at sign to Tunworth. Medium-sized garden; shrubs, lawns, yew hedges, herbaceous borders; fine beech trees and ilex. Interesting beech-lined walk to church. Also pleached hornbeam small walk and lime avenue. House (not open) scheduled as Ancient Monument, part dating to 1210; in Domesday Book with adjacent farmhouse and church. TEAS. *Adm £1.50 Chd free (Share to Church Roof Fund All Saints Church Tunworth). Sun June 27 (2-5.30)*

Tylney Hall Hotel ఉ఻ From M3 Exit 5 Via A287 and Newnham, M4 Exit 11 via B3349 and Rotherwick. Large garden. 67 acres surrounding Tylney Hall Hotel with extensive Woodlands and fine vistas now being fully restored with new plantings; fine avenues of Wellingtonias; rhododendron and azaleas; Italian Garden; lakes; large water and rock garden and dry stone walls originally designed with assistance of Gertrude Jekyll. TEA. *Adm £1.50 Chd free. Suns April 4, May 16 (2-6)*

Vernon Hill House ఻ (Lady Newton) 1m from Bishop's Waltham. Turn off Beeches Hill. Attractive 6-acre spring and summer garden; wild garden with bulbs growing informally; fine trees, roses, unusual shrubs; kitchen garden. Picnickers welcome. *Adm £1 Chd 25p. Suns May 2, June 13, July 4, Mon May 3 (2-7) also by appt May to early July* **Tel 0489 892301**

Verona Cottage ఻఻ (David J Dickinson Esq) Webb Lane, Mengham, Hayling Island. 4m S of Havant. From A3023 fork L to Mengham; shops and free public car park 100yds. Entrance to garden opp Rose in June public house. L-shaped medium-sized garden entirely replanted since 1988 into 3 separate gardens with shrubs; roses and summer flowers, latest floribundas for year-round interest. TEA. *Adm 60p chd free. Sun May 30 (11-6)*

Veronica Cottage ఻ (Mr & Mrs E J Hartwell) East End. At Lymington follow signs to I.O.W. ferry. Continue E on this rd past the ferry for 2½m. Veronica Cottage is on the R just beyond the East End Arms. (O.S. ref 363969) Work began on this ⅓-acre garden in 1985. The cottage

well supplies several ponds and waterfalls which are surrounded by marginal plants, grasses and shrubs. Meandering borders contain many unusual and labelled shrubs and trees. Cream teas at East End Arms. *Adm £1 Chd free (Share to South Baddesley Church). Sat, Sun July 17, 18 (2-6)*

Vine Cottage ఉ఻ (Mr & Mrs C F Hoare & Mr R J Hoare) Ewshott, Farnham. NW of Farnham on B3013. Half way down Beacon Hill on L. Approx 1 acre facing north incl small orchard; collection of moisture loving plants on acid soil; small rockery and water garden; double herbaceous beds and shrubbery. TEAS. *Adm £1 Chd free. Suns April 25, May 2, 16 (2-6)*

The Vyne ఉ఻ (The National Trust) Sherborne St John, 4m N of Basingstoke. Between Sherborne St John and Bramley. From A340 turn E at NT signs. 17 acres with extensive lawns, lake, fine trees, herbaceous border. TEAS. *Adm house & garden £4 Chd £2; garden only £2 Chd £1.* ▲*Sun June 13 (12.30-5.30)*

Walhampton ఉ఻ (Walhampton School Trust) Lymington. 1m along B3054 to Beaulieu. 90 acres with azaleas; rhododendrons; lakes; shell grotto. TEAS. *Adm £1 Chd 50p. Sun May 23 (2-6)*

Westbrook House ఉ఻ (Andrew Lyndon-Skeggs Esq) Howards Lane, Holybourne. Turn N off roundabout at Farnham, end of Alton bypass A31 1st R, 1st L, 200yds on R. Mature 2½-acre garden backing onto stream and village pond. Being adapted stage by stage by owner; traditional kitchen garden; orchard; herbaceous and shrub borders; mature trees. *Adm £1.50 Chd free. Sun June 13 (2-5)*

West Silchester Hall ఉ఻ (Mrs Jenny Jowett) Bramley Rd, Silchester. Off A340 between Reading and Basingstoke. 1½ acres; Herbaceous and perennial borders, rhododendrons, azaleas, many unusual spring and summer plants; small pond and water garden; kitchen garden all owner maintained. Small exhibition of Mrs Jowett's botanical paintings. TEAS. *Adm £1 Chd 50p. Suns May 30, Aug 8 (2-6). Parties by appt March-Sept* **Tel 0734 700278**

West Tytherley Gardens 10m E of Salisbury; 10m NW of Romsey. From A30 4½m W of Stockbridge take turn S signed West Tytherley-Norman Court. **The Old School House** is in centre of village; for **The Drove** and **Moorlands** continue through village on road to West Dean, after ½m turn L signed to Frenchmoor. TEAS at **Moorlands**. *Combined adm £2 Chd 50p. Sun April 4 (2-6)*
    The Drove ఉ఻఻ (Mr & Mrs T H Faber) 3 acres informal garden, flowering shrubs, spring bulbs and ponds
    Moorlands ఉ఻ (Mr & Mrs M Fry) Approx 1 acre of informal garden; shrubs; bulbs; herbaceous and pond; lovely view of open farmland; garden made from pasture land 10 yrs ago. TEAS
    ¶**The Old School House** ఻ (Mr & Mrs P A Harris) ¼ acre. Spring bulbs, shrubs, rockery on 3 levels

Regular Openers. See head of county section.

¶**White Cottage** ✗ (Mr & Mrs A W Ferdinando) Speltham Hill, Hambledon. 8m SW of Petersfield. Speltham Hill is the lane between The George Inn and village grocer's shop. Garden is last but one on R, climbing. Parking in village or in small layby atop Speltham Hill. Small ornamental garden with oriental interest on steep hillside with good view of the village. The steepness of the garden has resulted in many steps to afford access to difficult areas, and to intensive planting of trees, shrubs and ground cover to retain soil and yet retain views. *Donations. Sun May 30 (2-6)*

White Windows ✗❀ (Mr & Mrs B Sterndale-Bennett) Longparish. 5m E of Andover off A303 to village centre on B3048. ⅔ acre with unusual range of hardy perennials, trees and shrubs planted for year round foliage interest and colour groupings. TEAS except June 14. *Adm £1 Chd free. Sun, Mon June 13, 14; Sun Sept 26 (2-6). Also by appt Weds April to Sept* **Tel 0264 72 222**

Wonston Lodge ᙖ (Mr & Mrs N J A Wood) Wonston. A34 or A30 to Sutton Scotney. At War Memorial turn to Wonston-Stoke Charity; ¾m in Wonston centre. 3 acres, owner maintained. Pond with aquatic plants; shrub roses; clematis; flowering shrubs; topiary. TEAS. *Adm £1.50 Chd free. Sun Sept 5 (2-6)*

Woodcote Manor ᙖ✗ (Mrs J S Morton) Bramdean, SE of Alresford. On A272 Winchester-Petersfield Rd, ½m E of Bramdean. Woodland garden; bulbs, shrubs. C17 manor house (not open). *Adm £1 Chd free. Sun April 11 (2-5)*

The Wylds ᙖ (Gulf International) Warren Rd, Liss Forest. 6m N of Petersfield; follow signs from Greatham on A325 and Rake on A3. 40 acres; 10-acre lake; 100 acres of woodland; rhododendrons, azaleas, heathers; many other shrubs and trees. TEA. *Adm £1.50 Chd 50p. Sun May 23 (2-6)*

Hereford & Worcester

Hon County Organisers:	(Hereford) Lady Richard Curtis, Tarrington Court, nr Hereford
	(Worcester) Mrs Graeme Anton, Summerway, Torton, nr Kidderminster Tel 0299 250388
Assistant County Organisers	(Worcester) Jeremy Hughes Esq. Hillwood Farm, Eastham, Tenbury Wells, Worcs WR15 8PA Tel 058479 366
	(Worcester) Mrs William Carr, Conderton Manor, nr Tewkesbury, Glos GL20 7PR
	(Hereford) Mr & Mrs Roger Norman, Marley Bank, Whitbourne, Worcester WR6 5RU Tel 0886 21576

DATES OF OPENING

By appointment

For telephone numbers and other details see garden descriptions

Arrow Cottage, nr Weobley
The Bannut, Bromyard
Barnard's Green House, Malvern
Bredon Pound, Ashton under Hill
Brilley Court, Whitney-on-Wye
Brookside, Bringsty
Chennels Gate, Eardisley
Conderton Manor, nr Tewkesbury
6 Elm Grove, nr Stourport-on-Severn
Frogmore, nr Ross-on-Wye
Grantsfield, nr Leominster
28 Hillgrove Crescent, Kidderminster
Kingstone Cottages, Ross-on-Wye
Longacre, Colwall Green
Lower Hope, Ullingswick
Marley Bank, Whitbourne
The Manor House, Birlingham
Stone House Cottage Gardens, Stone

Torwood, Whitchurch
Well Cottage, Blakemere
Westwood Farm, Hatfield
White Cottage, Stock Green, nr Inkberrow

Regular openings

For details see garden descriptions

Abbey Dore Court, Abbey Dore, nr Hereford. Daily Mar 20 to Oct 17 except Weds
Barnard's Green House, Malvern. Every Thurs April to Sept
Bredon Springs, Ashton-under-Hill. April 1 to Oct 31. For days see text
The Cottage Herbery, Boraston, Tenbury Wells. Every Sun April 25 to Sept 26. Bank Hol Mons May 3, 31
Eastgrove Cottage Garden Nursery. For dates see text

Dinmore Manor, Wellington. Open all year
Frogmore, nr Ross-on-Wye. Mons April to Sept
Hergest Croft Gardens, Kington. Daily April 9 to Oct 31
How Caple Court, Ross-on-Wye. Mon to Sat April 1 to Oct 31. Suns May to Sept 26
Kingstone Cottages, Ross-on-Wye. May 4 to June 25. Mon to Fri (except May 31)
Lingen Nursery, Lingen. Daily Feb to Oct
Marley Bank, Whitbourne. 1st and 3rd Sat April to Sept
The Manor House, Birlingham. Every Thurs May 6 to July 8 & Sept 2 to Oct 7 ‡
The Picton Garden at Old Court Nurseries, Colwall. Weds to Suns, April to Oct
The Priory, Kemerton. Every Thurs May 20 to Sept 30 ‡

Staunton Park, Staunton-on-Arrow.
Weds, Suns, Easter and Bank
Hols April to end Sept
Stone House Cottage Gardens,
Stone. Weds, Thurs, Fris and Sats
March to Oct
White Cottage, Stock Green, nr
Inkberrow. April 4 to Oct 10
closed Thurs and alternative Suns
(closed August). Nursery open
daily Mar 21 to Oct 11 (closed
Thurs)
Whitlenge House Cottage,
Hartlebury. Thurs, Fris, Sats and
some Suns March to Oct

March 21 Sunday
The Old Rectory, Leinthall Starkes
Robins End, Eastham
March 28 Sunday
Overbury Court, nr Tewkesbury
Whitlenge House Cottage,
Hartlebury
April 4 Sunday
Garnons, nr Hereford
Holland House, Cropthorne
Ripple Hall, nr Tewkesbury
Tedstone Court, nr Bromyard
White Cottage, Stock Green, nr
Inkberrow
Wormington Grange, nr Broadway
April 9 Friday
Spetchley Park, nr Worcester
April 11 Sunday
Arrow Cottage, nr Weobley
Lakeside, Whitbourne
Staunton Park, Staunton-on-Arrow
White Cottage, Stock Green, nr
Inkberrow
Whitlenge House Cottage,
Hartlebury
April 12 Monday
Stone House Cottage Gardens,
Stone ‡
White Cottage, Stock Green, nr
Inkberrow
Whitlenge House Cottage,
Hartlebury ‡
April 18 Sunday
Lower Hope, Ullingswick
White Cottage, Stock Green, nr
Inkberrow
Wichenford Court, Wichenford
Wind's Point, Malvern
April 22 Thursday
Conderton Manor, nr Tewksbury
April 25 Sunday
Barbers, Martley, nr Worcester
Brookside, Bringsty
Dinmore Manor, Wellington
Lingen Nursery, Lingen
Whitlenge House Cottage,
Hartlebury

May 2 Sunday
Arley House, Upper Arley, nr
Bewdley
Arrow Cottage, nr Weobley
Barnard's Green House,
Malvern
Brookside, Bringsty
Chennels Gate, Eardisley
The Hill Court, Ross-on-Wye
Stone House Cottage Gardens,
Stone ‡
Tedstone Court, nr Bromyard
White Cottage, Stock Green, nr
Inkberrow
Whitlenge House Cottage,
Hartlebury ‡
Windyridge, Kidderminster ‡
May 3 Monday
Brilley Court, nr Whitney-on-Wye
Chennels Gate, Eardisley
The Cottage Herbery, Boraston,
Tenbury Wells
Stone House Cottage Gardens,
Stone ‡
White Cottage, Stock Green, nr
Inkberrow
Whitlenge House Cottage,
Hartlebury ‡
May 6 Thursday
The Manor House, Birlingham
May 8 Saturday
Hergest Croft Gardens, Kington
May 9 Sunday
Spetchley Park, nr Worcester
Stone House Cottage Gardens,
Stone
May 13 Thursday
The Manor House, Birlingham
May 16 Sunday
Brookside, Bringsty
28 Hillgrove Crescent,
Kidderminster
Lingen Nursery, Lingen
Little Malvern Court, nr Malvern
Stone House Cottage Gardens,
Stone ‡
White Cottage, Stock Green, nr
Inkberrow
Windyridge, Kidderminster ‡
May 20 Thursday
The Manor House, Birlingham
May 23 Sunday
Bodenham Arboretum, Wolverley
Red House Farm, Bradley Green
Stone House Cottage Gardens,
Stone
Torwood, Whitchurch
May 27 Thursday
The Manor House, Birlingham
May 30 Sunday
Arrow Cottage, nr Weobley
Chennels Gate, Eardisley
Stone House Cottage Gardens,
Stone ‡

White Cottage, Stock Green, nr
Inkberrow
Whitlenge House Cottage,
Hartlebury ‡
May 31 Monday
Arrow Cottage, nr Weobley
The Cottage Herbery, Boraston,
Tenbury Wells
Chennels Gate, Eardisley
Stone House Cottage Gardens,
Stone
White Cottage, Stock Green, nr
Inkberrow
Whitlenge House Cottage,
Hartlebury
June 3 Thursday
Conderton Manor, nr Tewksbury ‡
The Manor House, Birlingham ‡
June 6 Sunday
Astley Horticultural Society,
Stourport-on-Severn
Hartlebury Castle, nr
Kidderminster ‡
Lingen Nursery, Lingen
Stone House Cottage Gardens,
Stone ‡
Torwood, Whitchurch
Whitfield, Wormbridge
June 10 Thursday
The Manor House, Birlingham
June 13 Sunday
Brookside, Bringsty
Frogmore, nr Ross-on-Wye
Holland House, Cropthorne ‡
How Caple Court, Ross-on-Wye
The Marsh Country Hotel, Eyton,
nr Leominster
Moccas Court, nr Hereford
Newcote, Moccas
Pershore College of Horticulture ‡
The Priory, Kemerton
Staunton Park,
Staunton-on-Arrow
Stone House Cottage Gardens,
Stone ‡
White Cottage, Stock Green, nr
Inkberrow
June 17 Thursday
The Manor House, Birlingham
June 20 Sunday
Arrow Cottage, nr Weobley
Barbers, Martley, nr Worcester
Bell's Castle, Kemerton ‡
Birtsmorton Court, nr Malvern
Colwall Green & Evendine Gardens
Gatley Park, Leinthall Earls
Grantsfield, nr Leominster
28 Hillgrove Crescent,
Kidderminster ‡‡
St Michael's Cottage, Broadway
Stone House Cottage Gardens,
Stone ‡‡
Torwood, Whitchurch
Upper Court, Kemerton ‡

June 24 Thursday
The Manor House, Birlingham
June 27 Sunday
Berrington Hall, Leominster
Brilley Court, nr Whitney-on-Wye
Chennels Gate, Eardisley
Croft Castle, Kingsland
Overbury Court, nr Tewkesbury
Stone House Cottage Gardens, Stone ‡
Summerway, Torton nr Kidderminster ‡
Westwood Farm, Hatfield
White Cottage, Stock Green, nr Inkberrow
Whitlenge House Cottage, Hartlebury ‡
Yew Tree House, Ombersley
June 28 Monday
Westwood Farm, Hatfield
July 1 Thursday
The Manor House, Birlingham
July 4 Sunday
Hanbury Hall, nr Droitwich
Spetchley Park, nr Worcester
Torwood, Whitchurch
July 8 Thursday
The Manor House, Birlingham
July 10 Saturday
28 Cornmeadow Lane, Claines, Worcester
July 11 Sunday
Arley Cottage, Upper Arley, nr Bewdley
Bredon Pound, Ashton under Hill
Bredenbury Court (St Richards), Bredenbury
Broadfield Court, Bodenham
Cedar Lodge, Blakeshall, nr Wolverley
6 Elm Grove, nr Stourport-on-Severn
The Hill Court, Ross-on-Wye
Lakeside, Whitbourne
Lower Hope, Ullingswick
The Orchard Farm, Broadway ‡
The Priory, Kemerton
White Cottage, Stock Green, nr Inkberrow
Wormington Grange, nr Broadway ‡
July 15 Thursday
Conderton Manor, nr Tewksbury
July 18 Sunday
Arrow Cottage, nr Weobley
The Bannut, Bromford
Chennels Gate, Eardisley
Torwood, Whitchurch
July 25 Sunday
White Cottage, Stock Green, nr Inkberrow
Whitlenge House Cottage, Hartlebury
August 1 Sunday
Torwood, Whitchurch
August 8 Sunday
28 Hillgrove Cresent, Kidderminster
The Priory, Kemerton
August 15 Sunday
Brookside, Bringsty
Chennels Gate, Eardisley
August 22 Sunday
The Bannut, Bromyard
August 26 Thursday
Conderton Manor, Tewksbury
August 28 Saturday
Monnington Court, Hereford
August 29 Sunday
Monnington Court, Hereford
The Priory, Kemerton
Stone House Cottage Gardens, Stone
White Cottage, Stock Green, nr Inkberrow
Whitlenge House Cottage, Hartlebury
August 30 Monday
Monnington Court, Hereford
Stone House Cottage Garden, Stone ‡
White Cottage, Stock Green, nr Inkberrow
Whitlenge House Cottage, Hartlebury ‡
September 2 Thursday
The Manor House, Birlingham
September 5 Sunday
Barnard's Green House, Malvern
September 9 Thursday
The Manor House, Birlingham
September 11 Saturday
Keepers Cottage, Alvechurch
September 12 Sunday
Brookside, Bringsty
Keepers Cottage, Alvechurch
Lingen Nursery, Lingen
The Priory, Kemerton
White Cottage, Stock Green, nr Inkberrow
September 16 Thursday
The Manor House, Birlingham
September 19 Sunday
The Old Rectory, Leintahll Starkes
Torwood, Whitchurch
September 23 Thursday
The Manor House, Birlingham
September 26 Sunday
White Cottage, Stock Green, nr Inkberrow
Whitlenge House Cottage, Hartlebury
September 30 Thursday
The Manor House, Birlingham
October 3 Sunday
Dinmore Manor, Wellington
October 7 Thursday
Conderton Manor, nr Tewksbury ‡
The Manor House, Birlingham ‡
October 10 Sunday
White Cottage, Stock Green, nr Inkberrow
October 17 Sunday
Nerine Nursery, Welland
October 31 Sunday
Whitlenge House Cottage, Harltebury

DESCRIPTIONS OF GARDENS

● **Abbey Dore Court** ♿✲❀ (Mrs C L Ward) 11m SW of Hereford. From A465 midway between Hereford-Abergavenny turn W, signed Abbey Dore; then 2½m. 4 acres bordered by R. Dore; constantly being extended to accommodate increasing number unusual plants and shrubs; herbaceous borders, circular herb garden, walled garden, fern border, small orchard; pond and rock garden made in field. Home of a National Euphorbia Collection. Many unusual plants for sale. Out of the ordinary gift gallery. Lunch and TEAS. Food from 11.30. *Adm £1.50 Chd 50p (Share to Mother Theresa). Sat March 20 to Sun Oct 17 daily except Weds (11-6)*

Arley Cottage ♿ (Woodward family) Upper Arley, nr Bewdley. 5m N of Kidderminster off A442. Small country garden with lawns bordered by interesting shrubs and collection of rare trees. TEAS. *Adm £1 Chd free (Share L-FRUPA). Sun July 11 (2-5)*

Arley House ✲ (R D Turner Esq) Upper Arley, 5m N of Kidderminster. A442. Arboretum containing specimen conifers and hardwoods, rhododendrons, camellias, magnolias, heathers; Italianate garden; greenhouses with orchids, alpines. Aviary with ornamental pheasants, budgerigars. TEA. *Adm £1.50 Chd free (Share to St Peter's, Upper Arley). Sun May 2 (2-7)*

Arrow Cottage ⚬⚬ (Mr & Mrs L Hattatt) 10m NW Hereford via Burghill and Tillington towards Weobley. Take Ledgmoor turning then R (No through Rd) 1st Hse on Left. A plantsman's garden of nearly 2 acres, arranged as a series of immaculately maintained garden rooms. White garden, red border, 19th century shrub roses, kitchen garden, rockery, pool and stream. Featured on Channel 4 television 1991. *Adm £1 Chd 20p. Suns April 11, May 2; Sun, Mon May 30, 31, Suns June 20, July 18 (2-5). Also by appointment* **Tel 0544 318468**

¶Astley Horticultural Society ⚬⚬ 3m W of Stourport on Severn on B4196 Worcester to Bewdley rd. A selection of mature and new country gardens at their best in early June. Start from the Astley Parish Room and drive around the Parish of Astley and Dunley. Several exceptional gardens included. TEAS. *Adm £2 Chd free. Sun June 6 (1-6)*

The Bannut ⚬⚬ (Mr Maurice & Mrs Daphne Everett) Bringsty. 3m E of Bromyard on A44 Worcester Rd. (½m E of entrance to National Trust, Brockhampton). A 1-acre garden, planted with all year colour in mind; mainly established by the present owners since 1984. Mixed borders of trees, shrubs and herbaceous plants, island beds and a small bog garden. A colourful heather garden designed around a Herefordshire cider mill and an unusual heather knot garden with water feature. Plants for sale. TEAS. *Adm £1 Chd free. Suns July 18, August 22 (2-5). Also by appt* **Tel 0885 482206**

Barbers ⚬⚬⚬ (Mr & the Hon Mrs Richard Webb) Martley 7m NW of Worcester on B4204. Medium-sized garden with lawns, trees, shrubs, pools and wild garden. Home-made TEAS. *Adm £1 Chd free (Share to Martley Church). Suns April 25, June 20 (2-6)*

Barnard's Green House ⚬⚬⚬ (Mr & Mrs Philip Nicholls) 10 Poolbrook Rd, Malvern. On E side of Malvern at junction of B4211 and B4208. 3-acre cultivated garden; herbaceous, rockeries, heather beds, woodland/water garden, vegetable plot; several unusual plants and shrubs; 2 fine cedars, lawns. Mrs Nicholls is a specialist on dried flowers, on which she has written a book. Half-timbered house (not open) dates from 1635; home of Sir Charles Hastings, founder of BMA. Coach parties by appt. TEAS. *Adm £1 Acc chd free (Share to Save the Children Fund). Suns May 2, Sept 5 and every Thursday April to Sept incl. (2-6). Also by appt* **Tel 0684 574446**

Bell's Castle ⚬ (Lady Holland-Martin) Kemerton, NE of Tewkesbury. 3 small terraces with battlements; wild garden outside wall. The small Gothic castellated folly was built by Edmund Bell (Smuggler) c1820; very fine views. TEAS. *Adm £1 Chd free. Sun June 20 (2.30-6)*

Berrington Hall ⚬⚬ (The National Trust) 3m N of Leominster on A49. Signposted. Bus Midland Red (W) x 92, 292 alight Luston, 2m. Extensive views over Capability Brown Park; formal garden with personal favourites; wall plants, unusual trees, camellia collection, herbaceous plants, wisteria. Woodland walk, recent rhododendron planting. Light lunches and TEAS. *Adm £3.20 Chd £1.60. Grounds only £1.50.* ▲*For NGS Sun June 27 (12.30-5.30)*

Birtsmorton Court ⚬⚬ (Mr & Mrs N G K Dawes) nr Malvern. 7m E of Ledbury on A438. Fortified manor house (not open) dating from C12; moat; Westminster pool, laid down in Henry V11's reign at time of consecration of Westminster Abbey; large tree under which Cardinal Wolsey reputedly slept in shadow of ragged stone. Topiary. Motor Museum extra. TEAS. *Adm £1 Chd 25p. Sun June 20 (2-6)*

Bodenham Arboretum (Mr & Mrs J D Binnian) 2m N of Wolverley; 5m N of Kidderminster. From Wolverley Church follow signs. 134 acres landscaped & planted during the past 20 years; 2 chains of lakes & pools; woods and glades with over 1200 species & shrubs; Laburnum tunnel; Grove & Swamp Cypress in shallows of 3-acre lake. Bring wellingtons or strong boots. TEA. NO COACHES. *Adm £1.50 Chd free (Share to The Kemp House Trust, Home Care Hospice). Sun May 23 (2-6) parties by appt at other times of the year* **Tel 0562 850382**

Bredenbury Court (St Richards) ⚬ (Headmaster: R E H Coghlan Esq) Bredenbury, 3m W of Bromyard. On A44 Bromyard- Leominster rd; entrance on right (N) side of rd. 5-acre garden; 15 acres parkland with fine views. Simple rose garden and herbaceous borders. Picnics allowed. Use of swimming pool 30p extra. TEAS. *Adm £1 Chd 50p (Share to St Richards Hospice). Sun July 11 (12-6)*

Bredon Pound ⚬⚬ (Mr & Mrs David King) Ashton under Hill. 6m down the Cheltenham Rd from Evesham. A recently landscaped garden at the foot of Bredon Hill with fine views over the Vale of Evesham to the Cotswold Hills. Shrub roses, heathers and an interesting collection of trees and shrubs. TEAS. *Adm £1 Chd free (Share to Spastics Society). Sun July 11 (12-5). Also by appt May to August.* **Tel 0386 881209**

Bredon Springs ⚬ (Ronald Sidwell Esq) Paris, Ashton-under-Hill, 6m SW of Evesham. Take Ashton turning off A435, turn R in village; then 1st L. Limited parking. Coach parties must alight at church (by the old cross) and walk through churchyard (6 mins), following the mown footpath over 2 fields. 1¾ acres; large plant collection in natural setting. DOGS welcome. *Adm £1 Chd free (Share to NCCPG). April 1 to Oct 31, every Sat Sun Wed & Thurs; also Bank Hol Mons & Tues following (10-dusk)*

Brilley Court ⚬⚬ (Mr & Mrs D Bulmer) nr Whitney-on-Wye 6m E Hay-on-Wye. 1½m off main A438 Hereford to Brecon Rd signposted to Brilley. Medium-sized walled garden spring and herbaceous. Valley stream garden; spring colour. New ornamental kitchen garden. Excellent views to Black Mountains. TEAS. *Adm £1.50 OAPs £1 Chd 50p (Share to CRMF). Mon May 3; Sun June 27 (2-6). Also by appt April to July* **Tel 04973 467**

Regular Openers. Too many days to include in diary. Usually there is a wide range of plants giving year-round interest. See head of county section for the name and garden description for times etc.

Broadfield Court ও❀ (Mr & Mrs Keith James) Bodenham 7m SE Leominster A49 from Leominster or Hereford & A417 to Bodenham; turn left to Risbury signposted at Bodenham. 4 acres of old English gardens; yew hedges; spacious lawn; rose garden; herbaceous. Picnic area. 17 acres of vineyard; wine tasting included in entrance charge. TEAS. *Adm £2 OAP £1.50 Chd 50p. Sun July 11 (11-4.30)*

Bromesberrow Place, see Gloucestershire

Brookside ❀❀ (Mr & Mrs John Dodd) Bringsty; 3m E of Bromyard via A44 10m W of Worcester; Bringsty Common turn down track to 'Live & Let Live'; at PH carpark bear left to Brookside. 1½-acres; specimen trees and shrubs in grass sloping to lake; mixed beds with all year interest; alpine collection, unusual plants; daffodils in spring. Parties by arrangement only. TEAS on terrace. *Adm £1 Chd 20p (Share to Save the Children Fund). Suns April 25, May 2, 16 June 13, Aug 15, Sept 12 (2-6). Also other times by appt* **Tel 0886 21835**

¶**Cedar Lodge** ❀❀ (Mr & Mrs Vivian Andrews) Blakeshall. 1½m from Wolverley. ½-acre plantsman's garden with extensive range of trees, shrubs and plants (some rare), in country setting adjoining Kinver Edge. The garden was the 1991/92 overall winner of Practical Gardening magazine's 'My Garden' competition. TEAS. *Adm £1 Chd free (Share to Motor Neurone Disease Association). Sun July 11 (2-5.30)*

¶**Chennels Gate** ও❀❀ (Mr & Mrs Kenneth Dawson) Eardisley. 5m S of Kington. ½m from Tram Inn on Woodseave Lane. Signposted. A 2-acre plantsman's cottage garden, set in 15 acres with newly planted woodland and orchards. Rose garden; herbaceous borders; water garden; conservatory; decorative garden birds and waterfowl. Large selection of plants for sale. TEAS. *Adm £1.20 Chd free. Suns May 2, 30, June 27, July 18, Aug 15, Mons May 3, 31 (2-6). Also by appt* **Tel 0544 327288**

Colwall Green & Evendine Gardens ❀❀ 3m SW Malvern and 3m E of Ledbury on B2048. TEAS at The Elms. *Combined adm £1.50 Chd free. Maps available showing parking. Sun June 20 (2-6)*

    Beyond (Mr & Mrs Gill) Medium-sized gardens containing large number of unusual plants

    Caves Folly ও❀❀ (Mrs S Evans) Evendine Lane, Off Colwall Green. Medium-sized garden of old converted stables; started from meadowland in 1977; shrubs and roses but mainly a selection of interesting and unusual alpines and herbaceous plants; unlimited parking. 300yds from **The Elms** *(2-6)*

    The Elms School ও❀ (L A C Ashby Esq, Headmaster) Colwall Green. Medium-sized garden, herbaceous borders, fine views of Malvern Hills. TEAS. *Also open in conjunction with Wyche and Colwall Horticultural Society Show Sat Aug 14 (2-6)*

    The Picton Garden at Old Court Nursery (Mr & Mrs Paul Picton) for details see Picton Garden

    Tustins (Mrs D Singleton) Medium-size garden containing large numbers of unusual plants

---

By Appointment Gardens. See head of county section

Conderton Manor ও❀ (Mr & Mrs William Carr) 5½m NE of Tewkesbury. Between A435 & B4079. Cotswold stone manor house (not open). 7-acre garden with magnificent views of Cotswolds; flowering cherries, bulbs, trees, shrubs and mixed borders, newly planted bed, formal terrace. Teas available at the Silk Shop. *Adm £2 Chd 25p. Thurs April 22, June 3, July 15, Aug 26, Oct 7 (2- 6). Visitors other times by appt* **Tel 0386 89 389**

28 Cornmeadow Lane ❀❀ (Rev P J Wedgwood) Claines is a northern suburb of Worcester; follow signpost Claines at roundabout junction of A449 and M/way link rd; R at church. House beside 3rd hall on L about ½m down Cornmeadow Lane. Parking in Church Hall grounds. Small town garden packed with rare and tropical plants with plenty of colour. TEAS in aid of Children of the Andes. *Adm £1 Chd free. Sat July 10 (2-6)*

The Cottage Herbery ❀❀ (Mr & Mrs R E Hurst) 1m E of Tenbury Wells on A456, turn for Boraston at Peacock Inn, turn R in village, signposted to garden. Half timbered C16 farmhouse with fast-flowing Cornbrook running close to its side and over ford at the bottom of garden. ½-acre of garden specializing in a wide range of herbs, aromatic and scented foliage plants, planted on a cottage garden theme; also unusual hardy perennial and variegated plants; early interest bulbs, pulmonarias, euphorbias, symphytums. Nursery sells large selection of herbs. Organic garden. Silver Medal Chelsea 1992. Featured in Central TV My Secret Garden shown earlier this year. No toilets. TEAS (served in garden). *Adm £1 Chd free. Every Sun April 25 to Sept 26, also Bank Hol Mons May 3, 31 (10-6)*

Croft Castle ও❀ (The National Trust) 5m NW of Leominster. On B4362 (off B4361, Leominster-Ludlow). Large garden; borders; walled garden; landscaped park and walks in Fishpool Valley; fine old avenues. Light lunches and Teas Berrington Hall. *Adm £2.80 Family £7.70 Chd £1.40. For NGS Sun June 27 (2-6)*

Dinmore Manor ও❀❀ (R G Murray Esq) Hereford, 6m N of Hereford. Route A49. Bus: Midland Red Hereford-Leominster, alight Manor turning 1m. Spectacular hillside location. A range of impressive architecture dating from C14-20; chapel; cloisters; Great hall (Music Room) and extensive roof walk giving panoramic views of countryside and beautiful gardens below; stained glass. TEAS for NGS Sun April 25, Oct 3, unusual plants for sale. *Adm £2 Acc chd free (Share to NSPCC). For NGS Sun April 25, Sun Oct 3 (10-5.30). Open throughout the year (10.30-5.30)*

Eastgrove Cottage Garden Nursery ❀❀ (Mr & Mrs J Malcolm Skinner) Sankyns Green, Shrawley. 8m NW of Worcester on rd between Shrawley (on B4196) and Great Witley (on A443). Set in 5 acres unspoilt meadow and woodland, this unique 1-acre garden and nursery is of particular interest to the plantsman. Expanding collection of hardy plants in old world country flower garden with much thought given to planting combinations both of colour and form. C17 half-timbered yeoman farmhouse (not open). Garden and nursery maintained by owners since 1970. Outstandingly wide range of well grown less usual plants for sale, all grown at Nursery. Help and advice always available from owners. *Adm £1 Chd 20p (Share to RNLI). Thurs to Mon April 1 to July 31 (2-5).* **Closed thoughout August. Not open Tues & Weds.** *Sept 2 to Oct 16 open Thurs, Fris, Sats only (2-5)*

6 Elm Grove ঙ঺ (Michael Ecob) Astley Cross. W of Stourport on Severn. Turn S on B4196 towards Worcester-Bewdley. ⅓-acre garden with mature trees, borders, patio area, pool and small conservatory. By late June the borders take on a cottage garden appearance with many unusual plants amongst old favourites: small vegetable area used for show produce. Several neighbouring gardens in The Grove will also be open in conjunction with No 6. TEAS. *Adm £1. Sun July 11(1-6). Also by appt* **Tel 0299 822167**

Frogmore ঙ঺঺ (Sir Jonathan & Lady North) Pontshill. 4m SE of Ross-on-Wye. 1m S of A40 through Pontshill. 2-acre garden with fine mature trees and many unusual young trees and shrubs. Mixed borders with nut walk and ha ha. Additional borders and plantings since last opened. Mown walk along stream and to spinney. TEAS (in aid of Hope Mansel Church), hardy geranium nursery, open Mons only 10-6 April to Sept or by appt **Tel 0989 750214.** *Adm £1.50 Chd free. Sun June 13 (2-6)*

Garnons ঙ঺ (Sir John & Lady Cotterell) 7m W of Hereford on A438; lodge gates on right; then fork left over cattle grid. Large park landscaped by Repton; attractive spring garden. House is remaining wing (1860) of house pulled down in 1957. TEA. *Adm part of house & garden £2 Chd free; garden only £1 Chd free (Share to Byford Church). Sun April 4 (2-5.30)*

Gatley Park (Capt & Mrs Thomas Dunne) Leinthall Earls, 9m NW of Leominster; 9m SW of Ludlow. Turn E off A4110 between Aymestrey and Wigmore follow signs to village, 1½m; drive ½m long. Medium-sized garden; terraced rose gardens; herbaceous borders; old clipped yew walk; Magnificent position and views. TEAS in Jacobean house in aid of Aymestrey & Leinthall Earles Churches. *Adm £1.50 Chd 50p (Share to Aymestry & Leinthall Earls Churches). Sun June 20 (2-6)*

Grantsfield ঙ঺঺ (Col & Mrs J G T Polley) nr Kimbolton, 3m NE of Leominster. A49 N from Leominster, turn right to Grantsfield. Car parking in field; not coaches which must drop and collect visitors at gate. Contrasting styles in gardens of old stone farmhouse; wide variety of unusual plants and shrubs, old roses, climbers; herbaceous borders; superb views. 4-acre orchard and kitchen garden with flowering and specimen trees. Spring bulbs. TEAS. *Adm £1 Chd 50p (Share to Hamnish Church). Sun June 20 (2-5.30). By appt April to end Sept* **Tel 0568 613338**

Hanbury Hall ঙ঺ (The National Trust) Hanbury, 3m NE of Droitwich, 6m S of Bromsgrove. Signed off B4090. Extensive lawns; shrubberies; Victorian forecourt with detailed planting. William & Mary style brick house of 1701 with murals by Thornhill; contemporary Orangery and Ice House. TEAS. *Adm house & garden £3 Chd £1.50 Sun July 4 (2-6)*

Hartlebury Castle ঙ঺ (The Rt Revd The Lord Bishop of Worcester) Medieval moated castle reconstructed 1675, restored 1964. Many Tudor and Hanoverian Royal connections. Rose garden in forecourt. Wheelchairs ground floor. *Adm gardens & state rooms 75p OAPs 50p Chd 25p. Sun June 6 (2-5)*

● **Hergest Croft Gardens** ঙ঺ (W L Banks Esq & R A Banks Esq) ½m off A44 on Welsh side of Kington, 20m NW of Hereford: Turn left at Rhayader end of bypass; then 1st right; gardens ¼m on left. 3 gardens owned by Banks' family for 4 generations. Edwardian garden surrounding house (not open); Park wood with rhododendrons up to 30ft tall; old fashioned kitchen garden with spring and herbaceous borders. One of finest private collections of trees and shrubs; now selected to hold National Collections Maples and Birches. TEAS for parties by arrangement **Tel Kington 230160.** *Adm £2.20 Chd under 15 free (Share to NCCPG). Fri April 9 to Sun Oct 31 daily. For NGS Sat May 8 (1.30-6.30)*

The Hill Court ঙ঺ (Christopher Rowley Esq) Ross-on-Wye. 2¾m SW of Ross-on Wye; take B4228 towards Walford; after ½m at Prince of Wales, bear right, lodge gates 1½m on right. C18 house Grade I (not open) approached by double avenue. Garden Centre with walled garden, yew walk and water garden open daily. Private gardens with bronze & silver fountain garden, herbaceous borders, flowering shrubs and woodland garden open for NGS. TEAS. *Adm £1.50 OAP/Chd 75p (Share to St Michaels Hospice, Hereford). Suns May 2, July 11 (2-5.30)*

28 Hillgrove Crescent ঺঺ (Mr & Mrs D Terry) Kidderminster. Crescent linking Chester Rd (A449) & Bromsgrove Rd (A448). Town garden containing a variety of plants (many unusual) including alpines, herbaceous, shrubs and ferns. *Adm £1 Chd free (Share to CRMF). Suns May 16, June 20, Aug 8 (2-6). Also by appt* **Tel 0562 751957**

Holland House ঺ (Warden: Mr Peter Middlemiss) Main St, Cropthorne, Pershore. Between Pershore and Evesham, off A44. Car park at rear of house. Gardens laid out by Lutyens in 1904; house dating back to 1636 (not open). TEAS. *Adm 70p Chd 30p (Share to USPG). Suns April 4, June 13 (2.30-5)*

How Caple Court ঺ (Mr & Mrs Peter Lee) How Caple, 5m N of Ross on Wye 10m S of Hereford on B4224; turn right at How Caple Xrds, garden 400 yds on left. 11 acres; mainly Edwardian gardens in process of replanting, set high above R. Wye in park and woodland; formal terraces: yew hedges, statues and pools; sunken florentine water garden under restoration; woodland walks; herbaceous and shrub borders, shrub roses, mature trees: Mediaeval Church with newly restored C16 Diptych. Nursery specialising in old rose varieties and apple varieties, unusual herbaceous plants. Fabric shop. *Adm £2 Chd £1. Open Mon to Sat, April 1 to Oct 31. Also Suns May to Sept 26 (10-5). For NGS Sun June 13 (10-5)*

> **Regular Openers.** Too many days to include in diary. Usually there is a wide range of plants giving year-round interest. See head of county section for the name and garden description for times etc.

Keepers Cottage ✿✸ (Mrs Diana Scott) Alvechurch. Take main A441 rd through Alvechurch towards Redditch. Turn opp sign to Cobley Hill and Bromsgrove for 1m over 2 humpback bridges. 3-acre garden at 600ft with fine views towards the Cotswolds; rhododendrons, camellias; old fashioned roses; unusual trees and shrubs; rock garden; 2 alpine houses; paddock with donkeys. Show jumping as seen on TV 1m away at Wharf Meadow. TEAS. *Adm £1 Chd 50p (Share to St Mary's Hospice). Sat, Sun Sept 11, 12 (2-6)*

Kingstone Cottages ✸ (Mr & Mrs M Hughes) A40 Ross/Glos, turn left at Weston Cross to Bollitree Castle, then left to Rudhall. Interesting cottage garden on the wild side containing National Collection of old pinks and carnations. Many other unusual plants. Features include terraced beds, ponds, grotto, summerhouse and lovely views, unusual plants and dianthus for sale. Garden furniture designed and made on premises. Featured in Channel 4 'Flowering Passions'. *Adm £1 Chd free. Mon to Fri May 4 to June 25 (except May 31) (9.30-4.30). Also by appt.* **Tel Ross 65267**

Lakeside ✿✸ (Mr D Gueroult & Mr C Philip) Gaines Rd, Whitbourne. 9m W of Worcester off A44 at County boundary sign (ignore sign to Whitbourne Village). 6-acres, large walled garden with many mixed beds and borders; spring bulbs, climbers, unusual shrubs and plants, heather garden, bog garden, newly extended lake walk, medieval carp lake with fountain. Uncommon plants for sale. Steep steps and slopes. TEAS in aid of Red Cross. *Adm £1.50 Chd free. Suns April 11, July 11 (2-6)*

Lingen Nursery and Garden ✿✸ (Mr Kim Davis) Lingen. 5m NE of Presteigne take B4362 E from Presteigne, 2m turn L for Lingen, 3m opposite Chapel in village. 2 acres of specialist alpine and herbaceous nursery and general garden intensively planted giving a long period of interest having large areas of rock garden and herbaceous borders, a peat bed, raised screes and an Alpine House and stock beds, together with 2 acres of developing garden where picnics are welcome. Many unusual plants with comprehensive labelling. Wide range of plants for sale from the nursery frames. Catalogue available. TEAS (NGS days only). *Adm £1 Chd free. Suns April 25, May 16, June 6, Sept 12 (2-6) for NGS. Also open Feb-Oct everyday (10-6). Coach parties by appt* **Tel 0544 267720**

Little Malvern Court ✿✸ (Mr & Mrs T M Berington) 4m S of Malvern on A4104 S of junc with A449. 10 acres attached to former Benedictine Priory, magnificent views over Severn valley. An intriguing layout of garden rooms, and terrace round house. Newly made and planted water garden below, feeding into chain of lakes. Wide variety of spring bulbs, flowering trees and shrubs. Notable collection of old-fashioned roses. TEAS. *Adm £2 Chd 50p (Share to SSAFA). Sun May 16 (2-6)*

Longacre ⅙✸ (Mr D M Pudsey & Mrs H Pudsey) Evendine Lane, Colwall Green. 3m SW Malvern and 3m E of Ledbury, turning off B2048 nr Yew Tree Inn. Well laid out garden of 1 acre started from an old orchard in 1970; over 100 small trees under-planted with shrubs, bulbs and perennials for all-year-round interest. *Adm 75p Chd free. May by appt* **Tel 0684 40377**

Lower Hope ⅙✸ (Mr & Mrs Clive Richards) Ullingswick. From Hereford take the A465 N to Bromyard. After 6m this road meets the A417 at Burley Gate roundabout. Turn L on the A417 signposted Leominster. After approx. 2m take the 3rd turning on the R signposted Lower Hope and Pencombe. Lower Hope is 0.6m on the L hand side. 5- acre garden facing S and W constitutes principally herbaceous borders, rose borders, water gardens, woodland walks; in addition other features include a Laburnum Walk, conservatories and greenhouses, a fruit and vegetable garden. Surrounding the gardens are paddocks in which the prize-winning Lower Hope Pedigree Poll Hereford Cattle are grazed. TEAS. *Adm £2 Chd £1. Sun April 18, July 11 (2-6). Also open by appt.*

The Manor House ✿✸ (Mr & Mrs David Williams-Thomas) Birlingham, nr Pershore. Very fine views of Bredon Hill and Malverns, frontaging on the River Avon. Walled white and silver garden and gazebo as featured in 'The White Garden' by Diana Grenfell and Roger Grounds and in 'Traditional Homes' July 1992. Visitors are invited to picnic by the river from noon onwards. TEAS. *Adm £1 Chd free. Every Thurs May 6 to July 8 incl and Sept 2 to Oct 7 incl (2-6) or by appt* **Tel 0386 750005**

Marley Bank ✿✸ (Mr & Mrs Roger Norman) From A44 (5m E Bromyard) follow Whitbourne & Clifton-on-Teme signs for 1.2m. 1½-acre garden, begun 1980 to give all year interest, set in 3.5 acres steeply sloping old orchard surrounded by unspoilt farmland. Steep paths and many steps. Trees, shrubs, mixed borders, alpine terraces, troughs, peat beds, naturalised snowdrops & daffodils. TEA. *Adm £1 Chd free. First and third Sat April to Sept inc (10.30-5.30). Also by appt all year* **Tel 0886 21576**

¶**The Marsh Country Hotel** ⅙✸ (Mr & Mrs Martin Gilleland) Eyton. 2m NW of Leominster. Signed Eyton and Lucton off B4361 Richard Castle Rd. A 1½-acre garden created over the past 5 years. Herbaceous borders, small orchard, lily pond, stream with planted bank and herb garden. C14 timbered Great Hall listed grade II* (not open). TEAS. *Adm £1 Chd 50p. Sun June 13 (1.30-5)*

Moccas Court (Richard Chester-Master Esq) 10m W of Hereford. 1m off B4352. 7-acres; Capability Brown parkland on S bank of R. Wye. House designed by Adam and built by Keck in 1775. TEAS in village hall. *Adm house & garden £2.50 Chd 50p (Share to Moccas Church). Sun June 13 (2-6)*

Monnington Court (Mr & Mrs John Bulmer) Monnington. The ¾m lane to Monnington on Wye to Monnington Court is on the A438 between Hereford and Hay 9m from either. Approx 5 acres. Lake, pond and river walk. Sculpture garden (Mrs Bulmer is the sculptor Angela Conner); various tree lined avenues including Monnington Walk, one of Britain's oldest, still complete mile long avenues of Scots pines and yews, made famous by Kilvert's Diary; collection of swans and ducks; foundation farm of the British Morgan Horse - a living replica of ancient horses seen in statues in Trafalgar Square, etc; working cider press; FREE horse and carriage display at 3.30 each of open days. The C13, C15, C17 house including Mediaeval Moot Hall is also open. Barbecue on fine days. TEAS

10.30-6.30. Indoor horse display and films on rainy days. *Adm house and garden £3.50 Chd £2.50, garden only £2.50 Chd £1.50 (Share to British Morgan Horse Society). Sat, Sun, Mon Aug 28, 29, 30 (10.30-7)*

Nerine Nursery &⚘☙ (Mr & Mrs C A Norris) Brookend House, Welland, ½m towards Upton-on-Severn from Welland Xrds (A4104 × B4208). Internationally famous reference collection of Nerines, 30 species and some 800 named varieties in 5 greenhouses and traditional walled garden with raised beds, hardy nerines. Coaches by appt only. *Adm £1 Chd 50p. Sun Oct 17 (2-5)*

Newcote & (Mr John & Lady Patricia Phipps). Moccas. From Moccas village, ⅓m on rd to Preston-on-Wye. 2½ acres including woodland garden. Speciality shrubs and exotic trees. Water garden and pond area. *Adm £1 Chd 50p. Sun June 13 (2-6)*

¶**The Old Rectory** ⚘☙ (Mr & Mrs Martin Rickard) Leinthall Starkes. 10m NW of Leominster, 6m SW of Ludlow. Turn E off A4110 in Wigmore by Old Oak Inn. The garden is 1½m on the R after the turning signposted Burrington. 1½-acre garden on steep hillside, slippery after rain. Herbaceous borders intensively planted with ferns and various winter flowering plants, especially hellebores. Victorian walk to folly at top of hill with commanding views of the Wigmore Basin. Nursery on site specialising in ferns and some hellebores. National Collections of polypodium, cystopteris and thelypteroid ferns. Featured on BBC TV 'Gardener's World' in 1991. TEA. *Adm £1 Chd 50p. Suns March 21 (11-4), Sept 19 (2-6)*

The Orchard Farm &☙ (Miss S Barrie) Broadway. On A44. At bottom of Fish Hill; 7-acres incl interesting trees, shrubs, mixed borders, topiary, yew hedges, kitchen garden, lake and paddock. House (not open) c1650. Free Car Park. Home-made TEAS. *Adm £1 Chd free. Sun July 11 (1-6)*

Overbury Court &☙ (Mr & Mrs Bruce Bossom) 5m NE of Tewkesbury, 2½m N of Teddington Hands Roundabout, where A438 crosses A435. Georgian house 1740 (not open); landscape gardening of same date with stream and pools. Daffodil bank and grotto. Plane trees, yew hedges. Shrub, cut flower, coloured foliage, gold and silver, shrub rose borders. Norman church adjoins garden. TEAS. *Adm £1 Chd free. Suns March 28, June 27 (2-6)*

Pershore College of Horticulture &☙ 1m S of Pershore on A44, 7m from M5 junction 7. 180-acre estate; ornamental grounds; arboretum; fruit, vegetables; amenity glasshouses; wholesale hardy stock nursery. Plant Centre open for sales. West Midlands Regional Centre for RHS. Plant Centre open for gardening advice. TEA. *Adm £1 Chd 50p. Sun June 13 (2-5.30)*

The Picton Garden at Old Court Nurseries &⚘☙ (Mr & Mrs Paul Picton) Walwyn Rd, Colwall. 3m W of Malvern on B4218. 1½-acres W of Malvern Hills. A plantsman's garden extensively renovated in recent years. Rock garden using Tufa. Moist garden. Rose garden with scented old and modern varieties. Mature interesting shrubs. Large herbaceous borders full of colour from early summer. NCCPG National Reference collection of asters, mi-

chaelmas daisies, occupies its own vast borders and gives a tapestry of colour from late Aug through Sept and Oct. If wet there will be a small display of Asters under cover. *Adm £1.50 Chd free. Open Wed to Sun April to Oct inc (10-1; 2.15-5.30). Also in conjuction with* **Colwall Green** *and* **Evendine Gardens**

The Priory &☙ (The Hon Mrs Peter Healing) Kemerton, NE of Tewkesbury B4080. Main features of this 4-acre garden are long herbaceous borders planned in colour groups; stream, fern and sunken gardens. Many unusual plants, shrubs and trees. Featured in BBC2 Gardeners' World and 'The Garden magazine'. Small nursery. TEAS Suns only *Adm £1.50 Chd over 7 yrs 50p. (Share to CRMF June 13, SSAFA July 11). May 20 to end Sept every Thurs; also Suns June 13, July 11, Aug 8, 29, Sept 12 (2-7)*

¶**Red House Farm** ⚘☙ (Mrs M M Weaver) Flying Horse Lane, Bradley Green. 7m W of Redditch on B4090 Alcester to Droitwich. Turn R opp Kipper House public house. Approx ½-acre plant enthusiast's cottage garden containing wide range of interesting herbaceous perennials; roses; shrubs; alpines. Small nursery open daily offering wide variety of plants mainly propogated from garden. *Adm £1 Chd free. Sun May 23 (10-5)*

Ripple Hall &⚘ (Sir Hugo Huntington-Whiteley) 4m N of Tewkesbury. Off A38 Worcester-Tewkesbury (nr junction with motorway); Ripple village well signed. 6 acres; lawns and paddocks with donkeys; walled vegetable garden; cork tree and orangery. TEAS. *Adm £1 Chd 50p. (Share to St. Richard's Hospice, Worcester). Sun April 4 (2-6)*

Robins End ⚘☙ (Mr & Mrs A Worsley) Eastham. 15m W of Worcester, turn L off A443 2m after Eardiston to Eastham. ½m turn R to Highwood, 1st gate on L. Queen Ann Rectory garden in peaceful surroundings. Splendid display of snowdrops and daffodils; interesting kitchen garden. TEAS. *Adm £1 Chd free (Share to Eastham Parish Church). Sun March 21 (2.30-5.30)*

St Michael's Cottage &☙ (Mr & Mrs K R Barling) Broadway. 5m SE of Evesham. Thatched cottage opp St Michael's Parish Church, 200yds along rd from The Green to Snowhill. (public car park nearby, via Church Close.) Approx ⅓rd-acre of intensively planted cottage style and herbaceous garden planned in colour groups, including a small white sunken garden. Modest informal fishpond; views to Cotswold Way. TEAS in garden. *Adm £1 Acc chd free. Sun June 20 (2-6)*

Spetchley Park &⚘☙ (R J Berkeley Esq) 2m E of Worcester on A422. 30-acre garden containing large collection of trees, shrubs and plants. Red and fallow deer in nearby park. TEAS. *Adm £2 Chd £1. Good Fri April 9 (11-5) & Suns May 9, July 4 (2-5)*

Staunton Park &☙ (Mr E J L & Miss A Savage) Staunton-on-Arrow. 3m from Pembridge; 6m from Kington on the Titley road. 18m from Hereford; 11m from Leominster; 16m from Ludlow. Signposted. 14-acres of garden, specimen trees, herbaceous borders, herb garden, rock garden, hosta border, lake, lakeside garden, woodland walk, spring bulbs. TEAS. *Adm £1 Chd 50p. Weds, Suns April to end Sept. Easter and Bank Holidays. For NGS Suns April 11, June 13 (2-6)*

● **Stone House Cottage Gardens** ර.ණ (Maj & the Hon Mrs Arbuthnott) Stone, 2m SE of Kidderminster via A448 towards Bromsgrove next to church, turn up drive. 1-acre sheltered walled plantsman's garden with towers; rare wall shrubs, climbers and interesting herbaceous plants. In adjacent nursery large selection of unusual shrubs and climbers for sale. Featured in The Garden, Country Life and Hortus. Coaches by appt only. *Adm £1.50 Chd free. Suns May 2, 9, 16, 23, 30; June 6, 13, 20, 27; Aug 29; Mons April 12, May 3, 31; Aug 30 (10-6); also open March to Oct every Wed, Thurs, Fri, Sat (10-6). By appt Nov* Tel 0562 69902

Summerway ර.ණ (Mr & Mrs Graeme Anton) Torton, 3m S of Kidderminster, A449 turn up Summerway Lane. 3-acre garden with lawns, colourful mixed borders, waterfall in rock bank and pools; interesting collection of trees and large vegetable garden. TEAS. *Adm £1 Chd free. Sun June 27 (2-5.30)*

Tedstone Court ර.ණ (Mrs N C Bellville) Approx 17m from Hereford. From Bromyard take road for Stourport B4203 for 3m. Turn R signed Whitbourne, Tedstone Delamere. Spring garden, daffodils, rhododendrons; rockery; kitchen garden; fine views. TEAS. *Adm £1.50 Chd 25p. Suns April 4, May 2 (2-6)*

Torwood ර.ණ (Mr & Mrs S G Woodward) Whitchurch. Ross-on-Wye to Monmouth A40 turn to Symonds Yat West. Garden next to school. ¾-acre interesting colourful cottage garden. Herbaceous plants, conifers, water features, containers etc. Featured by Central Television 'My Secret Garden' shown earlier this year. TEA. *Adm £1 Chd free. Suns May 23, June 6, 20, July 4, 18, Aug 1, Sept 19 (2-6). Any other times by appointment April to Oct* Tel 0600 890306

Upper Court ර.ණ (Mr & Mrs W Herford) Kemerton, NE of Tewkesbury B4080. Take turning to Parish Church from War Memorial; Manor behind church. Approx 13 acres of garden and grounds inc a 2-acre lake where visitors would be welcome to bring picnics. The garden was mostly landscaped and planted in 1930s. TEAS. *Adm £1 Chd 50p. Sun June 20 (2-6)*

Well Cottage ර.ණ (R S Edwards Esq) Blakemere. 10m due W of Hereford. Leave Hereford on A465 (Abergavenny) rd. After 3m turn R towards Hay B4349 (B4348). At Clehonger keep straight on the B4352 towards Bredwardine. Well Cottage is on L by phone box. ¾-acre garden of mixed planting plus ½ acre of wild flower meadow suitable for picnics. There is a natural pool with gunnera and primulae. Good views over local hills and fields. Featured in Diana Saville's book 'Gardens for Small Country Houses'. *Adm £1 Chd free. By appt only May to Aug* Tel 09817 475

Westwood Farm (Mr & Mrs Caspar Tremlett). From Bromyard take A44 towards Leominster. R turn to Hatfield and Bockleton 2m R turn down Westwood Lane. First Farm. From Leominster, take A44 toward Worcester 6m L to Hatfield and Bockleton. Map ref OS sheet 149 60.59. ¾ acre of cottage type garden with some unusual plants and trees, small conservatory and fish pond, planted up. Dogs can be exercised in car park field. *Adm £1 Chd free.*

Sun, Mon June 27, 28 (2-6). Also open by appt May to June Tel 08854 212

White Cottage ර.ණ (Mr & Mrs S M Bates) Earls Common Rd, Stock Green. A422 Worcester-Alcester; turn L at Red Hart PH (Dormston) 1½m to T junc in Stock Green. Turn L. 2-acre garden, developed since 1981; large herbaceous and shrub borders, many unusual varieties; specialist collection of hardy geraniums; stream and natural garden carpeted with primroses, cowslips and other wild flowers; nursery; featuring plants propagated from the garden. Teas at Jinny Ring Craft Centre at Hanbury. *Adm £1 OAPs 75p Chd free. April 4, to Oct 10 Daily (10-5). Closed Thurs and alternate Suns except Suns April 4, 11, 18; May 2, 16, 30; June 13, 27; July 11, 25; Aug 29; Sept 12, 26. Nursery open daily March 21 to Oct 10 and all Bank Hol Mons Aug by prior appt only* Tel 0386 792414

Whitfield ර (G M Clive Esq) Wormbridge, 8m SW of Hereford on A465 Hereford-Abergavenny Rd. Parkland, large garden, ponds, walled kitchen garden, 1780 gingko tree, 1½m woodland walk with 1851 Redwood grove. Picnic parties welcome. TEAS. *Adm £1.50 Chd 50p. Sun June 6 (2-6)*

Whitlenge House Cottage ර.ණ (Mr & Mrs K J Southall) Whitlenge Lane, Hartlebury. S of Kidderminster on A449. Take A442 (signposted Droitwich) over small island, ¼m, 1st R into Whitlenge Lane. Follow signs. Professional landscaper's own demonstration garden with over 400 varieties of trees, shrubs, conifers, herbaceous, heathers and alpines, giving year-round interest. Small water features, rustic work, gravel gardens surrounded by rockeries and stone walls. Evolved over 9 years into 2 acres of informal plantsman's garden and incorporating an adjacent nursery specialising in large specimen shrubs. *Adm £1.50 Chd free. Suns March 28 Apr 11, 25 May 2, 30 June 27 July 25 Aug 29 Sept 26 Oct 31 Every Thurs, Fri, Sat March to Oct (10-5) Bank Hol Mons April 12, May 3, 31, Aug 30 (10-6)*

Wichenford Court ර.ණ (Lt Col & Mrs P C Britten) Wichenford. 7m NW of Worcester; turn right off B4204 at Masons Arms pub; 1m on right. Medium-sized garden dating from 1975; interesting young trees; daffodils and spring bulbs; flowering cherries; clematis; flowering shrubs and shrub roses. House dating back to C11 (not open), parts of original moat still in existence. C17 dovecote (NT). Collection of carriages. Picnic area open at noon. TEA. *Adm £1.50 Chd 30p (Share to Wichenford Memorial Hall). Sun April 18 (2-6)*

Wind's Point ර (Cadbury Trustees) British Camp. 3m SW of Malvern on Ledbury Rd. Medium-sized garden; unusual setting, lovely views. Last home of great Swedish singer Jenny Lind and where she died 1887. TEAS in aid of St Richards Hospice. *Adm £1 Chd free. Sun April 18 (12-5)*

¶**Windyridge** ර (Mr P Brazier) Kidderminster. Turn off Chester Rd N (A449) into Hurcott Rd, then into Imperial Avenue. 1-acre spring garden containing azaleas, magnolias, camellias, rhododendrons, mature flowering cherries and davidia. Please wear sensible shoes. *Adm £1 Chd 50p. Suns May 2, 16 (2-5)*

Wormington Grange ఈ (The Evetts Family) 4m W of Broadway. A46 from Broadway-Cheltenham, take 2nd turning for Wormington. Large natural garden; herb garden, old-fashioned roses. Lovely trees. Large lake with wildfowl. Interesting arts and crafts gates. Croquet lawn, very good views. Exhibition of Lord Ismay's Life 50p, July only. Visitors may play croquet if they wish. Home-made TEAS. *Adm £1 Chd free (Share to St Catherine's Church). Suns April 4, July 11 (2-6)*

Yew Tree House ఈ (Mr & Mrs W D Moyle) Ombersley. Turn off A449 up Woodfield Lane R at T-junction. 2½-acre garden with many rare herbaceous plants and shrubs. Pretty walled garden with alpines and lily pond, numerous old-fashioned roses. New plantings of blue, pink and white borders around tennis court and other yellow and white beds. Orchard, copse and lawns with lovely views set around c1640 timber framed house. TEA. *Adm £1 Chd 50p. Sun June 27 (2-6)*

Hertfordshire

Hon County Organiser:	Mrs Antony Woodall, The Old Rectory, Wyddial, Buntingford SG9 0EN
Assistant Hon County Organisers:	Mrs Edward Harvey, Wickham Hall, Bishop's Stortford CM23 1JQ
	Mrs Hedley Newton, Moat Farm House Much Hadham SG10 6AE
Hon County Treasurer:	Mrs John Lancaster, Manor Cottage, Aspenden, Nr Buntingford SG9 9PB

DATES OF OPENING

By appointment
For telephone numbers and other details see garden descriptions

Deansmere, West Hyde, Rickmansworth
Dormers, Hadley Wood
Garden Cottage, Abbots Langley
1 Gernon Walk, Letchworth
Manor Cottage, Stanstead
Waterdell House, Croxley Green
West Lodge Park, Hadley Wood

Regular openings
For details see garden descriptions

Benington Lordship, nr Stevenage. Suns & Weds Feb, Suns April to Aug & Weds April to Sept. Bank Hol Mons
Capel Manor Gardens, Enfield. Open daily April to Oct. Weekdays only Nov to March. Farm weekends & school hols April to Oct
Hopleys (Garden & Nursery). Suns, Mons Weds, Thurs, Fris, Sats, excluding Jan & Aug
The Manor House, Ayot St Lawrence. Suns May to Aug

April 4 Sunday
Holwell Manor, nr Hatfield

April 18 Sunday
Hanbury Manor Hotel, nr Ware ‡
The Manor House, Bayford ‡
St Paul's Walden Bury, Hitchin

April 25 Sunday
Great Munden House, nr Ware
Odsey Park , Ashwell

May 9 Sunday
St Paul's Walden Bury, Hitchin

May 16 Sunday
Hipkins, Broxbourne
Wheathampstead Gardens, Wheathampstead

May 23 Sunday
The Abbots House, Abbots Langley
Wrotham Park, Barnet

May 25 Tuesday
The Abbots House, Abbots Langley

May 30 Sunday
Great Sarratt Hall, Rickmansworth ‡
Queenswood School, Hatfield
Street Farm, Bovingdon ‡

May 31 Monday
Queenswood School, Hatfield

June 6 Sunday
West Lodge Park, Hadley Wood

June 12 Saturday
Cockhamsted, Braughing

June 13 Sunday
Cockhamsted, Braughing ‡
Hill House, Stanstead Abbots ‡
Moor Place, Much Hadham ‡
St Paul's Walden Bury, Hitchin

June 20 Sunday
The Abbots House, Abbots Langley
Leverstock Green & Hill End Farm Gardens
Odsey Park, Ashwell

June 26 Saturday
Benington Lordship, nr Stevenage

June 27 Sunday
Benington Lordship, nr Stevenage
Hanbury Manor Hotel, nr Ware
Waterdell House, Croxley Green

July 3 Saturday
The Barn, Serge Hill, Abbots Langley ‡
St Paul's Walden Bury, Hitchin
Serge Hill, Abbots Langley ‡

July 11 Sunday
Deansmere, West Hyde, Rickmansworth

July 14 Wednesday
Deansmere, West Hyde, Rickmansworth

July 25 Sunday
The Gardens of the Rose, St Albans
Hopleys (Garden & Nursery), Much Hadham

August 1 Sunday
The Manor House, Ayot St Lawrence

August 29 Sunday
The Abbots House, Abbots Langley

September 26 Sunday
Hopleys (Garden & Nursery), Much Hadham

October 3 Sunday
Knebworth House, Stevenage

October 24 Sunday
Capel Manor Gardens, Enfield
West Lodge Park, Hadley Wood

DESCRIPTIONS OF GARDENS

The Abbots House ♿✿❀ (Dr & Mrs Peter Tomson) 10, High Street, Abbots Langley NW of Watford (5m from Watford). Junction 20 M25, junction 6 M1. Parking in free village car park. 1¾-acre garden with interesting trees; shrubs; mixed borders; sunken garden; ponds; conservatory. Nursery featuring plants propagated from the garden. TEAS. *Adm £1.50 Chd free (Share to Friends of St Lawrence Church, Abbots Langley). Suns, Tues, May 23, 25, June 20, 29 (2-5)*

¶**The Barn** ✿ (Tom Stuart-Smith Esq) Abbots Langley. ½m E of Bedmond in Serge Hill Lane. 1-acre plantsman's garden. Small sheltered courtyard planted with unusual shrubs and perennials, contrasts with more open formal garden with views over wild flower meadow. Tea at Serge Hill. *Combined adm £3 with* **Serge Hill** *(Share to Tibet Relief Fund UK). Sat July 3 (10-5)*

Benington Lordship ✿❀ (Mr & Mrs C H A Bott) 5m E of Stevenage, in Benington village. Terraced plantsman's garden overlooking lakes, formal rose garden; Victorian folly, Norman keep and moat; spring rock and water garden; spectacular double herbaceous borders. Small nursery. Snowdrops. *Adm £2.20 Chd free. Suns & Weds Feb (12-5). Easter, Spring and Summer Bank Holiday Mons (12-5) Weds. April to Sept 30 (12-5). Suns April to Aug 30 (2-5) (Share to St Peters Church). For NGS TEAS and Floral Festival in Church adjoining garden. Sat, Sun June 26, 27, (12-6)*

Capel Manor Farm and Gardens ♿ (Horticultural & Environmental Centre) Bullsmoor Lane, Enfield, Middx. 3 mins from M25 junction M25/A10. W at traffic lights. Nearest station Turkey Street-Liverpool St line. 30 acres of historical and modern theme gardens, C17 garden, large Italian style maze, rock and water features. 5-acre demonstration garden run by the Consumers Assoc. Walled garden with rose collection and display glasshouses, tree collection and woodland walks. TEAS. *Adm £2 Concessions OAP £1.50 Chd £1 (non-show rates). Open daily April to Oct, weekdays only Nov to March (10-4.30 (5.30 weekends). Farm; weekends and school hols. April to Oct only (1-5.30) located on neighbouring estate separate adm rate. For NGS Sun Oct 24 (10-Dusk). For details of special events, group rates and gardening courses Tel 0992 763849. For Myddelton House see London*

Cockhamsted ♿✿❀ (Mr & Mrs R W D Marques) Braughing. 2m E of village towards Braughing Friars (7m N of Ware). 2 acres; informal garden; shrub roses surrounded by open country. C14 moat. TEAS in aid of Leukaemia Research. *Adm £1.20 Chd free. Sat, Sun June 12, 13 (2-6)*

Regular Openers. See head of county section.

¶**Deansmere** ♿✿❀ (Mr & Mrs Derek Austen) Old Uxbridge Rd, West Hyde. 3m SW of Rickmansworth, off A412. Leaving M25 junction 17, follow the sign 'Maple Cross'. In 200 yds at roundabout take 2nd exit; across traffic lights at Maple Cross (A412), at mini roundabout turn L (signposted 'Harefield'), in 100yds at T junction turn L, 100yds. Deansmere is opposite St. Thomas's Church. 2-acre garden old, new and in the making, full of variety and interest. Perennials, bedding plants, containers, bulbs, heather, shrubs, trees: summerhouses; aviary; rhododendron bed; pergola; vegetables, fruit trees; two small ponds; dell; viola and penstemon collections; greenhouses and view of the lake. TEAS. *Adm £1 Chd 50p. Sun, Wed July 11, 14 (2-6). Also by appt in April* **Tel 0923 778817**

Dormers ♿✿❀ (Mrs Shirley Nicholas) 373 Cockfosters Rd. Hadley Wood. Leave M25 at junction 24. Take A111 (signposted Southgate & Cockfosters) S, and Dormers is on this rd about 1m on R handside. Park in drive. Approx 1½ acres with interesting and unusual plants and features. Shrubs, mixed borders, greenhouses with house plants and propagating from garden. Over 500 different varieties of plants, small shale garden with alpines. Best time July, but year round interest. Except for mature trees, everything developed and planted over last 5yrs. TEA. *Adm £1 Chd 50p. By appt all year round (except Dec & Jan)* **Tel 081 449 3006**

¶**Garden Cottage** (Anthony House) 85 Furtherfield, Abbots Langley. NW of Watford 5m from Watford junction 20 M25 junction 6 M1. A small plantsman's garden in total 100' long by 20' wide; planted in 1991, filled with unusual perennials and interesting features all year. TEAS. *Adm £1 Chd 50p. By appt only* **Tel 0923 260571**

The Gardens of the Rose ♿❀ (The Royal National Rose Society) Chiswell Green Lane, 2m S of St Albans on B4630, follow brown tourist signs. 12-acre display garden; with roses of every description. 30,000 plants of some 1,700 different varieties. Licensed cafeteria; TEAS. *Adm £3.50 Chd free. Registered disabled £2.50. For NGS Sun July 25 (10-6)*

1 Gernon Walk ✿ (Miss Rachel Crawshay) Letchworth (First Garden City). Tiny town garden (100ft long but only 8ft wide in middle) planned and planted since 1984 for year-round and horticultural interest. *Collecting box. By appt only* **Tel 0462 686399**

Great Munden House ✿❀ (Mr & Mrs D Wentworth-Stanley) 7m N of Ware. Off A10 on Puckeridge by-pass turn W; or turning off A602 via Dane End. 3½-acre informal garden with lawns, mixed shrub and herbaceous borders; variety shrub roses, trees; kitchen and herb garden. Plant stall. TEAS. *Adm £1.50 Chd 50p. Sun April 25 (2.30-5.30)*

Great Sarratt Hall ♿☙❀ (H M Neal Esq) Sarratt, N of Rickmansworth. From Watford N via A41 (or M1 Exit 5) to Kings Langley; and left (W) to Sarratt; garden is 1st on R after village sign. 4 acres; herbaceous and mixed shrub borders; pond, moisture-loving plants and trees; walled kitchen garden; rhododendrons, magnolias, camellias; new planting of specialist conifers and rare trees. TEAS. *Adm £1.50 Chd free (Share to Courtauld Institute of Art Fund). Sun May 30 (2-6)*

Hanbury Manor Hotel ☙ (Poles Ltd) Thundridge. 2m N of Ware on A10, turn L 100 yds past end of dual carriageway from London or turn R past 'Sow & Pigs' travelling S. Garden well known in Victorian times, now part of hotel grounds. Restoration work commenced 1989, now well under way. Walled garden with listed 'moongate', extensive herbaceous borders, herb garden and fruit houses; yew hedged walks with spring bulbs planted orchard and period rose garden; secret garden in woodland setting; pinetum. TEAS. *Adm £1.50 Chd 75p. Suns April 18 June 27 (2-6)*

Hill House ☙❀ (Mr & Mrs R Pilkington) Stanstead Abbotts, near Ware. From A10 turn E on to A414; then B181 for Stanstead Abbotts; left at end of High St, garden 1st R past Church. Ample car parking. 6 acres incl wood; species roses, herbaceous border, water garden, conservatory, aviary, woodland walk. Lovely view over Lea Valley. Modern Art Exhibition in loft gallery (20p extra). Unusual plants for sale. Home-made TEAS. *Adm £1.50 Chd 50p (Share to St Andrews Parish Church of Stanstead Abbotts). Sun June 13 (2-5.30)*

Hipkins ♿☙❀ (Stuart Douglas Hamilton Esq & Michael Goulding Esq) Broxbourne. From A10 to Broxbourne turn up Bell or Park Lane into Baas Lane, opposite Graham Avenue. 3-acre informal garden with spring fed ponds; azaleas and rhododendrons; shrub and herbaceous borders specialising in plants for flower arrangers; many unusual plants; fine trees and well kept kitchen garden. TEAS. *Adm £1 Chd 20p. Sun May 16 (2.30-6)*

Holwell Manor ☙❀ (Mr & Mrs J Gillum) Nr Hatfield. On W side of B1455, short lane linking A414 with B158 between Hatfield (3m) and Hertford (4m). B1455 joins the A414 roundabout and is signposted Essendon. Holwell is 500 yds from this roundabout. Natural garden with large pond, mature trees, river walks; approx 2-3 acres. Island in pond covered with daffodils and narcissi in spring. TEAS. *Adm £1 Chd 50p. Sun April 4 (2-5)*

Hopleys (Garden and Nursery) ♿☙❀ (Mr Aubrey Barker) 5m from Bishop's Stortford on B1004. M11 (exit 8) 7m or A10 (Puckeridge) 5m via A120. 50yds N of Bull public house in centre of Much Hadham. 3½ acres of constantly developing garden; trees, shrubs, herbaceous and alpines; island beds with mixed planting in parkland setting; pond and many unusual and rare (incl variegated) plants. *Open every Mon, Wed, Thurs, Fri, Sat (9-5) and Sun (2-5) excl Jan and Aug.* ▲*For NGS TEAS. Adm £1.50 Chd 50p. Suns July 25, Sept 26 (11-6)*

> **By Appointment Gardens.** See head of county section

Knebworth House ♿☙ (The Lord Cobbold) Knebworth. 28m N of London; direct access from A1(M) at Stevenage. Station and Bus stop: Stevenage 3m. Historic house, home of Bulwer Lytton; Victorian novelist and statesman. Lutyens garden designed for his brother-in-law, the Earl of Lytton, comprising pleached lime avenues, rose beds, herbaceous borders, yew hedges and various small gardens in process of restoration; Gertrude Jekyll herb garden. Restaurant and TEAS. *Adm £1.50 Chd £1.* ▲*For NGS Sun Oct 3 (12-5)*

Leverstock Green and Hill End Farm Gardens via A4147 mid-way between Hemel Hempstead/St Albans. Car parking free. *Combined adm £2 Chd free. Sun June 20 (11-5)*
   Hill End Farm ♿❀ (Mr & Mrs Alban Warwick) Beech Tree Lane, Gorhambury. Part dates back to 1275. Mature garden; herbaceous borders; pond; grass walk flanked by coniferous and deciduous specimen trees; sunken garden with C16 plants. Lunches and picnic facilities. Plant stall. TEAS in aid of Herts V S Schemes
   King Charles II Cottage ♿❀ (Mr & Mrs F S Cadman) Westwick Row. 1 acre; roses a special feature; small, well-stocked ornamental pond. Part house also open (weather permitting) with flower arrangements by Mrs Sheila Macqueen (no extra charge)
   Swedish Cottage (Doug & Barbara Wiles) Westwick Row. Young ½-acre garden specializing in scented and wild flowers, plants to attract bees, butterflies, birds etc. Aviaries with parakeets, owls and wild fowl
   Westwick Cottage ♿❀ (Mrs Sheila Macqueen) Westwick Row. Medium-sized garden specialising in plants for flower arranging: many unusual specimens. Flower arrangements in the house (weather permitting) by Mrs Sheila Macqueen (no extra charge). Plant stall. TEAS, coffee & light refreshments

¶**Manor Cottage** ☙❀ (Mrs Anne Thorlin) 33a Hoddesdon Rd, Stanstead St Margarets. From A10 turn E on to A414; then take B181 down hill to mini roundabout; turn R into Hoddesdon Rd. Garden 200yds on R just pass St Margarets Church. Parking along Hoddesdon Rd. Originally oldest part of C16 Grade 11 listed Manor House. Medium-sized plantsmans garden planted over past 5yrs for all year interest. Water feature and pond with Koi; ornamental urns. Plants for sale propagated from garden. *Adm 80p Chd free. By appt only all year round* **Tel 0920 870 332**

The Manor House Ayot St Lawrence ♿☙ (Mrs Peter Thwaites) Bear R into village from Bride Hall Lane, ruined Church on L and the Brocket Arms on R. On bend there is a pair of brick piers leading to drive - go through white iron gates. The Manor house is on your L. New garden, with formal garden, mixed borders and nut grove, large walled garden and orchard. TEA NGS days only. *Adm £2 OAP/Chd 75p (under ten free). Open every Sun May 1 to Aug 31. Also by appt for parties. For NGS Sun Aug 1 (2-6)*

¶**The Manor House, Bayford** ☙ (Mr & Mrs D Latham) 4m SW of Hertford via A414 and B158 signed off B158 to Bakford. 3½ acres Elizabethan property with old walls and walled garden; many unusual shrubs and trees, ancient oak and large natural lake. TEAS. *Adm £1 Chd 50p. Sun April 18 (2-5.30)*

Moor Place ♿ (Mr & Mrs Bryan Norman) Much Hadham. Entrance either at war memorial or at Hadham Cross. 2 C18 walled gardens. Herbaceous borders. Large area of shrubbery, lawns, hedges and trees. 2 ponds. Approx 10 acres. TEAS. *Adm £1.50 Chd 50p. Sun June 13 (2-5.30)*

Myddelton House see London

Odsey Park ♿✗ (Mr & The Hon Mrs Jeremy Fordham) Ashwell. Situated equidistant between Royston and Baldock 4½m each way. On N carriageway of A505 enter by Lodge and drive into park as signposted. Recently remade medium-sized garden originally dating from 1860 with walled garden, set in park with mature trees, spring bulbs, tulips; small colourful herbaceous border, roses, shrubs and small herb garden. Car parking free. TEAS June 20 only. *Adm £1.50 Chd free (Share to Ashwell Church Restoration Fund). Suns April 25 (12-5) June 20 (2-6)*

Queenswood School ✗❀ Shepherds Way. From S. M25 Junction 24 signposted Potters Bar. In ½m at lights turn R onto A1000 signposted Hatfield. In 2m turn R onto B157. School is ½m on the R. From N. A1000 from Hatfield 5m turn L on B157. 120 acres informal gardens and woodlands. Rhododendrons, fine specimen trees, shrubs and herbaceous borders. Glasshouses; fine views to Chiltern Hills. Picnic areas. Lunches & TEAS. *Adm £1.50 OAPs/Chd 75p. Sun, Mon May 30, 31 (11-6)*

St Paul's Walden Bury ❀ (Simon Bowes Lyon and family) Whitwell, on B651 5m S of Hitchin; ½m N of Whitwell. Formal woodland garden listed Grade 1. Laid out about 1730, influenced by French tastes. Long rides and avenues span about 40 acres, leading to temples, statues, lake and ponds. Also more recent flower gardens and woodland garden with rhododendrons, azaleas and magnolias. Dogs on leads. TEAS. *Adm £1.50 Chd 75p (Share to St Pauls Walden Church). Suns April 18, May 9, June 13 (2-7), Sat July 3 (2-6) followed by lakeside concert: Ystrad Mynach Male Voice Choir. Also other times by appt* **Tel 0438 871218 or 871229**

¶Serge Hill ♿✗❀ (Murray & Joan Stuart-Smith) Abbots Langley. ½m E of Bedmond. The house is marked on the OS map. Regency house in parkland setting with fine kitchen garden of ½ acre. A range of unusual wall plants, mixed border of 100yds. New small courtyard garden and wall garden planted with hot coloured flowers. TEAS. *Combined adm £3 with* **The Barn** *(Share to Herts Garden Trust). Sat July 3 (10-5)*

¶Street Farm ♿❀ (Mrs Penelope Shand) Bovingdon. Marked on ordnance survey map; on rd between Bovingdon and Chipperfield exactly 1m from the Chesham Rd entrance to Bovington High St. Approx 3 acres comprising extensive lawns, long herbaceous borders. A large pond with an island surrounded by decorative shrubs and boasting beautiful water lilies and various miscanthas. Also raised beds, island beds and shrubberies with unusual plants in an attractive sylvan setting. A miniature paved garden enclosed by a yew hedge with tiny clipped box hedges surrounding several beds containing herbs, auricula and alpine strawberries. *Adm £1.50 OAP's £1 Chd free (Share to RSPB). Sun May 30 (2-6)*

Waterdell House ♿✗❀ (Mr & Mrs Peter Ward) Croxley Green. 1½m from Rickmansworth. Exit 18 from M25. Direction R'worth to join A412 towards Watford. From A412 turn left signed Sarratt, along Croxley Green, fork right past Coach & Horses, cross Baldwins Lane into Little Green Lane, then left at top. 1½-acre walled garden developed and maintained over many years to accommodate growing family; mature and young trees, topiary holly hedge, herbaceous borders; modern island beds of shrubs, old-fashioned roses; vegetable and fruit garden. TEAS 60p. *Adm £1 OAPs/Chd 50p. Sun June 27 (2-6) and by appt May-mid July (2-6).* **Tel 0923 772775**

West Lodge Park ✗ (T Edward Beale Esq) Cockfosters Rd, Hadley Wood. On A111 between Potters Bar and Southgate. Exit 24 from M25 signed Cockfosters. Station: Cockfosters underground (Piccadilly Line); then bus 298 to Beech Hill. Beale Arboretum, set in 10-acre section of West Lodge Park, consists of splendid collection of trees, some 500 varieties, all labelled; many original and interesting specimens, some old-established as well as scores planted since 1965; magnificent leaf colour. TEA (or lunch if booked in advance in adjoining hotel). *Adm £1.50 Chd 30p (Share to GRBS). Suns June 6 (2-6); Oct 24 (12-4). Organised parties anytime by appt. Collecting box.* **Tel 081 440 8311**

Wheathampstead Gardens 6m N of St Albans on B651 or 3m from junction 4 of A1 on B653. Car parking free. Not within walking distance of each other. *Combined adm £2 Chd 50p. Sun May 16 (2-6)*

The Dell ✗ (Mr T & Mrs T H Regis) Rose Lane. Travel N down Wheathampstead High St on B651. At roundabout turn L onto B653 and Rose Lane is 50yds on R. Med-iumsized garden (approx 2½ acres) on chalk; part cottage part informal; mixed borders incl shady border; shrubs, roses, undulating lawns; mature trees. At best in spring. Pretty walled vegetable garden

Lamer Hill ✗❀ (Mr & Mrs Peter Flory) Lower Gustard Wood. Proceed N from Wheathampstead Village on B651 towards Kimpton for 1m then with entrance to Mid-Herts Golf Club on L and cottages by triangle of grass on R, turn R (private road). Proceed for 200yds. Lamer Hill is on the R just before wood. Old garden of several acres which was re-designed 7yrs ago. Incl mature and young trees; pleached hornbeams, borders, shrub roses, cottage garden, small woodland. TEAS

Lamer Lodge ♿✗ (Mr & Mrs J Wilson) Lamer Lane. From roundabout N of Wheathampstead continue N towards Kimpton on Lamer Lane (B651) for ½m; 1st (Lodge) house on R on blind L bend. 2½ acres of informal garden, woodland paths, lawns, varied trees, shrubs and old roses; paved pond area with summer display in tubs; countryside surroundings

Wrotham Park ♿❀ (Mr & Mrs J Byng) M25 Junction 23, take A1081 towards Barnet, first left to Bentley Heath into Dancers Hill Rd. Lodge in village 1½m on R opp church. 30 acres in Parkland setting. Woodland, rhododendrons, azaleas, herbaceous. Picnic area. TEA. *Adm £1.50 OAPs/Chd 50p. Sun May 23 (2-6)*

Humberside

Hon County Organiser: Peter Carver Esq., The Croft, North Cave, East Yorkshire HU15 2NG
Tel 0430 422203

DATES OF OPENING

By appointment
For telephone numbers and other details see garden descriptions

The Cottages, Barrow Haven, nr
  Barton
Lanhydrock Cottage, Skerne
8 Welton Old Road, Welton

Regular openings
For details see garden descriptions

Burton Agnes Hall, Driffield. April 1
to Oct 31

April 11 Sunday
  The Croft, North Cave
April 12 Monday
  Croft House, Ulceby
  The White Cottage,
    Halsham

April 25 Sunday
  Lanhydrock Cottage, Skerne
May 2 Sunday
  The Cottages, Barrow Haven, nr
    Barton
  Il Giardino, Bilton
May 3 Monday
  The Cottages, Barrow Haven, nr
    Barton
May 16 Sunday
  Lanhydrock Cottage, Skerne
May 30 Sunday
  Castle Farm, Barmby Moor
  Il Giardino, Bilton
  8 Welton Old Road, Welton
June 2 Wednesday
  Castle Farm, Barmby Moor
June 6 Sunday
  Croft House, Ulceby
June 13 Sunday
  Boynton Hall, nr Bridlington
  Lanhydrock Cottage, Skerne
  Saltmarshe Hall, Saltmarshe
June 20 Sunday
  Chatt House, Burton Pidsea ‡‡

The Croft, North Cave ‡
Il Giardino, Bilton
Parkview, South Cave ‡
The White Cottage, Halsham ‡‡
June 27 Sunday
  Grange Cottage, Cadney
  The Green, Lund ‡
  5 Lockington Road, Lund ‡
July 11 Sunday
  Lanhydrock Cottage, Skerne
August 8 Sunday
  Houghton Hall, Market
    Weighton
  Lanhyrdrock Cottage, Skerne
August 29 Sunday
  The Cottages, Barrow Haven, nr
    Barton
August 30 Monday
  The Cottages, Barrow Haven, nr
    Barton
September 5 Sunday
  Lanhydrock Cottage, Skerne
September 12 Sunday
  The White Cottage, Halsham

DESCRIPTIONS OF GARDENS

¶**Boynton Hall** & (Mr & Mrs R Marriott) Bridlington. On B1253 2m W of Bridlington S from Boynton Xroads. Lawn and yew hedge around Elizabethan house and lovely old walled garden with shrubs and roses; also gate house and knot garden (recently created). TEAS in aid of church. *Adm £1.50 Chd £1. Sun June 13 (1.30-5)*

Burton Agnes Hall &⊗❀ (Mr & Mrs N Cunliffe-Lister) nr Driffield. Burton Agnes is on A166 between Driffield & Bridlington. 8 acres of gardens incl lawns with clipped yew and fountains, woodland gardens and a walled garden which has been recently redeveloped, it contains a potager, herbaceous and mixed borders; maze with a thyme garden; jungle garden; campanula collection garden and coloured gardens containing giant games boards. TEAS. *Adm £1.50 Chd 50p. April 1 to Oct 31 (11-5)*

¶**Castle Farm Nurseries** &⊗ (Mr & Mrs K Wilson) Barmby Moor. Turn off A1079 Hull/York rd, ¾m from Barmby Moor at Hewson & Robinson's Garage, towards Thornton; ½m on R is sign for nursery. 12yr-old garden of 1 acre created and maintained by owners; incl trees, mixed borders, herbaceous border, rock garden, rhododendrons and pool; emphasis on heather and conifer beds. Nursery open. Cream TEAS in aid of local Methodist Church. *Adm £1 Chd free. Sun May 30, (2-6) Wed June 2 (1.30-5.30)*

Chatt House &❀ (Mrs Harrison) Burton Pidsea. In mid-Holderness, approx 10m Hull via Hedon and Burstwick. Old-established garden with much re-organisation taking place in the pond area. Walled garden, lawns, arboretum, herbaceous, kitchen garden and greenhouse. TEAS. *Adm £1.50 Chd 50p. Sun June 20 (2-5)*

The Cottages ⊗❀ (Mr & Mrs E C Walsh) 4m due E of Barton-on-Humber, adjacent to Barrow-Haven Railway Station. Turn L 3m E of Barton. Variable shrub-lined walks adjacent to reed bed hides. Large range of trees, shrubs, perennials, insects, birds and butterflies abound. Organic vegetable garden, photographic hides. An all-the-year-round garden created in 10yrs on 1¼ acres, of a once derelict tile yard. Runner up in 'Birdwatching' Large Garden Competition in 1989. Large selection of plants for sale, hostas, lobelia etc. Partly suitable for wheelchairs. TEAS. *Adm £1 Chd & OAP free. Suns, Mons May 2, 3; Aug 29, 30, (11-5). Also by appt* **Tel 0469 31614**

The Croft &⊗❀ (Mr & Mrs Peter Carver) North Cave. On B1230 (1½m from exit 38, M62). Entrance 100yds S War Memorial in village centre (towards South Cave). Stewardship by same family since Queen Victoria's reign pervades this large garden of much pleasure and permanence. Recent additions include jardin potager, yew hedging (1985) and 'Tapis Vert' statue garden (1991). Featured on BBC TV with Geoffrey Smith and ITV with Susan Hampshire. Private car parking. TEAS. *Adm £1.50 Chd free (Share to St John Ambulance). Weds May 26, June 23, July 21. Also for NGS Suns April 11, June 20 (2-5)*

Croft House ♦❀☘ (Mr & Mrs Peter Sandberg) Ulceby. Immingham exit off A180 L to Ulceby. At War Memorial L into Front Street follow sign to Pit Moor Lane. 2 acres plantswoman's garden largely created and solely maintained by present owners. Mixed borders; bulbs; lawns, fine trees; hedging. Victorian greenhouses. TEAS. *Adm £1.50 Chd free. Mon April 12, Sun June 6 (2-5)*

¶**Grange Cottage** ❀☘ (Mr & Mrs D Hoy) Cadney. 3m S of Brigg. In Brigg turn L into Elwes St; follow rd to Cadney. From Market Rasen to Brigg Rd, turn L in Howsham on to Cadney Rd. ⅓-acre cottage garden; many unusual and old-fashioned plants; old roses; pond; orchard; conservatory with interesting tender plants. TEAS. *Adm £1 Chd free. Sun June 27 (2-6)*

The Green ♦❀☘ (Mr & Mrs Hugh Helm) Lund. 7m N of Beverley. Off B1248 Beverley Malton Rd. ¼-acre cottage garden; pool, rockery; climbing roses; shrubs; herbaceous plants, natural gravel garden. Established 8 years in this delightful award winning "Britain in Bloom" village. Also open **5 Lockington Road**. *Adm 75p Chd free. Sun June 27 (2-5)*

Houghton Hall ♦ (Lord & Lady Manton) Market Weighton. 1m (on N Cave Rd) from Market Weighton (due S). 4m N from N Cave. Drive entrance on R. Roses; shrubs; lawns and lake. Approx 2 acres, set in attractive parkland around Georgian Mansion (not open). High hedges and some topiary. TEA. *Adm £1 Chd free. Sun 8 Aug (2-5)*

¶**Il Guardino** ♦❀☘ (Peter & Marian Fowler) Bilton. 5m E of Hull City Centre. Take A165 Hull to Bridlington Rd. Turn off; take B1238 to Bilton Village. Turn L opp. St Peter's Church. "Il Guardino" is at bottom of Limetree Lane on L. Park in church car park or Church Lane. Once neglected garden approx ⅓ acre redesigned and revived over last 5yrs by present owners. Features incl mixed borders and island beds stocked with many unusual plants, shrubs and trees. Attractive beech hedge, small allotment, herb garden, orchard of old apple trees; pears; cherries; medlar and filberts; cedarwood greenhouse with many pelargoniums; fuchsias; grapevine; fig tree; meyer lemon and other less common plants. TEAS. *Adm 75p Chd free. Suns May 2, 30 June 20 (1-5)*

Lanhydrock Cottage ❀☘ (Mrs Jan Joyce) Skerne. 3m SE Driffield; follow signs to Skerne. Delightful small cottage garden of much interest, started by present owner, containing old-fashioned roses, herbs and many fragrant perennials and wild flowers grown together naturally to provide a habitat for butterflies and wild life. TEAS. *Adm 75p Chd free. Suns April 25, May 16, June 13, July 11, Aug 8, Sept 5 (11-5). Also by appt* **Tel 0377 43727**

5 Lockington Road ♦❀ (Miss E Stephenson) Lund. Lund is off B1248 Beverley-Malton Rd. Small walled garden converted from old fold yard on edge of village with old-fashioned roses and cottage garden plants. "Charmingly English". *Adm 75p Chd free. Sun June 27 (2-5)*

Parkview ♦❀☘ 45 Church Street (Mr & Mrs Christopher Powell) South Cave. 12m W of Hull on A63 turn N to S Cave on A1034. In centre of village turn L by chemists. 250yds on L black gates under arch. Plantsman's sheltered garden of approx ⅓-acre. Island beds packed with perennials & shrubs, spring garden area. Yorkstone terrace with sinks, pots and urns. Organic fruit & vegetable plot. Greenhouse & compost bins, pond & bog garden. Yorkshire cream TEAS 65p. *Adm 70p Chd 25p. (Share to PCC Church Yard Plant Fund). Sun June 20 (2-5)*

Saltmarshe Hall ♦❀ (Mr & Mrs Philip Bean) Howden. N bank of R Ouse, Approx 3½m E of Howden. Follow signs to Laxton through Howdendyke and then signs to Saltmarshe. House in park west of Saltmarshe village. Approx 10 acres beautifully situated on the banks of the R Ouse. Fine old trees, woodland, walled garden and courtyards. Recent planting includes herbaceous borders and old roses. TEAS in aid of Laxton Church. *Adm £1.50 Chd free. Sun June 13 (2-6)*

¶**8 Welton Old Road** ♦ (Dr & Mrs O G Jones) Welton. In village of Welton 10m W of Hull off A63. Coming E turn L to village past church, turn R along Parliament St. and up hill. House 50yds on R opp. Temple Close. From E take A63 and turn off at flyover to Brough; turn R for Welton and follow above instructions. Roadside parking in village. Informal 1-acre garden developed by owners over 30yrs. Imaginative planting with unusual shrubs, plants and less common trees; natural pond and lily pond. *Adm £1 Chd 20p. Sun May 30 (2-6). Open by appt. May to July* **Tel 0482 667488**

The White Cottage ❀ (Mr & Mrs John Oldham) Halsham. 1m E of Halsham Arms on B1362, Concealed wooded entrance on R. Parking available in grounds. The garden was created by its owners 20yrs ago and is surrounded by open countryside. Delightful specialised and unusual planting in island beds. Natural pond; vegetable and herb garden; architect designed sunken conservatory. An inspiration to all gardeners. Featured with Geoffrey Smith on BBC2 in 1992. TEAS. *Adm £1.50 Chd free (Share to Hull Hospice Dove House). Suns June 20, Sep 12, Mon April 12 (2-5)*

By Appointment Gardens. These owners do not have a fixed opening day usually because they do not like crowds or have insufficient parking space. Owner will often give guided tour.

Regular Openers. Too many days to include in diary. Usually there is a wide range of plants giving year-round interest. See head of county section for the name and garden description for times etc.

Isle of Wight

Hon County Organiser: Mrs John Harrison, North Court, Shorwell I.O.W. PO30 3JG
Hon County Treasurer: Mrs S Robak, Little Mead, Everard Close, Freshwater Bay, I.O.W. PO40 9PT

DATES OF OPENING

By appointment
For telephone numbers and other details see garden descriptions

North Court, Shorwell
Owl Cottage, Mottistone
Westport Cottage, Tennyson Close,
  Yarmouth

Easter Monday April 12
  Fountain Cottage,
  Bonchurch

April 18 Sunday
  Woolverton House, St Lawrence,
  Nr Ventnor
May 2 Sunday
  Yaffles, Bonchurch
May 9 Sunday
  North Court, Shorwell
May 23 Sunday
  The Watch House, Bembridge
May 30 Sunday
  The Three North Court Gardens,
  Shorwell
June 9 Wednesday
  Mottistone Manor Gardens,
  Mottistone

June 23 Wednesday
  The Five Gardens of Cranmore,
  Cranmore
June 27 Sunday
  Hamstead Grange, Yarmouth
July 4 Sunday
  Nunwell House, Brading
July 25 Sunday
  Conifers, 23 Witbank Gardens,
  Shanklin
September 26 Sunday
  Brook Edge, Binstead

DESCRIPTIONS OF GARDENS

¶**Brook Edge** ⚆ (Dr & Mrs Philip Goodwin) Binstead, at the bottom of Binstead Hill to Ryde rd. Parking available at factory car-park. 2½ acres of undulating garden on edge of old quarry with two streams flowing through. Fine woodland trees, waterside plants and shrubs. TEAS. *Adm £1 Chd 20p. Sun Sept 26 (2.30-5)*

Conifers ⬥⚆❀ (Mr & Mrs J Horrocks) 23 Witbank Gardens. From Shanklin centre take the Languard rd. to Languard Manor rd, turn R at Green Lane, turn R at Spar shop to Witbank Gardens. 1-acre semi-formal ornamental garden with varied and colourful selection of trees, shrubs, perennials and bedding plants; small aviary with exotic birds. Sale of plants by Haylands Farm. *Adm 75p Chd free. Sun July 25 (2-5)*

¶**The Five Gardens of Cranmore** ⬥⚆❀ Cranmore Ave is approx halfway between the town of Yarmouth and the village of Shalfleet on the A3054. From Yarmouth the turning is on the L hand side, opp a bus shelter approx 3m out of Yarmouth on an unmade rd. TEAS at Highwood. *Combined adm £1.50 Chd 50p. Wed June 23 (2-7)*
  ¶**Cranmore Lodge** (Mr & Mrs W Dicken). This is a garden in the making. Approx 1 acre with perennials, shrub roses and climbers. A small pond and woodland area. Plant stall
  ¶**Funakoshi** (Mr & Mrs D Self) A 1-acre garden divided by an aviary, patio, greenhouses, tunnels and vegetable plot into areas with shrubs, perennials, climbers and conifers
  ¶**Freshfields** (Mr & Mrs O Butchers) Approx 1-acre garden, patio, pond with marginal planting, raised bed and an interesting display of fuschias and a wild garden
  ¶**Highwood** (Mr & Mrs Cooper) 10-acre site with approx 4 acres under cultivation; woodland area, pond with marginal planting with many unusual trees, shrubs and perennials

  ¶**Halcyon** A smaller garden consisting of a conservatory of unusual plants and colourful shrubs and perennials

Fountain Cottage ⚆ (Mr & Mrs P I Dodds) Bonchurch. Approx ½m E from central Ventnor at junction of Bonchurch Village Rd, Trinity Rd and St Boniface Rd. Reasonable parking in these rds and on forecourt of garage/stable opposite. Originally a gardener's cottage with approx 2 acres formerly part of a country estate landscaped in the 1830's with ponds, stream, waterfalls and fountains being a feature. South facing slope, partly wooded and terraced. Really a spring garden but with hydrangea and roses providing colour later in the year. TEAS. *Adm £1 Chd free. Mon April 12 (2-5)*

Hamstead Grange ⬥❀ (Lt Col & Mrs C R H Kindersley) Yarmouth. Entrance to drive on A3054 between Shalfleet and Ningwood. Rose garden with shrubs, fine lawns and trees. Swimming pool. Superb views of Newtown Creek and Solent. Plant stall in aid of Haylands Farm. TEAS. *Adm £1 Chd free. Sun June 27 (2.30-5)*

Mottistone Manor Gardens ❀ (The National Trust: Sir John Nicholson) Mottistone. 8m SW Newport on B3399 between Brighstone and Brook. Medium-sized formal terraced garden, backing onto mediaeval and Elizabethan manor house, set in wooded valley with fine views of English Channel and coast between Needles and St Catherine's Point. TEAS. *Adm £1.80 Chd 90p. Wed June 9 (2-5.30)*

North Court ⬥⚆❀ (Mr & Mrs J R Harrison) Shorwell 4m S of Newport on B3323 entrance on R after rustic bridge opp thatched cottage; 8 acres, landscaped terraces, stream, water garden, shrubs and trees. Jacobean Manor House (part open) TEAS *Adm £1 Chd 20p. Sun May 9 (2.30-5.30) and Sun May 30 with The Three North Court Gardens, also by appt Tel **0983 740415** except April, July and Aug*

Nunwell House ✗✿ (Col & Mrs J A Aylmer) Brading. 3m S of Ryde; signed off A3055 in Brading into Coach Lane. 5 acres beautifully set formal and shrub gardens with fountains. Exceptional view of Solent. House developed over 5 centuries, full of architectural interest. Coaches by appt only. TEAS. *Adm £1 Chd 10p; House £1.30 Chd 50p extra. Sun July 4 (2-5)*

Owl Cottage ♿✿ (Mrs A L Hutchinson & Miss S L Leaning) Hoxall Lane, Mottistone. 9m SW of Newport, from B3399 at Mottistone turn down Hoxall Lane for 200yds. Interesting cottage garden, view of sea. Home-made TEAS. Plant sale. *Adm £1 Chd 20p. Visits by appointment only May, June, July, Aug, parties of 10 or more (2.30-5.30)* **Tel after 6pm 0983 740433**

The Three North Court Gardens ♿✗✿ (Mrs C D Harrison, Mr & Mrs J Harrison, Mr & Mrs L Harrison) Shorwell 4m S of Newport on B3323, entrance on right after rustic bridge, opp thatched cottage. 14 acres; 3 varied gardens consisting of landscaped terraces, stream and water garden, woodland, walled rose garden, herbaceous borders, shrubs and walled kitchen garden, surrounding Jacobean Manor House (part open). TEAS. *Combined adm £1.20 Chd 20p. Sun May 30 (2.30-5.30)*

¶**The Watch House** (Sir William Mallinson) Bembridge. Most easterly part of I of W. St Helens-Bembridge. Before ascending hill by Pilot Inn turn L to Silver Beach Cafe. Last house on R. ¾-acre garden best known for its garden architecture and sea views (house built for the Admiralty). Formal garden at rear of house with fruit trees, rose arches and box hedges. TEAS. *Adm £1 Chd 20p. Sun May 23 (2-5)*

¶**Westport Cottage** ✗✿ (Kitty Fisher & K R Sharp) Cottage is 100 yds SE up Tennyson Close off Tennyson Rd, Yarmouth. This is the main rd through the town. Entrance is to the R of the metal gate and footpath into the walled yard with parking. Westport Cottage was built in the 1860's as a coach house and stables with a ½-acre walled vegetable garden laid out in quarters facing SW. This area now contains in the NE quarter a lawn and pond with terrace, small borders with shade shrubs, roses, creepers and climbers, grasses and a general mixture of alkaline and sea wind tolerant plants. The NW corner is paved and the quarter is given over to a swimming pool; a humpted ground geranium bed, surrounded by greys, roses, apple treees from original planting and a carbon insulated greenhouse. The SE quarter is an orchard, cob nuts, pears, apples and walnut plus border of shrubs; the SW quarter is a vegetable plot. The garden contains many unusual features and is home to a vast mixture. *Adm £1 Chd 20p. By appointment all year* **Tel 0983 760751**

Woolverton House (Mr & Mrs S H G Twining) St Lawrence. 3m W of Ventnor; Bus 16 from Ryde, Sandown, Shanklin. Flowering shrubs, bulbs, fine position. Homemade TEAS. *Adm £1 Chd 20p (Share to St Lawrence Village Hall). Sun April 18 (2-5)*

Yaffles ✿ (Mrs Wolfenden) The Pitts. The garden may be approached through Bonchurch Village, up the hill past the parish church 1st on L or from the top rd (Shanklin 2m to the E) turn L down the Bonchurch Shute, garden is immediately above St Boniface Church and next to the cul de sac The Pitts. Park in the rd. A 60' flowering cliff sculptured into glades; it is full of interesting plants and commands excellent views of the channel. Only suitable for wheelchairs on the top level where the teas and toilet are situated. Joan Wolfenden's book the Year from Yaffles is sold in aid of the NGS. TEAS *Adm £1 Chd free. Sun May 2 (2.30-5)*

Kent

Hon County Organiser:	Mrs Valentine Fleming, Stonewall Park, Edenbridge TN8 7DG
Assistant Hon County Organisers:	Mrs Jeremy Gibbs, Upper Kennards, Leigh, Tonbridge TN11 8RE
	Mrs Nicolas Irwin, Hoo Farmhouse, Minster, Ramsgate CT12 4JB
	Mrs Richard Latham, Stowting Hill House, nr Ashford TN25 6BE
	Miss E Napier, 447 Wateringbury Road, East Malling ME19 6JQ
	The Hon Mrs Oldfield, Doddington Place, nr Sittingbourne ME9 OBB
	Mrs M R Streatfeild, Hoath House, Chiddingstone Hoath, Edenbridge TN8 7DB
	Mrs Simon Toynbee, Old Tong Farm, Brenchley TN12 7HT
Hon County Treasurer:	Valentine Fleming Esq, Stonewall Park, Edenbridge TN8 7DG

DATES OF OPENING

By appointment
For telephone number and other details see garden descriptions

Beech Court, Challock

Bog Farm, Brabourne Lees
Brewhouse, Boughton Aluph
Church Hill Cottage, Charing Heath
Church House, High Halden
Close Farm, Crockham Hill
The Coach House, Eastling
The Conifers, New Barn, Longfield

Field Farm, Iden Green, nr Benenden
Greenways, Berry's Green, nr Downe
115 Hadlow Road, Tonbridge
Kypp Cottage, Biddenden
Ladham House, Goudhurst
43 Layhams Road, West Wickham
Little Trafalgar, Selling

Longacre, Selling
Oswalds, Bishopsbourne
The Pear House, Sellindge
Peddars Wood, St Michaels
Tenterden
Pevington Farm, Pluckley
Saltwood Castle, nr Hythe
Southfarthing, Hawkenbury,
Staplehurst
Stoneacre, Otham, Maidstone
2 Thorndale Close, Chatham
39 Warwick Crescent, Borstal,
Rochester
Westview, Hempstead, Gillingham
Woodpeckers, Hythe

Regular openings
For details see garden descriptions

Cobham Hall, Cobham
Doddington Place, nr Sittingbourne
Goodnestone Park, nr Wingham,
Canterbury
Great Comp Charitable Trust,
Borough Green
Groombridge Place, Groombridge
Hever Castle, nr Edenbridge
Marle Place, Brenchley
Mount Ephraim, Hernhill,
Faversham
Penshurst Place, Penshurst
The Pines Garden & The Bay
Museum, St Margaret's Bay
Quex Gardens & Cotton – Powell
Museum, Birchington
Riverhill House, Sevenoaks
Squerryes Court, Westerham
Walnut Tree Gardens, Little Chart

February 14 Sunday
Woodlands Manor, Adisham
March 14 Sunday
Great Comp, Borough Green
March 21 Sunday
Great Comp, Borough Green
March 28 Sunday
Church Hill Cottage, Charing
Heath
Copton Ash, Faversham
Crittenden House, Matfield
Great Comp, Borough Green
Hole Park, Rolvenden
Woodlands Manor, Adisham
March 31 Wednesday
Woodlands Manor, Adisham
April 4 Sunday
Hole Park, Rolvenden
Spilsill Court, Staplehurst
2 Thorndale Close, Chatham
Yalding Gardens
April 6 Tuesday
Penshurst Place, Penshurst

April 9 Good Friday
Street End Place, nr Canterbury
April 11 Easter Sunday
Church Hill Cottage, Charing
Heath
Copton Ash, Faversham
Crittenden House, Matfield
Godinton Park, nr Ashford
Jessups, Mark Beech, nr
Edenbridge
Ladham House, Goudhurst
Longacre, Selling
Mere House, Mereworth
Oswalds, Bishopsbourne
The Pines Garden & The Bay
Museum, St Margaret's Bay
Southfarthing, Hawkenbury,
Staplehurst
Street End Place, nr Canterbury
39 Warwick Crescent, Borstal
April 12 Easter Monday
Church Hill Cottage, Charing
Heath
Copton Ash, Faversham
Crittenden House, Matfield
Longacre, Selling
Oswalds, Bishopsbourne
Southfarthing, Hawkenbury,
Staplehurst
April 14 Wednesday
Hole Park, Rolvenden
April 17 Saturday
Glassenbury Park, nr Cranbrook
April 18 Sunday
The Beehive, Lydd ‡
Church Hill Cottage, Charing
Heath
Cobham Hall, Cobham
Edenbridge House, Edenbridge
Egypt Farm, Hamptons, Plaxtol ‡‡
Glassenbury Park, nr Cranbrook
Godmersham Park, nr Ashford
Hamptons Farm House, Plaxtol ‡‡
2 Thorndale Close, Chatham
Vine House, Lydd ‡
April 21 Wednesday
Westview, Hempstead, Gillingham
April 24 Saturday
Pett Place, Charing
Westview, Hempstead, Gillingham
April 25 Sunday
Brewhouse, Boughton Aluph
Church Hill Cottage, Charing
Heath
Collingwood Grange, Benenden
Crittenden House, Matfield
Hole Park, Rolvenden
Longacre, Selling
Manor House, Upper Hardres
Mount Ephraim, Hernhill,
Faversham
New Barns House, West Malling
Pett Place, Charing
Stoneacre, Otham, Maidstone

Torry Hill, nr Sittingbourne
Withersdane Hall, Wye
April 28 Wednesday
Bog Farm, Brabourne Lees
Sissinghurst Garden,
Sissinghurst
May 1 Saturday
Riverhill House, Sevenoaks
May 2 Sunday
Church Hill Cottage, Charing
Heath
Coldham, Little Chart Forstal
Copton Ash, Faversham
Doddington Place, nr
Sittingbourne
Elvey Farmhouse, Westwell,
Ashford
Hole Park, Rolvenden
Ladham House, Goudhurst
Longacre, Selling ‡
Luton House, Selling ‡
Maurice House, Broadstairs
Northbourne Court, nr Deal
Southfarthing, Hawkenbury,
Staplehurst
Updown Farm, Betteshanger
39 Warwick Close, Borstal
Woodlands Manor, Adisham
May 3 (Bank Hol) Monday
Brewhouse, Boughton Aluph
Church Hill Cottage, Charing
Heath
Copton Ash, Faversham
Crittenden House, Matfield
Elvey Farmhouse, Westwell,
Ashford
Longacre, Selling
Southfarthing, Hawkenbury,
Staplehurst
May 5 Wednesday
Woodlands Manor, Adisham
May 8 Saturday
Peddars Wood, St Michaels,
Tenterden
Rock Farm, Nettlestead
May 9 Sunday
Court Lodge, Groombridge
Doddington Place, nr
Sittingbourne
Edenbridge House, Edenbridge
Meadow Wood, Penshurst
Stonewall Park, nr Edenbridge
2 Thorndale Close, Chatham
Thornham Friars, Thurnham
May 12 Wednesday
Petham House, Petham
Rock Farm, Nettlestead
May 13 Thursday
Beech Court, Challock
May 15 Saturday
Charts Edge, Westerham
Emmetts Garden, Ide Hill
Glassenbury Park, nr Cranbrook
Rock Farm, Nettlestead

May 16 Sunday
Beech Court, Challock
Bilting House, nr Ashford
Brewhouse, Boughton Aluph
Church Hill Cottage, Charing
   Heath
Coldharbour Oast, Tenterden
Crittenden House, Matfield
Doddington Place, nr
   Sittingbourne
Glassenbury Park, nr Cranbrook
Greencroft, Hildenborough
Hole Park, Rolvenden
Larksfield, Crockham Hill ‡
Larksfield Cottage, Crockham
   Hill ‡
Long Barn, Weald, Sevenoaks
Longacre, Selling
Pevington Farm, Pluckley
The Red House, Crockham Hill ‡
Torry Hill, nr Sittingbourne
Ulcombe Place, nr Maidstone

May 19 Wednesday
Rock Farm, Nettlestead
Waystrode Manor, Cowden
Westview, Hempstead, Gillingham

May 22 Saturday
Charts Edge, Westerham
Rock Farm, Nettlestead
Westview, Hempstead, Gillingham

May 23 Sunday
Brenchley Gardens ‡‡
Church Hill Cottage, Charing
   Heath
Doddington Place, nr
   Sittingbourne
Forest Gate, Pluckley
Goudhurst Gardens
Hole Park, Rolvenden
Kypp Cottage, Biddenden
Larksfield, Crockham Hill ‡
Larksfield Cottage, Crockham
   Hill ‡
Marle Place, Brenchley ‡‡
Ramhurst Manor, Leigh,
   Tonbridge
The Red House, Crockham Hill ‡
2 Thorndale Close, Chatham

May 24 Monday
Kypp Cottage, Biddenden

May 25 Tuesday
Kypp Cottage, Biddenden

May 26 Wednesday
Belmont, Throwley, nr Faversham
Edenbridge House, Edenbridge
Kypp Cottage, Biddenden
Rock Farm, Nettlestead
Whitehurst, Chainhurst, Marden

May 29 Saturday
Riverhill House, Sevenoaks
Rock Farm, Nettlestead

May 30 Sunday
Church Hill Cottage, Charing
   Heath

Copton Ash, Faversham
Flint Cottage, Bishopsbourne
Kypp Cottage, Biddenden
Ladham House, Goudhurst
Little Trafalgar, Selling ‡
Longacre, Selling ‡
Northbourne Court, nr Deal
Olantigh, Wye
Oxon Hoath, nr Hadlow
The Pines Garden & The Bay
   Museum, St Margaret's Bay
29 The Precincts, Canterbury
St Michaels House, Roydon,
   Peckham Bush
Sea Close, Hythe
Town Hill Cottage, West Malling
Updown Farm, Betteshanger
Walnut Tree Gardens, Little Chart
Waystrode Manor, Cowden

May 31 (Bank Hol) Monday
Brewhouse, Boughton Aluph
Church Hill Cottage, Charing
   Heath
Copton Ash, Faversham
Crittenden House, Matfield
Flint Cottage, Bishopsbourne
Kypp Cottage, Biddenden
Little Trafalgar, Selling ‡
Longacre, Selling ‡
Scotney Castle, Lamberhurst
Stoneacre, Otham, Maidstone
Whitehurst, Chainhurst,
   Marden

June 1 Tuesday
Kypp Cottage, Biddenden

June 2 Wednesday
Hole Park, Rolvenden
Knole, Sevenoaks
Kypp Cottage, Biddenden
29 The Precincts, Canterbury
Rock Farm, Nettlestead

June 5 Saturday
Peddars Wood, St Michaels,
   Tenterden
29 The Precincts, Canterbury
Rock Farm, Nettlestead
Sissinghurst Place Gardens,
   Sissinghurst

June 6 Sunday
The Anchorage, West Wickham
Beech Court, Challock
Brenchley Manor, Brenchley ‡
Congelow House, Yalding
Crittenden House, Matfield
Field Farm, Iden Green, Benenden
Kypp Cottage, Biddenden
Portobello, Brenchley ‡
29 The Precincts, Canterbury
Ringfield, Knockholt
Sissinghurst Place Gardens,
   Sissinghurst
2 Thorndale Close, Chatham

June 7 Monday
Kypp Cottage, Biddenden

June 8 Tuesday
Kypp Cottage, Biddenden

June 9 Wednesday
Bog Farm, Brabourne Lees
Kypp Cottage, Biddenden
Rock Farm, Nettlestead
Sissinghurst Garden, Sissinghurst
Upper Pryors, Cowden ‡
Waystrode Manor, Cowden ‡

June 11 Friday
Rosefarm, Chilham

June 12 Saturday
Rock Farm, Nettlestead
Rosefarm, Chilham

June 13 Sunday
Chiddingstone Gardens, nr
   Edenbridge
Church Hill Cottage, Charing
   Heath
Field Farm, Iden Green,
   Benenden
Forest Gate, Pluckley ‡
Groome Farm, Egerton
Horton Priory, Sellindge
Kypp Cottage, Biddenden
Little Trafalgar, Selling ‡‡
Longacre, Selling ‡‡
Mill House, Hildenborough
Northbourne Court, nr Deal
Old Tong Farm, Brenchley
Pevington Farm, Pluckley ‡
Town Hill Cottage, West
   Malling ‡‡‡
Walnut Tree Gardens, Little
   Chart ‡
Went House, West Malling ‡‡‡

June 14 Monday
Kypp Cottage, Biddenden
Penshurst Place, Penshurst

June 15 Tuesday
Kypp Cottage, Biddenden

June 16 Wednesday
Cares Cross, Chiddingstone
   Hoath ‡
Coach House, Mereworth Lawn
Kypp Cottage, Biddenden
Old Tong Farm, Brenchley
Rock Farm, Nettlestead
Stonewall Park, nr Edenbridge ‡

June 17 Thursday
Copton Ash, Faversham
Walnut Tree Gardens, Little Chart

June 18 Friday
Rosefarm, Chilham

June 19 Saturday
Petham House, Petham
Pett Place, Charing
Rock Farm, Nettlestead
Rosefarm, Chilham
Whitehurst, Chainhurst, Marden

June 20 Sunday
The Anchorage, West Wickham
Battel Hall, Leeds, nr Maidstone
Brewhouse, Boughton Aluph ‡

Coldham, Little Chart Forstal
Crittenden House, Matfield
Downs Court, Boughton Aluph ‡
Edenbridge House, Edenbridge
Godinton Park, nr Ashford
Goudhurst Gardens
Hartlip Gardens, nr Sittingbourne
Kypp Cottage, Biddenden
Little Crampton Farm, High
   Halden
Long Barn, Weald, Sevenoaks
Lullingstone Castle, Eynsford
The Manor House, Upper Hardres
Nettlestead Place, Nettlestead
The Old Parsonage, Sutton
   Valence
Old Place Farm, High Halden
Pett Place, Charing
St Clere, Kemsing
St Michaels House, Roydon,
   Peckham Bush
2 Thorndale Close, Chatham

June 21 Monday
Kypp Cottage, Biddenden

June 22 Tuesday
Kypp Cottage, Biddenden
Little Crampton Farm, High
   Halden
The Old Parsonage, Sutton
   Valence

June 23 Wednesday
Coach House, Mereworth Lawn
Kypp Cottage, Biddenden
Rock Farm, Nettlestead
The Silver Spray, Sellindge

June 24 Thursday
The Old Parsonage, Sutton
   Valence
Walnut Tree Gardens, Little Chart

June 26 Saturday
Charing Heath Gardens
The Old Parsonage, Sutton
   Valence
Peddars Wood, St Michaels,
   Tenterden
Rock Farm, Nettlestead

June 27 Sunday
Charing Heath Gardens
115 Hadlow Road, Tonbridge
Kypp Cottage, Biddenden
Little Trafalgar, Selling ‡
Longacre, Selling ‡
Marle Place, Brenchley
Northbourne Court, nr Deal
Placketts Hole, Bicknor, nr
   Sittingbourne
Plaxtol Gardens
Upper Mill Cottage, Loose
Waystrode Manor, Cowden
Went House, West Malling
West Farleigh Hall, nr
   Maidstone

June 28 Monday
Kypp Cottage, Biddenden

June 29 Tuesday
Kypp Cottage, Biddenden

June 30 Wednesday
Kypp Cottage, Biddenden
Rock Farm, Nettlestead
Upper Mill Cottage, Loose

July 1 Thursday
Walnut Tree Gardens, Little Chart

July 3 Saturday
Quex Gardens & Powell – Cotton
   Museum, Birchington
Rock Farm, Nettlestead

July 4 Sunday
Bluebonnets, Sevenoaks
Kypp Cottage, Biddenden
Luton House, Selling
Olantigh, Wye
South Hill Farm, Hastingleigh
Tanners, Brasted
Torry Hill, nr Sittingbourne
Upper Mill Cottage, Loose
Worth Gardens

July 5 Monday
Kypp Cottage, Biddenden

July 6 Tuesday
Kypp Cottage, Biddenden

July 7 Wednesday
Chartwell, Westerham
Kypp Cottage, Biddenden
Rock Farm, Nettlestead
The Silver Spray, Sellindge
Sissinghurst Garden, Sissinghurst

July 10 Saturday
Rock Farm, Nettlestead
The Silver Spray, Sellindge

July 11 Sunday
Bilting House, nr Ashford
Brewhouse, Boughton Aluph
Field House, Staplehurst
Kypp Cottage, Biddenden
Ladham House, Goudhurst
Little Trafalgar, Selling ‡
Longacre, Selling ‡
Mere House, Mereworth
Northbourne Court, nr Deal
Ringfield, Knockholt
Squerryes Court, Westerham
2 Thorndale Close, Chatham
Walnut Tree Gardens, Little Chart
Withersdane Hall, Wye

July 12 Monday
Kypp Cottage, Biddenden

July 13 Tuesday
Kypp Cottage, Biddenden

July 14 Wednesday
185 Borden Lane, Sittingbourne
Kypp Cottage, Biddenden
Peddars Wood, St Michaels,
   Tenterden
Rock Farm, Nettlestead

July 15 Thursday
Walnut Tree Gardens, Little Chart

July 17 Saturday
Rock Farm, Nettlestead

July 18 Sunday
The Beehive, Lydd ‡
Charing Heath Gardens
Edenbridge House, Edenbridge
Goodnestone Park, Wingham,
   Canterbury
Long Barn, Weald, Sevenoaks
The Rectory, Fairseat
Sea Close, Hythe
Vine House, Lydd ‡

July 19 Monday
The Beehive, Lydd ‡
Vine House, Lydd ‡

July 21 Wednesday
Groombridge Place,
   Groombridge
The Rectory, Fairseat
Rock Farm, Nettlestead
The Silver Spray, Sellindge

July 24 Saturday
Rock Farm, Nettlestead
The Silver Spray, Sellindge

July 25 Sunday
Brewhouse, Boughton Aluph
Copton Ash, Faversham
Little Trafalgar, Selling ‡
Longacre, Selling ‡
Northbourne Court, nr Deal
Spilsill Court, Staplehurst
2 Thorndale Close, Chatham

July 28 Wednesday
Rock Farm, Nettlestead

July 31 Saturday
Rock Farm, Nettlestead

August 1 Sunday
185 Borden Lane, Sittingbourne
Withersdane Hall, Wye
Woodpeckers, Hythe

August 4 Wednesday
185 Borden Lane, Sittingbourne
Cobham Hall, Cobham
Knole, Sevenoaks
Rock Farm, Nettlestead

August 7 Saturday
Peddars Wood, St Michaels,
   Tenterden
Rock Farm, Nettlestead

August 8 Sunday
Field House, Staplehurst
Groome Farm, Egerton
Little Trafalgar, Selling
Walnut Tree Gardens, Little Cha

August 15 Sunday
Chevening, Sevenoaks
Marle Place, Brenchley
Northbourne Court, nr Deal

August 22 Sunday
Goodnestone Park, Wingham,
   Canterbury
Walnut Tree Gardens, Little Cha
West Studdal Farm, nr Dover
Whitehurst, Chainhurst, Marden

August 25 Wednesday
The Silver Spray, Sellindge

August 29 Sunday
Copton Ash, Faversham
115 Hadlow Road, Tonbridge
Little Trafalgar, Selling ‡
Longacre, Selling ‡
Northbourne Court, nr Deal
The Pines Garden & Bay
  Museum, St Margaret's Bay
Sea Close, Hythe
August 30 (Bank Hol) Monday
Copton Ash, Faversham
Little Trafalgar, Selling ‡
Longacre, Selling ‡
The Silver Spray, Sellindge
September 4 Saturday
Whitehurst, Chainhurst, Marden
September 5 Sunday
185 Borden Lane, Sittingbourne

Nettlestead Place, Nettlestead
Withersdane Hall, Wye
September 12 Sunday
Coldharbour Oast, Tenterden
Horton Priory, Sellindge
Little Trafalgar, Selling ‡
Longacre, Selling ‡
Northbourne Court, nr Deal
Squerryes Court, Westerham
September 26 Sunday
Copton Ash, Faversham
Little Trafalgar, Selling
Mount Ephraim, Hernhill,
  Faversham
Northbourne Court, nr Deal
Oswalds, Bishopsbourne
October 2 Saturday
Quex Gardens & Powell – Cotton

Museum, Birchington
October 3 Sunday
Sea Close, Hythe
October 9 Saturday
Emmetts Garden, Ide Hill
October 10 Sunday
Hole Park, Rolvenden
Marle Place, Brenchley
October 16 Saturday
Copton Ash, Faversham
October 17 Sunday
Collingwood Grange, Benenden
Copton Ash, Faversham
Hole Park, Rolvenden
November 7 Sunday
Great Comp, Borough Green

DESCRIPTIONS OF GARDENS

The Anchorage ✿✾ (Mr & Mrs G Francis) 8 Croydon Road, W Wickham. 4m SW of Bromley. 100yds from A232 and A2022 roundabout; enter from A232 opp Manor House public house, as rd is one way. ⅓-acre garden, lovingly created since 1988, inspired by Sissinghurst, comprising small compartments individually designed for colour within recently-planted hedges; old-fashioned roses, irises & large collection of unusual perennials; herb garden, walled garden, vegetables, trained fruit trees; conservation & wild-life area incl pond, woodland & meadow flowers. TEAS. *Adm £1 Chd 25p (Share to Coney Hill School Appeal; Shaftesbury Society). Suns June 6, 20 (2-6)*

Battel Hall ఉ✾ (John D Money Esq) Leeds, Maidstone. From A20 Hollingbourne roundabouts take B2163 S (signed Leeds Castle), at top of hill take Burberry Lane, house 100yds on R. Garden of approx 1 acre created since 1954 around medieval house; roses, herbaceous plants, shrubs and ancient wisteria. TEAS. *Adm £1.50 Chd £1. Sun June 20 (2-6)*

Beech Court ఉ✾✿ (Mr & Mrs Vyvyan Harmsworth) Challock, 7m N of Ashford; entrance on A252, Challock being midway between Charing and Chilham, informal garden inspired by Inverewe garden Wester Ross. Fine collection of acers, rhododendrons, azaleas, conifers and shrubs set in 4 acres of lawns. TEAS on NGS days. *Adm £1.50 Chd 50p. Open May 6, 9, 20, 23, 30, 31; June 3, 10, 13, 17, 20. For NGS Thurs May 13; Suns May 16, June 6 (2-5.30); also by appt Tel 0233 740641*

The Beehive ✾ (C G Brown Esq) 10 High Street, Lydd. S of New Romney on B2075, in centre of Lydd opp Church. Small walled garden, tucked behind village street house dating from 1550, with over 200 varieties of plants. There are paths and cosy corners in this cottage garden with pond and pergola; a pool of seclusion; the busy world outside unnoticed passes by. Teas usually available in the church. *Adm £1 Chd 50p (Share to Horder Centre for Arthritis, Crowborough). Suns April 18, July 18; Mon Jul 19 (2.30-5.30)*

Belmont ఉ✿ (the Harris (Belmont) Charity) Throwley 4m SW of Faversham. Take A251 (Faversham-Ashford Rd), from Badlesmere follow brown tourist signs. Walled pleasure garden and orangery; small pinetum and walled kitchen garden; long yew walk and folly; Victorian grotto; pets' cemetery. House by Samuel Wyatt c.1792. TEAS. ▲*Adm £1.50 Chd 50p (Share to St Michaels Church, Throwley). Wed May 26 (2-5)*

Bilting House ఉ✾ (John Erle-Drax Esq) A28, 5m NE of Ashford, 9m from Canterbury. Wye 1½m. Old-fashioned garden with ha-ha; rhododendrons, azaleas; shrubs. In beautiful part of Stour Valley. TEAS £1. *Adm £1 Chd 30p (Share to BRCS). Suns May 16, July 11 (2-5.30)*

Bluebonnets ✾ (Mr & Mrs Alan Hissey) 138 Kippington Road, Sevenoaks. Opp entrance to Knole and Sevenoaks School, from A225 turn W down Oak Lane, third R into Kippington Road. 1½-acre pretty, informal garden with interesting plants, created for year-round interest and easy care, maintained entirely by owners. TEAS in aid of Macmillan Nurses. *Adm £1.50 Acc chd free. Sun July 4 (3-6.30)*

Bog Farm ఉ✾✿ (Mr & Mrs K J Hewitt) Brabourne Lees, 4m E of Ashford; via M20 junction 10 (Ashford), 3m S of Ashford on A20 turn E in Smeeth, proceed ½m to Woolpack Inn; bear R, continue 700yds following sign to garden on R down single track lane. 1-acre garden, planned and planted by owners since 1959 around small Kentish farmhouse (not open); good collection of shrubs, trees, species plants, ferns, bulbs arranged to give interest to each season; mixed borders; moisture plants; old roses; herb garden. *Adm £1 Chd 20p. Weds April 28, June 9 (2-7); also by appt*

185 Borden Lane ఉ✾✿ (Mr & Mrs P A Boyce) ½m S of Sittingbourne. 1m from Sittingbourne side of A2/A249 junction. Small informal garden with many varieties of fuchsia; hardy perennials; shrubs; pond; fruit, vegetable and herb garden. Home-made TEAS. *Adm £1 Acc chd free. Suns Aug 1, Sept 5; Weds July 14, Aug 4 (2-6)*

Brenchley Gardens 6m SE of Tonbridge. From A21 1m S of Pembury turn N on to B2160, turn R at Xrds in Matfield signposted Brenchley. *Combined adm £2 Acc chd free. Sun May 23 (2-6)*

Holmbush ♿✗ (Brian & Cathy Worden Hodge) 1½-acre informal garden, mainly lawns, trees and shrub borders, planted since 1960

Portobello (Barry M Williams Esq) 1½ acres, lawn, trees, shrubs incl azaleas and shrub roses; walled garden. C17 barn containing 1936 Dennis fire engine in running order. House (not open) built by Monckton family 1739

Puxted House ♿❀ (P J Oliver-Smith Esq) 1½ acres with rare and coloured foliage shrubs, water and woodland plants. Alpine and rose garden all labelled. Present owner cleared 20yrs of brambles in 1981 before replanting. TEA

¶Brenchley Manor ♿✗ (Mr & Mrs Barry Bruckmann) Brenchley, 6m SE of Tonbridge; from A21 at 1m S of Pembury turn N onto B2160; at Matfield Xrds turn R, sign-posted Brenchley. Medium-sized garden, currently being restored; ornamental yew hedge; knot garden; herbaceous borders; Domesday oak; pond & woodland. Early timber-framed house with fine renaissance arch. TEAS. *Adm £1.50 Acc chd free. Sun June 6 (2-6)*

Brewhouse ♿✗❀ (Mr & Mrs J A H Nicholson) Malthouse Lane, Boughton Aluph, 3m N of Ashford. Garden off Pilgrims Way. ¼m N and signed from Boughton Lees village green, on A251 Ashford-Faversham. 1-acre plantsman's garden with new features this year. C16 farmhouse (not open) with fine views of open chalkland. Collections of old roses, other old-fashioned flowers, herbaceous and foliage plants. TEAS (in aid of All Saints Church; not April & June). *Adm £1 Chd 25p. Suns April 25, May 16, June 20, July 11, 25; Mons May 3, 31 (2-6); also by appt throughout season* **Tel 0233 623748**

Cares Cross ♿❀ (Mr & Mrs R L Wadsworth) Chiddingstone Hoath. (Ordnance Survey Grid ref. TQ 496 431.) Landscaped garden around C16 house (not open). Dramatic views to N Downs over fields with old oaks, restored hedgerows, wildfowl lake and vineyard. Garden features old roses; water garden; innovative ground cover; rare shrubs and trees; speciality American plants. Featured on BBC Gardeners World 1990. TEAS. *Adm £2 OAPs £1 Acc chd free. Wed June 16 (2-6); also by appt to groups of 10 plus, weekdays only May 15 to July 15*

¶Charing Heath Gardens 10m NW of Ashford to W of A20. Proceed to Charing Heath; at Red Lion take Egerton Rd and, after crossing M20 both gardens are ¼m on. *Combined adm £2 Acc chd free. Sat June 26; Suns June 27, July 18 (2-6)*

¶Horseshoe Cottage ✗❀ (Mr & Mrs P Robinson) Garden set in elevated position which affords views of rural countryside. Terraced lower garden has a variety of unusual plants; the main garden of approx 1 acre has island beds and mature shrubs and conifers. From this garden an entrance gives access to:

By Appointment Gardens. See head of county section

¶High Banks ♿✗❀ (Mr & Mrs P Salter) 2-acre garden containing a wide variety of conifers, trees, plants and shrubs for all-year interest, and featuring rose, water and fuchsia gardens and a pergola walk. Also a display of tools and implements of bygone years. TEAS in aid of The Lord Whisky Animal Sanctuary Fund.

¶Charts Edge ♿ (Mr & Mrs John Bigwood) Westerham, ½m S of Westerham on B2026 towards Chartwell. 7-acre hillside garden being restored by present owners; large collection of rhododendrons, azaleas, acers & magnolias; specimen trees & newly-planted mixed borders; Victorian folly; walled vegetable garden. Fine views over North Downs. Dressage display at 3.30pm. TEAS. *Adm £1.50 Chd 25p (Share to BHS Dressage Group) Sats May 15, 22 (2-6)*

Chartwell ❀ (The National Trust) 2m S of Westerham, fork L off B2026 after 1½m, well signed. 12-acre informal gardens on a hillside with glorious views over Weald of Kent. Fishpools and lakes together with red-brick wall built by Sir Winston Churchill, the former owner of Chartwell. The avenue of golden roses given by the family on Sir Winston's golden wedding anniversary will be at its best. Self-service restaurant serving coffee, lunches and teas. *Adm £2 Chd £1. ▲Wed July 7 (12-5.30 last adm 5)*

Chevening ♿ (By permission of the Board of Trustees of Chevening Estate and the Rt Hon Douglas Hurd) 4m NW of Sevenoaks. Turn N off A25 at Sundridge traffic lights on to B2211; at Chevening Xrds 1½m turn L. 27 acres with lawns and woodland garden, lake, maze, formal rides, parterre. Garden being restored. TEAS in aid of Kent Church Social Work and overseas charities. *Adm £1.50 OAPs £1 Chd 50p. Sun Aug 15 (2-6)*

Chiddingstone Gardens 4m E of Edenbridge, via B2026, at Cowden Pound turn E to Mark Beech. Old Buckhurst is 1st house on R after leaving Mark Beech on Penshurst Rd. Maps will be provided. Teas in Chiddingstone village. *Combined adm £2.50 OAPs £2 Acc chd free (Share to St Mary's Church). Sun June 13 (2-5.30)*

Old Buckhurst (Mr & Mrs J Gladstone) Chiddingstone Hoath Rd, Mark Beech. 1-acre garden surrounding C15 farmhouse (not open). Part walled ornamental & kitchen gardens designed & planted 1988 onwards. 'New English' shrub roses; range of clematis, shrubs & herbaceous plants. Parking in 1-acre paddock

Hill Hoath House ♿ (Mr Anthony Hook) Hill Hoath Road. Medium-sized garden created by owners over the last ten years. Roses; herbaceous border & pond

The Old Rectory ♿✗ (Mr & Mrs Anthony Wood) 5 acres of lawns, trees, water & woodland garden; formal garden around house; mown path in glebe with outstanding views

Church Hill Cottage ♿✗❀ (Mr & Mrs Michael Metianu) Charing Heath, 10m NW of Ashford. Leave M20 at junction 8 (Lenham) if Folkestone-bound or junction 9 (Ashford West) if London-bound: then leave A20 dual carriageway ½m W of Charing signed Charing Heath and Egerton. After 1m fork R at Red Lion, then R again; cottage 250yds on R. C16 cottage surrounded by garden of 1½ acres, developed & planted by present owners since 1981. Several separate connected areas each containing island beds & borders planted with extensive range of perennials, shrubs, spring bulbs & foliage plants. Picnic area. *Adm £1 Chd 50p (Share to Canterbury Pilgrims Hospice). Suns March 28, April 11, 18, 25, May 2, 16, 23, 30, June 13; Mons April 12, May 3, 31 (2-5); also by appt* **Tel 0233 712522**

Church House ৬⚘ (Mr & Mrs Robin Carnegie) High Halden, 3m E of Tenterden. From A28 turn off in centre of village leaving Green on L. Church House at end on L. Medium-sized garden of C16 vicarage, planted since 1985. Mixed borders, large ponds, small bog garden, wildfowl. *Adm £1 Chd 50p. By appt only, April to Sept* **Tel 0233 850287**

¶**Close Farm** ৬⚘⚘ (Joan & Geoffrey Williams) Crockham Hill, 2½ N of Edenbridge on B2026. Turn into narrow private lane immediately adjacent to PO/antique shop. Close Farm is first house ½m along lane by grass triangle. Garden approx 1 acre, partly terraced, established in 1930s on Greensand ridge. Natural springs, watercourses and pond. Early flowering naturalised bulbs, hellebores, many summer perennials, shrub roses. Autumn colour. High path walk with good views. *Adm £1.50 Chd 50p. By appt only Feb to Nov incl* **Tel 0732 866228**

The Coach House, Eastling ৬⚘⚘ (Mr & Mrs Roger Turner) Faversham. From A2 in Faversham take Brogdale Rd, continue S to Eastling, house on right after Meesons Close. Informally planted ⅓-acre garden on chalk; mixed borders incl climbing and shrub roses; sheltered paved courtyard with formal fishpond; moisture loving plants contrast with sun loving species. *Adm £1 Chd 20p. By appt only, May 4 to July 9* **Tel 0795 890304**

The Coach House, Mereworth Lawn ⚘⚘ (Mr & Mrs J Frisby) 3m E of Borough Green. On E side of B2016 (Seven Mile Lane) 2½m from both A20 at Wrotham Heath & A26 at Mereworth roundabout. ½-acre converted Victorian walled kitchen garden, redesigned after 1987 hurricane; many specialist plants. Limited parking. TEAS. *Adm £1 Acc chd free (Share to St Christopher's Hospice). Weds June 16, 23 (2-6)*

¶**Cobham Hall** ৬ (Westwood Educational Trust), Cobham. next to A2/M2 8m E of junction 2 of M25, midway between Gravesend and Rochester on B2009. Beautiful Elizabethan mansion in 150 acres landscaped by Humphry Repton at end of C18. Acres of daffodils and flowering trees planted in 1930s; garden now being restored by Cobham Hall Heritage Trust. TEAS. *Adm House £2 Chd £1 Garden £1 (Share to Cobham Hall Heritage Trust). Open April 4, 9, 11, 12, 14, 15, 21, 22; July 25, 28, 29; Aug all Weds, Thurs, Suns (2-5) For NGS Sun April 18; Wed Aug 4 (2-5)*

Coldham ৬⚘⚘ (Dr & Mrs J G Elliott) Little Chart Forstal, 5m NW of Ashford. Leave M20 at junction 8 (Lenham) if Folkestone-bound or junction 9 (Ashford West) if London-bound: then leave A20 at Charing by road signposted to Little Chart, turn E in village, ¼m. Small garden developed since 1970 in setting of old walls; good collection of rare plants, bulbs, alpines, mixed borders. C16 Kent farmhouse (not open). TEA. *Adm £1.50 Chd 50p. Suns May 2, June 20 (2-5.30)*

Coldharbour Oast ৬⚘ (Mr & Mrs A J A Pearson) Tenterden. 300yds SW of Tenterden High St (A28), take lane signed West View Hospital, after 200yds bear R on to concrete lane signed Coldharbour, proceed for 600yds. Garden started in late 1987 from ¾-acre field in exposed position. Pond; dry stream; unusual shrubs and perennials maintained by owners aiming to triumph over adversities of wind and drought. TEA in aid of Steam Locomotive Restoration. *Adm £1 Acc chd free. Suns May 16, Sept 12 (12.30-5.30)*

¶**Collingwood Grange** ৬⚘⚘ (Mrs Linda Fennell), Benenden, SE of Cranbrook 100yds on E of rd to Iden Green from village centre. Bus: Cranbrook-Tenterden. Flowering cherries; rhododendrons, incl large collection of dwarf kinds; autumn colour. Former home of the late Capt Collingwood 'Cherry' Ingram. Special botanical interest. TEAS. *Adm £1.50 Acc chd free. Suns April 25 (2-6), Oct 17 (2-5)*

Congelow House ৬⚘ (Mrs D J Cooper) Yalding, 8m SW of Maidstone. Approx mid-way between Tonbridge and Maidstone, and S of Yalding. 4-acre garden created from an orchard since 1973; backbone of interesting ornamental trees planted about 1850, with recent plantings; walled vegetable garden; pleasure gardens incl rhododendrons, azaleas, irises, roses, shrub roses. Vegetables, organically grown, on sale. TEAS. *Adm £1.50 Chd 50p (Share to Henry Doubleday Research Ass). Sun June 6 (2-5.30). Also April 4 with* **Yalding Gardens**

The Conifers ⚘⚘ (Mr & Mrs P Bowler) 17 Festival Ave, New Barn, 6m SE Dartford, 4m S Gravesend. From A2 or A227 take B260 to Longfield. Turn N, signed New Barn, take 3rd R into Fawkham Ave, L to Nurstead Ave (unmade rd but suitable for minibuses) in 100yds L into Festival Ave. ⅓-acre garden designed & created by present owners since 1980. Fully labelled plant collection incl over 100 varieties of conifers, with water garden, dovecote, west country slate feature; fern, hosta, herbaceous and lily borders reached by rose and clematis-covered walkways. *Adm £1 Acc chd free. By appt only from June 6 to Sept 5* **Tel 0474 706570**

Copton Ash ৬⚘⚘ (Mr & Mrs John Ingram & Drs Tim & Gillian Ingram) 105 Ashford Rd, Faversham, 1m. On A251 Faversham-Ashford rd opp E-bound junction with M2. 1½-acre plantsman's garden developed since 1978 on site of old cherry orchard. Wide range of plants in mixed borders and informal island beds; incl spring bulbs, alpine and herbaceous plants, shrubs, young trees and collection of fruit varieties. Good autumn colour. TEAS. *Adm £1 Acc chd free (Share to National Schizophrenia Fellowship, Canterbury Group). Suns March 28, April 11, May 2, 30, July 25, Aug 29, Sept 26, Oct 17; Mons April 12, May 3, 31, Aug 30; Thurs June 17; Sat Oct 16 (2-6; 2-7.30 in June & July)*

¶**Court Lodge** ৬ (Mr & Mrs T C V Packman) Groombridge, 4½m SW of Tunbridge Wells. C15 house (not open) removed from Udimore in 1912. 7-acre garden with rhododendrons, pergola, pond and rockery. Distant views. TEAS. *Adm £1 Chd 25p. Sun May 9 (2-6)*

Crittenden House ⚔ (B P Tompsett Esq) Matfield, 6m SE of Tonbridge. Bus: MD 6 or 297, alight Standings Cross, Matfield, 1m. Garden around early C17 house completely planned and planted since 1956 on labour-saving lines. Featuring spring shrubs (rhododendrons, magnolias), roses, lilies, foliage, waterside planting of ponds in old iron workings, of interest from early spring bulbs to autumn colour. Rare young trees mentioned in Collins Guide to Trees in UK and Europe, by Alan Mitchell. Subject of article in *R.H.S. Journal*, 1990. Tea Cherry-trees, Matfield Green. Free car park. *Adm £1.25 Chd (under 12) 25p. Suns March 28, April 11, 25, May 16, June 6, 20; Mons April 12, May 3, 31 (2-6)*

Doddington Place ₺❀ (Mr Richard & the Hon Mrs Oldfield) 6m SE of Sittingbourne. From A20 turn N opp Lenham or from A2 turn S at Teynham or Ospringe (Faversham) (all 4m). Large garden, landscaped with wide views; trees and yew hedges; woodland garden with azaleas and rhododendrons, Edwardian rock garden; formal garden planted for late summer interest. TEAS, restaurant, shop. *Adm £1.50 Chd 25p (Share to Kent Assoc for the Blind and Doddington Church). Every Wed and Bank Holiday Mon from Easter to end Sept; Suns in May only. For NGS, Suns May 2, 9, 16, 23 (11-6)*

¶Downs Court ₺⚔ (Mr & Mrs M J B Green) Boughton Aluph, 4m NE of Ashford off A28. Take lane on L signposted Boughton Aluph church, fork R at pillar box, garden is next drive on R. Approx 3 acres with fine downland views, sweeping lawns and some mature trees and yew hedges. Mixed borders largely replanted by owners in last 10 years; shrub roses. TEAS in aid of Multiple Sclerosis Research. *Adm £1 Chd 50p Sun June 20 (2-6)*

Edenbridge House ₺❀ (Mrs M T Lloyd) Crockham Hill Rd, 1½m N of Edenbridge, nr Marlpit Hill, on B2026. 5-acre garden of bulbs, spring shrubs, herbaceous borders, alpines, roses and water garden. House part C16 (not open). TEAS. *Adm £1 Chd 25p. Suns April 18, May 9, June 20, July 18; Wed May 26 (2-6); also by appt for groups* Tel 0732 862122

Egypt Farm ⚔ (Mr & Mrs Francis Bullock) Hamptons, 6m N of Tonbridge, equidistant from Plaxtol & Hadlow. From Hadlow take Carpenters Lane, after ½m turn L at T-junction, R at next Xrds; next turning L (Pillar Box Lane), R at next junction, oast house on L 100yds N of Artichoke Inn. Undulating garden of 4 acres, designed by owners; spring bulbs, terrace, water garden. **Hamptons Farm** open same day. TEA. *Adm £1 Acc chd free (Share to West Peckham Church). Sun April 18 (2-6)*

Elvey Farmhouse ₺⚔❀ (Mr & Mrs P J C Canney) Kingsland Lane, Westwell. 1½m W of Ashford, from A20, turn N into Sandyhurst Lane at Potters Corner by Hare & Hounds, turn W after ¼m opp Ashford Golf Course, turn 1st R, N after 200yds, garden ½m. Small informal garden surrounding C16 farmhouse (not open). Approx 1½ acres with lovely views. TEAS in aid of Westwell Church. *Adm £1.50 Acc chd free. Sun, Mon May 2, 3 (2.30-6)*

Emmetts Garden ₺ (The National Trust) Ide Hill, 5m SW of Sevenoaks. 1½m S of A25 on Sundridge-Ide Hill Rd. 1½m N of Ide Hill off B2042. 5-acre hillside garden. One of the highest gardens in Kent, noted for its fine collection of rare trees and shrubs; lovely spring and autumn colour. TEAS. *Adm £2.50 Chd £1.30. April to end Oct every Wed, Thur, Fri, Sat & Sun. Open Bank Hol Mons. For NGS Sats May 15, Oct 9 (1-6) last adm 5, or sunset if earlier*

Field Farm ⚔❀ (Mr & Mrs Simon Gault) Iden Green, halfway between Sandhurst and Benenden, 5m SE of Cranbrook, 5m NE of Hawkhurst. Turn N off A263 at Sandhurst, or S off B2086 at Benenden, both signed Iden Green; at Xrds follow sign to Scullsgate and Nineveh, entrance 200yds. Medium-sized young garden surrounding C16 farmhouse (not open), with lovely views across the High Weald. Terraces, walls, steps and sunken garden created by owners from sloping site. Informal planting with mixed borders and masses of old roses. *Adm £1 Chd 50p. Suns June 6, 13 (2-6); also by appt May & June* Tel 0580 240771

Field House ₺⚔❀ (Mr & Mrs N J Hori) Clapper Lane, Staplehurst. W of A229, 9m S of Maidstone and 1½m N of Staplehurst village centre. Garden approx 1½ acres on Wealden clay developed by owners over 30 yrs. Interesting mixed borders and island beds; water gardens; secret garden and one acre of wild life meadow with pond. TEAS. *Adm £1 Chd 50p. Suns July 11, Aug 8 (2-5.30)*

Flint Cottage ⚔❀ (Mr & Mrs P J Sinnock) Bourne Park, Bishopsbourne, 4m S of Canterbury turn off A2 to Bridge, through village turn W at church, follow garden signs. Small garden; alpines in gravel beds, sink gardens; water feature; mixed borders and small heather beds; herb garden. TEAS. *Adm £1 Chd 40p (Share to Foundation for the Study of Infant Death). Sun May 30, Mon May 31 (2-5.30)*

Forest Gate ₺⚔❀ (Sir Robert & Lady Johnson) Pluckley, 8m W of Ashford. From A20 at Charing take B2077 to Pluckley village; turn L signed Bethersden, follow 1m to garden 100yds S of Pluckley station. 2-acre garden on heavy clay; well stocked mixed borders, new laburnum tunnel, ponds and interesting herb collection. Many plants labelled. C17 house (not open). Picnics allowed in meadow. Close to **Walnut Tree Gardens.** TEAS. *Adm £1.10 Acc chd free (Share to Cystic Fibrosis Research Trust). Suns May 23, June 13 (2-6)*

Glassenbury Park ⚔❀ (Mr & Mrs C J de Jong) Between Goudhurst and Cranbrook. A21 from Tunbridge Wells direction Hastings. Past AA Station turn L A262 signed Goudhurst-Cranbrook. 1m after Goudhurst turn R B2085 at Peacock Inn. Entrance gate ½m on R. 50 acres rolling parkland. Newly planted daffodils and tulips. Specimen trees, rhododendrons, azaleas. Wide variety newly planted trees. Ponds and lakes. TEAS. *Adm £2 Chd 50p. Sats, Suns April 17, 18, May 15, 16 (11-4)*

Godinton Park (Alan Wyndham Green Esq) Entrance 1½m W of Ashford at Potter's Corner on A20. Bus: MD/EK 10, 10A, 10B Folkestone-Ashford-Maidstone, alight Hare & Hounds, Potter's Corner. Formal and wild gardens. Topiary. Jacobean mansion with elaborate woodwork. Unique frieze in drawing room depicting arms drill of Kent Halbardiers 1630. *Adm garden only 70p, house & garden £2, Chd under 16 70p.* ▲*Suns April 11, June 20 (2-5)*

¶**Godmersham Park** ㊉ (John B Sunley Esq) off A28 midway between Canterbury and Ashford; garden signed from either end of Park loop rd. Early Georgian mansion (not shown) in beautiful downland setting. 24 acres formal and landscape gardens, superb daffodils, restored wilderness; topiary; rose beds; herbaceous borders. Associations with Jane Austen. TEAS. *Adm £1.50 Chd 75p (Share to Relate). Sun April 18 (11-6)*

Goodnestone Park ㊉✿❀ (The Lady FitzWalter) nr Wingham, Canterbury. Village lies S of B2046 rd from A2 to Wingham. Sign off B2046 says Goodnestone. Village St is 'No Through Rd', but house and garden at the terminus. Bus: EK13, 14 Canterbury-Deal; bus stop: Wingham, 2m. 5 to 6 acres; good trees; woodland garden, walled garden with old-fashioned roses. Connections with Jane Austen who stayed here. Picnics allowed. TEAS Weds & Suns from May 23 to Aug 29. *Adm £2 OAP £1.60 Chd under 12 20p (Disabled people in wheelchair £1). Suns April 4 to Oct 3 (12-6); Mons, Weds to Fris March 29 to Oct 29 (11-5) For NGS Suns July 18, Aug 22 (12-6)*

Goudhurst Gardens 4m W of Cranbrook on A262. TEAS. *Combined adm £2 Acc chd free. Suns May 23, June 20 (2-6)*

¶**Crowbourne Farm House** (Mrs Stephanie Coleman) 2-acre farmhouse garden in which replanting started in 1989. Established cottage garden; shrub roses; vegetable garden; and areas newly planted with trees and shrubs. Former horse pond now stocked with ornamental fish.

Tara ㊉❀ (Mr & Mrs Peter Coombs) 1¼ acres redesigned in 1982 into a number of linked garden areas, including a formal herb garden, each providing a different atmosphere, using an interesting range of plants and shrubs

Tulip Tree Cottage ✿❀ (Mr & Mrs K A Owen) 1 acre with sweeping lawn, established trees in herbaceous and shrub borders; 80ft Liriodendron tulipifera, said to be one of finest in country, also fine Cedrus atlantica glauca. In May azalea garden of ½-acre, established 1902

Great Comp Charitable Trust ㊉✿❀ (R Cameron Esq) 2m E of Borough Green. A20 at Wrotham Heath, take Seven Mile Lane, B2016; at 1st Xrds turn R; garden on L ½m. Delightful 7-acre garden skilfully designed by the Camerons since 1957 for low maintenance and year round interest. Spacious setting of well-maintained lawns and paths lead visitors through a plantsman's collection of trees, shrubs, heathers and herbaceous plants. From woodland planting to more formal terraces good use is made of views to plants, ornaments and ruins. Good autumn colour. Early C17 house (not shown). TEAS on Suns, Bank Hols and NGS days (2-5) *Adm £2.50 Chd £1 Open every day April 1 to Oct 31 (11-6). Opening for NGS (Share to Tradescant Trust) Suns Mar 14, 21, 28 (for hellebores, heathers and snowflakes); Nov 7 (for autumn colour)*

Greencroft ✿❀ (Dr & Mrs A Marr) Nizels Lane, Hildenborough, 3½m S of Sevenoaks. Take A225, at Riverhill roundabout take B245, Nizels Lane 1st R. 2-acre plantsman's garden. Trees, shrubs, mixed borders, interesting planting to screen Tonbridge by-pass, water and woodland garden. TEA. *Adm £1.25 Acc chd free. Sun May 16 (2-6)*

Greenways ㊉✿❀ (Mr & Mrs S Lord) Single Street, Berry's Green, nr Downe. 1½m S of Downe village on W side of country rd (Single Street) between Downe and Biggin Hill. Gardener's garden; interesting design ideas; willows, jasmines, honeysuckles and alpines; large collection of bonsai; gardens combining fruit and vegetables, trees, shrubs and flowers; small pool, conservatory and pottery. *Adm £1 Chd 50p (Share to Save the Children Fund). By appt only, anytime, please phone Tel 0959 574691*

¶**Groombridge Place** ㊉✿ 4m SW of Tunbridge Wells on B2110: Groombridge Place is on L, past the church. Historic walled gardens, including 'drunken' topiary garden, oriental garden and wild English garden surrounding C17 moated house. TEAS and light refreshments. ▲*Adm £3 Chd under 17 £1.50. Open from April 11 to Oct 11 (11-6)* Tel 0892 863999. *For NGS Wed July 21 (11-6)*

Groome Farm ✿❀ (Mr & Mrs Michael Swatland) Egerton, 10m W of Ashford. From A20 at Charing Xrds take B2077 Biddenden Rd. Past Pluckley turn R at Blacksmiths Arms; R again, until Newland Green sign on L, house 1st on L. 1½ acres; still being developed around C15 farmhouse and oast (not open). Interesting collection trees, shrubs, roses and herbaceous plants; also water, heather and rock gardens. TEAS. *Adm £1 Acc chd free. Suns June 13, Aug 8 (2-6)*

115 Hadlow Road ✿ (Mr & Mrs Richard Esdale) in Tonbridge. Take A26 from N end of High St signed Maidstone, house 1m on L in service rd. ¼-acre unusual terraced garden with roses, herbaceous borders, clematis, hardy fuchsias, shrubs, alpines, kitchen garden and pond; well labelled. TEA. *Adm £1 Acc chd free. Suns June 27, Aug 29 (2-6); also by appt Tel 0732 353738*

Hamptons Farm House ㊉✿ (Mr & Mrs Brian Pearce) Plaxtol. Between Plaxtol, Hadlow, Shipbourne & West Peckham. In a hamlet opp Artichoke Inn; signed from nearby villages. Garden of 3 acres; stream and pond; trees, shrubs, old barn; fine views. **Egypt Farm** open same day. *Adm £1 Acc chd free. Sun April 18 (2-6)*

Hartlip Gardens 6m W of Sittingbourne, 1m S of A2 midway between Rainham and Newington. Parking for Craiglea in village hall car park and The Street. TEAS at Hartlip Place. *Combined adm £2 Acc chd free. Sun June 20 (2-6)*

Craiglea ✿ (Mrs Ruth Bellord) The Street. Small cottage garden crammed with interesting shrubs and plants; vegetable garden; tiny pond

Hartlip Place ✿ (Lt-Col & Mrs J R Yerburgh) Secret garden concealed by rhododendrons, planted with old-fashioned roses; shrub borders; wilderness walk; sloping lawns; pond

● **Hever Castle** ⬤⬤ (Broadland Properties Ltd) 3m SE of Edenbridge, between Sevenoaks and East Grinstead. Signed from junctions 5 and 6 of M25, from A21 and from A264. Formal Italian gardens with statuary, sculpture and fountains; large lake; rose garden and Tudor style gardens with topiary and maze. Romantic moated castle, the childhood home of Anne Boleyn, also open. No dogs in castle, on lead only in gardens. Refreshments available. *Open every day from March 16 to Nov 7 (11-6 last adm 5.15 Castle opens 12 noon) Adm Castle and gardens £5 OAPs £4.50 Chd £2.50 Family (2 adults 2 chds) £12.50; Gdns only £3.60 OAPs £3 Chd £2.10 Family £9.30*

Hole Park ⬤⬤ (D G W Barham Esq) Rolvenden-Cranbrook on B2086. Beautiful parkland; formal garden with mixed borders, roses, yew hedges and topiary a feature, many fine trees. Natural garden with rhododendrons, azaleas, daffodils, conifers, dell and water gardens; bluebell wood. Autumn colour. *Adm £2 Chd under 12 50p (Share to Friends of Kent Churches and Rolvenden Church Council). Suns March 28, April 4, 25, May 2, 16, 23, Oct 10, 17; Weds April 14, June 2 (2-6)*

Horton Priory ⬤ (Mrs A C Gore) Sellindge, 6m SE of Ashford. From A20 Ashford-Folkestone, 1m from Sellindge, turn E along Moorstock Lane, signed Horton Priory. Bus: EK/MD 10, 10A, 10B Maidstone-Ashford-Folkestone; alight Sellindge, 1m. Herbaceous and rose border, lawn, pond and rock garden. Priory dates back to C12; church destroyed in reign of Henry VIII, but remains of W doorway and staircase to S aisle of nave can be seen by front door. Along W front Norman buttresses (all genuine) and C14 windows (some restored); one genuine small Norman window. Outer hall only open to visitors. Parking for cars in front of house, along drive and garage areas. *Adm £1 Chd 50p. Suns June 13, Sept 12 (2-6)*

Jessups ⬤ (The Hon Robin Denison-Pender) Mark Beech. 3m S of Edenbridge. From B2026 Edenbridge-Hartfield road turn L opp Queens Arms signed Mark Beech, 100yds on L. Small established garden, spring bulbs and shrubs, fine views to Sevenoaks Weald. Small wood. Wildfowl pond (25 different breeds). Car park in adjacent field. TEAS. *Adm £1 Chd 50p. Sun April 11 (2-5)*

Knole ⬤⬤ (The Lord Sackville; The National Trust) Sevenoaks. **This year will be celebrating 60 years of opening for the NGS.** Station: Sevenoaks. Pleasance, deer park, landscape garden, herb garden. TEAS. *Adm Car park £2.50: garden 50p Chd 30p; house £4 Chd £2.* ▲*Weds June 2, Aug 4 (11-5 last adm 4)*

Kypp Cottage ⬤⬤ (Mrs Zena Grant) Woolpack Corner, Biddenden. At Tenterden Rd A262 junction with Benenden Rd. Cottage garden (planted and maintained by owner) started about 1964 from rough ground; extensive collection of interesting plants; enjoy perfumed, shady nooks provided by over 200 climbing and shrub roses, intertwined with clematis; variety of geraniums and other ground cover plants. Good examples of trees suitable for small gardens. Morning coffee & home-made TEAS. *Adm £1 Chd 30p (Share to NSPCC). Suns, Mons, Tues, Weds May 23, 24, 25, 26, 30, 31; June 1, 2, 6, 7, 8, 9, 13, 14, 15, 16, 20, 21, 22, 23, 27, 28, 29, 30; July 4, 5, 6, 7, 11, 12, 13, 14 (Suns 2-6), weekdays 10.30-6); also by appt all summer* Tel 0580 291480

Ladham House ⬤⬤ (Betty, Lady Jessel) Goudhurst. On NE of village, off A262. 10 acres with rolling lawns, fine specimen trees, rhododendrons, camellias, azaleas, shrubs and magnolias. Newly planted arboretum. Spectacular twin mixed borders; fountain and bog gardens. Fine view. Car park free. TEAS. *Adm £2 Chd under 12 50p. Suns April 11, May 2, 30, July 11 (11-6); open other times by appt & for coaches*

Larksfield ⬤⬤ (Mr & Mrs P Dickinson) Crockham Hill, 3m N of Edenbridge, on B269 (Limpsfield-Oxted). Octavia Hill, a founder of the NT, lived here and helped create the original garden; fine collection of azaleas, shrubs, herbaceous plants, rose beds and woodlands; views over Weald and Ashdown Forest. **The Red House** and **Larksfield Cottage** gardens open same days. TEAS at The Red House. *Combined adm £2 OAPs £1.50 Chd 50p. Suns May 16, 23 (2-6)*

Larksfield Cottage ⬤⬤ (Mrs M J Johnston) Crockham Hill, 3m N of Edenbridge, on B269. An enchanting garden redesigned in 1981 with attractive lawns and shrubs. Views over the Weald and Ashdown Forest. **Larksfield** and **The Red House** gardens also open same days. *Combined adm £2 OAPs £1.50 Chd 50p. Suns May 16, 23 (2-6)*

43 Layhams Road ⬤⬤ (Mrs Dolly Robertson) West Wickham. Semi-detached house recognisable by small sunken flower garden in the front. Opp Wickham Court Farm. A raised vegetable garden, purpose-built for the disabled owner with easy access to wide terraced walkways. The owner, who maintains the entire 24ft × 70ft area herself, would be pleased to pass on her experiences as a disabled gardener so that others may share her joy and interest. *Collecting box. By appt only all year* Tel 081-462 4196

Little Crampton Farm ⬤⬤ (Mr & Mrs David Spry) High Halden. 3m NW of Tenterden on A262 towards Biddenden, after 500yds turn R at Man of Kent inn, after 1m turn L at fork signed Biddenden, entrance on R. 2½ acres of garden created by owners since 1977 from fields and farmyard; shrub roses; large shrubbery and herbaceous borders; large pond; kitchen garden. TEAS. *Adm £1 Chd 50p (Share to Gardening for the Disabled Trust). Sun June 20; Tues June 22 (2-5)*

Little Trafalgar ⬤⬤⬤ (Mr & Mrs R J Dunnett) Selling, 4m SE of Faversham. From A2 (M2) or A251 make for Selling Church, then follow signs to garden. ¾-acre garden of great interest both for its wealth of attractive and unusual plants, and its intimate, restful design. Emphasis is placed on the creative and artistic use of plants. TEAS. *Adm £1 Acc chd free. Suns May 30, June 13, 27, July 11, 25, Aug 8, 29, Sept 12, 26; Mons May 31, Aug 30 (2-6); also by appt* Tel 0227 752219

Long Barn ⬤ (Brandon & Sarah Gough) Weald, 3m S of Sevenoaks. Signed to Weald at junction of A21 & B245. Garden at W end of village. 1st garden of Harold Nicolson and Vita Sackville-West. 3 acres with terraces and slopes, giving considerable variety. Dutch garden designed by Lutyens, features mixed planting in raised beds. Teas in village. *Adm £1.50 OAPs £1 Chd 30p under 5 free (Share to Hospice at Home). Suns May 16, June 20, July 18 (2-6)*

Longacre &*❀ (Dr & Mrs G Thomas) Perry Wood, Selling, 5m SE of Faversham. From A2 (M2) or A251 follow signs for Selling, passing White Lion on L, 2nd R and immediately L, continue for ¼m. From A252 at Chilham, take turning signed Selling at Badgers Hill Fruit Farm. L at 2nd Xrds, next R, L and then R. Small plantsman's garden with wide variety of interesting plants, created and maintained entirely by owners. Most trees and shrubs planted in 1964; recently added herbaceous plants also alpines in gravel beds. Lovely walks in Perry Woods adjacent to garden. TEAS in aid of local charities. *Adm £1 Acc chd free (Share to Canterbury Pilgrims Hospice). Suns April 11, 25, May 2, 16, 30, June 13, 27, July 11, 25, Aug 29, Sept 12; Mons April 12, May 3, 31, Aug 30 (2-5); also by appt* Tel 0227 752254

Lullingstone Castle &*❀ (Mr & Mrs Guy Hart Dyke) In the Darenth Valley via Eynsford on A225. Eynsford Station ½m. All cars and coaches via Roman Villa. Lawns, woodland and lake, mixed border, small herb garden. Henry VII gateway; Church on the lawn open. TEAS. *Adm garden £1.50 OAPs/Chd £1; house 50p extra. Sun June 20 (2-6)*

Luton House *❀ (Sir John & Lady Swire) Selling, 4m SE of Faversham. From A2 (M2) or A251 make for White Lion, entrance 30yds E on same side of rd. 4 acres; C19 landscaped garden; ornamental ponds; trees underplanted with azaleas, camellias, woodland plants. *Adm £1 Chd 50p. Suns May 2, July 4 (2-6)*

The Manor House (Mr & Mrs John Shipton) Upper Hardres, 7m S of Canterbury. Take B2068, turn L at Street End (Granville public house), after 2m Upper Hardres Church on R, S-bend in rd, ½m on are white gates with yellow house set back. From A2 at Bridge turn W to Petts Bottom, past Duck Inn, 1m on turn R at stables, house on L at top of steep hill behind white gates. 8 acres of fine old trees; walled garden; rose, laburnum and wisteria walks; woodland bulb walk in spring; vegetables and small orchard. TEAS on June 20. *Adm £1.50 Chd 50p. Suns April 25 (2-5.30), June 20 (2-6.30)*

Marle Place &*❀ (Mr & Mrs Gerald Williams) Brenchley, 8m SE of Tonbridge. On B2162, 1m S of Horsmonden and 1½m NW of Lamberhurst. Turn W on Marle Place Rd. Victorian gazebo; plantsman's shrub borders; walled scented garden, large herb rockery and herb nursery. Woodland walk; collection of bantams. C17 listed House (not open). TEAS. *Adm £2 OAP/Chd £1.50. Every day April 1 to Oct 31 (10-5.30). For NGS Suns May 23, June 27, Aug 15, Oct 10 (10-6)*

Maurice House & (The Royal British Legion Residential Home) Callis Court Rd, Broadstairs. From Broadstairs Broadway take St Peter's Park Rd; turn R under railway arch into Baird's Hill; join Callis Court Rd entrance on R, 100yds beyond Lanthorne Rd turning. Well-maintained 8-acre garden; lawns, flowering trees, shrubs; formal flower beds; rose and water gardens; orchard. Spring bedding displays of wallflowers, tulips, polyanthus; wide variety of herbaceous plants and shrubs especially suited to coastal conditions. TEA. *Adm £1 Chd 25p (Share to the Royal British Legion). Sun May 2 (2-5.30)*

¶**Meadow Wood** &❀ (Mr & Mrs James Lee) Penshurst. 1¼m SE of Penshurst on B2176 in direction of Bidborough. 1920s garden, on edge of wood with long southerly views over the Weald, and with interesting trees and shrubs; azaleas, rhododendrons and naturalised bulbs in woods with mown walks. TEAS. *Adm £1.50 Chd £1 (Share to Relate). Sun May 9 (2-6)*

Mere House &*❀ (Mr & Mrs Andrew Wells) Mereworth, midway between Tonbridge & Maidstone. From A26 turn N on to B2016 and then into Mereworth village. 6-acre garden with C18 lake; ornamental shrubs and trees with foliage contrast; lawns, daffodils; Kentish cobnut plat. TEAS. *Adm £1 Chd 25p. Suns April 11, July 11 (2.30-6)*

Mill House &❀ (Dr & Mrs Brian Glaisher) Mill Lane, ½m N of Hildenborough, 5m S of Sevenoaks. From B245 turn into Mill Lane at Mill garage. 3-acre garden laid out in 1906; herbaceous and mixed borders; new secluded herb garden; old shrub roses and climbers; clematis and many fine trees. Formal garden with topiary; ruins of windmill and conservatory with exotics. TEAS. *Adm £1 Chd 25p. Sun June 13 (2-6)*

Mount Ephraim (Mrs M N Dawes and Mr & Mrs E S Dawes) Hernhill, Faversham. From M2 and A299 take Hernhill turning at Duke of Kent. Herbaceous border; topiary; daffodils and rhododendrons; rose terraces leading to a small lake; Japanese rock garden with pools; water garden; small vineyard. TEAS daily; lunches only Bank Hol Suns & Mons. *Adm £1.75 Chd 25p. Open April to Sept (2-6). For NGS Suns April 25, Sept 26 (2-6)*

Nettlestead Place &*❀ (Mr & Mrs Roy Tucker) Nettlestead, 6m W/SW of Maidstone. Turn S off A26 onto B2015 then 1m on L (next to Nettlestead Church). C13 manor house set in 7-acre garden; garden on different levels, defined by ragstone walls and yew hedges with fine views of open countryside; garden in course of further development, including pond garden, new terraces and plant collections. TEAS in June only. *Adm £1.50 Acc chd free (Share to St Mary's Church, Nettlestead). Suns June 20, Sept 5 (2-6)*

New Barns House &*❀ (Mr & Mrs P H Byam-Cook) West Malling. Leave M20 at Exit 4 to West Malling. In High Street turn E down Waters Lane. At T-junction turn R, take bridge over by-pass, follow lane 400yds to New Barns House. 1-acre garden with fine trees and flowering cherries. Walled garden, mixed borders and shrubs. TEAS. *Adm £1 Acc chd free. Sun April 25 (2-6)*

Northbourne Court *❀ (The Hon Charles James) W of Deal. Signs in village. Great brick terraces, belonging to an earlier Elizabethan mansion, provide a picturesque setting for a wide range of shrubs and plants on chalk soil; geraniums, fuchsias and grey-leaved plants. *Adm £2.50 OAPs/Chd £1.50 Suns May 2, 30, June 13, 27, July 11, 25, Aug 15, 29, Sept 12, 26 (2-6)*

By Appointment Gardens. Avoid the crowds. Good chance of a tour by owner. See garden description for telephone number.

Olantigh &% (J R H Loudon Esq) Wye, 6m NE of Ashford. Turn off A28 either to Wye or at Godmersham; ¾m from Wye on rd to Godmersham. Beautiful setting; water garden, rockery, shrubbery. Bring picnic. *Adm £1.25 Chd 30p. Suns May 30, July 4 (2-5)*

The Old Parsonage &%❀ (Dr & Mrs Richard Perks) Sutton Valence, 6m SE of Maidstone. A274 from Maidstone or Headcorn, turn E into village at King's Head Inn and proceed on upper rd through village; climb Tumblers Hill and entrance at top on R. 4-acre labour-saving garden planted since 1959 with emphasis on ground cover; trees, shrubs and mixed borders; cranesbills and shrub roses. Ancient nut plat now developed as a wild garden. Fine views over Low Weald. In grounds is Sutton castle, C12 ruined keep, permanently open to the public. *Adm £1 Chd 50p. Sun June 20, Tue 22, Thur 24, Sat 26 (2-6)*

Old Place Farm &% (Mr & Mrs Jeffrey Eker) High Halden, 3m NE of Tenterden. From A28 take Woodchurch Rd (opp Chequers public house) in High Halden, and follow for ½m. 3½-acre garden surrounding period farmhouse & buildings with paved herb garden & parterres, small lake, ponds, lawns, mixed borders, cutting garden, old shrub roses, lilies & foliage plants; all created since 1969 & still developing. Featured in *Country Life,* & *House & Garden* in 1990. TEAS in aid of St Mary's Church, High Halden. *Adm £1.50 Chd 50p. Sun June 20 (2-6)*

Old Tong Farm %❀ (Mr & Mrs Simon Toynbee) Brenchley. 8m SE of Tonbridge, 1¼m S of Brenchley. From Brenchley follow road to Horsmonden, take first turning R into Fairman's Rd, becoming Tong Rd. Medium-sized garden still being created around C15 house (not open); rose garden; pond; terrace; herb parterre; nut plat; wild woodland walk. Adj cottage with newly planted garden. TEAS. *Adm £1 Acc chd free. Sun June 13, Wed June 16 (2-6)*

Oswalds &%❀ (Mr & Mrs J C Davidson) Bishopsbourne, 4m S of Canterbury. Turn off A2 at B2065, follow signs to Bishopsbourne, house next to church. 3-acre plantsman's garden created since 1972 by present owners. Year-round interest includes bulbs; spring garden; mixed borders; rockeries; pools; bog garden; potager; pergola; old roses; and many fruit varieties. NCCPG National Collections of *Photinia* and *Zantedeschia.* House (not open) has interesting literary connections. Teas at village hall nearby. *Adm £1.50 Chd 50p (Share to Kent Gardens Trust). Suns April 11, Sept 26; Mon April 12 (2-5.30); also by appt Tel 0227 830340*

Oxon Hoath &% (Mr & Mrs Henry Bayne-Powell) nr Hadlow, 5m NE of Tonbridge. *Car essential.* Via A20, turn off S at Wrotham Heath onto Seven Mile Lane (B2016); at Mereworth Xrds turn W, through West Peckham. Or via A26, in Hadlow turn off N along Carpenters Lane. 10 acres, landscaped with fine trees, rhododendrons and azaleas; woodland walk; replanted cedar avenue; formal parterre rose garden by Nesfield; peacocks. Large Kentish ragstone house (not shown) principally Georgian but dating back to C14; Victorian additions by Salvin. Once owned by Culpeppers, grandparents of Catherine Howard. View over C18 lake to Hadlow Folly. TEAS in picnic area if fine. *Adm £1.50 Chd 50p. Sun May 30 (2-7)*

The Pear House %❀ (Mr & Mrs Nicholas Snowden) Sellindge, 6m E of Ashford. Turn L off A20 at Sellindge Church towards Brabourne into Stone Hill. ⅔ acre developed by present owners; still evolving. Contains smaller gardens with informal planting; bulbs, roses (mostly old-fashioned), shrubs, small orchard with climbing roses, pond garden, shady areas. *Adm £1 Chd 40p. By appt only May 1 to July 11 Tel 0303 812147*

Peddars Wood &%❀ (Mr & Mrs B J Honeysett) 14 Orchard Rd, St Michaels, Tenterden. From A28, 1m N of Tenterden, turn W into Grange Rd at Crown Hotel, take 2nd R into Orchard Rd. Small plantsman's garden created by present owner since 1984. One of the best collections of rare and interesting plants in the area, incl over 100 clematis, 50 climbing roses and lilies. TEAS. *Adm £1 Chd 20p (Share to Baptist Minister's Help Society). Sats May 8, June 5, 26, Aug 7; Wed July 14 (2-6); also by appt Tel 05806 3994*

Penshurst Place % (Viscount De L'Isle), S of Tonbridge on B2176, N of Tunbridge Wells on A26. 10 acres of garden dating back to C14; garden divided into series of 'rooms' by over a mile of clipped yew hedge; profusion of spring bulbs: herbaceous borders; formal rose garden; famous peony border. All year interest. TEAS and light refreshments. *Adm House & Gardens £4.50 OAPs £3.75 Chd £2.50: Gardens £3 OAPs £2.50 Chd £2.00. Open daily March 27 to Oct 3. For NGS Tues April 6; Mon June 14 (11-6)*

¶Petham House %❀ (Mr & Mrs Nicholas Graham) Petham, 6m S of Canterbury. From B2068 turn R, signposted Petham village at Chequers public house, down steep hill past church to T-junction in centre of Petham, turn L; continue up slight incline & fork L into Duck Pit, a minor rd, entrance on R. Garden mainly lawns with recently planted trees and shrubs for foliage effect; woodland strip; walled garden undergoing extensive restoration; vine house. House (not open) in Italianate style c. 1848 by Robert Palmer Browne. *Adm £1.50 Chd 50p. Wed May 12; Sat June 19 (1.30-6)*

Pett Place %❀ (Mrs I Mills, Mr C I Richmond-Watson & Mr A Rolla) Charing, 6m NW of Ashford. From A20 turn N into Charing High St. At end turn R into Pett Lane towards Westwell. Four walled gardens covering nearly 4 acres. Within formal framework of old walls, much planting has been carried out since 1981 to make a garden of different, pleasing vistas and secret places. A ruined C13 chapel is a romantic feature beside the manor house (not open), which was re-fronted about 1700 and which Pevsner describes as 'presenting grandiloquently towards the road.' TEAS. *Adm £1 Chd 50p (Share to Kent Gardens Trust). Suns April 25, June 20, Sats April 24, June 19 (2.30-5)*

Pevington Farm &❀ (Mr & Mrs David Mure) Pluckley, 3m SW of Charing. From Charing take B2077 towards Pluckley, before Pluckley turn R towards Egerton. Pevington Farm ½m on. From SW go through Pluckley, turn L for Egerton. ¾-acre garden with wonderful views over the Weald. Mixed borders with many interesting plants. TEAS in aid of St Nicholas Church, Pluckley, and Ashford

Independent Youth Club for the Handicapped. *Adm £1 Chd 50p. Suns May 16, June 13 (2-5.30); also by appt* Tel 0233 840317

The Pines Garden & The Bay Museum ৬৯ (The St Margaret's Bay Trust) Beach Rd, St Margaret's Bay, 4½m NE of Dover. Beautiful 6-acre seaside garden. Water garden. Statue of Sir Winston Churchill complemented by the Bay Museum opposite. Fascinating maritime and local interest. TEAS. *Adm £1 Chd 50p. Gardens open daily except Christmas Day. Museum open May to end Aug (closed Mon and Fri). For NGS Suns April 11, May 30, Aug 29 (10-6)*

Placketts Hole ৬৯৯ (Mr & Mrs D P Wainman) Bicknor 5m S of Sittingbourne, and W of B2163. Owners have designed and planted 2-acre informal garden, incl building walls around charming old house (C16 with Georgian additions); interesting mix of shrubs, large borders, formal rose garden, lots of herbs and sweet-smelling plants. TEAS. *Adm £1.50 Acc chd free (Share to Bicknor Church). Sun June 27 (2-6.30)*

Plaxtol Gardens 5m N of Tonbridge, 6m E of Sevenoaks, turn E off A227 to Plaxtol village. TEAS. Tickets and maps available at all gardens. *Combined adm £2.50 Acc chd free (Share to Friends of Plaxtol Church). Sun June 27 (2-6)*
 Malling Well House (Mr & Mrs Cedric Harris) The Street, Plaxtol; next to Papermakers Arms. An open garden of about 1¼ acres, created over last 15yrs by present owners; herbaceous border, pond, marsh garden and large vegetable plot
 ¶Pippins ৬৯ (Mr & Mrs Ken Blagrove) The Street. About ½ acre of open garden, with contrasting shrubs and trees. Garden created and maintained by the present owners
 ¶Schoolfield (Mr & Mrs Colin Creed) Turn L at the church, entrance 300 yds on L. 2½-acre garden created in the last 7 years, with ponds, a variety of borders and vegetable garden. Lovely views
 Spoute Cottage ৬৯ (Mr & Mrs Donald Forbes) situated at the bottom of Plaxtol St on L side opp Hyders Wrought Iron Works. ¾ acre of mixed borders of contrasting flowering and foliage plants, especially for flower arranging; small pond & stream. Japanese garden under construction. Plant nursery attached
 Stonewold House (Mr & Mrs John Young) The Street, Plaxtol. 5-acre small-holding with flower and vegetable garden; variety of animals: ponies, donkey, goat, chicken and geese; lovely views

Portobello (Barry M Williams Esq) Brenchley, 6m SE of Tonbridge. From A21, 1m S of Pembury turn onto B2160, turn R at Xrds in Matfield sign-posted Brenchley. For garden description see under **Brenchley Gardens** May 23, when this garden is open again. *Adm £1 Acc chd free. Sun June 6 (2-6)*

Regular Openers. Too many days to include in diary. Usually there is a wide range of plants giving year-round interest. See head of county section for the name and garden description for times etc.

¶29 The Precincts ৯৯ (The Archdeacon of Canterbury & Mrs T Till) Canterbury. Enter Cathedral Precincts by main (Christ Church) gate, follow path round W end of Cathedral into cloister, entry through gate N side of cloister. **No access for cars; please use public car parks**. ¾-acre of medieval walled garden with perpetual presence of the Cathedral soaring above. Enter Cellarer's Hall beneath earliest known carving of Thomas Becket, past a noble descendant of the mulberry tree in whose shade (allegedly) Becket's murderers washed their hands. TEAS. *Adm £1 Chd 50p Suns May 30, June 6; Wed June 2; Sat June 5 (2-6)*

¶Quex Gardens ৬৯৯ (The Powell-Cotton Museum Trust), Birchington, 10m E of Canterbury on A28. Entrance from Park Lane. Or take A253 Ramsgate rd and turn N for Acol. 17 acres of woodland and informal gardens with fine specimen trees, naturalised spring bulbs; old wisteria walk, shrub borders, old figs and mulberries and long herbaceous border. Garden incl Victorian walled kitchen garden being extensively restored. TEAS in aid of Quex Gardens Restoration Fund. ▲*Adm £1 Chd 50p. For NGS (Share to Quex Gardens Restoration Fund) Sats July 3, Oct 2 (2.15-6)*

Ramhurst Manor ৬ (The Lady Rosie Kindersley) Powder Mill Lane, Leigh, Tonbridge. Historic property once belonged to the Black Prince and Culpepper family. Formal gardens; roses, azaleas, rhododendrons, wild flowers. *Adm £1 Acc chd free. Sun May 23 (2.30-6)*

The Rectory ৬৯৯ (Revd & Mrs David Clark) Fairseat, ½m off A227 (at Vigo public house) 1½m N of Wrotham. Small, colourful, plantsman's garden; many foliage and ground-cover plants; salvias, campanulas, lilies. 14 island and hedge-backed beds, incl small colourful rockery. TEAS in aid of Maidstone Hospice. *Adm £1.50 Chd 50p. Sun July 18, Wed July 21 (2-5.30)*

The Red House ৬৯৯ (K C L Webb Esq) Crockham Hill, 3m N of Edenbridge. On Limpsfield-Oxted Rd, B269. Formal features of this large garden are kept to a minimum; rose walk leads on to 3 acres of rolling lawns flanked by fine trees and shrubs incl rhododendrons, azaleas and magnolias. Views over the Weald and Ashdown Forest. TEAS. **Larksfield** and **Larksfield Cottage** gardens also open same days. *Combined adm £2 OAPs £1.50 Chd 50p (Share to The Schizophrenia Association of Great Britain). Suns May 16, 23 (2-6)*

Ringfield ৬ (Prof Sir David Smithers) Knockholt. Via A21 London-Sevenoaks; from London turn at Pratts Bottom roundabout, also reached from Orpington-Bromley turn off from M25 or from Sevenoaks at Dunton Green (Rose & Crown). Rhododendrons, over 4,000 rose trees, incl recent varieties, and wide vistas. TEAS. *Adm £1 Chd 50p. Suns June 6, July 11 (2-6)*

Riverhill House ৯৯ (The Rogers family) 2m S of Sevenoaks on A225. Mature hillside garden with extensive views; specimen trees, sheltered terraces with roses and choice shrubs; bluebell wood with rhododendrons and azaleas; picnics allowed. TEAS. *Adm £1.50 Chd 50p. Every Sunday from April 1 to June 30 and Bank Hol Weekends in this period (12-6). For NGS Sats May 1, 29 (12-6)*

Rock Farm ৬✿❀ (Mrs P A Corfe) Nettlestead. 6m W of Maidstone. Turn S off A26 onto B2015 then 1m S of Wateringbury turn R. 1½-acre garden, skilfully set out around old farm buildings; planted since 1968 and maintained by owner; plantsman's collection of shrubs, herbaceous plants, ornamental pond. Plant nursery adjoining garden. Tea Nettlestead village. *Adm £1.50 Chd 50p (Share to St Mary's Church, Nettlestead). Weds May 12, 19, 26, June 2, 9, 16, 23, 30, July 7, 14, 21, 28, Aug 4; Sats May 8, 15, 22, 29, June 5, 12, 19, 26, July 3, 10, 17, 24, 31, Aug 7 (11-5)*

Rosefarm ৬✿❀ (Dr D J Polton) 1m NW of Chilham. 6m equidistant Canterbury and Faversham. ¼m along narrow lane. Signed 'Denne Manor' at Shottenden Xrds. Half-acre garden with interesting and unusual plants. *Adm £1 Acc chd free. Fris June 11, 18; Sats June 12, 19 (2-6)*

St Clere ৬✿ (Mr & Mrs Ronnie Norman) Kemsing, 6m NE of Sevenoaks. Take A25 from Sevenoaks toward Ightham; 1m past Seal turn L signed Heaverham and Kemsing; in Heaverham take rd to R signed Wrotham and West Kingsdown; in 75yds straight ahead marked Private rd; 1st L and follow rd to house. 4-acre garden with herbaceous borders, shrubs, rare trees. C17 mansion (not open). TEAS. *Adm £1.50 Chd 50p. Sun June 20 (2-6)*

St Michael's House ৬❀ (Brig & Mrs W Magan) Roydon, Peckham Bush. 5m NE Tonbridge, 5m SW Maidstone. On A26 at Mereworth roundabout take S exit (B2016) signposted Paddock Wood, after 1m turn L at top of rise (signed Roydon). Gardens ¼m up hill on L. Old vicarage garden of ¾ acre round house & enclosed by shaped yew hedge; roses, climbing roses, iris border, rock roses, herbaceous; courtyard and 6-acre meadow with extensive views. Original oil paintings and watercolours for sale. TEAS. *Adm £1.50 Chd 50p. Sun May 30, June 20 (2-6)*

● **Saltwood Castle** ৬ (The Rt Hon Alan Clark) 2m NW of Hythe, 4m W of Folkestone; from A20 turn S at sign to Saltwood. Medieval castle, subject of quarrel between Thomas a Becket and Henry II. C13 crypt and dungeons; armoury; battlement walks and watch towers. Lovely views; spacious lawns and borders; courtyard walls covered with roses. Picnics allowed. Saltwood Castle closed to the general public in 1993. *Private parties of 20 or more by appt weekdays only* Tel 0303 267190

Scotney Castle ৬✿ (Mrs Christopher Hussey; The National Trust) On A21 London-Hastings, 1¼m S of Lamberhurst. Bus: (Mon to Sat) M & D 246 & 256, Tunbridge Wells-Hawkhurst; alight Spray Hill. Famous picturesque landscape garden, created by the Hussey family in the 1840s surrounding moated C14 Castle. House (not open) by Salvin, 1837. Old Castle open May – end Aug (same times as garden). Gift Shop. Picnic area in car park. Tea Goudhurst. *Adm £3.20 Chd £1.60; Pre-booked parties of 15 or more (Wed-Fri) £2 Chd £1; April – Nov 7, daily except Mons & Tues, but open Bank Hol Mons (closed Good Fri). Wed-Fri 11-6, Sats & Suns 2-6 or sunset if earlier; Bank Hol Mons & Suns preceeding 12-6. For NGS (Share to Trinity Hospice, Clapham Common) Bank Hol Mon May 31 (12-6)*

Sea Close ✿❀ (Maj & Mrs R H Blizard) Cannongate Rd, Hythe. A259 Hythe-Folkestone; ½m from Hythe, signed. A plantsman's garden; 1¼ acres on steep slope overlooking the sea; designed, laid out & maintained by present owners since 1966. Approx 1000 named plants & shrubs, planted for visual effect in many varied style beds of individual character. Light refreshments. *Adm £1 Acc chd free (Share to Royal Signals Benevolent Fund). Suns May 30, July 18, Aug 29 (2-5.30), Oct 3 (2-4.30)*

The Silver Spray ৬✿❀ (Mr & Mrs C T Orsbourne) Sellindge. 7m SE of Ashford on A20 opposite school. 1-acre garden developed and planted since 1983 and maintained by owners. Attractively laid out gardens and wild area combine a keen interest in conservation (especially butterflies) with a love of unusual hardy and tender plants. TEAS. *Adm £1 Acc chd free (Share to St Mary's Church, Sellindge). Weds June 23, July 7, 21, Aug 25; Sats July 10, 24; Mon Aug 30 (2-5)*

Sissinghurst Garden ৬✿❀ (Nigel Nicolson Esq; The National Trust) Cranbrook. Station: Staplehurst. Bus: MD5 from Maidstone 14m; 297 Tunbridge Wells (not Suns) 15m. Garden created by the late V. Sackville-West and Sir Harold Nicolson. Spring garden, herb garden. Tudor building and tower, partly open to public. Moat. **Because of the limited capacity of the garden, visitors may often have to wait before entry. The Property is liable to be closed at short notice once it has reached its visitor capacity for the day.** Lunches and TEAS. *Adm £5 Chd £2.50 (Share to Charleston Farmhouse Trust). Garden open April 1 to Oct 15. (Closed Mons incl Bank Hols). Tues to Fri 1-6.30 (last adm 6pm); Sats and Suns 10-5.30 (last adm 5pm). For NGS Weds April 28, June 9, July 7 (1-6.30)*

Sissinghurst Place Gardens ৬✿❀ Sissinghurst, 2m N of Cranbrook, E of village on A262. TEAS. *Combined adm £1.25 Chd 25p. Sat, Sun June 5, 6 (12-6)*
   Sissinghurst Place (Mr & Mrs Simon MacLachlan) Large garden of herbaceous beds, lawns, rhododendrons, fine trees, shrubs and roses; herbs and climbers in ruin of original house, wild garden and pond
   The Coach House (Mr & Mrs Michael Sykes) House and garden adjacent and originally part of Sissinghurst Place. In 1983, the owners designed and planted a new garden within established yew hedges. Many unusual trees, shrubs and plants

South Hill Farm ৬✿ (Sir Charles Jessel Bt) Hastingleigh, E of Ashford. Turn off A28 to Wye, go through village and ascend Wye Downs, in 2m turn R at Xrds marked Brabourne and South Hill, then first L. Or from Stone Street (B2068) turn W opp Stelling Minnis, follow signs to Hastingleigh, continue towards Wye and turn L at Xrds marked Brabourne and South Hill, then first L. 2 acres high up on North Downs, C18 house (not open); old walls; ha-ha; formal water garden; old and new roses; unusual shrubs, perennials and foliage plants. TEAS. *Adm £1 Chd 25p. Sun July 4 (2-6)*

Southfarthing ✿❀ (Mr & Mrs Ivan Smith) Hawkenbury, Staplehurst, 2m W of Headcorn. From A229 Staplehurst Xrd turn E, 2m, or from A274 1m S of Sutton Valence turn W signed Hawkenbury-Staplehurst, 1m. Very small formal garden, remade spring 1987. Mainly alpines and small bulbs on rockery; peat bed; raised beds and sinks. Tiny orchard of old apple varieties; organic, no dig vegetable patch. *Adm £1 Acc chd free. Suns April 11, May 2; Mons April 12, May 3 (2-5.30); also by appt March to June* Tel 0580 892140

¶**Spilsill Court** &・& (Mr & Mrs C G Marshall) Frittenden Road, Staplehurst. Proceed to Staplehurst on A229 (Maidstone/Hastings). From S enter village, turn R immediately after Elf garage on R & just before 30mph sign, into Frittenden Rd; garden ½m on, on L. From N go through village to 40mph sign, immediately turn L into Frittenden Rd. Approx 4 acres of garden, orchard and paddock; series of gardens including those in blue, white and silver; roses; lawns; shrubs, trees and ponds. Small private chapel. Jacob sheep & unusual poultry. TEA. *Adm £1.50 Chd under 16 50p (Share to Gardening for the Disabled Trust). Suns April 4, July 25 (11-5)*

Squerryes Court & (Mr & Mrs John Warde) ½m W of Westerham signed from A25 Edenbridge Rd. 15 acres incl lake & woodland; well documented historic garden laid out in 1689; owners restoring the formal garden in William & Mary style; parterres, borders, 300-yr-old lime trees, dovecot, gazebo, cenotaph commemorating Gen Wolfe. TEAS. Weds, Sats, Suns from April 1 to Sept 30 (2-6). *Adm £1.80 Chd 90p (House & garden £3 Chd £1.50). For NGS (Share to St Mary's Church, Westerham) Suns July 11, Sept 12 (2-6)*

Stoneacre &・※ (Mrs Rosemary Alexander; The National Trust) Otham, 4m SE of Maidstone, between A2020 and A274. Old world garden undergoing extensive replanting. Yew hedges; herbaceous borders; ginkgo tree. Timber-framed Hall House dated 1480. Subject of newspaper and magazine articles. (National Trust members please note that this opening in aid of the NGS is on a day when the property would not normally be open, therefore adm charges apply). TEA. *Adm £1.50 Chd 50p. Sun April 25; Mon May 31 (2-5); also by appt* Tel 0622 862871

Stonewall Park (Mr & Mrs V P Fleming) Chiddingstone Hoath, 5m SE of Edenbridge. ½-way between Mark Beech and Penshurst. Large walled garden with herbaceous borders, extensive woodland garden, featuring species and hybrid rhododendrons and azaleas; wandering paths, lake. Also open at no extra charge **North Lodge** (Mrs Dorothy Michie) traditional cottage garden full of interest. TEA. *Adm £1.50 Acc chd free. Sun May 9; Wed June 16 (2-5)*

Street End Place & (Mr & Mrs R Baker White) Street End. 3m S of Canterbury-Hythe rd (Stone St). Drive gates at Granville Inn. Long established garden incl walled garden, in pleasant setting; large area of naturalised daffodils with lawns of flowering shrubs; fine trees. *Adm £1 Chd 50p. Fri April 9, Sun April 11 (2-4.30)*

Tanners ※ (Sir Michael & Lady Nolan) Brasted, 2m E of Westerham. A25 to Brasted; in Brasted turn off alongside the Green & up the hill to the top; 1st drive on R opp Coles Lane. Bus stop Brasted Green & White Hart 200yds. 5 acres; mature trees & shrubs; maples, magnolias, rhododendrons & foliage trees; water garden; interesting new planting. TEAS. *Adm £1.50 Chd 25p. Sun July 4 (2-6)*

2 Thorndale Close &・※※ (Mr & Mrs L O Miles) Chatham. From A229 Chatham-Maidstone rd turn E opp Crest Hotel into Watson Ave, next R to Thorndale Close. Minute front and rear gardens of 11 × 18ft and 20 × 22ft. Plantsman's garden with alpines, pool, bog garden, rockery, peat and herbaceous beds. *Adm £1 Acc chd free. Suns April 4, 18, May 9, 23, June 6, 20, July 11, 25 (2-6); also by appt* Tel 0634 863329

Thornham Friars &・※ (Geoffrey Fletcher Esq) Pilgrims Way, Thurnham, 4m NE of Maidstone. From M20 or M2 take A249, at bottom of Detling Hill turn into Detling and 1m along Pilgrims Way to garden. 2-acre garden on chalk. Distant views across parkland. Many unusual shrubs; trees; lawns with special beds for ericaceous shrubs. Tudor house. *Adm £1 Chd 25p. Sun May 9 (2-5.30)*

Torry Hill &・※※ (Mr & Mrs Leigh-Pemberton) 5m S of Sittingbourne. Situated in triangle formed by Frinsted, Milstead and Doddington. Leave M 20 at junction 8 for A20, at Lenham turn N for Doddington; at Great Danes N for Hollingbourne and Frinsted (B2163). From M2 Intersection 5 via Bredgar and Milstead. From A2 and E turn S at Ospringe via Newnham and Doddington. 8 acres; large lawns, specimen trees, flowering cherries, rhododendrons, azaleas and naturalised daffodils; walled gardens with lawns, shrubs, roses, herbaceous borders, wild flower areas and vegetables. Extensive views to Medway and Thames estuaries. TEA. *Adm £1 Chd 50p (Share to St Dunstan's Church, Frinsted). Suns April 25, May 16, July 4 (2-5)*

Town Hill Cottage ※※ (Mr & Mrs P Cosier) 58 Town Hill, West Malling. From A20 6m W of Maidstone, turn S onto A228. Top of Town Hill at N end of High St. Part walled small village garden of C16-C18 house, with many interesting plants. Hardy ferns for sale. TEAS. *Adm £1 Chd 50p. Suns May 30, June 13 (2-5)*

Ulcombe Place ※ (Mr & Mrs H H Villiers) Ulcombe, 8m SE of Maidstone. Turn off A20 between Leeds Castle and Harrietsham, signed Ulcombe. 2m to Xrds with garage, straight over, Ulcombe Place on R just after village sign. Gardens on different levels with fine view over the Weald. Interesting trees and shrubs, some rarities, lilacs and magnolias. TEAS. *Adm £1.20 Chd 60p (Share to Ulcombe Church Restoration Fund). Sun May 16 (2-6)*

Updown Farm &・※ (Mr & the Hon Mrs Willis-Fleming) Betteshanger, 3m S of Sandwich. From A256 Sandwich-Dover, turn L off Eastry by-pass SE of Eastry, signed Northbourne, Finglesham. Again 1st L; house 1st on R. 3-acre garden begun in 1975 and still in the making, round Tudor and C18 farmhouse. One of the most extensive fish-geries in East Kent; cherry and plum orchards with old roses and climbers; terrace garden; herbaceous borders, unusual trees and shrubs. TEAS in aid of NSPCC. *Adm £1 OAPs 70p Chd 30p. Suns May 2, 30 (2-6)*

By Appointment Gardens. These owners do not have a fixed opening day usually because they do not like crowds or have insufficient parking space. Owner will often give guided tour.

Upper Mill Cottage ⚭❀ (Mr & Mrs D Seeney) Salts Lane, Loose, 3½m S of Maidstone. Turn W off A229 to Loose. Parking in village; proceed 300yds on foot up Salts Lane. 1½-acre cottage garden created and maintained by owners since 1972, on site of old water mill with natural stream. Plantsman's garden with many unusual varieties incl water plants, herbaceous, alpines, roses, clematis, foliage and ground-cover plants. *Adm £1.50 Chd 50p. Suns June 27, July 4; Wed 30 June (2-5.30)*

¶**Upper Pryors** ⚭⚭ (Mr & Mrs S G Smith) Cowden, 4½m SE of Edenbridge. From B2026 Edenbridge-Hartfield, turn R at Cowden Xrds and take 1st drive on R. 10-acres recently redesigned to incorporate parkland and a water garden. The terrace, with courtyard and wisteria walkway leads out onto large lawns, borders and open views. TEAS. *Adm £1.50 Chd 50p. Wed June 9 (2-6)*

Vine House ⚭❀ (Dr & Mrs Peter Huxley-Williams) 62 High St, Lydd. S of New Romney on B2075, past the church in High St on R-hand side. Informal gardens of about 1 acre surrounding C16 farmhouse; many unusual small trees & shrubs; ponds with waterfall; vineyard; new planting of old-fashioned roses. Teas usually available in the church. *Adm £1 Acc chd free (Share to Spastics on April 18, to All Saints Church, Lydd on July 18, 19). Suns April 18, July 18; Mon July 19 (2.30-5.30)*

Walnut Tree Gardens ⚭⚭❀ (Mr & Mrs M Oldaker) Swan Lane, Little Chart. 6m NW of Ashford. Leave A20 at Charing signed to Little Chart. At Swan public house turn W for Pluckley, gardens 500yds on L. 5-acre gardens planted by owners since 1986. Extensive range of unusual young trees, shrubs and herbaceous plants; large collection of old fashioned roses; walled garden; bog and dry shade areas. Teas at Pluckley Church. *Adm £1.50 OAPs £1 (Share to Green Wicket Animal Sanctuary). Every Sun from May 30 to Aug 22 (2-5). For NGS Suns May 30, June 13, July 11, Aug 8, 22; Thurs June 17, 24, July 1, 15 (2-5) Coaches by appt* Tel 0233 840214

39 Warwick Crescent ⚭❀ (Mr & Mrs J G Sastre) Borstal, Rochester. From A229 Maidstone-Chatham at 2nd roundabout turn W into B2097 Borstal-Rochester rd; turn L at Priestfields, follow Borstal St to Wouldham Way, 3rd turning on R is Warwick Cres. Small front & rear plantsperson's gardens; most plants labelled; alpine terraces, peat & herbaceous beds; rockery with cascade & pool, bog garden, borders. *Adm £1 Acc chd free. Suns April 11, May 2 (2-6); also by appt* Tel 0634 401636

Waystrode Manor ⚭⚭❀ (Mr & Mrs Peter Wright) Cowden, 4½m S of Edenbridge. From B2026 Edenbridge-Hartfield, turn off at Cowden Pound. Station: Weekdays Cowden; Suns Oxted or East Grinstead. 8 acres; large lawns, small grey garden, borders, ponds, bulbs, shrub roses and clematis. Subject of many magazine articles. All plants and shrubs labelled. House C15 (not open). Last entry ½-hour before closing time. TEAS. Gift shop. *Adm £2 Chd 50p. Suns May 30, June 27 (2-6), Weds May 19, June 9 (1.30-5.30); also by appt for groups*

Went House ⚭❀ (Mr & Mrs Robin Baring) Swan Street, West Malling. From A20, 6m W of Maidstone turn S onto A228. Turn E off High Street in village towards station. Queen Anne house with secret garden surrounded by high wall. Interesting plants, water gardens and new parterre. TEAS. *Adm £1 Acc chd free (Share to Lane-Fox Respiratory Patients Assoc, St Thomas's Hospital). Suns June 13, 27 (2-6)*

West Farleigh Hall ⚭ (Mr and Mrs Stephen Norman) 4½m W of Maidstone, turn S off A26 Maidstone-Tonbridge rd at Teston Bridge turn W at T-junction, garden on L. Roses, herbaceous borders, woodland walk. TEA. *Adm £1.50 Acc chd free. Sun June 27 (2-6)*

West Studdal Farm ⚭❀ (Mr & Mrs Peter Lumsden) West Studdal, N of Dover half-way between Eastry and Whitfield. From Eastry take A256, after 2½m pass Plough & Harrow, then 2nd L and 1st R, entrance ¼m on L. From Whitfield roundabout take A256, after 2½m pass High & Dry public house, ¼m fork R at 3-way junction, entrance ½m on R. Medium-sized garden around old farmhouse set by itself in small valley; herbaceous borders, roses and fine lawns protected by old walls and beech hedges. TEAS in Duodecagonal folly. *Adm £1.25 Chd 50p. Sun Aug 22 (2-6)*

Westview ❀ (Mr & Mrs J G Jackson) Spekes Rd, Hempstead. From M2 take A278 to Gillingham; at 1st roundabout follow sign to Wigmore, proceed to junction with Fairview Av, turn L & park on motorway link rd bridge, walk into Spekes Rd, Westview 3rd on L. ¼-acre town garden on very sloping site with many steps; good collection of plants & shrubs suitable for a chalk soil; designed by owners for all-year interest and low maintenance. Good autumn colour. TEAS. *Adm £1 Acc chd free. Weds April 21, May 19; Sats April 24, May 22 (2-5); also by appt* Tel 0634 230987

Whitehurst ⚭⚭ (Mr & Mrs John Mercy) Chainhurst, 3m N of Marden. From Marden station turn R into Pattenden Lane and under railway bridge; at T-junction turn L; at next fork bear R to Chainhurst, then second turning on L. 1½ acres of trees, roses & water garden. Tree walk. TEA. *Adm £1 Chd 50p (Share to Chest, Heart, & Stroke Assoc). Sun Aug 22, Mon May 31, Wed May 26, Sats June 19, Sept 4 (2-6)*

Withersdane Hall ⚭⚭❀ (University of London) Wye College,Wye, NE of Ashford. A28 take fork signed Wye. Bus EK 601 Ashford-Canterbury via Wye. Well-labelled garden of educational and botanical interest, containing several small carefully designed gardens; flower borders and alpines; spring bulbs; early flowering shrubs especially suited to chalk; herb garden. Commemorative Garden created 1980 in honour of a visit by HM Queen Elizabeth The Queen Mother. New rain-fed garden. Illustrated guide book available. TEAS. *Adm £1 Chd 50p. Suns April 25, July 11, Aug 1, Sept 5 (2- 5.30)*

Woodlands Manor ⚭❀ (Mr & Mrs Colin B George) Adisham, 5m SE of Canterbury. On A2 Canterbury-Dover, 4m from Canterbury, ignore sign to Adisham, 1m further on leave A2 at sign to Elham B2065; at bottom of exit rd

---

Regular Openers. See head of county section.

turn sharp L, follow signs marking 6½ft rd to house, 1m. Approaching from E, from Adisham village turn R at end of The Street; at Woodlands Farm, ¾m on, follow signs. Station: Adisham. Buses: 16 or 17 Canterbury-Folkestone or 15 Canterbury-Dover; alight Bishopsbourne turn (request); pass under concrete bridge, signs to house, 1m. Small Georgian house of architectural interest (not open) set in old walled gardens. Spring garden a speciality; pleached lime and woodland walks; sunny corners; rose garden; gazebo. Good vistas; park. TEAS. *Adm £1 Acc chd free (Share to Clive Pare Memorial Fund, Friends of Adisham Church). Suns Feb 14 (snowdrop opening, 2-5), March 28 (2-5), May 2 (2-6); Weds March 31 (2-5), May 5 (2-6)*

Woodpeckers ⚘❀ (Mrs J Cronk & Mr D Dyer) Cannongate Road, Hythe. A259 Hythe-Folkestone rd ½m from Hythe, N end of Cannongate Road. ⅓-acre cliff top garden with views over Hythe Bay, well stocked with collection of plants specially suited to coastal conditions. Refreshments. *Adm £1 Chd 25p. Sun Aug 1 (2-6). Other times by appt* Tel 0303 266735

> By Appointment Gardens. See head of
> county section

Worth Gardens ⚘❀ 2m SE of Sandwich and 5m NW of Deal, from A258 signed Worth. A group of cottage gardens in wide variety in peaceful village setting. Maps and tickets available at each garden. TEAS. *Combined adm £1.50 Chd 25p. Sun July 4 (2-5)*

Yalding Gardens ⚘ 6m SW of Maidstone, three gardens S & W of village. *Combined adm £2 Chd £1. Sun April 4 (2-5.30)*

Congelow House ❀ (Mrs D J Cooper) S of village on B2162. For garden description see individual entry
¶**Long Acre** ⚘❀ (Mr & Mrs G P Fyson) is on L in Cheveney Farm Lane, just off Yalding/Hunton rd (Vicarage Road) ⅓m from Yalding War Memorial. Long, narrow garden comprising shrubberies, lawns, a vegetable and fruit garden and a paddock with young specimen trees. Shrubberies have been recently developed to eliminate the work in maintaining flower beds
Parsonage Oasts (Mr & the Hon Mrs Raikes) Between Yalding village and station turn off at Anchor public house over bridge over canal, continue 100yds up the lane. ¾-acre riverside garden with walls, shrubs, daffodils. TEAS in aid of Thorndene Home for Mentally Handicapped (in heated barn)

Lancashire, Merseyside & Greater Manchester

Hon County Organiser: David Cheetham Esq, 191 Liverpool Road South, Maghull, L31 8AB Tel 051 531 9233
Assistant Hon County Organisers: J Bowker Esq, Swiss Cottage, 8 Hammond Drive, Read, Burnley

DATES OF OPENING

By appointment
For telephone numbers and other details see garden descriptions

Anglian House, Leyland
Cross Gaits Cottage, Blacko
Dun Cow Rib Farm, Longridge
Swiss Cottage, Read

Regular openings
For details see garden descriptions

Catforth Gardens, Catforth. Daily March 13 to Sept 12. Adjacent nursery open
Sellet Hall Herb Garden, Whittington. Daily March to end Sept

April 18 Sunday
Lindeth Dene, Silverdale

May 2 Sunday
Bank House, Borwick
May 9 Sunday
Anglian House, Leyland
Spring Bank House, Cow Ark
May 16 Sunday
Linden Hall, Borwick
Swiss Cottage, Read
May 23 Sunday
191 Liverpool Road South, Maghull
Old Barn Cottage, Turton
May 29 Saturday
17 Poplar Grove, Sale
May 30 Sunday
Catforth Gardens, Catforth
Cross Gaits Cottage, Blacko
Dun Cow Rib Farm, Longridge
Lindeth Dene, Silverdale
191 Liverpool Road South, Maghull
17 Poplar Grove, Sale
Stonestack, nr Turton
May 31 Monday
Cross Gaits Cottage, Blacko

Dun Cow Rib Farm, Longridge
Stonestack, nr Turton
June 2 Sunday
Speke Hall, The Walk, Liverpool
June 6 Sunday
Bank House, Borwick
Mill Barn, Samlesbury Bottoms
Spring Bank House, Cow Ark
June 13 Sunday
Swiss Cottage, Read
June 20 Sunday
Anglian House, Leyland
Linden Hall, Borwick
June 26 Saturday
Clearbeck House, Tatham Green
June 27 Sunday
Catforth Gardens, Catforth
Clearbeck House, Tatham Green
Mill Barn, Samlesbury Bottoms
July 4 Sunday
Bank House, Borwick
Lindeth Dene, Silverdale
Windle Hall, St Helens
July 11 Sunday
Dun Cow Rib Farm, Longridge

Linden Hall, Borwick
Weeping Ash, Glazebury

July 18 Sunday
Cross Gaits Cottage, Blacko
Montford Cottage, Fence

July 25 Sunday
Catforth Gardens, Catforth

August 1 Sunday
Bank House, Borwick

Beechfield, Yealand Conyers, nr
Carnforth
Greyfriars, Fulwood

August 15 Sunday
Old Barn Cottage, Turton

August 29 Sunday
Stonestack, nr Turton

August 30 Monday
Stonestack, nr Turton

September 5 Sunday
Bank House, Borwick
Windle Hall, St Helens

September 12 Sunday
Weeping Ash, Glazebury

October 3 Sunday
Bank House, Borwick
Mill Barn, Samlesbury Bottoms

DESCRIPTIONS OF GARDENS

Anglian House &❀ (Ken & Sara Linford) Leyland. 22 Wyresdale Dr is off Langdale Rd, off Church Rd junction 28, M6. ⅕-acre garden comprising water spout pond, herbaceous bed; sunken garden, heather garden; raised beds. Used as landscape designer's demonstration area. TEAS. *Adm £1 Chd free. Suns May 9, June 20 (10-5); also by appt March to Aug* Tel 0772 433492

Bank House ❀❀ (Mr & Mrs R G McBurnie) Borwick. 2m NE of Carnforth off A6. Leave M6 at junction 35. Plantsman's garden of 2 acres designed to provide all year round shape, colour and form. Divided into different areas of interest including shady borders, sunny gravel area with old-fashioned roses, arboretum, fruit and vegetables. Island beds, silver and gold borders. Collection of carnivorous plants. Featured in 'English Private Gardens'. TEAS. *Adm £1 Chd 25p. Suns May 2, June 6, July 4, Aug 1, Sept 5, Oct 3 (2-6)*

¶Beechfield &❀ (Dr & Mrs R A Paine) Carnforth. 3m N of Carnforth junction 35 M6 onto A6 Carnforth to Milnthorpe rd. Turn to Milnthorpe, 1m on A6. Take L turn to Yealand Conyers (2 turnings off A6 if you miss the 1st). 1½-acre walled garden with box and yew hedges; shrub and herbaceous borders; old fruit trees; small sunken garden pond. Old garden reclaimed and developed by present owners with several plants and shrubs not usually surviving in the North. TEAS. *Adm £1 Chd free. Sun Aug 1 (2-6)*

Catforth Gardens &❀ Leave M6 at junction 32 turning N on A6. Turn L at 1st set of traffic lights; 2m to T-junction, turn R. Turn L at sign for Catforth, L at next T-junction, 1st R into Benson Lane. Bear L at church into Roots Lane. Includes adjoining garden of Willowbridge Farm with access through Catforth Gardens Nursery. TEAS NGS days only. *Combined adm £1 Chd 10p. Suns May 30, June 27, July 25 (12-5) adjacent nursery open March 13 to Sept 12 (10.30-5). Parties by appt* Tel 0772 690561/690269
Catforth Gardens Nursery (Mr & Mrs T A Bradshaw) 1-acre informal country garden, planted for year round interest and colour. Wide variety of unusual shrubs; trees; rhododendrons, azaleas; unusual and rare herbaceous plants including euphorbias, dicentras, pulmonarias; ground cover plants; national collection of hardy geraniums; 2 ponds with bog gardens, large rockery and woodland garden
Willow Bridge Farm (Mr & Mrs W Moore) ¼-acre garden planted with a wide variety of herbaceous perennials (many rare & unusual). Planted with particular attention to colour from spring to autumn, giving a cottage garden effect

Clearbeck House &❀ (Peter & Bronwen Osborne) Tatham Green about 12m E of Lancaster. Follow A683 then B6480 to Wray, turn R on by-road up the pretty Hindburn Valley through Millhouses. Turn R again and follow signs. From terraces and borders near the house, vistas lead into surrounding meadows and hills. Varied planting in the still developing garden includes bog, rose and herbaceous areas. A pyramid grotto within a symbolic garden and wildlife lakes are new additions. This is essentially a garden to walk in and has its surprises. TEAS in aid of Save the Children Fund. *Adm 80p Chd 30p. Sat, Sun, June 26, 27 (10.30-5)*

Cross Gaits Cottage ❀❀ (Mr & Mrs S J Gude) Take M65 exit junction 13. Follow Barrowford signs then Barnoldswick signs. Garden 1½m on Barnoldswick Road opp Cross Gaits Inn. ⅔-acre walled cottage garden, shrub and herbaceous borders. 2 ornamental ponds. 700ft above sea level; fine view of Pennines. TEA/coffee. *Adm £1 Chd 50p. Suns May 30, July 18, Mon May 31 (12-5). Also by appointment* Tel 0282 67163

Dun Cow Rib Farm &❀❀ (Mr & Mrs J Eastham) Longridge. Leave M6 at junction 32 (keeping hard L) follow signs for Preston/Garstang. Turn N onto A6 to traffic lights at Broughton, turn R onto B5269 for approx 6m passing through villages of Goosnargh & Cumeragh (Whittingham). After 30mph sign (on outskirts of Longridge) turn L onto Halfpenny Lane. Newly designed gardens of approx 1-acre around a Yeomans Cottage built by Adam de Houghton in 1616. Old-fashioned front walled garden with herb ring. Formal side garden on two levels with arbour, pergola, newly planted pond and bog garden. Cottage garden style planting with wide variety of plants, shrubs, trees, heathers, roses, clematis and other climbing plants. Lawns, paved areas and courtyards. TEA. *Adm £1 Chd 50p (Share to Lee House Mission Group). Suns, Mon May 30, 31, July 11 (1.30-5). Also by appt May & July* Tel 0772 782824

Greyfriars &❀ (Mr & Mrs William Harrison) Walker Lane, Fulwood, 2m N of Preston. junction 32 off M6 (M55); S to Preston; at Black Bull Xrds right to Boys Lane Xrds ½m entrance on R. 8 acres; lawns, rose beds, fuchsias; 5 greenhouses with hybrid begonias, geraniums and carnations; fountains and water display. TEAS. *Adm £1.50 Chd 30p. Sun Aug 1 (2-5.30)*

> **Regular Openers.** Too many days to include in diary. Usually there is a wide range of plants giving year-round interest. See head of county section for the name and garden description for times etc.

Linden Hall ✲❀ (Mr & Mrs E P Sharp) Borwick, 3m NE of Carnforth. Leave M6 exit 35; take A6 to Milnthorpe. House in centre of Borwick village. C19 garden of 5 acres, wide range of trees, shrubs and old-fashioned roses; ornamental lake with Chinese pagoda, herbaceous borders and knot garden; kitchen garden. TEA. *Adm £1 Chd under 14 free (Share to St Mary's Church, Borwick). Suns May 16, June 20, July 11 (2-5.30)*

Lindeth Dene ✲❀ (Mrs B M Kershaw) 38 Lindeth Rd, Silverdale. 13m N of Lancaster. Take M6 to junction 35, turn L (S) on A6 to Carnforth traffic lights. Turn R follow signs Silverdale. After level crossing ¼m uphill turn L down Hollins Lane. At T junction turn R into Lindeth Rd. Garden is 4th gateway on L, park in rd. Approx 1¼ acres overlooking Morecombe Bay on W facing slope. Large limestone rock garden, trees, shrubs, hardy perennials, troughs, heather garden, veganic kitchen garden with raised beds. Collections of saxifrages, geraniums, New Zealand plants. 1987 A G S Gold Medal Rock Garden Award, shown on BBC Gardener's World 1989. Teas and toilets available in village. *Adm £1 Chd free. Suns April 18, May 30, July 4 (2-5)*

191 Liverpool Rd South ♿❀ (Mr & Mrs D Cheetham) Maghull. A59 Liverpool-Preston rd: from Ormskirk or Liverpool take B5422. Garden ½ mile along. ½-acre suburban garden; rhododendrons, azaleas, camellias, rockery, pool, sink gardens, primulas, a variety of shrubs, bulbs, trees and herbaceous plants for all year colour in the smaller garden. TEA or coffee. *Adm £1 Acc chd free. Suns May 23, 30 (11-6)*

Mill Barn ♿❀ (Dr C J Mortimer) Goose Foot Close, Samlesbury Bottoms, Preston. 6m E of Preston. From M6 junction 31 2½m on A59/A677 B/burn. Turn S. Nabs Head Lane, then Goose Foot Lane 1m. 1-acre tranquil, terraced garden on banks of R Darwen. Mixed planting with many uncommon perennial plants on the site of C18 corn and cotton mills. A garden which is still developing. TEAS. *Adm £1 Chd free. Suns June 6, 27, Oct 3 (2-6)*

Montford Cottage ✲ (C Bullock & A P Morris) Fence, nr Burnley. Situated on the B6248 between Brierfield & Fence. From the M65 junction 13, take the A6068 (signs for Fence) and in 2m turn L onto the B6248 (signs for Brierfield). Proceed down the hill for ½m, entrance to garden is on L (near dangerous bend-drivers please take care). Comparatively young walled garden ⅔-acre developed over last 8 yrs and now maturing, with many unusual plants of particular interest to flower arrangers and plantsmen, particular emphasis on variety of foliage, with varied shrubs, trees, herbaceous plants and pools. TEAS. *Adm £1 Chd 50p. Suns July 18 (1-6)*

Old Barn Cottage ♿❀ (Mr & Mrs R Doldon) Green Arms Rd, Turton. Midway between Bolton and Darwen on B6391 off A666, or through Chapeltown Village High St (B6391). 1-acre developing garden on moorland site. Spring flowering trees; shrubs; azaleas, rhododendrons; water garden; heathers; conifers, herbaceous beds; moorland views. TEAS in aid of Birtenshaw Hall Special School for Handicapped (May), Beacon Counselling Service (Aug). *Adm 50p Chd free. Suns May 23, Aug 15 (1-6)*

17 Poplar Grove ✲❀ (Gordon Cooke) Sale. From the A6144 at Brooklands station turn down Hope Rd. Poplar Grove 3rd on R. This small town garden has been created in 4 yrs by the owner who is a potter and landscape designer. It has a special collection of unusual plants in an artistic setting with many interesting design features and details. TEA. *Adm £1 Chd 50p (Share to North Manchester General Hospital). Sat, Sun May 29, 30 (2-6)*

● **Sellet Hall Gardens** ♿✲❀ (Mr & Mrs Gray) 1m SW of Kirkby Lonsdale. From A65 take turning signed Burton & Hutton Roof follow rd up until brown tourist signs indicate the garden. Garden approx 3½ acres including a herb garden formally laid out. Wild garden, bog area, parterre, shrub and herbaceous borders. The garden has a nursery open all year. TEA. *Adm 70p Acc chd free. The garden is open daily from March to end Sept*

Speke Hall ♿✲ (The National Trust) Liverpool. 8m SE of Liverpool adjacent to Liverpool Airport. Follow signs for Liverpool Airport. A formal garden with herbaceous border, rose garden; moated area with formal lawns. A wild wood is included. Approx size of estate 35 acres. TEAS. *Adm 70p Chd 35p. Sun June 2 (12-5.30)*

Spring Bank House ✲❀ (Joan & Philip Lord) Cow Ark. Situated 6m NW of Clitheroe and within ½m of Browsholme Hall, which is well signposted. A country garden of 6½-acres, situated in the beautiful Hodder Valley, an area of outstanding natural beauty, made and maintained by the owners since 1975 and still developing. Stretching away from the house, 2 acres of informal garden are planted with a large variety of trees, shrubs and herbaceous perennials to provide all-the-year-round interest; while the remaining 4½ acres make up the woodland garden. This steeply wooded valley with stream is planted with species rhododendrons, acers and many other woodland plants, together with many native wild flowers. TEAS in aid of St Michael's Church, Whitewell. *Adm £1 Chd 50p. Suns May 9, June 6 (1.30-5.30)*

Stonestack ♿✲❀ (Frank Smith Esq) 283 Chapeltown Rd, Turton; 4½m N of Bolton, via A666 leading to B6391 nr Turton Tower. 2-acre garden; shrubs, rhododendrons, azaleas; herbaceous border; rockeries, waterfall, ornamental fishpond, fountain, rose borders, bog garden, fuchsias a special feature; greenhouses. As seen on BBC Gardener's World 1985 and BBC Look North TV Aug 88. TEA (Tea/plant sales to Bleakholt Animal Sanctuary). *Adm 50p Chd 25p. Suns, Mons May 30, 31; Aug 29, 30 (2-6)*

Swiss Cottage ✲❀ (James & Doreen Bowker) 8 Hammond Drive, Read, Burnley. 3m SE of Whalley on A671 Whalley to Burnley Road, turn by Pollards Garage, up George Lane to T junction, L into Private Rd past Tables Restaurant. 1½-acre Hillside Garden designed on two levels in mature woodland setting, outstanding views. Variety of shrubs, trees, rhododendrons, azaleas, perennials and alpines. Stream and bog garden feature. Featured in Lancashire Life. TEAS. *Adm £1 Chd free. Suns May 16, June 13 (1-5). Also by appt* **Tel 0282 774853**

¶**Weeping Ash** ⅋✿ (John Bent Esq) Glazebury. ¼m S A580 (East Lancs Rd Greyhound roundabout, Leigh) on A574 Glazebury/Leigh Boundary. ½-acre garden of year long interest on heavy soil. A broad sweep of lawn surrounded by deep mixed borders of shrubs and herbaceous perennials gives way to secret areas with a wide range of planting. A pool with candelabra primulas; a rose bed with gazebo; island beds of penstemons, conifers and heathers. Rhododendrons and sorbus are just a few of the features of this garden undergoing continuous review and development. TEAS. *Adm £1 Chd 50p (Share to Macmillan Lee Home Care Unit). Suns July 11, Sept 12 (2-6)*

Windle Hall ⅋✿ (The Lady Pilkington) N of E Lancs Rd, St Helens. 5m W of M6 via E Lancs Rd, nr Southport junction. Entrance by bridge over E Lancs Rd. 200yr-old walled garden surrounded by 5-acres of lawns and woodland full of spring flowers; Douglas Knight rock and water garden; Victorian thatched cottage. Tufa stone grotto; herbaceous borders, pergola and rose gardens containing exhibition blooms, miniature ornamental ponies, pheasants; greenhouses. TEAS. *Adm 80p Chd 30p. Suns July 4, Sept 5 (2-5)*

> **By Appointment Gardens.** See head of county section

Leicestershire & Rutland

Hon County Organisers: (Leicestershire) Mr John Oakland, Old School Cottage, Oaks-in-Charnwood, nr Loughborough LE12 9YD Tel 0509 502676
(Rutland) Mrs R Wheatley, Clipsham House, Oakham LE15 7SE Tel 0780 410238

Hon County Treasurer (Rutland): A Whitamore Esq., The Stockyard, West Street, Eaton-on-the-Hill, Stamford, Lincs PE9 3LS

DATES OF OPENING

By appointment
For telephone number and other details see garden descriptions

7 Hall Rd, Burbage Gardens
6 Denis Road, Burbage Gardens
Long Close, Woodhouse Eaves
Orchards, Walton, nr Lutterworth
Paddocks, Shelbrook,
 Ashby-de-la-Zouch
18 Park Road, Birstall
Stepping Stones Old Farm, Little
 Beeby
Vine Cottage, Sheepy Magna
 Gardens

Regular openings
Whatton House, Loughborough.
Suns, Weds and Bank Hol Mons
Easter to end August

March 18 Thursday
6 Denis Road, Burbage Gardens
April 4 Sunday
Long Close, Woodhouse Eaves
April 12 Monday
Gunthorpe, Oakham

April 13 Tuesday
Whatton House, Loughborough
April 15 Thursday
6 Denis Road, Burbage Gardens
April 18 Sunday
Paddocks, Shelbrook,
 Ashby-de-la-Zouch
April 21 Wednesday
Paddocks, Shelbrook,
 Ashby-de-la-Zouch
April 25 Sunday
Ashwell Lodge, Oakham
May 2 Sunday
Hoby Gardens, Hoby, nr Melton
 Mowbray
May 9 Sunday
Wakerley Manor, Uppingham
May 13 Thursday
6 Denis Road, Burbage Gardens
18 Park Road, Birstall
May 16 Sunday
Derwen, Coalville
18 Park Road, Birstall
May 23 Sunday
Owston Gardens, nr Oakham
May 30 Sunday
Long Close, Woodhouse Eaves
Paddocks, Shelbrook,
 Ashby-de-la-Zouch
June 1 Tuesday
Whatton House, Loughborough

June 2 Wednesday
Paddocks, Shelbrook,
 Ashby-de-la-Zouch
June 6 Sunday
Prebendal House, Empingham
Park Farm, Normanton,
 Bottesford (see
 Nottinghamshire)
June 9 Wednesday
Paddocks, Shelbrook,
 Ashby-de-la-Zouch
June 13 Sunday
Burbage Gardens, Burbage
Wartnaby, nr Melton
 Mowbray
June 15 Tuesday
Arthingworth Manor, Market
 Harborough
June 16 Wednesday
Arthingworth Manor, Market
 Harborough
Manton Gardens, Oakham
June 17 Thursday
Arthingworth Manor, Market
 Harborough
June 19 Saturday
The Old Barn Gardens,
 Plungar
Sheepy Magna Gardens
June 20 Sunday
Beeby Manor, Beeby

Belvoir Lodge, nr Grantham ‡
Market Overton Gardens
The Old Barn Gardens, Plungar ‡
Reservoir Cottage, Knipton ‡
Sheepy Magna Gardens

June 23 Wednesday
Beeby Manor, Beeby

June 27 Sunday
Barkby Hall, nr Syston ‡
Derwen, Coalville
Hoby Gardens, Hoby, nr Melton
   Mowbray ‡
Orchards, Walton, nr Lutterworth
South Luffenham Hall, nr
   Stamford
Sutton Bonington Hall, Sutton
   Bonington

July 4 Sunday
Brooksby College, nr Melton
Mowbray

July 11 Sunday
Ashwell House, Oakham
Stoke Albany House, Market
   Harborough
Wartnaby, nr Melton Mowbray

July 13 Tuesday
Stoke Albany House, Market
   Harborough

July 14 Wednesday
Stoke Albany House, Market
   Harborough

July 18 Sunday
Paddocks, Shelbrook,
   Ashby-de-la-Zouch

July 21 Wednesday
Paddocks, Shelbrook,
   Ashby-de-la-Zouch

July 25 Sunday
Carlton Village Gardens
The Gables, Thringstone

University of Leicester Botanic
   Garden, Oadby

August 1 Sunday
Market Bosworth Gardens

August 15 Sunday
Paddocks, Shelbrook,
   Ashby-de-la-Zouch

August 18 Wednesday
Paddocks, Shelbrook,
   Ashby-de-la-Zouch

September 19 Sunday
Whatton House, Loughborough

October 3 Sunday
1700 Melton Road, Rearsby

October 10 Sunday
Whatton House, Loughborough

DESCRIPTIONS OF GARDENS

Arthingworth Manor &❀ (Mr & Mrs W Guinness) 5m S of Market Harborough. From Market Harborough via A508 at 4m L to Arthingworth; from Northampton via A508. At Kelmarsh turn R at bottom of hill for Arthingworth. In village turn R at church 1st L. 6 to 7-acre beautiful garden; collection shrub roses; white garden; delphiniums, herbaceous and mixed borders; greenhouses. Newly planted 3-acre arboretum. Original house now being restored. *Adm £1.20 Chd 50p (Share to St John Ambulance, Northants). Tues, Wed, Thurs June 15, 16, 17 (2-5)*

Ashwell House &❀ (Mr & Mrs S D Pettifer) 3m N of Oakham, via B668 towards Cottesmore, turn L for Ashwell. 1½-acre vicarage garden, 1812; vegetable garden; almost original format partly given over to specialist flowers for drying. Pleasure garden with summer pavilion in classical style and architectural features by George Carter. TEAS. Home-made produce stall. *Adm £1 Chd 50p (Share to St Mary's Church). Sun July 11 (2-6)*

Ashwell Lodge &❀❀ (Mrs B V Eve) Ashwell, 3m N of Oakham. From Al, 10m N of Stamford, turn W through Greetham and Cottesmore; then turn R for Ashwell. Park in village st. Medium-sized garden redesigned by Percy Cane c.1973; spring bulbs; herbaceous borders, paved rose garden, shrubs, greenhouse. As featured in 'Country Life' Nov 1990. TEAS. *Adm £1 Chd free (Share to Forces Help Soc & Lord Roberts Workshops). Sun April 25 (2-6)*

Barkby Hall &❀ (Mr & Mrs A J Pochin) Barkby, nr Syston. 5m NE of Leicester. Woodland garden; azaleas, rhododendrons, ericas, conifers, roses, herbaceous, shrubs; mature trees; scented garden; interesting church nearby. TEAS. *Adm £1 Chd 25p (Share to Barkby Church Fabric Fund). Sun June 27 (3-6)*

Beeby Manor &❀❀ (Mr & Mrs Philip Bland) Beeby. 8m E of Leicester. Turn off A47 in Thurnby and follow signs through Scraptoft. 3-acre mature garden with venerable yew hedges, walled herbaceous border, lily ponds, rose towers and box parterre. Plus the start of a 1-acre ar-

boretum. C16 and C18 house (not open). TEAS. *Adm £1.60 Chd 30p (Share to Village Tree Project). Sun, Wed June 20, 23 (2-6)*

Belvoir Lodge &❀ (J S Wood Esq) 7m W of Grantham. Between A52 and A607, nr Belvoir Castle. Medium-sized garden; roses and delphiniums. TEAS. *Adm £1 Chd 30p. Sun June 20 (2-6)*

Brooksby College &❀❀ (by permission of Leicestershire County Council) 6m SW of Melton Mowbray. From A607 (9m from Leicester or 6m from Melton Mowbray) turn at Brooksby; entrance 100yds. Bus: Leicester-Melton Mowbray-Grantham; alight Brooksby turn, 100yds. Grounds inc extensive lawns, lake, ornamental brook, flowering shrub borders, heather bed, large collection young trees; other ornamental features; glasshouses. Church built 1220 open. TEA. *Adm £1 Chd free. Sun July 4 (1-5)*

Burbage Gardens ❀❀ From M69 junction 1, take A447 signed Hinckley. *Combined adm £1.20 Chd 20p (Share to LOROS). Sun June 13 (11-5)*
   6 Denis Road (Mr & Mrs D A Dawkins) 1st L after roundabout. Small garden planted for scent with alpine house, scree area, alpines in troughs, herbaceous borders with old roses; collection of clematis and spring bulbs. *Also open Thurs March 18, April 15 & May 13 (2-5). TEA Thurs only. Also by appt Tel 0455 230509*
   7 Hall Road Burbage (Mr & Mrs D R Baker) From Hinckley; 1st roundabout 1st L to Sketchley Lane; 1st R; 1st R; 1st R again; 1st L to Hall Rd. Medium-sized garden; mixed borders; alpines; sink gardens; scree area; collection of hellebores and hosta; unusual plants; foliage plants. *Also by appt Tel 0455 635616*
   34 Lutterworth Road (Mr & Mrs J Niave) 1st R to Burbage, into Coventry Rd which continues into Windsor St. Opp the Bull's Head turn R into Strutt Rd, then R into Lutterworth Rd. Medium-sized environmentally friendly garden. Mixed hedging to encourage wildlife, herbaceous borders and ornamental pond. Runner-up in local newspaper gardening competition

11 Primrose Drive (Mr & Mrs D Leach) Take 2nd turning on R into Sketchley Rd. 1st L into Azalea Drive, 1st R into Marigold Drive, 1st L Begonia Drive, 1st R into Primrose Drive. No 11 is on L on bend. Small cottage garden, large collection of clematis and paeonies. Plants and pressed flower work for sale

The Long Close ⅍ (Mr & Mrs A J Hopewell) Bullfurlong Lane, Burbage. From Hinckley, 1st R onto Coventry Road 2nd R onto Bullfurlong Lane, garden on L. Limited parking, park if poss on Coventry Rd. ½-acre family garden. Mixed borders; 'natural' ponds; vegetable plot; greenhouse and cool orchid house. Local orchid society in attendance. Cream TEAS, ploughman's lunches

Carlton Village Gardens ⅍ ✿❀ 1½m N of Market Bosworth off A447 Coalville-Hinckley Rd. Map/guide. TEAS. *Combined adm £1.50 Chd free. Flower festival in church (Share to Carlton Parish Amenities Fund). Sun July 25 (2-6)*

¶**Barnswood** (Mr & Mrs R W Wilkin) Developing informal garden with pond, beds, patio under construction

¶**Cartland House** (Mr & Mrs L Dearing) Empty plot with incipient pond; work beginning on new design

The Cheese Barn (Mr & Mrs C J Sinclair) Courtyard garden with containers and hanging baskets

¶**Fox Covert** (Mr & Mrs J A Orton) Conservation area and large pond under construction

¶**The Granary** (Mr & Mrs B Hunt) Former farmyard; ground preparation just begun

The Green (Mr & Mrs G K Zuger) 3-yr-old garden, pond and bog garden, mixed borders

Home Farm House (Mr & Mrs C J Peat) Small walled garden, family garden with flowers, vegetables and herbs

Kirkfield (Mr & Mrs W R Sharp) Informal family garden with flowers, fruit and vegetables

Saint Andrew's Church Flower festival

Treetops (Mr D Jackson) Informal garden with lawns, trees and shrubs

Whimbury (Mr & Mrs S Spencer) Mixed borders with interesting shrubs, perennials, pond

¶**York House** (Mr & Mrs D Swallow) Low maintenance family garden, mixed borders, containers

Derwen ✿❀ (Dr & Mrs Martin Wenham) 68a Greenhill Rd, Coalville. From A50 (Coalville by-pass) take the turning to Shepshed, then fork R at St David's Church, ½m on R. From B587 turn into top of Greenhill Road near Bull's Head, 1m on L. Town garden, largely redesigned and reconstructed during 1988-9 to give a wide variety of shape and texture using simple local materials. Planting is of perennials and shrubs with an emphasis on form and foliage. *Adm 60p Chd 15p (Share to Army Benevolent Fund). Suns May 16, June 27 (2-6)*

¶**The Gables** ⅍✿❀ (Mr & Mrs P J Baker) Main Street, Thringstone. Leave A512 Loughborough to Ashby de la Zouch rd at Bull's Head, sign-posted Thringstone. Main St is off the village green. ⅓-acre country garden. Herbaceous borders, many unusual plants, containers, clematis and old roses. Grade II listed cottage not open. TEAS. *Adm £1 Chd 25p. Sun July 25 (2-6)*

Gunthorpe ⅍ (A T C Haywood Esq) 2m S of Oakham. On Uppingham Rd; entrance by 3 cottages, on R going S. Medium-sized garden; springs flowers and flowering trees in good setting. TEAS. *Adm £1 Chd free (Share to Cancer Relief). Easter Mon Apr 12 (2-5.30)*

¶**Hoby Gardens** ✿ 8m NE of Leicester, 1m NW of A607 Leicester-Melton rd. Turn at Brooksby Agricultural College. *Combined adm £1.25 Chd free (Share to St John's Ambulance and Riding for the Disabled). Suns May 2, June 27 (2-6)*

¶**Glebe House** ⅍❀ (Mr & Mrs J M Peck) Church Lane. 1 acre of shrubs and herbaceous mixed borders, created since 1977, mainly within lovely C18 wall; paddock, vegetable garden. Pleasing views over glebe land. TEAS

¶**Rooftree Cottage** (D Headly Esq) Main Street. Small garden to a medieval cruck cottage. The site slopes down towards the R Wreake and the garden is planned to lead to pastoral views across the valley. Traditional and indigenous plantings

Long Close ❀ (Mrs George Johnson) 60 Main St, Woodhouse Eaves, S of Loughborough. From A6, W in Quorn B59l. Bus: Leicester-Loughborough, alight at gates (nr playing fields). 5 acres rhododendrons (many varieties), azaleas, flowering shrubs, old shrub roses, many rare shrubs, trees, heathers, conifers, forest trees; lily pools; fountain; terraced lawns. Featured in *Country Life* Dec 1984. *Adm £1.30 Chd 30p. TEA Sun April 4 (special rare plant sale) (2-5); TEAS Sun May 30 (2-6). Also by appt March to June* **Tel 0509 890616** *business hrs*

¶**Manton Gardens** ❀ Turn off A6003 halfway between Uppingham and Oakham to Manton village. TEAS. *Combined adm £1.50 Chd 25p. Sun June 13 (2-6)*

¶**The Barn House** ✿ (Mr & Mrs R A Diamant) Small irregular shaped plantsman's garden created from stable yard and started in 1986. Wide variety of plant associations set in gravelled areas. As featured on TV 'Gardeners World' and 'The Gardener' magazine

¶**Foxfields** ⅍✿ (Mr & Mrs D Hunt) Garden established in last 9 years, wonderful views of Rutland Water. Foliage shrubs and many varieties of roses. UK Britain in Bloom winner 1988

¶**Manton Grange** ⅍ (Mr & Mrs M Taylor) Recently redesigned garden. Good mix of foliage shrubs; rose garden with gazebo and fountain. Good trees and spectacular view

Market Bosworth Gardens ⅍❀ 1m off A447 Coalville to Hinckley Rd, 3m off A444. Pay on Market Bosworth Market Place. Village plan available. Other gardens will also open. TEAS. *Combined adm £1.50 Chd 50p. Sun Aug 1 (2-6)*

¶**1 & 2 Home Farm Mews** (Mr I Langley & Mr R Towers) Converted 100-yr-old farm buildings and woodland

¶**2 Lancaster Avenue** (Mrs E G Peacey) Flowers and shrubs maintained by a retired lady

¶**16 Northumberland Avenue** (Mr & Mrs K McCarthy) Newly landscaped garden

¶**24 Northumberland Avenue** (Mr & Mrs E G Watkins) Flowers, shrubs and lawns

¶4 Rectory Lane (Mr & Mrs P W Bonsell) A cottage garden

¶11 Stanley Road (Mrs O Caldwell) Garden with flowers and shrubs

¶273 Station Road (Mrs R J Baker) Flower garden and model village

¶8 Weston Drive (Mr & Mrs J Earl-Davies) Flower garden, fuchsias a speciality

¶Witherstitch Farm (Ann Carter) Farm garden with rockery

▌Market Overton Gardens ⚜ 6m N of Oakham beyond Cottesmore; 5m from the A1 via Thistleton; 10m E from Melton Mowbray via Wymondham. TEAS. *Combined adm £2 Chd 50p (Share to Market Overton Play Area Assoc). Sun June 20 (2-6)*

¶31 Bowling Green Lane (Richard Hirst) Secluded cottage garden, approx ⅓-acre, varied plants and shrubs

¶Church Cottage ♿⚜ (Mr & Mrs W M Cox) Well hidden partly-walled ½-acre old-fashioned garden surrounding thatched cottage; climbing and shrub roses; clematis paeonies; shrubs; perennials; lawns

¶The Old Hall ♿ (Mr & Mrs T Hart) Newly designed S facing 3-acre garden. Lovely views; flowing lawns on 2 levels; herbaceous borders; climbing roses; pond; unusual trees

¶Hill House (Brian & Judith Taylor) A ½-acre plantsman's garden, mainly of herbaceous beds for year round colour and texture, and comprising many uncommon hardy and half-hardy perennials

700 Melton Road ⚜❀ (Mr & Mrs J Kaye) Rearsby, N of Leicester on A607. In Rearsby, on L.H. side from Leicester. 1-acre developing garden with wide range of interesting herbaceous plants; some shrubs and trees. Nursery. *Adm 25p Chd 10p. Daily March to Oct (Wed to Sat 10-5.30, Sun 10-12). Also SPECIAL OPEN DAY Sun Oct 3 (2-5.30). Adm 80p Chd 30p (Share to St Michael's and All Angels Church, Rearsby). TEAS Oct 3 only*

▌he Old Barn Gardens ♿❀ (G W Miller Esq & Mr & Mrs E Pear) Church Lane, Plungar. 16m E of Nottingham ake A52, turn R 1m after Bingham. 12m N of Melton Mowbray via Scalford, Eastwell and Stathern. Farm buildings converted to 2 dwellings with own gardens. 1 acre with trees, shrubs, lawns, mixed borders; view. Plant stall. Art exhibition in Church. TEAS. *Adm £1 Chd free Share to St Helen's Church, Plungar). Sat, Sun June 19, 20 (11-6)*

▌rchards ❀❀ (Mr & Mrs G Cousins) Hall Lane, Walton, r Lutterworth. 8m S of Leicester via the A50 take a R urn just after Shearsby (sign-posted Bruntingthorpe); thereafter follow signs for Walton. 1-acre garden; courtyard with many unusual plants on the walls; orchard, ose, pool and wild gardens with a wide range of trees and shrubs. View over countryside. Featured on TV's Garden Club. TEAS. *Adm £1.20 Chd free. Sun June 27 (2-6). Also by appt June to Sept Tel Lutterworth 556958*

▌wston Gardens ♿ 6m W of Oakham via Knossington, m S of Somerby. From Leicester turn L 2m E of Tilton. lants and sundries stalls. TEAS. *Combined adm £1 Chd ee (Share to Owston Church). Sun May 23 (2-6)*

Homestead (Mr & Mrs D Penny) Recently developed ⅓-acre; collection of clematis and alpines being established; pond

Rose Cottage ❀(Mr & Mrs J D Buchanan) Undulating 1¾-acres; shrub and flower borders; spring bulbs, roses, alpines; ponds, waterfall; fine views

Paddocks ♿❀❀ (Mrs Ailsa Jackson) Shelbrook. 1½m W of Ashby-de-la-Zouch on B5003 towards Moira. 1-acre garden. Large collection and wide range of the more unusual herbaceous plants and shrubs. NCCPG collection of old named double and single primulas. Silver medallist at Chelsea and Vincent Square. TEA. *Adm £1 Chd free. Suns and Weds April 18, 21; May 30, June 2; July 18, 21; Aug 15, 18 (2-5). Also by appt Tel 0530 412606*

18 Park Road ♿❀ (Dr & Mrs D R Ives) Birstall. Turn off A6 into Park Road at crown of the hill on Leicester side of Birstall. Local buses stop at end of Park Road. About 1 acre of lawn, trees, shrubs and other mixed planting including hellebores, aquilegias, bluebells etc with emphasis on foliage and scent. TEAS. *Adm £1 Chd 25p (Share to COPE Thurs 13 May only). Thurs, Sun May 13, 16 (2-5.30). Also by appt in April, May and June Tel 0533 675118*

Prebendal House ♿ (Mr & Mrs J Partridge) Empingham. Between Stanford & Oakham on A606. House built in 1688; summer palace for the Bishop of Lincoln. Recently improved old-fashioned gardens incl water garden, topiary and kitchen gardens. TEAS. *Adm £1 Chd 50p. Sun June 6 (2-6)*

Reservoir Cottage ♿ (Lord & Lady John Manners) Knipton, 7m W of Grantham. W of A1; between A52 and A607; nr Belvoir Castle. Medium-sized country garden with lovely views over the lake. TEA. *Adm £1 Chd free. Sun June 20 (2-6)*

¶**Sheepy Magna Gardens** ♿❀ B4116 2 ½m N of Atherstone on Atherstone to Twycross Rd. Teas in aid of Sheepy Magna Church in Rectory garden. *Combined adm £2 Chd 30p (Share to Sheepy Church). Sat, Sun June 19, 20 (2-6)*

¶**Gate Cottage** ❀ (Mr & Mrs O P Hall) Church Lane. Opp church. Approx ½-acre cottage garden; mixed herbaceous borders; greenhouse; vegetable garden; several specimen trees; lawns and patio

¶**The Grange** (Mr & Mrs V Wetton) Main Rd. ¼m from shop towards Twycross opp entrance to trout ponds farm. Spacious Edwardian garden redeveloped since 1989. Extensive lawns; mature specimen trees; ponds; massed roses; heather beds; mixed borders

Vine Cottage ❀ (Mr & Mrs T Clark) 26 Main Rd. Opp shop. Approx ¾-acre cottage garden; mixed herbaceous borders; alpine gardens; ponds; vegetable plot with greenhouse. TEAS. *Also by appt Adm £1. May to Sept.. Tel 0827 880529*

By Appointment Gardens. These owners do not have a fixed opening day usually because they do not like crowds or have insufficient parking space. Owner will often give guided tour.

¶**South Luffenham Hall** &.&& (Mr & Mrs R A Butterfield) South Luffenham on A6121 between Stamford and Uppingham. Turn off A47 at Morcot. 3-acre garden around 1630 house (not open), featured in 'The Perfect English Country House'. Shrubs, roses, herbaceous borders, lawns, pleached lime hedge and terrace with alpines and lilies. TEAS. *Adm £1.50 Chd 50p. (Share to St Marys Church, S Luffenham). Sun June 27 (2-6)*

Stepping Stones Old Farm (Mr Clem Adkin) Little Beeby. 8m E of Leicester. Off A47 at Thurnby, through Scraptoft. R at Beeby Xrds. 1st R on Hungarton Lane. 1-acre garden on site of medieval deserted village, part excavated. Stream, small arboretum, shrub roses, spring bulbs in variety, spring blossom. Surprise features. Lovely countryside. TEA. *Adm £1 Chd 50p. By appt only March to July* **Tel 053 750 677**

Stoke Albany House &. (Mr & Mrs A M Vinton) 4m E of Market Harborough via A427 to Corby; turn to Stoke Albany; right at the White Horse (B669); garden ½m on L. Large garden with fine trees; shrubs; herbaceous borders and grey garden. TEAS on July 11 only. *Adm £1.20 Chd 30p. Sun July 11 (2-6); Tues, Weds July 13, 14 (2-5)*

Sutton Bonington Hall &. (Anne, Lady Elton) Sutton Bonington, 5m NW of Loughborough; take A6 to Hathern; turn R (E) onto A6006; 1st L (N) for Sutton Bonington. Conservatory, formal white garden, variegated leaf borders. Queen Anne house (not open). Picnics. TEA. *Adm £1.20 Chd 25p (Share to St Michael's and St Ann's Church, Sutton Bonington). Sun June 27 (12-5.30)*

Regular Openers. See head of county section.

University of Leicester Botanic Garden &.&& Stoughton Drive South, Oadby, Leicester. On SE outskirt of Leicester, opp Oadby race course. Bus, Midland Red Garden incorporates grounds of Beaumont Hall, Southmeade, Hastings House and The Knoll. 16 acres; trees rose, rock, water and sunken gardens; botanical green houses; herbaceous borders; heather garden. Open July (2-5) TEA. *Adm £1 Chd free (Share to BRCS & St Joh Ambulance). For NGS Sun July 25 (2-5)*

Wakerley Manor &.& (A D A W Forbes Esq) 6m Upping ham, right off A47 Uppingham-Peterborough through Bar rowden, or from A43 Stamford to Corby rd betwee Duddington and Bulwick. 4 acres lawns, shrubs, herba ceous; kitchen garden; three greenhouses. TEAS. *Adm £ Chd 10p. Sun May 9 (2-6)*

Wartnaby &.& (Lord & Lady King) Wartnaby 4m NW o Melton Mowbray. From A606 turn W in Ab Kettley, fron A46 at Durham Ox turn E on A676. Medium-sized garder shrubs, herbaceous borders, a good collection of old fashioned roses, a small aboretum and a newly designe vegetable garden. TEAS. *Adm £1.50 Chd 30p. Suns Jur 13, July 11 (2-6)*

Whatton House &.& (Lord Crawshaw) 4m NE of Lough borough on A6 between Hathern and Kegworth; 2½m S of junc 24 on M1. 15 acres; shrub and herbaceous bor ders, lawns, rose and wild gardens, pools; arboretun Chinese/Japanese garden is unique feature. Nurser open. TEAS. Teas in Old Dining Room. Catering arrange ments for pre-booked parties any day or evening. *Adi £1.50 OAP/Chd 75p. Open Suns and Weds from Easter end August. Also Bank Hol Mons. For NGS Tues April 1 June 1 (2-6). Special plant sales Suns Sept 19, Oct 1 Also by appt* **Tel 0509 842268**

&&

Lincolnshire

Hon County Organiser: Mrs Patrick Dean, East Mere House, Lincoln LN4 2JB Tel 0522 791371
Assistant Hon County Organisers: Lady Bruce-Gardyne, The Old Rectory, Aswardby, Spilsby, Lincs PE23 4JS Tel 0790 52652
Mrs Julian Gorst, Oxcombe Manor, Horncastle, Lincs LN9 6LU Tel 0507 533227

DATES OF OPENING

By appointment
For telephone numbers and other details see garden descriptions

21 Chapel Street, Hacconby
Wheelwrights Cottage, Oasby
58 Watery Lane, Butterwick

Regular openings
For details see garden descriptions

The Orchard, Foston, nr Grantham.
  March 1 to Sept 1

February 4 Thursday
  21 Chapel Street, Hacconby
March 4 Thursday
  21 Chapel Street, Hacconby

April 4 Sunday
  21 Chapel Street, Hacconby
  Fulbeck Hall, nr Grantham
  The Old Rectory, Fulbeck, nr
    Grantham
April 11 Sunday
  Little Ponton Hall, Grantham
April 18 Sunday
  Aubourn Hall, Aubourn nr
    Lincoln
  Stocks Farm, Leadenham

May 6 Thursday
21 Chapel Street, Hacconby
May 9 Sunday
Grimsthorpe Castle Gardens,
Bourne
May 13 Thursday
Grimsthorpe Castle Gardens,
Bourne
May 16 Sunday
Doddington Hall, nr Lincoln
The Orchard, Foston, nr Grantham
May 23 Sunday
Belton House, Grantham
Luskentyre, Roman Bank,
Saracens Head, nr Spalding
May 24 Monday
58 Watery Lane, Butterwick
May 25 Tuesday
58 Watery Lane, Butterwick
May 26 Wednesday
58 Watery Lane, Butterwick
May 27 Thursday
58 Watery Lane, Butterwick
May 28 Friday
58 Watery Lane, Butterwick

May 29 Saturday
58 Watery Lane, Butterwick
May 30 Sunday
Grantham House, Grantham
Stenigot House, nr Louth
58 Watery Lane, Butterwick
May 31 Monday
58 Watery Lane, Butterwick
June 6 Sunday
21 Chapel Street, Hacconby
Park Farm, Normanton,
Bottesford (see Notts for
details)
June 13 Sunday
Hall Farm, Harpswell
June 20 Sunday
Luskentyre, Roman Bank,
Saracens Head, nr
Spalding
Marston Hall, nr Grantham
Park House Farm, Walcott
June 27 Sunday
Gunby Hall, Burgh-le-Marsh
July 1 Thursday
21 Chapel Street, Hacconby

July 4 Sunday
Aubourn Hall, Aubourn nr Lincoln
July 11 Sunday
East Mere House, nr Lincoln
July 17 Saturday
Belton House, Grantham
August 1 Sunday
The Orchard, Foston, nr
Grantham
August 5 Thursday
21 Chapel Street, Hacconby
September 2 Thursday
21 Chapel Street, Hacconby
September 5 Sunday
Hall Farm, Harpswell
The Orchard, Foston, nr
Grantham
Sausthorpe Old Hall, nr Spilsby
September 12 Sunday
The Villa, South Somercotes,
Louth
October 7 Thursday
21 Chapel Street, Hacconby

DESCRIPTIONS OF GARDENS

Aubourn Hall &% (Sir Henry Nevile) Aubourn. 7m SW of Lincoln. Signposted off A606 at Harmston. Approx 3-acres. Lawns, mature trees, shrubs, roses, mixed borders. C11 church adjoining. Wheelchairs in dry weather only. TEAS. *Adm £1 Chd 50p. (Share to St. Peters Church Aubourn-repairs). Suns April 18, July 4 (2-6)*

Belton House &% (The National Trust) 3m NE of Grantham on the A607 Grantham to Lincoln road. Easily reached and signed from the A1 (Grantham north junction). 32 acres of garden incl formal Italian and Dutch gardens, and orangery by Sir Jeffrey Wyatville. TEAS. *Adm house & garden £4 Chd £2. ▲Sun May 23, Sat July 17 (11-5.30)*

Burghley House see Cambridgeshire

21 Chapel Street &% (Cliff & Joan Curtis) A15 3m N of Bourne, turn E at Xrds into Hacconby. Small village garden with alpine house, rockeries, scree bed, old stone troughs planted as miniature gardens. Herbaceous borders with climbing roses and numerous clematis, collections of snowdrops, primula allionii, lewisia, rhodohypoxis. Featured on TV. TEAS. *Adm 80p Chd 20p. (Share to Marie Curie Memorial Foundation). Suns April 4, June 6 (11-6). Also Thurs Feb 4, March 4, May 6, July 1, Aug 5, Sept 2, Oct 7 (2-dusk). Collecting box. Open by appt. Parties welcomed.* Tel 0778 570314

Doddington Hall &% (Antony Jarvis Esq) 5m SW of Lincoln. From Lincoln via A46, turn W on to B1190 for Doddington. Superb walled gardens; thousands of spring bulbs; wild gardens; mature trees; Elizabethan mansion. Free Car Park. Lunches and TEAS available from 12 noon in fully licensed garden restaurant. *Adm house & garden*

£3.40 Chd £1.70. Garden only £1.70 Chd 85p (Share to Lincolnshire Old Churches Trust). ▲Sun May 16 (2-6)

East Mere House &%& (Mr & Mrs Patrick Dean) Lincoln. 3m S of Lincoln on A15. 1m E on B1178. Mixed shrubs, roses and herbaceous borders vegetable and herb gardens. TEAS. *Adm £1 Chd 25p. Sun July 11 (2-6)*

Fulbeck Hall &% (Mrs M Fry) Grantham. On A607 14m S of Lincoln, 11m N of Grantham. 1m S of X-roads of A17 at Leadenham. 11-acres incl formal Edwardian garden with yew hedges, tulip tree, cedars and venetian well head; spring bulbs. There has been much recent planting of unusual trees, shrubs and herbaceous plants. TEAS. *Combined adm with* **The Old Rectory** *£2.50 Chd £1. Sun April 4 (2-5)*

Grantham house &% (Lady Wyldbore-Smith) Castlegate, opp St Wulframs Church, Grantham. An old English garden of approx 5 acres of bulbs, many unusual shrubs and trees; river walk and water garden. TEAS. *Adm £1 Chd 50p. Sun May 30 (2-6)*

Grimsthorpe Castle Gardens & (Grimsthorpe and Drummond Castle Trust) 8m E of A1 on the A151 from the Colsterworth junction, 4m W of Bourne. 15 acres of formal and woodland gardens which incl bulbs and wild flowers. The formal gardens encompass fine topiary, roses, herbaceous borders and an unusual ornamental kitchen garden. TEAS. *Adm £1 Chd 50p. ▲Sun, Thurs May 9, 13 (12-6)*

Regular Openers. Too many days to include in diary. Usually there is a wide range of plants giving year-round interest. See head of county section for the name and garden description for times etc.

Gunby Hall ර්🌢 (Mr & Mrs J D Wrisdale; The National Trust) 2½m NW of Burgh-le-Marsh; S of A158. 7 acres of formal and walled gardens; old roses, herbaceous borders; herb garden; kitchen garden with fruit trees and vegetables. Tennyson's 'Haunt of Ancient Peace'. House built by Sir William Massingberd 1700. Plant centre TEAS. *Adm garden only £1.50 Chd 70p (Share to St Barnabas Hospice (Lincoln).* ▲*Sun June 27 (2-6)*

Hall Farm ර්🌢 (Pam & Mark Tatam) Harpswell. 7m E of Gainsborough on A631. 1½m W of Caenby Corner. ¾-acre garden with mixed borders of trees, shrubs, roses and perennials (many of the plants are unusual). Over 80 varieties of rose - mainly old varieties. Recently constructed sunken garden and pond. Short walk to old moat and woodland. TEAS. *Adm £1 Chd 25p. Suns June 13, Sept 5 (2-6)*

Little Ponton Hall ර්🌢 (Mr & Mrs A McCorquodale) Grantham 3m. ½m E of A1 at S end of Grantham bypass. 3 to 4-acre garden. Spacious lawns with cedar tree over 200yrs old. Many varieties of old shrub roses; borders and young trees. Stream with spring garden; bulbs and river walk. Kitchen garden and listed dovecote. Adjacent to Little Ponton Hall is St Guthlacs Church which will be decorated and all visitors welcome. TEAS. *Adm £1 Chd under 12 free (Share to St Guthlacs Church, Little Ponton). Sun April 11 (2-6)*

Luskentyre ⚸ (Mr & Mrs C Harris) 7m E of Spalding signed from A17 at Saracen's Head. Attractive small garden extensively planted with a wide range of interesting plants mainly chosen for their ability to withstand dry conditions and give year-round interest. *Adm 80p Chd 20p. Suns May 23, June 20 (1-5)*

The Manor House ⚸ (John Richardson Esq) Bitchfield; 6m SE of Grantham, close to Irnham and Rippingale. A52 out of Grantham to Spital Gate Hill roundabout; take B1176 to Bitchfield; House on right after public house. 1½-acres entirely re-created in 1972; essentially a shrub rose garden (96 varieties) with shrubs and other perennials; 50 by 40ft pond planted spring 1985; small box hedged formal garden; ha-ha, new large garden room with fountain and over 100 plants. *Adm £2. Parties of 20 or more by appt only after June 1 to mid-July.* **Tel Ingoldsby 261**

Marston Hall ර්🌢 (The Rev Henry Thorold) 6m N of Grantham. Turn off A1, 4½m N of Grantham; on 1½m to Marston. Station: Grantham. Notable trees; wych elm and laburnum of exceptional size. House C16 continuously owned by the Thorold family. Interesting pictures and furniture. TEAS *Adm house & garden £2 Chd £1 (Share to Marston Church Restoration Fund).* ▲*Sun June 20 (2-6)*

¶**The Old Rectory** ⚸ (Mr & Mrs N O S Brown) Fulbeck. On A607 11m N of Grantham and 15m S of Lincoln. Adjoining the church with views across the Trent Valley. Spring bulbs, shrubs and roses are planted within the last 10 years. Signposted from Fulbeck Hall through the churchyard. *Combined adm with* **Fulbeck Hall** *£2.50 Chd £1. Sun April 4 (2-5)*

The Orchard ර්⚸🌢 (Janet and Richard Blenkinship) Foston, 6m NW of Grantham. Turn off A1 for Foston. Garden on narrow one way street nr Coopers Arms. 1-acre garden and nursery featuring extensive herbaceous borders with interesting plant associations. Small bog garden, hedgerow planting, meadow and raised beds. A wide range of the more unusual plants grown incl hostas, hardy geraniums, clematis and penstemon. TEA. *Adm 75p Chd free. Suns May 16, Aug 1, Sept 5 (10-5). Also March 1 to Sept 1 with NGS collecting box.*

Park House Farm ර්⚸🌢 (Mr & Mrs Geoffrey Grantham) Walcott. 16m S of Lincoln on B1189 between Billinghay and Metheringham. Traditional farm buildings have been adapted to enclose 1 acre of informal gardens with mixed borders; white garden, alpine and scree beds; climbers a speciality. Wild garden with pond; old orchard and mini nature reserve. TEAS. *Adm £1 Chd 50p (Share to Walcott Village Hall). Sun June 20 (2-6)*

Sausthorpe Old Hall ර් (Mrs W F Kochan) Sausthorpe, NW of Spilsby, A158 Lincoln-Skegness. Old garden, lawns, shrubberies, trees. TEAS. *Adm £1 Chd 50p (Share to The Old Churches Trust). Sun Sept 5 (2-6)*

Stenigot House ⚸🌢 (Mr & Mrs Peter Dennis) nr Louth. 6m S of Louth. Turn W off A153 at sign to Stenigot, 2m. Spacious lawns with lovely view over Wolds. Water garden with several varieties of astilbes; shrub roses and borders; kitchen garden. TEAS. *Adm £1.50 Chd 30p (Share to St Nicholas Church). Sun May 30 (2-6)*

Stocks Farm ර්⚸🌢 (Mr & Mrs P Booth & Mr & Mrs R Booth) Leadenham. On A607 13m S of Lincoln. Two adjacent village gardens with extensive views. One newly established with shrub borders of interest to flower arrangers. One farmhouse garden with vines and mature mixed borders. TEAS. *Adm £1 Chd 20p. Sun April 18 (2-6)*

¶**The Villa** ⚸🌢 (Michael & Judy Harry) South Somercotes. 8m E of Louth. Leave Louth by Eastfield Rd. Follow signs to S Cockerington. Take rd signposted to North & South Somercotes. House on L 100 yds before church. ¼-acre densely planted in the cottage style; large collection of herbs, old-fashioned and unusual perennials; orchard with interesting old varieties of fruit trees. Livestock incl flock of Lincoln Longwool Sheep. TEAS. *Adm £1 Chd free. Sun Sept 12 (2-6)*

58 Watery Lane ර්⚸🌢 (Mr & Mrs F Jervis) Butterwick. Take the A52 Skegness Rd out of Boston. Butterwick turn about 5m on the R. Carry on into the village keeping the Five Bells Inn on your R. Watery Lane 2nd turning L. We are the 2nd bungalow on the R. The garden is approx ¼-acre consisting of mainly alpines, over 300 grown. Rockery and raised beds, also containers; alpine house; 2 small ponds. *Adm 80p Chd free. Mon May 24 to Mon May 31. By appt April, May, June, (10.30-6.30)* **Tel 0205 760795**

By Appointment Gardens. Avoid the crowds. Good chance of a tour by owner. See garden description for telephone number.

Wheelwrights Cottage ✐☙ (Mr Ian & Mrs Annice Whittle) 7m E of Grantham signposted Oasby from A52 and B6403. Garden just inside the village street on R. Park where you can. Small cottage garden densely planted with interesting and unusual herbaceous plants. Winding paths and secret corners. Special interest in snowdrops, hellebores, spring bulbs, grasses, campanulas, clematis, asters and chrysanthemum. TEA. *Adm £1 Chd Free (Share to Heydour Church). By appt only.* **Tel 05295 379**

London (Greater London Area)

Hon County Organiser: Mrs Maurice Snell, Moleshill House, Fairmile, Cobham, Surrey KT11 1BG
Tel 0932 864532

Assistant Hon County Organisers: Mrs Stuart Pollard, 17 St Alban's Rd, Kingston-upon-Thames, Surrey
Tel 081 546 6657
Miss Alanna Wilson, 38 Ornan Road, London NW3 4QB Tel 071 794 4071

DATES OF OPENING

By appointment
For telephone numbers and other details see garden descriptions

24 Grove Terrace, NW5
33 Mundania Road, SE22
Flat 1, 1F Oval Road, NW1
7 St George's Road,
  Twickenham
81B St Peters Street, Islington
Tarn, Oxhey Drive
42 Woodville Gardens, Ealing

Regular openings
For details see garden descriptions

Barbican Conservatory EC2, Sats,
  Suns, Bank Hols all year
Chelsea Physic Garden SW3, Suns
  April 4 to Oct 31, Weds April 7 to
  Oct 27, Mon to Friday May 24 to
  May 28 , Mon to Friday June 14
  to June 18
Myddelton House, EN2 Weekday
  except Bank Hols and last Sun in
  the month Feb to Oct

20 March Saturday
The Elms, Kingston-on-Thames
21 March Sunday
The Elms, Kingston-on-Thames
3 April Saturday
Lambeth Palace, SE1
4 April Sunday
Chelsea Physic Garden, SW3

12 April Monday
Highgate Village 1, N6
Myddelton House, EN2
17 April Saturday
The Elms, Kingston-on-Thames
18 April Sunday
46 Canonbury Square, Canonbury
  Gardens
60 St Pauls Road, Canonbury
  Gardens
Eccleston Square, SW1
The Elms, Kingston-on-Thames
Fenton House, NW3
24 April Saturday
Trinity Hospice, SW4
25 April Sunday
Chiswick Mall, W4
29 Deodar Road, SW15
Edwardes Square, W8
24 Grove Terrace, NW5
St Mary's Convent & Nursing
  Home, Chiswick, W4
Tarn, Oxhey Drive
Trinity Hospice, SW4
7 Woodstock Road, W4
1 May Saturday
30 Hercies Road,
  Hillingdon
2 May Sunday
Harewood, Chalfont St Giles see
  Bucks
1 Hocroft Avenue, NW2
Flat 1, 1 F Oval Road
3 May Monday
1 Hocroft Avenue, NW2
5 May Wednesday
Frogmore Gardens, Windsor, see
  Berkshire
12 Lansdowne Rd, W11

6 May Thursday
Frogmore Gardens, Windsor, see
  Berkshire
8 May Saturday
The Elms, Kingston-on-Thames
9 May Sunday
39 Boundary Road NW8
The Elms, Kingston-on-Thames
5 Greenaway Gardens, NW3
Malvern Terrace, N1
2 Millfield Place, N6
17 Park Place Villas, Little
  Venice, W2
Southwood Lodge, N6
The Water Garden,
  Kingston-on-Thames
16 May Sunday
77 Copers Cope Road,
  Beckenham
Hall Grange, Shirley, Croydon
37 Heath Drive, NW3
Hornbeams, Stanmore
3 Radnor Gardens, TW1
40 St Margaret's Road, E12
South London Botanical
  Institute, SE24
36 Staveley Road, W4
22 May Saturday
Highwood Ash, NW7
23 May Sunday
Chiswick Mall, W4
49 & 51 Etchingham Park Road,
  N3
17 Fulham Park Gardens, SW6
117 Hamilton Terrace, NW8
133 Haverstock Hill, NW3
Highwood Ash, NW7
22 Loudoun Road, NW8
15 Norcott Road, N16

30 May Sunday
29 Deodar Road, SW15
Myddelton House, EN2
33 Upper Park Road, Kingston
66 Wallingford Avenue, W10
31 May Monday
Tarn, Oxhey Drive
5 June Saturday
Lambeth Community Care
Centre
Trinity Hospice, SW4
6 June Sunday
Barbican Conservatory EC2
Barnes Gardens, Barnes, SW13
54 Burnfoot Avenue, SW6
Cecil Road Gardens, N10
The Coach House, SW6
Eccleston Square, SW1
Highgate Village 1, N6
Lambeth Community Care Centre
26 Loughborough Park, SW9
52 Mount Park Road, W5
7 St George's Road, Twickenham
Trinity Hospice, SW4
Trumpeters' House and Lodge
Garden
10 June Thursday
12a Selwood Place, SW7
13 June Sunday
Barbican Conservatory, EC2
43 Brodrick Road, Wandsworth
Common, SW17
108 Camden Mews, NW1
Canonbury Gardens, N1
4 Cliff Road, NW1
43 Hill Top, NW11
10 Lawn Road, NW3
Little Lodge, Thames Ditton
4 Macaulay Road, SW4
Museum of Garden History,
Tradescant Trust, SE1
40 St Margaret's Road, E12
Southwood Lodge, N6
17 June Thursday
The Bow House, Barnet
18 June Friday
The Bow House, Barnet
19 June Saturday
The Bow House, Barnet

14 & 15 Lawrence Street, SW3
20 June Sunday
28 Barnsbury Square, N1
The Bow House, Barnet
15a Buckland Crescent, NW3
101 Cheyne Walk, SW10
82 Evelyn Avenue, Ruislip
17 Fulham Park Gardens, SW6
22 Gayton Road, NW3
Highgate Village 11, N6
Leyborne Park Gardens
Ruislip Gardens, Ruislip
7 St Albans Grove, W8
7 St George's Road,
Twickenham
33 Upper Park Road, Kingston
3 Wellgarth Road, NW11
24 June Thursday
The Bow House, Barnet.
25 June Friday
The Bow House, Barnet
26 June Saturday
The Bow House, Barnet
27 June Sunday
The Bow House, Barnet
Goldsborough, 112 Westcombe
Park Road, Blackheath
21a The Little Boltons, SW10
95 North Road, Kew
Ormeley Lodge, Richmond
Regents College, NW1
Trumpeters' House & Lodge
Garden
1 July Thursday
The Bow House, Barnet
2 July Friday
The Bow House, Barnet
3 July Saturday
The Bow House, Barnet
4 July Sunday
The Bow House, Barnet
24 Grove Terrace, NW5
8 July Thursday
The Bow House, Barnet
9 July Friday
The Bow House, Barnet
10 July Saturday
The Bow House, Barnet
29 Mostyn Road, SW19

11 July Sunday
The Bow House, Barnet
17 Fulham Park Gardens, SW6
22 Gayton Road, NW3
5 Greenaway Gardens, NW3
15 Langbourne Avenue, N6
29 Mostyn Road, SW19
Flat 1, 1F Oval Road
35 Perrymead Street, SW6
3 Radnor Gardens, TW1
15 Upper Grotto Road,
Strawberry Hill
7 West Eaton Place, SW1
10 Wildwood Road, NW11
17 July Saturday
27 Wood Vale, N10
18 July Sunday
15 Norcott Road, N16
11 Ranulf Road, NW2
27 Wood Vale, N10
24 July Saturday
239a Hook Road, Chessington
Trinity Hospice, SW4
25 July Sunday
29 Addison Avenue, W11
37 Heath Drive, NW3
239a Hook Road, Chessington
Trinity Hospice, SW4
31 July Saturday
30 Hercies Road, Hillingdon
1 August Sunday
30 Hercies Road, Hillingdon
57 St Quintin Avenue, W10
22 August Sunday
1 Lister Road, E11
29 August Sunday
Myddelton House, EN2
South London Botanical Institute,
SE24
18 September Saturday
Trinity Hospice, SW4
19 September Sunday
17 Fulham Park Gardens, SW6
Trinity Hospice, SW4
3 October Sunday
The Water Gardens,
Kingston-on-Thames
31 October Sunday
Chelsea Physic Garden, SW3

DESCRIPTIONS OF GARDENS

29 Addison Avenue, W11 ✗ (Mr & Mrs D B Nicholson)
No entry for cars from Holland Park Avenue; approach via
Norland Square and Queensdale Rd. Station: Holland
Park. Bus 12, 94. Prizewinning garden 30ft × 40ft, dense-
ly planted; phlox a speciality. Subject of articles in Tradi-
tional Homes 1990 and Living Magazine 1991. Adm £1
Chd 50p (Share to the Tradescant Trust). Sun July 25
(2-6)

The Anchorage see Kent

Barbican Conservatory, EC2 &✗ Silk Street, nearest
tube station Barbican and Moorgate. City of London's largest conservatory, part of the Barbican Centre; collection
of temporate plants including palms, orchids and climbers. Large collection of cactus and succulents with many
rare varieties. Time allowed approx 1½ hours, but many
other gardens with interesting plants to be seen in the locality. TEAS in restaurant. Adm 80p OAP/Chd 60p Family
(2 adults, up to 4 chd) £2.25. Sats, Suns, Bank Hols all
year. Telephone Operational Services Department 071 638
4141 for opening times. For NGS Suns June 6, 13
(12-5.30)

Barnes Gardens Barnes, SW13. *Adm £4 for 5 gardens of £1 each garden, OAP £2 for 5 gardens or 50p each garden, Chd free each garden. Sun June 6 (2-5)*

¶65 Castelnau, Barnes ✲ (Prof & Mrs George Teeling Smith) Underground to Hammersmith, the Buses 9A, 33, 72, 283 to Castelnau Library. No 65 Castelnau is 100yds S of library and on the same side of the rd. Two Londoners' idea of a country garden. Herbaceous border, roses, shrubs and lawn, creeper clad boundary walls, and, behind a tall clipped hedge, a little kitchen garden with narrow box edged beds where vegetables and flowers for cutting are grown.

29 Lonsdale Road ✲ (Mr & Mrs R Morris) Over Hammersmith Bridge first R or Underground Hammersmith. Bus 9, 33, 72. ⅓-acre south facing walled garden with York terrace. Designed to give all year interest. A plantsman's garden with herbaceous borders. Old English roses, clematis, peonies, iris, lilies and flowering shrubs, lavender walk with spring bulbs and hostas. *(2-5.30)*

26 Nassau Road ♿❀ (Captain & Mrs Anthony Hallett) 26 Nassau Road lies midway between the Thames and Barnes Pond and is approached via Lonsdale Road or Church Road in Barnes. Long, slim, terraced garden with tallest wisteria in Barnes, shrouded on all sides by weigela, philadelphus, pittosporum, chaemomeles, ceanothus with borders of hebe, cistus, rose, delphiniums, potentilla and spiraea. 200ft of dense green and gold but freaks of misplanted colour add to the confusion. Plants for sale

8 Queen's Ride ♿✲ (His Honour Judge White & Mrs White) Train: Barnes Station, turn R down Rocks Lane, then L along Queen's Ride. Bus, 22 terminus at Putney Hospital; 3 minutes walk W along Queen's Ride. House is at the junction of Queen's Ride and St Mary's Grove. ⅔-acre garden facing Barnes Common. Croquet lawn with herbaceous and mixed borders and a small history of the rose garden. TEA

¶23 Westmorland Road, Barnes ✲❀ (Mr & Mrs Norman Moore). From Hammersmith take Bus 9, 33 or 72 to the Red Lion. Turn L into Ferry Rd then L at the Xrds. Small harrow garden relying on flowering shrubs to provide year round interest and harmonious colour. Raised terrace and steps leading to lawn. *(Share to St Mary's Barnes Churchyard)*

28 Barnsbury Square, N1 ✲ (F T Gardner Esq) Islington N. 1¾m N of King's Cross off Thornhill Rd. Bus stop: Islington Town Hall, Upper St or Offord Rd, Caledonian Rd, 10 mins. Small prize-winning Victorian garden; gazebo; pond; grotto; roses, shrubs, plants of interest throughout year. *Adm £1 Chd free (Share to Homerton Hospital, CMRF). Sun June 20 (2-6)*

39 Boundary Road, NW8 ✲ (Hermoine Berton) St John's Wood. Between Finchley Rd and Abbey Rd. Buses 13, 113, 82, 46, 159; ask for Boundary Rd or 6 min walk between Swiss Cottage and St John's Wood station. Unusual walled garden closely planted to provide wild life sanctuary for birds, frogs, newts, toads, squirrels; accent on foliage, texture, fern and perfume; includes ponds, waterfall and rocks. As seen on Gardeners World. *Adm £1 Chd 20p (Share to London Lighthouse Aids Centre). Sun May 9 (2-6)*

The Bow House ♿✲ (Pauline & John Brown) 35, Wood Street, Barnet. In the centre of town, close to the Parish Church. Nearest underground – High Barnet, Northern Line. Buses to door (84a, 107, 234, 263, 307). Delightful old world walled garden of C17 listed house, ornamental pool. York stone terrace, pergola with roses and wide selection of plants and shrubs. An exhibition and sale of sculpture for the garden and paintings in the Bow House Gallery. *Adm £1 OAPs/Chd 50p. Thurs to Suns June 17 to July 11 (Thurs to Sats 10-5) (Suns 2-5)*

¶43 Brodrick Road, SW17 ✲ (Helen Yemm) Wandsworth Common. Brodrick Rd is approx 1m due S of Wandsworth Bridge, running across Trinity Rd just beyond the traffic lights at Bellvue Rd, and the end of Wandsworth Common. Some 110ft in length this tranquil town garden is surrounded by mature trees. Its length is broken by a bank of shrubs and a pond, overhung by an ancient apple tree. Elsewhere there is a mixture of flowering shrubs, herbaceous planting and colourful pots with clematis and rambling roses everywhere you look. The garden feels distinctly un-urban and there are some interesting examples of shade planting. *Adm £1 Chd 50p. Sun June 13 (2-6)*

15a Buckland Crescent, NW3 ♿✲❀ (Lady Barbirolli) Swiss Cottage Tube. Bus: 46, 13 (6 mins) or Hampstead Hoppa (request stop nearby). ⅓-acre; interesting collection of shrubs and trees in well-designed garden featured in Country Life Nov 88, also in books 'Private Gardens of London' by Arabella Lennox Boyd and 'Town Gardens' by Caroline Boisset. *Adm £1 Chd over 12 50p (Share to Befrienders International, the Samaritans Worldwide). Sun June 20 (2.30-6.30)*

54 Burnfoot Avenue, SW6 ✲ (Lady Jocelyn) nearest tube Parson's Green, then walk W on Fulham Rd, R up Munster Rd, 3rd street on L of Munster Rd. 14 bus along Fulham Rd. directions as above; 11 bus along Dawes Rd and walk down through Filmer Rd. 74 bus along Fulham Palace Rd walk through to Burnfoot Ave. Small walled paved garden 20′ × 30′ with raised beds, the emphasis on leaf shapes and colours; fruit trees; climbing plants; frequently changing due to deaths and new ideas; the garden is used as an extra room of the house. *Adm 70p (Share to St Joseph's Hospice Hackney). Sun June 6 (2-5)*

108 Camden Mews, NW1 ♿✲❀ (A Dougall) Located off York Way but beware of one way system. Distant tube stations; Camden and Caledonian Rd. Buses C12 10 29 253; designed on 3 levels this miniature garden is laid with York stone to provide floors, seating and a table; mirrors reflect light into dark corners and a small lawn accommodates one supine sunbather. Alpines, climbers and assorted thymes carry out their duties valiantly. TEAS (inc waffles). *Combined adm with* **4 Cliff Rd** *£1.50 Chd free. Sun June 13 (2.30-6)*

Canonbury Gardens ✲❀ Station: Highbury & Islington. Bus: 4, 19, 30, 43, 104, 279 to Highbury Corner or Islington Town Hall. A1 runs through Canonbury Sq. *Combined adm £3 or 90p each garden Chd £1.50 or 45p each garden. Sun June 13 (2-6)*

37 Alwyne Road &☆✿ (Mr & Mrs J Lambert) Bordering the New River Walk, surprisingly rural views and enclosed formal garden; old-fashioned roses, lilies, unpredictable pots. A garden writer's garden. TEAS (Share to TEAR Fund)

Canonbury House & (John Addey Esq) Canonbury Place. Replanted over the last five years the garden is maturing well; mulberry tree planted in 1619 by Sir Francis Bacon; most historic setting in Islington

46 Canonbury Square (Miss Peggy Carter) Walled garden lying behind 2 end-of-terrace Georgian houses with statuary; pool; waterfall; spring blossom. *Adm £1.50 Chd 75p for 2 gardens; 90p Chd 45p per garden. Also on Sun April 18 (1.30-5.30)*

60 St Paul's Road ☆✿ (John & Pat Wardroper) Typical back-of-terrace walled garden, planted chiefly for shade, and to create a quiet, green enclosed atmosphere just off a busy street; designed on 3 levels with paved patios, border of flowering shrubs. *Adm £1.50 Chd 75p for 2 gardens; 90p Chd 45p per garden. Also open Sun April 18 (1.30-5.30)*

¶81B St Peters Street, N1 ☆ (Gay Richardson) A1 to Islington at the triangular Green, turn down narrow street between the public house and petrol station on the S side of the green. Over the bump and the house is on L side of the rd just after the shops. An enclosed courtyard garden turned into a tiny haven with an oriental flavour; strong use of ericaceous plants in pots full of scents, shapes and textures. Unusual specimens incl several iris, japonicas and dwarf species rhododendrons. Winner of Angel Association garden prize and prize winner in Islington Gardeners Courtyard section, 1992. By appt **Tel 071 359 5329**

Capel Manor Farm and Gardens see Hertfordshire

Cecil Road, N10 ☆ Muswell Hill. Just off Alexandra Park Rd between Muswell Hill and the North Circular Rd. Teas in aid of St Andrew's church, vicarage garden or church hall if wet. *Combined adm 70p Chd free. Sun June 6 (2-5)*
> **5 Cecil Road** (Ben Loftus Esq) 70' × 20' garden designer's peaceful garden; old apple trees, roses, species foxgloves, masses of lilies, paeonies, unusual hellebores, ferns, bulbs and evergreens; many scented plants, rich and varied foliage
> **52 Cecil Road** (Mr & Mrs A Pask) Family garden with 2 long raised beds. Many climbing plants, clematis, jasmines, akebia, passiflora etc, variegated foliage for flower arranging; flowering shrubs and perennials. Also very small pond

Chelsea Physic Garden, SW3 &☆✿ (Trustees of the Garden) 66 Royal Hospital Rd, Chelsea. Bus 239 (Mon-Sat) alight outside garden (Cheyne Court). Station: Sloane Square (10-mins); Cars: restricted parking nr garden weekdays; free Sundays; or in Battersea Park (across river) weekdays. Entrance in Swan Walk. Second oldest Botanic Garden in UK; 3.8 acres; medicinal and herb garden, perfumery border; family order beds; collection of over 5,000 trees, shrubs and herbaceous plants, many rare or unusual. TEAS. *Adm £2.50 Students/Chd £1.30. Suns April 4 to Oct 31 (2-5); Weds April 7 to Oct 27 (2-5); also in Chelsea Flower Show week Mon-Fri May 24-28 and in Chelsea Festival Week Mon-Fri June 14-18 (12-5). For NGS Suns April 4, Oct 31 (2-5)*

101 Cheyne Walk, SW10 ☆ (Malcolm Hillier Esq) The garden is situated just to the W of Battersea Bridge on Cheyne Walk. Parking on Sunday is possible in Millman St, Beaufort St and in the wider parts of Cheyne Walk with a single yellow line or on residents spaces. The garden, in three sections, is long and narrow 115ft × 18ft with a terrace leading up through ferns and topiary to a winding path and then onto a raised pillared arbour. There is a mixture of old roses, shrubs and hardy perennials with many interesting container plantings. TEAS. *Adm £1 Chd free. Sun June 20 (1-6)*

Chiswick Mall, W4 ☆✿ Station: Stamford Brook (District Line). Bus: 290 to Young's Corner from Hammersmith. By car A4 Westbound turn off at Eyot Gdns S, then right into Chiswick Mall. *Suns April 25 (2-6), May 23 (2-6.30)*
> **16 Eyot Gardens** ☆ (Dianne Farris) Between Great West Road and river, at junction of Chiswick Mall and Hammersmith Terrace. If coming from outside London go down to river at Hogarth roundabout. Very small town garden at end of terrace of houses. Front has mostly yellow, blue and white flowers, a lot of pink in the back garden with raised beds and a little terrace, wisteria and camellias. Many unusual plants. TEAS. *Adm £1 Chd free*
> **Walpole House** ☆✿ (Mr & Mrs Jeremy Benson) Plantsman's garden; specie and tree peonies; water garden; spring flowers. Features in 'The Englishmans Garden'. Mid C16 to early C18 house, once home of Barbara Villiers, Duchess of Cleveland. Seeds and some plants for sale. *Adm £1 Chd 20p (Share to St Mary's Convent & Nursing Home, The Abbeyfield Chiswick Society Ltd)*

4 Cliff Road, NW1 ☆ (Ewen Henderson Esq) Cliff Road is between Camden Park Rd and York Way. A 60' × 20' garden of tone, texture and ambiguity; containing owner's sculpture and found objects. *Combined adm £1.50 with* **108 Camden Mews**. *Sun June 13 (2.30-6)*

The Coach House, SW6 ☆✿ (Dr John Newton) Landridge Rd. Nearest underground station Putney Bridge. Across New Kings Rd into Burlington Rd, R into Rigault Rd. The garden is at the end of Rigualt Rd behind the white wall. Small 34' × 36' walled garden with pond, fountain; herbaceous borders, surrounding small lawn designed to have a year round flowering. *Adm 70p Chd 30p. Sun June 6 (2-6)*

¶77 Copers Cope Road ☆✿ (Dr H F Oakeley) Beckenham. Opp the end of Brackley Rd. Nearest BR Station (3 min walk) is New Beckenham (Charing Cross to Hayes Line). Small town garden with rhododendrons, acers, azaleas, mixed with herbaceous and rockery plants 40' × 200'. Large greenhouse with National Collection of lycastes and anguloas. 3 gold medal displays at Chelsea Flower Show. TEA. *Adm £1 Chd 50p. Sun May 16 (2-6)*

> **Regular Openers.** Too many days to include in diary. Usually there is a wide range of plants giving year-round interest. See head of county section for the name and garden description for times etc.

29 Deodar Road, SW15 ᴥ᪷ (Peter & Marigold Assinder) Putney. Off Putney Bridge Rd Bus: 14, 22, 37, 74, 80, 85, 93, 220. Tubes: Putney Bridge and East Putney. Small garden 130ft × 25ft running down to Thames with lovely view. Camellias, wide range of variegated shrubs, hardy geraniums. Featured in Private Gardens of London by Arabella Lennox Boyd 1990. Cuttings and visits at other times by arrangement **Tel 081 788 7976**. TEA. *Adm £1 Chd 50p (Share to Royal Hospital & Home Putney SW15). Suns April 25, May 30 (2-5)*

Eccleston Square, SW1 ᴥ᪷ Central London; just off Belgrave Road near Victoria Station, parking allowed on Suns. 3-acre square was planned by Cubitt in 1828. The present Garden Committee have worked intensively over the last 12 years to see what can be created despite the inner city problems of drought, dust, fumes, shade and developers. Within the formal structure the garden is sub-divided into mini-gardens inc camellia, iris, rose, fern, and herb garden. TEAS. *Adm £1 Chd 50p. Suns April 18, June 6 (2-5.30)*

Edwardes Sq, W8 ᴥ᪷ (Edwardes Sq Garden Committee) Edwardes Sq is off Kensington High Street. Accessible by bus and underground. Car parking is allowed on Sundays. 3-acres laid out circa 1815. Spring flowering trees, shrubs and bulbs. *Adm £1 Chd 50p. Sun April 25 (2-6)*

The Elms ᴥ᪷ (Dr & Mrs R Rawlings) Kingston-on-Thames entry via Manorgate Road. 1m E Kingston on A308. Buses to Kingston Hospital: LT 213, 85, 57, 71; G line 714, 715, 718. BR Norbiton Station 100yds. Enter via garages in Manorgate Rd which is off A308 at foot of Kingston Hill. Small (55' × 25') compact town-house rear garden, of special interest to horticulturists and plant lovers. Truly a collector's garden with numerous rare and unusual plants, particularly featuring rhododendrons, magnolias, camellias, dwarf conifers and a wide range of evergreen and deciduous shrubs. Small trees, herbaceous, ground cover plants, a two-level pool with geyser and well planted margins, roses, clematis and other choice and tender climbers, alpine trays are also featured. This small garden even bears some fruit namely, plum, pear, and soft fruits. Seeds and plants available. The garden has been featured on the radio and in various publications. TEAS in aid of Home Farm Trust and Princess Alice Hospice. *Adm £1 Chd 50p. Sats, Suns March 20, 21; April 17, 18; May 8, 9 (2-5). Groups by appt* **Tel 081 546 7624**

49 & 51 Etchingham Park Rd, N3 ᴥ᪷ (Robert Double, Gilbert Cook and Diane & Alan Langleben) Finchley. Off Ballards Lane overlooking Victoria Park. Station: Finchley Central. 2 rear gardens. ⅝-acre; lawn, small orchard, shrubs, large selection of hostas. Sculpture by Wm Mitchell. Exhibition and sale of water colour paintings by Robert Double. TEAS. *Adm 50p Chd free. Sun May 23 (2-6)*

Fenton House, NW3 ᴥ (The National Trust) 300yds NNW of Hampstead Underground Station. 600yds S of Heath by Jack Straw's Castle. 1½-acre walled garden in its first decade of development. It is on three levels with compartments concealed by yew hedges and containing different plantings, some still in the experimental stage. The herbaceous borders are being planned to give year-round interest while the recently brick paved sunken rose garden is already donning the patina of age. The formal lawn area contrasts agreeably with the rustic charm of the orchard and kitchen garden. *Adm £1.50 Chd 50p. Sun April 18 (11-6)*

Frogmore Gardens see Berkshire

17 Fulham Park Gardens, SW6 ᴥ (A Noel Esq) Putney Bridge Tube. Refer to A-Z. Up Kings Road L at Threshers Off-licence, (Elysium St.) into Fulham Park Gardens. Turn R, on R hand side. 40ft × 17ft romantic silver and white garden, with interesting variety of plants in harmoniously designed form. An oasis of peace in a hostile environment. Featured in Sunday Times and on ITV. *Adm £1.50. Suns May 23, June 20, July 11, Sept 19 (2.30-6)*

¶22 Gayton Road, NW3 ᴥ (Mr & Mrs C Newman) Nearest Tube Hampstead, then down Hampstead High Street L into Gayton Rd. A long narrow Victorian garden, approx 60ft long. Brick paved. Shrubs, roses and unusual perennials. *Adm £1. Suns June 20, July 11 (1-5)*

¶Goldsborough, Blackheath, SE3 ᴥ᪷ 112 Westcombe Park Rd. Located between Greenwich Village Centre and The Standard Blackheath. N of Blackheath Heath and E of Greenwich Park. Nearest BR Westcombe Park (10 mins walk) or Maze Hill (15 mins walk). Buses to the Standard from Central London and surrounding areas. Hoppa buses stop directly outside. Westcombe Park Rd situated in A-Z of London. Car parking available. Community garden for close care and nursing home residents. Approx ½ acre of landscaped gardens, incl walkways of rose-covered pergolas; fish ponds; herbaceous borders and colourful annuals. A very sheltered and peaceful garden. TEAS. *Adm £1 Chd 50p. Sun June 27 (1.30-5)*

5 Greenaway Gardens, NW3 ᴥ (Mrs Marcus) Tube equidistant (½ mile) Hampstead or Finchley Road Stations. Buses: Finchley Road, West End Lane stop, nos. 13, 2, 113. From Finchley Road, turn up Frognal Lane, 2nd on left. Unusually large and varied London garden interestingly landscaped on three levels. York stone terrace with variety of climbing plants on sunny back wall of house; 2-level water feature; swimming pool; steps to large lawn surrounded by borders with wide variety of trees, shrubs and herbaceous perennials, decorative urns and furniture. Partially suitable for wheelchairs. TEAS July 11 only. *Adm 80p Chd 30p. Suns May 9, July 11 (2-6)*

24 Grove Terrace, NW5 ᴥ (Lucy Gent & Malcolm Turner) N Kentish Town; off Highgate Rd, E side. Entry to garden via Grove Terrace Mews. Long narrow garden (16' × 120') with a wide range of plants especially for shade behind well known Georgian terrace. *Adm £1 Chd 50p. Sun April 25, July 4 (2-6). Also by appt* **Tel 071 485 4764**

By Appointment Gardens. See head of county section

¶**Hall Grange** &✿ (Methodist Home for the Aged) Croydon. Situated in Shirley Church Rd near to junction with Upper Shirley Rd. From N leave A232 at junction of Shirley Rd and Wickham Rd. From S leave A212 at junction of Gravell Hill and Shirley Hills Rd. The garden was laid out circa 1913 by Rev William Wilkes secretary to the RHS and breeder of the Shirley Poppy. Approx 5 acres of natural heathland is planted with azaleas, rhododendrons, heathers and shrubs and remains unchanged. A grassy area contains many wild flowers and is mown only once a year to permit natural reproduction. No parking at garden. TEAS. *Adm £1 Chd free. Sun May 16 (2-6)*

117 Hamilton Terrace, NW8 &✿ (Mrs K Herbert and the Tenants Association). Hamilton Terrace is parallel with Maida Vale to the E. Buses from Marble Arch 16, 16a, 8, go up Edgeware Road to Maida Vale. Alight at Elgin Avenue, cross Maida Vale and go up Abercorn Place. 117 is to the L. There is room in Hamilton Terrace to park cars. 117 is the opp end of Hamilton Terrace from Lords nearly opp St Mark's Church. This is a large garden for London. It has been opened in May and July. This year it is being opened again in May. The lawn at the back is kept partly wild with different grasses and wild flowers. There is a tiny garden in memory of Dame Anna Neagle who lived in the house. There is a standard rose near the house given in her memory. TEA. *Adm £1 Chd 20p (Share to the Spastics Society). Sun May 23 (2-6)*

Harewood, Chalfont St Giles, see Buckinghamshire

133 Haverstock Hill, NW3 ✿❀ (Mrs Catherine Horwood). Belsize Park Tube Station turn L out of station. Buses C11, 168 (Haverstock Arms stop). Prizewinning 120ft long narrow garden divided into rooms; shrubs; old roses; herbaceous; climbers with an emphasis on scented plants; pond. Featured in Country Life and Wonderful Window-boxes. Highly Commended in The Gardener Magazine Gardener of the Year competition. *Adm £1 Chd free. Sun May 23 (2.30-5.30)*

37 Heath Drive, NW3 &✿❀ (Mr & Mrs C Caplin) Station: Finchley Rd; buses: 2, 13 & 113 Heath Drive. Many uncommon plants; lawn; pond; rockery; ferns. Unusual treatment of fruit trees, greenhouse and conservatory. 1982, 1983, 1987, 1988, 1989, 1991 winner of Frankland Moore Trophy. Featured in Arabella Lennox-Boyd's Private Gardens of London. TEAS. *Adm £1 Chd 50p. Suns May 16, July 25 (2.30-6)*

30 Hercies Road &✿❀ (Mr & Mrs J Gates) Hillingdon. From London West on A40 to Master Brewer Motel, N Hillingdon 1st L after traffic lights No 30 is on the R.h.s. From Oxford E on A40 to Uxbridge, roundabout past junc 1 Swakeleys turn R onto B483 Park Rd. 1st L Honeycroft Hill continue into Hercies Rd. By tube Hillingdon (Swakeleys) turn R over bridge. Front garden: New parterre and screed garden, leading to a long narrow mature cottage style back garden, patio with tubs and vine; herbaceous planting, wild garden with trees, shrubs and rhododendrons. TEAS. *Adm 50p Chd 10p. Sats May 1, July 31; Sun Aug 1 (10-5)*

Highgate Village I, N6 &✿ The Grove is between Highgate West Hill & Hampstead Lane. Stations: Archway or Highgate (Northern Line, Barnet trains) Bus: 210, 271 to Highgate Village. TEAS June 6 only. *Combined adm £1 OAPs/Chd 50p. Mon April 12, Sun June 6 (2-5)*
  6 The Grove (Mr & Mrs G Minden) ⅓-acre lawn, raised border, spectacular views from Elizabethan 'round' over Hampstead Heath
  7 The Grove ✿ (The Hon Mrs Judith Lyttelton) ½-acre designed for maximum all-year-round interest with minimum upkeep

Highgate Village II, N6 ✿ The Grove is between Highgate West Hill & Hampstead Lane Stations: Archway or Highgate (Northern Line, Barnet trains). Bus: 210, 271 to Highgate Village. Tea Lauderdale House & Kenwood. *Adm 75p each garden Chd free. Sun June 20 (2-5)*
  4 The Grove (Cob Stenham Esq) 2-tiered with formal upper garden; view across Heath; orchard in lower garden
  5 The Grove (Mr & Mrs A J Hines) Newly-designed garden on 2 levels

Highwood Ash, NW7 ❀ (Mr & Mrs R Gluckstein) Highwood Hill, Mill Hill. From London via A41 (Watford Way) to Mill Hill Circus; turn right up Lawrence St; at top bear left up Highwood Hill; house at top on right. Station: Edgware (Northern Line) Bus 251 (Sat only). 3¼-acre inc rose garden, shrub and herbaceous borders, rhododendrons, azaleas, lake with waterfall, a mixture of formal and informal. TEAS. *Adm £1 Chd 50p. Sat, Sun, May 22, 23 (2-6)*

43 Hill Top, NW11 ✿❀ (Prof & Mrs J E Webb) Golders Green 1m N, Bus: 102 alight Midholm. ⅓-acre garden, lawns; with small pond; large rockery; herbaceous border; rose bed and shrubbery. Productive vegetable and fruit garden. TEAS. *Adm £1 Chd free (Share to North London Hospice). Sun June 13 (2-6)*

1 Hocroft Avenue, NW2 &✿❀ (Dr & Mrs Derek Bunn) 113 bus (stop at Cricklewood Lane) Travelling N from the Finchley Road on the Hendon Way (A41), take the third turn on the L. This is Hocroft Avenue. Easy parking. Interesting front garden with new black and white bed featured in 'the Independent'. Prizewinning plantsman's garden with all year round interest. Mixed borders with wide variety of planting against a background of trees. Unusual plants for sale. Home-made TEAS. *Adm £1 Chd free (Share to Hampstead Church Music Trust). Sun, Mon May 2, 3 (2-6)*

239a Hook Road &✿ (Derek & Dawn St Romaine) Chessington. A3 from London, turn L at Hook underpass onto A243 Hook Rd, Garden is approx 300yds on L. parking available. Bus 71 from Kingston and Surbiton to North Star public house. A ¼-acre developing garden divided into two parts. The potager is now complete and has been featured in Country Living and the Gardener magazines; the flower garden; pond and rockery are to be redesigned. TEAS. *Adm £1 OAP's/Chd 50p (Share Leatherhead Night Shelter). Sat, Sun July 24, 25 (2-6)*

Hornbeams &% (Dr & Mrs R B Stalbow) Priory Drive, Stanmore. 5m SE of Watford; underground: Stanmore; Priory Drive private rd off Stanmore Hill (A4140 Stanmore-Bushey Heath Rd). ½ acre; flowering shrubs, alpines, hardy cyclamen, species tulips; unusual plants; vegetable garden; vine; pool; greenhouse, conservatory. Lemonade & biscuits. *Adm £1 Chd free (Plant proceeds to Jerusalem Botanic Garden). Sun May 16 (2.30-6)*

Lambeth Community Care Centre, SE11 &% Monkton Street. Lambeth North tube, turn onto Kennington Rd until Brook Drive, then R between bakery and office and through passage to Monkton St or drive through St Mary's Gardens. Elephant & Castle tube, cut through behind swimming baths to opposite end of Brook Drive, L into passage through Sullivan Rd. Buses: 3, 159, 109 Kennington Rd; 176, 12, 63, 68 Elephant & Castle. ⅔-acre garden ideal for people in wheelchairs to see all aspects of garden. Mixed shrubs, trees, small rose garden, herbs, interesting walkways and mixed borders. Part of award winning hospital designed by Edward Cullinan Architects. Indoor planted area also open. 1992 winner in London Hospital Gardens Competition. TEAS. *Adm 75p OAP/Chd 75p (Share to St. Thomas's Trustees for the garden). Sat, Sun June 5, 6 (2-5)*

Lambeth Palace, SE1 &% (The Archbishop of Canterbury & Mrs Carey) Waterloo main line and underground, Westminster, Lambeth and Vauxhall tubes all about 10 mins walk. 3, 10, 44, 76, 77, 159, 170, 507 buses go near garden. Entry to garden on Lambeth Palace Rd (not at gatehouse) 2nd largest private garden in London. Land in hand of Archbishops of Canterbury since end C12. Work in garden carried out over last 100 years but significant renewal has taken place during last 6 years; restored rose walk, new border beneath wall by Beth Chatto, herb garden, shrub border, wild garden, rhododendrons, spring bulbs and camellias. TEA in aid of Lambeth Boy Scouts. *Adm £2 OAP/Chd 10-16 £1 (Share to Lambeth Fund). Sat April 3 (2-5)*

5 Langbourne Avenue, N6 % (R P St J Partridge) Holly Lodge Estate. Off Highgate West Hill. Entrance by car via Swains Lane. A steeply rising garden behind a semi-detached house, full of dramatic foliage interspersed with flowers; large leaved plants such as bergenia, ciliata, melianthus, hydrangea aspera, gunnera and many others, create an impression of seclusion and mystery in a small garden. *Adm £1. Sun July 11 (2.30-5.30)*

2 Lansdowne Rd, W11 & (The Lady Amabel Lindsay) Holland Park. Turn N off Holland Park Ave nr Holland Park Station; or W off Ladbroke Grove ½-way along. Bus: 2, 88, GL 711, 715. Bus stop & station: Holland Park, 4 mins. Medium-sized fairly wild garden; border, climbing roses, shrubs; mulberry tree 200 yrs old. *Adm 80p Chd 10p. Wed May 5 (2-6)*

0 Lawn Road, NW3 &% (Mrs P Findlay) Tube to Belsize Park or go up Haverstock Hill. Turn R at Haverstock Arms then L. House 200yds on R, with blue door. ⅓-acre approx; uniquely curvaceous design of intersecting circles, set in rectangular format. Garden very heavily stocked; many unusual plants. *Adm £1 Chd 50p. Sun June 13 (2.30-6)*

14 & 15 Lawrence Street, SW3 (Miss Esther Darlington & John Casson Esq) Between King's Road and the river down Old Church Street S from King's Road, turn L round the statue of Sir Thomas More then L (behind garden) into Lawrence Street. Gardens at top of hill on L. Nearest tubes: Sloane Square and South Kensington. Prize winning small Chelsea cottage type gardens, old-fashioned flowers, clematis, roses and some unusual plants. Plants to cover each season. House built c1790, not open except for access to garden. *Combined adm £1.50 Chd 75p (Share to Chelsea Physic Garden). Sat June 19 (2-6)*

Leyborne Park Gardens % Two minute walk from Kew Gardens station. Take exit signposted Kew Gardens. On leaving station forecourt bear R past shops. Leyborne Park is 1st rd on R. Bus 391 to Kew Gdns station. Bus 65, to Kew Gdns. Victoria Gate. Access by car is from Sandycombe Rd. TEAS. *Combined adm £1 Chd free (Share to Arthritis and Rheumatism Council for Research). Sun June 20 (2-5.30)*
> **36 Leyborne Park** (David & Frances Hopwood) 120ft long mature, family garden; architect designed for minimum upkeep with maximum foliage effects; patio; imaginative children's play area; huge eucalyptus. TEAS
> **38 Leyborne Park** & (Mr & Mrs A Sandall) 120ft long organic family garden; lawn with mixed borders; containers; long established vine; alliums, euphorbias, eryngiums, scented pelargoniums, bamboos; small vegetable plot
> **40 Leyborne Park** (Debbie Pointon-Taylor) 120ft long garden; heather and conifer garden; lawn and mixed borders; mature shrubs; patio with containers and herbs

1 Lister Road, E11 %& (Myles Challis Esq) Leytonstone underground station (central line). 5mins to High Rd Leytonstone. Hills garage marks cnr of Lister Rd which is directly off High Rd. Garden designer's unexpected, densely planted sub-tropical garden containing a mixture of tender plants such as Daturas, gingers, cannas, tree ferns, bananas and hardy exotics including gunneras, bamboos, cordylines, phormiums and large leaved perennials in a space unbelievably only 40' × 20'. TEAS. *Adm £1 Chd 50p. Sun Aug 22 (11-5)*

21a The Little Boltons, SW10 %& (Mrs D Capron) Between Fulham and Old Brompton Rd off Tregunter Rd, next to The Boltons. Nearest tube Earls Court, buses 30, 14, 74. 70ft prize winning herbaceous plant collection. Portrayed in the book 'Private Gardens of London' by Arabella Lennox-Boyd. *Adm £1 Chd 25p. Sun June 27 (12-6)*

Little Lodge &% (Mr & Mrs P Hickman) Watts Rd, Thames Ditton (Station 5 mins). A3 from London; after Hook underpass turn left to Esher; at Scilly Isles turn right towards Kingston; after 2nd railway bridge turn left to Thames Ditton village; house opp library after Giggs Hill Green. A cottage style informal garden within 15 miles of central London. Many British native plants. Garden has an atmosphere of tranquillity, featuring plants with subtle colours and fragrance; small brick-pathed vegetable plot. TEAS. *Adm £1 Chd free (Share to Cancer Research). Sun June 13 (11.30-6)*

'There is no doubt that the Yellow Book is invaluable (buy two, one for the car, one for the bedside table); it will make many friends, discover the distilled essence of English gardens, and enjoy traipsing around otherwise totally closed, private domanis' ... *David Wheeler, Hortus*

'For visits to privately-owned gardens, The National Gardens Scheme's famous Yellow Book is undoubtedly the 'Bible' ...'
House & Garden

'Charity begins in the back Garden....I felt a debt of gratitude to the yellow book. We often put our bikes on the train and go into the country to visit two or three gardens on a summer Sunday..'
Anthea Masey, the Independent

'I'm going round other folks' gardens and I advise you to do the same....with the invaluable Yellow Book tucked under your arm....'
Alan Titchmarsh The Daily Mail

'Garden visiting armed with Yellow Book is the summer-long, number one hobby for many of us. Where would we go in the car without it? ...
Harold Lewis, The Citizen

'The season for visiting gardens open to the public is upon us....plan ahead with your diary and the best source of reference ... the little yellow book'
Roddy Llewellyn, The Mail on Sunday

'No car should be without a copy of The Yellow Book...'
Motoring and Leisure

Below Holehird Gardens, Cumbria.
Photograph by Val Corbett.

Right Ivy Cottage,
Glamorgan. *Photograph by
Eric Crichton.*
Below Howard's House, Beds.
Photograph by Juliette Wade.

Opposite Docton Mill, Devon. *Photograph by Juliette Wade.*
Left Hodsock Priory, Notts. *Photograph by Eric Crichton.*
Below and bottom Castle House, Gwent. *Photographs by Eric Crichton and Hugh Palmer.*

Right Knole, Kent. *Photograph by Sheila Orme.*
1993 sees Knole's 60th year of opening for the Scheme.
Below Benington Lordship, Herts. *Photograph by Brian Chapple.*
Opposite top Little Ponton Hall, Lincs. *Photograph by Eric Crichton.*
Opposite bottom Docwra's Manor, Cambs. *Photograph by Hugh Palmer.*

Below Ashwell Lodge, Leicestershire and Rutland. *Photograph by Eric Crichton.*

2 Loudoun Road, NW8 (Ruth Barclay) 3 to 4 min walk ɔ St. John's Wood tube station. Lies between Abbey oad and Finchley Rd serviced by buses, minutes from us stop. Small front garden, well matured, started from cratch 9 years ago. A strong emphasis on design with eaf and flowers subtle colour combination, water, arbour arden within a garden. Back Italianate courtyard, romanc and mysterious. Prizewinner for 4 consecutive years. eatured in a number of gardening books. Most recently own Gardens'. TEAS. *Adm £1 Chd 25p. Sun May 23 2-6.30)*

6 Loughborough Park, SW9 &&& (Marcus Grant & icky Meadows) Off Coldharbour Lane at Loughborough unction. Buses 35, 45 and P4 to end of rd. Tube Brixton. 0 × 30ft garden, westerley aspect, divided into three ections. Circular lawn with mixed borders and some ineresting plants; small wild garden with chickens; vegetble patch. Featured on Gardeners World June 92. TEAS. *dm £1 Chd free (Share to OXFAM). Sun June 6 (2-6)*

Macaulay Road, SW4 &&& (Mr & Mrs Jonathan oss) Clapham Common tube. Buses 88, 77, 77A, 137, 7, 45. Formal shape containing and restraining an exberant plantswoman's amateur collection of unusual and aried shrubs, including many old-fashioned roses, clenatis, silver/grey shrubs, hostas and cistus. Size 80' × 0'. *Adm £1 OAP 50p. Sun June 13 (2-6)*

Malvern Terrace, Barnsbury, N1 & Approach from S via entonville Rd into Penton St, Barnsbury Rd; from N via hornhill Rd opp Albion pub. Tube: Highbury & Islington. us: 19, 30 to Upper St Town Hall. Unique London terace of 1830s houses built on site of Thos Oldfield's dairy nd cricket field. Cottage-style gardens in cobbled cul-deac; music. Home-made TEAS. *Combined adm £1 Chd ree. Sun May 9 (2-5.30)*
  1 Malvern Terrace (Mr & Mrs Martin Leman)
  2 Malvern Terrace (Mr & Mrs K McDowall)
  3 Malvern Terrace (Mr & Mrs A Robertson)
  4 Malvern Terrace (Mr & Mrs P Dacre)
  5 Malvern Terrace (Mr & Mrs J Broad)
  6 Malvern Terrace (Mrs Angela Carr)
  7 Malvern Terrace (Joanna Smith & Mark Vanhegan)
  8 Malvern Terrace (Mr & Mrs R Le Fanu)
  10 Malvern Terrace (Dr & Mrs P Sherwood)

Millfield Place, N6 && Garden is off Highgate West Iill E side of Hampstead Heath. Buses 210, 271 to Highate Village or C2, C12, 214 to Parliament Hill Fields terninus. Nearest train stations Kentish Town, Tufnall Park nd North London BR line to Gospel Oak. 1½-acre spring nd woodland garden with camellias and rhododendrons. ong mixed herbaceous border with some formal bedding chemes; small orchard. TEAS. *Adm £1 Chd 50p. Sun May 9 (2-6)*

29 Mostyn Road SW19 && (Chris & Sue Spencer) Merton Park is 1m N of Wimbledon. From London cross Wimbledon Common, through Wimbledon Village, down Wimbledon Hill into The Broadway. Follow one-way sysem after Wimbledon Station following it round to the R before turning L into Hartfield Rd. Turn R at the end of Hartfield Rd cross level crossing. Mostyn Rd is 3rd on R. Greystones is 200 metres on R. ⅕-acre small garden laid

out by Gertrude Jekyll in 1913 with further plantings added by her between 1913 and 1922. The garden has been restored by the present owners. Re-planting was carried out in 1992 using Jekyll's original plant lists. The garden is far from mature and the owners are still in the process of trying to arrange plantings to Jekyllian principles. The garden has been featured in Traditional Homes and Period House and Its Garden. Also BBC Television's Gardeners' World. TEA. *Adm £1 Chd 50p. Sat, Sun July 10, 11 (2-6)*

52 Mount Park Road, W5 && (Mr & Mrs Paddy O'Hagan) Ealing. 7min walk N from Ealing Broadway station. No 52 is opposite No 71. 100ft × 50ft triangular garden on 2 levels. Designed for wildlife in 1989 by Chris Baines; woodland, pond and bog area. Terrace with interesting pots and architectural plants; dry stream and glass fountain; classical music; conservatory. TEAS in aid of SATFA. *Adm 80p Chd 30p. Sun June 6 (2-6)*

33 Mundania Road, SE22 && (Ms Helen Penn) 63 bus to Honor Oak. Nearest BR station Peckham Rye. 40' × 15' N facing front garden, woodland plants; 100' × 40' S facing back garden. Wide range of herbaceous plants and shrubs, some unusual, herbs and fruit; small pond with native grasses; lax planting style; conservatory with tender plants. *Adm £1 Chd free (Share to National Childcare Campaign). By appt May to June Tel 081 693 4741*

Museum of Garden History, The Tradescant Trust &&& St Mary-at-Lambeth, Lambeth Palace Road, SE1. Bus: 507 Red Arrow from Victoria or Waterloo, alight Lambeth Palace. 7,450 sq ft. replica of C17 garden planted in churchyard with flowers known and grown by John Tradescant. Tombs of the Tradescants and Admiral Bligh of the 'Bounty' in the garden. Opened by HM the Queen Mother in 1983. Museum being established in restored church of St Mary-at-Lambeth saved from demolition by The Trust. TEAS. *Adm £1 OAPs/Chd 50p (Share to Museum of Garden History).* ▲*Sun June 13 (10.30-5)*

Myddelton House &&& (Lee Valley Regional Authority) Enfield. A short distance from A10 Great Cambridge Rd and Bullsmore Lane junction which is 100yds S of junction 25 of M25. Station: Turkey St on Liverpool St Line. The 4-acres of garden were created by Edward A Bowles, author of gardening trilogy 'My Garden in Spring, Summer, Autumn and Winter'. The gardens feature a diverse and unusual plant collection including a large selection of many species and varieties of naturalised bulbs, as well as the National Collection of Award Winning Bearded Irises. The grounds have a large pond with terrace, two conservatories and interesting historical artefacts. TEA and plants for sale on NGS days and Suns only. *Adm £1.50 Concessions 75p. Open every weekday except April 9, May 31, Aug 30, Dec 27 to 31 (10-3.30) and last Sunday in the month (2-5) Feb to Oct. NGS days Mon April 12, Suns May 30, Aug 29 (1-5). No concessions on NGS days and Suns*

> **Regular Openers.** Too many days to include in diary. Usually there is a wide range of plants giving year-round interest. See head of county section for the name and garden description for times etc.

15 Norcott Road, N16 ✿✿ (Amanda & John Welch) Buses 73, 149, 76, 67, 243 (see bus map and A to Z) Clapton or Stoke Newington Stations (Rectory Rd closed Suns). Largish (for Hackney) walled back garden. Pond, fruit trees, herbs, tubs, herbaceous plants especially irises, geraniums and campanulas. TEAS. *Adm 70p Chd 50p (Share to St Josephs Hospice). Suns May 23, July 18 (2-6)*

¶**95 North Road** ✿✿ (Michael Le Fleming Esq) Kew. 500yds S of Kew Gardens Station (District Line & North London Link) on its eastern, down-line side. Exit in North Rd. Buses 391, R68. 100ft garden on a flowing plan with a high wall and interesting mixed planting to disguise the basic plot. Old roses and wisteria; irises; good foliage; a small pond and paved area with urns, pots and conservatory. TEA. *Adm £1 Chd 50p. Sun June 27 (11-6)*

Ormeley Lodge ✿ (Lady Annabel Goldsmith) Ham Gate Avenue, Richmond. From Richmond Park, exit at Ham Gate into Ham Gate Avenue. First house on R. From Richmond A307, 1½m past New Inn on R, first turning on L. House is last on L. Bus: 65. Large walled garden in delightful rural setting on Ham Common. Newly designed formal garden, wide herbaceous borders, box hedges. Walk through to newly planted orchard with wild flowers. Vegetable garden. Secluded swimming pool area, trellised tennis court with roses and climbers. TEA. *Adm £1 Chd 20p. Sun June 27 (3-6)*

Flat 1, 1F Oval Road, NW1 ✿ (Sheila Jackson) Tube station Camden Town. Buses: any bus to Camden Town, Camden High Street C2 and 274 stop very near. Parking can be difficult near centre on Sunday. A small side garden approaches an illustrator's very small hidden back garden approx 24ft × 20ft which abuts the Euston railway line. The garden is stuffed with a great variety of plants, many in pots banked to create interesting shapes and compositions, making use of a variety of levels. *Adm £1 Chd 50p. Suns May 2, July 11 (2-6). Also by appt* Tel **071 267 0655**

17 Park Place Villas, W2 (Little Venice) ✿ (H C Seigal Esq) Park Place Villas is off Maida Ave which runs along Regent's Canal from Maida Vale to Warwick Ave. Station: Warwick Ave. Garden (⅛-acre) is one of an internal square of small gardens each belonging to a single house; rhododendrons, azaleas, woodland plants, alpines in raised beds and sinks; small pond with aquatic and bog plants; grass. *Adm 50p OAPs/Chd free. Sun May 9 (2-6)*

35 Perrymead St, SW6 ✿ (Mr & Mrs Richard Chilton) Fulham. New King's Rd W from Chelsea; 1st on left after Wandsworth Bridge Rd. Stations: Fulham Broadway or Parsons Green; bus 22 from Chelsea; 28 from Kensington. Small paved garden with ornamental feature; surrounded by mature trees. Shrubs, climbers (especially clematis) interspersed with summer planting suitable for shade. *Adm £1 Chd 50p. Sun July 11 (2-6)*

> **By Appointment Gardens.** These owners do not have a fixed opening day usually because they do not like crowds or have insufficient parking space. Owner will often give guided tour.

3 Radnor Gardens ✿✿ (Ms Jill Payne) Twickenham Turn off Heath Rd into Radnor Rd by Tamplins garag and R into Radnor gardens. Small garden of an 11' 6 wide terraced house owned by a compulsive plant collec tor. Front garden – raised bed and terracotta pots. Bac garden – 45' long, 6' × 6' patio, winding brick path an two tiny ponds. Garden crammed with a motley collectio ranging from native wild flowers to tender plants. Sma conservatory. *Adm 50p Chd 20p. Suns May 16, July 1 (10-5)*

11 Ranulf Road, NW2 ✿ (Mr & Mrs Jonathan Bates) 13 82, or 113 bus to Platts Lane from Golders Green o Swiss Cottage; 28 from Golders Green or West Hamp stead. Nearest stations Finchley Rd, W Hampstead an Golders Green. Take Ardwick Rd at junc of Finchley R and Fortune Green Rd, bear L into Ranulf Rd. No 11 is o L at brow of hill. Medium-sized garden, surrounded by trees, full of colour; herbaceous borders, roses, lilies fuchsias, bedding plants and many geranium fille pots. Home-made TEAS. *Adm 80p Chd free. Sun July 1 (2-6)*

¶**Regents College**, NW1 ♿✿ Regents Park. Regent College is located at the junction of York Bridge and th Inner Circle opp Queen Mary's Rose Garden in Regent Park. Baker Street tube is on the Bakerloo, Jubilee, Met ropolitan, Hammersmith & City and Circle line and is ' minutes walk. Buses: 1, 2, 2B, 13, 18, 27, 30, 74, 159 The college and grounds occupy a site of approx 1 acres. The large lawns, wild flower areas and mature trees echo the surrounding parkland. This landscape give way to more ornamental planting near the buildings spe cial features incl the quadrangle garden with many shade tolerant plants; a gold border; a large wisteria growing u through boston ivy; herb area with bee hives; a folly gar den; grass tennis courts; greenhouses and the more inti mate former Botany garden. Development of the grounds continues. TEA. *Adm £1 Cons/Chd 50p. Sun June 2 (10-4)*

¶**Ruislip Gardens** Ruislip, Middlesex. *Combined adm £1.50 Chd free. Sun June 20 (2-5)*
235 Eastcote Road ✿✿ (Tony & Jim Hall) From Ruislip High Street take the B466 (Eastcote Road) nearest tube Ruislip Manor. Parking off Eastcote Rd ir Evelyn Ave please. Medium sized suburban garden 115ft × 80ft. Contains a wide variety of herbaceous perennials and shrubs, shady patio area and ponds TEA
82 Evelyn Avenue ✿ (Jan & Ken Morgan) Refer to A- Z. Nearest Underground Station – Ruislip Manor. Turr R out of Station. Continue up and over the hill; cross the Eastcote Rd and turn 1st R into Evelyn Ave. Surbu ban garden 40ft × 170ft. Curving borders and island beds planted with shrubs and herbaceous plants tc give year round interests. Lawns and mature trees

7 St Albans Grove (Mrs E Norman Butler) Stations Kensington High St or Gloucester Rd. Bus Milestone for 9, 46, 52, 72; Gloucester Rd for 49, 74. From Gloucester Rd turn into Victoria Grove then into St Albans Grove. A country garden designed for all seasons and one pair of hands. *Adm 80p Chd 40p. Sun June 20 (2-5.30)*

7 St George's Rd ✿❀ (Mr & Mrs Richard Raworth) St Margaret's, Twickenham. Off A316 between Twickenham Bridge and St Margarets roundabout. ½-acre maturing town garden backing onto private parkland. Garden divided into 'rooms' by yew, thuja and hornbeam hedges. Unusual shrubs, clematis and old English roses. Large conservatory with rare plants and climbers. Knot garden with herbs. Sink garden. Pergola covered in solanum jas. alba, roses and honeysuckle. New sunken paved garden with Pithari pot and planting. Small gravel garden. Mist propagation. Propagated specimens for sale. Featured in several books including Penelope Hobhouse's 'Garden Style' and 'Private Gardens of London' by Arabella Lennox Boyd, and Homes & Garden. TEA. *Adm £1 Chd free. Suns June 6, 20 (2-6) or by appt* **Tel 081 892 3713**

40 St Margaret's Road, E12 ✿❀ (Mr & Mrs K Mines) Wanstead. Off Aldersbrook Rd opp Wanstead Flats. Nearby underground station Wanstead, Central line, Eastham, District Line. Bus 101 from stations BR station Manor Park, leave station turn L then ½m alongside Wanstead flats. 100ft informal cottage garden with some unusual plants, pond, tree house and mouldering carvings rescued from a Victorian East London Church. Secluded and shady. TEAS. *Adm £1 Chd free. Suns May 16, June 13 (2-6)*

¶St Mary's Convent & Nursing Home, W4 ♿✿❀ (Sister Jennifer Anne) Chiswick. Exit W from London on A4 to Hogarth roundabout. Take A316 signposted Richmond. St Mary's is 500yds down on L. Parking in Corney Rd, 1st turning L after Convent. 2½-acre walled garden with fine specimen trees; herbaceous borders and shrub borders being planted for all-year-round interest, incl spring flowering shrubs and bulbs. TEAS. *Adm £1 Chd 50p. Sun April 25 (2-5)*

57 St Quintin Avenue, W10 ✿❀ (H Groffman Esq) 1m from Ladbroke Grove/White City Underground. Turn into North Pole Rd from Wood Lane (White City, Shepherds Bush or Harrow Road approaches) or left into Cambridge Gdns, right into St Marks Rd from Ladbroke Grove station. Bus; 7, 220 to North Pole Road, or 72, 283 to Du Cane Road. 30ft × 40ft walled garden; year-round selection of shrubs, perennials, summer bedding schemes. Patio; small pond; hanging baskets. 11 times winner Brighter Kensington & Chelsea Gardens competition. Featured in Channel 4's 'Flowering Passions'. 3 silver medals from London Gardens Society in 1992. Photos to be shown in future series of LWT's Gardening Roadshow. TEAS. *Adm £1.20 Chd 80p. Sun Aug 1 (2-6.30)*

12a Selwood Place, SW7 ♿ (Mrs Anthony Crossley) South Kensington, adjacent to 92 Onslow Gardens (cul-de-sac). South Kensington tube 8 mins walk, no. 14 bus down Fulham Rd (Elm Place request stop). Long green and white border; pink border in L-shaped walled garden; collection of roses, peonies, camellias, iris, lilies, poppies, vegetables; terraced herb garden. Suitable for wheelchairs only if dry. *Adm 70p Chd 35p. Thurs June 10 (2.30-6)*

South London Botanical Institute, SE24 ✿❀ 323 Norwood Rd. From South Circular Rd (A205) at Tulse Hill,

turn N into Norwood Rd; Institute is 100yds on right. Small botanic garden, formally laid out; many rare and interesting species; over 200 labelled plants. TEA. *Adm £1 Chd 50p (Share to South London Botanical Institute). Suns May 16, Aug 29 (2-5)*

Southwood Lodge, N6 ✿❀ (Mr & Mrs C Whittington) 33 Kingsley Place. Off Southwood Lane where it forms part of the Highgate Village one-way system. Buses 210, 271. Tube Highgate. Unusual densely planted garden on steeply sloping site (regret unsuitable for wheelchairs). *Adm £1 Chd 40p. Suns May 9, June 13 (2-6)*

36 Staveley Rd ♿✿ (J G Luke Esq) Chiswick, W4. Off Great Chertsey Rd (A316). Shrub garden with inter and under planting of perennials, overlooked by trees of adjacent Chiswick House Grounds. TEAS. *Adm 80p Chd 30p (Share to Chiswick House Friends). Sun May 16 (2-6)*

Tarn ✿❀ (Mr & Mrs R Solley) Oxhey Drive South, Northwood. From Northwood Station turn R into Green Lane. At mini roundabout (singposted NATO Headquarters) follow sign turning L into Watford Rd, take 3rd R into Sandy Lane; at top U-turn into Oxhey Drive South, 2nd house on L. Approx ⅓-acre garden of special interest to horticulturists and plant lovers. (Visited by International Camellia Society 1991). Many rare and unusual shrubs, trees and plants; large collection of rhododendrons; camellias; magnolias and allied species. Spring blossom, drifts of bulbs including wild cyclamen, anemones, erythronium; bluebells; primroses etc. Greenhouse with tender rhododendrons and camellias etc. Large collection of clematis and climbing roses growing informally through trees. Old world terrace with pond. Very old standard wisteria. Much of the garden was 'tree lifted' by present owner from Hampstead in 1970 where it had a mention by the late Lanning Roper in the 'Sunday Times'. *Adm £1 Chd 50p. Sun April 25, Mon May 31 (2-5.30). Also open by appt end Feb to end June* **Tel 0923 828373**

Trinity Hospice ♿✿❀ 30 Clapham Common North Side, SW4. Tube: Clapham Common. Bus: 37, 137 stop outside. 2-acre park-like garden restored by Lanning Roper's friends as a memorial to him and designed by John Medhurst. Ricky's sculpture is a feature. TEAS. *Adm 50p Chd free. Sats, Suns April 24, 25; June 5, 6; July 24, 25; Sept 18, 19 (2-5)*

Trumpeters' House (Miss Sarah Franklyn) **& Trumpeters' Lodge** ♿✿❀ (Mrs Pamela Franklyn) Old Palace Yard, Richmond. Off Richmond Green on the S side. Car parking on the green, and in car parks. About 3 acres, lawns, established old trees. Many old roses; shrubs; ponds; knot garden; mixed borders; aviary for doves. Featured in House & Garden and Country Life. NCCPG collection of old-fashioned pinks (Dianthus). TEAS only June 27. *Adm £1.50 OAPs £1 Chd 50p. Suns June 6, 27 (2.30-6)*

Regular Openers. Too many days to include in diary. Usually there is a wide range of plants giving year-round interest. See head of county section for the name and garden description for times etc.

15 Upper Grotto Road ⚘❀ (Ms Jeane Rankin) Strawberry Hill, Twickenham. Stations Strawberry Hill or Twickenham. Buses R68, 33 to Pope's Grotto, then Pope's Grove 1st R into Radnor Rd, 1st L Upper Grotto Rd or 90B, 267, 281, 290 to Heath Rd, into Radnor Rd, 2nd L into Upper Grotto Rd. Small sunken suntrap courtyard garden designed and constructed with advancing age and arthritis in mind; raised borders with small shrubs, herbaceous perennials, self sown annuals and some half-hardy annuals for infill; wall shrubs, clematis and other climbers; plants in pots and tiny fountain over pebbles. TEA. *Adm 50p Chd 25p. Sun July 11 (2-6)*

¶33 Upper Park Road ⚘❀ (Mr & Mrs Kopij) Kingston upon Thames. Close to Richmond Park. On leaving Richmond Park through Kingston Gate turn 1st R into Kings Rd 1st R into Park Rd and 1st R into Bertran Rd which leads to Upper Park Rd. British Rail Norbiton or Kingston (both 12 mins walk) LT 371 bus. Approx 120 × 25 created over last 3 yrs. Carefully designed with informal planting and soft colour schemes. Raised patio; small lawn with borders; bible garden with pergola. Small shady woodland area. TEAS. *Adm £1 Chd free (Share to Royal Marsden Hospital & St Paul's Church Kingston Reordering Fund). Suns May 30, June 20 (2-6)*

66 Wallingford Avenue, W10 ⚘ (Mrs R Andrups). Nearest underground station: Latimer Rd (Met Line). Nearest bus stop Oxford Gdns (7) or Ladbroke Grove (7, 15, 52). Small garden 20′ × 40′. Raised beds, mixed borders, ponds, conservatory. All-year-round garden. 7 times winner Brighter Kensington & Chelsea Gardens Competition. Refreshments 20p. *Adm £1 Chd 50p. Sun May 30 (2-5)*

The Water Gardens ⚘ Warren Road, Kingston (Octagon Developments Ltd). From Kingston take the A308 (Kingston Hill) towards London about ½m on R turn R into Warren Road. Japanese landscaped garden originally part of the Coombe Wood Nursery, approx 9 acres with water cascade features. *Adm £1 Chd 50p. Suns May 9, Oct 3 (2-5)*

3 Wellgarth Road, NW11 ⚘❀ (Mr & Mrs A M Gear) Hampstead Garden Suburb. Approx 4m N of London centre. Turning off the North End Road which runs between Hampstead and Golders Green (buses 268, 210 stop quite near). Golders Green tube station (Northern Line) is the nearest, 7 minutes walk and is also a terminal for buses from many parts of London. Medium-size garden. A walk all round the house, swathe of grass with long borders of bushes, trees and climbers now established and not too difficult to maintain. Close planting, herbaceous beds, roses, heathers and lavenders: herbs and mints, some uncommon plants. Paving, pots, tubs and old oak tree, and now newly added a small pond with bubbling water. Hampstead Gardens Competition Winner in 1989, 90, 91 & 92, and 1st in class in the London Gardens Society '92. Home-made TEAS. *Adm £1. Sun June 20 (2-6.30)*

7 West Eaton Place, SW1 ⚘❀ (Ann Bogod) Nearest tube Sloane Square, turn into Eaton Terrace or Eaton Place, behind Eaton Square. A narrow basement and porch of 1830 listed house; transformed into glowing garden imaginatively composed with many varieties bursting with colour, fragrance and unusual greenery, winning awards in 1986/87/88/89/90/91, featured in numerous publications here and abroad. Winning premier awards over last 6 years. Featured on TV. *Collection box. Suns July 11 (11-6)*

10 Wildwood Rd, NW11 ♿⚘ (Dr J W McLean) Hampstead. Wildwood Rd is between Hampstead Golf Course and N end of Hampstead Heath. From North End Rd turn by Manor House Hospital into Hampstead Way, then fork right. Garden planned and maintained by owner; one of finest herbaceous borders in North London, pond, HT roses; owner-grown prize winning delphiniums and seedlings. TEA. *Adm £1 Chd free. Sun July 11 (2-7)*

27 Wood Vale, N10 ⚘❀ (Mr & Mrs A W Dallman) Muswell Hill 1m. A1 to Woodman Pub; signed Muswell Hill; Muswell Hill Rd sharp right Wood Lane leading to Wood Vale; Highgate tube station. ¾-acre garden with herbaceous borders; ponds; orchard and kitchen garden. Unusual layout full of surprises. Numerous shrubs, roses, trees and conifers; greenhouses. Visitors may also wander in neighbouring gardens, all of which are of high standard. TEAS. *Adm £1 Chd under 14 free (Share to British Legion and St John's Ambulance, London District). Sat, Sun July 17, 18 (2-6)*

7 Woodstock Road, W4 ⚘ (Mr & Mrs L A Darke) Buses 94, 27. Underground district line to Turnham Green. (Piccadilly line stops Sunday). Turn R from station and over zebra crossing into Woodstock Rd. No. 7 is on L side beyond Sydney House flats and Bedford Rd. Victorian garden with large original rockery behind Norman Shaw house in Bedford Park, the earliest garden suburb. Wide selection of fine flowering trees; shrubs; herbaceous plants, roses and bulbs made over 40 years by present owners. Featured in 'London's Pride', the 1990 exhibition of the history of the capital's gardens in the Museum of London. *Adm 80p Chd free. Sun April 25 (2-5)*

42 Woodville Gardens, Ealing W5 ❀ (J Welfare) Off Hanger Lane (A406) approx half way between junctions with A40 and A4020. Large town garden with alpine area and herbaceous borders, paving plants, beds of shade and sun-loving plants, bog garden, shrubs, many euphorbias, pulmonarias, geums eryngiums, hellebores, etc. Plantsman's garden with many unusual plants. Seedlings and cuttings for sale. *Collection box. By appt only April to Sept* **Tel 081 998 4134**

✿

Norfolk

Hon County Organisers:	Mrs Clive Hardcastle, The Old Rectory, Southacre, King's Lynn, PE32 2AD
	Tel 0760 755469
	Lady Blofeld, Hoveton House, Nr Wroxham, Norwich NR12 8JE
	Tel 0603 782202
Assistant County Organisers:	Mrs Neil Foster, Lexham Hall, King's Lynn PE32 2QJ
	Mrs David Mcleod, Park House, Old Hunstanton, King's Lynn PE36 6JS
Hon Treasurer:	Denzil Newton Esq, Briar House, Gt Dunham, King's Lynn PE32 2LX

DATES OF OPENING

By appointment
For telephone numbers and other details see garden descriptions

Besthorpe Hall, Attleborough
Cubitt Cottage, Sloley
Dell Farm, Aylsham Gardens
Lanehead, Garboldisham
10 St Michael's Close, Aylsham
Wretham Lodge, East Wretham

Regular openings
For details see garden descriptions

Hoveton Hall Gardens, nr Wroxham.
 Every Wed, Fri, Sun, Bank Hols,
 Easter Sun to Sept 12
Norfolk Lavender Ltd, Heacham.
 Daily (Closed 3 weeks at
 Christmas)
The Plantation Garden, Norwich.
 Suns April to Oct
Raveningham Hall, Norwich. Suns,
 Bank Hols March 12 to Sept 12
Sandringham Grounds. Daily April
 11 to Oct 3 but see text for
 exceptions

April 11 Sunday
Lake House, Brundall
April 12 Monday
Lake House, Brundall
April 18 Sunday
Hoveton Hall Gardens, nr
 Wroxham
April 25 Sunday
The Birches, Wreningham
Rainthorpe Hall, Tasburgh
May 2 Sunday
Dunburgh House, Geldeston

May 3 Monday
Dunburgh House, Geldeston
May 9 Sunday
Grove House, Erpingham
The Old Rectory, Southacre
Raveningham Hall, Norwich
May 16 Sunday
How Hill Farm, Ludham
Rippon Hall, Hevingham
Wretham Lodge, East Wretham
May 23 Sunday
Barwick House, Stanhoe
Elmham House, North Elmham
Wolterton Park, nr Aylsham
May 30 Sunday
Aylsham Gardens
Cubitt Cottage, Sloley
Lexham Hall, nr Swaffham
Sheringham Park, Upper
 Sheringham
May 31 Monday
Swafield Old House, North
 Walsham
June 6 Sunday
Besthorpe Hall, Attleborough
Hoveton House, nr Wroxham
Letheringsett Gardens
June 9 Wednesday
Hoveton Hall Gardens, nr
 Wroxham
June 13 Sunday
Conifer Hill, Starston
The Garden in an Orchard, Bergh
 Apton
King's Lynn Old Town Gardens
Mannington Hall, Norwich
Raveningham Hall, Norwich
Sheringham Park, Upper
 Sheringham
June 20 Sunday
Elsing Hall, nr Dereham
Grove House, Erpingham
Oak Tree House, 6 Cotman Rd,
 Thorpe

Wicken House, Castleacre
June 27 Sunday
Bayfield Hall, nr Holt
72 Branthill Cottages,
 Wells-next-the-Sea ‡
Cubitt Cottage, Sloley
Felbrigg Hall, Norwich
Gayton Hall, King's Lynn
4 Green Lane, Munford ‡‡
Intwood Hall, Norwich
Lanehead, Garboldisham ‡‡
Ludham Gardens
Southgate Barn, South Creake ‡
Wretham Lodge, East
 Wretham ‡‡
July 11 Sunday
Blickling Hall, Aylsham
Horstead House, nr Norwich
Kettle Hill, Blakeney
July 18 Sunday
Easton Lodge, Easton
Oxburgh Hall Garden, Oxburgh
July 23 Friday
Park House, Old Hunstanton
July 24 Saturday
Park House, Old Hunstanton
July 25 Sunday
Cubitt Cottage, Sloley
Felbrigg Hall, Norwich
Oak Tree House, 6 Cotman Rd,
 Thorpe
Park House, Old Hunstanton
July 26 Monday
Park House, Old Hunstanton
July 29 Thursday
Holkham Hall, Wells-next-the-Sea
August 1 Sunday
Oxburgh Hall Garden, Oxburgh
The Plantation Garden, Norwich
Wickmere House, Wickmere
August 8 Sunday
Blickling Hall, Aylsham
August 29 Sunday
Barningham Hall, Matlaske

DESCRIPTIONS OF GARDENS

Aylsham Gardens
 5 Cromer Road &⚘ (Dr & Mrs James) Aylsham.
100yds N of Aylsham Parish Church down old Cromer
Rd on L hand side. Approx 1 acre of semi-wild garden
nr town centre with large willow trees and grass.
Shrubs and small natural pond. Mixed borders, heathers and vegetable garden. *Adm £1 Chd free. Sun
May 30 (2-6)*

Dell Farm ♿🌢🏵 (Mrs M J Monk) Aylsham. Approx ¼m W of centre of Aylsham turn L off Blickling Rd on to Heydon Rd (signposted Oulton). 400yds on to copper beech arching rd. Turn R through gate onto gravelled yard. 4-acre garden, 20 acres of meadows. Magnificent mature trees and shrubs. Various rose collections, rhododendrons, azaleas, heathers. Spring bulbs, primroses etc in old orchard and wild flower garden. TEAS. *Adm £1 Chd 50p. Sun May 30 (2-6). Also by appt especially for spring bulbs* **Tel 0263 732 277**

10 St Michael's Close 🌢🏵 (M I Davies Esq) Aylsham NW on B1354 towards Blickling Hall; 500yds from market place, turn R, Rawlinsons Lane, then R again. Front gravelled area with mixed shrub and herbaceous border; small rockery. Back garden with large variety of shrubs, herbaceous plants, bulbs, small lawn, roses, azaleas. Plant, pond. Aviary, guinea pigs. TEAS. *Adm £1. Sun May 30 (11-6). Also by appt* **Tel 0263 732174**

West Lodge ♿ (Mr & Mrs Jonathan Hirst) Aylsham. ¼m NW of market square on N side of B1354 (entrance in Rawlinsons Lane) Large 9-acre garden with lawns, mature trees, rose garden, herbaceous borders, ornamental pond and walled kitchen garden; Georgian House (not open) and outbuildings incl a well-stocked toolshed (open) and greenhouses. TEAS. *Adm £2 Chd free (Share to Aylsham Church Restoration Fund). Sun May 30 (2-5)*

Barningham Hall ♿🏵 (Lady Mott-Radclyffe) Matlaske, NW of Aylsham. Medium-sized garden, vistas, lake. TEAS. *Adm £2 Chd free. Sun Aug 29 (2-6.30)*

Barwick House ♿🌢 (Mrs R Ralli) Stanhoe. 10m NW of Fakenham off B1155. Large garden surrounded by park with many mature trees; mixed borders; woodland walk; azaleas and rhododendrons. TEAS. *Adm £1 Chd 50p (Share to St John Ambulance). Sun May 23 (2-5)*

Bayfield Hall (Mr & Mrs R H Combe) 1m N of Holt, off A148. Formal but simple pleasure gardens with medieval church ruin. Old-fashioned roses, herbaceous and shrub borders; magnificent view over lake and park. Wildflower centre adjacent to garden. Church Fete stalls in aid of St Martins Church, Glandford. TEAS. *Adm £1.50 Chd 50p. Sun June 27 (2-5)*

Besthorpe Hall ♿🌢🏵 (John Alston Esq) 1m E of Attleborough. On Attleborough-Bunwell Rd; adjacent to Besthorpe Church. Garden with shrubs, trees and herbaceous borders within Tudor enclosures; walled kitchen garden; tilting ground. Coach parties by appt. TEAS. *Adm £2 Chd free (Share to Besthorpe Church). Sun June 6 (2-5). Also by appt* **Tel 0953 452138**

¶**The Birches** ♿🌢🏵 (Mrs J McCarthy) Top Row. 8m S of Norwich on B1113 Norwich-New Buckenham Road. Take 1st turning L ¼m after Bird in Hand Restaurant. 1¼-acre garden landscaped with lawns, herbaceous, shrub and rose beds. Rockery, pond and alpine scree garden, orchard with naturlized bulbs. Vegetable garden, greenhouses and conservatory. TEAS. *Adm £1.50 Chd free. Sun April 25 (1-6)*

Blickling Hall ♿🌢🏵 (The National Trust) 1¼ miles NW of Aylsham on N side of B1354. 15m N of Norwich (A140). Large garden, orangery, crescent lake, azaleas, rhododendrons, herbaceous borders. Historic Jacobean house. Wheelchairs available. TEAS and lunches. *Adm £2.50 Chd £1.25. Suns July 11, Aug 8 (12-5)*

72 Branthill Cottages 🌢 (Timothy Leese Esq.) Wells-next-the-Sea. 6m from Fakenham, 2m from Wells. Off Fakenham-Wells road. Posters at unmarked crossroads, opp. driveway to Branthill Farm. ¼-acre cottage garden created by owner over 8 years with densely planted borders of roses, shrubs and herbaceous plants. Fine views over surrounding farmland. TEAS at Southgate Barn. *Adm £1 Chd free (Share to Wells Cottage Hospital). Sun June 27 (2-6)*

¶**Conifer Hill** ♿🏵 (Mr & Mrs Richard Lombe Taylor) Starston, Harleston. 18m S of Norwich. A140 to Pulham Xrds. Turn L to B1134. 1m NW of Harleston, off B1134. Take Redenhall Rd out of Starston. Conifer Hill on L ½m out of village. Steep bend and white gates. 4-acre Victorian garden. Lawns, shrubs, roses, herbaceous and kitchen garden. ½-acre pinetum, magnificent trees in steep escarpment of old quarry. TEAS. *Adm £1.50 Chd free. Sun June 13 (2-6)*

Cubitt Cottage ♿🌢🏵 (Mrs Janie Foulkes) Sloley. 11m N of Norwich just off B1150 Coltishall to North Walsham Rd. 2nd R after Three Horseshoes public house at Scottow. Into village, then Low Street, R at next signpost. 1-acre garden with lawns, herbaceous and shrub border, over 100 varieties of old roses, clematis and unusual plants; wildflower meadow; wild life pond and bog garden; vegetable garden and greenhouses. TEAS. *Adm £1.50 Chd free. Suns May 30, June 27, July 25 (2-6). Plus some other Sundays in June, July, Aug and Sept. Also by appt* **Tel 0692 69295**

Dunburgh House ♿🏵 (Major & Mrs Lorimer Mason) Geldeston. 2m N of Beccles just off Norwich Rd A146 6m E of Bungay off the Yarmouth Rd A143. 3¾ acres of an all-year round garden of interest; mature and recently planted, thousands of bulbs; shrubs, herbaceous and rose garden; very large kitchen garden, vegetable, fruit, greenhouses and conservatory. TEAS in aid of the restoration fund of Gillingham Church. *Adm £1.50 Chd free. Sun, Mon, May 2, 3 (2-5.30)*

Easton Lodge (J M Rampton Esq) Easton, 6m W Norwich. Cross the new Southern Norwich Bypass at the Easton Roundabout and take the Ringland Rd. Entrance at the W gate approx 1m from EC bus stop 'The Dog' on the old A47. Large garden in magnificent setting above river surrounded by fine trees; walks amongst interesting shrubs, roses, plants; herbaceous border; walled kitchen garden. Late Georgian house with Jacobean centre portion (not open). TEAS. *Adm £1.50 Chd free. Sun July 18 (2.30-5.30)*

Regular Openers. Too many days to include in diary. Usually there is a wide range of plants giving year-round interest. See head of county section for the name and garden description for times etc.

Elmham House &❀❀ (Mr & Mrs R S Don) North Elmham, 5m N of East Dereham, on B1110. Entrance opp Church. Medium-sized garden; wild garden; C18 walled garden; view of park and lake; vineyard, tours of winery. TEAS. *Adm £1.50 Chd free (Share to St Mary's Church N Elmham). Sun May 23 (2-6)*

Elsing Hall ❀❀ (Mrs D Cargill) Dereham. 2m E of Dereham off A47; sign to Elsing. Medieval house surrounded by moat. Over 200 varieties of old-fashioned roses; wild flower lawn, walled kitchen garden with roses, fruit trees & clematis. Many water plants by moat and fish stew. Rare and interesting trees in arboretum; newly planted formal garden with clipped box, lavender, sage, santolina and thyme. Suitable wheelchairs in places. TEAS. *Adm £1.50 Chd free (Share to Norfolk Gardens Trust). Sun June 20 (2-6)*

Felbrigg Hall &❀ (The National Trust) Roughton, 2½m SW of Cromer, S of A148; main entrance from B1436; signed from Felbrigg village. Large pleasure gardens; mainly lawns and shrubs; orangery with camellias; large walled garden restored and restocked as fruit, vegetable and flower garden; vine house; dovecote; dahlias; superb colchichum; wooded parks. Wheelchairs available. Lunches, pre booking essential. TEAS. *Adm £1.70 Chd 80p.* ▲*For NGS Suns June 27, July 25 (11-5)*

¶**The Garden in an Orchard** &❀ (Mr & Mrs R W Boardman) Bergh Apton, Norwich. 6m SE of Norwich off A146 at Hellington Corner signed to Bergh Apton. Down Mill Rd 300 yds. 3½-acre garden set in an old orchard. Many rare and unusual plants set out in an informal pattern of wandering paths. ½-acre of wild flower meadows, many bamboos, specie roses, 9 species of eucalyptus. In all a plantsman's garden. TEAS. *Adm £1.50 Chd free. Sun June 13 (11-6)*

Gayton Hall &❀ (Julian Marsham Esq) 6m E of King's Lynn off B1145; signs in Gayton village. 20 acres; wild woodland, water garden. Fete stalls in aid of Gayton Church. TEAS. *Adm 50p Chd free & Collecting Box (Share to St Nicholas Church, Gayton). Sun June 27 (2-5)*

¶**4 Green Lane** &❀❀(Mr & Mrs Dennis Cooper) Munford. From main Munford roundabout take A47 to Swaffham. After ¼m turn L down Green Lane. A bungalow garden with many island beds intensively planted with unusual perennial and cottage garden plants. Small pond and interesting gravel garden. *Adm £1 Chd free. Sun June 27 (2-6)*

¶**Grove House** &❀ (Mrs Valerie Alston) Erpingham. On A140 4m N Aylsham to Alby Crafts, parking in Alby Crafts car park. 4-acre garden. Primroses, spring bulbs, irises, old-fashioned roses, mixed borders, 4 ponds (1 with wild flower and conservation area). Plantsman's garden. TEAS. *Adm £1.50 Chd free. Suns May 9, June 20 (10-5)*

Holkham Hall &❀ (The Viscount Coke) Wells-next-the-Sea. 2m W of Wells off A149. Arboretum with many rare specimens of trees and shrubs; shell house. TEAS. *Adm 50p Chd 20p.* ▲*For NGS Thurs July 29 (1.30-4.45)*

Horstead House ❀ (Dr & Mrs David Nolan) Horstead. 7m from Norwich. Off B1150 N Walsham Rd opp 'Recruiting Sergeant'; drive gate by Horstead Mill Pool; bus 736 from Norwich. Landscaped garden on riverbank; walled garden; exceptionally good toolhouse. Home-made TEAS. *Adm £1.50 Chd free. Sun July 11 (2-5)*

Hoveton Hall Gardens &❀❀ (Mr & Mrs Andrew Buxton) nr Wroxham. 8m N of Norwich; 1m N of Wroxham Bridge on A1151 Stalham Road. Approx 10-acre gardens and grounds featuring principally daffodils, azaleas, rhododendrons and hydrangeas in a woodland setting and a large, mature, walled herbaceous garden. Water plants, a lakeside walk and walled kitchen garden provide additional interest. Early C19 house (not open). TEAS. *Adm £1.75 Chd 25p. Gardens open, every Wed, Fri, Sun and Bank Hols Easter Sun to Sept 12 incl (2-5.30). For NGS Sun April 18, Wed June 9 (2-5.30)*

Hoveton House &❀ (Sir John & Lady Blofeld) 9m N Norwich, ½m Wroxham on B1062, Horning-Ludham Rd. Interesting old-fashioned walled garden; herbaceous and other borders; rock garden; many unusual plants and bulbs. Established rhododendron grove. Kitchen garden. Lawns, walks etc. William & Mary House (not open.) TEAS. *Adm £2 Chd free. Sun June 6 (2-6)*

How Hill Farm & (P D S Boardman Esq) 2m W of Ludham on A1062; then follow signs to How Hill; Farm Garden – S of How Hill. Very pretty garden started in 1968 in water garden setting with three ponds; recent 3-acre broad (dug as conservation project) with variety of water lilies and view over the R. Ant; fine old mill. Winding paths through rare conifers (mainly dwarf); unusual and rare rhododendrons with massed azaleas; other ornamental trees and shrubs; a few herbaceous plants and lilies; collection of English holly, ilex aquifolium (over 50 varieties). Partly suitable for wheelchairs. TEAS. *Adm £1.50 Chd free (Share to How Hill Trust). Sun May 16 (2-5)*

Intwood Hall ❀ (The Hon Julian & Mrs Darling) 3½m SW of Norwich. Via A11 to Cringleford; fork left (avoid dual carriageway); over Cringleford Bridge, turn left; over Xrds and level Xing for ½m. 2 walled flower gardens (one Tudor); walled vegetable garden, greenhouses, roses; lovely trees. Saxon Church in grounds. TEAS. *Adm £1.50 Chd free. Sun June 27 (2-6)*

¶**Kettle Hill** &❀❀ (Mr & Mrs Richard Winch) Blakeney. ¼m from Blakeney on the B1388 Blakeney to Langham Rd. A new coastal and walled garden designed by Mark Rummary and planted in 1991/2. Long herbaceous borders, a terrace and grass paths through arboretum, planted after the 1987 hurricane, lead to a shrub rose garden deep in old wood. The lawns look out to a fabulous view of the sea over Morston and Skiffkey. TEAS. *Adm £1.50 Chd free (Share to Glaven Caring Trust). Sun July 11 (2-6)*

¶**Kings Lynn Old Town Gardens** &❀❀ Situated in the historic centre of the town nr St Margret's Priory Church and Sat market place. Partially suitable for wheelchairs. TEAS and stalls. *Combined adm £1.50 Chd 50p. Sun June 13 (2-6)*

¶**Ladybridge House, Nelson St** (Mr & Mrs A Williams) A secluded garden behind high C18 walls. With roses, shrubs and many ground cover plants

¶**May Cottages, Nelson St** (Mr & Mrs R Cooke & Mr & Mrs R Brown) Passageway flanked by C18 cottages, filled with climbing roses and containers of many bedding plants

St Margaret's Vicarage (Canon & Mrs M L Yorke) King's Lynn. Opp St Margaret's Church on Saturday Market Place. Old walled garden overlooked by twin towers of C12 Priory Church. Largely replanted 4 years ago with shrub and herbaceous borders and small old rose garden leading through courtyards into

2 St Margarets Place (Dr & Mrs D Bartlett) Old walled garden overlooked by towers of C12 Priory Church. Shrub and herbaceous borders and old rose garden leading to small C15 garden with many unusual climbing plants

¶**17-29 Queen St** (Mr & Mrs C D M Johnston & The Hon Mrs A Davidson) Recently created courtyard gardens behind listed buildings with interesting trees, shrubs and climbing plants

¶**262 Wotton Rd** (Mr & Mrs L Dyer) 1m NW from centre of King's Lyn. Small garden with over 250 varieties of trees, pond and wide variety of plants. Map available from vicarage

Lake House ❀ (Mr & Mrs Garry Muter) Brundall. Approx 5m E of Norwich on A47; take Brundall turn at Roundabout. Turn R into Postwick Lane at T-junction. An acre of water gardens set among magnificent trees in a steep cleft in the river escarpment. Informal flower beds with interesting plants; a naturalist's paradise; unsuitable for young children or the infirm. Wellingtons advisable. 'Unusual plants for sale.' TEAS. *Adm £1.50 Chd free (Share to Wateraid). Easter Sun & Mon (11-5)*

Lanehead ♿ (Mrs N A Laurie) Garboldisham, 8m W of Diss off A1066. Medium-sized garden created by owner; featured in a television programme, visited by many horticultural groups; well designed natural walks with shrubs and specimen trees; colour co-ordinated borders for all-year interest; water and bog garden; roses and woodland. Coffee, TEAS. *Adm £1.50 Chd free (Share to Garboldisham Church Fabric Fund). Sun June 27 (10.30-6). Also open by appt* **Tel 0953 81380**

Letheringsett Gardens ♿ 1m W of Holt on A148. Car park King's Head, Letheringsett. Following 5 gardens will be open. TEAS at The Glebe. *Combined adm £1.25 Chd 25p. Easter Sun June 6 (2-5.30)*

¶**Foundry House** (Peter Millar Esq) Small unusual garden. Roses

The Glebe ♿❀ (Hon Beryl Cozens-Hardy) Medium-sized riverside garden, with island, wild flowers, water garden, shrub borders, clematis

Hall Cottage (Mr David Mayes) Small riverside garden; two pools, interesting water plants, shrubs

Letheringsett Hall (Mrs English) Home for the Elderly; medium-sized garden

Letheringsett Estate Garden (Mr & Mrs Robert Carter) Large garden; wooded walks, fountain, lake, water plants, wild flowers. Hydraulic rams 1852 and 1905

Lexham Hall ♿✂❀ (Mr & Mrs Neil Foster) 2m W of Litcham off B1145. 3-acre woodland garden with azaleas and rhododendrons; walled garden, shrubs, roses; lake and parkland. TEAS. *Adm £2 Chd free (Share to St Andrews Church, E. Lexham). Sun May 30 (2-6)*

¶**Ludham Gardens** B1062 Wroxham to Ludham 7m. Turn R by Ludham village church into Staithe Road. Gardens ¼m from village. TEAS. *Adm £1.50 Chd free. Sun June 27 (2-6)*

¶**The Dutch House** ✂ (Mrs Peter Seymour) Long narrow garden designed and planted by the painter Edward Seago, leading through marsh to Womack Water. Approx 2½ acres

¶**The Mowle** ✂❀ (Mrs N N Green) Approx 2½ acres running down to marshes. Interesting shrub borders, unusual trees etc including tulip trees and a golden catalpa

Mannington Hall ♿✂❀ (The Lord & Lady Walpole) 2m N of Saxthorpe; 18m NW of Norwich via B1149 towards Holt. At Saxthorpe (B1149 & B1354) turn NE signed Mannington. 20 acres feature roses, shrubs, lake and trees. Heritage rose, scented and walled gardens. Extensive countryside walks and trails. C15 moated manor house (not open). Saxon church with C19 follies. TEAS and lunches. *Adm £2 OAPs/students £1.50 Chd free (Share to Itteringham Church). Sun June 13 (12-5)*

Norfolk Lavender Ltd ♿❀ (Caley Mill) Heacham. On A149 13m N of Kings Lynn. National collection of lavenders set in 2-acres (lavender harvest July-Aug); herb garden with many varieties of native herbs; rose garden. TEAS. *Adm free. Collecting box (Share to Heacham Parish Church). Daily to Christmas (10-5) Closed for three weeks Christmas holiday*

Oak Tree House ✂ (W R S Giles Esq) 6 Cotman Rd, Thorpe. E of Norwich off A47 Thorpe Rd. ¼m from Norwich Thorpe Station. From Yarmouth direction follow one way system towards City Centre, turn R at traffic lights opposite Min. of Fisheries & Agric. Approx 300yds on, turn L opposite Barclays Bank. Approx ½-acre town garden; mixed borders with Mediterranean influence; many unusual plants including palm trees. Conservatory containing tree ferns etc. Plantsman's garden. TEAS. *Adm £1.50 Chd 50p. Suns June 20, July 25 (1.30-5.30)*

The Old Rectory, Southacre ♿❀ (Mr & Mrs C Hardcastle) Southacre. 3m NW of Swaffham off the A1065 opp Southacre church. Medium-sized garden with splendid views of Castleacre Priory. Mixed borders, shrubs; small vineyard; herb garden; pool and many bulbs. TEAS. *Adm £1.25 Chd 25p (Share to Southacre Church Restoration Fund). Sun May 9 (2-6)*

Oxburgh Hall Garden ♿✂ (The National Trust) 7m SW of Swaffham, at Oxburgh on Stoke Ferry rd. Hall and moat surrounded by lawns, fine trees, colourful borders; charming parterre garden of French design. Lunches, cream TEAS. *Adm £1 Chd 50p. Suns July 18, Aug 1 (12-5)*

By Appointment Gardens. See head of county section

Park House &✿ (Mr & Mrs D McLeod) 1m E of Hunstanton off A149. Drive opp St Mary's Church, Old Hunstanton. 3-acre garden with walled rose garden, herbaceous and shrub borders, flowering trees; model railway. *Adm £1 Chd free (Share to St Mary's Church, Old Hunstanton). Fri, Sat, Sun, Mon, July 23 to 26 (10-5)*

The Plantation Garden &✿✿ (Plantation Garden Preservation Trust) 4 Earlham Rd, Norwich. Entrance between Crofters and Beeches Hotels, nr St John's R C Cathedral. 3-acre Victorian town garden created 1856-96 in former medieval chalk quarry. Still undergoing restoration by volunteers, remarkable architectural features include 60ft Italianate terrace and unique 30ft Gothic fountain. Surrounded by mature trees. 10 min walk city centre, beautifully tranquil atmosphere. *Adm £1.50 Chd free (Share to Plantation Garden Preservation Trust). Suns April to Oct (2-5.30). For NGS TEAS Sun Aug 1 (2-5.30)*

Rainthorpe Hall &✿ (G F Hastings Esq) 8m S of Norwich, 1m SW of Newton Flotman to Tasburgh. From Norwich take A140 for 7m; at Newton Flotman, by garage, fork right; on 1m to red brick gates on left. Large garden; fine trees; botanical interest, inc a collection of bamboos. Nursery Garden. Newly developed 4-acre Conservation Lake. Elizabethan house (open by appt) connected with Amy Robsart. TEAS. *Adm £1.50 Chd 75p. Sun April 25 (10-5)*

Raveningham Hall &✿ (Sir Nicholas Bacon) 14m SE of Norwich, 4m from Beccles off B1136. Large garden specialising in rare shrubs, herbaceous plants, especially euphorbia, agapanthus and shrub roses. Victorian conservatory and walled vegetable garden, newly planted Arboretum. *Adm £2 Chd free (Share to Priscilla Bacon Lodge). Nursery open 9-4 every day except weekends in November, December, January, February. Garden open every Sunday, Bank Hols and Weds March 23 to September 12 (2-5.30) Weds (1-4). For NGS TEAS Suns May 9, June 13 (2-5.30)*

Rippon Hall & (Miss Diana Birkbeck) Hevingham, 8m N of Norwich. From A140 Norwich-Aylsham rd, turn right (E) at Xrds just N of Hevingham Church. Rhododendrons and azalea borders. Large herd of rare breed of British White Cattle. TEAS. *Adm £1.50 Chd 25p. Sun May 16 (2-5.30)*

Sandringham Grounds &✿✿ By gracious permission of H.M. The Queen, the House and Grounds at Sandringham will be open (except when H.M. The Queen or any member of the Royal Family is in residence). Donations are given from the Estate to various charities. For further information see p 13. TEAS. *Adm House and Grounds £3 OAPs £2 Chd £1.50; Grounds only £2 OAPs £1.50 Chd £1. April 11 to Oct 3 daily. House closed July 19 to Aug 7 incl & Grounds closed July 23 to Aug 4 incl. Hours House 11 (Sun 12 noon) to 4.45; Grounds 10.30 (Sun 11.30) to 5*

Sheringham Park &✿ (The National Trust) 2m SW of Sheringham. Access for cars off A148 Cromer to Holt Road, 5m W of Cromer, 6m E of Holt (signs in Sheringham Town). 50-acres of species rhododendron, azalea and magnolia. Also numerous specimen trees including handkerchief tree. Viewing towers, waymarked walks, sea and parkland views. Special walk way and WCs for disabled. Teas at Felbrigg Hall nearby. *Adm £2.20 per car. Suns May 30, June 13 (10-5)*

Southgate Barn ✿ (Mrs Philip Anley) South Creake. 5m N of Fakenham off B1355 to Burnham Market. 100yds past turning to R signed Waterden turn L down lane. Entrance 100yds on L. Small garden of approx 2 acres made 9 years ago around a converted barn. Shrubs and trees in front. At back large terrace, roses, pergola, herbaceous border. Cream TEAS. *Adm £1 Chd free (Share to Rumanian Relief for Children in Orphanages). Sun June 27 (2-6)*

Swafield Old House &✿✿ (Sir Johan & Lady Steyn) Swafield. From N Walsham take the by-pass to Mundesley Cromer. Less than 1m turn R to Swafield. At end of village, just before sharp R hand bend, turn R up drive. 2½-acre linked gardens bordered by mature shrubberies and lovely trees. Handsome yew hedges surround a 'secret' garden with herbaceous borders. Thyme bed, wide variety of azaleas and rhododendrons; ornamental pond. Wheelchairs only in dry weather. TEAS. *Adm £1.50 Chd free. Mon May 31 (2-6)*

Wicken House &✿✿ (Lord & Lady Keith) Castle Acre, 5m N of Swaffham off A1065; W at Newton to Castle Acre; then 2m N off the rd to Massingham. Large walled garden planted in sections with many roses and unusual herbaceous plants; gravel paths and greenhouses; swimming pool garden; spring and wild gardens. Fine views. Approx 6 acres. Rare plants for sale. Cream TEAS. *Adm £1.50 Chd free. Sun June 20 (2-6)*

¶**Wickmere House** &✿ (Mr & Mrs Noel Bolingbroke-Kent) 6m N of Aylsham, 5m S of Cromer. Take A140 to Matlaske turning, on 3m, turn L to Wickmere and Round Church Tower. 3 acres of gardens. 2 Italianate walled gardens featuring many unusual plants, 1 designed by Lanning Roper; small Japaneses garden; lawns and shrubs; peacocks; mediaeval church with interesting monuments at entrance (open). TEAS. *Adm £1.50 chd 50p (Share to St Andrews Church, Wickmere). Sun Aug 1 (2-6)*

Wolterton Park ✿✿ (The Lord & Lady Walpole) Wolterton is signposted W from Norwich to Cromer Road (A410) via Erpingham. Approx 8m from Cromer, 6m from Aylsham. Historic park of 340-acres with lake. Gardens at present being redeveloped. Shrubs, borders, large kitchen garden. TEAS. *Adm £2 Students/OAPs £1.50 Chd free (Share to Wolterton Church Tower Appeal). Sun May 23 (2-5)*

Wretham Lodge &✿✿ (Mrs Anne Hoellering) East Wretham. All E from Thetford; left up A1075; left by village sign; right at Xrds then bear left. In May masses of spring flowers and apple blossom; bluebell walk. June hundreds of old, specie and climbing roses, walled garden, trained fruit trees, extensive lawns. Fine old trees. TEAS. *Adm £1.50 Chd free (Share to Norfolk Churches Trust in May, and to Wretham Church in June). Suns May 16, June 27 (2.30-5.30). Also by appt Tel 0953 498 366*

Northamptonshire

Hon County Organiser:	Mrs John Boughey, Butts Close, Farthinghoe, Brackley NN13 5NY Tel 0295 710411
Asst Hon County Organiser:	Mrs John Bussens, Glebe Cottage, Titchmarsh, Kettering NN14 3DB Mrs R H N Dashwood, Farthinghoe Lodge, Nr Brackley, Northants NN13 5NX
Hon County Treasurer:	R H N Dashwood, Esq Farthinghoe Lodge, nr Brackley, Northants NN13 5NX Tel 0295 710377

DATES OF OPENING

By appointment
For telephone numbers and other details see garden descriptions

Harpole Gardens, 19 Manor Close,
72 Larkhall Lane
Maidwell Hall, Northampton
The Spring House, Chipping Warden

Regular openings
For details see garden descriptions

Coton Manor, Guilsborough. Open
Weds, Suns & Bank Hols Easter
to end of Sept. Thurs July & Aug
Cottesbrooke Hall, nr Creaton.
Open Bank Hol Mons, Thurs April
15 to Sept 30

April 4 Sunday
Charlton, nr Banbury
Finedon Gardens, nr
Wellingborough
April 12 Monday
Titchmarsh Gardens, nr Thrapston
April 18 Sunday
Great Brington Gardens, nr
Northampton
Newham Hall, Daventry
April 25 Sunday
Castle Ashby House, nr
Northampton
Maidwell Hall, Northampton
May 2 Sunday
The Haddonstone Show Garden,
nr Northampton
May 3 Monday
The Haddonstone Show Garden,
nr Northampton
May 9 Sunday
Barnwell Manor, nr Peterborough
Holdenby House, Northampton

Irthlingborough Gardens, nr
Wellingborough
May 16 Sunday
Deene Park, nr Corby
May 20 Thursday
Coton Manor, Guilsborough
May 23 Sunday
Barnwell Manor, nr Peterborough
Chacombe Gardens, nr Banbury
Guilsbororugh & Hollowell
Gardens
May 30 Sunday
Aldwincle Gardens, nr Thrapston
Cottesbrooke Hall, nr Creaton ‡
Gamekeepers Cottage,
Cottesbrooke, nr Creaton ‡
Irchester, 68, High St, nr
Wellingborough
Preston Capes Gardens
Sholebroke Lodge, Whittlebury,
Towcester
May 31 Monday
Irchester, 68, High St, nr
Wellingborough
Lois Weedon House, Weedon
Lois, Towcester
Titchmarsh Gardens, nr Thrapston
June 6 Sunday
Benefield House, Lower
Benefield, nr Oundle ‡
Litchborough Gardens, Towcester
Pilton & Stoke Doyle Gardens, nr
Oundle ‡
Stoke Park, Stoke Bruerne,
Towcester
Versions Farm, nr Brackley
June 12 Saturday
Canons Ashby House, Daventry
June 13 Sunday
Bulwick Park, nr Corby
Dolphins, Great Harrowden
Evenley Gardens, Brackley
Weedon Lois Gardens, nr
Towcester

June 14 Monday
Evenley Gardens, Brackley
June 19 Saturday
Flore Gardens, nr Northampton
June 20 Sunday
Creaton Gardens, nr Northampton
Flore Gardens, nr Northampton
Geddington Gardens, nr Kettering
The Menagerie, Horton, nr
Northampton
Turweston Gardens, Brackley
June 27 Sunday
Bulwick Rectory, Bulwick, nr Corby
Easton Neston, Towcester
Fotheringhay Gardens, nr Oundle
Harpole Gardens, Northampton
Wilby Gardens, nr
Wellingborough
July 4 Sunday
Guilsborough Court, Guilsborough
West Haddon Gardens, nr
Northampton
July 11 Sunday
Cranford Gardens, nr Kettering
Guilsborough Court, Guilsborough
Kilsby Gardens, nr Rugby
Pytchley House, nr Kettering
August 15 Sunday
The Menagerie, Horton, nr
Northampton
August 17 Tuesday
Coton Manor, Guilsborough
September 5 Sunday
Cottesbrooke Hall, nr Creaton ‡
Gamekeepers Cottage,
Cottesbrooke, nr Creaton ‡
The Haddonstone Show Garden,
nr Northampton
September 19 Sunday
Canons Ashby House, nr Daventry
Finedon Gardens, nr
Wellingborough
September 26 Sunday
Bulwick Rectory, Bulwick, nr Corby

DESCRIPTIONS OF GARDENS

Aldwincle Gardens ✿ 4m S of Oundle; 3m N of Thrapston on A605. Turn at The Fox at Thorpe Waterville. Aldwincle village 1½m. TEAS at Little Acre 6 Cross Lane in aid of St Peter's Church Aldwincle. *Combined adm £1.50 Chd free. Sun May 30 (2-6)*

All Saints View &✿ (Mr & Mrs D Welman) Small garden surrounding modern house built 5 years ago; mainly perennials with some annuals; vegetable garden in old allotment
Little Acre & (Mr & Mrs E P Bamford) Informal garden of about an acre with mature trees and shrubs; productive vegetable garden; water features and some new planting

The Maltings &⚭ (Mr & Mrs N Faulkner) ¾-acre old farm house walled garden replanned since 1983; lawns, mixed borders, scree bed, tender wall shrubs and spring bulbs

Old School House (Mr & Mrs R Raymond-Anderson) Small secluded mainly walled garden. Previously a rough lawn and vegetable patch; present design started in 1989, care being taken to preserve old box hedge and trees

Barnwell Manor & (HRH Princess Alice Duchess of Gloucester & The Duke & Duchess of Gloucester) nr Peterborough. 2m S of Oundle; 4½m NE of Thrapston on A605. Pleasant grounds, spring flowers. C13 castle ruins. Car park free. TEAS. *Adm £1 Chd Free. Suns May 9, 23 (2.30-6)*

Benefield House &⚭ ❀ (Mr & Mrs John Nicholson) Lower Benefield. 3m W Oundle off A427. Oundle-Corby rd. 2½-acre garden with large herbaceous border with interesting plants. Shrubbery laid out in 1992. Old walled kitchen gardens containing vegetables and flowers. TEA. *Adm £1.50 Chd free (Share to St Mary's Church). Sun June 6 (2-6)*

Bulwick Park &❀ (Mr & Mrs G T G Conant) 8m NE of Corby; 13m NE of Kettering; in Bulwick Village turn into Red Lodge Rd; enter park over cattle grid. Large garden, beautifully set; formal terrace; some fine mature trees, pleasant walks; C19 orangery. TEAS. *Adm £1.20 Chd free (Share to Action Research Multiple Sclerosis). Sun June 13 (2-5.30)*

Bulwick Rectory &⚭❀ (Revd & Mrs Mervyn Wilson) Bulwick. 8m NE of Corby; 13m NE of Kettering; next to Bulwick Church. 1½-acre old rectory garden largely remade and replanted since 1978 as a number of gardens with vistas and surprises. Dovecote; folly; stonewalls. Shrubs, old roses, mixed borders with wide variety of plants. Fruit trees 30 varieties of apple, 15 of pear and 12 of plum in various forms of training and quince medlar and vegetables. TEAS. *Adm 70p Chd 30p (Share to St Nicholas Church). Suns June 27, Sept 26 (2-5)*

Canons Ashby House &⚭ (The National Trust) nr Daventry. Formal gardens enclosed by walls being developed. Gate piers from 1710; fine topiary; axial arrangement of paths and terraces; wild flowers, old varieties of fruit trees, newly planted gardens. Home of the Dryden family since C16, Manor House 1550 with contemporary wall paintings and Jacobean plastering. TEAS. *Adm £3 Chd £1.50 (includes house). Reduced party rate. For NGS Sats June 12, Sun Sept 19 (12-5.30)*

Castle Ashby House &⚭ (The Marquis of Northampton) 6m E of Northampton. 1½m N of A428 Northampton-Bedford; turn off between Denton and Yardley Hastings. Parkland incl avenue planted at suggestion of William III in 1695; lakes etc by Capability Brown; Italian gardens with orangery; extensive lawns and trees. Nature trail. Elizabethan house (not open). TEA. *Adm £2 Chd & OAPs £1. For NGS Sun April 25 (11-6)*

Chacombe Gardens 4m NE of Banbury. On A361 from Banbury centre turn R signed to Chacombe. TEAS **17 Silver St**. *Combined adm £1.50 Chd free (Share to St Peter & St Paul Church). Sun May 23 (2-6)*

Cartmel ⚭ (Mr & Mrs J B Willis) Small informal garden with mixed borders, rockery and pond

The Old Vicarage (The Lady Sophia Schilizzi) 2½ acres; flowering shrubs, daffodils, spring bulbs, lawns, orchard, small kitchen garden, herbaceous border and four new raised beds

Poplars Farm &❀ (Mr & Mrs Geoff Jones) 4 acres mixed borders; streamside borders with ferns, species primulas and bog plants; kitchen garden; dry garden with alpines; wild areas with some growing willow for fuel, spring and summer meadow areas being developed, greenhouse with cacti and carnivorous plants. Thatched 1654 farmhouse (not open); stone barns, interesting cacti, carnivorous and herbaceous plants raised in the gardens for sale

17 Silver St ⚭ (Mr & Mrs Stephen Large) 2-acres under development; paddocks with shetland ponies; wild stream-side; mixed borders; rose garden with wall plantings; small court

Charlton 7m SE of Banbury, 5m W of Brackley. From A41 turn off N at Aynho; or from A422 turn off S at Farthinghoe. Home-made TEAS **the Cottage**. *Combined adm £1.50 Chd 75p (Share to Charlton Village Hall). Sun April 4 (2-6)*

The Cottage ⚭ (Lady Juliet Townsend) Flowering shrubs, spring bulbs, roses, lawns, woodland walk, stream and lakes. House in village street

Holly House (The Hon Nicholas Berry) Walled garden with beautiful views. C18 house (not open)

Coton Manor &❀ (Mr & Mrs Ian Pasley-Tyler) 10m N of Northampton. 11m SE of Rugby nr Ravensthorpe Reservoir. From A428 & A50 follow Tourist signs. C17 stone manor house with water gardens, herbaceous borders, rose garden, old holly and yew hedges; interesting variety of foliage plants; collection of ornamental waterfowl, cranes and flamingoes. Home-made TEAS. *Adm £2.50 OAPs £2 Chd 50p. Open Weds, Suns & Bank Hols. Easter to end Sept; also Thurs July & Aug. For NGS Thurs May 20, Tues Aug 17 (2-6)*

Cottesbrooke Hall &⚭❀ (Capt & Mrs J Macdonald-Buchanan) 10m N of Northampton. Nr Creaton on A50; nr Brixworth on A508. Car park free. Large formal and wild gardens; herbaceous borders, fine old cedars, greenhouses. (Brixworth Church, 2½m, dates back to C7, is well worth a visit). *Adm £3.50. Gardens only £1.50. House and Gardens, but not greenhouses, open Bank Hol Mons and Thurs April 15 to Sept 30 (2-5.30) Adm £1.50 Chd 50p (Share to All Saints Church). For NGS Suns May 30, Sept 5 (2-6)*

Cranford Gardens &⚭ 4½m E of Kettering. A14 Kettering-Thrapston. TEAS, Station House, Oakrise. Car parking available. *Combined adm £1.50 Chd 25p (Share to Cranford Churches Restoration Fund). Sun July 11 (2-6)*

¶**Butchers Farm House** (Mr & Mrs R J Stonebridge) Cottage garden with terrace. Variety of trees, conifers, shrubs and a natural pond

Cranford Hall (Sir John & Lady Robinson) Large garden incl lawns, herbaceous borders, mature woodland and young trees

¶**16 Duck End** (Miss Margaret Thomson) Very small cottage garden overlooking the church. Borders of perennials and shrubs

¶**Ivy Cottage** (Mrs P Stonebridge) A small ornamental country cottage garden. Interesting variety of minature conifers, shrubs, annuals and climbing plants

The Manor House &. (Mr & Mrs J M Bentley) Very interesting large stone walled traditional Manor House garden

Oakrise &. (Mr & Mrs G T Oakes) 5 The Green. ½ acre with variety of shrubs, perennials, dwarf conifers; Japanese water garden with Koi Carp and water plants; lovely view

¶**Station House** (Mr & Mrs A Bates) Garden created from the original railway station. Old platform now a walled patio with fish pond and rockery. Many varieties of trees, new planting of shrubs, herbaceous perennials. Natural wildlife pond

Creaton Gardens &.⚘ 8m N of Northampton on A50. Turn R into village onto village green. Teas at Creaton House in aid of St Michael & All Angels Church. *Combined adm £1.25 Acc chd free. Sun June 20 (2-6)*

Creaton Lodge (Mrs R T Gibbs) 2-acres well established garden with lawns, fine mature trees, shrubs, herbaceous borders and conifer banks. New water garden

¶**11 Home Farm Close** ⚘ (Daphne & Patrick Clark) ¼ acre, newly designed garden for all seasons, surrounding modern house. Vegetable plot; herb garden; greenhouse; ponds; informal patios

Stoneacre (Mr & Mrs R J E Hopewell) ⅓-acre, slightly sloping, mainly walled garden but with open views. A cottage garden with lawns, ponds, summerhouse, greenhouse, vegetable and fruit plots and containing some less usual trees, flowering shrubs and herbaceous plants in the mixed borders. Plant stall in aid of St. Michael & All Angels Church

Deene Park &.⚘ (Edmund Brudenell Esq) 5m N of Corby on A43 Stamford-Kettering Rd. Large garden; long mixed borders, old-fashioned roses, rare mature trees, shrubs, natural garden, large lake and waterside walks. New parterre designed by David Hicks echoing the C16 decoration on the porch stonework. Interesting Church and Brudenell Chapel with fine tombs and brasses. TEAS. *Adm £1.50 Chd 50p. Sun May 16 (2-5)*

Dolphins &.⚘ ⚘ (Mr & Mrs R C Handley) Great Harrowden. On A509 2m N of Wellingborough on the L. 5m S of Kettering on the R. 2-acre country garden surrounding old stone house. Many old roses grown among interesting trees, shrubs and a wide range of hardy perennials. TEAS in aid of Harrowlands Rehablitation Centre. *Adm £1 Chd free. Sun June 13 (2-6)*

Easton Neston &.⚘⚘ (The Lord & Lady Hesketh) Towcester. Entrance on Northampton Rd (old A43). Hawkesmoor's only Private house. Large formal garden; ornamental water, topiary; walled garden; woodland walk with C14 church (not open) in grounds not suitable for wheelchairs. TEA. *Adm £2 Chd 50p. Sun June 27 (2-6)*

Evenley Gardens &.⚘⚘ From Brackley 1m S on A43 Teas at Evenley Hall. *Combined adm £1.40 Chd 40p. Sun Mon June 13, 14 (2-6)*

¶**15 Church Lane** (Mr & Mrs K O'Regan) ⅓-acre garden, newly built terrace pond, mixed borders and vegetable garden

Five Gables ⚘⚘ (Mr & Mrs M Bosher) SE facing sloping garden of 1½ acres. Designed in 'compartments' and still being developed

Hill Grounds &.⚘ (Mr & Mrs C F Cropley) 2-acres facing sheltered garden re-developed since 1982; mature trees, 200 yds of yew hedge; terrace; old roses winter garden; wide range of unusual plants

The Manor House (Mr & Mrs H Bentley) Church Lane, just off NW corner of village green. Established garden on ½-acre sloping site; topiary and an ambience in harmony with fine Elizabethan Manor House (not open)

Finedon Gardens &.⚘⚘ Wellingborough. 2m NE of Wellingborough on the A510, 6m SE Kettering on the A6 TEAS at **Thingden Cottage** April 4; at Church Flower Festival Sept 19. *Combined adm £1.50 Chd free. Sun April 4, Sept 19 (2-6)*

4 Harrowden Lane (Mr & Mrs D J West) ½-acre garden on a steep slope, created in last 10 years from waste land; lawns, rose and flower beds; ornamental fish pond with cascade fountain, aviary and green houses

¶**Thingden Cottage** &.⚘ (Mrs M A Leach) 4½ acre of garden, originally Finedon Hall grounds. Lawns, ancient trees, shrubs, spring flowers, brook, hillside pasture with unique view of Finedon Hall and Church

Flore Gardens 7m W of Northampton, 5 m E of Daventry on A45. Flower Festival at All Saints Church and U.R Chapel inc. Teas, plants, etc. *Combined adm £2 Chd free (Shore to Flower Festival). Sat, Sun June 19, 20 (2-6)*

Beech Hill ⚘ (Dr & Mrs R B White) The garden of approx 1 acre is on a hillside facing S over the Nene Valley. It is laid out to lawns, herbaceous and shrub borders with mature trees. There is a vegetable garden and an orchard, an alpine house and cool green house. The terrace has hanging baskets and tubs

The Croft (John & Dorothy Boast) ⅓-acre garden of C17 cottage with mature trees, shrubs, lawns and interesting perennials

The Old Manor ⚘ (Mr & Mrs Keith Boyd) Early C1 house (not shown) with medium-sized garden, comprising lawn, herbaceous border, rose garden, vegetables and fruit. Pleasant views over the Nene valley Also paddock with pond and shrubs

The Manor House ⚘ (Richard & Wendy Amos) 1 acre garden with established lawns and herbaceous border surrounded by mature trees. Formal pond and kitchen garden. Partly suitable for wheelchairs

¶**21 Spring Lane** (Mr & Mrs T W Measures) An informal garden of just under 1 acre comprising lawns, shrub borders with mature trees, herbaceous borders Vegetable garden, pool and wild life area

6 Thornton Close (Mr & Mrs D L Lobb) Medium-size garden; trees, shrubs, herbaceous plants, conifers and alpines. 2 small ponds with fish

The White Cottage ♿✿ (Mr & Mrs G Menzies) Large cottage garden. Approx 1 acre; lawns, shrubs, perennial beds; fruit trees and vegetable garden

Fotheringhay Gardens ♿✿ 4m NE of Oundle signposted from A605 3m S of Wansford from A47 and A1. Teas available in village hall. *Combined adm £1.50 Chd free (Share to Fotheringhay Church Restoration Committee). Sun June 27 (11-6)*
  The Blacksmith's Cottage ✿✿ (Mr & Mrs G M B Wilson) ⅓-acre with recently constructed raised terrace; many trees and shrubs planted since 1986; 'Compost heaps a speciality with wormery'
  Chestnut Tree Cottage ♿✿ ✿ (Mr & Mrs John Ingram) ¼ acre country cottage garden; roses, flowering shrubs, large vegetable garden and greenhouse
  Lodge Lawn ♿✿ (Mrs R Blake) Medium-sized informal cottage garden. Developed since 1984
  The Old Vicarage ✿ (Mr & Mrs Peter Fryer) 1-acre of well established gardens, herbaceous borders shrubs, old roses and mature trees, unusual plants
  Willow House (Mr & Mrs C M Saunders) A 10yr-old-house and garden of ⅔-acre; mixed fruit and vegetables, herbaceous plants, shrubs and family play area

Gamekeepers Cottage Garden (Mr & Mrs D Daw) Cottesbrooke. 10m W of Northampton, nr Creaton on A50; nr Brixworth on A508. Cottage garden featuring unusual herbaceous plants, flowers for drying, fruit, vegetables. TEAS. *Combined adm £1.50 Chd 50p with Cottesbrooke Hall. Suns May 30, Sept 5 (2-6)*

Geddington Gardens 3m N of Kettering on the A43 Northampton-Stamford Rd. Attractive village with C13 Eleanor Cross. TEAS at **Long Barn**. *Combined adm £1.50 Chd free (Share to Geddington Village Hall Building Fund). Sun June 20 (2-6)*
  ¶**Grange Farmhouse** ♿✿ (Mr & Mrs D Slater) 1m from village on Grange Rd. ⅓-acre informal country garden. Lawns, mixed borders, climbing roses, reclaimed orchard
  The Long Barn ♿✿ (Mr & Mrs A Gordon) 2-acre garden with fine mature trees, shrubs, herbaceous borders and lawns sweeping down to the river
  ¶**Priory Cottage** ✿ (Mr & Mrs G Johns) Medium-sized, informal garden on 3 levels. Large variety of plants and shrubs
  ¶**7 West Street** ♿ (Mr & Mrs D Brown) Informal wildlife garden encouraging birds, butterflies, frogs and newts. Mainly organic, it has small pond, mixed borders, vegetables and fruit
  40 West Street ✿ (Mr & Mrs P Spence) Interesting garden constructed on the site of an old farmyard. Wide variety of unusual plants, shrubs and climbers
  ¶**Willow View** ♿✿ ✿ (Mr & Mrs R Sallabanks) ⅕-acre garden, newly developed; lawns, flower beds, vegetables, herb garden and patio. Access to **Wisteria Cottage** garden
  ¶**Wisteria Cottage** ✿ (Mr & Mrs Charles Lockwood) 1½-acre cottage garden with adjoining paddock under development, bordered by the Ise Brook. Access from Willow View

¶**Great Brington Gardens** 7m NW of Northampton off A428 Rugby rd. 1st L turn past main gates of Althorp. Tickets/maps at church. Gardens signed in village. Parking facilities. Ploughman's lunches, TEAS. Exhibition and plant stall at various village venues in aid of the Brington Appeal, St Mary's Church restoration fund. *Combined adm £1.50 Chd free. Sun April 19 (11-5)*
  ¶**Brington Lodge** ♿✿ (Mr & Mrs P J Cooch) An old garden on the edge of the village, approx ¾ acre, partially walled with a number of spring flowering trees and shrubs
  ¶**Folly House** ✿ ✿ (Capt & Mrs L G Bellamy) Early C18 house (not shown) 1-acre garden, lawns, herbaceous, shrubs and vegetable garden. Interesting setting using different levels with the church as background
  ¶**30 Great Brington** ♿✿ (Mr & Mrs John Kimbell) Interesting small garden attached to old stone cottage, well-stocked with shrubs, climbers and perennials. Small pond with bog area, secret garden
  ¶**The Last Straw** ♿✿ (Mr & Mrs A Johnson) C15 thatched cottage with cottage garden. Pleasent views of Althorp. Many spring-flowering bulbs, summer hut
  ¶**The Old Rectory** ♿✿ (Mr & Mrs R Thomas) 3-acre garden, with mature trees, yew hedging, formal rose garden, vegetable and small herb gardens. ½ acre of orchard
  ¶**Ridgway House** ✿ (Mr & Mrs John Gale) 1½ acres with lawns, herbaceous borders and many spring-flowering shrubs and bulbs

Guilsborough Court ♿✿ (Mr & Mrs John Lowther) Guilsborough. 10m N of Northampton off A50. 10m NE of Daventry; 10m E of Rugby; ¼m outside Guilsborough on Cold Ashby rd. 4-acre garden, many fine mature trees, beautiful views, interesting shrubs, large lawn and herbaceous border. TEAS. *Adm £1 Chd free. Suns July 4, 11 (2-6)*

Guilsborough and Hollowell Gardens 10m NW of Northampton between A50 - A428. 10m E of Rugby. Cream Teas at **Dripwell House** by Guilsborough WI. TEAS at Hollowell Village Hall. *Combined adm £1.50 Chd 50p. Sun May 23 (2-6)*
  Dripwell House ✿✿ Guilsborough (Mr & Mrs J W Langfield, Dr C Moss, Mr & Mrs P G Moss) 2½-acre mature garden; many fine trees and shrubs on partly terraced slope. Rock garden, herbaceous border, herb garden. Some unusual shrubs and many rhododendrons and azaleas in woodland garden. Cream teas in garden
  Manor House Farm, Nortoft, Guilsborough ♿✿✿ (Mr & Mrs J M Clissold) Plantsman's 1-acre garden surrounding old stone farmhouse. Herbaceous borders with shrub roses, silver & white garden, heather bank, naturalised small narcissi. New formal vegetable garden, leading from tunnel with herbs and climbers
  Rosemount, Hollowell ✿✿ (Mr & Mrs J Leatherland) In centre of village, up hill behind bus shelter towards Church, entrance 100yds on R. ½-acre plantsman's garden reconstructed about 7 yrs ago, unusual plants and shrubs, alpine garden, fish pond, small collections of clematis, conifers, camellias, daphne and abutilons. Partly suitable for wheelchairs. Car parking and teas at village hall behind Church

The Haddonstone Show Garden, East Haddon Manor &❀ (Mr & Mrs R Barrow) 10m N of Northampton, 12m S of Rugby, from A50. Walled garden on different levels, old shrub roses, ground cover plants, conifers, clematis and climbers; swimming pool surrounded by Haddonstone Colonnade, over 30 planted pots and containers. Refreshments. *Adm £2 Chd free (Share to NSPCC) Garden Festival Weekend Sun, Mon, May 2, 3, (10-5) Adm £1.50 Chd free Sun Sept 5 (2-5)* TEAS. Special autumn plant sale

Harpole Gardens 4m W Northampton on A45 towards Weedon; turn right at 'The Turnpike' into Harpole. TEAS at **The Grange**. *Combined adm £1.50 Chd free. Sun June 27 (2-6)*

    The Close &❀ (Mr & Mrs Orton Jones) 68 High Street. Old-fashioned English country garden with large lawns, herbaceous borders and mature trees; stone house, various plant stalls

    The Grange & 55 Upper High St; 2-acre garden with interesting shrubberies, walks, herbaceous borders, fruit trees, kitchen garden; C18 family home (not open)

    72 Larkhall Lane (Mr & Mrs R G Murton) ⅙-acre well designed garden for all seasons; a flower to bloom everyday of the year; shrubs; variety of conifers and alpines. *Also by appt* **Tel 0604 830680**

    19 Manor Close ✗ (Mr & Mrs E Kemshed) 40yd × 10yd flower arranger's garden on new estate; cultivated by present owners since 1975. *Also by appt* **Tel 0604 830512**

    32 School Lane ✗ (Mr & Mrs A C Digby) Small 40′ × 25′ sun-lovers walled garden featuring potted and wall trained fruit; sunken garden with rockeries; herbs; tubs and alpine sinks. Lovely views over open countryside

Holdenby House ✗❀ (James Lowther Esq) 7m W of Northampton. Signposted from A50 and A428. Impressive remains of terrace gardens of Holdenby Palace, where Charles I was imprisoned; Elizabethan garden; fragrant and silver borders. Rare breeds farm animals; museum, falconry centre. TEAS. *Adm £2.50 (groups of 25 or more £2) Chd £1.50.* ▲*For NGS Sun May 9 (2-6). House open by appt Adm £3.50 (groups of 25 or more)*

Irchester, 68 High Street &✗❀ (Mr & Mrs R G Parker) 3m SE of Wellingborough, off A45. If coming from S then turn R off the A509. The garden is down a drive almost opposite St Katharine's Church. Please park in High St. ½-acre informal and interesting mixed garden developed over a 15-year period. There are flowering trees, shrubs, conifers, herbaceous plants, alpines and planted sinks. Some unusual plants. TEA. *Adm £1 Sun, Mon May 30, 31 (2-6)*

¶**Irthlingborough Gardens** &✗ 5m E of Wellingborough, off the A6. TEAS. *Combined adm £1 Chd free. Sun May 9 (2-6)*

    ¶**45 Finedon Road** (Mr & Mrs G Brown) 40′ × 70′ garden of formal design with informal planting of trees, shrubs, bulbs, climbers and perennials. Pond and courtyard

49 Finedon Road &✗ (Mr & Mrs D Ingall) A garden full of interest and unusual plants which includes spring bulbs, herbaceous border, shrubs, pools, gravel bed and rock, wild and scented areas. Also fruit and vegetables

Kilsby Gardens ✗ 5m SE of Rugby on A428 turn R on B4038 through village. 6m N of Daventry on A361. Flower Festival at St Faith's Church and UR Chapel. Teas in village hall. *Combined adm £1.50 Chd free. Sun July 11 (2-6)*

    Croft Close (Mr & Mrs P Couldrey) Rugby Rd. Herbaceous beds, shrubs, pond and rockery. Productive vegetable garden, soft fruit, greenhouse

    The Haven & (Mr & Mrs Arthur Old) Essen Lane. ½-acre walled garden of listed cottage

    Lawn House (Mr & Mrs B Morris) 7 The Lawns. Small walled garden with no grass (despite name of house); formal pond; mixture of surfaces: paving, cobbles, shingle; climbing and rock plants; variety of containers

    Pytchley &❀ (Mr & Mrs T F Clay) 14 Main Rd. 1-acre mature garden; lawns; trees; island beds; vegetable garden; 3 fish ponds; wild garden

    The Old Vicarage & (Mr & Mrs P G B Jackson) On A5 opp George Hotel. 1-acre; lawns, mature trees, shrubs, herbaceous border, small water garden, vegetable garden

    ¶**Rainbow's End** & (Mr & Mrs J J Madigan) Middle St. Approx ⅛-acre mixed garden with large pond feature and own design of pergola patio

    ¶**1 Smarts Estate** & (Mr & Mrs Sheasby) Decorative front garden with climbers and bedding. Back garden vegetables and flowers grown for showing. Greenhouses

    15 Smarts Estate (Mr & Mrs A R Collins) Mature, small garden with shrubs, climbers, herbaceous border, pond and vegetable garden, fruit. Greenhouse

Litchborough Gardens ✗ Towcester, Litchborough village is on B4525 mid-way between Northampton and Banbury. Teas in WI Hall, Farthingstone Rd. *Combined adm £1 Chd free (Share to St Martins Church). Sun June 6 (2-6)*

    The Hall & (A R Heygate Esq) Large garden with open views of parkland; laid to lawns and borders with clipped hedges around the house; the extensive wild garden has large numbers of specimen trees and shrubs; walks wind through this area and round the lakes

    Orchard House ❀ (Mr & Mrs B Smith) Banbury Rd, Landscape architects country garden designed for low maintenance; orchard, pools, conservatory and working pump

Lois Weedon House ❀ (Mr & Mrs John Greenaway) Weedon Lois. 7m from Towcester on the edge of Weedon Lois village. Pass through village going E towards Wappenham; as you leave village Lois Weedon House next entrance on R, further on is second entrance which has a lodge. Medium-sized garden with terraces and fine views; lawns; pergola; water garden; mature yew hedges. TEAS. *Adm £1.50 Chd free (Share to Lois Weedon PCC). Mon May 31 (2-6)*

Maidwell Hall ⚘ (Mr & Mrs J H Paul, of Maidwell Hall School) A508 N from Northampton, 6m S of Market Harborough, entrance via cattle grid on S fringe of Maidwell village. 45 acres of lawns, playing fields, woodland. Colourful display of spring bulbs, magnolias and early flowering shrubs; mature rose garden; lake and arboretum. TEA. *Adm £1.50 Chd free (Share to St Mary's Church, Maidwell). Sun April 25 (2-6) also by appt April to July, Sept to Oct* **Tel 060128 234**

¶**The Menagerie** ⚘ (Mr G Jackson-Stop & Mr I Kirby) Horton. 6m S of Northampton. On B526 turn L 1m S of Horton. An C18 folly with Rococo plasterwork room (open). A garden in the making. Designed as an architectural journey, with formal water gardens, informal wetlands. Rose garden and a spiral mound. 4.5 acres. TEAS. *Adm £2 Chd 50p. Suns June 20, August 15 (2-6)*

Newnham Hall ⚘ (Lt Colonel John Chandos-Pole) 1½m S of Daventry, 4-acres facing S over Nene Valley; topiary walk; walled kitchen garden; mixed borders; wild garden and roses. TEAS. *Adm £1 Chd 50p (Share to Northampton and County Association for the Blind). Sun April 18 (2-6)*

Pilton & Stoke Doyle Nr Oundle ⚘ Take A605 and midway between Oundle and Thrapston turn W at cross roads to go past Lilford Park to Pilton. For Stoke Doyle continue to next crossroads and turn R. Teas available at Wadenhoe Village Hall. *Combined adm £1.20 Chd free. Sun June 6 (2-6)*
Elmes House (Mr and Mrs J H Otter) Pilton. Two walled gardens with various perennial and shrub borders. Grass tennis court leading to over 2-acres of rough ground with woodland walk. Trees planted in 1973
Mill House (Mr & Mrs H Faure Walker) Stoke Doyle. Medium-sized walled garden, mixed borders; vegetable garden; area from field leading to stream recently planted with trees, yews and shrub roses. Plant stall

¶**Preston Capes Gardens** ⚘ Approx 7m S of Daventry, 3m N of Canon's Ashby. TEAS. *Comb adm £2 Chd 50p (Share to St Peter's & St Paul's Church). Sun May 30 (2-6)*
¶**Archway Cottage** (Mr & Mrs King) Approx ½-acre garden, with outstanding views over Northants countryside. Lawns with specimen shrubs, herbaceous borders and ornamental fish pond. Sloping plot being converted to nature garden, with natural pond, marginal plants and berry-bearing trees and shrubs
¶**City Cottage** ⚘ (Mr & Mrs Gavin Cowen) A mature garden in the middle of an attractive village, with a walled herbaceous border, rose beds, flowering shrubs, wisteria and magnificent magnolia tree
¶**Old West Farm** ⚘ (Mr & Mrs Gerard Hoare) Little Preston. Between Charwelton (A361) and Maidford. 2-acre garden re-designed since 1980. Small woodland area with bulbs, borders, roses and flowering shrubs for year round interest

Pytchley House ⚘ (Lady Glover) Pytchley, 3m S of Kettering. Between A43 & A509. Rose garden, lawns, fine trees and topiary; Temple of Zeus. House 1633. **Essential** dogs kept on leads. Produce stall. TEAS. *Adm 75p Chd 25p (Share to NSPCC). Sun July 11 (2.30-6)*

Sholebroke Lodge ⚘ (A B X Fenwick Esq) Whittlebury, 3m S of Towcester. Turn off A413 Towcester end of Whittlebury village. 5-acres informal garden; large new planting of shrubs, bulbs, wild flowers and interesting plants in established setting. Garden shop. Home-made TEAS. *Adm £1 Chd 50p. Sun May 30 (2-6)*

The Spring House (Mr & Mrs C Shepley-Cuthbert) Mill Lane Chipping Warden on A361 between Banbury and Daventry. Garden originally laid out by Miss Kitty Lloyd Jones in the thirties and now mature. Approx 3 acres app through a 16′ tapestry hedge. April-May spring flowers, bulbs and blossom. June-Sept bog and water garden at its most colourful. Other times unconventional borders, shrub roses and specimen trees with many new plantings. Ploughmans lunches and Teas available for groups & clubs by arrangement. *Open by appt* **Tel 0295 86261**

Stoke Park ⚘ (R D Chancellor Esq) Stoke Bruerne Towcester. Stoke Bruerne village lies 1m off A508 between Northampton and Stony Stratford. Stoke Park is down a private road ¾m, first turning left, ¼m beyond village. Approx 3-acres. Terraced lawn with ornamental basin, orchard, herb garden, shrub and other borders, as setting to two C17 pavillions and colonnade. TEA. *Adm £1, Chd 50p.* ▲*Sun June 6 (2-6)*

Titchmarsh Gardens ⚘ 2m N of Thrapston, 6m S of Oundle on A605, Titchmarsh signposted as turning to E. TEAS. *Combined adm £1.50 Chd free (Share to St Marys Church, Titchmarsh). Mons April 12, May 31 (2-6)*
Crown Cottage (Rev & Mrs H W Williams) 28, Church Street. ⅓ acre. Old cottage garden established trees and shrubs mixed borders, wide views. *April 12*
Glebe Cottage ⚘ (Mr & Mrs J Bussens) ⅓ acre; NE aspect; informal herbaceous and shrub borders and beds. Clematis in a variety of situations
The Manor House ⚘ (Mr Leonard Harper) A one-acre garden comprising a wide range of well-matured flowering shrubs and rose beds. Paddock with spring flowers and good views of countryside
16 Polopit (Mr & Mrs C Millard) ½ acre. Developed since 1984; rockeries, ornamental and herbaceous borders; fruit decorative shrubs
Titchmarsh House ⚘ (Mr & Mrs Ewan Harper) 3½ acres extended and laid out since 1972; cherries, magnolias, herbaceous irises; shrub roses, clematis, range of shrubs, walled borders

Turweston Gardens A43 from Oxford, in Brackley turn R at traffic lights. A422 towards Buckingham, 1m turn L signposted Turweston. TEAS in village hall. *Combined adm £2 Chd 50p (Share to St Mary's Restoration Fund). Sun June 20 (2-6)*
Spring Valley (Mr & Mrs A Wildish) 1-acre terraced garden with ponds
Turweston Barn (Mr & Mrs Anthony Kirkland) 2 acres informal planting, mixed herbaceous and shrub borders, lawns, woodland and walled garden
Turweston House (Mrs Octavian von Hofmannsthal) 5½ acres landscaped garden; walled garden and lake
Turweston Mill (Mr & Mrs H Leventis) 5 acres, mill stream, water garden, lawns

Versions Farm &✿❀ (Mrs E T Smyth-Osbourne) Brackley 2m N of Brackley on the Turweston Rd. 3-acres plantsmans garden; old stone walls; terraces; rose garden; shrubs and trees some unusual, newly laid out pond and knot garden Conservatory. TEAS. *Adm £1.20 Chd free (Share to Whitfield Church). Sun June 6 (2-6)*

Weedon Lois Gardens ✿❀ Nr Towcester. 8m W of Towcester. TEAS. *Combined adm £1.50 Chd free. Sun June 13 (2-6)*
¶**Elizabeth House** & (Mr & Mrs A Cartwright & Mr & Mrs N Cartwright) A C17 vicarage garden now divided into two. 2½ acres with herbaceous beds, unusual shrubs, a walled vegetable garden and wild wooded area
The Old Barn (Mr & Mrs John Gregory) Small ⅓-acre plantsman's garden designed by the owners to compliment converted C18 barn; on a sloping site with interesting selection of herbaceous perennials, climbing plants, shrub roses and gravel gardens

West Haddon Gardens ✿❀ As seen on BBC TV in 1992. The village is on the A428 between Rugby and Northampton and lies 4m E of M1 exit 18. TEAS. *Combined adm £1.50 Chd free (Share to West Haddon Parish Church and West Haddon Baptist Church). Sun July 4 (2-6)*
The Bungalow West Haddon Hall (John and Jean Terry) Small secluded informal garden surrounded by mature trees with rockery; lawns; mixed borders; two aviaries and pond
Crystal House & (Pat and Dick Hughes) ¼-acre of landscaped garden, mostly walled, informal terrace areas, lawn and mixed borders, many containers and hanging baskets, new summerhouse and vegetable garden

> **Regular Openers.** See head of county section.

Hardays House & (Ian and Anne Ballantyne) 1½-acres, lawns and shrubbery on sloping ground with south- facing views, pond, vegetable garden, new flower beds
Lime House (Leslie and David Roberts) ⅓-acre of sloping garden with rockeries, shrubbery, rose garden, croquet lawn, summerhouse and greenhouse
The Mews (Rob and Jane Dadley) ½-acre of secluded walled garden including lawns, secret garden, herbaceous border, formal and informal ponds, statuary and pergolas
Well Cottage (Rosemary Wright) Very small walled garden on various levels displaying many containers, pond and a variety of plants
West Cottages & (Geoff and Rosemary Sage) ⅔-acre of mixed borders and lawns; informal pond; lawn tennis court and kitchen garden. Newly acquired additional land; garden under construction. Open views

Wilby Gardens. 3m SW of Wellingborough on the A4500 to Northampton signposted Wilby. TEAS at **Wilby House**. *Combined adm £1.50 Chd free. Sun June 27 (2-6)*
¶**Glebe Farmhouse** &✿ (Mr & Mrs K B Shipp) Medium-sized garden with shrub and herbaceous borders
¶**7 Mears Ashby Road** ✿ (Mr & Mrs K H Coleman) Small garden containing shrubs and herbaceous borders. Variety of plants in containers, plenty of colour
Wilby Cottage &✿ (Mr & Mrs B K Gale) Well established cottage garden, surrounded by walls and hedge, shrubs, herbaceous border, rockery and tubs, a plantsman's garden
Wilby House &✿ (Mr & Mrs W Barker) 5 acres of garden with some established trees and old stone walls; formal rose garden with box hedges, herbaceous borders, shrubs and trees planted within the last 10 years; lawns and kitchen garden

Northumberland

Hon County Organiser: Mrs G Baker Cresswell, Preston Tower, Chathill, Northumberland NE67 5DH
Tel 0665 89210
Assistant Hon County Organiser: Mrs T Sale, Ilderton Glebe, Ilderton, Alnwick, Northumberland NE66 4YD
Tel 06687 293

DATES OF OPENING

April 18 Sunday
Belsay Hall Gardens, nr Ponteland
Preston Tower, Chathill
May 16 Sunday
Wallington, Cambo
May 23 Sunday
Lilburn Tower, Alnwick

June 13 Sunday
Berryburn, Ancroft
Chillingham Castle, Chillingham
Meldon Park, Morpeth
June 17 Thursday
Herterton House, Morpeth
June 26 Saturday
Kirkley Hall College, Ponteland
June 27 Sunday
Bradley Gardens, Wylam

Chesters Walled Garden, nr
Hexham
Kirkley Hall College, Ponteland
Loughbrow House, Hexham
Mindrum, Cornhill on Tweed
July 4 Sunday
Belsay Hall Gardens, nr
Ponteland
July 8 Thursday
Herterton House, Morpeth

July 14 Wednesday
Bridge House, Ponteland
July 18 Saturday
Cragside, Rothbury
Kiwi Cottage, Scremerston

July 21 Wednesday
Bridge House, Ponteland
July 25 Sunday
Blenkinsopp Hall,
Haltwhistle

July 28 Wednesday
Bridge House, Ponteland
August 5 Thursday
Herterton House, Morpeth

DESCRIPTIONS OF GARDENS

Belsay Hall, Castle & Gardens ♿❀ (English Heritage) Ponteland. Belsay village lies 14m NW of Newcastle-upon-Tyne, on the A696 OS map 88. Ref NZ 082785. 30-acres newly restored C19 garden incl formal terraces; large heather garden; rhododendrons, rare trees & shrubs. Quarry garden covering several acres. Belsay Hall & Castle within the grounds. TEAS and refreshments. *Adm (incl Hall and Castle) £2.20 Concessions £1.60 Chd £1.25. Suns April 18, July 4 (10-6)*

Berryburn ✗ (Mr & Mrs W J Rogers-Coltman) Ancroft. 5m S of Berwick. Take Ancroft Mill Rd off A1 for 1m; drive entrance 2nd turn on R beside council bridge. 4 acres created from wilderness since 1981. Mixed borders; shrubs; shrub roses; woodland walk alongside burn with progressive tree planting. TEAS and stalls in aid of CRMF. *Adm £1.50 Chd free. Sun June 13 (2-5)*

¶Blenkinsopp Hall ♿ (Mrs J E Joicey) Haltwhistle. Entrance off A69, ½m W of Haltwhistle. Herbaceous borders, rockery, kitchen garden. Grounds with lake and woodland walk. TEAS. *Adm £1 Chd free. Sun July 25 (2-6)*

Bradley Gardens ♿❀ (Mr & Mrs J Hick) Sled Lane, Wylam. Along A695 between Crawcrook and Prudhoe. Approx ½m W from Crawcrook, R.A.C. signposted. A69 through Wylam, over bridge S of R Tyne, 3rd turning R, ¼m up lane. Signposted from Wylam. Approx 2 acres walled garden formerly kitchen garden to Bradley Hall. We specialise in herbs, both pot grown and fresh cut. Display beds of herbs, herbaceous border, childrens play area and greenhouse to view. Cottage garden plants and a selection of shrubs and bedding also available. Scented garden and shop. TEA. *Adm £1 Chd free. Sun June 27 (9-5)*

Bridge House ♿❀✗ (Dr & Mrs J C White) Fox Covert Lane, Ponteland. 8m NW of Newcastle. Just off A696, last L turn before leaving Ponteland village (travelling W). ¼m down Fox Covert Lane. 1¼-acre garden, only 6 yrs old. Includes riverside planting, vegetable garden, herbs, mixed borders and summer meadow. TEAS. *Adm £1 Chd free. Weds July 14, 21, 28 (2-5)*

Chesters ♿✗ (Major & Mrs J E Benson) Humshaugh. 5m N of Hexham. ½m W of Chollerford on B6318. Curved terraced border in front of C18 house with 1891 wings designed by Norman Shaw. Herbaceous borders, rock garden, lawns overlooking ha-ha and parkland with fine views over the North Tyne. TEAS. *Combined adm with* **Chesters Walled Garden** *£1.50 Chd under 10 free. Sun June 27 (1-5)*

Chesters Walled Garden ♿❀❀ (Hexham Herbs) Chollerford. 6m N of Hexham, just off the B6318. ½m W of Chollerford roundabout, past the entrance to Chesters Roman Fort, take L turning signposted Fourstones and immediately L through stone gateposts. 2-acre walled garden containing a very extensive collection of herbs. Raised thyme bank, home to the National Thyme Collection, Roman garden, Elizabethan-style knot garden, gold and silver garden and collection of dye plants. Herbaceous borders contain many unusual plants and old-fashioned roses. Outside the walled garden is a newly-planted wildflower meadow and woodland walk. Hexham Herbs won a large gold medal at National Garden Festival, Gateshead 1990 and featured on BBC2's 'Gardener's World'. Shop. *Combined adm with* **Chesters** *£1.50 Chd under 10 free. Sun June 27 (1-5)*

Chillingham Castle ✗ (Sir Humphry Wakefield) Chillingham. N from Alnwick, S from Berwick-upon-Tweed. Parkland landscaped with avenues and lodges by Sir Geoffrey de Wyattville fresh from his Royal triumph at Windsor in 1828. Lake and woodland walks with finest specimen trees in the region. Moats removed and gardens brought up to castle 1752. Italian and French topiary garden with largest herbaceous border in Northern England all restored with urns and fountains. TEAS. *Adm £3 OAPs £2.50 Chd £2. Sun June 13 (1.30-5)*

Cragside ✗ (The National Trust) Rothbury, 13m SW of Alnwick (B6341); 15m NW of Morpeth (B6344). Open for the first time in 1992 Lord Armstrong's original formal garden, incl orchard house, fernery, terraces and rose loggia. Extensive grounds of over 1000 acres on S edge of Alnwick Moor; famous for magnificent trees; rhododendrons and beautiful lakes. House designed by Richard Norman Shaw, famous Victorian architect; built 1864-1895; contains much original furniture designed by Shaw; also pictures and experimental scientific apparatus (it was 1st house in the world to be lit by electricity generated by water power). Café. Shop. Grounds, Power Circuit and Armstrong Energy Centre. TEAS. *Adm House, Garden & Grounds £5.40; Garden & Grounds £3.30 Chd half price. Family ticket House, Garden & Grounds (2 adults & 2 chd) £14. For NGS Sun July 18 (10.30-7)*

Herterton House ✗❀ (Frank Lawley Esq) Hartington. Cambo, Morpeth. 2m N of Cambo on the B6342 signposted to Hartington. (23m NW of Newcastle-on-Tyne). 1 acre of formal garden in stone walls around a C16 farmhouse. Incl a small topiary garden, physic garden, flower garden and a nursery garden. Planted since 1976. *Adm £1.10 Chd free.* ▲*For NGS Thurs June 17, July 8, Aug 5 (1.30-5.30)*

By Appointment Gardens. These owners do not have a fixed opening day usually because they do not like crowds or have insufficient parking space. Owner will often give guided tour.

Kirkley Hall College &✕❀ (Dr R McParlin) Ponteland. 2½m N of Ponteland. Off A696 Newcastle upon Tyne to Jedburgh Rd. 4m S of B6524 Morpeth to Belsay Rd, 8m W of A1 Newcastle upon Tyne to Morpeth Rd RAC signposted. Turn L at main drive gates, travel W for approx ¼m turn R at Horticultural Centre signboard. 10-acre garden and grounds, plantsman's paradise, plants labelled; trees, shrubs, ornamental borders, herbaceous perennials, sunken garden, wide range of dwarf conifers, alpines, wall trained fruit, greenhouses, propagation. Free car and coach parking. TEAS. *Adm £1.50 OAPs & Chd over 8 70p, under 8 free. ▲For NGS Sat, Sun June 26, 27 (10-5). For information Tel 0661 860808*

¶**Kiwi Cottage** &❀ (Col J I M Smail) Scremerston. Kiwi Cottage is in the village of Scremerston, about 2½m due S of Berwick-upon-Tweed. It is the 1st house on the R hand side of the village, off the A1 rd coming from the S and the last house on the L hand side of the village when travelling S from Berwick-upon-Tweed. Entrance through gateway next to War Memorial. Please drive in and do not park on the rd. 3-acre garden with lawns, annuals, herbaceous plants, providing colour and interest throughout the year. Shrubs, orchard and large vegetable garden TEA. *Adm £1. Sat July 18 (2-5)*

Lilburn Tower ✕ (Mr & Mrs D Davidson) Alnwick. 3m S of Wooler on A697. 10 acres of walled and formal gardens including conservatory and large glass house. About 30 acres of woodland with walks and pond garden. Also ruins of Pele Tower and C15 Chapel. Rhododendrons and azaleas. TEAS. *Adm £1 Chd 25p under 5 free. Sun May 23 (2-6)*

Loughbrow House &✕❀ (Mrs K A Clark) Hexham. Take B6306 from Hexham fork R, lodge gates in intersection of 2nd fork, ½m up drive. 5 acres; woodland garden; herbaceous borders, roses, wide lawns; kitchen garden. Homemade TEAS. *Adm £1 Chd 25p. Sun June 27 (2-6)*

Meldon Park &✕ (M J B Cookson Esq) Morpeth. Situated 6m W of Morpeth on B6343. Victorian and Edwardian laid out garden, with walled kitchen garden, herbaceous borders, roses and woodland walk with azaleas and rhododendrons. TEAS. *Adm £1 Chd 50p. Sun June 13 (2-5)*

Mindrum ✕❀ (Hon P J Fairfax) Cornhill on Tweed. On B6352, 4m from Yetholm, 5m from Cornhill on Tweed. Old-fashioned roses; rock and water garden; shrub borders. Wonderful views along Bowmont Valley. Approx 2 acres. TEAS. *Adm £1 Chd 50p. Sun June 27 (2-6)*

Preston Tower &✕❀ (Maj & Mrs T Baker Cresswell) Chathill. 7m N of Alnwick, take the turn to the R ¼m beyond Esso garage and Little Chef, signed to Preston and Chathill. Preston Tower is at the top of a hill, in 1¼m. Mostly shrubs and woodland; daffodils and azaleas. C14 Pele Tower with great views from the top. TEAS. *Adm £1 Chd 50p. Sun April 18 (2-5)*

Wallington &❀ (The National Trust) Cambo. From N 12m W of Morpeth (B6343); from S via A696 from Newcastle, 6m W of Belsay, B6342 to Cambo. Walled, terraced garden with fine shrubs and species roses; conservatory with magnificent fuchsias; 100 acres woodland and lakes. House dates from 1688 but altered and interior greatly changed c.1740; exceptional rococo plasterwork by Francini brothers; fine porcelain, furniture, pictures, needlework, dolls' houses, museum, display of coaches. Café. Shop. *Adm to House and Garden £4; Grounds only £2. Chd half price. Last admission (5). For NGS Sun May 16 (10-7)*

Regular Openers. Too many days to include in diary. Usually there is a wide range of plants giving year-round interest. See head of county section for the name and garden description for times etc.

Nottinghamshire

Hon County Organisers: Mr & Mrs A R Hill, The White House, Nicker Hill, Keyworth, Nottinghamshire NG12 5EA Tel 0602 372049

Assistant Hon County Organisers: Mr & Mrs J Nicholson, 38 Green Lane, Lambley, Nottingham Tel 0602 312998

Hon County Treasurer: Mr J Gray, 43 Cliffway, Radcliffe-on-Trent, Nottinghamshire NG12 1AQ Tel 0602 334272

DATES OF OPENING

By appointment
For telephone number and other details see garden descriptions

17 Bridle Rd, Burton Joyce

Holmes Villa, Walkeringham
Mill Hill House, East Stoke
The Old Mill House, Cuckney
St Helens Croft, Halam

Regular openings
For details see garden descriptions
Felley Priory, Underwood. For dates see text
Hodsock Priory, Blyth. For dates see text

April 4 Sunday
Gateford Hill Nursing Home
Fulbeck Hall, nr Grantham (see
Lincs for details)
The Old Rectory, Fulbeck, nr
Grantham (see Lincs for
details)
April 7 Wednesday
The Willows, Radcliffe-on-Trent
April 11 Sunday
Felley Priory, Underwood
Hodsock Priory, Blyth
St Helens Croft, Halam
April 12 Monday
St Helens Croft, Halam
April 14 Wednesday
Springwell House, Brinkley
April 18 Sunday
Morton Hall, Retford
Stocks Farm, Leadenham (see
Lincs for details)
April 21 Wednesday
38 Green Lane, Lambley
Rose Cottage, Underwood
May 2 Sunday
Mill Hill House, East Stoke
Morton Hall, Retford
Trent Farm House, Fiskerton
May 3 Monday
Thurlby Farm, Stanton on the
Wolds ‡
The White House, Keyworth ‡
May 4 Tuesday
St Helens Croft, Halam
May 5 Wednesday
The Willows, Radcliffe-on-Trent
May 9 Sunday
Gringley on the Hill Gardens
May 16 Sunday
Morton Hall, Retford
May 19 Wednesday
38 Green Lane, Lambley
16 Prince Edward Crescent,
Radcliffe-on-Trent
May 22 Saturday
Epperstone Gardens
May 23 Sunday
Epperstone Gardens

Field House Nursing Home
May 30 Sunday
Burton Joyce Gardens
Gardeners Cottage, Papplewick ‡
Mill Hill House, East Stoke
Papplewick Gardens, Papplewick ‡
June 2 Wednesday
Gardeners Cottage, Papplewick
The Willows, Radcliffe-on-Trent
June 6 Sunday
5 Long Row, Kingston on Soar
The Old Slaughterhouse, Shipley
Gate (see Derbyshire for
details)
Park Farm, Normanton, Bottesford
Rose Cottage, Underwood
Southwell Gardens
June 13 Sunday
6 Cherwell Court, Bulwell
Felley Priory, Underwood
Hazel Cottage, Treswell, nr
Retford
Mill Hill House, East Stoke
June 16 Wednesday
38 Green Lane, Lambley
June 19 Saturday
The Old Barn Gdns, Plungar (see
Leics for details)
June 20 Sunday
Flintham Hall, Flintham, nr
Newark
Marston Hall, nr Grantham (see
Lincs for details)
The Old Barn Gdns, Plungar (see
Leics for details)
St Helens Croft, Halam
June 23 Wednesday
Hodsock Priory, Blyth
June 26 Saturday
Colwick Gardens
June 27 Sunday
Gamston Gardens
Green Mile, Babworth
Holmes Villa, Walkeringham
Mattersey House, Mattersey
Skreton Cottage, Screveton
July 4 Sunday
Epperstone Festival Gardens

The Old Slaughterhouse, Shipley
Gate (see Derbyshire for
details)
Sutton Bonington Hall, Sutton
Bonington
Thrumpton Hall, Nottingham
Upton Gardens
July 6 Tuesday
St Helens Croft, Halam
July 7 Wednesday
The Willows, Radcliffe-on-Trent
July 11 Sunday
Gringley on the Hill Gardens
Mill Hill House, East Stoke
July 18 Sunday
Greenways, Bathley
14 Temple Drive, Nuthall
July 25 Sunday
Thurlby Farm, Stanton on the
Wolds ‡
The White House, Keyworth ‡
August 1 Sunday
St Helens Croft, Halam
August 4 Wednesday
The Willows, Radcliffe-on-Trent
August 15 Sunday
Rose Cottage, Underwood
August 22 Sunday
14 Temple Drive, Nuthall
September 1 Wednesday
The Willows, Radcliffe-on-Trent
September 5 Sunday
St Helens Croft, Halam
September 7 Tuesday
Thurlby Farm, Stanton on the
Wolds ‡
The White House. Keyworth ‡
September 12 Sunday
Mill Hill House, East Stoke
Rose Cottage, Underwood
September 19 Sunday
St Helens Croft, Halam
September 22 Wednesday
Springwell House, Brinkley
October 10 Sunday
Morton Hall, Retford
October 24 Sunday
St Helens Croft, Halam

DESCRIPTIONS OF GARDENS

Burton Joyce Gardens Situated about 6m NE of Nottingham off A612 to Southwell. In Burton Joyce turn L onto Main St at 1st Xrds. L again within 100yds onto Lambley Lane. Bridle Rd is ½m on R and is an impassable-looking rd. *Combined adm £1.60 Chd 50p. Sun May 30 (2-6)*

17 Bridle Road &⚹❀ (Mr & Mrs C P Bates) Burton Joyce, Nottingham. 1-acre mixed borders, woodland slopes, stream and water garden with naturalised ferns, primulas, hostas and moisture loving plants. Terrace and orchard with spring and summer bulbs in grass. TEAS. *Also by appt* Tel 0602 313725

¶**61 Lambley Lane** &⚹ (Mr & Mrs R B Powell) Approx ⅔-acre of spring flowering plants; shrubs; azaleas; bulbs and trees

6 Cherwell Court ⚹❀ (Louise & Roger Whittle) Meadow Rise. Leave M1 junction 26 E towards Nottingham on A610. At 1st roundabout take 2nd L A611 towards Hucknall. 2nd R and down Hempshill Lane, 2nd L into Meadow Rise, 2nd R into Cherwell Court. Small garden designed to encourage wildlife, 2 small ponds, sunken garden with old roses and ferns, conservatory, many unusual plants and shrubs, restricted parking. TEA. *Adm 75p Chd free (Share to Nottinghamshire Wildlife Trust). Sun June 13 (2-6)*

¶**Colwick Gardens** From Nottingham take B686 to Colwick. Bear L at 1st traffic lights after Midland Caravans. St John's Church 50yds on R, corner of Rectory Rd. Admission tickets and map to gardens at St John's Church. Tea at Church. *Combined adm £1.50 Chd 50p (Share to St John's Church, Colwick). Sat June 26 (2-6)*

¶**1 First Avenue** ✗ (Mr & Mrs H A G Roberts) Small garden incl flower beds; tubs; patio; conifers; trellis. Ivy covered arches; small vegetable patch

¶**10, New Vale Road** ✗ (The Rev Basil Hobbs) Interestingly designed long, narrow garden incl formal and wild life ponds, many interesting plants and features. Climbing plants and secret areas

¶**The Old Rectory** ᕲ✗ (Mr & Mrs R A Northern) A walled garden with variety of shrubs; pergola; summerhouse; gravelled areas

¶**20 Ramblers Close** ᕲ✗ (L A Ashurst Esq) Garden developed over last 5 yrs incl interesting shrubs; perennials; heathers; large pond, many fish; extensive fruit and vegetables

¶**8 Vale Gardens** ✗ (Mr & Mrs B Thompson) Garden approx 500 sq yds, open plan. Lawn; pond with wishing well. Patio and herbaceous borders; colourful containers

Epperstone Festival Gardens ᕲ✗❀ 8m NE of Nottingham off A6097 between Lowdham and Oxton. Lunches, strawberry TEAS, plants, stalls in aid of the Village Festival Funds. *Combined adm £2 Chd 50p. Sun July 4 (12-6)*
Epperstone House (Col & Mrs James Gunn) 2½ acres; roses; herb garden; shrubbery; trees; vegetables; magnificent yew hedge
Hazelwych: for description see **Epperstone Gardens** below
Hill House (Mrs J M Sketchley) 1½ acres incl herbaceous border; formal rose garden; shrub roses and herb garden
Sunny Mead for description see **Epperstone Gardens** below

Epperstone Gardens ᕲ 8m NE Nottingham off A6097 between Lowdham and Oxton. Parking opp Cross Keys and opp White Gates. TEAS, adjoining **Hazelwych**. *Combined adm £1.50 Chd free (Share to Epperstone Village Hall Fund). Sat, Sun May 22, 23 (2-6)*
Hazelwych (Mr & Mrs P J Clark) ½-acre, trees, shrubbery, pond and alpine terrace. Also open with **Epperstone Festival Gardens** *Sun July 4 (12-6)*
Sunny Mead (Mr & Mrs F Stokes) ½-acre garden facing S with view over Dover Beck. Azaleas, rhododendrons, and spring garden. *Also open with* **Epperstone Festival Gardens** *Sun July 4 (12-6)*
White Gates ❀ (Mrs V Pilsworth) 2 acres rhododendrons, azaleas, heathers, shrubbery, herbs and orchard

Felley Priory ᕲ❀ (The Hon Mrs Chaworth Musters) Underwood. 8m SW Mansfield. leave M1 junction 27, take A608, entrance is ½m W of M1. Old-fashioned garden round Elizabethan House. Orchard of daffodils, herbaceous borders, pond, topiary, unusual plants for sale. TEAS. *Adm £1 Chd 25p. Weds March 10, 24, April 14, 28, May 12, 26, June 9, 23, July 14, 28, Aug 11, 25, Sept 8, 29, Oct 13, 27. TEAS for NGS Suns April 11, June 13 (2-5.30)*

Field House Nursing Home ᕲ❀ (Mr & Mrs R C Pring) 11 Main Road, Radcliffe-on-Trent. 6m E Nottingham. Follow A52 and turn N into Radcliffe-on-Trent. Opp Co-op supermarket, turn into Radcliffe Health Centre car park. Nursing Home adjoins car park. 1-acre garden with many specimen conifers and rare shrubs. Large conservatory, colourful bedding schemes; thatched cottage reconstructed from old materials in 1987 within grounds; and set in a typical cottage garden; garden opening will include plant stall. Cream TEAS. *Adm £1 Chd 25p (Share to Residents' Comfort Fund). Sun May 23 (2.30-6)*

Flintham Hall ✗❀ (Myles Thoroton Hildyard Esq) 6m SW of Newark on A46. Fine trees, park and lake, walled garden with borders and wilderness, aviary, glasshouses, unique conservatory, herbaceous borders, woodland walk. Featured 'Country Life' Sept 89. Picnics allowed. TEAS. *Adm £1.50 OAPs £1 Chd 50p (Share to St Augustines Church Flintham PCC). Sun June 20 (2-6)*

Gamston Gardens ᕲ 3m S of Retford; A638 Retford-Markham Moor Rd. Combined gardens, near river bridge. TEAS. *Adm £1.50. Sun June 27 (2-6)*
Brewery House Cottage ❀ (C M D Polhill Esq) Collection of old and modern shrub roses, interesting shrubs, trees and plants. Featured in 'The Rose Gardens of England'
West Bank ✗ (Mr & Mrs M Sutton) Approx ⅔-acre small garden containing hybrid tea, shrub and climbing roses; evergreen beds; herbaceous border and beds; old fruit trees

Gardeners Cottage ᕲ✗❀ (Mr & Mrs J Hildyard) Papplewick; nr Papplewick Hall. 6m N of Nottingham off A60. Interesting old-fashioned garden of ½ acre with 150yd long border, shrub and rhododendrons; garden shrub roses. Large rockery and water feature; scree beds. Many unusual plants. *Adm £1 Chd 25p (Share to St. James Church Window Fund). Sun May 30 (2-6), Wed June 2 (2-6)*

Gateford Hill Nursing Home ᕲ❀ 1m N of Worksop on the A57. Nursing home is well signed from main rd. Impressive house built 1860. Large walled garden, putting green and extensive grounds. Spectacular display of daffodils of many varieties. TEAS. *Adm £1 Chd 25p. Sun April 4 (1.30-5)*

38 Green Lane ✗❀ (Mr & Mrs J E Nicholson) Lambley. 6m N of Nottingham. Take B684 Woodborough Rd turn R to Lambley. Main St turn L into Church St, R into Green Lane. Small cottage garden densely planted, spring bulbs, herbaceous beds, shrub roses, varied climbers, secret corners and surprises. Separate formal vegetable garden. Beautiful views across open countryside. Exhibition and sale of paintings by Nottinghamshire artists in April. TEA. *Adm £1 OAPs 50p Chd free. Weds April 21, May 19, June 16 (1-5)*

By Appointment Gardens. These owners do not have a fixed opening day usually because they do not like crowds or have insufficient parking space. Owner will often give guided tour.

Green Mile も (Mr & Mrs Anthony Scott) Babworth. Babworth 2½m W of Retford. Turn off A620 alongside Prison or off A638 at Barnby Moor. 8 acres of unusual trees and shrubs; impressive hedges in yew and beech. Large display of HT, floribunda and old-fashioned roses. Woodland with rhododendrons and azaleas bordering small lake. Heather garden; walks through wild winter garden. Picnics. *Adm £1 Chd 25p. Sun June 27 (2-6)*

Greenways も (Mr & Mrs D Smith) Bathley. 1m A1. B6325 North Newark. 1½-acre, mixed trees; shrubs; enclosed rose garden; formal beds; orchard and vegetables. Newly planted pergola; alpine troughs. TEAS. *Adm 75p Chd 25p (Share to Arthritis & Rheumatism Council, Newark Branch). Sun July 18 (2-6)*

¶**Gringley On The Hill Gardens** 6m E of Bawtry, 5m W of Gainsborough on A631. TEAS and Plants in aid of Gringley Village Church. *Combined adm £1.50 Chd 50p. Suns May 9, July 11 (2-6)*

¶**Colley Hill Cottage** (Mrs Sue Tallents) A densely planted, small cottage garden, created by the owner with flower arranging and nature in mind; raised beds; small pond and herbaceous area; some unusual plants and shrubs. Also alpines, spring bulbs and ferns

Gringley Hall も (Dulce Threlfall) 2-acre English country garden with mixed borders; old and new roses; water garden and some interesting young trees ¶**Honeysuckle Cottage** (Miss J E Towler) Approx ¼-acre traditional small terraced cottage garden with rose beds; herbaceous and shrub borders. Interesting loose laid chevron brick wall; paths of river boulders and brick

¶**South Beeches** (Dr & Mrs G R Fenton) ½-acre part of an old garden with interesting mature and young trees. Unusual plants and old stone troughs are a feature of the garden; keen vegetable gardener

¶**Hazel Cottage** も (Mr & Mrs M J Rush) Treswell. Treswell is approx 6m E of Retford; 4½m NW of A57 at Dunham-on-Trent. Parking in village st and at Church Hall. ½-acre packed plantsman's garden developed and designed since 1986 to give pleasure in every season. The garden contains many unusual trees, shrubs and herbaceous plants; also collection of old roses, clematis and climbing plants on pergolas; small pond and gravelled areas. Teas and plants sales in aid of village church at village hall 400yds from Hazel Cottage. *Adm £1 Chd free. Sun June 13 (2-6)*

Hodsock Priory も (Sir Andrew & Lady Buchanan) Blyth. Off B6045, Blyth-Worksop rd approx 2m from A1. 5 acres bounded by dry moat. Grade 1 listed gatehouse circa 1500. Victorian Mansion (not open). Mature trees incl large specimen of cornus, indian bean, tulip tree, swamp cypress; small lake; bog garden; bulbs; mixed borders; hostas, roses old and new. Established holly hedges, good autumn colour, featured in 'Shell Garden Guide', 'Country Life, magazine, 'Good Garden Guide' and article in 'Sunday Times' by Graham Rose. TEAS in Orangery. *Adm £1.80 Wheelchairs/Acc Chd free. Suns March 21, May 16, 23, June 13, 27, July 11, Aug 15; Weds April 21, May 12, 19, every Wed in June, Weds July 7, 14, Aug 11, 18. For NGS Sun April 11, Wed June 23 (1-5)*

Holmes Villa も (Sheila & Peter Clark) Holmes Lane, Walkeringham; NE Retford and within 4m Gainsborough. Take A620 from Retford and A161 to Walkeringham and then towards Misterton. Follow yellow boards for last mile. Interesting garden created since 1985 from a potato field; flower arrangers' plants incl collections of ivies, alliums and many unusual herbaceous plants; alpine filled troughs. TEAS. *Adm £1 Chd free (Share to Lincs. Trust for Nature Conservation). Sun June 27 (2-6). Also by appt* **Tel 0427 890233**

¶**5 Long Row** (Mrs Claire & Dr Andy Sparrow) Kingston-on-Soar. Junction 24 off M1 towards Kegworth. 1st L to Kingston - turn R under railway bridge signed Kingston-on-Soar. Parking on green. 1-acre expanding cottage garden incl herb wheel; organic vegetable plot; extensive fruit; interesting greenhouse which includes cacti grown from seed. Open vistas; friendly pig, rare breed of hens, turkeys, cockerel, ducks and Palomino pony. Cream TEAS. *Adm £1 Chd 25p. Sun June 6 (2-6)*

Mattersey House も (Mr & Mrs T P O'Connor-Fenton) Mattersey, 6m N of Retford, 4m SE of Bawtry; from A636 at Ranskill turn E on to B6045 for Mattersey; Buses from Retford and Bawtry. Medium-sized; walled garden; shrub roses, herbaceous borders. TEA. *Adm £1 Chd 20p. Sun June 27 (2-6)*

Mill Hill House も (Mr & Mrs R J Gregory) Elston Lane, East Stoke. 5m S of Newark on A46 turn E on Elston Lane. Garden ½m on R. Entrance through nursery car park. ½-acre plantsmans garden for all seasons, wide selection of unusual hardy plants; mixed borders, alpines, shade plants. *Adm £1 (Share to NCCPG). Suns, May 2, 30; June 13; July 11; Sept 12 (2-6). Also by appt daily April 1 to Oct 31* **Tel 0636 525 460**

Morton Hall (Lady Mason) Ranby, 4m W of Retford. Entrance on Link Rd from A620 to S bound A1. Medium-sized woodland garden, flowering shrubs, rhododendrons, azaleas, specimen trees; pinetum in park, cedars and cypresses. Bulbs, autumn colour. Picnics. Partly suitable for wheelchairs. TEAS. *Adm £2 per car or 75p per person whichever is the least (Share to Ranby Church). Suns April 18, May 2, 16, Oct 10 (2-6)*

The Old Mill House も (Dr E A Nicoll) Cuckney. 6m N of Mansfield. On A60 Worksop-Mansfield rd. 2-acres. Superb water garden featured in 'English Water Gardens' (Weidenfeld & Nicolson). Waterside and bog plants; heather rockeries bordering waterfalls; wild garden and butterfly meadow; over 200 trees, all planted since 1969. Restoration of ancient woodland and shrubbery. Riverside walk with old mill pond and trout. Abundant wildlife. *Adm £1 Chd free. By appt only for special groups in months May to August*

Papplewick Gardens も North end of Papplewick Village on B683, 7m N of Nottingham off the A60. Parking at Hall only. *Combined adm £1.50 Chd free (Share to St James Church, Papplewick). Sun May 30 (2-6)*

Regular Openers. See head of county section.

Altham Lodge (C G Hill Esq) Lovely garden of rhododendrons; azaleas and spring flowers

Papplewick Hall (Dr & Mrs R B Godwin-Austen) Woodland garden of approx 8 acres underplanted with rhododendrons; spring bulbs and hostas

¶**Park Farm** &✿✿ (Mr & Mrs John E Rose) Normanton, Bottesford. Park Farm is half way between Bottesford and Long Bennington on A1 side of Normanton village and sited on the old Normanton Airfield. 2½-acre garden, developed since 1987 comprising formal and mixed borders; natural and formal ponds; scree gardens and small woodland area. Mature trees moved by JCB to flat open field prior to the creation of this garden. TEA. *Adm £1 Chd free. Sun June 6 (11-6)*

16 Prince Edward Crescent ✿ (Mr Geoff Denman) Radcliffe-on-Trent. From RSPCA shelter, take 2nd R (St Lawrence Boulevard) and 1st L. Very small garden with accent on foliage plants. TEA. *Adm 70p Chd free (Share to PDSA Nottingham). Weds May 19 (2-6)*

¶**Rose Cottage** ✿✿ (Mr & Mrs Allan Lowe) Underwood. 1½m from junction 27 M1. Take B608 to Heanor. Join B600; after about 200-300 yds turn R into Main Rd by large sign for 'the Hole in the Wall' Inn. Flower arrangers cottage garden with ponds; shrubs; small secret garden. Rear garden of approx 1,000 sq yds with surprise features, partly developed from a field very recently; goat and other animals. Bed of show spray chrysanthemums; greenhouses. TEAS. *Adm £1 Chd 25p. Suns June 6, Aug 15, Sept 12 (2-6)*

Skreton Cottage &✿ (Mr & Mrs J S Taylor) Screveton, 8m SW of Newark, 12m E of Nottingham. From A46 Fosse Rd turn E to Car Colston; left at green and on for 1m. Bus: Nottingham-Newark, alight Red Lodge Inn (1m walk). 1¾-acre garden, now mature, designed to be of interest throughout year. Landscaped to create separate gardens each with its own character, containing unusual & interesting trees, plants and shrubs. Set in delightful unspoilt country village. TEAS. *Adm £1 Chd free (Share to St. Wilfrid's Church, Screveton). Sun June 27 (2-6)*

Southwell Gardens End of Bishops Drive on S side of Minster. Turn right for free parking on recreation ground. TEAS. *Combined adm £2 Chd 50p. Sun June 6 (2-6)*

　　Bishops Manor &✿ (The Rt. Rev the Lord Bishop of Southwell and Mrs Harris) The house is built into a part of the old medieval Summer Palace of the Archbishops of York. The ruins form a delightful enclosed garden, lawns, 4 seasons tree garden, orchard and vegetable garden. Rose beds and attractive borders in an unusual setting. *(Share to Mirasol Charitable Trust)*

　　Clyde House &✿✿ (Mr & Mrs Graham H Edwards) Westgate. ⅔-acre walled garden organically managed. Vegetables; fruit; mixed borders; pond; compost area; greenhouse. Guided tours. *(Share to Foresight)*

By Appointment Gardens. These owners do not have a fixed opening day usually because they do not like crowds or have insufficient parking space. Owner will often give guided tour.

¶**Springwell House** ✿✿ (Mrs Celia Steven) Brinkley. In Southwell turn off A612 by White Lion Pub towards Fiskerton. Springwell House ¾m on right hand side. Approx 2 acres, many unusual trees and shrubs; perennials. Restored wild life pond; waterfall; varied pond plants; view. Collection of daffodils featuring local names supplied by world famous specialist. Autumn foliage colour; selection of plants; climbers and trees available from adjoining nursery. *Adm £1 Chd 25p. Weds April 14, Sept 22 (9-5). Also groups by appt* Tel 0636 814501

St Helen's Croft ✿ (Mrs E Ninnis) Halam. A614 Nottingham-Doncaster, turn off at White Post roundabout to Southwell and Halam. 3m from Southwell Minster. ¾-acre garden. Alpine path by mixed herbaceous and shrub border. New rose and delphinium area. Adjoining 7-acre field planted as conservation area with cowslips, fritillaries, primroses etc. Trees for autumn colour; acers, sorbus liquidambar and parrotias. *Adm £1 wheelchairs free. Suns April 11, June 20, Aug 1, Sept 5, 19, Oct 24, Mon April 12, Tues May 4, July 6 (2-5). Also by appt* Tel 0636 813219

Sutton Bonington Hall & (Anne, Lady Elton) 5m NW of Loughborough, take A6 to Kegworth, turn R (E) onto A6006. 1st left (N) for Sutton Bonington into Main St. Conservatory, formal white garden, variegated leaf borders. Queen Anne house (not open). Picnics. TEA. *Adm £1.20 Chd 25p (Share to St Michael's & St Ann's Church, Sutton Bonington). Sun July 4 (12-5.30) Also open for Leicestershire, Sun June 27 (12-5)*

14 Temple Drive &✿✿ (Mr & Mrs T Leafe) Nuthall. 4m N W of Nottingham. From M1 leave at junction 26 and take A610 towards Nottingham. Circle 1st roundabout in A6002 lane and leave on minor rd marked 'Cedarlands and Horsendale'. From Nottingham take A610, turning off at the Broxtowe Inn, Cinderhill. Parking restricted, use Nottingham rd. ⅓- acre garden with herbaceous borders; informal island beds, ornamental trees and shrubs; troughs; old-fashioned roses; clematis. Mostly labelled. Fruit and vegetable gardens. TEAS and cake stall in aid of the Cats Protection League. *Adm £1 Chd 50p. Suns July 18, Aug 22 (2-5.30)*

Thrumpton Hall & (George Seymour Esq) 8m SW of Nottingham. W of A453; 3m from M1 at Exit 24. Large lawns; massive yew hedges; rare shrubs; C17 larches, cedars, planted to commemorate historic events since George III. Lake. Early Jacobean house shown. NO DOGS in house. TEA. *Adm to Garden £1 Chd 50p; House £2 extra Chd £1 (Share to The Tradescant Trust, London). Sun July 4 (2.30-6)*

Thurlby Farm &✿ (Mr & Mrs M J Hemphrey) Stanton on the Wolds. 9m S of Nottingham. On A606 turn R by Shell garage, along Browns Lane, Thurlby Lane L at junction after 1m. Ample parking on site. 1 acre created in a field since 1976; varied shrubs; trees; herbaceous borders; woodland walk, spring flowers and bulbs. 5-acre rose field to be seen in season. TEA. *Adm £1 Chd free. Mon May 3, Sun July 25, Tues Sept 7 (2-6)*

¶**Trent Farm House** ⬥❀ (Mr & Mrs G Hubbard) Fiskerton. Fiskerton village, approx 6m W of Newark and 2m from Southwell. The house is situated on Main St adjacent to village shop and Bromley Arms Inn. ⅓-acre cottage type garden fronting River Trent with heather beds; numerous conifers; herbaceous beds; mature and specimen trees, shrubs and hostas. Small woodland area. 60yd walk along riverbank to Bromley Arms who serve afternoon teas. *Adm £1 Chd 25p. Sun May 2 (2-6). Also groups by appt* **Tel 0636 830134**

Upton Gardens ❀ South Retford on A638 or in Eaton village, turn L to Upton. TEAS at **Willowholme Herb Farm**. *Combined adm £1.25 Chd 20p (Share to Headon Church PCC). Sun July 4 (2-6)*
    Manor Farm ⬥ (Mr & Mrs Walker) Cottage garden with mixed borders, old orchard and vegetables
    Willowholme Herb Farm (Mr & Mrs Farr) Cottage garden, with established herb garden containing culinary, aromatic and medicinal herbs

The White House ⌀❀ (Mr & Mrs A R Hill) Nicker Hill, Keyworth. Approx 8 miles SE Nottingham. From A606 at Stanton-on-the-Wolds, by Shell Garage, turn into Browns Lane. Follow Keyworth signs into Stanton Lane, and continue into Nicker Hill. ¾-acre garden, designed and largely developed since 1987. Extensive water & bog garden, pergola; mixed borders with many unusual trees; shrubs and perennials especially bulbs, primulas, euphorbias, grasses, penstemon, asters and tender perennials. Many of the unusual plants seen in garden available on plant stall. *Adm £1 Chd free. Mon May 3, Sun July 25, Tues Sept 7 (2-6). Also groups by appt* **Tel 0602 372049**

The Willows ⌀❀ (Mr & Mrs R A Grout) 5 Rockley Ave, Radcliffe-on-Trent. Radcliffe-on-Trent is N of A52; from High St PO turn into Shelford Rd; over railway bridge, 300yds opp green seat turn left into Cliff Way, then 2nd right. Restricted parking. Designed 1982 62yds × 12yds garden; a quart in a pint plot; featured 'Gardeners World' TV 1986 and Yorks TV 'Great Little Gardens' 1992. Many rare and unusual plants; collections of hostas, hellebores, pulmonarias, paeonias, snowdrops. Holders of National Collection of Crocus Chrysanthus Cultivars. Colour planned island beds throughout the year. Coaches strictly by appt **Tel 0602 333621**. TEA. Weds April 7, May 5, Sept 1. TEAS Weds June 2, July 7 Aug 4 (2-5.30). *Adm £1 (Share to National Council for Conservation of Plants & Gardens)*

Oxfordshire (including Vale of the White Horse)

Hon County Organisers:	Col & Mrs J C M Baker, Hartford Greys, Sandy Lane, Boars Hill Oxford, OX1 5HN Tel 0865 739360
Hon County Treasurer:	Col J C M Baker
Assistant Hon County Organisers:	
Vale of the White Horse (Abingdon, Wantage & Faringdon areas)	Mrs D J Faulkner, Haugh House, Longworth, Abingdon, Oxon OX13 5DX Tel 0865 820286
N Oxon (Chipping Norton & Banbury areas)	Mrs A D Loehnis, Haughton House, Churchill, nr Chipping Norton, Oxon OX7 6NU Tel 0608 658212
S Oxon (Henley, Wallingford & Thame areas)	Mrs J Kimberley, Madhuban, Hinksey Hill, Oxford OX1 5BE Tel 0865 735521
E Oxon (Oxford & Bicester areas)	Mrs P F Naccache, 376 Woodstock Road, Oxford OX2 8AF Tel 0865 513736
W Oxon (Bampton, Burford & Steeple Aston areas)	Mrs H H Atkinson, Ampney Lodge High Street, Bampton OX18 2JN Tel 0993 850120

DATES OF OPENING

By appointment
For telephone numbers and other details see garden descriptions

23 Beech Croft Road, Summertown
Broadwell House, nr Lechlade
Brook Cottage, Alkerton, nr Banbury
Carinya, Goring Rd, Woodcote
The Clock House, Coleshill

Greystone Cottage, Kingwood Common, nr Henley
Hearns House, Gallows Tree Common
Holywell Manor, Oxford
Home Farm, Balscote, nr Banbury
Home Farm House, Steeple Aston & Middle Aston Gardens
Mount Skippet, Ramsden ‡
4 Northfield Cottages, Oxford
Nutford Lodge, nr Faringdon

Seven Bells, Garsington Gardens
Sparrow Hall, Swalcliffe
Stansfield, Stanford-in-the-Vale
Wilcote House, nr Finstock ‡
Yeomans, Tadmarton

Regular openings
For details see garden descriptions

Brook Cottage, Alkerton nr Banbury.
    Mon to Fri April 1 to Oct 31

Kingston Bagpuize House. Suns, Bank
Hols mons April 1 to Sept 30
Old Rectory, Salford, nr Chipping
Norton. 1st Tues of every month
April to Sept
Stansfield, Stanford-in-the-Vale.
Every Tues April 6 to Sept 21
Stanton Harcourt Manor, for various
days see text

March 7 Sunday
Greystone Cottage, Kingwood
Common, nr Henley
March 28 Sunday
Ashbrook House, Blewbury
Taynton House, nr Burford
April 4 Sunday
Bampton & Weald Gardens ‡
Buckland, nr Faringdon ‡
Epwell Mill, nr Banbury ‡‡
Haseley Court & Coach House, nr
SE Oxford
Home Farm, Balscote, nr
Banbury ‡‡
The Mill House, Sutton Courtenay
Quarry Bank House, Gibraltar Hill,
nr Tackley
Sarsden Glebe, Churchill
Souldern Gardens, Bicester
Wadham College, Oxford
Wootton Place, nr Woodstock
April 11 Sunday
Bignell House, Chesterton
Clifton Hampden Manor ‡
Faringdon House
Little Place, Clifton Hampden
Milton Hill House, Abingdon
April 12 Monday
Broadwell Gardens and Kencot
Gardens, nr Lechlade
Dry Sandford Gardens, nr
Abingdon
April 18 Sunday
Broughton Poggs & Filkins
Gardens
Lime Close, Drayton
The Mill House, Stadhampton
The Old Rectory, Coleshill
Shotover House, nr Wheatley
Steeple Aston & Middle Aston
Gardens
Swyncombe House, nr Nettlebed
Wardington Gardens, nr Banbury
April 25 Sunday
St Hugh's College, Oxford
Kingston Bagpuize House
Loreto, Ewelme
Stanton Harcourt Manor
Wick Hall & Nurseries, nr
Abingdon
May 2 Sunday
The Old Rectory, Albury, nr
Tiddington

Westwell Gardens, nr Burford
May 3 Monday
Denton House, Denton
Garsington Manor, nr Wheatley
Kingston Lisle Park, Wantage ‡
Sparsholt Manor, nr Wantage ‡
May 9 Sunday
Checkendon Court, nr Reading ‡
Dogwood, Kennington
The Grange, Bampton
Green End, Sutton Courtenay
Greystone Cottage, Kingwood
Common, nr Henley ‡
The Manor House, Sutton
Courtenay
40 Osler Rd, Headington
Gardens, Oxford
Wolfson College, Oxford
May 14 Friday
Hearns House, Gallows Tree
Common
May 16 Sunday
Barton Abbey, Steeple Barton
Chivel Farm, Heythrop, nr
Chipping Norton ‡
Epwell Mill, nr Banbury ‡
Hearns House, Gallows Tree
Common
Hill Farm, Elsfield, nr Oxford ‡‡
Longworth Gardens, nr Abingdon
Nuffield Place, nr Nettlebed
Woodperry House, nr Beckley
Oxford ‡‡
May 22 Saturday
Greys Court, nr Henley
May 23 Sunday
Balscote Gardens, nr Banbury
Foxcombe End, Boars Hill ‡
Headington Gardens, Oxford
Manor Farm, Old Minster Lovell
Wardington Gardens, nr Banbury
Wood Croft, Boars Hill ‡
May 30 Sunday
Adwell House, nr Tetsworth
Friars Court, nr Faringdon
Hornton Gardens, nr Banbury
Nutford Lodge, nr Faringdon
University Arboretum, Nuneham
Courtenay
The Yews, Swerford, nr Chipping
Norton
May 31 Monday
Broadwell House, Broadwell
Gardens nr Lechlade
The Old Vicarage,
Weston-on-the-Green
Swerford Park, nr Chipping
Norton ‡
Wroxton Gardens
The Yews, Swerford, nr Chipping
Norton ‡
June 6 Sunday
Charlbury Gardens
Kingston Blount Gardens

Lime Close, Drayton
The Malt House, Henley
South Newington Gardens, nr
Banbury
Stansfield, Stanford-in-the-Vale
Stratton Audley Gardens
Waterperry Gardens, nr Wheatley
June 9 Wednesday
Stratton Audley Gardens
June 13 Sunday
Bloxham Gardens
Kiddington Hall, nr Woodstock
Sibford Ferris Gardens
Swinbrook House, nr Burford ‡
Taynton House, nr Burford ‡
White's Farm House, Letcombe
Bassett
June 16 Wednesday
Sibford Ferris Gardens
June 19 Saturday
Hill Court, Tackley
Thame Cottage, Warborough
June 20 Sunday
Adderbury Gardens
Clock House, Coleshill
Dry Sandford Gardens, nr
Abingdon
Gaunt Mill, Standlake
Green College, Oxford
Goring-on-Thames Gardens
Haseley Court & Coach House
Hill Court, Tackley
Iffley Gardens, S Oxford
Kingston Lisle Park, Wantage
Sibford Gower Gardens
Thame Cottage, Warborough
June 27 Sunday
Dundon House, Minster Lovell
Greys Green Gardens, nr
Henley-on-Thames
Heron's Reach, Whitchurch
Hook Norton Gardens ‡
Kencot House, nr Lechlade
The Mill House, Sutton Courtenay
Salford Gardens, nr Chipping
Norton
Swalcliffe Gardens ‡
Towersey Manor, nr Thames
Westwell Gardens, nr Burford
July 2 Friday
Hearns House, Gallows Tree
Common
July 4 Sunday
Great Rollright Gardens, nr
Chipping Norton
Exeter & New Colleges, Oxford
Hearns House, Gallows Tree
Common
Shucklets, Ramsden
July 11 Sunday
Benson Gardens
Garsington Gardens, nr Wheatley
Home Farm, Balscote, nr
Banbury ‡

Magdalen College, Oxford
Manor Barn House, Wendlebury,
nr Bicester
Shutford Gardens ‡
Stanton Harcourt Manor
July 18 Sunday
Adwell House, nr Tetsworth
Nutford Lodge, Nr Faringdon
Rewley House, Oxford
Sibford Gower Gardens, nr
Banbury
Stonewalls, Hempton, Banbury
Swinbrook Gardens, nr Burford
Tusmore Park, nr Bicester &
Brackley
White's Farm House, Letcombe
Bassett
July 25 Sunday
Chastleton Gardens, nr
Moreton-in-Marsh
The Grange, Bampton
Headington Gardens, Oxford
Queen's & Wadham Colleges,
Oxford
August 1 Sunday
Ashbrook House, Blewbury
Broughton Castle, nr Banbury ‡
East Oxford Gardens

Laurels Farm, Wroxton ‡
August 8 Sunday
Haughton House, Churchill
Stansfield, Stanford-in-the-Vale
Waterperry Gardens, Wheatley
August 15 Sunday
Christ Church, Corpus Christi &
Trinity Colleges, Oxford
Colegrave Seeds Ltd, Adderbury
Thames-Side Court, Shiplake
Wardington Manor, nr Banbury
August 22 Sunday
Woodperry House, nr Beckley
August 29 Sunday
Blenheim Palace, Woodstock
Loreto, Ewelme
August 30 Monday
Blenheim Palace, Woodstock
Loreto, Ewelme
The Old Vicarage,
Weston-on-the-Green
September 5 Sunday
Benson Gardens
Charlbury Gardens
Chastleton Glebe, Chastleton
Gardens, nr Moreton-in-Marsh
Faringdon House
Worcester College, Oxford

September 11 Saturday
Alkerton House, nr Banbury ‡
Brook Cottage, Alkerton nr
Banbury ‡
September 12 Sunday
Alkerton House, nr Banbury ‡
Bottom House, Bix, nr Henley
Broadwell House, Broadwell
Gardens and Kencot Gardens,
nr Lechdale
Brook Cottage, Alkerton nr
Banbury ‡
Clock House, Coleshill ‡‡
Epwell Mill, nr Banbury ‡
Kencot Gardens, nr Lechlade
Nutford Lodge, nr Faringdon
The Old Rectory, Coleshill ‡‡
Rofford Manor, Little Milton
September 19 Sunday
Evelegh's, Long Wittenham, nr
Abingdon
Little Place, Clifton Hampden
October 3 Sunday
Garsington Manor, nr Wheatley
Hook Norton Manor, Banbury
The Mill House, Sutton Courtenay
St Catherine's College Oxford
Wilcote House, nr Finstock

DESCRIPTIONS OF GARDENS

Adderbury Gardens On A4260, 3m S of Banbury. A large village with many quaint lanes and a beautiful church. TEAS. *Combined adm £1.50 Chd free. Sun June 20 (2-6)*
West of A423
Berry Hill House ♿⚘ (Mr & Mrs J P Pollard) Berry Hill Rd, off A4260 signed Milton, Bloxham, W Adderbury. 2-acre garden reclaimed since 1982. Mature trees; lawns; shrubbery; mixed herbaceous and shrub borders. Kitchen garden
Briarwood ⚘ (Mr & Mrs J W Johnson) Berry Hill Rd. ¼-acre cottage style garden with interesting collection of shrubs and herbaceous plants
Crosshill House (Mr & Mrs Gurth Hoyer Millar) Manor Rd. 4-acre classic Victorian walled gardens around stone Georgian House
Fleet Farm House ⚘ (Mr & Mrs R P Bratt) Aynho Rd. On A4100 E of A423. Cottage garden with herbaceous borders, roses, vegetables, fruit, farmyard with container plants

Adwell House ♿⚘ (Mr & Mrs W R A Birch Reynardson) Nr Tetsworth, 4m SW of Thame. From London leave M40 at exit 6, turn L in Lewknor. From Oxford A40, turn R in Tetsworth. Roses, formal and water gardens, ornamental lakes, fine trees, lawns; new tree and shrub planting. Commemorative garden with monument. Recently designed potager. TEAS. Plant sale (subject to availability). *Adm £1.50 Chd free (Share to Adwell Church PCC). Suns May 30, July 18 (2.30-5.30)*

Alkerton House (Mr & Mrs H Ewer) Alkerton (For direction see **Brook Cottage**). 2½ acres of trees, shrubs and conifers. *Combined adm with **Brook Cottage** at extra charge of 50p. Sat, Sun Sept 11, 12 (2-7)*

Arboretum see Oxford University Gardens

Ashbrook House ♿⚘❀ (Mr & Mrs S A Barrett) Blewbury. 4m SE of Didcot on A417; 3½-acre chalk garden with small lake, stream, spring bulbs. Teas Lantern Cafe. *Adm £1 Chd free. Suns Mar 28, Aug 1 (2-6)*

Balscote Gardens ♿❀ Pretty hill village ½m off A422 5m W of Banbury. TEAS May only at a nearby garden in aid of Church (C14 St Mary Magdalene). *Adm £1. Suns April 4, July 11. Combined adm £1.50 Chd free. Sun May 23 (2-6)*
Home Farm (Mr & Mrs G C Royle) C17 house and barn with attractive views from ½-acre closely planted elevated garden designed for year-round interest with contrasting foliage, flowering shrubs, bulbs, heathers, alpines, herbaceous, roses, young trees. Featured in Maison et Jardin, No 19 Spring 1992 and R.H.S. The Garden July 1992. *Also open April 4, July 11. Adm £1. Also by appt Tel 0295 738194*
Homeland (Dr & Mrs J S Rivers) ¾-acre, developed since 1982 with shrubs, roses, perennials and rock garden, includes field adjacent to church, planted with trees. *Open only May 23*

Bampton & Weald Gardens On A4095 Witney-Faringdon rd. TEAS at **Weald Manor**. *Combined adm £1.50 Chd free. Sun April 4 (2-5.30)*

Bampton Manor &✿ (Earl & Countess of Donoughmore) Interesting wild spring garden with beautiful views of church. Masses of varied spring flowers. *(Share to Dr Clark Memorial Fund)*
Weald Manor & (Maj & Mrs R A Colvile) Medium-sized old garden; woodland area with many daffodils; topiary and shrub borders; fine trees; small lake *(Share to Lord Roberts Workshops)*

Barton Abbey &✕✿ (Mrs R Fleming) On B4030; 1m Middle Barton; ½m from junction of A4260 and B4030. 4 acres lawns; 3 acres of lake; fine trees; kitchen garden and glasshouses; prize rosette display. Plants and home produce stall. TEAS. *Adm £1 Chd free. Sun May 16 (2-6)*

23 Beech Croft Road ✕ (Mrs A Dexter) Summertown, Oxford. A 23yd by 7yd, south-facing, plant lover's paved garden of a terraced house has been made secluded by planting evergreen shrubs, roses and clematis all round the brick walls; the 2 herbaceous, 2 alpine, 2 shady beds all contain many unusual plants, shrubs, ferns; troughs filled with small alpines. NO push-chairs. *Adm £2. By appt only April to Sept 30* **Tel 0865 56020**

Benson Gardens ✿ Off High St. Benson off A423 Oxford-Henley, 2m from Wallingford. TEAS at **Mill Lane House**. *Combined adm £1.50. Suns July 11, Sept 5 (2-6)*
  Hethersett (Dr Anne Millar) ½-acre garden on natural chalk stream; climbing plants and bog area; colour co-ordination and plant-form a feature of mixed beds
  Mill Lane House (Marion & Geoff Heywood) ¼-acre garden with alpine rockeries and banks sloping to stream, pond, bog garden, small island and spring. Dried flower crafts display and weather permitting, chair caning demonstration

Bignell House ✿ (Mr & Mrs P J Gordon) Chesterton. On A4095 2m SW Bicester. 16-acre traditional English country house garden; lawns leading to lake system with rock pool; stone arches; bridge to daffodil island; fine mature trees inc wellingtonia and spruce; aconites; primroses; variety of wild species; woodland plants. House designed by Wm Wilkinson mid C19 (one wing only remains). Stall and TEAS in aid of Bicester Friends of the Earth. *Adm £1 Chd free. Easter Sun April 11 (2-6)*

Blenheim Palace ✿ (His Grace the Duke of Marlborough) Woodstock, 8m N of Oxford. Bus: 44 Oxford-Chipping Norton-Stratford, alight Woodstock. Original grounds and garden plan by Henry Wise. Park landscaped and lake created by 'Capability' Brown in late C18. Maze; butterfly house; cafeteria; adventure play area; *Adm charge not available on going to press. For NGS Sun, Mon, Aug 29, 30 (11-5)*

Bloxham Gardens ✕ A large village near Banbury on A361 to Chipping Norton. Has a fine church with a 198ft spire. TEAS at S. Newington. *Combined adm £1.50 Chd free. Sun June 13 (2-6)*
  25 The Avenue (Miss E Bell-Walker) A small informal garden with emphasis on small shrubs; sub shrubs and herbaceous plants
  71 Courtington Lane ✿ (Mr P Sheasby) About ⅓ acre with herbaceous borders, shrubs, rockeries and

small peat beds; there is a small pond and a series of alpine troughs; the greenhouse contains cacti and a large succulent collection especially Lithops, Haworthia and Echeveria; a wide range of herbaceous species are grown
Rose Cottage ✿ (Mr & Mrs David Willmott) Small cottage garden developed in recent yrs. Concentration of alpines; shrubs and roses on elevated site

Bottom House &✕✿ (Mrs G Scouller) Bix, 1½m NW of Henley-on-Thames on A423 (dual carriageway) 2-acre family garden with good mixed autumn borders, many unusual plants. Small formal garden with topiary; silver and yellow garden. TEAS. *Adm £1 Sun Sept 12 (2-6)*

Broadwell Gardens 5m NE Lechlade, E of A361 to Burford. Delightful Cotswold village with interesting church. TEAS (not May). *Combined adm with* **Kencot** *£2 Chd free. Mon April 12, Sun Sept 12.* **Broadwell House** *only £1.50 Chd free. Mon May 31 (2-6)*
  Broadwell House &✿ (Brigadier & Mrs C F Cox) Mature 2-acre garden planted for colour throughout the year. Many interesting trees and shrubs including wellingtonia, ginkgo, acers, aralias, salix, cornus, clematis. Topiary, rare plants, many golden, silver and variegated; unusual grasses, penstemons and osteospermums, also many hardy geraniums. Featured in 'Over the Hills from Broadway'. Listed house and old barn. Gardening clubs welcome. *Mon April 12, Sun Sept 12 (2-6). Also solo opening Mon May 31 (2-5). Adm £1.50. Also by appt* **Tel 0367 860230**
  Broadwell Old Manor ✕ (Mr & Mrs M Chinnery) 1-acre garden with listed house. Shrub borders, courtyard and topiary garden. Pleached lime hedge, old mulberry tree, young tulip and sorbus trees. *April 12 only*

Brook Cottage ✿ (Mr & Mrs D Hodges) Alkerton, 6m W of Banbury. From A422, Banbury-Stratford, turn W at sign to Alkerton, L opp Alkerton War Memorial, into Well Lane, R at fork. 4-acre hillside garden, formed since 1964, surrounding C17 house. Wide variety of trees, shrubs and plants of all kinds in areas of differing character; water garden; alpine scree; one-colour borders; over 200 shrub and climbing roses; many clematis. Interesting throughout season. TEAS in aid of Shenington Nursery Sept 11, 12 and for groups on other dates by appt. DIY Tea & Coffee on all open weekdays. *Adm £1.50 OAPs £1 Chd free. Mon to Fri April 1 to Oct 31 (9-6). Sat, Sun Sept 11, 12 (2-7). Evenings, other weekends and all group visits by appt* **Tel 0295 87303** *or* **87590**

Broughton Castle &✿ (Lord Saye & Sele) 2½m W of Banbury on Shipston-on-Stour rd (B4035). 1-acre shrub, herbaceous borders, walled garden, roses, climbers seen against background of C13-C16 castle surrounded by moat in open parkland. House also open, extra charge. TEAS. *Adm Garden only £1.50 Chd 75p.* ▲*For NGS Sun Aug 1 (2-5)*

Regular Openers. Too many days to include in diary. Usually there is a wide range of plants giving year-round interest. See head of county section for the name and garden description for times etc.

Broughton Poggs & Filkins Gardens &❀ Enchanting limestone villages between Burford and Lechlade, just E of A361. A number of gardens varying in size from traditional cottage garden to over 2 acres, growing wide variety of plants. Mill in process of restoration. TEAS. *Combined adm £2 Chd free. Tickets from* **The Court House, Broughton Hall** *or* **Little Peacocks** *(Share to Broughton & Filkins Church Funds). Sun April 18 (2-5.30)*

Broughton Poggs:
    Broughton Hall (Mr & Mrs C B S Dobson)
    Broughton Mill (J Huggins Esq)
    Corner Cottage (Mr & Mrs E Stephenson)
    The Court House (Richard Burls Esq)
    The Old Rectory (Mrs E Wansbrough)
    Rose Cottage (Mr & Mrs R Groves)
Filkins:
    Fox House (Sir John & Lady Cripps)
    Little Peacocks (Colvin & Moggridge, Landscape Consultants)
    The Old Smithy (Mrs Frances Fynn)
    St Peter's House (J Cambridge Esq)
    The Vicarage (Rev & Mrs W L Glazebrook)

Buckland ❀ (Mrs Richard Wellesley) Signposted to Buckland off A420, lane between two churches. Beautiful lakeside walk; fine trees; daffodils; shrubs. Norman church adjoins garden. TEAS. *Adm £1 Chd free. Sun April 4 (2-7)*

¶**Carinya** ✄❀ (Mrs S J Parsons) Goring Rd, Woodcote. 8m NW of Reading; 5m SE of Wallingford on SW edge of Village on B471. ⅓-acre cottage style garden planted for all year interest, trees, shrubs, herbaceous, bulbs, alpines, clematis and old roses, etc. *Adm £1 Chd free. By appt only May to Sept Tel 0491 680663*

Charlbury Gardens ❀ Large historic village on B4022 Witney-Enstone. TEAS. *Combined adm £1.50 Chd free (Share to Wytham Hall Sick Bay for Medical Care of Homeless). Suns June 6, Sept 5 (2-6)*
    Gothic House (Mr & Mrs Andrew Lawson) Near Bell Hotel. ⅓-acre walled garden, planted for sculpture display and colour association. False perspective, pleached lime walk with bulbs, trellis, alpine pyramid, terrace pots
    The Priory & (Dr D El Kabir and others) Adjacent church. A collector's garden in the making. Over 1 acre planted with many fine specimens of trees and shrubs in a formal topiary garden with terraced beds incorporating colour scheme foliage

Chastleton Gardens 3m SE of Moreton-in-Marsh. From Chipping Norton W on A44, turn L at Chastleton, R at T-junction, 1m. From M-in-Marsh: E on A44, R after 3m. TEAS in aid of Chastleton Church. *Combined adm £1.50 Chd free. Sun July 25 (2-6). Chastleton Glebe only. Adm £1. Sun Sept 5*
    Chastleton Glebe &❀ (Prue Leith) 5 acres; old trees; terraces (one all red); small lake, island; Chinese-style bridge, pagoda; formal vegetable garden; Cotswold house; views; new rose tunnel
    Kitebrook End Farm & (Mr & Mrs W G Bamford) ½-acre garden four years old, converted from derelict farm yard. Designed to be labour-saving; walls; paving and shaped borders around a lawn. Massed shrubs and herbaceous planting for ground cover and colour, southerly aspect, opened up with raised ha-ha wall

Checkendon Court &✄ (Sir Nigel & Lady Broackes) Checkendon, NW of Reading. 2m NE of Woodcote on B479 nr Checkendon church. 15 acres, attractively laid out with yew hedges, large herbaceous borders, roses, kitchen garden; work continues to woodland areas. New rhododendrons and azalea planting and new laburnum pergola walk. TEAS at **Greystone Cottage**. *Adm £2 Chd free. Sun May 9 (2-5)*

Chivel Farm &✄❀ (Mr & Mrs J D Sword) Heythrop, 4m E of Chipping Norton, off A34 or A361. High and open to extensive view, 1½-acre garden designed for continuous interest; many island beds framing wide lawn. Unusual shrubs and herbaceous plants; small formal white garden. TEAS. *Adm £1 Chd free. Sun May 16 (2-6)*

Christ Church See Oxford University Gardens

Clifton Hampden Manor &✄❀ (Mr C Gibbs) 4m E of Abingdon on A415. 4-acre romantic C19 garden above R. Thames with statuary and far-reaching views; long pergola, new lime tunnel, herbaceous borders, bulbs, wild riverside walks, much new planting in progress. TEA. *Combined adm with* **Little Place** *£1.50 Chd free (Share to St Michael's and All Angels' Church). Sun April 11 (2.30-5.30)*

Clock House &✄❀ (Michael & Denny Wickham & Peter Fox) Coleshill, 3½m SW of Faringdon N of B4019. Garden at top of village. Planted around site of Coleshill House, which was burnt down in the 50's, the main floor plan has been laid out and is being planted as a memorial to this famous house. Walled garden in old laundry drying ground; unusual plants, vegetables and herbs; good views across Vale of the White Horse and parkland. Toilets not suitable disabled. TEAS. *Adm £1 Chd free. Suns June 20, Sept 12 (2-6) and by appt June/July Tel 0793 762476*

Colegrave Seeds Ltd &✄ Milton Rd, West Adderbury, 3m S of Banbury. Turn off A423 Banbury-Oxford at sign Milton-Bloxham. Trial grounds ½m on right. Seed trials grounds and new display gardens containing thousands of summer flowering annuals and perennials. Many new items in trial prior to introduction. A festival of colour unique in Oxfordshire. Covered display area of hanging baskets and containers. (Note strictly wholesale; no retail sales). Parking. Light lunches and TEAS. *Adm £1.50 Chd free (Share to RNLI). Sun Aug 15 (11-5)*

Corpus Christi College (see Oxford University Gardens)

Denton House ✄❀ (Mr & Mrs J Luke) Denton SE of Oxford. 1m E of Garsington between A40 and B480. 3-acre walled garden; large lawns; many mature trees and shrubs; spring bulbs incl fritillaria; wild garden; walled vegetable garden; interesting stable yard. Gothic windows from Brasenose Chapel in high stone wall surrounding garden. TEAS in aid of Cuddesdon Church and Village Hall. *Adm £1 Chd free. Mon May 3 (2-6)*

By Appointment Gardens. Avoid the crowds. Good chance of a tour by owner. See garden description for telephone number.

Dogwood ఉ*ఈ*❀ (Mr & Mrs D Rogers) Kennington. Signposted S of Oxford ring road at A34 junction for Abingdon. 95 The Avenue. Plantsman's garden on 200ft plot designed on several levels, including water feature, planted for year round interest with approx 1,500 plants, all labelled. Featured in Sept 89 Practical Gardening magazine and on 'Garden Club', TV, June 1991. Large plant stalls. TEAS in aid of Guide Dogs. *Adm 80p Chd free. Sun May 9 (2-6)*

Dry Sandford Gardens ఉ*ఈ*❀ Dry Sandford 3m NW of Abingdon, off A420 at Besselsleigh, or A34 at Marcham Rd, nr Abingdon Airport. TEAS. *Combined adm £1.50 Chd 20p (Share to Dry Sandford Church). Mon April 12, Sun June 20 (2-6)*

   Church Farm House (Mr & Mrs C Rudge) 1 acre surrounding listed C17/18 farmhouse and barns. Mixed borders; including shrubs; roses; bulbs; herbaceous; silver leaved and alpine plants suitable for dry soil on limestone, herb garden and pond

   The Manor House (Mr David & Lady Daphne Bailey) 3½-acre walled garden; borders; shrubs; unusual plants; large old-fashioned shrub rose garden; herbs; 3-acre woodland garden; lake; bulbs

Dundon House ఉ*ఈ*❀ (Mr & Mrs C M Pack) In Old Minster Lovell, charming Cotswold village on R Windrush. Off B4047 Witney-Burford Rd opp White Hart, signed to Minster Lovell Hall, 1st drive on R, parking in field to L. Mainly C16 house, (not open), owned in C18 by the Dundons, a notorious family of highwaymen; moved in 1930s to old quarry. Beautiful views across Windrush valley. 4-acre terraced garden built over last 10yrs. Yew hedges and stone walls enclose flower, shrub rose and wild gardens. Planted pool and new woodland gardens. TEAS in aid of WI. *Adm £1.50 Chd free. Sun June 27 (2-5)*

East Oxford Gardens. Off Cowley Rd, Oxford 1m E from the Plain. Parking and TEAS at **Restore**. *Combined Adm £1 (Share to Restore and St John's Home). Sun Aug 1 (2-5)*

   Restore ఉ❀ Manzil Way N off Cowley Rd leading to E Oxford Health Centre. A town garden and plant nursery run as a mental health rehabilitation project. Sample beds of shrubs, perennials, herbs, alpines and annuals. Large range of plants for sale, also handmade crafts and cards

   St John's Home ఉ St Mary's Rd, off Leopold St S of Cowley Rd. 3-acre grounds of All Saints Convent and St John's Home for the Elderly. Mature trees, lawns, secluded prayer garden; cherry orchard and vegetable garden

Epwell Mill ❀ (Mr R A Withers) Epwell, 7m W of Banbury, between Shutford and Epwell. Medium-sized garden, interestingly landscaped in open country, based on former water-mill; terraced pools; bulbs; azaleas. TEAS. *Adm £1 Chd free (Share to Epwell Church Restoration Fund). Suns April 4, May 16, Sept 12 (2-6). Please apply in writing for groups*

Evelegh's ఉ*ఈ*❀ (Mr & Mrs J H Rose) High St, Long Wittenham. 4m NE of Didcot. From A415 turn S at Clifton Hampden or N from B4016 to Long Wittenham. Long narrow 1-acre garden leading to backwater of R. Thames.

Character changes from borders to informal woodland by river. Interesting plantings; herbaceous, shrubs, roses, small herb garden, alpines in scree, annuals to give long season of colour. *Combined adm with* **Little Place, Clifton Hampden** *£1.50 Chd free. Sun Sept 19 (2-6)*

Exeter College see Oxford University Gardens

Faringdon House ఉ (Miss S Zinovieff) Faringdon. Large garden; spring bulbs; autumn borders; orangery; park; lakeside walk; fine trees; Norman church adjoining. TEAS in aid of All Saints Church & NGS April 11, Save the Children Fund June 6. *Adm £1 Chd free. Suns April 11, Sept 5 (2-5)*

¶Foxcombe End ఉ❀ (Mr & Mrs R Stevens) Boars Hill, 3 m S of Oxford. From Ring Rd follow signs to Wotton and Boars Hill. From Junction at top Hinksey Hill, Foxcombe Lane 1st on L. 11 acres of natural garden, incl a nature trail, a pasture with two donkeys and an abundance of wild flowers, particularly orchids. Extensive oak woodlands, within which are magnolia and azalea gardens and rhododendrons. Yew walk and ornamental yew hedges around the house. TEAS in aid of Sobell House Hospice. *Adm £1 Chd 20p Sun May 23 (2-6)*

Friars Court ఉ❀ (Mr & Mrs J M Willmer) Clanfield. On A4095 Witney to Faringdon Rd S of Clanfield. Listed part moated farmhouse. Garden and copses, many mature trees and shrubs, new planting for colour and wildlife. Conducted nature trail. TEAS in attractive old farm room. *Adm £1.25 Chd free (Share to British Red Cross). Sun May 30 (2-6)*

Garsington Gardens SE of Oxford, N of B480. TEAS in village hall in aid of St Mary's Church. *Combined adm £1.50. Sun July 11 (2-6)*

   Seven Bells Cottage ఉ*ఈ*❀ (Dr Michael & Mrs Lesley Pusey) Southend. 1-acre garden of surprises, developed since 1986, with views to Berkshire Downs and the Chilterns. A diversity of interesting trees, shrubs, plants, vegetables and herbs. Herbaceous border, island beds, wildlife areas, ponds and bog garden. Garden sculptures. Small C16 thatched farmhouse. *Also by appt April 1 to Sept 30* **Tel 086736 488**. *Adm 70p*

   Home Close *ఈ* (Mrs M Baker) Southend. 1½-acre garden, being redeveloped, surrounding C17 listed bailiff's house and granary. Mixed borders; walled garden with water feature; herb garden; pergola; kitchen garden; orchard; woodland area

   ¶The Old Kennels (Mr & Mrs Tony Bagnall Smith). Top of Oxford Rd 'Hill' opp Red Lion. ½-acre walled garden subdivided into 4 separate walled gardens. C17 ex-farmhouse with barn was home to Christ Church Beagles for 120 yrs. Lawn, parterre, vines, fig, herbaceous and major shrub rose bank

Garsington Manor ❀ (Mr & Mrs L V Ingrams) SE of Oxford N of B480. House C16 of architectural interest (not open). Monastic fish ponds, water garden, dovecot c.1700; flower parterre and Italian garden laid out by Philip and Lady Ottoline Morrell; fine trees and yew hedges. Free car park. TEAS. *Adm £1.50 Chd free. Mon May 3, Sun Oct 3 (2-6)*

Gaunt Mill (Mr & Mrs Michael Belmont) Standlake 6m SE Witney 1½m E of village on B4449. Partly suitable for wheelchairs 3 acres on 1000-yr-old mill site with 2 arms of R. Windrush, bridge over weir leads to 2-acre island with unusual trees; shrubs, rose garden. TEAS in aid of Northmoor Church. *Adm £1.50 Chd free. Sun June 20 (2-6)*

Goring-on-Thames Gardens ✿ 5m S of Wallingford, where B4009 crosses wooden bridge over Thames, a beautiful old village backed by steep wooded hills. TEAS. *Combined adm £2 Chd free. Sun June 20 (2-6)*
 Coney Berry ✾✿ (Mr & Mrs H F Armstrong) Elvendon Road, running E from B4009 N of Goring, parallel to B4626 Goring-Crays Pond Rd. Informal garden with woodland backing on thin soiled chalk hill. Trees and hedges planted at turn of century, shrubs, roses, ground cover for easy maintenance; white border, large herb border, old-fashioned roses. *(Share to Arthritis & Rheumatism Council)*
 Manor Field ⚭✾✿ (Mr & Mrs D L Watts) An interesting ½-acre garden of modern bungalow. Collection of rock plants, some in troughs. Unusual shrubs and tender plants, vegetable garden. *(Share to Sport for Disabled in the South)*
 The Mill Cottage ⚭✾ (Mr & Mrs M J H Weedon) By St Thomas Church. 1-acre riverside garden of C17 timbered cottage with its own small bridge and island, dramatic views over the Thames. Children's entertainment corner. *(Share to Westminster Pastoral Foundation)*
 The Old Farmhouse ⚭ (Mr & Mrs J F Denny) Station Road. A walled village garden of approx 1 acre. It surrounds square 1809 house and incl lawns, herbaceous, roses, shrubs; swimming pool; kitchen garden; lily pond and attractive varied layout. *(Share to St John Ambulance)*

The Grange ⚭✿ (Mrs R Johnston & Mr & Mrs P Taylor) Bampton. Entrance in High St. Large garden: lovely specimen trees, interesting shrubs and borders, pond, walled ornamental kitchen garden. Homemade TEAS in beautiful courtyard. *Adm £1.50 Chd free. Suns May 9, July 25 (2-6)*

Great Rollright Gardens 3m N of Chipping Norton, off A34 or A361. TEAS at **Old Rectory** in aid of St Andrews Church Restoration Fund. *Adm £1.50 Chd free. Sun July 4 (2-6)*
 Barston House ⚭✾ (Miss E L Jackson) 1-acre, formal garden with herbaceous borders, shrubs; kitchen garden; views
 Duck End ✾ (Mr & Mrs J Lively) Informal ½-acre cottage garden, surrounding listed C17 farmhouse with dovecote; streams, yew hedges, shrub roses; parking available in adjoining paddock only
 Great Rollright Manor ⚭✾ (Mr & Mrs K Seel) Lawns surrounded by trees and shrubs leading to small lake; walled kitchen garden; views
 The Old Beer House (Mr & Mrs B A Tucker) ½-acre village garden with small knot garden and conservatory; orchard
 The Old Rectory ⚭✾ (Mr Michael & Lady Joanna Stourton) 3 acres with beautiful views to south. Herbaceous border, lawns, knot garden; tree walk; water

garden with brook, small lake; many specimen trees
 Rectory Cottage (Mrs J Lawrence) ¼-acre of C17 cottage. Sheltered, S facing, divided by trellis. Small woodland garden; pond

Green College See Oxford University Gardens

Green End ⚭✾ (Dr & Mrs J Conway) 15 The Green, Sutton Courtenay, 2m S of Abingdon, opp Manor House, facing car park with large yew tree in front garden. 1-acre garden with raised beds, spring flowers and trees; small ornamental ponds; small herb garden. *Adm 50p Chd free. Sun May 9 (2-6)*

Greenlands ⚭✾✿ (Henley Management College) See Bucks

Greys Court ✾✿ (Lady Brunner; The National Trust) Rotherfield Greys, 3m W of Henley-on-Thames on rd to Peppard. 8 acres amongst which are the ruined walls and buildings of original fortified manor. Rose, cherry, wisteria and white gardens; lawns; kitchen garden; Archbishop's maze. Jacobean house open with C18 alterations on site of original C13 house fortified by Lord Grey in C14. Donkey wheel and tower. Large sale of unusual plants. TEAS. *Adm garden £2.80 Chd £1.40 House £1 extra, Chd 50p extra. For NGS Sat May 22 (2-5.30)*

Greys Green Gardens ⚭✾ Rotherfield Greys, 3m W of Henley-on-Thames. Two secluded gardens close to Greys Green War memorial. *Combined adm £1. Sun June 27 (2-6)*
 Greys House (Mr & Mrs K S Barker) Informal garden in 1¼ acres designed by Robin Williams. Interesting flowering shrubs, roses, and herbaceous borders, large lawn, pond with Koi, apple walk, open views, parking
 Green Place (Mr & Mrs R P Tatman) 1-acre garden with extensive views towards the East. Roses, fuchsias and herbaceous borders

Greystone Cottage ⚭✾✿ (Mr & Mrs W Roxburgh) Colmore Lane, Kingwood Common. Between B481 Nettlebed-Reading rd and Sonning Common-Stoke Row rd; turn N at 'Unicorn'. 2-acre garden in woodland setting. Many unusual shrubs and plants, including varied collection of hostas, geraniums, grasses, fritillary species, ferns and old fashioned roses. Woodland walk with azaleas, narcissus, hellebores, bilberries and cistus. 80-year-old arched pear tree walk, wildlife ponds, sink gardens, small Mediterranean garden, golden garden. Planted for year round interest. Featured in 'Practical Gardening'. Small nursery. TEAS. *Adm £1 Chd free. Suns March 7, May 9 (2-6). Also by appt March 1 to Sept 1* **Tel** 0491 628559

Haseley Court & Coach House ⚭✾✿ SE of Oxford. From London M40 exit 7, L to A329, 1st L to Great Haseley then to Little Haseley. From Oxford A40, L on A418 to Aylesbury, 1st R onto A329 and over M40. TEAS. *Combined adm £1.50 Chd free Suns April 4, June 20 (2-6)*
 The Coach House (Mrs C G Lancaster) Hornbeam and laburnum tunnels, orchard, spring bulbs; courtyard borders; walled garden with box hedges; summer-house; large collection of old roses and herbaceous plants; Rosa mundi hedge; potager; white garden

Haseley Court (Mr & Mrs D Heyward) Topiary chess set in box and yew; mixed borders planted in 1990; woodlands with many spring flowers; ornamental canal

¶**Haughton House** &☀ (Mr & Mrs A D Loehnis) Churchill. 3m SW of Chipping Norton on B450. From Burford via A361. W for Churchill. Medium-sized garden recently reclaimed. Terrace with fine views, borders, formal white garden, meadow. All season interest. Also fine kneelers in nearby church. TEAS in aid of village church. *Adm £1 Chd free. Sun Aug 8 (2-6)*

Headington Gardens ☀☀ East Oxford, off London Road, ¾m W of ring road. TEAS in parish hall, Dunston Rd. TEAS (except May 9). *Adm 70p. Sun May 9,* **40 Osler Rd** *only. Suns May 23, July 25. Combined adm £1.60 Chd free (2-6)*

    2 Fortnam Close (Mr & Mrs D Holt) Off Headley Way. Winner best back garden, Oxford in Bloom 1991. Featured on TV. ¼-acre garden on 3 levels, trees, shrubs including heathers, azaleas and a large wisteria. Roses, bearded iris and other herbaceous plants in a planned layout which includes a pond and pergola. There are watercolour paintings and pressed flower arrangements to view if you wish

    Mary Marlborough Lodge & (Nuffield Orthopaedic Centre) Windmill Rd. 2 easy-to-manage gardens with raised beds featuring herbaceous plants and vegetables; roses; raised cold frames; array of hanging baskets; display of lightweight tools. A splendid source of ideas for less able gardeners and those wishing to simplify garden work. Ample parking. *25 July only (Share to MML)*

    40 Osler Road (Mr & Mrs N Coote) ⅔-acre 'secret garden' in built-up area on the edge of old Headington. Semi-formal design with statuary and extensive use of decorative pots with tender shrubs and plants supporting Mediterranean atmosphere of house. Plants for dry soil (neutral sand), some rare or unusual, many chosen for foliage effect. Luxuriant spring display. Featured in 'English Private Gardens' (1991) and on TV. TEA. No plant stall May 9 only

    Pumpkin Cottage &☀ (Mr & Mrs M Davis) 6 St Andrew's Lane, Old Headington, off St Andrew's Rd, nr to Church. Small garden, 20m × 16m, enclosed within stone walls situated at rear of Grade II listed cottage. Small pool and rockery; mixed planting; paved areas with some container grown plants. Small cobble paved front garden. Wheelchair access possible by arrangement

    1 Stoke Place & (Mr & Mrs E McCabe) The garden takes its shape from a network of old stone walls which happen to have survived in the area. A scattering of trees blending with the stonework provides a framework for a linked series of paths and flowerbeds which gives an atmosphere of seclusion. A number of small pools and many contrasting shrubs and plants provide variety but do not diminish the sense of privacy of the whole garden. The area is just short of an acre. *Not open in July (Share to Motor Neurone Disease Assoc)*

Hearns House &☀ (Mr & Mrs J Pumfrey) Gallowstree Common, 5m N of Reading, 5m W of Henley. From A4074 turn E at The Fox, Cane End. Limited car parking in the garden so additional Friday openings. Architects house in 2-acre expanding garden in woodland setting. Emphasis on design, good foliage and single colour areas with paved courtyard and shady walks. Unusual plants for sale. Concert if wet July 4. TEAS or coffee in aid of Water Aid. *Adm £1 Chd free. Fris, Suns May 14, 16; July 2, 4 (10-12; 2-5); also by appt in Sept* Tel **0734 722848**

Heron's Reach ☀ (Mr & Mrs B Vorhaus) Eastfield Lane, Whitchurch. From Pangbourne take tollbridge rd over Thames to Whitchurch; at The Greyhound turn R into Eastfield Lane. 1 acre in beautiful Thames-side setting with views to the Chiltern hills; woodland garden with pond, stream and waterfall; shrubs, and herbaceous borders. TEA. *Adm £1 Chd free. Sun June 27 (2-6)*

Hill Court &☀☀ (Mr & Mrs Andrew Peake) Tackley. 9m N of Oxford. Turn off A4260 at Sturdy's Castle. Walled garden of 2 acres with clipped yew cones at the top of the terrace as a design feature by Russell Page in the 1960s. Terraces incl silver, pink and blue plantings, white garden, herbaceous borders, shrubberies, replanted orangery. Many rare and unusual plants. Entry incl History Trail (not suitable for wheelchairs) round village green, through Hill Court park to church, with illustrated leaflet giving notes on unique geometric fishponds (1620), C17 stables and pigeon house, C18 lakes, icehouse etc (stroll of at least 1hr). TEAS. *Adm £1.50 Chd free (Share to Tackley Local History Group). Sat, Sun June 19, 20 (2-6)*

Hill Farm &☀☀ (Mr & Mrs J Garson) Elsfield. 5m N of Oxford. A40 flyover signed Marston and Elsfield. Mixed borders, shrubs, trees; good view of Oxford. TEAS. *Adm £1 Chd free (Share to Elsfield Church). Sun May 16 (2-6)*

Hook Norton Gardens ☀ 4m NE of Chipping Norton off A361. TEAS in aid of St Peter's Church. *Combined adm £1 Chd free. Sun June 27 (2-6)*

    Springside (Mrs R Rye) Brewery Lane, ¼-acre sloping to stream. Trees, shrubs, perennial and rock plants; bog garden and troughs, an interesting collection; unusual ornaments inc small water wheel

    Talbot House ☀ (Mr & Mrs George Hummer) Queens St. nr church, ½-acre old-fashioned cottage garden on 2 levels, many different plants, herbaceous, annual, plenty of colour and interest; potager

Hook Norton Manor ☀ (Mr & Mrs N Holmes) SW of Banbury. From A361, 1m from Chipping Norton turn N and follow signs. 2½-acres terraced lawns leading down to streams; trees, shrubs and bog garden. TEAS in aid of St Peter's Church. *Adm 80p Chd free. Sun Oct 3 (2-5.30)*

Hornton Gardens 6m NW of Banbury. Between A422 and B4100. An attractive village known for its quarry which produced Hornton stone for the neighbourhood. Fine old buildings around the village green. TEAS in aid of Hornton School. *Combined adm £1.50 Chd free. Sun May 30 (2-6)*

Bellevue ✿✿ (Mr & Mrs E W Turner) Bell St. Approx 1½-acre hillside garden of many aspects. Bordered walks; a 'surprise' garden leading to water falling to pools, flower beds and the finest views of Hornton Village. Added attraction miniature windmill ⅓ scale of original at Hornton

Hornton Hall ✿✿ (Mr & Mrs A H Fraser) Out of the village on the Horley-Edge Hill Rd. Hornton stone house with excellent views. Well established 2½-acre garden with mature trees; formal yew hedges; herbaceous borders; magnolias and an ancient wisteria

Sunnyside ✿✿✿ (Philip Williams Esq) A cottage garden of approx ½-acre with attractive borders of mixed perennials; shrub planting and pond area. Created from rough ground over 5 years and still adding

West End House ✿✿ (The Hon William & Mrs Buchan) Small, well stocked garden developed over 10yrs; interesting layout; spring bulbs, flowering shrubs and herb garden

Iffley Gardens ✿✿ S Oxford. Secluded old village within Oxford's ring road, off A4158 from Magdalen Bridge to Littlemore roundabout. Renowned Norman church, featured on cover of Pevsner's Oxon guide. Short footpath from Mill Lane leads to scenic Iffley Lock and Sandford-Oxford towpath. TEAS from 3-5 at thatched village hall, Church Way. Plant stall in aid of the White House Nursery. *Combined adm £1 Chd free. Sun June 20 (2-6)*

 8 Abberbury Road (F S Tordoff Esq) Off Church Way. ½-acre plantsman's garden developed since 1971. Mature trees, shrubs, coloured and variegated foliage, many old and modern shrub roses and climbers

 24 Abberbury Road (Mr & Mrs E Townsend-Coles) ½-acre family garden with fruit, flowers and vegetables

 71 Church Way (Mr & Mrs R D Harrison) A small, low maintenance front garden with mixed shrubs and herbaceous plantings

 Rosedale ✿ (Mrs T Bennett) Mill Lane, off Church Way. ½-acre garden on different levels, hidden behind walls. A mixture of trees, shrubs, roses and herbaceous plants with a large rockery and tiny woodland garden

Kencot Gardens ✿✿✿ 5m NE of Lechlade, E of A361 to Burford. A most charming Cotswold village with interesting church. TEAS. Combined adm with **Broadwell** £2 Chd free. Mon April 12, Sun Sept 12 (2-6).

 Kencot House only £1.50 Chd free

 De Rougemont (Mr D Portergill) ½-acre garden with very varied planting: over 150 named plants; beds for perennials, conifers, fuchsias, herbs and roses; vegetables and fruit trees. *Mon April 12, Sun Sept 12*

 The Gardens (Lt-Col & Mrs J Barstow) ¼-acre cottage garden featuring spring bulbs, iris, roses, herbaceous, rock plants, old apple trees and a well. *Mon April 12, Sun Sept 12*

 Ivy Nook (Mr & Mrs W Gasson) Cottage garden; rockeries, lawns, mixed borders. *Sun Sept 12 only*

 Kencot Cottage (Mrs M Foster) Very small garden with spring bulbs and bedding, also bonsai trees. *Mon April 12, Sun Sept 12*

 Kencot House (Mr & Mrs A Patrick) 2-acre garden with lawns, trees, borders; quantities of daffodils and other spring bulbs; roses and over 50 different clematis; notable ginkgo tree. Interesting carved C13 archway. *Mon April 12, Sun Sept 12. Solo opening Sun June 27 (Share to RSPB) £1.50*

 Kencot Manor (Mrs A Davies) 2-acre family garden with some mature plants and trees, incl grape vines, yew hedge, glaucous cedar. Much replanting in the last 3yrs to give all round colour. *Sun Sept 12 only*

 Manor Farm (Mr & Mrs J R Fyson) 2-acre garden with lawns; naturalised spring bulbs; fritillaries a speciality; clipped yew, lime pleach in the making; C17 listed farmhouse. *Mon April 12 only*

 The Old Rectory (Mr & Mrs A Lamburn) 1-acre family garden with lawns, trees and bulbs. *Mon April 12, Sun Sept 12*

Kiddington Hall ✿ (Hon Maurice & Mrs Robson) 4m NW of Woodstock. From A44 Oxford-Stratford, R at Xrds in Kiddington and down hill; entrance on L. Partly suitable for wheelchairs. Large grounds with lake, parkland designed by Capability Brown; terraced rose garden and orangery beside house designed by Sir Charles Barry; C12 church, C16 dovecote and large walled kitchen garden. TEAS in aid of St Nicholas Church, Kiddington. *Adm £1.50 Chd free. Sun June 13 (2-6)*

Kingston Bagpuize House ✿✿✿ (Lady Tweedsmuir) Kingston Bagpuize, A415/A420, 5½m W of Abingdon. Flowering shrubs, bulbs; woodland garden; herbaceous plants; hydrangeas. Charles II Manor house. House not suitable wheelchairs. TEAS. *Adm house & garden adults £2.50, OAPs £2, Chd £1.50 (under 5 not admitted to house). Garden only 50p, under 5's free (Share to British Red Cross and Lucy Faithful home). Suns, Bank Hols Mons April 1 to Sept 30 (2.30-5.30). For NGS April 25 (2.30-5.30). Last adm 5pm*

Kingston Blount Gardens ✿✿ 4m S of Thame, 4m NE of Watlington 1½m NE of junction 6, M40. Kingston Blount is on the B4009. TEAS at **Town Farm Cottage.** *Combined adm £1 Chd free. Sun June 6 (2-6)*

 ¶**Moat Manor** (Mr & Mrs A O Hunt) Pretty 1½-acre garden surrounding C17 listed house. Herbaceous; roses; lawns and small lake

 Town Farm Cottage (Mr & Mrs J Clark) 5 yr old colourful ¾-acre garden, small lake walk, pergola, well stocked rockery, scree bed, herbaceous beds with many unusual plants

Kingston Lisle Park ✿✿ (Mr & Mrs James Lonsdale) Wantage. Approx 6m from Wantage off the B4507. 15 acres of trees, lawns and herbaceous borders, tree nursery and 2 lakes. TEAS. *Adm £1 Chd free. Mon May 3, Sun June 20 (2-5)*

Lime Close ✿✿ (Miss de Laubarede) 35 Henleys Lane, Drayton. 2m S of Abingdon. 3-acre mature garden with very rare and unusual trees, shrubs, perennials and bulbs. Raised beds, rock garden and troughs with alpines, Creation of new borders and much new planting in progress. New ornamental kitchen garden with pergola under construction and herb garden designed by Rosemary Verey. Listed C16 house (not open). Unusual plants for sale. TEAS. *Adm £1.50 Chd free. Suns April 18, June 6 (2-6.30)*

Little Place ❀ (His Honour Judge & Mrs Medd) Clifton Hampden. 5m E of Abingdon. Leaving Abingdon on A415, At Clifton Hampden turn R at traffic lights and take 1st turning R. Garden 200yds on R. 1½-acre terraced garden originally made at turn of century (part possibly designed by Gertrude Jekyll) but replanned by present owners; recently planted small woodland walk. *Adm £1.50 Chd free (Share to Barristers Benevolent Association). Combined adm with* **Clifton Hampden Manor** *Sun April 11 (2.30-5.30). Combined adm with* **Evelegh's, Long Wittenham** *Sun Sept 19 (2-6)*

Longworth Gardens ❀❀ nr Kingston Bagpuize 7m W of Abingdon N of A420 Oxford Faringdon Rd. TEAS (at **Longworth Manor**) in aid of St Mary's Church. *Combined adm £2 Chd free. Sun May 16 (2-6)*
   Haugh House (Mrs D Faulkner) 2 acres old shrub roses, mixed borders; unusual plants
   Longworth Manor ❀ (Lt-Col & Mrs J Walton) Medium-size garden with tulips and borders; shrubs and ornamental ponds. C17 Cotswold stone house with good views over R. Thames. A wild flower meadow is now established.

Loreto ❀❀❀ (Mr & Mrs R J Styles) Between Ewelme and Benson off B4009 NE of Wallingford. 5 acres; extensively replanted and developed since 1974. Emphasis on water gardens, shrubs and conifers, herbaceous and bedding plants. TEAS. *Adm £2 Chd free. Suns April 25, Aug 29, Mon Aug 30 (2-6)*

Magdalen College. See Oxford University Gardens

The Malt House ❀ (Mr & Mrs D F K Welsh) 59 Market Place, Henley-on-Thames, nr Town Hall. ½-acre unusual, imaginatively-designed town garden, featuring C16 malthouse, round lawn, beds of less common plants and shrubs. (Unsuitable for pushchairs or young children). TEAS in aid of Samaritans. *Adm £1 Chd free. Sun June 6 (2-6)*

Manor Barn House ❀❀❀ (Mr & Mrs Charles Swallow) Wendlebury. 12m NE of Oxford off A421 to Bicester. Small barn converted in 1979. Garden and field 3½ acres developed over last 12 years from neglected farmyard and adjoining land. Large pond, dug in 1985 and fed from roofs and high water table. Variety of rushes and aquatic plants, trout, crayfish. Rose walk, specimen trees and shrubs. Homemade TEAS, ice cream and plants for sale in aid of Wendlebury Church. *Adm £1 Chd 50p. Sun July 11 (2-6)*

Manor Farm ❀❀ (Sir Peter & Lady Parker) Old Minster Lovell, beautiful Cotswold village in Windrush valley. Off B4047 Witney-Burford rd; turn R at sign to Old Minster Lovell and Leafield; in ¼m cross Windrush bridge, turn R at Old Swan; no parking in village, follow signs to large free car park. 5-acre garden around small Cotswold farmhouse adjoining churchyard and ruins of Minster (open); mediaeval barns divide garden into sections; pools, informal herbaceous areas; shrubs and specie roses. C14 dovecote. Owner is author of book about her garden: 'Purest of Pleasures'. TEAS by WI. *Adm £1.50 Chd free (Share to Chiswick Family Rescue). Sun May 23 (2-5)*

The Manor House ❀ (The Hon David Astor) Sutton Courtenay. 4m S of Abingdon. Out of Abingdon on the A415. From M40 N to Abingdon, turn off A415 to Culham – Sutton Courtenay. From A34 going N come into Milton Village take last rd on R to Sutton Courtenay. 10 acres of garden approx 100 acres of land. ½m R Thames Bank. TEAS. *Adm £1.50 Chd 50p. Sun May 9 (2-6)*

The Mill House, Stadhampton ❀❀ (Mr & Mrs F A Peet) A329/B480, 8m SE of Oxford. 1-acre family garden with old mill and stream. Mill not working but machinery largely intact and wheel turning with pumped water. Parking on green; parking for disabled only at house. TEAS. *Adm £1 Chd free (Share to Stodhampton Church Restoration Fund). Adm £1. Sun April 18 (2-5.30)*

The Mill House, Sutton Courtenay ❀❀❀ (Mrs J Stevens) S of Abingdon. Approx 8½ acres; R Thames runs through garden which is on several islands with mill pond and old paper mill. TEAS. *Adm £2 Chd £1; under 4's free. Suns April 4, June 27, Oct 3 (2-6)*

Milton Hill House ❀❀ (W H Smith Personnel Division) A34 to Milton Trading Estate Roundabout, take A4130 to Chilton Harwell Rd. ½m from roundabout nr Pack Horse Inn. 54 acres varied collection of trees; shrubs; herbaceous borders; ha-ha; wooded walk; rose garden. TEAS. *Adm £1 Chd free. Sun April 11 (2-6)*

Mount Skippet ❀❀ (Dr & Mrs M A T Rogers) Ramsden, 4m N of Witney. At Xrds turn E towards Finstock; after 30yds, turn R (sign-post Mount Skippet). After 400yds turn L (No Through Way sign) for 75yds. 2 acres; 2 rock gardens; alpine house; stone troughs; shrubs; herbaceous beds; primulas; conservatory; many rare plants. Fine views. Cotswold stone house largely C17. Teas for groups by prior arrangement; also picnic area. *Adm £1 Chd free. By appt only April 1 to Sept 30* Tel 0993 868253

New College. See Oxford University Gardens

4 Northfield Cottages ❀❀ (Miss S E Bedwell) Water Eaton, nr Kidlington. A cottage garden of approx ¼-acre designed and planted over the last 5 years. Mainly herbaceous with some unusual plants and large greenhouse. *Adm 70p Chd free. Open by appt only all year round* Tel 08675 78910

¶**Nuffield Place** ❀❀❀ (By kind permission of the Warden & Fellows of Nuffield College) Huntercombe. Signposted off A423 midway between Henley-on-Thames & Wallingford. Former home of Lord Nuffield, the founder of Morris Motors. 4-acre garden with mature trees, yew hedges, rose pergola and rockery. Laid out during and just after the First World War. Adjoining bluebell woods. Morris and Wolseley cars on display. TEAS. *Adm £1.50 Chd free. Sun May 16 (2-5)*

Nutford Lodge ❀❀ (Mrs P Elmore) In Longcot Village next to The King & Queen public house. 1m S of A420 between Faringdon and Shrivenham. 1½ acres with ornamental vegetable plot, herb and alpine rockeries, colour schemed borders, sculpture trail with many interesting features. An indoor gallery. *Adm 75p Chd free (Share to Headway in Oxford). Suns May 30, July 18, Sept 12 (2-6). Also by appt* Tel 0793 782258

The Old Rectory, Albury &*❀ (Mr & Mrs J Nowell-Smith). Nr Tiddington. 4m W of Thame, at end of cul-de-sac off A418 Wheatley-Thame rd. Approx 5 acres incl lawns and borders wooded walk around lake. TEAS and plants in aid of St Helens Church. *Adm £1 Chd free. Sun May 2 (2-6)*

The Old Rectory, Coleshill & (Mr & Mrs Martin) 3m W of Faringdon. Coleshill (a Nat Trust village) is on B4019, midway between Faringdon and Highworth. Medium-sized garden; lawns and informal shrub beds; wide variety shrubs, inc old-fashioned roses; 40-yr-old standard wisteria. Distant views of Berkshire and Wiltshire Downs. House dates from late C14. TEAS. *Adm £1 Chd free. Suns April 18 (2-6), Sept 12 (2-5)*

The Old Rectory, Farnborough nr Wantage. See Berkshire

The Old Vicarage &❀ (Mrs T A Laurie) Weston-on-the-Green 4½m SW of Bicester, take Bletchingdon turn into village centre. 2½-acre old-fashioned vicarage garden imaginatively restored keeping its tranquil secluded atmosphere. Many unusual plants and colour combinations. Stream in a woodland walk and lily ponds. Something of interest for everyone. TEAS in aid of St Mary's Church. *Adm £1 Chd free. Mons May 31, Aug 30 (2-6)*

Oxford University Gardens
  Christ Church &* **Masters' Garden** Entrance on Christ Church Meadow (through War Memorial garden on St Aldates). Created in 1926, has herbaceous borders and a new border with some unusual shrubs. A walk past Pocock's Plane, an oriental plane planted 1636, leads through Cathedral garden to Deanery garden where Lewis Carroll's Alice played; Cheshire Cat's chestnut tree. *Adm 75p Chd free. Sun Aug 15 (2-5)*
  Corpus Christi &* Entrance from Merton St or Christchurch **Fellows garden**. Several small gardens and courtyards overlooking Christchurch meadows. Fellows private garden not normally open to the public. *Adm 75p. Sun Aug 15 (2-5)*
  Exeter College * **Rector's Lodgings** The Turl, between High & Broad Sts, Oxford. Small enclosed garden, recently replanted, herbaceous and shrubs, especially clematis. *Combined adm with **New College** £1.50 Chd free. Sun July 4 (2-5)*
  Green College &* Woodstock Rd, next to Radcliffe Infirmary. 3 acres; lawns, herbaceous borders, medicinal garden with notes on traditional usage of plants. Radcliffe Observatory (Tower of the Winds) open for views of Oxford and TEA. *Adm £1 OAPs 50p Chd free (incl Observatory). Sun June 20 (2-6)*
  Holywell Manor * (Balliol College) Central Oxford at corner of Manor Rd and St Cross Rd on L of St Cross Church opp law library. College garden of about 1 acre, not normally open to the public. Imaginatively laid out 50 yrs ago around horse chestnut to give formal and informal areas. Mature ginkgo avenue, spinney with spring flowers and bulbs. *Adm 75p Chd free. Please tel or call at Porters lodge any time of the year.* **Tel 0865 271501**
  Magdalen College &* High Street Oxford. Entrance in High St. 60 acres including deer park, college lawns,

Fellows Garden and **President's Gardens** not normally open to the public; numerous trees 150-200 yrs old, notable herbaceous and shrub plantings; Magdalen Meadows containing the deer herd is surrounded by Addison's Walk, a tree lined circuit by the R Cherwell developed since the late C18. TEAS. *Adm £1.50 Child £1. Sun July 11 (12-6)*
  New College * **Warden's Garden** Entered from New College Lane, off Catte St. Secret walled garden, replanted 1988 with interesting mix of herbaceous and shrubs. *Combined adm with* **Exeter College** *£1.50 Chd free. Sun July 4 (2-5)*
  Queen's College * **Fellows' Garden** High St. ½-acre with splendid herbaceous borders seen against high old stone walls; large ilex tree. Teas 43 St Giles in the garden if fine. *Combined adm with* **Wadham College** *£1.50 Chd free. Sun July 25 (2-5)*
  Rewley House &* (Oxford University Dept of Continuing Education) Wellington Sq., St John Street. Roof Garden, 60ft × 26ft, and courtyard gardens, planted by townscaper, Jeanne Bliss, with variegated shrubs, climbers, trailing plants in mobile boxes on wheels. Maintained by Oxford Gardeners under the direction of Christopher Herdman. TEAS. *Adm 75p Chd free. Sun July 18 (2-5)*
  St Catherine's College &*❀ Manor Rd, nr St Cross & Longwall Sts., Oxford. Garden planted around new college 1963-65 designed by late Prof Arne Jacobsen to link modern architecture with river meadow site; water garden; wide range of trees and shrubs planted for autumn colour. Large plant sale in aid of BHF. TEA. *Adm 75p Chd free. Sun Oct 3 (2-5)*
  St Hugh's College &*❀ At intersection of St Margaret's Rd and Banbury Rd, N of city centre. 10 acres comprising main garden, Principal's and Fellows' gardens largely developed from grounds of 3 early C19 houses with some original features remaining. Fine trees, many shrubs, herbaceous plants; dell garden developed from Victorian fernery; large terrace with rock beds. TEAS. *Adm 75p Chd free. Sun April 25 (2-5.30)*
  Trinity College &*❀ **President's Garden** Entrance in Broad St. Surrounded by high old stone walls, recently re-designed, has mixed borders of herbaceous and shrubs, and statuary. Historic main college gardens with specimen trees inc 200-yr-old forked catalpa and splendid fraxinus, fine long herbaceous border and handsome garden quad originally designed by Wren. *Adm 75p Chd free. Sun Aug 15 (2-5)*
  University Arboretum *❀ 6m S of Oxford on A423, 400yds S of Nuneham Courtenay. 55 acres incl informal rhododendron walks, camellia, bamboo and acer collections, natural woodland and oak woodland, meadow with pond and associated aquatics and marginals; fine collection of mature conifers; many 150 yrs old. Staff available to answer queries. Plant stall in aid of Oxford University Botanic Garden. *Adm £1 Chd free. Sun May 30 (2-6)*

Regular Openers. Too many days to include in diary. Usually there is a wide range of plants giving year-round interest. See head of county section for the name and garden description for times etc.

Wadham College: ♿✗ **Fellows' Private Garden & Warden's Garden** Parks Rd. 5 acres, best known for trees and herbaceous borders. In the Fellows' main garden superb purple beech, fine ginkgo and Magnolia acuminata, etc; in the Back Quadrangle very large Tilia tomentosa 'Petiolaris'; in the Warden's garden an ancient tulip tree; in the Fellows' private garden Civil War embankment with period fruit tree cultivars, recently established shrubbery with unusual trees and ground cover amongst older plantings. Teas 43 St Giles (July 25 only, in garden if fine). *Adm 75p Chd free. Sun April 4. Combined adm with* **Queen's College** *£1.50, Sun July 25 (2-5)*

Wolfson College ♿✿ End of Linton Rd, off Banbury Rd, between city centre and Summertown shops. 9 acres by R Cherwell; garden developed in recent years with comprehensive plant collection tolerant of alkaline soils, grown in interesting and varied habitats both formal and informal, around a framework of fine mature trees; award winning building designed by Powel & Moya; Presidents garden. TEAS. *Adm 75p Chd free. Sun May 9 (2-6)*

Worcester College ✗ **Provost's Garden** Entrance through lodge at junction of Beaumont St and Walton St. The college has 26 acres of grounds, landscaped in early C19 with a large naturalised lake. The garden is not normally open to the public and comprises a rose garden, wooded lakeside walk and orchards. *Adm 75p Chd free. Sun Sept 5 (2-6)*

Quarry Bank House ♿✗ (Mr & Mrs D J Smith) nr Tackley. 2m E of Woodstock. From A423 take A4095 to Bicester; entrance at bottom of Gibraltar Hill on sharp bend of river bridge. 4¾ acres with abundance of early spring flowers in sheltered situation on R. Cherwell; lawns, fine cedar, orchard and banks of trees and shrubs; attractive walks in natural quarry setting. TEAS in aid of Bletchingdon Church. *Adm £1 Chd free. Sun April 4 (2-6)*

Queen's College see Oxford University Gardens

Rewley House see Oxford University Gardens

Rofford Manor ♿✗✿ (Mr & Mrs J L Mogford) Little Milton. 10m SE of Oxford. 1m from Little Milton on Chalgrove Rd. Signposted Rofford only. 2 acres of gardens, within old walls laid out since 1985. Vegetable, herb, rose and swimming pool gardens. Box garden with raised pool. Yew hedges and pleached limes. Twin herbaceous borders planted Autumn 1989 flanking lawn leading to recently constructed ha-ha. TEAS. *Adm £1.50 Chd free. Sun Sept 12 (2-6)*

St Catherine's College see Oxford University Gardens

St Hugh's College see Oxford University Gardens

Salford Gardens ✗ 2m W of Chipping Norton. Off A44 Oxford-Worcester. TEAS. *Combined adm £1.50 Chd free. Sun June 27 (2-6)*

    Old Rectory ♿✿ (Mr & Mrs N M Chambers) Shrub roses, herbaceous and foliage plants; shrubs; ground cover. Kitchen garden. *Also open 1st Tuesday of month April to Sept (10-4). Adm £1*

Willow Tree Cottage ✿ (Mr & Mrs J Shapley) Small walled twin gardens; one created by owners since 1979 with shrub and herbaceous borders, many clematis; other created 1985 from old farmyard with heathers and large alpine garden. Featured in 'Successful Gardening'

Sarsden Glebe ✿ (Mr & Mrs Rupert Ponsonby) Churchill. 3m SW of Chipping Norton. Via B4450 to Churchill; from Burford via A361 and W for Churchill. Medium-sized garden by Repton; fine trees, anemones, bulbs; herbaceous border. TEAS in aid of British Red Cross. *Adm £1 Chd free. Sun April 4 (2-6)*

Shotover House ♿✿ (Lt-Col Sir John Miller) Wheatley, 6m E of Oxford on A40. Bus: Oxford-Thame or Oxford-High Wycombe-London; alight Islip turn. Large unaltered landscape garden with ornamental temples, lawns and specimen trees. Also small collection of rare cattle, sheep and birds. TEAS (in arcade with view of lake). *Adm £1 Chd free. Sun April 18 (2-6)*

Shucklets ✗✿ (Dr & Mrs G Garton) High Street Ramsden. 3m N of Witney off B4022, near centre of village. Plantsman's garden of 2 acres, with a variety of different areas: rock garden, raised beds, troughs; foliage plants, shrubs, old-fashioned roses; ornamental vegetable garden, small vineyard. TEAS by W.I. *Adm £1 Chd free. Sun July 4 (2-6)*

Shutford Gardens ✗✿ An unspoilt village 5m W of Banbury, between A422 to Stratford and B4035 to Shipston. TEAS. *Combined adm £1 Chd free. Sun July 11 (2-6)*

    Fiveways Cottage (Dr & Mrs M R Aldous) Just over ½ acre in present form started 1986. Essentially cottage garden style, with shrubs, roses and many herbaceous plants, small fish pond edged by alpine bed and troughs, many trees still immature

    Shutford Manor ♿ (Mr & Mrs N D Cadbury) 1½-acre walled garden of dramatic C16 house with pastoral view. Yellow and white border; formal beds with old-fashioned and modern shrubs roses; avenue of poplars

Sibford Ferris Gardens ✗ Near the Warwickshire border, S of B4035 (Banbury 6½m, Shipston-on-Stour 7½m). TEAS in aid of Sibford Primary School. *Combined adm £1 Chd free. Sun, Wed, June 13, 16 (2-6)*

    Back Acre ✿ (Mr & Mrs F A Lamb) Almost an acre, much of which is wild woodland and rough grass with wild flowers; rockery and pond, constructed about 100 years ago and restored over the last few years

    Home Close (Mr & Mrs P A Randall) Cotswold stone house fronting formal 1¼-acre garden designed by Baillie-Scott in 1911, under restoration. Courtyard with ornamental fountain and Roman-style stone recesses. Terraced garden, large variety of shrubs including rare species

    The Old Court House (Mr & Mrs R Springate) A small garden of unusual design and sub-divisions. Hidden courtyard, many pot plants and other decorative features

    The Small House ♿ (Mr & Mrs R H Franke) 1¾-acres with interesting trees. *Open only June 13*

Sibford Gower Gardens Near the Warwickshire border, S of B4035 (Banbury 7m, Shipston-on-Stour 7m) Superlative views and numerous intriguing tucked away lanes are features of this village. TEAS

Sun June 20 *(2-6) Combined adm £1 chd free*

¶**Handywater Farm** ⚅✿ (Mr & Mrs W B Colquhoun) ½m N of Sibford Gower on rd leading to Epwell; 1½ acre family garden in process of creation since 1980. Lovely setting in open rolling countryside. Westerly sloping lawns, stream and ponds, shrub and herbaceous beds

Meadow Cottage ⚅⚅✿ (Mr & Mrs Roger Powell) 6 The Colony. At S end of village. A 1.3-acre garden started from a field in 1988. Large 'shrubaceous' borders; over 1300 different plants; many unusual. Conifers; shrub roses and alpines in raised beds; budding arboretum leading to stream. Views

Sun July 18 *(2-6) Combined adm £1.50 Chd free*

Carters Yard (Mr & Mrs W J S Clutterbuck) Next to Wykeham Arms. ⅓-acre very private cottage garden. Various beds and rockeries in soft colours

The Manor House ⚅ (Mr & Mrs M Edwards) Opp Wykeham Arms. Completely reconstructed May 1989, the gardens (under 1 acre) are already well established and complement the romantic atmosphere of this recently renovated rambling thatched manor house

Meadow Cottage (as described for earlier date)

Temple Close ⚅✿ (Mr & Mrs E Jones) E of Wykeham Arms. 1¼ acres with rockery, various beds of shrubs, roses, perennials and herbs; paved stream-side walk running through extensive water garden between two ponds with fountains; pets paddock; good view

Souldern Gardens ✿ Between Banbury (8m) and Bicester (7m) off A41. 5 gardens in picturesque 'Best Kept' prizewinning village. TEAS. *Combined adm £1.50 Chd free (Share to Souldern Trust).* **Sun April 4** *(2-6)*

The Barn ⚅ (Mr & Mrs J Talbot) Sheltered garden with pond; wide mixed borders

Great House Close ⚅ (Mrs C E Thornton) Long, varied garden and orchard framed by old farm buildings

The Old Forge (Mr & Mrs D Duthie) Resourceful, densely planted cottage garden with stone walling

Souldern House ⚅ (Maj & Mrs A H Gray) Walled garden round C17 house; gazebo dated 1706, ancient yew hedge; bantams

Souldern Manor ⚅ (Mr & Dr C Sanders) 25 acres of C17 house with much fresh development. Linked ponds, rock garden, waterfall, fountains, temple, pavilions and view of Cherwell valley are enhanced by many newly planted mature trees. Children's play area and pony rides

South Newington Gardens A small village 1½m from Bloxham, nr Banbury on A361 to Chipping Norton. It has a fine church, with superb mediaeval wall paintings. TEA at The Barn. 3 gardens within easy walking distance. *Combined adm £1.* **Sun June 6** *(2-6)*

Applegarth ⚅✿ (Mr & Mrs Kenneth Butcher) ¾-acre cottage garden with a rose walk featuring old-fashioned roses and lavenders; herbaceous borders and mixed borders with some unusual shrubs and young trees; small water garden and pond

¶**The Barn** ⚅✿ (Mrs Rosemary Clark) Green Lane. 1 acre of lawns and mixed borders with outdoor chess game, croquet lawn, vine walk and vegetable patch

The Little Forge ⚅ (Mr M B Pritchard) Small garden with shrubs; trees and vegetable patch

Sparsholt Manor (Sir Adrian & Lady Judith Swire) Off B4507 Ashbury Rd 3½m W of Wantage. Spring garden, lakes and wilderness. *Adm £1 Chd free (Share to St John Ambulance, Wantage division).* **Mon May 3** *(2-6)*

Stansfield ⚅⚅✿ (Mr & Mrs D Keeble) 49 High St, Stanford-in-the-Vale. 3½m SE of Faringdon. Turn off A417 opp Vale Garage into High St, 300yds. Park in street. 1¼-acre plantsman's garden started in 1979. Scree bed, damp garden, alpines in troughs, developing copse underplanted with shrubs, hellebores, bulbs and shade plants, bed of ornamental grasses contrasted with bold foliage plants. TEAS. *Adm £1 Chd free. Open every Tues April 6 to Sept 21 (10-4) Suns June 6, Aug 8 (2-6); also by appt* Tel 0367 710340

Stanton Harcourt Manor ⚅✿ (Mr Crispin & The Hon Mrs Gascoigne) W of Oxford on B4449. Formal woodland & water gardens. C15 chapel & medieval kitchen in grounds. TEAS. *Adm House and garden £3 Chd/OAP's £2. Garden only £1.50 Chd/OAP's £1.* Thurs April 22, 29, May 13, 27, June 10, 24, July 8, 22, Aug 5, 19, 26, Sept 9, 23, Suns April 11, 25, May 2, 16, 30, June 13, 27, July 11, 25, Aug 8, 22, 29, Sept 12, 26, Bank hol Mons April 12, May 3, 31, Aug 30. For NGS Suns April 25, July 11 (2-6)

Steeple & Middle Aston Gardens. Beautiful stone villages midway between Oxford & Banbury, ½m off A423. Incl in price, by kind permission of Mr & Mrs B C Box, are grounds of **Middle Aston House**, with Lakes designed by William Kent. TEAS. *Combined adm £2 Chd free.* **Sun April 18** *(2-6)*

Cedar Lodge ⚅ (Mr & Mrs G Croft) North Side. Large terraced garden in later stages of restoration. Several herbaceous borders with colour themes; mature and newly planted unusual trees; thousands of bulbs in spring

Home Farm House ⚅✿ (Mrs T J G Parsons) Middle Aston, ¾m N of Steeple Aston, opp Middle Aston House. 1-acre informal garden surrounding C17 farmhouse (not open), fine view. Mixed planting, incl bulbs, unusual perennials, shrubs and roses. Kitchen garden and Jacob sheep. Interesting small nursery open by appt May to Sept Tel 0869 40666

Kralingen (Mr & Mrs Roderick Nicholson) 2-acre informal garden designed for low maintenance. Great variety of interesting trees and shrubs; water garden and wild flower area

The Longbyre ⚅✿ (Mr & Mrs V Billings) Hornton stone house in ¼ acre. Garden on different levels recently constructed out of old orchard. Water feature, mixed perennials, shrubs, bulbs in beds and tubs

¶**Rowans** ⚅⚅✿ (Mr & Mrs M J Clist) The Dickredge, opp White Lion. An acre of orchard and mixed garden, incl shrubs, herbaceous borders, alpines, vegetables and small streamside area

Willow Cottage ❀ (Mr & Mrs M Vivian) The Dickredge, opposite White Lion. Hornton stone cottage with ½-acre garden. Old-fashioned shrub roses, many unusual plants in garden and conservatory. Fish pond with Koi

Stratton Audley Gardens &❀❀ 3m NE of Bicester, off A421 to Buckingham. Village dates from Roman times. Church is largely mediaeval with spectacular late C17 tomb. TEAS. *Combined adm £1.50 Chd free (Share to Helen House Hospice). Sun June 6, Wed June 9 (2-6)*
  1 Church Cottages (Mr & Mrs L Sweetman) About ½-acre. A proper country cottage garden with rockery pools and stonework, vegetables, seasonal bedding, orchids
  Mallories (Mr P Boyd) Mainly walled garden of ¾ acre behind row of C17 cottages converted to house. Sunny and shady herbaceous borders, old roses and other shrubs, wall plants and climbers, small conservatory
  ¶**Manor Farm** & (Mrs H M Gosling) A recently constructed garden at Old Manor Farm House of approx ¾ acre. Shrub borders, raised beds and tree plantings, a small pond with running water and a nice view southwards into the hills
  St George's &❀❀ (Mrs R Wigley) A walled garden of ½ acre at end of cul-de-sac in Cavendish Place. Walls clothed with variety of climbers incl many clematis. Several unusual shrubs in this interesting garden. Formal pond spanned by a bridge and stocked with ornamental fish
  Stratton House &❀ (Mr & Mrs P J Bailey) A quiet and peaceful walled garden, set in ¾ acre, with terraces, paved area with fountain, herbaceous border, shrubs, heathers, ornamental pond, topiary, a black walnut tree and a yew, said to be over 400 yrs old

Stonewalls &❀ (Mr & Mrs B Shafighian) Hempton. 1½m W of Deddington on B4031. A plantsman's garden of ¾ acre divided into many interesting areas, incl shrubbery, herbaceous border, conifer and heather bed, nearly 200 clematis and climbers. Sunken pool. *Adm 50p Chd free. Sun July 18 (2-6)*

Swalcliffe Gardens W of Banbury on B4035 halfway between Banbury and Shipston-on-Stour. TEAS *Adm £1 Chd free. Sun June 27 (2-6)*
  ¶**The Manor House** ❀ (Mr & Mrs F Hitching) Swalcliffe next to church. Large garden around C13 Manor house (not open). Mixed borders, interesting plants, sunken garden with shrub roses, walled herb garden. Fine church, all pre C15, early tithe barn housing farm implement collection adjacent. Parking at Tithe Barn.
  Sparrow Hall &❀ (Mrs J Panks) ½-acre walled garden, planted for easy care with wide collection minitature conifers, heathers and alpines; English/Japanese effect. Large Patio with stone troughs, etc planted for seasonal display. *By appt all year round* Tel **0295 78433**

Swerford Park ❀ (Mr & Mrs J W Law) 4m NE of Chipping Norton, just off A361 to Banbury, ½m W of Swerford Church. Partly suitable for wheelchairs. In extensive parkland setting with lakeside walks, small garden of Georgian house overlooks spectacular wooded valley with series of lakes linked by waterfalls. Approach along front drive where signed; parking at rear only, may not be very close. TEAS at **The Yews**, ½m E of Church. *Adm £1 Chd free. Mon May 31 (2-6)*

Swinbrook Gardens &❀ 2½m E of Burford, off A40. Unspoilt Cotswold village in Windrush Valley with interesting church. TEAS. *Combined adm £1.50 or £1 each garden Chd free (Share to Swinbrook with Widford Churches Trust). Suns June 13, July 18 (2-6)*
  Swinbrook House (Mr & Mrs J D Mackinnon) 1½m N of Swinbrook on Shipton-under-Wychwood Rd. Large garden; herbaceous border; shrubs; shrub roses; large kitchen garden; fine views. Picnics allowed. *Open Suns June 13, July 18 (2-6)*
  Swinbrook Manor (Mrs S Freund) Medium-sized garden in exceptionally pretty surroundings next to church; mixed shrub and herbaceous planting against old stone walls. *Open Sun July 18 only*

Swyncombe House &❀ (Mr W J Christie-Miller) Cookley Green on B481 Nettlebed-Watlington. Tranquil setting in a large park; rare trees; many mature flowering shrubs and spring bulbs in woodland. C11 church in grounds. TEA (in aid of St Botolph's Church). *Adm £1 Chd free. Sun April 18 (2-7)*

Taynton House (Mr & Mrs David Mackenzie) Taynton, off A424 Burford to Stow-on-the-Wold. Medium-sized garden behind listed stone house in delightful Cotswold village with interesting church. Stream and copse with thousands of daffodils and spring flowers. Roses and mixed planting in summer. TEAS. *Adm £1 Chd free (Share to St John's Church, Taynton). Suns March 28, June 13 (2-6)*

Thame Cottage ❀❀ (Mr & Mrs D Atkinson) Warborough. 12m SE of Oxford on A329 Wallingford (2m) to Thame (12m) rd, nr centre of village next to Greet Hall. 1½-acre garden completely redesigned by owners and featured in several books and magazine articles. Wide variety of unusual plants and shrubs; old-fashioned and climbing roses, cottage garden plants and plants for scent., colour and shape of foliage; incl walled garden and natural pond. Plants and pots for sale. TEAS in aid of Warborough Church. *Adm £1 Chd free. Sat, Sun June 19, 20 (2-6)*

¶**Thames-Side Court** &❀ (Mr U E Schwarzenbach) Shiplake. Take A4155 (Reading Rd) out of Henley-on-Thames to Shiplake memorial (approx 2 mls). Turn into Station Rd go over level Xing. Turn immed L into Bolney Rd, and continue to the end of this rd. Spend hrs in these 25 acres of outstanding riverside gardens; sunken, Japanese and water gardens, dramatic tropical glasshouse, greenhouses. Children and adults are invited to ride on superb steam trains along a magnificiently landscaped track and to have the chance to play croquet and boule. TEAS. *Adm £4 Chd £2. Sun Aug 15 (11-5)*

Towersey Manor & (Mr & Mrs U D Barnett) Towersey, 1½m SE of Thame, 300 yds down Manor Rd from Xrds in middle of village. Main 2-acre garden lying behind house, has all been laid out and planted within last 17 years. Formal hornbeam hedges frame smaller informal areas incorporating many shrubs, trees and old-fashioned and modern shrub roses. TEAS in fine old timbered barn. *Adm £1 Chd free. Sun June 27 (2-6)*

Trinity College see Oxford University Gardens

Tusmore Park &❀ (Tusmore Park Holdings) On A43, Baynards Green 2m, Brackley 3½m. About 20-acres of lawns, herbaceous borders, woodland garden and terraces; 6-acre lake, 3 greenhouses. TEAS. *Adm £1 Chd free. Sun July 18 (2-6)*

University Arboretum see Oxford University Gardens

Wadham College see Oxford University Gardens

Wardington Gardens 5m NE of Banbury. TEAS. *Combined adm £2.50 Chd free. Suns April 18, May 23 (2-5.30)*
  Pettifers &❀❀ (Mr J & the Hon Mrs Price) Lower Wardington C17 village house looking on to Wardington church. Unusual and interesting plants, particularly foliage plants; the 1-acre garden frames an exceptional view of sheep pastures and wooded hills
  Wardington Manor &❀ (The Lord Wardington) 5-acre garden with topiary, rock garden, flowering shrub walk to pond. Carolean manor house 1665. *Also Sun Aug 15 Adm £1.50*

Waterperry Gardens &❀❀ 2½m from Wheatley M40 Junction 8. 50m from London, 62m from Birmingham, 9m E of Oxford. Gardens well signed locally with Tourist Board 'rose' symbol. 20-acres; ornamental gardens, nurseries, parkland; many interesting plants; shrub, herbaceous and alpine nurseries; glasshouses and comprehensive fruit section. High quality plant centre, garden shop (**Tel 0844 339226**). TEA SHOP. Saxon church with famous glasses and brasses in grounds. *Adm Gardens & Nurseries £1.95 OAPs £1.50 Chd 95p. Coach parties by appt only* **Tel 0844 339254.** ▲*For NGS (Share to NCCPG). Suns June 6, Aug 8 (10-6)*

Weald Manor see Bampton & Weald Gardens

Westwell Gardens 2m SW of Burford; from A40 Burford-Cheltenham, turn L after ½m on narrow rd signposted Westwell. Unspoilt hamlet with delightful church. *TEAS. Combined adm £2 Chd 50p (Share to St Mary's Church Westwell). Suns May 2, June 27 (2-6.30)*
  The Dower House ❀❀ (Mrs Pamela Moore) Incl box garden; orchard; young arboretum of specialist trees; river bed; tubs; hanging baskets and herbaceous borders
  Westwell Manor ❀❀ (Mr & Mrs T H Gibson) 6 acres surrounding old Cotswold manor house; knot and water gardens; potager; shrub roses; herbaceous borders; topiary; moonlight garden

White's Farm House &❀ (Dr & Mrs M Shone) Letcombe Bassett 3m SW of Wantage. Take B4507 signed Ashbury, then through Letcombe Regis. 2½ acres; mixed borders; wild garden with 30 yrs growth of chalk-tolerant trees, shrubs, unusual herbaceous plants, summer bulbs. Gravel scree bed, plants in pots and tubs, pond, playground and monster walk. TEAS in C18 barn. *Adm £1 Chd free Suns June 13, July 18, (2-6)*

Wick Hall & Nurseries &❀❀ (Mr & Mrs P Drysdale) Between Abingdon & Radley on Audlett Drive. Parking for disabled at house, some off-street parking. Approx 10 acres lawns and wild garden; topiary; ericaceous bed; pond garden; rockeries; walled garden enclosing knot garden. Young arboretum. Early C18 house, barn and greenhouses garden restored and developed since 1982. TEAS. *Adm £1 Chd free. Sun April 25 (2-5)*

Wilcote House &❀ (The Hon C E Cecil) Finstock. Between Finstock & North Leigh. East of B4022 Witney-Charlbury Road. 4 acres set in parkland surrounding an early C17-C19 Cotswold stone house. Shrub and herbaceous borders, old-fashioned rose garden and 40yd laburnum walk (planted 1984). Old orchard being replanted as an arboretum. Spring bulbs, flowering trees, sheep and lovely views. TEAS. *Adm £1 Chd free (Share to DGAA & Katherine House Hospice). Sun May 30. For NGS Sun Oct 3 (2-5.30). Also by appt Mr Pollard* **Tel 0993 868 606**

Wolfson College see Oxford University Gardens

Wood Croft ❀❀ (St Cross College) Foxcombe Lane, Boars Hill, S of Oxford. From ring rd follow signs to Wootton and Boars Hill. From junction at top Hinksey Hill, house first on L. 1½ acres designed and planted by the late Prof G E Blackman FRS. Rhododendrons, camellias, azaleas, many varieties primula in woodland and surrounding natural pond; fine trees. TEA. *Adm £1 Chd free (Share to Royal Marsden Hospital Development Appeal). Sun May 23 (2-6)*

Woodperry House ❀❀ (Mr & Mrs Robert Lush) nr Stanton St John. 4m E of Oxford off B4027 on road from Headington to Horton-cum-Studley. Approx 5 acres including lime tree avenue, formal garden under construction, 1 acre of walled vegetable garden (being restored). Large herbaceous and shrub borders. Good views and Country walks (Aug). TEAS in aid of Oxford Playhouse (May) in aid of Westham House (Aug). *Adm £1.50 Chd free. Suns May 16, Aug 22 (2-5)*

Wootton Place &❀❀ (Mr & Mrs H Dyer) 3m N of Woodstock off A34, next to Church. Laid out by Capability Brown; 150 varieties of daffodil, very fine trees incl huge ancient walnut; walled garden. TEAS. *Adm £1.50 Chd free (Share to Sir Michael Sobell House Hospice). Sun April 4 (2-5.30)*

Worcester College see Oxford University Gardens.

Wroxton Gardens 3m NW of Banbury off A422. Grounds of Wroxton Abbey open free. Teas at village fete May. TEAS **Laurels Farm** only. *Combined adm £1. Mon May 31 (2-6)*
  ¶**6 The Firs** Stratford Rd &❀❀ (Mr & Mrs D J Allen) Approx ⅓-acre family garden with island beds, shrubs, herbaceous perennials and rockery
  Laurels Farm ❀ (Mr & Mrs R Fox) ½-acre with island beds, shrubs, old roses and herbaceous perennials. TEAS. *Adm 80p. Also open Sun Aug 1*

Regular Openers. See head of county section.

Yeomans ✿❀ (Mrs A E Pedder) Tadmarton 5m SW of Banbury on B4035. Small garden on 4 levels, featured in 'Easy Plants for Difficult Places' by Geoffrey Smith; C16 thatched cottage. Colourful from spring to autumn; wide variety annuals, perennials, shrubs; many climbers inc roses, clematis; shrub roses with hips. *Adm 70p Chd free (Share to Katharine House Hospice Trust). April to Sept by appointment only.* **Tel 0295 78285**

The Yews ♿✿❀ (Mr & Mrs F W Timms) Swerford, a pretty village 5m NE of Chipping Norton, just off A361 to Banbury. 2-acre walled garden with mature trees and many flowering shrubs; water gardens, waterfall, fountains; swimming pool. TEAS from 2pm in aid of Katherine House Hospice. *Adm £1 Chd free under 12yrs.* Sun, Mon May 30, (2-6) 31 (12-6)

Powys

See separate Welsh section beginning on page 274

Rutland

See Leicestershire

Shropshire

Hon County Organisers: Mrs J H M Stafford, The Old Rectory, Fitz, Shrewsbury SY4 3AS
Tel 0743 850555
Mr & Mrs James Goodall, Glazeley Old Rectory, Glazeley, Bridgnorth, Shropshire WV16 4JF

Hon County Treasurer: Mrs P Trevor-Jones, Preen Manor, Church Preen, nr Church Stretton SY6 7LG

DATES OF OPENING

By appointment
For telephone numbers and other details see garden descriptions

Acton Round, Morville, nr Bridgnorth
Adcote School, Little Ness, nr Shrewsbury
Ashford Manor, nr Ludlow
Bakers House, Bromley, nr Bridgnorth
Brownhill House, Ruyton XI Towns
Church Bank, Westbury
Farley House, Much Wenlock
Glazeley Old Rectory, Glazeley
Haye House, Eardington
Limeburners, Ironbridge
Lower Hall, Worfield
Moortown, nr Wellington
Ruthall Manor, Ditton Priors

Regular openings
For details see garden descriptions

Nordybank Nurseries, nr Ludlow.
Suns, Mons, Weds May 16 to August 29
Weston Park, Shifnal. Easter to Sept
Wollerton Old Hall, Market Drayton.
Every Fri June 5 to Sept 25

February 28 Sunday
Erway Farm House, Dudleston Heath
March 28 Sunday
Erway Farm House, Dudleston Heath
April 4 Sunday
New Hall, Eaton-under-Heywood
April 10 Saturday
Erway Farm House, Dudleston Heath

April 11 Sunday
Erway Farm House, Dudleston Heath
April 12 Monday
Badger Farmhouse, nr Shifnal
Erway Farm House, Dudleston Heath
April 18 Sunday
Astley Abbotts House, Bridgnorth
April 21 Wednesday
Swallow Hayes, Albrighton
April 25 Sunday
Adcote School, Little Ness, nr Shrewsbury
Erway Farm House, Dudleston Heath
New Hall, Eaton-under-Heywood
May 2 Sunday
Morville Hall Gardens, nr Bridgnorth
Swallow Hayes, Albrighton

May 3 Monday
Millichope Park, Munslow
May 9 Sunday
Adcote School, Little Ness, nr
Shrewsbury
May 12 Wednesday
Swallow Hayes, Albrighton
May 16 Sunday
Gatacre Park, nr Bridgnorth
May 17 Monday
Mawley Hall, Cleobury Mortimer
May 23 Sunday
Adcote School, Little Ness, nr
Shrewsbury
Bitterley Court, Ludlow
Brownhill House, Ruyton XI
Towns
Gatacre Park, nr Bridgnorth
Willey Park, Broseley
May 26 Wednesday
Swallow Hayes, Albrighton
May 30 Sunday
Erway Farm House, Dudleston
Heath
Hatton Grange, Shifnal
Longnor Hall, nr Dorrington
Lower Hall, Worfield
Peplow Hall, Hodnet
Upper Shelderton House,
Clungunford
Walcot Hall, Lydbury North
May 31 Monday
Dudmaston, nr Bridgnorth
Hatton Grange, Shifnal
Longnor Hall, nr Dorrington
Oteley, Ellesmere
Walcot Hall, Lydbury North
June 3 Thursday
Preen Manor, nr Church Stretton
June 5 Saturday
Brownhill House, Ruyton XI
Towns
Ruthall Manor, Ditton Priors
June 6 Sunday
Adcote School, Little Ness, nr
Shrewsbury
Brownhill House, Ruyton XI
Towns
Limeburners, Ironbridge
The Lyth, Ellesmere
The Old Vicarage, Cardington
5 Park Lane, Oswestry &
Byeways, Whittington
Swallow Hayes, Albrighton
June 13 Sunday
The Old Vicarage, Cardington
June 15 Tuesday
Weston Park, Shifnal
June 17 Thursday
Preen Manor, nr Church Stretton
June 20 Sunday
Bitterley Court, Ludlow

Lower Hall, Worfield
Millichope Park, Munslow
The Old Vicarage, Cardington
June 21 Monday
Mawley Hall, Cleobury Mortimer
June 23 Wednesday
Morville Hall Gardens, nr
Bridgnorth
June 26 Saturday
Whittington Village Gardens, nr
Oswestry
June 27 Sunday
Benthall Hall, Broseley
Brownhill House, Ruyton XI
Towns
Carpenters Cottage, Clee St
Margaret, nr Ludlow ‡
David Austin Roses Ltd, nr
Wolverhampton
Erway Farm House, Dudleston
Heath
Field House, Clee St Margaret, nr
Ludlow ‡
Glazeley Old Rectory, Glazeley
Moortown, nr Wellington
The Old Vicarage, Cardington
Whittington Village Gardens, nr
Oswestry
Wollerton Old Hall, Market
Drayton
July 1 Thursday
Preen Manor, nr Church Stretton
July 3 Saturday
Acton Round, Morville, nr
Bridgnorth
July 4 Sunday
Acton Round, Morville, nr
Bridgnorth ‡
2 Beacon Hill, Monkhopton ‡
Herbert Lewis Garden, Merton
Nurseries, Bicton
The Old Rectory, Fitz
The Old Vicarage, Cardington
July 7 Wednesday
Herbert Lewis Garden, Merton
Nurseries, Bicton
July 11 Sunday
Harnage Farm, Cound,
Shrewsbury ‡
The Mill Cottage, Cound,
Shrewsbury ‡
The Old Vicarage, Cardington
Peplow Hall, Hodnet
July 14 Wednesday
Burford House Gardens, nr
Tenbury Wells
July 15 Thursday
Preen Manor, nr Church Stretton
July 18 Sunday
The Old Vicarage, Cardington
July 19 Monday
Mawley Hall, Cleobury Mortimer

July 24 Saturday
Brownhill House, Ruyton XI
Towns
July 25 Sunday
Astley Abbotts House, Bridgnorth
Brownhill House, Ruyton XI
Towns
Erway Farm House, Dudleston
Heath
Herbert Lewis Garden, Merton
Nurseries, Bicton
July 29 Thursday
Preen Manor, nr Church Stretton
July 31 Saturday
Church Bank, Westbury
August 1 Sunday
Church Bank, Westbury
Herbert Lewis Garden, Merton
Nurseries, Bicton
Wollerton Old Hall, Market
Drayton
August 4 Wednesday
Herbert Lewis Garden, Merton
Nurseries, Bicton
August 5 Thursday
Hawkstone Hall, nr Market
Drayton
August 6 Friday
Hawkstone Hall, nr Market
Drayton
August 7 Saturday
Hodnet Hall Gardens, nr Market
Drayton
August 8 Sunday
Herbert Lewis Garden, Merton
Nurseries, Bicton
August 11 Wednesday
Burford House Gardens, nr
Tenbury Wells
August 14 Saturday
Hodnet Hall Gardens, nr Market
Drayton
August 22 Sunday
Herbert Lewis Garden, Merton
Nurseries, Bicton
August 29 Sunday
Erway Farm House, Dudleston
Heath
September 5 Sunday
Herbert Lewis Garden, Merton
Nurseries, Bicton
September 8 Wednesday
Burford House Gardens, nr
Tenbury Wells
September 26 Sunday
Erway Farm House, Dudleston
Heath
Preen Manor, nr Church Stretton
October 6 Wednesday
Swallow Hayes, Albrighton

DESCRIPTIONS OF GARDENS

Acton Round ⚘❀ (Mr & Mrs Hew Kennedy) 6m W of Bridgnorth. A458 Morville-Shrewsbury, 2m after Morville turn L (W). 1½-acre garden with yew hedges; rose, herbaceous and newly planted borders; various follies; attractive church and beautiful early Georgian house (not open). TEAS. *Adm £1.50 Chd £1 (Share to Acton Round Church). Sat, Sun July 3, 4 (2-6.30). Garden also open by appt* Tel 0746 31203

Adcote School ⚘ (Adcote School Educational Trust Ltd) Little Ness, 8m NW of Shrewsbury via A5 to Montford Bridge, turn off NE follow signs to Little Ness. 20-acres; fine trees inc beeches, tulip trees, oaks (American and Evergreen); atlas cedars, Wellingtonia etc; rhododendrons, azaleas; small lake; landscaped garden. House (part shown) designed by Norman Shaw RA; Grade 1 listed building; William Morris windows; De Morgan tiles. TEAS. *Adm £1 Acc chd free. Suns April 25, May 9, 23 June 6 (2-5). Other times strictly by appt only* Tel Baschurch 260202

Ashford Manor ☂❀ (Kit Hall Esq) Ashford Carbonel, 2¾m S of Ludlow. E of A49 Ludlow-Leominster. Garden of 2-acres, herbaceous foliage and shrubs grown in the hope of maintaining interest through the entire year, hence very few flowers. Worked entirely by owner. *Adm 50p. Picnic area – Dogs welcomed. Reasonably level ground. By appt all year.* Tel Ludlow 872100

Astley Abbotts House ☂❀ (Mrs H E Hodgson) 3m NW of Bridgnorth. B4373 from Bridgnorth turn R at Cross Lane Head. Bus: Bridgnorth-Broseley or the Smithies; alight Cross Lane Head ½m. 10 acres, 5 acres lavender, PYO at July opening; bee village; herbs; wild woodland garden; fine trees; lawns; rhododendrons. TEAS. *Adm £1 Chd free (Share to Wolverhampton Eye Infirmary, July only). Suns April 18, July 25 (2-6)*

¶**Badger Farmhouse** (Mr & Mrs N J D Foster) Badger. From A464 Shifnal to Wolverhampton Rd turn S to Burnhill Green. In Burnhill Green turn W to Beckbury. At T junction in Beckbury turn S, ¾m on R. 3-acre garden. Over 100 varieties of daffodils and narcissi in a mature setting. Mainly in three orchards, one of apple one pear and plum and one of cherry. Also fine trees, shrubs and roses. TEAS. *Adm £1.20 Chd free (Share to St Giles' Church, Badger). Mon April 12 (2-6)*

¶**Bakers House** ☂⚘❀ (Miss L M North) Bromley. 2m from Bridgnorth. From Bridgnorth to Wolverhampton Rd (A454) signposted Bromley approx 1m from B'th or Bridgnorth to Telford Rd (A442) signposted Bromley approx 2m from Bridgnorth, Timbered cottage opp phone box. Approx ½-acre cottage garden with unusual and interesting perennials, shrubs and old roses. Scree garden for alpines, alpine house; peat bed and stone troughs; informal planting in cottage garden style in a very pretty rural setting. Best months May & June. *Adm £1 Chd 25p. Parties welcome. By appt only April to July* Tel Bridgnorth 763296

¶**2 Beacon Hill** ⚘ (Mr & Mrs J Link) Monkhopton. 5¾m W of Bridgnorth on Bridgnorth-Craven Arms rd. From Bridgnorth take A458 (Shrewsbury); turn L at Morville B4386 situated on L at 1st Xrds 2¾m. Small garden with fish pools; small conifers; shrubs; perennials. TEA. *Adm £1 Chd 50p. Sun July 4 (2-6)*

Benthall Hall ☂⚘ (Mr & Mrs James Benthall; The National Trust) 1m NW of Broseley, 4m NE of Much Wenlock (B4375); turning up lane marked with brown sign. Garden 3-acres; shrub roses; rockery banks; lawns; former kitchen garden; wild garden. Interesting plants and fine trees. C16 house also open. *Adm £1.50 Chd £1 (House & Garden £2.50 Chd £1). Sun June 27 (1.30-5.30)*

Bitterley Court ☂⚘❀ (Mr & Mrs J V T Wheeler) Ludlow. Next to Bitterley Church. Follow A4117 E from Ludlow and turn off to Bitterley after about 2m. 5m from Ludlow altogether. A 6-acre garden comprising mainly lawns, specimen trees and shrubs, shrub roses and some borders. TEAS. *Adm £1 Chd 50p. Suns May 23, June 20 (2-6)*

Brownhill House ⚘❀ (Roger & Yoland Brown) Ruyton XI Towns. 10m NW of Shrewsbury on B4397, in village. Park at Bridge Inn. Unusual and distinctive hillside garden bordering River Perry; which has been shown on BBC2 'Gardeners World'. Great variety of features and style including laburnum walk; parterre; formal terraces; extensive shrub planting; woodland paths; glasshouses; fruit and large kitchen garden. New developments every year. TEAS. *Adm £1.20 Chd free. Sun May 23; Sats, Suns June 5, 6 Sun June 27, Sat, Sun July 24, 25 (2-6). By appt May to Aug.* Tel Baschurch 260626

Burford House Gardens ☂⚘❀ (John Treasure Esq) 1m W of Tenbury Wells. 400yds S of A456. Bus: CM Ludlow-Tenbury Wells. 4-acre garden designed in 1954 by owner in beautiful surroundings on R Teme. Flowering shrubs, herbaceous plants, extensive lawns. National Clematis Collection (held on behalf of NCCPG). Nursery specializing in clematis, herbaceous, many unusual shrubs and climbers. Fine church adjacent containing Cornwall monuments. Gift shop. DOGS on lead, nursery only. TEAS; salad lunches. *Adm £1.95 Chd 80p. Season ticket £7.50, Family Season £15. Parties (by appt); 25 or more £1.60 each.* ▲ *Wed July 14, Aug 11, Sept 8 (10-5)*

¶**Carpenters Cottage** ⚘❀ (Mr & Mrs A R Mitchell) Clee St Margaret, 8m NE of Ludlow. Turning to Stoke St Milborough and Clee St Margaret. 5m from Ludlow, 10m from Bridgnorth along B4364. Through Stoke St Milborough to Clee St Margaret. Ignore turn to R to village, carry on to Field House on L. Carpenters Cottage down hill. Turn R; 3rd house on L. (Parking only at Field House). 1-acre garden created since 1988 on old cottage garden site. Orchard with shrub roses, stream and bog garden. Borders with many unusual plants and shrubs. *Combined adm with* **Field House** *£1.50 Chd 50p. Sun June 27 (12-6)*

Church Bank ⚘❀ (Mr & Mrs B P Kavanagh) Rowley 12m SW of Shrewsbury on B4386 Montgomery Rd continuing through Westbury. After ⅓m turn R for Rowley. After

3½m turn L at Xrds for Brockton. Church Bank is on L after 120yds. A plant enthusiasts, S facing garden set in a beautiful and little known part of the county, begun 5 years ago and continuing to develop and change. *Adm £1 Chd free. Sat, Sun July 31, Aug 1 (2-6); also by appt May to Sept* Tel 0743 891661

David Austin Roses &❀ (Mr & Mrs David Austin) Bowling Green Lane, Albrighton, 8m NW of Wolverhampton. 4m from Shifnal (A464) left into Bowling Green Lane; or junc 3, M54 to Albrighton, right at sign 'Roses & Shrubs', Bowling Green Lane 2nd R. Famous nursery and gardens; 700 varieties old roses, shrub, species and climbing roses; rose breeding trials; rose fields; small herbaceous display garden. Private garden recently redesigned with many plants. Sculpture. TEAS. *Adm £1.20 Chd free. Sun June 27 (2-6)*

Dudmaston &✗❀ (Sir George & Lady Labouchere; The National Trust) 4m SE of Bridgnorth on A442. Bus stop at gates ½m. 8 acres with fine trees, shrubs; lovely views over Dudmaston Pool and surrounding country. Dingle walk. TEAS. *Adm £1.50 Chd 50p. Mon May 31 (2-6)*

Erway Farm House ✗❀ (Mr & Mrs A A Palmer) 3m N of Ellesmere, 2m S of Overton on Dee. Signposted from B5068 Ellesmere-St Martins Road and B5069 Overton-Oswestry Road. 1-acre Plantswoman's garden in light woodland, packed with rare and interesting plants. (Featured on TV, 'Gardeners World'). Hellebores in profusion, many varieties of snowdrop. Later, daphnes, hardy geranium, peaonia, and other shade loving plants. Plants and unusual seeds from garden for sale. *Adm £1 Chd free. Sat April 10, Sun April 11, Mon April 12 (2-6), also last Sun in every month Feb to Sept*

Farley House ✗ (Mr & Mrs R W Collingwood) From A458 at Much Wenlock turn N on to A4169 signed Ironbridge; house 1m on L. 1-acre garden made since 1980 by owners; alpines, herbaceous island beds, shrubs and trees. Gardening clubs and WI welcome. *Adm £1 Chd free. By appt only April-Oct* Tel Much Wenlock 727017

¶Field House &✗❀ (Dr & Mrs John Bell) Clee St Margaret. 8m NE of Ludlow. Turning to Stoke St Milborough and Clee St Margaret. 5m from Ludlow, 10m from Bridgnorth along B4364. Through Stoke St Milborough to Clee St Margaret. Ignore R turn to Clee Village. Carry on to Field House on L. Parking. 1-acre garden created since 1982 for yr-round interest. Mixed borders; rose walk; pool garden; herbaceous borders; organic vegetable garden; spring bulbs and autumn colours. TEAS. *Combined adm with* **Carpenters Cottage** *£1.50 Chd 50p. Sun June 27 (12-6)*

Gatacre Park &❀ (Lady Thompson) Six Ashes, 6m SE of Bridgnorth on A458. Stourbridge-Bridgnorth Rd. 8 acres. Originally a Victorian garden partly redeveloped over the last 56 years by present owner. Flowering shrubs, fine trees, inc 100ft tulip tree and manna ash; topiary walk; large woodland garden with pieris, azaleas, rhododendrons inc many interesting species now fully grown. Lovely views over Park. TEA. *Adm £1 Chd free. Suns May 16, 23 (2-6)*

Glazeley Old Rectory &✗❀ (Mr & Mrs J A Goodall) 3½m S of Bridgnorth on B4363 Bridgnorth-Cleobury Mortimer rd. 2½-acre garden; soil pH 6.5; largely herbaceous borders with some cottage beds; bulbs; shrubs; old-fashioned roses, shady, paved and moisture gardens. Very beautiful, natural setting. Award winning garden 1990. TEAS. *Adm £1 Chd 50p. Sun June 27 (2-6); also by appt* Tel 074 635 221

¶Harnage Farm &✗ (Mr & Mrs Ken Cooke). Cound. 8m SE of Shrewsbury on A458. Turn to Cound 1m S of Cross Houses. Harnage Farm 1m, bearing L past church. ½-acre farmhouse garden; well stocked with unusual herbaceous plants, shrubs and climbers. Extensive views over beautiful Severn Valley. TEAS. *Combined adm with* **The Mill Cottage** *£1.50 Chd 50p. Sun July 11 (2-6)*

Hatton Grange &❀ (Mrs Peter Afia) Shifnal. Lodge gate entrance on A464, 2m S of Shifnal. 1m up drive. Large dingle with pools, rhododendrons, azaleas, fine old trees; shrubbery; rose-garden; lily pond garden. TEAS. *Adm £1.20 Chd 50p (Share to Cancer Relief Macmillan Fund). Sun, Mon May 30, 31 (2-7)*

Hawkstone Hall &✗ (Redemptorist Study Centre) 13m NE of Shrewsbury. 6m SW of Market Drayton on A442. Entrance from Marchamley. Large formally laid out garden. Features include ornamental flower beds; herbaceous border; rockery; pools and magnificent trees. Georgian mansion (open) with courtyard garden and winter garden. TEAS. *Adm garden only £1 Chd 50p reduced rates for pre-booked parties of 20 or more.* ▲*Thurs, Fri Aug 5, 6 (2-5)* Tel 063084 242

Haye House ✗❀ (Mrs Paradise) Eardington. 2m S of Bridgnorth, sign Highley B4555. 1m through village Eardington. 1-acre garden especially planted by the owner, for her work as a National & International flower demonstrator. Grade 2 listed house (not open). TEAS. *Adm £1 Chd 30p. By appt only* Tel 0746 764884

Herbert Lewis Garden, Merton Nurseries &✗❀ (Herbert Lewis & Family). Bicton. 3m NW of Shrewsbury on B4380 (old A5) towards Oswestry. The Herbert Lewis is attached to Merton Nurseries. The acre of garden is a plantsman's collection of widely available and unusual plants. It is a garden for all seasons containing over 200 varieties of conifers and heathers for autumn and winter interest. However the outstanding feature is the vast collection of herbaceous perennials growing in borders and island beds. A woodland garden contains rhododendrons and azaleas as well as a selection of moisture and shade loving plants incl magnificent specimens of gunnera manicata. Open for hospice rest of the year. Guided tours if required; coach parties. TEAS in aid of Shropshire Hospice. *Adm £1.50 Chd 50p. Weds, Suns July 4, 7, 25; Aug 1, 4, 8, 22; Sept 5 (11-6). Evenings by appt* Tel 0743 850773

By Appointment Gardens. These owners do not have a fixed opening day usually because they do not like crowds or have insufficient parking space. Owner will often give guided tour.

Hodnet Hall Gardens &# (Mr & the Hon Mrs A Heber-Percy) 5½m SW of Market Drayton; 12m NE Shrewsbury; at junc of A53 and A442. 60-acre landscaped garden with series of lakes and pools; magnificent forest trees, great variety of flowers, shrubs providing colour throughout season; featured on TV and Radio. Unique collection of big-game trophies in C17 tearooms. Gift shop and kitchen garden. TEAS; parties to pre-book. Free car-coach park. *Adm £2.50 OAP £2 Chd £1. April 1 to end of Sept (Mon to Sat 2-5; Suns & Bank Hols 12-5.30). Reduced rates for organised parties of 25 or over* **Tel Hodnet 202**. *For NGS Sats Aug 7, 14 (2-5)*

Limeburners &# (Mr & Mrs J E Derry) Lincoln Hill. On outskirts of Ironbridge, Telford. From Traffic Island in Ironbridge take Church Hill and proceed up hill for ½m, garden on L 300yds below The Beeches Hospital. Prize Winning garden formerly site of a rubbish tip developed by owners as a Nature garden to attract wildlife. Many unusual shrubs giving year round interest. TEAS in aid of Arthritis & Rheumatism Council for Research. *Adm £1.25 Chd 25p. Sun June 6 (2-6). Open by appt April to Sept* **Tel 0952 433715**

Longnor Hall &## (Mr & Mrs A V Nicholson) Longnor. Take A49 road S of Shrewsbury to Longnor. Entry to Longnor Hall garden through grounds of Longnor Church. 70-acre garden and parkland. Interesting varieties of trees; herbaceous borders, yew and beech hedges; walled kitchen garden; stable yard and C17 house (not open); sheep and deer; Cound Brook; views of The Lawley and Caer Caradoc hills. Adjacent C13 Longnor Church. TEAS. *Adm £1.50 Chd 50p (Share to St. Mary's Church, Longnor). Sun, Mon May 30, 31 (2-6)*

Lower Hall &# (Mr & Mrs C F Dumbell) Worfield, E of Bridgnorth, ½m N of A454 in village centre. 4 acres on R Worfe; stream, pool; shrub and woodland garden. Tudor half-timbered house (not open). Plant sales to local charity. TEAS. *Adm £2 OAPs £1.50 Chd free. Suns May 30, June 20 (2-6) By appt – Coach parties May to Aug and evening parties with local catering.* **Tel 074 64607**

The Lyth &## (Mr & Mrs L R Jebb) 1m SE of Ellesmere; entrance between Whitemere and junc of A528/A495. 2-acre garden; rhododendrons, azaleas; good outlook on park-land; heath bed, shrub borders. Regency colonial house (not open), birthplace of founder of Save The Children, Eglantyne Jebb. Meres nearby worth a visit. TEAS by local Save the Children Fund. *Adm £1.50 Chd 50p. Sun June 6 (2-6)*

Mawley Hall (Mr & Mrs R A Galliers-Pratt) 2m NE of Cleobury Mortimer. On A4117 Bewdley-Ludlow Rd. Bus: X92, alight at gate. A natural garden in beautiful country with magnificent views; designed for wandering amongst roses, herbs, flowering shrubs; fine old trees. *Adm £1 Chd 50p. Mons May 17, June 21, July 19 (2-6)*

¶**The Mill Cottage** &## (Mrs A J Wisden & Miss J M Hawkes) Cound. 8m SE of Shrewsbury on A458. Turn to Cound 1m S of Cross Houses. Mill Cottage 300yds on L. ¼-acre cottage garden. Many unusual & lovely herbaceous & alpine plants. Large collection of clematis. Good

& varied collection of hostas. *Combined adm with* **Harnage Farm** *£1.50 Chd 50p. Sun July 11 (2-6)*

Millichope Park (Mr & Mrs L Bury) Munslow, 8m NE of Craven Arms. From Ludlow (11m) turn L off B4368, ¾m out of Munslow. 13-acre garden with lakes; woodland walks; fine specimen trees, wild flowers; herbaceous borders. TEAS. *Adm £1.50 Chd 50p. Mon May 3, Sun June 20 (2-6)*

Moortown &## (David Bromley Esq) 5m N of Wellington. Take B5062 signed Moortown 1m between High Ercall and Crudgington. Approx 1-acre plantsman's garden. Here may be found the old-fashioned, the unusual and even the oddities of plant life, in mixed borders of 'controlled' confusion – special collections of snowdrops, daffodils, Old English Florist's Tulips and old roses are of particular interest. TEA. *Adm £1.50 Chd 50p. Sun June 27 (2-5.30). By appt only, March, April and May* **Tel High Ercall 770205**

Morville Hall Gardens &# nr Bridgnorth. 3m NW of Bridgnorth on A458 at junction with B4368. TEA. *Combined adm £1.50 Chd 50p. Sun May 2, Wed June 23 (2-6)*

> **Morville Hall** (Mr & Mrs John Norbury & The National Trust) Recently restored 2-acre garden with newly planted parterre and vineyard; C12 Church, Elizabethan House (not open) in fine setting
>
> **The Dower House** (Dr K Swift) 1½-acre formal garden begun 1989; ornamental kitchen garden
>
> **The Gate House** (Mr & Mrs A Rowe) Cottage garden with small vineyard.

New Hall (Mrs R H Treasure) Eaton-under-Heywood, 4m SE of Church Stretton. Between B4368 and B4371. 10 acres of woodland with grass walks, pools, wild flowers, streams. Garden suitable for wheelchairs only in dry weather. *Adm £1 Chd 10p. Suns April 4, 25 (2-5)*

Nordybank Nurseries # (Polly Bolton) Clee St. Margaret. 7½m NE of Ludlow. Turning to Stoke St Milborough and Clee St Margaret 5m from Ludlow, 10m from Bridgnorth along B4364, through Stoke St Milborough on the Lane to Clee St Margaret. 1-acre cottage garden; trees, shrubs & unusual herbaceous plants with cottage garden favourites. Also 'field garden' displaying approx 500 varieties of herbaceous plants; daffodil & narcissi bulbs in May; shrubs and roses June/July; buddleias July/Aug. TEAS. *Adm £1 OAP 50p Chd 20p. Open every Sun, Mons, & Weds May 16 until Aug 29 (11-6)*

The Old Rectory ## (Mrs J H M Stafford) Fitz; A5 NW of Shrewsbury; turn off at Montford Bridge, follow signs; from B5067 turn off at Leaton, follow signs. 1¼-acre botanists garden; shrub roses, vegetables; water garden. TEAS. *Adm £1.20 Chd 20p. Sun July 4 (12-6)*

The Old Vicarage & (W B Hutchinson Esq) Cardington, 3m N of B4371 Church Stretton-Much Wenlock Rd, signed, or turn off A49 Shrewsbury-Ludlow Rd at Leebotwood, 2½-acre scenic garden; trees, shrubs, roses, primulas, alpines, water garden. Lunch and tea picnics allowed; on site parking. *Adm £1 Chd free. Suns June 6, 13, 20, 27; July 4, 11, 18 (12-5.30)*

Oteley &❀ (Mr & Mrs R K Mainwaring) Ellesmere 1m. Entrance out of Ellesmere past Mere, opp Convent nr to A528/495 junc. 10 acres running down to Mere, inc walled kitchen garden; architectural features many interesting trees, rhododendrons and azaleas, views across Mere to Ellesmere Church. TEAS (For NSPCC). *Adm £1 Chd 50p. Mon May 31 (2-6)*

5 Park Lane, Oswestry & Byeways, Whittington ❀❀ TEAS at 5 Park Lane. *Combined adm £1.50. Sun June 6 (12-5.30)*

> **Byeways** &❀ (Mr & Mrs D Molesworth) Whittington. 2½m NE of Oswestry. Turn off B5009, 150 yds NW of church, into Top St. Then into Daisy Lane. Parking at Whittington Castle and Top St. Modern cottage garden specializing in herbaceous plants, traditional, new and unusual species. Collections of hardy geraniums, campanulas and plants for gritty areas
> **5 Park Lane** (Mrs J Jones) Turn L off A495 Oswestry to Whittington rd at black & white lodge, continue down Burma Rd for 300yds to marked car park. A Victorian grotto with arches & caves. In the process of being restored and planted. TEAS

Peplow Hall &❀ (The Hon & Mrs R V Wynn) 3m S of Hodnet via A442; turn off E. 10-acre garden with lawns, azaleas, rhododendrons, etc; roses, herbaceous borders; walled kitchen garden; 7-acre lake. TEAS. *Adm £1.50 Chd 50p. Suns May 30, July 11 (2-5.30)*

Preen Manor ❀❀ (Mr & Mrs P Trevor-Jones) Church Preen, nr Church Stretton; 5m SW of Much Wenlock. On B4371 3m turn R for Church Preen and Hughley; after 1½m turn L for Church Preen; over Xrds, ½m drive on R. 6 acres on site of C12 Cluniac monastery, later Norman Shaw mansion (now demolished); garden restored and replanned now contains a variety of different gardens; walled, terraced, wild, water, kitchen and chess gardens; fine trees in park; woodland walks. C12 monastic church with oldest yew tree in Europe. TEAS (except Sept 26). *Adm £1.50 Chd 50p. Thurs June 3, 17, July 1, 15, 29 (2-7); Sun Sept 26 (2-5). Coach parties by appt June & July only* **Tel 0694 771207**

Ruthall Manor &❀❀ (Mr & Mrs G T Clarke) Ditton Priors, Bridgnorth. Weston rd from village church 2nd L, garden ¾m. 1-acre garden with pool and specimen trees. Designed for easy maintenance with lots of ground-covering and unusual plants. Old Shires Tea Room in village open (10-5) daily except Weds. *Adm £1.50 Chd free. Sat June 5 (2-6). By appt April to Sept* **Tel Ditton Priors 608**

Swallow Hayes &❀ (Mrs P Edwards) Rectory Rd, Albrighton WV7, 7m NW of Wolverhampton. M54 exit 3 Rectory Rd 1m towards Wolverhampton off A41 just past Roses and Shrubs Garden Centre. 2-acres; planted since 1968 with emphasis on all-the-year interest and ease of maintenance; National collection of Hamamellis and Russell Lupins, over 1500 different plants labelled. TEAS. *Adm £1 Chd 10p (Share to Compton Hospice). Weds, Suns April 21; May 2, 12, 26; June 6; Oct 6 (2-6); also by appt for parties* **Tel 0902 372624**

Upper Shelderton House ❀❀ (Mr & Mrs G W McKelvie) 3m SW of Craven Arms. From A49 turn W at Craven Arms or at Bromfield, sign posted. From Clungunford on B4367 turn E. Azaleas, rhododendrons, trees and shrubs approx 4½ acres. Beautiful views. TEAS in aid of St Cuthbert's Church. *Adm £1 Chd 50p. Sun May 30 (2-6)*

Walcot Hall &❀ (The Hon Mrs E C Parish) Bishops Castle 3m. B4385 Craven Arms to Bishops Castle, turn L by Powis Arms, in Lydbury N. Arboretum planted by Lord Clive of India's son, now undergoing restoration. Cascades of rhododendrons, azaleas amongst specimen trees and pools. Fine views of Sir William Chambers Clock Towers, with lake and hills beyond. TEAS. *Adm £1.50 Chd 15 and under free. Sun, Mon May 30, 31 (2-6)*

Weston Park & (The Weston Park Foundation) Shifnal. 7m E of Telford on the A5 in the village of Weston-under-Lizard. Easy access junction 12 M6 and junction 3 M54. Free car/coach park. 28 acres Capability Brown landscaped gardens and arboretum, incl fine collection of nothofagus, rhododendrons and azaleas. Formal gardens of SW terrace recently restored to orginal C18 design, together with colourful adjacent Broderie Garden. Wide variety of trees, shrubs and flowers provides colour throughout the season. C17 house (open adm £1). TEAS and light meals available in The Old Stables restaurant. *Adm £3 OAPs/Chd £2 reduced rates for parties of 20 or more. Open Easter to September (enquiries for dates & times* **Tel 095276 207**). *For NGS Tues June 15 (11-5)*

Whittington Village Gardens &❀ Daisy Lane Whittington. 2½m NE of Oswestry. Turn off B5009 150yds NW of church into Top St then into Daisy Lane. Car parking at Whittington Castle and Top St. Group of adjoining gardens; many good design ideas; grit garden for silver and grey foliage, a recently restored well, new ideas for the mount garden and a range of garden pools. TEAS at Cedarville, Daisy Lane. *Combined adm £1.50 Chd free. Sat, Sun June 26, 27 (1-5.30)*

Willey Park ❀ (The Lord & Lady Forester) Broseley 5m NW of Bridgnorth. Turn W off B4373. Formal garden with ½m woodland-rhododendron walk; spectacular azalea bed near house. TEAS. *Adm £1.20 Chd 50p (Share to St John Ambulance, Shropshire). Sun May 23 (2-6.30)*

Wollerton Old Hall ❀❀ (John & Lesley Jenkins) Wollerton. From Shrewsbury take A53 to Hodnet 13m. Follow same road out towards Market Drayton. Turn R just after 'Wollerton' sign. Go 300 yards over a bridge to a brick pound. Garden ahead on L. 2-acre garden created around a C16 house (not open). A combination of formal design, plant associations, and intensive cultivation of perennials; a number of separate gardens with different atmospheres. Wide range of plants, some unusual and rare. Continuing expansion of garden. Partly suitable wheelchairs. TEAS. *Adm £1.50 Chd 50p. Suns June 27, Aug 1, open every Fri June 4 to Sept 24 (2-5)*

Regular Openers. Too many days to include in diary. Usually there is a wide range of plants giving year-round interest. See head of county section for the name and garden description for times etc.

Somerset

Hon County Organiser:	Mrs David Wood, Bittescombe Manor, Upton, Nr. Wiveliscombe, Taunton TA4 2DA Tel 039 87240
Assistant Hon County Organisers:	Miss P Davies-Gilbert, Coombe Quarry, West Monkton, Taunton
	Mrs Antony Robb, East Combe, Huish Champflower, Wiveliscombe, Taunton
	Mrs K Spencer Mills, Hoopers Holdings, High Street, Hinton St George
Somerset Leaflet:	Mrs Richard Windsor Clive, c/o Mrs Wood.
Hon County Treasurer:	John A Spurrier Esq, 28 Jeffries Way, Stonegallows, Taunton

DATES OF OPENING

By appointment
For telephone numbers and other details see garden descriptions

Broadview, Crewkerne
Butleigh House, Butleigh
Cobbleside, Milverton Gardens
Elworthy Cottage, Elworthy
Fig Tree Cottage, Hinton St George Gardens
Garden Cottage, Milverton Garden
Greencombe, Porlock
Hadspen House, nr Castle Cary
Hoopers Holdings, Hinton St George Gardens
Landacre Farm, Withypool
Littlecourt, West Bagborough
Manor Farm, Stone Allerton Gardens
The Mill, Cannington
Mill House, Stone Allerton Gardens
The Mount, Wincanton
The Red House, Cannington
Watermeadows, Clapton
Withey Lane Farmhouse, Barton St David

Regular openings
For details see garden descriptions

Clapton Court Gardens, Crewkerne. March to Oct daily except Sats. Other dates see text
East Lambrook Manor Gardens, South Pertherton. Daily Mon to Sat. Closed Nov 1 to Feb 28
Greencombe, Porlock. Sats to Tues, April to July
Hadspen House, nr Castle Cary. Thurs to Suns & Bank Hol Mons, March 1 to Oct 1
Hatch Court, Hatch Beauchamp Gardens. Thurs and Fris June 3 to Sept 24 incl Aug Bank Hol Mon
Milton Lodge, Wells. Daily except Sats, Easter to end of Oct
Watermeadows, Clapton. April to Sept except Suns

March 28 Sunday
Peart Hall, Spaxton
April 4 Sunday
Smocombe House, Enmore
April 9 Friday
Beryl, Wells
Broadview, Crewkerne
April 11 Sunday
Broadview, Crewkerne
Fairfield, Stogursey
Wayford Manor, Crewkerne
April 12 Monday
Broadview, Crewkerne
April 17 Saturday
Greencombe, Porlock
April 18 Sunday
Barrington Court, Ilminster
Hangeridge Farm, Wellington Gardens
Wootton House, Butleigh Wootton
April 22 Thursday
Elworthy Cottage, Elworthy
April 24 Saturday
The Mount, Wincanton
April 25 Sunday
Landacre Farm, Withypool
The Mount, Wincanton
April 28 Wednesday
The Mill, Cannington
The Mount, Wincanton
April 29 Thursday
Elworthy Cottage, Elworthy
May 1 Saturday
Kingsdon, Somerton
May 2 Sunday
Broadview, Crewkerne
Kingsdon, Somerton
Seithe, Godney
Spaxton Gardens, Spaxton
Stowell Hill, Templeton
Wayford Manor, Crewkerne
May 3 Monday
Broadview, Crewkerne
Dodington Hall, Nether Stowey, Bridgwater
May 5 Wednesday
Withey Lane Farmhouse, Barton St David
May 6 Thursday
Elworthy Cottage, Elworthy

May 8 Saturday
Pear Tree Cottage, Stapley
May 9 Sunday
Barn Elms, Milverton
Elworthy Cottage, Elworthy
Lovibonds Farm, Burrowbridge
Pear Tree Cottage, Stapley
Stowell Hill, Templeton
West Bradley House, Glastonbury
May 12 Wednesday
Withey Lane Farmhouse, Barton St David
May 13 Thursday
Elworthy Cottage, Elworthy
May 16 Sunday
Court House, East Quantoxhead
Kites Croft, Westbury-sub-Mendip
Milton Lodge, Wells
Smocombe House, Enmore
Stowell Hill, Templeton
Wayford Manor, Crewkerne
37 Whitmore Road, Taunton
May 19 Wednesday
Kites Croft, Westbury-sub-Mendip
Withey Lane Farmhouse, Barton St David
37 Whitmore Road, Taunton
May 22 Saturday
The Mount, Wincanton
May 23 Sunday
Cannington College Gardens
Field Farm, Shepton Mallet
Hapsford House, Great Elm
Landacre Farm, Withypool
Stowell Hill, Templeton
Westhay, Kingston St Mary
May 26 Wednesday
The Mount, Wincanton
Withey Lane Farmhouse, Barton St David
May 30 Sunday
Bittiscombe Manor, Upton
Broadview, Crewkerne
Chinnock House, Middle Chinnock
East Lambrook Manor Garden, South Petherton
Greencombe, Porlock
Hestercombe Garden, Cheddon Fitzpaine
Hinton St George Gardens, Crewkerne

Milton Lodge, Wells
Peart Hall, Spaxton
Stone Allerton Gardens, nr
  Axbridge
Wambrook Gardens, nr Chard
Wayford Manor, Crewkerne

May 31 Sunday
Bittiscombe Manor, Upton
Broadview, Crewkerne
Chinnock House, Middle Chinnock
Dodington Hall, Nether Stowey,
  Bridgwater
Hinton St George Gardens,
  Crewkerne
Stone Allerton Gardens, nr
  Axbridge

June 2 Wednesday
Withey Lane Farmhouse, Barton
  St David

June 5 Saturday
East Horrington Gardens
Kingsdon, Somerton
The Mount, Wincanton

June 6 Sunday
East Horrington Gardens
Kingsdon, Somerton
Lovibonds Farm, Burrowbridge
The Mill, Cannington
The Mill House, Castle Cary
Montacute House, Montacute
Rose Cottage, Creech Heathfield

June 9 Wednesday
Broadview, Crewkerne
The Mill, Cannington
The Mount, Wincanton
Withey Lane Farmhouse, Barton
  St David

June 13 Sunday
Broadview, Crewkerne
Lower Severalls, Crewkerne
Marsh Mill House, Over Stowey
Milton Lodge, Wells

June 16 Wednesday
Withey Lane Farmhouse, Barton
  St David

June 17 Thursday
Elworthy Cottage, Elworthy

The Red House, Cannington

June 18 Friday
Broadview, Crewkerne
The Red House, Cannington

June 19 Saturday
The Mount, Wincanton
The Red House, Cannington

June 20 Sunday
Hassage House, Faulkland
Hatch Beauchamp Gardens
Montacute Gardens, nr Yeovil
Stogumber & Kingswood
  Gardens, Taunton

June 23 Wednesday
Withey Lane Farmhouse, Barton
  St David

June 24 Thursday
Elworthy Cottage, Elworthy
Gaulden Manor, Tolland
The Mount, Wincanton

June 26 Saturday
Bruton Gardens
Greencombe, Porlock

June 27 Sunday
Ash House, Rimpton, Yeovil
Bruton Gardens
Butleigh House, Butleigh
Cherry Bolbury Farm, Henstridge
Landacre Farm, Withypool
Littlecourt, West Bagborough
Stratton House, Stoney Stratton

June 30 Wednesday
Stratton House, Stoney Stratton
Withey Lane Farmhouse, Barton
  St David

July 3 Saturday
Wellington Gardens

July 4 Sunday
Batcombe Gardens, Bruton
Stapleton Manor, Martock
Wellington Gardens

July 8 Thursday
Elworthy Cottage, Elworthy

July 11 Sunday
Hadspen House, nr Castle Cary
Lower Severalls, Crewkerne
Milton Lodge, Wells

Sutton Hosey Manor, Langport

July 15 Thursday
Broadview, Crewkerne
Elworthy Cottage, Elworthy

July 18 Sunday
Brent Knoll Gardens, Highbridge
Greencombe, Porlock

July 22 Thursday
Elworthy Cottage, Elworthy

July 24 Saturday
Kingsdon, Somerton

July 25 Sunday
Barrington Court, Ilminster
Kingsdon, Somerton
Milverton Gardens, Taunton

August 1 Sunday
Stapleton Manor, Martock
Tintinhull House, nr Yeovil

August 5 Thursday
Dunster Castle, nr Minehead

August 8 Sunday
The Mill, Cannington

August 11 Wednesday
Broadview, Crewkerne
The Mill, Cannington

August 15 Sunday
Hatch Beauchamp Gardens
Seithe, Godney

August 29 Sunday
Broadview, Crewkerne

August 30 Monday
Beryl, Wells
Broadview, Crewkerne

September 9 Thursday
Elworthy Cottage, Elworthy

September 12 Sunday
Kites Croft, Westbury-sub-Mendip

September 15 Wednesday
Kites Croft, Westbury-sub-Mendip

September 16 Thursday
Elworthy Cottage, Elworthy

September 23 Thursday
Elworthy Cottage, Elworthy

September 30 Thursday
Elworthy Cottage, Elworthy

DESCRIPTIONS OF GARDENS

Ash House & (Mr & Mrs Malcolm Shennan) Rimpton. 4m NE of Sherborne turn off B3148 Marston Magna Rd at White Post Inn to Rimpton ½m. 1¼-acre of newly laid out garden in 1988. Mixed shrub herbaceous perennial and roses. Many rare and interesting plants. TEAS. *Adm £1 Chd free. Sun June 27 (2-6)*

Barn Elms ✗ (Mrs Pauline Dodd) 9m W of Taunton on new B3227 (old A361). L at roundabout to Milverton. L at Glebe Inn down Roebank Rd. R at Houndsmoor Lane. 1-acre wild garden and ponds. Small formal garden; many interesting plants; imaginative design. *Adm £1 Chd free. Sun May 9 (2-5.30)*

Barrington Court & ✗ ❀ (The National Trust) Ilminster. NE of Ilminster. Well known garden constructed in 1920 by Col Arthur Lyle from derelict farmland (the C19 cattle stalls still exist). Gertrude Jekyll approved of the design and layout; paved paths with walled iris, white and lily gardens, large kitchen garden. Licensed restaurant, plant sales and garden shop. TEAS. *Adm £3 Chd £1.50. Suns April 18, July 25 (12-5)*

Batcombe Gardens 2½m N of Bruton, W of A359 Bruton-Frome; S of A361 Shepton Mallet-Frome via Cranmore; E of A371 via Evercreech. TEAS at Rockwells House. *Combined adm £1.50 Chd free. Sun July 4 (2-6)*

Boxbush Farm ✗ (Mrs Anne Nicholson) Batcombe. With your back to Rockwells, turn R 3rd House on L. Approx ¾-acre cottage garden with herbaceous beds, shrubs, rockery and small lily pond
Ravenswood ❀ (Mr & Mrs Bryan) Baileys Lane ¾-acre garden with scrub and herbaceous borders, ponds and excellent views
Rockwells ❀ (Mr & Mrs F J Dupays) 2½-acres with herbaceous border, shrubs, terraces and pools below Jacobean & Georgian house

Beryl ♿ (Mr & Mrs E Nowell) ½m N of Wells off B3139 to Bath. Left at Hawkers Lane. Victorian park created in 1842. Walled vegetable garden broken into quadrangles with box hedging and double flower picking borders. More recent planting of trees and shrubs and creation of walks and vistas. TEAS. *Adm £1 OAP/Chd 50p. Good Fri April 9, Mon Aug 30 (11-5.30)*

Bittescombe Manor ♿❀ (Mr & Mrs D Wood) Upton 6m from Dulverton and Wiveliscombe. On B3227 Taunton to Wiveliscombe, follow signs to Huish Champflower, L at Castle Inn, L at B3190 to Upton. The 5-acre garden is 950 ft up on Brendon Hills. Formal walled rose garden, shrubbery, water garden and herbaceous borders. TEAS in aid of Upton Church. *Adm £1.50 Chd free. Sun May 30, Mon 31 (2-5.30)*

Bodden Gardens ✗❀ Take A361 Frome Rd from Shepton Mallet. 1m further on opp Charlton House Hotel, turn L up lane. TEAS. *Combined adm £1.50 Chd 50p. Sun July 19 (11-6)*
Grassroots (Mr & Mrs M Meadows) Small cottage garden (40 × 60 yds) planted with old-fashioned perennials, old roses, interesting foliage; all year interest

Brent Knoll Gardens off A38 2m N of Highbridge and M5 exit 22. A mixture of 3 colourful country gardens. TEAS at Copse Hall. *Combined adm £2 Chd free. Sun July 18 (2-6)*
Copse Hall ❀ (Mrs S Boss & Mrs N Hill) Terraced gardens, crinkle crankle kitchen garden wall, kiwi fruit. Display and sale of fuchsias by Brent Knoll Friendly Fuschia Society
¶Greystones (Mr & Mrs Hugh Gilpin)
¶Tableland (Drs Gavin & Meg Stoddart)

Broadview ✗❀ (Mr & Mrs R Swann) 43a East Street, Crewkerne. Take the A30 Yeovil Rd out of Crewkerne approx 200 yds on the left hand side. Please enter drive by turning R from the E Yeovil side. 1-acre terraced garden on elevated site with panoramic views over Crewkerne. Interesting plants and shrubs, many for sale. TEAS. *Adm £1 Chd free. Fri, Suns, Mons, April 9, 11, 12; May 2, 3, 30, 31; Wed, Sun, Fri June 9, 13, 18; Thurs July 15; Wed, Sun, Mon Aug 11, 29, 30 (11-6). Also by appt Tel 0460 73424*

¶Bruton Gardens TEAS. *Combined adm £2 Chd free. Sat, Sun June 26, 27 (2-6)*
¶14 Burowfield ✗❀ (Mr & Mrs D Atkins) N of Bruton on the A359 to Frome. Semi-detached house with small front garden and beautifully maintained back garden with aviary, flowers and vegetables

¶Leaside ♿❀ (Mr & Mrs M Heddderwick) 1m SE of Bruton on B3081 (signposted Wincanton) turn E to Stourton 1st cottage on R. 1-acre field transformed into a nature garden with many fragrant shrubs and nearly 1000 trees. Informal pond and old-fashioned roses. *(Share to British Kidney Fund)*
¶Tolbury Farm ✗❀ (Mr & Mrs M King) In Bruton turn N at Blue Bell Inn. 200 yds to public car park on L. Follow signs thereafter on foot. 1 acre of well-designed hillside garden with imaginative planting, good herbaceous borders, trees and rockery

Butleigh House ♿❀ (Sir Dawson & Lady Bates) Butleigh, 4m SE of Glastonbury and N of B3153 at Kingweston. Turn down High Street in centre of village. About 3-acres of well laid out garden. Large herbaceous borders with chosen colours; fine trees; high semi-circular yew hedge; many roses and other good plants. TEAS in aid of St Leonards Church, Butleigh. *Adm £1.50 Chd free. Sun June 27 (2-6). Also by appt June & July*

Cannington College Gardens ♿✗❀ Cannington, 3m NW of Bridgwater. On A39 Bridgwater-Minehead Rd. Old College: Benedictine Priory 1138; fine Elizabethan W front; 7 old sandstone walled gardens protect wide range of plants, inc many less hardy subjects, ceanothus, Fremontias, Wistarias etc; 10 very large greenhouses contain exceptionally wide range of ornamental plants. New College (built 1970); magnificent views to Quantocks; tree and shrub collections; ground cover plantings; lawn grass collection and trials; horticultural science garden; one of the largest collections of ornamental plants in SW England including 8 national plant collections. TEAS. *Adm for both College grounds £1.50 Chd (& organised parties of OAPs) 75p. Special rates for party bookings. For NGS Sun May 23 (2-6)*

Cherry Bolbury Farm ♿ (Mr & Mrs C Raymond) Henstridge. From Henstridge traffic lights continue on A357 through Henstridge towards Stalbridge. In centre of Henstridge turn R at small Xrd signed Furge Lane. Farm at end of lane. 5m E of Sherborne, 7m S of Wincanton. ¾-acre owner-designed young garden planted for year round interest. Nature ponds, small fish pond, extensive views. TEAS. *Adm £1. Sun June 27 (2.30-5.30)*

Chinnock House ♿✗❀ (Guy & Charmian Smith) Middle Chinnock. Off A30 between Crewkerne and Yeovil. 1½-acre walled gardens, silver, white and herbaceous; recently redesigned. TEAS. *Adm £1.50 Chd free. Sun May 30, Mon, 31 (2-5.30)*

● **Clapton Court** ✗❀ (Capt S J Loder) 3m S of Crewkerne on B3165 to Lyme Regis. 10 acres; worth visiting at all seasons; many rare and unusual plants, shrubs and trees of botanical interest in lovely formal and woodland settings; largest and oldest ash in Great Britain; newly designed rose garden. Plant Centre selling choice, rare clematis, herbaceous, shrubs and trees. LUNCHES (licensed) and TEAS April to Sept. *Adm £3 Chd (4-14) £1. (apply for party tariff). March to Oct daily ex Sats. (Weekdays 10.30-5; Suns 2-5); also Sats April 10 (2-5), April 24 (11-5) Tel 0460 73220/72200*

Court House &⚘ (Col & Mrs Walter Luttrell) East Quantoxhead 12m W of Bridgwater off A39; house at end of village past duck pond. Lovely 5-acre garden; trees, shrubs, roses and herbaceous. Views to sea and Quantocks. Partly suitable for wheelchairs. Teas in Village Hall. *Adm £2 Chd free. Sun May 16 (2-5.30)*

¶**Dodington Hall** ⚘ (Grania & Paul Quinn) A39 Bridgwater-Minehead. 2m W of Nether Stowey turn at signpost opp Castle of Comfort. ¼m turn R. Entrance through churchyard. Reclaimed 1½-acre terrace garden; clematis, shrub roses, bulbs; Tudor house (part open). TEAS. *Adm £1 Chd free. Mons May 3, 31 (2-6)*

Dunster Castle ⚘ (The National Trust) On A396 3m SE of Minehead. Terraces of sub-tropical plants, shrubs and camellias surrounding the fortified house of the Luttrells for 600 years; fine views. Self-drive battery operated car available. Teas in village. *Adm Garden Only £2.50 Chd £1.20. For NGS Thurs Aug 5 (11-5)*

East Horrington Gardens ⚘⚘ 2m NE of Wells. Turn E off B3139 either at Mendip Hospital or at W/E Horrington Xrds above school. 3 very different gardens, from small cottage through to herbaceous borders and rock garden, 4 acres of conifers, shrubs and ponds. TEAS at Springfield House. *Combined adm £1.50 Chd free. Sat, Sun June 5, 6 (2-6)*
    Ashmount (Mr & Mrs Gordon Cox)
    Hillside Cottage (Mr & Mrs W A L Mackay)
    Springfield House (Mrs S J Cross)

East Lambrook Manor Garden ⚘⚘ (Mr & Mrs A Norton) 2m NE of South Petherton. Off A303 to S Petherton; Martock Rd, then left to E Lambrook at bottom of hill. Traditional 'cottage style' garden created by the late Margery Fish and made famous by her many gardening books. Many unusual and now rare plants, trees and shrubs. The Margery Fish Nursery sells plants from the garden. TEAS (May 30 only). *Adm £2 OAPs £1.80 Chd 50p. Open Mon-Sat (10-5). Closed Nov 1 to Feb 28. For NGS Sun May 30 (10-5); parties by appt only Tel 0460 40328 Fax 0460 42344*

Elworthy Cottage ⚘⚘ (Mike & Jenny Spiller) Elworthy, 12m NW of Taunton on B3188 5m N of Wiveliscombe. 1-acre informal garden, all year round, mixed planting. Bulbs, alpines, unusual herbaceous plants. Large collection of hardy geraniums; penstemons; grasses and plants for foliage effect, many of which are for sale in adjoining nursery. Teas in next village. *Adm 75p Chd free (Share to Cancer & Leukaemia in Childhood Trust). Thurs April 22, 29; May 6, 13; Sun May 9 (12-5); Thus June 17, 24; July 8, 15, 22; Sept 9, 16, 23, 30 (2-5). Also by appt Tel Stogumber 56427*

Fairfield & (Lady Gass) Stogursey, 11m NW of Bridgwater 7m E of Williton. From A39 Bridgwater-Minehead turn N; garden 1½m W of Stogursey. Woodland garden with bulbs and shrubs. Views of Quantocks. Dogs in park and field only. TEA. *Adm £1.50 Chd free (Share to Stogursey Church). Easter Sun April 11 (2-5.30)*

Farleigh Hungerford Gardens (see Wiltshire)

Field Farm ⚘⚘ (Mr & Mrs D R Vagg) ½m S Shepton Mallet on A371 Cannards Grave Rd. Large farmhouse garden with lovely mixed planting; old and climbing roses, variegated plants, water garden, large rockery; many old stone features. TEAS. *Adm £1.50 Chd free (Share to Doulting Church). Sun May 23 (2-6)*

Gauldon Manor ⚘⚘ (Mr & Mrs J Le G Starkie) Tolland. Nr Lydeard St Lawrence. 9m NW Taunton off A358. Medium-sized garden made by owners. Herb; bog; scent and butterfly gardens. Bog plants, primulas and scented geraniums. Partly suitable for wheelchairs. Cream TEAS. *Adm house & garden £2.80, garden only £1.25, Chd £1.25. Thurs June 24 (2-5.30)*

Greencombe &⚘⚘ (Miss Joan Loraine Greencombe Garden Trust) ½m W of Porlock, left off road to Porlock Weir. 46 year old garden on edge of ancient woodland, overlooking Porlock Bay. Choice rhododendrons, azaleas, camellias, maples, roses, hydrangeas, ferns and small woodland plants. National collection of Polystichum the 'thumbs up' fern, and of Erythronium, Vaccinium and Gaultheria. Completely organic, with compost heaps on show. *Adm £2 Chd 50p. Sats, Suns, Mons, Tues April, May, June & July (2-6); also by appt Tel Porlock 862363. For NGS Sats April 17, June 26, Suns May 30, July 18 (2-6)*

Hadspen House &⚘⚘ (N Pope) 2m SE of Castle Cary on A371 to Wincanton. 8-acre Edwardian garden housing the National Rodgersia Collection and featuring a curved, walled garden of herbaceous borders planted with particular attention to colour; woodland area of fine, mature, specimen trees and shrubs border; a meadow garden with naturalised, native flowers and grasses. TEAS Suns. *Adm £2 Chd 50p. Garden and Nursery open; Thurs, Fris, Sats, Suns, and Bank Hol Mons (9-6) March 1 to Oct 1; also by appt Tel Castle Cary 50939. For NGS Sun July 11 (2-6)*

¶**Hapsford House** ⚘ (Mr & Mrs R Enthoren) Great Elm. From Frome take A362 NW to Radstock. Turn L to Great Elm after 1m, ¼m to house. Partly suitable for wheelchairs. 8-acre garden runs from Regency House (not open) to the River Mels. Laburnum walk to meadow, rich with damsel flies. Woodland paths to riverside walks across bridges to island of wildflowers with unrestored grotto. After 40 years of neglect garden 3 years into a programme of restoration and replanting including mainly hardy geraniums, some for sale. TEAS *Adm £1.50 Chd 75p. Sun May 23 (2-6)*

Hassage House ⚘⚘ (Mr & Mrs J Donnithorne) Faulkland. 8m S of Bath on Trowbridge-Radstock Rd A 366, 1½m West Norton St Philip, 1m E Faulkland. Turn off at Tuckers Grave Inn. 300yds turn R, house at end of lane. 1½-acres of informal garden; shrubs, herbaceous, roses; lily pond; conservatory. TEAS. *Adm £1 Chd free. Sun June 20 (1.30-6)*

¶**Hatch Beauchamp Gardens** 5m SE of Taunton (M5 junction 25) off A358 to Ilminster. Turn L in village of Hatch Beauchamp at Hatch Inn. Parking at Hatch Court. TEAS. *Combined adm £2 Chd £1 under 12 free. Suns June 20, Aug 15 (2.30-5.30)*

Hatch Court &☙ (Dr & Mrs Robin Odgers) Turn L in village at Hatch Inn. 5-acre garden with 30 acres of parkland and deer park surrounding a perfect 1750 Palladian mansion. Extensive, recent and continuing restoration, redesign and replanting. Breathtaking walled kitchen garden, fine display of roses, shrubs, clematis and many young trees. Glorious views and a lovely setting. TEAS. *Adm Garden only £1.50, Chd £1.00 under 12 free, house and garden £2.50 Thurs (house also open) and Fridays June 3 to Sept 24 incl Aug Bank Hol Mon (2.30-5.30). For NGS Suns June 20, Aug 15*

¶**Hatch Court Farm** &☙ (John Townson Esq) ⅓-acre walled garden created over the past 5 years from derelict farm buildings. Mixed borders and wild area with large pond surrounded by wood and parkland

¶**Hestercombe Garden** (Somerset County Council) Cheddon Fitzpaine. Signposted from Monkton-Heathfield off the A371. Historic gardens designed by Sir Edwin Luytens and Miss Gertrude Jekyll (this year marks the 150th anniversary of her birth). The multi-level garden features much attractive stone work and a sunken plot. Long pergola and pleasing orangery. TEAS. *Adm £1.50. Sun May 30 (2-6)*

Hinton St George Gardens 2m NW of Crewkerne. N of A30 Crewkerne-Chard; S of A303 taking old Ilminster Rd, not new Ilminster By-Pass, at roundabout signed Lopen & Merriott, then right to one of Somerset's prettiest villages. TEAS & dog park provided at Hooper's Holding. *Combined adm £2 Chd free. Sun, Mon May 30, 31 (2-6)*
  Fig Tree Cottage ☙ (Mr & Mrs Whitworth) Old walled cottage garden and courtyard of stables made from kitchen garden of neighbouring rectory, over the past 12 years by owners inspired by Margery Fish. Ground covers, shrubs, old-fashioned roses. Three giant fig trees, all perennials. *Other dates by appt Tel 0460 73548*
  ¶**Holly Oak House** (Mr & Mrs Michael O'Loughlin) Gas Lane. ½-acre garden with terraced lawns and south facing views. A mixture of flower beds, shrubs and herbaceous borders
  Hooper's Holding &☙ (Mr & Mrs K Spencer-Mills) High St. ¼-acre 'young' garden, in a formal design; lily pool; dwarf conifers, rare herbaceous and shrubby plants; NCCPG National Collection of Hedychiums; fancy poultry. TEAS in aid of Cats Protection League. *Other dates by appt (Hedychiums flowering Sept and Oct) Tel 0460 76389*
  Springfield House & (Capt & Mrs T Hardy) 1½-acres; semi-wild wooded dell, mature trees framing view to Mendips, shrubs, herbaceous plants, bulbs

Iford Manor see Wiltshire

Kingsdon &☙☙ (Mr & Mrs Charles Marrow) 2m SE of Somerton off B3151 Ilchester Rd. From Ilchester roundabout on A303 follow NT signs to Lytes Cary; left opp gates ½m to Kingsdon. 2-acre plantsman's garden and nursery garden. Over 500 varieties of unusual plants for sale. Teas in Village Hall. *Adm £1.50 Chd free. Sats, Suns May 1, 2; June 5, 6; July 24, 25 (2-7.30)*

Kites Croft ☙☙ (Dr & Mrs W I Stanton) Westbury-sub-Mendip 5m NW of Wells. At Westbury Cross on A371 turn uphill, right to square and left up Free Hill to Kites Croft 2-acre garden with fine views to Glastonbury Tor. Winding paths lead from the terrace to different levels; lawn, pond, rockery, herbaceous borders, shrubs and wood. Many unusual plants of interest to the flower arranger and cottage gardener. TEAS. *Adm £1 Chd 30p (Share to Westbury Village Hall). Suns May 16, Sept 12, Weds May 12, Sept 15 (2-5); also by appt for groups Tel 0749 870328. No coaches*

¶**Landacre Farm** ☙☙ (Mr & Mrs Peter Hudson) Withypool, nr Minehead. On the B3223 Exford/S. Molton Rd 3m W of Exford not in Withypool village. 9m NW of Dulverton ¼m above Landacre Bridge. ½-acre terraced garden 1000ft up on Exmoor. Developed from a field over past 17yrs by present owners; rockery, stream and bog garden, octagonal pergola, rhododendrons and shrub roses. Exposed position with fantastic views of Barle Valley and open moorland; specializing in climbers and hardy perennials. TEAS. *Adm £1. Chd free. Suns April 25, May 23, June 27 (2-.5.30). Also by appt Tel 064 383 223*

Littlecourt &☙☙ (Jane Kimber & John Clothier) West Bagborough. 7m N of Taunton signed from A358. 6-acre garden in fine setting with woodland and water; spectacular new borders, interesting and extensive planting; wonderful views and good plant stall. TEAS. *Adm £1.50 Chd free. Sun June 27 (2-6). Also by appt at anytime Tel 0823 432281*

Lovibonds Farm &☙☙ (Mr & Mrs J A Griffiths) Burrowbridge. A361 from Taunton to Glastonbury, in village of Burrowbridge turn L immediately over bridge ½m on. 3-acre garden reclaimed 5yrs ago from derelict farmyard; herbaceous; shrub; bog garden; ponds and woodland walk; small lake with ornamental duck and geese. TEAS in aid of Burrowbridge WI. *Adm £1.50 Chd free. Suns May 9, June 6 (2-6)*

Lower Severalls &☙☙ (Howard & Mary Pring) 1½m NE of Crewkerne. Turning for Merriott off A30; or Haselbury Rd from B3165. 1-acre plantsman's garden beside early Ham stone farmhouse. Herbaceous borders inc collection of salvias and herbaceous geraniums. Herb garden. Nursery (open daily March 1 to Oct 31 10-5, Suns 2-5). Closed all day Thurs. Sells herbs, unusual herbaceous plants and half-hardy conservatory plants. TEAS. *Adm £1 Chd free. Suns June 13, July 11 (2-5.30)*

Marsh Mill House &☙☙ (Mr & Mrs J H McWilliam) Over Stowey. A39 Bridgwater to Minehead, bear L at Cottage Inn. 8m W of Bridgwater. 9m N of Taunton through Kingston St Mary. 1½-acre garden, bordered by stream, crisscrossed with box-edged paths and rose covered arches. Colour themed shrubs and hosta walk; vine covered pergola and peacocks. TEAS in aid of Over Stowey Parish Church. *Adm Adult £1.50. Sun June 13 (2-6)*

The Mill ☙☙ (Mr & Mrs J E Hudson) 21 Mill Lane, Cannington. 4m W of Bridgwater on A39. Turn opposite Rose & Crown. ¼-acre cottage type plantsman's garden with waterfall and pond, over 70 clematis and National Caltha Collection. TEA in aid of Cannington W.I. *Adm £1.50 Chd free (Share to NCCPG). Weds, Suns April 28, June 9, Aug 11 (2-5), June 6, Aug 8 (11-5). Also by appt* Tel **0278 652304**

The Mill House 🅰🅱 (Mr & Mrs P J Davies) Castle Cary. Do not go into Castle Cary Town Centre, but follow signs to Torbay Rd Industrial Estate (W). Entrances to Trading Estate on L proceed E along Torbay Rd to 30mph sign. Garden on the R. Approximately 1-acre terraced sloping garden, with streams and waterfalls. Emphasis on Natural look. Many interesting plants mingled with native flora. Bog garden; small orchard and vegetable plot. TEAS and plants in aid of Oncology Centre BRI Bristol. *Adm £1 Chd 50p. Sun June 6 (2-6)*

Milton Lodge 🅰🅱 (D C Tudway Quilter Esq) ½m N of Wells. From A39 Bristol-Wells, turn N up Old Bristol Rd; car park first gate on L. Mature terraced garden with outstanding views of Wells Cathedral and Vale of Avalon. Mixed borders; roses; fine trees. Separate 7-acre arboretum. TEAS: Suns & Bank Hol Mons April to Sept. *Adm £2 Chd under 14 free (Share to Wells Museum). Open daily (2-6) ex Sats, Easter to end Oct; parties by arrangement. For NGS Suns May 16, 30, June 13, July 11 (2-6)*

Milverton Gardens 9m W of Taunton on the new B3227 (old A361) L at roundabout to Milverton. *Combined adm £1.50 Chd free. Sun July 25 (2-6)*
 ¶**Cobbleside** 🅰🅱 (Mr & Mrs C Pine) ¾-acre walled garden incl newly laid out herb garden and potagere. Completely redesigned, with photographs illustrating the old layout. *Also by appt weekends from July 25* Tel **0823 400404**
 3 The College 🅰 (Mr Eric Thresher) Small interesting garden, featuring fireplaces amongst shrubs and borders
 Garden Cottage 🅱🅰🅱 (Mr & Mrs R Masters) Interesting plantsman garden with many unusual plants for sale. TEAS in aid of Milverton Surgery Defibrillator Fund. Primroses in variety and other spring flowers for visitors by appt. *Also welcome May to Sept* Tel **0823 400601**

Montacute Gardens 4m from Yeovil follow A3088, take slip road to Montacute, turn L at T-junction into village. *Combined adm £2 Chd free. Sun June 20 (2-5.30)*
 Abbey Farm 🅱 (Mr & Mrs G Jenkins) Turn R between Church and Kings Arms (no through Rd). 2½-acre of mainly walled gardens on sloping site provide setting for mediaeval Priory gatehouse. Garden laid out in 1966 and now being improved and extended. About half the garden suitable for wheelchairs. Parking available. TEAS in aid of St Catherine's Church Fund

Park House 🅱 (Mr & Mrs Ian McNab) Turn L (signposted Tintinhull) after red brick Council Houses and immediately R. Approx. 2-acre walled garden with herbaceous borders and vegetable garden. Spacious lawns some shrubs. The literary Powys family lived here during their father's lifetime. Cream TEAS proceeds to St Catherines Church Fund

Montacute House 🅱🅰🅱 (The National Trust) Montacute. NT signs off A3088 4m W of Yeovil and A303 nr Ilchester. Magnificent Tudor House with contemporary garden layout. Fine stonework provides setting for informally planted mixed borders and old roses; range of garden features illustrates its long history. TEAS. *Adm Garden only £2.50 Chd £1.20. For NGS Sun June 6 (11.30-5.30)*

The Mount 🅱 (Alison & Peter Kelly) Wincanton. Follow one-way system round lower half of town, bare L at signposted Castle Cary, on up hill, house on L. 1¼-acre. Plantswomans garden with hidden surprises. Alpine lawn and garden, half terraced shrub borders, gravel bed, rockery and pond. TEAS at weekends. *Adm £1.50 Chd free. Sats April 24, May 22, June 6, 20; Suns April 25; Weds April 28, May 26, June 9; Thurs June 24 (2-6). Also by appt April* Tel **0963 32487** *sundown*

¶**Pear Tree Cottage** 🅱🅰🅱 (Mr & Mrs C R Parry) Stapley. 9m S of Taunton nr Churchingford. Charming cottage garden leading to 2½-acre newly made park; well planted with interesting trees and shrubs leading to old peat and mill pond. TEAS. *Adm £1. Sat, Sun, May 8, 9 (2-6)*

Peart Hall 🅱🅰🅱 (Mr & Mrs J Lawrence-Mills) Spaxton. Bridgwater 6m. Take A39 and Spaxton Rd W from Bridgwater. In village, take Splatt Lane opp school, then L to church and garden. Extensive gardens include rockeries sloping to trout stream, riverside walk with weirs, waterfalls; Victorian herb garden; daffodils; many rare trees. TEAS in aid of Red Cross *Adm £1.50 Chd free. Suns March 28 (2-5), May 30 (2-6)*

The Red House 🅱🅰🅱 (Mr & Mrs James Lloyd) High Street, Cannington, Bridgwater. M5 exits 23 or 24. Take A38 to Bridgwater. From Bridgwater take the Minehead Rd. Cannington is 3m. The Red House is 300yds past War Memorial on the R. 3-acre garden on level site, created from a field since 1976. Walled garden (1710); good cross section of trees and shrubs; interesting herbaceous, perennials and bedding. TEAS. *Adm. £1.50 Chd 50p. Thurs, Fri, Sat June 17, 18, 19 (2-5). Also by appt June and July (2-3.30)* Tel **0278 652239**

Rose Cottage 🅰🅱 (Mr & Mrs R M Hughes) Creech Heathfield. 4m NE of Taunton from A38, A358 or A361 turn off for Creech St Michael. Follow signs for Creech Heathfield. ⅔-acre plantsman's informal garden; wide variety of shrubs, perennials and climbers, many unusual and tender, pergola, small bog and fernery. *Adm £1 Chd free. Sun June 6 (2-6)*

By Appointment Gardens. These owners do not have a fixed opening day usually because they do not like crowds or have insufficient parking space. Owner will often give guided tour.

Regular Openers. See head of county section.

Seithe ᕃ☞❀ (John & Renata White) Godney. 5m W of Wells on B3139 turn L at Panborough 5m NW from Glastonbury on B3151, R from Glastonbury B3151 E from Westhay. B3151 E from Blakeway. 2½-acres on Somerset levels in area designated of special scientific interest surrounded by peat diggings, 1-acre cultivated garden, comprising large all organic vegetable gardens, surrounded by herbaceous and cottage garden flowers; orchard and pond garden; new features, pergola arches. Many mature unusual trees and plants. TEAS in aid of Godney New Village Hall. *Adm £1 Chd free. Suns May 2 (Dried flower & material for sale Aug opening), Aug 15 (drawings by garden owner for sale) (2-6)*

Smocombe House ᕃ☞❀ (Mr & Mrs Frank Paton) Enmore. 4m W of Bridgwater take Enmore Rd, 3rd L after Tynte Arms. 5-acres S facing in Quantock Hills. Lovely woodland garden rising up hill behind the house; views down to stream and pool below; rhododendron woodland and waterside stocked with wide variety of interesting plants for spring display; 100 tree arboretum designed by Roy Lancaster; charming old kitchen garden. TEAS in aid of Enmore Parish Church. *Adm £1.50 Chd free. Suns April 4, May 16 (2-6)*

Spaxton Gardens ❀ Take A39 and Spaxton Rd W from Bridgwater. In village take Splatt Lane opp school. TEAS in aid of Spaxton Church. *Combined adm £1.50 Chd free. Sun May 2 (2.30-5.30)*

    Tuckers ☞ (Mrs John Denton) ½-acre delightful cottage garden with orchard leading over leat to Old Mill House. One way system to Old Mill House from Tuckers

    Old Mill House ☞ (Mr & Mrs W Bryant) 2-acre beautiful, peaceful plantsman's garden beside a weir and trout stream. Many interesting plants. *(Plant stall in aid of RAF Benevolent Fund)*

Stapleton Manor ᕃ☞❀ (Mr & Mrs G E L Sant) 1m N of Martock on B3165 Long Sutton Rd. 2½-acres of roses, shrubs; herbaceous and mixed borders; pool/bog garden; dahlia walk; grass area with small trees and shrubs; fine mature trees. Scheduled Georgian Hamstone house (not open). *Adm £1 Chd free. Suns July 4, Aug 1 (12-6)*

Stogumber and Kingswood Gardens ☞❀ A358 NW from Taunton for 11m. Sign to Stogumber W near Crowcombe; R after railway bridge. Five smallish plantsmen's gardens in lovely edge of Quantocks settings. TEAS in aid of Red Cross at Hill Farm. *Combined adm £2 Chd free. Sun June 20 (2-6)*

Stogumber

    Brook Cottage ᕃ☞ (Mrs M Field) Stogumber. Good plants, lilies, water

    ¶**Butts Cottage** (Mr & Mrs J A Morrison) Cottage garden with old roses, old-fashioned perennials, alpines, pond, small vine house and vegetable garden

    Hill Farm ☞❀ (Mr & Mrs J S H Illingworth) Beautifully laid out medium-sized gardens on 3 levels. Bog garden with primulas etc. Herbaceous and Roses. TEAS in aid of Red Cross

    Orchard Deane ☞❀ (Mr & Mrs P H Wilson) Stogumber. Mixed borders, wide variety of hardy plants, bulbs and alpines

Wynes ☞ (Mr & Mrs L Simms) Country garden with orchard; shrubs; ponds; alpines and vegetable garden

Kingswood

    Cridlands ☞ (Mr & Mrs A M Janssenswillen) Kingswood. Terraced with named perennials, roses & shrubs

    Kingswood Farm ☞ (M H and D H Leonard) Hillside cottage garden, named plants and small wood

Stone Allerton Gardens 11m NW of Wells, 2m from A38, signposted from Lower Weare. TEAS. *Combined adm £1.50 Chd free. Sun May 30, Mon May 31 (2-6)*

    Berries Brook ☞ (Mr & Mrs D J Searle) ½-acre cottage garden. Roses, shrubs, pond

    Fallowdene ☞ (Prof. & Mrs G H Arthur) ½-acre of walled gardens surrounding C18 house (not open). Rose and honeysuckle pergola, mixed shrub and herbaceous borders, lawns, vegetable garden and splendid view to the Quantocks

    Greenfield House ☞ (Mr & Mrs D K Bull) Walled garden with Climbers and mixed planting. House listed 1741 (not open). TEAS on Monday in aid of Allerton Harvest Home

    Manor Farm ᕃ☞❀ (Mr & Mrs P Coate) 1-acre of mixed herbaceous and shrub beds, foliage bed, borders, water garden. Old orchard and many climbing plants, a painter's garden. Listed C18 House (not open). TEAS on Sunday in aid of Calcutta Rescue Fund. *Also by appt* Tel 0934 713015

    Mill House ☞❀ (Mr & Mrs B W Metcalf) ¼-acre cottage style, Plantsman's garden with unusual and a great variety of plants. Extensive views over levels to Quantocks. *Also by appt* Tel 0934 712459

Stowell Hill ☞ (Mr & Mrs Robert McCreery) NE of Sherborne. Turn at Stowell, ½m N of Templecombe on A357. Spring bulbs; collection of flowering shrubs; inc rhododendrons, azaleas, magnolias, Japanese cherries. TEA in aid of Lord Roberts Workshops. *Adm £1 Chd free. Suns May 2, 9, 16, 23 (2-5.30)*

¶**Stratton House** ᕃ☞ (Mr & Mrs G Denman) Stoney Stratton. ¾m E of Evercreech on the Balcombe rd. Interesting and unusual shrubs in a 2 acre garden which is backed by a 20' wall. Planted from scratch 87-88; shrub roses. *Adm £1.50. Sun, Wed June, 27, 30 (2-6)*

Sutton Hosey Manor ᕃ☞ (Roger Bramble Esq) On A372 just E of Long Sutton. 2-acres; ornamental kitchen garden, lily pond, pleached limes leading to amelanchier walk to duck pond; rose and juniper walk from Italian terrace. TEA. *Adm £1.50 Chd over 3 yrs 50p (Share to Marie Curie Cancer Research). Sun July 11 (2.30-6.30)*

Tintinhull House ᕃ☞ (The National Trust) NW of Yeovil. NT signs on A303, W of Ilchester. Famous 2-acre garden in compartments, developed 1900-1960, influenced by Gertrude Jekyll and Hidcote; many good and uncommon plants. C17 & C18 house (not open). TEAS in aid of St Andrews Church. *Adm £1 Chd 25p. For NGS Sun Aug 1 (2-6)*

Regular Openers. See head of county section.

Wambrook Gardens & 2m SW Chard. Turn off A30 Honiton rd 1m W of Chard at top of hill. 6 gardens in beautiful wooded countryside; romantic views. TEAS/ Plants in aid of Wambrook Church Fabric Fund. *Combined adm £2 or 50p per garden Chd free. Sun May 30 (2-6)*

¶**Broad Oak** (Mr & Mrs D Eames) Oak woods lead up to 2 acres of mainly pre-1914 azaleas and rhododendrons. TEA

The Cotley Inn & (Mr & Mrs D R Livingstone) Pub garden approx 1-acre created in the last 2 years comprising of large lawn area with fishpond, shrubs, young trees and long flower border

¶**Dennetts Farm** ✿✿ (Mr & Mrs F J Stubbings) Working cottage garden with many herbs and vegetables grown for sale. Emphasis on ease of working and use of salvaged materials

The Old Rectory &✿✿ (Mr & Mrs T P Jackson) Hillside garden in beautiful setting. Rose terrace; young rhododendrons, camellias, azaleas and heathers; water garden and ponds. Vegetable garden

Wambrook House ✿✿ (Brig & Mrs Guy Wheeler) 2-acre organically run garden surrounding Regency rectory (not open); mature trees, mixed borders, roses; rockery, small water garden, walled vegetable garden with small vineyard

Yew Tree Cottage ✿✿ (Ron & Joan White) A picture book Thatched Cottage surrounded by lawns; herbaceous borders; shrubbery and productive organic vegetable garden

Watermeadows ✿✿ (Mr & Mrs R Gawen) Clapton is to be found 200 yds down the road from Clapton Court. A sophisticated cottage garden made from a field over 15yrs. There is something of everything including one hundred and twenty of the old-fashioned roses. Car park. *Adm £1 Chd free. Open April to Sept (9-5). Parties by appt* **Tel 0460 74421**

Wayford Manor ✿ (Mr & Mrs Robin L Goffe) SW of Crewkerne. Turning on B3165 at Clapton; or on A30 Chard-Crewkerne. 3 acres, noted for magnolias and acers. Bulbs; flowering trees, shrubs; rhododendrons. Garden redesigned by Harold Peto in 1902. Fine Elizabethan manor house (not open). TEAS. *Adm £1.50 Chd 50p. Suns April 11, May 2, 16, 30 (2-6); also by appt for parties only*

¶**Wellington Gardens** ✿ W of Wellington 1m off A38 bypass signposted Wrangway. 1st L towards Wellington Monument over motorway bridge 1st R. TEAS *Combined adm £1.50 Sat, Sun July 3, July 4 (2-6)*

¶**Hangeridge Farm** &✿ (Mr & Mrs J M Chave) Wrangway. 1-acre garden, large lawns, herbaceous borders, flowering shrubs and heathers, raised rockeries, spring bulbs. Lovely setting under Blackdown Hills. *Also April 18 (2-6)*

¶**Marlpit Cottage** ✿ (Mr & Mrs John Manning) Wrangway. An 8yr-old ½-acre garden. Informal mixed herbaceous borders, many interesting plants

¶**The Mount** (Jim & Gilly Tilden) Chelston. Off M5 1m NW of junction 26. At A38 Chelston roundabout take Wellington rd. After 200yds turn R to Chelston. 1st house on R. Enclosed garden with herbaceous borders and shrubs; trees, old roses, more shrubs and pond outside. 1 acre altogether. Cream TEAS in aid of Wellington Stroke Club

West Bradley House & (Mr & Mrs E Clifton-Brown) Glastonbury. 2½m due E of Glastonbury. Turn S off A361 (Shepton Mallet/Glastonbury Rd) at W Pennard. House is next to church in scattered village of W Bradley. 3-acre open garden lying alongside 3 old carp ponds. 70 acres of apple orchards around house, hopefully in full blossom when garden open. Visitors welcome to walk (or even drive) through orchards. Parking available. TEAS in aid of W Bradley Church. *Adm garden & orchards £1 Chd 50p (Share to National Listening Library). Sun May 9 (2-6)*

Westhay &✿ (Mr & Mrs T Thompson) Kingston St Mary Taunton. 1st house on the R up the hill after the White Swan Inn, Kingston St Mary. Landscaped walled garden, bog garden, small lake; wood walk; spring daffodil lawn; streams and informal shrubberies. Suitable for wheelchairs in parts. Cream TEAS. *Adm £1 Chd free. Sun May 23 (2-6)*

37 Whitmore Rd ✿✿ (Mr & Mrs E Goldsmith) Taunton. Leave Taunton following signs to Kingston; turn 1st left past Bishop Fox School; turn 2nd right into Whitmore rd. ⅓-acre flower garden with herbaceous and perennial plants laid out to make maximum use of space for pleasure garden, fruit and vegetable garden. Tea Taunton. *Adm 50p Chd 20p. Sun May 16, Wed May 19 (2-5)*

Withey Lane Farmhouse &✿✿ (Sqn Ldr & Mrs H C Tomblin) Barton St David. 4m E of Somerton, turn off B3153 in Keinton Mandeville, turn R in village opp Old Chapel Restaurant. 200yds turn L at Manor House. 300yds turn R into small lane; farmhouse 300yds on right. ⅓-acre plantsman's garden with many unusual and interesting plants; herbaceous beds with shrubs; raised alpine beds; old roses; climbing plants; vegetables grown organically in deep beds 1½-acre old cider orchard. TEA. *Adm £1 Chd 50p. Weds, May 5, 12, 19, 26, June 2, 9, 16, 23, 30 (2-6); also by appt* **Tel 0458 50875**

Wootton House & (The Hon Mrs John Acland-Hood) Butleigh Wootton, 3m S of Glastonbury. Herbaceous borders; rose garden; shrubs, trees, bulbs; rock garden; woodland garden. C17 house (not open). TEA. *Adm £1.50 Chd under 5 free (Share to British Red Cross Society). Sun Sept 18 (2-5.30)*

Staffordshire & part of West Midlands

Hon County Organisers: Mr & Mrs D K Hewitt, Arbour Cottage, Napley, Market Drayton, Shropshire TF9 4AJ Tel 063087 2852

DATES OF OPENING

By appointment
For telephone numbers and other details see garden descriptions

Arbour Cottage, Napley
12 Darges Lane, Great Wyrley
Grafton Cottage,
   Barton-under-Needwood, Lichfield
Heath House, nr Eccleshall
Littlewood Farm Nursery, Cheddleton
Lower House, Sugnall Parva
Manor Cottage, Chapel Chorlton
Wedgwood Memorial College,
   Barlaston

Regular openings
For details see garden descriptions

Dorothy Clive Garden,
   Willoughbridge. April 1 to
   October 31
Littlewood Farm Nursery,
   Cheddleton. Tues to Fri April 9 to
   June 30
Manor Cottage, Chapel Chorlton.
   Mons May 3 to Sept 27

April 18 Sunday
   Eccleshall Castle Gardens
April 24 Saturday
   Dorothy Clive Garden,
     Willoughbridge
May 15 Saturday
   Lower House, Sugnall Parva
May 16 Sunday
   Heath House, nr Eccleshall
   Little Onn Hall, Church Eaton
   Lower House, Sugnall Parva
   Wightwick Manor, Compton
May 23 Sunday
   Fradswell Hall, Fradswell
   Wedgwood Memorial College,
     Barlaston
May 30 Sunday
   The Wombourne Wodehouse,
     Wolverhampton
June 6 Sunday
   The Garth, Milford, Stafford
June 13 Sunday
   12 Darges Lane, Great Wyrley
   26 Fold Lane, Biddulph
   Little Onn Hall, Church Eaton
June 19 Saturday
   Shugborough, Milford
June 20 Sunday
   The Covert, nr Market Drayton
   Moseley Old Hall, Fordhouses,
     Wolverhampton

June 25 Friday
   Farley Hall, Oakamoor
June 27 Sunday
   The Garth, Milford, Stafford
   Grafton Cottage,
     Barton-under-Needwood,
     Lichfield
July 4 Sunday
   41 Fallowfield Drive,
     Barton-under-Needwood ‡
   Grafton Cottage,
     Barton-under-Needwood,
     Lichfield ‡
July 11 Sunday
   12 Darges Lane, Great Wyrley
August 1 Sunday
   Grafton Cottage,
     Barton-under-Needwood,
     Lichfield
   Heath House, nr Eccleshall
   The Willows, Trysull
September 4 Saturday
   Dorothy Clive Garden,
     Willoughbridge
September 26 Sunday
   Biddulph Grange Garden,
     Biddulph
October 17 Sunday
   Wedgwood Memorial College,
     Barlaston

DESCRIPTIONS OF GARDENS

Arbour Cottage ق ⋌ ❀ (Mr & Mrs D K Hewitt) Napley. 4m N of Market Drayton. Take A53 then B5415 signed Woore, turn L 1¾m at telephone box. Cottage garden 2 acres of alpine gardens, grasses, shrub roses and many paeonias, bamboos etc. Colour all the year round from shrubs and trees of many species. TEAS. *£1.50 Chd 50p. By appt Fris and Sats. May 18 to June 29* **Tel 063087 2852**

Biddulph Grange Garden ⋌ (The National Trust) Biddulph. 5m SE of Congleton, 7m N of Stoke-on-Trent on A527, turn into Grange Rd, car park signposted. An exciting and rare survival of a high Victorian garden, acquired by the National Trust in 1988. The garden has undergone an extensive restoration project which will continue for a number of years. Conceived by James Bateman, the 15 acres are divided into a number of smaller gardens which were designed to house specimens from his extensive and wide ranging plant collection. An Egyptian Court; Chinese Pagoda, Willow Pattern Bridge; Pinetum and Arboretum together with many other settings all combine to make the garden a miniature tour of the world. TEAS. *Adm £3.70 Chd £1.85 Family £9.25. Sun Sept 26 (11-6)*

¶The Covert ق ⋌ ❀ (Mr & Mrs L Standeven) Burntwood. Turn off A53 Newcastle-Market Drayton Rd onto Burntwood at Loggerheads Xrds. A developing cottage garden in modern surroundings, approx ¾ acre. Mixed border/beds, pond, bog gardens featuring many unusual shrubs, trees and plants. TEAS. *Adm £1.50 Chd 50p. Sun June 20 (2-6)*

12 Darges Lane ⋌ ❀ (Ann and Ken Hackett) 12 Darges Lane, Great Wyrley. From A5 (Churchbridge Junction) take A34 towards Walsall. Darges Lane is 1st turning on R (over brow of hill). House on R on corner of Cherrington Drive. Approx 2m SW of Cannock. Small ¼-acre well stocked plantsmans and flower arrangers garden. Foliage plants a special feature. Well maintained mixed borders including trees, shrubs and rare plants giving year round interest. West Midlands Gardener of the Year 1990. TEAS *Adm £1 Chd 50p. Suns June 13, July 11 (2-6). Also by appt* **Tel 0922 415064**

Dorothy Clive Garden ق Willoughbridge. On A51 between Stone and Nantwich. 8-acre garden: woodland with rhododendrons and azaleas, spring bulbs, shrub roses; water garden and large scree in fine landscaped setting.

Colourful flower borders in late summer and autumn are a feature. Car park. TEAS. *Adm £2 Chd 50p. April 1 to Oct 31. For NGS Sats April 24, Sept 4 (10-5.30)*

Eccleshall Castle Gardens & (Mr & Mrs Mark Carter) ½m N of Eccleshall on A519; 6m from M6, junction 14 (Stafford); 10m from junction 15 (Stoke-on-Trent). 20 acres incl wooded garden with moat lawns around William and Mary mansion house; herbaceous, rose garden, wide variety of trees and shrubs; also recently renovated C14 tower. Home-made cream TEAS. Free car/coach parking. *Adm £1 Chd 50p.* ▲*For NGS Sun April 18 (2-5.30)*

¶**41 Fallowfield Drive** &※❀ (Mrs S Webster) Barton-under-Needwood. Take B5016 from Barton-under-Needwood to Yoxall. Turn L before leaving Barton onto Park Drive, leading to Fallowfield Drive. ¼-acre colourful garden of summer flowers and shrubs with pool. TEAS. *Adm £1.50 Chd 50p. Sun July 4 (1-6)*

¶**Farley Hall** &※ (Lady Bamford) Oakamoor. From Uttoxeter follow signs to Alton Towers. On R 200 yds past Alton Towers entrance. Walled vegetable, fruit and perennial gardens; formal lawn containing pleached limes and yew hedges. *Adm £1.50 Chd 50p. Fri June 25 (2-5.30)*

¶**26 Fold Lane** &※❀ (Mr & Mrs D Machin) Biddulph. 5m SE Congleton off the A527. Follow the signs for Biddulph Grange Gardens, turn into Grange Rd pass the entrance for Grange Gardens. 2nd L into Fold Lane, parking in garden & lane. 2-acre garden with herbaceous border. Informal cottage garden. Wild life pond area and old herb garden. TEAS. *Adm £1.25 Chd 50p. Sun June 13 (1-6)*

¶**Fradswell Hall** (Mr & Mrs Gerald Tams) Fradswell. Take B5027 from Stone, through Milwich to Coton. Turn R by Wheatsheaf inn & follow lane, 1st turning on L to Fradswell. Or take R off A51 from Rugeley at Weston & follow signs to Gayton, then take 2nd R to Fradswell. Hall is next to village church. 7 acres of trees and shrubs, cedars, rhododendrons, azaleas, lawns and ponds. TEA. *Adm £1.50 Chd 50p. Sun May 23 (1.30-5.30)*

The Garth ❀ (Mr & Mrs David Wright) 2 Broc Hill Way, Milford, 4½m SE of Stafford. A513 Stafford-Rugeley Rd; at Barley Mow turn R (S) to Brocton; L after 1m. ½-acre; shrubs, rhododendrons, azaleas, mixed herbaceous borders, naturalized bulbs; plants of interest to flower arrangers. Rock hewn caves. Fine landscape setting. Coach parties by appt. TEAS. *Adm £1 Chd 50p. Suns June 6, 27 (2-6)*

Grafton Cottage ※ (Mr & Mrs Peter Hargreaves) Bar Lane, Barton-under-Needwood. 5m N of Lichfield, 3m S of Burton-on-Trent on A38. Take B5016 between Barton-under-Needwood and Yoxall. Bar Lane is ½m W of Top Bell public house. Grafton Cottage ¾m along lane. ¼-acre colourful cottage garden. Replanted 1984 with mixed borders, wide range of perennials, old roses and stream. TEAS. *Adm £1.50 Chd 25p (Share to Royal National Institute for the Blind, Midlands Branch). Suns June 27, July 4, Aug 1 (1-6). Also by appt Tel 0283 713639*

Heath House ※❀ (Dr & Mrs D W Eyre-Walker) Nr Eccleshall. 3m W of Eccleshall. Take B5026 towards Woore. At Sugnall turn L, after 1½m turn R immediately by stone garden wall. After 1m straight across crossroads. 1½-acre garden. Borders, bog garden, woodland garden. Many unusual plants. Car parking limited and difficult if wet. TEAS. *Adm £1.50 Chd free (Share to Parish Church). Sun May 16, Aug 1 (2-6). Also by appt Tel 0785 280318*

Little Onn Hall & (Mr & Mrs I H Kidson) Church Eaton, 6m SW of Stafford. A449 Wolverhampton-Stafford; at Gailey roundabout turn W on to A5 for 1¼m; turn R to Stretton; 200yds turn L for Church Eaton; or Bradford Arms - Wheaton Aston & Marston 1¼m. 6-acre garden; herbaceous lined drive; abundance of rhododendrons; formal paved rose garden with pavilions at front; large lawns with lily pond around house; old moat garden with fish tanks and small ruin; fine trees; walkways. Paddock open for picnics. TEAS. *Adm £1.50 Chd 50p (Share to Marie Curie Cancer Care). Suns May 16, June 13 (2-6)*

Littlewood Farm Nursery &※❀ (Mr & Mrs R Donovan Bloore) Cheddleton. W towards Stoke-on-Trent from A52/520 Xrds. 2nd R into Rownall Rd, after 2m turn R into marked drive. From Stoke-on-Trent take A52 towards Ashbourne; at top of long hill take 2nd L after 'Red Cow', proceed as above. Garden approx 6m from Leek, 6m from Stoke-on-Trent. A developing, tranquil, 1-acre cottage garden with extensive views over Pennine foothills. Unusual perennials, primulas, bog plants, hostas, border geraniums; flowering shrubs; natural ponds; streamlet; woodland and picnic area. TEA. *Adm £1.50. April 9 to June 30 Tues to Fri (10-6). Also by appt Tel 0538 360478*

Lower House &❀ (Mrs J M Treanor) Sugnall Parva. 2m W of Eccleshall. On B5026 Loggerheads Rd turn R at sharp double bend. House ½m on L. Approx 1 acre in open countryside of mixed borders; pond; shrubs and rockery gradually being shaped from originally flat lawn areas. TEAS. *Adm £1.50 Chd free. Sat, Sun May 15, 16 (2-6). Also by appt Tel 0785 851 378*

Manor Cottage &※❀ (Mrs Joyce Heywood) Chapel Chorlton. 6m S of Newcastle-U-Lyme. On A51 Nantwich to Stone Rd turn behind Cock Inn at Stableford; white house on village green. ⅔-acre unusual plants in flower arrangers cottage garden, of special interest, ferns and grasses. TEAS. *Adm £1.50 Chd 50p. Mons May 3 to Sept 27 (2-5) also by appt Tel 0782 680206 before 9.30 a.m.*

Moseley Old Hall &※❀ (The National Trust) Fordhouses, 4m N of Wolverhampton, between A460 & A444 south of M54 motorway; follow signs. Small modern reconstruction of C17 garden with formal box parterre; mainly includes plants grown in England before 1700; old roses, herbaceous plants, small herb garden, arbour. Late Elizabethan house. TEAS. *Adm House & Garden £3 Chd £1.50; Garden £1.50 Chd 75p. Sun June 20 (2-5.30)*

By Appointment Gardens. Avoid the crowds. Good chance of a tour by owner. See garden description for telephone number.

¶**Shugborough** &✿❀ (Staffordshire County Council) Shugborough lies about 6m E of Stafford, car access being through the lodge gates at Milford on the A513 Stafford-Lichfield Rd. Car Parking at both main site & farm is available. Grade 1 listed gardens with riverside walk, monuments incl a Chinese House, Doric Temple and Shepherds Monument. Formal terraces, Victorian rose garden and woodland trials. Tours 2pm, 3pm, 4pm. Separate charges for Mansion House; restored original servant's quarters and working farm. TEAS. *Adm £1 per car incls entry to parkland & gardens. £3 per head for tours. Sat June 19* Tel **0889 881388**

Wedgwood Memorial College ❀ Station Rd, Barlaston. In centre of Barlaston village (200 yds uphill from the railway level-crossing). Barlaston is 5m S of Stoke-on-Trent. Leave M6 at junctions 14 or 15 and take A34. The village is 1m E of this rd (Grid ref: SJ 8900-3839). Approx 10 acres grounds and gardens including a late Victorian formal garden, shrubberies, a spinney, lawns, a tennis court, an orchard, a water garden and a sports field. The main feature is the developing arboretum with nearly 400 species of tree (a particularly good collection of cherry, sorbus and maple). All are labelled with notes for visitors. A developing wild flower meadow and a sculpture garden are now incorporated in the grounds and arboretum. TEAS. *Adm £1.50 Chd 50p. Suns May 23 (2-5.30), Oct 17 (2-5); also by appt May to Oct* Tel **0782 372105**

Weston Park see Shropshire

Wightwick Manor & (The National Trust) Compton, 3m W of Wolverhampton A454, Wolverhampton-Bridgnorth, just to N of rd, up Wightwick Bank, beside Mermaid Inn. Partly suitable for wheelchairs. 17-acre, Victorian-style garden laid out by Thomas Mawson; yew hedges; topiary; terraces; 2 pools; rhododendrons; azaleas. House closed. Coffee & biscuits. *Adm £1.50 Chd 75p. For NGS Sun May 16 (2-6)*

¶**The Willows** &✿❀ (Mr & Mrs Nigel Hanson) Trysull. 7m SW of Wolverhampton. From A449 at Himley B4176 towards Bridgnorth, 2¼m turn R to Trysull. ¾m on L. 2-acre garden created and maintained by present owners since 1981. Designed for all-year-round interest. Natural pool, hostas, wide range shrubs and perennials. *Adm £1 Chd 25p. Sun Aug 1 (2-6)*

The Wombourne Wodehouse &✿❀ (Mr & Mrs J Phillips) 4m S of Wolverhampton just off A449 on A463 to Sedgley. 18-acre garden laid out in 1750. Mainly rhododendrons, herbaceous and iris border, woodland walk, water garden. TEAS. *Adm £1.50 Chd free (Share to Cancer Research). Sun May 30 (2-6); also by appt for parties* Tel **0902 892202**

Suffolk

Hon County Organisers:

(East)	Mrs Robert Stone, Washbrook Grange, Washbrook, Nr Ipswich Tel 0473 730244
(West)	Lady Mowbray, Hill House, Glemsford, Nr Sudbury Tel 0787 281 930

Assistant Hon County Organiser:

(West)	Mrs M Pampanini, The Old Rectory, Hawstead, Bury St Edmunds IP29 5NT
(East)	Mrs B R Jenkins, SRN, SCM, Paigles, 6 The Street, Holton-St-Peter, Halesworth 1P19 8PH Tel 0986 873731
	Mrs R I Johnson, The Old Farmhouse, Flixton Road, Bungay NR35 1PD

Hon County Treasurer (West): Sir John Mowbray

DATES OF OPENING

By appointment
For telephone numbers and other details see garden descriptions

Bucklesham Hall, Bucklesham
4 Church Street, Hadleigh
13 Drapers Lane, Ditchingham
Gable House, Redisham
Pippin Cottage, Woodditton, nr Newmarket
Rosemary, East Bergholt
Rumah Kita, Bedfield
St Stephens Cottage, Spexhall

Thrift Farm, Cowlinge, nr Newmarket
25, Westbury Avenue, Bury St Edmunds
West Stow Hall, Bury St Edmunds
Whepstead Hall, Bury St Edmunds

Regular openings
For details see garden descriptions

Akenfield, 1 Park Lane May 3 to end of Sept
Blakenham Woodland Garden, nr Ipswich. Weds, Thurs, Suns, Bank Hol Mons April to Sept

Euston Hall, nr Thetford. June 3 to Sept 30, Thurs & 2 Suns

March 21 Sunday
25, Westbury Avenue, Bury St Edmunds

March 28 Sunday
Barham Hall, Barham, Ipswich

April 4 Sunday
Great Thurlow Hall, Haverhill

April 12 Monday
Whepstead Hall, Bury St Edmunds

April 18 Sunday
Gifford's Hall, Wickhambrook

Nedging Hall, nr Hadleigh
April 25 Sunday
The Abbey, Eye
Blakenham Woodland Garden, nr
Ipswich
Hawstead Gardens, Hawstead
May 2 Sunday
13 Drapers Lane, Ditchingham
Dunburgh House, Geldeston
May 3 Monday
13 Drapers Lane, Ditchingham
Dunburgh House, Geldeston
May 9 Sunday
Hartshall Farm, Walsham le
Willows
Riverside House, Clare
May 16 Sunday
The Abbey, Eye
Keepers Cottage, Lawshall
The Rookery, Eyke
St Stephens Cottage, Spexhall
Woottens, Wenhaston
May 23 Sunday
Battlies House, Rougham
Blakenham Woodland Garden, nr
Ipswich
Ruggs Cottage, Raydon
May 24 Monday
Ruggs Cottage, Raydon
May 25 Sunday
Ruggs Cottage, Raydon
May 30 Sunday
Grundisburgh Hall, Woodbridge
The Priory, Stoke by Nayland
June 5 Saturday
Orchard End, Rishangles
June 6 Sunday
The Old Rectory, Brinkley, nr
Newmarket
Orchard End, Rishangles
Thrift Farm, Cowlinge, nr
Newmarket
Wyken Hall, Stanton

June 13 Sunday
The Abbey, Eye
21 Bederic Close, Bury St
Edmunds
Gable House, Redisham
Garden House, Moulton, nr
Newmarket
Pippin Cottage, Woodditton, nr
Newmarket
Rosemary, East Bergholt
Somerleyton Hall, Lowestoft
The Spong, Groton
Stour Cottage, East Bergholt
Woottens, Wenhaston
June 19 Saturday
Orchard End, Rishangles
June 20 Sunday
Hillwatering Farmhouse, Langham
The Lawn, Walsham le Willows
Little Thurlow Hall, Haverhill
Moat Cottage, Great Green,
Cockfield
The Old Rectory, Cockfield
Orchard End, Rishangles
Playford Hall, Ipswich
The Rookery, Eyke
Ruggs Cottage, Raydon
Rumah Kita, Bedfield
June 21 Monday
Ruggs Cottage, Raydon
June 22 Tuesday
Ruggs Cottage, Raydon
June 27 Sunday
Cavendish Hall, Cavendish
Euston Hall, nr Thetford
Grundisburgh Hall, Woodbridge
Pippin Cottage, Woodditton, nr
Newmarket
July 3 Saturday
Orchard End, Rishangles
July 4 Sunday
Fort Henry, Martlesham Heath
Gifford's Hall, Wickhambrook

Long Melford Gardens
Magnolia House, Yoxford
Orchard End, Rishangles
July 11 Sunday
Felsham House, Bury St Edmunds
Holbecks, Hadleigh
North Cove Hall, Beccles
Redisham Hall, Beccles
Woottens, Wenhaston
August 8 Sunday
Akenfield, 1 Park Lane, Charsfield
Ruggs Cottage, Raydon
August 9 Monday
Akenfield, 1 Park Lane, Charsfield
Ruggs Cottage, Raydon
August 10 Tuesday
Akenfield, 1 Park Lane, Charsfield
August 11 Wednesday
Akenfield, 1 Park Lane, Charsfield
August 12 Thursday
Akenfield, 1 Park Lane, Charsfield
August 13 Friday
Akenfield, 1 Park Lane, Charsfield
August 14 Saturday
Akenfield, 1 Park Lane, Charsfield
August 15 Sunday
West Stow Hall, Bury St Edmunds
Woottens, Wenhaston
August 22 Sunday
21 Bederic Close, Bury St
Edmunds
September 5 Sunday
Euston Hall, nr Thetford
Fort Henry, Martlesham Heath
Rumah Kita, Bedfield
September 19 Sunday
Chequers, Boxford
The Rotunda, Ickworth Park,
Bury St Edmunds
September 26 Sunday
St Stephens Cottage, Spexhall

DESCRIPTIONS OF GARDENS

The Abbey ⅙⅍❀ (Mrs K Campbell) Eye. 6m S of Diss, Norfolk. Leaving Eye on B1117 passing Eye Church on L cross River Dove and The Abbey is immediately on the L with ample parking. Marked remains of Benedictine Priory on some maps. The garden is approx. 3 acres and surrounds a red brick and flint timber framed house incorporating a Benedictine Abbey founded in the 11th century. The remains of the church such as are above ground make for interesting gardening with walls and courtyards. Raised beds and sink gardens and 2 large glasshouses. Unusual plants, many double primroses and auriculas, iris and roses and a large herbaceous collection. Minature geraniums and succulents are in the glasshouses. Ample parking. TEAS. *Adm £1 OAP & Chd 70p. Suns April 25, May 16, June 13 (2-5.30)*

Akenfield, 1 Park Lane ⅍❀ (Mrs E E Cole) Charsfield, 6m N of Woodbridge. On B1078, 3m W of Wickham Market. ¼-acre council house garden; vegetables, flowers for drying, 2 greenhouses; small fishponds with water wheel; many pot plants etc. In village of Charsfield (known to many readers and viewers as Akenfield). TEAS Sunday only. *Adm £1 OAPs 75p Chd free.* ▲*For NGS Sun Aug 8 daily to Sat Aug 14 (10.30-7)*

By Appointment Gardens. These owners do not have a fixed opening day usually because they do not like crowds or have insufficient parking space. Owner will often give guided tour.

Barham Hall &⌂▨ (Mr & Mrs Richard Burrows) Barham. Ipswich to A45 going W. 4m sign Great Blakenham to roundabout beneath motorway. Leave by 3rd turning to Claydon. Through Claydon, after decontrolled signs turn R up Church Lane to Barham Green. ½m up Church Lane. Barham church on L.h.s Barham Hall behind long brick wall. 7 acres of undulating gardens mainly recreated during the last 5yrs. 3 herbaceous borders, a lake surrounded by azaleas and bog plants, a woodland shrub garden full of spring flowers; a very considerable collection of victorian roses set in well kept lawns with mature trees; a water garden and many other interesting features. TEAS. *Adm £1 OAPs 75p Chd 25p (Share to St Mary's & St Peters Church Barham). Sun March 28 (2-5)*

Battlies House &▨ (Mr & Mrs John Barrell) Bury St Edmunds. Turn N off the A45 at the GT Barton and Rougham industrial estate turning, 3m E of Bury St Edmunds. In ½m turn R by the lodge. 8-acre garden laid out to lawns; shrubberies; woodland walk with a variety of old trees; rhododendrons; elms and conifers. TEAS. *Adm £1 Chd free. Sun May 23 (2-6)*

¶**21 Bederic Close** ▨▧ (Mrs S Robinson) Bury St Edmunds. Leave A45 at exit for Bury St Edmunds (E) and Sudbury. Proceed N and at 1st roundabout (Sainsbury's entrance) turn L into Symonds Rd. After R angled turn at end take 1st R into Bederic Close. ⅙ acre surbuban garden enthusiastically developed over 10yrs with rockery and water garden. Over 500 old-fashioned, unusual rare plants and shrubs. Emphases on conservation to encourage wildlife. Finalist in Gardener of the Year Competition. *Adm £1.50 Chd free.* ▲*For NGS Suns June 13, Aug 22 (2.30-6)* Tel **0284 764310**

Blakenham Woodland Garden ▨ Little Blakenham. 4m NW of Ipswich. Follow signs from 'The Beeches' at Lt Blakenham, 1m off the old A1100, now called B1113. 5-acre bluebell wood densely planted with fine collection of trees and shrubs; camellias, magnolias, cornus, azaleas, rhododendrons, roses, hydrangeas. *Adm £1. Weds, Thurs, Suns, Bank Hol Mons April to Sept (1-5). For NGS Suns Apr 25, May 23 (1-5)*

Bucklesham Hall &⌂▨ (Mr & Mrs P A Ravenshear) Bucklesham 6m SE of Ipswich, 1m E of village opp to Bucklesham Village School. 7 acres; created and maintained by owners since 1973; unusual plants, shrubs, trees; shrub/rose garden; water and woodland gardens. *Adm £2 Chd free. Reduction for large parties. By appt* Tel **0473 659263**

¶**Cavendish Hall** &▨ (Mrs T S Matthews) Cavendish. Entrance on A1092 midway between Cavendish and Clare, approx 9m NW of Sudbury. Fine views overlooking Stour Valley. Woodland walks, old roses, peonies, shrubs in encircling borders. TEAS. *Adm £1.25 Chd 50p. Sun June 27 (2-6.30)*

Chequers & (Miss J Robinson) Boxford, 5m W of Hadleigh via A1071. From Sudbury A134 then A1071. From Ipswich A1071, from Colchester A134. 2-3-acre plantsman's walled and stream gardens full of rare plants. TEA. *Adm £1.25 Chd free. Sun Sept 19 (2-6)*

¶**4 Church Street** ▨▧ (Lewis Hart) Hadleigh. Approx 6m W of Ipswich on the A1071. 25yds from St Mary's Church. ⅓-acre old walled garden. Wide range of lesser known plants. Many clematis, penstemon, iris, euphorbia, alpines; trees and shrubs incl. sorbus, skimmia, indigofera. Collection of plants in sinks and tubs. *Donation box. Open by appt* Tel **0473 822418**

13 Drapers Lane ▨▧ (Mr & Mrs Borrett) Ditchingham. 1¼m Bungay off the B1332 towards Norwich. ⅓-acre containing many interesting, unusual plants including 80 plus varieties of hardy geraniums, climbers and shrubs. Herbaceous perennials a speciality. Owner maintained. TEAS. *Adm 60p Chd free. Sun, Mon May 2, 3 (10-4). Also any time by appt* Tel **0986 893366**

Dunburgh House &▧ (Major & Mrs Lorimer Mason) Geldeston. 2m N of Beccles just off Norwich Rd A146 6m E of Bungay off the Yarmouth Rd A143. 3¾ acres of an all-year round garden of interest; mature and recently planted; thousands of bulbs; shrubs, herbaceous and rose garden; very large kitchen garden, vegetable, fruit, greenhouses and conservatory. TEAS in aid of the restoration fund of Gillingham Church *Adm £1.50 Chd free. Sun, Mon, May 2, 3 (2-5.30)*

Euston Hall ▨ (The Duke & Duchess of Grafton) on the A1088 12m N of Bury St Edmunds. 3m S of Thetford. Terraced lawns; herbaceous borders, rose garden, C17 pleasure grounds, lake. C18 house open; famous collection of paintings. C17 church; temple by William Kent. Craft shop. Wheelchair access to gardens, tea-room and shop only. TEAS in Old Kitchen. *Adm house & garden £2.25 OAPs £1.50, Chd 50p Parties of 12 or more £1.50 per head (Share to NGS). Thurs June 3 to Sept 30; Suns June 27 & Sept 5 (2.30-5)*

Felsham House &▨ (The Hon David & Mrs Erskine) Felsham 7m SE of Bury St Edmunds off A134, 8m W of Stowmarket via Rattlesden. 5 acres incl meadow with wild flowers, established trees, shrubs, roses; herb garden. TEAS. *Adm £1.20 Chd 50p. Sun July 11 (2-6)*

¶**Fort Henry** &▨ (Gerald Ashton Esq) Martlesham Heath. Turn L at Telecom roundabout into Eagle Way, approx ¼m turn 2nd L into Lancaster Rd which leads into York Rd. Small interesting garden planted with box parterres, roses and bedding. Deep pond and fountains. Medusa's Grotto. (Unsuitable for small children). *Adm £1 (Share to Ipswich Diabetic Centre). Suns July 4, Sept 5 (2-6)*

Gable House &⌂▨ (Mr & Mrs John Foster) Redisham. 3½m S of Beccles. Mid-way between Beccles and Halesworth on Ringsfield-Ilketshall St Lawrence Rd. Garden of 1 acre, mixed borders, fruit and vegetables. Home-made TEAS. *Adm £1 (Share to St Peters Church Redisham, Beccles, Suffolk). Sun June 13 (2-5.30). Suns from May to Sept by appt* Tel **0502 79298**

¶**Garden House** &⌂▨ (Mr & Mrs J F Maskelyne) Moulton. 3m E of Newmarket. Follow signs for Gazeley. In Moulton village turn R down Brookside bordering the village green. 9m from Bury St Edmunds. A very interesting ¾-acre garden maintained by owners with clematis,

...ses, small woodland area and alpines near the house. ...EAS. *Adm £1 Chd 50p. Sun June 13 (2-5.30)*

...ifford's Hall ✗ (Mrs J M Gardner) Wickhambrook; 10m ...W of Bury St Edmunds, 10m NE of Haverhill, ¾m from ...umbers' Arms, Wickhambrook in direction of Bury St ...dmunds on A143, garden ¾m up lane. Medium-sized ...arden; roses; herbaceous borders. C15 moated manor ...ouse (not open). TEA. *Adm £1 Chd 25p (under 14). Suns ...pril 18, July 4 (2-5.30)*

...reat Thurlow Hall ও (Mr & Mrs George Vestey) Haver-...ll. N of Haverhill. Great Thurlow village on B1061 from ...ewmarket; 3½m N of junction with A143 Haverhill-Bury ...Edmunds rd. 20 acres. Walled kitchen garden, herba-...ous borders, shrubs, roses, spacious lawns, river walk, ...out lake. Daffodils and blossom. TEA. *Adm £1.50 Chd ...ee. Sun April 4 (2-5)*

...rundisburgh Hall ও✗❀ (Lady Cranworth) 3m W of ...oodbridge on B1079, ¼m S of Grundisburgh on Grun-...sburgh to Ipswich Rd. Approx 5 acres walled garden ...th yew hedges; wisteria walk and mixed borders. Old ...se garden; lawns and ponds. TEAS. *Adm £1.50 Chd free ...hare to St Marys Grundisburgh, St Botolphs Culpho). ...ns May 30, June 27 (2-6)*

...artshall Farm ✗❀ (Mr & Mrs J D L Wight) Walsham-...-Willows, 12m NE of Bury St Edmunds. Take Westhorpe ...from Walsham-le-Willows; signed 2m on left. Gardens, ...boretum, woodland (shelter, ornamental), created since ...68, on 16 acres round farmstead. Around 2,000 var-...ies of rare and beautiful trees, shrubs, conifers, peren-...als, bulbs, alpines and roses. TEAS *Adm £1 Chd 50p. ...n May 9 (2-6) Coach parties by appt.* **Tel 0359 259 ...8**

...wstead Gardens ✗❀ 4m S of Bury St. Edmunds, ...gnposted from 2nd roundabout at Southgate Green. In ...wstead turn L by telephone box onto village green. ...rdens on L hand side. TEA. *Combined adm £1 Chd 50p. ...n April 25 (2-6)*

Beech Cottage (Major & Mrs Carr) Cottage type gar-den with small stream and excellent spring rockery. Previously fuchsia nursery and many varieties still grown, both outdoors and under glass. Small meadow with livestock and magnificent beech trees. Shown in conjunction with South View

South View (Glyn David Hammond) 11 acres, com-prising garden with perennial borders, shrubs, water garden, kitchen garden and orchard. Walk through pastured field and brookside wood, mainly native trees and shrubs, wildlife pond, all maintained with em-phasis on wildlife conservation

...illwatering Farmhouse ও✗ (Sir Patrick & Lady Salt) ...ngham. Approx 9m NE Bury St Edmunds. Leave A143 ...Ixworth by-pass at roundabout signed Walsham-le-...llows. Farmhouse is 2m along on R handside. DO NOT ...rn down into Langham. Young (15yrs old) garden of 1 ...re with water garden, large variety of roses, shrubs and ...rennials. *Combined adm with* **The Lawn** *£1.50 OAPs £1 ...d free. Sun June 20 (2.30-6)*

Holbecks ❀ (Sir Joshua & Lady Rowley) Hadleigh. From Hadleigh High St turn into Duke St signed to Lower Lay-ham; immediately over bridge go right up concrete rd to top of hill. 3 acres; early C19 landscape terraced and walled gardens, flowerbeds, roses and ornamental shrubs. TEA. *Adm £1 Chd 25p (Share to Suffolk Historic Churches Trust). Sun July 11 (2-5.30)*

Keepers Cottage ও✗ (Mr & Mrs P Coy) Bury Rd Law-shall. 6m S of Bury St Edmunds; from A134 Bury St Ed-munds to Sudbury turn R at Lawshall signpost; proceed for 2½m through village to T junction turn R on Bury Road and proceed for ½m. ½-acre garden surrounding a C15 thatched cottage; many mixed borders of shrubs; perennials; roses and bulbs; backing on to woodland. TEAS. *Adm £1 Chd free. Sun May 16 (2-6)*

The Lawn ও (Mr & Mrs R Martineau) Walsham-le-Willows. 10m NE of Bury St Edmunds. Leave A143 on Ix-worth by-pass at sign Walsham-le-Willows. House on R ½m short of village. 3-acres, herbaceous borders, lawns, small walled garden. The main garden overlooks parkland. Woodland walk, short circuit 5-10 mins. Large circuit 10-15 mins. TEAS. *Combined adm with* **Hillwatering Farm** *£1.50 OAPs £1 Chd free. Sun June 20 (2.30-6)*

Little Thurlow Hall ও❀ (Mr & Mrs E Vestey) Haverhill. On B1061 between Newmarket and Haverhill, 6m from Haverhill, in middle of village. 6 acres. A re-made garden started in 1987; herbaceous and lily borders; sunken gar-den; ancient canals; formal box edged herb and kitchen gardens, greenhouses and conservatory, woodland walk and wildflower area. Paddocks with horses. TEA. *Adm £1.50 Chd 50p. Sun June 20 (2-6)*

Long Melford Gardens Gardens on Long Melford Village Green. Ely House, Church Walk, 100yds N and Conduit House 100yds S of Clare Road A1092. 2 Pound Cottages 100yds S of Conduit House. Sun House in centre at vil-lage opp the Cock and Bell. TEAS at Sun House. Long Melford is 3½m N of Sudbury on A134. *Combined adm £2 or 80p per garden Chd free. Sun July 4 (2-6)*

Conduit House ও (Sir Harold & Lady Atcherley) Ap-prox. 1-acre partly walled garden with old trees; old-fashioned roses and mixed borders

Ely House ও (Miss Jean M Clark) Small walled gar-den; mixed borders; ponds and fountains

2 Pound Cottages ✗❀ (Dr Jack Litchfield) A small front garden and a long narrow back garden of approx ¼-acre; informally planted with a wide variety of shrub and herbaceous plants including many lilies and unusual plants.

¶**Sun House** ✗ (Mr & Mrs John Thompson) Two at-tractive adjacent walled gardens with roses, shrubs and herbaceous borders. Interesting collection of cle-matis. Water and architectural features

Magnolia House ✗ (Mr Mark Rumary) On A1120 in centre of Yoxford. Small, completely walled village gar-den. Mixed borders with flowering trees, shrubs, climbers, bulbs, hardy and tender plants. *Adm £1 Chd free. Sun July 4 (2.30-6)*

¶**Moat Cottage** ⚥ (Mr Stephen Ingerson) Great Green. Cockfield. Take A134 S from Bury St Edmunds. After Sicklesmore village turn sharp L for Cockfield Green and R at 1st Xrds. Follow winding rd through Bradfield St Clare. At Great Green fork L Moat Cottage is opp garage at far end. 1 acre of enchanting cottage garden created over the last 6yrs and forever changing. The garden is divided into smaller areas incl white, herb and rose gardens, herbaceous borders, with a kitchen garden that provides the owners with all year round vegetables. Teas at Old Rectory (½m). Combined adm with **The Old Rectory** £1.50 OAPs £1 Chd free. Sun June 20 (2-6)

Nedging Hall &⚥ (Mr & Mrs Brian Buckle) Nedging. 4m N of Hadleigh via A1141 towards Bildeston. House on R (E) side of road. 15 acres of park- like garden, especially good in spring with bulbs. Lake and many fine trees; baby lambs. TEAS. Adm £1 Chd 50p. Sun April 18 (2-5)

North Cove Hall &❀ (Mr & Mrs B Blower) Beccles. Just off A146 3½m E of Beccles on Lowestoft Rd. Take sign to North Cove. 5 acres of garden; large pond; mature and interesting young trees. Walled kitchen garden; shrub roses; herbaceous borders; woodland walks. TEAS. Adm £1.50 Chd free. Sun July 11 (2.30-6)

The Old Rectory, Brinkley ⚥ (Mr & Mrs Mark Coley) 6m S of Newmarket B1051, then B1052. After Brinkley post office, 1st left down Hall Lane, Old Rectory at bottom on R with white gates. 2-acre garden created over last 15yrs; mixed borders and some interesting trees. TEA. Adm £1 Chd 50p. Sun June 6 (2-6)

¶**The Old Rectory, Parsonage Green** & (Mr & Mrs David Marshall) Cockfield. Take A134 S from Bury St Edmunds. After 5 ½m turn SE onto A1141, signposted Lavenham. 1 ¼m turn L (E) signposted Cockfield and Stowmarket. Old Rectory 1m on R by small green. ½m to Moat Cottage. Approx 8 acres with moat, lawns, mature trees and walled garden with herbaceous beds. TEA. Combined adm with **Moat Cottage** £1.50 OAPS £1 Chd free. Sun June 20 (2-6)

¶**Orchard End** &⚥❀ (Mr & Mrs N C Cass) Rishangles. 3m S of Eye on rd between Occold and Bedingfield. ½-acre recently created garden with island beds and water feature. Mostly perennials and shrubs but also extensive and interesting geranium collection. 2 acres being developed for wildlife. TEAS. Adm £1.50 OAPs £1 Chd free. Sats, Suns June 5, 6, 19, 20, July 3, 4 (2-6)

Pippin Cottage &❀ (Mr & Mrs Sanders) Woodditton. Leave E end of Newmarket on B1061 for Haverhill, almost immediately fork L (signpost Woodditton) continue approx 3m and at 2nd Xroads turn R. Garden is 2nd thatched cottage on L nearly opposite Three Blackbirds public house. 1½-acre garden designed and planted by owners, surrounding a C17 cottage; large collection of trees, shrubs, hardy perennials, shrub roses etc; natural pond and paved areas covered with alpines, paddock and small wooded area; TEAS. Adm £1 Chd 30p. Suns June 13, 27 (2-6). Also open by appointment Tel 0638 730857

¶**Playford Hall** & (Mrs R D Innes). Edge of Playford Village, situated between Ipswich and Woodbridge. Moated

Elizabethan house surrounded by 10-acre garden wi⟨th⟩ lake, lawns, fine trees, herbaceous borders enclosed ⟨by⟩ yew hedges, shrub borders with many rare shrubs and in⟨te⟩resting selection of shrub and climbing roses. TEA⟨S⟩ Adm £1.50 Chd free. Sun June 20 (2-6)

The Priory &❀ (Mr & Mrs H F A Engleheart) Stoke-b⟨y⟩ Nayland (1m); 8m N of Colchester, entrance on B1068 ⟨⟩ to Sudbury. Interesting 9-acre garden with fine vie⟨w⟩ over Constable countryside, with lawns sloping down ⟨⟩ small lakes & water garden; fine trees, rhododendrons ⟨⟩ azaleas; walled rose garden; mixed borders & ornament⟨⟩ greenhouse. Wide variety of plants; peafowl. TEAS. Ad⟨m⟩ £1.50 Chd free. Sun May 30 (2-6)

Redisham Hall &⚥ (Mr Palgrave Brown) SW of Beccle⟨s⟩ From A145 1½m S of Beccles, turn W on to Ringsfiel⟨d⟩ Bungay Rd. Beccles, Halesworth or Bungay, all within 6⟨m⟩ 5 acres; parkland and woods 400 acres. Georgian hou⟨se⟩ C18 (not shown). Safari rides. TEAS (3.30-5 only). Ad⟨m⟩ £1.50 Chd free (Share to East Suffolk Macmillan Nurse⟨s⟩) Sun July 11 (2-6)

¶**Riverside House** ⚥ (Mr & Mrs A C W Bone) Clare. C⟨on⟩ the A1092 leading out of Clare towards Haverhill; almo⟨st⟩ opp the Dalgety grain silo. Approx 1 acre riverside ga⟨r⟩den, mainly walled, laid out with lawns, trees, shrub⟨s⟩ bulbs and herbaceous borders. Teas at 'Kate's Kitchen' Clare. Adm £1.50 Chd free. Sun May 9 (2-6)

The Rookery &⚥❀ (Captain & Mrs Sheepshanks) Eyk⟨e⟩ 5m E of Woodbridge turn N off B1084 Woodbridge-Orfo⟨rd⟩ Rd when sign says Rendlesham. 10-acre garden; plante⟨d⟩ as an arboretum with many rare specimen trees a⟨nd⟩ shrubs; landscaped on differing levels, providing view⟨s⟩ and vistas; the visitor's curiosity is constantly aroused ⟨by⟩ what is round the next corner; ponds, bog garden, shru⟨b⟩bery, alpines, garden stream, bulbs, herbaceous borde⟨rs⟩ and a 1-acre vineyard. TEAS. Adm £1.50 Chd 50p. Su⟨ns⟩ May 16, June 20 (2-6)

Rosemary &⚥❀ (Mrs N E M Finch) Rectory Hill. Turn ⟨off⟩ the A12 at East Bergholt and follow rd round to chur⟨ch⟩ Rosemary is 100yds down from the church on L. Matu⟨re⟩ 1-acre garden adapted over 20yrs from an old orcha⟨rd⟩ loosely divided into several smaller gardens; mixed bo⟨r⟩ders; herb garden; over 50 old roses, unusual plant⟨s⟩ TEAS. Adm £1 Chd free. Sun June 13 (2-6) and by ap⟨pt⟩ May & June Tel 0206 298241

The Rotunda, Ickworth Park &⚥ (The National Trus⟨t⟩) Horringer. 3m SW of Bury St. Edmunds on W side ⟨⟩ A143 (155:TL8161) 30 acres of garden. South gardens r⟨e⟩stored to stylized Italian landscape to reflect extraor⟨di⟩nary design of the Rotunda. Fine orangery, agapanth⟨us⟩ geraniums and fatsias. North gardens informal wild flow⟨er⟩ lawns with wooded walk; the Buxus collection, great va⟨r⟩iety of evergreens and Victorian stumpery. New planti⟨ngs⟩ of cedars. TEAS. Adm £1.50 (park and garden) Chd 5⟨0p⟩ Sun Sept 19 (10-4.30)

By Appointment Gardens. Avoid the crowds. Good chance of a tour by owner. See garden description for telephone number.

Ruggs Cottage &✿❀ (Mrs Patricia Short) Raydon. 12m NE of Colchester and 11m S of Ipswich, off A12 between Colchester and Ipswich. Turn N on B1070 towards Hadleigh. Raydon is 2m from A12. Car park available at Chequers Inn. Ruggs Cottage is on R just before Chequers Inn. ¾-acre designer plantsman's garden with wide selection of flowering shrubs and trees, herbaceous and unusual plants, small herb garden, grassy walks, roses and bulbs, small greenhouse with mimosa. TEAS by PCC Suns only. No plants Aug 8. *Adm £1.50 Chd free. Suns May 23, June 20, Aug 8, (2-6) Mons May 24, June 21, Aug 9, Tues May 25, June 22 (11-3)*

Rumah Kita & (Mr & Mrs I R Dickings) (O/S map ref TM223665) Bedfield is situated 2½m NW of the A1120 on secondary rd turning between Earl Soham and Saxted Green. 2-acre garden designed and planted by owners since 1978. Contains many rare and interesting plants; mixed borders, formal and informal; parterre for spring and summer effect; blue white and silver pond garden. Extensive collection of half hardy perennials. TEAS. *Adm £1 Chd free. Suns June 20, Sept 5 (2-6) and by appt until end Oct* Tel 0728 628401

St Stephens Cottage &✿❀ (Mr & Mrs D Gibbs) Spexhall, 2m N of Halesworth. Approx 1-acre garden. Features inc natural pond leading to bog, herb and white garden. Many established deciduous and coniferous trees and shrubs; rockeries; herbaceous borders and island beds containing interesting and unusual plants, many for sale. Members of the Cottage Garden Society and Hardy Plant Society. Conservatory featured on Gardeners World. TEAS if dry. *Adm £1 Chd free. Suns May 16, Sept 26 (10-5), also by appt all year* Tel 0986 873394

Somerleyton Hall & (The Lord & Lady Somerleyton) 5m NW of Lowestoft. Off B1074. Large garden; famous maze; beautiful trees and avenue. House C16 added to 1844. Grinling Gibbons' carving, library, tapestries. Mentioned in Domesday Book. Miniature railway. Light lunches & TEAS. *Adm £3.50 OAPs £2.70 Chd £1.60. House open 2-5 Gardens 12.30-5: Easter Sun to end Sept, Thurs, Suns, Bank Hol Mons; Tues, Weds, July and Aug; in addition miniature railway will be running on most days. For NGS (Share to Samaritans) Sun June 13*

The Spong ❀ (Joseph Barrett Esq & John Kirby Esq) Groton, Boxford. 5m W of Hadleigh on A1071. Leave Boxford via Swan Street, bear R at Fox and Hounds follow main road past Groton Church, take next R. The Spong is the pink house at the bottom of the hill. 7-yr-old garden of ⅔-acre; approached over stream; planned as a series of small gardens due to irregular shape; mixed herbaceous/shrubs; ponds; pergola. TEA. *Adm £1 Chd 50p. Sun June 13 (2-6)*

Stour Cottage ✿ (Mr J H Gill) East Bergholt. Halfway between Ipswich and Colchester on the A12, turn at the sign for E Bergholt, follow rd around to the R towards the village centre. Car parking in the centre of the village. Take the lane to the R by the post office and Stour Cottage Garden entrance is the first large gate on the L side

of lane. Formal walled garden of about ⅓-acre, Italianate in feeling. Many unusual half hardy shrubs and climbers. Features include fountain water garden and greenhouse with interesting collection of tender plants. *Adm £1 Chd free. Sun June 13 (2-6)*

¶**Thrift Farm** &✿❀ (Mr & Mrs H A Oddy) Cowlinge. 7m SE of Newmarket, centrally between Cowlinge, Kirtling and Gt Bradley. On the Gt Bradley rd from Kirtling. Picturesque thatched house set in a cottage style garden extending to approx 1½ acres. After the 1987 storm the garden took on its new mantle of island beds filled with herbaceous plants amongst shrubs and ornamental trees in great variety. It is a garden which encourages you to walk round but many will just sit and enjoy the vistas. TEAS. *Adm £1 Chd 50p. Sun June 6 (2-6). Also by appt* Tel 0440 83274

25 Westbury Avenue &✿❀ (Mr & Mrs D J Payne) Bury St Edmunds. 1m West of town centre. Parkway roundabout (Kings Rd)-Queens Rd-Westbury Ave. ½-acre to lawns, shrubs and trees, many spring flowers and bulbs. Heathers, conifers, fuschias, roses. Patio and sunken garden. Water features, seasonal beds and borders, greenhouse. TEA. *Adm £1 Chd under 14 free. Sun March 21 (12-5) also by appt* Tel 0284 755 374

West Stow Hall & (Mrs M I C M Barrère) West Stow. Take A1101 NE from Bury St Edmunds to Mildenhall. Turn R between Lackford and Icklingham, for West Stow and Anglo-Saxon village, 2m on L. 7-acre garden created in 1980; mixed borders; walled and gravel gardens; orchard; wild gardens including meadow, woodland and stream; dovecote and outbuildings. C16 gatehouse and C16-C19 House (not open). TEAS *Adm £1 Chd 50p (Share to National Association for Colitis and Crohn's disease). Sun Aug 15 (12-6); also by appointment* Tel 0284 728771

Whepstead Hall &✿❀ (Mr & Mrs A J Root) Brockley Rd. From Bury St Edmunds take A143 Haverhill Rd turn L onto B1066 approx 4m on R. Oak gates and red macadam drive. 6½ acres of daffodils, spring flowers, ornamental fish ponds and fine views over Suffolk countryside. TEAS. *Adm £1.25 Chd 50p. Mon April 12 (12-5). Also by appt* Tel 0284 735746

Woottens &✿❀ (M Loftus) Blackheath Rd. Woottens is situated between A12 and B1123 follow signposts to Wenhaston. Woottens is a small romantic garden with attached cottage nursery, in all about ¾-acre; scented leafed pelargoniums, old-fashioned pinks, violas, cranesbills, lilies, salvias, osteospermums, penstemons primulas, etc. TEAS. *Adm 70p OAPs 50p Chd 20p. Suns May 16, June 13, July 11, Aug 15 (2-6)*

Wyken Hall &❀ (Mr & Mrs K Carlisle) Stanton, 9m NE from Bury St Edmunds along A143; leave A143 between Ixworth and Stanton. 4-acre garden much developed recently; with knot and herb gardens; old-fashioned rose garden; wild garden; lawns and gazebo; shrubs and trees. Woodland walk, vineyard. TEA. *Adm £2 OAPs £1 Chd free. Sun June 6 (2-6)*

Surrey

Hon County Organiser:	Lady Heald, Chilworth Manor, Guildford GU4 8NL Tel 0483 61414
Assistant Hon County Organisers:	Mrs J Foulsham, Vale End, Albury, Guildford GU5 9BE Tel 048 641 2594
	Mrs D Hargreaves, The Old Rectory, Albury, Guildford GU5 9AX Tel 048 641 3463
	Mrs P Karslake, Oakfield Cottage, Guildford Road, Cranleigh GU6 8PF Tel 0483 273010
	Mrs J Pearcy, Far End, Pilgrims Way, Guildford GU4 8AD Tel 0483 63093
Hon County Treasurer:	Lt Cdr D J Dampier, Chipperfield, Dedeswell Drive, West Clandon, Guildford GU4 7TQ Tel 0483 222472

DATES OF OPENING

By appointment
For telephone number and other details see garden descriptions

Brookwell, Bramley. May to Sept
Chauffeur's Flat, Tandridge. May 16-31, June 20 to July 4
Chilworth Manor, Guildford
The Coppice, Reigate
2 Court Avenue, Old Coulsdon
Coverwood Lakes, Ewhurst
High Meadow, Churt
Hookwood Farm House, West Horsley. May to July
Knightsmead, Chipstead
Pinewood House, Worplesdon Hill, Woking. April to Oct
Postford House, Chilworth
Rise Top Cottage, (2 The Cottage) Mayford. May & June
South Park Farm, South Godstone. April, May & June
Spring Cottage, Cranleigh
Unicorns, Farnham. End of April to end of Aug
Vann, Hambledon
Walton Poor, Ranmore Common
Woodside, Send. May only
Woodyers, Wonersh
Yew Tree Cottage, Haslemere. June & July
67 York Road, Cheam

Regular openers
For details see garden descriptions

Coverwood Lakes, Ewhurst. Various dates April, May & Oct
Crosswater Farm, Churt. Daily May 1 to June 13
25 Little Woodcote Estate, Wallington. Weds Sats April 3 to Sat Sept 25
Painshill, Cobham. Suns April 11 to Oct 17
Ramster, Chiddingfold. April 24 to June 6

Tilgates, Bletchingley. Daily from March 1 except Christmas Day.
Walton Poor, Ranmore Common. Wed to Sun Easter to Sept 30

March 14 Sunday
Maryland, Worplesdon
April 3 Saturday to April 7 Wednesday
Chilworth Manor, Guildford
April 4 Sunday
Tilgates, Bletchingley
Whinfold, Hascombe
April 7 Wednesday
Brook Lodge Farm Cottage, Blackbrook
April 11 Sunday
Hascombe Court, Godalming
High Meadow, Churt
Walton Poor, Ranmore Common
Wintershall, Bramley
April 12 Monday
High Meadow, Churt
Vann, Hambledon
April 13 Tuesday to April 18 Sunday
Vann, Hambledon
April 14 Wednesday
Applegarth Cottage, Westcott
April 17 Saturday
Claygate Gardens
April 18 Sunday
Applegarth Cottage, Westcott
Highlands, Givons Grove, Leatherhead
Lodkin, Hascombe
April 21 Wednesday
The Coppice, Reigate
April 25 Sunday
Applegarth Cottage, Westcott
Claygate Gardens
Street House, Thursley
Woodside, Send
May 2 Sunday to May 7 Friday
Malthouse Farm, Hambledon ‡
May 2 Sunday
Compton Lodge, Moor Park, Farnham

Feathercombe, nr Hambledon ‡
Tilgates, Bletchingley
May 3 Monday
Feathercombe, nr Hambledon ‡
Vann, Hambledon ‡
May 4 Tuesday to May 9 Sunday
Vann, Hambledon ‡
May 8 Saturday to May 12 Wednesday
Chilworth Manor, Guildford
May 9 Sunday
Coverwood Lakes, Ewhurst
Hascombe Court, Godalming
Highlands, Givons Grove, Leatherhead
Wintershall, Bramley
May 15 Saturday
Claremont Landscape Garden, Esher
Pyrford Court, nr Woking
May 16 Sunday
Compton Lodge, Moor Park, Farnham
Coverwood Lakes, Ewhurst
Fidlers Grove, South Godstone
Lime Tree Cottage, Weybridge
Montfleury, Virginia Water ‡
Postford House, Chilworth
Pyrford Court, nr Woking
87 Upland Road, Sutton
Westbourn, Virginia Water ‡
Whinfold, Hascombe ‡‡
Winkworth Arboretum, Hascombe ‡‡
May 19 Wednesday
Broom House, Headley, nr Leatherhead
Lime Tree Cottage, Weybridge
Postford House, Chilworth
Rise Top Cottage, (2 The Cottage) Mayford,
May 23 Sunday
Munstead Wood, nr Godalming
Postford House, Chilworth
Windlesham Park, nr Bagshot
May 26 Wednesday
Rise Top Cottage, (2 The Cottage) Mayford,

May 29 Saturday
Crosswater Farm, Churt
Merrist Wood College,
Worplesdon
May 30 Sunday
Brook Lodge Farm Cottage,
Blackbrook
Crosswater Farm, Churt ‡
Feathercombe, nr Hambledon
High Meadow, Churt ‡
15 Highview Road, Lightwater
Hookwood Farm House, West
Horsley
Merrist Wood College,
Worplesdon
Munstead Wood, Godalming
Street House, Thursley
May 31 Monday
Crosswater Farm, Churt ‡
Feathercombe, nr Hambledon
High Meadow, Churt ‡
June 2 Wednesday
Hookwood Farm House, West
Horsley
**June 6 Sunday to June 12
Saturday**
Spring Cottage, Cranleigh
Tilgates, Bletchingley
June 6 Sunday
2 Chinthurst Lodge, Wonersh ‡
Tilgates, Bletchingley
Vann, Hambledon
Walton Poor, Ranmore Common
Woodyers, Wonersh ‡
**June 7 Monday to June 12
Saturday**
Vann, Hambledon
**June 12 Saturday to June 16
Wednesday**
Chilworth Manor, Guildford
June 12 Saturday
Brookwell, Bramley
Claygate Gardens
Knightsmead, Chipstead
June 13 Sunday
Brookwell, Bramley
Hampton, Seale, Farnham
Hascombe Court, Godalming ‡
Haslehurst, Haslemere ‡‡
High Hazard, Blackheath
Knightsmead, Chipstead
Lodkin, Hascombe ‡
Yew Tree Cottage, Haslemere ‡‡
June 19 Saturday
Brook Lodge Farm Cottage,
Blackbrook
The Round House, Hascombe
South Park, Bletchingley

June 20 Sunday
Brook Lodge Farm Cottage,
Blackbrook
Claygate Gardens
East Clandon Gardens
Merrist Wood College,
Worplesdon
The Round House, Hascombe
South Park, Bletchingley
Street House, Thursley
Thanescroft, Shamley Green
June 26 Saturday
The Moorings, Horley
June 27 Sunday
Moleshill House, Cobham
The Moorings, Horley
Vale End, Albury
June 30 Wednesday
The Coppice, Reigate
July 3 Saturday
South Park Farm, South Godstone
July 4 Sunday
High Meadow, Churt
Maryland, Worplesdon ‡
South Park Farm, South
Godstone ‡‡
Tilgates, Bletchingley ‡‡
White House, nr Guildford ‡
July 5 Monday
High Meadow, Churt
South Park Farm, South Godstone
July 7 Wednesday
Broom House, Headley, nr
Leatherhead
July 10 Saturday
2 Court Avenue, Old Coulsdon
Little Mynthurst Farm, Norwood
Hill
41 Shelvers Way, Tadworth
July 11 Sunday
Little Mynthurst Farm, Norwood
Hill
41 Shelvers Way, Tadworth
**July 17 Saturday to July 21
Wednesday**
Chilworth Manor, Guildford
July 17 Saturday
2 Court Avenue, Old Cousldon
July 18 Sunday
Polesden Lacey, Bookham
67 York Road, Cheam
July 21 Wednesday
Brook Lodge Farm Cottage,
Blackbrook
67 York Road, Cheam
July 25 Sunday
Street House, Thursley

July 28 Wednesday
The Coppice, Reigate
August 1 Sunday
Tilgates, Bletchingley
Vale End, Albury
**August 7 Saturday to August
11 Wednesday**
Chilworth Manor, Guildford
August 8 Sunday
Chiddingfold House. Chiddingfold
The Coppice, Reigate
Odstock, Bletchingley
August 15 Sunday
Brook Lodge Farm Cottage,
Blackbrook
Hay Place, Ripley
August 22 Sunday
Dunsborough Park, Ripley
August 29 Sunday
Annesley & Springfold, Haslemere
East Clandon Gardens
High Meadow, Churt
Street House, Thursley
August 30 Monday
East Clandon Gardens
High Meadow, Churt
September 5 Sunday
Tilgates, Bletchingley
September 19 Sunday
Haslehurst, Haslemere
September 26 Sunday
Claremont Landscape Garden,
Esher
Maryland, Worplesdon
Street House, Thursley
October 3 Sunday
Painshill, Cobham
Tilgates, Bletchingley
White House, nr Guildford
October 10 Sunday
Walton Poor, Ranmore Common
October 17 Sunday
Pyrford Court, nr Woking
October 31 Sunday
Lodkin, Hascombe
November 7 Sunday
Tilgates, Bletchingley
December 5 Sunday
Tilgates, Bletchingley

1994
January 2 Sunday
Tilgates, Bletchingley
February 6 Sunday
Tilgates, Bletchingley
March 6 Sunday
Tilgates, Bletchingley

DESCRIPTIONS OF GARDENS

Annesley ⅙❀ (Capt & Mrs Trechman) Three Gates Lane, Haslemere. First right from Haslemere High St (A286), ¼m down lane on right. 3 acres; shrubs, roses, annuals and items of interest to flower arrangers. Also open, entrance from Annesley, **Springfold** ⅙ (Mrs G St G Kelton) 18 acres overlooking Sussex Weald with magnificent views; mainly shrubs & woodland. Home-made TEAS. *Combined adm £1 Chd 20p. Sun Aug 29 (2-6)*

Applegarth Cottage ✿❀ (Mr & Mrs K P A Mathews) Westcott. Westcott is 2m on Guildford Rd (A25) from Dorking. Turn up Longmore Lane by Cricketers public house, past church on R. Take 1st L down Hildens, Applegarth Cottage is 8th house on R. 2-acre specialist camellia garden, also magnolias, rhododendrons and azaleas. Fine views towards Ranmore and Leith Hill; lawns; bulbs etc. Part of garden suitable for wheelchairs. Cream TEAS. *Adm £1 Chd 50p (Share to Age Concern, Basingstoke & Westcott Church Fund). Wed April 14, Suns Apr 18, 25 Cake stall on Suns April 18, 25 Madrigals with the Frensham Choir on Sun April 25 (3-5.30)*

Brook Lodge Farm Cottage ঊ✿❀ (Mrs Basil Kingham) Blackbrook, 3m S of Dorking. Take left hand turning for Blackbrook off A24, 1m S of Dorking 500yds past Plough Inn. 3-acre 45 year old plantsman's garden with wide selection of flowering trees, shrubs, herbaceous plants; large greenhouse, kitchen garden and herb garden. TEAS. *Adm £1.50 Chd free (Share to St Catherine's Hospice, Crawley). Weds April 7, July 21 (11-3), Sat June 19, Suns May 30, June 20, Aug 15 (2-6)*

Brookwell ঊ✿❀ (Mr & Mrs P R Styles) 1½m S of Bramley on A281; turn R into private road-bridleway in Birtley Green. 2-acre garden with lake and woodland. Mixed borders, sunken garden, and knot garden planted with scented flowers and herbs. Collection of old roses, fruit tunnel and vegetable garden; greenhouses and conservatory. TEA. *Adm £1 Chd free (Share to St Andrew's Church, Grafham Restoration Fund). Sat June 12, Sun June 13, by appt May-Sept (2-6)* **Tel 0483 893423**

Broom House ✿❀ (Mr & Mrs G A Cannon) Headley. From Leatherhead by-pass (A24) take B2033 to Headley. Travel 1.6m. At bottom of Tot Hill turn R into lay-by next to Hyde Farm. Park in lay-by. Short walk along Crabtree Lane (a bridle path) to house. Situated on edge of Headley Heath. 2 acres of sloping lawns; mature trees and conifers, shrubs, rhododendrons and azaleas, herbaceous borders; sandstone rockery; alpine sinks. Japanese water garden. Developed and maintained by owners since 1984. TEAS. *Adm £1 Chd free. Weds May 19, July 7 (2-5)*

¶Chauffeur's Flat ✿ (Mr & Mrs Richins) Tandridge. Tandridge Lane lies 1m W of Oxted off the A25. Drive adjacent to church ½m from A25. Pass Lodge to your R. Fork R. Continue through to Courtyard. This fascinating and romantic garden set in just under 1 acre of land with superb views. Uses an abundant variety of trees and shrubs intermingled with wild and cultivated plants. Mainly set on two levels as a series of mini gardens the upper having a more natural woodland feel, the lower using informal planting within a formal framework. Use has been made of old building materials. Only for the surefooted. *Adm £1 Chd 25p (Share to Waylands Special Needs Unit). By appt only May 16-31, June 20-July 4 (10-5)* **Tel 0883 715937** *before 9 am*

¶Chiddingfold House ✿ (Mr & Mrs J R Morrison) Chiddingfold. In Chiddingfold turn E at top of village green on rd marked to Dunsfold. Chiddingfold House about 500 yds from green on N side of rd. A large and interesting garden divided into many smaller ones incl a beautifully underplanted Pergola; rose garden; fish pond. Very fine lawns. *Adm £1 Chd 50p. Sun Aug 8 (2-5)*

Chilworth Manor ঊ✿ (Lady Heald) 3½m SE of Guildford. From A248, in centre of Chilworth village, turn up Blacksmith Lane. Bus: LC 425 Guildford-Dorking; alight Blacksmith Lane. Station: Chilworth. Garden laid out in C17; C18 walled garden added by Sarah, Duchess of Marlborough; spring flowers; flowering shrubs; herbaceous border. House C17 with C18 wing on site of C17 monastery recorded in Domesday Book; stewponds in garden date from monastic period. Flower decorations in house (Sats, Suns): April 3-7 Chobham Floral Club, May 8-12 Guildford Floral Decoration Society, June 12-16 Oxshott Flower Arrangement Society, July 17-21 St John's Floral Art Group, Aug 7-11 Ashtead Flower Arrangement Group. Free car park in attractive surroundings open from 12.30 for picnicking. TEAS (Sat, Sun, only). *Adm to garden £1.50 Chd free. Adm to house £1 Sat & Sun only (Share to Marie Curie Foundation Guildford Branch); Open Sats to Weds April 3-7, May 8-12, June 12-16, July 17-21 Aug 7-11 (2-6); also by appt* **Tel 0483 61414**

¶2 Chinthurst Lodge ঊ✿❀ (Mr & Mrs M R Goodridge) Wonersh. 4m S Guildford, A281 Guildford-Horsham. A Shalford turn E onto B2128 towards Wonersh. Just after Wonersh rd sign, before village, garden on R. 1-acre all year-round garden, herbaceous borders, large variety specimen trees and shrubs including Parrotia Persica; kitchen garden; fruit cage; two wells; ornamental pond and conservatory. See **Woodyers**. TEAS. *Adm £1 Chd free (Share to Guildford Branch Arthritis & Rheumatism Council). Sun June 6 (2-6)*

Claremont Landscape Garden ঊ✿ (The National Trust) ½m SE of Esher; on E side of A307 (No access from A3 by-pass). Station: Esher. Bus GL 415, alight at entrance gates. Earliest surviving English landscape garden; begun by Vanbrugh and Bridgeman before 1720; extended and naturalized by Kent; lake; island with pavilion, grotto and turf amphitheatre; viewpoints and avenues. TEAS 11-5.30. *Sat adm £1.70 Chd 85p, Sun adm £2.50 Chd £1.25 ▲For NGS Sat May 15, Sun Sept 26 (10-7)*

¶Claygate Gardens ✿ Drive into Claygate from Esher, Hinchley Wood, Hook or Chessington, look for the posters and arrows and pick up a local map at the 1st garden you call upon. Please start at any point especially on April 25. Teas at Foley Arms on April 25. *Combined Adm £2 Chd free Sun April 25 (4 gardens) £1.50 Sats April 17, June 12, Sun June 20 (Share to National Schizophrenia Fellowship June 12, 20)*

¶8 Dalmore Avenue (Miss P Greenwood). An ancient 80 year old hawthorn is a feature of this delightful small garden, designed, developed and maintained over the last 7 yrs by its loving owner. *Sun April 25 (2-6), Sat June 12 (11-5)*

¶27 Foley Road (Mr & Mrs D Love). Small, informal garden with some unusual plants and ornamental grasses of particular interest to the flower arranger. *Suns April 25 (2-6), June 20 (11-5)*

¶90 Foley Road (Mr & Mrs B Mathew). A plantsman's garden specialising in bulbs. The owner is the author of 13 bulb books. Collection of species irises. *Sat Apr 17 (11-5), Sun April 25 (2-6)*

21 Glenavon Close (Mr & Mrs P Barton). Some unusual shrubs and specimen trees. Informal layout and being gradually altered with a view to easier future management. *Sat April 17 (11-5), Sun April 25 (2-6)*

¶**37 Hare Lane** (Mr & Mrs C Ingram). Parking and entrance in Loseberry Rd. Originally a narrow garden, and designed by the owner to overcome this, more land was acquired a year ago and is being incorporated for fruit and vegetables; hardy geraniums, cistus, roses; some interesting green ideas. TEA. *Suns June 12, 20 (11-5)*

Cooksbridge, Fernhurst (See Sussex)

¶**Compton Lodge** ✿✿ (Mr & Mrs K J Kent) Farnham. 2m E of Farnham along A31 Hogs Back turn S down Crooksbury Rd at Barfield School signposted Milford & Elstead. 1m on R Compton Way, Compton Lodge 2nd house on R. 1 ¼-acre south facing sloping garden. Extensively renovated over the last 8 yrs by owners. Mature rhododendrons and azaleas; mature trees; raised herbaceous border with rose and clematis trellis; rose border. 2 ponds; heather bed and mixed beds; conservatory. *Adm £1 Chd 50p. Suns May 2, 16 (2-6)*

The Coppice ✿✿ (Mr & Mrs Bob Bushby) Reigate. M25 to junction 8. A217 (direction Reigate) down Reigate Hill immediately before level Xing turn R into Somers Rd cont as Manor Rd. At very end turn R into Coppice Lane 'The Coppice' approx 200yds on L. Partly suitable wheelchairs. 5½ acres redeveloped in last 4yrs. Mixed borders with interesting and unusual plants giving yr round interest. Pergola and conservatory, 2 large ornamental ponds. Frillarias and spring bulbs. April to May. Cream TEAS. *Adm £1.50 Chd 50p (Share to Winged Fellowship). Weds April 21, June 30, July 28, Sun Aug 8 (2-5); also by appt April to May Tel 0737 243158*

Copyhold, Fernhurst (See Sussex)

The Cottage see **Rise Top Cottage**.

Court Avenue ✿✿✿ (Dr K Heber) Old Coulsdon. Approach from London-Brighton Rd. A23 from south or M23/25, turn R B276 Old Coulsdon, from N after leaving Purley turn L B2030 Old Coulsdon. Follow rd to top of hill, immediately past parade of shops. Garden opposite Tudor Rose public house (food available). Flat compact garden approx ⅓-acre filled with herbaceous plants and shrubs in cottage garden layout; small ponds; good selection of unusual plants. Gives ideas for small gardens and use of foliage. TEA. *Adm £1 Chd 50p (Share to Coulsdon Rotary International Charities). Sats July 10, 17 (10-4.30); also by appt Tel 07375 54721*

Coverwood Lakes ✿✿✿ (Mr & Mrs C G Metson) Peaslake Rd, Ewhurst. 7m SW of Dorking. From A25 follow signs for Peaslake; garden ½m beyond Peaslake. Landscaped water and cottage gardens in lovely setting between Holmbury Hill and Pitch Hill; rhododendrons, azaleas, primulas, fine trees, both mature and young. 3½-acre Arboretum planted March 1990. Herd of pedigree Poll Hereford cattle and flock of sheep. (Mr & Mrs Nigel Metson). TEAS. *Adm (Gardens only) £1.50 Chd £1. (Farm and Gardens) £2 Chd £1 car park and Chd under 5 free. Gardens, Suns May 9, 16. Farm & gardens Wed May 26, Suns April 25, May 2, 23, 30 (2-6.30) Oct 24 hot soup and sandwiches (11-4.30). For NGS Suns May 9, 16 (2-5.30). Also by appt Tel 0306 731103*

Crosswater Farm ✿✿✿ (Mr & Mrs E G Millais) Churt. Farnham and Haslemere 6m, from A287 turn E into Jumps Road ½m N of Churt village centre. After ¼m turn acute left into Crosswater Lane and follow signs for Millais Nurseries. 6-acre woodland garden surrounded by NT Property. Plantsmans collection of rhododendrons and azaleas including many rare species collected in the Himalayas, and hybrids raised by the owners. Ponds, stream and companion plantings. Plants for sale from specialist Rhododendron nursery. TEAS in aid of Frensham Church Restoration on NGS days only. *Adm £1.50 Chd free. Daily May 1 to June 13 For NGS Sat, Sun, Mon May 29, 30, 31 (10-5) Tel 0252 792698*

Dunsborough Park ✿ (C F Hughesdon Esq) Ripley; entrance across Ripley Green. Bus: GL 715 alight Ripley village. Extensive rose gardens, herbaceous borders, greenhouses with tropical plants, water garden, parts suitable for wheelchair. Home-made TEAS. *Adm £1 Chd 50p. Sun Aug 22 (2-6)*

East Clandon Gardens ✿✿ Situated 4m E of Guildford on A246. This C16 hamlet, public house and C12 church is well worth a visit. From M25 turn S on A3, 1m L to Ripley. Turn L in Ripley, Rose Lane, then 2nd R. East Clandon is 4m. Home-made TEAS. Combined *Adm £1 Chd free. (Share to Cherry Trees, respite care for handicapped children). Sun June 20, Sun, Mon Aug 29,30 (2-6)*

> **Stuart Cottage** (Mr & Mrs J M Leader). ½-acre garden comprising rose walk, herbaceous beds, some unusual planting; small fountain and paved garden area. Old apple trees and a collection of chimney pots providing raised planting blend with the charm of the C16 flint and brick cottage
>
> **3 The Tithe Barn** (Mr & Mrs L Wharrad). As a contrast to the Stuart Cottage garden, No 3 The Tithe Barn in Ripley Rd provides a fine example of a small walled courtyard garden. The clever use of setts in circular patterns which lead to a small fountain and the many containers of plants are particularly worth noting. The owners are both artists and will be showing a collection of paintings in August

The Elms Kingston-on-Thames (see London)

Feathercombe ✿ (Miss Parker) nr Hambledon, S of Godalming. 2m from Milford Station on Hambledon Rd, turn to Feathercombe off rd between Hydestile Xrds and Merry Harriers. Fine view; flowering shrubs, trees, heathers. Garden designed and made by Eric Parker. Picnic area at garden. Tea Winkworth Arboretum. *Adm £1 Chd 10p (Share to Order of St John, Surrey). Suns, Mons May 2, 3, 30, 31 (2-6)*

¶**Fidlers Grove** ✿✿✿ (Miss Dunkels) South Godstone. Follow the A22 from South Godstone, S towards East Grinstead for 1m. Turn R into Carlton Rd opp Walkers Garden Centre. Take the 1st R then turn next R, then next L. This is a gravel lane between two fields leading to the entrance gate. Medium-sized country garden approx 1 acre containing an established border; small pond and newly planted shrubbery. The 'Studio Garden' is newer with small pond; vines and bonsai house. Scattered throughout the gardens is the work of Neil Godfrey, Sculptor. TEAS. *Adm £1 Chd 25p. Sun May 16 (2-6)*

Hall Grange, Croydon (see London)

Hampton &⚘ (Mr & Mrs Richard Thornton) Hampton. Situated S of A31 Hogs Back mid-way between Farnham & Guildford, approach from Seale, Puttenham or Elstead following rd to Cutt Mill ponds. Parkland and lakes unaltered from Humphrey Repton's original design of early C19; extensive lawns; summer flowering herbaceous borders; traditional walled garden. TEAS. *Adm £1 Chd free. Sun June 13 (2-6)*

Hascombe Court ⚘ (Mr & Mrs O Poulsen) 2½m SE of Godalming. Off B2130 between Hascombe and Godalming. Large garden with Jekyll influences, mostly designed by Percy Cane. Woodlands; rhododendrons; views; herbaceous border; terrace and rose garden. Japanese rock and water garden now restored; walled garden redesigned. TEAS. *Adm £1.50 Chd free. Suns April 11, May 9, June 13 (2-5)*

Haslehurst &⚘ (Mrs W H Whitbread) Bunch Lane, Haslemere. Turn off High St into Church Lane, leave church on left, carry on to T-junction, turn R, Hazelhurst, 2nd on L. 2½ acres; lawns, superb trees, rhododendrons, azaleas; various shrubs; paved rose garden, double herbaceous border; woodland rockery & waterfall. C15 Barn. See **Yew Tree Cottage**. TEA. *Adm £1 Chd 50p (Share to Queen Mary's Clothing Guild). Suns June 13, Sept 19 (2.15-6)*

Hay Place &⚘⚘ (Mr & Mrs H L Powell-Cullingford) Ripley. Going S on A3 take access rd B2215 through Ripley village 1m going S, L after Jovial Sailor Public House. Going N on A3 take access Rd B2215 across Burnt Common roundabout, pass Mitsubishi Garage on L. 220yds on R is Kiln Lane. Hay Place is situated 200yds up on L. Parking in field on R. Almost at entrance to Kiln Lane and in Hay Place. 2-acre garden created by owners since 1953. Heavy soil, many varieties of trees and shrubs. Small pond and rockery; extensive lawns and paths; kitchen garden. Pleasant views. Home-made TEAS. *Adm £1 Chd 50p (Share to Cherry Trees). Sun Aug 15 (2-6)*

¶**High Hazard** &⚘ (Mr & Mrs P C Venning) Blackheath, Guildford. 3½m SE of Guildford from B2128 at entry to Wonersh, turn L into Blackheath Lane, straight on at Xrds in village. Rear access to garden is 300 yds on R. Park in Heath car park a further 150 yds up lane. (No access to front of house which faces the cricket ground in use). ½-acre garden designed and laid out by the present owners 10 years ago. Herbaceous and mixed borders containing interesting and some unusual herbaceous perennial plants, a large number of which are for sale on the premises. TEAS. *Adm £1 Chd free (Share to St Joseph's Centre for Addiction, Holy Cross Hospital, Haslemere). Sun June 13 (2-6)*

Highlands ⚘⚘ (Mr & Mrs R B McDaniel) Givons Grove, Leatherhead. From Leatherhead By-pass (A24) at roundabout by Texaco garage 1m S of Leatherhead turn into Givons Grove and proceed up hill (The Downs) for ¾m, ignoring side turnings. Highlands is on the R. Chalk garden of 1 acre on a steep slope. Large rock garden, alpine house and sinks; mixed borders; orchard; pond; fruit and vegetable garden. Fine views over Mole Valley. TEAS in

aid of Cystic Fibrosis. *Adm £1 Chd free. Suns April 18, May 9 (2-6)*

High Meadow ⚘⚘ (Mr & Mrs J Humphries) Tilford Rd, Churt. From Hindhead A3 Xrds take A287 signposted Farnham. After ½m take R fork signposted Tilford. 1.9m to Avalon PYO farm. Park here, short walk to garden. Disabled visitors park on grass verge in drive. Approx 1 acre maintained by owners. Spring bulbs; rhododendrons; small peatbank; sinks for alpines. Large collection of old and modern shrub roses and David Austin English roses. Colour coordinated borders. Sunken garden with pond. TEAS. *Adm £1 Chd free (Share to Chibolya Mission). Suns Mons April 11, 12, May 30, 31, July 4, 5, Aug 29, 30 (2-6) and by appt* Tel 0428 606129

15 Highview Road ⚘ (Mr & Mrs J Pearce) Lightwater. Camberley 4m Chobham 4m 1½m S of junction (3) M3 off Macdonald Road Lightwater. ½-acre garden on hillside including rock; water; heather and Japanese garden. A good example of a steeply terraced layout. (Many steps). TEAS. *Adm £1 Chd free. Sun May 30 (2-6)*

239a Hook Road, Chessington (see London)

Hookwood Farm House &⚘⚘ (Mr & Mrs E W Mason) West Horsley. Approx 7m E of Guildford off A246 Guildford-Leatherhead Rd. From Guildford turn R into Staple Lane (sign-posted Shere) at end of dual carriageway. At top of Staple Lane turn L and then take 1st L into Shere Rd. (sign-posted West Horsley) then L into Fullers Farm Rd. From Leatherhead turn L into Greendene (signposted Shere) follow this for approx 2½m then R into Shere Rd. The garden made and maintained by the owners over the last 15yrs approx 1½ acres in size, is situated on a south facing slope of the North Downs. Large variety of interesting and unusual plants including alpines; herbaceous plants particularly geraniums; trees and shrubs. The garden also features a wild area with pond, a small kitchen garden and a Victorian style conservatory. Home-made TEAS in aid of Cystic Fibrosis Research Trust. *Adm £1.50 Chd free (Share to Spastics Society). Sun May 30, Wed June 2 (2-6); also by appt* Tel 04865 4760 *May to July*

Knightsmead ⚘⚘ (Mrs Jones & Miss Collins) Rickman Hill Rd, Chipstead. 1m SW of Coulsdon. 3m SE of Banstead. From A23 in Coulsdon turn W onto B2032. Through traffic lights, left fork into Portnalls Rd. Top of hill at Xroads, turn R into Holymead Rd. R into Lissoms Rd. R into Bouverie Rd. ½-acre plantsman's garden, designed and maintained entirely by owners. Wide variety of shrubs and perennials for year round interest; pond; scented roses; raised alpine and peat beds, clematis, hostas, hardy geraniums etc. New vertical garden. Small craft exhibition. Home-made TEAS in aid of Surrey Wildlife Trust in conservatory. *Adm £1 Chd 50p. Sat, Sun June 12, 13 (2-5.30) and by appt* Tel 0737 551694

Lime Tree Cottage ⚘⚘ (Mrs P Sinclair) 25 Ellesmere Rd. 1½m from Weybridge; Ellesmere Rd turn off Queens Rd. A317 immediately W of junction with Seven Hills Rd B365. Garden is at top of Ellesmere Rd. Design and planting combine to make this small (70' × 70' inc house) cottage garden. TEA. *Adm 75p Chd free. Sun May 16, Wed May 19 (10-4)*

Little Lodge, Thames Ditton (see London)

Little Mynthurst Farm &✿❀ (Mr & Mrs M Stone) Norwood Hill. Between Leigh (2m) and Charlwood (3m); from Reigate take A217 to Horley; after 2m turn R just after river bridge at Sidlowbridge; 1st R signed Leigh; then L at T junction. 12-acre garden; walled old-fashioned roses, herbaceous borders and shrubs around old farm house (not open). Kitchen garden with greenhouses and secret garden. TEAS. *Adm £1.50 Chd free (Share to St Catherine's Hospice, Crawley). Sat, Sun July 10, 11 (2-6)*

25 Little Woodcote Estate &✿❀ (Mr & Mrs Brian Hiley) Wallington. Private Rd off Woodmansterne Lane. Signed SCC Smallholdings. Woodmansterne Lane joins B278 and A237. An exciting 1-acre plantsmans garden full of many rare unusual, tender and interesting plants; rock garden; several large herbaceous borders; annual border; extensive collection of stone sinks; washing line garden and bog garden. A good collection of plant containers, garden and farm bygones. Suitable in parts for wheelchairs. *Adm £1.20 Chd free (Share to Motor Neurone Disease Association). Every Wed & Sat April 3 to Sept 25 (9-5). Also open for parties by appt Tel 081 647 9679*

Lodkin ❀ (Mr & Mrs W N Bolt) Lodkin Hill, Hascombe, 3m S of Godalming. Just off B2130 Godalming-Cranleigh, on outskirts of Hascombe; take narrow lane off signposted Thorncombe Street. About 5½ acres including woodland, stream and prolific daffodils and cherries. 4 old Victorian greenhouses have been completely rebuilt and are in full use to produce fruit, flowers and vegetables. Chrysanthemums in October. Much of the old cast staging etc has been retained. In parts suitable for wheel chairs. TEAS. *Adm £1 Chd 30p. Suns April 18, June 13, (2-6), Oct 31 Adm 75p that day (2-4)*

Malthouse Farm ❀ (Mr & Mrs George Pitt) Hambledon. 3½m S of Godalming. Take A283 through Witley, after 1m at bottom of long downhill straight turn L to Hambledon; house ⅝m on R. (Suitable for & with strong helper. Please use back entrance.) 2 to 3 acres; overlooking fields with views to S downs. Rhododendrons, azaleas; flowering trees and shrubs; spring bulbs; roses; small water garden; woodland walk leading to lake under restoration. House (not open) C17 with later additions. C18 granary on staddle stones. Small selection of Edwardian and vintage cars. Home-made TEAS (Sun-Mon only). *Adm £1.50 Chd free (honesty box Tues-Fri) (Share to Cruse Bereavement Care). Sun May 2 to Fri May 7 (2-6)*

Maryland &✿❀ (Mrs J Woodroffe) Worplesdon. From Guildford (A3) take A322 Bagshot Road. 4-acre mixed garden including woodland area; large herbaceous border, lawns; mature specimen trees; climbing and wall shrubs and many less common plants. Snowdrops in March, NCCPG National Collection of Veratrum. TEA. *Adm £1 Chd free. Suns, Mar 14 (2-5), July 4, Sept 26 (2-6)*

By Appointment Gardens. These owners do not have a fixed opening day usually because they do not like crowds or have insufficient parking space. Owner will often give guided tour.

Merrist Wood College &✿❀ Worplesdon 4m NW of Guildford. 40 acres of amenity areas, landscape demonstration gardens, 16 acres nursery stock, house a listed building (Norman Shaw 1877). Only reception hall open. One of the largest colleges of agriculture and horticulture in the UK with students from many countries. Information available for courses in Nursery, Landscape, Agriculture, Arboriculture, Countryside, Equestrian and Golf Studies. TEA. *Adm no charge. Rare plants for sale. Percentage of Plant Shop takings to NGS. For NGS Sat, Sun, May 29, 30, June 20 (10-6) with Surrey Horticultural Federation Summer Flower Show June 20 only*

Moleshill House &✿❀ (Mr & Mrs Maurice Snell) Cobham. House is on A307 Esher to Cobham Road nr A3 bridge. Parking in free car park. 1-acre flower arranger's garden. Informal planting around circular lawn; wild garden with bog; dovecote. Silver and green garden. Paving and pots. TEAS. *Adm £1 Chd 50p. Sun June 27 (2-5.30)*

Montfleury ✿❀ (Cdr & Mrs Innes Hamilton) Christchurch Rd, Virginia Water. From A30 at Virginia Water, opp Wheatsheaf Restaurant, turn down B389. Over roundabout. Last house on R before village. Former National Award Winners' new small garden. Propagation. Substantial, interesting plant sales. Also nursery stock for immediate effect. Unlimited parking. TEA. *Adm £1 Chd 10p. Sun May 16 (2-6)*

The Moorings &✿❀ (Dr & Mrs C J F L Williamson) 14 Russells Cres., Horley. Nr town centre between A23 and B2036; 400 yds from the railway station. 1-acre secluded country garden in centre of small town; contains all sorts of rare plants, interesting trees, many roses, pleasant vistas. An escapist's garden! See Collins Book of British Gardens. TEA. *Adm £1 Chd 25p. Sat, Sun June 26, 27 (2-6)*

29 Mostyn Road, Merton Park (see London)

Munstead Wood &✿❀ (Sir Robert & Lady Clark) nr Godalming. Take B2130 Brighton Rd out of Godalming towards Horsham. After 1m church on R, Heath Lane just thereafter on L. 400yds on R is entrance to Munstead Wood. Limited parking. 10 acres of rhododendrons, azaleas, woods and shrub and flower beds. Home until 1931 of Gertrude Jekyll; parts of garden in course of refurbishment. The architect for the house (not open) was Edwin Lutyens. TEAS. *Adm £1.50 OAP/Chd £1. Suns May 23, 30 (2-6)*

¶Odstock ✿❀ (Mr & Mrs J F H Trott) Bletchingley. Between Godstone 2m and Redhill 3m on A25. Junc 6 off M25 to Godstone. A25 towards Redhill. In Bletchingley from Whyte Harte up hill - Castle Square on L at top of hill. Parking in village. No parking in Castle Square. Bus 409 from Redhill Station alight at Red Lion public house. ⅔ of an acre maintained by owners and continually being developed for all year interest. Covered walk created by training old apple trees plus other climbers. Interesting variety of plants and shrubs with imaginative complementary and contrasting groupings of form and colour. Japanese features; dahlias. No dig, low maintenance vegetable garden. TEAS. *Adm £1 Chd free (Share to NSPCC). Sun Aug 8 (12-5)*

Painshill ♿ ✿ (Painshill Park Trust) 1m W Cobham on A245. Entrance on R, 200yds E of A3/A245 roundabout. Painshill contemporary with Stourhead & Stowe, is one of Europe's finest C18 landscape gardens. Created by the Hon Charles Hamilton between 1738-1773. Barren heathland transformed to ornamental pleasure grounds and parkland of dramatic beauty and contrasting scenery, dominated by 14-acre lake fed from river by immense waterwheel; grotto, ruined Abbey, Temple, Chinese Bridge, castellated Tower, Mausoleum. In 1948, after 200yrs of private ownership, the Park was neglected and in 1981 the Painshill Park Trust was formed to restore the gardens. Suitable for wheelchairs with exceptions. TEA. *Adm £3, disabled, students and OAPs £2.50 Chd free (Share to Painshill Park Trust). Suns only April 11 to Oct 17 (11-6). Private groups on other days. For NGS Sun Oct 3 (11-6)*

Pinewood House ♿ ✿ (Mr & Mrs J Van Zwanenberg) Heath House Rd, Worplesdon Hill. 3m Woking, 5m Guildford off A322 opp Brookwood Cemetery Wall. 4 acres. Newly planted Victorian clematis border. Walled garden and arboretum; water garden; bulbs in April. Interesting new house finished in Dec '86 with indoor plants. Home-made TEAS £1.50, TEA £1. *House & gardens adm £1 (Share to Action Research). Parties of 2-20 by appt only April to Oct* Tel 0483 473241

Polesden Lacey ♿ ✿ (The National Trust) Bookham, nr Dorking. 1½m S of Great Bookham off A246 Leatherhead-Guildford rd. 60 acres formal gardens; extensive grounds, walled rose garden, winter garden, lavender garden, iris garden, lawns; good views. House originally a Regency villa dating early 1820's, remodelled after 1906 by the Hon Mrs Ronald Greville, well-known Edwardian hostess; fine paintings, furniture, porcelain and silver, also many photographs from Mrs Greville's albums on display. King George VI and Queen Elizabeth (now the Queen Mother) spent part of their honeymoon here. For wheelchair details contact Administrator Tel 0372 458203. Gift shop. Lunch and TEAS in licensed restaurant in grounds (11-6). *Adm garden £2.50, house £3.50 extra; Chd £1.75. For NGS garden only Sun July 18 (11-6)*

Postford House ♿ ✿ (Mrs R Litler-Jones) Chilworth. 4m SE Guildford Route A248 Bus LC 425 Guildford-Dorking alight nr entrance. 25 acres woodland; water garden; stream; rose garden; vegetable garden; rhododendrons, azaleas and shrubs; swimming pool open. Home-made TEAS. *Adm £1 Chd free (Share to Cruse Bereavement Care May 23). Suns May 16, 23 Wed May 19 (2-6). Also by appt* Tel 0486 412657

Pyrford Court ♿ Pyrford Common Rd, 2m E of Woking. B367 junction with Upshott Lane; M25 exit 10 onto A3 towards Guildford off into Ripley signed Pyrford. 20 acres; wild gardens; extensive lawns; azaleas, rhododendrons, wisterias, autumn colour. TEAS. *Adm £2, Chd 70p (Share to Cancer Research Campaign). Sat, Suns May 15, 16 (2-6.30), Oct 17 (12-4)*

Ramster ♿ ✿ (Mr & Mrs Paul Gunn) Chiddingfold. On A283, 1½m S of Chiddingfold; large iron gates on R. Mature 20-acre woodland garden of exceptional interest with lakes, ponds and new woodland walk. Laid out by Gauntlett Nurseries of Chiddingfold in early 1900s. Fine rhododendrons, azaleas, camellias, magnolias, trees and shrubs. Picnic area. TEAS (Sats, Suns, Bank Hols May only). *Adm £1.50 Chd under 16 free (Share to NGS). April 24 to June 6 daily (2-6). Special early morning opening for photographers from 7am May 14, 15. Parties by appt.* Tel 0428 644422

Rise Top Cottage (formerly 2 The Cottage) ✿✿ (Trevor Bath Esq) Off Maybourne Rise, Mayford. 3m S of Woking, off the A320. On entering Maybourne Rise, take immediate L turn. At the top of the rise, the garden is approached along a rough track (about 100yds). Please park tactfully in Maybourne Rise. ⅓-acre, closely planted with many cottage garden plants, and some surprises. Special interests — white flowers, hardy geraniums, pulmonarias, aquilegias. Included in Good Housekeeping feature on Cottage Gardens. Home-made TEAS all day. *Adm 80p Chd free. (Share to Arthritis Care) Weds May 19 (10-5) May 26 (2-6); also by appt May and June.* Tel 0483 764958

The Round House ♿ ✿✿ (Mr & Mrs V Taylor) Hascombe. On B2130 Cranleigh-Godalming Rd, 1m S of Hascombe. 2½-acre Victorian walled garden in a lovely setting below Hascombe Hill. Run as small market garden specialising in pick-your-own fruit and dried flowers. Paths and lawns bordered with lavender, roses, delphiniums and many herbaceous plants, flowering and foliage shrubs. More than 70 varieties of flowers and foliage are dried in garden shed which is open for viewing. TEAS. *Adm £1.20 Chd 10p (Share to Waverley Family Support Service). Sat, Sun June 19, 20 (2-6)*

¶**41 Shelvers Way** ✿✿ (Mr & Mrs K G Lewis) Tadworth. 6m S of Sutton off the A217. 1st turning on R after Burgh Heath traffic lights heading S. 400 yds down Shelvers Way on L. ⅓-acre suburban style with a difference. Cobbled area with bubble fountain and shingle scree leading to mixed herb and herbaceous plantings. Designed and developed entirely by owners for year round interest. TEA. *Adm £1 Chd 30p. Sat, Sun July 10, 11 (2-6)*

South Park ♿ ✿ (Mr & Mrs T F Goad) Bletchingley. Bletchingley lies between Redhill and Oxted on the A25. From Bletchingley going E on A25 take R fork out of the village on to Rabies Heath Rd, continue approx ½m and take 1st R turn down cul de sac marked Wychcroft and South Park. Approx 4-acre Edwardian garden with work by Jim Russell in late 60s. Mixed border and shrubbery; gazebo and yew walks; long vistas. C17 chapel open. TEAS. *Adm £1.50 OAPs £1 Chd 50p. Sat, Sun June 19 (2-6), June 20 (12-5)*

South Park Farm ♿ ✿ (Mr & Mrs E B Stewart-Smith) South Godstone, 1m S of railway bridge over A22 at South Godstone; turn R into Carlton Rd opp. Walker's Garden Centre; follow signs for 1m. Medium-sized garden; wide variety of roses; herbaceous border; fine trees and landscape; small lake. C17 (listed) farm house (not open). Peacocks. Home-made TEAS till 6 in large C17 barn. *Adm £1.50 Chd free. Sat, Sun Mon July 3, 4, 5 (2-6). Also by appt April May June* Tel 0342 892141

Spring Cottage ♿✂❀ (Mr & Mrs D E Norman) Cranleigh. A281 from Guildford turn L 1m out of Bramley. Turn R at roundabout then immediately L, signposted Cranleigh School & Smithwood Common; garden 1m on R. 1-acre with lovely view, incl cottage garden; interesting shrubs and woodland garden. TEA. *Adm £1 Chd free. Sun June 6 to Sat June 12 (2-6) and by prior appt* **Tel 0483 272620**

Spur Point, nr Fernhurst (See Sussex)

Street House ❀ (Mr & Mrs B M Francis) Thursley village ½m off A3 between Milford and Hindhead. From A3 100yds past Three Horse Shoes public house. House is on L. Car park is on recreation ground past PO in centre of village. Please park carefully in wet weather. Street House, a listed Regency building and childhood home of Sir Edwin Lutyens where he first met Gertrude Jekyll (not open). Garden of 1¼ acres divided into three separate and individual gardens. Beautiful views towards Devils Punch Bowl. Ancient wall; special features include magnificent specimen cornus kousa; Japanese snowball tree; rare old roses; special rhododendrons and camellias; rubus tridel and many surprises. Special feature Astrological Garden now completed. Home-made TEAS. *Adm £1.50 Chd 50p (Share to Thursley Horticultural Soc). Suns April 25, May 30, June 20, July 25, Aug 29, Sept 26 (11-5)*

¶**Thanescroft** ♿✂ (Mr & Mrs Peter Talbot-Willcox) Shamley Green. 5m S of Guildford, A281 Guildford-Horsham rd, at Shalford turn E onto B2128 to Wonersh and Shamley Green. At Shamley Green Village sign turn R to Lord's Hill, ¾m on L. 4-acres mixed formal and informal garden, incl vegetables; lawns; roses; herbaceous; shrubs and specialist trees. Interesting icehouse swimming pool. TEAS. *Adm £1 Chd 25p. Sun June 20 (2-6)*

Tilgates ♿✂❀ (David Clulow, Esq) Bletchingley. A25 from Redhill towards Godstone, immediately after crossing motorway bridge 1st L, into Big Common Lane, then 1st R into Little Common Lane. Tilgates 50yds on. Plantsman's 7-acre garden with water and young arboretum. National Collection of Magnolias (400 different types). Over 3,500 accurately labelled rare trees, shrubs, rhododendrons & alpines; 30,000 unusual daffodils. TEAS (Soup in Jan) (Share to The Tree Register of the British Isles). *Adm £1.50. Open every day from March 1 except Christmas Day (10-5). For NGS Suns April 4, May 2, June 6, July 4, Aug 1, Sept 5, Oct 3, Nov 7, Dec 5 (10-5). Jan 2, Feb 6, March 6, 1994 (10-4)*

¶**Unicorns** ✂ (Mr & Mrs Eric Roberts) Long Hill Farnham. Approx 4 ½m E of Farnham take A31 towards Guildford. After ¾m turn R into Crooksbury Rd through 's' bend then L turn to The Sands through village past Barley Mow public house on R. Long Hill 1st turning on R. A woodland garden on a sloping site, rhododendrons, azaleas, ferns, plants for ground cover. Teas at Manor Farm Seale. *Adm £1 (Share to Hydestile Wildlife Hospital). Open by appointment only end of April to end of August* **Tel 02518 2778**. *Due to terrain 2 to 15 adults only*

37 Upland Road ♿✂❀ (Mr & Mrs David Nunn) 50yds S Carshalton Beeches station into Waverley Way, at shops into Downside Rd, then 1st on L. 0.4-acre secluded suburban plantsman's garden overlaying chalk. Shrubs; herbaceous; pond; orchard; fruit and vegetable garden. Developed and maintained by owners. Exhibition of botanical watercolour paintings. TEAS. *Adm £1 Chd free. Sun May 16 (2-6)*

Vale End ❀ (Mr & Mrs John Foulsham) Albury, 4½m SE of Guildford. From Albury take A248 W for ¼m. 1-acre walled interesting garden in beautiful setting; views from terrace across sloping lawns to mill pond and woodland; wide variety herbaceous plants; old roses, ornamental pond; attractive courtyard, fruit and vegetable garden featured in 'Gardeners World' 1992. Morning coffee and home-made TEAS in aid of Guildford BC Riverside Meadows Nature Project. *Adm £1.50 Chd free. Suns June 27, Aug 1 (10-5)*

Vann ✂❀ (Mr & Mrs M B Caroe) ✂ Hambledon, 6m S of Godalming. A283 to Wormley. Turn left at Hambledon Xrds signed 'Vann Lane'. Follow yellow 'Vann' signs for 2m. House on left. GPO box on gate. 4½ acres surrounding Tudor, William & Mary house with later additions and alterations incorporating old farm buildings by W D Caroe 1907-1909. Formal yew walk, recently replanted ¼-acre pond, Gertrude Jekyll water garden 1911, pergola, old cottage garden. Spring bulbs, woodland, azaleas, roses. Featured in *Country Life, Field, Monocle, Surrey Magazine, Mon Jardin Ma Maison, BBC Time Watch 1989, Practical Gardening 1990, Architectural Digest 1991*. Maintained by family with 14 hours assistance per week. Part of garden suitable for wheelchairs. Party bookings, guided tours, morning coffee, lunches, home-made teas in house from Easter-July by prior arrangement. TEAS. Easter Mon April 12, Bank Hol Mon May 3, Sun June 6 only. *Adm £1.50 Chd 30p (Share to Hambledon Village Hall). Easter Mon April 12 (2-7) Tues-Sun April 13-18 (10-6). Bank Hol Mon May 3 (2-7), Tues-Sun May 4-9 (10-6), Sun June 6 (2-7), Mon-Sat June 7-12 (10-6) and by appt* **Tel 0428 683413**

Walton Poor ♿✂❀ (Mr & Mrs Nicholas Calvert) From N off A246 on outskirts of East Horsley take Shere Rd, 1st fork L Crocknorth Rd. From S take A2003 to Ranmore Rd from Dorking to E Horsley. Approx 3 acres; tranquil, rather secret garden; paths winding between areas of ornamental shrubs; landscaped sunken garden; pond; herb garden. Autumn colour. Extensive range of foliage, scented plants and herbs for sale; garden immediately adjacent to miles of forest paths leading to North Downs with fine views over Tillingbourne valley. TEAS (May and June) (from 3pm) *Adm £1 Chd 30p (Share to Leukaemia Research). Suns April 11, June 6 (11-6) Oct 10 (11-5). Herb garden open daily Wed to Sun Easter to Sept 30. Main garden open by appt* **Tel 04865 2273**

Regular Openers. Too many days to include in diary. Usually there is a wide range of plants giving year-round interest. See head of county section for the name and garden description for times etc.

By Appointment Gardens. These owners do not have a fixed opening day usually because they do not like crowds or have insufficient parking space. Owner will often give guided tour.

Westbourn ✍ (Mr & Mrs John Camden) Virginia Water. From Egham 3m S on A30. Turn L into Christchurch Rd opp the Wheatsheaf Hotel. After 200 yds turn R into Pinewood Rd; Westbourn is 50 yds on the R. 4 acres landscaped woodland on two levels extensively planted with unusual trees and shrubs. Rhododendrons and azaleas predominate with over 80 different species and as many hybrids. Other notable collections well represented include acer, prunus, sorbus, hydrangea, ferns, ornamental cherries and hosta. The River Bourne, a narrow winding rivulet, forms the southern boundary of the garden. Soft drinks & biscuits. *Adm £1 Chd free. Sun May 16 (2-6)*

Whinfold ᵴ✍❀ (Mr & Mrs A Gash) Hascombe. 3½m SE of Godalming. Turn off B2130 at top of Winkworth Hill between Godalming and Hascombe. Woodland garden about 15 acres originally planned by Gertrude Jerkyll in 1897. The garden is maintained by the owners with weekend help and includes a pond, herb garden, specimen trees, magnolias, rhododendrons, azaleas and camellias with spring bulbs followed by masses of bluebells. TEA. *Adm £1 Chd free (Share to Hydon Hill Cheshire Home). Suns April 4, May 16 (2-5)*

White House ᵴ❀ (Lt Cdr & Mrs Michael Lethbridge). Stringers Common Guildford. On A 320 Guildford to Woking Rd 2m N of Guildford centre just beyond junction with Jacob's Well Rd. 3 acres, shrubs and herbaceous borders in setting of stone walls, roses, old orchard special emphasis given to managing the whole ecologically to become small nature reserve including pond life. TEA. *Adm £1 Chd free. (Share to Jacobs Well Ecological Society) Suns July 4 (2-6), Oct 3 (2-5.30)*

Windlesham Park ᵴ✍ (Mr & Mrs Peter Dimmock) Woodlands Lane. 2m E of Bagshot. S of Sunningdale, NW of Chobham; from Windlesham Church S to T-junction, turn left into Thorndown Lane becoming Woodlands Lane over M3; entrance 100yds on right, white pillars. 9-acre parkland setting with many and varied well established azaleas and rhododendrons. Fine cedars and mature trees; wet areas. TEAS. *Adm £1 Chd 25p (Share to St John the Baptist Church). Sun May 23 (2-6)*

Winkworth Arboretum (The National Trust) Hascombe, Godalming. Entrances with car parks; Upper 3m SE of Godalming on E side of B2130; Lower 2¼m S of Bramley on Bramley-Hascombe rd, turn R off A281 from Guildford by Bramley Grange Hotel, up Snowdenham Lane. Coaches (by strict arrangement) should use Upper car park on B2130. Station: Godalming 3m. 95 acres of hillside planted with rare trees and shrubs; 2 lakes; many wild birds; view over N Downs. Limited suitability for wheelchairs. TEAS 11-6. *Adm £2. ▲Sun May 16 (dawn-dusk)*

Wintershall ✍ (Mr & Mrs Peter Hutley) 2½m S of Bramley village on A281 turn R, then next R. Wintershall drive next on L. Bus: AV 33 Guildford-Horsham; alight Palmers Cross, 1m. 2½-acre garden and 100 acres of park and woodland; bluebell walks in spring; banks of wild daffodils; rhododendrons; pheasantry, specimen trees, ornamental pools and ponds; several acres of lakes and flight ponds; Domesday yew tree. St Francis Chapel by Chapel Lake. Path passes Stations of the Cross to Chapel of St. Mary, Queen of Peace at top of the hill. TEA from 3.30 pm. Picnic area. *Adm £1.50 Chd under 15 free. Suns April 11, May 9 (2-5.30)*

Woodside ✍❀ (Mr & Mrs J A Colmer) Send Barns Lane, Send, nr Ripley, 4m NE of Guildford; on A247 (Woking/Dorking Rd) 200 yds west (Send side) at junc with B2215 (Old A3). If travelling via M25 leave at junction 10. ⅓-acre garden; main feature rock garden and alpine house; many shrubs incl rhododendrons, ericaceous species etc; herbaceous planting; specialist collection of alpines. *Adm £1 Chd free. Sun April 25 (2-6) and during May by appt only* Tel 0483 223073

Woodyers ᵴ❀ (Brig & Mrs Fraser Scott) Wonersh, 4m S Guildford; A281 Guildford-Horsham; at Shalford turn E onto B2128 to Wonersh; in village centre (opp. car park of Grantley Arms public house) take road to Shamley Green. ¾-acre traditional, owner-maintained, walled garden; lawns, roses, herbaceous, bedding and shrubs; kitchen garden; greenhouses, swimming. Refreshments. See **Chinthurst Lodge** *Adm £1 Chd free (Share to Wonersh Church Green Trust). Sun June 6 (2-6). Also by appt* Tel 0483 893086

Yew Tree Cottage ✍❀ (Mr & Mrs E E Bowyer) Bunch Lane, Haslemere. Turn off High St into Church Lane, leave church on L, carry on to T junction, turn L, 1st house on L. 2-acre garden created by owners since 1976 on hillside. Large variety of trees and shrubs, water garden, kitchen garden, Jacob and Shetland sheep, Chinese geese, Shetland pony in paddock beyond garden. See **Haslehurst.** Tea at Haslehurst. *Adm £1 Chd 50p (Share to Haslemere Educational Museum). Sun June 13 (2.30-6). Also by appt June & July* Tel 0428 644130

67 York Rd ᵴ✍❀ (F A Wood Esq) Cheam. York Rd is situated in the Sutton Cheam area and runs between Cheam Rd and Dorset Rd. 67 is located at the S end of York Rd, towards the junction with Dorset Rd, which is a turning off Belmont Rise A217. Mainly walled suburban garden just under 0.2 acres, laid out and developed by the present owner over the past 5-6yrs. The layout comprises two lawned terraces with interesting hard landscaping and footpath patterns, incl raised shrub, heather and flower beds. Good range of plants, incl viburnums, hollies, ferns, ivies and conifers, plus 75' herbaceous border with wide range of hardy plants. Two raised ponds, one comprising an open roofed water pavilion. Good selection of wall climbers. Dried flowers for sale. TEAS in aid of Salvation Army. *Adm £1 Chd free. Sun, Wed July 18, 21 (10-4); also by appt* Tel 081 642 4260

Sussex

Hon County Organisers:
(East & Mid-Sussex)

Mrs Michael Toynbee, Westerleigh, Mayfield Lane, Wadhurst TN5 6JE
Tel 0892 783238

(West Sussex)

Mrs Nigel Azis, Coke's Barn, West Burton, Pulborough RH20 1HD
Tel 0798 831636

Assistant Hon County Organisers:
(East & Mid-Sussex)
(West Sussex)
(West Sussex)
(West Sussex)

Mrs J Charlesworth, Snape Cottage, Snape Lane, Wadhurst
Mrs Michael Burton, Church Farmhouse, Lavant, nr Chichester
Mrs Jane Newdick, Dale House, West Burton, Pulborough
Mrs A Tuck, New Barn, Egdean, Pulborough

Hon County Treasurers:
(East & Mid-Sussex)
(West Sussex)

A C W Hunter Esq, Cottenden Oast, Stonegate, Wadhurst
W M Caldwell Esq, The Grange, Fittleworth, Pulborough

DATES OF OPENING

By appointment
*For telephone number and other
details see garden descriptions*

Bates Green Farm, nr Hailsham
Chidmere, Chidham
Casters Brooks, Cocking, nr
  Midhurst
Coates Manor, Fittleworth
Cooke's House, West Burton
Combehurst, Frant
Coombland, Coneyhurst,
  Billingshurst
Crawley Down Gardens
Crossgate House, Crossgates,
  Amberley
Duckyls, Sharpthorne
116 Findon Road, Worthing
Ketches, Newick
Kings John's Lodge, Etchingham
Malthouse, Chithurst, nr Rogate
Mill House, Nutbourne
Moorlands, nr Crowborough
Spur Point, nr Kingsley Green. May
  only
Telegraph House, North Marden, nr
  Chichester. May to Aug
Whitehouse Cottage, Staplefield
  Lane, Haywards Heath

Regular openings
For details see garden descriptions

Borde Hill Gardens, nr Haywards
  Heath. Suns March 7 to April 4.
  Daily April 9 to Oct 31
Cobblers, Crowborough. See text for
  dates
Denmans, Fontwell, nr Arundel.
  Daily, March 1 to Dec 24 incl
  Bank Hols
Great Dixter, Northiam. Daily April 1
  to Oct 10 EXCEPT see text

High Beeches Garden, Handcross.
  Open April 12 to June 27 & Sept
  4 to Oct 30. Closed Weds & Suns
Merriments Gardens, Hurst Green
Parham House & Gardens,
  Pulborough
West Dean Gardens, nr Chichester.
  Daily March 1 to Oct 31

March 8 Monday
Denmans, Fontwell, nr Arundel
March 21 Sunday
Champs Hill, Coldwaltham, nr
  Pulborough
Sennicotts, nr Chichester
March 27 Saturday
Champs Hill, Coldwaltham, nr
  Pulborough
The Manor of Dean, Tillington,
  Petworth
March 28 Sunday
Champs Hill, Coldwaltham, nr
  Pulborough ‡
The Manor of Dean, Tillington,
  Petworth
The Upper Lodge, Stopham, nr
  Pulborough ‡
March 29 Monday
The Manor of Dean, Tillington,
  Petworth
March 31 Wednesday
West Dean Gardens, nr Chichester
April 4 Sunday
Berri Court, Yapton, nr Arundel
Fitzhall, Iping, nr Midhurst
Rymans, Apuldram, nr Chichester
The Upper Lodge, Stopham, nr
  Pulborough
April 5 Monday
Berri Court, Yapton, nr Arundel
Little Thakeham, Merrywood
  Lane, Storrington
April 9 Friday
Houghton Farm, nr Arundel ‡
Merriments Gardens, Hurst Green

The Upper Lodge, Stopham, nr
  Pulborough ‡
April 11 Sunday
Chidmere House, Chidham
The Upper Lodge, Stopham, nr
  Pulborough
April 12 Monday
Chidmere House, Chidham
Highdown Gardens, Goring-by-Sea
Merriments Gardens, Hurst Green
The Old Rectory Fittleworth ‡
Stonehurst, Ardingly
The Upper Lodge, Stopham, nr
  Pulborough ‡
April 17 Saturday
The Manor of Dean, Tillington,
  Petworth
April 18 Sunday
Buckham Hill Gardens, nr Uckfield
Cooke's House, West Burton ‡
Hurst Mill, nr Petersfield
The Manor of Dean, Tillington,
  Petworth
Northwood Farmhouse,
  Pulborough
The Upper Lodge, Stopham, nr
  Pulborough ‡
April 19 Monday
Cooke's House, West Burton
The Manor of Dean, Tillington,
  Petworth
Northwood Farmhouse,
  Pulborough
April 20 Tuesday
Cooke's House, West Burton
April 25 Sunday
Cooke's House, West Burton
Highdown Gardens, Goring-by-Sea
Malt House, Chithurst, nr Rogate
Newtimber Place, Newtimber
Rymans, Apuldram, nr Chichester
Stonehurst, Ardingly
April 26 Monday
Cooke's House, West Burton
April 27 Tuesday
Cooke's House, West Burton

May 1 Saturday
Bignor Park, nr Sutton,
  Pulborough
Cedar Tree Cottage, Washington
Cooksbridge, Fernhurst

May 2 Sunday
Bignor Park, nr Sutton,
  Pulborough ‡
Bumble Cottage, Monkmead
  Lane, W Chiltington ‡
Cooksbridge, Fernhurst
Duckyls, Sharpthorne
116 Findon Road, Worthing
Malt House, Chithurst, nr Rogate
Mereworth, Nyetimber Lane,
  West Chiltington ‡‡
Merriments Gardens, Hurst Green
Offham House, Offham
The Upper Lodge, Stopham, nr
  Pulborough ‡‡

May 3 Monday
Bignor Park, nr Sutton,
  Pulborough ‡
Bumble Cottage, Monkmead
  Lane, W Chiltington ‡‡
Duckyls, Sharpthorne
116 Findon Road, Worthing
Malt House, Chithurst, nr Rogate
Mereworth, Nyetimber Lane,
  West Chiltington ‡‡
Merriments Gardens, Hurst Green
The Upper Lodge, Stopham, nr
  Pulborough ‡‡

May 5 Wednesday
Cedar Tree Cottage, Washington

May 8 Saturday
Cedar Tree Cottage, Washington
High Beeches Gardens,
  Handcross
Hurst House, Sedlescombe

May 9 Sunday
Berri Court, Yapton, nr Arundel
Hammerwood House, Iping ‡
Malt House, Chithurst, nr
  Rogate ‡
Nymans, Handcross
Standen, East Grinstead

May 10 Monday
Berri Court, Yapton, nr Arundel
Houghton Farm, nr Arundel

May 11 Tuesday
Houghton Farm, nr Arundel

May 15 Saturday
Champs Hill, Coldwaltham, nr
  Pulborough
The Manor of Dean, Tillington,
  Petworth
Middle Coombe, East Grinstead

May 16 Sunday
Champs Hill, Coldwaltham, nr
  Pulborough ‡
Chelwood Vachery, Nutley
Cowdray Park Gardens,
  Midhurst ‡‡‡

Crossgate House, Crossgates,
  Amberley ‡
East Lymden, Ticehurst
Ghyll Farm, Crowborough ‡
Hammerwood House, Iping ‡‡
Hurst Mill, nr Petersfield
Malt House, Chithurst, nr
  Rogate ‡‡
The Manor of Dean, Tillington,
  Petworth ‡‡‡
Middle Coombe, East Grinstead
Moorlands, nr Crowborough ‡
Mountfield Court, nr
  Robertsbridge
New Grove, Petworth ‡‡‡
North Springs, Fittleworth
Selehurst, Lower Breeding, nr
  Horsham
Stonehurst, Ardingly
Three Oaks, West Broyle,
  Chichester ‡‡‡‡
Trotton Gardens, nr Rogate ‡‡
The Upper Lodge, Stopham, nr
  Pulborough ‡
Woodstock, West Broyle,
  Chichester ‡‡‡‡

May 17 Monday
The Manor of Dean, Tillington,
  Petworth
Mountfield Court, nr
  Robertsbridge

May 19 Wednesday
Ashburnham Place, Battle
Crossgate House, Crossgates,
  Amberley ‡
Parham House & Gardens,
  Pulborough ‡
Sheffield Park Garden, nr Uckfield

May 20 Thursday
Parham House & Gardens,
  Pulborough

May 22 Saturday
Champs Hill, Coldwaltham, nr
  Pulborough ‡
Crossgate House, Crossgates,
  Amberley ‡
Fittleworth Gardens, Pulborough ‡
Lane End, Midhurst

May 23 Sunday
Champs Hill, Coldwaltham, nr
  Pulborough ‡
Chidmere House, Chidham
Cobblers, Crowborough
Cowbeech Farm, nr Hailsham
Fittleworth Gardens, Pulborough ‡
Lane End, Midhurst ‡‡
Legsheath Farm, East Grinstead
Malt House, Chithurst, nr
  Rogate ‡‡
Merriments Gardens, Hurst
  Green ‡‡‡
New Barn, Egdean, nr Petworth ‡
Pashley Manor, Ticehurst ‡‡‡
Stanbridge House, Staplefield

The Upper Lodge, Stopham, nr
  Pulborough ‡
Wadhurst Park ‡‡‡

May 24 Monday
Chidmere House, Chidham
Lane End, Midhurst
New Barn, Egdean, nr Petworth

May 26 Wednesday
Ashburnham Place, Battle

May 29 Saturday
Crossgate House, Crossgates,
  Amberley ‡
Gaywood Farm, Gay Street, nr
  Pulborough ‡
Lane End, Midhurst
Whitehouse Cottage, Staplefield
  Lane, Haywards Heath

May 30 Sunday
Ardingly Gardens
Baker's Farm, Shipley, nr
  Horsham
Bates Green Farm, nr Hailsham
Champs Hill, Coldwaltham, nr
  Pulborough ‡
Crossgate House, Crossgates,
  Amberley ‡
The Garden in Mind, Stansted
  Park, Rowlands Castle ‡‡‡‡
Gaywood Farm, Gay Street, nr
  Pulborough ‡
Ghyll Farm, Crowborough ‡‡‡
Houghton Farm, nr Arundel ‡
Lane End, Midhurst ‡‡
Lye Green House, Lye ‡‡‡
Malt House, Chithurst, nr
  Rogate ‡‡
Manvilles Field, Fittleworth
Moorlands, nr Crowborough ‡‡‡
Sennicotts, nr Chichester ‡‡‡‡
Tappington Grange, Wadhurst
Whitehouse Cottage, Staplefield
  Lane, Haywards Heath

May 31 Monday
Ardingly Gardens
Cobblers, Crowborough
Gaywood Farm, Gay Street, nr
  Pulborough ‡
Highdown Gardens, Goring-by-Sea
Houghton Farm, nr Arundel ‡
Lane End, Midhurst ‡‡
Malt House, Chithurst, nr
  Rogate ‡‡
Manvilles Field, Fittleworth
Penns in the Rocks, Groombridge

June 1 Tuesday
Crossgate House, Crossgates,
  Amberley

June 6 Sunday
Cobblers, Crowborough
Combehurst, Frant ‡
Crossgate House, Crossgates,
  Amberley ‡
Fitzhall, Iping, nr Midhurst ‡
Hailsham Grange, Hailsham

Ketches, Newick
Merriments Gardens, Hurst Green
Nymans, Handcross
Offham House, Offham
The Old Rectory, Fittleworth ‡
Pembury, Clayton, nr Brighton
Sherburne House, Eartham, nr
 Chichester
Whiligh, Wadhurst ‡

June 7 Monday
Whiligh, Wadhurst

June 9 Wednesday
Bateman's, Burwash
Pashley Manor, Ticehurst

June 11 Friday
Crossgate House, Crossgates,
 Amberley

June 12 Saturday
Bignor Park Cottage, Sutton, nr
 Petworth ‡
Buckhurst Park, Withyham
Coombland, Coneyhurst,
 Billingshurst
Frith Hill, Northchapel ‡‡
Frith Lodge, Northchapel ‡‡
Lilac Cottage, Duncton, nr
 Petworth ‡
Somerset Lodge, Petworth ‡

June 13 Sunday
Bignor Park Cottage, Sutton, nr
 Petworth ‡‡
Clinton Lodge, Fletching ‡
Coates Manor, Fittleworth ‡‡
Frith Hill, Northchapel ‡‡‡
Frith Lodge, Northchapel ‡‡‡
Hurst Mill, nr Petersfield ‡‡‡
Kingston Gardens, nr Lewes
Knabbs Farmhouse, Fletching ‡
Lilac Cottage, Duncton, nr
 Petworth ‡‡
Nyewood House, Nyewood, nr
 Rogate ‡‡‡
Rogate Gardens, nr Petersfield
Somerset Lodge, Petworth ‡‡
The White House, Burpham, nr
 Arundel

June 14 Monday
Bignor Park Cottage, Sutton, nr
 Petworth
Clinton Lodge, Fletching
Little Thakeham, Merrywood
 Lane, Storrington

June 15 Tuesday
Little Thakeham, Merrywood
 Lane, Storrington

June 16 Wednesday
Coates Manor, Fittleworth ‡
Lilac Cottage, Duncton, nr
 Petworth ‡
Somerset Lodge, Petworth ‡

June 19 Saturday
Chilsham House, nr Hailsham
Crossgate House, Crossgates,
 Amberley

King John's Lodge, Etchingham ‡
Little Hutchings, Etchingham ‡
Telegraph House, North Marden,
 nr Chichester
Winchelsea Gardens

June 20 Sunday
Ambrose Place Back Gardens,
 Worthing
Baker's Farm, Shipley, nr Horsham
Buckham Hill Gardens, nr Uckfield
Casters Brook, Cocking, nr
 Midhurst
Chilsham House, nr Hailsham
Cobblers, Crowborough
Crossgate House, Crossgates,
 Amberley ‡
Framfield Gardens
The Garden in Mind, Stansted
 Park, Rowlands Castle
Houghton Farm, nr Arundel ‡
King John's Lodge,
 Etchingham ‡‡
Little Hutchings, Etchingham ‡‡
Mayfield Cottage Gardens, nr
 Tunbridge Wells ‡‡
Moat Mill Farm, Mayfield, nr
 Tunbridge Wells ‡‡
Merriments Gardens, Hurst Green
New Barn, Egdean, nr
 Petworth ‡‡‡
Northwood Farmhouse,
 Pulborough
Northsprings, Fittleworth ‡‡‡
Rogate Gardens, nr Petersfield
Rymans, Apuldram, nr Chichester
Rye Gardens
Telegraph House, North Marden,
 nr Chichester
The White House, Burpham, nr
 Arundel ‡

June 21 Monday
Clinton Lodge, Fletching
Houghton Farm, nr Arundel
New Barn, Egdean, nr Petworth
Northwood Farmhouse,
 Pulborough

June 22 Tuesday
Houghton Farm, nr Arundel
New Barn, Egdean, nr Petworth

June 23 Wednesday
Great Allfields, Balls Cross
Houghton Farm, nr Arundel

June 25 Friday
Crossgate House, Crossgates,
 Amberley
Down Place, Sourth Harting

June 26 Saturday
Coombland, Coneyhurst,
 Billingshurst
Crawley Down Gardens
Down Place, South Harting
The Old Rectory, Sutton

June 27 Sunday
Bates Green Farm, nr Hailsham

Berri Court, Yapton, nr Arundel
Casters Brook, Cocking, nr
 Midhurst
Chidmere House, Chidham
Cobblers, Crowborough
Crawley Down Gardens
Crossgate House, Crossgates,
 Amberley ‡
Down Place, South Harting ‡‡
Ketches, Newick ‡‡‡
Manor Farmhouse, Ripe, nr
 Lewes
Nutbourne Gardens, nr
 Pulborough ‡
The Old Rectory, Sutton ‡
Pheasants Hatch, Newick ‡‡‡
Pyramids, South Harting ‡‡
Trotton Gardens, nr Rogate ‡‡
Wilderness Farm, Hadlow Down

June 28 Monday
Berri Court, Yapton, nr Arundel
Chidmere House, Chidham
Clinton Lodge, Fletching
Nutbourne Gardens, nr
 Pulborough
Pheasants Hatch, Newick

July 4 Sunday
Merriments Gardens, Hurst Green

July 7 Wednesday
Merriments Gardens, Hurst Green

July 10 Saturday
Crown House, Eridge
North Springs, Fittleworth
Palmer's Lodge, West Chiltington
 Village

July 11 Sunday
Brickwall, Northiam
Cobblers, Crowborough
Crown House, Eridge
Fitzhall, Iping, nr Midhurst
North Springs, Fittleworth
Palmer's Lodge, West Chiltington
 Village

July 16 Friday
Wakehurst Place, Ardingly

July 17 Saturday
The Manor of Dean, Tillington,
 Petworth
Palmer's Lodge, West Chiltington
 Village
Telegraph House, North Marden,
 nr Chichester

July 18 Sunday
Chilsham House, nr Hailsham
The Garden in Mind, Stansted
 Park, Rowlands Castle
The Manor of Dean, Tillington,
 Petworth
Merriments Gardens, Hurst Green
Nyewood House, Nyewood, nr
 Rogate
Palmer's Lodge, West Chiltington
 Village
Rymans, Apuldram, nr Chichester

Telegraph House, North Marden,
nr Chichester
July 19 Monday
The Manor of Dean, Tillington,
Petworth
July 20 Tuesday
Houghton Farm, nr Arundel
July 21 Wednesday
Houghton Farm, nr Arundel
Merriments Gardens, Hurst Green
July 24 Saturday
116 Findon Road, Worthing
Middle Coombe, East Grinstead
July 25 Sunday
Bates Green Farm, nr Hailsham
Cobblers, Crowborough
116 Findon Road, Worthing
Middle Coombe, East Grinstead
July 30 Friday
St Mary's House, Bramber
July 31 Saturday
Cooksbridge, Fernhurst
August 1 Sunday
Cobblers, Crowborough
Cooksbridge, Fernhurst
Hailsham Grange, Hailsham
Kingston Gardens, nr Lewes
Merriments Gardens, Hurst
Green
August 6 Friday
St Mary's House, Bramber
August 7 Saturday
Champs Hill, Coldwaltham, nr
Pulborough
August 8 Sunday
Champs Hill, Coldwaltham, nr
Pulborough
East Lymden, Ticehurst ‡
Millstones, Wadhurst ‡
August 14 Saturday
The Manor of Dean, Tillington,
Petworth
August 15 Sunday
Cobblers, Crowborough
The Manor of Dean, Tillington,
Petworth
Merriments Gardens, Hurst Green

Wilderness Farm, Hadlow Down
August 16 Monday
The Manor of Dean, Tillington,
Petworth
August 18 Wednesday
Merriments Gardens, Hurst Green
August 21 Saturday
Bumble Cottage, Monkmead
Lane, W Chiltington ‡
Champs Hill, Coldwaltham, nr
Pulborough ‡
Mereworth, Nyetimber Lane,
West Chiltington ‡
August 22 Sunday
Bumble Cottage, Monkmead
Lane, W Chiltington ‡
Champs Hill, Coldwaltham, nr
Pulborough ‡
Mereworth, Nyetimber Lane,
West Chiltington ‡
August 28 Saturday
Bumble Cottage, Monkmead
Lane, W Chiltington ‡
Mereworth, Nyetimber Lane,
West Chiltington ‡
August 29 Sunday
Ardingly Gardens
Bumble Cottage, Monkmead
Lane, W Chiltington ‡
Chidmere House, Chidham ‡‡
Houghton Farm, nr Arundel
Mereworth, Nyetimber Lane,
West Chiltington ‡
Merriments Gardens, Hurst Green
Newtimber Place, Newtimber
Rymans, Apuldram, nr
Chichester ‡‡
August 30 Monday
Ardingly Gardens
Chidmere House, Chidham
Houghton Farm, nr Arundel
Penns in the Rocks, Groombridge
September 1 Wednesday
Merriments Gardens, Hurst Green
West Dean Gardens, nr Chichester
September 4 Saturday
High Beeches Gardens, Handcross

September 5 Sunday
Fitzhall, Iping, nr Midhurst
Merriments Gardens, Hurst Green
Wilderness Farm, Hadlow Down
September 11 Saturday
The Manor of Dean, Tillington,
Petworth
September 12 Sunday
The Manor of Dean, Tillington,
Petworth
Merriments Gardens, Hurst Green
Standen, East Grinstead
September 13 Monday
The Manor of Dean, Tillington,
Petworth
September 19 Sunday
Cowbeech Farm, nr Hailsham
September 23 Thursday
Houghton Farm, nr Arundel
September 24 Friday
Houghton Farm, nr Arundel
September 26 Sunday
The Garden in Mind, Stansted
Park, Rowlands Castle
Mereworth, Nyetimber Lane,
West Chiltington
September 27 Monday
Mereworth, Nyetimber Lane,
West Chiltington
October 2 Saturday
The Manor of Dean, Tillington,
Petworth
October 3 Sunday
The Manor of Dean, Tillington,
Petworth
October 4 Monday
The Manor of Dean, Tillington,
Petworth
October 17 Sunday
Long House, Cowfold
October 20 Wednesday
Sheffield Park Garden, nr Uckfield
October 24 Sunday
Berri Court, Yapton, nr Arundel
October 25 Monday
Berri Court, Yapton, nr Arundel ‡
Denmans, Fontwell, nr Arundel ‡

DESCRIPTIONS OF GARDENS

Ambrose Place Back Gardens, Richmond Rd &✿❀
Worthing 10m E of Bognor, 7m W of Brighton. Take
Broadwater Rd into town centre, turn R at traffic lights
into Richmond Rd opp Library; small town gardens with
entrances on left; parking in rds. TEAS. *Combined adm £1
Chd 25p (Share to St Paul's Church Worthing). Sun June
20 (11-1, 2-5)*
  No 1 (Mrs M M Rosenberg) Walled garden; shrubs,
pond, climbing plants
  No 3 (Mr & Mrs M Smyth) Paved garden with climbing
plants and lawn

No 4 (Mr & Mrs T J Worley) Paved garden with raised
herbaceous borders, lawn and flowering summer
plants
No 6 (Mr & Mrs Leslie Roberts) Attractive garden with
conservatory
No 7 (Mr & Mrs R Phillpot) Patio garden, with conservatory
No 8 (Mr & Mrs P McMonagle) Summer flowering
plants and lawn
No 10 (Mr & Mrs C F Demuth) Paved garden with
roses and interesting trees
No 11 (Mrs M Stewart) Roses, summerhouse, flowering plants

No 12 (Mr & Mrs P Bennett) Newly created paved small garden

No 14 (Mr & Mrs A H P Humphrey) Roses, flowering plants, greenhouse and bonsai collection

Ambrose Villa (Mr & Mrs Frank Leocadi) Italian style small town garden

68 Richmond Road (Mr & Mrs Denis Hayden) Worthing. ¼m W down Richmond Road (10m walk). Small walled town garden, perennials, shrubs and containers

Ardingly Gardens &✗ 1m West of Ardingly on Street Lane (Balcombe Road) Entrance through Knowles. Gardens are interconnecting. Teas at Church Rooms nearby. *Combined Adm £1.50 Chd free (Share to Chailey Heritage). Suns, Mons May 30, 31, Aug 29, 30 (2-5.30)*
  Knowles ❀ (The Michell Family) 7-acre garden reconstructed after storm; water garden; wood. Acid loving trees and shrubs; some unusual plants. Fine views; formal and informal areas
  Jordans (Mr & Mrs K Waistell) 2 acres of gardens, some large mature trees (Gingko, Tulip, Wellington). Herbaceous and shrub borders

Ashburnham Place &✗❀ (Ashburnham Christian Trust) Battle. 5m W of Battle on B2204. 220 acres of beautiful woodland and grassland; gardens landscaped by George Dance and Capability Brown, whose 1777 orangery houses the two oldest camellias in the country. Woodland walks, 3 large lakes and features from several centuries. TEAS. *Adm £2 Chd 75p Reduction for OAPs. Weds May 19, 26 (11-5)*

Baker's Farm ✗❀ (Mr & Mrs Mark Burrell) Shipley, 5m S of Horsham. Take A24 then A272 W, 2nd turn to Dragon's Green, L at George and Dragon then 300 yds on L. Large Wealden garden; lake; laburnum tunnel; shrubs, trees, rose walks of old-fashioned roses; scented knot garden and bog gardens. TEAS. *Adm £1.30 Chd 30p (Share to St Mary the Virgin, Shipley). Suns May 30, June 20 (2-6)*

Bateman's &✗ (The National Trust) Burwash ½m S (A265). From rd leading S from W end of village. Home of Rudyard Kipling from 1902-1936. Garden laid out before he lived in house and planted yew hedges, rose garden, laid paths and made pond. Bridge to mill which grinds local wheat into flour. LUNCHES & TEAS. *Adm £3.50 Chd £1.80. Wed June 9 (11-5.30)*

Bates Green Farm &✗❀ (Mr & Mrs J R McCutchan) Arlington. 2½m SW of A22 at Hailsham and 2m S Michelham Priory, Upper Dicker. Approach Arlington passing the 'Old Oak Inn' on R continue for 350yds then turn R along a small lane. (TQ5507). Plantsman's tranquil garden of over 1-acre gives year-round interest; rockery; water; mixed borders with colour themes, and shaded foliage garden. B & B accommodation. TEAS. *Adm £1.50 Chd free. Suns May 30, June 27, July 25 (2.30-5). Also by appt* **Tel 0323 482039**

Berri Court & (Mr & Mrs J C Turner) Yapton, 5m SW of Arundel. In centre of village between PO & Black Dog public house. A2024 Littlehampton-Chichester rd passes. Intensely planted 3-acre garden of wide interest; trees,

flowering shrubs, heathers, eucalyptus, daffodils, shrub roses, hydrangeas and lily ponds. *Adm £1 Chd 30p. Suns, Mons April 4, 5; May 9, 10; June 27, 28, (2-5) Oct 24, 25 (12-4)*

Bignor Park (The Viscount & Viscountess Mersey) Pulborough, 5m from Petworth on West Burton rd. Nearest village Sutton (Sussex). 11 acres of trees, shrubs and magnificent views of the South Downs, from Chanctonbury Ring to Bignor Hill. Music in the temple. TEAS. *Adm £1 Chd 25p. Sat, Sun, Mon May 1, 2, 3 (2-5)*

Bignor Park Cottage &✗ (Dr & Mrs D Rudd-Jones) Bignor 4m S of Petworth on the West Burton Rd, on S side of Coates Common. 2 to 3 acres with rhododendrons, azaleas, shrubs, specimen trees and wild garden. Large pond with wildfowl. TEA. *Adm £1 Chd 20p. Sat, Sun Mon June 12, 13, 14 (2-6)*

● **Borde Hill Garden** &❀ (The Borde Hill Garden Co. Ltd.) 1½m. N of Haywards Heath on Balcombe Rd. Large informal garden of great botanical interest and beauty; rare trees and shrubs; extensive views; woodland walks, rhododendrons, azaleas, camellias, magnolias, at its best in the spring. Picnic area. Licensed restaurant. *Adm £3 Chd £1 parties of 20+ and OAPs £2.50. Open Bank Hol weekends April & May, Suns March 7 to April 4, daily April 9 to Oct 31 (10-6) May & June (10-8)*

Brickwall & (Frewen Charitable Trust), Northiam. 8m NW of Rye on B2088. Tudor home of Frewen family since 1666. Gardens and walls built and laid out by Jane Frewen c.1680; chess and lavender gardens; arboretum. *Adm £1.50 Chd under 12 free. Sun July 11 (2-5)*

Buckham Hill Gardens nr Uckfield; Uckfield-Isfield Back Rd. *Combined adm £1 Chd 20p. Suns April 18, June 20 (2-5)*
  Beeches Farm ✗ (Mrs Vera Thomas) Sunken garden; roses, borders; planted for winter colour. TEA. *(Share to Royal Agricultural Benevolent Institution)*
  Home Farm House ✗ (Mrs P Cooper) 500yds S of Beeches on the Isfield Rd. Small attractive gardens

¶**Buckhurst Park** ✗❀ (Earl & Countess De La Warr) Withyham. On B 2110 between Hartfield and Groombridge. Drive adjacent to Dorset Arms public house. Lutyens, Jekyll terraces, Repton park and lake. Waterfall with rocks all currently being restored by James Pulham. TEAS. *Adm £1.50 Chd 50p. Sat June 12 (2-5.30)*

Bumble Cottage ✗ (Mr & Mrs D Salisbury-Jones) West Chiltington. 2m E of Pulborough, 2m N of Storrington. From Pulborough turn off A283 E of Pulborough into W Chiltington Rd then R into Monkmead Lane (signed Roundabout Hotel) follow yellow signs. From Storrington take B2139 W into Greenhurst Lane, R at T Junc. 100yds fork L into Monkmead Lane then 2nd entrance after Hotel. Charming 'all seasons' garden of just under 1 acre created from a sandy slope. Wide variety of interesting trees, shrubs and plants combined with ponds all set off by very fine lawn. *Adm £1 Chd 25p. Sun, Mon, May 2, 3, Sats, Sun Aug, 21, 22, 28, 29 (2-6)*

Cabbages & Kings see Wilderness Farm

Casters Brook ✿ (Mr & Mrs John Whitehorn) Cocking; 3m S of Midhurst at Cocking PO on A286 take sharp turn E; garden is 100 yds to right. Interesting 2-acre chalk garden full of surprises; slopes to old mill pond, good collection of old roses; fine downland setting. TEAS. *Adm £1 Chd free (Share to Cocking Church). Suns June 20, 27 (2-6). Also by appt* **Tel 0730 813537**

Cedar Tree Cottage ᚖ✿✿ (Mr & Mrs G Goatcher) Rock Rd, Washington. Turn W off A24 ¼m N. of Washington Roundabout. Park in 'Old Nursery' Car Park. Mixed borders with plants for the connoisseur; mature and rare specimens in adjoining old Nursery re-developed as 5-acre garden/arboretum. Fine views of S Downs. Picnics welcome. *Adm £1 Chd 25p. Sat May 1, Wed May 5, Sat May 8 (2-6)*

Champs Hill ᚖ✿✿ (Mr & Mrs David Bowerman) Coldwaltham, S of Pulborough. From Pulborough on A29, in Coldwaltham turn R to Fittleworth Rd; garden 300yds on R. From Petworth turn off B2138 just S of Fittleworth to Coldwaltham, garden approx ½m on L. 27 acres of formal garden and woodland walks around old sand pit. Conifers and acid-loving plants, many specie heathers labelled. Superb views across Arun valley. Special features. March - Winter heathers and spring flowers. May - rhododendrons, azaleas, wild flowers. August - heathers and other specialities. TEAS (not March). *Adm £1.50 Chd free. Sats, Suns March 21, 27, 28; May 15, 16, 22, 23, 30; Aug 7, 8, 21, 22 (Sat 11-5, Sun 1-5)*

Chelwood Vachery ᚖ✿ (BAT Industries plc) Nutley, nr Uckfield on A22 3m S of Forest Row. 102 acres inc woodland and 24 acres formal gardens of great charm with rare heathers, rhododendrons, original bog garden and Zen garden of meditation. Homemade TEAS. *Adm £2 OAPs £1 Chd 80p. Sun May 16 (12-5)*

Chidmere House ᚖ (Thomas Baxendale Esq) Chidham, 6m W of Chichester. A259 1m Bus: SD276/200 Chichester-Emsworth. Interesting garden; with subject of article in 'Country Life'; yew and hornbeam hedges; bulbs, and flowering shrubs bounded by large mere, now a private nature reserve. C15 house (not open). *Adm £1.20 Chd 40p. Suns, Mons April 11, 12; May 23, 24; June 27, 28; Aug 29, 30 (2-7). Also by appt for parties only* **Tel 0243 572287 or 573096**

Chilsham House ᚖ✿ (Mr & Mrs P E B Cutler) Herstmonceux. 5m NE of Hailsham. From A271 in Herstmonceux take turning by Woolpack Inn towards Cowbeech after approx ¾m turn R into Chilsham Lane, ¾m on the left. 1½-acre garden, herbaceous border, water garden, old fashioned roses. Small gardens in colour harmony, many unusual plants. Victorian garden. TEAS. *Adm £1 Chd 20p. Sat, Sun June 19, 20; Sun July 18 (2-5.30)*

Clinton Lodge ✿✿ (Mr & Mrs H Collum) Fletching, 4m NW of Uckfield; from A272 turn N at Piltdown for Fletching, 1½m. 6-acre formal and romantic garden overlooking parkland with old roses, double herbaceous borders, yew hedges, pleached lime walks, copy of C17 scented herb garden, medieval-style potager, vine and rose allée, wild flower garden. Carolean and Georgian house (not open). TEAS. *Adm £2 Chd 50p (Share to Fletching Church Fabric Fund). Sun June 13; Mons, 14, 21, 28 (2-6)*

Coates Manor ᚖ✿✿ (Mrs G H Thorp) nr Fittleworth. ½m S of Fittleworth; turn off B2138 at signpost marked 'Coates'. 1 acre, mainly shrubs and foliage of special interest. elizabethan house (not open) scheduled of historic interest. TEAS. *Adm £1.25 Chd 20p. Sun, Wed June 13, 16 (11-6). Also by appt*

Cobblers ᚖ✿✿ (Mr & Mrs Martin Furniss) Mount Pleasant, Jarvis Brook, Crowborough. A26, at Crowborough Cross take B2100 towards Crowborough Station. At 2nd Xrds turn into Tollwood Rd for ¼m. 2-acre sloping site designed by present owners since 1968 to display outstanding range of herbaceous and shrub species and water garden, giving all season colour. Subject of numerous articles and TVS 'That's Gardening' programme June 1991. TEAS. *Adm £2.50 Chd £1 (incl home-made Teas). Sun, Mon May 23, 31; Suns June 6, 20, 27, July 11, 25, Aug 1, 15 (2.30-5.30)*

Combehurst ᚖ✿ (Mrs E E Roberts) 3m S of Tunbridge Wells off A267, 400 yds S of B2099. 2½-acre beautifully laid out garden; shrubs, trees, plants. TEAS. *Adm £1 Chd free. Sun June 6 (2-6). Also by appt* **Tel Frant 750367**

Cooke's House ᚖ✿ (Miss J B Courtauld) West Burton, 5m SW of Pulborough. Turn off A29 at White Horse, Bury, ¾m. Old garden with views of the Downs, round Elizabethan house (not open); varied interest incl spring flowers, topiary, herbaceous borders, herbs. Free car park. *Adm £1 Chd free under 14. Suns, Mons, Tues April 18, 19, 20, 25, 26, 27 (2-6). Also by appt*

Cooksbridge ✿ (Mr & Mrs N Tonkin) Fernhurst. On A286 between Haslemere and Midhurst, ¾m S of Fernhurst X-roads. 6 acres, landscaped garden with glade and woodland. Pictured in the GRBS 1993 Gardens to remember calendar this plantsman's garden is situated in a fold of the downs beside the river Lodd. Features include the herbaceous border, vine and ornamental plant houses, lily pond and well stocked shrubberies. The main lawn sweeps down from the terrace to the lake which has an island with weeping willow and several species of waterfowl. TEAS. *Adm £1 Chd 50p 5 and under free. Sats, Suns May 1, 2, July 31, Aug 1 (2-6)*

Coombland ✿✿ (Mr & Mrs Neville Lee) Coneyhurst. In Billingshurst turn off A29 onto A272 to Haywards Heath; approx 2m, in Coneyhurst, turn S for further ¾m. Large garden of 5 acres developed since 1981 with the help and advice of Graham Stuart Thomas. Undulating site on heavy clay. Old shrub-rose beds, rose species and ramblers scrambling up ageing fruit trees; extensive planting of hardy geraniums; herbaceous border with interesting planting. Oak woodland; orchard dell with hybrid rhododendrons; hostas; primulas and meconopsis. Nightingale wood with water area under development, water wheel recently added leading to 1-acre arboretum. National collection of hardy geraniums held here. TEAS. *Adm £1.50 Chd 50p. Sats June 12, 26 (10-5). Nursery open by appt only Mon to Fri (2-4)* **Tel 040387 549**

By Appointment Gardens. Avoid the crowds. Good chance of a tour by owner. See garden description for telephone number.

Cowbeech Farm ✿❀ (Mrs M Huiskamp) Cowbeech. 4m NE of Hailsham. A271 to Amberstone turn off N for Cowbeech. 5-acre garden, woodland walk, herb garden. Attractive Japanese garden, shrubs, trees. Picnic area, morning coffee, farmhouse TEAS. *Adm £1.25 Chd 75p. Suns May 23, Sept 19 (10-12) (2-5)*

Cowdray Park Gardens ♿✿ (The Viscount Cowdray). S of A272. 1m E of Midhurst. Entrance by East Front. Avenue of Wellingtonias; rhododendrons, azaleas; sunken garden with large variety trees and shrubs, Lebanon cedar 300 yrs old; pleasure garden surrounded by ha-ha. *Adm £1. Sun May 16 (2-7)*

Crawley Down Gardens ✿ B2028 8m N of Haywards Heath, 4m W of E Grinstead. 2½m E of M23 (junction 10). TEAS at **Bankton Cottage**. *Combined adm £1.50 Chd free. Sat, Sun June 26, 27 (2-6)*

Bankton Cottage ♿❀ (Mr & Mrs Robin Lloyd) 3½-acre garden, herbaceous borders, shrub and climbing roses. Large 1-acre pond, many terracotta pots planted up round house. Large range on sale. Featured 'Country Living' 1990. *Also open by appt* **Tel 0342 714793**

Yew Tree Cottage ❀ (Mrs K Hudson) ¼-acre garden planted for all year round interest and easy management. Featured in RHS 1989 and book 'Cottage Garden'. *Also open by appt* **Tel 0342 714633**

Crossgate House ✿❀ (Jean Taylor & Andrew Muggeridge) Amberley. 4m S of Storrington on B2139 turn R into Amberley. R by Black Horse and follow rd for approx ¾m garden on L past Sportsman Inn. Small exposed garden over dry alkaline soil. Designed to please a plantsman and an artist. Many unusual herbaceous perennials. White flowered Judas tree blooming in May. Beautiful views over Amberley wildbrooks. Unsuitable for wheelchairs and pushchairs. Garden liable to over-crowding early afternoon. *Adm £1 Chd 50p. Sun May 16 (2-5), Wed May 19 (2-9), Sats, Suns May 22, 29, 30, June 6, 19, 20, 27(2-5), Tues June 1 (2-9), Fris June 11, 25 (2-9). Also by appt* **Tel 0798 831317**

Crown House ♿✿❀ (Maj L Cave) Eridge, 3m SW of Tunbridge Wells. A26 Tunbridge Wells-Crowborough rd; in Eridge take Rotherfield turn S; house 1st on right. 1½ acres with pools; alpine garden; herbaceous border; herb garden; aviary. Full size croquet lawn. Prize winner in Sunday Express garden of the year competition. Produce stalls. TEAS. *Adm £1.25 Chd free (Share to Multiple Sclerosis). Sat, Sun July 10, 11 (2-6)*

Denmans ♿✿❀ (Mrs J H Robinson) Denmans Lane, Fontwell. Chichester and Arundel 5m. Turn S on A27 at Denmans Lane, W of Fontwell Racecourse. Renowned gardens extravagantly planted for overall, all-year interest in form, colour and texture; areas of glass for tender species. Plant Centre. TEAS. *Adm £2.25 OAPs £1.85 Chd £1.25. Groups over 15 persons £1.65. Open daily from March 1 to Dec 24 incl. Bank Hols. Coaches by appt. For NGS Mons March 8, Oct 25 (9-5)*

¶Down Place ✿❀ (Mr & Mrs D M Thistleton-Smith) South Harting. ¼m E down unmarked lane below top of hill. 1m SE of South Harting on B2141 towards Chichester. From Petersfield E via B2146 to South Harting. From Chichester via A286 for 4m, N of Lavant turn NW on to B2141. 7-acre hillside chalk garden on N slope of South Downs. Terraced herbaceous and shrub borders, walks through woodland and natural wild flower meadow. Fine views over South Harting. TEAS. *Adm £1.20 Chd 50p (Share to National Asthma Campaign). Fri, Sat, Sun June 25, 26, 27 (2-6)*

Duckyls ❀ (Lady Taylor) Sharpthorne. 4m SW of E Grinstead. 6m E of Crawley. At Turners Hill take B2028 S 1m fork left to W Hoathly, turn L signed Gravetye Manor. 12-acre large terraced garden being gradually restored with collection of azaleas, rhododendrons, camellias, fine views. Interesting primrose collection. TEAS. *Adm £2 Chd 50p (Share to Sackville College, St Margaret's Church West Hoathly). Sun, Mon May 2, 3. Also parties by appt (2-6)* **Tel Sharpthorne 810352**

¶East Lymden ✿❀ (Mrs V G FitzGerald) Ticehurst. Turn W off A21 at Flimwell. 1¼m after Ticehurst. 7-acre garden with rhododendrons, azaleas and specimen trees. New herbaceous borders; large walled kitchen garden. B & B accommodation. TEAS. *Adm £1 Chd 50p. Open every Wed May to Sept for NGS. Suns May 16, Aug 8 (2-6)*

116 Findon Road ✿❀ (Mr Charles R Noble) Worthing. Do not park on the A24, but use side roads. 500 yds N of A24/A27 junc (Offfington Corner) on E side of Findon Rd. ¼-acre garden, containing many plants of a less common nature incl lime haters growing on chalky subsoil, unusual in this area. A plantsman's garden of considerable charm. TEAS. *Adm 70p Chd 30p. Sats, Suns May 2, 3; July 24, 25 (2-6). Also by appt May-Oct* **Tel 09032 63282**

Fittleworth Gardens ♿✿❀ Fittleworth A282 midway Petworth-Pulborough; in Fittleworth turn onto B2138 then turn W at Swan. Park near Swan as parking is limited. TEAS. Plants in aid of NSPCC. *Combined Adm £1.50 Chd free. Sat, Sun May 22, 23 (2-6)*

The Grange ♿ (Mr & Mrs W M Caldwell) 3-acre garden with island beds of azaleas, rhododendrons and other shrubs, sloping to river Rother

The Hermitage (Mr & Mrs P F Dutton) Charming informal garden; azaleas, rhododendrons, flowering shrubs; with lovely views to the river and S Downs

Lowerstreet House (L J Holloway Esq) Small garden with shrubs, bulbs, herbaceous

Fitzhall ✿❀ (Mr & Mrs G F Bridger) Iping, 3m W of Midhurst. 1m off A272, signposted Harting Elsted. 9 acres; herb garden; herbaceous and shrub borders; vegetable garden. Farm adjoining. House (not open) originally built 1550. Garden and teas all year round. *Adm £1.50p OAPs £1.25 Chd 75p. For NGS Suns April 4, June, 6, July 11, Sept 5 (2-6)*

Regular Openers. Too many days to include in diary. Usually there is a wide range of plants giving year-round interest. See head of county section for the name and garden description for times etc.

By Appointment Gardens. See head of county section

Framfield Gardens ◊✿ At S end of Uckfield bypass (A22) turn NE to Framfield (2½m). TEAS at Hobbs Barton. *Combined adm £2 Chd 30p. Sun June 20 (2-6)*

  Hailwell House ✿ (Lady Elizabeth Baxendale). On L, B2102 towards Uckfield, ½m from church. 4-acres of shrubs and borders with lake

  Hobbs Barton (Mr & Mrs Jeremy Clark) ¼m E of church turn L off B2102. ½m turn L again, house ¾m on L. 2½ acres of undulating lawns, shrubs, specimen trees; roses and herbaceous; ornamental water; walled vegetable and fruit garden. TEAS in C16 Barn room

Frith Hill ✿✿ (Mr & Mrs Peter Warne) Northchapel 7m N of Petworth on A283 turn E in centre of Northchapel into Pipers Lane (by Deep Well Inn) after ¾m turn L into bridleway immed past Peacocks Farm. 1-acre garden, comprising walled gardens with herbaceous border; shrubbery; pond; old-fashioned rose garden and arbour. Herb garden leading to white garden with gazebo. TEAS. *Adm £1 Chd 25p (Share to Cystic Fibrosis Research Fund). Sat, Sun June 12, 13 (2-6)*

Frith Lodge ✿ (Mr & Mrs Geoffrey Cridland) Northchapel. 7m N of Petworth on A283 turn E in centre of Northchapel into Pipers Lane (by Deep Well Inn) after ¾m turn L into bridleway immediately past Peacocks Farm. 1-acre cottage style garden recently created around pair of Victorian game-keepers cottages. Undulating ground with roses, informal planting with paved and hedged areas; outstanding views of Sussex Weald. TEA. *Adm £1 Chd 50p. Sat, Sun June 12, 13 (2-6)*

¶**The Garden in Mind** ✿✿ (Mr & Mrs Ivan Hicks - Stansted Park Foundation) Stansted Park, Rowlands Castle. From A3 at Horndean follow brown signs for Stansted House. From A27M at Havant follow Stansted House brown signs. Stansted House is 3m NE of Havant. Set within a ½-acre walled garden at Stansted House. A deliberate, theatrical, whimsical exercise in creating a fantasy, magic, dream garden (or nightmare!). Visitors should visit with an open mind. Original brief (1991) was to create in 4 months on a tiny budget, a surreal, symbolic dream garden. The longer term plan is to develop this theme. Whilst children are welcome they must be firmly under control as garden is a gallery and cannot be played in. Beware as objects are only balanced. Overall design based on the concept of 'The World Tree' but the garden can also be seen as a maze, mandala or journey through life. TEAS. *Adm £1.01 Chd donation. Suns May 30, June 20, July 18, Sept 26 (2-6)*

¶**Gaywood Farm** ◊✿✿ (Mrs Anthony Charles) nr Pulborough. 3m S of Billingshurst turn L off A29 into Gay Street Lane. After railway bridge at 2nd junction fork L and at T junction turn L signed 'no through rd'. 2-acre garden, fine weeping Ash, black Mulberry, Irish yews and extravagantly planted borders with interesting plant assoc. Large pond surrounded by good planting. TEAS. *Adm £1 Chd 25p. Sat, Sun, Mon May 29, 30, 31 (2-6)*

¶**Ghyll Farm** ✿✿ (Mr & Mrs I Ball) Crowborough. 1m S of Crowborough centre on A26. L into Sheep Plain Lane immed R Sweethaws ½m. 'The Permissive Garden' planted by the late Lady Pearce. 1-acre, azaleas, camellias, woodland bluebell walk; spectacular views. TEAS in

aid of Rocking Horse Appeal. *Adm £1 Chd 50p. Suns May 16, 30 (2-6)*

¶**Great Allfields** ✿ (Lord & Lady Birkett) Balls Cross. 3m N of Petworth. Take 283 out of Petworth, turn 2nd R signed Balls Cross, Kirdford. At Balls Cross take L turn after Stag Inn to Ebernoe, Northchapel (Pipers Lane) 250yds entrance on R. A cottage garden with exotic tastes and territorial ambitions of approx an acre, old walls and barns covered with many interesting climbers. *Adm 80p Chd free. Wed June 23 (10-6)*

● **Great Dixter** ✿✿ (Quentin Lloyd) Northiam, ½m N of Northiam, off A28 8m NW of Rye. Buses infrequent 340, 342, 348. Hastings & District. Alight Northiam P. Office 500 yds. Topiary; wide variety of plants. Historical house open (2-5). TEAS. *Adm house & garden £3.30 Chd 50p OAPs & NT members (Fris only) £2.70; garden only £2.20 Chd 25p. April 1 to Oct 10 daily except Mons but open on Bank Hols; (2-5) Sats, Suns Oct 16, 17, 23, 24 (2- 5); garden open May 29, 30, 31; also Suns in July, Aug; Mon Aug 30 (11-5)*

¶**Hailsham Grange** ◊✿✿ (John Macdonald Esq) Hailsham. Turn off Hailsham High St into Vicarage Rd, park in public car park. Formal garden designed and planted since 1988 in grounds of former C17 Vicarage (not open). A series of garden areas representing a modern interpretation of C18 formality; Gothic summerhouse; pleached hedges; herbaceous borders, romantic planting in separate garden compartments. Teas in adjacent church in aid of The Children's Society. *Adm £1.50. Suns June 6, Aug 1 (2-5.30)*

Hammerwood House ◊ (The Hon Mrs J Lakin) Iping, 1m N of A272 Midhurst to Petersfield Rd. Approx 3m W of Midhurst. Well signposted. Large informal garden; fine trees, rhododendrons, azaleas, acers, cornus, magnolias; wild garden (¼m away), bluebells, stream. TEAS. *Adm £1.50 Chd free. Suns May 9, 16 (1.30-6)*

● **High Beeches Gardens** ✿ (High Beeches Gardens Conservation Trust) Situated on B2110 1m E of A23 at Handcross. 20-acres of enchanting landscaped woodland and water gardens; spring daffodils; bluebell and azalea walks; many rare and beautiful plants; wild flower meadows, glorious autumn colours. Picnic area. Car park. Lunches and TEAS only on special events days April 12, May 3, 31, Aug 22, Oct 24 (10-5). *Daily April 12 to Oct 30 (1-5) closed June 27 to Sept 4 and on Weds and Suns. Adm £2.50 Acc chd free (Share to St Mary's Church, Slaugham). For NGS Sats May 8, Sept 4 (1-5). Also by appt for organised groups at any time*

Highdown, Goring-by-Sea ◊✿ (Worthing Borough Council) Littlehampton Rd (A259), 3m W of Worthing. Station: Goring-by-Sea, 1m. Famous garden created by Sir F Stern situated in chalk pit and downland area containing a wide collection of plants. Spring bulbs, paeonies, shrubs and trees. Many plants were raised from seed brought from China by great collectors like Wilson, Farrer and Kingdon-Ward. TEAS. *Collecting box. ▲Mon April 12; Sun April 25; Mon May 31 (10-6)*

Houghton Farm ✿✤ (Mr & Mrs Michael Lock) Arundel. Turn E off A29 at top of Bury Hill onto B2139 or W from Storrington onto B2139 to Houghton. 1-acre garden with wide variety of shrubs and plants, interesting corners and beautiful views. Tea Houghton Bridge Tea Gardens. *Adm £1 Chd free. Fri April 9; Mon, Tues May 10, 11; Sun, Mon May 30, 31; Sun, Mon, Tues, Wed June 20, 21, 22, 23; Tues, Wed July 20, 21; Sun, Mon Aug 29, 30; Thurs, Fri Sept 23, 24 (2-5)*

Hurst House ♿✤ (Mr & Mrs J Keeling) Hurst Lane. From Sedlescombe take lane towards Brede; take 1st lane on left, 600 yds, garden on R. 6 acres; rhododendrons, azaleas, camellias, bulbs; herbaceous borders; rose garden; greenhouses with houseplants. TEAS. *Adm £1.20 Chd 20p (Share to Arthritis Care Hastings Branch). Sat May 8 (2-5.30)*

¶**Hurst Mill** ✿ (Mr & Mrs Peter Simon) Hurst. 2m SE of Petersfield on B2146 mid-way between Petersfield and S Harting 8-acre garden on many levels in lovely position overlooking 4-acre lake in wooded valley with wildfowl. Waterfall and Japanese water garden beside historic mill. Bog garden; large rock garden with orientally inspired plantings; acers, camellias, rhododendrons, azaleas, magnolias, hydrangeas and ferns; shrubs and climbing roses; forest and ornamental trees. TEAS. *Adm £1.50 Chd 50p. Suns April 18, May 16, June 13 (2-6)*

Ketches ♿✿ (David Manwaring Robertson Esq) Newick, 5m W of Uckfield on A272. Take Barcombe Rd S out of Newick, house is on right opp turning to Newick Church. 3 acres; old-fashioned roses; specimen trees; shrub and herbaceous borders. TEAS. *Adm £1 Chd free. Suns June 6, 27 (2-6). Also by appt mid May to mid July* Tel 082 572 2679

¶**King John's Lodge** ♿✿✤ (Mr & Mrs R A Cunningham) Etchingham. Burwash to Etchingham on the A265 turn L before Etchingham Church into Church Lane which leads into Sheepstreet Lane after ½m. L after 1m. A romantic garden of over 3 acres surrounding a listed house. Formal garden with fountain and lily pond leading to a wild garden and rose walk. Large herbaceous borders with old shrub roses; secret garden and shaded white garden. B & B accommodation. Garden Statuary and plants for sale. TEAS. *Adm £1.20 Chd free. Sat, Sun June 19, 20 (11-5). Also by appt* Tel 0580 819 232

Kingston Gardens ✤ 2½m SW of Lewes. Turn off A27 signposted Kingston at roundabout; at 30 mph sign turn R. Home-made TEAS **Nightingales**. *Combined adm (payable at **Nightingales** only) £1.50 Chd free. Suns June 13, Aug 1 (2-6)*

    Nightingales (Geoff & Jean Hudson) The Avenue. Informal sloping ½-acre garden for all-year interest; wide range of plants incl shrub roses, hardy geraniums, perennials, ground cover. Mediterranean plants. Childrens play area. Short steep rough walk or drive, parking limited, to:-

    The White House ♿ (John & Sheila Maynard Smith) The Ridge. ½-acre garden on a chalk ridge. Shrubs, herbaceous border, alpines; greenhouse with unusual plants

Knabbs Farmhouse ✤ (Mr & Mrs W G Graham) 4m NW of Uckfield; from A272 turn N at Piltdown for Fletching, (TQ430/240) 1½m. Garden at N-end of village and farm. ½-acre informal garden; mixed beds and borders; shrubs, roses, perennials, foliage plants. Good views over ha-ha. TEAS at **Clinton Lodge**. *Adm 80p Chd 20p. Sun June 13 (2-6)*

Lane End ✿ (Mrs C J Epril) Sheep Lane, Midhurst. In North St turn L at Knock-hundred Row, L into Sheep lane, L to garden. Park at church or in lane. 2 acres incl wild garden; alpine rockery with pools; rhododendrons, azaleas, heath border. Below ramparts of original castle with fine views over water meadows to ruins of Cowdray House. Tea Midhurst. *Adm £1 Chd free. Sats, Suns, Mons May 22, 23, 24, 29, 30, 31 (11-6)*

Legsheath Farm ✤ (Michael Neal Esq) Legsheath Lane. 2m W of Forest Row, 1m S of Weirwood Reservoir. Panoramic views with woodland and water garden walks. Fine davidia, acers and rhododendrons. TEAS. *Adm £1.50 Chd free. Sun May 23 (2-5.30)*

¶**Lilac Cottage** ✿ (Mrs G A Hawkins) Willet Close, Duncton. 3m S of Petworth on the W side of A285 opp St Michaels School. Park in Close where signed. Small village garden on several levels with shrubs, small trees and approx 90 varieties of shrub and climbing roses and herb garden. TEA. *Adm 75p. Sat, Sun, Wed June 12, 13, 16 (2-6)*

Little Hutchings ✿✤ (Mr & Mrs P Hayes) Fontridge Lane, Etchingham. (TQ 708248). Take A265 to Etchingham off A21 at Hurst Green. Signposted. 1½-acre old-fashioned garden laid out over 17 years. Over 230 different varieties of shrub and old roses. Extensive tightly packed herbaceous borders, incl large collection clematis. TEAS. *Adm £1.20 Chd free. Sat, Sun June 19, 20 (2-6)*

¶**Little Thakeham** ✿✤ (Mr & Mrs T Ratcliff) Storrington. Take A24 S to Worthing and at roundabout 2m S of Ashington return N up A24 for 200yds. Turn L into Rock Rd for 1m. At staggered Xrds turn R into Merrywood Lane and garden is 300yds on R. From Storrington take B2139 to Thakeham. After 1m turn R into Merrywood Lane and garden is 400yds on L. 4-acre garden with paved walks, rose pergola, flowering shrubs, specimen trees, herbaceous borders and carpets of daffodils in spring. The garden laid out to the basic design of Sir Edward Lutyens in 1902 is entering its 3rd and final year of restoration. All surrounding one of the finest examples of a Sir Edward Lutyens manor house now a luxurious country house hotel. *Adm £1 Chd 25p. Mons, Tues April 5 (2-5) June 14, 15 (2-6)*

¶**Long House** ✤ (Mr & Mrs V A Gordon Tregear) Cowfold. 1m N of A272, Cowfold-Bolney Rd; 1st turning L after Cowfold. A unique opportunity to view a garden in the process of being restored after a period of decline. Comprising 2½ acres within walls surrounding house dating from early C16 (house not open). TEA. *Donation on entry. Sun Oct 17 (12-4)*

¶**Lye Green House** ✗ (Mrs Hynes) Lye. Lye Green is situated on the B2188 between Groombridge and Crowborough, 7m SW of Tunbridge Wells. 6-acre garden restored over 3 yrs after long neglect. 4 large ponds, woodland and rockeries; 7 enclosed gardens, herbaceous borders, rose garden, kitchen garden and lime walk. TEA. *Adm £1.50 Chd free. Sun May 30 (2-6)*

Malt House ❀ (Mr & Mrs Graham Ferguson) Chithurst, Rogate. From A272, 3½m W of Midhurst turn N signposted Chithurst then 1½m; or from A3 2m S of Liphook, turn SE to Milland, then follow signs to Chithurst for 1½m. 5 acres; flowering shrubs incl exceptional rhododendrons and azaleas, leading to 50 acres of lovely woodland walks. TEA. *Adm £1.50 Chd 50p. Suns April 25, May 2, 9, 16, 23, 30; Mons May 3, 31 (2-6); also by appt for parties or plant sales* Tel 0730 821433

Manor Farmhouse ৬✗ (Mr & Mrs M Clark) Ripe. In centre of village opp 'The Lamb'. From Lewes take A27 Eastbourne rd and after about 5m turn L to Ripe. About 1¼ acres, featuring an old walled rose garden and pond with ornamental ducks. TEAS. *Adm £1.25 Chd 50p. Sun June 27 (2-6)*

The Manor of Dean ৬✗ (Miss S M Mitford) Tillington, 2m W of Petworth. Turn off A272 N at NGS sign. Flowers, shrubs, specimen trees, bulbs in all seasons. A miniature pony, 2 pigmy goats, Vietnamese pigs, tame lambs. House (not open) 1400-1613. TEA 50p. *Adm £1 Chd over 5 50p. Sats, Suns, Mons March 27, 28, 29; April 17, 18, 19; May 15, 16, 17; July 17, 18, 19; Aug 14, 15, 16; Sept 11, 12, 13; Oct 2, 3, 4 (2-6)*

Manvilles Field ৬✗❀ (Mrs P J Aschan & Mrs J M Wilson) 2m W of Pulborough take A283 to Fittleworth, turn R on double bend. 1½ acres with many interesting shrubs, clematis, roses, other herbaceous plants. Beautiful views surrounding garden. TEAS. *Adm £1 Chd 40p. Sun Mon 30, 31 (2-6)*

Mayfield Cottage Gardens ✗ 8m S of Tunbridge Wells on A267. *Combined adm £1 Chd 20p. Sun June 20 (2-5.30)* **Moat Mill Farm, Mayfield** *also open*

Hopton (E Stuart Ogg Esq) Fletching St. ½-acre, delphinium specialist
Knowle Way (J Freeman Esq) West St. S of High St by Barclays Bank. ¼-acre plantsman's garden
The Oast ❀ (Mr & Mrs R G F Henderson) Fletching St. Turn off A267 by garage towards Witherenden ¼m. Charming ½-acre sloping garden, fine views. TEAS

Mereworth ✗ (Mrs H C Wiffen) Silverwood, Nyetimber Lane, West Chiltington, 3m E of Pulborough. From A283 turn N to Nutbourne & West Chiltington; cross junction; stay on lower rd, 2nd L; 1st L. 1-acre garden, trees, conifers, heathers; small herbaceous shrub borders. TEA. *Adm £1 Chd 40p. Sun, Mon May 2, 3, Sats, Suns, Aug 21, 22, 28, 29; Sun, Mon, Sept 26, 27 (2-6)*

Merriments Gardens ৬✗❀ (Mark & Mandy Buchele) Hawkhurst Rd, Hurst Green. Situated between Hawkhurst and Hurst Green. 2m SW Hawkhurst. A new garden created Autumn 1991 from open field; water gardens; mixed borders; many unusual plants displayed; wood and orchard in infancy. TEAS. *Adm £1 Chd free. Fri, Mon, April 9, 12; Suns, Mon May 2, 3, 23; Suns June 6, 20; Suns Weds, July 4, 7, 18, 21, Aug 1, 15, 18, 29, Sept 1, 5, 12 (12-5)*

Middle Coombe ৬✗❀ (Andrew & Ann Kennedy) East Grinstead. From E Grinstead 1½m SW on B2110. Turn L into Coombe Hill Rd. ¼m on L. 7½-acre garden and woodland walk with small lake. The garden was created in 16 weeks in 1990. Designed in Victorian rooms using Agriframes. Formal and informal planting to give all year colour. Light lunches and TEAS. *Adm £2 Chd free. Sats, Suns May 15, 16, July 24 25 (12-5)*

Millstones ✗❀ (Mr & Mrs H W Johnson) Tapsells Lane, Wadhurst. 6m SE of Tunbridge Wells. Tapsells Lane turns off B2099 at NW end of Wadhurst. ½-acre plantsman's garden featuring an exceptionally wide range of shrubs and perennial plants. *Adm £1 Chd free. Sun Aug 8 (2-6)*

¶**Moat Mill Farm** ✗ (Mr & Mrs C Marshall) Newick Lane, Mayfield. 1m S on Mayfield-Broadoak Rd. 8 acres, formal garden, herbaceous border and wild gardens. TEAS. *Adm £1 Chd 20p. Sun June 20 (2-5.30). Also open* **Mayfield Cottage Gardens**

Moorlands ❀ (Dr & Mrs Steven Smith) Friar's Gate, 2m N of Crowborough. St Johns Rd to Friar's Gate. Or turn L off B2188 at Friar's Gate. 3 acres set in lush valley adjoining Ashdown Forest; water garden with ponds and streams; primulas, rhododendrons, azaleas, many unusual trees and shrubs. TEAS. *Adm £1.50 Chd 30p. Suns May 16, 30 (2-6) and by appt only April to Oct* Tel **0892 652474**

Mountfield Court ৬ (T Egerton Esq) 2m S of Robertsbridge. On A21 London-Hastings; ½m from Johns Cross. 2-3-acre wild garden; flowering shrubs, rhododendrons, azaleas and camellias; fine trees. Homemade TEAS. *Adm £1 Chd 50p (Share to All Saints Church Mountfield). Sun, Mon May 16, 17 (2-6)*

New Barn ৬✗ (Mr & Mrs A Tuck) Egdean 1m S of Petworth turn L off A285, at 2nd Xrds turn R into lane or 1m W of Fittleworth take L fork to Midhurst off A283. 200yds turn L. 2 acres, owner maintained informal garden round converted C18 barn in beautiful farmland setting. Large natural pond and stream. Irises, roses, clematis, shrubs and herbaceous; foliage and bark interest; woodland area with bluebells. Picnic area. Soft drinks and biscuits. *Adm £1 Chd 20p. Sun, Mon, Tues, May 23 (11-5.30), 24 (12.30-6), June 20 (11-5.30), 21 (12.30-6), 22 (11-5.30)*

New Grove ৬✗ (Mr & Mrs Robert de Pass) Petworth. 1m S of Petworth turn L off A285 and take next L. Follow signs. From the N at Xrds in Petworth straight across into Middle Street then L into High Street follow signs. A mature garden of about 3 acres. Mainly composed of shrubs with all year interest incl magnolias, camellias, azaleas, cornuses, roses etc. lovely views to the South Downs. TEAS. *Adm £1 Chd free. Sun May 16 (2-6)*

Newtimber Place &⚘ (His Honour & Mrs John Clay) Newtimber. 7m N of Brighton off A281 between Poynings and Pyecombe. C17 moated house. Wild garden, roses, mixed borders and water plants. TEAS in aid of Newtimber Church. *Adm £1.20 Chd 30p. Suns April 25, Aug 29 (2-6)*

North Springs ⚘ (Mr & Mrs Michael Waring) Fittleworth. Garden situated between Fittleworth and Wisborough Green. Approach either from A272 outside Wisborough Green or A283 at Fittleworth and follow signs. Steep hillside garden of approx 2½ acres with spectacular views set in 40 acres woodland. Rhododendrons, camellias and other acid-loving shrubs, large mixed borders, clematis, old and modern roses, springfed pools and pond stocked with golden carp. TEAS (Suns only). *Adm £1.50 Chd 75p. Sun June 20; Sat, Sun July 10, 11 (2-6)*

Northwood Farmhouse &⚘⚘ (Mrs P Hill) Pulborough. 1m N of Pulborough on A29. Turn NW into Blackgate Lane and follow lane for 2m then follow the signs. Cottage Garden with bulbs, roses, pasture with wild flowers and pond all on Wealded clay surrounding Sussex farmhouse dating from 1420. TEAS. *Adm £1 Chd 50p. Suns, Mons April 18, 19; June 20, 21 (2-5)*

Nutbourne Gardens ⚘⚘ nr Pulborough. Take A283 E from junction with A29 (Swan Corner) 2m with 2 L forks signposted Nutbourne. Pass Rising Sun and follow signs to gardens. TEAS. *Combined adm £1.50 Chd 25p. Sun, Mon June 27, 28 (2-6)*

    Ebbsworth (Mrs F Lambert) Charming, well-planted, owner maintained cottage garden, surrounding old cottage. Roses and lilies, together with herbaceous borders. Man-made stream and ponds planted with water plants

    Manor Farm & (Mrs A M Rhys Jones) Pleasant ½-acre garden with interesting roses surrounding modern house

    Mill House (Sir Francis & Lady Avery Jones) ¾-acre surrounding old miller's house; and wild flower banks; cottage frontage with interesting walled herb garden; sloping down to water garden with stream, spring-fed pools and nearby mill pond. *(also by appt)*

    The Old Manor Cottage (Mr & Mrs J H A Lang) Steeply terraced small garden, with wide range of plants, trees and lily pond

Nyewood House &⚘ (Mr & Mrs Timothy Woodall) Nyewood. From A272 at Rogate take rd signposted Nyewood, S for approx 1¼m. At 40 mph sign on outskirts of Nyewood, turn L signposted Trotton. Garden approx 500 yds on R. 3-acre S facing garden recently renovated, with herbaceous borders, newly planted knot garden, pleaching, rose walk and water feature. TEAS. *Adm £1 Chd 25p. Suns June 13, July 18 (2-5.30)*

Nymans &⚘⚘ (The National Trust) Handcross. On B2114 at Handcross signposted off M23/A23 London-Brighton rd, SE of Handcross. Bus: 137 from Crawley & Haywards Heath (TQ265294). Rare trees and shrubs. Botanical interest. New rose garden. Wheelchairs available at the garden. TEA. *Adm £3.30 Chd £1.65. Suns May 9, June 6 (11-7)*

Offham House &⚘ (Mr & Mrs H N A Goodman; Mrs H S Taylor) Offham, 2m N of Lewes on A275. Cooksbridge station ½m. Fountains; flowering trees; double herbaceous border; long paeony bed. Queen Anne house (not open) 1676 with well-knapped flint facade. Featured in George Plumptre's Guide to 200 Gardens in Britain. Home-made TEAS. *Adm £1 Chd over 14 25p. Suns May 2, June 6 (2-6)*

The Old Rectory, Fittleworth ⚘⚘ (Mr & Mrs G Salmon) 2m W of Pulborough on A283 and next to Fittleworth church (parking in Church Lane and Bedham Rd). 2 acres of varied garden informally divided with interesting corners and walks. Spring bulbs; herbaceous borders; good variety of shrub roses. TEAS. *Adm 80p Chd 40p. Suns April 12, June 6 (2-5.30)*

The Old Rectory, Sutton &⚘ (Mr & Mrs Michael Boreham) Take A285 4m S of Petworth follow signs on L to Coates and Sutton Garden is R at top of hill into Sutton. From A29 turn W at foot of Bury Hill signposted Bignor; Sutton lies 1m W of Bignor. 2½ acres of medium-sized mixed garden of old trees; roses; herbaceous border with lovely views. House dates from 1320 (not open). Cream TEAS (in aid of the Church Repair Fund) *Adm £1 Chd free. Sat, Sun June 26, 27 (2-6)*

Palmer's Lodge ⚘ (R Hodgson Esq) West Chiltington Village. At Xroads in centre of West Chiltington Village opp Queens Head. 2m E of Pulborough 3m N Storrington. A charming plantsman's ½-acre garden with herbaceous and shrub borders. *Adm £1 Chd free. Sats, Suns, July 10, 11, 17, 18 (2-6)*

Parham House and Gardens & (gdns) ⚘ (Hse) ⚘ 4m SE of Pulborough on A283 Pulborough-Storrington Rd. Beautiful Elizabethan House with fine collection of portraits, furniture, rare needlework. 4 acres of walled garden; 7 acres pleasure grounds with lake. 'Veronica's Maze' a brick and turf maze designed with the young visitor in mind. Picnic area. New potager and rose garden planned for 1992; also plant sales in converted old mower shed. Light refreshments in Big Kitchen. Shop. St Peter's Church nearby. *Open Easter Sun to first Sun in Oct; Weds, Thurs, Suns & Bank Hols. Adm House & garden (1992 rates) £3.20 OAPs £2.50 Chd £1.50. Garden £1.60 Chd 75p. For NGS. Wed, Thurs May 19, 20 (Garden & picnic area 1-6, House 2-6 last adm 5.30)*

¶**Pashley Manor** ⚘⚘ (J Sellick Esq) Ticehurst. 10m S of Tunbridge Wells. 1½m SE Ticehurst on B2099. Pashley Manor is a grade 1 Tudor timber-framed ironmaster's house dating from 1550 with a Queen Anne rear elevation of 1720. Standing in a well timbered park with magnificent views across to Brightling Beacon. 8 acres of formal garden, dating from the C18, were created in true English romantic style and are planted with many ancient trees and fine shrubs, new plantings over the past decade give additional interest and subtle colouring throughout the year. Waterfalls, ponds and a moat which encircled the original house built 1262. Delightful views, peaceful environment and the sound of running water. TEAS on fine days. *Adm £2.50 OAP/Chd £2 (Share to St Michael's Hospice, Hastings). Tues, Wed, Thurs, Sat and Bank Hols April 10 to Oct 16. For NGS Sun May 23, Wed June 9 (11-5)*

Pembury &❀ (Nick & Jane Baker) Clayton. 6m N of Brighton. On B2112, 100yds from junction with A273. 2-acre informal, developing garden on heavy clay at foot of South Downs. Fine views; young and mature trees, shrubs, old-fashioned roses and herbaceous planting. Owner maintained; designed for year round interest. Saxon Church with restored wall paintings. Childrens' play area. Parking for wheelchairs in garden. Teas in village hall in aid of Clayton Church Fund. *Adm £1.25 Chd free. Sun June 6 (11-6)*

Penns in the Rocks ✖ (Lord & Lady Gibson) Groombridge. 7m SW of Tunbridge Wells on Groombridge-Crowborough Rd just S of Plumeyfeather corner. Bus: MD 291 Tunbridge Wells-East Grinstead, alight Plumeyfeather corner, ¾m. Large wild garden with rocks; lake; C18 temple; old walled garden. House (not shown) part C18. Dogs allowed in park. TEAS. *Adm £1.50 – Up to two chd 50p each, further chd free. Mons May 31, Aug 30 (2.30-5.30)*

Pheasants Hatch & (Mrs G E Thubron) Piltdown. 3m NW of Uckfield on A272. 2 acres, rose gardens with ponds and fountains; herbaceous borders; foliage; wild garden; peacocks. TEAS. *Adm £1 Chd free. Sun, Mon June 27, 28 (2-6)*

Pyramids &❀ (Gillian Jacomb-Hood) South Harting. 4m SE of Petersfield from B2146 take turning signed Nyewood-Rogate, 200yds on R after Harting stores. ½-acre created by owner with mainly chalk loving plants, interesting modern house (designed by Stout & Lichfield) linked to garden by paved areas; pool; spring bulbs; old-fashioned roses; shrubs; trees. Fine views of South Downs. TEAS. *Adm £1 Chd 30p. Sun June 27 (2-6)*

Rogate Gardens ✖❀ Rogate 5m W of Midhurst, 4m E of Petersfield on A272. Turn off N at Rogate Xroads. ½m up hill turn L at 'S' bend for both gardens. TEAS at Village Hall. *Combined adm £1.50 (Share to Rogate Village Hall Trust). Suns, June 13, 20 (2-6)*
> **Hunters Lodge** (Mr & Mrs S Rimmer) well stocked S facing owner maintained garden of ½ acre overlooking Rother valley with views to S Downs; providing all year round colour and interest from a variety of interesting trees, shrubs and herbaceous plants
> **Slade Lane Cottage** (Mrs R Brodrick) S facing ¾-acre garden on sloping site overlooking Rother valley to S Downs; good collection of shrub roses, cistus and wide variety of trees, shrubs, and herbaceous plants on sandy soil enriched by home-made compost. Garden is maintained by 2 dedicated women with help for hedges, grass and heavy work. All plants for sale are home grown

Rye Gardens ✖ Adjacent to church and town hall. Cars must be left in nearby town car parks. TEAS at **11 High St.** *Combined adm £1 Chd 25p. Sun June 20 (2-6)*
> **11 High Street** (Mr & Mrs C Festing) One-way street on R hand side, next door to Midland Bank. ⅓-acre old walled garden; many flowering shrubs and trees inc Ginkgo tree by fish pond. Vinery; herbaceous borders
> **Lamb House** (Mr & Mrs W S Martin) On West St nr church. Approx 1-acre walled garden; variety herbaceous plants; shrubs; trees; herbs. Home of Henry James 1898-1916 and E F Benson 1918-1940.

Rymans &✖ (Lord & Lady Claud Phillimore) Apuldram, 1½m SW of Chichester. Witterings Rd out of Chichester; at 1½m SW turn R signposted Apuldram; garden down rd on L. Walled and other gardens surrounding lovely C15 stone house (not open); bulbs, flowering shrubs, roses. Tea shops in Chichester. *Adm £1 Chd 30p. Suns April 4, 25 (2-5.30); June 20, July 18, Aug 29 (2-6.30)*

St Marys House &✖ (Mr Peter Thorogood) Bramber. 10m NW of Brighton in Bramber Village off A283 or 1m E of Steyning. Medium-sized formal gardens with amusing topiary, large example of living-fossil Gingko tree and Magnolia Grandiflora; pools, waterfalls and fountains, ancient ivy-clad 'Monk's Walk', all surrounding listed Grade I C15th timber-framed medieval house, once a monastic inn. TEAS. *(House open but not in aid of NGS) Easter to Sept 30, Suns and Thurs (2-6) Bank Hol Mons (2-6) also Mons in July, Aug, Sept (2-6). For NGS garden only Adm £1 Chd 50p. Fris July 30, Aug 6 (2-6)*

Selehurst &✖❀ (Mr & Mrs M Prideaux) Lower Beeding, 4½m S of Horsham on A281 opp Leonardslee. Large woodland garden recently extended with a chain of five ponds and a romantic bridge. Fine collection of camellia, azaleas, rhododendrons; walled garden, 60' laburnum tunnel underplanted with cream and silver, fine views. TEAS. *Adm £1.25 Chd 25p (Share to St. John's Church, Coolhurst). Sun May 16 (1-5)*

Sennicotts &❀ (John Rank Esq) Chichester. From Chichester take B2178 signposted to Funtington for 2m NW. Blind entrance at beginning of open stretch. Long drive ample parking near house. From Portsmouth A27, Havant roundabout take A259 to Emsworth, in Fishborne turn N marked Roman Palace then straight on until a T junction. Entrance opposite. 6-acre mature garden with intriguing spaces, lawns, shrubs, rhododendrons, daffodils (March opening). Large walled kitchen and cutting garden; greenhouses and orchard. *Adm £1.20 Chd free. Suns March 21 (10-2), May 30 (2-6)*

Sheffield Park Garden &✖ (The National Trust) Midway between E Grinstead and Lewes, 5m NW of Uckfield; E of A275. The garden, with 5 lakes, was laid out by Capability Brown in C18, greatly modified early in the C20. Many rare trees, shrubs and fine waterlilies; the garden is beautiful at all times of year. Teas Oak Hall (not NT). *Adm £4 Chd £2. For NGS Weds May 19, Oct 20 (11-6)*

¶**Sherburne House** &✖ (Mr & Mrs Angus Hewat) Eartham, 6m NE of Chichester, approach from A27 Chichester-Arundel Rd or A285 Chichester-Petworth Rd nr centre of village, 200yds S of church. Chalk garden of about 2 acres facing SW. Shrub and climbing roses; lime-tolerant shrubs; herbaceous, grey-leaved and foliage plants, pots, small herb garden, kitchen garden potager and conservatory. TEAS. *Adm £1 Chd 50p. Sun June 6 (2-6)*

By Appointment Gardens. These owners do not have a fixed opening day usually because they do not like crowds or have insufficient parking space. Owner will often give guided tour.

Somerset Lodge (Mr & Mrs R Harris) Petworth. 7m S of Northchapel on A283. 15m N of Chichester on A285 garden on A283 100 yds N of church. Parking in town car park. Charming ½-acre new garden with ponds and walled kitchen garden, small collections of old and English roses and wildflower garden. Cleverly landscaped on slope with beautiful views. *Adm 80p Chd 20p. Sat, Sun, Wed June 12, 13, 16 (2-6)*

Spur Point ⚙ (Mr & Mrs T D Bishop) nr Fernhurst. 3 acres of S facing terraced gardens, created by owners since 1970. Well planted with rhododendrons, azaleas, shrubs and mixed borders. Outstanding views to South Downs. *Adm £2 Chd 50p. By appt only during May. Tel 0483 211535*

¶**Stanbridge House** ♿⚙ (Marion and Bruce Porter) Staplefield Lane. Staplefield 2m S of Handcross. Take B2114 at Handcross signposted off M23/A23 London-Brighton Rd. At Staplefield village green opp the Jolly Tanners, fork R. At Xrds straight ahead. ½m entrance on right. 5 acres of mature trees, shrubs, herbaceous, ornamental and wildlife ponds, wildflower meadow, greenhouses and vegetable garden. The acid soil favours some fine acres, rhododendrons and azaleas. Gardens only suitable for wheelchairs with pushers. TEAS. *Adm £1 Chd 25p. Sun May 23 (2-6)*

Standen ⚙ (The National Trust) 1½m from East Grinstead. Signed from B2110 and A22 at Felbridge. Hillside garden of 10½-acres with beautiful views over the Medway Valley. TEAS. *Adm £2.30 Chd £1.15.* ▲*Suns May 9, Sept 12 (12.30-5.30. Last adm 5pm)*

Stonehurst ❀ (Mr D R Strauss) Ardingly. 1m N of Ardingly. Entrance 800yds N of S of England showground, on B2028. 30-acre garden set in secluded woodland valley. Many interesting and unusual landscape features; chain of man made lakes and waterfalls; natural sandstone rock outcrops and a fine collection of trees and shrubs. TEAS. *Adm £2 Chd £1 (Share to Homelife). Mon April 12; Suns April 25, May 16 (11-5)*

Tappington Grange ♿⚙❀ (Mr & Mrs Peter Kininmonth) Wadhurst. 4m SE Tunbridge Wells. Sharp turning almost opp Wadhurst Station. 3 acres; herbaceous and shrub borders; ornamental wildfowl; extensive water garden. Parking in station car park. TEAS. *Adm £1.50 Chd free. Sun May 30 (2-6)*

Telegraph House (Mr & Mrs David Gault) North Marden, 9 m. NW of Chichester. Entrance on B2141. From Petersfield to South Harting for 2m. From Chichester via A286 for 4m N of Lavant turn W on to B2l4l. 1-acre enclosed chalk garden 700 ft asl; chalk-tolerant shrubs, shrub roses, herbaceous plants; 1m avenue of copper beeches; walks through 150-acre yew wood; lovely views. House (not shown) in small park, built on site of semaphore keeper's cottage. TEAS. *Adm £1.50 Chd 75p. Sats, Suns June 19, 20; July 17, 18 (2-6). Also by appt May to Aug (2-5)* **Tel Harting 825206**

Three Oaks ♿⚙❀ (Mr & Mrs J C A Mudford) West Broyle. From roundabout N of Chichester take B2178 (Funtingdon) Rd NW for about 1⅓m. Turn L into Pine Grove and after a 100yds R into West Way. Small cottage garden. TEAS available at The Spinney. *Combined adm £1.30 with* **Woodstock**. *Sun May 16 (1.30-6)*

Trotton Gardens ⚙❀ 3½m W of Midhurst on A272. All parking and plant stall at Trotton Old Rectory. TEAS at Trotton Place. *Combined adm £2 Chd 50p. Suns May 16, June 27 (2-6)*

> **Trotton Old Rectory** (Mr & Mrs John Pilley) Medium-sized garden, old-fashioned roses, interesting shrubs, herbaceous borders, lake, water and vegetable gardens
> **Trotton Place** (Mr & Mrs N J F Cartwright) Entrance next to church. Large garden extending to over 4 acres surrounding C18 house (not open). Walled fruit and vegetable garden; C17 dovecote with small knot garden. Fine trees; mature borders with shrub roses; lake and woodland walk

The Upper Lodge ⚙❀ (J W Harrington Esq) Stopham, 1m W of Pulborough; via A283 towards Petworth; Lodge is on L by telephone kiosk at Stopham. A plant connoisseur's garden with mainly rhododendrons and azaleas; wide selection of shrubs for acid soil. *Adm £1 Chd 20p. Suns March 28, April 4; Easter Fri, Sun, Mon, April 9, 11, 12; Sun April 18 (2-5); Suns, Mons May 2, 3, 16, 23 (2-6)*

Wadhurst Park ♿⚙ (Dr & Mrs H Rausing) Wadhurst. 6m SE of Tunbridge Wells. Turn R along Mayfield Lane off B2099 at NW end of Wadhurst. L by Best Beech public house, L at Riseden Rd. 800-acres park with 7 different species of deer. Re-created garden on C19 site; restored C19 conservatories. Trailer rides into park. TEAS. *Adm £1.50 Chd 50p. Sun May 23 (2-5.30)*

Wakehurst Place ♿⚙ (National Trust & Royal Botanic Gardens, Kew) Ardingly, 5m N of Haywards Heath on B2028. National botanic garden noted for one of the finest collections of rare trees and flowering shrubs amidst exceptional natural beauty. Walled gardens, heath garden, Pinetum, scenic walks through steep wooded valley with lakes, attractive water courses and large bog garden. Guided tours 11.30 & 2.30 most weekends, also prebooked tours. The ranger **Tel 0444 892701**. TEAS. *Adm £3.30 OAPs/Students £1.70 Chd £1.10. Fri July 16 (10-7)*

West Dean Gardens ♿⚙❀ (Edward James Foundation) On A286, 5m. N of Chichester. Extensive garden in downland setting with specimen trees; 300′ pergola; gazebo; summer-houses; borders, old roses and wild garden, large walled garden under restoration. Circuit walk (2¼m) through park and 35-acre St Roche's Arboretum. TEA. *Adm £2.25 OAPs £2 Chd £1 parties £1.70 per person. March 1 to Oct 31 daily (11-6) last adm 5. For NGS Weds March 31, Sept 1 (11-6)*

¶**Whiligh** ⚙❀ (Mr & Mrs J Hardcastle) Wadhurst. On N side of B2099 between Wadhurst and Ticehurst. Old 4-acre garden, with mature trees and a variety of planting for colour interest. TEAS. *Adm £1.25 Chd under 14 free. Sun, Mon June 6, 7 (2-5.30)*

Regular Openers. See head of county section.

The White House ✍✿ (Elizabeth Woodhouse) Burpham. Turn off A27 Arundel-Worthing Rd ½ S of Arundel. Proceed through Wepham to Burpham for 2m. Garden is at far end of village. Charming garden, planned and planted by botanic artist. Great attention to plant forms and colour arrrangements. TEAS. *Adm 80p Chd 25p (Share to Burpham Church Restoration Fund). Suns June 13, 20 (2.30-6)*

Whitehouse Cottage (Barry Gray Esq) Staplefield Lane, Staplefield 5m NW of Haywards Heath. Garden is ⅓m. E of A23; and 2m S of Handcross. In Staplefield at Xroads by cricket pavilion take turning marked Staplefield Lane for 1m. Large garden with mixed shrubs, old roses; woodland path beside stream linked by ponds; interesting paved and planted areas around house. TEAS. *Adm £1 Chd 10p. Sat, Sun May 29, 30 (2-6). Also by appt* **Tel 0444 85229**

Wilderness Farm, Cabbages & Kings Garden (Mr & Mrs Andrew Nowell) Hadlow Down, ½m S of A272 from village. A contemporary ½ acre courtyard garden, designed and planted by Ryl Nowell to demonstrate design ideas; renovated farm buildings against the backdrop of the High Weald, the garden contains interesting construction details and a wealth of plants. Featured in 'Gardeners World' July 1991. TEAS. *Adm £1 Chd 50p. Sun June 27, Aug 15, Sept 5 (2-6)*

> **By Appointment Gardens.** Avoid the crowds. Good chance of a tour by owner. See garden description for telephone number.

Winchelsea Gardens ✍ S of Rye. *Combined adm £1.50 Chd 75p. Sat June 19 (2-6)*

    Cleveland House (Mr & Mrs S Jempson) 1½-acre semi-formal walled garden; many varied plants, ornamental trees, water feature, beautiful views, swimming in heated pool

    ¶**Cooks Garden** (Roger & Tina Neaves) Cottage garden with views to Rye Bay

    Nesbit (Mr & Mrs G Botterell) Formal enclosed ¼-acre garden; many and varied plants

    Old Castle House (Mr & Mrs Packard) Walled garden with roses and varied trees and shrubs. TEAS

    The Old Rectory (June & Denis Hyson) ½ acre of open lawn garden with views overlooking the Brede Valley

    ¶**Periteau House** (John and Robbie Gooders) Walled garden

    Three Wishes (Mrs M Fuller) Higham Green. Cottage garden

    ¶**Trojans Plat** (Mr & Mrs Norman Turner) Small cottage garden

    Well House (Misses Barbara & Nancy Lyle) Small enclosed town garden

Woodstock ✍ (Group Captain A R Gordon-Cumming) West Broyle. From roundabout N of Chichester take B2178 (Funtingdon) rd NW for 1⅓m. Turn L into Pine Grove and after 100yds R into Westway. Woodstock is at far end. ⅔-acre mainly woodland garden specialising in ground cover plants especially asiatic primulas and hostas (over 20 varieties of each). TEAS at The Spinney in aid of Save the Children Fund. *Combined adm with* **Three Oaks**. *£1.30 Chd free. Sun May 16 (1.30-6)*

Warwickshire & West Midlands

Hon County Organiser: Mrs D L Burbidge, Cedar House, Wasperton, Warwick CV35 8EB
Assistant Hon County Organiser: Miss Helen Syme, Puddocks, Frog Lane, Ilmington, Shipston-on-Stour CV36 4LQ
                                 Mrs C R King-Farlow, 8 Vicarage Road, Edgbaston, Birmingham B15 3EF
                                 Mrs Michael Perry, Sherbourne Manor, Sherbourne, Warwick CV35 8AP
Hon County Treasurer: Michael Pitts, Hickecroft, Mill Lane, Rowington, Warwickshire CV35 7DQ

DATES OF OPENING

By appointment

For telephone numbers and other details see garden descriptions

Brook Farm, Abbots Salford
Ilmington Manor, Shipston-on-Stour
Ivy Lodge, Warwick
The Mill Garden, Warwick
Sherbourne Park, nr Warwick
8 Vicarage Road, Edgbaston

Vine Cottage, Sheepy Magna (see Leicestershire & Rutland for details)
Woodpeckers, Bidford-on-Avon

March 7 Sunday
    Birmingham Botanical Gardens & Glasshouses, Edgbaston
March 30 Tuesday
    Woodpeckers, Bidford-on-Avon
April 4 Sunday
    Hunningham Village Gardens

Sherbourne Manor, nr Warwick

April 11 Sunday
Alveston Gardens,
Stratford-upon-Avon
59 Hazelwood Road, Acocks
Green
The Mill Garden, Warwick
April 12 Monday
59 Hazelwood Road, Acocks
Green
April 13 Tuesday
Woodpeckers, Bidford-on-Avon
April 17 Saturday
Castle Bromwich Hall Garden
Trust
April 18 Sunday
Ilmington Gardens,
Shipston-on-Stour
Ivy Lodge, Radway
Moseley Gardens
April 25 Sunday
Idlicote Gardens, nr
Shipston-on-Stour
May 2 Sunday
55 Elizabeth Road, Moseley,
Birmingham
May 4 Tuesday
Woodpeckers, Bidford-on-Avon
May 9 Sunday
Brook Farm, Abbots Salford
The Mill Garden, Warwick
May 16 Sunday
Compton Scorpion Farm,
Shipston-on-Stour
Greenlands, Wellesbourne
Ilmington Manor,
Shipston-on-Stour
Maxstoke Castle, nr Coleshill
Pear Tree Cottage, Ilmington
Wroxall Abbey School, nr Warwick
May 23 Sunday
Cedar House, Wasperton, nr
Warwick
Dorsington Gardens,
Stratford-on-Avon
May 30 Sunday
55 Elizabeth Road, Moseley,
Birmingham
Loxley Hall, nr Stratford-on-Avon
26 Sunnybank Road, Wylde Green
June 1 Tuesday
Woodpeckers, Bidford-on-Avon

June 6 Sunday
Baddesley Clinton Gardens
The Mill Garden, Warwick
8 Vicarage Road, Edgbaston
June 13 Sunday
Alscot Park, nr Stratford-on-Avon
Brook Farm, Abbots Salford
Crossways, Shrewley, nr Warwick
Greenlands, Wellesbourne
Holywell Gardens, nr Claverdon
Wroxall Abbey School, nr Warwick
June 16 Wednesday
Greenlands, Wellesbourne
June 19 Saturday
17 Gerrard Street, Warwick
Vine Cottage, Sheepy Magna (see
Leicestershire & Rutland for
details)
June 20 Sunday
Avon Dassett Gardens
17 Gerrard Street, Warwick
Vine Cottage, Sheepy Magna (see
Leicestershire & Rutland for
details)
50 Wellington Road, Edgbaston
Whichford & Ascott Gardens
June 22 Tuesday
Woodpeckers, Bidford-on-Avon
June 26 Saturday
Compton Scorpion Farm,
Shipston-on-Stour
Rowington Gardens
June 27 Sunday
Compton Scorpion Farm,
Shipston-on-Stour
Honington Village Gardens
Ilmington Manor,
Shipston-on-Stour
Ivy Lodge, Radway
Loxley Hall, nr Stratford-on-Avon
Pereira Road Gardens, Harborne
Roseberry Cottage, Fillongley
Rowington Gardens
July 4 Sunday
Alscot Park, nr Stratford-on-Avon
The Butchers Arms, Priors
Hardwick, nr Rugby
Harborne Follies, Birmingham
Packwood House, nr Hockley
Heath
July 11 Sunday
Ashorne House, Warwick

Fieldgate Lane Gardens,
Kenilworth
Ilmington Manor,
Shipston-on-Stour
Moseley Gardens
July 12 Monday
Ashorne House, Warwick
July 18 Sunday
Brook Farm, Abbots Salford
Hall Green Gardens, Birmingham
59 Hazelwood Road, Acocks
Green
Martineau Centre Gardens,
Edgbaston
Warmington Village Gardens
July 25 Sunday
Hill Top Farm, Avon Dassett
The Mill Garden, Warwick
Old Mill Cottage, Avon Dassett
26 Sunnybank Road, Wylde Green
July 27 Tuesday
Woodpeckers, Bidford-on-Avon
August 1 Sunday
55 Elizabeth Road, Moseley,
Birmingham
Hunningham Village Gardens
August 16 Monday
Ryton Gardens, nr Coventry
August 24 Tuesday
Woodpeckers, Bidford-on-Avon
August 29 Sunday
The Mill Garden, Warwick
September 4 Saturday
Ryton Gardens, nr Coventry
September 12 Sunday
59 Hazelwood Road, Acocks
Green
Tysoe Manor, nr Warwick
September 19 Sunday
The Mill Garden, Warwick
September 25 Saturday
Castle Bromwich Hall Garden
Trust
September 26 Sunday
Birmingham Botanical Gardens &
Glasshouses, Edgbaston
October 10 Sunday
The Mill Garden, Warwick

DESCRIPTIONS OF GARDENS

Alscot Park &⚘ (Mrs James West) 2½m S of Stratford-on-Avon A34. Fairly large garden; extensive lawns, shrub roses, fine trees, orangery, with C18 Gothic house (not open), river, deer park, lakes. Coach parties by appt. Home-made TEAS. *Adm £1 Chd free (Share to Warwickshire Assoc. of Boys' Clubs). Suns June 13, July 4 (2-6)*

Alveston Gardens &⚘❀ 2m NE of Stratford-upon-Avon. Turn left at War Memorial off B4086 Stratford-Wellesbourne rd; Alveston ¼m. TEAS at The Malt House in aid of Alveston WI. *Combined adm £1 Chd 20p. Sun April 11 (2-6)*

The Bower House & (Mr & Mrs P S Hart) 1 acre, owner-designed, unusual trees, water garden and rockeries. Pergolas, alpine sinks, choice shrubs

Court Leys (Mr & Mrs E Barnard) 1 acre; shrubs, trees and herbaceous borders, circular raised brick planters, conservatory

Long Acre (Dr & Mrs N A Woodward) Owner designed, 1 acre; interesting trees, shrubs and roses; rockery, barbecue area, pergola, terraces and ponds

Parham Lodge &✿❀ (Mr & Mrs K C Edwards) 1 acre; designed and maintained by owners. Choice trees, shrubs; plants, bulbs; island beds with heathers, large pond, patios, tubs, rose garden

Ashorne House & (Mr & Mrs A J Sidwell) Ashorne 5m S of Warwick. 1½m W of junction of A41 Warwick-Banbury, signed Ashorne. Entrance and car park in adjacent cricket pitch. 8 acres; typical English country garden; small lake. TEAS (in aid of Village Hall fund). *Adm £1.50 Chd free. Sun July 11; collecting box Mon July 12 (2-6)*

Avon Dassett Gardens &✿ 7m N of Banbury off B4100 (use Exit 12 of M40). Car parking in the village and in car park at top of hill. TEAS at **Old Mill Cottage**. *Combined adm £1.50 Chd free (Share to Myton Hamlet Hospice). Sun June 20 (2-6)*

Hill Top Farm (Mrs N & Mr D Hicks) 1-acre garden. Dramatic display of bedding plants, perennials and roses. Extensive kitchen garden. Greenhouses. *Also open July 25 (2-6)*

¶Home Farm House (Mr & Mrs M J Appleton) Cottage garden with shrubs and herbaceous plants

The Limes (Mr & Mrs C J Baylis) Large garden with mature trees, herbaceous borders, shrubs and lawns. Collection of herbs

Old Mill Cottage (Mr & Mrs M Lewis) Conservation garden of ½ acre with shrub, perennial borders and rockeries. Collection alpines and herbs. Two ponds and kitchen garden. *Also open Sun July 25 (2-6)*

The Old New House (Mr & Mrs M G Potts) Established garden with specimen trees and shrubs; lawns and rose garden

The Old Pumphouse (Mr & Mrs W Wormell) Cottage garden with mixed borders featuring varieties of pinks and shrub roses and clematis. Kitchen garden and greenhouse

The Old Rectory (Mrs L Hope-Frost) 2-acre garden surrounding listed building mentioned in Doomsday Book (not open). Large variety of fine trees and shrubs. Small wood

The Old Schoolhouse (Mr & Mrs P Fletcher) Small garden with interesting plants and shrubs; pond; views over parkland

Baddesley Clinton &✿ (The National Trust) ¾m W off A4141 Warwick-Birmingham road near Chadwick End. 7½m NW of Warwick. Mediaeval moated manor house little changed since 1633; walled garden and herbaceous borders; natural areas; lakeside walk. Lunches and TEAS. *Adm Grounds only £2. Shop and restaurant open from 12.30.* ▲*For NGS Sun June 6 (12.30-6)*

Birmingham Botanical Gardens & Glasshouses &✿❀ 2m SW of Birmingham City Centre, signposted from Hagley Rd (A456). 15 acres; Tropical House with large lily pond and many economic plants. Palm House; Orangery; Cactus House. Outside bedding displays; rhododendrons and azaleas; rose garden; rock garden; 200 trees. Theme, herb and cottage gardens. Fun area for children. Plant centre. Bands play every Sun afternoon. TEAS in the Pavilion. *Adm £3.20 Chd, Students & OAPs £1.60. Open daily. For NGS Suns March 7, Sept 26 (10-6)*

Brook Farm &✿ (Mr & Mrs R B Hughes) Abbots Salford, Salford Priors 5m N of Evesham on B439. 1½ acres; large mixed borders, island beds, pond; bog, scree and peat gardens. TEAS. *Adm £1 Chd Free. Suns May 9, June 13, July 18 (2-6). Also by appt all year* **Tel 0386 871122**

The Butchers Arms &✿ (Mr & Mrs L Pires) Priors Hardwick, S of Rugby. 6m SE of Southam. From Southam turn R off Daventry rd. 4-acre garden started 1977 (parts very new) informal garden made from S sloping field; island beds with shrubs, trees, old-fashioned shrub roses, hedges, conifers, natural stream and lake. Swimming pool, patio, pergola. C15 stone-built cottage (not open). On 'Gardener's World' BBC2 Aug 1990. TEAS. *Adm £1 Chd free. Sun July 4 (2-5)*

Castle Bromwich Hall Garden Trust Chester Rd. &✿ 4m E of Birmingham. 1m from junction 5 of the M6 (exit Northbound). An example of the Formal English Garden of the C18. The ongoing restoration, started 6yrs ago now provides visitors, academics and horticulturalists opportunity of seeing a unique collection of historic plants, shrubs, medicinal and culinary herbs and a fascinating vegetable collection. Guided tours Weds, Sats & Suns. Shop. TEAS only by prior arrangement. *Adm £2 OAPs £1 Chd 50p & OAPs £1. Mons to Thur April to Sept (1.30-4.30) Sats & Suns Bank Hols (2-6). For NGS Sats April 17, Sept 25 (2-6)*

Cedar House &✿ (Mr & Mrs D L Burbidge) Wasperton. 4m S of Warwick on A429, turn right between Barford and Wellesbourne, Cedar House at end of village. 3-acre mixed garden; shrubs, herbaceous borders, ornamental trees, woodland walk. TEAS. *Adm £1.50 Chd free (Share to St John's Church, Wasperton). Mon May 23 (2.30-5.30)*

Compton Scorpion Farm (Mrs T M Karlsen) nr Ilmington. As for Ilmington Manor then fork L at village hall; after 1m down steep narrow lane, house on L. Garden designed and created by owners 5yrs ago from meadow hillside, aiming at Jekyll single colour schemes. TEAS. *Adm £1 Chd free. Sun, May 16, Sat, Sun June 26, 27 (2-6)*

¶Crossways &✿❀ (Mr & Mrs M P Andrews) Shrewley. 5m NW of Warwick. 16m SE of Birmingham on B4439 between Hockley Heath and Hatton at Shrewley Xrds. ¾-acre traditional flower garden; cottage garden; flowers, old roses, orchard. Organically managed and designed to encourage wildlife. TEA. *Adm £1 Chd free. Sun June 13 (2-5)*

Dorsington Gardens &✿ 7m SW of Stratford-on-Avon. On A439 from Stratford turn left to Welford-on-Avon, then right to Dorsington. TEAS. *Combined adm £2 Chd free (Share to St Peter's Church, Dorsington). Suns May 23 (2-5.30)*

Knowle Thatch (Mr & Mrs P W Turner)

Milfield (Mr & Mrs P Carey)

The Moat House (Mr & Mrs I Kolodotschko)
¶New House Farm (Mr & Mrs G Wood-Hill)
The Old Manor (Mr F Dennis) TEAS
The Old Rectory (Mr & Mrs N Phillips)
White Gates (Mrs A G Turner)
Windrush (Mrs M B Mills)

55 Elizabeth Rd ✿❀ (Rob & Diane Cole) Moseley. 4m S of Birmingham City centre, halfway between Kings Heath Centre & Edgbaston Cricket Ground. Off Moor Green Lane. Plantsman's garden 100′ × 30′ on 3 levels, with scree area and mixed borders of alpines, rhododendrons, primulas and many unusual plants. Alpine House & troughs. TEAS in aid of Guide Dogs for the Blind. *Adm 80p Chd 20p. Suns May 2, 30, Aug 1 (2-6)*

¶Fieldgate Lane Gardens ♿ N end of Kenilworth on the A452. *Adm £1 Chd free. Sun July 11 (2-6)*

¶12 Fieldgate Lane (Mrs P Taylor) Kenilworth. ½ acre of informal planting. Shrubs and borders for easy maintenance; small pond

¶16 Fieldgate Lane (Mr & Mrs T Brayson) 1-acre garden with naturalised areas. Trees as main interest

17 Gerrard Street ✿ (Miss P M & Mr T K Meredith) Warwick. 100yds from castle main gate. Car park at St Nicholas. Small town garden with interesting plants. *Adm 40p Chd free. Sat, Sun June 19, 20 (11-1 & 2-6)*

Greenlands ♿❀ (Mr Eric T Bartlett) Wellesbourne. Leave Statford-upon-Avon due E on the B4086. Garden on Xrds at Loxley/Charlecote by airfield. An acre of mature trees; shrubs; shrub roses and herbaceous borders. TEAS. *Adm 80p Chd 20p. Suns May 16, June 13, Wed June 16 (11-5)*

¶Hall Green Gardens ✿❀ *Adm £1 Chd free. Sun July 18 (2-5)*

¶120 Russell Rd ✿❀ (Mr D Worthington) Turn off A34 E at Swithland Motors, Hall Green, down York Rd then L into Russell Rd. Small suburban garden designed by owner; shrubs, herbaceous, climbers, old roses and fountain; tubs, hanging baskets and window boxes. TEA

¶63 Green Rd (Mrs M Wilkes) Green Rd is W off A34 Hall Green Parade. (Nr Hall Green Station). Narrow suburban garden; 4 pools, bedding plants, herbaceous, shrubs, several distinctive features made by owner

Harborne Follies ✿❀ Birmingham A-Z Ref page 87.1H. 3m from Birmingham City centre to W on A456 (Hagley Rd W). 3rd on L past Kings Head public house, 2nd L into Sir Richards Drive. Parking in Sir Richards Drive & Fitzroy Ave (on the rd). TEAS at **Hagley Rd W** in aid of St John Ambulance. *Combined adm £1.50 Chd free. Sun July 4 (2-6)*

9 Sir Richards Drive ✿❀ (Dr & Mrs D Collier). ⅕-acre garden with mixed planting of trees, shrubs and herbaceous perennials. Large paved terrace with numerous containers for more tender plants. Plants for sale in aid of St John Ambulance

31 Fitzroy Ave (Mr P Thompson) ¼-acre garden, containing trees and shrubs as a background to a splendid display of annual bedding plants & hanging baskets

159 Hagley Rd West (Mr & Mrs M Edwards) ¼-acre garden, mixed shrubs, trees and herbaceous perennials, many of the latter grown especially for dried flower arrangements. Pond and attractive terrace

59 Hazelwood Rd ♿✿❀ (Mrs J M Dudley) Acocks Green. 4m SE of Birmingham just off A41 at Acocks Green. 1st R up Shirley Rd opp Methodist Church. ⅕-acre colourful garden with spring bulbs, shrubs, trees, bedding plants, fuchsias, geraniums and chrysanthemums. Large well stocked greenhouse. See the owls. TEAS. *Adm £1 Chd 20p. Easter Sun, Mon April 11, 12, Suns July 18, Sept 12 (11-5)*

Holywell Gardens ♿✿❀ 5m E of Henley-in-Arden, nearest village Claverdon. TEAS in aid of Myton Hospice. *Combined adm £1.50 Chd free. Sun June 13 (11-6)*

Holywell Farm (Mr & Mrs Ian Harper) 2¼-acre natural garden; lawn, trees, shrubs. Laid out in 1963 for easy maintenance, surrounding C16 half timbered house

Holywell Manor Farm (Mr & Mrs Donald Hanson) Cottage type garden round C16 half timbered farmhouse, all within moated outer boundary incl natural duck pond

Honington Village Gardens ♿✿❀ 1½m N of Shipston-on-Stour. Take A34 towards Stratford then right signed Honington. TEAS **Honington Hall**. *Combined adm £2 Chd free (Share to All Saints Church, Honington Restoration Fund). Sun June 27 (2.15-6)*

Honington Hall (Lady Wiggin) Extensive lawns; fine trees. Carolean house (not open); Parish Church adjoining house

Honington Glebe (Mr & Mrs John Orchard) Over 2 acres of informal garden interesting ornamental trees; shrubs and foliage. Parterre and raised lily pool recently laid out in old walled garden

Holts Cottage (Mr & Mrs L Goodman)
Honington Lodge (Lord & Lady Tombs)
The Old Cottage (Mrs Wigington)
Old Mullions (Mr & Mrs R Lawton)

Hunningham Village Gardens ♿✿❀ Hunningham. From Leamington Spa B4453 to Rugby. Signposted Hunningham R after Weston-under-Wetherley. Or A425 to Southam at Fosseway (B4455) turn L. At Hunningham Hill turn L then follow signs to church. 3 village gardens all with wonderful views. Plants & Tea April 4, Teas Aug 1 near the church. *Combined adm £1.50 Chd free (Share to St Margarets Church). Suns April 4 (2-5), Aug 1 (2-5.30)*

The Bungalow (Mr & Miss Rouse) A cottage garden with large vegetable plot

The Olde School House (Mr & Mrs G Longstaff) A new owner-designed and maintained 1-acre garden. Borders, shrubs, pond/wildlife area

Highcross (Mr & Mrs T Chalk) A secluded garden, with alpines

By Appointment Gardens. These owners do not have a fixed opening day usually because they do not like crowds or have insufficient parking space. Owner will often give guided tour.

Idlicote Gardens &⚶🏵 3m E of Shipston-on-Stour. TEAS. *Combined adm £1.50 OAPs £1 Chd free (Share to Parish Church of St James the Great). Sun April 25 (2-6)*
  Idlicote House (Maj & Mrs R P G Dill) About 4 acres. Fine views. Small Norman church in grounds also statuary and follies. Garden being improved each year. House C18 (not open) listed Grade II partly attributed to Sir John Soane. Exterior recently restored
  Badgers Cottage (Dr & Mrs D R N Custance)
  Badgers Farm (Sir Derek & Lady Hornby)
  1 Bickerstaff Cottages (Mr & Mrs C Balchin)
  Bickerstaff Farm (Sir John & Lady Owen)
  Mews Cottage (Mr & Mrs D Colton)
  The Old Rectory (Mr & Mrs D Higgs)
  Woodlands (Capt & Mrs P R Doyne)

Ilmington Gardens ⚶🏵 8m S of Stratford-on-Avon, 4m NW of Shipston-on-Stour. Ilmington Morris dancers. TEAS in the Village Hall. *Combined adm £2 OAPs £1.50 Chd free (Share to Ellen Badger Hospital). Sun April 18 (2-6)*
  The Bevingtons (Mrs Bishop)
  Crab Mill (Prof D C Hodgkin)
  ¶Crab Mill Cottage (Mrs M Greathead)
  Foxcote Hill (Mr & Mrs M Dingley)
  Foxcote Hill Cottage (Miss A Terry)
  Frog Orchard (Mrs C Naish)
  The Manor (Mr D & Lady Flower)
  Pear Tree Cottage (Dr & Mrs A Hobson)
  Puddocks (Miss H Syme)
  The Rectory (The Rev. & Mrs V Story)

Ilmington Manor &🏵 (Mr D & Lady Flower). 4m NW of Shipston-on-Stour, 8m S of Stratford-on-Avon. Daffodils in profusion (April). Hundreds of old and new roses, ornamental trees, shrub and herbaceous borders, rock garden, pond garden, topiary, fish ponds with geese and ducks. House (not open) built 1600. TEAS (June 27, July 11) TEA (May 16). *Adm £1.50 OAPs £1 Chd free. Suns May 16, June 27, July 11 (2-6). Also by appt Tel 060882 230*

Ivy Lodge & (Mrs M A Willis) Radway 7m NW of Banbury via A41 and B4086, turn right down Edgehill; 14m SE of Stratford via A422. Left below Edgehill. 4-acres; spring bulbs and blossom; wildflower area; climbing roses; site Battle of Edgehill. TEAS. *Adm £1 Chd free (Share to St Catherine's Hospice, Banbury). Sun April 18, June 27 (2-6). Also by appt in Oct Tel 0295 87371*

Loxley Hall (Col A Gregory-Hood) 4m SE of Stratford-on-Avon. Turn N off A422 or W off A429 1½m SW of Wellesbourne. Modern sculpture, iris, shrubs, roses, trees. Small Japanese Garden. Old church adjacent can be visited. TEAS. *Adm £1 Chd 20p. Suns May 30, June 27 (2-7)*

Martineau Centre Gardens &⚶🏵 (City of Birmingham Education Dept) Priory Rd, Edgbaston. From Birmingham S via A38; R at Priory Rd (lights and box junction); entrance 100yds on right opp Priory Hospital. 2-acre demonstration gardens; hardy ornamentals, vegetables, small orchard; glasshouses; nature reserve/wild garden. Mown field for picnics. TEAS. *Adm £1 Chd 50p. Sun July 18 (10.30-6)*

Maxstoke Castle &⚶ (Mr & Mrs M C Fetherston-Dilke) nr Coleshill, E of Birmingham, 2½m E of Coleshill on B4114 take R turn down Castle Lane; Castle Dr 1¼m on R. 4 to 5 acres of garden and pleasure grounds with flowers, shrubs and trees in the immediate surroundings of the castle and inside courtyard; water-filled moat round castle. *Adm £2 OAP/Chd £1 under 6 free. Sun May 16 (2-5)*

The Mill Garden &⚶🏵 (Mr A B Measures) 55 Mill St, Warwick off A425 beside castle gate. 1 acre; series of informal, partially enclosed areas, on river next to castle. Superb setting; herb garden; raised alpine beds; small trees, shrubs, cottage plants and some unusual plants. Use St Nicholas Car Park. Tea in Warwick. *Collecting box. Open for NGS and other charities Suns & Bank Hols April 11, May 9, June 6, July 25, Aug 29, Sept 19, Oct 10. Other times when possible (2-6). By appt Tel 0926 492877*

Moseley Gardens ⚶🏵 Approx 3m from Birmingham City Centre halfway between Kings Heath Centre & Moseley Village. TEAS. *Combined adm £1.20 Chd 20p. Suns April 18, July 11 (2-6)*
  No 16 Prospect Rd 🏵 (Mrs S M & Mr R J Londesborough) Small garden with wide range of plants. Registered wildlife garden. *Also by appt all year Tel 021 449 8457*
  No 17 Prospect Rd (Mr & Mrs A Packer) Small family garden, fruit and vegetables, greenhouse, mixed borders
  No 19 Prospect Rd (Mr K White) Well planted spring suburban garden. *April 18 only*
  No 30 Prospect Rd (Mrs J Taylor) South-facing terraced garden incorporating rockery-covered air-raid shelter.
  No 33 School Rd (Ms J Warr-Arnold) Mixed garden containing plants with interesting histories. *Sun July 11 only*
  No 65 School Rd (Mrs W Weston) Small shady garden with patio and pergola. *Sun July 11 only*
  No 14A Clarence Rd (Ms C Fahy) West-facing garden with year round interest. *Sun July 11 only*

Packwood House &⚶ (The National Trust) 11m SE of Birmingham. 2m E of Hockley Heath. Carolean yew garden representing the Sermon on the Mount. Tudor house with tapestries, needlework and furniture of the period. Teas at Baddesley Clinton (NT) Henley in Arden or Knowle. *Adm garden only £2. ▲For NGS Sun July 4 (2-6)*

Pear Tree Cottage &🏵 (Dr & Mrs A F Hobson) Ilmington 8m S of Stratford-on-Avon, 4m NW of Shipston-on-Stour. Cottage garden with many interesting plants and bulbs. Designed and maintained by owners; rock garden and terrace. TEA at **Ilmington Manor**. *Adm 50p Chd 20p. Sun May 16 (2-6)*

Pereira Road Gardens ⚶🏵 Birmingham A-Z 5c p.72 between Gillhurst Rd and Margaret Grove, ¼m from Hagley Rd or ½m Harborne High St. TEAS at **No. 84** in aid of St Mary's Hospice. *Combined adm £1.50 Chd 30p. Sun June 27 (2-5)*

No. 50 ✿ (Prof M Peil) About ⅕ acre, with a wide range of shrubs and perennials for all seasons; fruit and vegetables. Large bed of plants with African connections, pond. (Plants sold in aid of Catholic Fund for Overseas Development.)

No. 45 (Wyn & Alfred White) Harborne. ⅕ acre on four levels. Spring bulbs, rhododendrons, roses, shrubs, herbaceous borders, ornamental and fruit trees in formal and informal areas. Sale of gifts in aid of Break Through Trust for the Deaf

No. 84 ૐ (Mr R E Barnett) ⅕ acre with 30 degree sloping concreted bank, now extensive rockery, interesting shrubs, herbaceous borders

Roseberry Cottage ૐ⚘✿ (Mr & Mrs Richard G. Bastow) Fillongley. 6m N of Coventry on B4098 Tamworth Road. Go under motorway bridge to top of hill, take Woodend Lane, sign on R. Turn L into Sandy Lane, opp triangle of beech trees. 1st house on right in Sandy Lane. Please use one way system due to restricted parking. Garden of 1¾ acres including herbaceous border, rock garden, pool, peat and bog area, scree and small herb garden. Stone troughs, orchard with wild flowers, organically grown fruit and vegetables. Herbs for sale, thymes a speciality. TEA. *Adm £1 Chd 30p (Share to NCCPG). Sun June 27 (2-6)*

¶**Rowington Gardens** ૐ⚘✿ 6m NW of Warwick. 15m SE of Birmingham on B4439 between Hockley Heath and Hatton. Turn into Finwood Rd (signed Lowsonford); at Rowington Xrds 1st L into Mill Lane. TEA. *Combined adm £1.50 Chd 50p (Share to St Laurence's Church Rowington). Sat, Sun June 26, 27 (2-5.30)*
  Hickecroft (Mr & Mrs J M Pitts) 2-acre garden re designed and replanted; some interesting plants, mixed borders. Home to part of the NCCPG Digitalis collection
  ¶**Woodlands** (Mr & Mrs M J O Morley) A medium-sized English country garden surrounding C16 farmhouse. Recent tree planting on large scale. Interesting use of former swimming pool

Ryton Gardens ૐ⚘✿ (The Nat Centre for Organic Gardening) 5m SE of Coventry on B4029 (off A45 to Wolston). 8-acre site demonstrating organic gardening methods as seen on Channel 4's 'All Muck and Magic' series: composting display, herb, rose and bee garden; shrub borders; vegetable plots and fruit; garden for the blind and partially sighted; conservation area with pond and wild flowers meadow. Shop; childrens play area; award winning cafe serving organically grown food. Guide dogs allowed. TEAS. *Adm £3 Concessions £2, Chd free. Open daily except Christmas period. April-Sept (10-6); Oct-Mar (10-4). For NGS Mon Aug 16, Sat Sept 4 (9-5)*

Sherbourne Manor ૐ✿ (Mr & Mrs M Perry) 2m S of Warwick just off A429 Barford Rd. Large garden contains herbaceous borders; lawns; stream; one small lake and large variety of established trees. Paddocks with rare breed sheep. TEAS in aid of All Saints Church, Sherbourne. *Adm £2 OAP's £1 Chd free. Sun April 4 (2-6)*

Sherbourne Park ૐ (The Hon Lady Smith-Ryland) 3m S of Warwick off A429; ½m N of Barford. Medium-sized garden; lawns, shrubs, borders, roses, lilies; lake; temple;

church by Gilbert Scott 1863 adjacent to early Georgian House (not open) 1730. Featured in 'New Englishwoman's Garden' (R Verey) and 'English Gardens' (P Coats). Featured in 1991 & 1992 Gardeners Royal Benevolent Society Calendar. Lunches for private tours by arrangement. Free car park. *Adm £2 OAPs and Chd (13-16) £1, under 12 free (Share to All Saints Church, Sherbourne). Open for private tours and by appt only.* **Tel 0926 624255 624506**

26 Sunnybank Road ⚘✿ (Chris & Margaret Jones) Wylde Green. ¾m S of Sutton Coldfield. Turn off A5127 towards Wylde Green Station then; 2nd L. ⅕-acre town garden on sandy soil, redesigned in mid-80's by present owners as a series of 'rooms'. Year-long interest achieved by use of bulbs, shrubs and herbaceous plants. TEAS in aid of Leprosy Mission. *Adm £1 OAPs 50p Chd free. Suns May 30, July 25 (2-6)*

Tysoe Manor ૐ✿ (Mr & Mrs W A C Wield) Tysoe. 5m NE of Shipston-on-Stour. Take the 4035 to Banbury. In Brailes turn L to Tysoe. The Manor is the first house on the L after reaching Upper Tysoe. 4-acre garden, large lawns with stone walls, herbaceous and flower borders; rose beds and mature ornamental and fruit trees. TEAS in aid of Tysoe Church. *Adm £1.50 Chd free. Sun Sept 12 (2-6)*

8 Vicarage Rd ૐ⚘✿ (Charles & Tessa King-Farlow) Edgbaston, 1½m W of City Centre off A456 (Hagley Rd). ¾-acre retaining in part its Victorian layout but informally planted with mixed borders of interesting and unusual plants; shrub rose border; walled kitchen garden and conservatory. TEAS. *Adm £1 Chd free (Share to St George's Church). Sun June 6 (2-6). Also by appt* **Tel 021 455 0902**

Warmington Village Gardens ૐ✿ 5m NW of Banbury on B4100. TEAS at The Glebe House. *Combined adm £1.50 Chd free (Share to Warmington PCC Restoration Fund). Sun July 18 (2-6)*
  Berka (Mr & Mrs B J Castle) Chapel Street
  The Glebe House (Mr & Mrs G Thornton) Village Road
  Holly Cottage (Dr & Mrs T W Martin) The Green
  Mews Cottage (Mr & Mrs E J Squire) The Green
  Poynters (Mrs F Ingram) School Lane
  Rotherwood (Miss E M Kirkpatrick & Miss M R Goodison) Soot Lane
  Underedge (Mr & Mrs J Dixon) 1 Church Hill

50 Wellington Rd ૐ⚘✿ (Mrs Anne Lee) Edgbaston. 200yds NE of Edgbaston Old Church on the corner of Ampton Rd & Wellington Rd. 1-acre walled town garden, partly replanted in 1985. Terrace, paving, brick paths & some architectural features. 100-yr-old rhododendrons & large trees. Two long mixed borders round large lawn, fountain. TEAS. *Adm £1 Chd 20p. Sun June 20 (2-6)*

Whichford & Ascott Gardens ✿ 6m SE of Shipston-on-Stour. Turn E off A34 at Long Compton for Whichford. TEAS at The Old Chapel House on Sat. Cream TEAS Sun at Whichford House. *Combined adm £1.80 Chd free (Share to Katherine House Hospice). Sun June 20, (2-6)*

Brook Hollow (Mr & Mrs J A Round) Garden on a bank, recently planted; stream and water garden
Combe House (Mr & Mrs D C Seel) Hidden garden surrounding house; mature fine trees.
The Old House (Mr & Mrs T A Maher) Undulating, newly planted garden. Natural ponds and wildflower meadow.
Rightons Cottage (Col & Mrs C R Bourne) Medium-sized garden planted for quiet enjoyment with minimal upkeep in retirement
Stone Walls (Mrs J Scott-Cockburn) Walled garden; paved garden in foundations of old stable
Whichford House (Mr & Mrs J W Oakes) Large garden with extensive views
The Whichford Pottery (Mr & Mrs J B M Keeling) Secret walled garden, unusual plants, large vegetable garden and rambling cottage garden. Adjoining pottery

---

Regular Openers. See head of county section.

Woodpeckers &. &% (Dr & Mrs A J Cox) The Bank, Marlcliff, nr Bidford-on-Avon 7m SW of Stratford-on-Avon. Off the B4085 Between Bidford-on-Avon and Cleeve Prior. 2½-acre plantsman's garden designed and maintained by owners; colour-schemed herbaceous and mixed borders, old roses, meadow garden, alpines in troughs and gravel, pool, knot garden, ornamental kitchen garden. Featured on BBC2 'Gardener's World'. *Adm £1.20 Chd free. Tues March 30, April 13, May 4, June 1, 22, July 27, Aug 24 (2-5). Also by appt all year* Tel 0789 773416

Wroxall Abbey School &. &% (Mrs I D M Iles, Principal) Wroxall 6m NW of Warwick. Nr Fiveways junc on A4141. 27 acres; spring flowers, shrubs, rhododendrons, small enclosed flower garden. 'Nature trail' incl comments on plants, flowers, etc. Work in progress on surveying and re-instatement of historical pleasure grounds, by Warwickshire Garden Trust. Evensong in Chapel 5pm. TEA. *Adm £1.50 Chd 50p (Share to St Leonard's Church, Wroxall). Suns May 16, June 13 (2-5)*

Wiltshire

Hon County Organiser: Brigadier Arthur Gooch, Manor Farmhouse, Chitterne, Warminster BA12 OLG
Assistant Hon County Organisers: Mrs David Armytage, Sharcott Manor, Pewsey
Mrs Anthony Heywood, Monkton House, Monkton Deverell

DATES OF OPENING

By appointment
For telephone numbers and other details see garden descriptions

Andover House, nr Malmesbury
Ashtree Cottage, Kilmington Common
Bryher, Bromham
Chisenbury Priory, Pewsey
Fitz House, Teffont Magna
Home Covert, Devizes
Kellaways, nr Chippenham
Lower Farm House, Milton Lilbourne
7 Norton Bavant, nr Warminster
Sharcott Manor, nr Pewsey

Regular openings
For details see garden descriptions

Broadleas, nr Devizes. Every Sun, Wed & Thurs April 1 to Oct 30
Chisenbury Priory. Every Wed May to Sept Sun May to Aug and Bank Hol Mons

The Courts, nr Bradford-on-Avon. Open every day except Sat April to Oct
Easton Grey House, nr Malmesbury. Daily. For exceptions see text.
Fitz House, Teffont Magna. Every Sat & Sun May to Sept
Hazelbury Manor, nr Box. Daily May 1 to Sept 30, April and Oct Suns only
Heale Gardens & Plant Centre, Middle Woodford. Open all year
Iford Manor, nr Bradford-on-Avon. Daily May to Sept except Mons & Fris. April & Oct Suns only
Lackham Gardens, nr Chippenham. Open daily March 20 to Nov 7
Long Hall, Stockton, nr Warminster. Every Wed March to Sept
Manningford Gardens & Nurseries, nr Pewsey. Daily all year except Dec 25 to Jan 2. Closed Weds
Sheldon Manor, nr Chippenham. Easter Sun & Mon. Every Suns, Thurs & Bank Hols April 11 to Oct 3
Stourhead Garden, Stourton, Mere. Daily

Stourton House, Mere. Suns, Weds, Thurs, & Bank Hols, April 1 to Nov 28
Waterdale House, East Knoyle. Suns April 11 to June 6
West Kington Gardens, Pound Hill House. Wed to Sun & Bank Hols April 9 to Sept 26

February 21 Sunday
Lacock Abbey Gardens, nr Chippenham
February 28 Sunday
Lacock Abbey Gardens, nr Chippenham
March 7 Sunday
Lacock Abbey Gardens, nr Chippenham
March 20 Saturday
The Botanic Nursery, Atworth
March 21 Sunday
The Botanic Nursery, Atworth
March 28 Sunday
Crudwell Court Hotel, nr Malmesbury

April 4 Sunday
Kingfisher Mill, Gt Durnford, Woodford
Long Hall, Stockton, nr Warminster
Manor House Farm, Hanging Langford
April 7 Wednesday
Sharcott Manor, nr Pewsey
April 11 Sunday
Andover House, nr Malmesbury
Lockeridge House, nr Marlborough
The Manor, Manningford Bruce
West Kington Gardens, Pound Hill
April 18 Sunday
Easton Grey House, nr Malmesbury
Fonthill House, nr Tisbury
April 25 Sunday
Broadleas, nr Devizes
Iford Manor, nr Bradford-on-Avon
Oare House, nr Pewsey
May 1 Saturday
Hazelbury Manor Gardens, nr Box
May 2 Sunday
Hazelbury Manor Gardens, nr Box
Hyde's House, Dinton, nr Salisbury
Lackham Gardens, nr Chippenham
Little Durnford Manor, nr Salisbury
May 5 Wednesday
Sharcott Manor, nr Pewsey
May 8 Saturday
Stourton House, Mere
May 9 Sunday
Corsham Court, nr Chippenham
Inwoods, nr Bradford-on-Avon
Ridleys Cheer, Mountain Bower
Spye Park, nr Chippenham
Stourton House, Mere
May 12 Wednesday
Bryher, Bromham
May 16 Sunday
Beech Knoll House, Aldbourne
Fitz House, Teffont Magna
Luckington Court, nr Chippenham
Stourhead Garden, Stourton, Mere
Waterdale House, East Knoyle
May 19 Wednesday
Bryher, Bromham
May 23 Sunday
Alderbury House, nr Salisbury
Ashtree Cottage, Kilmington Common
Bowden Park, Lacock, Chippenham
Conock Manor, nr Devizes
Snarlton House, nr Trowbridge
May 26 Wednesday
Bryher, Bromham
May 30 Sunday
The Old Rectory, Stockton

West Kington Gardens
June 2 Wednesday
Bryher, Bromham
Sharcott Manor, nr Pewsey
June 5 Saturday
The Botanic Nursery, Atworth
June 6 Sunday
The Botanic Nursery, Atworth
Bradley House, nr Warminster
Foscote Gardens, Grittleton
Landford Lodge, nr Salisbury
Waterdale House, East Knoyle
June 9 Wednesday
Bryher, Bromham
June 13 Sunday
Avebury Manor, Avebury
Fitz House, Teffont Magna
Kellaways, nr Chippenham ‡
Langley House, Chippenham ‡
Sheldon Manor, nr Chippenham
Sherston Gardens ‡‡
Stonehenge Gardens, Amesbury
Thompson's Hill, Sherston ‡‡
June 16 Wednesday
Bryher, Bromham
June 20 Sunday
Andover House, nr Malmesbury
Ashtree Cottage, Kilmington Common
Biddestone Manor, nr Corsham
Edington and Coulston Gardens
Great Chalfield Manor, nr Melksham
Job's Mill, Crockerton, nr Warminster
Ridleys Cheer, Mountain Bower
June 26 Saturday
Castle Combe Gardens, nr Chippenham
June 27 Sunday
Castle Combe Gardens, nr Chippenham
Cheverell Gardens
Hillbarn House, Great Bedwyn
Little Durnford Manor, nr Salisbury
Manningford Bruce House, nr Pewsey ‡
The Manor, Manningford Bruce ‡
Upper Seagry Gardens, Chippenham
July 4 Sunday
Courtlands, nr Chippenham
Crudwell Court Hotel, nr Malmesbury
East Kennett Manor, nr Marlborough ‡
Hoddinotts House, Tisbury
Lockeridge Down, nr Marlborough ‡
July 7 Wednesday
Sharcott Manor, nr Pewsey
July 11 Sunday
Ashtree Cottage, Kilmington

Common
Corsham Court, nr Chippenham
Lackham Gardens, nr Chippenham
Long Hall, Stockton, nr Warminster
Manningford Gardens & Nurseries, nr Pewsey
July 18 Sunday
Bolehyde Manor, nr Chippenham
Chisenbury Priory nr Pewsey ‡
The Courts, nr Bradford-on-Avon
Enford Grange, Pewsey ‡
Middlehill House, Box
Wedhampton Manor, nr Devizes
West Kington Gardens Pound Hill
July 21 Wednesday
Home Covert, Devizes
July 24 Saturday
Hazelbury Manor Gardens, nr Box
July 25 Sunday
Hazelbury Manor Gardens, nr Box
Luckington Manor, nr Chippenham
Oare House, nr Pewsey
August 1 Sunday
Heale Gardens & Plant Centre, Middle Woodford
Lower Farm House, Milton Lilbourne ‡
The Old Bakery, Milton Lilbourne ‡
Wylye Gardens, nr Warminster
August 4 Wednesday
Sharcott Manor, nr Pewsey
August 8 Sunday
Chisenbury Priory nr Pewsey
August 15 Sunday
Broadleas, nr Devizes
August 22 Sunday
Ashtree Cottage, Kilmington Common
The Courts, nr Bradford-on-Avon
Home Covert, Devizes
August 29 Sunday
Hyde's House, Dinton, nr Salisbury
September 1 Wednesday
Sharcott Manor, nr Pewsey
September 5 Sunday
Mompesson House, The Close, Salisbury
West Kington Gardens
September 11 Saturday
Stourton House, Mere
September 12 Sunday
Ashtree Cottage, Kilmington Common ‡
The Manor, Manningford Bruce
Stourton House, Mere ‡
September 19 Sunday
Hillbarn House, Great Bedwyn
September 26 Sunday
Avebury Manor, Avebury

October 3 Sunday
Ashtree Cottage, Kilmington
Common
Lackham Gardens, nr
Chippenham
October 6 Wednesday
Sharcott Manor, nr Pewsey

October 30 Saturday
The Botanic Nursery, Atworth
October 31 Sunday
The Botanic Nursery, Atworth
1994
February 20 Sunday
Lacock Abbey Gardens, nr
Chippenham

February 27 Sunday
Lacock Abbey Gardens, nr
Chippenham
March 6 Sunday
Lacock Abbey Gardens, nr
Chippenham

DESCRIPTIONS OF GARDENS

Alderbury House &❀ (Mr & Mrs R Cookson) Alderbury. 3m SE of Salisbury on A36; turn W to Alderbury. After 1m Green Dragon on L; R at 2nd Xrds down Folly Lane; R at T-junction; house on L opp church. 10-acre garden and park laid out by Peter Coats. Park runs down to lake and small island; pretty walk round lake. Many fine specimen trees; azaleas; rhododendrons and flowering shrub borders; bog garden. Walled garden with herbaceous, well laid out fruit and vegetables; 2 greenhouses. C18 listed house (not open) built by James Wyatt for Fort family of stone from bell tower of Salisbury Cathedral which Wyatt demolished. TEAS in aid of St Mary's Church. *Adm £1 Chd 50p (age 2-12). Sun May 23 (1-5)*

Andover House &❀❀ (Earl & Countess of Suffolk and Berkshire) Charlton Park. 2m from Malmesbury on A429 take North Lodge entrance to Charlton Park. 5-acre garden with parkland and arboretum. A series of gardens within the garden with many fine trees, shrubs, herbaceous, herb and rose gardens. Drifts of spring bulbs inc many varieties, many newly planted. C18 Dower House (not shown) with stable yard. *Adm £1.50 Chd free. Suns April 11, June 20 (2-6) also by written appt - Andover House, Charlton Park, Malmesbury SN16 9DG*

Ashtree Cottage ❀❀ (Mr & Mrs L J Lauderdale) Kilmington Common. 3½m NW of Mere (A303) on B3092, ½m N of Stourhead Garden. turn W at sign for Alfred's Tower and follow NGS signs. 1-acre garden created since 1984 by owners, a series of gardens surrounding thatched cottage, with densely planted mixed borders of shrubs, roses and perennials and unusual plants, many of which are available for sale in the garden nursery. TEAS except Oct 3. *Adm £1 Chd 50p (Share to St Margaret's Somerset Hospice & Woodgreen Animal Shelter). Suns May 23, June 20, July 11, Aug 22, Sept 12, Oct 3 (2-6). Also daily by appt Tel 0985 844740*

¶**Avebury Manor Garden** &❀ (The National Trust) Avebury. On A361 9m N of Devizes 2m from Beckhampton roundabout on A4. Entrance to Manor and car park N of the village. This 4-acre garden is undergoing restoration to planting, hedges and walls. Ancient walled garden on site of former priory, divided by stone walls and topiary hedges, incl a rose garden; topiary garden, herb garden. Italian walk and half moon garden. Late mediaeval manor house under restoration (not open). Teas available in Red Lion & Stones Restaurant. *Adm £2 Chd £1.30.* ▲*Suns June 13, Sept 26 (11-5)*

Beech Knoll House ❀❀ (Mr & Mrs Richard Price) Aldbourne. 8m NW of Hungerford, 8m NE of Marlborough M4 exit 14 via Baydon or Hungerford. Park in centre of village by pond and 'Crown' pub. Walk to Church then up lane to R of Church around 'Crooked Corner'. Beech Knoll is on the R. Signs from Church. 2-acre garden has an enclosed London style entrance garden. Large terraced lawns with huge specimen purple beech trees. East facing planting examples and colourful bulbs and tree peonies. Restoration work recently undertaken in walled Victorian kitchen garden where there is a large fruit cage and swimming pool (not open). Beautiful plants tumbling over sarsen stone walls near the small conservatory. Clipped hedges dotted about add a note of eccentricity. TEAS. *Adm £1 Chd free (Share to Home Farm Trust). Sun May 16 (2-6)*

Biddestone Manor &❀ (Mr N Astrup) Biddestone, nr Corsham, 5m W of Chippenham, 3m N of Corsham. On A4 between Chippenham and Corsham turn N; or from A420, 5m W of Chippenham, turn S. Large garden with extensive lawns; small lake; topiary; swimming pool set in attractive rose garden; newly planted orchard and herb garden. Fine C17 manor house (not open) with interesting older outbuildings. TEAS. *Adm £1 Chd 50p. Sun June 20 (2-6)*

Bolehyde Manor &❀ (Earl and Countess Cairns) Allington. 1½m W of Chippenham on Bristol Rd (A420). Turn N at Allington crossroads. ½m on R. Parking in field. A series of gardens around C16 Manor House; enclosed by walls and Topiary, densely planted with many interesting shrubs and climbers, mixed rose and herbaceous beds; inner courtyard with troughs full of tender plants; wild flower orchard, vegetable, fruit garden and greenhouse yard. TEAS. *Adm £1.50 Chd 50p (Share to Kingston St Michael Church). Sun July 18 (2.30-6)*

The Botanic Nursery ❀❀ (Terence & Mary Baker) Rookery Nurseries, Atworth. 1m W of Atworth 4m from Melksham on the A365 Bath rd to Atworth. At clock tower turn L, continue along rd for 1m to Xrds, turn R to Rookery Nurseries and Stonar school. Display Nursery garden devoted to cultivation and propagation of a unique range of hardy lime tolerant garden plants inc flowering shrubs and perennials, many of which are not available elsewhere in Wilts. Large glasshouse planted with hardy and tender flowering plants and climbers. Holders of National Digitalis (foxglove) collection. Gardens still being developed. Partially suitable for wheelchairs. *Adm 50p Chd free. Plant centre open daily in village behind clock tower Tel 0225 706631 (10-5). Garden for NGS only. Sats, Suns March 20, 21; June 5, 6; Oct 30, 31 (10-4) (Production nurseries, display garden & glass houses only open for NGS days)*

Bowden Park ♿✿❀ (Bowden Park Estate) Lacock, 5m S of Chippenham. From Lacock village take rd to Bowden Hill, Sandy Lane and Devizes; proceed up hill; (entrance and parking top lodge opposite Spye Arch). 12 acres incl horticultural areas, shrubberies; borders; fountains; follies; woodland and water gardens. *Adm £1 Chd 50p. Sun May 23 (2-6)*

Bradley House ♿✿ (The Duke & Duchess of Somerset) Maiden Bradley; 7m SW of Warminster, 1m Longleat, 3m Stourhead. Large garden; lawn; trees; herbaceous borders; extensive views. Early C18 house (not open). Church C11 (open). TEA. Games and Stalls. *Adm £2 Chd 50p. (Share to Maiden Bradley Church). Sun June 6 (2.30-5)*

Broadleas ❀ (Lady Anne Cowdray) S of Devizes. Bus: Devizes-Salisbury, alight Potterne Rd. Medium-sized garden; attractive dell planted with unusual trees, shrubs, azaleas and rhododendrons; many rare plants in secret and winter gardens. Home-made TEAS (on Sundays). *Adm £1.50 Chd 50p. April 1 to Oct 30 every Sun, Wed & Thurs. For NGS (Share to Wilts Gardens Trust). Suns April 25, Aug 15 (2-6)*

Bryher ♿✿❀ (Mr & Mrs Richard Packham) Yard Lane Bromham. 4m N of Devizes on A342 to Chippenham turn R into Yard Lane at Xrds. A compact level garden, approx ⅔ acre created around a bungalow home. Borders planted mainly for foliage effect using a wide range of red, gold, silver and variegated plants, with many unusual varieties; short wildlife walk; display greenhouses with small nursery beds. *Adm 75p Chd free. Weds May 12, 19, 26, June 2, 9, 16 (11-5). Also by appt Tel 0380 850455*

Castle Combe Gardens ♿ Chippenham 5m M4 exit 17 S B4039 Chippenham Burton. Large car park clearly signed at top of hill. Originally Norman, now mostly C15, one of England's prettiest villages. Map of gardens available. TEAS in village. *Combined adm £1 Chd free. Sat, Sun June 26, 27 (2-6)*

Dower House (Margaret, Viscountess Long of Wraxhall). The house is an architectural feature in the centre of the village, with 4½ acres of terrace garden largely in the course of restoration; trees, herbaceous borders; shrub roses. Good view from top

¶**Hillside House** (Mr & Mrs Edward Walton) Walled hillside garden with courtyard and terraces behind an attractive Georgian house. Small herbaceous borders, roses and rockery

Preedy's Cottage (Mr & Mrs J A L Timpson) Roses, herbaceous border, summer bedding, lawns, swimming pool (not open)

61 Whitegate ❀ (Mr & Mrs C J Pratt) Small garden with all-year-round planting. An example of care and initiative in achieving variety in a small garden. Potted plants for sale

Cheverell Gardens ♿✿❀ 5m S of Devizes; turn W off A360 Salisbury-Devizes Rd. Take any rd into Great Cheverell; follow signs to gardens. TEAS **Cheverell Mill** (in aid of Great & Little Cheverell Churches). *Combined adm £2 Chd free. Sun June 27 (2-6)*

The Manor House (Mrs Oliver Brooke) Great Cheverell, take lane beside Bell Inn. Medium-sized garden; herbaceous borders; roses; interesting very old yew and box hedges

Cheverell Mill ❀ (Brigadier & Mrs Robert Flood) Little Cheverell. 2 acres created from wilderness since 1972; based on original mill features; shrubs, shrub roses, waterplants beside stream running through garden. Courtyard, conservatory and restored barns. Iron water wheel

Glebe House (Mr & Mrs L W J Clark) Great Cheverell. 1-acre partly walled garden with roses, shrubs and herbaceous. Lovely position with far reaching views over Avon vale

Hilliers Cottage (Mrs M L Wort) Little Cheverell. Cottage garden planted by owner since 1964. Stream. Many shrubs, roses and unusual plants

Chisenbury Priory ♿✿❀ (Mr & Mrs Alastair Robb) 6m SW of Pewsey, turn E from A345 at Enford then N to East Chisenbury, main gates 1m on right. Medieval Priory with Queen Anne face (not open) in middle of 5-acre garden on chalk; walled gardens; mature trees; shrubs; lawns; water; fine herbaceous borders; vineyard. Many unusual plants. TEAS. *Adm £2 Chd free (Share to Romanian Orphans, July, Enford Church, Aug). Every Wed May to Sept, Sun May to Aug & Bank Hol Mons. For NGS Suns July 18, Aug 8 (2-6). Parties welcome by appt Tel 0980 70406*

Conock Manor ♿✿❀ (Mr & Mrs Bonar Sykes) 5m SE of Devizes off A342. Mixed borders, flowering shrubs; extensive replanting including new arboretum and woodland walk. C18 house in Bath stone (not shown). TEAS. *Adm £1 Chd 20p free under 5 (Share to Chirton Church, Chirton, nr Devizes). Sun May 23 (2-6)*

Corsham Court ♿ (The Lord Methuen) 4m W of Chippenham. S of A4. Park and gardens laid out by Capability Brown and Repton; trees, flowering shrubs; some rare specimens of flowering trees. Elizabethan mansion; famous Old Masters in C18 state rooms and C18 furniture by Adam etc shown. *Adm gardens £1.50 Chd £1; house & garden £3 Chd £1.50 (Share to RNLI).* ▲*For NGS Suns May 9, July 11 (2-6)*

Courtlands ♿✿ (Mr Julius Silman) 4m S of Chippenham on Corsham-Lacock Road, 2m E of Corsham. 4-acre formal garden divided by splendid yew hedges into three connecting lawned gardens. Features include 2 gazebos; sunken lily pond with fountain, large fish pond with waterfall; walled kitchen garden; greenhouse with vines. Use of heated swimming pool available. TEA. *Adm £1 Chd under 10 free. Sun July 4 (2-6.30)*

The Courts ♿✿ (National Trust) Holt, 2m W of Bradford-on-Avon, S of B3107 to Melksham. In Holt follow National Trust signs, park at Village Hall. 3½-acres different formal gardens divided by yew hedges, raised terraces and shrubberies. Features incl conservatory, lily pond, herbaceous borders, pleached limes with interesting stone pillars, venetian gates and stone ornaments. 3½-acres wildflower and arboretum; many fine trees. NT C15 House (not shown) open every day except Sat April to Oct. TEAS (on NGS days only). *Adm £2.50 Chd £1.50. For NGS Suns July 18, Aug 22 (2-5)*

¶**Crudwell Court Hotel** & (Nicholas Bristow Esq) Crudwell. On the A429 between Cirencester and Malmesbury. E of the rd, beside the church. 2½-acre garden surrounding C17 Rectory (now a hotel). Fine specimen 'rivers' beech, blue atlas cedar, magnolias, C12 dovecote surrounded by ancient yew hedges; Victorian sunken pond with wrought iron surround and lavender hedging. Newly planted rose garden and spring colour border outside conservatory. Herbaceous; shrub and herb borders; climbing roses; espaliered fruit trees and an Edwardian wooded walk in process of restoration. Swimming pool available in July. Coffee, lunch TEAS. *Adm £1 Chd free. Suns March 28, July 4 (11-5)*

East Kennett Manor & ✿✾ (Dr & Mrs C B Cameron) 5m W of Marlborough; ½m S of A4, approach via West Overton. 3-acre sarsen stone walled garden, featuring long herbaceous border; shrubs; herbs and several small gardens divided by hedges. C18 house (not open) with stable block and dovecote. Plant sale in aid Christchurch Restoration Fund. Teas at Lockeridge Down. *Adm £1 Chd free. Sun July 4 (2-6)*

Easton Grey House & (Mrs Diane P Saunders) 3½m W of Malmesbury on B4040. Intensively cultivated 9-acre garden of beautiful C18 house. Also contains Easton Grey Church with its interesting Norman tower, font etc. Superb situation overlooking R. Avon and surrounding countryside; lime-tolerant shrubs; tremendous display of spring bulbs, clematis, many roses; large walled garden containing traditional kitchen garden, large greenhouses, rose garden and borders. Home-made TEAS in garden; produce, cake, and other stalls (in aid of Easton Grey Parish Church). *For NGS - Adm £1.50 Chd free - Sun April 18 (2-6). Also open all the year except Sundays, Good Friday & Christmas/New Year period) Adm 50p per person - collecting box - for the NGS and Easton Grey Parish Church*

Edington and Coulston Gardens 4m Westbury on B3098 halfway between Westbury and West Lavington. Follow signs and park outside Monastery garden or in Church car park for the Old Vicarage and walk up to B3098. TEAS at **Monastery Garden**. *Combined adm £2 Chd free (Share to Wiltshire Garden Trust). Sun June 20 (2-6)*

    Bonshommes Cottage (Michael Jones Esq). Through Old Vicarage Garden. ¼-acre garden, formally part of the Vicarage garden with mixed herbaceous, roses, shrubs. An interesting feature is the control of Japanese knotweed, which divides the garden into different areas

    ¶**Font House** ✾ (Mr & Mrs R S Hicks) Coulston. 1½m E of Edington on B3098 take 1st L to Coulston, 1st house on L. 1-acre garden on two levels with courtyard and raised alpine bed; herbaceous borders, shrubs, herb garden and some newly planted trees amongst older ones. A small avenue of malus floribunda leads to small orchard

    The Monastery Garden & (The Hon Mrs Douglas Vivian) 2½-acre garden with many varieties of spring bulbs; orchard and shrub roses; mediaeval walls of national importance

The Old Vicarage & ✾✿ (J N d'Arcy Esq) A 1½-acre garden on greensand situated on hillside with fine views; intensively planted with herbaceous borders; shrubs; a small arboretum with a growing range of trees; woodland plants; bulbs; lilies and recently introduced species from abroad. NCCPG National Collection of Evening primroses, over 20 species

Enford Grange & ✿ (Maj & Mrs A M Everett) Pewsey. 6m S of Pewsey. From A345 at Enford across Avon bridge; turn R 300yds. Garden on R Avon surrounding Queen Anne farmhouse; ornamental pool; trout streams; walled gardens; water-loving plants; large conservatory; climbing plants and shrubs. TEAS in aid of local church. *Adm £1 Chd free. Sun July 18 (2-6)*

● **Fitz House** ✾ (Maj & Mrs Mordaunt-Hare) Teffont Magna village on B3089, 10m W of Salisbury. Hillside terraced gardens frame listed group of stone buildings in one of Wiltshire's prettiest villages. C16-C17 house (not open) admired by Nikolaus Pevsner in his Wiltshire Guide. The gardens, bordered by yew, beech hedges and stream, are haven of tranquillity planted with spring bulbs, blossom, azaleas, profusion of roses, clematis, honeysuckles, vines and mixed borders. Many scented plants. Featured in 'Country Life' July 1990, the book 'English Private Gardens' May 1991 and TV programme 'Thats Gardening 1992'. Teas on NGS Suns only in village hall in aid of Fight for Sight. *Adm £2 Chd £1. Sats, Suns May to Sept. For NGS Suns May 16, June 13 (2-5.30). Parties by appt Tel 0722 716257*

Fonthill House ✿ (The Lord Margadale) 3m N of Tisbury. W of Salisbury via B3089 in Fonthill Bishop. Large woodland garden; daffodils, rhododendrons, azaleas, shrubs, bulbs; magnificent views; formal garden, limited for wheelchairs. TEAS. *Adm £1.50 Chd 30p (Share to Wiltshire Wildlife Trust). Sun April 18 (2-6)*

Foscote Gardens ✾✿ Grittleton, 5m NW of Chippenham. A420 Chippenham-Bristol; after 2m turn right on B4039 to Yatton Keynell, fork right for Grittleton; in village for 2m, just over motorway turn right at Xrds; house on right. Home-made TEAS. *Combined adm £1.50 Chd 30p. Sun June 6 (2-6)*

    Foscote Stables ✾✿ (Mr & Mrs Barry Ratcliffe) 2½-acres; many clematis; shrub roses; unusual shrubs, trees; small collection ornamental ducks

    Foscote Stables Cottage ✿ (Mrs Beresford Worswick) This adjoining garden has been re-designed and replanted but still retains its cottage character

Great Chalfield Manor ✾✿ (The National Trust) 4m from Melksham. Take B3107 from Melksham then 1st R to Broughton Gifford signed Atworth, turn L for 1m to Manor. Park on grass outside. Garden and grounds of 7 acres laid out 1905-12 by Robert Fuller and his wife; given to NT in 1943, it remains the home of his family. Garden paths, steps, dry walls relaid and rebuilt in 1985 and roses replanted; daffodils, spring flowers; topiary houses, borders, terraces, gazebo, orchard, autumn border. C15 moated manor (not open) and adjoining Church. TEA in aid of All Saints Church. *Adm £1 Chd 50p.* ▲*For NGS Sun June 20 (2-6)*

Hazelbury Manor Gardens &⚘❀ (Hazelbury Manor Ltd) nr Box. 5m SW of Chippenham; 5m NE of Bath; 3m N of Bradford-on-Avon. From A4 at Box, take A365 to Melksham, L onto B3109; L again at Chapel Plaister; drive immediately on R. 8 acres of Grade II landscaped formal gardens surrounding a charming C15 fortified manor house. An impressive yew topiary and clipped beeches surround the large lawn; herbaceous and mixed borders blaze in summer; laburnums and limes form splendid walkways. Other features include rose garden, stone ring ponds, an enchanting fountain and rockery. Beyond the house is a new plantation of specimen trees. TEA. *Adm Gardens only £2.80 OAPs £2 Chd £1. Open daily May 1 to Sept 30. April & Oct Suns only. For NGS Sats, Suns May 1, 2, July 24, 25 (2-6)*

Heale Gardens & Plant Centre &❀ (Maj David & Lady Anne Rasch) Middle Woodford, 4m N of Salisbury on Woodford Valley Rd between A360 and A345. 8-acres beside R Avon; interesting and varied collection of plants, shrubs; and roses in formal setting of clipped hedges and mellow stonework surrounding C17 manorhouse where Charles II hid after the battle of Worcester. Water garden with magnolia and acer frames, an authentic Japanese Tea House and Nikki bridge. Well stocked plant centre. Gift shop. Open all year. TEAS in the house on NGS Sunday only. *Adm £2 Accompanied chd under 14 free. For NGS Sun Aug 1 (10-5)*

Hillbarn House✗ (Mr & Mrs A J Buchanan) Great Bedwyn, SW of Hungerford. S of A4 Hungerford-Marlborough. Medium-sized garden on chalk with hornbeam tunnel, pleached limes, herb garden; some planting by Lanning Roper; a series of gardens within a garden. Swimming pool may be used (under 12) Topiary. TEA. *Adm £2 Chd 50p. Suns June 27, Sept 19 (2-6)*

¶**Hoddinotts House** &⚘❀ (Mr & Mrs George Medley) Tisbury. 1m N of Tisbury on the rd to Hindon. Signposted from B3089 at Fonthill Bishop. 3m from the A303. 1-acre garden developed from a field since 1974 by two horticulturists. Ornamental borders with shrubs and trees; fruit garden, vegetable garden, greenhouses and frames in an attractive rural setting. Ample parking. *Adm £1 Chd 50p (Share to WWF UK). Sun July 4 (2-6)*

Hodges Barn Shipton Moyne, See Gloucestershire

Home Covert &❀ (Mr & Mrs John F Phillips) Roundway Devizes. 1m N of Devizes on minor rd signed Roundway linking A361 to A342. 1m from each main road, house signed. An extensive garden developed since 1960 by present owners, with many unusual trees, shrubs, and hardy plants. Formal herbaceous borders and water gardens 80ft below with waterfall, streams and a small lake planted with bog primulas and various waterside plants. Also many shrub roses and clematis. TEAS on August 22 only in aid of St James Church Repair Fund. *Adm £1.50 Chd free. By appt (£2). Wed July 21, Sun Aug 22 (2-6).* Tel Devizes 723407

Hyde's House ❀ (George Cruddas Esq) Dinton. 5m W of Wilton, off B3089, next to church. 2 acres of wild and formal garden in beautiful situation with series of hedged garden rooms and numerous shrub and herbaceous borders. Many bulbs and new planting. Large walled kitchen garden, herb garden and C11 dovecote (open). Charming C16/18 Grade 1 listed house (not open), with lovely courtyard; short walk to lake; TEAS in adjacent thatched 'old school room'. *Adm £1.50 Chd free (Share to Dinton Village Hall Fund). Suns May 2, Aug 29 (2-5)*

Iford Manor (Mrs Cartwright-Hignett) Off A36 7 miles south of Bath − sign to Iford 1 mile or from Bradford-on-Avon/Trowbridge via Lower Westwood village (Brown Signs). Entrance & free parking at Iford Bridge. Italian style terraced garden, listed Grade 1, home of Harold Peto between 1898 and 1933. House not shown. *Adm £2 OAPs/Student/Chd 10+ £1.50. Open daily May to Sept (except Mons & Fris) (2-5). TEAS on Suns and Bank Hols (including Easter Mon & NGS). April & Oct Suns only no teas. For NGS open Sun April 25 (2-5)*

Inwoods & (Mr & Mrs D S Whitehead) Farleigh Wick, 3m NW of Bradford-on-Avon. From Bath via A363 towards Bradford-on-Avon; at Farleigh Wick, 100yds past Fox & Hounds, right into drive. 5 acres with lawns, borders, flowering shrubs, wild garden, bluebell wood. TEAS. *Adm £1 Chd 40p. Sun May 9 (2-6)*

Job's Mill ❀ (Virginia, Marchioness of Bath) Crockerton, 1½m S of Warminster. Bus: Salisbury-Bath, alight Warminster. Medium-sized garden; small terraced garden, through which R. Wylye flows; swimming pool; kitchen garden. TEAS. *Adm £1 Chd 30p (Share to WWF). Sun June 20 (2-6)*

Kellaways &⚘❀ (Mrs D Hoskins) 3m N of Chippenham. A420 from Chippenham, 1st right through Langley Burrell on East Tytherton Rd. From M4, exit 17 (Chippenham-Cirencester) follow signs to Sutton Benger thence right to East Tytherton and Calne. 2 acres; early C17 Cotswold stone house; walled garden; herbaceous borders; irises, roses, shrubs; rock garden; collection old roses, many unusual plants. TEAS. *Adm £1 Chd 50p. Sun June 13 (2-7); also by appt March to Nov with Teas by arrangement* Tel Kellaways 203

Kingfisher Mill & (The Hon Aylmer Tryon) Gt Durnford. 2m Amesbury. From A345 turn W at High Post. Or 1m from Bridge Inn at Upper Woodford. Park in Village Road. Down short avenue of poplars. 3-acres very watery garden on R. Avon with primulas and wild garden to encourage butterflies and show beauty of wild flowers. Good daffodils from Lionel Richardson's nursery in Waterford. Spring bulbs and variety of magnolias. In June many athletic roses up willows. Garden begun 1962 from old water meadow by enthusiastic amateur. Teas at Black Horse in village. *Adm £1 Chd free. Sun April 4 (2-5.30)*

By Appointment Gardens. These owners do not have a fixed opening day usually because they do not like crowds or have insufficient parking space. Owner will often give guided tour.

Regular Openers. See head of county section.

Lackham Gardens &⚘❀ (Lackham College Principal Peter Morris) Lacock, 2m S of Chippenham. Signposted N of Notton on A350. Few mins S of junction 17 on M4. Station: Chippenham. Bus: Chippenham-Trowbridge, alight drive entrance, 1m. Large gardens; walled garden with greenhouses, carnations, alstroemeria, pot plants, warm greenhouse plants, giant fruited Citron tree, propagating house, fuchsias, begonias; lawn paths separating plots well laid out, labelled with great variety of interesting shrubs, usual and unusual vegetables, herbaceous plants, fruit. Modern style Bradstone paved garden and gazebo. Willow pattern bridge and pool. Sculpture exhibition in the gardens. Pleasure gardens featuring a major historical collection of roses depicting the development of the modern rose; mixed borders, herbs, shrubs, lawns; woodland walks down to river; large bird viewing hide. Raffle drawn shortly after demonstrations at 3.30pm; in walled garden (May 2) aspects of garden design, (July 11), cuttings from leaves, (Oct 3) autumn flowers from shrubs. Particulars of Lackham full and part-time courses available. Museum of Agricultural Equipment, RARE breeds. Adventure playground. Coffee shop; TEAS Bookable menu etc on request within coach party organiser pack (11-4). *Adm £3 Chd £1 (Share to Horticultural Therapy of Frome, Somerset). Open daily Mar 20 to Nov 7. For NGS Suns May 2, July 11, Oct 3 (2-6)*

Lacock Abbey Gardens &⚘ (National Trust) Chippenham. A350 midway between Melksham-Chippenham Road. Follow National Trust signs. Use public car park just outside the Abbey. 9 acres of parkland surrounding the Abbey with a lake and lovely trees. Display of early spring flowers with carpets of aconites; snowdrops; crocuses and daffodils. C13-C18 Abbey (not open till April). Teas available in village. *Adm £1 Chd free. Suns Feb 21, 28, Mar 7 (2-5). 1994 Suns Feb 20, 27, Mar 6*

Landford Lodge &❀ (Mr & Mrs Christopher Pilkington) 9m SE of Salisbury turn W off A36; garden ½m N of Landford. C18 House (not open) in lovely parkland overlooking lake; many fine trees. Special feature 3-acre wood with rhododendrons and azaleas. Herbaceous; ornamental terrace and swimming pool (open). Tree nursery. 500 varieties of trees planted in alphabetical order in walled garden. TEAS. *Adm £1 Chd 50p. Sun June 6 (2-5)*

Langley House &⚘❀ (Mrs A L Scott-Ashe) Langley Burrell. 2m NE of Chippenham on A420; 300yds from Langley Burrell rd junction. 5-acre formal garden and parkland; magnificent old trees; mainly herbaceous with shrubs, old-fashioned roses and lily pool. Lovely old coach house and stabling. C18 Georgian Manor (not open); C12 Saxon Church with Kilvert the diarist connections (open). TEAS. *Adm £1 Chd free (Share to ARMS). Sun June 13 (2-6)*

Little Durnford Manor & (Earl & Countess of Chichester) 3m N of Salisbury, just beyond Stratford-sub-Castle. Extensive lawns with cedars; walled gardens, fruit trees, large vegetable garden; small knot and herb gardens, terraces, borders, gravel garden, water garden, lake with islands, river walks. Cottage Garden also on view. Home-made TEAS. *Adm £1 Chd 50p (Share to Wessex Medical School Trust). Suns May 2, June 27 (2-6)*

Lockeridge Down &⚘ (Mr & Mrs J W Ritchie) Lockeridge. 3m W of Marlborough along A4 turn L to Lockeridge village. R at the school along West Overton Rd for 400yds. Approx 1½ acres. House (not open) set among lawns amidst well established trees; shrub border. Inner walled garden, containing herbaceous borders with a variety of roses, clematis and shrubs. TEAS. *Adm £1 Chd free. Sun July 4 (2-6)*

Lockeridge House &⚘❀ (Mr & Mrs P Lowsley-Williams) Lockeridge. 2m W of Marlborough via A4 turn S, ¼m on R. 2 acres with R Kennet running through; herbaceous rose garden, shrub roses. Ornamental vegetable, herb garden and spring bulbs. TEAS. *Adm £1.50 Chd free. Sun April 11 (2-5)*

Long Hall &⚘❀ (Mr & Mrs N H Yeatman-Biggs) Stockton 7m SE of Warminster; S of A36; W of A303 Wylye interchange. Follow signs to church in Stockton. 4-acre mainly formal garden; a series of gardens within a garden; herbaceous gardens, shrub rose gardens; clipped yews; flowering shrubs, fine old trees; masses of spring bulbs; fine hellebore walk. C13 Hall with later additions (not open). Unusual plants for sale. TEAS Suns only. *Adm £2 Chd free (Share to Horticultural Therapy). Every Wed March to Sept (10.30-4.30). For NGS Suns April 4, July 11 (2-6)*

Lower Farm House &⚘❀ (Major & Mrs John Agate) Milton Lilbourne. Milton Lilbourne E of Pewsey on B3087. Turn down village street by garage at Xrds. Leave shop on R and Lower Farm House is 75yds beyond on L opposite farm yard. An enlarged and developing 7-acre landscaped garden designed by Tim Rees and planted over the last three years. The garden faces south with views to Salisbury Plain over two ponds and a connecting stream. Water garden; spring bulbs; shrubs and herbaceous borders; extensive lawns; mature trees; gazebo; kitchen garden. Conservatory with exhibition of plans and photographs showing garden development. Teas at The Old Bakery, Milton Lilbourne. *Adm £1 Chd free (Share to The Life-Anew Trust, East Knoyle). Sun Aug 1 (2-6). Also by appt March to Sept* **Tel Marlborough 62911**

Luckington Court &❀ (The Hon Mrs Trevor Horn) Luckington village, 10m NW of Chippenham; 6m W of Malmesbury. Turn S off B4040 Malmesbury-Bristol. Bus: Bristol-Swindon, alight Luckington. Medium-sized garden, mainly formal, well-designed, amid exquisite group of ancient buildings; fine collection of ornamental cherries; other flowering shrubs. House much altered in Queen Anne times but ancient origins evident; Queen Anne hall and drawing-room shown. TEAS in aid of Luckington Parish Church. *Collecting box. Sun May 16 (2.30-6)*

Luckington Manor &⚘❀ (Mr & Mrs Trevor Knight) N.W. of Chippenham 7½ S.W. of Malmesbury on the B4040 Malmesbury-Bristol. 3 acres, 3 walled flower gardens; shrubberies; a young arboretum. C17 Manor House (not open) Home-made TEAS in garden. Plants, cake and other stalls in aid of St Mary & St Ethelbert Luckington Parish Church Roof Fund. *Adm £1 Chd 25p. Sun July 25 (2-5)*

Manningford Bruce House ও ⚫ (Maj & Mrs Robert Ferguson) Manningford Bruce 2m SW of Pewsey on A345 on right after Manningford Bruce sign. From Upavon to Devizes 1m after Woodbridge Inn on left. 1½ acres; lawns, shrubbery and walled garden of C17/C18 Rectory (not open). Herbaceous borders with many unusual plants, shrubs and a folly. Small kitchen garden. Owner maintained. *Adm £1 Chd free. Sun June 27 (2-6)*

Manningford Gardens and Nursery ও ⚫⚫ (Mr & Mrs Peter Jones) 2m SW of Pewsey on A345. Turn right at Nursery sign to Manningford Bruce; through village and over railway, nursery on right. Display gardens, featuring exciting colour combinations of white/yellow, pink/red, blue/orange. An astrological garden and patchwork quilt garden are under construction. There is a box maze planted to celebrate the International Year of the Maze in 1991. The nursery specialises in cottage garden plants. *The gardens are open daily except Dec 25 to Jan 2. Closed Weds. Adm free but donations welcome, these are divided equally between the NGS and maintenance of the gardens. For the NGS when the private garden is open. TEAS. Adm £1 Chd free. Sun July 11 (10.30-6)*

The Manor ও (Mr & Mrs N De Brito E Cunha) Manningford Bruce 2m SW of Pewsey on A345 on R after Manningford Bruce sign from Upavon-Devizes 1m after Woodbridge Inn on left. 4-acre garden recently refurbished, including large walled garden with herbaceous borders and great variety of shrubs and plants; tennis court; croquet lawn; conservatory and herb garden. Swimming pool and rustic arbour. *Adm £1 Chd free. Suns April 11, June 27, Sept 12 (2-6)*

Manor House Farm ও ⚫ (Miss Anne Dixon) Hanging Langford. 9m NW of Salisbury S of A36 Salisbury-Warminster. 3m SE of A303 Wylye interchange. Follow signs from Steeple Langford. Series of walled gardens with masses of bulbs; herbaceous plants; many shrubs; old-fashioned roses; collection of clematis; paeonies and delphiniums. Ornamental pond; secret garden in walls of old shearing barn, superb walnut, C14/16 Wiltshire manor house (not open). Opening coincides with exhibition of Langford pedigree lambs and sheep ¼m down the road. Teas Hanging Langford Village Hall in aid of Village Hall Fund. *Adm £1.50 Chd free. Sun April 4 (2-6)*

Middlehill House ও ⚫⚫ (Mr & Mrs Ronald Banks) nr Box, turn W from A4 at Northey Arms, signed 'Middlehill, Ditteridge and Colerne'. Buses from Bath and Chippenham, alight Northey Arms, 5 mins. Intensive garden created around C18 Regency-fronted house with glass-covered Italian verandah. Cultivated herbaceous borders, lawns, many roses and shrubs leading to natural woodland. Pools containing ornamental fish. TEAS & cake stall for Ditteridge Church. *Adm £1 Chd free (Share to British Heart Foundation). Sun July 18 (2-6)*

¶**Mompesson House** ও ⚫⚫ (The National Trust) The Close. Enter Cathedral Close via High St gate and Mompesson House is on the R. NGS visitors use Stable Gate. Free car parking in close. The appeal of this comparatively small but attractive garden is the lovely setting in Salisbury Cathedral Close and with a well-known Queen Anne House. Planting as for an old English garden with raised rose and herbaceous beds around the lawn. Climbers on pergola and walls; shrubs and small lavender walk. TEAS. *Adm £1 Chd free.* ▲*Sun Sept 5 (12-5.30)*

7 Norton Bavant ও ⚫⚫ (Mr & Mrs J M Royds) nr Warminster. 2m E of Warminster turn S to Sutton Veny at Heytesbury roundabout, then R to Norton Bavant. Turn R in village 1st house on R after tall conifer hedge. Unusual alpine plant collector's garden with over 300 varieties of a 30 year collection. Alpine house, several troughs and specialised collection of daphnes. Members of AGS especially welcome. TEA. *Adm 75p Chd free. By appt April to July Tel 0985 40491*

Oare House ও (Henry Keswick Esq) 2m N of Pewsey on Marlborough Rd (A345). Fine house (not open) in large garden with fine trees, hedges, spring flowers, woodlands; extensive lawns and kitchen garden. TEA. *Adm £1 Chd 20p (Share to The Order of St John). Suns April 25, July 25 (2-6)*

The Old Bakery ও ⚫⚫ (Joyce, Lady Crossley) Milton Lilbourne E of Pewsey on B3087. Turn down village street by garage at X-rds. The Old Bakery is opp churchyard. Fairly intensive 1-acre garden. Mixed shrub and herbaceous plantings. 3 small glasshouses; small rock garden; some rare plants. Home-made TEAS. *Adm £1 Chd free. Sun Aug 1 (2-6)*

¶**The Old Rectory** ও ⚫ (Mr & Mrs David Harrison) Stockton. 7m SE of Warminster, S of A36 W of A303 Wylye interchange. The Old Rectory is just beyond the church. The 2-acre garden surrounds an attractive C18 house, with lawns and some fine old trees incl a cedar and a magnificent beech, in the front. To the S it splits into several smaller gardens; an entirely walled herb garden with a variety of herbs, leavened with climbers and some fine roses and vines; and the orchard, dominated by a stunning walnut tree, leads to three separate smaller walled gardens with a great variety of plants incl roses and peonies. *Adm £1 Chd free. Sun May 30 (2.30-6)*

Ridleys Cheer ও ⚫⚫ (Mr & Mrs A J Young) Mountain Bower, N Wraxall. 8m NW of Chppenham. At 'The Shoe' on A420 8m W of Chippenham turn N then take 2nd L and 1st R. 1½-acre informal garden containing interesting and unusual trees and shrubs; many shrub roses including hybrid musks and spring flowers; planted progressively over past 20 yrs; also 2-acres woodland planted 1989 including a number of less common oaks; TEAS in aid of N Wraxall Church and Orchard Vale Trust. *Adm £1 OAPs 75p Chd free. Suns May 9, June 20 (2-6.30)*

Sharcott Manor ও ⚫⚫ (Capt & Mrs David Armytage) 1m SW of Pewsey via A345. 5 acres with water; redesigned since 1977 with a lot of new planting for all-year interest; many young trees; shrubs, old roses, foliage plants. Small collection of ornamental water-fowl. TEAS. *Adm £1 Chd free (Share to IFAW). First Weds in every month from April to Oct (11-5) all for NGS. Also by appt Tel 067 263485*

Sheldon Manor &❀ (Maj M A Gibbs) 1½m W of Chippenham turn S off A420 at Allington Xrds. Eastbound traffic signed also from A4. Formal garden around C13 house (700-yrs-old); collection of old-fashioned roses in profusion; very old yew trees; many rare, interesting trees and shrubs. Homemade BUFFET LUNCHES (licensed) and cream TEAS. *Adm house & garden £3 OAPs £2.75p; Chd over 11 £1. Garden only £2.50, OAPs £1.75. Easter Sunday & Mon then every Sun, Thur & Bank Hol to Oct 3. For NGS Sun June 13 (12.30-6)*

Sherston Gardens ❀❀ High Street, Sherston. 5m from Malmesbury. *Combined adm £1 Chd free (Share to Multiple Sclerosis). Sun June 13 (2-6)*
   Balcony House (Mrs E M J Byrne) Oldest house in Sherston. Small garden with old-fashioned roses, some topiary, small white garden with yew hedge separating it from coloured garden. Acid bed with azaleas, rhododendrons, acres etc. Some plants from Turkey and Greece in conservatory
   Foresters House & (R Creed Esq) Cotswold stone walled garden. Professionally designed for enthusiastic owner, planted 1984. Many interesting plants, particularly herbaceous; pond; pergola. TEAS in aid of Sherston Parish Church

Snarlton House ❀ (Mr & Mrs Adrian Butler) Wingfield. On A366 2½m Trowbridge-Bradford. Midway between Wingfield Xrds and Farleigh Hungerford; opp pair of cottages, turn down farm track. 1½-acres informal riverside gardens created by owners in last ten years, planned to give all year round interest. Large variety plants, shrubs, alpines. Conservatory. Coffee, TEAS, plants in aid of Dorothy House Foundation. *Adm £1 Chd free. Sun May 23 (10.30-5)*

¶**Spye Park** ❀ (Mr & Mrs Simon Spicer) Take A342 Chippenham and Devizes rd, turn E at Sandy Lane opp 'The George' public house. Turn S after ½m at White Lodge. Follow signs to car park. Exit only through the village of Chittoe. 25-acre woodland walk through carpets of bluebells with paths cut through the wood. Some fine old trees mostly oak and beech, survivors of the 1989 hurricane, incl the remnants of 1000 yr old King Oak with the 900-yr-old Queen still alive. *Adm £1 Chd free. Sun May 9 (11.30-5)*

Stonehenge Gardens Amesbury S of A303. From centre of town follow separate directions for each garden. *Adm £1 per garden Chd free. Sun June 13 (2-6)*
   Amesbury Abbey Garden & Grounds &❀ (Mr & Mrs John Cornelius Reid) Amesbury. From centre of Amesbury take Stonehenge Road. R immediately beyond Parish Church and before R. Avon. 20-acres landscaped park and woodland with magnificent old trees including some fine cedars. Special features are the C18 Baluster Bridge over River Avon and Chinese Summer house (recently restored) and garden on the far side of the river. Recently planted shrub and herbaceous gardens. Rebuilt C19 Abbey based on C17 original Mansion (not open). Visitors are requested to keep to the paths round buildings
   South Mill &❀ (Commander & Mrs Ronald Hay) Amesbury. S Amesbury off Salisbury Rd signed by

Police Station. C17 converted Mill (not open) in most attractive setting on R. Avon with wildfowl. 2-acre garden, divided into 2 islands featuring lawn, shrubs and rose garden; a wild garden and vegetable garden with orchard and apiary

Stourhead Garden &❀ (The National Trust) Stourton, 3m NW of Mere on B3092. One of earliest and greatest landscape gardens in the world; creation of banker Henry Hoare in 1740s on his return from the Grand Tour, inspired by paintings of Claude and Poussin; planted with rare trees, rhododendrons and azaleas over last 240yrs. Open every day of year. Lunch, tea and supper Spread Eagle Inn at entrance. NT shop. Teas (Buffet service Village Hall). *Adm March to October £4 Chd £2 parties of 15 or over £3.20. Nov to Feb Adult £2.60 Chd 1.30. For NGS Sun May 16 (8-7)*

Stourton House &❀❀ (Anthony & Elizabeth Bullivant) Stourton, 3m NW of Mere (A303) on rd to Stourhead. Park in Nat Trust car park. 4½-acres informal gardens; much to attract plantsmen and idea seekers. Interesting bulbs, plants and shrubs through all seasons. Speciality daffodils and hydrangeas. Well known for 'Stourton Dried Flowers' whose production interests visitors (BBC Gardeners World '81 and '92). Coffee, lunch, TEAS in Stourton House Garden. *April 1 to November 28 every Sun, Wed, Thurs and Bank Hols. For NGS Adm £2 Chd 50p (Share St Peters Church, Stourton). Sats and Suns May 8, 9; Sept 11, 12 (11-6)*

Thompson's Hill ❀❀ (Mr & Mrs J C Cooper) Sherston. 5m Malmesbury-Tetbury. In Sherston village turn left at Church down hill, bear right up Thompson's Hill. ½-acre fully planted, interestingly designed garden made since 1980. Pretty conservatory added to house 1992. Illustrated in 'House & Garden' Magazine, new issue 'The Englishwoman's Garden' and 'The English Garden' by Peter Coates just published. *Adm £1.50 Chd 50p (Share to Cancer Research). Sun June 13 (2-6.30)*

Upper Seagry Gardens &❀ From A420 Swindon-Chippenham Rd turn N at Sutton Benger Church over M4. Hungerdown House is at the first junction where you turn into Upper Seagry for Seagry House (which has a separate car park). TEAS at **Hungerdown House**. *Combined adm £2 Chd free. Sun June 27 (2-6)*
   Hungerdown House ❀ (Mr & Mrs John Beaven) Picturesque 4-acre garden with many interesting features designed by Percy Cane. A series of gardens on different levels with Courtyards; a 200ft terrace flanked by 12ft borders and a circular pool; flowering shrubs; herbaceous plants and shrubberies in mixed borders; a fine arboretum provides autumn colour
   Seagry House ❀ (Mr & Mrs Thomas May) Approx 4 acres of cultivated garden approached by a long drive with listed gates; divided into four main sections by yew hedges and walks, containing water garden designed by Gertrude Jerkyl, herbaceous, swimming pool (which may be used) and tennis court; walks break up the four sections with a fish pond as the focal point. Much of the garden and the walks have been restored and recently planted; the future project is the recovery of a two level water garden with some fine trees and lawns

Waterdale House ❀ (Mr & Mrs Julian Seymour) Milton, East Knoyle. North of East Knoyle on A350 turn westwards signed Milton, garden signed from village. 4-acre mature woodland garden with rhododendrons, azaleas, camellias, maples, magnolias, ornamental water and bog garden; herbaceous borders and hydrangeas. New gravelled pot garden. TEAS if fine. *Adm £1.50 Chd free. Suns April 11 to June 6. Teas in East Knoyle Village Hall combined with Flower Festival in Parish Church in aid of Church Roof Appeal Sun May 16 only. For NGS Suns May 16, June 6 (2-5.30)*

Wedhampton Manor ♿✂❀ (C V C Harris Esq) 5m SE of Devizes. Off N side of A342 (nr junction with B3098) 2½ acres informal gardens with new and developing borders amongst the long-established. Many fine old and new trees incl remarkable rare cut leaf lime. Herbaceous border, interesting variety of shrubs, herb, vegetable and fruit gardens incl medlar, mulberry, quince and espaliered apple and pear. Greenhouses and fine William and Mary house (not open). Sale of trees and plants. TEAS. *Adm £1 Chd free (Share to Order of St John). Sun July 18 (2-6)*

West Kington Gardens West Kington, 8m NNW of Chippenham, 2m NE of Marshfield exit 18 on M4 take A420 Chippenham-Bristol road N signed West Kington. At village take No Through Road at Xrds. TEAS at **Pound Hill House** (May) in aid of St Mary's Church, W Kington and at **Manor Farm** (Sept) in aid of Dorothy House Foundation, Bath. *Combined adm £2 OAPs £1.50 Chd free. Suns May 30, Sept 5 (2-6)*

Manor Farm ♿ (Sir Michael & Lady Farquhar) Lovely setting, interesting design many unusual features. Wide border herbaceous and mixed planting. Rose walk, Pergolas & walls covered with large variety of clematis, Honeysuckle, roses and Fremontodendron. Wild garden with trees and shrubs. Courtyard with many tender plants in tubs. Garden created since 1979

Pound Hill House ♿✂❀ (Mr & Mrs P Stockitt) Around C15 Cotswold Stone House 2-acre garden in charming setting. The garden is made up of small gardens, an old-fashioned rose garden with clipped box, a small Victorian vegetable garden, pergola with wisteria, roses, clematis; a grass walk with large shrub roses, herbaceous border backed by clipped yew hedges, re-designed shade and water garden. Courtyard garden with clipped yews and box, paved area with interesting plants in tubs, raised alpine beds. Very extensive retail plant area with plants drawn from adjacent nursery with 2000 varieties. *Open Wed to Sun and bank hols April 9 to Sept 26. For NGS Adm £1.50 OAP £1. TEAS in aid of BB Cancer Research Sun April 11. TEAS in aid of Orchard Vale Trust Sun July 18 (2-6)*

Wylye Gardens ♿ 10m NW of Salisbury and SE of Warminster at A36/A303 interchange for Wylye. The 2 gardens share one entrance opp the village hall, in a picturesque village. Attractive river walk beside the Wylye. TEAS at Riverside in aid of Yarnbury WI. *Combined adm £1 Chd free. Sun Aug 1 (2-5.30)*

Perrior House (Mrs Bilbe-Robinson) ⅓-acre walled garden with fine yew hedges and colourful lay-out of herbaceous plants

Riverside ❀ (Mrs & Mrs Robert Martin) ½-acre garden bordering River Wylye, created from old orchard. Cleverly subdivided giving secluded areas and interesting character changes. Extravagantly planted with climbers, outstanding variety of trees, shrubs, herbaceous and ground cover plants. Fruit and vegetables

Another garden may join this group

Worcestershire

See Hereford

Yorkshire

Hon County Organisers:
(N Yorks - Districts of Hambleton, Richmond, Ryedale, Scarborough & Cleveland)

Mrs William Baldwin, Riverside Farm, Sinnington, York YO6 6RY
Tel 0751 31764

(West & South Yorks & North Yorks Districts of Craven, Harrogate, Selby & York)

Mrs Roger Marshall, The Old Vicarage, Whixley, York YO5 8AR
Tel 0423 330474

DATES OF OPENING

By appointment
For telephone numbers and other details see garden descriptions

Beacon Hill House, nr Ilkley
Briery Wood, Ilkley
Brookfield, Oxenhope
Deanswood, Littlethorpe
50 Hollins Lane, Hampsthwaite
Holly Cottage, Leas Gardens, Scholes
78 Leeds Road, Selby
Ling Beeches, Scarcroft, nr Leeds
The Mews Cottage, 1 Brunswick Drive, Harrogate
Nawton Tower, Nawton
Old Sleningford, Mickley
Otterington Hall, Northallerton
Ryedale House, Helmsley
Silver Birches, Scarcroft
Sleightholme Dale Lodge, Fadmoor
St Nicholas, Richmond
Stonegate Cottage, nr Keighley
Tan Cottage, Cononley, nr Skipton
Victoria Cottage, Stainland
York Gate, Adel, Leeds 16
York House, Claxton

Regular openings
For details see garden descriptions

Castle Howard, nr York. Daily March 19 to Oct 31
Constable Burton Hall, Leyburn. Daily April 1 to Sept 1
Gilling Castle, Gilling East. Daily July & Aug
Land Farm, nr Hebden Bridge. May 1 to Aug 31 Sats, Suns, Bank Hol Mons
Newby Hall, Ripon. Daily April to Sept except Mons
Shandy Hall, Coxwold. Open every Wed & Sun June 1 to Sept 30
Stockeld Park, Wetherby. Thurs only April 1 to Oct 7

April 4 Sunday
Otterington Hall, Northallerton

Shandy Hall, Coxwold
April 11 Sunday
Netherwood House, Ilkley
April 17 Saturday
Victoria Cottage, Stainland
April 18 Sunday
Bolton Percy Gardens, Tadcaster
Victoria Cottage, Stainland
April 25 Sunday
Parcevall Hall, nr Skipton
Wytherstone House, nr Helmsley
May 1 Saturday
St Nicholas, Richmond
May 2 Sunday
The Old Rectory, Wath, nr Ripon
Stonegate Cottage, nr Keighley
May 9 Sunday
Ling Beeches, Scarcroft, nr Leeds ‡
Silver Birches, Scarcroft ‡
Sinnington Gardens, nr Pickering
York House, Claxton
May 16 Sunday
Hemble Hill Farm, Guisborough
78 Leeds Road, Selby
Norton Conyers, nr Ripon
May 22 Saturday
Victoria Cottage, Stainland
May 23 Sunday
Goddards, York
Silver Birches, Scarcroft
Stillingfleet Lodge, nr York
Victoria Cottage, Stainland
May 29 Saturday
Nawton Tower, Nawton
Old Sleningford, Mickley
May 30 Sunday
Bolton Percy Gardens, Tadcaster
Creskeld Hall, Arthington
Nawton Tower, Nawton
Old Sleningford, Mickley
May 31 Monday
Nawton Tower, Nawton
Old Sleningford, Mickley
Shandy Hall, Coxwold
June 5 Saturday
Pennyholme, Fadmoor
York Gate, Adel, Leeds 16
June 6 Sunday
Brookfield, Oxenhope
Elvington Gardens, nr York
Pennyholme, Fadmoor

The Riddings, Long Preston
Sleightholme Dale Lodge, Fadmoor
Snilesworth, Northallerton
York Gate, Adel, Leeds 16
June 12 Saturday
Pennyholme, Fadmoor
Ryedale House, Helmsley
June 13 Sunday
Blackbird Cottage, Scampston
Derwent House, Osbaldwick
Inglemere Lodge, Ilkley
78 Leeds Road, Selby
Littlethorpe Gardens, Nr Ripon
Parcevall Hall, nr Skipton
Pennyholme, Fadmoor
Wytherstone House, nr Helmsley
The Willows, nr Brighouse
June 20 Sunday
St Nicholas, Richmond
Shandy Hall, Coxwold
Sinnington Gardens, nr Pickering
Thornton Stud Gardens, Thirsk
June 27 Sunday
Bishopscroft, Sheffield
Bossall Gardens, Bossall
Hillbark, Bardsey
32 Hollybank Road, York
Kelberdale, Knaresborough
Low Askew, Cropton, Pickering
Millgate House, Richmond
Skipwith Hall, nr Selby ‡
Stillingfleet Lodge, nr York ‡
Stockeld Park, Wetherby
Victoria Cottage, Stainland
York House, Claxton
July 4 Sunday
8 Dunstarn Lane, Adel
Thornton Stud Gardens, Thirsk
July 8 Wednesday
Shandy Hall, Coxwold
July 11 Sunday
Bennet Grange, nr Sheffield ‡
61 Carsick Hill Crescent, Sheffield ‡
Grimston Gardens, Gilling East
30 Latchmere Rd, Leeds 16
78 Leeds Road, Selby
Norton Conyers, nr Ripon ‡
The Old Rectory, Wath, nr Ripon ‡
Otterington Hall, Northallerton

Shandy Hall, Coxwold
Springfield House, Tockwith, nr
York
July 15 Thursday
Grimston Gardens, Gilling East
July 17 Saturday
Sleightholme Dale Lodge,
Fadmoor
July 18 Sunday
Beamsley Hall, nr Skipton
8 Dunstarn Lane, Adel ‡
Hovingham Hall, Hovingham

30 Latchmere Rd, Leeds 16 ‡
Leas Gardens, Scholes
Sleightholme Dale Lodge,
Fadmoor
5 Wharfe Close, Leeds 16 ‡
Wytherstone House, nr Helmsley
July 25 Sunday
30 Latchmere Rd, Leeds 16
August 1 Sunday
30 Latchmere Rd, Leeds 16
August 8 Sunday
Sedbury Hall, nr Richmond

August 22 Sunday
The Old Rectory, Mirfield
Parcevall Hall, nr Skipton
August 29 Sunday
The White House, Husthwaite
September 19 Sunday
The Dower House, Great
Thirkleby
Maspin House, Hillam, nr Selby
October 3 Sunday
Bolton Percy Gardens, Tadcaster

DESCRIPTIONS OF GARDENS

¶**Beacon Hill House** ⚘❀ (Mr & Mrs D H Boyle) Langbar. 4m NW of Ilkley. 1¼m E of A59 nr Bolton Abbey. A large garden of interest to garden historians, situated at 900' on the southern slope of Beamsley Beacon. Sheltered by established woodland and retaining many original Victorian features. Interesting plantings and tender wall shrubs. Rhododendrons, Eucryphias, unusual bulbs and hardy plants. TEAS. *Adm £2. Groups and parties by written appointment only*

Beamsley Hall ♿❀ (Marquess & Marchioness of Hartington) Beamsley. 5m E of Skipton. 6-acre traditional English garden with new plantings; including extensive herbaceous border and kitchen garden. Minor restrictions for wheelchairs. TEAS. Also at Bolton Abbey or at Devonshire Arms. *Adm £1.50 OAPs £1 Chd under 15 free. Sun July 18 (1.30-5.30)*

¶**Bennet Grange** (Mr & Mrs Milton-Davis) Fulwood. From Sheffield centre take A57 Glossop and Manchester, through Broomhill and Crosspool. After ½m turn L (Coldwell Lane) R at Xrds (Sandygate Rd). Pass Hallamshire Golf Club. L at Xrds (Blackbrook Rd) turn R at the top (Harrison Lane). House on L in wood. A large established sheltered garden, set in lovely location with beautiful views to Derbyshire Peaks. Long herbaceous border, shrubs, and natural woodland. TEAS in aid of WI. *Adm £1 Chd 50p. Sun July 11 (1.30-5)*

Bishopscroft ❀ (Bishop of Sheffield) Sheffield. 3m W of centre of Sheffield. Follow A57 (signposted Glossop) to Broomhill then along Fulwood Road to traffic lights past Ranmoor Church. Turn Right up Gladstone Rd and then L into Snaithing Lane. Bishopscroft on R at top of hill. 1¼-acres of well-established suburban woodland garden. Small lake and stream; the aim is to present something of the feeling of countryside in the nearby Rivelin Valley; a good variety of elders, brambles and hollies; herbaceous, shrub and rose borders. TEAS. *Adm £1 Chd free (Share to the Church Urban Fund). Sun June 27 (2-6)*

Blackbird Cottage ♿❀ (Mr & Mrs R H Hoad) Scampston. 5m from Malton off A64 to Scarborough through Rillington turn L signposted Scampston only, follow signs. ⅓-acre plantswoman's garden made from scratch since 1986. A great wealth of interesting plants, with shrub, herbaceous border. Alpines are a speciality. Please visit throughout the day to ease pressure on a small but in-spirational garden. Unusual plants for sale. Morning coffee and TEAS. *Adm £1 Chd free (Share to Scampston Village Hall). Sun June 13 (10.30-5)*

Bolton Percy Gardens ⚘❀ Tadcaster. 10m SW of York. Turn S off A64 immediately next to Q8 garage. Gardens not adjacent. Light lunches and TEAS in aid of church. *Combined adm £1 Chd free. Suns April 18, May 30, Oct 3 (1-5)*
  Betula & Bolton Percy Cemetery (Roger Brook Esq) An acre of old village churchyard gardened by Roger Brook, in which garden plants are naturalised and grow wild. The National Dicentra Collection will be on view in Roger Brook's garden and allotment
  Windy Ridge (Mr & Mrs J S Giles) A natural garden evolving on a ¾ acre site sloping down to the Ings with new plantings of unusual hardy plants. Large collection of primulas and Barnhaven primroses grown from seed

Bossall Gardens ♿⚘ From York proceed in NE direction on A64 (York to Malton & Scarborough) for 7m and turn R at signpost marked Claxton & Bossall. Go straight across the Xrds in Claxton and you come to Bossall (2m). Gardens adjacent. C12 church will be open. TEA. *Adm £1.50 Chd free. Sun June 27 (2-5)*
  ¶**Bossall Hall** (Brig I D & Lady Susan Watson) 6-acre garden with moat surrounding C17 hall. Many old trees, lawns, orchard, walled kitchen garden, shrub and rose borders
  ¶**The Old Vicarage** (Mr & Mrs E A K Denison) Approx 2 acres. The garden consists of lawns, borders, shrubs, herbaceous plants and a rose garden all of which has been created in the last 20 yrs.

Briery Wood ⚘ (Mrs M B Marshall) Hebers Ghyll Drive, Ilkley. S at traffic lights in town centre; Brook St, turn right into The Grove; then left up Grove Rd; Briery Wood last on R up Hebers Ghyll Drive. 6 acres; fine rhododendrons, azaleas, spring shrubs, conifers. Fine views over Blue Bell woods up Wharfedale. *Adm £1.50 Chd free. By written appt only for groups, societies and private parties*

Regular Openers. Too many days to include in diary. Usually there is a wide range of plants giving year-round interest. See head of county section for the name and garden description for times etc.

Brookfield ✿✤ (Dr & Mrs R L Belsey) Oxenhope. 5m SW of Keighley, take A629 towards Halifax. Fork R onto A6033 towards Haworth. Follow signs to Oxenhope. Turn L at Xrds in village. 200yds after P O fork R, Jew Lane. A little over 1 acre, intimate garden, including large pond with island and mallards. Many varieties of candelabra primulas and florindaes, azaleas, rhododendrons. Unusual trees and shrubs; screes; greenhouse and conservatory. TEA. *Adm £1 Chd free. Sun June 6 (2-6). Also by appt* Tel 0535 643070

¶**61 Carsick Hill Crescent** (Mrs J Atkinson) Sheffield. From Sheffield centre take A57 Glossop and Manchester through Broomhill and Crosspool. After ½m turn L up Coldwell Lane to Xrds. Straight over Sandygate Rd, down Carsick Hill Rd. Carsick Hill Crescent, third turning on L. An established ¾-acre garden with interesting plantings. Good use of a sloping site incorporating; two small ponds, rockery, mixed shrub and herbaceous borders. TEA. *Adm £1 Chd free. Sun July 11 (11-2)*

● **Castle Howard** ✤ (The Hon. Simon Howard & Castle Howard Estate Ltd) York. 15m NE of York off the A64. 6m W of Malton. Partially suitable for wheelchairs. 300 acres of formal and woodland gardens laid out from the C18 to present day, including fountains, lakes, cascades and waterfalls. Ray Wood covers 50 acres and has a large and increasing collection of rhododendron species and hybrids amounting to 600 varieties. There is also a notable collection of acers, nothofagus, arbutus, styrax, magnolia and a number of conifers. There are walks covering spring, summer and autumn. Two formal rose gardens planted in the mid 1970's include a large assembly of old roses, china roses, bourbon roses, hybrid teas and floribunda. Refreshments are available in the House Restaurant and also in the Lakeside Cafe. During the summer months there are boat trips on the lake in an electric launch. There is a gift shop in the House and a plant centre by the car park. TEAS. *Adm £4 Chd £2. Every day March 19 to Oct 31 (10-4.30)*

● **Constable Burton Hall Gardens** ♿ (Charles Wyvill Esq) 3m E of Leyburn on A684, 6m W of A1. Bus: United No. 72 from Northallerton alight at gate. Large garden, woodland walks; something of interest all spring and summer; splendid display of daffodils; rockery with fine selection of alpines (some rare); extensive shrubs and roses. Beautiful John Carr house (not open) in C18 park; small lake with wildfowl. Beautiful countryside at entrance to Wensleydale. *Adm £1 Chd 50p; reduction for large parties* Tel Bedale 50428. *April 1 to Sept 1 daily (9-5.30)*

Creskeld Hall ♿✿✤ (The Exors of Lady Stoddart-Scott) Arthington. 5m E of Otley on A659. Well established 3-4-acre large garden with woodland plantings; rhododendrons, azaleas, attractive water garden with canals, walled kitchen and flower garden. TEAS. *Adm £1.50 Chd free. Sun May 30 (12-5)*

By Appointment Gardens. Avoid the crowds. Good chance of a tour by owner. See garden description for telephone number.

Derwent House ♿✿✤ (Dr & Mrs D G Lethem) Osbaldwick. On village green at Osbaldwick. 2m E of York City centre off A1079. Approx ¾ acre, a village garden extended in 1984 to provide a new walled garden with yew hedges and box parterres. Conservatories, terraces and herbaceous borders. TEAS. *Adm £1 Chd free. Sun June 13 (1.30-5)*

The Dower House ♿✤ (Mrs H Coupe) Great Thirkleby. 4m from Thirsk on A19 on alternative route avoiding Sutton Bank. Smallholding run as a nature reserve bounded by a stream with ponds, wildflowers, birds, fish, donkeys. Rare trees with autumn colour, fruit and rose hips. TEAS. *Adm £1 Chd free (Share to Ripon Choral Soc and St Leonards Hospice). Sun Sept 19 (2-6)*

¶**8 Dunstarn Lane** ♿✗ (Mr & Mrs R Wainwright) Adel. From Leeds ring rd A6120 exit Adel, up Long Causeway. 4th junction R into Dunstarn Lane, entrance 1st R. 28 bus from Leeds centre stops near gate. Entire garden formerly known as The Heath. 2 acres of long herbaceous and rose borders incl 60 varieties of delphiniums. Large lawns for picnics. *Adm £1 Chd free. Suns July 4, 18 (2-6)*

Elvington Gardens ✗✤ 8m SE of York. From A1079, immed. after leaving York's outer ring road turn S onto B1228 for Elvington. Light lunches and Teas in Village Hall in aid of village hall. Large free car park. *Combined adm £2 Chd free. Sun June 6 (11-5)*
 Elvington Hall (Mr & Mrs Pontefract) 3-4-acre garden; terrace overlooking lawns with fine trees and views; sanctuary with fish pond
 Brook House (Mr & Mrs Christopher Bundy) Old established garden with fine trees; herb garden with rustic summer house; kitchen garden
 Red House Farm (Dr & Mrs Euan Macphail) Entirely new garden created from a field 9 years ago. Courtyard with interesting plantings and half-acre young wood
 Eversfield (David & Helga Hopkinson) Modest sized garden with a wide variety of unusual perennials; grasses and ferns divided by curved lawns and gravel beds

Gilling Castle ✗ (The Rt Revd the Abbot of Ampleforth) Gilling East, 18m N of York. Medium-sized terraced garden with steep steps overlooking golf course. *Adm 80p Chd free. For NGS July & Aug daily (10-dusk)*

Goddards ♿✗ (The National Trust Yorkshire Regional Office) 27 Tadcaster Rd, Dringhouses. 2m from York centre on A64, next to Chase Hotel. 1920s garden designed by George Dillistone, herbaceous borders, yew hedges, terraces with aromatic plants, rock gardens, pond. Guided tours, TEAS. *Adm £1.50 incl NT members. Sun May 23 (2-5) No coaches please*

Grimston Gardens ✗✤ Gilling East: 17m N of York; 7m S of Helmsley on B1363. Follow sign 1m S of Gilling East. TEA. *Adm £1.50 Chd free (Share to Camphill Trust 15 July only). Sun July 11, Thurs July 15 (2-6)*
 Grimston Manor Farm (Richard & Heather Kelsey) ½-acre garden (originally our field) offering all year interest. An intricate design profusely planted with a wide collection of herbaceous plants; trees and shrubs of particular interest to the flower arranger

Grimston Chase (Mr & Mrs R Clarke) A wooded hillside incorporating a 3-acre woodland garden, flower beds surrounding mature trees and lawns with a stream dividing up the woodland. Variety of flowers with rhododendrons along a woodland path. Magnificent views

Grimston Cottage (Mr & Mrs J Dent) A garden in the making with water feature; aromatic plants in paving; wild flower lawn; organically grown vegetables in raised beds. Some mature shrubs

Hemble Hill Farm &♣ (Miss S K Edwards) Guisborough, on A171 between Nunthorpe and Guisborough opp the Cross Keys Inn. Dogs welcome, 7-acre garden facing the Cleveland Hills with formal and informal areas inc lake; young arboretum; heather, rhododendrons, large conservatory. TEAS. *Adm £1 Chd free. Sun May 16 (2-6)*

Hillbark ✿♣ (M D Simm & T P Gittins) Bardsey. 4m SW of Wetherby, turn W off A58 into Church Lane. The garden is 150yds on L just before Church. Please use village hall car park (turn R opp Church into Woodacre Lane). A young country garden of almost 1 acre, initially planted in 1987 and still evolving. Interesting design on 3 levels to take advantage of sloping S facing site. Mixed planting of shrubs, herbaceous and foliage plants; paved terraces with small pond; some English roses; stream with bridges to small woodland garden planted amongst mature trees; large horseshoe pond with ducks and marginal planting. Sunday Express 'Large Garden of the Year' 1990. TEA. *Adm £1 Chd 50p (Share to Cookridge Hospital Cancer Research). Sun June 27 (11-5)*

50 Hollins Lane ✿ (Mr & Mrs G Ellison) Hampsthwaite. 2m W of Harrogate, turn R off A59 Harrogate-Skipton rd. Small ¼-acre garden with limestone rockeries; rhododendrons; azaleas and climbers. Pergola and pool. Many unusual plants and alpines. TEA. *Adm £1.50. By appointment only for groups or societies* Tel 0423 770503

¶**32 Hollybank Road** ✿ (Mr & Mrs D Matthews) Holgate. A 59 (Harrogate Rd). From York centre. Cross iron bridge, turn L after Kilima hotel (Hamilton Drive East). Fork slightly L (Hollybank Rd) after 400yds. A small town garden 7yds × 28yds planted for year-round interest. Shrubs, small trees, climbing plants, roses, clematis and plants in containers. Cobbled fountain feature, 4 separate patio areas, 2 small ponds, wooden bridge leading to pergola. TEA. *Adm £1 Chd free. Sun June 27 (11-5)*

Hovingham Hall & (Sir Marcus & Lady Worsley) 8m W of Malton. House in Hovingham village, 20m N of York; on B1257 midway between Malton and Helmsley. Medium-sized garden; yew hedges, shrubs and herbaceous borders. C18 dovecote; riding school; cricket ground. TEAS in aid of Hovingham Church. *Adm £1 Chd 50p. Sun July 18 (2-6)*

Inglemere Lodge ✿♣ (Mr & Mrs Peter Walker-Sharp) Ilkley. From Ilkley centre A65 towards Skipton. After ¾m opp post box turn L into Easby Dr. Owner-built and maintained ⅙-acre garden surrounding L-shaped bungalow. Unusual layout on sloping site with small pond and larged raised bed. Full of colour and interesting plants well displayed and labelled, many of which are for sale during the summer. TEAS. *Adm £1 Chd free (Share to Wheatfields Hospice). Sun June 13 (1.30-5)*

¶**Kelberdale** ✿♣ (Stan & Chris Abbott) Knaresborough. 1m from Knaresborough on B6164 Wetherby Rd. House on L immed after new ring rd roundabout. An attractive, owner made and maintained, medium-sized garden with river views. Planted for year-round interest with large herbaceous border, conifer and colour beds. Alpines and pond. TEA. *Adm £1 Chd free. Sun June 27 (10-6)*

Land Farm ✿♣ (J Williams Esq) Colden, nr Hebden Bridge. From Halifax at Hebden Bridge go through 2 sets traffic lights; take turning circle to Heptonstall. Follow signs to Colden. After 2¾m turn R at 'no thru' road, follow signs to garden. 2 acres incl alpine; herbaceous, formal, heather. Elevation 1000ft N facing. Has featured in 'Gardeners' World'. C17 house (not open). *Adm £1.50. May 1 to end Aug; Sats, Suns, Bank Hol Mons (10-5)*

30 Latchmere Rd ✿♣ (Mr & Mrs Joe Brown) Leeds 16. A660 from City Centre to Lawnswood Ring Rd roundabout; turn sharp left on to ring rd A6120 for ⅓m to 3rd opening on left Fillingfir Drive; right to top of hill, turn right at top by pillar box, then left almost opposite into Latchmere Road, 3rd house on left. Bus stop at gate (Bus every 15 mins); 74 & 76 from City Centre; 54 from Briggate; 73 from Greenthorpe. A small garden full of interest; fern garden; herbaceous borders; alpine garden; glade; camomile walk; 2 pools; patio built of local York stone; sink gardens; collection of 80 clematis. Featured Sunday Telegraph Magazine & TV with Yehudi Menuhin in *'Fiddling with Nature'* 1985. Gardeners' World, screened 1989. *Adm 75p Chd 30p (Share to GRBS). Suns July 11, 18, 25; Aug 1 (2.30-5.30)*

Leas Gardens ✿♣ 8m S of Huddersfield on A616. Turn W at signpost to Scholes. Adjacent properties in Leas Gardens with gardens of interest individually created from a field in 1988. TEA. *Combined adm £1 Chd free. Sun July 18 (2-5)*

Hawthorn Cottage (Mr & Mrs N Walshe) ½-acre garden; ponds with bog garden, lawns, rose arbour, mixed borders and rock gardens; good views

Holly Cottage & (Mr & Mrs John Dixon) ½-acre sloping garden with raised alpine bed and paved area with troughs; pond with small bog garden, rockery and herbaceous borders with good selection of plants. *Also by appt* Tel 0484 684083

78 Leeds Rd ✿♣ (Mrs E Marshall) Selby. 1m from Selby on A63 Leeds rd (approachable from M62 or A1; Selby turn off). ½-acre suburban garden, of particular interest to plant lovers; mature clematis, conifers, roses, small shrubs, herbaceous border, several alpine troughs, small pool and rockery. TEA. *Adm 50p Chd free. Suns May 16, June 13, July 11 (2-6); also by appt* Tel 0757 708645

Regular Openers. See head of county section.

By Appointment Gardens. See head of county section

Ling Beeches 👤♿❀ (Mrs Arnold Rakusen) Ling Lane, Scarcroft 7m NE of Leeds. A58 mid-way between Leeds and Wetherby; at Scarcroft turn W into Ling Lane, signed to Wike on brow of hill; garden ⅓m on right. 2-acre woodland garden designed by owner emphasis on labour-saving planting; unusual trees and shrubs; ericaceous plants, but some species roses, conifers, ferns and interesting climbers. Featured in The English Woman's Garden and Gardens of Yorkshire and Humberside (Batsford Series). TEA. *Adm £1.50. Sun May 9 (2-5); also by appt* **Tel Leeds (0532) 892450**

Littlethorpe Gardens 👤♿❀ nr Ripon. Littlethorpe lies 1½m SE of Ripon indicated by signpost close to Ripon Racecourse on the B6265 twixt Ripon and the A1. TEAS at **Littlethorpe Hall**. *Combined adm £2 Chd free. Sun June 13 (1.30-5.30)*

Deanswood (Mr & Mrs R J Barber) Garden of approx 1½ acres created during the last 8 years. Herbaceous borders; shrubs; special features streamside garden; 3 ponds with many unusual bog/marginal plants. Adjacent nursery open. *Also by appt* **Tel 0765 603441**

Littlethorpe Hall (Mr & Mrs D I'Anson) Mature garden (Victorian). 2 acres of lawns with specimen trees, azaleas; heathers and herbaceous beds. Small lake stocked with fish and a number of interesting waterside plants

Littlethorpe House (Mr & Mrs James Hare) 2 acres with old-fashioned roses; established mixed herbaceous and shrub borders

Low Askew ♿❀ (Mr & Mrs Martin Dawson-Brown) Cropton. 5m NW of Pickering between the villages of Cropton and Lastingham. Plantsman's garden full of interest incl scree, borders, roses & shrubs. Situated in beautiful countryside with stream and walk to River Seven. Troughs & pots are a speciality, filled with rare & species pelargoniums. Plant stall by local nurserymen. Morning coffee & teas in aid of Red Cross. *Adm £1 Chd free (Share to Red Cross, & NSPCC). Sun June 27 (11.30-5)*

¶Maspin House 👤♿❀ (Mr & Mrs H Ferguson) Hillam Common Lane. 4m E of A1 on A63 direction Selby. Turn R in Monk Fryston after Texaco Garage. L at T junction. Maspin House 1m on L. Garden evolving since 1985 over 1 acre. Owner made and maintained. Unusual varieties of hardy plants and annuals giving good late colour. Ponds, alpines and mixed island beds. Newly planted orchard with shrub roses. TEAS in aid of Monk Fryston School. *Adm £1 Chd free. Sun Sept 19 (2-6)*

¶The Mews Cottage ♿❀ (Mrs Pat Clarke) 1 Brunswick Dr, Harrogate. W of town centre. From Cornwall Rd, N side of Valley Gardens, 1st R (Clarence Dr), 1st L (York Rd), first L (Brunswick Dr). A small garden on a sloping site of particular interest to hardy planters. Full of unusual and familiar plants but retaining a feeling of restfulness. A courtyard with trompe l'oeil and a gravelled area enclosed by trellising, providing sites for part of a large collection of clematis. *Adm £1 Chd 50p. Open for groups, Societies, and private parties by appt only* **Tel 0423 566292**

¶Millgate House ♿ (Austin Lynch & Tim Culkin) Richmond Market Place. House is located at bottom of Market Place opp Barclays Bank. SE walled town garden overlooking the R Swale. Although small the garden is full of character, enchantingly secluded with plants and shrubs. Foliage plants incl ferns, hostas; old roses and interesting selection of clematis, small trees and shrubs. Featured in 'Homes & Gardens'. Full of ideas for the small gardener. *Adm £1 Chd 50p. Sun June 27 (8am-8pm)*

Nawton Tower 👤♿ (Mr & Mrs D Ward) Nawton, 5m NE of Helmsley. From A170, between Helmsley and Nawton village, at Beadlam turn N 2½m to Nawton Tower. Large garden; heathers, rhododendrons, azaleas, shrubs. Tea Helmsley and Kirbymoorside. *Adm £1 Chd 50p. Sat, Sun, Mon May 29, 30, 31 (2-6); also open by appt* **Tel 0439 71218**

Netherwood House ❀ (Mr & Mrs Peter Marshall) 1m W of Ilkley on A65 towards Skipton; drive on L, clearly marked Netherwood House. Daffodils, spring flowering shrubs, duck pond; new rockery, bulb and stream plantings. TEAS. *Adm £1 Chd free. Sun April 11 (2-5.30)*

● Newby Hall & Gardens 👤♿❀ (R E J Compton Esq) Ripon. 40-acres extensive gardens laid out in 1920s; full of rare and beautiful plants. Winner of HHA/Christie's Garden of the Year Award 1987. Formal seasonal gardens, reputed longest double herbaceous borders to R. Ure and National Collection holder Genus Cornus. C19 statue walk; woodland discovery walk. Miniature railway and adventure gardens for children. Lunches & TEAS in licensed Garden Restaurant. The Newby shop and plant stall. *Adm House & garden £5 OAPs £4 Disabled/Chd £2.90, Garden only £3, OAPs £2.50, Disabled/Chd £2. April to Sept daily ex Mons (Open Bank Hols) (Gardens 11-5.30; House 12-5). Group bookings and further details from Administrator* **Tel 0423 322583**

Norton Conyers 👤❀ (Sir James Graham) 3½m N of Ripon. Take Wath sign off A61 Ripon-Thirsk. Large C18 walled garden in full cultivation; interesting borders and orangery; old-fashioned and unusual hardy plants a speciality, many for sale. Jacobean house also open. TEAS. *Collecting box for NGS (Share to Camphill Village Trust, Botton Village, Danby, Whitby).* ▲*For NGS Suns May 16, July 11 (2-5.30)*

The Old Rectory, Mirfield 👤♿❀ (G Bottomley Esq) Exit 25 of M62; take A62 then A644 thru Mirfield Village; after approx ½m turn L up Blake Hall Drive, then 1st L, Rectory at top of hill. 1-acre garden surrounding Elizabethan Rectory. Mixed borders, Mulberry tree dating from C16; well, pergola and small ornamental pond. TEAS. *Adm £1 Chd free. Sun Aug 22 (2-5)*

The Old Rectory, Wath 👤❀ (Mrs Tulip Bemrose) 5m from Ripon off the A61 Ripon-Thirsk rd, 1½ m off the A1. 6½ acres of grounds inc lawns, unusual shrubs and climbers, walled garden and terrace; formal rose garden and woodland walk. TEA. *Adm £1 Chd 50p. Suns May 2, July 11 (2-5.30)*

Old Sleningford &❀ (Mr & Mrs James Ramsden) 5m W of Ripon, off B6108. After North Stainley take 1st or 2nd left; follow sign to Mickley for 1m from main rd. Unusual, interesting 3-acre garden with extensive lawns, interesting trees; woodland walk; exceptionally lovely lake and islands and recently planted stream-side walk; mediaeval mill; walled kitchen garden; herbaceous border, yew hedges, huge beech hedge, Victorian fernery; flowers and grasses grown for drying. Home-made TEAS. *Adm £1.50 Chd 50p (Share to Spennithorne, Home of Healing). Sat, Sun, Mon May 29, 30, 31 (1-5). Groups catered for, also by appt all year* **Tel Ripon 635229**

Otterington Hall &❀ (Sir Stephen & Lady Furness) Northallerton. 4m S of Northallerton. On A167 just N of South Otterington village. 7 acres of garden and woodland which originally opened for the NGS in 1935; outstanding topiary and yew hedges, woodland walks, shrubs, artists studio will be open July 11 only. TEAS. *Adm £1 Chd 20p. Suns April 4 (2-5), July 11 (2-6) parties by appt April to Sept* **Tel 0609 772061**

Parcevall Hall Gardens ❀ (Walsingham College (Yorkshire Properties) Ltd) Skyreholme, 12m N of Skipton. From Grassington on B6265 turn S at Hebden Xrds, follow signs to Burnsall, Appletreewick to Parcevall Hall. 20-acres in Wharfedale; shelter belts of mixed woodland, fine trees; terraces; fishponds; rock garden; tender shrubs inc Desfontainea; Crinodendron; camellia; bulbs; rhododendrons; orchard for picnics, old varieties of apples; autumn colour; birds in woodland; splendid views. TEAS. *Adm £2 Chd 50p.* ▲*for NGS Suns April 25, June 13, Aug 22 (10-6)*

Pennyholme (Mr C J Wills) Fadmoor, 5m NW of Kirbymoorside. From A170 between Kirbymoorside and Nawton, turn N, ½m before Fadmoor turn left, signed 'Sleightholmedale only' continue N up dale, across 3 cattlegrids, to garden. No Buses. Large, wild garden on edge of moor with rhododendrons, azaleas, primulas, shrubs. TEAS. *Adm £1 Chd 50p (Share to All Saints, Kirkbymoorside). Sats, Suns June 5, 6, 12, 13, (11.30-5)*

¶**The Riddings** ❀❀ (Mr & Mrs T Hague) Long Preston. ¼m W of Long Preston on A65. Turn R over cattle grid up private rd. Parking adjacent to house. Designated wild-life gardens. 10 acres of grounds with mature trees, hollies and conifers. A small formal garden with heathers, alpines and some topiary; a traditional walled kitchen garden with ornamental pond; a delightful walk through rhododendron wood with beck, small waterfalls and bog garden undergoing restoration. TEAS. *Adm £1 Chd 50p. Sun June 6 (10-5)*

Ryedale House & (Dr & Mrs J A Storrow) 41 Bridge Street, Helmsley. On A170, 3rd house on R after bridge into Helmsley from Thirsk and York. ¼-acre walled garden; varieties of flowers, shrubs, trees, herbs. Teashops in Helmsley. *Adm 75p Chd 35p. Sat June 12 (2-6) also by appt May to July* **Tel 0439 70231**

St Nicholas (The Lady Serena James) 1m S of Richmond. On Brompton Catterick Bridge rd, ½ way down hill after leaving Maison Dieu. Bus: Darlington-Richmond; alight The Avenue, 500yds. Medium-large garden of horticultural interest; shrubs, topiary work. *Adm 50p Chd 25p. Sat, Sun May 1, June 20 (all day), also by appt parties only*

¶**Sedbury Hall** &❀ (Mr & Mrs W G Baker Baker) Richmond. A66 ½m W of Scotch Corner. Turn L immed after Sedbury Layby. Large established garden in approx 10 acres of grounds and parkland. Herbaceous border and roses leading to a secret garden. Wall shrubs & many varieties of climbing roses. Walled kitchen garden. Woodland walk with magnificent view over Swaledale. *Adm £1.50 Chd free. Sun Aug 8 (2.30-5.30)*

Shandy Hall ❀❀ (The Laurence Sterne Trust) Coxwold, N of York. From A19. 7m from both Easingwold and Thirsk turn E signed Coxwold. C18 walled garden, unusual plants; old roses. 1-acre, with low-walled beds. Newly opened 1-acre wild garden in Quarry adjoining garden. Home of C18 author, Laurence Sterne, who made the house famous. Craft shop in grounds. Unusual plants for sale. Wheelchairs with help. Tea Coxwold (Schoolhouse Tea Room; home baking). *Adm £1 Chd 50p (Share to Laurence Sterne Trust). Garden or house open every Wed and Sun (2.30-4.30) from June 1 to Sept 30: also groups by appt. on other days or evenings during the same period. For NGS Suns April 4, June 20, July 11, Mon May 31, Wed July 8 (2-5)*

Silver Birches &❀ (Stanley Thomson Esq) Ling Lane, Scarcroft, 7m NE of Leeds. A58 mid-way between Leeds-Wetherby; at Scarcroft turn W into Ling Lane, signed Wike; garden ½m. 2½-acre woodland garden; foliage trees and shrubs; many conifers, rhododendrons, azaleas; good collection of heaths and heathers; attractive water feature, climbers and roses. TEAS. *Adm £1.50 Chd free (Share to Northern Horticultural Society). Suns May 9, 23 (2-6) also by appt June to Oct for parties* **Tel Leeds 0532 892335**

Sinnington Gardens ❀ 4m W of Pickering on A170. A group of gardens which featured in Channel 4 series 'Nature Perfected', will be open in picturesque village. Tickets and parking on village green. Morning coffee and TEAS. *Combined adm £2 Chd free. Suns May 9, June 20 (11-6)*

Skipwith Hall &❀ (Mr & Mrs Nigel Forbes Adam) Selby. From York take A19 to Selby (fork L at Escrick, 4m to Skipwith). From Selby take A19 to York turn R onto A163 to Market Weighton, turn L to Skipwith after approx 2m. An interesting 3-acre garden with well established shrub roses, trees, mixed borders and wall shrubs, large traditional walled kitchen garden. TEAS. *Adm £1.50 Chd free. Sun June 27 (2-5.30)*

Regular Openers. Too many days to include in diary. Usually there is a wide range of plants giving year-round interest. See head of county section for the name and garden description for times etc.

By Appointment Gardens. See head of county section

Sleightholme Dale Lodge ❀ (Mrs Gordon Foster; Dr & Mrs O James) Fadmoor, 3m N of Kirkbymoorside. 1m from Fadmoor. Hillside garden; walled rose garden; herbaceous borders. *Not* suitable for wheelchairs. No coaches. TEAS (Teas and plants not available June 6). *Adm £1.25 Chd 40p. Sun June 6 (11.30-5) Sat, Sun July 17, 18 (2-7); also by appt*

Snilesworth ὁ (Viscount & Viscountess Ingleby) Northallerton. Halfway between Osmotherley and Hawnby. From Osmotherley bear L sign posted Snilesworth, continue for 4½m across the moor. 4½m from Hawnby on Osmotherley Rd. Turn R at top of hill. Garden created from moorland in 1957 by present owners father; rhododendrons and azaleas in a 30 acre woodland setting with magnificent views of the Hambleton and Cleveland hills; snowgums grown from seed flourish in a sheltered corner. TEAS. *Adm £1 Chd 20p. Sun June 6 (2-5)*

Springfield House ὁ ✿❀ (Mr & Mrs S B Milner) Tockwith. 5m E of Wetherby; 1m off B1224. Garden at west end of village. 1½ acres. Well established walled garden with herbaceous borders, water and rock gardens. Rose and conifer garden; shrub walk. Wide variety of plants. TEA. *Adm £1.20 Chd free. Sun July 11 (2-6)*

Stillingfleet Lodge ὁ ✿❀ (Mr & Mrs J Cook) Stillingfleet 6m S of York, from A19 York-Selby take B1222 signed Sherburn in Elmet. ½-acre plantsman's garden subdivided into smaller gardens, each one based on a colour theme with emphasis on the use of foliage plants, holders of National Collection of Pulmonaria. Adjacent nursery will be open. Homemade Teas in village hall in aid of local church. *Adm £1 Chd free. Suns May 23, June 27 (1.30-5.30)*

Stockeld Park ὁ (Mr & Mrs P G F Grant) 2m NW of Wetherby. On A661 Wetherby-Harrogate Rd; from Wetherby after 2m entrance 2nd lodge on left. Bus: Wetherby-Harrogate, alight Stockeld lodge gates (¼m drive). Listed grade 1 house and garden. 4-acres with lawns, grove and flowers, fine trees and roses. House built 1758 for Col Middleton by James Paine (listed Grade 1). C18 pigeon cote. Chapel 1890. *Open Thurs only April 1 to Oct 7 (2-5)* ▲*For NGS Sun June 27. Gardens only* TEAS *Adm £1.50 Chd 50p (2-5)*

Stonegate Cottage ✿❀ (Mrs B Smith) Farnhill. 2m W Silsden. From Silsden or A629, follow directions to Farnhill. Stonegate Cottage is situated above Kildwick Church. Cottage garden of approx 1 acre, on sloping site. Small pool and rockery. Unusual trees & shrubs. Wide variety of plants incl spring bulbs, herbaceous and roses. TEAS. *Adm £1 Chd free. Sun May 2 (2-5.30). Also by appt* **Tel 0535 632388**

Tan Cottage ✿❀ (Mr & Mrs D L Shaw) West Lane, Cononley. Take A629; turn off to Cononley 2¾m out of Skipton; top of village turn right onto Skipton rd. ¾-acre plantsmans garden adjoining C17 house (not open). Interesting plants, many old varieties; national collection of primroses. *Adm £1.50. Open only by appt* **Tel 0535 32030**

Thornton Stud Gardens ὁ (Lord Howard De Walden) 2½m N of Thirsk on the Thirsk to Northallerton rd, A168. Turn L in Thornton le Street. 8 acres of lawns with herbaceous borders, rose beds, many fine trees, lakeside walk, with unusual thatched summer house. TEA. *Adm 75p Chd 25p. Sun June 20, July 4 (2-5.30)*

Victoria Cottage ✿ (John Bearder Esq) Stainland. 6m SW of Halifax. Take the A629 (Huddersfield) from Halifax and fork R on the B6112 (Stainland) Rd. Turn R at 2nd set of traffic lights the B6114. After 1m fork L onto Branch Rd (sign), after 1m turn L by Mills up a hill. Victoria Cottage is the 1st house on the R bend. Approaching from Huddersfield take A640 Outlane, Sowood, Stainland (sign) ¾-acre plantsman garden, created by the owner from a NE sloping field since 1950. Daffodils; roses, flowering shrubs, some unusual for a hilly and wild part of the Pennines. Scenic setting. *Adm £1 Chd 30p. By appt only on these days for parking reasons, Sat, Sun April 17, 18; Sat, Sun May 22, 23; Sun June 27 (10-5)* **Tel 0422 365215/374280**

5 Wharfe Close ✿❀ (Mr & Mrs C V Lightman) Adel. Adel signposted off Leeds ring rd A6120 ¼m E of A660 Leeds-Otley Rd. Follow Long Causeway into Sir George Martin Drive. Wharfe Close adjacent to bus terminus. Please park on main rd. A medium-sized well stocked garden created from a sloping site incorporating pools, rock garden, trellis work and small woodland walk using a wide variety of plantings; some unusual plants grown on a predominately acid soil. TEAS. *Adm £1 Chd free. Sun July 18 (2-5)*

The White House ὁ ✿❀ (Dr & Mrs A H Raper) Husthwaite. 3m N of Easingwold. Turn R off A19 signposted Husthwaite 1½m to centre of village opposite parish church. 1-acre garden created from scratch in 5 years and of particular interest to the plantswoman, containing herb garden, conservatory, gardens within the garden, herbaceous; shrubs; borders and many fascinating unusual plants; do visit throughout the day please to ease pressure. Morning coffee & TEAS. *Adm £1 Chd 10p (Share to Church of St Nicholas, Husthwaite). Sun Aug 29 (11-5)*

¶**The Willows** ὁ ✿❀ (Mr & Mrs Fleetwood) 172 Towngate, Clifton. From M62 exit 25, take A644 towards Brighouse. 1st R to Clifton. L at T junction; house approx 250 yds on L. ¾ acre owner created and maintained garden. Oriental features with pools and waterfalls. Herbaceous border, rockeries, containers and sink gardens. A wide variety of plantings in old orchard surrounding modern house. TEAS. *Adm £1 Chd 50p under 12 free. Sun June 13 (1-6)*

Wytherstone House ❀ (Maj & Lady Clarissa Collin) Pockley, 3m NE of Helmsley from A170 signpost. Large garden, tremendously improved recently, consisting of shrubs (some choice and hard to find) shrub roses, perennials, terracotta pots, herb garden, mediterranean garden, beech hedges and magnificent views; hopefully by summer 93 there will be a pond and water garden in a recently planted small arboretum with interesting and rare trees. Hard to find rare plants will be for sale in newly opened nursery. TEAS. *Adm £1.50 Chd under 12 free over 12 50p. Sun April 25, June 13, July 18 (2-6)*

rk Gate ⌀❀ (Mrs Sybil B Spencer) Back Church Lane, lel, Leeds 16. Behind Adel Church on Otley Rd out of eds (A660). Bus: WY 34 Leeds-Ilkley; alight Lawnswood ms, ½m. A family garden created by father, son and other, now maintained by Mrs Spencer and her 2 days week gardener. 1 acre of particular interest to the antsman and containing orchard with pool, an arbour, niature pinetum, dell with stream, Folly, nutwalk, ony bed, iris borders, fern border, herb garden, sumerhouse, alley, white and silver garden, vegetable rden, pavement maze, Sybil's garden, all within 1-acre!

NO COACHES. TEA. *Adm £2 Chd free. Sat, Sun June 5, 6 (2-6). Also by appt* Tel **0532 678240**

York House ❀ (Mr & Mrs W H Pridmore) Claxton, 8m E of York, off A64. 1-acre plantsmans garden, created by owners since 1975; old roses, herbaceous, shrubs, fruit. Loose gravel drive could be difficult for wheelchairs. TEAS at Old forge, Sand Hutton (1m). *Adm £1 Chd 20p (Share to Northern Horticultural Society). Suns May 9, June 27 (2-6); also by appt* Tel **Flaxton Moor 986360**

WALES

Clwyd

Hon County Organisers:	Mrs Richard Heaton, Plas Heaton, Trefnant, Denbigh LL16 5AF
North:	Tel 0745-730229
	Mrs Sebastian Rathbone, Bryn Celyn, Ruthin LL15 1TT Tel 08242-2077
South:	Mrs J R Forbes, Pen-y-Wern, Pontblyddyn, nr Mold CH7 4HN Tel 0978-760531
Hon County Treasurer:	A Challoner Esq., 13 The Village, Bodelwyddan LL18 5UR

DATES OF OPENING

By appointment
*For telephone numbers and other
details see garden descriptions*

Bryn Derwen, Mold
Byrgoed, Llandderfel
Dolhyfryd, Denbigh
Donadea Lodge, Babell
15 Faenol Avenue, Abergele
Glyn Arthur, Llandyrnog
Hartsheath, Pontblyddyn
Merlyn, Moelfre, Abergele
Tir-y-Fron, Ruabon
Trem-Ar-For, Dyserth
Tynant, Moelfre

April 4 Sunday
Hawarden Castle, Hawarden
April 25 Sunday
Hartsheath, Pontblyddyn
April 30 Friday
Tir-y-Fron, Ruabon
May 2 Sunday
Castanwydden, Llandyrnog
May 8 Saturday
Chirk Castle, nr Wrexham
May 9 Sunday
Bryniau Gardens
Plas Ffordd Ddwr, Llandyrnog
Plas yn Rhos, Gellifor
Rug, Corwen
Three Chimneys, Rhostyllen

May 15 Saturday
Erddig Park, Wrexham
May 16 Sunday
Dolhyfryd, Denbigh
Hawarden Castle, Hawarden
Tyn-y-Craig, Llandrillo ‡‡‡
Yr Hen Ardd, Llandderfel, nr
Bala ‡‡‡
May 23 Sunday
Argoed Cottage, Overton-on-Dee
Hilbre, Wrexham Rd,
Overton-on-Dee
Orchard House, Wrexham Rd,
Overton-on-Dee
May 28 Friday
Tir-y-Fron, Ruabon
May 30 Sunday
Bryn Derwen, Mold
Eyarth House, nr Ruthin
Plas Nantlglyn, nr Denbigh
May 31 Monday
Plas Nantlglyn, nr Denbigh
June 6 Sunday
The Old Rectory, Llangynhafel
June 13 Sunday
Abercregan, Llangollen
Byrgoed, Llandderfel
June 16 Wednesday
Byrgoed, Llandderfel
June 19 Saturday
Greenfield, Trefnant ‡‡
Plas Heaton & Cottage,
Trefnant ‡‡
June 20 Sunday
Gwaenynog, Denbigh

Pen-y-Wern, Pontblyddyn
June 25 Friday
Tir-y-Fron, Ruabon
June 26 Saturday
Cerrigllwydion Hall, Llandyrnog
June 27 Sunday
Bryn Celyn, Llanbedr
The Mount, Higher Kinnerton, nr
Chester
July 3 Saturday
Welsh College of Horticulture,
Northop
July 4 Sunday
Gofer, Llannefydd ‡
Pen Swch, Llanefydd ‡
Tyn yr Odyn, Llannefydd
July 11 Sunday
Donadea Lodge, Babell
Gwysaney Hall, Mold
Merlyn, Moelfre, Abergele
July 18 Sunday
Howells School, Denbigh
July 25 Sunday
Henllan Village Gardens, Denbigh
July 30 Friday
Tir-y-Fron, Ruabon
August 27 Friday
Tir-y-Fron, Ruabon
September 24 Friday
Tir-y-Fron, Ruabon
October 17 Sunday
Hartsheath, Pontblyddyn
October 24 Sunday
Three Chimneys, Rhostyllen

DESCRIPTIONS OF GARDENS

Abercregan &❀ (Mr & Mrs V Whitworth) Llangollen. A5 150yds Chirk side Llangollen Golf Club. 2½-acre water garden designed by Douglas Knight in 1985. Roses; herbaceous garden; rhododendrons. Magnificent views of Vale of Llangollen. TEAS and plant stall in aid of Clwyd Special Riding Trust. *Adm £1 Chd 50p. Sun June 13 (2-6)*

Argoed Cottage &❀ (Mr & Mrs C J Billington) Overton-on-Dee. App Overton-on-Dee from Wrexham on A5 cross over Overton Bridge and in about ¾m on brow hill turn L into Argoed Lane. 1¾-acre garden, part old and part newly created. Interesting trees and shrubs. Herbaceous border; roses and vegetable garden. *Adm £1 Chd free. Sun May 23 (2-6)*

Bryn Celyn &*&* (Mr & Mrs S Rathbone) Llanbedr. (OS Ref SJ 133 603). From Ruthin take A494 towards Mold. After 1½m at the Griffin Inn turn L onto B5429. 1¼m house and garden on R. 1-acre garden; mixed borders; walled garden; old-fashioned roses. TEAS. *Adm £1 Chd 50p. Sun June 27 (2-6)*

Bryn Derwen *&* (Roger & Janet Williams) Wrexham Road, Mold. ½m from Mold Cross on Mold-Wrexham rd B5444; opp Alun School and Sports Centre (large car park). ½-acre old walled garden with large sunken area. Plantsmans garden with wide variety of plants for sun and shade, giving interest from spring to autumn; allium, cistus, euphorbia, ferns, hostas, grasses, etc. Japanese garden. Featured on BBC Radio Wales Garddio. TEA. *Adm £1 Chd 25p. Sun May 30 (2-5.30). Also by appt* **Tel Mold 756662**

Bryniau Gardens *&* 2m from Dyserth on A5151 towards Trelawnyd. First L out of Dyserth after lay-by on R. TEAS at **Craig-y-Castell**. *Combined adm £2 OAP's £1 Chd free. Sun May 9 (2-6)*

> **Appletree Cottage** & (Mr & Mrs R L Owen) Approx 1½ acres of landscaped gardens with trees; shrubs; alpines; roses and herbaceous plants. Some parts in the process of development and replanting. Features incl a rock quarry garden and natural hillside with spring flowers and bulbs
>
> **Craig-y-Castell** (Mr & Mrs M D Watchorn) Site of Dyserth Castle (1241/1263) 4 acres bounded by dry moat and vallum, featuring mature trees; shrubs; rockeries; rose garden. Beautiful views towards Snowdonia. ¾m beyond **Appletree Cottage**
>
> **2 Craig-y-Castell Cottages** *&* (Mr & Mrs A Williams) Garden with open views of Dyserth and the Vale of Clwyd. 1 acre of reclaimed wilderness populated by a variety of conifers and shrubs that can withstand ignorant malpractice and planted by the 'ad hoc Topsy' school of garden design, and without the aid of squared paper. ¾m beyond **Appletree Cottage**

Byrgoed *&* (Alan & Joy Byrne) Llandderfel. 4½m NE Bala. Off B4401 Bala-Corwen Rd. L into village 1st R over stream and up hill. Fork R at old chapel, Byrgoed is ⅝m on L (OS 125 990 372). Small well stocked terraced cottage garden. Thyme lawn, rockery and spring bulbs. TEA. *Adm £1 Chd 50p (Share to Llandderfel Parish Church). Sun June 13, Wed June 16 (3-6). By appt anytime. Tel* **06783 270**

Castanwydden &*&* (A M Burrows Esq) Fforddlas, Llandyrnog. Take rd from Denbigh due E to Llandyrnog approx 4m. From Ruthin take B5429 due N to Llandyrnog. OS ref 1264 (sheet 116). Approx 1-acre cottage garden with a considerable variety of plants and bulbs. TEAS. *Adm £1 OAP/Chd 50p (Share to Llangynhafal Parish Church). Sun May 2 (2-6)*

Cerrigllwydion Hall *&* (Mr & Mrs D Howard) Llanrhydd. E of Denbigh. B5429 ½m from Llandyrnog village on Ruthin Road. Extensive grounds with mature trees; herbaceous borders; vegetables and greenhouses. TEAS. *Adm £1.50 Chd free (Share to Llanynys Church). Sat June 26 (2-6)*

Chirk Castle *&* (The National Trust) Chirk 7m SE of Llangollen. Off A5 in Chirk by War Memorial. 4½ acres trees and flowering shrubs, rhododendrons, azaleas, rockery, yew topiary. TEA. *Adm to garden £1.50 OAPs/Chd 75p. Sat May 8 (12-5)*

Dolhyfryd &*&* (Capt & Mrs H M C Cunningham) The Lawnt, 1m from Denbigh on B5401 to Nantglyn. Several acres of park, woodland and shrub garden with river; magnificent native trees, many azaleas, rhododendrons and bulbs. TEA. *Adm £1 Chd 50p (Share to Henshaw's Society for the Blind). Crocuses end of Feb and beginning March. Sun May 16 (2-6) and by appt* **Tel 0745 814805**

Donadea Lodge &*&* (Mr & Mrs Patrick Beaumont) Babell. Turn off A541 Mold to Denbigh at Afonwen, signposted Babell; T junction turn L. A55 Chester to St Asaph take B5122 to Caerwys, 3rd turn on L. Mature shady garden with unusual plants, shrubs, shrub roses and climbers; over 50 different clematis; pink, yellow and white beds. Featured on BBC Radio Wales & recommended by The Good Gardens Guide 1991. Cream TEAS. *Adm £1 Chd 50p (Share to RNLI) Sun July 11 (2-6). By appt from June 12 to Aug 12* **Tel 0352 720204**

Erddig Park &*&* (The National Trust) 2m S of Wrexham. Signed from A483/A5125 Oswestry Road; also from A525 Whitchurch Road. Garden restored to its C18 formal design incl varieties of fruit known to have been grown there during that period and now includes the National Ivy Collection. Light lunches & TEAS. Tours of the garden by Head Gardener at 12 and 4.00. *Adm House incl Family Rooms and garden £5 Chd £2.50 Group £4; Adm to Below Stairs only and garden £3 Chd £1.50 Group £2.40, Family £7.50 (2 adults and 2 children). For NGS Sat May 15 (11-6)*

Eyarth House *&* (Mrs J T Fleming) 2m S of Ruthin off A525. Bus: Ruthin-Corwen, Ruthin-Wrexham. Large garden; rock garden; shrubs and ornamental trees. TEA. *Adm £1 Chd 50p (Share to St Mary's Church). Sun May 30 (2.30-6)*

15 Faenol Avenue &*&* (Mr & Mrs A Carr) Abergele. A55 W take slip rd Abergele, Rhuddlan. Turn L at Roundabout, 150yds turn R into Faenol Ave. A55 E slip rd Prestatyn, Rhuddlan R at roundabout towards Abergele. 150yds R into Faenol Ave. Small but delightful garden, town gardeners wishing to create a cottage garden will find lots of ideas here. Alpine plants in stone sinks. *Adm 50p Chd 25p. April to Sept by appt* **Tel 0745 832059**

Glyn Arthur *&* (Mr & Mrs Rowley Williams) Llandyrnog, 5m E of Denbigh, 6m N of Ruthin. A541 off B5429. 2 acres; azaleas, rhododendrons; short walk to landscaped trout pool. *Adm £1 Chd 50p (Share to Llangwyfan Church). By appt April 1 to end Sept. No coaches.* **Tel 0824 790323**

Gofer &*&* (Mr & Mrs J M J Whellens) Llannefydd. 8m from Denbigh B5328 to Henllan. Bear R at top of hill leaving church on L signed Llannefydd. Through village then 1st L signed Llansannan 1½m house on L. (OS sheet 116 961E 697N.) ½-acre with bog garden, shrubs and herbaceous borders. Extensive views. TEA. *Adm 75p Chd 25p (Share to Llannefydd Parish Church). Sun July 4 (2-6)*

Greenfield &✗ (Mr & Mrs E M W Griffiths) Trefnant. 3m N of Denbigh. From Denbigh A525 St Asaph rd, at traffic lights in Trefnant turn L into B5428 Henllan rd; house 400yds on L opp church. 2-acre informal garden; good roses; interesting plants in gazebo; extensive views of Vale of Clwyd. TEA. *Adm £1 Chd free (Share to Holy Trinity Church Trefnant). Sat June 19 (2-6)*

Gwaenynog &✗❀ (Maj & Mrs Tom Smith & Mrs Richard Williams) Denbigh. 1m W of Denbigh on A543, Lodge on left. 2-acre garden incl the restored kitchen garden where Beatrix Potter wrote the Tale of the Flopsy Bunnies. Small exhibition of some of her work. C16 house visited by Samuel Johnson during his Tour of Wales. Coffee and biscuits 11-12.30pm. TEAS. *Adm £1.50 OAPs £1 Chd 25p (Share to Nantglyn Church). Sun June 20 (11-12.30) (2-6)*

Gwysaney Hall &✗ (Captain & Mrs P Davies-Cooke) Mold. 1½m NW of Mold via A541; 400yds after end of 30 mph limit, entrance on R (from Mold). Early Jacobean house (not open) set in picturesque park with many mature trees; extensive walks through gardens, shrubberies, pinetum and water garden, fine views. TEA. *Adm £1 OAP/Chd 50p. Sun July 11 (2-6)*

Hartsheath ✗ (Dr M C Jones-Mortimer) Pontblyddyn. ½m S of intersection with A5104. Red brick lodge on E side of A541. Large woodland garden; many varieties of flowering cherries and crab apples. Tidy picnic lunchers welcomed. Lunch & Tea at Bridge Inn, Pontblyddyn. *Adm £1 Chd £1 (Share to Pontblyddyn Church). Suns April 25, Oct 17 (12-5). Also weekdays March to May by appt* **Tel 0352 770 204**

Hawarden Castle &✗ (Sir William & Lady Gladstone) On B5125 just E of Hawarden village. Large garden and picturesque ruined castle. *Adm £1 Chd/OAPs 50p. Suns April 4, May 16 (2-6)*

Henllan Village Gardens ✗ From Denbigh take B5382 signed Henllan approx 2m. From Trefnant B5428 signed Henllan approx 3m. Car parks in village, map provided. Teas in Church Institute. *Combined adm £2 OAPs £1 Chd free. Sun July 25 (2-6)*
¶**Bryn Teg** &✗ (Mr & Mrs C J Williams) Lawn at front of bungalow, borders containing bedding plants. Dahlias of exhibition standard. Rear of bungalow will contain exhibition onions, cabbages, cauliflowers, carrots, etc. 2 small greenhouses, one containing tomatoes
34 Glasfryn (Mrs Joyce Robertson) Secluded garden with conifers, shrubs and roses, lawns and small ponds with fountains and waterfall
¶**Gwyndy** ✗ (Mr & Mrs Harry Davies) Small intensively planted terraced garden with vegetables and many annuals
Gwynfa, 43 Glasfryn & (Mr Gwilym Rothero) Small garden, lawns, shrubs, roses and small pool; soft fruit
Hafan Glyd, 16 Glasfryn & (Mr & Mrs C Bent) Roses, shrubs, trees. A homely country garden of interest with water feature and pleasant herbaceous borders

¶**Merddyn** &✗ (Mr & Mrs Ivor Aled Jones) An L-shaped garden in three sections of pool and patio area; lawn with mixed border of shrubs, herbaceous and spring and summer bedding; cultivated area o vegetables, soft fruit, chrysanthemums and gladioli Shaded area for exhibition fuchsias. Small front garden of lawn, rose bed, summer bedding, small area o conifers and heathers

Hilbre &✗ (Mr & Mrs W Story) Wrexham Rd, Overtor on Dee, 6½m from Wrexham on A528. Adjoining Orchard House. Parking in Argoed Lane. 1-acre garden witl shrubs, bulbs and conifers. TEAS. *Adm £1 Chd free. Su May 23 (2.30-6)*

Howells School &✗❀ (Headmistress, Mrs M Steel Head Gardener, Mr E Yates) Denbigh. A525 from S Asaph, 1st R after traffic lights. School on L. Approx (acres of formal gardens, trees; shrubs; walled garden an greenhouses around C19 school. TEAS. *Adm £1 Chd 25p (Share to North Wales Friends of Medical Aid to Tam Nadu). Sun July 18 (2-6)*

Merlyn &❀ (Drs J E & B E J Riding) Moelfre, Abergele Leave A55 (Conwy or Chester direction) at Bodelwyddan Castle, proceed uphill by castle wall 1m to Xrds. 0.1m to T-junction. (white bungalow) R B5381 towards Betws y Rhos for 2m, then fork L (signed Llanfair TH) garden 0.4m on R. 2-acre garden developed from a field since 1987. Long mixed border; damp and gravel garden; many shrubs and old roses; rhododendrons and azaleas; spring garden. Views of sea. Teas and lunches available a Wheatsheaf, Betws yn Rhos. *Adm £1 Chd 50p. Sun Ju 11 (2-6) also by appt Feb to Nov incl.* **Tel 0745 824435**

The Mount &✗❀ (Mr & Mrs J Major) Higher Kinnerton 6m W of Chester, L off A5104 just after it crosses A55 Approx 2-acre garden with mature trees; shrubs an lawns; kitchen garden, variety of perennial plants som interesting and unusual. TEAS. *Adm £1.50 Chd fre (Share to All Saints Church Higher Kinnerton). Sun Jun 27 (2-6)*

The Old Rectory &✗❀ (Mr & Mrs John Arbuthnott Llangynhafal, SE of Denbigh. N of Ruthin and E of B5429 signed at Cyffion Xrds. Medium-sized terrace country gar den, herbaceous borders, shrubs and wall plants. TEAS *Adm £1 Chd 50p (Share to St Cynhafal's Church, Llangyr hafal). Sun June 6 (2-6)*

Orchard House &✗ (Mrs Kington) Wrexham Rd, Over ton on Dee, 6½m from Wrexham on A528. Adjoining Hil bre. Parking in Argoed Lane. 1½-acres; topiary hedge shrubs; bulbs; garden geared for easy maintenance. *Adr 75p Chd free. Sun May 23 (2.30-6)*

Pen Swch & (Mrs M & Miss M E Glaze) Llannefydc From Denbigh take B5382 signed Henllan and Llansan nan. In Bryn-Rhyd-Yr-Arian sharp R signed Llannefydc House on R 2m. Small mountain garden approx ½ acr with a collection of specie rhododendrons. Well stocke rockeries, vegetable garden, conservatory and new wate garden. Parking as for Gofer. *Adm 75p Chd 25p. Sun Ju 4 (2-6)*

Pen-y-Wern と✕❀ (Dr & Mrs Forbes) Pontblyddyn, 5m SE of Mold, 7m NW of Wrexham. On E side of A541, ½ way between Pontblyddyn and Caergwrle. 2½-acre terraced country-house garden incl interesting small gardens. New formal rose garden. Shrubs and herbaceous borders; wild fowl and ponds. Magnificent copper beech with canopy circumference of 250ft. TEAS. *Adm £1 Chd 25p (Share to Hope Parish Church). Sun June 20 (2-6)*

Plas Ffordd Ddwr と✕❀ (Mr & Mrs D Thomas) Llandyrnog. 2m E of Denbigh. Follow signs to Llandyrnog from roundabout at Ruthin end of Denbigh by-pass A525, house 2m on R. 2½-acre country garden, elevated position in Vale of Clwyd. Est shrubs, lawns and mature trees. Also small woodland and pond restoration being undertaken – bring wellies if wet. TEAS. *Adm £1 Chd 25p (Share to Llandyrnog Church). Sun May 9 (2-6)*

Plas Heaton と✕ (Mr & Mrs R J Heaton) Trefnant 2½m N of Denbigh on B5428. From Denbigh take Henllan rd , then turn R. Med-sized garden. Interesting trees and woodland walk. TEA at Greenfield. *Adm £1 Chd free. Sat June 19 (2-6)*

Plas Heaton Cottage と✕ (Miss A M H Spiller) Trefnant 2½m N of Denbigh on B5428. From Denbigh take Henllan rd, then turn R. An informal walled cottage garden. Climbing plants and rose bed with herbaceous border the length of small garden. Donations. *Open with* **Plas Heaton** *Sat June 19 (2-6)*

Plas Nantglyn と✕❀ (Janette & Richard Welch) Nantglyn. From Denbigh follow signs for Nantglyn in SW direction; near phone box in Nantglyn straight over Xrds and bear R at fork, house 300yds on L. (OS Ref 116 003 613). Large old-established gardens with azaleas, rhododendrons, topiary, roses and herbaceous borders; fine trees; good views. TEAS. *Adm £1 Chd 25p. Sun, Mon, May 30, 31 (2-6)*

Plas-Yn-Rhos と❀ (Miss M E Graham) Gellifor. 3m N of Ruthin A494. L at Llanbedr DC on B5429 2¼m house on R. ¾-acre garden with wide views of the Clwydian range; herbaceous borders; lawns with croquet; new young wood. (Gift stall in aid of Clwyd Special Riding Centre) Large car park. *Adm £1 Chd 25p. Sun May 9 (2-6)*

Rug と✕❀ (Lord & Lady Newborough) Corwen. Follow via A5 over river bridge to traffic lights about ¼m turn off A5 on R by lodge. 5 acres still being developed after reduction of C18 house to its original size 1972-1976. Mainly shrubs, bulbs and wild woodland garden with dogs cemetery. Victorian conservatory with family crests on pillars. 7-acre lake with RNLI and other model boats being sailed. Restored 100-guinea gate from Glynllifon; cannon from Belan Fort; sundial from Bodfean. (All Wynn Houses of former days.) TEAS. *Adm £1 OAP's and Chd 50p (Share to RNLI and Orthopaedic Hospital, Gobowen). Sun May 9 (2-6)*

Three Chimneys ✕❀ (Mr & Mrs Hollington) 3m SW of Wrexham via Rhostyllen. From Wrexham A5152 fork R at Black Lion onto B5097. From Ruabon B5605 turn L onto B5426 signed Minera. Turn R ½m over bridge, L at Water Tower. Garden ¼m on L opp post box. Forester's garden of 1 acre; maples, conifers, cornus and sorbus species and varieties. Many small trees used in the manner of a herbaceous border. Very unusual and interesting. *Adm £1 Chd 25p. Suns May 9 (2-6), Oct 24 (1-5)*

Tir-y-Fron と✕❀ (Mr & Mrs P R Manuel) Llangollen Road, Ruabon. 5m from Wrexham, take A539 from Ruabon By-Pass, signed Llangollen, turn R on brow of hill after 200yds. 1¾-acre garden with shrubs and herbaceous plants surrounded by mature trees with quarry. Offa's Dyke separates garden from drive. TEAS. *Adm £1 Chd free (Share to Llangollen Canal Boat Trust). Open last Fri of every month April to Sept incl (2-6). Other times by appt only Tel 0978 821633*

Trem-Ar-For ✕❀ (Mr & Mrs L Whittaker) 125 Cwm Rd, Dyserth. From Dyserth to Rhuddlan rd A5151. Turn L at Xrds signed Cwm, fork L and at traffic de-restriction sign house on L. ¾-acre limestone terraced hillside garden with dramatic views towards Snowdon and Anglesey. A highly specialised garden with many rare and interesting plants with special emphasis on alpines, daphnes and specie paeonies. TEA. *Adm £1 Chd 50p (Share to North Wales Wildlife Trust). By appt April to Sept Tel 0745 570349*

Tynant (Mr & Mrs D J Williams) Moelfre, 8m W of Oswestry. From Oswestry take B4580 to Llansilin, thence follow signs to Moelfre. Signs in Moelfre to Tynant. 5-acre cottage garden with streams, pools, vegetable and fruit gardens. Areas of interesting trees and shrubs. Walk through wild woodland garden with stream below, in pretty Welsh valley, only suitable in parts for wheelchairs. *Adm £1 OAPs/Chd 50p (Share to Horticultural Therapy). By appt all year Tel 0691 70 381*

Tyn-Y-Craig ✕❀ (Maj & Mrs Harry Robertson) Llandrillo. Grid ref: 117 377008 1½m from Llandrillo towards Bala off the B4401 Corwen to Bala Rd. Developed over 20 yrs, a hillside garden approx 1½ acres, incorporating 6 descending landscaped pools. TEA. *Adm £1 Chd 50p (Share to Royal Marsden Hospital Cancer Appeal). Sun May 16 (2-5.30)*

Tyn Yr Odin と❀ (Mr & Mrs J S Buchanan) Llanefydd. 8m from Denbigh. B5382 signed Henllan and Llansannan. In Bryn Rhyd yr Arian turn sharp R signed Llanefydd. Garden ½m on L. Approx ⅔-acre cottage garden on the bank of the River Aled. With stream, ponds and alpine garden. Conifers, heathers, roses, shrubs, greenhouses and alpine house. *Adm 75p Chd 25p (Share to St Kentigerns Hospice). Sun July 4 (2-6)*

Welsh College of Horticulture と✕❀ Northop. Village of Northop is 3m from Mold and close to the A55 expressway. Mature gardens incorporating many national award winning features. Commercial sections. Garden Centre and retail sections where produce and garden sundries can be purchased. A Golf Course is being constructed for the teaching of Greenkeeping Skills. Many local trade and craft skills are on display, vintage machinery set out by proud owners and a model railway. Student demonstrations showing various horticultural, floristry and engineering skills. TEAS. Car parking. *Adm £1 OAP's & Chd 50p families £2.50. Sat July 3 (10-5)*

Yr Hen Ardd ⚘ (Mr & Mrs T Willsher) Llandderfel. 4½m E of Bala. Take A494 from Bala towards Corwen after 1m take B4401 on R, approx 3m further turn L onto B4402, 1st R into square, cross stream 200yds Chapel on R. Garden beyond Chapel. From Corwen B4401 via Cynwyd and Llandrillo to Llandderfel. Well stocked plantsman's terraced cottage garden. TEA. *Adm £1 Chd 25p (Share to Amnesty International). Sun May 16 (2-6)*

Dyfed

Hon County Organisers:
North (Ceredigion District)   Mrs P A Latham, Garreg Farm, Glandyfi, Machynlleth SY20 8SS
South (Carmarthen, Dinefwr,   The Lady Jean Philipps, Slebech Hall, Haverfordwest SA 62 4AX
Pembroke & Preseli Districts)

DATES OF OPENING

By appointment
For telephone numbers and other details see garden descriptions

Blaengwrfach Isaf, nr Llandyssul
Hean Castle, Saundersfoot
Living Garden, Bryn
Llanllyr, Talsarn
Old Cilgwyn Gardens, Newcastle
   Emlyn
Penrallt Ffynnon, nr Newcastle Emlyn
Winllan, nr Lampeter

Regular openings
For details see garden descriptions

Bro Meigan Gardens, Boncath. April
   to Nov except Tues
Cae Hir, Cribyn. Open daily except
   Mons April to Oct
The Dingle, Crundale. Daily March
   14 to Oct 17 except Tues
Hilton Court Nurseries, Roch. Daily
   March to Oct

Saundersfoot Bay Leisure Park. Daily
   March 30 to April 29
Winllan, nr Lampeter. Daily except
   Fri May & June

April 4 Sunday
   The Forge, Landshipping,
      Narberth
   Llanllyr, Talsarn
April 18 Sunday
   Bro Meigan Gardens, Boncath
April 25 Sunday
   Pant-yr-Holiad, Rhydlewis
May 2 Sunday
   Four Ashes, Cosheston
May 16 Sunday
   Pant-yr-Holiad, Rhydlewis
May 23 Sunday
   Post House, nr Whitland
   Slebech Hall,
      Haverfordwest
May 30 Sunday
   Ffynone, Boncath
   Hean Castle, Saundersfoot
June 6 Sunday
   Cae Hir, Cribyn

June 13 Sunday
   Caermaenau Fawr,
      Clynderwen
   Pant-yr-Holiad, Rhydlewis
June 20 Sunday
   Bro Meigan Gardens, Boncath
   Carrog, nr Llanrhystyd
   The Forge, Landshipping,
      Narberth
   Living Garden, Bryn
June 27 Sunday
   Llanllyr, Talsarn
July 18 Sunday
   Pant-yr-Holiad, Rhydlewis
July 25 Sunday
   Blaencilgoed House,
      Ludchurch
July 28 Wednesday
   7 Maes yr Awel, Ponterwyd
August 15 Sunday
   Pant-yr-Holiad, Rhydlewis
September 5 Sunday
   Cae Hir, Cribyn
September 12 Sunday
   Pant-yr-Holiad, Rhydlewis
October 3 Sunday
   Llanllyr, Talsarn

DESCRIPTIONS OF GARDENS

¶**Blaencilgoed House** ⚘⚘ (Mr & Mrs Wyn Jones) Ludchurch. 4m SE of Narberth taking the B4314 to Princes Gate. 1-acre garden created over 25yrs. Herbaceous borders, shrubs, vegetables, conservatory. TEAS. *Adm £1. Chd free. Sun July 25 (11.30-6)*

Blaengwrfach Isaf ⚘⚘ (Mrs Gail M Farmer) Bancyffordd, 2m W of Llandysul. Leaving Llandysul on Cardigan rd, by Half Moon pub fork left; continue on this road; approx 1½m, after village sign Bancyffordd farm track on right. ¾-acre garden incorporating woodland, wild and cottage garden aspects within a secluded and sheltered

area. Created by present owners over the past 20 years. Many specie and shrub roses; old fashioned and scented plants grown in variety of ways amongst unusual trees planted for all year interest. Areas specially created with bees, butterflies and birds in mind; new pathway bordered by wild-flower meadow open 1991. Adjacent craft workshops. Teas in village 1m. *Adm 75p Chd free. By appt April, May, June, Oct (10-4)* Tel Llandysul 362604

Bro Meigan Gardens ♿⚘ (Mr & Mrs L R Toms) 6m S of Cardigan, 2m W of Boncath. From Cardigan take A487 to Eglwyswrw. L on B4332 2m on R. Or from Tenby A478 L at B4332 2m on L. 6½-acre garden created by owners since 1986. Formal gardens, orchard, turf maze, wild dingle, physic garden, pergola, dragons nest. Wide range of herbaceous plants, shrubs, trees and bulbs for all year interest. Many unusual plants, the collection growing all the time. Approx 100 varieties of trees; new gardens for 1993. Plenty of seats to enjoy the gardens and the glorious views of the Preselis. TEAS. *Adm £1.25 Chd 50p. Open April to Nov (11-6). Closed Tuesdays. For NGS Suns April 18, June 20 (11-6)*

Cae Hir ※❀ (Mr Wil Akkermans) Cribyn. W on A482 from Lampeter. After 5m turn S on B4337. Cae Hir is 2m on L. Beautiful and peaceful 6-acre garden on exposed W facing slope. Entirely created and maintained by owner from 4 overgrown fields of rough grazing. Started in 1985. Many unusual features found unexpectedly around each corner including red, yellow and blue sub-gardens, bonsai 'room', stonework, ponds, lovely views. Water garden being developed. As featured on radio and TV. TEA. *Adm £1.50 Chd 50p. Open daily except Mons April to Oct, (1-6pm). For NGS Suns June 6, Sept 5 (10-6) (Share to Cafod)*

¶**Caermaenau Fawr** (Mr & Mrs Richard Lewis) Clynderwen. Turn off A40 at Penbluyn roundabout coming from Carmarthen on to Cardigan Rd; drive is 1st on R. Enchanting old farmhouse garden. Gypsy caravan created by owner. TEAS. *Adm £1 Chd free. Sun June 13 (2-6)*

Carrog ᝐ❀ (Mr & Mrs Geoffrey Williams) Llanddeiniol, NE of Llanrhystyd. From A487 Aberystwyth-Aberaeron Rd, 6m S of Aberystwyth, 1m beyond Blaenplwyf TV mast. Bus stop (Aberystwyth Aberaeron) ¼m from house. 5-acres in setting of mature trees, reclaimed, replanted and maintained entirely by owners; walled garden; lawns; shrubs; young ornamental trees; pond with bog and water plants; shrub roses; conservatory with orchids. TEAS. *Adm £1 Chd 30p. Sun June 20 (2-6)*

The Dingle ᝐ※ (Mrs A J Jones) Crundale. On approaching Haverfordwest, take R turn at 1st roundabout signed Fishguard & Cardigan. At next roundabout take R turn on to B4329. ½m on fork R opp General Picton; then 1st right into Dingle Lane. 3-acres plantsman's garden; rose garden; formal beds; scree; herbaceous border; unusual shrubs; water garden; woodland walk. Picturesque and secluded; free roaming peacocks. Nursery adjoining. Tearoom. *Adm £1 Chd 50p (Share to Cancer Relief Macmillan Nurses Fund). Daily (except Tues) March 14 to Oct 17 (10-6)*

Ffynone (Earl & Countess Lloyd George of Dwyfor) Boncath. From Newcastle Emlyn take A487 to Cenarth, turn left on B4332, turn left again at crossroads just before Newchapel. Large woodland garden in process of restoration. Lovely views, fine specimen trees, rhododendrons, azaleas. Ask for descriptive leaflet. House by John Nash (1793), not shown. Later additions and garden terraces by F. Inigo Thomas c.1904. TEA. *Adm £1 Chd free. Sun May 30 (2-6)*

¶**The Forge** ᝐ※❀ (I & S Mcleod-Baikie) Landshipping. Nearest town Narberth. Landshipping well sign posted. Pass New Parc with pillar box; 200yds further on, gates on R. Approx 9 acres recently planted woodland garden with many varieties of bulbs, trees and shrub roses. TEAS. *Adm £1 Chd 50p. Suns April 4, (2-5), June 20 (2-6)*

Four Ashes (Mr & Mrs Richard Hayes) Cosheston. Follow M4 to its most westerly point, then A48 to join A40 W to St Clears. Follow A477 from St Clears towards Pembroke Dock. After passing through Sageston and Milton hamlets, continue along A477 and turn R immediately after the garden centre on L, follow signpost to Cosheston; up a steep hill, straight over Xrds and continue along unclassified rd for ½ to 1m, then take L turn at the signpost for Four Ashes. This 5-acre medium-sized riverside garden was planned for year round beauty. It has a simple, natural layout of trees, rare shrubs, rhododendrons, azaleas, camellias, conifers and heathers as well as herbaceous plants, ornamental trees and roses; alpines and rockery; ground flowering plants and mixed borders. There are over 1,000 different varieties of trees and shrubs within the garden. TEA. *Adm £1.50 OAP/Chd £1. Sun May 2 (2-6)*

Hean Castle ᝐ※❀ (Mr & Mrs T Lewis) Saundersfoot. 1m N of Saundersfoot. 1½m SE of Kilgetty. Take Amroth road from Saundersfoot or the Sardis road from Kilgetty. 2-acres; mixed borders with some unusual plants and shrubs; rose garden; walled garden and greenhouse; conifers; pot plants and troughs. Good view. TEAS. *Adm £1.50 Chd free. Suns May 30 (11-5). Also by appt* Tel 0834 812222

Hilton Court Nurseries ᝐ※❀ (Mrs Cheryl Lynch) Roch. From Haverfordwest take the A487 to St Davids. 6m from Haverfordwest signs L to Hilton Court Nurseries. 4 acres of garden with superb setting overlooking ponds and woodlands. Spectacular lily ponds in July and August; wild flower walks; unusual trees and shrubs giving colour throughout the year. Nursery adjoining. TEAS. *Collecting box. Daily March to October 1 (9.30-5.30), October (10.30-4)*

Living Garden ※❀ (Alan C Clarke Esq) 4a Brynmorlais Bryn, Llanelli; 2½m NE of town on B4297. Parking 'Royal Oak' Bryn. Garden near by (signed). Long, slim plantsman's garden subdivided for interest. Wide range of plants; terracotta ware, pools and water features. TEAS in aid of Hall St. Church. *Adm £1 Chd 25p. Sun June 20 (2-5.30); also by appt* Tel 0554 821274 *April to Oct*

Llanllyr ᝐ※❀ (Mr & Mrs Robert Gee) Talsarn 6m NW of Lampeter in B4337 to Llanrhystud. Garden of about 4 acres, originally laid out in 1830's, renovated, replanted and extended since 1986. Mixed borders; lawns; bulbs; large fish pond with bog and water plants. Formal water garden. Shrub rose borders; foliage, species and old-fashioned plants. TEAS *Adm £1 Chd 50p. (Share to St Hilary's Church Fund, Trefilan). Suns April 4, June 27, Oct 3 (2-6) Also by appt April to Oct. Please write*

¶**7 Maes yr Awel** ※❀ (Mrs Beryl Birch) Ponterwyd. From Aberystwyth take A44 towards Llangurig. At Ponterwyd Village, turn R on to A4120 Devil's Bridge rd, then turn 1st L almost immed. Small hillside garden in mountainous surroundings. 15yrs challenging gardening on steep acid meadowland at an altitude of approx 800ft have resulted in sheltered 'hidden' gardens with pools and fountain, herbaceous plantings, flowering shrubs and specimen trees. Ample seating; large conservatory for refreshments in inclement weather. TEA. *Adm 50p Accom Chd free. Wed July 28 (10-4)*

¶Old Cilgwyn Gardens ♿ (Mr & Mrs E Fitzwilliams) Newcastle Emlyn. Situated 1m N of Newcastle Emlyn on the B4571, turn R into entrance gates in dip in rd. 12-acre woodland garden set in parkland, 100 acres of which are Sites of Special Scientific Interest; snowdrops, daffodils, bluebells, azaleas, rhododendrons etc; ponds and Chinese bridge. For those prepared to walk, a 100yr-old tulip tree can be seen on the S.S.S.I. land. *Adm £1. By appt all year* **Tel 0239 710244**

Pant-yr-Holiad ✗❀ (Mr & Mrs G H Taylor) Rhydlewis, 12m NW Llandysul. NE Cardigan. From coast rd take B4334 at Brynhoffnant S towards Rhydlewis; after 1m turn left; driveway 2nd L. 5-acres embracing distinctive herb garden, alpine beds, water features, rare trees & shrubs in woodland setting; extensive collection rhododendron species; fancy water-fowl. Recently completed area with collections of birch and unusual herbaceous plants. TEA. *Adm £1 Chd 50p (Share to Rhydlewis Village Hall). Only open Sun April 25, May 16, June 13, July 18, Aug 15, Sept 12 (2-5)*

Penrallt Ffynnon ✗ (Mr R D Lord & Ms Jane Lord) Cwm-cou, 3m NW of Newcastle Emlyn. Follow Cwm-cou to Cardigan rd (B4570) up long hill for 1¼m; turn right for 150yds; ignore sharp left bend, bear right along narrow lane for 400yds. 4½-acres trees, shrubs; good views, made by owner since 1971 for all-year interest; Camellia hedge, daffodils in very great variety; Japanese and other cherries; eucalypts; magnolias, sorbus, acer, malus, willow species; shrub roses, rhododendrons; conifers; many other trees, shrubs, herbaceous plants, some uncommon; autumn colour and berries. *Collecting box. Visitors welcome by appt all year* **Tel Newcastle Emlyn 710654**

Post House ✗❀ (Mrs Jo Kenaghan) Cwmbach 6m N of St Clears. From Carmarthen W on A40. Take B4298 through Meidrim; leave by centre lane signed Llanboidy. Turn right at Xrds signed Blaenwaun; right at Xrds to Cwmbach; garden bottom of hill. From Whitland E on A40, left at Ivydean nurseries, right at 3rd Xrds signed Cwmbach. 4-acre valley garden in the making; rhododendrons, azaleas, camellias, unusual trees and shrubs underplanted with hardy orchids, anemonies, trilliums, wild snowdrops, bluebells, etc. Large pool newly developed bog garden. Old roses, herbaceous plants. Greenhouses and conservatory. Plants for sale in season. TEAS. *Adm £1.50 OAP's & Chd £1. Sun May 23 (2pm onwards)*

Saundersfoot Bay Leisure Park ♿❀ (Ian Shuttleworth Esq) Broadfield, Saundersfoot. On B4316, ¾m S from centre of Saundersfoot. Interesting layout of lawns, shrubs and herbaceous borders with many plants of botanical interest in 20-acre modern holiday leisure park. Large rock garden and water feature; laburnum walk. Holders of a National collection of Pontentilla fruticosa. Tea Saundersfoot. *Adm 50p Chd free (Share to Rotary Club of Tenby). March 30 to Sept 28 daily (10-5)*

Slebech Hall ♿❀ (The Lady Jean Philipps) 6m E of Haverfordwest. From Carmarthen via A40, take 1st turn left after Canaston Bridge, signed The Rhos; drive on left, about ½m with 1 white lodge. Bus: Haverfordwest-Tenby or Haverfordwest-Carmarthen; bus stop 3m. Large garden; fine position on bank of the Cleddau; picturesque ruins of Church of St. John of Jerusalem in garden. TEAS. *Adm £1 Chd free (Share to Uzmaston Church Restoration Fund). Sun May 23 (2-7)*

Winllan (Mr & Mrs Ian Callan) Talsarn. 8m NNW of Lampeter on B4342, Talsarn-Llangeitho Rd. 6-acres wildlife garden with large pond, herb-rich meadow, small woodland and 600 yds of river bank walk. Over 200 species of wildflowers with attendant butterflies, dragonflies and birds. Limited suitability for wheelchairs. *Adm £1 Chd 50p (under 12 free). Open May & June daily excl Fris. (12-6). Also by appt July & Aug* **Tel 0570-470612**

The Glamorgans

Hon County Organisers: Mrs A D Arnold, Woodside Cottage, Wenvoe, Cardiff Tel 0222 594434
Mrs Christopher Cory, Penllyn Castle, Cowbridge, South Glamorgan Tel 0446 772780

DATES OF OPENING

By appointment
for telephone numbers and other details see garden descriptions

11, Arno Road, Little Coldbrook, Barry
24 Elm Grove Place, Dinas Powis
Newcastle House Gardens, Bridgend
19 Westfield Road, Glyncoch, Pontypridd
9 Willowbrook Gardens, Mayals, Swansea
Woodside Cottage, Wenvoe

March 28 Sunday
Penllyn Castle, Cowbridge

April 18 Sunday
Dumgoyne, Radyr

April 25 Sunday
Pendoylan & Peterston-super-Ely
Gardens
May 2 Sunday
Dumgoyne, Radyr
Ewenney Priory, nr Bridgend
May 9 Sunday
Ewenny Priory
May 16 Sunday
Dumgoyne, Radyr
Llanvithyn House, Llancarfan
Newcastle House Gardens,
Bridgend

9 Willowbrook Gardens, Mayals,
Swansea
May 23 Sunday
Coedarhydyglyn, Cardiff
June 5 Saturday
Cwmpennar Gardens
June 6 Sunday
Cwmpennar Gardens
June 20 Sunday
The Clock House, Llandaff
Gelly Farm, Cymmer
Merthyr Mawr House,
Bridgend

June 27 Sunday
11 Eastcliff, Southgate, Swansea
Newcastle House Gardens,
Bridgend
July 4 Sunday
Pontygwaith Farm, Edwardsville
July 18 Sunday
29 Min-y-Coed, Radyr
August 1 Sunday
Pontygwaith Farm, Edwardsville
August 8 Sunday
29 Min-y-Coed, Radyr

DESCRIPTIONS OF GARDENS

¶**11 Arno Road** ⚗ (Mrs D Palmer) Little Coldbrook. From A4050 Cardiff to Barry, take roundabout marked Barry Docks and Sully. Then 2nd R into Coldbrook Rd, 2nd L then 6th R into Norwood Cresc; 1st L into Arno Rd. 40ft × 30ft informal garden with ponds, herbaceous plants, some unusual; gravelled area planted with low growing plants. Hardy geraniums a speciality. TEAS. *Adm £1 Chd 30p. By appt at weekends May to Oct* **Tel 0446 743642**

The Clock House ♿⚗❀ (Prof & Mrs Bryan Hibbard) Cathedral Close, Llandaff, 2m W of Cardiff. Follow signs to Cathedral via A4119. Bus: Cardiff Corp-Western Welsh, alight Maltsters Arms. Small walled garden; fine old trees; wide variety of shrubs and plants; important collection of shrub, species and old roses. NT stall. TEAS. *Adm £1.50 Accom chd free. Sun June 20 (2-6)*

Coedarhydyglyn (Sir Cennydd Traherne) 5m W of Cardiff. Bus: Western Welsh, Cardiff-Cowbridge, alight gates. Natural terrain, pleasant situation; lawns, flowering shrubs, good collection of conifers; Japanese garden, fine trees. TEA. *Adm £1 Chd 10p (Share to Cardiff and District Samaritans). Sun May 23 (2.30-6)*

Cwmpennar Gardens ⚗❀ Mountain Ash 1m. From A4059 turn R 100yds past the traffic lights; follow sign to Cefnpennar, follow rd uphill through woods for ¾m, bear right sharply uphill before bus shelter, gardens 200 yds. Car park 100yds past bus shelter. Mixture of formal and informal gardens with some natural woodland in all three of conservation interest. Variety of shrubs, rhododendrons and azaleas, rockeries, shrub roses; new plantings of shrubs and roses, small pond. Rich in bird life, with nest boxes usually occupied. Gardens high on mountain side in secluded rural surroundings of coal mining valley. Gardens filmed for BBC WALES 'Down to Earth' 1992. TEAS. Plant stall and Glamorgan Wildlife Trust Sales stall. *Combined adm £1 Chd 50p (Share to St Margarets Church Restoration Fund). Sat, Sun June 5, 6 (2-6)*
  The Cottage (Judge & Mrs Hugh Jones)
  Ivy Cottage (Mr & Mrs D H Phillips)
  Woodview (Mrs V Bebb)

Dumgoyne ⚗❀ (Mr & Mrs Hubert Jackson) 90 Heol Isaf, Radyr. A4119 Cardiff-Llantrisant Rd; 2m W of Llandaff turn right on to B4262 for Radyr. Rhondda buses: alight at Radyr turning. Cardiff bus service 88 stops near house. Small, immaculate, Chelsea-inspired garden; large glasshouse with superb collection of pelargoniums. *Adm free. Only open for plant sales. For NGS, special plant sale days Suns April 18, May 2, 16, (2.30-5)*

11 Eastcliff ♿⚗❀ (Mrs Gill James) Southgate. Take the Swansea to Gower road and travel 6m to Pennard. Go through the village of Southgate and take the 2nd exit off the roundabout. Garden 200yds on the L. Seaside garden approx ⅓ acre and developed in a series of island and bordered beds for spring and summer interest. A large number of white and silver plants. Unusual plants and shrubs. TEA. *Adm £1 Chd free. Sun June 27 (2-5)*

¶**24 Elm Grove Place** ♿⚗❀ (Mr & Mrs J Brockhurst) Dinas Powis. Elm Grove Place is a cul-de-sac 200yds E of Dinas Powis Railway Station on the Cardiff to Barry rd (A4055) under railway bridge, 4m from Cardiff, 3m from Barry. Plantsman's garden 60m × 30m, herbaceous, shrubs, greenhouse and several alpine and scree beds; patio area with some unusual container plants; pergola with clematis, wistaria and jasmine. TEA. *Adm £1 Chd free. By appt anytime between April to end Sept* **Tel 0222 513681**

Ewenny Priory ♿⚗❀ (R C Q Picton Turbervill Esq) Ewenny, 2m S of Bridgend. Bus: Bridgend-Ogmore, alight Ewenny Bridge, ½m. Medium-sized garden; plants of interest. Old walled priory dating from 1137 and Church (house not open). NT, plant/produce stalls. NO DOGS. TEAS. *Adm £1.50 Chd 50p. Sun May 9 (2-6)*

Gelly Farm ⚗❀ (Mrs A Appleton, Mrs L Howells, Mrs S Howells) Cymmer. 10m N E of Port Talbot, on A4107, ½m beyond Cymmer, towards Treorchy, turning off rd on R. 4 small varied gardens and 1 vegetable garden grouped around the farmyard of a historically listed working hill farmstead on the slopes of a steep valley. TEA 50p. *Adm £1.50 Chd 50p (Share to The Royal Agricultural Benevolent Institution.) Sun June 20 (2-6)*

Llanvithyn House ⚗❀ (Mr & Mrs L H W Williams) Llancarfan 1.8m S of A48 at Bonvilston, sign for Llancarfan 100yds W of Bonvilston Garage, 1m N of Llancarfan. Medium size garden on site of C6 monastery. C17 gatehouse. Lawns, interesting trees, shrubs, borders. TEAS if fine. *Adm £1.50 Chd 25p. Sun May 16 (2-6)*

Merthyr Mawr House ⚘❀ (Mr & Mrs Murray McLaggan) Merthyr Mawr. 2m SW of Bridgend. Large garden with flowering borders, shrubs, scree garden; wood garden with chapel ruin C14 on site of Iron Age fort. TEA. *Adm £1.50 Chd £1 (Share to The Samaritans). Sun June 21 (2-6)*

29 Min-y-Coed ⚘❀ (Mr & Mrs J H Taylor) Radyr, 6m from Cardiff. On A4119 2m W of Llandaff turn R on B4262 towards Morganstown. From M4 junction 32 on A470 to Taffs Well turn L, then L to B4262 for Radyr. Hillside terraced informal garden with year round colour. TEAS. *Adm 50p Chd free. Suns July 18, Aug 8 (2-5.30)*

Newcastle House Gardens ❀ (C D Fraser Jenkins Esq) West Road, Bridgend. From town centre 400yds up Park St turn R up St Leonards Rd, 2nd R into West Rd. Small town garden completely surrounded by walls; tender plants grown in unheated greenhouses; rare trees, shrubs and herbaceous plants. TEAS in aid of St Illtyd's. *Adm £1.50 Chd 50p Acc children under 14 free (Share to St Illtyd's Church, Newcastle, Bridgend). Suns May 16, June 27 (2-5). Also by appt* **Tel 0656 766880**

Pendoylan and Peterston-Super-Ely Gardens Cowbridge 4½m. A48 Cardiff to Cowbridge. From Cardiff turn R at Sycamore Cross (½-way between St Nicholas and Bonvilston) to Peterston-Super-Ely; take 2nd L to Pendoylan; gardens ½m on L and ¾m on R. Continue towards Welsh St Donats, garden ½m further on L, another on R. *Combined adm £2 Acc Chd free (Share to Pendoylan Church Tower Fund.). Sun April 25 (2-6)*
Trehedyn House (Mr & Mrs D I Williams) Peterston-Super-Ely. ½-acre informal country garden, lawn; newly planted mixed border and old shrub roses, with walks through 1½-acre paddock with established and newly planted trees. TEAS and stalls
Ffynnon Deilo (Mr & Mrs John Lloyd) Pendoylan. Small cottage garden with fish pond and Holy well; interesting plants. Difficult for wheelchairs
¶**Long Acre** ⚘ (Mr & Mrs Howard Tombs) Pendoylan. A wildlife garden. A walk through conifer wood underplanted with daffodils, bluebells, azaleas and camellias to a dell with rhododendrons and shrubs. Fine views
¶**The Old Vicarage** ⚘❀ (Mr & Mrs Michael Gardner) Pendoylan. About 2 acres of cultivated gardens; large water garden, lawns, rhododendrons, azaleas and other shrubs. Stalls

Penllyn Castle ⚘❀ (Mrs Christopher Cory) 3m NW of Cowbridge. From A48 turn N at Pentre Meyrick. Turn R at T-junction straight ahead through gate, leaving church on L. Large garden with fine views; old trees and some new planting; spring shrubs (rhododendrons and magnolias) and bulbs. TEA. *Adm £1.50 Chd 50p. Sun March 28 (2-6)*

¶**Pontygwaith Farm** ⚘❀ (Mr & Mrs R J G Pearce) Edwardsville. Take A4054 Old Cardiff to Merthyr Rd. Travel N for approx 3m through Quaker's Yard and Edwardsville. 1m out of Edwardsville turn sharp L by old bus shelter. Garden at bottom of hill. Medium-sized garden; fish pond, lawns, perennial borders. TEAS. *Adm £1 Chd 50p. Suns July 4, Aug 1 (2-6)*

19 Westfield Road ⚘❀ (Mr & Mrs Brian Dockerill) Glyncoch Pontypridd. From Pontypridd travel 1½m N along B4273 and take L turn by school. At top of hill follow road to L then take first R and R again into Westfield Rd. ½-acre garden divided by hedges and dry stone walls into smaller areas each with a separate character. Differing habitats including pools, rock garden and peat beds allow a wide range of plants to be grown extending the season of interest through the year. TEAS. *Adm £1 Chd 50p. Visitors welcome by appt* **Tel 0443 402999**

9 Willowbrook Gardens ⚘ (Dr & Mrs Gallagher) Mayals, 4m W of Swansea on A4067 (Mumbles) rd to Blackpill; take B4436 (Mayals) rd; 1st R leads to Westport Ave along W boundary of Clyne Park; 1st L into cul-de-sac. ½-acre informal garden designed to give natural effect with balance of form and colour between various areas linked by lawns; unusual trees suited to small suburban garden, esp conifers and maples; rock and water garden. TEAS. *Adm £1.20 Chd 30p. Sun May 16 (1-6) also by appt* **Tel 0792 403268**

¶**Woodside Cottage** ⚘❀ (Mrs A D Arnold) Wenvoe. From Culverhouse Cross to Barry Rd, turn into village of Wenvoe, on Walston Rd between church and public house; 2nd L, Church Rise; 5th house with flag pole. Very, very small walled cottage garden, small pond and herbaceous border. *Adm £1 Chd free. By appt May to July inclusive.* **Tel 0222 594434**

Regular Openers. See head of county section.

———————— ————————

Gwent

Hon County Organiser: Mrs Glynne Clay, Lower House Farm, Nantyderry, Abergavenny NP7 9DP
Tel 0873 880257

Asst Hon County Organiser: Mrs R L Thompson, Llangwilym House, Llanfihangel Gobion, Abergavenny

DATES OF OPENING

By appointment
For telephone numbers and other details see garden descriptions

Castle House, Usk
The Chain Garden, Abergavenny
Edge Hill, nr Trelleck
Harvest Hill, The Narth, nr Trelleck
Lower House Farm, Nantyderry
Orchard House, Coed Morgan, nr Abergavenny
Tir Coppi Cottage, West End, Abercarn
Wern Farm, Glascoed

Regular openings
For details see garden description

Penpergwm Lodge, nr Abergavenny.
   Thurs to Sats April 1 to July 24
   except June 26
Tredegar House & Park, Newport.
   Easter to end of Oct

April 24 Saturday
   Penpergwm Lodge, nr
   Abergavenny
May 1 Saturday
   Penpergwm Lodge, nr
   Abergavenny
May 2 Sunday
   Lower House Farm,
   Nantyderry
May 3 Monday
   Lower House Farm, Nantyderry
May 8 Saturday
   Penpergwm Lodge, nr
   Abergavenny

May 15 Saturday
   Penpergwm Lodge, nr
   Abergavenny
May 16 Sunday
   Brynderwen Court, Bettws
   Newydd, nr Usk
May 22 Saturday
   Penpergwm Lodge, nr
   Abergavenny
May 23 Sunday
   Oakgrove, St Arvans,
   Chepstow
May 29 Saturday
   Penpergwm Lodge, nr
   Abergavenny
May 30 Sunday
   Traligael, Whitebrook
May 31 Monday
   Clytha Park, nr
   Abergavenny ‡
   Trostrey Lodge, Bettws Newydd,
   nr Usk ‡
June 5 Saturday
   Penpergwm Lodge, nr
   Abergavenny
June 6 Sunday
   The Graig, nr Raglan
June 12 Saturday
   Penperpgwm Lodge, nr
   Abergavenny
June 13 Sunday
   Penpergwm Lodge, nr
   Abergavenny
June 19 Saturday
   Penpergwm Lodge, nr
   Abergavenny
June 20 Sunday
   Wern Farm, Glascoed
June 27 Sunday
   Great Campston, Llanfihangel
   Crucorney

July 3 Saturday
   Penpergwm Lodge, nr
   Abergavenny
July 4 Sunday
   Court St Lawrence, nr Usk
   Llanfair Court, nr
   Abergavenny
July 10 Saturday
   Penpergwm Lodge, nr
   Abergavenny
July 11 Sunday
   Great Killough, nr Abergavenny ‡
   Orchard House, Coed Morgan, nr
   Abergavenny ‡
July 17 Saturday
   Penpergwm Lodge, nr
   Abergavenny
July 18 Sunday
   Tredegar House & Park, Newport
July 24 Saturday
   Penpergwm Lodge, nr
   Abergavenny
July 25 Sunday
   Llan-y-Nant, Coed Morgan, nr
   Abergavenny
August 1 Sunday
   Harvest Hill, The Narth, nr
   Trelleck
August 22 Sunday
   Charters, Nantyderry
August 29 Sunday
   Lower House Farm, Nantyderry
August 30 Monday
   Lower House Farm, Nantyderry
September 5 Sunday
   Castle House, Usk
September 12 Sunday
   Tredegar House & Park,
   Newport
October 10 Sunday
   Llanover, nr Abergavenny

DESCRIPTIONS OF GARDENS

¶**Brynderwen Court** &⚘ (Dr & Mrs P Williams) Bettws Newydd. From Usk take Abergavenny rd B4598; after 2m fork R to Bettws Newydd. Garden on L ½m after 'Black Bear' Inn. 7-acre garden plus 3 acres woodland in country park setting. Herbaceous borders; lily ponds, fountains, naturalised daffodils and other bulbs; flowering shrubs, rhododendrons, azaleas; rose garden in walled enclosure; terraces overlooking R. Usk and 'Usk Valley Walk'. Limited parking in wet weather. Cream TEAS in aid of A.R.C. *Adm £2 OAP £1 Chd free. Sun May 16 (2-6)*

Castle House ⚘⚘ (Mr & Mrs J H L Humphreys) Usk; 200yds from Usk centre; turn up lane by fire station. Medium-sized garden; a flower garden of orderly disorder around ruins of Usk Castle. TEAS. *Adm £1 Chd free. Sun Sept 5 (2-6) and also by appt* **Tel 029167 2563**

The Chain Garden ⚘ (Mr & Mrs C F R Price) Chapel Rd, 1m N of Abergavenny. Turn off A40 (on Brecon side of town) into Chapel Rd, garden at top of rd. 2 acres with stream; lawns; rhododendrons; shrubs, fruit and vegetables. *Adm £1 Chd free. By appt only April 1 to Sept 30* **Tel 0873 853825**

Charters &⚘ (Mr & Mrs Peter Lang) Nant-y-derry, Abergavenny. From B4598 Usk to Abergavenny turn off at Chain Bridge, after 1m garden opp Foxhunter Inn. Approx 2½-acre garden. Mixed borders, shrubs and herbaceous. Kitchen garden, vegetables organically grown. Flowers for drying, dried arrangements and bunches for sale. TEAS. *Adm £1 Chd 50p. Sun Aug 22 (2-6)*

Clytha Park & (R Hanbury-Tenison Esq) ½ way between Abergavenny and Raglan on old rd (not A40). 5 acres; C18 layout; trees, shrubs; lake. Plants etc at Trostrey Lodge, 1m. TEAS. *Adm £1 Chd 50p. Sun May 31 (2-6)*

Court St Lawrence &*🏵 (Lt. Col & Mrs G D Inkin) Llangovan, 6m SW of Monmouth, 5m NE of Usk, between Pen-y-Clawdd and Llangovan. 5 acres of garden and woodland with trees, shrubs, lake, roses etc. TEAS, plants and produce stalls. *Adm £1 Chd 25p. Sun July 4 (2-6)*

Edge Hill *✻* (Mr & Mrs J A Shearston) 1½m W of Trelleck. Ring for instructions. 1-acre garden on difficult site over 900 ft high on steep hillside facing NE. Mixed trees, conifers, shrubs, herbaceous, climbers, etc; small conservation pond, formal lily pool; peafowl, aviaries, glorious views to Black Mountains. Limited parking. TEA. *Adm £1 Chd 25p. By appt only (Garden Clubs & W.I. welcome)* **Tel 0600 860473**

The Graig *✻🏵* (Mrs Rainforth) Pen-y-Clawdd, SW of Monmouth. Turn S from Raglan-Monmouth Rd (not Motorway) at sign to Pen-y-Clawdd. Bus: Newport-Monmouth, alight Keen's shop, ½m. Mixed cottage garden with interesting shrubs & roses. TEAS. *Adm £1 Chd 20p. Sun June 6 (2-6)*

Great Campston 🏵 (Mr & Mrs A D Gill) 7m NE of Abergavenny; 2m towards Grosmont off A465 at Llanfihangel Crucorney. Drive on R just before brow of hill. Pretty 2-acre garden set in wonderful surroundings. Designed and planted from scratch by Mrs Gill, a garden designer; wide variety of interesting plants and trees enhanced by lovely stone walls, paving and summer house with fantastic views. The house stands 750ft above sea level on s. facing hillside with spring fed stream feeding 2 ponds. TEAS. *Adm £1 Chd 50p. Sun June 27 (2-6)*

Great Killough &*✻* (Mr & Mrs John F Ingledew) Llantilio Crossenny, 6m E of Abergavenny. S of B4233. 3-acre garden created in the 1960s to complement mediaeval house. TEAS. *Adm £1 Chd free (Share to Barnardos). Sun July 11 (2-6)*

Harvest Hill &*✻🏵* (Mr & Mrs Richard Sadler) The Narth, nr Monmouth. 2m E of Trelleck on B4293 on Monmouth to Chepstow rd. 1-acre mixed garden with flowers, fruit and vegetables. Cream TEAS. *Adm £1 Chd 25p (Share to Hospice of the Marches, Torrington). Sun Aug 1 (2-6). Also by appt* **Tel Trelleck 860 527**

Llanfair Court & (Sir William Crawshay) 5m SE of Abergavenny. Route old A40 and B4598. Medium-sized garden, herbaceous border, flowering shrubs, roses, water garden; modern sculpture. TEAS. *Adm £1 Chd 50p. Sun July 4 (2-6)*

Llanover & (R A E Herbert, Esq) S of Abergavenny. Bus: Abergavenny-Pontypool, alight drive gates. Large water garden; some rare plants, autumn colour. TEAS. *Adm £1 Chd 50p. Sun Oct 10 (2-6)*

Llan-y-Nant &*✻* (Mr & Mrs Charles Pitchford) Coed Morgan. 4m from Abergavenny, 5m from Raglan on old A40 (now B4598) Raglan to Abergavenny rd. Turn up lane opp 'Chart House' inn; pass Monmouthshire Hunt Kennels 500 yds on R. 3 acres of garden and woodlands. Lawn, beds, shrubs, herbs, alpines and kitchen garden. Small lake with wild life. TEAS. *Adm £1 Chd 50p. Sun July 25 (2-6)*

Lower House Farm *✻🏵* (Mr & Mrs Glynne Clay) Nantyderry, 7m SE of Abergavenny. From Usk-Abergavenny rd, B4598, turn off at Chain Bridge. Medium-sized garden designed for all year interest; mixed borders, fern island, bog garden, herb bed, paved area, unusual plants. Late flowering perennials. Featured in magazines and on T.V. TEAS. *Adm £1 Chd 50p. Suns, Mons, May 2, 3; Aug 29, 30 (2-6); also by appt* **Tel Nantyderry 880257**

Oakgrove &*✻🏵* (Mr & Mrs C Hughes Davies) St Arvans. 1½m from Chepstow on A466 towards Monmouth, drive on L after Racecourse. 2½ acres; fine beech trees, herbaceous borders, shrub roses; grey and silver border; recently established collection of fagus and nothofagus; wild garden. TEAS. *Adm £1 Chd 50p. Sun May 23 (2-6)*

Orchard House &*✻🏵* (Mr & Mrs B R Hood) Coed Morgan. 1½m of old Raglan-Abergavenny rd. Approx 6m from Abergavenny. Turn opposite King of Prussia or The Charthouse. A garden of approx 1 acre with mixed borders of unusual herbaceous plants and shrubs, rosebeds and lawn. TEAS in aid of St David's Church. *Adm £1 Chd 30p. Sun July 11 (2-6). Also by appt April to Sept* **Tel 0873 840289**

Penpergwm Lodge &🏵 (Mr & Mrs Simon Boyle) 3m SE of Abergavenny. From Abergavenny take B 4598 towards Usk, after 2½m turn L opp King of Prussia Inn. Entrance 300yds on L. 3-acre mixed garden with unusual vegetable and flower garden; lawns, borders; terraces and fine mature trees. Small nursery of special plants. TEAS (Sun only) in aid of St Cadoc's Church. *Adm £1 Chd 20p. April 1 to July 24 Thurs-Sats (2-6). For NGS Sun June 13 and every Sat April 24 to July 24 except Sat June 26 (2-6)*

Tir Coppi Cottage *✻🏵* (Mr & Mrs Peter Davenport) West End. 2m NW of Abercarn. 8½-acre small holding designed and managed to attract wild life. 700ft up on Mynydd Islwyn with views of Ebbw Valley. Pretty plant-packed cottage garden, organic orchard and vegetables. Wildlife habitats incl mature woodland, hedges, ponds and ditches. Free-range poultry, Angora goats, Soay sheep, donkeys. Wild flower plants for sale. TEAS. *Adm £1 Chd free (Share to Donkey Sanctuary, Sidmouth, Devon). By appt only May 15 to July 31* **Tel 0495 245288**

Traligael (Mr & Mrs E C Lysaght) 4m S of Monmouth via B4293 turn left for Whitebrook, or 3½m from A466 at Bigsweir Bridge past Whitebrook; garden alongside lane. 3-acre garden in woodland setting with water garden; rhododendrons and shrubs. *Adm £1 Chd free. Sun May 30 (2-6)*

Tredegar House & Park &*✻🏵* (Newport Borough Council) 2m SW of Newport Town Centre. Signposted from A48 (Cardiff road) and M4 junction 28. Set in 90 acres of historic parkland surrounding a magnificent late C17 house (also open) are a series of C17 & C18 formal walled gardens. The early C18 Orangery Garden is currently being recreated following extensive archaeological and research work. The orangery is also open. The central Cedar Garden has wide recently revived herbaceous borders. On NGS days the private gardens around the Curator's Cottage and Home Farm Cottage are also open.

Away from the house is an Edwardian sunken garden restored mid 1980s. Spectacular rhododendrons border the lake. TEAS. *Adm £1 Chd 50p (Share to The Friends of Tredegar House and Park). For NGS Suns July 18, Sept 12 (11-6). House, Gardens etc open Easter to end of Oct ring for details* **Tel 0633 815880**

¶**Trostrey Lodge** ⚘⚘ (Mr & Mrs R Pemberton) Bettws Newydd. Half way between Raglan and Abergavenny on old road (not A40). Turning to Bettws Newydd opposite Clytha gates 1m on R. Pretty walled garden and small orchard in fine landscape; interesting plants; bring and buy plant sale. Teas at Clytha Park 1m. *Adm £1 Chd 50p. Mon May 31 (2-6)*

Wern Farm ⚘⚘ (Mr & Mrs W A Harris) Between Usk and Little Mill on A472. Turn at signpost for Glascoed village, 1m from main rd (Beaufort Inn or Monkswood Garage). 1½-acres completely new garden created since 1984 following natural contours of ground; trees, shrubs, herbaceous plants, alpines, shrub roses; rockery; herbs; veg garden; small aviary; ¼ acre of flowers grown for drying. Demonstration of Bee-keeping by professional keeper and demonstration of wool spinning with organically dyed wool. TEAS. *Adm £1 Chd 30p. Sun June 20 (2-6); also by appt* **Tel 0495 28 363**

Regular Openers. See head of county section.

Gwynedd & Anglesey

Hon County Organisers:
(Anglesey & North Gwynedd)
(South Gwynedd)

Mrs B S Osborne, Foxbrush, Aber Pwll, Port Dinorwic, Gwynedd LL56 4JZ
Tel 0248 670463
Mrs W N Jones, Waen Fechan, Islaw'r Dref, Dolgellau, LL40 1TS
Tel 0341 423479

DATES OF OPENING

By appointment
For telephone numbers and other details see garden descriptions

Bont Fechan Farm, Llanystumdwy
Bryn Golygfa, Bontddu
Bryniau, Boduan
Brynmelyn, Ffestiniog
Bryn-y-Bont, Nantmor
Cefn Bere, Dolgellau
Foxbrush, Aber Pwll, Port Dinorwic
Fronheulog, Llanfrothen
Glandderwen, Bontddu
Gwyndy Bach, Llandrygarn
Hafod Garregog
Hen Ysgoldy, Llanfrothen
Henllys Lodge, Beaumaris
Mur Cwymp, Garndolbenmaen
Pencarreg, Glyn Garth, Menai Bridge

Regular openings
For details see garden descriptions

Bryn Meifod, Glan Conwy. Thurs in May & Sept, Suns in June & Aug
Crug Farm, nr Caernarfon. Thurs to Suns & Bank Hols March 4 to Oct 3
Plas Muriau, Betws-y-Coed. Tues to Suns March 1 to Oct 31

Plas Penhelig, Aberdovey. Wed to Sun May 1 to Mid Oct
Sychnant, Capelulo. Thurs, May 6 to Sept 30

March 28 Sunday
Plas Penhelig, Aberdovey
April 4 Sunday
Bryniau, Boduan
April 11 Sunday
Bont Fechan Farm, Llanystumdwy
Crug Farm, nr Caernarfon
Foxbrush, Aber Pwll, Port Dinorwic
April 12 Monday
Crug Farm, nr Caernarfon
April 18 Sunday
Plas Penhelig, Aberdovey
May 2 Sunday
Gilfach, Rowen , nr Conwy
May 9 Sunday
Hafod Garregog
May 13 Thursday
Plas Newydd, Llanfair Pwll
May 16 Sunday
Bont Fechan Farm, Llanystumdwy
Farchynys Cottage, Bontddu
May 23 Sunday
Maenan Hall, Llanrwst
Pen-y-Parc, Beaumaris
Farchynys Cottage, Bontddu

May 29 Saturday
Coleg Glynllifon, Caernarfon
May 30 Sunday
Bryn Eisteddfod, Glan Conwy
Bryn Golygfa, Bontddu
Bryniau, Boduan
Crug Farm, nr Caernarfon
Foxbrush, Aber Pwll, Port Dinorwic
Penrhyn Castle, nr Bangor
May 31 Monday
Bryn Golygfa, Bontddu
Crug Farm, nr Caernarfon
June 19 Saturday
Henllys Lodge, Beaumaris
June 20 Sunday
Gilfach, Rowen , nr Conwy
Henllys Lodge, Beaumaris
June 27 Sunday
Bryniau, Boduan
July 3 Saturday
Gwyndy Bach, Llandrygarn
July 4 Sunday
Bont Fechan Farm, Llanystumdwy
Gwyndy Bach, Llandrygarn
July 18 Sunday
Crug Farm, nr Caernarfon
August 8 Sunday
Bryniau, Boduan
August 14 Saturday
Gilfach, Rowen , nr Conwy

August 22 Sunday
Bont Fechan Farm, Llanystumdwy
August 29 Sunday
Crug Farm, nr Caernarfon

Foxbrush, Aber Pwll, Port
Dinorwic
Glandderwen, Bontddu
Maenan Hall, Llanrwst

August 30 Monday
Crug Farm, nr Caernarfon

DESCRIPTIONS OF GARDENS

¶**Bont Fechan Farm** ൟ⚶❀ (Mr & Mrs J D Bean) Llanystumdwy. 2 m from Criccieth on the A487 to Pwllheli on the L-hand side of the main rd. Small garden with rockery, pond, herbaceous border, steps to river, large variety of plants. Nicely planted tubs. Tea. *Adm 50p Chd 25p. Suns April 11, May 16, July 4, Aug 22 (11-7) By appt* **Tel 0766 522604**

¶**Bryn Eisteddfod** (Dr Michael Senior) Glan Conwy. 3½m SE Llandudno 3m W Colwyn Bay; up the hill (Bryn-y-Maen direction) from Glan Conwy Corner where A470 joins A55. 8 acres of landscaped grounds incl mature shrubbery, arboretum, old walled 'Dutch' garden, large lawn with ha-ha. Extensive views over Conwy Valley, Snowdonia National Park, Conwy Castle, town and estuary. *Adm £1 Chd 50p. Sun May 30 (2-5)*

¶**Bryn Golygfa** ⚶ (Mrs K & Mr R Alexander) Dolgellau. 5m W of Dolgellau. Take A496 to Bontddu; garden is N 100yds past Bontddu Hall Hotel. Small garden on steep hillside; mixed planting incl rhododendrons and alpines. *Adm 50p Chd 25p. Sun, Mon May 30, 31 (11-5). Also by appt mid-May to mid-Aug*

¶**Bryniau** ⚶❀ (P W Wright & J E Humphreys) Boduan. ½m down lane opp. St Buan's Church, Boduan, which is halfway between Nefyn and Pwllheli on the A497. New garden created since 1988 on almost pure sand. Over 60 types of trees; hundreds of shrubs, many unusual, showing that with a little effort, one can grow virtually anything anywhere. TEA. *Adm 75p Chd free. Suns April 4, May 30, June 27, Aug 8, (11-6) and by appt* **Tel 0758 7213 38**

Brynmelyn ⚶ (Mr & Mrs A S Taylor) Cymerau Isaf. About 2m SW of Blaenau Ffestiniog, on A496 Maentwrog-Blaenau Ffestiniog Rd. Enter by lower gate in layby opp junction to Manod, by footpath sign. After 100yds leave car at garage and follow small footpath to R of garage, descending to stone bridge and Cymerau Falls. Continue over bridge and up hill, follow footpath L; garden about ¼m from garage. Cultivated garden under 1 acre, divided into smaller gardens, each with separate character; variety of shrubs and perennial plants for different habitats, providing interest throughout season. Surrounded by nature reserve woodland; bluebells late May, early June. Good Autumn colours. *Collecting Box (Share to The National Osteoporosis Society). By appt May 1 to Oct 15* **Tel Ffestiniog 076 676 2684**. *Please telephone before 9.30 am or after dusk.*

Bryn-y-Bont ❀ (The Misses Davis & Entwisle) Nantmor. 2½m S of Beddgelert, turn L over Aberglaslyn Bridge into A4085, 500yds turn L up hill, 2nd house on R. Small garden created since 1978 on S facing wooded hillside over

looking Glaslyn Vale (As featured on Radio Wales 'Get Gardening' in 1990). *Adm £1 Chd free. Open by appt mid April to mid Sept (11-5pm) Parties welcome* **Tel 076 686 448**

¶**Bryn Meifod** ⚶❀ (Dr & Mrs K Lever) Graig. Just off A470 1½m S of Glan Conwy. Follow signs for Aberconwy Nursery. ¾-acre garden developed over 25yrs but extensively replanted in the last 3yrs. Unusual trees and shrubs, scree and peat beds. Good autumn colours. Wide ranging collection of alpines especially autumn gentians and saxifrages. *Adm £1 Chd 25p. Thurs in May and Sept; Suns in June and Aug (2-5)*

Cefn Bere ⚶ (Mr & Mrs Maldwyn Thomas) Cae Deintur, Dolgellau. Turn L at top of main bridge on Bala-Barmouth Rd (not the by-pass); turn R within 20yds; 2nd R behind school and up hill. Small garden; extensive collection of alpines, bulbs and rare plants. Tea Dolgellau. *Collecting box. By appt only, spring & summer months* **Tel Dolgellau 422768**

¶**Coleg Glynllifon** ൟ⚶❀ (The Principal) Caernarfon. Situated at Coleg Glynllifon, approx 7m from Caernarfon on the A499 to Pwllheli. The garden being developed is part of the old east-walled garden. This redevelopment is part of facilities for College's Special Needs Dept. and is undertaken with the assistance of the Welsh Historic Garden Trust. Research being undertaken on Glynllifon family records at County Archive Dept. gives guidance to original garden layout. Tearoom at Park Glynllifon. *Adm 50p Chd free. Sat May 29 (10-4)*

Crug Farm ⚶❀ (Mr & Mrs B Wynn-Jones) Griffiths Crossing. 2m NE of Caernarfon ¼m off main A487 Caernarfon to Bangor Road. Follow signs 'Crug Farm Plants'. Plantsmans garden; ideally situated; 2 to 3 acres grounds to old country house. Gardens filled with choice, unusual collections of plants incl many climbers, hardy geraniums, epimediums, daphnes and numerous others. Only partly suitable wheelchairs. TEAS in aid of RNLI and local charities. *Collecting box for walled display garden open Thurs, Fri, Sat, Suns & Bank Hols March 4 to Oct 30 (10-6). See calendar for openings of private gardens. Adm £1 Chd 50p. Natural Rock garden only open Suns & Mons April 11, 12, May 30, 31 July 18, Aug 29, 30 (10-6)*

Farchynys Cottage ⚶❀ (Mrs G Townshend) Bontddu. On A496 Dolgellau-Barmouth rd; well signed W of Bontddu village. 4 acres; partly well-established garden, with attractive, unusual shrubs and trees; partly natural woodland first extensive planting in 1982, new plantings each year. Silver Cup winner 'Wales in Bloom' 1987 Committee Award 1985, 1986 and 1989. Car park. TEAS. *Adm 50p Chd 25p.* ▲*For NGS Suns May 16, 23 (11-6)*

Foxbrush ♿✂❀ (Mr & Mrs B S Osborne) Aber Pwll, Port Dinorwic. On Bangor Rd, approach to Port Dinorwic opp W lodge to Vaynol Estate; signposted. Fascinating 3-acre country garden on site of old mill and created around winding river; rare and interesting plants; ponds and small wooded area. Extensive plant collections incl rhododendrons, ferns, primula, alpines, clematis and roses; 45ft long pergola; fan-shaped knot garden with traditional and unusual herbs; coaches welcome. Craft sudio with jewellery, gifts. TEA. *Adm £1 Chd free. Suns April 11, May 30, Aug 29 (11-5). Also by appt* **Tel 0248 670463**

Fronheulog ✂ (Mr & Mrs J Baily Gibson) Llanfrothen. From Llanfrothen via B4410, after ½m turn L; after 200yds left again; opp Hen Ysgoldy (below). Wild rocky hillside made into garden by owners since 1973; mainly heathers, shrubs and ground cover. *Collecting box. By appt only mid April to mid Sept* **Tel 0766 770558**

¶Gilfach ✂ (James & Isoline Greenhalgh) Rowen. At Xrds 100yds E of Rowen (4m S of Conwy) S towards Llanrwst, past Rowen School on L; turn up 2nd drive on L, signposted. 1-acre country garden on S facing slope overlooking Conwy Valley; set in 35 acres farm and woodland; mature shrubs; herbaceous border; small pool. Partly suitable wheelchairs which are welcome. Magnificent views of River Conwy and mountains. TEAS. *Adm £1 Chd 10p. Suns May 2, June 20, Sat Aug 14 (11-5)*

Glandderwen ✂ (A M Reynolds Esq) 5m W of Dolgellau. Take A496 to Bontddu. Garden is on S 100yds past Bontddu Hall Hotel; large white wooden gates. ½-acre on N bank of Mawddach Estuary facing Cader Idris; set amid large oaks; shrubs, trees; steep and rocky nature. *Adm 50p Chd 25p. Sun, Aug 29, (11-5). By appt May 1 to Sept 30* **Tel 0341 49229**

Gwyndy Bach ♿✂❀ (Keith & Rosa Andrew) Llandrygarn. From Llangefni take the B5109 towards Bodedern, the cottage is exactly 5m out on the L. A ¾-acre artist's garden set amidst rugged Anglesey landscape. Romantically planted in intimate 'rooms' with interesting plants and shrubs, old roses and secluded lily pond. Studio attached. TEAS. *Adm £1 Chd free. Sat, Sun July 3, 4 (11-5.30. Also by appt* **Tel 0407 720651**

Hafod Garregog ❀ (Mr & Mrs Hugh Mason) Nantmor, 5m N of Penrhyndeudraeth on A4085 towards Aberglaslyn. Garden in woodland setting with fine mountain views; trees, shrubs, flowers and vegetables; woodland bluebell walk. Shown on BBC's 'Gardener's World'. Home of Rhys Goch Eryri AD 1430. Situated above R. Hafod. Parties welcome. New garden being made. TEAS. *Adm £1 Chd free. Sun May 9 (11-5). By appt April to Sept* **Tel 076 686 282**

Henllys Lodge ♿✂❀ (Mr & Mrs K H Lane) Beaumaris. Past Beaumaris Castle, ½m turn L, 1st L again. Lodge at entrance to Henllys Hall Hotel drive. Approx 1-acre country garden, planted in traditional cottage style featuring extensive collection of hardy geraniums. Small woodland area. Stunning views across Menai Straits. TEAS. *Adm 50p. Sat, Sun June 19, 20 (2-5.30). Also by appt* **Tel 0248 810106**

Hen Ysgoldy ✂ (Mr & Mrs Michael Jenkins) Llanfrothen. From Garreg via B4410, after ½m L; garden 200yds on R. Natural garden with streams and established trees, incl magnolias, eucalyptus and embothrium. Shrubs incl a variety of azaleas and rhododendrons, mixed borders planted for colour and interest most of the year round. *Collecting box. By appt April 1 to Sept 30* **Tel 0766 771231**

Maenan Hall ❀ (The Hon Christopher McLaren) Exactly 2m N of Llanrwst on E side of A470, ¼m S of Maenan Abbey Hotel. Gardens created since 1956 by the late Christabel, Lady Aberconway and then present owner; 10 acres; lawns, shrub, rose and walled gardens; rhododendron dell; many species of beautiful and interesting plants, shrubs and trees set amongst mature oaks and other hardwoods; fine views of mountains across Conway valley. Home-made TEAS. *Adm £1.50 Chd 50p (Share to Child Line Wales Sun May 23 & Margaret Mee Amazon Trust Aug 29). Suns May 23, Aug 29 (10-5) Last entry 4pm*

Mur Cwymp ✂❀ (Mrs I E Hepher) Garndolbenmaen lies 5m E of Criccieth ¾m from Porthmadog-Caernarfon A487 Rd. Turn E into Village signposted near cafe. In village turn sharp L by Chapel, 1st R opposite PO Box in wall 3rd gate on R. 1½-acre garden, within 9-acre small holding, contains many unusual trees and shrubs. Pergolas, screens, garden pots, lanterns and sculptures designed and handmade here are features of the garden. Splendid views. Visitors personally welcomed and escorted. TEA. *Adm £1 Chd 50p (Share to Multiple Sclerosis Society). April 15 to Sept 15. By appt only* **Tel Garndolbenmaen (076 675) 383**

Pencarreg ♿✂❀ (Miss G Jones) Glyn Garth. 1½m NE of Menai Bridge towards Beaumaris on A545 on R down Glan y Menai Drive. Park in lay-by on rd, in drive for disabled. 1-acre lawns, variety of shrubs, stream and rock garden overlooking Menai Straits. Fine views of Carneddi. Garden featured BBC TV 'Gardening Together' and 'Palu Mlaen' Aug '86. TEA (Share to Rescue Dogs, Wales). *Collecting Box. By appt only all year* **Tel 0248 713545**

Penrhyn Castle ♿❀ (The National Trust) 3m E of Bangor on A5122. Buses from Llandudno, Caernarvon. Bettws-y-Coed; alight: Grand Lodge Gate. Large gardens; fine trees, shrubs, wild garden, good views. Castle was rebuilt in 1830 for 1st Lord Penrhyn, incorporating part of C15 building on C8 site of home of Welsh Princes. Museum of dolls; museum of locomotives and quarry rolling stock. NT Shop. TEAS and light lunches. Guide dogs admitted into Castle. *Adm £2 Chd £1. For NGS Sun, May 30 (12-5). Last adm ½ hr prior to closing*

Pen-y-Parc (Mrs E E Marsh) Beaumaris. A545 Menai Bridge-Beaumaris rd; after Anglesey Boatyard 1st left; after Golf Club 1st drive on left. NOT very easy for wheelchairs. 6 acres; beautiful grounds, magnificent views over Menai Strait; azaleas, rhododendrons and heathers; interesting terrain with rock outcrops used to advantage for recently planted conifer and rock gardens; small lake in natural setting; 2 further enclosed gardens. We would like to share the pleasure of this garden. TEA. *Adm £1 Chd 25p. Sun May 23 (11-5)*

¶Plas Muriau *⚘⚘* (Lorna & Tony Scharer) Bettws-y-Coed. On A470 approx ¼m N of Waterloo Bridge, Bettws-y-Coed; entrance by minor junction to Capel Garnon. Large neglected Victorian garden undergoing restoration and replanting with approx 1 acre open to visitors; emphasis on recreating a structured garden within its woodland setting and magnificent views, using perennials, herbs, native plants, bulbs and roses. Many unusual plants for sale at adjacent nursery. *Collecting Box. Tues to Sun incl March 1 to Oct 31 (11-6)*

Plas Newydd *⚘* (The Marquess of Anglesey; The National Trust) Isle of Anglesey. 1m SW of Llanfairpwll and A5, on A4080. Gardens with massed shrubs, fine trees, and lawns sloping down to Menai Strait. Magnificent views to Snowdonia. C18 house by James Wyatt contains Rex Whistler's largest wall painting; also Military Museum. TEAS and light lunches. *Adm house & garden £3.50 Group £2.80 Chd £1.75, garden only £1.75 Chd 90p, Family Adm £8.80. For NGS Thurs May 13 (12-5)*

Plas Penhelig *⚘* (Mr & Mrs A C Richardson) Aberdovey, between 2 railway bridges. Driveway to hotel by island and car park. 14 acres overlooking estuary, exceptional views. Particularly lovely in spring: bulbs, daffodils, rhododendrons, azaleas; rock and water gardens, mature tree heathers, magnolias, euphorbias; herbaceous borders, rose garden; wild and woodland flowers encouraged in large orchard; walled kitchen garden, large range of greenhouses, peaches, herbs. TEAS. *Adm £1 Chd 50p. Suns March 28, April 18 (2.30-5.30); also Wed to Sun inc May 1 to mid-Oct. Collecting box*

Sychnant *⚘⚘* (Chandler & A Williamson) Penmaenmawr. Situated on and 200 metres from the foot of the Sychnant Pass in Dwygyfylchi. Between Conwy and Penmaenmawr. OS Sheet SH 745768. Over ½-acre steep terraced dry garden under renovation, containing many rare and unusual plants. Large collection of pinks, geraniums, erodiums and grasses. Flat shoes recommended. Adjacent nursery open. *Collecting Box. Thurs May 6 to Sept 30 (10-6)*

Powys

Hon County Organisers:
(North – Montgomeryshire) Captain R Watson, Westwinds, Kerry, Newtown, Powys Tel 068688 605
(South – Brecknock & Radnor) Mrs C R C Inglis, Llansantffraed House, Bwlch Brecon Tel 087487 229
Assistant County Organiser:
S. Powys Miss Shan Egerton, Pen-y-Maes, Hay on Wye, Via Hereford Tel 0497 820 423
Hon County Treasurer: North Elwyn Pugh Esq, Post Office, Kerry, Newtown Tel 068688 221
South Mr C.R.C. Inglis, Llansantffraed House, Bwlch, Brecon Tel 087 487 229

DATES OF OPENING

By appointment
For telephone numbers and other details see garden descriptions

Ashford House, Talybont on Usk
Bryn Glas, Llanfair Caereinion
Craig-y-Bwla, nr Crickhowell
Diamond Cottage, Buttington
Fraithwen, Tregynon, Newtown
Glebe House, Welshpool
Maenllwyd Isaf, Abermule
The Old Vicarage, Llangorse
The Walled Garden, Knill, nr
   Presteigne

April 18 Sunday
Gliffaes Country House Hotel,
   Crickhowell
April 25 Sunday
Moor Park, nr Crickhowell

April 28 Wednesday
Diamond Cottage, Buttington
May 2 Sunday
Maesllwch Castle, Glasbury
May 8 Saturday
Cae Hywel,
   Llansantffraid-ym-Mechain
May 9 Sunday
Cae Hywel,
   Llansantffraid-ym-Mechain
Penmyarth, Crickhowell
May 16 Sunday
Trawscoed Hall, Welshpool
May 22 Saturday
Craig-y-Bwla, nr
   Crickhowell
May 23 Sunday
Bronhyddon,
   Llansantffraid-ym-Mechain
Craig-y-Bwla, nr Crickhowell
Glanwye, Builth Wells
May 26 Wednesday
Diamond Cottage, Buttington

May 29 Saturday
Bodynfoel Hall, Llanfechain
May 30 Sunday
Bodynfoel Hall, Llanfechain
Bryn Glas, Llanfair Caereinion
Llysdinam, Newbridge-on-Wye
May 31 Monday
Garth House, Garth
June 1 Tuesday
Powis Castle Gardens,
   Welshpool
June 6 Sunday
Ashford House, Talybont on Usk
Craig Llyn, Rhayader,
   Llanwrthwl
Gregynog, Tregynon
June 13 Sunday
Llangorse Gardens, Brecon
Lower Cefn Perfa, Kerry, nr
   Newtown
Parc Gwynne, Glasbury-on-Wye
June 16 Wednesday
Llangorse Gardens, Brecon

June 19 Saturday
Upper Dolley, Dolley Green,
Presteigne

June 20 Sunday
Llanstephan House, Llyswen
Upper Dolley, Dolley Green,
Presteigne

June 27 Sunday
Fraithwen, Tregynon, Newtown
Tretower House, Crickhowell

June 30 Wednesday
Diamond Cottage, Buttington

July 4 Sunday
Manascin, Pencelli, Brecon

July 10 Saturday
Argoed Fawr, Llanwrthwl
Upper Dolley, Dolley Green,
Presteigne

July 11 Sunday
Argoed Fawr, Llanwrthwl
Treberfydd, nr Bwlch
Upper Dolley, Dolley Green,
Presteigne

July 28 Wednesday
Diamond Cottage, Buttington

August 1 Sunday
Station Road Gardens, Talybont
on Usk

Talybont on Usk Gardens,
Talybont on Usk

August 8 Sunday
Craig Llyn, Rhayader, Llanwrthwl
Kerry Gardens, Kerry, nr Newtown

August 22 Sunday
Llysdinam, Newbridge-on-Wye

October 3 Sunday
Bodynfoel Hall, Llanfechain

October 17 Sunday
Gliffaes Country House Hotel,
Crickhowell

DESCRIPTIONS OF GARDENS

¶**Argoed Fawr** ✿❀ (Mr & Mrs M J Maltley) Llanwrthwl. 7m N of Builth Wells on A470. 5m S of Rhayader. ½-acre cultivated garden with small shrubbery; rock garden; pergola; vegetable garden; fruit trees and bushes. Herbaceous border, climbing roses, and clematis, extending to 3 acres of conservation area with stream where new plantings of trees and hedges have been grown to encourage wildlife. TEAS. *Adm £1 Chd over 16, 50p. Sat, Sun July 10, 11 (10-5)*

Ashford House &✿❀ (Mr & Mrs D A Anderson) Brecon. ¾m E of Talybont on Usk on B4558 signed from A40 through village. Walled garden of about 1 acre surrounded by woodland and wild garden approx 4 acres altogether. Mixed shrub and herbaceous borders; new small formal garden; meadow garden and pond; alpine house and beds; vegetables. The whole garden has gradually been restored and developed over the last 12yrs. TEAS. *Adm £1 Chd free (Share to Action Research). Sun June 6 (2-6). Also by appt* **Tel 087 487 271**

Bodynfoel Hall &✿❀ (Maj & Mrs Bonnor-Maurice) Llanfechain, 10m N of Welshpool. Via A490 to Llanfyllin. Take B4393 to Llanfechain, follow signs to Bodynfoel. 3½ acres; gardens and woodland; new lake; young and mature trees; shrub roses and heather bank. TEAS. *Adm £1 OAPs 50p Chd free. Sat, Sun May 29, 30 (2-6); Sun Oct 3 (2-5).* **Tel 069184 486**

Bronhyddon ❀ (Mr & Mrs R Jones-Perrott) Llansantffraid-ym-Mechain. 10m N Welshpool on A495 on E side in centre of village. Long drive; parking in fields below house. Wood having been almost clear felled now planted with choice young trees & shrubs on acid soil on S facing slope. Grass rides have been made and in spring is a mass of bluebells and foxgloves; a mature stand has anemones, snowdrops & primroses. Both areas lead out of small garden in front of house with elegant Regency verandahs & balconies. TEAS. *Adm £1 Chd free. Sun May 23 (2-6)*

Bryn Glas ❀ (Dr & Mrs Milton Jones) B4389 Llanfair Caereinion going S to A485 Newtown-Welshpool rd. ¼m from village 1st R opp garage; then 1st L, over cattle grid, by Bryn Glas Lodge. Parking below house. A large garden; many mature shrubs & trees on a sloping site; winding drive leads to house. Mixed beds around the house & buildings give added interest. TEAS. *Adm £1 Chd free. Sun May 30 (1.30-6). Also by appt* **Tel 0938 810338**

Cae Hywel ❀ (Miss Judith M Jones) Llansantffraid-ym-Mechain, 10m N of Welshpool. On A495; on E (Oswestry) side of village. Car park in village. 1 acre; S facing slope on different levels; rock garden; herb garden; interesting shrubs, trees and plants. Partly suitable for wheelchairs. TEAS. *Adm £1 Chd 10p. Sat, Sun May 8, 9 (2-6)*

Craig-y-Bwla ❀ (Mr & Mrs George Williams) 5m NE Crickhowell on Llanthony to Fforest Coal Pit Road. Signed from Crickhowell Fire Station 30-acres mainly woodland garden. Laburnum arch. Small lakes. River walks. Picnic area. Autumn foliage. TEAS. *Adm £1.50 Chd free (Share to Brecon Mountain Rescue). Sat, Sun May 22, 23 (2-6). Also by appt May to Oct* **Tel 0873 811810** *or* **0873 810413**

¶**Craig Llyn** (Mrs M Munday) Llanwrthwl. 4m out of Rhayader towards Builth Wells on A470 sign-posted Llanwrthwl. ¾m up lane is Craig Llyn. Limited parking by Craig Llyn gardens, pleasant walk up R. Wye leaving car in village. Nearly 2 acres of steep hillside garden overlooking R. Wye and valley. Mostly planted with heathers, shrubs, rhododendrons, azaleas, sloping lawns, woodland and vegetable garden. Special features are natural stone paths (very uneven), that represent waterways in the Fen tradition. TEAS in aid of Llanwrthwl Church. *Adm £1 Chd 25p. Suns June 6, Aug 8 (11-4)*

Diamond Cottage ✿❀ (Mr & Mrs D T Dorril) Buttington. 4½m NE of Welshpool. From Welshpool take A458 Shrewsbury Rd. Turn R into Heldre Lane, R at next junction, R at Xrds up the hill. From Shrewsbury, turn L 100yds past 'Little Chef' into Sale Lane, L at next junction, R at Xrds. Parking in lane above cottage. 1.7-acre garden created since 1988 on N facing slope of Long Mountain at 700ft. Unusual herbaceous plants and shrubs; natural wooded dingle with small stream; large vegetable garden, patio and pool. Extensive views to Berwyn Mountains. TEAS. *Adm £1 Chd free. Weds April 28, May 26, June 30, July 28 (2-6). By appt* **Tel Trewern 570**

¶**Fraithwen** &@ (Mr & Mrs D Thomas) Tregynon. 6m N of Newton on B4389 midway between villages of Bettws, Cedewain and Tregynon. 1-acre garden created in the last 10yrs; herbaceous borders, rockeries and ponds packed with interesting, unusual and rare plants and shrubs for colour throughout the year. Also on display antique horse-drawn machinery and implements. TEAS. *Adm £1 Chd free (Share to Bettws Community Hall). Sun June 27 (2-6). Also by appt*

Garth House & (Mr & Mrs F A Wilson) Garth on A483 6m W of Builth Wells. Drive gates in village of Garth by Garth Inn. Large wood with azaleas and rhododendrons; water and shrub garden; herbaceous garden; fine views. Historic connection with Charles Wesley & the Gwynne family. TEAS. *Adm £1 Chd free. Mon May 31 (2-6)*

Glanwye &@ (Mr & Mrs David Vaughan, G & H Kidston) 2m SE Builth Wells on A470. Large garden, rhododendrons, azaleas; newly sown wild flower meadow. Good views of R. Wye. Cream TEAS. *Adm £1 Chd free (Share to Llanddewi Cwm Church). Sun May 23 (2-6)*

Glebe House & (Mrs Jenkins & Mrs Habberley) Guilsfield, 3m N of Welshpool. A490 (Llanfyllin) rd from Welshpool for 2m; fork right for Guilsfield. 1½ acres; magnificent spring bulb display; unusual clematis and climbers; several gardens within a garden. *Adm £1 Chd free. By appt only* **Tel 0938 553602**

Gliffaes Country House Hotel & (Mr & Mrs Brabner) 3m W of Crickhowell. Large garden; spring bulbs; azaleas & rhododendrons, new ornamental pond; heathers; shrubs; ornamental trees; fine maples; autumn colour; fine position high above R. Usk. *April to Dec. For NGS Adm £1 Chd 50p (collecting box). Suns April 18, Oct 17 (2-5)*

Gregynog &@ (University of Wales) Tregynon, 7m N of Newtown. A483 Welshpool to Newtown Rd, turn W at B4389 for Bettws Cedewain, 1m through village gates on left. Large garden; fine banks, rhododendrons and azaleas; dell with specimen shrubs; formal garden; colour-coded walks starting from car park. Descriptive leaflet available. Early C19 black and white house; site inhabited since C12. TEAS. *Adm £1 Chd 10p. Sun June 6 (2-6)*

Kerry Gardens & 3m S of Newtown. Take A489 to Craven Arms. Some gardens featured on BBC TV Wales. Start from Kerry Lamb car park. TEAS in aid of village hall. *Combined adm £1 Chd 10p. Sun Aug 8 (2-6)*
   Mar-Jon Dolforgan View (Mrs O Hughes) Interesting garden; wide variety of annuals, plants and shrubs
   Post Office (Mr & Mrs E Pugh) Leeks, spray chrysanthemums and fuchsias grown for exhibition also small colourful garden
   Westwinds (Captain & Mrs R Watson) Colourful garden; rockery, pools, shrubs, flower beds. TEAS

¶**Llangorse Gardens** @ Llangorse is on B4560 4m off A40 at Bwlch, 6½m from Brecon and 4½m from Talgarth. Park in village. TEAS. *Combined adm £1.50. Sun June 13, Wed June 16 (2-6)*
   ¶**The Neuadd** (Mr & Mrs Paul Johnson) Informal garden of about 1 acre maintained by owners. Mixed borders with the emphasis on interesting trees, shrubs and foliage plants; small vegetable and fruit garden; wild garden and copse to encourage wild life
   The Old Vicarage && (Major & Mrs J B Anderson) Small family garden maintained by owners with interesting herbaceous and shrub borders; lawns, trees and vegetables. *Spring to Oct by appt* **Tel 087484 639**

Llanstephan House &&@ (Hon Hugo & Mrs Philipps) Llanstephan. Cross R.Wye on suspension bridge off A470 (Brecon-Builth Wells rd) between Llyswen and Erwood. R at T-junction then follow signs. Large old garden in process of extensive restoration and replanting. Walled kitchen garden with young fruit trees, vegetables, roses, herbs and herbaceous plants. Shrubs, woodlands, beautiful views of Black Mountains. TEAS. *Adm £1 Chd free. Sun June 20 (2-6)*

Llysdinam &@ (Lady Delia Venables-Llewelyn & Llysdinam Charitable Trust) Newbridge-on-Wye, SW of Llandrindod Wells. Turn W off A479 at Newbridge-on-Wye; right immediately after crossing R. Wye; entrance up hill. Large garden. Azaleas; rhododendrons, water garden and herbaceous borders; shrubs; woodland garden; kitchen garden; fine view of Wye Valley. TEAS. *Adm £1 Chd free (Share to NSPCC). Suns May 30, Aug 22 (2-6.30)*

Lower Cefn Perfa &@ (Mr & Mrs J Dugdale) Kerry, Newtown. Follow signs off A489. Medium-sized easily maintained garden with R. Mule running through it. TEAS in aid of Powys Branch British Red Cross Soc. Holiday for the disabled. *Adm £1 Chd free. Sun June 13 (2-6)*

Maenllwyd Isaf &&& (Mrs Denise Hatchard) Abermule, 5m NE of Newtown & 10m S of Welshpool. On B4368 Abermule to Craven Arms, 1½m from Abermule. 3 acres; unusual shrubs and plants; goldfish pool; 'wild' pool; R. Mule. C16 listed house also open by appt. *Adm £1 Chd free (Share to Winged Fellowship Trust). Only by appt all year. Gardening clubs etc welcome* **Tel 0686 630204**

Maesllwch Castle (Walter de Winton Esq) Glasbury-on-Wye. Turn off A438 immediately N of Glasbury bridge. Through Glasbury ½m turn R at Church. Medium-sized, garden owner maintained. Exceptional views from terrace across R. Wye to Black Mountains. Old walled garden, woodland walk, fine trees. TEA. *Adm £1 Chd 30p (Share to All Saints Church, Glasbury). Sun May 2 (2-5)*

Manascin &&(Lady Watson) Pencelli. 3m SE of Brecon on B4558 pink house in Pencelli Village. Small garden, many features; small pond with water lilies and fountain; shrubs; roses, lilies and vegetable patch. Teas in village. *Adm £1 Chd free. Sun July 4 (2-6)*

Moor Park & (Mr & the Hon Mrs L Price) Llanbedr. Turn off A40 at Fire Station in Crickhowell; continue 2m, signed Llanbedr. 5 acres; roses, borders, trees and walled kitchen garden. Lake, water garden under construction; woodland walk. TEAS. *Adm £1 Chd free. Sun April 25 (2-6.30)*

Parc Gwynne &&& (Mr & Mrs W Windham) Glasbury on Wye. From Brecon towards Hereford on A438 cross Glasbury Bridge, 1st L sign-posted Boughrood and 1st L at War Memorial. Entrance across green. Small riverside garden, mainly herbaceous with white and apricot borders. *Adm £1 Chd free (Share to Queen Mary's Clothing Guild). Sun June 13 (2-6)*

Penmyarth & (Mr & The Hon Mrs Legge-Bourke) Glanusk Park. 2m W of Crickhowell. A40, 12m from Brecon, 8m from Abergavenny. 11-acre rose, rock and wild garden with bluebells, azaleas, rhododendrons and pond. TEAS. *Adm £1. Sun May 9 (2-6)*

Powis Castle Gardens ✕❀ (The National Trust) Welshpool. Turn off A483 ¾m out of Welshpool, up Red Lane for ¼m. Gardens laid out in 1720 with most famous hanging terraces in the world; enormous yew hedges; lead statuary, large wild garden. Part of garden suitable for wheelchairs, top terrace only. TEA. The date shown below is a *Special opening* for NGS; garden only. *Adm gardens only (Castle closed) £3 Chd £1 N.T. members also pay.* ▲*Tues June 1 (2-6)*

Station Road Gardens &✕ Talybont-on-Usk. ½m from turning off A40. 6m E of Brecon, signposted Talybont. Teas in village. *Combined adm £1.50 Chd free. Sun Aug 1 (2-6)*
>   **Cartrefle** (Mr & Mrs J F Fox) Small compact garden with variety of trees, shrubs, vegetables and an abundance of flowers in pots and tubs as well as the normal flower beds. Also a water garden feature
>   **Lonicera** (Mr & Mrs G Davies) A garden of varied interest incorporating several small feature gardens extending to approx ¼ acre. These include a modern rose garden; landscaped heather garden with dwarf conifers; herbaceous and woody perennials; colourful summer bedding displays; window boxes, hanging baskets and patio tubs forming extensive house frontage display; greenhouses

Trawscoed Hall ✕❀ (Mr & Mrs J T K Trevor) 3m N of Welshpool on Llanfyllin Road. Long drive through woodlands, lovely panoramic views from S facing sloping gardens with interesting plants. 2 acres. Magnificent wisteria covering front of fine Georgian house (not open) built 1777. Granary dating from 1772. Nature trails through prize-winning woodlands. TEAS (in aid of Asthma Research). *Adm £1 Chd free. Sun May 16 (2-6)*

Treberfydd (Lt Col & Mrs D Garnons Williams) Bwlch. 2¼m W of Bwlch. From A40 at Bwlch turning marked Llangorse then L for Pennorth. From Brecon, leave A40 at Llanhamlach. 2¼m to sign Llangasty Church but go over cattle grid to house. Large garden; lawns, roses, trees, rock garden. TEAS. *Adm £1 Chd free (Share to Llangasty Church). Sun July 11 (2-6)*

Tretower House &❀ (Lt Col & Mrs P K Cracroft) Leave Crickhowell on A40 towards Brecon. Take R fork for Builth Wells. Garden 1m in Tretower village. 2½-acre family garden maintained by owners. Mainly herbaceous. Views of Black Mountains and Tretower Castle. TEAS. *Adm £1 Chd free (Share to Tretower Church). Sun June 27 (2-6)*

¶**Upper Dolley** ✕❀ (Mrs B P Muggleton) Dolley Green. Take B4356 W out of Presteigne towards Whitton. At Dolly Green, 2m from Presteigne, turn L down 'No Through Road' by red brick church; Upper Dolley is 100yds on L. From Knighton take B4355 to turning for Whitton, B4357. Turn L at Whitton B4356 to brick church; turn R. 2-acre country garden with open views of Lugg Valley; variety of borders with many shrub roses and large natural pond; C16 Grade 2 listed house (not open). TEAS weather permitting. *Adm £1 Chd 50p (Share to The Bible Society). Sats, Suns June 19, 20, July 10, 11 (2-6)*

The Walled Garden & (Miss C M Mills) Knill, 3m from Kington and Presteigne. Off B4362 Walton-Presteigne rd to Knill village; right over cattle grid; keep right down drive. 3 acres; walled garden; stream; bog garden; primulas; shrub roses. Nr C13 Church in lovely valley. *Adm £1 Chd 50p. By appt any day (10-7)* **Tel 0544 267411**

STOP PRESS

¶**'Natural Hands' Massage** ♿☙ Aardseweg 17. On route N19 find Ten Aard (not on all maps), between Geel and Kasterlee. At traffic lights in Ten Aard turn into Aardseweg (between British/Flemish war memorial and school). 'Natural Hands' is a white house with small horse on chimney, 250 metres from lights on right. 2,500 square metres all organic, includes wide variety of vegetables outside and under glass, soft fruits, flowers, flowering trees/shrubs, lawn, three stocked ponds and indoor garden. Some produce available. Flower season commences with 20,000 bulbs from January to June, annuals, perennials. In an area with plenty of interesting sightseeing. Guided tour in English, Dutch, French and German. Several good hotels and restaurants in the area. TEAS. *Adm £1 or BFr 50 Chd free. By appt every day April 1 to September 7 (10 to dusk)*

THE COUNTIES OF ENGLAND AND WALES

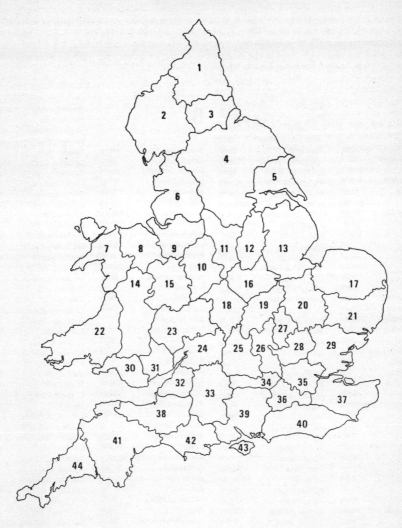

KEY TO MAP

1 Northumberland	12 Nottinghamshire	23 Hereford & Worcester	34 Berkshire
2 Cumbria	13 Lincolnshire	24 Bedfordshire	35 Greater London
3 Durham	14 Powys	25 Gloucestershire	36 Surrey
4 Yorkshire	15 Shropshire	26 Oxfordshire	37 Kent
5 Humberside	16 Leicestershire	27 Buckinghamshire	38 Somerset
6 Lancashire	17 Norfolk	28 Hertfordshire	39 Hampshire
7 Gwynned	18 Warwickshire	29 Essex	40 Sussex
8 Clwyd	19 Northamptonshire	30 Glamorgan	41 Devon
9 Cheshire	20 Cambridgeshire	31 Gwent	42 Dorset
10 Staffordshire	21 Suffolk	32 Avon	43 Isle of Wight
11 Derbyshire	22 Dyfed	33 Wiltshire	44 Cornwall

Index to Gardens

This index lists all gardens alphabetically and gives the counties in which they are to be found. Refer to the relevant county pages where the garden and its details will be found, again in alphabetical order. The following unorthodox county abbreviations are used: C & W—Cheshire and Wirral; L & R—Leicestershire and Rutland; G & A—Gwynedd and Anglesey. An * denotes a garden which will not be in its normal alphabetical order as it is a group garden and will be found under the Group Garden name but still within the county indicated.

NOTES

NOTES

Index to Advertisers

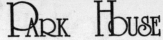

314

LAWN WISE

SPECIALISED LAWN CARE
EXPERT ADVICE AND WRITTEN REPORTS
Individual treatment programmes designed for your lawns, courts and pitches, country wide.

61 Oxford Road, Abingdon, Oxon OX14 2AA
Tel: 0235-520596
Member of the Institute of Groundmanship

HOUSE NAMES OF DISTINCTION

The Cottage

- We are specialists in ENGRAVED GOLD LEAF LETTERING ON WELSH SLATE.
- We manufacture PROFESSIONAL & TRADE PLAQUES IN SLATE.
- We have a unique process for engraving, crests, company logos and coloured pictures of your choice on Slate.
- Our SLATE NAME PLATES will not rot, warp or rust, we guarantee them for 100 years!
- Orders dispatched throughout UK and abroad.

Send s.a.e. or phone for brochure
J WILLIAMS & CO, The Slate Yard, Sand St.
Pwllheli, N Wales LL53 5ES
Est. 1850   Tel: 0758 612645

BRITISH WILD PLANTS
Largest selection of Coir fibre Nursery grown plants at lowest prices. Illustrated A4 Guide to Garden Use and Price list (Trade list available): 3 x 24p stamps:
M. Gould, Stockerton Nursery, Kirkcudbright, Galloway DG6 4XS. (GW)

Large Field Grown Herbaceous Perennials including Primulas, Herbs and Wildflowers.

Send two stamps for latest catalogue to:
R Moss & Sons (NG), Astley Road, Irlam, Manchester M30 5LN

Philip Hind Tours

- Cornwall's Spring Gardens (and Scillies option) 16-19 April
- North Cornwall Houses & Gardens 21-24 May
- Herefordshire Historic Houses 1-4 May
- Devon Houses 10 & 11 July
- Derbyshire Houses 10-13 September

Telephone 0840 - 770695

Mac Pennys

LONG LIFE PLANT LABEL
THE UNIQUE ANSWER TO A GARDENING PROBLEM!
a non fade, permanent record, plant label. Simply 'engrave' on the specially coated black side, your plant name using the 'scriber' provided.
Details from:
Mac Penny Products, Burley Rd, Bransgore, Christchurch, Dorset BH23 8DB
Tel: 0425 72348

BROOKBRAE SUNDIALS
A range of artist designed, craftsmen made traditional and sculptural sundials including plinths.
Sent for free leaflet to:
Brookbrae Limited, 53 St. Leonard's Road London SW14 7NQ. Tel: 081 876 9238

FROM PALMS TO POPPIES
from
The Palm Farm
an unusual range of plants from subtropical species to hardy trees and shrubs from one nursery in South Humberside. Mail order service (18p stamp for list) or nursery customers welcome. Open 7 days, 2-5pm (Ring ahead in winter)
STATION ROAD, THORNTON CURTIS, Nr ULCEBY SOUTH HUMBERSIDE DN39 6XF TEL: 0469 31232

Sue Pack
Garden Design
Offers a friendly and efficient service. From planting plans to complete garden designs. Initial consultation free of charge.

Contact Sue on Milton Keynes 0908 317029

SOUTH AFRICA
Join a small party visiting private gardens, wine estates and historical houses of the Western Cape. Staying in country house hotels we explore at leisure this beautiful area.
Departing November 11, 1993 and February 1994.

Alternatively, independent itineraries and travel arrangements to suit the individual.

Accompanied Cape Tours, Hill House, Much Marcle, Ledbury, Herefordshire HR8 2NX Tel: 0531 84210

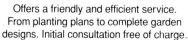

323

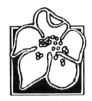

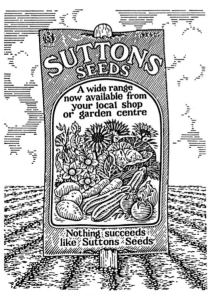

Westminster Abbey Gardens

College Garden, once the monks' herb garden, has been in continuous cultivation for over 900 years.

Discover the hidden garden at the heart of the Little Cloister and from there the new garden on the site of St. Catherine's Chapel.

Open every Thursday–free–10.00 to 18.00 hrs (Oct to March closing 16.00 hrs)

Thompson & Morgan
The Seedsmen Est. 1855

Since the first seed catalogue in 1855, Thompson & Morgan have been offering to gardeners world wide, some of the most popular, rare and interesting plants from seed. In the latest catalogue, you'll find on offer an extensive range of annuals, perennials, biennials, alpines, house and conservatory plants, cacti, trees, shrubs and vegetables — it's a treasure store of garden gems!

Take the opportunity to browse at your leisure through the world's largest illustrated seed catalogue — almost 2,000 pictures of glorious flowers and mouth watering vegetables. Use the coupon below to request your copy today.

In association with the National Garden Scheme you may deduct £3 OFF the value of your T&M order. Simply cut out the special exclusive voucher on this page and attach to your order.

Michauxia tchihatcheffii

Tomato Sungold – the Sweetest

£3 off

see over page for details

CATALOGUE REQUEST
complete details over page

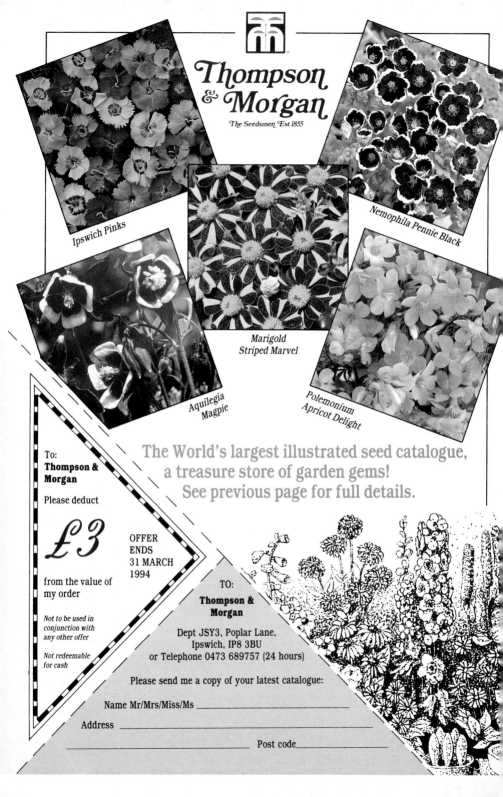

Gardens of England and Wales

A 55 minute documentary produced in association with
the *National Gardens Scheme.*

BBC TV Presenter Sara Edwards visits fifteen beautiful private gardens
which open for the *National Gardens Scheme* Charitable Trust.

Programme 1 features:-

Abbey Dore Court	Birtsmorton Court
Chilworth Manor	Clipsham House
Coverwood lakes	Edge Hill
Greatham Mill	Greencombe
Jenkyn Place	Lower House Farm
The Mill, Cannington	Mwyndy House
Preen Manor	Trevi Gardens

The '*Gardens of England and Wales*' Video is available on VHS format
price £11.95 plus £1.80 post and packing. U.K. & Europe

Send a cheque/PO for £13.75
payable to:
S.E.E.R TV & Video Productions Ltd.,
2 Larch Grove, Lisvane, Cardiff. CF4 5TH

If you prefer to pay by Visa ☐ Access ☐

quote no. ☐☐☐☐ ☐☐☐☐ ☐☐☐☐ ☐☐☐☐

Expiry date . . . .

Signed . . . .

Please state below name & address to which video should be sent.

. . . .

. . . .

. . . .

. . . . Postcode . . . .

Or phone Cardiff 0222 - 751159 (24 hours) for credit card orders.

Overseas orders welcome, all prices include shipping
Australia A$40, New Zealand NZ$53, USA $65.00
Trade enquiries welcome.

A percentage of the profits from this video will be presented to the NGS Charitable Trust.

GARDENS
OF ENGLAND & WALES **1994**

PUBLISHED MARCH

Price: £3.75 including UK postage. Airmail to Europe £4.25; Australia A$15.50 and New Zealand NZ$19.50

To The National Gardens Scheme, Hatchlands Park, East Clandon, Guildford, Surrey, GU4 7RT. Tel 0483 211535

Please send _____ copy/copies of *Gardens of England and Wales* for which I enclose PO/cheque for _____
Postal orders and cheques should be made payable to The National Gardens Scheme and crossed.
If sending money from abroad please use an international money order or add $1 to cheques for clearance.

Name Mr/Mrs/Miss (Block letters)

Address

The books will be posted on publication. If you wish to receive an acknowledgement of your order, please enclose an s.a.e.
North American Agents Green Shade Inc, Cape Neddick, Maine 03902-0547 – $12.00 plus $3 post & packing (Canada – $15.00 + $4.00)
Trade terms Supplies of this book on sale or return should be ordered direct from our trade distributors:
Seymour, 1270 London Road, Norbury, London, SW16 4DH (Tel 081-679 1899)   REG CHARITY NO 279284

TO ADVERTISE IN

GARDENS OF ENGLAND AND WALES 1994

CONTACT:

AW PUBLISHING, PO BOX 38, ASHFORD, KENT TN25 6PR

TELEPHONE: 0303 813803 FAX: 0303 813737

Authoritative and wide-ranging, Batsford
horticulture books cover a variety of
gardening interests.
Look out for our books in your local bookshop
or send off today for our full horticulture list.

NEW TITLES FOR 1993

March   **Helleborus** £19.99
             Propagation of Hardy Perennials £19.99

June   **Primula** £60.00

July   **Cultivation of Rhododendrons** £35.00
             Dianthus £25.00
             Poppies £29.99

September   **Gardening with Exotics** £25.00

BEST-SELLERS OF 1992

The Vegetable Garden Displayed £10.95
Creative Propagation £17.99
Alliums £17.99
The Rustic Garden £35.00

Batsford books are available from all good bookshops.
For full details of our complete horticulture list, please
contact the Publicity Department at the address below.

B a t s f o r d

4 Fitzhardinge Street
London W1H 0AH

READ THE BEST
GARDENING
BOOKS

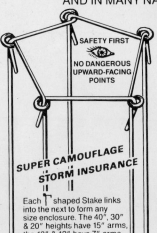

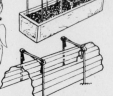

ISBN 0-900558-25-3

Cover illustration of Dallam Tower, Milnthorpe, Cumbria, by Val Biro (by courtesy of Brigadier & Mrs. C. E. Tryon-Wilson).

ISBN 0-900558-25-3

ISSN 0141-2361

9 780900 558252